Crying the News

Crying the News

A History of America's Newsboys

VINCENT DIGIROLAMO

Furthermore:
a program of the J.M. Kaplan Fund

OXFORD
UNIVERSITY PRESS

OXFORD
UNIVERSITY PRESS

Oxford University Press is a department of the University of Oxford. It furthers the University's objective of excellence in research, scholarship, and education by publishing worldwide. Oxford is a registered trade mark of Oxford University Press in the UK and certain other countries.

Published in the United States of America by Oxford University Press
198 Madison Avenue, New York, NY 10016, United States of America.

Library of Congress Cataloging-in-Publication Data
Names: DiGirolamo, Vincent, author.
Title: Crying the news : a history of America's Newsboys / Vincent DiGirolamo.
Description: Oxford, UK : New York, NY : Oxford University Press, 2019. |
Includes index.
Identifiers: LCCN 2018032434 | ISBN 9780195320251 (hardcover) |
ISBN 9780199717729 (epub)
Subjects: LCSH: Paperboys—United States—History. |
Poor children—United States—History. | Child labor—United States—History. |
Newspaper carriers—United States—History.
Classification: LCC HD8039.N422 U637 2019 | DDC 381/.45071—dc23
LC record available at https://lccn.loc.gov/2018032434

7 9 8 6

Printed by Sheridan Books, Inc., United States of America

For April Masten, partner in time

And in recognition of my father, George, and uncles Tony, Johnny, Angelo, Toto, and Andrew DiGirolamo, and Charma Ferreira—news criers all

A Boston police detective interrogates runaways Andrew DiGirolamo, Vincent Serafino, and George DiGirolamo, 1931.

Many shall run to and fro, and knowledge shall be increased.
—Daniel 12:4

CONTENTS

ACKNOWLEDGMENTS

Peddling newspapers was usually a transitional form of labor, a bridge over which children—boys in particular—crossed to more stable, better-paid, grown-up occupations. Yet in some cases, mostly sad, it turned into a lifelong career. Only now, on the eve of publication, does it occur to me that I have spent more time studying the news trade than most of my subjects spent working in it. There is something sad about that too, though the work has sustained me in many ways over the years. While it did not start out as such, this book evolved into a critique of the notion of the self-made man. Its very existence is a case in point, as it is the result of time, money, faith, favors, and ideas proffered by many individuals and institutions.

I will always be indebted to Herbert Gutman whose National Endowment for the Humanities summer seminar for trade unionists led me from labor journalism to labor history, and to the US Department of Education Jacob K. Javits Fellowship that emboldened me to pursue an academic career. I want to acknowledge Rod Holmgren and Thomas C. Leonard, who introduced me to the history of journalism at Monterey Peninsula College and the University of California, Berkeley, respectively, and Edmund (Terry) Burke III, Lisbeth Haas, Susan Mann, Robert G. Moeller, Page Smith, and Tyler Stovall who modeled excellence at UC Santa Cruz.

At Princeton University I had the good fortune to work with Christine Stansell, Daniel Rodgers, and Elizabeth Lunbeck. They and Michael B. Katz of the University of Pennsylvania encouraged me to keep the big questions in mind as I pursued my small subjects. John Murrin, James McPherson, Reid Mitchell, Nell Irvin Painter, Gail Pemberton, Gyan Prakash, and Sean Wilentz critiqued my earliest drafts while Robert Darnton offered sound advice on doing cultural history: "Start with a strong demographic base." George Kateb made me think harder about the moral implications of my work during my stint at the University Center for Human Values. The Woodrow Wilson Foundation funded a stimulating year of research and writing, and the Peter B. Lewis Fund at the Center of International Studies underwrote an important research trip to England.

History is a collective enterprise, especially as practiced by scholars in and of Great Britain. I would like to thank John Charleton, Leonore Davidoff, Anna Davin, Joe and Sally Foster, John Gillis, Sally Mitchison, Deborah Nord, Tammy Proctor, Julia Reid, Carolyn Steedman, Randolph Trumbach, Dror Wahrman, Richard Whiting, Tom Woodhouse, and Gill Redfern. A special *ta* to Leslie Tuttle, Noa Wahrman, and Dov Ber Kerler for their translations of Latin and Yiddish.

As the inaugural J. N. G. Finley Postdoctoral Fellow in the History Department at George Mason University I had the chance to bounce ideas off Roy Rosenzweig and Lawrence Levine, as well as Michael O'Malley and John Cheng. While at Colgate University I received a Picker Research Fellowship and close readings from Margaret Darby and Bruce Pegg.

I got critical support from the National Endowment for the Humanities in the form of a research fellowship to the American Antiquarian Society. I thank Georgia Barnhill, Nancy Burkett, Joanne Chaison, John Hench, John Keenum, Marie Lameroux, Dennis Laurie, Russell Martin, Jim Moran, Carolyn Sloat, Laura Wascowic, and Richard and Judith Collins for making the AAS such a warm and productive refuge for me. The other residents and fellows were equally important, especially Gretchen Adams, Dennis Brutus, Kathy Corman, Joseph Cullen, Richard Wightman Fox, Melissa Homestead, Helen Lefkowitz Horowitz, Kristen Moon, Sarah Roth, Alan Taylor, and Karen Woods Wierman.

As a lecturer at Princeton I benefited from a Humanities Division Research Grant, the research assistance of Kate Mulry, and the generosity of David Goldschmidt and Cherie Campbell. I am obliged to the Bentley Historical Library at the University of Michigan for a Mark C. Stevens Research Fellowship, and to AnnaLee Pauls at Princeton's Firestone Library and Victor Remer at the New York Children's Aid Society.

I have also enjoyed the support of Dena Ferreira, Ana Calero, and my colleagues in the History Department at Baruch College. Additional aid was provided by a Eugene M. Lang Junior Faculty Research Fellowship, three PSC-CUNY Research Awards, and the Dean's Office of the Weissman School of Arts and Sciences. Thanks are also due the poets—Emily Brandt, Ricky Ray, Esther Smith, and Lisa Jarnot for Lisa's manuscript workshop; Mark Noonan and the participants of the NEH's City of Print seminar; and Lisa Keller, Ian K. Shin, and members of the Columbia University Seminar on the City. The seminar's Leonard Hastings Schoff Trust Fund Publications Award helped underwrite the illustrations. Additional production costs were fabulously met by a Furthermore Grant from the J. M. Kaplan Fund and a 2018 CUNY Office of Research Book Completion Award.

I am grateful to colleagues throughout the academy who read my work. Ruth Alexander, Herman Beavers, Peter Benes, Burton Bledstein, Dani Botsman, Miriam Forman-Brunell, Timothy Gilfoyle, Michael A. Gordon, Kristine Lindenmeyer, John C. Nerone, Scott Sandage, Susan Schweik, Marjatta Rahikainen, and Laurel Thatcher Ulrich offered valuable comments on conference papers. Joshua Brown, Laura Coyle, Cara DiGirolamo, Eric Love, James Marten, Julie Miller, Janis Mimura, David Nasaw, Donna Rilling, Lisa Rubens, Harry Stein, Barbara Young Welke, and Molly Williams read individual chapters. I owe special thanks to Nancy Cott, Martha Hoppin, Alane Salierno Mason, April Masten, Harvey Schwartz, and Kathleen Thompson who read multiple chapters; to Marilyn Schwartz and Madeleine Adams for their editorial advice; to editors Susan Ferber, Alexandra Dauler, Hayley Singer, Macey Fairchild, and Cheryl Merritt at Oxford University Press, and to literary agents Jill Kneerim and Brettne Bloom for putting us together. The staff of the National Humanities Center and its copyeditor Karen Carroll made the final push a pleasure.

I also appreciate the many folks who passed on references. These include Ben Alpers, Ken Appollo, Sharon Bloch, Laurie Block, Susan Chambre, Martha Dennis Burns, Marcus Daniel, Moshe Dann, Jennifer Delton, T. J. Desch-Obi, Maribel Dietz, Anthony Di Renzo, Faye Dudden, Jonathon Earle, John Giggie, Gayle Goodman, Sally Gordon, and especially Bert Hansen. Others who shared sources with me are Grace Hale, Diane Harrigan, Shamil Jeppie, Walter Johnson, Kate Joyce, Stephen Kantrowitz, Philip Katz, Jordan Kellman, Sue Kim, Felicia Kornbluh, Jennifer Luff, Linda Lierheimer, Michael Millender, Sally Mills, James A. Newton, Dennis Northcott, Kathleen Nutter, Geoffrey Plank, Robin Schore, Brian Shovers, Harry Stein, Kristine Stilwell, Brad Verter, Su Wolfe, Diane Winston, Henry Yu, and no doubt others whose discoveries I now selfishly count as my own.

No one was more generous with sources than Peter J. Eckel. Inspired by the life of Father John Drumgoole, director of St. Vincent's Newsboys' Home in New York, Peter amassesd a singular collection of newsboy books, prints, objects, and ephemera, which is now part of Princeton University Library's Department of Rare Books and Special Collections. Peter and his wife, Sally, were essential in making this book a cultural as well as a social history.

My only greater debt is to family, especially my parents, George and Diane DiGirolamo. In some ways this book is family history as it grew out of the stories my father and uncles told about selling papers and shining shoes on the streets of Somerville, Massachusetts, and Monterey, California, during the Great Depression. They and my aunts taught me to take pride in being a hard-working family. They gave me my first job at age 8 busing tables at Angelo's Restaurant on the wharf in Monterey on Sundays from 11:00 to 7:00 for a dollar an hour, plus tips. I didn't know then that I was contributing to the family economy, but I liked being called a good worker and earning more money in a day than my paperboy friends earned in a week.

Most of all I wish to thank April Masten, who wrote her own works of history while I wrote mine. April, our daughter Cara, and nephew Ric Masten know more than anyone else just what a long route it has been. My thanks to them and the others for seeing me through it and collectively debunking all nonsense about self-made men.

Introduction

Echoes Down the Alleys of History

For centuries no sound was more urgent, exasperating, or quintessentially American than the cry of the newsboy: "Here is your bloody news! Here is your fine, bloody news!" yelled "peg-legged Jemmy McCoy" as he trod the cobbled streets of Philadelphia in September 1776, just days after New York had fallen to the British.

Eighty-five years later a scamp in Providence, Rhode Island, created a commotion crying, "Fort Sumter is *vaccinated* and blown up! extra *Traveller*—extra *Journal*." The trouble was, he made it up; the bombardment that commenced the Civil War in April 1861 would not occur for another two weeks.

In May 1898, at the height of the Spanish-American War, 13-year-old Lillian Hadley of Hoboken, New Jersey, was arrested for crying papers in Manhattan's theater district after dark. Her mother and out-of-work father had given her a dime to buy the papers, but charity officers detained her as a beggar. When told she was better off with them than at home, Lillian replied, "Excuse me for contradicting, but I don't think I am."

Skip ahead to June 1937 and we hear Chester and a pal shouting through the streets of New Orleans, "Louis K.O.s Braddock!," excited that a Negro like themselves had won the heavyweight boxing championship of the world. But pride curdled into fear when a white man told them to shut up, put a gun to their backs, and marched them out of the neighborhood.[1]

So it went for America's news peddlers. They carried vital intelligence to a young nation of readers, bamboozled them if opportunity arose, received unwanted attention from authorities, and met violent rebuke from those who disliked their message. Even if they were sometimes unreliable, obnoxious, or endangered, newsboys and newsgirls provided an indispensable service retailing the breaking news that would become America's history.

Yet their role in that history has escaped serious inquiry. "Humblest of the journalists were the newsboys," wrote historian Frank Luther Mott in 1962. "The unwritten story of their rise would be a romantic chapter in the history of American journalism."[2] No one rushed to write that story, romantic or otherwise. This neglect is surprising because newsboys—from the brilliant Benjamin Franklin to the dauntless Ragged Dick, created by novelist Horatio Alger Jr., and the high-kicking Jack Kelly, hero of the Disney musical *Newsies*—have long fascinated us as symbols of struggle and achievement. But what do we really know about them? Who were these children? Where did they come from? And what can they tell us about the American experience?

While often regarded as indigenous to American soil, America's newsboys are direct descendants of the ballad singers, "mercurie girls," and "flying stationers" who first appeared on the streets of London, Paris, and other European cities in the sixteenth century. They arose not just with Johannes Gutenberg's invention of movable type but also with the transition from a feudal to a capitalist society in which production for profit created new social classes. The men and women who peddled the world's first broadsides, gazettes, and folios were people of low station whose wares were subject to high taxes that made them unaffordable to the masses, most of whom couldn't read anyway.[3]

In the New World, by contrast, literacy rates were high and children dominated the news trade. Contemporaries hailed them as both products and producers of press freedom, popular democracy, and national character, never mind that they were also scorned as "street Arabs and guttersnipes."[4] Theirs was a gritty, gregarious, and precarious world that existed together with, and yet separate from, the world of adults. *Crying the News* reconstructs that world and deconstructs the enduring myths it spawned. A history of print capitalism from the pavement up, this book chronicles the rise of the American press from the perspective of its most marginal workers. Their ranks included not just boys but, as New York strike leader Dave Simons said in 1899, "niggers, goils, cripples, old women, fakirs, beggars an' sich."[5] This is their story.

Exactly how many children sold or delivered papers is hard to say. People entered and left the trade as the weather turned or headlines shrank. The best estimates of journalists, social workers, and circulation managers suggest that newsboys multiplied throughout the industrial age. In 1839 in New York there were 150 newsboys between the ages of 6 and 16. They increased to 500 or 600 by 1854. Newsboys proliferated everywhere during the Civil War. Buffalo and Atlanta counted 200 "bonafide" newsboys in the 1870s. Boston licensed 400, and Philadelphia hosted 750, rising to 1,200 in the early 1880s. Detroit's newsboys doubled to 1,600 during that decade.[6]

With the outbreak of the war with Spain in 1898, Chicago's newsboys jumped from 2,000 to 8,000. New York's shot up from 5,000 to 15,000. Rochester relied on 700 newsboys, Grand Rapids 1,200, and Cincinnati 1,900 in the early 1900s. Despite a decline in other forms of child labor, newsboys' ranks swelled throughout the 1920s. Pittsburgh had about 1,200 and Buffalo 1,500. Enid, Oklahoma, with a fraction of those other cities' populations, tallied more than 800 newsboys. According to conservative industry estimates, juvenile hawkers and carriers together totaled 570,000 in the 1930s. Constant turnover required many more individuals to sustain these averages. However imprecise, the numbers suggest that distributing newspapers was one of the first and most formative occupational experiences of America's youth.[7]

Although they have all but disappeared from city streets, newsboys remain familiar figures in American culture. Yet they are historical enigmas. There are two reasons for this paradox. First, they were part of a casual labor force whose experiences have proved easier to romanticize than to recover. With few exceptions, circulation managers did not keep track of the boys' names and ages. Nor did most municipalities. Newsboys, as we will see, affiliated with the Knights of Labor, the American Federation of Labor, and, in the West, the Industrial Workers of the World, but records of their activities take up little space in union archives.

An abundance of sources has nevertheless survived to tell their history. The industry's very product recounts their exploits, albeit filtered through human interest stories and other journalistic conventions. Newsboys were also the focus of documentary photographs, muckraking novels, and sociological studies. They appeared in comic strips, memoirs, minstrel shows, movies, paintings, poems, postcards, sculptures, sermons, songs, trade cards, and travelers' accounts. These sources enable this book to trace the changing experience of newsboys and illuminate the process by which they and their work acquired new social meanings. The illustrations herein are a case in point: while most reflect how newsboys actually looked and acted in various periods, they document even more reliably how conceptions of childhood, attitudes about labor, and modes of representation changed over time.

The second reason newsboys eluded scholars so long is that their pervasive presence on city streets rendered them invisible. Child labor investigator Edward N. Clopper termed this phenomenon the "illusion of the near." "Street workers have always been far more conspicuous than any other child laborers," he wrote in 1912, "and it seems that this very proximity has been their misfortune. If we could have focused our attention upon them as we did upon children in factories, they would have been banished from the streets long ago. But they were too close to us."[8] The "illusion of the near" still makes it hard to consider newsboys with fresh eyes and ears. Outworn myths of success and self-flattering notions of national character continue to skew our understanding of these children.

My approach is to recognize that newsboys were both historical and archetypal figures. They lived and worked in specific times and places, yet they also
came to personify American character and exemplify the Franklinian virtues of
honesty, industry, and thrift. From the colonial period onward, American artists
and poets associated news carriers with Mercury, the youthful fleet-footed messenger of the gods. Known as Hermes in the Greek pantheon, he is the god of
roads and commerce, luck and cunning, music and theft.

Like his mythological forebear, the American newsboy represents a bundle
of contradictions. He was at once an exploited worker and an independent
merchant, a spreader of truths and a trafficker in lies. Part hero and part villain, he was as likely to shortchange a customer as to return his lost billfold—
both acts calculated to achieve maximum gain. He prided himself on being
a breadwinner but would stay away from home for days and risk everything
shooting craps. He usually worked for profits, not wages, yet identified with
the interests of labor more than with capital. He was quick to strike and even
quicker to abandon the trade altogether. He was a voracious reader who had
little time for school, a stylish dresser who made do with castoffs, and a believer in fair play who felt a moral obligation to fleece any fool who crossed
his path. He despised all things rural yet often came from the countryside. He
was a symbol of individuality, yet a representative of his class; a model of independence, yet dependent on the kindness of strangers. It's no wonder that he
captured America's imagination, representing capitalism's manifest evils and
its by-your-bootstraps appeal.

It's certainly ironic that industrial capitalism's most woeful victims became its
chief proponents—its vox populi. I intend to show how this happened. My aim
is not simply to distinguish history from myth but to explore the dialectical relationship between the two—to dissect how newsboys' dual careers as workers
and symbols shaped each other, creating wealth for some and meaning for many.

Newsboys, I argue, came to personify the spirit of capitalism in America
because of their low-rung ubiquity, not in spite of it. Their mythic, Algeresque
ability to rise "upward and onward," to overcome and even benefit from poverty,
has served to reinforce the legitimacy of the capitalist order. The myth holds
that individual character, not social class, shapes the structure of opportunity
in America. The list of illustrious ex-newsies reads like a who's who in the world
of business (Thomas Edison, Walt Disney, Warren Buffett), politics (Al Smith,
Warren Harding, Herbert Hoover), entertainment (Harry Houdini, W. C.
Fields, Frank Capra), sports (Jack Dempsey, Knute Rockne, Jackie Robinson),
literature (Jack London, Sherwood Anderson, Thomas Wolfe), and journalism
(Adolph Ochs, Walter Winchell, Theodore White). According to the myth,
these great men did not just happen to be newsboys but were great *because* they
were newsboys; the work itself brought out their latent genius.[9]

No one has subscribed to this myth more ardently than some of the boys who lived it. Boston mayor John "Honey Fitz" Fitzgerald, who peddled papers in the 1870s and later published a weekly newspaper, said that his newsboy experience taught him "more about the business of publishing than any of those fancy colleges across the river." Likewise, filmmaker Mervyn LeRoy, who quit school in 1913 at age 13 to sell papers, explained in his autobiography, "I saw life in the raw on the streets of San Francisco. I met the cops and the whores and the reporters and the bartenders and the Chinese and the fishermen and the shopkeepers. . . . When it came time for me to make motion pictures, I made movies that were real, because I knew first hand how real people behaved."[10]

To call certain stories myths is not to say they are false, only to recognize that they have struck a chord in the culture. Myths arise to explain social or natural phenomena. The newsboy myth accounts for individual success and national progress. The problem with such myths, warned historian Christopher Lasch, is that they invite nostalgia at the expense of memory. Strictly speaking, "nostalgia does not entail the exercise of memory at all," he said, "since the past it idealizes stands outside time, frozen in unchanging perfection."[11] In America, nostalgia often takes the form of a pastoral longing for a lost country life, such as that associated with the Old South or the Old West. This abstract longing finds expression in stereotypes such as the happy darky or the noble savage, which serve to suppress the horrors of slavery and conquest. The newsboy myth represents a rare form of urban nostalgia. It, too, appears harmless, but it distorts our understanding of the past, notably the wrenching costs of industrial capitalism.

Children handled a variety of newspapers, including labor, radical, religious, ethnic, and woman's suffrage papers. They were thus integral to the expansion and diversification of American print culture. This book tells this story, but it deals mainly with the distribution of general circulation English-language dailies. These papers constitute what is generally called the commercial, popular, or mainstream press. I prefer the term *capitalist press* because it highlights the economic underpinnings of the industry, the cultural milieu in which it operated, and the ideological influence it exerted. This is not to say that the press was a monolithic institution; the editorial position of American newspapers ran the gamut on social and political questions. Nevertheless, most newspapers were privately owned, profit-seeking enterprises that employed or otherwise engaged thousands of people to transform the raw material of life into a tangible commodity called news that required shipping, schlepping, and selling.

In conducting its business, the capitalist press relied more extensively on children's labor than any other sector of the economy except agriculture. Newspapers developed the most innovative methods of recruiting, disciplining, and retaining that labor. They took the lead in defining child news peddling as an essential public service, refuting reformers' claims that it was a veritable social evil. Throughout this debate, the news trade served as a point of contact in which working-class youth—both immigrant and native-born—came face-to-face with capitalism, not abstractly but in the person of editors, publishers, customers, and competitors. As the jaded Gilded Age newspaper editor in E. L. Doctorow's 1994 novel *The Waterworks* observed, "No publisher wanted to admit that his weighty estate was carried on the small, rounded shoulders of an eight-year-old boy," but it was true nonetheless.[12] Indeed, newsboys' labor facilitated the learning and leisure of their more privileged peers; not only did carriers deliver the papers that better-off families read at home, but they generated the revenue that publishers pocketed or paid out in salaries. These earnings helped buy their children books and toys, birthday parties and vacations, tutors and prep schools. Joseph Pulitzer and William Randolph Hearst's pampered progeny, like those of other press barons—and the retinue of editors, accountants, and attorneys they employed—all benefited from the surplus value of newsboy labor.

Acclaimed by the *Chicago Tribune* in 1869 as "young toilers in the cause of truth," newsboys merit a place in the histories of labor, childhood, and journalism.[13] They bring with them a capacity to shake up these fields. In labor history, for example, their experience challenges convenient yet dubious distinctions between child labor and adult labor, work and play, wages and profit, opportunity and exploitation. They can also expand our understanding of various paid and unpaid labor regimes, having distributed papers as wage earners, pieceworkers, indentured servants, and chattel slaves. Indeed, America's first newsboy was not Benjamin Franklin, as is usually asserted, but an anonymous slave. Franklin delivered his brother's newspaper, the *New England Courant*, as a 15-year-old apprentice in 1721. "After having work'd in composing the Types & printing off the Sheets," he recalled in his *Autobiography*, "I was employ'd to carry the papers thro' the Streets to the Customers." His apprenticeship began three years earlier, during which time he also wrote and peddled topical broadsides, which his father ridiculed, saying, "Verse-makers were generally Beggars." Josiah Franklin was not uniquely cranky on the subject. Peddlers of all types were held in low regard. Criminal law, dating back to sixteenth-century England, equated them with beggars and vagabonds, and compelled them to work or face dire consequences. Those who peddled broadsides were considered the worst of the lot, but their enterprise helped transform reading from a private devotional practice to a public secular one.[14] Six years before Franklin carried the *Courant*, however, a slave owned by Boston postmaster John Campbell, publisher of the *Boston News-Letter*, the first successful newspaper in the colonies, disseminated that paper. Written in the margin of a yellowed copy owned by abolitionist judge Samuel Sewall and now preserved at the New-York Historical Society is a note saying, "Mr. Campbell's negro gave me this, May 24, 1705."[15]

Crying the News takes juvenile street peddling seriously as work, and not just as an object of romance or reform. This approach seeks to liberate labor history from the tyranny of adult wage labor and to show how "penny capitalism"—the small-scale enterprises undertaken by working people to make ends meet—was integral to the welfare of their families, the socialization of their children, and the fortunes of a major industry.[16] This study is no antiquarian exercise. Independent contractors are still prevalent in the trade and even more common in the economy at large. Today, more than forty-two million "gig workers," accounting for one-third of the US workforce, are independent contractors. They are projected to exceed 40 percent by 2020, and their numbers are climbing worldwide.[17]

One way to shatter the "illusion of the near" is to see newsboy labor as part of a complex informal or "shadow" economy (also called a "hidden" or "dual" economy) closely related to formal economies and labor markets. The terms refer to the wide range of commercial exchanges that are usually overlooked by official measures of economic activity. They are modest labor-intensive enterprises that take place on a local, face-to-face basis, such as selling one's own fish or vegetables or taking in laundry or boarders. Such activities tend to be household-centered, but they are linked to big industries and imbedded in national, even international commodity and labor markets. Although the word *informal* connotes an unstable or fragile kind of trade, there is no more enduring form of economic activity.[18]

By conceptualizing child newswork as part of a shadow economy embedded in the history of capitalism and submitting it to a micro (street-level) and macro (industrywide) analysis, we begin to see it not just as a survival strategy of the poor but also as a tacit policy of the state to ease the effects of poverty. The lack of effective child labor laws is usually viewed as evidence of a weak state's inability to protect the welfare of its children, but the story of America's newsboys suggests that the absence of such legislation was a deliberate policy of granting children's labor to certain industries. The press was a major beneficiary of this policy. Newspapers emerge in this book as some of the most relentless exploiters of children's labor and innovative promoters of their welfare via newsboys' homes, schools, clubs, courts, and "republics." The children, meanwhile, show themselves to be active agents of their own lives: they formed unions, led strikes, and created a distinct youth subculture with their own argot, dress, rituals, and ethics.

Historians of childhood have done much to enlarge our understanding of the evolving experience of young people and diverse ideologies of childhood. In so doing they have illuminated the process of social change.[19] *Crying the News* seeks to contribute to this enterprise by highlighting working-class youth, who have been much less studied in the American context than middle-class youth,

ostensibly because they left fewer records. Girls, too, have suffered relative neglect in the field compared to boys, whose gender-specific experiences are sometimes passed off as representative of childhood in general. This book deals more
with boys than girls, but not because boys naturally dominated the trade. Rather,
it inquires into the origins and implications of this sexual division of labor and
asks how girls fared in a wageless masculine work culture that was often hostile
to their presence. It also sheds light on the political lives of children and their
role as consumers. Despite their hand-to-mouth existence, news sellers often
had more money and freedom than other children to buy the food and entertainment they liked, including the many novels, plays, and movies that featured
themselves as protagonists.

With regard to the history of journalism, we might ask if it really matters how
people get their news. What difference does it make whether it is printed on low-
grade paper and cried in the streets, converted into electromagnetic signals and
broadcast over airwaves, or captured in code and streamed over the internet?
I argue that it does matter, particularly to the people doing the crying, broad-
casting, or streaming, but also to those on the receiving end. Whatever form it
takes, mass communication is a social interaction. The means of interaction are
products of specific political and economic arrangements, which in turn shape
the communication itself.

A history of journalism, then, that focuses on distribution—on the commercial, technological, and human process by which newspapers got from press to
people—focuses on one of the most, not least, important aspects of their power
and influence. "Circulation is what makes a newspaper a newspaper," wrote sociologist Robert Park in 1923, "because its power is mainly based on the number
of people who read it." Writing at the height of the frenzied tabloid-style journalism immortalized in Ben Hecht and Charles MacArthur's play *The Front Page*,
Park argued that newspapers were not the rational creations of thinking men but
products of a remorseless struggle for existence in a changing environment. That
prodigious quantities of kids once played a key role in this struggle is hardly in-
cidental to understanding their lives and times and the industry in which they
worked. Indeed, as perennial sources of knowledge, income, recreation, and discipline, newspapers must be counted among the most formative institutions of
American childhood.[20]

In addition to weaving together the histories of labor, childhood, and journalism, *Crying the News* incorporates aural history, with its attention to news
crying as an aspect of the urban soundscape that blurs the boundaries between
the oral and the written; disability history, with its recognition of news peddling as a potentially disabling occupation that also accommodated people with
disabilities; and the histories of education and philanthropy, with its discussion
of newsboy schools, charities, and welfare work.

The chapters that follow examine the shared experience of five generations of newsboys —ten if we count by what one veteran hawker called "newsboy generations."[21] Part One, "Children of the Penny, 1833–1865," reveals how class politics underlay newsboys' fabled rise to prominence with the penny press, examines how they survived the financial panics of the 1850s huddled together on streets, in lodging houses, and aboard orphan trains, and shows how newsboys north and south, enslaved and free, met the crisis over slavery and influenced the outcome of the Civil War.

Part Two, "Children of the Breach, 1866–1899," places newsboys at the center of the social upheavals of the Gilded Age. It recovers their role in Reconstruction politics, the mass strikes of the 1870s and 1880s, the expansion of the railroads, and the settlement of the West. It analyzes the changes wrought in the trade by the arrival of Europe's yearning masses, the rise of giant word-hurling media corporations, and the interventions of reformers armed with flash cameras and the Social Gospel. Lastly, it tells how newsboys navigated the economic whirlpools of the 1890s and amplified the tumult of yellow journalism.

Part Three, "Children of the State, 1900–1940," investigates how newsboys in the early twentieth century became crucial measures of progress and targets of reform movements that pitted parents, publishers, and activists against one another. It shows how newsies answered competing calls to duty during the Great War, epitomized the crassness of the tabloid twenties, and were forever marked by the headlines and breadlines of the Great Depression. The conclusion sketches their home front service in World War II and the Cold War, tracks their fate in suburbia, and ponders their historical legacy in what may well be the waning days of paper-and-ink journalism.

If the day ever comes when newspapers exist only in archives, the memory of people such as Jemmy McCoy in Philadelphia, the little liar in Providence, Lillian Hadley in New York, and the ill-treated Chester in New Orleans will sink deeper into the sands of time. Let us now follow their footsteps and heed their voices while they can still be heard, as former newsboy Lawrence Ferlinghetti put it, "echoing down the alleys of history."[22]

PART ONE

CHILDREN OF THE PENNY, 1833–1865

1

Rising with the *Sun*

In September 1833, a handful of boys—including Bill Lovell, age 9; Bernard Flaherty, 10; Henry Lewis Gassert, 11; and Sam Messenger, age unknown—responded to a want ad placed among the theatrical notices in an odd little newspaper in New York City. "TO THE UNEMPLOYED," it read. "A number of steady men can find employment by vending this paper. A liberal discount is allowed to those who buy and sell again."[1] The advertisement's appearance in the second issue of the *Sun* was an open invitation to follow in Benjamin Franklin's proverbial footsteps and yet blaze a new occupational trail in a modern age of steam and scandal, panic and panaceas.

The ad did not bode well for the *Sun's* future, as its 23-year-old publisher, Benjamin Day, had priced copies of the paper at the ridiculously low sum of a penny and now sought to thrust it upon an indifferent public unaccustomed to buying newspapers in the street. Philadelphia's Jemmy McCoy notwithstanding, few carriers peddled papers on their rounds no matter how dramatic the news. Down-on-their-luck printers occasionally did so in the early republic, but they were denounced for stooping so low. *Pennsylvania Evening Post* editor Benjamin Towne, who became a Tory the minute redcoats occupied Philadelphia, exposed himself to further scorn in the 1780s when he printed and peddled occasional handbills entitled "All the News, for two coppers." Later, Richard Folwell, founder of the *Spirit of the Press* in Philadelphia, gained notoriety and a "scanty pittance" when he "hawked his paper about the streets himself." He died penniless and received a proper burial only after a collection was taken up at a local coffeehouse.[2]

Reputable printers, by contrast, required the steady patronage of subscribers, and they did not expect random pedestrians to part with hard coin for papers they could read and discuss in taverns and coffeehouses. Measuring just 8½ by 11 inches at a time when other newspapers were double or triple in size, the four-page *Sun* changed all that. What possessed Day to think he could succeed in offering his paper so cheaply and so boldly? And what drove Lovell, Flaherty, Gassert, Messenger, and others to head down to the *Sun's* office to investigate the offer? Ambition, perhaps. Curiosity, to be sure. But poverty and politics provide even better explanations for the rise of the penny press and America's newsboys.

Aside from playing an indispensable role in the development of popular journalism, this founding generation of street newsboys witnessed, and indeed hastened, major shifts in the way Americans came to know each other, earn their living, and govern their affairs. Newsboys stood at the crossroads, literally and figuratively, of a country undergoing revolutionary changes in communication, transportation, market capitalism, and mass democracy. Poised to pounce on the next main chance, these children offer incomparable insight into an industry and a nation on the move. Some knew it at the time. "The newsboy," declared a journalist in 1843, "is destined to fix the period which gave him birth, in the niche of history."[3]

Heralds of a Noisy World

Newsboys of the 1830s differed from their predecessors in fundamental ways. Carriers in the colonial era belonged to a very small fraternity. No more than forty newspapers existed on the continent before the Revolution. Most were four-page weeklies and none appeared more often than three times a week. Their circulation ranged from 600 (the minimum an editor needed to survive) to 2,000. Copies were mainly sent through the mail or picked up at print shops, some of which doubled as general stores. A news-hungry visitor to the offices of the *American Weekly Mercury* in eighteenth-century Philadelphia would find molasses by the barrel, rum, tea, peas, chocolates, patent medicines, snuff, spectacles, beaver hats, goose feathers, and "very good Pickled Sturgeon." Because newspapers were the most perishable products on the premises, printers also had them delivered to subscribers' homes or offices. Many printers delegated the job to their apprentices, who were also known as "printer's devils" due to their ink-smudged faces and mischievous tendencies. Delivering papers was just one of the many duties spelled out in their bonds of indenture. One boy's contract listed his responsibilities as "riding post, sawing wood, feeding pigs, and learning to print."[4]

Some printers had to look no further for an apprentice than to their own son or sibling. James Franklin held his brother Benjamin to a nine-year bond of indenture. Benjamin was integral to the short-lived success of James's *New England Courant*, especially after James was jailed for insulting officials and clergymen. Yet after enduring what he considered to be the "harsh and tyrannical treatment" of his brother for three years, the 17-year-old Benjamin ran off to seek his fortune. Labor shortages emboldened many apprentices to strike out on their own.

Rare is the edition of a colonial newspaper that did not carry advertisements offering rewards for the return of runaway apprentices.[5]

Apprenticeship was not the only labor system used in the distribution of colonial newspapers. News carrying was also casual paid employment, as indicated by an advertisement in the *New York Mercury* in 1761 for a "nice boy" to deliver papers to city patrons two hours every Monday morning. Ten years later the *Mercury* sought "a clever honest fellow" for similar work four hours every Monday. The increased hours reflected the *Mercury*'s rising circulation, but it was still a part-time job that likely supplemented rather than supplanted bound labor.[6]

Carriers generally distributed newspapers on foot in or near the towns where they were printed, while postriders delivered them farther afield, often traveling by horse, wagon, or coach. In addition to working for printers, both contracted directly with subscribers or served postmasters, delivering newspapers and mail, which consisted mainly of newspapers. Post boys were of such practical and symbolic importance that newspapers around the world took their names from them. London, Dublin, New York, Boston, New Haven, and Wilmington, North Carolina, all spawned daily or weekly *Post-Boys*. The *American Weekly Mercury* adorned its head with a woodcut of its namesake, accompanied by a postrider and a fleet of ships (Figure 1.1). German-language newspapers in Pennsylvania also relied on *Herumtragers* (round carriers) or *Zeitungstragers* (news carriers) in

Figure 1.1. Like many colonial newspapers, the *American Weekly Mercury*, founded in Philadelphia in 1719, highlighted the speed of communication in its name and nameplate. Courtesy American Antiquarian Society.

the 1760s and issued annual appeals on their behalf, a custom that did not exist in Germany.[7]

These printed appeals, or carrier's addresses, proved to be a lasting legacy to modern newsboys. The first such address dates back to January 1, 1720, when Aquilla Rose, a 25-year-old printer and aspiring poet in Philadelphia, gave the "boys" who distributed the *American Weekly Mercury* a broadside for their subscribers. New Year's Day, not Christmas, was the traditional day of gift giving in the colonies, and Rose reasonably expected that the carriers' gesture would be rewarded. Assuming the voice of a carrier, he wrote:

> Full fifty Times have roul'd their Changes on,
> And all the Year's Transactions now are done;
> Full fifty Times I've trod, with eager Haste,
> To bring you weekly News of all Things past.
> Some grateful Thing is due for such a Task,
> Tho' Modesty itself forbids to ask;
> A Silver Thought, express'd in ill-shap'd Ore,
> Is all I wish; nor would I ask for more.[8]

In setting down these lines, Rose invented an enduring journalistic tradition. Having grown up in England, he had seen bell ringers, lamplighters, and bakers' lads distribute similar sheets on New Year's Day, but the custom had not yet spread to news carriers or crossed the Atlantic until Rose took the initiative. Americans would compose thousands of these annuals over the next three hundred years. They were the world's first greeting cards and, like those cards, are rarely acclaimed for their literary merit. Yet their authors have included such venerable wordsmiths as Longfellow, Whittier, Hawthorne, and Poe. Most carriers' addresses begin with a deferential greeting, recap the year's events in rhyme, and close with a subtle—or not so subtle—appeal for a tip. Many doubled as editorials offering stinging criticism of policies and policymakers.[9]

Although most carriers' addresses refer to their bearers as boys—carrier boys, post boys, printers' boys, and newsboys—the word *boy* did not necessarily signify a child; it could refer to an unmarried male in his twenties or a servant of any age. At the same time, many addresses specifically identify carriers as "lads," "shavers," or "striplings" and describe them as "small," "bashful," or "callow." An 1805 address issued by the *Farmer's Cabinet* in Amherst, New Hampshire, begins, "Though in my teens, unskill'd in learned lore," which is a rare early reference to the teen years as a distinct stage of life. Other addresses, by contrast, were expressly written for "news-men" and allude to their "sage experience." It is difficult to speculate about the average age of news carriers; half the population was under 16, and children and adults often worked in the same trades. As in most agrarian societies, children took on adult responsibilities early. They were expected to contribute to the family's support by age 7, enter college at 13, and begin military training at 16. Youth was defined more by one's social and economic dependence than by years lived.[10]

Women also carried papers in the early republic, as is evident in the carrier's address of the *American Telegraphic* in Newfield, Connecticut, of 1799:

> To you, generous patrons, see Polly appear,
> To congratulate you on the birth of the year.
> A song—a mixture of humor and folly,
> At a season like this, is expected from Polly.
> For carriers must sing, whether female or male,
> On New Year's Day, or their purses will fail.[11]

The fact that some addresses were "humbly adress'd to the Gentlemen and Ladies" suggests that women, including Benjamin's sister Jane Franklin, were also readers of newspapers and potential tippers of carriers (Figure 1.2). An ever-increasing majority of white women in the colonies and early republic could read. Judging from the content of newspapers—including the letters, poems, and articles addressing domestic as well as political concerns—they likely read the copies that came into their homes. Nevertheless, they and Polly were interlopers in the affairs of men. In producing, distributing, and even reading newspapers, women entered an implicitly masculine public sphere.[12]

In England, women, not boys or men, dominated the news trade in the early 1600s. Known as "mercurie girls," they hawked unlicensed ballads, broadsheets, and news books through the streets of London. Bookseller Nathaniel Butter reputedly hired them for their buxomness and lung power. By 1750 women controlled a good share of the London news market, which consisted of five dailies, five weeklies, and several thrice-weeklies with a combined circulation of 100,000. It was still a risky business, and two veterans, Mrs. Nutt and Mrs. Dodd, were regularly jailed well into their seventies for selling proscribed papers.[13]

In addition to newspapers, colonial printers issued a barrage of fiery tracts, pamphlets, and broadsides as they felt increasingly aggrieved by imperial power. Boys were particularly useful for distributing seditious material because, as minors, they would not incur the full wrath of the Crown if caught. Thus they were notoriously cheeky: if questioned about the source of their stock, carriers typically replied that it "dropped from the moon."[14]

The pamphlet war became a shooting war in April 1775 when American militia fought British soldiers at Lexington and Concord. Among those who spread the word was Israel Bissell, a 23-year-old postrider from Watertown, Massachusetts, who rode for four days and nights, covering the 345 miles to

Figure 1.2. A printer's devil makes his rounds, from "Verses from the Year 1790," a carrier's address of the *New-York Weekly Museum.* Courtesy American Antiquarian Society.

Philadelphia, crying, "To arms, to arms, the war has begun." But the war of words continued. Newspaper publishers divided into patriot and loyalist camps; there was no middle ground. Some seventy-five newspapers appeared and disappeared in this period. All were plagued by paper shortages, unreliable sources, and erratic distribution. Some introduced midweek supplements or "extraordinaries" to provide late-arriving news and advertisements.[15]

The Revolution hastened the development of independent methods of distributing newspapers in the colonies. Before the war most subscribers received copies via the Royal Post, which was expensive and liable to ban any publication that was critical of colonial authorities. The *Boston Gazette* expressed widespread fears in 1774 when it said, "Our News-Papers, those necessary and important Alarms in Time of public Danger, may be rendered of little Consequence for want of Circulation." Chafing under such "oppressive dictation," the Continental Congress instituted a Constitutional Post—a free mail service not intended to generate tax revenues—in 1775, and named Benjamin

Franklin the postmaster general. The British system disintegrated in the face of this competition and its postriders were discharged for lack of funds. In their stead galloped patriotic American post boys, whose work was deemed so vital that in 1777 the Continental Congress exempted them from military service. Postmaster General Richard Bache, Franklin's successor and son-in-law, failed to establish an effective postal network during the war, however, forcing army commanders George Washington and Nathanael Greene to set up their own teams of postriders to keep communication lines open.[16]

As the war dragged on, some newspaper subscribers offset the unreliability of the post by forming "clubs," "companies," or "classes" and distributing their papers cooperatively. Their children often helped out. In 1780 Isaiah Thomas's brother in Lancaster, Massachusetts, secured fifty-two subscribers to the *Massachusetts Spy*, which they took turns fetching in Worcester, sixteen miles away. When it was his turn he mounted his 8-year-old son Alexander on horseback and sent him off on the two-day journey.[17]

By 1800 the number of newspapers in America rose to 235, of which 24 were dailies. Ten years later the total topped 350 and by 1820 had reached 512. This proliferation prompted observers to dub America "a nation of newspaper readers."[18] English traveler John Lambert marveled at the cheapness and availability of American newspapers, noting that "there is scarcely a poor owner of a miserable log hut, who lives on the border of the stage road, but has a newspaper left at his door." Lambert's visit in 1808 coincided with the expanded use of stagecoaches, yet readers who were on the stage line sometimes had to satisfy themselves with papers that agreed with the politics of their coachman. One of the drivers he encountered was a Federalist who refused to cater to the Democratic-Republicans on his route. "No sooner did he blow his horn than up scampered men, women, and children to the coach, eagerly begging for their favourite paper," said Lambert. "If they wanted a democratic one, they must either take a federalist, or go without. He had a few of the others with him, but he never would deliver them if he could avoid it."[19]

The War of 1812 gave carriers and postriders an opportunity to demonstrate that their courage matched that of their revolutionary forebears. Fought in part over British impressment of American sailors and seizure of American ships, this second war for independence reminded Americans that commerce was the source of enterprise, progress, and liberty. News carriers embodied these attributes, especially those who worked in the two theaters of war along the Great Lakes and the Atlantic seaboard. One carrier remembered for his stalwart service was Paul Drinkwater, who delivered the *Buffalo Gazette* to American settlers in Upper Canada. The area received no mail until he fixed up a route from "a little village called Buffalo" to the head of Lake Ontario, a sixty-mile loop, which he traveled weekly from January to June 1812. Rumors of war had filtered back and forth across the border, but real news was scarce until Drinkwater appeared, wading through snow almost to his knees. He stood "six feet four in his stockings" and was "slender out of all proportions," recalled Eber Howe, whose father was one of the settlers. "His advent and passage through the country was an era of much moment to boys and girls." Drinkwater subsisted on hardtack and cider, which he carried with him, and offerings of metheglin—Welsh liquor made from boiled honey and herbs.[20]

Hostilities curtailed Drinkwater's delivery career but enhanced that of Charles O'Conor, who distributed his father's paper, the *Military Monitor*, as an 8-year-old in New York throughout the war. He walked the length of Manhattan to Harlem every Saturday and then rowed a skiff down the Hudson River to Hoboken, New Jersey. O'Conor felt himself a true patriot carrying the anti-British weekly. "Sometimes the publication was delayed," he recalled, "and to get through my circuit of delivery would take all night; but I boldly went up doorsteps, chucking papers under the doors; plunged into areas and down through alleyways, fearless of the police and every body, for my bundle of papers was a perfect safeguard, as good to me as the aegis and crested helmet to Hector."[21]

In a rare depiction of a post boy at work, Philadelphia artist John Lewis Krimmel showed the arrival of a coach and carrier in rural Pennsylvania as a truly democratic moment in his 1814 painting *Village Tavern* (Plate 1). The boy no sooner crosses the sunlit threshold carrying the locked leather mail pouch over his shoulder and a basket of bundled papers under his arm than he is beckoned to a table to share tidings with the locals. The tavern–post office is bustling with villagers, including convivial artisans, a pleading wife and child, and two engrossed newspaper readers, young and old. Past editions hang on rods beside war prints and an 1814 almanac. The hubbub fails to stir the dog lying under the table, but a Quaker gentleman standing by the bar is clearly uneasy about the free flow of ale and information.[22]

Historians often observe that communication was slow in early America because news traveled only as fast as a person could walk, ride, or row. They point out that it took postriders two days to travel from New York to Philadelphia, a week to go from New York to Boston, and a fortnight to reach the southern states—even longer in winter, when roads were bad.[23] But speed is relative; Americans in the early republic were more often thrilled by the arrival of carriers than disappointed by their delay. John Greenleaf Whittier captured the sheer wonder of a world glimpsed through weeks-old newspapers in his poem "Snow-Bound: A Winter Idyll":

> At last the floundering carrier bore
> The village paper to our door. . . .
> We felt the stir of hall and street,
> The pulse of life that round us beat.[24]

These forgotten intermediaries of journalism played an indispensable role in that world-shaking explosion of letters, literacy, and democracy known as the "print revolution." As both producers and products of this revolution, these seemingly marginal figures helped generate the political tumult that transformed British subjects into American citizens. Their successors would go on to define the nature of that citizenship.[25]

Conditions Fair

Newsboys' reincarnation in New York was no chance occurrence. With a population of more than 200,000, "Gotham" was the largest city in North America. Its year-round harbor had long made it a bustling port, but the opening of the Erie Canal in 1825 transformed it into a continental center of trade, finance, and manufacture. Goods flowed up and down the Hudson River to the Great Lakes and Mississippi Valley, and back and forth across the Atlantic. Called the "Empire City," New York thrived on the exchange of information as well as commodities. It was home to thirty-six weekly newspapers and eleven dailies with an average circulation of 1,700 copies.[26]

Day's appeal to the unemployed made sense, as unemployment was a recurring condition in urban America, especially among those who had not yet reached or were already past their prime. Street peddling offered many families their only means of subsistence. Men, women, and children had hawked a variety of goods and services on the streets of New York before 1833; they sold hot corn, fresh eels, and hominy. They cut wood, sharpened knives, and swept chimneys. But they didn't cry papers. At 6¢ a copy, the leading journals were too expensive to find casual buyers. Dubbed "blanket sheets," these papers unfolded to a four-foot width and required a library table or countinghouse desk to be read. With a blend of commercial news and high-flown opinion, they held little appeal for the working classes, for whom 6¢ represented a half day's wage, or the equivalent of a pound of sugar or block of cheese. Nor was their business sought, as most publishers considered it undignified to pander to new subscribers. One in New York boasted that his great circulation of 2,000 had come unsolicited. Another in Brooklyn, when asked why he waited twenty years to send boys out to hawk his paper, replied with a scowl, "Do you think that I would disgrace the Star by selling it in the streets?" In Boston, the cofounder of the semiweekly *Traveller* heard about Day's scheme and gave some papers to boys to peddle in the South End. His partner happened upon them and was so embarrassed that he bought up their entire stock.[27]

The *Sun* was not the first cheap daily in the country, just the first to succeed. Dr. Christopher Columbus Conwell started the *Cent* in Philadelphia in 1830, but it disappeared without a trace. James Gordon Bennett, an "ill looking, squinting" Scotsman with a caustic editorial style, issued the *New York Globe* in 1832 at 2¢ a copy, but it was undercapitalized and lasted only a month. And on New Year's Day 1833, Dr. Horatio David Sheppard founded the 2¢ *Morning Post* in New York with the backing of a young printer from New Hampshire named Horace Greeley. Its debut coincided with a blizzard that kept peddlers and pedestrians off the streets. Sheppard cut the price to a penny, but the *Post* never recovered.[28]

Unlike these earlier experiments in penny journalism, Day's paper was greeted by good weather and a burgeoning labor movement. A member of the New York Typographical Association, Day worked as a compositor for several of the blanket sheets, whose shameless fawning to the upper classes he and his associates abhorred. Their discontent found expression in the New York Workingmen's Party, a coalition of mechanics and small masters known as "Workies" who felt that many new entrepreneurs were reducing independent tradesmen to groveling wage earners and thus destroying the Republic. To promote their views, Day helped found the *Daily Sentinel* in February 1830. It soon changed hands when the party collapsed, but its successor and several weeklies in the state continued to agitate on behalf of workingmen.[29]

Day rebounded from the party's collapse by opening a small print shop on the ground floor of a three-story brick building at 222 William Street. Business was good until the summer of 1832, when an outbreak of cholera killed 3,500 New Yorkers—mostly slum dwellers—and set off an exodus among the well-to-do. Some of the city's poor earned money hawking "cholera extras" issued by the *Courier and Enquirer*, but the epidemic caused a business slump that idled many and nearly wiped Day out. To get his press working again and realize his dream of a radical daily for the masses, Day took a chance on the *Sun*, giving it the motto "It shines for All." The *Sun* focused on local news—not just business affairs, but crime reports and theater reviews, all written with such verve that a "sort of *gamin* sprightliness characterized the paper."[30]

Day's intended readers were wage earners and mechanics like himself. To reach them, he offered subscriptions at a low $3 per year, payable up front. The sixpenny dailies charged $10 a year, payable after six months; by trusting their subscribers—extending them credit, as it were—some of these papers carried arrears totaling $10,000 to $50,000. Day broke with custom by operating on a cash basis. The only problem was that profits on the penny sheet looked to be so low that men could not be persuaded to hawk them. Desperate to disseminate his first issues, Day turned to the city's most abundant resource: its children. Almost half of New Yorkers were under 20, and boys between 5 and 15—the age group of most of his recruits—numbered 19,000, about 10 percent of the population. Scores had been orphaned by the epidemic and were already hustling or begging in the streets.[31]

Day engaged the venturesome Lovell, the affable Flaherty, the energetic Gassert, the capable Messenger, and a half dozen other boys at $2 a week. Born in England in 1824, Lovell had been in the United States for less than a year. He and Flaherty, a native of Cork, Ireland, were among the 540,000 immigrants, more than 40 percent of them Irish, who came to the United States in the 1830s. Flaherty's father operated a grocery, or tavern, on the Bowery, and his mother ran a boardinghouse. In addition to hustling papers, he picked up odd jobs and small roles at a local theater.[32]

Gassert was born in Kurnbach, Germany, in 1822. His father was an artist and scholar who settled on the Lower East Side of Manhattan, an area then patched with cornfields. "It was the custom in those days to subscribe to the newspaper, which were delivered by storekeepers and others," recalled the 80-year-old Gassert in 1902. "The custom started by me of running about with an armful of papers taken from a nearby book store and shouting aloud the leading features of the news of the day was taken up by the other boys in their neighborhood and gradually extended until newsboys were common enough."[33]

Little is known about Sam Messenger except that he was old enough to be listed as a "papercarrier" in city directories, sold 700 copies of the *Sun* a day in the Fulton Market district, and organized routes and carriers that proved to be quite lucrative.[34]

Day assigned districts to all the boys, which he instructed them not to desert until they had sold 125 copies. Otherwise, they had complete control of their areas; they could stroll for customers, which was Lovell and Flaherty's approach, or build subscription routes, which was Messenger's method. Or, like Gassert, they could do both. Day offered additional copies at 9¢ a dozen, which many boys requested after just a few hours. At first he bought back unsold copies, but he stopped when he learned that the boys were returning papers they had rented out. These first newsboys worked for a combination of wages and profits and exercised a kind of artisanal autonomy. The "active boys" in the squad earned $5 a week, which compared well to the incomes of others in the industry; reporters earned $3 a week and journeymen printers $7.[35]

Adults soon saw the potential for profit. Joshua Southwick, a shoemaker and part-time carrier, signed up 600 subscribers on a 25 percent commission, which netted him $8.65 a week, more than twice what he had earned distributing one of the blanket sheets. He then bought copies of the *Sun* outright at ⅔¢ per copy, increasing his take to $13.50 a week. Messenger bought out Southwick's interest in 1835, thereby establishing the principle of routes as property. The *Sun*'s daily circulation rapidly reached 10,000, and routes sold for $30 to $60. By 1840 it would rely on the services of a hundred carriers of all ages.[36]

Some historians insist that the *Sun*'s prime innovation was cash payments, not newsboys, since it sold most of its print run to subscribers through dealers and carriers rather than to pedestrians via hawkers. In 1835 the *Sun* reported a daily circulation of 19,000, with 16,000 copies (84 percent) delivered to subscribers, 2,000 (11 percent) sold on the streets, and the remaining 1,000 (5 percent) mailed out of town. Yet this breakdown obscures the fact that many dealers relied on boys to service their routes and hawk on the side.[37]

Hawkers also were indispensable in getting new ventures off the ground. In 1834 Mordecai Noah hired nine carriers at $2.50 a week to launch the *Evening Star* in New York, though it had no more than fifty subscribers. Account books show that the boys sold 677 copies the first day of publication, 258 copies the next day, about 75 on the third day, and between 20 and 30 copies thereafter. Street sales dwindled, but not before stimulating subscriptions; the peddlers' piercing cries begat the carriers' quiet labors. If the peddlers received undue credit over the years, it began early on because of their utility as icons of enterprise and symbols of speculation—prime virtues in this age of "Go Ahead."[38]

These virtues are exhibited in a painting from the late 1830s that documents the newsboy's arrival as an economic actor (Plate 2). It also calls attention to the proliferation of print that was changing the meaning of commerce from a series of discrete, personal, morally tinged relationships to a pervasive, impersonal form of commodity exchange. The painting, *7½ Bowery, N.Y.C.*, depicts an orange-colored four-story flatiron building decked with giant business signs and ornamented with clocks and hats visible from afar. Below, the corner of Bowery and Division Street bustles with shoppers and merchants; soft goods are displayed under the awning, a victualer tends her stand, and a barefoot newsboy offers the *Sun* to a passing soldier. Road traffic consists of delivery wagons, a packed omnibus, and a fire pump pulled by a brigade of firefighters. The streets are immaculate except for an outlaw pig—swine were useful trash-eaters that officials were nevertheless trying to ban. The picture, probably by resident sign painter W. Riley, represents commerce as a traditional face-to-face activity that was ascending to new heights with the profusion of texts in public space.[39]

Integral to this cultural and commercial boom, penny papers created work for hundreds of boys and wealth for those who excelled, such as Mark Maguire, the first "King of the Newsboys." Born in 1814 on a ship bound from Ireland to America, Maguire began carrying papers in New York in 1831 at age 17. He counted President Andrew Jackson and senators Henry Clay, Daniel Webster, John Calhoun, and Thomas Hart Benton among his customers. Maguire established routes and pitches all over the city and, by his own Bunyonesque telling, employed five hundred boys, including Flaherty and his pals Edward Walsh, John Jourdan, and Joseph Dowling, to work them. Young vagrants overran the streets of New York in this era of aqueduct building. Maguire gave boys papers to hawk even when they were "bursted up," or broke. He offered them straight pay or a share of the profits, and let them settle up at night. Maguire was a businessman, not a philanthropist, but his easy terms provided a kind of social welfare that paid dividends. Walsh matured into a police captain, Jourdan a police superintendent, and Dowling a police court justice. Maguire prospered as well and became so popular that his ward thought of running him for alderman. Instead, he became a sportswriter for the *Sun* and opened several roadhouses, operated a baseball ground and half-mile trotting track up on 106th Street, and raced his own horses, including a swift gray gelding named after himself.[40]

Another wide-awake lad, 18-year-old Sinclair Tousey, arrived in New York in 1833 and rose to become a giant in the trade. Born in New Haven, Connecticut, in 1815 and orphaned at age 11, Tousey left school to take a job at a cotton mill in Dutchess County. He stayed for two years, flaying his fingers on the machinery and filling his lungs with cotton dust. From age 13 to 16 he bound himself out to a farmer, who paid him 12¢ for three years' toil. Hitting the road again, he supported himself as a farm hand, carpenter, and grocer. In 1833 he transported a load of quinces to market in Manhattan and decided to stay. He supported himself by delivering Noah's *Star*, a Whig paper, the *Jeffersonian*, a Democratic daily, and American reprints of English quarterlies. Between rounds he collected payments from advertisers and letters from privately owned mailboxes. Two New York dailies hired him to drum up subscriptions in New Haven and Philadelphia, but he failed and returned to New York in 1835 to become, at age 20, one of the first carriers of James Gordon Bennett's *Morning Herald*. Tousey left the news trade the next year. He dabbled in patent medicines and published the *Louisville Daily Times*, the first penny paper west of the Alleghenies. By 1840 he had settled in upstate New York to farm and raise a family, never imagining he would later return to Manhattan and found a company that would dominate newspaper distribution throughout North America.[41]

Two distinct methods of newspaper circulation emerged at this time. The London Plan, patterned after British dailies, relied on independent distributors, be they hawkers, carriers, or dealers. Day and Bennett favored this method because it ensured them a regular cash flow and freed them from the chore of keeping accounts and collecting from subscribers. It also gave vendors incentive to hustle, since their earnings grew with their sales. Other penny publishers shunned middlemen and developed their own delivery systems. The *Philadelphia Ledger*, founded in 1836 by three of Day's old workie associates, did not trust that its message would reach the right people through random street sales. So they developed what became known as the Philadelphia Plan. The partners divided the city into districts, hired young men to solicit subscriptions, and oversaw door-to-door delivery. The owners, not the carriers, retained possession of the subscription lists and allowed no papers to be sold to independent dealers or hawkers until an hour after the last carrier left on his route. Street sales accounted for a fraction of the *Ledger*'s circulation, which soared beyond all expectations.[42]

Engines of Change

While class politics and financial need were the twin engines that drove the penny press, many new inventions helped publishers meet the demand for their product. The hand-cranked flatbed press that Day used to put out his first issue was not far removed from the one Benjamin Franklin had operated a century earlier. It was capable of producing two hundred copies an hour. Day acquired a double-cylinder press that could turn out two thousand copies per hour, and in 1835 powered it with steam. At the same time, newly improved machines for reducing rags to pulp slashed paper prices and stimulated another street trade: rag picking.[43]

Publishers and peddlers also profited from the mass production of eyeglasses and the invention of kerosene lamps and "phosphorized pine sticks," or matches. The lamps doubled the reading day, while the matches provided income and convenience for the poor. "The cheap matches and the cheap newspapers were sold in every street," recalled one editor. "Families before this, had borrowed coals of fire and newspapers of their richer neighbors. With the reduced prices, each family had a pride in keeping its own match-box, and in taking its favorite daily journal."[44]

Newsboys and match sellers also served as useful political operatives. They tended to align with either Whig or Democratic dailies and were always available to help bust up a meeting or tear down a candidate's posters. One faction of radical Democrats acquired their name from a popular brand of matches, Loco Focos, after rivals extinguished their lamps during a meeting, only to see them continue by match light. Artists tapped the boys' propaganda potential. In 1836 Whig printer Henry R. Robinson issued a lithograph depicting Whigs and Loco-focos as scuffling street urchins. (Figure 1.3). Entitled *A Gone Case*, it shows several newsboys and a black-faced chimney sweep standing before the Custom House, a traditional Democratic stronghold, watching a valiant Whig carrier defeat a ragged, sniveling matchboy. "I'll loco poke you," declares the Whig as he punches the boy in the nose. "Oh! you d——d Whiggy," cries the matchboy. "I told him he had better not fight," says one of the three cowering Loco-foco ragamuffins. They are carrying the Democratic dailies *New Era* and the *Evening Post* and a lecture by Scottish-born labor radical and abolitionist Fanny Wright. "Does Fanny know you're out?" taunts the chimney sweep. Meanwhile, four confident, neatly dressed Whig newsboys, each holding party papers (the *Transcript*,

Figure 1.3. Newsboys, match sellers, and chimney sweeps quickly entered the vernacular of political humor in Jacksonian America. *A Gone Case. A Scene in Wall-street.* Printed and published by Henry R. Robinson, 1836. Lithograph on wove paper, 26.5 cm × 36.5 cm, Library of Congress, Prints and Photographs Division, Washington, DC. LC-USZ62-5869.

Gazette, Courier, and *Evening Star*), urge on their comrade: "Hurrah! the Whigs; that's the Ticket," "I'll be blow'd if that aint a smasher," and "Pitch into the loafer." Thus did America's newsboys enter the political fray.[45]

Finally, railroads and telegraphs, the greatest technological marvels of the age, enabled news and newspapers to travel far beyond their home cities and keep boys busy throughout the region. A few weeks after its first issue, the *Herald* was available, via agents, in Newark and Paterson, New Jersey, as well as Providence, Philadelphia, Poughkeepsie, Hudson, Albany, and Troy. Twelve-year-old Charles Crocker, the eldest of six children, was sole agent of the penny *Transcript* in Troy, a privilege secured from an Albany newsagent for $200 on credit. He started selling papers in 1834 after his father went bankrupt and headed west for a fresh start. Crocker built the circulation to 700 copies within six months, selling or delivering each one himself. He paid 62½¢ per hundred, earning an average daily profit of $2.63, more than enough to support his family. When his father summoned them to a farm in Indiana two years later, Crocker had paid off the loan and saved $400. His precocious grasp of commerce found ready application on the frontier. He acquired an iron forge in Indiana, mined gold and opened a dry goods store in California, established a string of banks, and became a founding partner of the Central Pacific Railroad, the western link of the trans-continental railroad.[46]

Trains were also important sites of retail exchange, which produced specialists known as "news butchers." As with the street hawkers, several boys claim to have been the first. One was William Henry Williams, who sold on board Cornelius Vanderbilt's New York and Harlem Railroad, established in 1832. Legend holds that Vanderbilt wanted some remuneration for the privilege, but Williams said all he could offer was service to the passengers. As a compromise, Vanderbilt required him to carry a bucket and a dipper and offer passengers free drinks of water. Williams went on to make millions buying up railroad newsstands in depots all across the country and consolidating them into the Union News Company.[47]

Another pioneer train boy, Harry Ashby, worked the Hudson River Road between New York and Albany in the mid-1840s. He was reputedly "educated in all the branches of a New York hoodlum's trade" when he persuaded Charles Bash, the line's first conductor, to let him sell on board. Ashby took a thousand copies of the *Herald* and the *Tribune* on his first trip and sold every one. "He thought he was a rich man, and when he returned to New York he bought a new suit of clothes and went on quite a spree." As a result, he missed the next trip and his friend "Lucky" Baldwin, a peddler of secondhand books, took over the business and his place in retail history. Ashby became a colonel in the Union Army and proprietor of the Metropolitan Hotel in Chicago, while Baldwin went on to renown in horse racing circles.[48]

A fourth candidate for the title of America's first news butcher is Billy Skelly, who sold his wares on the New York & Erie at an unspecified "early date." Chartered in 1831 and finished in 1851, the railroad ran from the Hudson River port of Piermont, twenty miles north of Manhattan, to Dunkirk, a hamlet on the banks of Lake Erie. Skelly secured a monopoly on the 144-mile line. Exclusive rights to sell on such well-traveled commuter routes went as high as $5,000 per year and paid big dividends. Train boys marked up their papers 50 percent and routinely sold 2,000 copies a day. Skelly would end up selling his rights to the New York & Erie in 1864 at a "thumping big profit" to Williams, who merged with Tousey's new firm, the American News Company.[49]

Blacks and girls had a harder time entering the trade. African Americans were sometimes allowed to vend on cars in the South. A Negro brakeman in Petersburg, Virginia, did it as a sideline in 1857 and retailed pickled fish at several stations. Girls, on the other hand, could serve passengers only if they passed as boys. In 1858 a "good looking" boy peddled papers on the line between Cairo and Centralia, Illinois, until she was discovered to be a woman in her twenties. "She traveled with other boys, played billiards, smoked segars, swore and drank whiskey as easily and naturally as a newsboy might be expected to do," reported the *Cairo Times*. Nevertheless, her career came to an abrupt end.[50]

No less immediate was the impact of telegraphy on newsboys, who profited even before inventor Samuel F. B. Morse unveiled it at the US Supreme Court on May 24, 1844, tapping out the immortal words "What hath God wrought." Several weeks earlier, with wires not yet in place between Baltimore and the capital, Morse had his associate in Annapolis Junction send him a message from rail passengers who were delegates to the Whig convention that had nominated Henry Clay for president. When they arrived in Washington seventy-five minutes later they were astonished to hear newsboys crying extras containing the news. The magazine *Yankee Doodle* predicted that Morse's talking wires would soon render newspapers and vendors redundant. Instead, they multiplied.[51]

Moon Tales

Beyond political scoops, penny papers vied for readers with sensational tales of murder, scandal, and scientific discovery. One of the most lucrative stories for newsboys was the murder trial of Matthias the Prophet, aka Robert Matthews, a charismatic New York City street preacher of Scottish ancestry who dressed in astrological robes, wore a long beard, and claimed to be Jesus Christ. Matthias won converts among prominent New Yorkers, one of whom signed over his Westchester County estate to serve as a commune, where nude rituals and "spiritual marriage" were practiced. Their benefactor's sudden death led to the murder charge. Day hired the *Courier and Enquirer*'s best writer, a Scotsman named Richard Adams Locke, to secretly supply him with copy, which he published on the front page of the *Sun* and repackaged in pamphlet form after Mathias's acquittal. Newsboys sold more than 6,000 copies of the 3¢ pamphlet in one day, probably earning them a penny apiece and a lifelong fondness for fakirs.[52]

Their next windfall was a series of articles on the lunar explorations of the world's most prominent astronomer, Sir John Herschel of England. The *Sun*, with Locke now in the editor's chair, nearly doubled its sales in August when it ran the reports, purportedly based on a supplement to the *Edinburgh Journal of Science*, detailing Herschel's telescopic discovery of life on the moon. In precise, luminous prose Herschel described seeing oceans, beaches, trees, and such astonishing creatures as tiny bison, single-horned blue goats, and giant beavers that walked upright. The most amazing finding came in the fourth installment, where Herschel reported spotting a new species of furry, winged bat-like humans that dwelled in cliffs, worshipped at a golden temple, and fornicated in public.

Newsboys made a killing with these stories. They sold all the copies they could get their hands on, often at fancy prices. During the entire week of publication they had to fight their way through the crowds that besieged the *Sun*'s offices from dawn to midnight. On the day of the last installment, Day had the whole series ready in a pamphlet. Newsboys quickly sold out the entire edition of 20,000 copies. They also peddled 25¢ woodcuts depicting the creatures described in the story. Only in mid-September, when a delegation of Yale professors set out to inspect the supplement and a ladies' club in Springfield, Massachusetts, started raising money to send missionaries to the moon, did Locke reveal the series to be a hoax, or rather a satire of pseudoscientific writing. Locke's admission outraged rival publishers, especially Bennett, but did not dampen the public's appetite for the story; the Bowery Theatre soon mounted an "extravaganza" entitled *Moonshine, or Lunar Discoveries*. Nor did readers punish the *Sun* for its splendid deception, as this was an age of hoaxes and humbug exemplified by the rise of showman Phineas T. Barnum. His incredible exhibits encouraged a kind of cultural democracy in which truth rested not with authorities but with the majority. The *Sun*'s circulation continued to climb and by 1836 claimed average daily sales of 27,000 copies, greater than any other newspaper in the world and more than all the New York blanket sheets combined. The *Sun*'s distribution zones grew, too, and could not be purchased for less than $600. The best routes rose in value to $2,000 each and were bought up by young men who founded wholesale news agencies and reading emporiums that bore names such as Parthenon and Athenaeum, linking them to the birthplace of democracy.[53]

Not to be outdone, Bennett unleashed the *Herald*'s already scurrilous brand of journalism. It reported crime and scandal, exposed Wall Street chicaneries, and ridiculed the blanket sheets at every opportunity: "Shake down your petticoats, ye old ladies of the Times—the very boys in the streets are laughing at you." The six-penny papers retaliated in kind, denouncing the *Herald* as a vile sheet that trafficked in "Obscenity," "Blasphemy," and "Humbug." Then the rough stuff began. Bennett suffered a public beating, caning, and horsewhipping. His enemies also pressured Congress to prohibit the bulk shipment of newspapers through the mail, another distribution method he relied upon.[54]

Through it all, the *Herald*'s circulation grew. Stories about crimes of passion and prostitution not only enthralled readers but also exposed the foibles of the upper classes and the biases of the legal system. The most infamous of these stories followed the 1836 murder of prostitute Helen Jewett and the acquittal of the young clerk accused of the crime. This running story spiked the *Herald*'s circulation by 10,000 to 15,000 copies a day and won the *Sun* 1,300 new subscribers. Newspapers across the country covered the story for months, enabling newsboys to sell scarce issues for a shilling apiece (12½¢) and lithographs of the principals. "And in this manner," noted one editor, "the children of many poor people are kept from starvation—nay, find profitable employment."[55]

New York newsboys became ever more aggressive as publishers started issuing "extraordinary" editions, also known as extras or "extrees," to beat competitors. "The first thing you hear in the morning is the newsboy's cry, and the last thing at night is the importunity of the Chronicle carrier," noted the *Spirit of the Times* in 1837. "They waylay you as you go down Wall-street, up Broadway, into the Theatre, on board or away from the steamboat, and even as you go into church. One lives, while in New York, in a complete rustle of newspapers." News criers created a similar sensation in Buffalo, where they cried the *Western Star*, a penny paper that featured a crude woodcut of a newsboy blowing a horn, with the legend "Be it our object to please." New Orleans's first newsboys, by contrast, conducted their business quietly from stands or benches. Yet shortly did their "peals of violent cachination ring out upon the morning air."[56]

Not all urbanites welcomed this assault on their senses. Former New York City mayor Philip Hone felt that the children should be seen and not heard. He railed against the penny papers, which he said "are hawked about the streets by a gang of troublesome, ragged boys, and in which scandal is retailed to all who delight in it, at that moderate price." Gassert was one of those boys, and he never forgot how the local constable "would chase me over the hills for presuming to yell the leading news of the day in the streets." Authorities coined a term for such troublemakers: "juvenile delinquents."[57]

The Politics of Panic

New York's thundering presses suddenly grew quiet in May 1837 when a financial panic pitched the nation into a six-year depression. Nine out of ten factories in America closed down within six months, unemployment hovered between 30 and 50 percent, and the budding trade union movement collapsed. Bread riots broke out in New York, where "mere boys" helped break into warehouses and dump hundreds of barrels of flour to protest "monopolies."[58] The *Sun* had denounced those monopolies and was pilloried as an instigator of the violence. Advertising revenue evaporated, and all of New York's thirty-five penny papers failed except the *Sun* and *Herald*. Day was so shaken that he sold the *Sun* to his brother-in-law, Moses Beach, for $40,000, which he later said was "the silliest thing I ever did in my life."[59]

While the depression quieted many a newsboy, it had serious repercussions for other young workers as well. Manufacturers reorganized production so that low-skill, low-wage operatives—often women and children—could turn out goods. But their availability as a labor source weakened the collective power of artisans and reduced apprenticeship to a mere euphemism for child labor. Apprentices had little opportunity to learn the dwindling mysteries of their craft and even less chance to attain journeyman status, let alone the status of master. Many apprentices lived apart from their masters, who naturally wielded less authority over them, contributing to a rise in "street lounging" and youth gangs. Clerics and freethinkers alike decried their behavior. "The great school of juvenile vice is the STREET," declared the Rev. James W. Alexander in 1838. "Here the urchin, while he 'knuckles down at taw' (shoots marbles), learns the vulgar oath, or the putrid obscenity." The much-maligned Fanny Wright agreed that children picked up "vicious habits" on the street, but she recognized that many poor families could not get by without their earnings. This dilemma would trouble child labor reformers for years to come.[60]

Devastating though it was, the depression prompted legal protections for the nation's most vulnerable children and workers. In the 1838 case of *Ex parte Crouse*, a Pennsylvania court outlined the doctrine of *parens patriae*, which held that the state possessed ultimate parental authority and could remove abused or disorderly children over their parents' objections. State and private agencies founded reformatories, almshouses, asylums, penitentiaries, and police forces during these years. In 1842, in *Commonwealth v. Hunt*, a Massachusetts court upheld the right to strike, ruling that unions were not criminal conspiracies and that workers could withhold their labor if they wished. States in New England also enacted the first legislation to make school attendance mandatory and restrict the employment of children under 12 to ten hours a day in many industries.[61]

Schooling was sporadic for most children in America, including newsboys, but literacy rates were high compared to other countries, partly because of the emphasis placed on Bible reading. Between 60 and 80 percent of white adults in the northern states claimed some command of the written word. Newspapers were instigators as well as the beneficiaries of mass literacy. "Among newspapers, the penny press is the same as common schools among seminaries of education," declared Walt Whitman, now Loco-foco editor of the 1¢ *Aurora*, in 1842. "They carry light and knowledge in among those who most need it."[62]

Fellow Democrat Francis Edmonds examined the press's impact in his widely exhibited but now lost painting of 1838, *The Penny Paper*. Also called *The Newspaper Boy*, it depicted "a large room thronged with men, women, and children, into the midst of whom a ragged boy has entered to sell his Sunday morning papers." Edmonds considered it to be his most ambitious effort, as did critic Henry Tuckerman. "Almost every subject delineated, even to the old shoe that hangs upon the wall, is a legitimate imitation," he said. Edmonds extolled the virtues of ordinary citizens in his paintings. His newsboy conveyed the sense of shared interest that, the depression notwithstanding, could unite a disparate people scattered over a vast continent. He intuited what political scientist

Benedict Anderson would later theorize: that only the rise of print capitalism could create an "imagined community" called a nation.[63]

There were limits to this community, as blacks, Indians, and women were excluded from full participation in public affairs. But they founded—and distributed—their own newspapers to build communities and assert their rights. *Freedom's Journal*, the nation's first African American newspaper, started in New York in 1827; the *Cherokee Phoenix and Indian Advocate* began the following year in New Echota, Georgia; Fanny Wright's "infidel paper," the *Free Enquiry*, moved from New Harmony, Indiana, to New York in 1829; and William Lloyd Garrison's abolitionist weekly, the *Liberator*, debuted in Boston in 1831. "Reform is commotion," Garrison liked to say, and the *Liberator* was his chief means of raising it. Abolitionist papers circulated through the mail and via carriers, but black seamen also smuggled them into southern states by stitching them inside the lining of their coats.[64]

The *Liberator's* most famous carrier was Lewis Howard Latimer, the son of a fugitive slave from Virginia whose cause Garrison championed in 1842 when the man's owner tried to reclaim him in Boston. The case led to passage of a law forbidding the use of Massachusetts's jails for detaining runaways. Born in Chelsea, Massachusetts, in 1848, Latimer was the youngest of four children. He attended grammar school and did well enough to skip a grade, but his schooling ended at age 10 when he started working in his father's barbershop, helping out on his wallpaper-hanging jobs, and distributing the *Liberator*. Latimer joined the navy at age 16 and served in the Civil War. Afterward he worked as an assistant to Alexander Graham Bell and Thomas Edison, inventing the carbon filament used in Edison's lightbulb.[65]

C'est la Guerre

The conduct and character of newsboys became of paramount concern in 1839 when four penny dailies—the *Sun, Dispatch, Whig,* and *Tattler* (founded by Day)—threatened to cut off all the regular boys because of their alleged "profanity, ribaldry, and indecency." The boys rioted in protest, leading to several "amusing arrests." The *Herald* rushed to the defense of this "very numerous body of youth," which it said comprised about 130 to 150 "young fellows, from six years of age to sixteen." The *Herald* admitted that the newsboys were "partly reprobates," but it said they had gained respectability much faster than even the penny press itself. "There may be some bad chaps among them, as there is among every class of persons; but we doubt very much whether the proprietors, editors, reporters, and *employes* of the penny press do not contain a much larger percentage of pure wickedness than the whole class of newsboys."[66]

The *Herald*'s praise was partially motivated by self-interest, as its boys had recently sold in one morning 4,000 copies of an extra describing the capture of the slave ship *Amistad*. Yet the paper stressed only their selfless devotion to family. "Many of these boys—indeed most of them, are the solace and support of widowed mothers, bereaved sisters, and other helpless relations," said the *Herald*, estimating that their dependents numbered at least five hundred. "The attempt, therefore, of the penny press to deprive these industrious little fellows of a living in these hard times, is the most revolting species of monopoly and arrogance that we remember to have heard of." Their work was their salvation, insisted the *Herald*: "Like all American boys of their age, they are lively, active, industrious, witty and independent. They rise in the morning at 3 or 4 o'clock, dispose of their wares before 3 o'clock in the afternoon, and while other boys are rioting about the theatres, and screaming 'fire' at the top of their lungs, the newsboys are quietly retiring to rest, in order to be ready to rise before the next morning's sun." The *Herald* reported that some of these boys had amassed savings of between $100 and $1,000, which attested to their "rational habits of decency and good behavior. To say, therefore, that this business of the newsboys is a 'prolific source of vice,' is exactly the reverse of the truth."[67]

Bennett later published figures showing how this "laughable little campaign" or "la Petite Guerre" resulted in a net loss of around 14,000 copies per day for the crusading dailies and a net gain of 2,500 copies for the *Herald*. He predicted that his competitors' advertising revenue would suffer, and suggested that the newsboys would be well within their rights to boycott the Saturday weeklies issued by each of these newspapers. The editorial closed by asking that the "larger newsboys read this article to the smaller" and together disprove the slanderous remarks of the penny press by their good behavior: "Let the newsboys stick to right principles—behave decently—make no riot—and they will have a moral as well as a personal and pecuniary triumph. Hurrah! for the little rascals of newsboys! Like all sinners, they will become saints by persecution. Wash your hands and faces, my chaps, and go ahead—to virtue and victory."[68] Victory of a sort was achieved. The penny *Whig* spent itself out the following year, the *Dispatch* and *Tattler* survived a few more years by merging, and the chastened *Sun* rebounded after declaring a truce with its newsboys.

This would not be the end of it. The physical assaults, editorial sniping, social ostracism, and political bushwhacking were preliminary skirmishes in the Great Moral War of 1840, in which an alliance of publishers, politicians, merchants, and ministers sought to drive the *Herald* and its boys out of business. They urged carriers, advertisers, and readers to boycott the paper and withhold custom from any vendor who carried the *Herald*. The Rev. David Hale, a prominent Whig reformer and co-owner of the *Journal of Commerce*, called newsboys an "intoler-able nuisance," and proposed that the Common Council license them. Bennett issued a "memorial" from the newsboys blasting Hale and the Wall Street papers as the real nuisances. It was signed by "Pat Macbeth, chairman of the newsboys," and "Little Pickle, secretary," but it dripped with the kind of invective that came from Bennett's pen. Newsboys gathered at the *Herald* office on Ann Street and petitioned city officials to grant the *Courier and Enquirer* and *Journal of Commerce* special licenses "to retail bombast and folly" and "humbug and hypocrisy," and suggested that the license numbers be stamped on "their d——d impudent foreheads."[69]

City officials stayed out of the dispute, but the insults flew back and forth. The Wall Street papers lambasted Bennett as a "loathsome and leprous slan-derer and libeler," and charged that he had once been a lowly peddler in the streets of Glasgow. Bennett embraced the slur as he would peerage. "Yes, I have been a pedler, and am still a pedler of the thoughts, and feelings, and high im-aginings of the past and present ages," he said. "I peddle my wares as Homer did his—as Shakespeare did his—as every great intellectual and mighty pedler of the past did—and when I shall have finished my peddling in this world, I trust I shall be permitted to peddle in a better and happier region for ever and ever." It was a brilliant comeback, enabling Bennett to identify in one breath with the most towering figures in Western literature and the lowliest urchins of the metropolis.[70]

Although both sides blew smoke over principle and propriety, the Moral War was, at bottom, a circulation war. It raged for several months and caused the *Herald* and its 150 newsboys to lose about a third of their average daily sales of 17,000 copies, and about half that over the next two years, as well as much adver-tising revenue.[71] Bennett felt that the war was fueled by jealousy of his business success and bigotry toward his Catholicism rather than his penchant for vitriol. He nevertheless curbed his editorial tongue, and hostilities subsided. He soon announced the purchase of a splendid granite-and-brick building on the corner of Fulton and Nassau Streets, which would have—in addition to a spacious press room, paper vaults, and offices—an apartment reserved for newsmen and newsboys. It was intended, he said, to "keep the young rascals out of the street, and thus preserve the quiet of the neighborhood." The blankets adjusted as well; one by one they cut their prices, spiced up their columns, and secured the serv-ices of newsboys.[72]

The eccentric idealist Horace Greeley now took center stage to redefine the tone and politics of penny journalism. In 1841, at age 30, he founded the *New York Tribune* as a "respectable" cheap paper. He had previously started the *New-Yorker*, an unpromising literary digest, and edited two campaign papers, the

Jeffersonian and the *Log Cabin*, which helped elect the Whig politician William Seward governor of New York and William Henry Harrison US president in the groundbreaking "Hard Cider and Log Cabin" campaign of 1840, the first in which both parties used campaign buttons, blankets, and tea sets to appeal to voters. Greeley wanted to publish a low-priced Whig paper to compete with the Democratic dailies and prove that cheap did not mean nasty. With $3,000 in capital, a third of it borrowed, he issued the first number of the *Tribune* on April 10. His associates David Peck Rhoades, future president of the New-York News Company, and George Jones, later cofounder of the *New York Times*, and probably Greeley himself, in his homespun clothes and a wispy beard, peddled the first edition (Figure 1.4). Yet they mainly distributed it via the London Plan, selling discounted copies to newsboys such as 16-year-old John Hoey from Ireland.[73]

The most enterprising boys picked up papers from several newspaper offices and used City Hall Park as "a kind of Newspaper Exchange." But the *Herald* and

Figure 1.4. A young Horace Greeley flogs his own paper, the *New York Tribune* (founded 1841), n.d. New York Public Library, Humanities and Social Sciences Library/Print Collection, Miriam and Ira D. Wallach Division of Art, Prints and Photographs. ID 1247921.

the *Sun*, once sworn enemies, closed ranks against Greeley and these feisty free agents. Bennett and Beach refused to sell papers to any distributor, large or small, who handled the *Tribune*. Bennett tried to gain control of the *Herald*'s routes, but his carriers united and forced him to back down. Beach bribed some *Tribune* carriers and strong-armed those he could not buy off. He had *Sun* newsboys drive *Tribune* hawkers from their corners. Greeley responded in kind, and petty fighting followed in which Beach himself had to rescue a "youthful emissary." He accused Greeley of instigating the violence. "It is *false*," replied Greeley, "that any boys were sent, 'backed by men to fight it out,' until our boy had first been severely beaten with a cowhide by the minions of Beach. We then took measures, as a matter of course, to protect him." The public sided with Greeley, said his friend and biographer James Parton, "and this was *one* reason of the Tribune's speedy and striking success."* Ironically, when Jones and Henry Raymond founded the *New York Times* ten years later, Greeley responded to it just as Bennett and Beach had done to the *Tribune*; he told his carriers that they would forfeit all rights to carry the *Tribune* if they got up routes for the new paper. The *Times* survived nonetheless.[74]

The newsboy had clearly arrived, his voice and vices the subject of petty jests and mounting fears. There he stood at the point of sale, retailing news of the world's most historic and trivial events. His very existence was a testament to the swirling changes around him. He benefited from the web of turnpikes, canals, and rail lines that speeded and cheapened the flow of goods, people, and information across the country. He dispensed newspapers conveyed from afar and enjoyed mobility himself in an ever-expanding search for new opportunities and escape from old oppressions. Part patriot, part pest, the newsboy slew distance and ignorance with his legs, peace and quiet with his mouth, transforming political debates, neighborhood gossip, and the soundscape of America's cities.

Penny newspapers were one of the first mass-produced commodities in this newly industrializing nation, and they contained notices and advertisements that expanded the market for other goods and services. These papers made information affordable and fun, sometimes wickedly so, and fostered a sense of unity among a diverse people. Written and edited with street sales in mind, the

---

* Circulation disputes continued to flare up. In 1847 the *Tribune* challenged the *Herald* to submit to an independent audit, with the loser donating $100 to the city's two orphan asylums. Auditors found the *Herald*'s circulation was 28,946 and the *Tribune*'s 28,195. Greeley paid up. Irked anew twelve years later, he offered to donate $1,000 to charity if Bennett could prove his circulation exceeded the *Tribune*'s. Bennett bettered him again by spurning the challenge and calling Greeley an inveterate gambler who would one day be found matching pennies with the newsboys. See John Handy, "Praise from an Old Reader," *New York Tribune*, Aug. 30, 1915, 6.

penny press wallowed in stories of murder, adultery, and other topics formerly deemed unworthy of serious journals. Newsboys took this trend one step— and one octave—further by sensationalizing the sensational with their aggressive appeals. They created the market for these newspapers with their lusty voices, and made commonplace the practice of owning rather than borrowing the paper one read. By 1840 newsboys in New Orleans had even begun to influence the content of their papers by appealing to publishers to stop printing poetry, which they said depressed sales. They warned that if they saw capital letters beginning all the lines of an article, they knew it to be poetry, and would take only half the usual number of papers. Poetry in the columns fell off by 10 percent.[75]

Newsboys were also products of the social and political ferment of the era. Competition for readers led to the nation's first circulation wars, in which newsboys served as shock troops, bloodying their fists on behalf of publishers. While supposedly independent, penny newspapers represented the interests of Democrats, Whigs, or Workies, which made newsboys into enduring political actors and symbols.

But what became of the hundreds of boys who made up this cohort of news peddlers? The only ones who can be traced are those few who gained notoriety as adults and liked to remind people of how they got their start. The *Sun's* first four newsboys can be included among them. Lured to Australia by rumors of gold, Lovell "struck it rich" and, by his own telling, repeated his success in California. He returned to New York around 1860, bought the noted trotting mare American Girl, and became a prominent turfman. Flaherty (Figure 1.5) parlayed his talent for blarney and jig dancing into a theatrical career. Taking the stage name Barney Williams, he specialized in Irish dialect humor and became a great favorite at Barnum's American Museum, the National Theatre, and playhouses around the world. His wife, meanwhile, gained fame playing Dick, the Newsboy.[76] Gassert apprenticed as a cigar maker and then he, too, joined the gold rush to California, where he discovered there was more money to be made supplying miners with newspapers than panning for gold. Capitalizing on his New York connections, he wholesaled eastern papers for 25¢ apiece and opened news shops in San Francisco and Sacramento, where week-old papers fetched up to 50¢ and fresh ones sold for $1 each. On returning to New York, he went into the tobacco importing business.[77] Messenger became a rich livery-stable keeper, and Hoey took a job fetching papers in a pony cart for the Adams Express Company, eventually becoming its president.[78]

These boys lived lives of merit and accomplishment, no doubt aided by a dollop of self-invention. They saw their opportunities and took them, excelling

Figure 1.5. Bernard Flaherty, aka Barney Williams (1823–1876), the *New York Sun's* first newsboy. © National Portrait Gallery, London. By (Octavius) Charles Watkins, albumen print, arched top, 1850s, 7⅝ in. × 5⅞ in. (193 mm × 151 mm). Purchased, 2001. NPG P947.

in business, sports, entertainment, journalism, law, and science. There is no evidence that peddling papers had anything to do with their later successes, but the narrative of humble beginnings and unlimited opportunity served their purposes and the ascendant bourgeois orthodoxy.

Lovell, Flaherty, Gassert, Messenger, Southwick, Maguire, Walsh, Jourdan, Dowling, Tousey, Crocker, Williams, Ashby, Skelly, Latimer, Macbeth, Little Pickle, and John Hoey were agents as well as subjects of change, shaped by the same historical forces they unleashed on the world. That is why by 1843, ten years after its fretful appearance, the *Sun* alone, four times bigger than the original, required a hundred regular carriers in New York and Brooklyn, a hundred more in other cities and towns, and about two hundred local hawkers. The newsboy had doubtlessly emerged as "the type of the time—an incarnation of the spirit of the day," according to James C. Neal, the Philadelphia writer who predicted that the newsboy would "fix the period which gave him birth, in the niche of history." The newsboy, he explained, personified the new capitalist order whereby man—"commercial man, speculating man, financial man"—no longer rallied with sword and shield under gaudy banners to kill his neighbor but instead gathered round newspapers, "anxious to ascertain what his neighbor is about, that he may turn him and his doings to profitable account." "Our clarion now," he declared, "is the shrill voice of the newsboy, that modern Minerva, who leaped full blown from the o'erfraught head of journalism."[79]

The only question that remained was where this voice would lead.

2

Voice of Young America

"To see a News Boy in all his glory, you must get up an hour before day break," advised the *New York Sunday Morning Atlas* in 1840. "Direct your steps towards one of those profitable establishments called a cash paper. As you near it you will hear the hum of many voices, mixed with a deep bass rattling sound, to which they play a sort of falsetto. You come to the office and you are suddenly in the midst of a troop of Lilliputians. A number of them are gazing anxiously down a cellar from which a considerable quantity of steam ascends, through which steam appear several twinkling lights like stars in a fog."[1]

So begins one of the first journalistic descents into the world of the newsboy. It was a noisy, subterranean world shrouded in vapor, cloaked with romance, and now blurred by the mists of time. Our guide remains a mystery as well, perhaps one of the paper's three proprietors or an anonymous penny-a-liner who labored under flickering gaslight on the margins of fame and penury. Yet his reporting enables us to see and hear with astonishing clarity how a new occupational group came of age in "Young America" and became its principal symbol, embodying the exuberance and possibility of a republic that had survived its revolutionary infancy and was about to enter the next glorious stage of its national life.

In the seven years since Flaherty, Messenger, and Gassert first flogged the *Sun* on the streets of New York, newsboys had cropped up in most American cities and formed one of the nation's first urban youth subcultures. Their castoff clothing, unintelligible slang, and adolescent swagger alerted all who saw and heard them that they were lads who knew the tricks of their trade and the ways of the world. "Nature seems to have contemplated a peculiar race of juveniles expressly to become Newsboys!" mused one natural philosopher.[2]

To make good on his promise to "show the News Boy up in all his peculiarities," the *Atlas* man had to go no farther than his own office. As the newspaper's powerful presses rattled and belched in the cellar, he took in the scene. He saw several boys "indulging in a snooze" and noted that when the weather was fine "youthful snorers" could be heard occupying all the empty boxes and casks nearby. He listened to one group critiquing the latest stage shows and watched others "clubbing" their money to buy the coming edition in bulk. Copies bound for the mail had already been shipped off, as had those supplied to adult dealers for local subscribers. Only the boys remained to be served.[3]

A man shouldering several quires of newspapers suddenly emerged from the steamy cellar, followed by a helper. As they stepped into an office, a shout rang out and in rushed the boys who had been watching from atop the stairs. The theater critics followed and then the snoozers, rubbing their eyes and fumbling for a "ready rhino" (coin) in their pockets. "A hundred or more boys are assembled and each is struggling and striving to get served first, as though his life depended upon it. This is considered an important point . . . [as] the earliest sellers reap the richest harvest. The advantage of clubbing is now seen. One boy calls for one, two or three hundred papers—he is served and immediately retires, followed by his clique of creditors, to whom he at once discharges his debt by handing over twenty five or fifty papers as it may be, according to the sum with which each has invested." As soon as they got their papers, the boys ran off toward the piers and markets, filling the air with their cries: "'Ere's the Sunday Morning Atlas!" Many of these "little merchants" invested their whole capital in papers "and do not dream of taking breakfast till they have disposed of a good portion of their stock in trade."[4]

In describing this weekly ritual, the *Atlas* writer highlighted many important aspects of the trade. The invention of steam presses in the 1830s had made newspapers one of the first modern mass-produced commodities, yet their distribution required a host of Old World hawkers and carriers, mostly children. He conveyed the scale of this trade when he noted that the *Atlas*, which had a circulation of 3,500, or about 20 percent of the output of the city's five Sunday papers, relied on more than a hundred newsboys.[5] He documented the all-male makeup of the labor force and the masculine work culture untroubled by fighting, gambling, or sleeping out. He captured the sporadic nature of the work, requiring long periods of idleness followed by sudden bursts of activity. He touched on the industry's obsession with speed, which was fast becoming a moral imperative in the cosmology of modern journalism. And he attested to the relative autonomy of the boys and the boisterous blend of competition and cooperation that characterized their work.

The Sunday *Atlas* offered stimulating reading on a day reserved for church-going or quiet contemplation of scripture. It relied mainly on street sales generated by boys whose cries disturbed worshippers and provoked protests. The *Atlas* defended them, noting that they diffused useful knowledge to tens of thousands and acquired "an early independence of feeling." Theirs was honest labor, insisted the writer, and far preferable to idleness. Their "harmless noise" was a blessing, he said, as "the boys of 1840 [are] more quiet and better behaved than those of 1834." He attributed their bad reputations to their chief enemies, the credit papers, whose denunciations, he said, stemmed from their inability to compete against the cash papers.[6]

In case these words failed to convince, the *Atlas* ran an illustration by young Benson Lossing of a barefoot and threadbare *Atlas* newsboy counting his change (Figure 2.1). An accompanying poem suggested that he might one day become president. In article, illustration, and verse, the *Atlas*'s message was clear: to silence the newsboy was to halt the coming man.[7]

Figure 2.1. "He buys his goods with ready cash, / Then through the street he hies, / And crying constantly the while, / Makes money by his cries. . . . As yet on life's draftboard domain, / He's but a short time resident, / His enterprise, with all his faults / May make him one day President." Benson Lossing, "The News Boy." *Atlas Picture Gallery . . . 1840,* Jan. 24, 1841, 1. Courtesy American Antiquarian Society.

As allies of the new cash papers and enemies of the old credit papers, newsboys in Young America were embroiled in all the major conflicts of their day, becoming mixed metaphors for enterprise and annoyance. One's opinion of their work and character depended on one's opinion of the papers they sold—which was largely a matter of politics, since the cash papers were primarily Democratic while the credit papers were Whig. Even newspapers that claimed to be independent usually favored one party over another. Editors collaborated with party leaders to set policy, devise strategy, and enforce discipline. Their hawkers and carriers provided the arm, leg, and lung power necessary to trumpet certain candidates or causes and throttle others, specifically temperance, nativism, westward expansion, and war with Mexico. Newsboys' cultural influence stemmed from their frequent depiction in—and distribution of—the many novel publications of the period, including "mammoth" fiction weeklies, illustrated collections of city cries, didactic religious tracts, scandalous "flash" papers, and leather-bound annuals or "giftbooks." They simultaneously gained fame as sovereigns of the stage—irrepressible patrons of cheap theaters and familiar characters in melodramas and minstrel shows. They were, in short, part of the political vernacular of Young America.[8]

The term "Young America" embraced a diverse constituency, including working-class rowdies who felt that they, like the nation, could not submit to the dictates of their elders or "betters"; middle-class artists and writers who vowed to produce national works that could stand beside Europe's best; members of antislavery, anti-immigrant, and anti-liquor societies who strove to strengthen the moral fiber of the people; and Democrats who sought to expand democracy (and, paradoxically, slavery) by declaring war on Mexico in 1846 and electing General Zachary Taylor president in 1852. They were Young Americans all.[9]

References to children permeated the political rhetoric of the day. Images of newsboys cropped up in lithographs, paintings, plays, and periodicals. To be sure, other figures vied for recognition as emblems of the age. Andrew Jackson personified the common man. So, too, did frontiersman Davy Crockett, as well as purely fictional characters such as Uncle Sam, Brother Jonathan, and Major Jack Downing—all products of the humorists' pen. Newsboys differed from these "crafty democratic rascal-heroes" in that they represented America's urban future, not its agrarian past. Moreover, they articulated the self-interested commercial values of the rising generation, not the public-spiritedness of the founders.[10]

But who were these boys, really? Where did they come from? Where did they go at night? What were the codes and customs they lived by? And did their proliferation augur well or ill for the republic? To answer these questions, America's most celebrated writers, artists, and entertainers produced a carnival of works that promised, like the *Atlas*, "to expose the true character of the newsboy."[11]

What their efforts reveal is that the newsboy was himself a product of popular culture and mass politics whose insistent adolescent voice struck the keynote of the era.

The Buzzing Crowd

America at midcentury was distinguished by one indisputable demographic fact: children outnumbered adults. According to the 1850 US Census, 52 percent of the nation's population was under the age of 19; 41 percent was under 15. Newsboys made up a small but growing proportion of this cohort. Their numbers rose right along with the number and circulation of America's newspapers. Nationally, 116 dailies sprang up in the 1840s. Another 133 were founded over the next decade, culminating in 387 in 1860.[12] This expansion was most apparent in New York, whose fourteen to eighteen dailies emitted 60,000 copies by 1840 and rose to 300,000 by 1860. Several popular weeklies boosted this output: the *New York Ledger* (founded in 1851), *Frank Leslie's Illustrated Newspaper* (1855), and *Harper's Weekly* (1856). Altogether, counting weeklies and semiweeklies, Gotham's 104 newspapers claimed (and probably attained) a yearly circulation of 78 million, followed by Boston, whose 113 papers produced 54 million copies, and Philadelphia, whose 51 papers turned out 40 million.[13]

These publications circulated via news agencies and the mail but also by newsboys. In 1842 New York's weekly *Flash* estimated there were "some three hundred in the city, perhaps more." The *Herald* alone claimed 150 newsboys and carriers of all ages. In 1852 the *Clipper* counted "thousands of men, women, and children engaged in the retail newspaper trade in New York." Of these, between 500 and 600 were boys. The New York State Census of 1855 offered the least reliable head count, listing newsboys (probably adults only) among the 388 people engaged in "miscellaneous occupations."[14]

Lower Manhattan, particularly the maze of streets around City Hall Park, was the hub of journalistic enterprise in America. Park Row, Frankfort, Fulton, Nassau, and Ann Streets constituted what one writer called "newsboydom." The area was home not just to the city's daily papers but also to about eighty weeklies and monthlies, and virtually all the city's newspaper distribution agencies. Ann Street also housed print shops, type foundries, and booksellers. The neighborhood was part of the densely populated Sixth Ward, which swelled with poor families, over a third of whom were Irish. German immigrants made up 20 percent of the contiguous wards that stretched from the Bowery to the East River. By 1860 more than half of the city's population was foreign born. Their children, who "seemed to spring, mushroom fashion, out of the very ground," provided an ample labor pool for the burgeoning news trade.[15] A visiting Scotsman noted the dominance of the Irish: "Ragged, barefoot, and pertinacious, they are to be found in the streets from dawn till past dark, crying out 'The glorious news of the fall of Delhi!' The last 'terrible explosion on the Ohio—one hundred lives lost!' or the last 'Attempted assassination in a lager beer cellar!' They recall the memories of the old country by their garb, appearance, and accent, if not by their profession."[16]

Newsboys ranged in age from 6 to 16, but in 1842 the strolling newspaper columnist Lydia Maria Child found "a little ragged urchin, about four years old, with a heap of newspapers, 'more big as he could carry,' under his little arm, and another clenched in his small, red fist. The sweet voice of childhood was prematurely cracked into shrillness, by screaming street cries, at the top of his lungs: and he looked blue, cold, and disconsolate. May the angels guard him!" Child's 1831 child-rearing manual, A Mother's Book, had helped replace the Puritan idea of infant depravity with the notion of childhood innocence. She saw the pathetic "urchin" as a reminder of society's need to protect children while preparing them for a less-than-innocent world. Benjamin Day's Brother Jonathan contended, however, that "the best kind of private charity is employment."[17]

The Clipper also spotted newsboys as young as 5 and 6, and admitted that some were probably sent out by drunken parents to earn money for liquor. But it insisted that most were from decent and deserving families, and urged readers to support these "children of tender years." Joseph C. Neal took issue with this euphemism. "He has no tender years," he wrote of the newsboy, because of his early "collision with the world." The Boston Herald agreed, saying, "They are boys in years and stature, but men in precocious mind; Yorkshiremen, or Scotchmen, or Yankees. They owe nothing to common schools; everything to the rough school of the world."[18]

Years were not the only measure of a newsboy's age. The Atlas referred to their prepubescent falsetto voices. George D. Strong of New York's Knickerbocker Magazine categorized them by size, saying that the typical newsboy appeared "on the stage of action at the height of three-feet-six" and exited it upon reaching four feet three. Genre paintings suggest that some boys peddled papers well past the five-foot mark and into their mid-teens, but not much longer. Puberty, which then occurred around age 16 for boys, generally ended their vending careers. As Leslie's pointed out, "An old newsboy is a rarity not yet exhibited at Barnum's." Newsboys stayed in the trade anywhere from a few months to a few years. Afterward, "they are apprenticed out and their places supplied by new recruits," said the Atlas, or they "purchase a route and become regular carriers." Girls, women, and blacks soon joined their ranks as itinerant peddlers or tenders of plank-and-barrel stands (Plate 3).[19]

According to the Flash, newsboys came in two grades: speculators and worker bees. The speculators were erstwhile newsboys who had risen to become wholesale dealers or agents. They took large quantities of the papers on commission from the printing office and employed boys to vend them. Also known as "Chief Newsboys," "Foremen," and "small Capitalists," these middlemen helped newspapers reach boys throughout the city. Most speculators were "tight Irish lads," said the *Flash*, which lavished them with praise, as they were essential to the paper's distribution: "These young men have adopted news vending as a business, and being generally honest, acute and industrious, they make more money out of most of the cash papers than either editor or proprietor. Some of them are said to have laid up a competence, and may retire from the world when other youths of the same age are just preparing to enter it."[20]

Among those immortalized by the *Flash* were Jem G., Martin McG., Patrick W., Ned H., Santa Anna, and Dutch. Santa Anna, who probably shared some trait with the Mexican general who laid siege to the Alamo in 1836, was a "large and skilful dealer who knows the city like a book, and for a bantam cock, is a very expert boxer." Dutch belonged to a respectable family and could live without work, but he preferred "an honorable livelihood gained by his own efforts."[21]

Journalist George G. Foster, a radical Democrat, profiled several city newsdealers, depicting them in terms both flattering and derisive. He caught up with newsboy "king" Mark Maguire and his cronies at Butter-cake Dick's, an all-night cellar eatery on Spruce Street, just below the *Tribune* office. It was a newsboy hangout where 3¢ bought a cup of coffee and the heavy buttered biscuit that was the house specialty, and whose proprietor, Richard Marshall, was himself a "retired member of the craft." The boys "raised a muss" when printers and reporters sought admission, but they eventually gave in. Maguire's party that night included the hard-drinking, smoking, and swearing Mike Madden, who specialized in Sunday papers and commanded two hundred to three hundred newsboys; Pat Lyons, a "rollicking, aisy-going" family man who was as famously short and stout as his wife was tall and thin; and Tommy Ryan, Maguire's affable "prime minister," who bragged that all his sons would grow up to be Whigs. Financially secure, these dealers aspired to respectability. To attain it they held a newsboys' ball at Tammany Hall in 1853. Profiling them was a way to recognize local boys who had made good but also to poke fun at those whose social reach exceeded their grasp.[22]

Far outnumbering the speculators were the worker bees. "Some of them are the children of poor parents, forced into their occupation by privation and suffering, and they gain more by it on an average than grown men can by manual labor," said the *Flash*. The *Atlas* agreed that many boarded at home and took their profits there, but others picked up lodgings, about sixpence per night, and took their meals at cheap eating houses. Some received weekly wages, and about a dozen lived communally in a house rented for them by their dealer. Among those singled out by the *Flash* were "Dennis Antree, Peter Anderson, Bill Heals, and Kelly, at the corner of Chatham and Orange streets. Not less worthy of commendation are Butter-keg-Dick, Denny Mehan, and Tom McGinnis, who sells for Santa Anna. Charles Barton goes to Newburgh and other towns on the Hudson, and would effect his object if the devil stood in the way. Wee Johnnie, the Brothers Burns and Mat Mullen deserve our word. Pigeon, Lame Gainer and Larry O'Gaff are entitled to a niche in the temple of Fame." This honor roll affirms the Irish dominance of the trade and the *Flash*'s shameless use of flattery to keep vendors loyal.[23]

New York's worker bees bumbled their sheets wherever customers could be found. They swarmed around City Hall, the courthouse, and other public buildings. So many "vagabond newsboys and peddlers" lined the halls of the post office and filled it with their "vile and disgraceful language" in the winter of 1840 that a Masonic newspaper recommended they all be horsewhipped, an idea no doubt appalling to Lydia Maria Child. In 1843 a veritable "army of newsboys" daily beset the neighborhood around St. Paul's Chapel on Broadway. Presuming they were a passing fad, the *New Mirror* asked, "What is to become of them when the glut is over, and the people are surfeited with cheap and trashy publications?" Newsboys also serviced Wall Street and the surrounding mercantile blocks, whose sidewalks were choked with vendors—not just itinerants but also established dry-goods dealers and auction house proprietors whose goods and negotiations regularly spilled out of doors. Parks and squares were another good place to find customers. So were the omnibus stops along Broadway; boys even sold on the scarlet-and-yellow buses and sleighs, as well as in the cars of the steam-powered Harlem Railroad, which was not without risks. Newsboys who dared cry their papers in the cars on Sundays were locked up, while those who fell beneath the wheels, like young Patrick Hogan in 1843, lost their lives.[24]

Still, they persisted, and sales increased every year. Their customers were not just merchants but workers as well, a fact often remarked on by visitors. "Newspapers are seen everywhere in the hands of the labouring as well as the wealthy classes," noted another Scotsman in 1854. "In the streets, at the doors of hotels, and in railway-cars, boys are seen selling them in considerable numbers. Nobody ever seems to grudge buying a paper." Sales were so steady that some boys were able to secure credit from Wall Street banks. "What security can you offer?" asked a cautious director of a grubby applicant no older than 12. "He knows me," said the newsboy, pointing to the teller. The 25¢ loan was approved.[25]

Newsboys did not just ply their trade outdoors but boldly entered hotels, restaurants, and offices. On a visit in 1852–53, the English artist Eyre Crowe noted that the New York newsboy, unlike his London counterpart, was not content to "din with ear-shrieking sounds the latest news from the pavement; he simply made his way straight into drawing-room or hotel parlor with his batch of '*Eralds and Tribunes*,' which once handed to the purchasers, he went off, as a capitalist brat of eight years of age." Crowe's traveling companion, William Thackeray, found them to be "amazing, confident urchins with the most infectious grins."[26]

As these travelers' accounts suggest, tourism took off in the 1850s and stimulated newsboys' earnings. The opening of the glass-domed Crystal Palace exhibition hall near present-day Bryant Park in the summer of 1853 attracted six thousand visitors a day until destroyed by fire in 1858.[27]

Newsboys were thickest around New York's waterfront. The city had four ferry piers serving Brooklyn, Staten Island, and Jersey City, and six steam lines to Hartford, New Haven, Providence, Philadelphia, and Albany. Dockhands and shipbuilders also proved to be steady customers. The Brooklyn Navy Yard, busy producing sail and steam ships, employed so many immigrants that a nativist newspaper scoffed that the *Irish Volunteer* and *Boston Pilot* were "the most popular papers the newsboys can carry into this *Irish Navy Yard* in America."[28]

Newsboys also sold on board ships and ferries, often securing passage by slipping a paper to a crewman. Some boys proffered books, magazines, and fresh fruit as well, carrying enough stock under their arms "to load a commondray horse." On an excursion up the Hudson River, Whig writer N. P. Willis complained that these "varlets of newsboys" shattered the "customary repose of steamship travel" with "'Here's the Star!' 'Buy the old major's paper, sir?' 'Here's the Express!' 'Buy the New Ery!' 'Would you like a New Era, sir?' 'Take a Sun, miss?' And a hundred such deafening cries, to which New-York has of late years become subject." Willis called it the "babel of a metropolis," which hardly waned on the return trip, as the boys picked up local papers to sell on board and back in New York.[29]

Some newsboys regarded certain steamboats as their private property. "Let a strange boy make his appearance on any of these consecrated grounds," said the *Flash*, "and he fares worse than a wounded porpoise in the midst of a school." Newsboys also plied their trade aboard Mississippi riverboats, and some lost their lives when the engines blew; indeed, three died in the 1849 explosion of the *Louisiana* in New Orleans.[30]

Ships bringing newspapers and passengers from Europe also attracted "precocious urchins" like John Hoey, who rowed out to fetch and sell papers on the Norwich steamers before they docked. Charles Dickens's ship was similarly besieged in 1842, as was the protagonist of his novel, *The Life and Adventure of Martin Chuzzlewit*. A violent election, noted Chuzzlewit, "found fresh life and notoriety in the breath of the news-boys, who not only proclaimed them with shrill yells in all the highways and bye-ways of the town, upon the wharves and among the shipping, but on the deck and down in the cabins of the steam-boat; which, before she touched the shore, was boarded and over-run by a legion of

those young citizens." Among the fictional papers they cried were the New York
Sewer, Stabber, and *Family Spy.*[31]

Dickens's sarcasm was steeped in injury, as Greeley's *Tribune* and the mammoth *New World* had pirated his novel *Barnaby Rudge* the previous year. Harper
and Brothers would do the same a few months later with his *American Notes.*
Newsboys hawked uncopyrighted editions for a shilling apiece. Harper's Cliff
Street office "was literally blocked up with the newsboys," according to one
paper, "and the demand was greater than the supply." The *New World* and its
rival *Brother Jonathan,* founded by Benjamin Day after he sold the *Sun* and lost
the *Tattler,* later tried to beat book publishers at their own game by issuing
novels by Dickens and other European authors as "extras." These weeklies
sent messengers aboard steamships before they docked to secure copies of the
novels. Typesetters would work through the night resetting the books, "and
within twenty-four hours would have them on the streets, damp from the
presses, being cried by newsboys: 'Extry! Dickens' new novel! Only ten cents
a copy!' "[32]

The boys who hawked the flash papers parodied by Dickens were reputedly
the most degenerate of the lot. Part gossip sheets and part consumer guides,
these sensational weeklies catered to the "flash" lifestyle of "sporting men" who
drank, gambled, and whored openly in what otherwise was a period of religious
fervor. Some of these sheets dabbled in blackmail, threatening to print the names
of brothel-goers unless they paid hush money. But even without extortion they
generated nice incomes for their editors and publishers, the saloonkeepers who
stocked them, and the boys who peddled them for 6¢ apiece, plus cakes and
coffee furnished by the newspapers.[33]

Flash papers earned the condemnation of the respectable classes, who
launched obscenity and libel proceedings against their editors. *Polyanthos,*
founded by blackface minstrel George Washington Dixon, sought to avoid prosecution by claiming no editor or writer other than its carrier, Dixon's alter ego,
"the American Coco La Cour, Negro Dancer and Buffalo Singer."[34] The *Whip*
came under attack when its 16-year-old "roller-boy" and carrier was found
dead of exposure on an iron grate on New Street. The press reported that Brian
Carson had run away from home and lodged in a filthy cellar on Ann Street,
"where some forty or fifty newsboys sleep every night, and where they indulge
in all sorts of excesses."[35]

Although authorities suppressed the flash papers, a flood of "swill literature"
and "obscene prints" filled the breach. Much of this material found its way into
the hands of "vagrant newsboys," otherwise known as "emissaries of Satan." One
of these boys socked a cart horse in the face after the driver refused to buy his
wares, causing the driver's child to fall under the wheels. Foster blamed the grown
men who "seduced" newsboys into the trade and implored them to resist such

temptation: "Boys! you had better jump into a furnace at white heat, than have any thing more to do with this low and nasty traffic! Stick to the newspapers!"[36]

But still the traffic flourished. In January 1855 "several little newsboys" were arrested near City Hall Park for selling the inaugural edition of the racy *Broadway Belle*. Its proprietors, already in custody, were ordered to reimburse the boys for their unsold papers. A magistrate released them on the presumption that they did not know they were breaking any law, but newsboys were rarely innocent of such matters. Physician William Sanger described the "book bluffing" fraud favored by newsboys who loitered around New York's docks and depots. They would proffer obscene images tucked in the pages of their papers, but deftly remove them during the exchange to resell. Walt Whitman, who generally applauded the "blab of the pave," once spotted a 15-year-old with a drooping eye and "villainous low forehead" selling dirty books near the *Herald* office. "There," he told a friend, "is a New York reptile." The *Belle* responded with puff pieces and a penny song sheet "affectionately dedicated to the numerous and respectable and useful body of New York newsboys."[37]

Saucy by Design

Whichever kind of paper they sold, newsboys relied first and foremost on their voices. Two good legs were a luxury in a trade so amenable to the disabled. A cocked eye or humped back could boost business by generating sympathy. But a newsboy with weak pipes was a hopeless case. He risked losing his livelihood if he lost his voice and, according to writer Cornelius Mathews, might be considered "as pitiful as a bill sticker." His mates would be honor bound to take up a collection for him, as the newsboys in Mathews's 1842 novel, *The Career of Puffer Hopkins*, did for a hoarse colleague who had been "entirely too violent on the China question." Mathews was a literary nationalist dedicated to producing and promoting works that dealt with distinctly American subjects. He championed international copyright laws that would keep American publishers from purloining the works of English authors, thereby undercutting the market for native talent. Mathews created a furor in 1842 when, at a dinner in Dickens's honor, he called for the cancellation of America's "great debt" to British writers and the promotion of national "works of genius." Mathews's novel follows the initiation of an innocent country boy into the unscrupulous world of New York journalism and politics. Ironically, it is illustrated by "Phiz" (Hablot Knight Brown), Dickens's favorite illustrator and fellow countryman.[38]

George Foster also commented on newsboys' cries, suggesting that the cry's maker was generally the son of an oysterman, "from whom he derived his voice, and the free and self-possessed manner with which he employs it in the street."

The *Atlas* admitted that newsboys were "loud talking, impudent fellows" who delighted in tormenting each other, but defended their right to work unmuzzled:

> So let no men condemn the voice
> Of these same little boys;
> We can't pursue a call-ing,
> Unless we make a noise.[39]

In 1846 Frances Osgood's *Cries of New York with Fifteen Illustrations* became the first of this genre to depict a newsboy. Popular in England and the United States, City Cries were illustrated children's books that celebrated the distinctive cries of street vendors. Four years later another one graced the cover of William Croome's *City Cries; or, A Peep at Scenes in Town*, which proposed to decipher the "Babylonian confusion" of petty traders.[40]

Volume was not the only vocal quality a newsboy needed. He required a distinctive yell to set him apart from the herd. And he had to be both clever and stingy with his words; too much information would satisfy rather than whet the appetite for news. The line between clever and crooked was easily crossed. Even their staunchest defenders admitted that newsboys' cries could not be taken as gospel, as they sometimes brought on revolutions and dethroned kings at will.[41]

Shipping news was of special concern to merchants, seamen, and their families. Newsboys sometimes exploited their unease with alarming cries about overdue ships. When the *Atlantic* was overdue in February 1851, some of them yelled, "News of the Atlantic"—referring to the ocean, not the missing ship. "The little rascals well know how to touch the springs of anxiety in the public breast, and turn excitements to their pecuniary advantage," chided the *Brooklyn Eagle*. When the ship arrived a few days later, newsboys worked through the night. "But no one," said the *New York Tribune*, "could lose his temper at being awakened by the words: 'The Atlantic is safe!' " Real disasters, such as the sinking of the *Arctic* off Newfoundland in 1854 with a loss of more than 320 lives, generated profits exceeding $5 a day for the most obstreperous newsboys (Figure 2.2).[42]

While many city dwellers regarded newsboys' cries as the bane of modern life, others, particularly in the West, welcomed them as signs of civilization. A visitor to San Francisco in the 1850s was astounded to hear boys "crying their various papers with the latest intelligence from all parts of the world." So, too, was author Richard Henry Dana, who noted that the sleepy Spanish town where he had anchored twenty-four years earlier now featured "well-lighted streets, as alive as by day, where boys in high-keyed voices were already crying the latest New York papers." These boys might well have seen the Metropolitan Theatre's recent production of *Young America; or, The New York News Boy!* As early as 1852 a contingent of San Francisco newsboys joined firemen, teamsters, and butchers

Figure 2.2. News of shipwrecks created a sensation in the age of sail and steam. James McNeill Whistler, *Terrible Disaster! Loss of the Arctic!!* (1854). The Metropolitan Museum of Art, New York. Acc. No. 1970.121.43.

in marching in the city's annual Washington's Birthday parade. By 1855 the city had its own Newsboy's Sabbath School.[43]

Residents of Sacramento received their newspapers by steamboat, the arrival of which generated much hoopla in March 1851 when the agent of the New Orleans–based *California True Delta* illuminated his house at midnight with twelve star candles and awakened everybody in the neighborhood by crying, "Sound the tocsin, beat the drum, the True Delta, the True Delta's come!" The papers "went off at a half a dollar, like frost on a warm morning," reported the *Marysville Herald*, "and the newsboys were frisky and gleesome as rabbits in the frost." The city passed an ordinance licensing peddlers of out-of-state newspapers but then quickly repealed it. The newsboy would shortly leap to Hawaii and the Orient, mused another visitor, for he was a civilizing influence "more powerful than that of the missionary." A gang of American newsboys had indeed recently landed in Melbourne, Australia, reported the *Boston Courier*, and "created quite a jealousy amongst the newspaper folks by their eager business habits."[44]

The boy who introduced news crying to California was James Shain, a printer's devil for the *San Francisco Daily Alta California*, the first newspaper founded in the Bear Flag Republic in 1848. Born in Australia and raised in Chile, the young emigrant found work on the paper after arriving with his parents. He inked the type of the initial editions and hawked copies while on his rounds. "It didn't take long to supply the subscribers," he said. "I think we had about twenty-five patrons, all told"— including General John C. Frémont, "The Great Pathfinder." While hardly a scandal sheet, the *Alta California* occasionally carried hot news that fetched prices up to 50¢.[45]

In between their cries, newsboys communicated with each other in what sounded to many like a secret language. Some traced it to the boys' propensity for abbreviation or their absorption of all the catchphrases of the theater and the penny press, particularly insults ("Does your mother know you're out?") and thinly veiled threats ("Some things can be done as well as others"). Newsboys were notoriously insolent. "He opens his mouth," said Strong, "and out flies a winged army of proverbs calculated to ridicule wealth, and contemn station." However peculiar, newsboys' lingo (philologists later called it a dialect) tended to be infectious. Land speculators caught in the falling market of 1845 knowingly borrowed a newsboy term when they described their condition as "stuck."[46]

Next to their voices, newsboys were most distinguished by their appearance, which was at once flamboyant and ragtag. "In his dress," wrote Foster, "he does not affect the latest fashions.—No Newsboy, no legitimate Newsboy, has ever been seen in a whole suit. The uniform of his Craft is a slouched cloth cap, dilapidated roundabout and breeches, no shoes or stockings, and a dirty face with hands to match." Strong agreed: "The canons of fashion, the laws of dress, and the dictates of cleanliness, he especially eschews, averring that they are begot by pride from effeminacy, and totally unworthy [of] the regard of a lad of spirit." In other words, the newsboy intuitively recognized his disheveled appearance as a marker of masculinity.[47]

It was not just his choice or condition of clothes that was unique, but the manner in which he wore them. "Watch him daily," advised Strong, "and you will not detect a button-hole of his coat in conjunction with its lawfully-wedded button, nor any other part of his dress, in the position which the artist designed." His headgear, too, was arranged with the utmost casualness: "His fur cap in winter, and open-flapped beaver in summer, appear thrown upon his fertile cranium by the Genius of Disorder; now displaying its front to the left, anon to the right, and again to the rear." New York newsboys always wore their caps "perched on the extreme supporting point of their heads," observed another trend spotter, and pulled their hair over their eyes. Neal acknowledged that the newsboy was "somewhat uncouth in his externals," which consisted mainly of "soiled garments and patches," but credited him with applying those patches himself, as he generally had no mother at home.[48]

Theories abounded as to where the newsboys got their clothes. Most New Yorkers assumed they were acquired from the secondhand clothing stalls on Chatham Street or "fished out of the lowest depths of the pawnbroker's *omnium gatherum*." Some people said they chose their outfits from cast-off items found in the streets early in the morning. Still others speculated that the clothes grew on them like moss on a tree. "Find us the Tailor who makes the Newsboy's Uniform," said Foster, "and we will tell you when the American Union is going to be dissolved." For all these writers, descriptions of newsboys' "rigs or fit-outs" were opportunities for political commentary. While observers such as Lydia Maria Child expressed concern over the physical condition of newsboys, these men saw them as proletarian dandies, or "half-fledged b'hoys," who were as dapper and theatrical in their own way as their metaphorical—and sometimes biological—older brothers, the Bowery b'hoys.[49]

The Bowery b'hoy was a product of the street and the stage. He was a downwardly mobile young mechanic, cabdriver, or butcher boy who dressed like a peacock, favoring felt top hats, red flannel shirts, buttoned galluses or suspenders, and high black boots. A "soap lock" curling down his forehead completed the look. He worked when he could, but conspicuously loafed in saloons and on street corners. Although a quintessential New York type, he had counterparts in Philadelphia and Boston, for he was part of a vibrant youth culture created by a national economic shift away from craft production by skilled artisans and toward mass production by untaught wage earners. No longer secure in the property of his skill and labor, nor confident of his ability to become his own master, the b'hoy came to resent the merchants who profited from his humiliating decline. To make up for his diminishing status, the b'hoy affected a cocksure swagger and sought to define himself more by his pastimes than by his work. He attended cockfights and boxing matches, ran with volunteer fire companies, and voted Democratic or for the nativist American Party as soon as he came of age.[50]

Antebellum newsboys emulated Bowery b'hoys' speech, dress, attitude, and actions. They inhabited their bodies in ways that struck some observers as laughable but which mirrored the diverse ethnic and cultural influences of their polyglot cities. Strong's newsboy walked as though his knees, hips, and elbows had been well schooled in the sailor's hornpipe, the Irishman's jig, "and the 'double-shuffle' of old Virginia and 'come-it-strong' of Communipaw"—in other words, Negroes.[51] Together, their walk, talk, and dress constituted the outer signs of an inner quality or attitude, which could be summed up in a word: "sauciness." It was this attitude, along with his voice, that enabled the newsboy to seize public space.

One of the first artists to plumb the character of this new urban type was Henry Inman. He had made his name painting the noble scions of prominent Hudson River valley families, reinforcing in portraiture the view of childhood as a time of play and innocence. But in 1841, recalled his friend Mary Mapes Dodge, Inman went "sauntering slowly along Broadway in the hope of seeing some fine specimen of the newsboy race who would do for a 'subject.'" Most would not do. "Some had a squint," she said, "some looked vicious; some had straight red hair sticking out like bristles; some were badly formed, and some showed a deformed spirit within." Dodge, who edited *St. Nicholas Magazine* for children, said a boy named Joe, a "stalwart, roguish, noble-looking youngster" who fit Inman's image of a newsboy, finally approached him. "Begrimed though he was, " she said, referring to his portrait (Plate 4), "the fellow looks as if a king's heart were beating in his bosom. No one can look upon that bright, intelligent face, with its glowing cheeks and sparkling eyes, lit with energy and sturdy purpose, without feeling that the picture is no fancy sketch, but a veritable portrait of some rare prince among the newsboys." The twist in Dodge's tale is that Joe showed up for the sitting freshly bathed, with a new haircut, and wearing his Sunday best, all of which rendered him utterly inauthentic. Weeks had to pass before Inman could render the lad's "true" likeness.[52]

Dodge's story highlights the hazards of using art to reconstruct reality, but Inman's painting, beginning with the oval composition reserved for "fancy pieces"—sentimental portraits of women and children—remains a touchstone for probing the cultural significance of newsboys. It is a full-length study of a tattered yet dapper youth, about 10 years old, with red hair and a luminous complexion. He poses casually in front of an ebony sphinx on the balustrade of the Astor House Hotel on an otherwise deserted Broadway. The boy looks into the viewer's eyes as he would at a passerby, ready to pull a copy of the *Sun* from the stack under his arm. The New York press praised the painting as "true to nature" and a "clear perception of character." "His Newsboy seems to live and breathe," agreed the *Philadelphia Public Ledger*. Ralph Waldo Emerson admired it, too, in Philadelphia, where it had been sent for engraving in *The Gift* for 1843. Publisher Edward L. Carey commissioned humorist Seba Smith to write a story around it. The result was "Billy Snub, the Newsboy," a morality tale about a boy's efforts to support his saintly mother and elude his alcoholic father. Another lithographed version adorned the sheet music for "The Newsboy," a comic song written and performed in 1844 by William B. Chapman at the National theaters in Boston and New York. All in all, it wasn't a bad run for Joe.[53]*

---

* In sending "Billy Snub" to Carey, Smith wrote: "I shall express no opinion of its merits farther than to say that sundry little urchins to whom I have read it have teased me to read it over and over again, and are even more loud and decided in their praise of the story than they were of the 'tough yarn' [an earlier story]. This gives me hope . . . for I have often thought that children and illiterate people were better tests of the popularity of a story than learned critics." See Seba Smith to Carey & Hart, New York, Mar. 25, 1842, box 82, Edward Carey Gardiner Collection, Carey Section, Historical Society of Pennsylvania. Smith returned to the subject in 1844 in "The Young Traders," a story based

Inman's newsboy was emblematic of a new nation where democracy was achieved by the dissemination of knowledge, and opportunity could be attained through self-help. The painting contains references to other contemporary concerns as well. The sphinx, which never adorned the Astor House steps, attests to the period's vogue for ancient Egypt and the contrasting modernity of the newsboy. The partly eaten apple on the balustrade may signify the forbidden fruit that doomed humankind to labor or the hand-to-mouth existence of poor boys. The smoke billowing from a mansion in the background suggests the kind of warm home life that the boy lacks. An "OK" chalked on the wall (also evident in Page's *The Young Merchants*) alludes to the Democratic slogan of the recent Log Cabin campaign in which the Whigs first gained the White House by pitting the rough-hewn Indian fighter and Mexican war veteran William Henry Harrison against the elite New York Democrat Martin Van Buren, "Old Kinderhook." The painting represents Inman's projection of Whig values across the lowest stratum of society.[54]

This reading is supported by the painting's provenance. It was commissioned by, or a gift for, Inman's friend George D. Strong, author of an admiring 1840 essay on newsboys in *Knickerbocker Magazine*. "The newsboy is emphatically a creation of the new world," he wrote. "As the locomotive and the steam-boat are the mute heralds of its sway, so the newsboy may be termed its speaking representative."[55] Having grown up in the crowded immigrant wards of Five Points, Strong felt an affinity with street boys. He cut his political teeth as a Tammany Hall shoulder-hitter and once led a mob armed with bludgeons and daggers to break up a Whig meeting. But by 1840 Strong was himself a Whig, a bank president, and part of the influential literary circle associated with *Knickerbocker Magazine*.[56]

Whigs and Democrats still engaged in pitched battles in the 1840s, but they mostly clashed in print, where both parties claimed the newsboy as their own. Writing in *U.S. Magazine and Democratic Review*, Neal attributed many of the ideals of Jacksonian democracy to a composite Philadelphia newsboy named Tom Tibbs. "Compared to him, the sun itself is a sluggard," he wrote. "He looks upon the community as a collective trout—a universal fish, which must nibble at his bait, lie in his basket, and fill his frying pan. On this maxim, heroes have

---

on a painting by William Page. Art again preceded fiction. Page depicts a moment of reciprocity in City Hall Park between a handsome newsboy and pretty fruit peddler; he sits sampling her berries out of his straw hat, while she stands reading one of his papers. A belltower looms matrimonially in the background. See Seba Smith, "The Young Traders," in *The Gift: A Christmas and New Year's Present* (Philadelphia: Carey and Hart, 1844), 221–54; and William Page, *The Young Merchants* (1842), oil on canvas, 42 × 36 in., Pennsylvania Academy of Fine Arts, The Carey Collection, 1879.8.19.

overrun the world. It has been the foundation, not only of fortunes, but also of empires. Why should it not elevate Tibbs?"[57]

Excerpted in the *American Common-School Reader*, Neal's essay found wide readership. It was commissioned to illustrate the unflattering newsboy sketches of F. O. C. Darley. His newsboy is a gaunt, lumbering lad who can hardly muster the energy to peddle his papers, let alone overrun the world (Figure 2.3). The 21-year-old Darley came from a Main Line Philadelphia family and worked for

THE NEWS BOY.

Figure 2.3. "He looks upon the community as a collective trout—a universal fish, which must nibble at his bait, lie in his basket and fill his frying-pan." F. O. C. Darley, *The News Boy*, engraved by A. L. Dick, in Joseph C. Neal, "Pennings and Pencillings, In and About Town," *US Magazine and Democratic Review* 13, no. 61 (July 1843); 88. Eckel Collection, Princeton University Library.

a time in a countinghouse, but he made his name drawing the "engine boys, 'killers,' and loafers generally" he saw every day on the streets of Philadelphia. It was Neal's text in the magazine that transformed Darley's loafers into saucy dynamos. Neal addressed the issue in the scene in which a "starched gentleman of the old school" demands that the editor of the *National Pop-gun and Universal Valve Trumpet* restrain his impertinent newsboys. The editor erupts:

> Suppress sauciness! Why, my dear bungletonian, sauciness is the dis-covery of the age—the secret of advancement! We are saucy now, sir, not by the accident of constitution—temperament has nothing to do with it. We are saucy by calculation, by intention, by design. . . . Without sauciness, what is a news-boy? What is an editor? What are revolutions? What are people? Sauce is power, sauce is spirit, independence, victory, every thing. It is, in fact,—this sauce, or "sass," as the vulgar have it— steam to the great locomotive of affairs. Suppress, indeed! No, sir; you should regard it as part of your duty as a philanthropist and as a patriot, to encourage this essence of superiority in all your countrymen.[58]

There in the person of Tom Tibbs was the dynamic, hyperegalitarian spirit of Young America.

Musses and Mergers

Sauciness was clearly in the eye of the beholder. What some saw as spirit and independence, others regarded as aggression and criminality. Violence was en-demic to working-class life. All boys fought to settle differences, to prove their manhood, or just for fun. But such conflicts were more intense with economic interests at stake. Fighting, in short, was part of a newsboy's job; he had to fight to protect his turf, his stock, his earnings, and his honor. In 1843 a New York newsboy invoked his rights as a citizen by driving off a larger competitor from his hydrant on the corner of Pearl and Chatham Streets: "I don't like to hurt not no one a mite," he said, "but this *is* the U-nited States, and Bob Morris is mayor." In 1851 a ragged newsboy beat *New York Evening Mirror* editor Hiram Fuller after he said, "Vamose you little jack-ass." The boy replied between punches, "I aint a jack-ass—a jack-ass is *fuller* in the face, *fuller* in the ears, and a *fuller* all over." Newsboys were also known to assault editors who failed to get their paper out on time, as such delays cut into their sales.[59]

While newsboys got into plenty of spontaneous scuffles, they also arranged formal bouts and elaborate gang fights to resolve differences. "A Disgraceful Fight . . . occurred in Spruce-st., near the office of *The Tribune* yester day afternoon," reported the paper in 1848, "in which a large number of news-boys were participants." Some boys preferred to settle disputes on neutral ground across the Hudson or East River. In 1844 the *Herald* issued a "Caution to Newsboy Rioters, Fire Engine Rowdies, &c" who made Hoboken, New Jersey, their point of designation. It reported that two *Sun* newsboys, Daniel Daly and James Edmonds, had been arrested for creating a disturbance and throwing stones, and were committed to a New Jersey prison "until they know how to behave." New York boys would find the Jersey prison "very different in comfort and accommodation from our city prison," warned the *Herald*. A similar case occurred in 1851 when police in Red Hook, Brooklyn, got wind of a gang fight to take place on a Sunday morning between rival newsboys in Manhattan. The boys thought Red Hook was beyond the reach of the law, but officers met their flotilla of skiffs at daybreak and turned them away. Still determined to settle scores, the belligerents rowed off toward Weehawken, New Jersey.[60]

The press covered and thereby encouraged such dustups. In April 1843 the *Evening Tattler* and the *Spirit of the Times* gave a round-by-round account of the "Great Fight" between newsboy Matthew Mullin and a challenger named Belford in a ring in Red Hook before a huge crowd. The fight went eight rounds before Belford "guv in." Similarly, in June 1853, the *Clipper* devoted ten column inches to a back-alley "muss" between two feuding newsboys, Jack and English: "Both *men* on hand, but puffing rather hard and looking wicked; Jack sent in his one on English's conk, but received in return a stunner on the right ogle, making it see more Suns and Stars than he had sold that day." Editors knew that the boys liked to see their exploits in print, and no doubt hoped such stories would increase their paper's appeal among them.[61]

The press also reported on newsboy walking bouts and other contests. In 1843 the *New York Sporting Whip* advertised the "queer feat and funny challenge" of M. Gillan, a newsboy who devoured "two stone" (28 lbs.) of potatoes and a pound and a half of butter in two hours, washed down by a half pint of castor oil. He bet $25 no one could equal him. "*Vivé la* newsboy," said the *Sporting Whip*. In 1854 the *Clipper* ran a notice from Philadelphia newsboys challenging their New York counterparts to a newspaper-folding contest for a friendly wager of $250. New York newsboy E. H. "Extra" Kendric proposed upping the ante to $500, specifying that competitors would fold 6,000 weekly papers (about a day's work) "mail fashion, each paper six folds." It's not clear if the match took place, but the blustering was good for morale.[62]

Boasts and challenges were part of working-class saloon culture, but some ended tragically. One January night in 1849 18-year-old Michael Driscoll entered Butter-cake Dick's with several other newsboys. They were drunk and started throwing plates at each other. Cornelius Cuddey, a small boy left in charge, tried to restore order, but the gang threatened him. He seized a large dirk and stabbed

Driscoll in the heart. The gang beat Cuddey senseless before the police arrived. Driscoll's murder made national news; the religious press in particular decried "the depraved and irregular habits of the class of youths known as newsboys."[63]

Newsboy culture entailed cooperation as well as conflict. In addition to clubbing their money, they extended credit to newcomers, generally respected each other's turf, and ganged up against those who didn't. Cheating was rare, said the *Atlas*, as "fistic law" applied. Pittsburgh artist David Gilmour Blythe captured the wiliness of two newsboys settling accounts atop a hinged box (Plate 5). The shorter one has the fleshy face, demanding disposition, and rumpled suit of a prosperous merchant. He holds a silver coin in one hand and points at his stack of pro-Whig *Commercial Journals* with the other. The taller, more ragged boy carries the rival *Dispatch*, the first penny paper in western Pennsylvania, and displays several gold pieces. He wears a ratty straw hat and puffs unperturbed on a cheroot. The narrative of the painting is uncommon; the boys do not wave or shout their papers, scan the horizon for customers, or steadfastly meet the viewer's gaze. Instead, they are preoccupied with their filthy lucre and the prospect of bettering or getting bettered by the other. Pittsburgh was a city of 47,000 people in 1850. Its iron, coal, and glass industries grew large, yet did not supply enough jobs for its swelling population, 85 percent of whom were propertyless and two-thirds foreign born, mainly German and Irish. The painting reflects Blythe's antipathy toward immigrants and contempt for the crass commercial values that passed for patriotism.[64]

One example of cooperation among newsboys occurred in Philadelphia in 1851 when peddlers of the *New York Weekly Herald* got so fed up at having to fetch their papers at the downtown Exchange along with the big dealers and shopkeepers that they arranged to take delivery themselves at the Kensington depot almost two miles away and run them downtown via an "Indian Express"— that is, a relay. No boy was allowed to run more than three blocks before being relieved. They gained over thirty minutes on their competitors, who cried foul. The Democratic press defended the city's nearly one thousand newsboys and brokered a "Guadalupe Hidalgo adjustment" in their favor.[65*]

Newsboys also conspired to raise prices when conditions warranted. Brooklyn boys who showed up at the ferry and found papers in short supply were known to sell the 1¢ *Sun* for 4¢ and the 2¢ *Herald* for 10 pence or a shilling. Carriers further boosted earnings by supplying copies of the *Sun* to *Herald* subscribers or renting papers by the hour.[66]

---

* Newsboys in Saratoga, New York, organized a similar system of fetching papers from the train, but some of the smaller ones hired a real Indian from a nearby village to help them keep up. They paid him 25¢ for each day he arrived first. See "Newsboy Enterprise," *Sarotaga Whig*, in *Union Democrat*, Aug. 23, 1854, 1.

Even worse for publishers was the crime of stealing newspapers from doorsteps. The *New-York Mirror* complained of it in 1838 and expressed shock on discovering the culprits were newsboys who then sold the papers as their own. The *Mirror* urged vigilance against these "young candidates for the House of Refuge." The *New York Express* spent "large sums of money" to apprehend such thieves. Bowery firebrand Mike Walsh, founder of the *Subterranean*, promised a "sound kicking" to any "false-hearted, pilfering scoundrel" who claimed to take the paper but whose name did not appear in his subscription book. He was sure they stole their papers from porterhouses and barbershops since his newsboys usually sold out before 10:00 a.m. and seldom got far from the office. The boldest heist occurred in October 1842, when three newsboys stole the entire 2,000-copy edition of the *Flash*. Even small-time marauders faced jail time if they were unable to post bail of up to $300. The problem hit Baltimore in 1839 and spread to the Midwest by 1849. "Stealing newspapers is the basest form of depravity," howled the *Milwaukee Sentinel*. It called such thieves "monsters of iniquity." The *Sentinel* offered a $10 reward for the conviction of anyone caught in the act. The *Journal* in nearby Madison had its boys blow whistles upon dropping off a paper.[67]

The petty thievery practiced by newsboys occurred in an industry rife with chicanery. Hoaxes continued to entertain and exasperate the public. In March 1841, newsboys in Boston busily sold copies of President Harrison's inaugural address until it was discovered to be Thomas Jefferson's speech, to which had been affixed Harrison's signature. In the summer of 1842, newsboys in New York peddled ten thousand penny pamphlets depicting P. T. Barnum's Feejee Mermaid. And in April 1844 they profited from a hoax perpetrated by Edgar Allan Poe in the ever-receptive *Sun*. Poe fabricated a three-day crossing of the Atlantic by a balloonist. "I never witnessed more intense excitement to get possession of a newspaper," he bragged.[68]

Poe's friend George Lippard, a Philadelphia literary reformer, found newsboys to be useful figures to weigh in on social questions. His 1845 story "Jake Heydigger, The Newsboy of the Ledger Corner" follows a brash but industrious 12-year-old who foils his drunkard father's attempt to rob a Quaker, whose compassion shames the father into rectitude. A friend of labor and enemy of privilege, Lippard believed that brotherly love offered the best remedy for exploitation and injustice.[69]

Day in and day out, newsboys were more likely to be victims than perpetrators of theft. Many complained about nonpaying subscribers. The *Brooklyn Eagle* took up their cause in 1846, calling the nonpayers "mean men" who robbed children of their bread and butter. "We wish that they could receive reproof through the medium of cowhide from each of the lads who have been thus fleeced," said the *Eagle*. Some cheats (lawyers, typically) would take a paper, read the telegraphic dispatches, then hand it back to the boy and walk off.[70]

Most daily newspapers sold for a penny or two, the 6¢ dailies having gone extinct by the 1850s. Profit margins were small, with discounts averaging 30 percent on penny papers and 25 percent on 2¢ papers. The wholesale price to big dealers and small newsboys alike was 72¢ for a hundred 1¢ *Suns* and $1.50 for a hundred 2¢ *Heralds*, with no returns allowed. More profitable were the 6¢ Sunday papers, which generated earnings of $2 to $3 a day. "For their age, they make money very easily—more so than any other of the street boys," commented the *New York Independent* in 1854. The *Clipper* offered another measure of newsboys' earning power in response to a want ad for a library assistant at a salary of $4 a week. "Such munificence," said the editor, "would be laughed at by the alley boys."[71]

Given the ebb and flow of sales, scams, and sidelines, newsboys' incomes varied greatly. The *Brooklyn Eagle* said its boys typically earned 3 or 4 shillings (35¢ to 50¢) a day. *Cries of New York* reported 30¢ as the low end of the scale but said some boys made $1 profit on each hundred sold. Dick Lafferty, the lame newsboy in Joseph Holt Ingraham's 1843 temperance novel *Jemmy Daily; or, The Little News Vendor*, sometimes sold over a hundred papers a day and once earned $1 and 9 pence. The *Broadway Belle* told readers of a little boy on crutches who sold 170 *Belles* one rainy Friday in 1855 and brought $1.70 home to his mother. Mathews said that newsboys made $2 to $3 from a steamer's "extras," selling as many as 150 papers in an hour. Apparently these earnings did not suffice, as newsboys accounted for 40 to 50 percent of all minors arrested for theft in New York in the late 1840s.[72]

The alley boys who sold newspapers nonetheless enjoyed advantages over boys in other lines of work. One was the likelihood of tips, which were uncommon in service trades but accounted for half of a newsboy's income. They could pad their profits by shortchanging customers, crying false news, or passing off day-old papers as the latest edition. "We have no possible control over this matter, any more than a Bank has over the issue of counterfeit or altered notes in its name," explained Greeley. He urged buyers to beware, and to bring any "diddlers" to the nearest stationhouse, not to his office. In 1856 authorities in New York cracked down on boys who sold bogus editions "by pasting on to old ones proper dates." Yet newsboys engaged in legitimate sidelines as well. They chased down hats on windy days and rented space atop crates along parade routes. They hawked fans during heat waves and sold peeks through smoked glass during solar eclipses. John Ellard of Philadelphia became an expert in numismatics and "turned many a penny" trading old coins. San Francisco newsboys sold cough drops along with their papers.[73]

Boys of the Bowery Pit

What did newsboys do with their earnings? According to the *Atlas*, many of the "ragged little rascals" supported widowed mothers and helpless siblings. Within a year of his arrival in 1849, Chicago newsboy Knute Nelson, age 8, paid off the loan that had brought him and his mother to America from Norway. Of course, newsboys also frittered away their money on groundnuts, spruce beer, and other indulgences. Several in New York pooled their earnings and bought a horse and wagon at auction for $4.25—not for work, but for "sporting in afternoon rides on the Avenue, like so many young gentlemen of fortune."[74]

Newsboys also liked to gamble, which was common among the working class. Newsboys were particularly drawn to it because their entire livelihood was a game of chance: they wagered their initial outlay that they could sell their stock before day's end, after which it was worthless. A willingness to risk extended to their leisure pursuits. The typical newsboy was "scarcely ever without dice, small cards, and other implements of hazard in his pocket," noted Mathews. "He pitches pennies sometimes, like all other boys, or plays at marbles; but this he holds to be a small business. In general he disdains the common sports of youth."[75]

Despite their subsistence on the margins of the economy, newsboys achieved renown as prolific consumers of popular amusements. They had two things going for them that few of their peers could match: spending money and the freedom to go where they pleased. They frequented 3¢ porterhouses, dime museums, and shilling theaters. Indeed, one wit called New York "the City of Newsboys and Three-cent Stages." Newsboys packed the orchestra pits and upstairs galleries of Niblo's and the Bowery, National, Olympic, and Chatham theaters. The last of these served up "melodramas of the lowest and most demoralizing character," said the *National Era*, and could hold 1,500 patrons, most of whom were "Jews, newsboys, and sailors." The boys ranged in age from 6 to 18. Lossing caricatured one pit dweller as a grinning imp eagerly rubbing his hands between his knees, the upturned hat in his lap brimming with peanuts and handbills (Figure 2.4). "The newsboy works hard to acquire money," he said, "and still harder to pass it away."[76]

Ticket prices were scaled to attract working-class audiences, especially after the 1837 panic, when managers cut prices by half or more. The "rage of the town," noted the *Herald*, "seems to be . . . altogether in favor of the cheap penny cash system in theaters, as well as in newspapers." The Chatham charged 25¢ for a box seat, 1 shilling for bench space in the pit, and 6 pence for a perch in the gallery. Calculated in newspapers, admission to the gallery required the sale of eighteen 1¢ papers bought wholesale for 12¢. Tips sweetened the math nicely.[77]

THE NEWS-BOY,
In the Pit of the Chatham Theatre.

Figure 2.4. "The newsboy works hard to acquire money, and still harder to pass it away." Benson John Lossing, "The News-Boy, In the Pit of the Chatham Theatre," *Rural Repository* 23, no. 19 (May 23, 1846): 145–46. Eckel Collection, Princeton University Library.

So valued was newsboys' patronage that it influenced theaters' offerings. By newsboy standards, legitimate drama required five elements, said the *Atlas*: "a good deal of blood and murder"; terrific combats in which one man fights two or three at once; Negro dancing and minstrel songs; pretty costumes; and ghosts. Even the decor of theaters took newsboys' tastes into account. "That curtain is a wondrous one," noted a patron of the Chatham, and it was evidently "designed by an amateur news-boy; it is not a green curtain, neither blue, nor red but seems a mighty flourish of all colors; just the medly, to suit a news vendor."[78]

Antebellum theaters ranged from low dives to ornate palaces, the most sumptuous of which bedazzled poor slum children. The six Doric columns and stucco exterior of the Bowery Theatre resembled genuine marble. Separate swinging doors led to the pit and the gallery. Inside, box seats formed a horseshoe around a stage that stretched 84 feet behind a crimson curtain bordered in gold. Newly invented gaslights whispered overhead behind cut-glass globes. Newsboys did not sit in awed silence but carried on as if they owned the place. They ate, drank, smoked, snored, gambled, "chawed" tobacco, and talked throughout the shows.

Some called out their papers between acts. Others carved their names into the benches, said Mathews, "securing a right to the spot no less sacred than that guaranteed by the pew rents at Grace Church or St. Patrick's." Boys in the gallery at the Chatham threw coins and apple cores onto the stage during performances, prompting their pals in the pit to scramble among the actors to get the money or hurl the apples back upstairs.[79]

Newsboy audiences were most rambunctious during the holiday season, forcing managers to post policemen in the gallery. One December night in 1844 at a Bowery Theatre performance of Dickens's *A Christmas Carol*, three hundred newsboys, all guests of *Brother Jonathan*, engaged in a running battle with the police, "to the uproarious delight of the gods and goddesses of the gallery. . . . Several of the noisiest and most unmanageable of these amateurs, were, at length, snaked out by the police, and the scene of their exploits changed to the Tombs." Actors were used to such disruptions. They could expect the newsboys to call them by name, criticize their dress, and engage them in conversation. One instant a cast member would be "talking heroic poetry to some personage of the scene, and the next inquiring of Jake, in the pit, how he would trade his bull-terrier for a fighting-cock and a pair of pistols." Children in the audience, actors onstage, and even policemen sometimes—to their regret—fell asleep. One officer awoke to find that the newsboys had blackened his face with burnt cork, filled his boots with peanut-shells, and punched a hole in his hat for a lit candle.[80]

Such shenanigans characterized newsboy behavior in theaters from Boston to Mobile, Alabama. Boys in Philadelphia pioneered the practice of "passing their smaller comrades from hand to hand over their heads." William Mitchell, manager of the Olympic, threatened economic sanctions to maintain order. "Gentlemen of the pit," he addressed them one night, "you now pay one shilling for admittance; if this noise is not stopped, I shall raise the price to three shillings." Yet no manager could afford to alienate newsboys, who aided them simply by selling their papers, most of which contained theatrical news. The Bowery honored its newsboy patrons with a song, "The Boys of the Bowery Pit," which became the house specialty.[81]

Pit dwellers particularly enjoyed seeing themselves portrayed onstage. They first met newsboy characters singing and dancing in minstrel shows or as supernumeraries who filled out crowd scenes, brought news to advance the plot, or provided a bit of comic relief. They then rose to become protagonists in melodramas that transformed their humble lives into the stuff of legend. Newsboy heroes defeated dastardly villains, defended saintly mothers, and died glorious deaths. What could be more entertaining to a real newsboy?

Newsboy characters and entertainers were by-products of a cultural hubbub created by the penny press and blackface minstrelsy, both of which emerged in the working-class districts of New York in the 1830s. Real newsboys watched

Long Island Negroes dance for eels at the Catherine Street market. They packed the belowground "cork theaters," where white men in blackface incorporated the steps and patter of blacks and Irish immigrants into skits. And they learned the songs and steps themselves to amuse their friends and earn extra money:

> The rain is fast falling the wind rushes cold,
> And all of these 'ere remain yet to be sold;
> So I'll warm up by dancing and cutting queer capers,
> For I'm Blowed if there's fun in being stuck upon papers.
> "Hey, jim-along, jim-along josey,
> Hey jim-along, jim-along jo."
> Here's the Brother Jonathan, Uncle Sam, Boston Notion, and Yankee
>   Nation,
> the largest paper in creation!

Such numbers appeared in "Negro songsters" and were often performed in blackface, but the makeup was optional, as newsboys were comic, subordinate, smut-faced figures to begin with.[82]

Stage newsboys were swift with sass but highly principled, which pleased real newsboys in the audience. In *The Fireman*, a melodrama staged at the National in 1849, a scoundrel recruits a newsboy to run an errand. "I can do any thing for a dollar," says the boy, "—swim under water, dance Juba, sing O, Susannah, or play on the bones," but he refuses to deceive a young woman.[83]

Newsboy characters eventually took center stage in hit shows such as *The Newsboy of New York*, which opened at the National in September 1851; *Young America; or, The New York News Boy!*, which played on both coasts in 1854; and George Christy's *The Magician*, which kept Barnum's American Museum packed through the summer of 1857. A specialist in blackface minstrelsy, Christy impersonated Sam Sharp, the newsboy. "Never was sable vender of hurried up literature so perplexed and bothered before, and never did newsboy extricate himself from his perplexities and botherations with half the cleverness," said a reviewer. In the finale, Sharp streaks high over the stage astride a fiery steed representing the dreaded world-ending comet of Charles V. These plays and ballets were not just diversions but dramatizations of the most pressing issues of the day: slavery, immigration, temperance, poverty, and woman's suffrage.[84]

Bringing Down the House

Newsboys were political actors in life as well as onstage or in the pit. Theirs was not just a colorful, alternative youth subculture but also at times a violent, oppositional one that reflected their growing sense of themselves as members of a disaffected working class. The "little merchants" paraded en masse through the streets of New York in 1844 on behalf of political causes or in response to perceived slights by their newspapers. "A number of News-Boys behaved improperly yesterday in the neighborhood of this office, and gave considerable annoyance to persons looking at the bulletin," admonished the *Herald*. "We give them only one hint. If they do not behave themselves with strict propriety, we shall prohibit the sale of any copies of the Herald to any News-Boy, and give the whole monopoly of supplying the public in this city to the regular carriers." It is not clear why the boys mistreated the bulletin readers; perhaps they saw them as cheapskates who were not willing to buy their own copies. In any case, the *Herald*'s threat proved to be an empty one: the newspaper boasted a circulation of 35,000, "the greatest in the world," and street sales played a major part.[85]

While newsboys could be annoying just for the fun of it, their misbehavior usually stemmed from specific grievances. When the Philadelphia *Public Ledger* instituted a new pricing policy in 1844, the boys balked and passed a resolution:

> Resolved, That the news boys is free news boys, entitled to sell papers according to free trade, as cheap as they can be printed.
>
> Resolved, That the news of Clay's election *oughn't* to be kept from the people, and we are opposed to all tricks to keep it from them wot buys our papers.
>
> Resolved, That we will open a room, spend one night a week, and smoke segars, and that we will lick any boy wot drinks any liquor.
>
> Resolved, That as the Ledger has violated the rights of man, in asking us poor boys with widowed mothers and desolated sisters to pay two cents for extras.[86]

The resolution is all that survives of their brief "two-penny strike," but it speaks volumes about their developing political consciousness. They claim their rights as "free news boys," which distinguished them not only from plantation slaves but also from "wage slaves" whose independence had been compromised by submission to an employer. They regard themselves as guardians of a free press that was essential to the well-being of the republic. They express pride in their sociability. They vow to police their own ranks. And they claim a masculine responsibility based on the "rights of man" to protect their female dependents.

As the depression eased around the middle of the decade, labor agitation erupted in many cities, especially New York. In 1844–45 printers, bookbinders, upholsterers, shoemakers, tailors, and tailoresses waged dramatic strikes, often with torchlight parades. Irish dockworkers and carpenters and German bakers and cabinetmakers also formed unions. Not surprisingly, New York newsboys engaged in their own strikes and protests. In 1845 they staged a massive street demonstration to denounce the policies of the *Evening Mirror* and the *Evening Express.* This dispute centered on the *Mirror*'s unwillingness to sell papers to them at an early hour and the *Express*'s unauthorized publication of a *Mirror* column. The boys held an "indignation meeting" and agreed to wage a campaign of "moral suasion." They passed a resolution stating, "We will indignantly frown down any such attempt at *gouging. . . .* To the fulfillment of the above threat we pledge our *lives,* our *fortunes,* and our *sacred honor!*" The boys then marched through the streets, some thirty or forty of them wearing "shocking bad hats" that bore large placards identifying themselves as "Mirror Newsboys" (Figure 2.5). They also carried muslin banners emblazoned with the mottoes "Fair play and no gouging!," "Honesty is the best policy!," and "This truth we will teach the Express."[87]

Serious business underlay this particular form of street theater. No paper could survive long without reliable distribution, as the *Express* found out again the next year when newsboys refused to buy copies at the new price of 25¢ per hundred and set off "Another Grand Flare Up!" The "damp and voiceless sheets" piled up for several days, which delighted rival publishers, who nonetheless

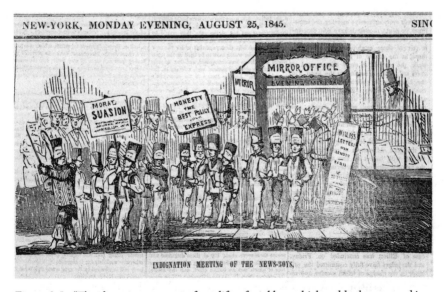

Figure 2.5. "The above is a true copy from life, of a *tableau* which suddenly appeared in front of our office on the morning after the arrival of the 'Great Britain.'" John Brougham, "Indignation Meeting of the News-Boys," *New York Evening Mirror,* Aug. 25, 1845, 1. Eckel Collection, Princeton University Library.

urged the *Express* to capitulate: "'Live and let live,' is a sound policy as well as duty. The poor newsboy works hard for his pennies."[88]

The most enterprising publishers sought to woo newsboys and increase readership by mounting their own demonstrations, excursions, and banquets. The mammoth weeklies *New World* and *Brother Jonathan*, which measured more than 8 feet square and required "two boys, at least, to hold it for perusal," vied for the services of newsboys. *New World* editor Park Benjamin bribed them with gloves and theater tickets. In March 1842 he outfitted "an army of newsboys" with banners and handbills and marched them to the music of fife and drum down Wall Street and Broadway to promote his latest issue. *Brother Jonathan*, meanwhile, inaugurated an annual procession of newsboys on Christmas Eve to announce its holiday editions. Preparations for the parade began the night before when editors sent large stocks of peanuts and bologna sausages to the Bowery, Olympic, and Chatham theaters. After the shows let out, the newsboys assembled at the corner of Nassau and Wall, "where the leaders were selected, their banners prepared, and the line of march settled upon for the next day." The boys stopped traffic in the morning as they paraded from City Hall Park up Chatham Street and the Bowery, across Grand Street, down Broadway to Wall, and then up Nassau to Ann Street. They passed the offices of several dozen newspapers and received greetings by printers and folding girls, the latter waving handkerchiefs and smiling at the boys "in the most bewitching manner." Many editors and publishers, including Greeley, popped their heads out of the high windows along the route. The boys responded with a series of "tremendous and even terrific" cheers. Afterward, the paper treated the marchers to a "splendid collation, with toasts and speeches, as is usual on such occasions." The mammoths were clearly adept at harnessing the energy of the newsboys.[89]

Cornelius Mathews parodied this relationship in his novel *Puffer Hopkins*. At one point, representatives of the fictional *Mammoth Mug*, edited by Piddleton Bloater, recruit Hopkins and others to sell their paper, even though it contains "pirated" material. But the boys draw the line when a party hack asks them to post placards of his candidate and destroy those of his opponent. "We are pledged contrarywise to the citizens of New-York," said one. "The city 'ud have a shock of the apoplexy, and go into fits regularly till we begun to cry again. The news-boys, sir, and we all knows it—but we're too modest to say it out of doors—is the moral lamplighters of this 'ere city." Mathews was poking fun at the idea of the press and its peddlers as paragons of virtue. In truth, editors in Young America had few qualms about using newsboys to "make the air sing" against their enemies. But the humor illustrates a serious point—that hollering papers gave newsboys a sense of being implicated in public affairs.[90]

Editors were not the only ones who tried to get newsboys to do their bidding. Political and religious figures also recruited them to circulate papers, posters, and other propaganda, including copies of President Tyler's veto messages. In 1841 the *Catholic Register* posted bills calling for newsboys to distribute extras in which Bishop John Hughes exhorted Irish Catholic Democrats to vote for Whig candidates who supported Governor William Seward's plan to aid parochial schools. In 1850 Sixth Ward rowdies, upset by the lack of election day libations, swung a congressional election to the Whigs by inducing 580 "thoughtless and vicious men" to abandon the Democratic choice and vote for Dominick McGrath, "a newsboy not of age!" And in New Orleans Irish American newsboys, with the support of parents and teachers, factored in the 1856 presidential election by refusing to carry the *Daily Creole*, the organ of the anti-immigrant, anti-Catholic American Party. The party controlled city government and hoped to elect Millard Fillmore president, but it could not win over the newsboys.[91]

Despite being competitors, newsboys considered themselves to be a labor fraternity that stood tight against interlopers. "They are mischievous, yet good natured," said the *Flash*, "but if you offend them, you had better have thrust your hand into a hornet's nest. They will hoot after and utterly banish you from Ann and Nassau streets, and moreover, their annoyance is not always confined to mere words. They make common cause, and to affront one is to affront all." Newsboys in Boston demonstrated solidarity by organizing a general indignation meeting on State Street in 1846 declaring state legislators "a bunch of humbugs" for passing a law requiring them to attend school three months a year. Boys in Albany, New York, went further, organizing a Newsboys Association in 1850. They elected officers, adopted a constitution, regulated prices, and mandated mutual support. Section 6 read: "Should any member of the society 'get into a muss,' the rest are bound to 'go in' and help him out, or pay a fine of twelve cents." In 1855 New Orleans newsboys joined union printers and pressmen in refusing to work until their dispute was settled. These youths may have symbolized the spirit of capitalism in Young America, but that spirit coexisted with a commitment to the rights of labor.[92]

Newsboys' solidarity sometimes extended beyond death. In 1846 a committee of the "allied powers" of New York newsboys, with Johnny McGowan as chairman, visited the *Mirror of Saturday* to solicit funds for the burial of one of their mates. "We saw, for the first time," said the editor, "a look of sadness struggling though their somewhat obscure faces, which showed that they too have human hearts beating under their ragged jackets, and tears to shed over the cold grave of their poor little dead companion, for whose coffin they were raising the means to pay." United in grief and poverty, newsboys would bury their own throughout the century.[93]

Rumors of War

Newsboys' importance to newspapers and prominence as political symbols peaked during the Mexican War. The war revolutionized the industry. For the first time American correspondents took to the field with the troops and wrote graphic accounts of battles. Soldiers sent long letters to newspapers, which transformed obscure officers into heroes and made terse battle commands ("A little more grape, Captain Bragg!") into national catchphrases. Penny papers were proclaimed the "national literature," and the boys who peddled them were attributed with an infectious strain of patriotism. "If our troops do but make as vigorous a charge upon the enemy as newsboys do upon the public with their extras," said a Boston reporter, "the victory will be ours without a doubt."[94]

The war triggered a second wave of cheap dailies in the West. Cincinnati gave birth to dozens of papers, making it the nation's fourth-largest publishing center, behind New York, Boston, and Philadelphia. Newspapers forged national links using steamers, railroads, telegraphs, and the Pony Express. James Gordon Bennett sought a further edge with his "pigeon post" to Washington and Albany. But as the war progressed he resorted to the more cutthroat tactic of cooperation. The *Herald* joined five other New York papers to procure telegraph reports of foreign events. Bennett later bought a ship, the *Naushon*, which he renamed *Newsboy*, and placed it in the service of the group to obtain news from incoming European vessels. The enterprise was a folly, but it led to the formation of the Associated Press in 1851.[95]

Because of their innovative newsgathering methods, newspapers routinely received word from the front ahead of government officials. The *Philadelphia Public Ledger* ran an express train from Pensacola, Florida, to Montgomery, Alabama, and regularly issued extras containing vital intelligence that had not yet reached the White House. The president and his generals sometimes learned the outcome of battles from the mouths of boys crying, "Great news, great news, by Telegraph!" New York newsboys tended to station themselves midway between the *Tribune* and *Herald* to "make a mad rush for whichever was first ready to supply them." Reports of victories led crowds to gather around the boys, resulting in spontaneous celebrations, parades, and fireworks. Yet by war's end, 50,000 Mexicans and 13,000 Americans had been killed. Because newspapers printed the names of American war dead before relatives had been officially notified, some newsboys brought inconsolable grief to their customers.[96]

Yet the reliability of war news was always suspect when filtered through the mouths of newsboys. One incredible cry—"Great victory! Two thousand Mexicans killed! Santy Anny's leg captured!"—inspired P. T. Barnum to exhibit what purported to be the Mexican general's wooden leg. Comedian Pete Morris, a regular at Barnum's museum, turned the newsboy into a vehicle of press criticism in his minstrel number, "Yes, Sir-ee!":

> There's news from Mexico come to-day,
> Which is awful horrifying,
> How 20,000 men were killed,
> And 10,000 more were dying,
> The Mexicans have run away,
> We'll show them to cut capers,
> Now all of this must be true,
> Yes, sir-ee! Hoss-fly,
> Bekase 'tis in the papers.[97]

Also critical is Napoleon Sarony's 1847 lithograph *One of the News-B'hoys*, which shows a reptilian figure stalking the streets with his newspapers held high like a cudgel and crying news of General Zachary Taylor's victory at the Battle of Buena Vista (Figure 2.6). Behind him two newsboys brawl in front of the *Herald* building.[98]

Another international story that thrust newsboys into the limelight broke in March 1848 when the *Herald*'s news boat met the British packet ship *Cambria* and received word of revolution in France. Within hours, *Herald* newsboys were on the streets announcing the abdication of King Louis Philippe and the proclamation of a new republic modeled on that of the United States. Louis Philippe's fall was especially sweet to Americans given his efforts to muzzle the press and install his son on the throne in Mexico. Bostonians welcomed the news as proof positive of the superiority of republicanism over monarchy. Some credited reports of the king's flight with making the hawking of extras respectable in Boston.[99]*

Stories about Louis Philippe's exile took a fanciful turn in May when newsboys noticed a "fat, waddly man" wearing a peaked wig and flourishing a large umbrella disembarking from a steamer in Jersey City in the company of a fine lady and a "pretentious number of attendants." According to the Democratic weekly *John-Donkey*, the well-heeled "above Bleecker newsboys" spread rumors that the former ruler had arrived in America. Frequent sightings followed, culminating in a rash of editorials,

---

* Although poorly enforced during the war, and denounced by Bostonians, an ordinance had prohibited boys from selling papers "out of doors" on pain of arrest, fine, and imprisonment. The law was repealed in January 1849, allowing minors to hawk papers if they obtained a license and attended school. See Frederic Hudson, *Journalism in the United States, from 1690 to 1872* (New York: Harper and Brothers, 1873), 383–84, and Edwin A. Perry, *The Boston "Herald" and Its History: How, When and Where It Was Founded* (Boston: Boston Herald, 1878), 31.

ONE OF THE NEWS-B'HOYS.
SKETCHES OF N.YORK, N°18.

Figure 2.6. "'Ere's the hextry 'Erald—got the 'orrible battle in Mexi-c-o-o-o-! and
defeat of Santy Anny! Victory of old Rough and Read-e-e-e at Bony Wisty! 'Ere they
are! (Put it to him Zack!)." Napoleon Sarony, *One of the News-B'hoys. Sketches of N. York,
No. 18.* Lithograph published by Sarony & Major, New York, 1847, Library of Congress,
Washington, DC. LC-USZ62-5217.

cartoons, and burlesques purporting to document the deposed sovereign's grand
reception by the hoi palloi of New York. Published by ex-newsboy George Dexter,
the *John-Donkey* reported on a fanciful parade led by comedian Pete Morris as a
brigadier general riding an "unimpeachable black charger," and Mark Maguire carrying a crimson cushion bearing the crown of France and a "Tribune hat"—the
flat-topped newspaper cap of the working class.[100]*

   While newsboys provided good fodder for satire, their rowdiness struck
many—Whigs and Democrats alike—as the rumblings of a dangerous

---

* Newsboys helped spread the republican fervor behind the 1848 revolutions, especially the
Young Italy movement, which advocated unification under republican rule. In *Roman Newsboys*
(1848–49), Pennsylvanian painter Martin Johnson Heade shows two urchins waving revolutionary
newsbills before a wall covered with posters and graffiti, the chief weapons of their cause. See
Theodore E. Stebbins, *The Life and Work of Martin Johnson Heade: A Critical Analysis and Catalogue
Raisonné* (New Haven, CT: Yale University Press, 2000), 50–52.

underclass. "How are these boys to acquire the knowledge and character necessary to exercise the rights of citizenship," asked *Young America*. "And how are they to get a living when they grow up? If society do not attend to these small matters, a day of retribution, of which flour riots, engine rows, and church burnings may afford a small foretaste, will surely come." New Yorkers' worst fears were realized during the Astor Place riot on May 10, 1849. It began when a crowd of nativist Bowery b'hoys protested the appearance of British thespian William Macready at the Astor Place Theatre and asserted the superior talents of their homegrown star Edwin Forrest. City police and state militia hastened to quell the riot but ended up firing on the crowd, killing twenty-two people and wounding thirty. It was the first fatal suppression of a civil disturbance since the nation's founding. Many saw it as the harbinger of class warfare. Speaking for the city's elite, N. P. Willis said that those who posed a real threat to the republic were not the supporters of Macready but the arrogant fire company runner, the speeding omnibus driver, the profane market woman, and the selfish newsboy "who disturbs the decent citizen with his cries in the early morning."[101]

New York artist Frederick Spencer also saw the riot as a dire portent and the newsboy as a potential threat. The artist could not ignore the class and ethnic tensions exploited by the penny press, whipped up by its saucy newsboys, and now culminating in riot. He explored these themes in his 1849 portrait *The News-Boy* (Figure 2.7), which depicts a robust youth seated on a fire hydrant (a b'hoy symbol) to which is affixed a Macready handbill. He holds a bundle of *Sun*s and *Herald*s under his arm. A dog lies at his feet. The boy's face and bearing suggest a dignity and manliness that may enable him to transcend his environment. He is framed as if onstage by two pilasters before a jumble of trompe l'oeil posters advertising a ship's passage to the Sierra gold fields, a 50¢ bounty on dogs, an art exhibit, a school for boys, and sales items such as hats, clothes, and pills. One poster offers a full account of the "RIOT" in bold red letters, above which reads an ominous legend: "SOMETHING COMEING." Spencer's newsboy is obviously the coming man, but it's not clear if he represents the promise or downfall of Young America.[102]

Yet another artist pointed the way out of this quandary: west. Thomas LeClear's 1853 portrait *Buffalo Newsboy* depicts the archetypal young man on the make, poised to profit from new markets linked by an expanding network of roads, rails, canals, and, of course, newspapers (Plate 6). Born in Oswego in 1818, LeClear was himself a product of the transportation and market revolution that brought prosperity to upstate New York. He got his start decorating panels on steamboats. A student of Henry Inman, LeClear painted several newsboy studies, but *Buffalo Newsboy* exudes greater confidence and physical prowess than his or Inman's earlier efforts. A strapping youth in his early teens, the newsboy sits on a railroad trunk in an alley eating the ever-tempting apple.

Figure 2.7. Newsboys became symbols of class resentment after New York's Astor Place riot in May 1849. Frederick R. Spencer, *The Newsboy*, 1849, oil on panel, 21 × 17 in. Courtesy Mr. and Mrs. Peter Rathbone.

Copies of the *Buffalo Express* lay on the ground and against the trunk, which bears the letters "OK." He wears battered boots, a handsome green coat, and a wide-brimmed hat called a "wideawake," which was also a term for people who were alert to moneymaking opportunities. The hat throws a shadow across his eyes, but the rest of his face is well lit, showing off his round, youthful features and alabaster skin. As in the other paintings, the walls and fences in the background are covered with posters, the largest of which reads: "Attention. 50 Boys Wanted." It is likely a call to his trade, reinforcing the message that time, territory, and the market are on his side.[103]

More than any other personification of the age, the newsboy represented the liberating potential of a democratic society driven by a wide-open market economy. Yet he also epitomized the bamboozlement of mass politics and the sham of self-interest masquerading as concern for the greater good. His flamboyant style alternately annoyed and amused his elders, but it also helped him to survive the hardships of street life. In the capable hands of Young America's cleverest writers, artists, and actors, newsboys elbowed their way into political and cultural debates over the relative influence of class or character in shaping individual and national destinies. No real consensus had been reached by 1853, but the terms of the debate and the experience of America's most vulnerable newsboys—the homeless—suddenly shifted as the economy faltered and a new generation of reformers arose to save them.

3

Johnny Morrow and the Dangerous Classes

Nine-year-old Johnny Morrow limped down the gangplank of the *Helen McGraw* in New York on November 23, 1850, with his father, stepmother, four younger siblings, and 18-year-old Mary Morrow, a poor relation pledged to service in exchange for her passage. Bound from Liverpool, the Morrows were among the ship's 256 steerage passengers, a mere droplet in the wave of famine Irish— nearly a million and a half people—who washed ashore between 1845 and 1855. Most were cotters (small tenant farmers), who had to adapt to city life with its crowded streets, cramped apartments, and capricious wages. Johnny's father worked erratically as a carpenter, his stepmother took in sewing, and he, though slowed by a diseased leg, peddled matches, scavenged for food and fuel, and hawked the little stools that his father made, charging 12¢ to 15¢ apiece. But the less his father worked, the more he drank, and the more likely he was to beat Johnny for his paltry earnings and growing appetite. Afraid to go home some nights, he and his brother Willie slept out—in parked stagecoaches or on the cabin seats of the Fulton Ferry—until they heard about a new place called the Newsboys' Lodging House.[1]

Morrow was one of countless children who foraged on the streets of New York in the 1850s, and one of almost nine thousand who found their way to the Newsboys' Lodging House during the decade.[2] Yet, unlike the others, he wrote about it in a memoir published in 1860 while he was still in his teens (Figure 3.1). *A Voice from the Newsboys* is a rare first-person account of life on the streets and under the wing of the Children's Aid Society (CAS), a fledgling organization that would become the preeminent child welfare agency in America. Like slave narratives of the era, Morrow's book allowed readers access to the life and mind of a person many presumed lacked the intelligence, if not the humanity, for articulate self-expression. Even those who ministered to street children deployed a menagerie of metaphors and an atlas of nomads to describe them. They were likened to "rats," "wolves," and "buzzards"; "Arabs," "Comanches," and

Figure 3.1. Johnny Morrow, poster child for the Children's Aid Society. William Momberger, engraved by Samuel J. Pinkney, frontispiece, Johnny Morrow, *A Voice from the Newsboys* (New York: A. S. Barnes & Burr, 1860).

"Hottentots." Collectively, they made up what Charles Loring Brace, founder of the CAS, called the "dangerous classes."[3]

Morrow rejected these terms; he did not see himself as a beast or savage. Rather, he identified as a member of the "newsboy class," in which he included "all those unfortunate children of poverty in cities, who have to live in the streets mostly by their own *wits* and *resources*, whether by *peddling newspapers, sweeping crossings, selling stationery*, or any other little traffic which they may carry on." Such a life, he said, "is spent by many a boy (or, with some unessential variations, by many a girl) in our great cities."[4]

Morrow's life and life story typify the transformation of the newsboy in the 1850s from an impish urban type to an alarming social problem. His experience of extreme poverty offers a unique perspective on the hardships of the working poor and their strategies for survival. News peddlers of all ages, races, and sexes provided essential support for themselves and their families at midcentury. They attracted the attention of artists and writers who wished to comment on social conditions. And they supplied the labor and ingenuity that built local news distribution links into an integrated national system. Some boys became clients of the innovative charities that were established by a new generation of reformers. Many more found themselves embroiled in campaigns to abolish chattel slavery, expand women's rights, and preserve Sunday as a day of rest. More than their exposed bodies, the very soul of America's newsboys seemed to be at risk in this turbulent era.

In the Face of Disaster

Truly a dismal decade, the 1850s saw not one but two economic recessions and the heaviest influx of impoverished immigrants in the nation's history. Financial downturns in 1853 and 1857 left thousands without work. In New York, poverty bred epidemics of cholera, typhus, and consumption, which raised the city's mortality rate to one in twenty-seven, higher than that of London or Paris. More than half of Gotham's children died before age 5; eight out of nine of those early childhood deaths occurred in immigrant families. "The times are so hard in New York," said newsboy Danny Sullivan, "that I couldn't break them with a sledge hammer." Born in England and raised in Louisville, Kentucky, Sullivan set out for New York in the winter of 1854–55 seeking opportunity and adventure. Instead, he found a city plagued by hunger, disease, and joblessness, and overrun with young wanderers like himself. Skilled white workers responded by founding the first national labor unions, while the less favored marched for bread and jobs. Public and private aid was meager in the best of times, and limited to the so-called deserving poor. Worthy by virtue of their youth, children filled New York's nine orphan asylums and, together with the ill, elderly, blind, and insane, made up a quarter of the city's almshouse inmates. Yet most poor youths preferred to take their chances on the street.[5]

Ironically, the 1857 crisis yielded "a great harvest" for New York's five to six hundred newsboys. "I wish the panic would last always," said a cartoon newsboy in the *Clipper*. "I made twenty shillin yesterday." These "shrewd financial knights of the curb stone" demanded 3¢ for their penny papers, said the *New York Tribune*, "and got it without any grumbling. People were perfectly willing to pay an extra price to see their own monetary ruination in print." One journalist credited newsboys with the "pluck, energy, perseverance and determined go-ahead-ism" that all New Yorkers needed to weather the crisis.[6]

Artists also saw newsboys as capitalist heroes. James Henry Cafferty placed two steadfast street merchants at the center of his masterpiece *Panic of 1857, Wall Street, Half Past 2 o'Clock, October 13, 1857*, which depicts the day all but one of the city's fifty-eight banks suspended specie payment (Plate 7). Wall Street, as Cafferty shows, became choked with businessmen, most wearing top hats, dark coats, and grave expressions. Of all the speculators milling about the sidewalk near Trinity Church, the newsboys are the only ones still engaged in business.[7]

Even more optimistic was a lithograph issued by the American Bank Note Company in 1858 (Figure 3.2). Possibly executed by Francis Edmonds, the firm's principal owner, it depicts a barefoot boy handing a paper to a commercial trader standing dockside amid barrels, bales, and other cargo. Both figures are prosperously plump. Ships and locomotives cross behind a bank in the background, further attesting to the soundness of the economy.[8]

Street urchins were clearly in vogue during the crisis. Winslow Homer included several news sellers in the Boston street scenes he drew for *Ballou's Pictorial*. These were promotional illustrations, which *Ballou's* published for a fee from the businesses pictured or as a favor to advertisers. In New York, the *Cosmopolitan Art Journal* reminded painters that they didn't have to travel to Italy to find eye-catching vagabonds: "We have lazzaroni in abundance, hanging about our public markets. Yet our artists rarely think it becoming in them to give us a glimpse of the loose fish that float in the turbid stream of our own social system." Rising to the challenge, artists submitted a record number of genre scenes to the National Academy's annual exhibition in 1860. "The pictures of New-York street life, of newsboys, etc., were numerous, and some of them were very good," adjudged the art journal.[9]

Figure 3.2. Who better to restore confidence in the economy? "The Paper," No. 93. American Bank Note Co., 1858. Library of Congress, Washington, DC.

Newsboy studies also came from the studios of George Yewell, William Winner, Moses Wight, John McRae McLenan, Charles Blauvelt, James Johnson, William Penn Morgan, John Mackie Falconer (Plate 8), and sculptor Franklin Simmons. The boys are usually depicted as lone figures, but they convey a variety of social messages depending on the artists' choice of setting or background (on thresholds or by wall posters), their insertion of symbols (fruit or debris), and their selection of poses, expressions, and clothing (slouched or erect, confident or wary, theatrical or naturalistic). Despite their variations, artists treated newsboys' poverty as picturesque. The face of the "dangerous classes" was sad, sleepy, or stoic, but never angry or threatening. Either the boys did not appear to them as such or the market demanded more reassuring portrayals.[10]

It was not altogether fanciful that newsboys should represent the promise of capitalism. Peddling papers was not just a stopgap to starvation or a last resort of the wretched but part of a booming industry that provided some people with much more than a subsistence living. Even during the depression, the ceaseless laying of telegraph lines and railroad tracks, coupled with the growth and consolidation of wholesale newspaper agencies, hastened the national distribution of newspapers and periodicals. "A traveler cannot visit a city, village, town or hamlet in any of the Northern, Middle, Western or Eastern States, accessible to railroad," said a reporter in 1858, "but that he hears the cry of the newsboy, ''Ere's the New-York 'Erald, Times and Tribune.'"[11]

Provincial papers also proliferated in response to new readers and technologies. America's dailies, like its population, increased by a third during the decade (from 254 to 387), and their circulation nearly doubled to 1.5 million. The number of weeklies grew by 40 percent, from 1,902 to 3,173. German immigrant and "Forty-Eighter" Johannes Adam Simon Oertel celebrated this march of progress in his 1853 lithograph *Things as They Were, and Things as They Are* (Figure 3.3). A statue of Johann Gutenberg, inventor of the printing press, stands atop a pedestal bisecting the scene. To the left, a monk sits before an hourglass copying a book with a feather quill. Ancient weapons and a crucifix hang on the wall behind him. To the right, a telegraph operator sits at his keys in view of a factory and telegraph wires, backed by a flag and liberty cap. A barefoot newsboy runs along a tree limb crying his extras.[12]

Even greater progress was afoot in 1858 when newsboys announced the laying of the transatlantic cable. "And by their lips spoke the Queen to President Buchanan," effused novelist Elizabeth Oakes Smith. "Boys in New York hawked their extras until nearly 2 a.m.," said the *Evening Post*, "awakening the sleepers and calling sober citizens who were about to retire, to the doors and windows to purchase the 'Queen's Message.'"[13]

More than just symbols of advancement, newsboys physically accomplished the national distribution of newspapers. Ex-newsboys Joseph Marsh in Detroit,

Figure 3.3. The newsboy, a symbol of modernity ushered in by Gutenberg. Johannes Adam Simon Oertel, *Things as They Were, and Things as They Are* (1853), lithograph, published by Nagel & Weingartner, New York. Library of Congress, Washington, DC. LC-USZ62-19456.

John Walsh in Chicago, and Sinclair Tousey, John Hamilton, Solomon Johnson, and Patrick Farrelly in New York founded wholesale distribution firms. They made fortunes speeding newspapers and magazines to the hinterland, as did Horace Greeley with his *Weekly Tribune* and Robert Bonner with the *New York Ledger*, a story paper that featured the writings of Louisa May Alcott, E. D. E. N. Southworth, and Harriet Beecher Stowe. By 1856 the *Ledger* had attained a weekly circulation of 80,000, most of which was handled by the firm of Ross & Tousey. Monday was "Ledger Day" at the firm, and it became a spectacle. Tourists gathered to watch newswomen, cartmen, and "scores of small boys" lay siege to the place. Newsboys crowded the counters three deep, eager to get their stock. Virtually every employee was requisitioned to wait on them. "These hundreds of thousands of Ledgers are seen moving off the shoulders of porters, and in the hands of newsboys, in drays and carts, in every direction," observed orator Edward Everett, but after twenty minutes "the throng is dispersed, and the ubiquitous journal is on its way to the remotest corners of the land." One by one, Tousey and associates absorbed their competitors, covering the continent with print.[14]

Scraping By

Unlike these titans of the trade, the great mass of newsboys in the 1850s were partners with poverty, living hand-to-mouth in the company of dirt and disease, wind and rain. It is easy to romanticize their struggles, but even easier to flit over them like so many clichéd images. Hunger—gut-rumbling, breath-souring, head-spinning hunger—was a fact of life among the urban poor at midcentury. Some boys went days without bread. Yet hunger was more than a physical sensation; it was a social force. Hunger shaped class relations by turning individuals of all ages into willing workers. Johnny Morrow called hunger "the tyrant of animal life" and the most compelling force behind his trade. His father denied him breakfast and supper so "that I might obtain food for myself from those of my customers who were charitably disposed." The eponymous hero of the 1859 novel *Hartley Norman: A Tale of the Times* also cited hunger as the impetus for selling papers. "The case is urgent—work or starve," he told his mother.[15]

To feed themselves, newsboys sometimes bartered papers or ran errands for victualers. A fresh paper might net a piece of bread or a scrap of meat. One elderly woman known as the "Fulton street cake aunty" kept accounts for boys who were short of cash. Newsboys also dined at cheap refectories such as the Nassau coffee saloon in the basement of the *Sun* building, where bare feet and ragged trousers were no grounds for being chucked out. "The Proprietor knows the Newsboys very well and makes considerable allowances for their *caste*," observed a visitor. "He sees them every day, industrious, and self-dependent, and if they happen to be unfortunate in the sale of papers or other speculations—he trusts them—and they very rarely 'step out.'"[16]

Antebellum cities were gastronomic emporiums, even for children who counted their earnings by the penny. Johnny Morrow said newsboys used to treat themselves to a cup of coffee and a dozen griddle cakes at a saloon for 9¢ after the rush for morning papers was over. And it was not uncommon after a good day for them "to march into a restaurant and order a dinner of venison or woodcock, with sauces, which would not be despised by an alderman." Such a feast could be had for 12¢ in New York, but prices were higher elsewhere. The well-traveled Danny Sullivan complained that a 6¢ beefsteak in New York cost 20¢ in Boston. Happily, his favorite dish was the more affordable mackerel— "splendid fish, that."[17]

Each city had its specialties. Newsboys in Philadelphia were notably fond of clam soup, cheesecake, and mint sticks. Boys in Buffalo liked "kümmelwecks," later known as donuts. A "great favorite with juvenilia" in New York were bolivars, tasty but usually stale gingerbread cakes sold at corner stands. Other popular sweets included jawbreakers, pulled molasses, popcorn balls, penny cups of ice cream, cylinders of lemon, wintergreen lozenges, and—in the summer— watermelon, a slice of which cost a cent or two. "The newsboys, especially, are much addicted to this juicy fruit," said the *Atlantic Monthly*, and vendors often set up their tables in front of newspaper offices. Some skeptics felt that cravings for "dainties," not real hunger, caused newsboys to eat rather than save their earnings.[18]

Newspapers themselves offered dining options. *Sun* publisher Moses Beach and Mordecai Noah of the evening *Union* teamed up in 1844 to open an oyster cellar and saloon below the *Sun* office. James Gordon Bennett, whose *Herald* stood across the street, suggested that their foray into seafood reflected their failings in the news business, but the *Herald*'s own cellar soon housed the Union Restaurant.[19] The *Tribune*'s basement was home to two eateries. The first, Butter-cake Dick's, was famous not only for its cakes and coffee but also for its easy credit. The proprietor, Dick Marshall, had a soft heart for "busted" boys but little patience for rowdies. "Take your ugly snout out of this ere coffee-shop sudden," he would tell them, "if yer don't want it spiled—dy'e hear." The menu included cold pork and beans, cold ham, boiled eggs, rice pudding, and Connecticut pies, most famously pumpkin. Marshall refused on principle to stock graham crackers, which were invented by anti-masturbation campaigner Sylvester Graham, who condemned "exciting" foods such as sweets, meats, and coffee. Serving up news and stews was not just a New York custom. In 1861 the *San Francisco Herald* sublet its basement to a man who operated a "low-down dive" that served whiskey along with more substantial fare, and in 1868 the *Montreal Witness* opened a newsboys' lunchroom in the rear of its office. These places may not have taken in much money, but they paid handsome dividends by keeping hawkers close at hand.[20]

Newsboys' gustatory obsessions are also evident in their nicknames. New York's ranks included "Oysters," "Chops," "Huckleberry," "Lozenges," and "Round-hearts," who was partial to small molasses cakes of that name. Among the Brooklynites were "Ham-and-eggs," "Turkey," "Lobster," and "Lollipop." Philadelphia claimed "Doughnuts," "Coffee," "Biscuit," and "Apples." Atlanta was home to "Long Hungry," who was famous for his perpetually famished expression. However silly, such names suggest that eating was a serious concern for newsboys. Even the many who lived at home needed to earn money to alleviate the harsh hierarchy of the family table, where wage-earning men, not growing children, got the best portions because the welfare of all depended on their health.[21]

Tobacco provided no nutritional value, but it helped newsboys alleviate hunger pangs. Their addiction to the "nauseous weed" was well known. The "smallest lads" in Philadelphia not only chewed it, said one observer, "but some of them actually *ate tobacco!*" Newsboys in Boston were notorious for rescuing cigar butts from spittoons, while those in New York would follow smokers for a mile to get their castoffs.[22] The smoking habit of Pittsburgh boys worried artist David Gilmour Blythe, a member of the anti-immigrant American or "Know-Nothing" Party whose incident-packed street, post office, and courtroom scenes feature cigar-chomping newsboys. *Street Urchins*, painted around 1857, suggests danger more than precocity as the leader crouches to light a short-fused fire-cracker near a powder keg marked with the Masonic symbol—a dot in a tri-angle in a circle. The city had suffered a wave of strikes and epidemics due to railroad fraud. Public funds were invested in the construction of new lines that never appeared, leading officials to raise taxes, landlords to hike rents, and the dispossessed to engage in riot, arson, and looting. The urchins that Blythe pictured so piteously exulted in these disturbances.[23]

Boys who worked and sometimes slept in the streets of American cities were not all orphans, outcasts, or runaways. Most had homes, even if unwelcoming. Morrow's family of eight lived in a one-room cellar that measured 30 by 20 feet. The children slept five to a bed in one corner, while his parents and a newborn slept in another corner. His father's carpenter bench occupied a third. Given such cramped conditions, a son who slept out was hardly missed, though his earnings might be. New York police chief George Matsell said that in warm weather even sons of respectable parents absented themselves from their families for weeks, returning home only for clean clothes or meals. Parents who allowed their sons—never their daughters—such freedom may have been remiss by middle-class standards, but their supposed neglect helped their children acquire the skills and networks necessary to survive in an unsparing urban economy.[24]

Newsboys' earnings fluctuated widely in the 1850s. They made anywhere from 75¢ to $5 a day, according to the *New York Dispatch*. Oakes Smith put the range between $1 and $3. Sunday papers alone could raise their income by $3 or $4. In one of his earliest stories, "The Gold Piece; or, The Newsboy's Temptation," Harvard Divinity student Horatio Alger Jr., a stickler for accurate details, allowed his hero only $3 a week. A homeless newsboy could get by on 6 shillings (75¢) a day, said the *New York Times*. "Active boys" made about $1 a day, but an execution in the city or a revolution in Europe would raise it to $2 or $3. The "Horrid Murder" of philanderer Harvey Burdell in 1857 and the trial of his lover were a "godsend" to them, said Oakes Smith, but a curse to those of-fended by the brutal blaring of the sordid details (Figure 3.4).[25]

BRUTAL NEWSBOY *to* NERVOUS OLD LADY. " Horrid Murder, M'm!"

Figure 3.4. "Brutal Newsboy to Nervous Old Lady. 'Horrid Murder, M'm!'" Publisher Frank Leslie said that hearing boys cry news of the Burdell murder convinced him to cover it in the "minutest detail," thereby saving his illustrated paper from financial ruin. *Harper's Weekly* 2, no. 99 (Nov. 20, 1858): 752. Eckel Collection, Princeton University Library.

Children who slept out raised more concerns in the 1850s than in earlier times, partly because they were more numerous. Journalists Walt Whitman and George Foster had routinely encountered slumbering children on their midnight rambles, but their accounts allayed rather than raised public fears. Leaving his office one night in April 1842, Whitman noticed a ragged boy fast asleep on the steps of a building near Tammany Hall. He stooped over him and saw in the glare of gaslight a boy 11 or 12 years old, "by no means deficient in beauty and intelligence." Whitman was about to wake him up when a watchman stepped out of the shadows and stopped him. He said the youth was a newsboy who lived uptown and often slept there after leaving the Chatham Theatre and before the morning papers came out. "We inwardly breathed a benison upon the slumbers and future lot of the poor devil," said Whitman, "and walked forward." Foster depicted street waifs even more benignly—as carefree campers in an urban glade. Having no home and not thinking it worthwhile to pay for lodgings, his composite character, Tom Newsboy, "takes up his quarters for the night in a box or bunk, under a stoop or in an entryway, where half a dozen of them frequently huddle together, heads and points, with a shaggy dog in their midst, as good a fellow as any of them."[26]

Children made their beds in an ingenious array of places—in old crates and hogsheads along the waterfront, under steps and bridges, on benches and barges, in stables and market stalls. Two newsboys, little warmed by the irony, slept one winter in a burned-out safe on Wall Street. Another choice location was over steam gratings, or "iron bedsteads." They provided warmth on cold nights but could burn exposed skin. The most convenient gratings were located above the giant steam presses of the dailies. Police routinely scared up thirty or forty boys sleeping along Nassau and Ann Streets.[27]

From Park Row in Manhattan to Lafayette Square in New Orleans, few publishers felt that such scenes reflected poorly on their enterprise. James Gordon Bennett used to complain to police about "the crowd of newsboys and loafers" who blocked the doors of the *Herald* office, but most of his counterparts thought they were providing a public service by giving children work and letting them bed down nearby. In 1856 *Leslie's Illustrated* endorsed sleeping out as a healthful activity: "On pleasant summer nights in the vicinity of our daily newspaper offices, may be seen from fifty to one hundred news-boys, distributed over the pavements and iron steps, asleep in every possible attitude, and resting so quietly, that all crowned heads and millionaires would look on with envy."[28]

Not everyone was so untroubled by newsboys' al fresco accommodations. It could be upsetting to see what appeared to be an empty sack or coiled rope on the sidewalk suddenly move, yawn, and rise up on a pair of thin legs. Sleeping on the streets was dangerous, as children were known to beat, rob, and abuse each other. One homeless youth who sought safe lodgings in New York in 1855 told a woeful tale to explain his broken nose: "I slept in boxes about the Herald office, and some of the boys were bad to me. They knocked me about nights and laughed at me; said I was never a doin' nothing." Street children also looked out for each other; a 12-year-old who lived in a box on 22nd Street said he got by only because "the boys fed him."

New York Tribune editor Horace Greeley sympathized with the plight of the "news gamins." He often shared a table with them at Oliver Hitchcock's, the all-night lunchroom on Park Row that replaced Butter-cake Dick's. Leaving his office late one night, Greeley saw a stir of newsboys shivering and stamping their feet over the steam gratings on Spruce Street. They told him they were waiting for the morning's steamship extras. Greeley ordered the doors of the pressroom thrown open so the boys could enjoy the full warmth of its boilers. The room became a refuge for newsboys on wintry nights. More than a few learned to read and write from kindly printers and editors. The *Tribune* benefited from having the boys on hand for the morning editions and occasional "midnight extras," such as the one issued after passage of the 1854 Kansas-Nebraska Act, which allowed slavery to spread to new regions by popular vote.[29]

Keeping clean posed a challenge to street boys. Baths were rare even for children who had homes, as few tenements had running water. Most New Yorkers made do with backyard privies, as a comprehensive underground sewage system was still on the drawing boards. A good soak could be had at the free or cheap public baths recently established in New York, Philadelphia, and other cities. Fountains also served the purpose, but the sight of urchins scrubbing themselves in public upset genteel urbanites and embarrassed some bathers. A reporter who once met his regular newsboy "disporting himself like a grampus" at a park pump remarked that the boy "blushed scarlet." "Had I caught him carrying the pump away, he could not have been more abashed."[30]

River bathing offered another alternative. Johnny Morrow and friends enjoyed summer dips in the East or Hudson River. Newsboys protested when authorities banned river swimming in the 1870s. "I am a news-boy, and a poor boy, and I know just how acceptible [*sic*] a bath is in the heat of summer," wrote one lad on behalf of his pals. "Can you not in some way use the influence of your paper so as to get us the privilege of making ourselves clean by bathing in the river? It would go far to make better citizens, at any rate more clean and healthy ones, of us, and we will not forget THE TIMES." A bit of scruffiness was good for business, generating both sympathy and sales. But the truly filthy invited ridicule. One who slept in a gashouse in Yonkers had a face so stained by smoke and tar that he was taken for a "colored boy." For he who lacked soap and water, the cry of "two (s)cents hath a double meaning," said one paper. "He scorcheth himself at the office stove and grinneth at the olfactory torments of the imprisoned editor."[31]

Branded as "bummers," the dirtiest newsboys risked not just losing business but also attracting the attention of police or charity workers, some of whom wielded a new weapon in their war on poverty: the camera. Samuel B. Halliday of the American Female Guardian Society showed its utility in the "rescue" of one Tommy Mack in 1859. "When I told him I wanted him to go with me, he refused," said Halliday, "and, throwing his arms around an awning post, manifested considerable determination not to quit the neighborhood. We, however, soon started, stopping first at the photographers, where Tommy in rags, sitting on a tea-chest, had his likeness taken, making a most emphatic picture." It showed a barefoot boy with windblown hair as "tarry" as his face, and a wound under his eye. The picture proved decisive when Mack's parents tried to regain custody. They argued in Superior Court that they were industrious, temperate people whose son was normally a clean, neatly dressed schoolboy who never begged. Halliday's attorney simply produced the photograph and the case was decided: custody to the society.[32]

Life in the Loft

Vagrants under 16 were usually sent to the House of Refuge for indefinite terms lasting up to age 21 for boys and 18 for girls. They slept in windowless cells and labored eight-plus hours a day, making nails and shoes or doing chores. Those who broke the silence or committed other infractions were whipped, placed in leg irons, or confined in solitary. Some New Yorkers found these conditions appalling and supported the creation of a separate institution for "morally exposed" but noncriminal children. The result was the New York Juvenile Asylum, founded in 1851. It sought to instill the habits of self-discipline in its inmates and indenture them to farmers or artisans. Even this facility failed to impress Charles Loring Brace, a recent graduate of Yale College and the Union Theological Seminary in New York. He felt that custodial institutions destroyed "the independent and manly vigor" necessary for practical life. "The family," he said, "was God's reformatory."[33]

While headed toward a promising career in the ministry, Brace grew to distrust theology that did not address people's material needs. In 1851 he took a grand tour of Europe, where he met with urban missionaries and saw firsthand the devastation caused by the 1848 revolutions. On returning to New York he surveyed the city's poverty wards and organized a series of "Boys' Meetings" on Sunday evenings. In 1853, at age 27, he founded the Children's Aid Society and served as its director for almost thirty-eight years.[34]

Brace's philosophy of reform was based on the twin gospels of Jesus Christ and Charles Darwin. He believed that it was his duty to aid the poor and spread the word of God, yet he felt that indiscriminate almsgiving and proselytizing had produced generations of paupers and prostitutes. He advocated a more scientific charity that encouraged self-sufficiency and adhered to the laws of nature. Brace understood urban poverty as an environmental problem that could be eradicated by draining the "stagnating pool" that had spawned this "ignorant, debased and permanently poor class." By emancipating children from their slum homes, Brace sought to avoid "an explosion from this class which might leave this city in ashes and blood."[35]

The Children's Aid Society's prime innovation was the placing-out system, which sent city children to live with foster families in the country, where they could breathe fresh air, learn honest work, and develop strong characters. Children were not indentured, as there were no formal contracts. The employing family agreed only to educate the child and give him or her $100 on turning 18. It was usually a him, as boys were placed out at rates more than three times that of girls. Farm families preferred boy labor, and city parents were reluctant to part with the more reliable earnings and domestic help of daughters.[36]

The CAS also supplied western manufacturers, including newspaper publishers, with boy labor. When the *Milwaukee Sentinel* solicited two "straight-forward, up and down boys" to sell and deliver papers in 1857, Brace drummed up two volunteers, "Yank" and "Little Eddie." Yank wrote back that he was "making money like blazes"—$10–$12 a week. He and Eddie typified the majority of CAS clients, who used the emigrant program to find steady work, not foster homes. By 1860 more than five thousand children had been placed out by the CAS. The *Sun* called the system "one of the most remarkable discoveries of the age."[37]

But praise was not unanimous. Forty percent of the children sent west on "orphan trains" had living parents, some of whom regarded Brace as a kidnapper. Westerners complained that their communities had become dumping grounds for delinquents. Others objected to the way the children were lined up for inspection at train stations. Brace replied that the system conformed to the laws of supply and demand since it transported children from places with surplus labor to places where it was scarce. Any dissatisfied children could simply leave, he said. Some did, complaining that they were unpaid farmhands; others stayed on to inherit the farm or, in the case of Andrew Burke and John Green Brady, 11-year-old seatmates on an 1859 orphan train, become the governors of North Dakota and the Alaska Territory, respectively.[38]

Brace felt early on that something had to be done with those who would not or could not leave the city. He failed to grasp how letting children huddle overnight around newspaper offices could pass for charity. What the boys needed most, he decided, was a suitable place to sleep. Cheap lodging houses charged 25¢ a bed, or 15¢ for half a bed. Brace felt he could do better. On March 18, 1854, he opened the Newsboys' Lodging House in the loft of the *Sun* building on Fulton Street. When *Sun* publisher Moses Beach donated the space, he pledged that the boys could stay there even if every tenant left. It was a generous act, but the near constant noise and vibration of the presses made renting the building difficult.[39]

Brace aimed not just to shelter homeless youth but to end urban poverty by instilling the values that would lead to settled Christian lives. Newspapers were important allies in this endeavor: they provided the space, support, and publicity necessary to open the lodging house, which—not incidentally—accommodated the itinerant labor needed to distribute their product. This was self-interested altruism at its midcentury best, and it led to the founding of newsboy homes in Philadelphia and Chicago four years later, and in scores of cities afterward.[40] Newsboys were not the only ones permitted to check in, but the homes were named for them because they represented the manly self-reliance that Brace and his imitators sought to foster. "There is no reason why newspaper selling should be a vagabond business," he said. Brace appointed as superintendent Christian C. Tracy, a carpenter who possessed the requisite blend of toughness and compassion. He was assisted by volunteers and a matron.[41]

Like most working-class youth, newsboys learned early on that living space was a commodity that required hard coin and acquiescence to their elders. Boys of "tender years," especially those from Irish and German families, commonly boarded away from home, sometimes in rooming houses that catered to specific occupations, such as sailors or clerks. The Newsboys' Lodging House was typical in this regard, but cheaper. It provided a bed for 6¢, supper for 4¢, and free baths. Some boys preferred their "*free dirt*," but they had no choice in the matter. House rules, all clearly posted, also proscribed fighting, drinking, smoking, and chewing tobacco. Lights-out was at nine o'clock. If a boy came in a bit later, he was fined a nickel; after ten, a dime. No one was admitted after eleven o'clock, although the curfew was eventually pushed to midnight. The wake-up call came at 6:30 a.m., often with the cry "Steamer's in!" The house lent needy lodgers shoeshine boxes or metal checks good for copies of the *Telegram* or *Daily News*. No other institution offered so much freedom to come and go.[42]

Boys came to the lodging house in many ways. When it first opened, Tracy placed notices in newspapers, distributed business cards, and passed the word among the leading newsboys. C. C. Wiegard, superintendent between 1856 and 1858, personally scoured the docks and markets for homeless boys. Municipal lodging houses, which catered to adults, also referred boys to the home. Police sometimes escorted young vagrants there instead of to jail. Parents would surrender their children to the CAS in times of duress, but most boys just walked in the door of their own accord.[43]

Johnny and Willie Morrow ventured up the stairs of the lodging house one December night in 1854. On entering, they were hit by the warmth of a potbellied stove. They saw a spacious drawing room with whitewashed walls and long strips of coir matting running down the aisles. A row of pegs near the door held the lodgers' hats, coats, and scarves in an array of colors, styles, and sizes. They saw the man in charge—Tracy—sitting behind a large desk bearing an inkstand, quill, and open ledger. Opposite was the classroom area, filled with writing desks and adorned with maps, prints, and two globes. There was a melodeon and other instruments, and hundreds of shelved books. Some boys sat quietly reading near the stove. The brothers were shown the washroom behind a sliding door and sleeping quarters upstairs containing fifty numbered bunks, each with a new straw mattress. As usual, Tracy asked the newcomers their names, ages, and occupations. He asked if they could read and write, and the whereabouts of their parents or previous lodgings. Afraid they might be turned out if they were known to have parents, Johnny said he and Willie were orphans. They signed the ledger under the name Moore.

The boys were also asked to turn in any weapons. They had none, but a murderous collection of knives, razors, rusty nails, slingshots, pistols, and a two-foot pickaxe piled up in the home's "war museum." Johnny and Willie then paid their money and received a cubby with lock and key. A later visitor to the home, Louisa May Alcott, noted that the cubbies made the boys "so happy because they feel that they *own* something." It mattered little, she said, that they had nothing but "an old rag of a cap or a dirty tippet [scarf]" to put in it. Boys actually acquired many little possessions—including marbles, pencils, and songbooks—which they would entrust to the superintendent before their obligatory bath. Others owned good clothes and shoes but preferred to go barefoot when extras came out because they could run faster.[44]

Most of the lodgers were between 6 and 18 years old, with 13 the median age. One report referred to them as "restless, untamed boy-men, whose experiences of hardships and suffering had made them old even in childhood." Tracy generally refused to admit applicants "if too old or too vicious," but in January 1856 he took pity on "Alick the Newsman" McDonnell, a veteran of the streets who was afflicted with "the rheumatiz" and partial to the numbing properties of rum. An admitted "wreck" in his mid-forties, Alick had peddled and delivered papers since coming from Ireland in 1835. "When I began business in the news-trade the times were good," he said, "but now there are so many in that way of living, that we old men are often short, and find the times press on us. The newsboys have a good many hard specimens among them now. It is no wonder as they are very numerous now. There are more daily papers now, but two generations ago (I count by newsboys generations) there were more weeklies in Ann street."[45]

Altogether, the lodging house sheltered 400 boys its first year and 4,000 a year in the latter part of the decade. In 1860 it provided 27,390 separate lodgings, served 16,837 meals, and ran up almost $3,500 in expenses, a third of which was covered by the boys. The difference was made up by municipal aid—mainly funds obtained from liquor licenses—and private donations of cash, coal, crackers, apples, soap, sheets, quilts, clothing, pens, and paper.[46]

Some boys lived at the house for months, while others spent a night or two. More than a few sold papers to support themselves while traveling. Danny Sullivan showed up carrying over his shoulders several carpetbags, which hung down so far they looked like a kilt over his bare legs. The bags bulged with toys, cards, newspapers, and other stock. A talented raconteur, he earned the nickname "The Professor" because he could lecture on any subject, especially life on the road. Asked how he got by during his four-month tour of New England, he replied, "I threw cards—peddled papers—killed Irishmen to sell them for soap-fat, and niggers to make blacking—any thing for an honest living." Ethnic jokes functioned as a kind of currency among the boys, enabling them to fit in by making fun of social inferiors. To his credit, Sullivan was also known for "doing the Samaratan," bringing penniless boys to the home.[47]

The place also accommodated boys with disabilities, notably the deaf, mute, and "short fingered." It was open to all races, yet admitted few African Americans in its early years. When the first Negro checked in, "two or three of the hard boys got up a conspiracy against him," said Brace, "and Mr Tracy had no little difficulty in quelling the mutiny, and winning them to a more kindly mood." Yet when another "young American Pariah" showed up in February 1856, he noted that the boys treated him kindly: "Tonight, they sit near the dark visaged stranger boy, they chat with him amicably; and sympathize with his story." The boy, David Johnson, had run away from a farm in New Jersey after a dispute with his employer. Tracy urged him to return, but before going he entertained the boys with a dance. Walter McAlpine, an Irish lad nicknamed "Lummydoo," patted out the beat on his thighs. That night, while Republican Party delegates met for the first time in Pittsburgh to oppose the spread of slavery, the Newsboys' Lodging House resounded with interracial harmony.[48]

One of the home's most novel innovations was its penny savings bank, a heavy walnut table with 110 numbered slits in the top. Tracy built it to encourage thrift and a "sense of property." Monthly deposits averaged $200. The drawer was opened for withdrawals once a week when roll was called. The home offered 5 percent interest, plus a $3 monthly prize to the largest depositor. While the aim was to discourage profligate spending and gambling, the monthly winners were expected to treat their friends to coffee or cakes. Such sharing was not unwise, as friends could provide a better hedge against hardship than savings. Besides, given the pitfalls of street life, not all boys survived to tap their accounts, as is evident in an 1855 roll call:

> "No. 3?"
> "Gone dead."
> "No. 4?"
> "At his country seat, gettin' his winter lodgin.'" (House of Refuge.)
> "No. 5?"
> "Gone to heaven!"[49]

Tracy attended to the boys' injuries and ailments by applying plasters and spooning out medicine as needed. The seriously ill were sent to city dispensaries, but children occasionally died on the premises, including "Mickety," the first boy to sign the ledger. "His disease was consumption," said Brace, "perhaps brought on by exposure in early days, when he slept in boxes or on the damp ground." The boys clubbed together and bought a handsome mahogany coffin to bury him in Brooklyn's Green-Wood Cemetery, one of the lush suburban "memorial gardens" that had begun to replace overcrowded churchyards.[50]

The lodging house held nondenominational services every Sunday night. Morrow claimed to be one of the few Protestants in the house, but virtually all famine Irish were Catholic, a fact he may have wished to conceal in his book, along with his Irish roots, to avoid fueling charges that the CAS was converting Catholic youth. Brace did not interfere with any child's creed, but he sought to make the scriptures relevant to their lives by pointing out that Christ had been a homeless workingman. The boys were keen on Bible stories and considered miracles "natural and proper," but the Golden Rule (do unto others as you would have them do unto you) struck them as impossible, especially when one was "stuck and short." The boys enjoyed singing most of all; they would take off their coats, roll up their sleeves, and pitch in with gusto. One lodger composed a special hymn for the house:

> See your children round you smiling,
> On your bosom, on your knee;
> Think upon the News boy's fortune
> When your homestead rings with glee.[51]

Although Brace held up newsboys as models of industry, he did not encourage them to stay in the trade. Nor did many lodgers wish to. "I don't like selling newspapers," a boy named George told him in 1858, "it is not the way to be somebody. I only sell them because I don't want to do worse." Some lodgers secured paper routes or became newspaper folders, yet Brace preferred them to acquire more marketable skills. To this end, the society had established eight industrial schools by 1860 that taught boys carpentry, cobbling, and printing, and offered girls instruction and employment in needlework, housekeeping, and the manufacture of paper bags. The CAS opened its first lodging house for girls in 1862. It discouraged street peddling in favor of the domestic arts, but Brace said the girls had a "foolish pride or prejudice against house-work" and frequently upset the place with their "petty quarrels and jealousies." The staff turned away any applicant who looked to be a prostitute for fear she would corrupt the younger girls.[52]

To strengthen the character of his lodgers, Brace invited a stream of speakers, including publishers, scientists, and churchwomen—anyone who could "bring a personal influence to bear on the children" and combat the separation of the classes, which Brace considered to be a "great evil." The tenor of their remarks, as perceived by the children, can be heard in a parody delivered one night by a newsboy nicknamed Fatty:

> "Boys, I want to speak a word to you. . . . I was once a boy myself. . . . I used to pitch pennies, and chew tobacco, and drink rum, and smoke cigars, just as you do.
>
> "Now boys! *Boys!*" rapping the table, "I want you to listen attentively, so that I can hear a pin drop. If I cannot hear a pin drop, I cannot speak at all.
>
> "O boys! I used to like rum once. Two thousand five hundred dollars, all but a cent, were pulled out of my pocket, in two years, by rum. Be men! Quit it!
>
> "There is another thing I want to speak to you about that is selling papers on Sunday. It's not right. You know it isn't. You ought to go to Sunday-school to *Sunday-school,* boys; and after you come out . . . maybe *you would find a purse of money!*"[53]

Fatty's speech brought down the house, and it suggests that the boys did not necessarily swallow the bromides they heard.

Yet concern over their drinking was not misplaced. Brace said the younger ones had more interest in ginger ale than gin, but he admitted that many of the older boys liked their beer and even hard spirits. Brace once ventured into a "gin shop" and found ten newsboys, about 18 or 19 years of age, "sitting around the stove, so stupefied with liquor, though it was only 9 o'clock in the morning, that they could not answer a question intelligently." Newsboys in Boston were known to consume "really astonishing" amounts of liquor. The temperance movement was potent in the 1850s, with a dozen states having passed "Maine laws" forbidding the sale of alcohol. Tracy usually tried to reform rather than expel intemperate lodgers; he kept Alick the Newsman around partly as an object lesson in dissipation. After going on a "burst" in April 1856, Alick and several boys signed pledges to abstain from liquor, at least until the Fourth of July. But this is the last mention of the old newsman in the house diary.[54]

Drink played a large and often ruinous role in working-class life. One reason is that it was so cheap; rum could be had for a penny a glass at grog shops, the lowest of which was warmer and better lit than the typical tenement apartment. Brace called alcohol a source of much misery, grief, and crime. Drunkards' homes were "nests in which young fledglings of misfortune and vice begin their flight," he said. Johnny Morrow portrayed his father's drinking as the cause of his family's undoing, but both he and Brace discounted the economic woes that made jobs so scarce and working people so desperate.[55]

Sinners and Slaves

As Fatty indicated, newsboys were also the focus of Sabbath reformers—those who believed that Sunday should be strictly observed as a day of rest. Sabbatarianism rivaled spiritualism, antislavery, and woman's suffrage as a mass movement in antebellum America. All were inspired by the moral fervor of the Second Great Awakening, or what one newsboy called "these revival times." Sabbatarians circulated petitions, endorsed candidates, and tilted the 1840 presidential election to William Henry Harrison and the Whigs. They pressured Congress to suspend mail trains and close post offices on Sundays, but they could not stem the tide of Sunday papers, whose coverage of vice and crime, they felt, represented an unholy threat to their congregants' and America's salvation. Dozens of Sunday newspapers sprang up in the 1850s. San Franciscans supported at least three and Philadelphians could choose from sixteen. Unable to suppress the papers themselves, sabbatarians lowered their sights on the children who peddled them and made "the day, or night, hideous with their noise."[56]

Agitation against the "*Sunday news-crying* nuisance" began in 1835 when complaints led to the arrest of "an unusually audacious boy" who dared to cry the *Sunday Morning News*, New York's first Sunday paper, at the door of a church. He was hauled off to the Tombs, though released by a magistrate. A lawsuit brought against the arresting officer turned the case into a cause célèbre. In 1838 a Whig alderman prohibited the sale of Sunday papers and mandated the jailing of boys who hawked them. A young lawyer made his name defending the boys, winning the loyalty of many Jewish clients who had a vested interest in striking down the law.[57]

The sabbatarian upsurge was particularly strong in Philadelphia, where the pious placed chairs in the street to prevent carriages from passing and disturbing their worship. Churchgoers had little tolerance for newsboys, fifteen of whom were jailed for two days in 1849. "Alas for our religion," declared the *Philadelphia Freeman*, "which imprisons poor news-boys for selling papers on Sunday . . . but tolerates . . . the traffic of humans beings." Police arrested several more boys in 1853 for violating the state's Sabbath or "blue" law by hawking the *Sunday Dispatch*. A judge fined them $4 each, which the paper promptly paid. The Democratic press in New York excoriated the judge. "What next?" asked the *Clipper*. "Won't he also punish infants for crying on Sunday! Their noise is more annoying than that of newsboys. Go it, Philadelphia. No wonder you are so far behind the age." In February 1855, Robert T. Conrad, a former newspaper editor and the first mayor to preside over a consolidated Philadelphia, ordered the arrest of several boys for crying papers through the streets. But as they told their pitiful tales of want, Conrad discharged them and gave them each $2.50 for their troubles.[58]

Despite their presumed sophistication, New Yorkers, too, tried to stop newsboys from desecrating the Sabbath with their cries. In February 1850, posters printed by one of the Sunday papers appeared in neighborhoods calling the boys to a mass meeting to defend their right to work. Some three hundred of them met in City Hall Park. They heard speeches from *Subterranean* publisher Mike Walsh and members of their own ranks, one of whom declared that their yearly pittance "would not buy the first month's outfit of a baby of the aristocracy." The conclave adopted fourteen resolutions, including a tax on clergy to compensate newsboys for lost income, and a ban on the ringing of church bells on Sunday. Afterward, they marched noisily down Ann Street and up Broadway. "Such a mighty host of ragged creatures I never beheld," said one observer. "The procession itself reminded one of going down stairs, the largest or boss newsboys being in the first platoon, and the others following according to their age—until the end, where was stationed a bare footed little fellow, about eight years of age with a cigar in his mouth, and his hands placed in the pockets of his unmentionables, as old-manified as possible."[59]

New York newsboys continued to face harassment. In June 1850 an alderman tried to subdue a "little urchin vendor" but retreated when residents of a boardinghouse came to the boy's aid. The incident reveals the major weakness of the sabbatarian cause: few people believed that reading Sunday papers was a sin. Their popularity increased every year, and at 6¢ apiece represented newsboys' best chance to "make a pile." Brace sympathized with the boys' need to earn their daily bread but urged them to suspend their labors on Sunday. As an incentive, he began providing refreshments after religious exercises. Sabbath reformers emulated the practice throughout the city, creating what one paper called the "Sunday-dinner-for-the-news-boys movement."[60]

Sabbatarians finally gained the upper hand in 1857 with the founding of the New York Sabbath Committee. It persuaded some publishers to switch their publication day to Saturday, and in 1858 it pressured Mayor Daniel Tiemann to order police to enforce the ban on Sunday news crying. But a backlash arose. The *New York Herald*, which had a Sunday circulation of 82,000, ridiculed the order as one of the greatest reforms since the expulsion of the Jews from Egypt. The newsboys themselves presented a remonstrance to the police commission, arguing that less than a quarter of the city's population attended church regularly, while half was accustomed to reading Sunday papers. "We are resolved to gird on the battle harness at once," vowed the boys, "and resist to the last the enthronement of this new fifth monarchy, this attempted Puritan dynasty."[61] A new drinking song at Hitchcock's Summer Garden became their anthem:

> There's Tiemann too, our model Mayor, to him I'll turn my song,
> To purify our city air he goes it rather strong;

He's stopped the newsboys' cries, I think on them he's quite severe,
He says on Sunday we shan't drink a drop of lager bier.
>The beer! the beer! our spirits for to cheer,
>The beer! the beer! we goes in for our lager beer.[62]

The *Clipper* backed them with a cartoon titled "War upon the Newsboys! The Majesty of the Law Signally Vindicated!" It shows a police squad rounding up newsboys in front of a busy saloon while a clergyman tolls his church bell (Figure 3.5).[63]

Newspapers without Sunday editions defended the crackdown as a necessary solution to a problem that "had annoyed a whole city for years." The *New York Times* dismissed charges that sabbatarians were ogres, hypocrites, and Pharisees. If authorities could not rid the city of the clamor that disturbed religious exercises, it said, then "all hope of 'ferreting out serious crimes and arresting their perpetrators' . . . must be in vain." The paper accused the largely

WAR UPON THE NEWSBOYS!
THE MAJESTY OF THE LAW SIGNALLY VINDICATED!

Figure 3.5. Sabbatarians hoped to win an easy victory by campaigning against the "Sunday news crying nuisance." "War upon the Newsboys! The Majesty of the Law Signally Vindicated!" *New York Clipper,* June 25, 1858, 80. Courtesy American Antiquarian Society.

Democratic Sunday press of "electioneering," trying to stir up class resentment and play down worse Sabbath violations, such as the rioting and bloodshed among Irish and Italians at Sunday beer gardens.[64]

In the midst of the controversy, the *Newark Daily Advertiser* recommended that some qualified person compile the names, ages, and parentage of all quondam newsboys, calculate the time spent in their "noisy vocation," and see if they tended to rise in respectability or sink into perdition. "Such a sketch would make a successful little brochure," said the paper, and "help to resolve the problem of whether their business ought to be patronized, or suffered; or whether it should, like slavery, be restricted to its present boundaries, and not be permitted to extend to places, where it has not yet taken root."[65]

The comparison with slavery sounds facetious to modern ears. Newsboys and slaves occupied separate spheres, as far removed from each other as North from South, city from country, and social mobility from perpetual servitude. Yet the two figures coexisted in antebellum America and were linked to the same labor markets, reform movements, and cultural works. In his 1857 novel *The Tenant-House*, Augustine Duganne described newsboys as "slaves of the Press"— dwarves held captive by the giant Steam. Their task, he said, "was to watch for earliest printed sheets, and scatter them far and wide through city streets; crying, meanwhile, in childish treble, the news of a mighty world . . . of which, too oft, their own poor share was cold and hunger." Newsboys' vaunted freedom to rise, suggests Duganne, was little more than empty rhetoric.[66]

Newsboys were also implicated in the slavery debate by virtue of the papers they carried and the stories they cried. Disseminating news of the sectional crisis could be dangerous, as both pro- and antislavery factions liked to blame the messenger for the message. Capitol Hill newsboys were beaten for circulating President Franklin Pierce's 1856 message to Congress maligning abolitionists and declaring the Kansas free state movement "treasonable" (Figure 3.6). Vendors of Greeley's antislavery *New York Tribune* also risked abuse if they approached a visiting southern planter or any of the resident merchants and manufacturers who relied on southern trade (Figure 3.7). Railroad newsboy David Hill avoided such problems by refusing to carry the *Tribune* on the New York Central's Albany-to-Buffalo route. "I wouldn't sell that Radical sheet, no matter what you'd give me for it," said the future New York governor. "I'm a Democrat and won't spread such nasty lies before the public as old Greeley writes."[67]

Most train boys lacked Hill's scruples and carried newspapers that spanned the political spectrum. The esteemed lecturer Ralph Waldo Emerson lauded them as symbols of modernity who embraced the sacred enterprise of knitting people together, thereby reshaping political alliances. "Look into the morning trains," he instructed, "which, from every suburb carry the business men into the city to their shops, counting-rooms, work-yards and warehouses. With them,

Figure 3.6. Disseminating news during the sectional crisis could by risky. "The Message—How It Was Delivered and How It Was Received," *Young America* 1, no. 2 (Feb. 1856): 27. Author's collection.

enters the car—the newsboy, that humble priest of politics, philosophy, and religion. He unfolds his magical sheets, twopence a head his bread of knowledge costs—and instantly the entire rectangular assembly, fresh from breakfast, are bending as one man to their second breakfast." Emerson's aim was not flattery but dissent; he proceeded to denounce passage of the Fugitive Slave Act, which, in requiring northerners to return fugitive slaves, made all Americans complicit in the "peculiar institution." Emerson seized on the figure of the news butcher to stress each person's capacity to remake his and the nation's destiny.[68]

Novels and plays also helped raise the consciousness of America's newsboys, especially *Uncle Tom's Cabin*, which appeared as a novel in 1852 and in play form opened at the National Theatre in 1853. Newsboys filled the pit as usual, but New Yorkers took a special interest in their reaction to its antislavery message. They noted that the boys—"the very dregs of the outcasts of our City"—cheered when Eliza and her baby escaped the slave hunters on a piece of pasteboard ice. They convulsed with delight when the Kentucky hero spat contemptuously on a wall poster for a runaway slave. And they cried real tears over Little Eva's death. "The effect of the representation is to elevate the black," observed the *Times*; "and we are very much mistaken, from the tone on this occasion, if the United

Boy—Tribune, Sir   Daily Tribune, Sir? only two cents?
Southerner —No, curse your Tribune'—don't you see I'm a *white* man?

Figure 3.7. A newsboy makes a mistake. "Boy—Tribune, Sir. Daily Tribune, Sir?
Only two cents? Southerner—No, curse your Tribune—don't you see I'm a *white*
man?," n.d. In Glyndon G. Van Deusen, *Horace Greeley: Nineteenth-Century Crusader*
(Philadelphia: University of Pennsylvania Press, 1953), 217.

States' officers ever get much assistance, in chasing runaways, from the 'Bowery-
boys.'" A club was formed for newsboys who promised to be good enough to
join Little Eva in heaven. It was called the "O-de-Ram Society" after the boys'
mispronunciation of the hymn Uncle Tom sang to Eva on her deathbed, "O, de
Lamb, de bressed Lamb." Thus did the "low" theater advance the moral and political education of New York's newsboys.[69]

African Americans, both enslaved and free, also worked in the antebellum
news trade. The relative autonomy of the work, along with its access to intelligence, made it an appealing job for a slave. In the case of Matthew Minnis, a
mulatto carrier in Louisville, it served as a springboard to freedom. Like many
slaveholders, Minnis's mistress hired him out. He delivered the *Louisville
Democrat* and the *Journal*, a Whig paper, for several years. But in 1854 the
Democrat became a "noisy popular sovereignty paper" that backed the Kansas-
Nebraska Act. Minnis's owner moved him exclusively to the *Journal*, which
opposed the act. "She supposed he was there to work," gloated the *Democrat*,
"but, on the contrary, we are informed that he loafed about the city for a few

days, and then made off to Canada." He wrote a "cool, saucy letter" to the paper announcing his safe arrival in Chatham, Ontario.[70]

It's not clear what kind of work Minnis secured as a free man, but some runaways found refuge in the news trade. One ex-slave, a double amputee, operated a stand on West Broadway, between Anthony and Leonard Streets, in New York. His name has been lost to history but his words still echo across the ages because of an interview he granted in March 1852 to a correspondent for *Frederick Douglass' Paper.* "He's none of your nomad criers in the literary world," wrote Communipaw. "He is a stationed vender, or, perhaps, like his class, the colored people, he noiselessly does his mission and leaves it to others to find out who and what he is." Communipaw—a reference to the militant interracial community of blacks, Indians, and Dutch in colonial New Jersey—was the pseudonym of black abolitionist James McCune Smith. He stood for some time watching the broad-chested, mixed-race vendor at work, noting the sympathetic treatment he received from his diverse clientele: "Many a 'b'hoy,' half covered from last night's debauch, staggers a square out of the way, to deal with him, and many a child, with half tearful eye-lid, runs across the way, passing a dozen vociferous newsboys, to buy a paper from the poor legless *man*; and many a dandy, who thinks, in a political sense, the negro almost a dog, snatches up a paper, and with half-averted face, throws down four times its worth, and rushes away from the human sympathy that has stolen away into his heart."[71]

Smith saw the disabled vendor as a unifying figure. "Merciful God! what a living fountain of human sympathy hast thou planted on that stone stoop, linking human creature to human creature, in spite of all the bars which society has vainly placed between them!" he exclaimed. When business slackened, Smith approached the vendor and learned that he was a sailor from Virginia who had lost his legs to frostbite after being shipwrecked off the coast of Maryland. He was married with children and operated two stands with his wife: "I sell more *Heralds* than any other paper; and of the Sunday papers, the *Despatch* and *Times* are most called for; next, the *Atlas*, &c. What papers are left unsold, I dispose of, at thirty-one cent a hundred, for waste paper. My profits on the dailies are from one-fourth, to a cent each; on the Sunday papers, one cent. My wife goes down in the mornings, to buy the papers, and I can judge very nearly, of the quantity that will sell."[72]

Smith saw him in a new light, not as a mendicant but as a merchant, not as a dependent but as a breadwinner. Given the recent passage of the Fugitive Slave Act, which made northern blacks vulnerable to kidnapping by slave hunters, Smith risked a sensitive question:

COM. —You *came* from Virginia—free, of course?
NEWS VENDER. —Why—yes—I—made myself free.

COM. —Have you no fears of being arrested and taken back!

NEWS VENDER. —Not now, (sadly looking at his maimed legs.) When I stood six
feet two in my stockings, and heard talk of Virginians hereabouts, I would go
straight to the dock, take ship, and be away two or three months; but now—
what would they want with me?[73]

One of a series of street interviews Smith published in the paper, his conversation with the vendor reinforced his opposition to slavery and caste. A practicing
physician who held degrees from the University of Glasgow, Smith believed in
the possibility of social and individual advancement, and idolized his editor, ex-
slave Frederick Douglass, as the epitome of the self-made man. Smith portrayed
the vendor in similar terms, reinforcing with a poignant twist the narrative of the
newsboy pulling himself up by his bootstraps. Yet his article reveals news selling
to be a genuine means of survival and hope for those at the bottom of society.[74]

In 1858 the Vermont-born white artist Thomas Waterman Wood captured
the precarious dignity of such a man in *Moses, the Baltimore News Vendor* (Plate
9). The subject stands on a cobbled street in worn but natty attire carrying a
sheaf of newspapers under one arm, with more tucked in his coat pocket. A free
black in a slave city, he doffs his hat and smiles, a threat to no one, a service to
all. A real person, Moses Small belonged to the publisher of the thrice-weekly
Federal Gazette, which he carried from 1813 to 1838. He also delivered its
successors, the pro-southern *Baltimore Patriot* and *Baltimore American*, until
1857, and was regarded for his excellent morals, manners, and reliability. A local
merchant commissioned Wood to paint Small's portrait, which later appeared
as a lithograph, the sale of which helped support the vendor after a stroke left
him paralyzed and blind. Small died in 1861 and was remembered as one of
the "monuments" of the city whose privilege it was to deliver papers to some
of the city's most prominent citizens: "Truly a *gentleman*—black, but very
comely in his walks and ways—students of the nicer graces of life found in his
unconscious elegance a model of deference without servility, urbanity without
smirk." However effusive, Moses Small's admirers never took the full measure of
the man.[75]

Heroes of the Heart

Literature, even more than art or journalism, played a crucial role in shaping
attitudes about newsboys. Johnny Morrow's memoir, Duganne's novel, and
even *Uncle Tom's Cabin* were part of a burgeoning market in sentimental
stories for readers of all ages. Produced and distributed by the American
Tract Society, American Sunday-School Union, and commercial publishers,

many of these volumes featured homeless newsboy protagonists.[76] Most successful was Elizabeth Oakes Smith's 1853 bestseller *The Newsboy*. It was not written for hire, as were her husband Seba Smith's earlier newsboy stories, but inspired by Oakes Smith's experience ministering to street children under the auspices of the Young Men's Christian Union. Founded in England in 1844, the union (later the Young Men's Christian Association, or YMCA) spread to North America in 1851. Its members established branches in New York, Philadelphia, Boston, Washington, and Montreal. They preached on street corners, on wharves, and in firehouses—wherever they could gather an audience. Before shifting its attention to children "from better homes," the union established Sabbath schools for newsboys in Cincinnati, San Francisco, and elsewhere. Oakes Smith read to the children at these schools. She wrote a story especially for them "meant to inculcate sobriety and industry." Although never published, it did "good service" during her thirty years of school visits.[77]

The Newsboy enjoyed a more illustrious fate. Mirroring the waif novels issued by the Sunday School Union in England, it is a rambling, 527-page melodrama about a boy whose innate goodness prevents him from doing wrong despite his debasing environment. Bob, the protagonist, adopts destitute little girls, sets up house with them in a deserted railroad car, and performs countless good works. The novel tries to convey the rough camaraderie of newsboys. It describes them sleeping in groups, huddled around bonfires, pitching pennies, rollicking in cheap theaters, and addressing each other by affectionate nicknames such as "Yoppy," "Squinty," and "Log Leg." Oakes Smith also rendered an initiation rite in which Bob is "broken in"—pummeled by another newsboy while the gang forms a cordon against prying eyes. Bob is then made to demonstrate his street cry. The other boys fling pennies at him until he has "a capital upon which to start." Bob didn't possess an inkling of class resentment. "He never dreams of fellowship out of his own ranks," wrote Oakes Smith. "All the rest of the people in the world are an enigma to him, and he sees the crowd go by with as little interest in the individuals which compose it as if they each and all belong to another race. The fine dresses of the women, the nice fixtures of the men scarcely arrest his eye."[78]

The Newsboy saw twelve editions its first year and received glowing reviews. Standing against this "great Gangetic tidal wave of laudation" was *Putnam's Weekly*: "As a history of fact, it is, of course absurd: as a romance, is slatternly in plot, entirely unsatisfactory in catastrophe, flatulently sentimental, tawdry and forced in diction, ragged and careless in delineating character, without any moral or point of any kind, one of the very emptiest and leanest of the horde of lean and empty books which have been so impertinently shoved before the public for a year or two."[79] Otherwise the reviewer liked it fine.

The critic was reacting not just to Oakes Smith's story but also to the plethora of juvenile and adult novels infused by melodrama. Many of them portrayed work as an act of heroism rather than a habit of discipline. News peddling, with its Franklinian heritage, was particularly amenable to such treatment. Fictional newsboys invariably entered the trade to support widowed mothers. According to literary critic Ann Douglas, such books reflect the "feminization of American culture," in which market capitalism emerged as an unforgiving masculine system that required the veneer of a soft, feminized culture to obfuscate its harshness. Whatever its faults, Oakes Smith's novel drew attention to newsboys as a neglected class.[80]

Serial fiction, such as the *Boston Herald*'s "Philip Mortimer, the Boston Newsboy; or, The Intellect of Rags," and fictionalized biographies such as F. Ratchford Starr's *Didley Dumps, or John Ellard, the Newsboy* also accomplished this aim. Ellard (Figure 3.8) was a small humpbacked boy who slept in newspaper bags in printing offices before church and business leaders founded the Newsboys' Aid Society and opened a home in 1858. Ellard lived there while

Figure 3.8. Illustrated novels, biographies, and tracts raised sympathy for newsboys and funds for their benefactors. John Ellard, aka "Didley Dumps," ca. 1858, in F. Ratchford Starr, *Didley Dumps or John Ellard, the Newsboy* (Philadelphia: American Sunday-School Union, 1860). Eckel Collection, Princeton University Library.

running a newsstand at the county building on Sixth and Chestnut. It was little more than a table in a niche decorated with posters, but it provided a living. According to Starr, a supporter of the home, Ellard was "a great favorite with the boys." He liked to roughhouse, tell stories, and extend small loans to his colleagues. On days when he was feeling poorly the boys would carry him to and from his stand. He died of consumption, brought on by exposure, in December 1869, at age 16. A cortege of fifty-six newsboys escorted his coffin from the home to the graveyard, passing his stand, which had been draped in black crepe and tied with a white ribbon. Accounts of their short, blameless lives fostered a "practical public sympathy" for the newsboys and the institutions that ministered to them.[81]

Real and fictional news peddlers advanced myriad causes beyond their own plight, including spiritualism and woman's rights. In 1854 New York Supreme Court Judge John Worth Edmonds, Francis's elder brother and the most prominent jurist in the state, published a tract entitled "Communication from a Newsboy Who Died of Cholera Last Fourth of July," which related his conversation with the spirit of 11-year-old Tim Peters, as channeled through his daughter Laura. The result is a conventionally colloquial account of newsboy life: "I made about a shilling a day, depending on the news and the brain of the editor. I tell you one thing, if any one of the boys didn't sell his papers, we'd go shucks with him, and each take one—that was among the good fellers. Tell you what I used to do—go 'long up Broadway, and see one of your fine-looking fellows, run agin' him, most knock his breath out, then ask, 'Have a paper, sir?' "[82]

Edmonds became a serious investigator of spiritualism after his wife died in 1851. He was at the height of his career when the tract appeared, but it led to his forced retirement from the bench after he admitted that he sometimes reached legal decisions in consultation with the spirits of dead jurists. Spiritualism, or ghostology, as cynics called it, also thrived in slum neighborhoods, where mediums charged 25¢ for interviews with deceased relatives. According to humorist Philander Doesticks, some "spirit knockers" used defunct newsboys to fetch requested souls and run other errands.[83]

The most popular news peddler of the era was the heroine of E. D. E. N. Southworth's 1859 novel *The Hidden Hand; or, Capitola the Madcap*. It was inspired by an item in a New York newspaper about a 9-year-old girl who had been found selling papers in boys' clothing and sent to an asylum in Westchester County. Southworth, an advocate of the woman's suffrage movement initiated in Seneca Falls, New York, in 1848, transformed the newsgirl into a precocious tomboy who exposed the systemic inequality that most Americans saw as natural. Thirteen-year-old Capitola Black is an heiress cheated of her birthright and forced to fend for herself on the streets of New York. Denied work because of her sex and subject to "danger from bad boys and bad men," Capitola dons boys' clothes ("the vestments of masculine privilege"), affects guttersnipe slang ("Oh crickey!"), and commences selling papers. Spared a traditional upbringing, she develops the masculine virtues of courage, candor, and self-reliance, only to be betrayed by her raven locks. At her hearing the court recorder asks:

"Boy—girl I should say—what tempted you to put yourself into male attire?"
"Sir?"
"In boy's clothes, then?"
"Oh, yes—want, sir—and—danger, sir."

Ragged boys could get little jobs to earn bread, she explained, but "I, because I was a girl, was not allowed to carry a gentleman's parcel, or black his boots, or shovel the snow off a shopkeeper's pavement, or put in coal, or do *any*thing that *I* could do just as well as *they*. And so because I was a girl, there seemed to be nothing but starvation or beggary before me." The cost of gender inequality had never before been stated so succinctly. The story found an adoring audience in serial form, as a book, and onstage well into the 1880s.[84]

Morrow's memoir was part of this surge of didactic literature for young readers. It is the story of his reformation, which began after he arrived at the Newsboys' Lodging House and told Tracy that he was not really an orphan. The superintendent regarded the confession as evidence of Morrow's true character. The story circulated in the press, and Morrow became a poster child for the Children's Aid Society. He learned to read and write at the evening classes, sang in the Newsboys' Choir, and attended Sunday school without fail. He hoped to become a minister himself and lodged for a time at the Union Theological Seminary to prepare for entry into Yale or Oberlin College. Meantime, his father died, and Morrow arranged for his brother Willie, now in the custody of the Juvenile Asylum, and sister Annie to be sent west on orphan trains. He also conspired with CAS agents to spirit his sister Jane and half brother Jonathan away from his improvident stepmother. Morrow resolved to write, publish, and peddle his life story to help defray the cost of his education. He may well have written the first draft in some of the two dozen copybooks donated to the lodging house in 1859 by his publisher, A. S. Barnes.[85]

The book is full of precisely remembered earnings and addresses, yet is less than reliable about important matters such as the author's age, religion, and nationality. It lacks the usual newsboy slang and includes some suspiciously orotund passages: "As the Indian vanishes toward the West, at the sound of the woodman's axe, and before the march of civilization, so vanishes the newsboys at the sound of the voices of good men, and before the march of intellectual culture." To alleviate any doubts about authorship, the editor, W. B. D. of Englewood, New Jersey, states that Morrow's memoir is "a daguerreotype of fact, untouched by art." He plays down his contribution as simply "putting it into a somewhat more correct and attractive shape than could possibly be expected of a boy of only sixteen years." W. B. D. was William B. Dwight, founder of Dwight's School for Girls in Englewood. His brother, the Rev. James H. Dwight, was pastor of the town's First Presbyterian Church and Morrow's "early" and "intimate friend." The brothers were descendants of a long line of preachers and teachers starting with Jonathan Edwards, Princeton University's first president. Contrary to Dwight's claim, immigration records indicate that Morrow was 18 when the book came out. He was small for his age and may have found it wise to shave off a few years. Or maybe he just lost track.[86]

A Voice from the Newsboys appeared in spring 1860. It received favorable notices in ladies' magazines and the religious press. The *Evangelist* called it "a new feature in our literature." It also won endorsements from the city's most prominent churchmen, including Henry Ward Beecher. Morrow flogged the book tirelessly. Even before it was published, he took orders for copies at talks he gave in Philadelphia and Baltimore on his way to Abraham Lincoln's inauguration. Morrow addressed Sunday schools and church congregations, including the Rev. Washington Gladden's First Congregational Methodist Church in Brooklyn.[87]

Morrow's self-invention included physical as well as moral regeneration. He submitted to an operation on his leg, which went well and buoyed his spirits. "I feel a new being already," he wrote to a friend, "and I have not the slightest doubt in regard to my future welfare in life." But Morrow bled to death after trying to change his bandages rather than troubling the doctor to do it. Death notices appeared in Christian, abolitionist, African American, and mainstream newspapers. "A Bright Spark Suddenly Extinguished," reported the *Brooklyn Eagle*. On the day of his funeral, Brooklyn's State Street Congregational Church was filled with thirteen hundred mourners, chiefly newsboys and Sunday school students. "Sobs sounded in the stillness," wrote Brace, "as the news boys, with voices hoarse with feeling, sang a favorite hymn, 'There's a rest for the weary.'" After eulogies by Brace, James Dwight, and others, the mourners marched to Evergreens Cemetery, where Morrow's remains were interred and marked with a gravestone that identified him by occupation: "Johnny Morrow, the Newsboy, died May 23, 1861, aged 17." His book continued to win friends for the CAS. A second edition appeared in 1870. Even in death Johnny Morrow was the Children's Aid Society's greatest success story.[88]

Recovering the lives and struggles of Johnny Morrow, Didley Dumps, Moses Small, and others corrects the prevailing image of newsboys as young, able-bodied, and white. Their diverse experiences also compel us to consider character, however tempered by misfortune, as a genuine quality of spirit rather than a moralistic construct wielded by elites to account for individual success or failure. Popular culture was full of such accountings—pictures and stories of persevering newsboys who became prominent businessmen or politicians, surpassing in wealth and reputation the men they once served. History, too, affirms their status as "living monuments to the 'ups and downs' of life!"[89]

Those boys who didn't survive their childhoods can also tell us much about their times. They were genuinely mourned by their peers and treated to humbly lavish funerals befitting honest tradesmen. Fellow members of the "newsboy class" asserted their solidarity, respectability, and humanity in burying them, and in sharing their food, money, and lodgings. They took advantage of the Children's Aid Society and helped shape its services to meet to their needs. Morrow, for example, saw its lodging house not just as a temporary shelter but also as an institution of upward mobility—in his case, an industrial school for the ministry. He also used its placing-out system to rescue his siblings from unpromising fates. His book stayed in print because it conveyed Brace's central message, and that of most slave narratives: "that there is a soul—solemn and immortal, which lives in the poorest outcast boy, as in the best and most cultured of society. Such lads as these are *worth saving*." Despite his blatant paternalism and doom-laden embrace of the term "dangerous classes," Brace took on and fairly met the challenge of providing aid, education, and training for thousands of outcast children. The Thanksgiving message delivered by the rector of Grace Church in 1890 after Brace's death is no less valid today than when he said it: "New York owes Brace a statue."[90]

There were certainly limits to his utopian vision and that of other evangelicals in antebellum America. Newsboys exposed those limits by standing up to authorities who tried to ban Sunday news crying. The boys won that battle as the circulation of Sunday papers soared in New York from 79,000 in 1850 to 280,000 in 1870. Some historians say that the sabbatarian movement stimulated the popularity of Sunday papers, but their spread had more to do with the Civil War. The *New York Times*, once a staunch supporter of the movement, started its Sunday edition on April 21, 1861, nine days after the attack on Fort Sumter. Many other dailies followed suit.[91] The *New York Sun* held firm and even urged generals not to fight battles on Sunday, but such demands were soon muffled by the roar of cannon and the cries of a new generation of newsboys serving a nation divided.

4

Battle Cries

Strolling down Broadway late one Saturday night after attending a new opera by Verdi, poet Walt Whitman heard newsboys hollering in the distance. They soon came "tearing and yelling up the street, rushing from side to side even more furiously than usual." It was April 13, 1861, and the news was astounding: secessionists in Charleston, South Carolina, had fired on Fort Sumter—had fired on the flag! The Civil War had begun. Whitman bought an extra, crossed over to where the lamps of the Metropolitan Hotel were blazing, and read the news. Thirty to forty people gathered, and someone read the story aloud while all listened silently. Some questioned its veracity, recalling that boys had cried bogus extras of a Sumter bombardment months earlier. But this report was true.[1]

Few Americans would ever forget where they were when they heard the news about Fort Sumter, and many heard it first, said the next day's *Herald*, from "swiftfooted news boys, ever ready to be on the wing, like the herald of the gods . . . There was scarcely a part of the city where their active forms were not to be seen or their shrill voices heard, proclaiming the announcement of internecine strife." This opening volley of the war was the first of many unthinkable events that newsboys hollered into reality over the next four years. Americans North and South came to crave and fear the news in equal measure. "What awful times we have fallen upon," wrote Abby Howland Woolsey to her sister. "The sound last night of the newsboys crying till after midnight with hoarse voices 'Bombardment of Fort Sumter,' was appalling." Yet the young New Yorker admitted she would get "into a perfect fever" if her papers were late. "Only *bread and the newspaper* we must have," noted future jurist Oliver Wendell Holmes Jr., "whatever else we do without."[2]

In their own way, Whitman, Woolsey, and Holmes noted how the momentous could come crashing in on the mundane. The nameless newsboys who made these exchanges possible scattered into the night. But their identities and stories reveal much about civilian life on the home front and army life in the field. Moreover, they show how the two were connected. Newsboys numbered among the few civilians who crossed back and forth between these points. Some undermined the Union cause as smugglers, spies, and rioters. Others defended it as drummer boys, soldiers, and messengers. Chicago newsboys even helped elect their obscure favorite-son candidate president by hawking *The Campaign Life of Lincoln*. Those in Milwaukee peddled his first inaugural address as extras.[3] The information they spread over the next four years proved to be so critical to morale and strategy that it sometimes meant the difference between victory and defeat. Some boys profited handsomely from the work. Others lost their lives to it. But they all helped convey the hazards and fortunes of war to their compatriots.

War Footing

As the biggest news story of its day, the Civil War transformed the way news was gathered, written, displayed, and disseminated. The use of the telegraph by far-flung correspondents led to a more concise style characterized by the summary lead. Illustrations and interviews appeared more frequently, and layouts featured less white space as the cost of newsprint shot up. But the biggest change was in the volume of sales. The Sumter crisis sparked a circulation boom throughout the North. New York papers set the pace, their daily output climbing from 300,000 to 425,000 between 1860 and 1865. The *Herald* led with as much as 100,000 sales a day, followed by the *Times* with 75,000. Even William Lloyd Garrison's abolitionist weekly the *Liberator*, with never more than 3,000 subscribers, sold 20,000 extras in the streets of Boston via newsboys.[4]

The war spawned two other innovations: multiple and evening editions. Newspapers previously had issued extras only when extraordinary news arrived after the day's paper had gone to press, but important cables were now received throughout the day, leading publishers to issue three or four editions and establish separate evening papers. Seven new evening sheets appeared in New York in the 1860s, bringing the total to twelve. Their presses produced 160,000 copies a day, most of which were sold on the streets. New Yorkers preferred street purchases over subscriptions so they could read at work and sample different papers each day. A visiting Scotsman decried the practice, claiming that this "chance circulation" encouraged "the sensation system of newspaper headings and paragraphs."[5]

More welcomed than disparaged, newsboys multiplied in northern cities during the war. In Detroit, they became "a noticeable feature of the town" with the Battle of Bull Run (First Manassas) in July 1861. Their ranks swelled so much that civic leaders tried to license them. Cincinnati established a school for twenty-five newsboys in 1861 led by the superintendent of public instruction.

Chicago's Common Council passed an ordinance in January 1862 requiring newsboys to take out a 50¢ license and wear a "tasty" leather badge. It limited the number of licenses to a hundred, though there were at least twice that many newsboys in the city. News sellers in New York totaled "many thousands," said one journalist, and spanned "all the seven ages of man." In 1862 the *Brooklyn Eagle* claimed that forty thousand "lively little newsboys" heralded its name abroad, but later referred more modestly to its "scores of Mercuries."[6]

Expansion of the trade was most pronounced in the nation's capital, which claimed a hundred cigar- or pipe-smoking young news hawkers. By June 1861 the demand for New York and Philadelphia newspapers grew so brisk that they organized "pony expresses" to run them from the train depot to Willard's Hotel on Pennsylvania Avenue, where most of the city's correspondents lodged. An inveterate newspaper reader, President Lincoln was sometimes spotted outside the Executive Mansion looking up and down the street for a newsboy. The flow of papers soon became constant. "Every morning at 6 o'clock," reported the *Chicago Tribune*,

> a hundred newsboys begin to peddle the Baltimore dailies—the *American, Sun,* and *Clipper. Intelligencer* and *Chronicle* make their appearance on the streets about 7 a.m. . . . At eleven . . . o'clock a.m., the Philadelphia train arrives, bringing the *Press* and *Inquirer.* . . . These furnish the populace and strangers "food for reflection" until three p.m., when the first edition of the *Republican* and *Star* make their appearance, followed every half hour by a later edition, until the New York train arrives at five p.m. bringing large supplies of the *Herald, Tribune,* and *Times,* and are howled about the streets, depots, landings, camps and hospitals till night.[7]

The work left lasting impressions on the boys. Seven-year-old Allen Clark's route took in Douglas Hospital on 2nd and I Streets, where surgeons worked in open tents. "I forget not the sights," he wrote sixty years later. William Calvin Chase, an African American, started peddling in 1863 at age 10 to aid his mother and five sisters after their father's murder. White newsboys did not let blacks work among them, but Chase got his papers from a black employee of the *Star.* Chase worked his way through Howard University and became a lawyer and editor of the *Washington Bee,* where he "shelled the citadel of race prejudice" for forty years.[8]

The proliferation of newsboys during the war was also a product of increased earnings. Carriers in New York made 3¢ a week on each subscriber. One who had 500 customers earned $15 a week, less what he paid his help. Hawkers took in $3 to $4 per day, reported the *Saturday Evening Post,* and up to $5 on Sundays.

"Battles and sieges, advances and retreats, victories and discomfitures, have been bread and butter, or rather 'coffee and cakes,' to the Newsboy," said the *New York Ledger*. "He waxes fat on exciting extras." Charles O'Connor, superintendent of the Newsboys' Lodging House, said some of the bigger boys could sell 500 or 600 papers in a few hours, realizing $11 to $12 profit. Lincoln's reelection earned Tom and Jack Collarton $35 and $37, respectively. Two other boys sold 2,400 papers after his assassination, and 2,000 papers announcing the capture of Confederate president Jefferson Davis.[9]

Newsboys had help attracting customers. Newspapers posted the latest news on bulletin boards outside their offices (Figure 4.1). These notices whetted the public's appetite for newspapers, but they could also hurt sales—and sometimes mysteriously went up in flames. Some events were so startling that the whole city seemed to trumpet the news. The "small lads" who swarmed from the newspaper offices of Park Row on April 2, 1865, crying, "Richmond has fallen!" made up a civic chorus backed by the triumphant pealing of church bells through every neighborhood, the salutary roar of artillery in City Hall Park, and the spontaneous cheering and singing of crowds on Wall Street. Newsboys easily found buyers amid such jubilation.[10]

Feverish sales were not unique to New York. Boston newsboys took full advantage of their license by crying their papers from church steps. The entrance and corridors of Milwaukee's post office likewise resounded with the shouts of newsboys who wormed through the crowds, making "intolerable nuisances" of themselves. Eleven-year-old Julius Bleyer sold 300 papers there after First Bull Run: "They were Sentinels, and I tell you we had to fight to get them, too. The

Figure 4.1. War news in the summer of 1862 drew large crowds and enterprising newsboys to the bulletin board outside the office of the *New York Evening Post*. New York Public Library, Stereoscope ID: g91f211_028f.

press was a slow old trap, and it seems to me that there were over a hundred of us street Arabs hanging around the office waiting our turns. We used to get all kinds of prices, from 5 cents up to a quarter, and a number of times some excited individual who had friends in an engagement, would hand me a dollar and forget his change." Bleyer enjoyed similar boom days after the fall of Atlanta and the Battle of Lookout Mountain. "I made more wealth than I have for weeks at a time since I have been operating in wheat and pork," he said. Some people worried that newsboys were becoming hardened by the news. "A military engagement, no matter how important in its consequences, was spurned in disgust," Bleyer admitted, "if its list of casualties was small." Newsboys in Philadelphia raised similar concerns, yet some of these "unprincipled monkies" would give away their entire stock when hospital ships laden with sick and wounded soldiers tied up at the Chestnut Street wharf.[11]

Ferry and train boys also did a thriving business, though not without risks. John Bowman of Staten Island sailed out every morning before light to meet the steamer carrying his papers in a waterproof bag, but in December 1861 he was run over by the ship off New Brighton and drowned. The more fortunate William Thompson sold 500 to 1,000 copies of the *Missouri Republican* and *St. Louis Democrat* on the North Missouri Railroad, often raising prices after major engagements. "On such occasions," he said, "the train generally would find the depot platform crowded with people, not passengers, but farmers and others who had come in to buy papers and learn about the battle. They would almost mob me, pushing their 15 and 25-cent scrip at me, and as they saw I didn't have time to make the change they'd let it go."[12]

Fifteen-year-old Thomas Edison capitalized on the massacre at Shiloh so shrewdly that it bordered on profiteering. He held exclusive rights to sell papers on the Grand Trunk Railroad between Detroit and his hometown of Port Huron, Michigan, and foresaw a windfall when he arrived in the city. Huge crowds had gathered outside the *Detroit Free Press*, where bulletin boards reported that 60,000 men had been killed or wounded in the battle.* Edison promised to supply the telegrapher at the depot free periodicals for months if he would wire a bulletin about the battle to the stations along the line. He then ordered 1,000 copies of the *Free Press*—ten times his usual number. The editor let him have the bulk on credit. Customers mobbed Edison at every stop. The papers went so fast he raised their price from 5¢ to 10¢ and then to 25¢ apiece. "I sold all out and made what to me then was an immense sum of money," he said.[13]

* Though less than originally reported, casualties at Shiloh were staggering: 13,000 Union and 11,000 Confederate soldiers were killed, wounded, or missing. This two-day total exceeded the number of Americans killed in all previous wars combined.

Detroit newsboys rose up in protest two years later when the *Free Press* and *Advertiser* raised their prices. The boys formed an ad hoc union, fired themselves up with diatribes against the rising cost of living, and voted with one voice to strike. "Banded together, a conquering host, the tatterdemalion legion paraded the streets," reported the *Cleveland Herald*, "proclaiming their terrible resolve to let the whole machinery of journalism stop, the presses grow rusty, and the world perish in ignorance, unless they were allowed their half cent." The strikers held out until suppertime, weakened by defections and the publishers' refusal to negotiate.[14]

Newsboys' desire for profits sometimes exceeded that of publishers, as was the case with three brothers in San Francisco. On December 24, 1864, newsboys Gustavus, 22, Charles, 19, and Michael Henry De Young, 15, printed 3,000 extras describing bogus Union victories for sale to the large crowd that daily formed outside the *Evening Bulletin*'s Montgomery Street office in anticipation of its five o'clock edition. At 4:45 a squad of boys suddenly appeared on the street crying papers containing what purported to be a Pony Express report: "Richmond Taken! Ben Butler Shot!" "You ought to have seen the rush for those extras, at two bits each!" recalled an old printer. "Crowds fairly smothered the newsboys. The excitement lasted ten minutes, and then couriers rode furiously through the streets proclaiming the extra a fraud." Thirteen boys and Gustavus De Young were arrested for the swindle. A year later the brothers founded the *San Francisco Chronicle*.[15]

Deceptions plagued suppliers as well as customers. A Pittsburgh newsboy used to pay for his papers with counterfeit bills known as "brown paper." Milwaukee's "Reddy the Sneak" perfected the art of folding two newspapers into one. It "worked for a long time," noted a friend, "but he was finally caught, and got a good flogging." Still, he managed to buy a shanty for his widowed mother. "Yes, indeed, many a family received its entire support during the war from newsboys—the father being in the army."[16]

Whether or not they were the sons of soldiers, Civil War–era newsboys received more sympathy than their predecessors. The most common way to help them was by tipping. *New York Herald* managing editor Frederic Hudson estimated that New York newsboys who dispensed carrier's addresses elicited no less than $5,000 "*in pourboires*" every New Year's Day between 1860 and 1865. Donations to the Newsboys' Lodging House also rose during the war.[17]

Stifling Dissent

Yet sympathy slid easily into anger when boys were caught hustling papers deemed to be disloyal to the Union. The War Department temporarily shut down ninety hostile papers, despite the grumblings of their vendors, and suspended the writ of habeas corpus, allowing authorities to detain citizens without charge. Baltimore newsboy David Smith was arrested in May 1861 for carrying secessionist propaganda and a loaded pistol but was released with a reprimand. Among those jailed in August and September were the editors of two Baltimore dailies (the *Exchange* and the *South*), a reporter for the *New York Daily News*, and several newsboys. Authorities charged them with "openly and zealously advocating the cause of the insurrection and largely contributing to unsettle and excite the public mind." Nicholas Lynch, who tried to sell the *New York Daily News* and the *World* on the day they were banned, "played the drop game" on his would-be detainer: "I got a bundle of papers in the office, and a soldier told me, presenting a musket with a fixed bayonet, to stop. I pushed the bayonet aside with my hand, darted out between his legs, upsetting him, and escaped amid the laughter of the other soldiers."[18]

Pat Murphy of Louisville also had no qualms about selling banned papers. Twelve years old when the war broke out, he raced his skiff against rivals to serve a Union camp in Jeffersonville, Indiana, and smuggled a suppressed Cincinnati paper to Copperheads (Peace Democrats) in Louisville. Murphy recruited a fireman on a mail boat to deliver two hundred copies of the paper each day. He bought them for 2½¢ each and sold them for 25¢ apiece, earning as much as $50 on his $5 outlay. To avoid suspicion, he would wrap the papers around his body under his clothes. One day a detective noticed his abnormal girth and seized the contraband. Murphy escaped by diving into the river and swimming away.[19]

The arrest of George A. Hubbell, 25, on Connecticut's Naugatuck Railroad created more ripples than usual. On September 20, 1861, a US marshal, acting on orders from the secretary of war, arrested Hubbell for selling the *Daily News*. He was accused of being a "noisy secessionist and doing great mischief by his treasonable talk." Many intervened on his behalf, including his older brother Nathan, who in a letter to Lincoln appealed rather too jocularly to "Honest Old Abe's" forgiving instincts. He pointed out that George had a spinal deformity and was "the sole help of his poor mother who is in the deepest sorrow." He said his brother was a "strong Union man" who sold the *Daily News* only at the request of railway president and Democratic congressman William D. Bishop, who he feared would replace him if he didn't do as he was told. As for George's "treasonable talk," Nathan blamed the people on the train who had "impertinently interfered with his business." The younger Hubbell was released a week later after taking an oath of allegiance.[20]

Clement Vallandigham, the foremost Copperhead in Congress, brought Hubbell's case and that of a 15-year-old newsboy to the attention of his colleagues. He said the boy was among the 640 political prisoners confined for treasonable practices at Camp Chase, near Columbus, Ohio, and slated for a military trial. The boy's only offense, he said, was that he owed 15¢ to his Negro washerwoman, who reported him to a provost marshal for engaging in disloyal practices. "And yet, for four weary months," railed Vallandigham, "the lad had lain in that foul and most loathsome prison, under military charge, lest, peradventure, he should overturn the Government of the United States; or, at least, the Administration of Abraham Lincoln!"[21]

Newsboys also figured in political cartoons critical of press censorship, including an 1863 lithograph lambasting General Ambrose Burnside's suspension of the *Chicago Times* and *New York World* for "disloyal and incendiary statements" (Figure 4.2). The *Times*, edited by southern sympathizer Wilbur Storey, was shut down for two days before a judge issued an injunction against the general's order. The cartoon portrays a tattered Burnside with a gavel on his bald head. He tells his black body servant that he was roughed up by the *Times*'s printer's devil and ordered to gaze on a statue of Columbia wielding the sword of civil liberty. Above, the words "Back out Ambrose—A. Lincoln" crackle over a telegraph wire, a reference to the president's rescindment of Burnside's order. To the right, a newsboy, symbol of a free and unfettered press, cries, "Eres the Times Morning Edition. dugham-stealers got Injunctioned."[22]

Figure 4.2. E. W. T. Nichols, "Oppression!! Suppressing the Press." Lithograph on wove paper, 24.1 × 31.5 cm (Boston, 1863). Library of Congress, Washington, DC.

In 1864 Democratic congressman James Brooks, publisher of the virulently Copperhead *New York Express*, made newsboys the centerpiece of his defense of civil liberties. In the debate over a bill incorporating the Newsboys' Home in the District of Columbia, Brooks questioned the need for the home if newspapers were to be suppressed. He proposed an amendment to prohibit the suppression of newspapers by military force, "thus depriving newsboys of their employment." He also demanded that the Magna Carta be posted on the Capitol walls, "not only in English but in the original Latin," and taught to Washington newsboys so that they might become "champions of human liberty." Brooks was ruled out of order and the bill passed without amendment. The *New York Times* feigned support for his Magna Carta idea, saying it would turn the boys into abolitionists.[23]

Artist J. G. Brown used an *Express* newsboy to comment on the pervasiveness of pro-Confederate and antiblack sentiment during the war. His 1863 painting *A Newspaper Boy Hitching a Ride*, or *Colored People Not Allowed on This Line*, shows three urchins, two white and one black, clinging to the rear step of an omnibus (Figure 4.3). The white *Express* seller is trying to knock

Figure 4.3. J. G. Brown, *A Newspaper Boy Hitching a Ride* (*Colored People Not Allowed on This Line*), 1863, oil on canvas, 15 × 12 in. Formerly Copley Newspapers Inc., The James S. Copley Library, La Jolla, CA.

the black boy off as a soldier riding inside the car looks on in amusement. The "light colored bully . . . believes that the black boy has no rights a white boy is bound to respect," noted a reviewer after the painting's exhibition in March 1863. Four months later newsboys and Negrophobia ran amok in the New York City draft riots, leaving at least 119 people dead.[24]

The violence broke out after a Conscription Act granted exemptions to anyone who could pay $300. Governor Horatio Seymour, a Democrat, called the draft "a terrible affliction" on New York's poor. The irregular pay given to soldiers did "not provide the necessary support to their families," he said, "and they are frequently broken up and ruined." *Harper's Weekly* estimated that boys between 8 and 18 were responsible for at least half the arson and theft. The *Round Table* claimed that in many instances boys under 14 were "pushed forward" on the presumption that the "defenders of the property would not shoot children."[25] Mobs attacked conscription centers, the homes of prominent Republicans, and the offices of two "woolly head" (antislavery) newspapers, the *Tribune* and the *Times*. *Tribune* editor James Parton said that "the fringe of the crowd nearest the Tribune building was composed of boys,—newsboys, apparently,—some of whom were not more than 12 years old." He placed them among the five thousand rioters who sang "Hang Horace Greeley to a sour apple tree!" while a smaller group destroyed property and set fire to the building. The *Tribune* became a fortress afterward, barricading its windows with bales of newsprint. Meanwhile, *Times* publisher Henry Raymond set up two Gatling guns in the front office and vowed to rake Chatham and Centre Streets should the mob descend again. Rioters also torched the Colored Orphan Asylum and lynched at least eleven black men. Eight-year-old newsboy Edwin Fitzgerald was repulsed by the violence, but not all his peers felt this way, according to the *Round Table*: "Boys, chiefly of Irish parentage, not over seven years of age, armed with clubs and pieces of iron hoops, were seen marshaling others older and younger than themselves to hunt 'the nagurs,' while lads above twelve years old were carrying revolvers to shoot the unfortunate victims of their hate."[26]

Sinclair Tousey and Charles Loring Brace were appalled by the bloodletting. Tousey papered the city with posters headed "Don't unchain the tiger," telling rioters to beware of public outrage and retaliation. He denounced Peace Democrats, endorsed freedmen's civil rights, and published *An Antislavery Alphabet* for young readers. Brace stepped up his work on behalf of New York's "dangerous classes." "The rioter of 1863 is merely the street-boy of 1853 grown up!" he said in a fundraising circular. Brace resolved to sponsor more orphan trains. He was relieved that his supporters did not abandon the Children's Aid Society after this "fire in the rear," as Lincoln called it, was quelled by Union troops from Gettysburg.[27]

Mustering Up

The war provided older newsboys with a new career option: soldiering. With the outbreak of hostilities, many of Mercury's children laced up the boots of Mars. Some were recruited right on the job. In Cleveland, the firing on Fort Sumter sparked a spontaneous meeting in the folding room of a local paper. James Wood, one of the city's fifteen or twenty newsboys, said a lawyer mounted a table and addressed the workers: "He lauded the Union cause to the skies, and urged those present to immediately respond to the call for troops that was sure to follow."[28]

Newsboys did respond, particularly residents of newsboys' homes. The prospect of steady pay and military glory was too great to pass up compared to the fitful existence of news selling. Privates earned $12 a month plus enlistment bounties of around $50. Peer pressure provided extra incentive, especially when generated by neighborhood recruitment drives. More than forty residents of the Philadelphia Newsboys' Home enlisted in 1861, many of whom had drilled in mock companies. So many boys departed that the home soon closed its doors. The Washington Newsboys' Home, established in March 1864 on Armory Square by a joint resolution of Congress, also saw mass desertions by older lodgers who either joined up or followed the army as sutlers. Enlistments at the Newsboys' Lodging House in New York similarly reduced the average age of its lodgers. Hundreds of former newsboys fought "manfully and heroically under the national flag," eulogized the *Christian Weekly*. "And many a brave fellow rescued from a life of shame by this Newsboys' Lodging House, sleeps upon the battle fields of Shiloh, Donaldson, Seven Pines, and the Wilderness."[29]

The army of the United States required volunteers to be at least 18 years old, but many youths bluffed their way past recruiting sergeants eager to form units. Worcester, Massachusetts, newsboy Patrick Courtney ran off and joined the 182nd New York Regiment in 1862 at age 17. He was captured at the Battle of Cold Harbor and spent time in Andersonville Prison. The best estimates are that by war's end anywhere between 5 and 20 percent of soldiers in the Union and Confederate armies were underage. Boys of 12 could lawfully serve as drummer boys and ambulance drivers. One New York newsboy and orphan train rider who distinguished himself as a drummer was Andrew Burke, future governor of North Dakota. Brace said that more than a thousand of the boys he sent west served in the national armies.* "Many have died in hospital or on the battle-field,"

---

* A supporter of the Liberty Party and defender of John Brown, Brace rejoiced at the outbreak of war, believing it would end slavery. He was 35 years old in 1861. Instead of enlisting, he joined the *New York Times* and the *Independent* as a Washington, DC–based correspondent, and in this capacity covered the Union defeat at Second Manassas. See Emma Brace, *The Life of Charles Loring Brace* (New York: Scribner's, 1894), 265.

he wrote in the annual report of 1865, but "we have yet to learn of a disgraceful action committed by one of them."[30]

Boston newsboys also sacrificed for the Union cause. Henry Morgan, founder of the city's newsboys' home and its Franklin Night School, lauded his pupil Barney Bartlett, who "rushed to the field a drummer boy." Wounded in action, he recovered and reenlisted as a soldier. Bartlett was killed in the Battle of Fredericksburg while letting a wounded comrade drink from his canteen. "Ah! there are noble, generous souls among street-boys," said Morgan.[31]

To instill patriotism, many newsboys' homes invited prominent Unionists to address their lodgers. Among the guest speakers at the Boston home was abolitionist Wendell Phillips. "Free schools make newsboys; without education, no one would buy a paper," he told them. The boys booed his emphasis on education, but Phillips persisted. "Who commands at Charleston?" he asked. "Gillmore," replied the boys. "Do you know about his guns?" There was no answer. "Well I will tell you," said Phillips. "They will send a shot five miles: Mr. Parrott, the inventor of them, was a poor New-Hampshire boy. His thoughts were worth fifty thousand men. You see then, that the character and brains make men."[32]

Although hustling papers on the home front was safer than shouldering a weapon in the army, newsboys sometimes encountered violent reactions to the news they cried. After First Bull Run, which most northern papers initially declared a Union victory, boys who shouted otherwise were run off the streets. "It was regarded as a smart commercial fraud," said the *New York Times*, "which ought to be put a stop to by the police." Carriers of the *Philadelphia Inquirer*, which called the battle a disaster, were kicked out of homes for serving the paper.[33]

Peddling war news was especially risky in border states. One reporter noted how St. Louis boys were alternately summoned and spurned as they rushed around selling extras about the fall of Fort Henry in February 1862: "I saw one of the venders of intelligence enter the store of a noted Secessionist, where he shouted the nature of the news at the highest note of his voice. A moment later he emerged from the door, bringing the impress of a Secessionist's boot."[34]

Newsboys were not just the victims of assaults but dished out their own abuse as well, especially in Washington, DC, where paroled Rebel officers often strutted about in uniform. "More than once," recalled a reporter, "I saw ultra-loyal newsboys or boot-blacks throw a lump of mud, or a brickbat, at the passing Confederate." Union officers also were subject to swindle and sass. One capital newsboy, hoping to avoid being "stuck" with unsold papers, planted himself at the entrance to the Metropolitan Hotel and shouted, "Extra STAR—Great battle in Alabama!" A passing officer took the bait, but after scanning the pages said, "You little rascal, I can't see any battle!" "No," answered the boy as he moved off,

"I reckon you don't and you never will see one if you loaf round this 'ere hotel *all* the time!"[35]

Southern newsboys took equal pride in bedeviling occupying forces and could get away with it more easily than adults, who risked arrest or worse for insulting Federals. General Benjamin Butler, commander of the Union Army in New Orleans, recalled that during the yellow fever epidemic in the summer of 1862 newsboys, who had previously organized themselves into a military company, helped spread fear among unacclimated Yankees. Two boys would hang on to the lamppost, he said, and call to each other within earshot of Union sentries: "Jimmy, have you heard the news?" "No; what is it?" "They have got the 'yeller' fever down in Frenchtown prime; eleven have died to-day, there, and it's spreading. The Yanks will catch it awful. I shall be glad, won't you, when they either die off or run away in their ships?" Southern newspapers could be suppressed, but apparently not southern newsboys.[36]

Rebel Yells

The fortunes of war differed for newsboys in the North and the South; while newspaper sales boomed throughout the loyal states, they plummeted in those that seceded. Southern newspapers were among the first and heaviest casualties of the rebellion. In 1861 the eleven states of the Confederacy published eighty dailies, barely twenty of which were still operating by war's end. In addition to rising production costs, falling advertising revenues, paper shortages, and postal problems, southern editors had to contend with the loss of labor and property because of volunteering personnel and the invading Federal troops. The difficulty of collecting on subscriptions also continued.[37]

Richmond was the center of Confederate journalism. Its four dailies—the *Dispatch, Enquirer, Whig,* and *Examiner,* later joined by the *Sentinel*—exerted much influence over the southern press. The city also produced the *Southern Illustrated News* in 1862 to fill the void left by the unavailability of *Harper's Weekly*. Cartoonist Thomas Nast mocked the mendacity of these papers in his drawing of a skeleton running through the streets of Richmond crying Confederate losses as victories (Figure 4.4). A British journalist offered a sadder, more sympathetic description of the "sealed city" six months later: "War looks at you from hospital churches and through the bright eyes of fever; it thrills you in the limp of cripples that beg at the wayside; it whispers sadly in the rustle of crape, and shouts its discontent in the yell of newsboys."[38]

New Orleans, under Union control after the first year of the war, published six dailies, including the loyal *Tribune*. Labeled a "nigger paper," it was not sold by any newsboy and was carried by just one dealer. Nor was Greeley's *Tribune* in

RICHMOND NEWSBOY ANNOUNCING THE REBEL SUCCESS!!!

Figure 4.4. "Richmond Newsboy Announcing the Rebel Success!!!" *Harper's Weekly* 7, no. 290 (July 19, 1862): 464. Library of Congress, Washington, DC

demand. "I wouldn't sell the *Tribune* if I was paid for it," said one New Orleans newsboy. "They say it's Abolition." New Orleans hawkers were nevertheless as prolific and annoying as those in the North. "The Crescent City has its newsboys and its juvenile lazzaroni," wrote a northern correspondent, "and between the two, the one either screaming his *Daily Era* or *Extra Delta* into your ear in the street, or constantly thrusting it under your nose in all other public places and the other assailing you at every turn for a five cent ticket to buy a loaf of bread, one's existence is rendered almost unbearable." General Nathaniel Banks, Butler's replacement, thinned their ranks when he ordered a draft in 1863, which gave Henrietta Newsham, a refugee from Vicksburg, the confidence to swap her newsboy disguise for a dress. She reportedly earned thousands of dollars selling papers before dying of smallpox in 1864.[39]

Atlanta, a city of 10,000 at the start of the war, was home to three papers, the *Register, Intelligencer,* and *Southern Confederacy.* Its population doubled during the hostilities, and several out-of-state papers relocated there. The *Knoxville Register, Chattanooga Daily Rebel,* and *Memphis Appeal* (nicknamed the *Moving Appeal*) moved in after Federals overran Tennessee. During the siege of Atlanta in July 1864, a shell whizzed through the *Appeal* office on Whitehall Street and exploded in the back alley, killing a newsboy. "We could not identify the little fellow," said the editor. "Every undertaker had fled the city. We coffined the boy rudely enough and buried him at night sorrowfully by moonlight in the rear of the building."[40]

The Richmond dailies were more readily available to the Army of Northern Virginia, while the *Chattanooga Rebel* and *Memphis Appeal* had the widest circulation among soldiers in the western armies. The agency serving General Braxton Bragg's Army of Mississippi and Army of Tennessee had a standing order of 5,000 of the *Rebel's* 9,000 daily circulation. Still, demand among soldiers and civilians exceeded supply. "At every station, on any road you may pass," reported a *Charleston Mercury* correspondent, "squads of from 10 to 20 men may be seen standing round while one reads the last paper, procured of some newsboy or passenger."[41]

The war ushered into the South many of the same journalistic practices that were new to the North. These included an increasing emphasis on telegraphic news, the evolution of cooperative news gathering, the use of special correspondents (particularly soldiers), and the recruitment of newsboys in cities to replace the old subscription trade. Southern newspapers also started issuing regular extras, but they were usually "mere slips of paper" containing a single column from a coming edition. They appeared almost every day and sold for 10¢ to newsboys, who retailed them for a quarter. Their high cost reflected the fact that their contents were based mainly on northern papers that had been run in through blockades. Nine-year-old Dick Brugman of Little Rock, Arkansas, earned $13.25 in Confederate shinplasters hawking one such extra issued by the *Arkansas State Gazette* after the Rebel victory in August 1861 at the Battle of Oak Hills. It was the first money he ever made.[42]

The prices of newspapers rose everywhere during the war but especially in the South, where shortages were acute. The Confederacy was home to just 24 of the nation's 555 paper factories, which drove the cost of newsprint from 8¢ per pound in 1861 to 25¢ or more in 1863. One- and two-penny papers now sold for 4¢ or 5¢ apiece, and subscription rates almost tripled. Some publishers were so uncertain about the future that they discontinued annual subscriptions or offered them for only three months at a time. A few halved their prices to soldiers but would accept no paper currency, only coin. More accommodating was the *Southern Watchman* of Athens, Georgia, which would exchange papers

for "corn, wheat, flour, oats, rye, butter, hay, shucks, fodder, chickens, eggs—
anything that can be eaten or worn, or that will answer for fuel." Desperate for
paper and ink, some publishers offered rag pickers high prices for clean cotton
and linen rags, while others bought up shoe blacking to use as ink. Dozens of
papers in Louisiana and Mississippi resorted to printing on ledger, wrapping,
or tissue paper. Instead of lamenting the high prices, newsboys upped them
even further. An 1863 issue of the *Vicksburg Citizen*, printed on wallpaper, urged
readers to resist being gouged: "The price of our paper at the office is twenty-five
cents. Newsboys who charge fifty cents on the streets are not authorized by us
to sell at that price."[43]

Newsboys in the Confederacy also had access to northern papers, which
commanded high prices. "Such is the scarcity of Northern intelligence that
ten, fifteen and even twenty dollars are freely paid for a single New York paper,"
declared a Richmond correspondent in June 1861. Prices dropped as enterprising newsmen found ways to collect northern papers by flag-of-truce boats
and various underground channels. In 1862 Richmond newsboys peddled
copies of the *New York Herald* for what one southern paper called "the moderate price of two dollars." By 1864 the Richmond press regularly received two-
day-old Baltimore, Philadelphia, and New York papers from across army lines.
Earnings from this trade were crucial; one 13-year-old supported his three sisters for months while their father was off fighting and their mother stewed in jail
for her part in the Richmond bread riot of 1863.[44]

With money to be made and hunger afoot, competition among southern
newsboys sometimes led to rock and fist fights. In March 1863 four Nashville
youths were arrested for brawling; two were fined $5 and one $1, plus costs.
"These newsboys are acquiring some very bad habits," said the *Nashville Dispatch*,
"of which they must be broken, or the city will be flooded with a growing generation of candidates for the Penitentiary. Many of the smallest of them use language perfectly shocking to persons not by any means sensitive on the subject,
and one-half of the fights among them originate in the calling of each other improper names."[45]

One hazard of the trade was the unreliability of currency. The Confederacy
introduced a full range of bills and coins in 1861, including copper and silver
pennies, a copper 5¢ piece, and a dime with Jefferson Davis's profile on it. Yet
the fluctuating value of this money heightened the risk of doing business and
led many boys to accept streetcar tickets as payment or to speculate in currency as a sideline. In April 1862 a newsboy in Fredericksburg, Virginia, sold
a $10 Richmond note to a Union soldier for 10¢. The boy thought the bill was
worthless, but the soldier wrote home saying that a local storekeeper had accepted it at full value after refusing his US treasury notes.[46] Newsboys' distrust
of Confederate money was nevertheless prudent, as its value plunged whenever

the Union army occupied a city. Memphis boys "respectfully declined" Rebel coins for the Rebel *Argus* a few months later because "they won't take it at the office." Toward the end of the war a Union soldier in Chattanooga reported, "Scrip is useless, a newsboy hesitating to sell a paper for $100.00 of it." Missouri train boy William Thompson once had his train stopped by Rebel guerrillas whose leader swapped him a thick roll of bills for his papers, saying, "You can keep the change, sonny." Thompson thought he had hit the jackpot but then saw it was Confederate scrip "worth about ten cents a barrel." Ever alert to an angle, northern newsboys sold counterfeit Confederate notes as curiosities for 3¢ to 5¢ on the dollar.[47]*

Both blacks and whites distributed newspapers in the South during the war. Blacks served as hawkers, carriers, and train boys. Thomas E. Miller, a light-skinned free black, worked the Charleston-to-Savannah line and listed it among his qualifications when he was elected to Congress and named president of the Colored Normal Industrial Agricultural and Mechanical College of South Carolina. William Sanders Scarborough, the 12-year-old son of a free black father and a slave mother, earned his first greenbacks selling the *Macon Telegraph* in 1864. Though enslaved himself, he learned to read and enjoyed much freedom as a child. He and his playmates, mostly Irish boys, were permitted to cross the lines and sell papers to Union soldiers. He brought his earnings home to his father, who placed the money in a fine walnut box with a lock and key. Peddling papers on the streets of Macon, Georgia, was risky, however, as blacks were often harassed by ruffians or impressed to work in the town's military hospitals. Scarborough was apprenticed to a shoemaker, at whose shop he secretly read the newspaper to enslaved workers and forged permits that enabled them to visit relatives.[48]

The practice of hiring out enslaved men, women, and children continued during the war, when the Confederacy's 3.5 million bondservants made up 40 percent of its population and a majority of its labor force. Nine out of ten Richmond newsboys were black, which bothered some whites. In 1863 the *Richmond Daily Whig* complained that there was a "large number of strong, able-bodied negroes engaged in vending newspapers about the streets, railroad depots, and places 'where men do most congregate.'" "A good deal of *muscle*

---

* Hoarding in the North led to shortages of copper-nickel "white" pennies, the newsboys' standby. In their place came privately issued 1¢ pieces, "very losable silver threepenny bits," and 25¢ bills. To compensate for the lack of silver, the US mint issued bronze Indian head pennies in 1864 and 2¢ coins bearing a bust of George Washington on one side and a new motto, "In God We Trust," on the other. See David Q. Bowers, *History of United States Coinage: As Illustrated by the Garrett Collection* (Wolfeboro, NH: Bowers and Merena Galleries, 1979), 242–45, and Len Buth, "The W. E. Tunis Token of Clifton, C.W.—Revisited," *Numismatica Canada* 2, no. 3 (Sept. 2003): 116–18.

is thus expended," said the paper, which "may be a source of considerable income to the darkies, or their employers," but did not profit the Confederacy.
"We need negro labor on the farms, to work on fortifications, and in other places
that will not only remunerate the owner of the negro, but be of some benefit to
the country at large." Moreover, the *Whig* charged that slaves crowded out the
hundreds of white boys in the city who needed to support widowed and indigent mothers. "We hope the spectacle of a 'big buck nigger,' going about the city
vending newspapers, will no more be seen, and that it will be abolished, if necessary, by the interposition of the police."[49]

Ironically, the paper's critique of the "peculiar institution" echoed the
arguments of Wilmot Democrats and free-soilers, whose main objection to
slavery was that farmers and tradesmen couldn't compete against it. Enslaved
news peddlers also cheapened the newsboy as a symbol of enterprise and upward mobility. The incessant shouting and insolent manner that was irritating
in white newsboys was terrifying in blacks. Nothing was more threatening to
white southerners than slaves who wished to better themselves, because that
goal meant one thing: freedom.

In Harm's Way

Northern newsboys served not just anxious civilians on the home front but also
active military stationed in forts, encamped in bivouacs, and entrenched on the
front lines. Twelve-year-old Cyrus Curtis got his start in journalism selling the
Courier at inflated prices to soldiers at Camp Preble in Portland Harbor, Maine.
Some boys stowed away amid the luggage on military trains or hid themselves
under soldiers' greatcoats. These youths became key links in a supply chain that
stretched from the basements of big-city newspapers to remote armies in the
field. So efficient were the *Philadelphia Inquirer*'s distribution channels that when
the Federal government wanted something known in the eastern and western
armies, it requested that a special edition be circulated free by the paper's agents.
These agents, said one correspondent, were "a modern addition to the camp fol-
lower that Napoleon did not have in his grand armies."[50]

With more than two million soldiers, the Union Army represented an immense market for newspapers. According to journalist-turned-soldier George
F. Williams, "Newspapers were always plentiful, the army newsboys being
a decided feature at the front. No sooner did an army halt within reach of
these enterprising fellows than they were to be seen galloping from brigade
to brigade, distributing daily papers to eager buyers." Both men and boys engaged in this work, but the *New York Herald* referred to them as "enterprising
juveniles."[51]

Soldiers' hunger for news was so great that they sometimes wrote home asking for information about the battles that they had just been in. On the eve of Gettysburg, an Indiana soldier complained in a letter that the train from Alexandria brought newspapers, but the rush for them was so great that it was impossible to get one. One commander responded to the chaos by arresting all the youths for not selling in proper order. During the siege of Vicksburg, a sergeant from Ohio noted that although newsboys were "thick in camp" shouting the *Chicago Times* and *Cincinnati Commercial*, the soldiers stuck to a cooperative system. "Here a single copy does for a whole company," he said, "and the one that buys it reads it aloud—a plan which suits the buyer very well, if not the seller."[52]

Newspaper artist Edwin Forbes recognized that army newsboys engaged in dangerous work, especially during active campaigns. Newspapers sometimes had to be brought up from the rear on horseback "through a country infested by bushwhackers" and distributed to troops that "might be engaged in battle and stretched out over miles of ground." Fear of rivals prevented them from waiting until the end of the battle, he said, "and out upon the danger-line they would go, to sell their stocks as soon as possible. Among the batteries where shells were bursting they would halt, and, surrounded by crowds of clamoring soldiers, would sell their papers and make change with the coolness of veterans—which indeed they quickly became."[53]

Soldiers also remarked on how close newsboys got to the action. In his report on the Battle of Gaines' Mill, Virginia, in June 1862, Colonel Richard Tylden Auchmuty noted that although fighting was imminent, newsboys went along the lines crying the New York and Philadelphia papers. Sure enough, the 57,000 Rebels under General Robert E. Lee's command launched an all-out assault, forcing Union soldiers and newsboys alike to retreat across the Chickahominy River. A hardened campaigner from Illinois shared a corroborating anecdote in a letter home: "A newsboy came along in the ditch, crying, 'Heer's your Cincinnati, Louisville and Nashville papers.' Crack! Crack!! Went two Rebel guns, and a Johnnie holloed 'There is your Atlanta *'Appeal*'!"[54]

Who were these fearless and foolhardy boys, and how did they find themselves at the front dodging bullets and making change? Some were city newsboys who seized the opportunity to make money by following the troops south. Others were adventure-seeking schoolboys who tagged along with their home-state units. Still others were young recruits charged with keeping their companies supplied with papers. All were part of a vast distribution system sustained by giant news agencies and lucrative government contracts.[55]

Ten-year-old Washington, DC, newsboy Robert Budd, an African American, drifted toward the battlefield because he could sell papers on both sides for a dollar apiece. He also discovered a market for back issues after Second Manassas, when officers offered him $5 for copies describing the battle. Budd realized that newspapers were not just perishable commodities but also durable data. After the war, he opened a shoeshine and newspaper stand in New York and became a dealer in old newspapers who was known to his customers as "Back-Number" Budd.[56]

Among the tag-alongs was William Cullen "Doc" Aubery, who fell into the job after following his four older brothers into the 2nd Vermont regiment in June 1861. Turned away because of his youth, he found work at $2 a week keeping a lieutenant's quarters neat, boots black, and sword sharp. Encamped in Arlington, Virginia, after the regiment's first engagement, Aubery took it upon himself to rustle up some papers for the men. "A happy thought came over me," he wrote in his memoirs. "I launched out into the newspaper business. Went out on to the Arlington Heights with a few copies of the New York Herald, Washington Chronicle and Philadelphia Inquirer and found that it was a good thing to do, and keep it up. Finally I got me a horse and went mounted every day, serving the various regiments then there."[57]

Aubery found that it was best to attach himself to a unit. He chose the Iron Brigade, made up of regiments from Wisconsin, Indiana, and Michigan. The hardest-fighting soldiers in the Union Army, they saw action at Bull Run, Antietam, Fredericksburg, Chancellorsville, Gettysburg, and two dozen other battles. Aubery supplied them with papers throughout their campaigns. He also provided sundry items including stockings, buttons, needles, postage stamps, and contraband liquor. "The boys seemed to take a friendly liking to the manner in which I did business with them," he said, especially his willingness to extend credit until payday. He claimed that the only person who ever stiffed him was Abraham Lincoln. Aubery said he was riding past the president's headquarters near Fredericksburg, Virginia, in April 1863 when an aide-de-camp waved him over and told him to give a paper to the president, who sat writing in the sand with the tip of an umbrella and joking with an aide. "With a quaint smile on his face, he quickly jerked the paper out of my hands."[58]

Like his peers, Aubery distributed papers not just in camp (Figure 4.5) but also on the battlefield. He considered himself "an uncontrollable coward," having twice come under fire. At Bull Run he lost his horse and survived a volley from the First Virginia Cavalry. "The zip, zip of their bullets was heard very plainly," he said. "I thought I was hit at first. A ball from one of their carbines hit the dry bark of a tree, scattered the dirt and dust so that my eyes were completely blurred for about half an hour." Aubery's other close call came on the third day at Gettysburg while distributing copies of the *Philadelphia Inquirer* on Cemetery Ridge during a two-hour truce. Suddenly cannon fire resumed on both sides, shaking the ground. "I didn't let that uncontrollable cowardly feeling that prevailed in me show itself until I had a good chance to get out of there," he said, "for the boys did want the Inquirers so badly."[59]

"THE NEWS BOY" AT CAMP WINFIELD SCOTT, NEAR YORKTOWN, VA. From a Sketch by our Special Artist.—See page 28.

Figure 4.5. Edwin Forbes, "News from the Front," in *Thirty Years After: An Artist's Story of the Great War* (New York: Fords, Howard & Hulbert, 1890).

The popularity of newspapers among Federal soldiers was partly due to the ample pay they received. "Never did I see an army so plentifully provided with pocket-money, and who found it burn so fiercely in their pockets," commented London *Daily Telegraph* correspondent George Augustus Sala. Confederate soldiers had much less spending money and access to print than their Union counterparts. Supplying their regiments with papers was not the lucrative undertaking it was in the North. In some cases it was a form of unpaid family labor in which a son served his father's company gratis.[60]

Given the dearth of paying customers in the Confederate Army, many southern newsboys crossed no-man's-land to try their luck in Union camps. On May 12, 1864, after three days of fighting at Spotsylvania Court House, two boys appeared in camp offering fresh Richmond papers to members of the cavalry corps of the Army of the Potomac. "For the balance of the day," reported the general, "we collected our wounded, buried our dead, grazed our horses, and read the Richmond papers, two small newsboys having, with commendable enterprise, entered our lines and sold to the officers and men." Some southern boys who ventured into Union camps were stripped of their wares. In either case, reading Confederate newspapers helped the Union Army not just to pass the time but also to win the war. The acquisition of Atlanta papers during the protracted Atlanta campaign provided General William Tecumseh Sherman with the important news that Jefferson Davis had replaced the cautious and elusive General Joseph Johnston with the aggressive and predictable General John Bell Hood. Sherman instructed his troops to expect an attack, and they were ready when it came.[61]

Trusted newsboys serving the Union Army did not just deliver newspapers but also acted as couriers. Infantrymen entrusted them with letters home, and officers sometimes enlisted them to carry dispatches to nearby commanders. Such versatility was the hallmark of the USS *Newsboy*, an all-purpose steamer that patrolled the Cumberland and Tennessee Rivers. Armed with a 12-pound gun and manned by a crew of artillerists, the ship transported troops, conveyed messages, ran reconnaissance, and hauled timber and salt until it was destroyed in April 1863 at the Battle of Irish Bend on the Atchafalaya River in Louisiana.[62]

Despite the dangers they faced, civilian newsboys rarely carried arms. Their best defense against the enemy was to mark themselves as noncombatants. They accomplished this goal by their dress. Union Army newsboys exhibited the same flamboyant style as city newsboys. Many observers commented on their dandified outfits as they scrambled behind breastworks or dispensed papers on horseback.[63]

Mounts were cheap during the war; condemned government mares sold for 37½¢ in Washington, DC. Even a broken-down horse provided newsboys with the means to exercise their preference for flight over fight. George Williams told of a "bright young fellow" who started one morning from Harpers Ferry to join the troops in the Shenandoah Valley under General Philip Sheridan. He had scarcely descended from the heights at the back of the town when he found himself pursued by a party of Mosby's Rangers. He galloped down the road clinging to his bundles of papers, hearing bullets whistle past his ears. He got away, but his customers found their papers riddled with holes. Such adventures were so common that "neither soldier nor newsboy thought much about them," said Williams.[64]

The crack guerrilla unit led by Virginian John Singleton Mosby was known for its humane treatment of captured newsboys. In one close shave, all prisoners had to draw lots to determine the seven who would be executed in retaliation for an equal number of rangers hung by General George Custer at Front Royal.

A newsboy was among the condemned, but when informed of his age and occupation, Mosby released him and ordered a second drawing to determine the
seventh slot.[65]

Spying and Other Sidelines

Because northern and southern newsboys moved about freely on trains and
between camps, they were sometimes suspected as spies. In September 1863 a
New York Herald reporter traveling with General George Meade's army along the
Rappahannock reported that "one Rebel came over the river within our lines,
under pretence of selling some things and distributing a few old papers. We seized
him as a spy." General Sheridan, once a State Street newsboy in Boston, took similar precautions after winning a tactical victory near Meadow Bridge outside
Richmond in May 1864. His cavalrymen were still on the battlefield collecting the
wounded, burying the dead, and grazing their horses when "two small newsboys
with commendable enterprise" crossed their lines from Richmond to sell their
papers. "They were sharp youngsters, and having come well supplied, they did a
thrifty business," recalled Sheridan. "When their stock in trade was all disposed
of they wished to return, but they were so intelligent and observant that I thought
their mission involved other purposes than the mere sale of newspapers, so they
were held till we crossed the Chickahominy and then turned loose."[66]

Such precautions were not unwise. A Union scout in Richmond informed his
commander that Robert E. Lee employed "two little boys trained as spies, who
give him all manner of information. They are very young and travel along our
lines in the character of newsboys. They have given General Lee much valuable
information, and traveling under this guise are little apt to be suspected as spies.
Their names are Smith." The boys' father joined Lee's staff "in acknowledgement
of their services."[67]

One of the most successful newsboy spies of the Confederacy was James
Kellan of Missouri. He was orphaned at age 5, and his guardians found him
work as a newsboy on the Baltimore & Ohio Railroad in 1855 when he turned
11. When war broke out he was a veteran news butcher of 17 and worked the
Missouri Pacific line between St. Louis and Jefferson City. A slender, "delicately
featured" boy with long raven locks, Kellan became a favorite of pro-secessionist
politicians who had to leave the state when the legislature voted not to secede.
He carried mail to and from the exiled Democrats in Memphis and passed
money to Missourians who joined the Rebel army. He was court-martialed in
St. Louis in 1861 but banished rather than imprisoned because of his youth. He
continued to spy for the Confederacy and narrowly escaped execution after a
second arrest.[68]

On the Union side, the Federal Secret Service used informants in the South, including an active spy ring in Richmond. The ringleader was John Y. Phillips, a New York press mechanic who was transferred there with his wife and four children on the eve of secession. His eldest son, Charlie, was a frail lad who looked much younger than his 14 years. A "pretty boy" like Kellan, he used his looks to his advantage. Charlie's father urged him to join the ranks of Richmond's newsboys, even though he knew his son would get roughed up at first. Charlie learned to fight and talk like the other boys and soon began to use news selling as a cover to gather information and pass messages between his father and other agents. " 'Newsies' can get in almost anywhere—you know that," he told a reporter years later in New York. "And once in, it wasn't so hard as you might think. Every one was thinking of nothing but the war, so, 'Gee!' I'd say, 'ain't ye got a lot o' cannons here!' An' workmen would say something like 'Ain't them the guns, though! Won't they just blow the Yanks to hell! Forty o' those six-inchers!' And that would be something worth remembering right there." Charlie's assignments took him to Petersburg, Lynchburg, and across enemy lines, and he often received aid and information from Negroes. We have only his word on it, but Charlie claimed he delivered messages personally to General Grant at Fort Donelson, stole Confederate dispatches, and shot two men in the line of duty. He "got the collar" once but escaped by walking out of the courthouse and telling the guards, "Ta, ta, boys—the judge said I was to go home an' grow some." The Phillipses survived the war undetected, but their associates were not so lucky: Charlie once witnessed the public hanging of a trusted contact.[69]

While most newsboy spies lived to tell their tales, at least one, William Richardson from Howard County, Maryland, paid with his life. He joined Company G of the 147th Regiment, Pennsylvania Volunteer Infantry, after its Chancellorsville campaign in 1863. Regimental historian M. S. Schroyer remembered him as a "bright, jovial and good looking young man" who used to ride through the camp with his papers spread unfolded over his horse's back. "We all liked him." Richardson stayed with the company on its Gettysburg campaign, making his headquarters with the army wagon train in Westminster and then Frederick City, Maryland. While there, General Hugh Judson Kilpatrick suspected him of spying and found him carrying a map of the defenses of Baltimore and Washington. Richardson confessed that he had been in contact with the Rebel cavalry. He was hanged from a locust tree just west of Frederick City on July 6, 1863, by order of General John Buford. Richardson's body swung for three days, until the whole army had marched by. "We saw him on the second day," wrote Schroyer. "He was entirely nude, his eyes protruded from their sockets and were wide open, the veins over his body were much swollen, in short, it was a horrible sight to behold. A poor, misguided, intelligent young man, who offered up his young life without honor to himself, his family or his country."[70]

In addition to spying, half-breeched newsboys were also used for propaganda purposes. After a devastating raid by Confederate general J. E. B. Stuart near White House, Virginia, in June 1862, a local newsboy appeared in the camp of the 95th Pennsylvania with fresh copies of the *Richmond Dispatch*. "He professes to have strolled unwarily into our lines," reported the *Herald*, "but there is reason to believe that he came purposely, at the instigation of the exultant rebels, who wished us to receive their version of the late incursion." The boy, "a sharp-eyed youth of twelve summers," sold his papers for a dime apiece as he was escorted to company headquarters, giving the last copies to the commanding officer. "The spry little fellow seemed gleeful and hopeful," said the *Herald*, "and as much of a cosmopolitan as if he had been a correspondent." However, reporter Joel Cook saw "traces of sorrow" in his eyes. The boy confessed that he had been recruited to carry news of Stuart's bold raid and France's imminent recognition of the Confederacy to the camp to demoralize the troops. His mission may have had some effect, as Cook heard "outspoken complaint that treason lurks in the army."[71]

The Union Army engaged in its own propaganda war by taking over local newspapers as soon as it occupied a city. "Memphis is full of newsboys," reported a Wisconsin infantryman in March 1863. "On every corner they are crying their papers." These papers sometimes gave work to freed children, such as the one *Harper's Weekly* depicted helping distribute the *Loyal Georgian* in Savannah three days after its fall in December 1864 (Figure 4.6).[72]

The capture of Rebel cities also meant the arrival of northern newsboys, who constituted the shock troops of occupation. James McBride, vice president of the Newsboys' Association in Chicago, sold papers in Memphis, Nashville, Natchez, New Orleans, Savannah, Augusta, and Charleston during the war, netting and saving $2,000. The fall of Richmond in April 1865 presented a boom market for Yankee newsboys, one of whom entered the city several minutes ahead of the Union Army. "He went dashing through the column on a little mule, neither turning to the right nor left, shouting at the hight [sic] of his voice," reported the *Chicago Tribune*. A boy who arrived later with a bundle of *New York Heralds* "sold them so fast he could not move about, after landing, for more than a few yards at a time." News-starved Atlantans scooped up the papers more swiftly than did the bluecoats. The *Herald* sold 4,000 copies a day in the city; the *Philadelphia Inquirer* and *Baltimore American* averaged 700; and the *New York Times* and *Tribune* disposed of 300 and 400. Vagabond northern newsboys known as "Ishmaels of the press" reaped the harvest.[73]

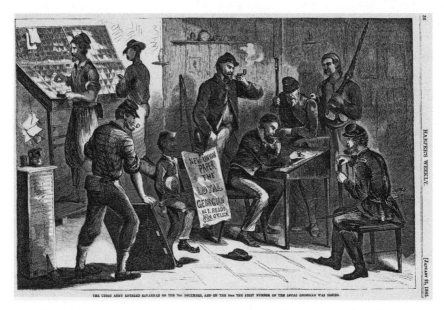

Figure 4.6. Federal troops relied on northern newsboys and former slaves to distribute pro-Union newspapers in occupied southern cities. "Issue of the 'Loyal Georgian,'" *Harper's Weekly* 9, no. 421 (Jan. 21, 1865): 36. Eckel Collection, Princeton University Library.

If newspapers were vital to maintaining soldiers' morale in the field, they were even more precious to those in prison. According to an official at Camp Morton, Indiana, "newsboys visited regularly with the leading papers." Many of them "did a good business in purchasing the rings made of cannel-coal, and breastpins made of bone, as well as small and curious articles carved out of wood by the prisoners, which they sold outside of camp, as relics." Guards at Camp Douglas in Chicago were not so lenient, but prisoners clubbed together to entice a boy to smuggle in the Copperhead *Chicago Times.* The scheme worked until the boy was found with copies in his boots.[74]

Newspapers were also available in Confederate prisons, where they were either smuggled in loaves of cornbread or openly delivered through bribery. New York congressman Alfred Ely enjoyed steady access to Richmond papers while held in Libby Prison after First Bull Run. They "are seized in the early morning on the arrival of the newsboys," he said, "and read by many even before they rise from their cots." Some boys accepted the soldiers' metal buttons as payment. One morning a ruckus ensued after a boy raised his price from 3¢ to 5¢. With time on their hands, the inmates debated the ethics of the price hike. Some quoted Shakespeare, Byron, and Tom Moore; others employed Latin, French, and Irish to support their arguments. Afterward, Ely ruled, to great exception, that the boy had a right to charge what he wanted.[75]

One young news merchant who found himself behind bars at Libby Prison was the ubiquitous Doc Aubery. He was imprisoned in November 1862 after being captured by two Rebel outposts while riding toward the front in northern Virginia. "I think I'm in the wrong pew," he told them. He had $380 hidden in his boot, but the soldiers never searched him. They turned him over to an officer who confiscated his horse and marched him and forty or fifty other prisoners twenty miles to Gordonsville, where they boarded a train to Richmond. Once paroled, Aubery boarded a truce boat bound for Annapolis and took the next train to Washington. He renewed his passes at the War Department, bought another 500 *Heralds*, and returned by boat down the Potomac to rejoin his brigade. The general rewarded him with the gift of a horse and instructed him to keep the newspapers coming.[76]

Heroes and Mutineers

Not surprisingly, heroic newsboys permeated the art and literature of the period. Among the latter were juvenile novels such as *Tom Brice, the News-Boy; or, Honesty Rewarded* (1862); Oliver Optic's *The Little Merchant: A Story for Little Folks* (1862); and Ann S. Stephens's *The Soldier's Orphans* (1866). Published by commercial and evangelical presses, these books barely mention the war but invariably cast "fatherless newsboys" as the least yet most deserving of God's children. They aimed to instill honesty in their readers, gratitude for their comfortable homes, and charity for those less fortunate. Many of the books doubled as advertisements for the Children's Aid Society. Some bear dedications to its founders and most include chapters offering "A Peep at the News-boys in the Lodging-house."[77]

Artists portrayed newsboys with a bit more dash than their literary counterparts. Thomas Nast placed one at the head of New York's 7th Regiment as it paraded down Broadway, 991 strong, on April 19, 1861, en route to its defense of Washington (Plate 10). The boy is shown leading a column of officers and troops in trim gray uniforms, bayonets glinting skyward. American flags billow in the wind from tall buildings overflowing with well-wishers. A staunch Republican and honorary member of the regiment, Nast shows Major Robert Anderson, the commander of Fort Sumter, reviewing the troops from the balcony pediment at the base of the foremost flag. Assisting him are the many boys perched atop lampposts.

Louis Lang, a German immigrant like Nast, placed child peddlers in his masterpiece *Return of the 69th Regiment, NYC* (1862–63) (Plate 11), including two fallen newsboys in the foreground, with hat and extras strewn across the cobbled street. It is the morning of July 27, 1861, a week after the debacle at Bull

Run, and all around them are soldiers—infantry, cavalry, drummer boys, and the wounded—debarking from the steamer *John Potter*, which has just docked at the foot of Battery Place. Castle Garden, the old fort and immigration depot, can be glimpsed in the background, a reminder of the immigrant origins of this celebrated Irish American regiment.

Less panoramic but even more flattering is William Winner's portrait of a rakish newsboy outside the office of the *North American* at 132 South 3rd Street in Philadelphia (Figure 4.7). He sits with regal self-assurance on a crate inscribed with the year 1864. This self-made merchant prince holds a batch of papers, most prominently the *North American*, a Republican daily, against his right leg, and gazes off to his left. Perhaps a transplanted farm lad, Winner's newsboy has acquired the urbane bohemian style of his trade. He is neither a

Figure 4.7. William E. Winner, *Newsboy*, 1865, oil on cardboard, 26 × 20 ¾ in. Philadelphia, Location unknown. Photograph courtesy of Historical Society of Pennsylvania.

comic nor a sentimental figure but a supremely knowing one—an astute observer of the bustling boulevard over which he presides. Winner and Lang each
donated works to raise funds for the US Sanitary Commission, a private relief
agency that helped care for sick and wounded soldiers. So, too, did Eastman
Johnson, who exhibited two newsboy paintings, *Morning News* and *The Post Boy*,
at sanitary fairs in Albany and Manhattan.[78]

The son of a Kentucky hemp farmer and manufacturer who employed slaves,
artist Thomas Satterwhite Noble fought for the Confederacy. But he abhorred
slavery and included a white newsboy among the ironic, liberty-loving figures
in his 1866 painting *The Last Sale of Slaves*, depicting a scene in St. Louis. Both
Kentucky and Missouri were loyal border states sharply divided over slavery.
Before its destruction by fire, Noble's large canvas depicted the tearful auction of
a beautiful girl and her family on the steps of the city courthouse. About seventy-
five people participate in or stand witness to the sale, including a pretty little
orange vendor, an Italian image peddler offering plaster busts of Washington,
Jefferson, Shakespeare, and Jesus Christ, and a newsboy who rushes among the
crowd "crying his papers in vain." Painted for a northern public just after passage
of the Thirteenth Amendment, the canvas was displayed in the rotunda of the
Capitol in Washington in 1867.[79]

Chromolithographs also depicted newsboys as symbols of free labor,
equality, and union—the very ideals over which the war was fought. A widely
circulated 1861 print by Belgian immigrant Dominique C. Fabronius shows celestial rays of light shining on a soaring eagle holding in its talons olive branches
and two American flags (Figure 4.8). The flags read "All Men Are Created Equal"
and "Stand by the Declaration." Hanging from them is a large wicker gondola
holding a black man and a white man. The former drops his shackles out of the
basket as the latter proclaims, "Break Every Yoke; Let the Oppressed Go Free."
The cheering crowd below consists of a Union soldier, a free black man, and
three newsboys selling the Democratic but abolitionist *Boston Herald*. Here, the
newsboys help make abolition a war aim two years before Lincoln would do so
via the Emancipation Proclamation.[80]

Despite the glorification of newsboys during the war, large firms dominated
the distribution of reading matter to Federal troops. "The sale of newspapers
and periodicals in the army was immense, and men who furnished them made
fortunes," said Edwin Forbes. "The work of distribution was in the hands of
general agents, who received them in bulk from the North. They placed them
with sub-agents in the field, who made final distribution with a large corps of
mounted newsboys."[81] Forbes's tidy description belies the chaos and controversy
surrounding the system. The scramble of newsagents and newsboys to serve the
military market in the first months of the war created much carping and confusion at train depots and military camps. Officers complained about the constant

Figure 4.8. Dominique C. Fabronius, *All Men Are Created Equal—Stand by the Declaration,* lithograph, 19½ × 16 in. (50 × 41 cm) (Boston: Thayer & Co., ca. 1861). The Library Company of Philadelphia (Reilly 1861-41) 7700.F.

requests for railroad passes. Newsagents objected to the arbitrary dismissal of their requests. And soldiers groused about the markup in prices.

In November 1862 General Herman Haupt wrote to Generals Burnside and Henry W. Halleck in Washington, saying, "We are annoyed by applications for passes, which are in all cases refused. It is desirable that an order should issue from your headquarters to regulate the transportation of suttlers [*sic*] and their supplies, news-carriers, and citizens." The full response came on February 7, 1863, from Major-General Joseph Hooker, who limited the number of newsboys to one for each division of the Army of the Potomac. Divisions numbered between 4,000 and 5,000 soldiers by 1863. The vendors struck on February 19, vowing to sell no newspapers to the army until the order was rescinded. The *New York Times* referred to the strike as a "mutiny of newsboys" and expressed outrage at their insubordination. "We are not at all surprised that the newsboys should have come to the conclusion that they had as good a right to command the army as Gen. Hooker," said an editorial. "He ought to get in the habit of submitting his orders for their approval, before issuing them." The strike collapsed after un-authorized newsboys were ordered out of the lines. In March more than fifty of them reached New York City, many having been with the army since its depar-ture the previous March.[82]

Hooker also called for bids from newsagents who wished to furnish newspapers to the army, and in June awarded the contract to John M. Lamb. Lamb offered $53.20 per day, or $1,800 a month, payable to the medical directors of the army, which then totaled 90,000 men. Under the plan, the provost-marshal of each corps kept a register of the names and locations of all newsagents and newsboys, and issued permits and passes only to those listed therein. The passes accorded them free passage on railroads and steamboats and across guarded bridges. Still, only one newsboy was allowed per division. The *New York Herald*, which had been temporarily suppressed, excoriated Hooker for his handling of the matter, saying, "Instead of vigilantly watching the enemy in his front, [the general] was busy day and night in regulating or suppressing the circulation of newspapers in a foolish campaign against the newsboys."[83]

The arrangement proved to be a boon to Lamb, who charged a fixed price of 5¢ per copy, magazines and illustrated papers excepted. Yet he undertook consider-able risk, not the least of which was the difficulty of supplying papers to an army on the move. Lamb also had to compete with independent agents (Figure 4.9) who continued to canvass the troops; some did so without documents and others with passes purchased on the black market. One New York boy named Jimmy smuggled himself across the river at Fredericksburg on a boat full of soldiers. "Being a favorite, the men did not put him out," reported the *Saturday Evening Post*. "You will find the New York newsboy in almost every army in the country, selling his newspapers or doing 'express business,'" wrote Brace in 1862. "One of them recently established a lodging-house for boys in Washington, where there was one bed for seven sleepers, at twenty-five cents a head, and the floor was let out for a shilling. He returned home with a handsome sum saved." A 15-year-old boy who served a Massachusetts regiment made $2,700 the first year of the war.

Figure 4.9. Alexander Gardner, *Virginia. Newspaper Vendor and Cart in Camp.*
Photograph from the main eastern theater of war, Meade in Virginia, August–November
1863. Library of Congress, Washington, DC.

He reinvested in tobacco and cigars, opened a grocery in Washington, and by
war's end had amassed a fortune of $30,000 to $40,000.[84]

Union Army guards on railroads were also known to turn exceptional profits
by allowing transport of newspapers without postal charge and then selling them
to newsboys at the end of the line. But by far the biggest beneficiaries of military
distribution were the New York firms of Ross & Tousey, Dexter & Brothers, and
Hamilton, Johnson & Farrelly, along with Chicago newsdealer John R. Walsh.
After acquiring rival news agencies, the three New York agencies merged operations in February 1864 under a new name, the American News Company,
with Tousey as president. He had realized early on that soldiers represented a
huge market, not just for daily and weekly papers but also for dime novels. He
collaborated with Beadle & Co. in 1863 to introduce two new series for shipment to the front. They were so popular that newsboys had to work quickly or
risk being stripped of them. Walsh, meanwhile, dominated the local and regional
distribution of Chicago newspapers through his Western News Company, which
also sold storybooks, songbooks, and stationery stamped with flags and other
patriotic motifs.[85]

When and where possible, newsagents set up stands in military camps or erected log shanties near railway stations. "Thus far, the system has worked far better than any that has preceded it," reported Provost-Marshal General M. R. Patrick to General Meade, who replaced Hooker as commanding officer of the Army of the Potomac at the end of June. The monopoly system proved to be so lucrative that exclusive rights to sell papers to the Army of the Potomac later went for $75,000 a year, the money again going to the hospitals. Commanders in other regions made similar arrangements for the distribution of newspapers to their troops. General Sherman had to address the issue during the battles for Atlanta. He refused to grant a monopoly to any newsagent yet allowed bundles of newspapers to be sent by military railroad along with other provisions, "but not their carriers. These are superfluous."[86]

Sherman's rebuke notwithstanding, newsboys provided a valuable service to their country. In supplying individual soldiers and entire units with newspapers and periodicals, newsboys did not just satisfy their hankering for news but stimulated a feeling of unity and common purpose among soldiers and sailors in distant theaters of war. So valuable were newsboys to the morale of Union troops in the West that a rare fortnight's absence caused concern. "The face of a newsboy has not gladdened the sight of the army for ten days," remarked a reporter with Grant's army in Mississippi in December 1862. "We had come to look upon these dirty but shrewd imps as synonyms for everything indicative of enterprise. Heretofore they have kept close in the wake of the army and were never many days behind."[87]

George Williams said newsboys formed "a bond of fellowship" between the eastern and western armies by keeping them apprised of each other's movements. He recalled one evening outside Petersburg, Virginia, when the boys galloped along the lines of entrenchment crying out that Sherman's troops had reached the sea. Tumultuous cheers erupted "until it seemed as if the whole army was uttering one mighty shout of gladness." On hearing the roar, Rebel pickets asked the cause, and when they were told, said Williams, "a deep silence fell on Lee's lines."[88]

Army newsboys also played an indispensable role in the 1864 elections, which was a referendum on the war and emancipation. Lincoln's Democratic opponent was his foot-dragging former general in chief, George McClellan, who ran on a peace platform. Never before had a nation at war held a general election, and the difference in many states proved to be the soldier vote. Nineteen northern states allowed their troops to vote by absentee ballot, to decide, in effect, if they would continue fighting. Of the dozen states that tabulated those ballots separately, Lincoln won 78 percent of the vote. Soldiers also provided the margin of victory in several congressional districts, voting four to one for Republicans.[89] It is doubtful that an army starved for news would have rewarded its commander in chief with such support.

So essential were newspapers to maintaining morale that some units assigned recruits to distribute them. One of the last Civil War soldiers so employed was Private Alfred Himes of Company C, 125th Regiment of the New York Volunteers. He was named "company newsboy" after he enlisted on January 9, 1865, in Troy. He took his newspaper duty seriously enough to have himself photographed holding a small stack of papers on his lap (Figure 4.10). He wears a military cap and tunic, and a plaid necktie. The only son of a single mother, Himes died in his first battle, near Boydton Plank Road, during the siege of Petersburg, Virginia, on March 31, 1865, nine days before Lee's surrender at Appomattox. His file reads, "Killed by a bullet passing through his chest while in the line of his duty as a soldier in action with the enemy." Sadly, his mother was denied his pension because she had remarried.[90]

Figure 4.10. Private Alfred Himes, Company C, 125th New York Volunteer Infantry Regiment, killed in the line of duty at the Battle of Boydton Plank Road, Virginia, Mar. 31, 1865. Ambrotype by C. C. Schoonmaker, Troy, NY, 1865. Courtesy Greg French, Early Photography.

Final Curtain

As with the attack on Fort Sumter, news of Lincoln's assassination on April 14, 1865, at Ford's Theater in Washington, sent shock waves through the nation. Abolitionist Sherman Booth was handling telegraph copy at the daily *Wisconsin* when the news came over the wire. "As he spread the sheet of 'manifold' telegraph paper out on one of the imposing stones, his exclamations of horror brought the entire force of the office to his side," recalled a colleague. "The boys paled at the agitation of their superiors, and some of the girl compositors wept. All was confusion for a time. But newspaper instinct triumphed and an 'extra' was soon under way. Matter was double-leaded, scare heads were written, column rules were turned, the press started up, and Milwaukee was plunged into a sea of gloom by the sad tidings which the newsboys proclaimed."[91]

A shrill-voiced newsboy outside Washington's Ebbitt House hotel shouted, "Daily Morning Chronicle—all about the assassination of president Lincoln!" A guest opened her window and called out, "Oh, it's so cruel to shout so! Please *don't!*" The boy obliged, and handed out his papers in silence. In New Orleans 13-year-old John Frazier sold a thousand *Picayunes* at the corner of Natchez Alley. In New York Charlie Craven, also 13, dispensed an untold number of *Heralds* but kept his last copy, wrapped in oilcloth, for the rest of his life.[92]

Conversely, some boys knew the assassin, actor John Wilkes Booth. "To newsboys Booth was always liberal," said one Pittsburgh boy, "not infrequently handing a dollar for a paper and saying: 'No change; buy something useful with the money.'" A New York newsboy who worked the ferry pier to Philadelphia claimed the dubious honor of informing Booth's mother that her son had been killed trying to escape capture.[93]

Newsboys also took part in the violence that erupted after the assassination. San Francisco's Toby Rosenthal joined a Unionist mob that occupied the offices of the *Daily Democratic Press*, "a 'secesh' 'rat' sheet [that] re-echoed the cry of the assassin, '*Sic semper tyrannis!*'" "A horrible tumult followed," said Rosenthal. "Tables, cupboards, papers, everything which was at hand flew out of the windows." Trapped inside when the militia stormed the building, Rosenthal was held at bayonet point by a soldier. "A hundred times I could feel the cold steel in my chest," he recalled, "and for a long time I could not see armed troops without shuddering." The *Press* did not publish another issue, but reemerged under a new name: the *Examiner*. The *San Francisco Monitor* suffered a similar attack and never recovered. A carrier sued the city for damages over the loss of his route, but a judge ruled against him claiming that routes were not property.[94]

Individually and as a group, Civil War–era newsboys became familiar figures in all American cities, not just those in the Northeast, and they assumed the role of

breadwinner in many of their families. Some northern newsboys defended the
Union as soldiers, while others risked their lives to supply the news that helped
keep their fighting spirit up and political commitments strong. Still others, including Nicholas Lynch, Pat Murphy, George Hubbell, and the New York draft
rioters, weakened the Union cause in pursuit of profit, sympathy for the Rebels,
or hatred of Negroes.

Their counterparts in the Confederacy bolstered and compromised its war
effort in similar ways and came away profoundly changed by the conflict. For
enslaved newsboys, that change meant freedom. Figuratively, newsboys of both
races and regions entered the popular arts and debates that raged over secession, emancipation, and violations of civil liberties, and in the process helped define their own and other people's political affinities and animosities. The city of
Buffalo memorialized their service by placing a barefoot newsboy—along with
Lincoln, his cabinet, and various soldiers and civilians—on the bas-relief drum
of its 1883 Civil War monument in Lafayette Park.[95]

Of those newsboys who survived the war, several, including Thomas Edison,
Toby Rosenthal, and Andrew Burke, went on to distinguish themselves in science, art, and politics. Newsboy spy Charlie Phillips became a New York City
police officer. A few remained in the news trade and prospered. Louisville smug-
gler Pat Murphy became known as "King of the Newsboys" and had amassed an
estate of twenty-two houses and $50,000 cash on his death in 1900.[96]

But what of the vast majority of newsboys whose names and careers have
been lost to history? Most commentators say they grew up to become laborers
or outlaws. "A dozen or two still cry papers on the street," wrote Boston's Henry
Morgan in 1866. A score or two became "cash boys" (clerks). Some found homes
on farms. One became a ship captain, but more than forty were "already under
lock and key." Junius Henri Brown of the New York Tribune noted in 1869 that
newsboys generally changed their calling before they were out of their teens,
becoming porters or mechanics. If he was lucky he married and bought a home;
if not he became "a pimp or blackleg, a thief or ruffian, a burglar or a murderer."
However accurate, such generalizations indicate that the wartime valorization of
newsboys quickly subsided.[97]

As for Walt Whitman, he devoted himself to nursing soldiers throughout the
war and never forgot the physical and emotional toll it took on the American
people. Yet he knew the memory of their sacrifice would fade with each generation. "Future years will never know the seething hell and black infernal background of countless minor scenes and interiors," he wrote, "and it is best they
should not—the real war will never get in the books."[98] Newsboys cried their
papers through that seething hell, and their voices punctuated the silence of
countless minor scenes and interiors. Theirs are some of the stories Whitman
knew would be lost. Civil War–era newsboys were admittedly minor players

in a drama not of their own making, but so were most Americans. In plying their trade, not only did they serve their families and customers, but many, in their own small way, also helped preserve the Union. Some of their voices were stilled, but a new generation arose to take their place. These children would find themselves embroiled in conflicts that pitted not North against South but labor against capital.

PART TWO

CHILDREN OF THE BREACH, 1866–1899

5

Disorder in the Air

The Union victory brought peace to the reunited states, but it also led to an economic crisis in which child vagrancy reached pestilential proportions. "Sparse are the locust of Algeria compared with these small Arabs of the streets," said the *Atlantic Monthly* in 1869. The postwar years saw roaring factory production and inflation, rampant crime and corruption, and great disparities of wealth and poverty. Few felt these social ills more keenly than the children who retailed news of their effects on a daily basis. They, along with widows, orphans, and ex-soldiers, suffered the most glaring hardships, which the pictorial press duly exploited. In 1868 *Harper's Weekly* depicted the arrest of a band of impecunious veterans, some still in military tunics, for obstructing the sidewalk with their advertising placards as a lone newsboy stands witness to their humiliation (Figure 5.1). Newsboys emerged during these hard times as a social problem with a unique capacity to hold a mirror to society. Writers and artists made them dual symbols of the uplifting potential of industrial capitalism and the savage struggle for existence that some believed underlay its operation. In the South, Democrats turned them into emblems of Republican misrule. A closer look, however, shows that real newsboys, unlike their idealized counterparts, rose up in the 1870s to expose and challenge the social inequities of their time.[1]

While lucky to have escaped the carnage of civil war, the post-1865 cohort of newsboys came of age in the midst of an escalating class war that took its own toll on working people. Laborers who had hoped to share the wealth generated by America's tremendous industrial growth now faced pay cuts, layoffs, and lockouts. Prospects were particularly grim for white yeomen farmers and former slaves who fell into a new kind of bondage contracted a year at a time as sharecroppers. Black youths who rejected onerous labor contracts and sought opportunity in cities fell afoul of new vagrancy laws that carried long sentences of hard labor. Meanwhile, business boomed for capitalists who sought to rebuild the nation's war-torn infrastructure and expand its industrial capacity. Taking advantage of unregulated financial and credit practices, they gobbled up

Figure 5.1. A newsboy stands witness to injustice in postbellum New York. Robert Weir
Jr., "Arrest of Placard-Bearers," *Harper's Weekly* 12, no. 586 (Mar. 21, 1868): 188.

competitors and tried to corner markets in coal, steel, oil, and gold. The winners
displayed their wealth in ostentatious mansions, carriages, and cotillions.

Thriving sectors of the newspaper industry showed a similar penchant for
monopoly and display. Sinclair Tousey's American News Company built on its
wartime success to dominate the nationwide distribution of print. The company kept a fleet of twenty delivery wagons and forty horses in its Franklin
Street stables, and in 1877 it erected a magnificent five-story building on
Chambers Street crowned with a white cast iron statue of a newsboy that
stood ten feet tall. Pictured on wagons, letterhead, and stock certificates, this
image became one of the first corporate trademarks in America. By 1887,

the year Tousey died, the firm owned or controlled more than twenty thousand newspaper agencies across North America, including hundreds of railroad newsstands, and posted annual revenues of $17 million. Known as the "Newsboy Giant," it became one of the most hated monopolies of its day, with the power to ruin dealers and kill periodicals by demanding extortionate rates or refusing to deal with them at all. Defenders excused its "sharp control" as having driven scoundrels out of the trade and protected the interests of honest merchants, including "the ragged newsboy, and the old woman dealing her wares from a doorstep or the head of a barrel." But critics likened the firm to an octopus, saying, "Not even the Standard Oil Company squeezes so great a number of people, nor so tightly."[2]

Newspaper publishers also erected monuments to their power and prestige. Flush from the wartime boom, owners of the *New York Herald, Tribune,* and *New-Yorker Staats-Zeitung* built grand edifices that transformed the city's skyline. Inside these palatial factories roared giant Hoe presses that in 1869 generated gross sales of $801,000, $514,000, and $217,000, respectively. The old guard was fast passing from the scene. *Sun* owner Moses Beach died in 1868, and his son promptly sold the paper. Henry Raymond of the *Times* succumbed in 1869, as did James Gordon Bennett of the *Herald* in 1872. (The *New York Evening Post* eulogized him as "a great news vendor.") Horace Greeley succumbed to a mental breakdown in 1872 after the death of his wife, a disastrous run for the presidency, and the loss of his beloved *Tribune.* The city, as if trying to lift the industry's spirits, dedicated a statue to Benjamin Franklin in Printing House Square (Figure 5.2). Then, almost overnight, the economy buckled, creating tribes of homeless "anti-rent newsboys" who nightly bedded down in Franklin's shadow.[3]

The newspaper industry in this "dreadful decade" relied more than ever on children to disseminate its goods, particularly the many competing evening and Sunday papers that sprang up. In so doing, publishers provided poor children and families with the means to survive the country's worst economic crisis to date. "Times have got so hard that nearly all the boys in town have got to peddling papers," complained a Chicago vendor. One young entrant, John Connors, drew customers with the cry "Evening Herald, one cent, To help my mother pay the rent." These boys—and some girls—enabled newspapers to remain profitable. The children, meanwhile, turned increasingly to the services of the Children's Aid Society and its sometime rival the Catholic Church, but avoided the more punitive Society for the Prevention of Cruelty to Children. Above all, the hard times compelled newsboys to pool their resources and take full advantage of their talents, not the least of which was their capacity to make noise. Some heard it as the hum of commerce, others as the rumble of revolution.[4]

Figure 5.2. A Founding Father and his progeny. "New York City.—The Statue of Franklin, in Printing-House Square, Unveiled January 17th," *Frank Leslie's Illustrated Newspaper*, Feb. 3, 1872, 332. Eckel Collection, Princeton University Library.

Enfants Terribles

Gilded Age newsboys were bastard children of a failing economy and a flour-ishing press. Set off by risky investments, trade imbalances, and the graft of Boss Tweed, Jay Gould, and the Grant administration, the Panic of 1873 threw the nation into a six-year spiral. Banks fell like dominoes, including the estimable Jay Cooke & Co. So stunning was its bust that a Philadelphia newsboy who shouted the news was arrested for slander. New York newsboys contributed to the panic by trumpeting the suspension of small-town "First Nationals" as if they were the Wall Street colossus. Police arrested several "knowing gamins" for the deception, but the crisis was real enough. Unemployment reached three million nationally, creating an army of tramps chasing cruel rumors of work. The boom in adver-tising and pictorial journalism that preceded the crash guaranteed its vivid cov-erage. Among the periodicals that emerged to compete with *Harper's* and *Leslie's* were *Galaxy* (1866), *Appleton's Journal* (1869), *Scribner's Monthly, Punchinello*

(1870), *Puck* (1871), and the *New York Daily Graphic* (1873). All employed new technology that could print photos directly onto woodblocks, metal plates, or lithographic stones, thus speeding the engraving process. "Street Arabs" hawked all these publications—and cavorted in their pages (Figure 5.3).[5]

New York newsboys also gained prominence in dime novels such as *The Bloody Footprint, or, The Adventures of a Newsboy* and the equally sensational urban guidebooks of the period. James D. McCabe's *Lights and Shadows of*

Figure 5.3. Fired streetcar conductor William Foster was hanged in the Tombs for murdering a passenger with an iron car hook. His case revived the debate over capital punishment. "The Newsboys Rush at the Office of 'The Daily Graphic' on the Day of Foster's Execution," *Daily Graphic* 1, no. 18 (Mar. 24, 1873): 1. Eckel Collection, Princeton University Library.

New York Life, Edward Crapsey's *The Nether Side of New York*, and similar titles saturated a market born of curiosity and fear. The authors alternately portrayed newsboys as "bright intelligent little fellows, who would make good and useful men if they could have a chance" and as *"enfants terrible* of civilization."[6]

Clergymen followed their lead by touring slum districts at night with police escorts and reporting back to rapt congregations. "There is nothing on the street that so moves me," said the Rev. Thomas De Witt Talmage in a widely circulated sermon at the Brooklyn Tabernacle, "as when on a wintry morning I see a newsboy with papers that he can't sell about one fourth clothed crying with the cold, his face or hands bleeding from a fall, or rubbing a knee that has been hit on the side of the car, selling newspapers that tell of railroad accidents, and boiler explosions, and the foundering of ships in the last storm, while he says nothing about that which was to himself greater than all other misfortunes and disasters—the fact that he was ever born at all."[7]

An equally woeful picture of newsboy life unalleviated by bourgeois concern emerged in Louisa May Alcott's "Our Little Newsboy" and other stories and poems that filled new juvenile magazines such as *Youth's Companion, Our Young Folks, Oliver Optic's Magazine*, and *St. Nicholas*.[8] The poetry in particular focused on self-sacrificing waifs who were shamefully neglected by their betters:

> Only a newsboy! weary and cold,
> Nursling of poverty, six years old;
> Why should we heed him, ragged and lorn?
> Leave him the fate to which he was born![9]

Accompanying these publications was a rash of kindred novels, including the anonymously written *Luke Darrell, the Chicago Newsboy* (1866); the Rev. Henry Morgan's *Ned Nevins, the Newsboy; or Street Life in Boston* (1866); and the Rev. Thomas March Clark's *John Whopper the Newsboy* (1871). By turns humorous, sentimental, and didactic, these books celebrated the camaraderie of newsboys and their preciousness in the eyes of God. Morgan based his book on his experience running the Franklin night school. Hawked from Maine to Oregon by disabled soldiers and schoolchildren, it became a bestseller. Ned's cloying motto "If I do no wrong, something good will come to me" became a national catchphrase. Clark's *John Whopper* was the much more plausible story of a Roxbury, Massachusetts, carrier who falls though a cave to China and then rides a draft up to the North Pole.[10]

Most influential were the comforting depictions of newsboys and bootblacks in the stories of Horatio Alger Jr. and the paintings of John George Brown. Beginning with *Ragged Dick; or, Street Life in New York with the Boot-Blacks* in 1866, Alger's novels presented street boys as good-hearted scamps whose character made success inevitable. So immediate was his influence that an 1868 profile of Sinclair Tousey bore the headline "A Real Alger Hero." Likewise, Brown, the most prolific and popular genre painter of his day, pictured poor children as rosy-cheeked cherubs who thrived on the streets (Plate 12). Having toiled in a glass factory as a child in Newcastle, England, he identified with his subjects. His first paintings are anecdotal scenes of street children smoking, fighting, or showing off. *The Beggars* (1863) depicts a winking *Herald* hawker paying two crossing sweeps for their services. Brown's urchins appealed to old elites such as the Vanderbilts and Astors and new-money industrialists, merchants, and financiers, earning him a "sumptuous income" of $50,000 a year and the envy of his peers. (They called him "Newsboy Brown.") Yet he and Alger advanced an explicit social agenda in the early 1870s, using their work to expose the pa-drone system, in which Italian and Italian American children —"little slaves of the harp"—were indentured as street performers. The campaign led to passage of the Padrone Act of 1874, which empowered police to apprehend mendicant children, including those who "disguised their purposes" by singing, dancing, tightrope walking, or playing instruments. News peddlers generally escaped suspicion.[11]

Alger and Brown considered themselves realists. "Art should express contemporaneous truth, which will be of interest to posterity," said Brown. "I want people a hundred years from now to know how the children I painted looked." He used caps, scarves, and other items fetched from the dress-up box in his studio, but only to convey the authenticity of his subjects. Brown worked on the third floor of the Old Studio Building on West 10th Street, where a stream of child models from the tenements came and went, occasionally chalking a door or breaking a pane. Such were the costs of doing business, for "boys that are well brought up are not picturesque," said Brown. He said he received five hundred boy sitters during his career.* Alger, too, preferred to introduce real boys into his stories. He routinely visited the Newsboys' Lodging House, where Superintendent Charles O'Connor let him interview the new arrivals. Thus did he meet Rufus, hero of *Rough and Ready; or, Life Among the New York Newsboys* (1869).[12]

Alger's claim to be a realist is partly substantiated by the journalistic record. The preposterous plots in which newsboys foil dastardly crimes, inherit fabulous fortunes, and rescue beautiful heiresses were the stuff of news columns.

---

* Brown's contemporaries also produced allegorical newsboy studies during the depression. Gilbert Gaul depicted a flower girl and a newsboy asleep in front of a bakery window under a yellow gaslight, while Seymour Guy's *Returning to Specie Payments* shows a newsboy whistling over a silver dime he has earned. Guy's painting was inspired by the Specie Resumption Act of 1875, which reinstated the gold standard, thereby worsening the crisis. See "Brooklyn Art Association," *New York Herald*, Dec. 2, 1877, 6, and "American Artists," *New York Commercial Advertiser*, Oct. 5, 1876, 1.

Real newsboys apparently demonstrated luck and pluck on a regular basis. In 1868 the *Chicago Tribune* reported that a newsboy working outside the Sherman House Hotel on Clark Street responded to cries of "Stop, thief!" and tackled a bank robber fleeing with $700 cash in hand. In 1871 the newspaper published a squib about Wm. A. W. White, a New York newsboy and bootblack, who on the death of his grandmother in Ireland inherited more than £23,000, the equivalent of $116,500. And New York newsboys Steve Brodie and William O'Neill saved so many people from drowning that they formed a lifeguard corps to patrol the East River (Figure 5.4).[13]

Whether they appeared in novels, newspapers, paintings, or as plaster statuettes (the last produced for the mass market by German immigrant Karl Mueller), valorous newsboys reassured Americans that despite the acquisitive individualism of the period, an irrepressible humanity had survived to overcome hardships in a modern society of strangers. The spirit of capitalism had not crushed the spirit of altruism; rather, it enabled the strong to survive. Even

Figure 5.4. William O'Neil, aka "Nan the Newsboy," used his celebrity to start a lifesaving corps in Manhattan. James Edward Kelly, *Nan Saves Three Boys from Drowning,* in *St. Nicholas* 6, no. 10 (Aug. 1879): 677. Gouache on illustration board. 7½ × 8¼ in. Delaware Art Museum. Acc. No. 83-151. Gift of Helen Farr Sloan, 1983.

English philosopher Herbert Spencer, father of social Darwinism, singled out "the newsboy who brings round the third edition with the latest telegrams" as integral to, and emblematic of, a free press. Spencer saw the press as "the spontaneous cooperation among private individuals, aiming to benefit themselves by ministering to the intellectual needs of their fellows." He stressed that it had not been developed by legislation but had "grown up in spite of many hindrances from the Government." This view conveniently ignores the web of party ties, printing contracts, postal privileges, transportation subsidies, public schools, and free speech protections that underpinned the press's singular influence in America.[14]

Alger, Brown, Spencer, and other bootstrap ideologues also disregarded the wide range of theories and institutions that working people embraced in their struggle to survive the effects of industrialization. Few newsboys grew up to become businessmen, editors, or advocates of laissez-faire economics. According to one study, most newspaper editors and executives in the nineteenth century belonged to "an elite blessed with considerable advantages by accident of birth." Newsboys typically remained in working-class occupations and held corresponding social views. James Hudson Maurer of Reading, Pennsylvania, called himself a lifelong rebel. He helped his brother deliver the *Reading Eagle* for two years before getting his own route in 1870 at age 6. Their policeman father died the following year and the boys' income was needed more than ever. Maurer went to work in a factory at age 9, became a machinists' apprentice at 15, and joined the Knights of Labor at 16. His time in school totaled less than thirteen months. "What education I did secure, I got, not on account of the State, but in spite of it," said Maurer. He discovered Henry George's *Progress and Poverty* at age 20 and became a Single-Taxer. He successively joined the Greenback Party, the Populist Party, and the Socialist Labor Party. He credited the *Communist Manifesto* for welding his inherent rebel spirit but said his mother's unstinting generosity to the poor and her fierce defense of underdogs had even more influence. "It was not from what I read," said Maurer, "because I was active in radical circles long before I could read. It came from what I lived."[15]

Whether or not they were aspiring capitalists, newsboys contributed to the financial health of the Gilded Age press. In 1869 New York boys helped distribute twenty-four daily papers—thirteen in the morning and eleven in the evening, including two French- and four German-language papers.* The city was home to another 126 weeklies, including religious, illustrated, humor, sporting, political,

---

* The English-language morning papers were the *Times, Tribune, Herald, Sun, World, Journal of Commerce, Star, Transcript,* and *Daily Bulletin;* the evening papers were the *Evening Post, Commercial Advertiser, Express, Evening Mail, Evening Commonwealth, Evening Telegram, Press and Globe, Daily News,* and *Democrat.*

professional, and foreign-language journals, many of which were hawked on the streets. Novelty publications also came and went; in 1870 newsboys played matchmaker by peddling the *Matrimonial News*, a British paper filled with ads for marriage partners. The industry emerged that year as one of the biggest employers in the city, with every major daily exceeding a hundred employees, not counting the countless hawkers and carriers who worked on their own hook. These children were always underfoot, jostling and bantering with reporters, editors, and illustrators; some of the children, like Salty, the fictional Chicago newsboy befriended by Luke Darrell, realized that the big printing offices "couldn't get 'long no how without us." Indeed, the existence of this large un-tapped labor source helped Gilded Age publishers acquire the capital necessary to start their papers.[16]

Mark Twain, a correspondent for the *Alta California* in 1867, was more impressed by Gotham's newsboys than by its newspapers. He found the boys to be a "wild independent lot" who would "make good desperado stuff to stock a mining camp with." He watched them pitch pennies and listened to them pro-fanely discuss national affairs. Twain, who delivered papers as a printer's devil in Hannibal, Missouri, paid tribute to these curb merchants in his 1889 novel *A Connecticut Yankee in King Arthur's Court*. A scathing satire on progress and civilization, the story follows manufacturer Henry Morgan—"Sir Boss"—into the age of chivalry. At one point he sits benumbed by the hokum of a royal ritual: "When outside there rang clear as a clarion note that enchanted my soul and tumbled thirteen worthless centuries about my ears: 'Camelot Weekly Hosannah and Literary Volcano—latest irruption—only two cents—all about the big miracle in the Valley of Holiness!' One greater than kings had arrived—the newsboy." Morgan alone "knew the meaning of this mighty birth, and what this imperial magician was come into the world to do." He dropped a nickel out the window and got his paper; "the Adam-newsboy of the world went around the corner to get my change; is around the corner yet."[17]

The importance of newsboy labor to American newspapers is evident in their own pages. In June 1867 the *Brooklyn Daily Programme* called for a thousand boys to sell its early morning edition. It got nowhere near that number and the paper died. Established papers liked to smother newborn competitors in their cradle by denying them the living breath of newsboys. In July James Gordon Bennett Jr. founded the *New York Evening Telegram* as a penny paper to crush the *Daily News*, recently converted to a 1¢ evening paper. Knowing that all great papers, including the *Herald*, had begun as cheap sheets, Bennett did not un-derestimate the *Daily News*. He sought new readers by using pink paper and giving the first week's edition free to newsboys. According to one observer, "The street opposite its doors used to be blocked up with scores and even hundreds of newsboys so that vehicles could hardly pass." The *Daily News* countered by offering to buy copies of the *Telegram* from the boys at the waste paper price of 5½¢ per pound, payable in copies of the *Daily News*. "In this way 8,000 of Bennett's papers were disposed of in one day," reported the neutral *Brooklyn Eagle*. "But still the war goes on."[18]*

Seven weeks later, the *Daily News* claimed to have beaten back the *Telegram's* attack. "Not one in fifty of the newsboys now carries it," said a correspondent, while the *Daily News* employed five hundred newsboys spread out in six branch offices who sold more than 40,000 copies a day. The *Daily News* "monopolized ninety-five hundredths of the newsboys of New York from 2 o'clock till dark!" By 1870 the paper boasted a circulation of 100,000, mainly in the tenement wards. Critics charged that its real secret to success was serving up murder, suicide, abduction, execution, and boxing "garnished with unctuous headlines and 'glib and oily speech.'" Some publishers maintained that it was a disgrace to be hawked by these "brazen throated members of the Fourth Estate," but not Bennett. The *Telegram* endured, essentially as an evening edition of the *Herald*, by keeping the price low to newsboys and coming out an hour earlier than the competition. Bennett soon sent reporter Henry Stanley on an expedition to Africa to find the missing explorer and missionary Dr. David Livingstone. Stanley found Livingstone in November 1871 and *Herald* and *Telegram* newsboys cried the story for weeks, lifting the *Herald's* circulation to the 100,000 mark. The *Hartford Courant* tried to top the stunt by publishing a mock letter from Livingstone thanking the *Courant* for sending one of its newsboys to Lake Tanganyika with the latest news.[19]

The pictorial press also experimented with new ways to manage its distribution force. The *New York Daily Graphic* appointed its quickest folder, 18-year-old Charles Frohman, as boss newsboy at a salary of $10 a week. He sought a "high type" of boy to sell the nickel daily, and succeeded so well that he expanded distribution to the 1876 Centennial International Exhibition in Philadelphia. The future theatrical producer opened a branch office on the exhibition grounds and devised myriad ways to increase circulation of the paper's Centennial supplements, including putting his vendors in uniform.[20]

Uniformed newsboys first appeared in London in the mid-1860s as an innovation of the radical *Daily Telegraph* and the half-penny *Echo*, which issued

---

* The *Eagle* found itself the target of a similar campaign the next year when several Manhattan papers tried to break into its Brooklyn market by selling newsboys six copies for a penny. But the boys were too smart for them, said the *Eagle*. They would buy a lot, tote it to the junkman, and invest their earnings in copies of the *Eagle*. So much waste paper flooded the market that its wholesale price fell half a cent. One recycler started posting placards all over the city saying, "Kash pade fur olde noose paprs at twenty-five Ann street." The misspellings attracted much attention and the proprietor soon hired newsboys to pass out a small newspaper carrying the same tortured message. See *Brooklyn Eagle*, Aug. 26, 1868, 2; *Minnesota Tribune*, May 4, 1868, 2.

caps to its boys. Military types in America embraced the idea. In 1869 Major Jack Stratman organized an army of well-drilled and uniformed newsboys to peddle his *Evening Tribune*, a short-lived, anti-Chinese daily in San Francisco. A few years later a Chicagoan proposed that a "neat and attractive uniform would do as much to civilize the newsboys of our city . . . Clothed in respectable garb, they would think more of themselves; their manners, if not conversation, would improve; and, in time, they would become more thrifty and provident." No one tested this theory in Chicago, but in Washington, DC, the *Daily Nation* outfitted its newsboys in black capes bearing the paper's name in red letters on the back. The effect on their deportment is unknown. Railroad news agencies believed unequivocally in the benefits of uniforms and required all employees to buy at least one set. Train boys came to resent the endless deductions from their pay envelopes and in one case accused the company president of fraud.[21]

Light Fingers and Stout Hearts

Although newsboys were notoriously hard to count, journalists, city officials, and census takers regularly tried to tally them up. In 1868 the *Brooklyn Eagle* estimated there were 2,000 newsboys and 300 newsgirls in New York City. Boston newsboys held steady at 400, the maximum allowed under its new licensing scheme. About 100 were "absolutely self-governed and self-supported," said the *Boston Daily Advertiser*. They slept in low lodging houses when they had funds and "anywheres"—in sheds, on stairways, and in pigsties—when they didn't. Philadelphia, said the *Inquirer*, was home to more than 300 newsboys, a quarter of whom attended Sunday afternoon lectures organized for them at the county courthouse in 1865. Indianapolis, St. Louis, and Buffalo put their newsboy totals at about 100. Out west, dozens of newsboys noisily distributed Cheyenne, Wyoming's two English- and one German-language newspaper in 1868, while Denver relied on 20 boys. Turnover was great everywhere, requiring a steady stream of replacements.[22]

Chicago kept the closest tabs on its juvenile workforce. The city licensed 400 newsboys and 700 bootblacks in 1866 but acknowledged that many more, including girls, followed these trades unlicensed. In 1868 the *Tribune* counted 500 newsboys and 120 bootblacks in the city, three-quarters of whom were homeless and motherless, which prompted the Chicago Sunday-School Union to establish a Newsboy Mission in the Board of Trade Hall.[23] They numbered 800 in the early 1870s, when the city took in $600 in license fees at $2 apiece. Critics objected to taxing "the little 'waifs' " and making them produce certificates of good moral character. Handling the *Post* or *Republican* was evidence to the contrary, they said, and even the city council couldn't produce such certificates.

Publishers advocated repealing the tax, as did the boys. They made their case at a benefit concert for the Newsboys' Home. Backed by a chorus of his peers, newsboy Gus Henderson sang:

> The town with fine tunnels and gay avenues
> Can never very much below par go
> And you'd think they might rest without a license at best
> From the poor "Shine-'em Ups" of Chicago.[24]

Licensing endured nonetheless, and by 1875 it had helped reduce the number of "legitimate" newsboys and bootblacks to 300 (plus three girls), average age 12. Two-thirds lived with their parents and the rest at the newsboys' home.[25]

New York, with an estimated 10,000 children under 14 "adrift in the streets," was the capital of newsboydom. If lined up double file three feet apart, they would form a procession eight miles long, calculated Edward Crapsey. Ten thousand was the figure cited by police, philanthropists, and clergy, none of whom ever explained how he arrived at the number. Crapsey broke them down into four subgroups: "hapless waifs," "infantile street beggars," "boy burglars," and the "self-helpful," who scoured the streets for a relatively honest living. Newsboys and bootblacks fell into the latter category. "Generally ragged, often hatless or shoeless, or both, unclean in person and language, the newsboys are a class by themselves," he said. "Nowhere else, and among no other human beings, is there so much energy, independence, effrontery, cunning, shiftlessness, and contentedness with the lot fortune sends." In an 1872 series on "Child-Life," a writer for the *Evening Telegram* consigned newsboys to the darkest realms: "Ordinarily speaking, he is a little vampire, with all the faults of a man, without any of his virtues—a precocious embodiment of vagabondage and sin—a little monster, the production of Poverty and Low Life. Yet for all that he is a child."[26]

To the federal government, newsboys were part of a burgeoning juvenile labor force created by the expansion of the factory system. The 1870 US Census, the first to count young workers, reported 740,000 gainfully employed youths between the ages of 10 and 15, representing one of every seventeen workers in the United States. Those grouped in trade and transportation numbered 15,000. Of these, 4,387 worked in the street trades as bill posters, bootblacks, chimney sweeps, hucksters, lamplighters, messengers, newspaper sellers, peddlers, rag pickers, and scavengers. The news sellers—criers and carriers—numbered 2,000 and made up the largest proportion, 46 percent. These figures are impossibly low when compared to municipal tallies, suggesting that parents were either reluctant to tell census takers that their children worked the streets or, more likely, did not feel that such casual work constituted an occupation. Another explanation is that many newsboys were under 10 and beneath the gaze of census takers. Regardless, the economy relied even more heavily on child labor over the next ten years. According to the 1880 US Census, the number of child workers increased 66 percent, with the biggest growth in trade and transportation.[27]

Census data also shed light on the ethnicity of newsboys. The 1870 tally reported that three out of four were American born. The remainder came mainly from Germany or Ireland. Most had immigrant parents, followed immigrant customs, and endured immigrant slurs. As a New York journalist noted in 1867, "The children of these people, though born here and technically called Americans, are as much foreigners in instinct, education and behavior as their parents." Another writer said the majority of newsboys were "children of the low Irish," who tended to stay where they first landed. They inherited their "parental inability to progress" and remained newsboys "to the end of their days," while those of "native American parentage" usually "get beyond their starting-point in life."[28]

Environment more than ancestry shaped the lives of these children. An intimate of the notorious Whyos street gang said that every one of its members, including the executed murderer Daniel Driscoll, started out as a newsboy and was instructed by older Fagins in the ways of pickpocketing through paper selling. George Washington Appo's career trajectory certainly fit this pattern. Born in 1856 to a Chinese father and an Irish mother in what would become New York's Chinatown, Appo had to fend for himself at age 11. His mother died when he was 4, and his father was mostly in jail. Appo lodged at a rooming house on Donovan's Lane, otherwise known as "Murderer's Alley." "I started out to sell newspapers for a living and remained at this occupation for two years," he said in a prison memoir. "During the course of that time, I made the acquaintance of two boys of my own age who always were well dressed and had plenty of money—as I believed, earned by selling papers. But I soon found out that they were picking pockets on Broadway and used the newspapers as a cover to work their crooked business. After watching them and several other boys, I soon learned the knack of how to pick a pocket."[29]

Appo tended to this business until he was arrested at age 15 and sentenced to the school ship *Mercury*. Charles Loring Brace visited the ship and found it an effective reformatory. He said half of the three hundred sailors had once been street boys, and almost all of these had stayed at the Newsboys' Lodging House. "Them's the things as keeps boys from the State's Prison, Sir," said one. "If I'd stuck to that lodge, Sir, I wouldn't ha' been took up for bumming." When the ship returned after eight months at sea, Appo fled rather than finish his bid at the Tombs. He found new lodgings in Donovan's Lane and resumed selling papers and picking pockets until rearrested in March 1874. An incorrigible thief, he would spend years in Sing Sing Penitentiary.[30]

African Americans also worked in the news trades, mainly in the South. "A negro newsboy would be as great a rarity in New York as a black swan," observed

Scribner's Monthly in 1870. Yet they were visible in Cincinnati, where they formed the Colored Newsboys' Union, and active in Richmond, Virginia, and Charleston, South Carolina. All peddlers of New York newspapers in Charleston were black, and the dozen or so carriers of the *News and Courier* were primarily "old trustworthy colored men," said the paper, along with the "sprightly" 60-year-old Aunt Jane, who served residents of Sullivan's Island.[31]

White and black newsboys caught the eye of the Charleston-born, Düsseldorf-trained William Aiken Walker, whose paintings reflected the blend of nostalgia and imitation that permeated the culture of the New South. A wounded Confederate veteran, Walker catered to the tourist trade and was known to set up his easel on street corners in Baltimore, New Orleans, and Jacksonville, Florida. His white newsboys personify self-assurance and the desire of many southerners to remake the region in the image of the commercial North (Figure 5.5). His black newsboys, by contrast, are ragged, one-shoed comic figures wearing straw hats and frightened expressions—urban equivalents of the fictional plantation darkies then popular in dialect stories (Figure 5.6).[32] Photographers were

Figures 5.5. and 5.6. The Old South meets the New in the work of William Aiken Walker. *Newsboy Selling the* Baltimore Sun (left), 1871. Oil on board, 12 × 8 in. Morris Museum of Art, Augusta, Georgia. Gift of the family of R. Roy Goodwin II. *Newsboy* (*POST NO BILLS*) (right), 1883. Oil on academy board, 11 × 6 in. Location unknown. Eckel Collection, Princeton University Library.

Figure 5.7. Peanut and news sellers in Jacksonville, Florida, had to contend with the occasional alligator on Main Street and itinerant Yankee photographer on the docks. Chandler Seaver Jr., "No. 46. Group of Natives. B," The Southern Series (Boston: Chas. Pollock, 1874). Courtesy Early Office Museum (officemuseum.com).

also drawn to the region and its newsboys. In 1874 the peripatetic Boston stereographer Chandler Seaver posed a group of African American newsboys and peanut vendors in Jacksonville, Florida, around waterfront barrels (Figure 5.7). However picturesque they may have appeared to northern eyes, these children sought income more than attention and probably got paid for posing.

Wherever they peddled, African Americans were more vulnerable to arrest and caricature than whites. With the passage of "black codes," any boy found to "loiter away his time" selling papers could be held as a vagrant and "apprenticed" against his will. Newly emancipated carriers and sellers also got caught in the crosshairs of Reconstruction politics. During the bitter election of 1866, state militiamen fired on blacks who dared distribute the *Missouri Republican*. In 1867 Negro youths who sold the *New Orleans Republican* suffered beatings by white newsboys, often under the tolerant eye of police. And in Mobile, Alabama, Democratic dailies enlisted hawkers to follow the Union Army–appointed mayor and cry articles critical of him. The mayor repeatedly arrested the most annoying crier, a disabled black youth named Archy Johnson, twice banishing him from the city and once jailing him for eighteen days. The mayor was convicted of violating the 1866 Civil Rights Act by serving as both complainant and judge and inflicting a punishment (banishment) that could not be imposed on a white person. White Mobilians rejoiced that a "trap made to catch the Southerner had first gobbled up a Yankee official." Yet they were hardly comforted to know that the law had put a "crippled half-idiot negro" on equal footing with the most powerful white man in the state.[33]

White newsboys, meanwhile, contributed in art and life to the racist backlash that ensued after black men got the right to vote in 1870. A cartoon in

the Democratic *Leslie's Illustrated Newspaper* shows two white newsboys—
Everymen in miniature—eyeing a Zip Coon character strutting in a checkered
suit, with top hat and walking stick (Figure 5.8). "Say, Bill, who's that?" asks the
first newsboy. "That! why, that there chap are the Fifteenth Amendment," replies
the other. In 1871 white newsboys in Louisville joined the campaign to stop
blacks from riding on streetcars by throwing them off the cars or pulling them
through the windows. Three years later, their colleagues in Atlanta demanded
that the *Herald* quit selling to blacks. "We won't run with 'em," explained the
leader. "The *Constitution* don't sell to niggers, and their boys laugh at us when we
have to holler the *Herald* 'long-sid o' black fellers."[34]

Figure 5.8. E. S. B., "There Goes the Fifteenth Amendment," *Frank Leslie's Illustrated
Newspaper,* Jan. 1, 1870, 272. Eckel Collection, Princeton University Library.

Northern whites were no more enlightened. Indianapolis youths excluded African Americans in 1878 when they formed a Newsboys' and Bootblacks' Association. "The colored gamins were on hand in full force," said one account, "and from the manner in which they hung together, it looked as though they were bent upon capturing the offices. Several of the white boys insisted on the appointment of a committee on credentials. This resulted in the elimination of about twenty colored boys from the room, it being clearly demonstrated they were not genuine newsboys and bootblacks, but had been rung in by an aspirant for the office of president. An all-white ticket was then nominated."[35]

To counter the pervasive racism of the period, the Boston–based African American artist Edward Mitchell Bannister offered another view of Negro character and citizenship. His 1869 portrait *Newspaper Boy* depicts a light-skinned mulatto with curly hair, full lips, and serious eyes (Plate 13). Dressed in a seaman's cap and fitted jacket, he stands holding copies of the venerable antislavery *Boston Evening Transcript*. Nothing is known about the sitter, but Bannister invested him with great dignity. A landscape specialist, he avoided political subjects, but a comment in the *New York Herald* that the "Negro seems to have an appreciation of art, while being manifestly unable to produce it" led him to paint the picture.[36]

As the *Brooklyn Eagle*'s 1868 estimate of three hundred newsgirls in New York suggests, taboos against girls in the trade broke down during the Civil War. Frequent sightings were also reported in Chicago, Philadelphia, and Detroit. Labor economist Virginia Penny endorsed the practice in her 1863 cyclopedia of female employment, which argued that women were well suited to news peddling and related occupations such as folding and addressing newspapers for the mail, selling subscriptions, soliciting ads, and distributing tracts. "Walking from house to house all day is very fatiguing to persons not accustomed to being much on their feet," she wrote. "It requires a person that has at heart the good of her fellow beings, and is willing to converse with all classes and ages. It calls for a person of piety, and one of tact and judgment." Penny recognized that men and boys dominated the news trade while women and girls mainly sold edibles, but she did not see this division of labor as natural or permanent. "Many, perhaps, cannot read, and do not wish to sell papers with whose contents they are unacquainted," she said. "Others may think they will be less likely to make any profit by their sale." Yet Penny reported that a mother and daughter who operated a stand outside a Broadway hotel earned 50¢ to $1 a day, including Sundays, when they delivered papers to subscribers' homes. "Contact with the world," she said, "does not always wear out the fineness and delicacy that we love in women."[37]

Suffragists and Salvationists agreed. In 1868 Elizabeth Cady Stanton and Susan B. Anthony dispatched little Irish girls in short "fenian-colored" (red) dresses to sell copies of their paper, the *Revolution*, urging the police to provide special protection. Peddling the paper could be risky. In 1869 a boy in Chicago got caught in a tug-of-war between a suffragist and an elderly man who objected to him crying that "incendiary" sheet outside his home. All three were hauled before a magistrate, who also felt that the woman's movement was "destructive of all good dinners and domestic peace." He dismissed the charges against the man but fined the suffragist $10 and ordered her to sew the boy's torn jacket. She said she did not know how to sew, which only affirmed the menace of woman's rights.[38]

Male and female members of the Salvation Army, from cadets to captains, peddled the *War Cry* on the streets of St. Louis and New York in the early 1880s and then in all states and territories. Some did so while singing hymns outside saloons. "The 'Hallelujah Lasses' are considered fully the equal of any of the male forces in efficiency," noted the *Cincinnati Gazette*, using a common epithet. Salvationists referred to themselves as "Women Warriors." Top sellers made the "War Cry Hustlers Honor Roll" and vied for the title of state champion (Figure 5.9).[39]

Figure 5.9. Honored *War Cry* hawkers sold 100 to 150 copies a week, often enduring requests for kisses and other taunts. Also displayed here is the Salvation Army's New York–based magazine *Conqueror*. Photographer unknown, tintype, ca. 1892. 3 7/16 × 2 5/16 in. (8.7 × 5.9 cm). International Center of Photography, New York. Gift of Steven Kasher and Susan Spungen Kasher, 2008. Acc. No. 2008.81.7.4.

Age mattered greatly in the reception of female news sellers. Derided as "ancient crones" and "old beldames," newswomen were often accused of obstructing sidewalks. The controversy led to a landmark case, *People vs. John Butler, a Newsboy, et al.*, which clarified the city's right to regulate its streets and sidewalks. Butler, 13, operated a stand (a propped-up board, five feet long) at the corner of New Church and Cortlandt Streets by permission of the Board of Aldermen. The mayor contested their authority, but the aldermen prevailed, enabling Butler and the women to stay in business.[40]

Another marginal figure, Mrs. Tom-Ri-Jon, aka Suzi Hanscom Donli Elliott, helped establish sartorial rights for news peddlers. She hawked her husband's paper, the *Volcano*, in Boston and New York in the 1870s wearing a hat with a half-moon-shaped sign bearing the paper's name. The *Volcano* advanced an array of causes, including labor rights and dress reform. A "stout, 'good looking' women of 25," Elliott also wore men's clothes. Officials at Trinity and St. Paul's Churches had her arrested several times for this affront. The courts always acquitted her, ruling that her dress was a legitimate means of advertising.[41]

Young girls, by contrast, mainly stirred sexual fears. The *New York Star* observed in 1871 that "bare-headed, bare-necked, bare-legged" newsgirls between 7 and 12 years old were "utterly depraved; the selling of newspapers is but a cloak to hide their infamous vocation; they are lost to all virtue while still in their childhood." None too worried, the *Washington Critic* welcomed its first newsgirl, Katie Howard, in 1874 with a risqué joke: "New York, Philadelphia, and Cincinnati, and Chicago have their newsgirls, why not Washington? 'Ray for The Critic, and for Katie! Price one cent—The Critic, not Katie." Newsboys in Cleveland offered their own moral critique of the "encroachment of the petticoat" when five newsgirls staked out the business corners of Third Street. "They are sent out by their mothers to get whisky for them," charged one boy, "and they make sixty cents or a dollar apiece each afternoon. Je! Christopher, but they do sell!"[42]

Newsgirls had their defenders as well. *Pomeroy's Democrat* admitted that they were the "most obtrusive of city Arabs," but it found them "indefatigable in their attendance to duty, neither heat nor cold interfering with the laudable, though childlike, desire to earn their own living." Some papers allotted them a portion of the pressroom, which they routinely overflowed. *Scribner's* predicted great success, noting that the "little girls, ragged in dress but stout of heart, sell papers every day in Printing House Square, with the gallant approval of chivalrous newsboys."[43]

Such attention soon propelled these modern mercuries into popular culture. They took center stage in *The New York News Girls*, which debuted at Tony Pastor's Theatre in 1869, and melted hearts with the song "Please Buy My Last Paper, I Want to Go Home." The composers said the song was based on a real

incident. Horatio Alger Jr. paid homage to newsgirls by making one the protagonist of his 1871 novel *Tattered Tom*. The eponymous heroine lives by her wits
on the streets disguised as a boy until she is reunited with her wealthy mother
and resumes life as a lady. E. D. E. N. Southworth's *The Hidden Hand*, featuring
disguised newsboy Capitola Black, was reprinted in the *Ledger* in 1868–69 and
again in 1883 before appearing in book form. It was also adapted for the stage,
making it the century's most effective proponent of "tomboyism" as a challenge
to the prevailing domestic ideology, which held that women's place was in the
home and their most cherished virtues were piety, purity, and submissiveness.
Southworth was justifiably proud that her readers included "some professors of
colleges, ministers of the gospel, and senators on the one hand. School boys and
girls and little street gamins on the other—and a vast multitude between."[44]

The most outspoken opponent of newsgirls and newsboys was Elbridge
T. Gerry, founder of the Society for the Prevention of Cruelty to Children.
Established in 1874, the SPCC focused first on Italian street musicians and
acrobats and secured passage of the federal Padrone Act, prohibiting the importation of any person for involuntary service. "The Cruelty," as it came to be
known, acquired police powers and targeted other "mendicant" or "wandering"
occupations, including news peddling. The word *peddling* in this period connoted
the distribution of ill-gotten goods. SPCC agents saw the small, ragged children
who sold papers at night and on streetcars as victims of neglectful parents and
routinely took them into custody. They also apprehended girls who tended their
mothers' stands during the day. News peddlers and their families resisted this interference, but the organization grew. By decade's end, the SPCC (with Sinclair
Tousey on its board of directors) had offices in thirty-four cities in the United
States and fifteen abroad. In the 1880s the SPCC joined forces with moral purity
campaigner Anthony Comstock, who mounted a crusade against dime novels
and other "flash" literature that glorified crime. This "sensational" material was
"one of the greatest obstacles in the way of our reforming the newsboys," said the
matron of a newsboys' home in Philadelphia. The rotund Comstock was known
to assault Park Row hawkers whose wares he found objectionable.[45]

Reformers in New York also cracked down on newsboys' leisure pursuits—
not just their street play and dice games, but a basement theater called the
Grand Duke's Opera House (Figure 5.10). Newsboys and bootblacks opened
it in the fall of 1871 at 21 Baxter Street. They put on a variety of entertainments
for their peers (boys only), attracting the attention of the press, professional
actors, and visiting dignitaries. They charged 3¢ to 10¢ admission and took in
about $40 a week. Proceeds often went to the poor of the Sixth Ward. But in
1874 the Association for Juvenile Delinquency closed down the theater on the
grounds that its proprietors had not paid the $500 license fee required of all the-
ater operators as compensation for the bad habits that boys ostensibly acquired

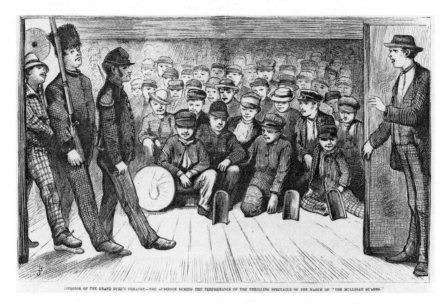

Figure 5.10. Joseph Becker, "Interior of the Grand Duke's Theatre—The Audience during the Performance of the Thrilling Spectacle of the March of the 'Mulligan Guards,'" *Frank Leslie's Illustrated Newspaper*, Jan. 17, 1874, 316. Library of Congress, Washington, DC.

there. Theater owners challenged the tax as infringing free speech, and the Grand Duke's reopened. Several of the performers enjoyed long theatrical careers.[46]

Census tables, genre paintings, news accounts, cyclopedias, and reformers' reports all confirm that the news trade attracted the full spectrum of humanity. As *New York Sun* managing editor Oliver Dyer put it in 1869: "What a variety of people—the extremely old, and the extremely young; the robust, the decrepit, and the blind, women as well as men—make their living by selling the morning papers." He marveled at the ability of the blind to adapt to an environment built for sighted people; one such vendor, a Scotsman named John Beith, made his way to the *Sun* office every morning before the streetcars ran by placing his canes into the grooves of the track (Figure 5.11). "But it seems a sad thing for a poor blind man thus to have to toil for his bread," said Dyer. "And the women and children, too! God pity them. But, after all, let us be thankful that there is even this way for them to earn wherewith to keep starvation at bay."[47]

Dyer's views reflected the consensus among bourgeois urbanites, the SPCC excepted. Most saw news peddling as a form of charity; some felt that it gave poor children an advantage in their struggle to succeed. In her 1871 book *Nature's Aristocracy*, Jenny Collins argued that the children's "street education" prepared them well for success in business, journalism, or politics. "As a class in the community," she asserted, "the bootblacks and newsboys are *naturally* the brightest,

PHOTO. ᵒᶠ JOHN WOOD, N.Y.   JOSEPH LAING.LITH. N.Y.

JOHN BEITH
THE BLIND, SCOTTISH NEWSMAN OF NEW YORK.
Scottish - American Poet.

1880

Figure 5.11. Joseph Laing, *John Beith, The Blind, Scottish Newsman of New York,* 1880, lithograph, 9 × 5½ in. After a photo by Bowery photographer John Wood. Museum of the City of New York.

the shrewdest, and the wittiest." The time and money spent rescuing them, she said, would be better "expended in missionary work among the wealthy."[48]

Though hardly an objective observer, the *New York Times* also defended child street peddlers. "They supply legitimate wants in the community and support themselves or their families by their labor," it said. "To cut them off from this would be to turn workers into paupers." The paper lamented the lack of class-room space in the city and a loophole (not closed until 1901) that exempted children in "lawful occupations" from attending school. It backed a bill requiring all child traders to attend a half-time or evening school at least four months a year, yet at the same time it downplayed concerns about their well-being. After watching a "flock" of Park Row newsboys stretch out on some steps one summer night, a *Times* reporter remarked:

> Poor little fellows, do you say? Humbug. Happy little rascals, say I, with no boss to bother them, no master to drive, with only one care on earth, the policeman, and he can't catch them! Poor fellows, indeed. They lead the life of a King. Whenever they get as much as a dime ahead they eat a meal that is royal to them; they are never scolded for reaching home late, for they never go home at all—indeed, have no home to go to; sleep where they will and when they will; swear without being flogged; steal without being caught; no Sunday-school lessons to learn; nobody to make them wash in ice-water on wintry mornings. Happy, careless, lucky little newsboys![49]

Those who best understood the reality of street life were its survivors. Yet they could gain the ear of the public only if they achieved some kind of success, which implicitly proved the point of Jennie Collins and other middle-class aficionados of poverty. Owen Kildare, for instance, grew up barefoot in the tenements of the heavily Irish Fourth Ward to become a prizefighter and author. His father was killed before he was born and his mother died in childbirth, so his neighbors took him in. Kildare collected coal, fetched buckets of beer for grown-ups ("rushing the growler"), and sold papers on the docks. The homeless newsboys and bootblacks became "personages of great interest to me," he said. "I watched their ways, and even found myself calculating their receipts." In 1871, when he was 7, his guardian kicked him out after an argument, and he ended up sleeping among the Park Row newsboys. He watched closely as a boy prepared his bed from newspapers in a dark hallway off Frankfort Street: "First, he spread a number of sheets on the floor; then built a pillow from the major part, and, at last, proceeded to cover himself with the remaining papers." When the boy invited Kildare to share the warmth, he was only too happy to oblige.[50]

Such ingenuity was not uncommon. The "peddling and poorest classes" put newspapers to myriad uses. They wore them under their clothes for warmth, stuffed them in their holey shoes, and folded them into work hats. They used them to fuel their barrel fires, wipe their bottoms, and make the balls, swords, and kites that sufficed as toys. More than a few foundlings were left on doorsteps swaddled only in newspaper. Newspapers were, in short, part of the material culture of working-class childhood, the equivalent of the cradles, nightgowns, and rocking horses of more privileged children. In Kildare's case, newspapers literally kept him alive. He fell in with a gang led by "Little Tim" Sullivan, who alone among them had a home. Sullivan "staked" him to a nickel. "I stuck to that business for over ten years," wrote Kildare in a memoir that tells the story of his coming to literacy with the help of a schoolteacher who became his wife. Kildare wrote four more books and was known as "the Kipling of the Bowery." At his death in 1911 he was director of a fledgling group called the Newsboys' National Association.[51]

Kildare's contemporary, future politician William Lorimer, started from an equally low rung. Born in Manchester, England, in 1861, he was 10 years old and living in Chicago when his father died. The eldest of six children, he began peddling Sunday papers, obtained a morning delivery route, and shined shoes. His mother taught him to read, and he brought a schoolbook with him on his rounds, studying it by the light of street lamps. Lorimer never went to school a day in his life, yet rose to become a West Side political boss, six-term congressman, and scandal-plagued senator, hounded by the newspapers he once delivered.[52]

Race Against Time

To grasp the day-to-day experience of news peddlers like Kildare and Lorimer it is necessary to understand how the industry worked. The process by which boys got their papers still seemed chaotic to many observers, but its efficiency had increased greatly during the war. Time was money in the news game, and speed was as much a commodity of the press as its stories and pictures. Workers in every department prided themselves on how fast their world spun and how cleverly they could shave seconds off the news gathering or distribution process via newsboats, carrier pigeons, pony express riders, telegraphs, railroads, or streetcars. Dyer rhapsodized about the way in which the 3:00 a.m. edition of the *Sun* came off the press at 250 copies a minute, then 500 copies a minute with a second press, and 750 copies a minute with a third. If necessary, he said, "the number can be forced up to 900." He lauded the virtuosity of the countermen who could count up to 400 copies a minute, "almost exactly as a pianist runs off arpeggios on his instrument, and with an equal precision and delicacy of touch."[53]

At the start of this period newspapers rolled off the press in whole sheets and had to be loaded into carts and hand-folded by newsboys, pressmen, or "fly boys." At the *Commercial Advertiser* in 1871 this last position was held by 8-year-old Tim Sullivan, the gang leader who staked Kildare to his first papers. "I was very small but the money was necessary at home," he said, "and I spent my time bringing bundles to a cart and meeting a man who had to serve the public with papers. And for which I received the large sum of $1.50 a week."[54]

As with counting, folding provided specialists with an opportunity to show off. House champions would challenge each other to matches for hefty bets.

In July 1871, *Boston Journal* folder John Carven met *Boston Post* wunderkind James Fitze for a head-to-head bout. Fitze folded 1,501 to Carven's 1,460, each making four folds to a paper, in one hour's time. Fitze's victory by forty-one papers was considered the fastest folding ever performed. But the introduction of folding machines the following year rendered such feats obsolete. Much improved from their prewar prototypes, the new machines could cut and fold 360 papers a minute, or 212,600 an hour, 140 times faster than the fastest man.[55]

Newsboys tended to gather early and play until their papers were ready. An 1867 article and engraving in *Leslie's Illustrated* depict the tumult of newsboys waiting for the five o'clock edition of the *New York Daily News* (Figure 5.12). They are shown fighting, tumbling, swinging sticks, and riding piggyback in the *News's* cavernous delivery room. Employing military lingo, *Leslie's* said that a "brigade of newsboys" takes the place by storm half an hour before the papers come out. After "posting pickets" to guard against interruption, "an impromptu ring is formed," and the exercises commence with a dextrous manoeuvre by Master Christie, a one-legged youth known for his gymnastic abilities. "He is

Figure 5.12. "Scene at the office of the *New York Daily News*—The news boys awaiting the issue of the five o'clock edition," *Frank Leslie's Illustrated Newspaper*, Dec. 28, 1867, 233. Eckel Collection, Princeton University Library.

held in high estimation by the 'entire company,' " says *Leslie's*, "and our picture shows them giving him a triumphal march." Several "nimble lads" cling to the bars of the pressroom while a "peeler" tries to keep order with his billy club as several scowling adults push through the crowd with thier papers.[56]

The accuracy of the scene is borne out by other illustrations and accounts of newsboys "cutting up shines" while waiting for papers. They liked to cross swords, pitch pennies, and play horseshoes, baseball, kickball, and a "perilous" new game called cat, which entailed hitting a stick in the air with another stick until it was caught. "The wonder is that eyes have not already been put out," said the *National Police Gazette*, "so prevalent has this game of hazard become in our most frequented thoroughfares." Newsboys also "guyed" passersby with absurd questions, particularly on All Fools' Day, which they claimed as their own. Some found sport in torturing animals (dogs, cats, rats, turtles), but more often they befriended strays and took their aggressions out on each other, as in a group wrestling match they called "Pile of Maggots."[57]

The *Brooklyn Eagle* said its newsboys were "as mischievous as monkeys, and as vicious as a Scotch terrier when not occupied in their legitimate calling." The conduct of newsboys was no better at the *Brooklyn Union*, where even the presence of the "awe-inspiring Chittenden" (*Union* publisher and congressman Simon B. Chittenden) in the counting room could not subdue their wild spirit. A reporter at the *Cincinnati Enquirer* said the spectacle of two hundred young men and little urchins "shouting, struggling, squeezing, screaming, swearing" for their papers recalled visions of the Black Hole of Calcutta. Unable to exit because of the inflowing crowd, boys whose heads scarcely reached the tabletops would stand in the corner and cry.[58]

Newspaper staff had no qualms about disciplining these children. Captain W. I. Whitwell, pressroom superintendent of the *Arkansas Gazette*, "spanked many of the boys and almost scared others to death when they attempted to get too gay," a colleague recalled. "A little of the Captain's 'strap oil,' as a licking with his strap was called, was a good thing to cure a boy of cutting up in the basement." Other papers employed security guards for the task. Edward Speich, who hawked the *Buffalo Times* in the 1870s, remembered "they had an old fellow, with a big club, stand around those long tables to make the boys preserve order." Monitors on Boston newspapers whipped the legs of boys who tried to push ahead in line. The most vulnerable in Philadelphia's news alley—the small and "colored"—incurred the expense themselves, paying William Herrity, aka "Billy, the Scrapper," a cent a day for protection. These "riotous imps of journalism" tended to be most disruptive when printing delays threatened their earnings, giving them less time to sell the papers they had purchased. Newspapers tolerated their outbursts because they had to, as the boys' labor was indispensable. Jacob Riis learned this lesson when he acquired the struggling *South Brooklyn News* in

1875 and had to be up every Saturday morning "with the first gleam of sunlight to skirmish for newsboys."[59]

Most newspapers and news agencies instituted a ticket or check system during this period to hasten distribution. Instead of paying cash for papers, newsboys bought tickets or metal checks the size of a two-cent piece stamped with the number of papers purchased. The *Sun's* smallest check called for three papers and its largest for eight thousand. When the papers were ready the boys would present the check to the circulator, who would hand over the required amount and deposit the check through a hole in the counter. This method saved time, enabling the entire 3:00 a.m. edition of 69,000 copies to get out the door in an hour and a half. It also reduced the number of employees handling money. Yet these tickets and checks functioned as currency among newsboys and were spent, traded, gambled, forged, and stolen, just like real money. In 1867 *Brooklyn Eagle* newsboy James Carr was arrested for picking a ticket worth 150 copies from the pocket of a fellow newsboy and spent fifteen days in jail. Proprietors were even less tolerant of the old crime of stealing newspapers off doorsteps, or the new variation, perfected in Chicago, of filching entire bundles dropped off in the wee hours.[60]

Supply men distributed the papers to boys throughout the city via wagons and streetcars. The *New York Democrat*, founded by Mark "Brick" Pomeroy, transformed its vendors and vehicles into advertisements. In 1869 Pomeroy and publisher Charles P. Sykes hired thirty-eight boys and one girl at $4 a week and outfitted them in uniforms with red caps in the shape of a brick. The paper then unveiled a handsome fleet of horse-drawn wagons painted red, white, and blue and adorned with a mural in which a mechanic reads the *Democrat* to coworkers as a newsboy circulates through the shop.[61]

The *Democrat* was one of nine evening papers in New York in the early 1870s. Priced from 1¢ to 5¢, they relied mainly on street sales and advertising revenue generated by ad agencies, another innovation of the period. Their daily circulations ranged from 7,000 to 10,000, or about half the amount needed to keep a morning paper afloat. On some days news wagons could be seen racing up the Bowery dropping free bundles of unsold editions to the crowds of children that trailed behind. "When a journal may be had so cheaply a large circulation is no great wonder," reproached the *Times*. German artist William Hahn captured the irony of barefoot boys, including a mumpy lad with a face compress, scrambling for newspapers from a delivery cart on Union Square as attentive mothers, sisters, and nursemaids stroll with their charges (Plate 14). Samuel Gompers of the Cigar Makers International Union also commented on the kite tail of boys—up to two hundred at a time—that chased the newspaper wagons. In 1883 he told the US Senate Committee on Education and Labor, "If the poor boys were on the point of starvation and their only hope of life was in that wagon

I do not believe they could run much faster or risk their lives much more than they do sometimes."[62]

Horsecar lines replaced omnibuses and stagecoaches in many American cities in the postwar years, and circulation bosses commandeered them in the early morning to transport papers. This practice was pioneered in Boston, which was among the first cities to install tracks, and perfected in New York, where uptown morning commuters shared space with women and boys who madly folded newspapers and threw them off in bundles to their carriers.[63]

Streetcars also served as popular retail sites. Newsboys learned to hop on and off with such ease that "flipping" cars became a recognized skill. "They climb up on the steps of the stage," wrote Edward Winslow Martin, "thrust their grim little faces in the windows, and almost bring nervous passengers to their feet by their yells; or, scrambling into a street car, they will offer you their papers in such an earnest, appealing way, that, nine times out of ten, you will buy them out of sheer pity for the boys." *Harper's Bazar* illustrator Jennie Brownscombe depicted one such lad piping his way through a car crammed with all classes of humanity (Figure 5.13).[64]

Streetcars presented newsboys with risks as well as profits. Countless young hawkers were ground up under their wheels, generating many inquests and lawsuits to determine who was responsible for their death or dismemberment. Notices of such accidents became staples of Gilded Age newspapers. "Every few days," said *Harper's Weekly*, "our city journals record an item under some such head as '*Child run over*,' '*Boy instantly Killed*,' '*Fatal Railroad Accident*,' or '*Reckless Driving*.' The number of children wounded or killed during the last twelve months by being run over by our city cars must be pretty large." In one prominent case, Francis Shields, a 13-year-old Irish-born newsboy, was killed instantly on July 22, 1867, when he fell under the wheels of a 42nd Street horsecar. Witnesses on the street said the driver hit the boy with the reins and kicked him before he fell, but the conductor and passengers could not corroborate the accusations and the driver was exonerated. "It is horrifying to read of youngsters employed in the peddling business, being driven off the street cars with unnecessary violence—sometimes to their fatal injury," editorialized the *New York Times*. "But it is scarcely less horrifying to see the way in which they risk their own lives, and alarm humane spectators by jumping on at the front of crowded cars while these are running at full speed." The *Times* broke rank with other papers and endorsed company efforts to ban newsboys from its cars.[65]

Newspapers usually came to the defense of their boys. "If there must be kicking and cuffing," warned the *Brooklyn Eagle* in 1869, "the New York conductors are themselves the proper subjects of the discipline." One New York newsboy was so upset over the beatings that he and his colleagues received from conductors that he appealed to the editor of the *Times*:

Figure 5.13. Newsboys were not always welcome on streetcars. Jennie Brownscombe, "A City Railroad Car," *Harper's Bazar* 6, no. 19 (May 10, 1873): 1. Eckel Collection, Princeton University Library.

You are undoubtedly aware of the fact that the newsboys are obliged to pay one dollar weekly to the Third Avenue Railroad Company for permission to enter their cars to sell their papers, and that those not having paid the above amount, (those having paid are furnished with a badge, which they received in the morning and return in the evening,) are most barbarously ill-treated when they attempt to jump on the cars. I myself was last month so ill-treated by a conductor of their cars, that I was confined to my room for two weeks. When nearly on the car I was seized by the conductor, received a few blows in my face, and was finally kicked into the middle of the street.[66]

The writer went on to request, on behalf of all the other newsboys, "the privilege of entering their cars, free of charge, to sell their papers." He signed himself "A Newsboy."

America's newsboys would continue to resist streetcar companies for decades, resulting in precious pennies earned and lives lost. The hazards increased as lines switched to steam, electric, and cable power in the 1880s, increasing the speed and volume of traffic. Yet this conflict was part of a much larger struggle to assert their right to work and play. Cincinnati newsboys appealed directly to the mayor in 1871 when an overzealous cop forbade them from sitting in the shade of the post office and importuning pedestrians. In 1876 Chicago newsboys took their beef with a downtown hotel and the local constabulary to the *Tribune*. Although letters to editors were rare then, they wrote:

> We, the newsboys and bootblacks of the City of Chicago, would earnestly ask you to be kind enough to insert this in your paper, whether we have to pay a license to hotel-porters for selling papers and blacking boots before the same, as the Commercial Hotel porters are against us staying around on the sidewalk in front of the said Commercial Hotel, either on Lake or Dearborn street. We try to make an honest living, but the police also drive us away. Please inform us if we have the right to stand on the sidewalk or not. By so doing you will oblige the poor
> Newsboys and Bootblacks.[67]

And in 1877 New Orleans newsboys asked a *Times* columnist for help in securing a holiday on December 26, "as we would like to have one very much, and we need one bad, as we ain't had one for three years."[68]

These solicitations attest, first, to the literacy of newsboys. Even if polished by editors, the letters are stirring cries for justice. The boys wisely seek sympathy by identifying themselves as honest and hardworking lads. They show their political savvy by simultaneously appealing to the public and applying for the intercession of influential newspapers, which had a vested interest in the welfare of their hawkers and carriers. The missives also reveal solidarity among the boys, as the writers explicitly claim to represent many others, if only by invoking the royal "we." In short, the letters suggest that the boys saw themselves not as powerless victims but as members of a respectable trade who operated in a moral economy that put their right to work unmolested or to take a day off above the right of railroad, hotel, or even newspaper owners to manage their property as they saw fit. Courts sometimes agreed, ordering streetcar and ferry companies to pay for the loss of a newsboy's legs, $3,000 on average.[69]

Freaks of Fortune

Newsboys' earnings varied greatly during the period. Many journalists inquired into the subject, but the boys had little incentive to tell the truth. At the low end of the scale is Martin's estimate that New York newsboys rarely earned more than 30¢ a day. The *New York Weekly Tribune* said they took in from 50¢ to $3 a day, "according to their age, activity, and capital." *Appleton's Journal* staked out the middle ground, saying their profits varied from 50¢ to $1.25. Crapsey thought 50¢ a day was about right, but that sum required fourteen-hour workdays. "Out of these scanty earnings," he said, "got at such a great cost, the newsboy can, if he will, live cleanly and comfortably." Those at the top even indulged in expensive cigars.[70]

More extravagant claims were made for newsboys in other cities. The *Buffalo Morning Express* reported in 1868 that newsboys who worked full-time earned between $7 and $10 a week. The *Indianapolis Sentinel* surveyed its newsboys in 1873 and found that most lived at home and earned from $3 to $8 or even $10 a week, blacking boots and doing odd jobs as well. In 1877 the *Chicago Daily News* claimed its boys earned from 50¢ to $5 per diem.[71]

Sales stalled wherever coins were in short supply. Such was the case after the Fourth Coinage Act curtailed the minting of silver. Labeled the "Crime of '73" by western miners and farmers, the law caused prices to fall and made debts harder to pay back. *Daily News* founder Melville Stone, a former *Tribune* carrier, responded by importing kegs of pennies from the Philadelphia mint and persuading merchants to mark items at odd prices, such as 99¢. Other publishers followed suit, but some newsboys still had to accept payment in stamps.[72]

Unlike wage workers, newsboys could look forward to boom days when the news was so compelling that they could jack up prices and make a killing. Superintendent O'Connor said he knew of instances when the bigger boys sold 500 to 600 papers in two hours, realizing $11 or $12 profit. On May 16, 1868, for example, New York newsboys sold thousands of extras announcing the Senate's acquittal of President Andrew Johnson on impeachment charges. And on February 1, 1871, Philadelphia newsboys helped distribute a record 104,000 copies of the *Evening Star* recounting the execution of a child murderer. In newsboy parlance, "extrys" were anything that "sells fuss rate." Some publishers started offering prizes to newsboys who sold the most papers. In 1872 the *Washington Daily Critic* promised a winter outfit at Christmas to the top seller and $10 to the runner-up.[73]

More attention, it seems, was paid to newsboys' earnings than to those of other workers. Interest can partly be attributed to their close association with the press and to their appeal as journalistic subjects. But many also believed that newsboys' ability to earn confirmed the regenerative power of capitalism. No one held this belief more strongly than Horace Greeley. In one of his last addresses to newsboys at the Park Place Lodging House in January 1869, Greeley told them that getting rich was a way of doing good in the world, while poverty was a cause of crime. He advised them to save their money, avoid drink, and learn a trade or become a farmer; but above all, be honest—not because it was the right thing to do, but because it would lead to wealth. "All the thieves in the city," he said, "never acquired as much wealth as John Jacob Astor." The boys were fond of Greeley and greeted him familiarly in the streets. When he died in 1872, "great numbers of newsboys" passed through City Hall, where his body lay in state. They also lined the funeral route, their shrill cries for once hushed. Enduring icons of republican virtue, portraits of Greeley and a *Tribune* newsboy by Augustus M. Friedlander hung side by side in the newspaper's counting room for years to come.[74]

Among the many skills needed to prosper in the trade was an ability to predict sales. One advantage of folding one's own papers was that it gave boys a chance to scan the edition and decide what to cry. Although it didn't deliver the windfall profits of the American Civil War, the Franco-Prussian War generated a flurry of street sales in 1870, especially among German Americans. Irish American newsboys in Milwaukee, however, refused to sing "Great Prussian Victory" because their sympathies lay with the French.[75]

Coverage of prizefights, horse races, and steamboat races continued to attract readers, especially gamblers. The race between the rival steamers *Lee* and *Natchez* in New Orleans in 1870 generated such excitement and heavy betting (even among the ladies) that newsboys at the *Picayune* leaped on the counter, waved their hats, and yelled "like so many young demons" for more extras. Yet the reading public also began to pay attention to novel pastimes such as chess, speed walking, and baseball. "On my way to town," remarked a befuddled Brooklynite in the summer of 1867, "the newsboys shout such and such a paper, with the account of the great baseball match." One of the first newspapers to report "all news and gossip of the sport" was the *Philadelphia City Item*, whose editor owned a team. When rival clubs started to pay players, the *Item* was "unsparing in its denunciation of the 'hired men.'" Newsboys' cries helped turn the players into celebrities, which aided the sport's efforts to professionalize. Newsboys from Philadelphia to Charleston formed their own teams as early as 1869.[76]

Athletics—boxing in particular—provided newsboys with a chance to rise above their circumstances. Like Kildare, those who rose highest were showmen as well as sportsmen, and their fame bordered on infamy. Known as "the Napoleon of newsboys [and] the G. Washington of bootblacks," Steve Brodie was born to a widowed mother in 1861 and started selling papers at age 6. One of seven brothers, he lived off and on at the Newsboys' Lodging House on Park Place and hung out on the waterfront. To supplement his income he started jumping from the decks—and then the eighty-foot-high crossbars—of ships while a pal passed the hat among the passengers. He spent so much time swimming in the river that he was said to be almost amphibious. He got his first press notice when he was appointed lieutenant of a Life Saving Corps, and made more news with his many rescues. Brodie's notoriety also stemmed from his success as a marathon speed walker. In one race he wore a blue flannel cap, which became all the rage among newsboys; they directly profited from his exploits, as news of walking match results could boost circulation by 30,000 copies. One magazine commented on the racing craze, saying, "The newsboys have caught the fever, and the epidemic rages among the small fry with all the virulence of the measles. When it comes to a point when we cannot have our morning paper because our carrier is trying to do one hundred miles in twenty-four hours, it is high time for the magistrates to interfere."[77]

Brodie's mentor in the news trade was George Washington Connors, nicknamed "Chuck" because he liked to cook chuck steak on a stick over trash fires. Born to Irish immigrant parents around 1852 and raised on Mott Street, Connors was the quintessential news b'hoy; he became a popular clog dancer, ballad singer, and boxer. Shanghaied on a British steamer, he fell in with London costermongers and adopted their slang and dress. Both he and Brodie would ascend to greater heights of athletic, theatrical, and political celebrity in the 1880s, although Brodie's greatest feat was a sham. In 1886 he took a bet to jump off the new Brooklyn Bridge. He faked it, but the stunt led to a theatrical career in which he reprised his jump nightly onstage at a dime museum (Figure 5.14). He became a highly paid vaudeville actor, playing himself in theatricals such as *On the Bowery*. His most lasting contribution to showbiz was to inspire the slang term *brodied*, meaning "flopped." He later opened his own saloon, operated a racetrack, and became a force in Tammany Hall.[78]

The third member of this Bowery triumvirate was Swipes the Newsboy. Born Simon K. Besser around 1868, Swipes launched his career in the news trade at age 4. Orphaned at 7, he moved into the Newsboys' Lodging House, where he lived until he turned 22. He operated a newsstand in the Bowery and trained as a boxer. Swipes stood 5 feet 2 inches tall and fought as a bantamweight (112–118 lbs.). Tragedy made him famous. In January 1888 he killed his friend Billy Dempsey in a hastily arranged smoker in the backroom of a hotel in Fort Hamilton, Brooklyn. Both men had been drinking and agreed to spar for four rounds and split the $25 prize money, but blows to the head sent Dempsey into convulsions. Bare-knuckle boxing was illegal in New York, yet all escaped prosecution because the fighters wore "skin tight gloves." Swipes tried to make amends by fighting benefit bouts for Dempsey's widow and child and the victims of the Johnstown flood. He boxed in

Figure 5.14. Steve Brodie demonstrates how he jumped off the Brooklyn Bridge in a publicity poster for his Bowery show. Photographer unknown. Tintype, ca. 1886. 3½ × 2 9/16 in. (8.9 × 6.5 cm). International Center of Photography, New York. Gift of Steven Kasher and Susan Spungen Kasher, 2008. Acc. No. 2008.81.6.

barns, bars, and other smalltime venues, sometimes under the name Tom White and often against bigger men. Some were "fights to the finish" that lasted more than twenty rounds. He earned purses ranging from $200 to $1,000, but he turned to show business after he married Minnie Rosenblatt in 1891. He taught his elfin bride to box, and she performed with him at Coney Island as "Little Swipesie," a 108-pounder "willing to meet all comers."[79]

Newsboys' most distinctive quality—their cries—gained new advocates and adversaries in Gilded Age America. In 1866 the New York literary magazine *Round Table* launched a campaign against them, saying, "All these traders help to make city life disagreeable with their noise, and we hope that something may yet be done to modify what is a very distinct and intolerable nuisance." Some cities instituted licensing schemes and limited the number of licenses issued to "these noisy little Immortals." Others passed noise ordinances, but enforcement was usually lax. Clerics in Washington, DC, pushed to abolish the Sunday newsboy in 1870, but the little "barefoots" appeared in the city council chambers with a huge remonstrance against the petition. Compulsory education and child labor laws were still rare; only four states required school attendance by 1873 and only six had set a minimum age for factory work, generally between 10 and 13. Fourteen states regulated the hours children could work, which were usually capped at ten per day. But, again, the laws applied only to factory work. The only party calling for child labor reform in 1872 was the Prohibition Party.[80]

The proliferation of afternoon dailies increased the vileness as well as the volume of newsboys' cries. These papers relied mainly on street sales and appealed to readers' most morbid curiosities. Newsboys typically spiced their broadcasts with teasers such as "'Nuther murder!" or "'Orrible haccident!" There was nothing subtle about their salesmanship. Martin observed that half a dozen newsboys "will sometimes surround a luckless pedestrian, thrusting their wares in his face, and literally forcing him to buy one to get rid of them. The moment he shows the least disposition to yield, they commence fighting amongst themselves for the 'honor' of serving him." Enterprising boys knew that certain editions were likely to sell best in certain locales, and made beelines to these spots. Where better to sell news of an ecclesiastical trial than on the steps of the accused pastor's church? Such was the thinking of a New York newsboy who found a ready market one Sunday morning in 1879 until removed by church officials.[81]

Whatever the words, some people heard newsboys' cries as a kind of music. "It is one of the pleasantest recreations of the Philadelphians," reported *Punchinello*, "to sit at their front windows, and listen to his thirty thousand newsboys sing together their vesper hymn—'Star of the Ee-e-e-vening! Doub-ull-sheet-Star!'" Where the writer came up with the figure is a mystery, since residents still relied less on hawkers than readers elsewhere because of an efficient citywide carrier system. In 1870 the *Public Ledger*, a morning paper, sold just 5 percent of its 72,000 daily circulation through hawkers. But the *Day*, an afternoon paper edited with street sales in mind—that is, packed with short, pungent stories on local topics—was peddled exclusively by "lusty-throated newsboys." *Harper's Bazar*'s 1873 woodcut "Life in Broadway, New York" celebrated such cries as the leitmotif of a glorious urban symphony (Figure 5.15).[82]

The esteemed Brooklyn cleric Henry Ward Beecher also lauded newsboys' lung power. "These newsboys stand at the head of a street," he proclaimed during the Civil War, "and send down their voice through it, as an athlete would roll a ball down an alley." By comparison, "pale and feeble-speaking" ministers could scarcely be heard by their congregation, and some lawyers could hardly fill a courtroom with their voices. Beecher advised men training for the "speaking-professions" to go into partnership with newsboys "till they got their mouths open, and their larynx nerved and toughened." Ironically, newsboys besmirched Beecher's name at the top of their lungs during his six-month adultery trial in 1874–75. The New York press covered the story in such excruciating detail that the activity outside the offices of the *Graphic* and other newspapers and distribution depots reminded some of wartime. A mess of newsboys had the audacity to peddle the story on the steps of Beecher's Plymouth Church as the congregation was leaving, until police dispersed them. The scandal found wide appeal; newsboys in Memphis, Tennessee, risked arrest by peddling extras purporting to contain Beecher's confession, while those in Virginia City, Nevada, found buyers by crying, "H'yar's yer Beecher-Tilton Gall of Bitterness!" *Leslie's* captured the frenzy with a cartoon showing hawkers accosting Beecher himself with their extras (Figure 5.16).[83]

Most offensive were cries of false news, which could be prosecuted under laws against "exciting the community" or "obtaining money by trick and device." Such were the charges pressed against a Philadelphia newsboy in 1867 for shouting "Assassination of President Johnson" and "Murder of General Grant." Newsboys in Hartford, Connecticut, concocted duels between the principals of Johnson's impeachment trial the following year. The *New York Times* denounced these "young reprobates" as corrupt Ring politicians in training. Yet newspapers sometimes cooked up their own canards, as when the death of a distinguished journalist and philosopher was shouted through the streets. Purchasers of the paper found a story in large type about the demise of an infant bearing the famous man's name. The *New York Herald* perpetrated an audacious hoax in 1874 when it sent newsboys howling through the city with a full-page report that all the animals of the Central Park Zoo—including rhinos, baboons, and jungle cats—had broken out and were ravaging the city, with great loss of life.[84]

Some newsboys held themselves to higher standards of veracity than did editors. Once on hearing a boy crying "Extry! Accident and terrible loss of life!" a bigger boy called him over and asked how many lives. Told there were only two dead, he informed the novice, "You can't holler on two." April Fools' Day was an exception, particularly in San Francisco, where mail coaches carrying eastern papers usually arrived after dark. Newsboys—"and a California newsboy is the sharpest of his race," said the British weekly *All the Year Round*—would hustle these precious imports on the streets for 25¢ apiece. Buyers had to beware, as the papers might be a year old.[85]

So constant were the cries of America's newsboys that their absence became noteworthy. One such instance occurred after the ferryboat *Westfield* exploded in its slip in July 1871. Nearly a hundred people perished, and for days afterward the Battery was "occupied with a silent, awe-struck crowd watching the work of men grappling for bodies. 'Even the newsboys and bootblacks, usually so vociferous,'" said *Harper's Weekly*, "'glided about among the crowd as if they had suddenly been struck dumb.'"[86]

The hush did not last long, as a national calamity soon restored their voices and generated sales, sympathy, and solidarity among newsboys. The Great Chicago Fire in October 1871 leveled an area four miles long and three-quarters of a mile wide. It killed three hundred people and left a hundred thousand— about a third of the population—homeless, including some sixty residents of

Figure 5.15. "We can almost hear the cry of the newsboy, the rush of feet, and the roar of wheels. Soldiers, policemen, women, beggars, negroes, all mingle in the whirling rush of life, too intense to last, too much in haste to stumble often." Sydney Hull, "Life in Broadway, New York," *Harper's Bazar*, 6, no. 5 (Feb. 1, 1873): 72–73. Author's collection.

Figure 5.16. Selling scandal to the scandalized. "Rev. Henry Ward Beecher Purchasing Extras from the Newsboys," *Frank Leslie's Illustrated Newspaper*, Aug. 8, 1874, n.p. New York Public Library.

the Newsboys' and Bootblacks' Home, which burned to the ground. Chicago's leading newspapers were burned out, too, but the national press issued a stream of extras as updates flashed over the wire, enabling readers to follow the advance of the flames from downtown to the residential North Division.[87]

Among those who took refuge in the LaSalle Street tunnel was a *Chicago Journal* newsboy. When the fire neared, a wall of heat and smoke came funneling through the tunnel, causing him to faint while everyone else ran for their lives. A policeman rescued the boy and revived him with a splash of water. Newsboys were proverbially "tough customers," wrote a journalist, "but this one must be a little salamander." He and his mates served as symbols of the city's resilient spirit. Some who resumed work were accused of extortion for charging a nickel, dime, or even 35¢ for their papers, yet most helped comfort survivors who read about the relief efforts on their behalf. Newsboys thus became national heroes, instantly celebrated in the pages of the 1871 dime novel *Will Waffles; or, The Freaks and Fortunes of a News Boy*.[88]

In reality, the grim prospect of earning a living after the fire forced thirty thousand Chicagoans to leave the city on free railroad passes. Among them were an untold number of newsboys and bootblacks whose plight elicited compassion from their colleagues. Newsboys in Brooklyn raised $20.50 "for their suffering associates in Chicago." Cincinnati newsboys voted to appropriate all of their profits for two days for the relief of boys affected by the fire. Meanwhile, residents of the Newsboys' Lodging House in New York hosted several groups of refugees, some of whom bore scorch marks or other disfigurements. "The New York boys gave their brothers of the West a very cordial reception," reported a contemporary chronicler, "and as far as their little means allowed, lavished upon them a generous welcome." The New York newsboys were much younger than the Chicagoans, who numbered eighteen and averaged between 16 and 19 years of age. The local boys treated them like celebrities, huddling around them at mealtime and showing them off at their favorite haunts.[89]

They also took the opportunity to talk business. The usual lodging house games were cancelled one Sunday evening so the boys could discuss the state of trade in their respective cities. They compared notes on earnings, tips, and turf rights. The bootblacks lamented a recent drop in prices but proposed that a "choker fee" would set things rights. They agreed it was no time for a strike, yet discussed other tactics. The Chicago boys said it was a shame that not all the fountains in New York were working, as they were inviting to customers. They urged their hosts to claim the fountain in City Hall Park as their headquarters and get more portable chairs, which were good for business. At the end of the meeting the regulars passed the hat for their guests and a boy named Billy proposed a resolution. "I move that we're awful sorry for the suffering of the newsboys and black-a-boots of Chicago," he said, "and that if they stay, we post 'em, and that anything we can do we'll do to help 'em, and that we're sorry it ain't more than $8.25." One of the Chicago youths rose and thanked the "gents" for their hospitality.[90]

For Want of Shelter

The postwar recession deepened the need for newsboy philanthropy. Charles Loring Brace responded by expanding his efforts to provide lodgings for them. In an 1865 editorial, the *New York Times* praised the "quiet labors" of the Children's Aid Society, which were "drying up the very sources and springs of childish misery and criminality." The springs flowed eternal, but such endorsements helped Brace secure more spacious accommodations, open five new lodging houses, and win public appropriations. In some years more than half of the society's funding came from state and local government. In 1868, when Moses Beach sold the *Sun*, the *Commercial Advertiser* took over the building's lease and proposed to raise another story for the boys, but the Fulton Street home was moved into a four-story building at 49–51 Park Place. (Figure 5.17) It, too,

THE THEATRE—
WHERE THEY SPEND THEIR MONEY.

WAITING FOR
THE PAPERS.

SUPPER.

THE BARBER.

GYMNASIUM.

SAVINGS BANK.—MAKING DEPOSITS.

THE NEWSBOYS' LODGING-HOUSE, NEW YORK.

Figure 5.17. Located over the *Sun* office on Fulton Street, the Newsboys' Lodging House offered meals, beds, baths, haircuts, recreation, and night classes. It sheltered more than 8,000 boys in 1866. Half were foreign-born, including 3,000 from Ireland. Most were between 12 and 15 years old, but one in five was under 11. Seventy percent were orphans or half-orphans; 80 percent could read and write. Charles G. Bush, "The Newsboys' Lodging-House, New York," *Harper's Weekly* 11, no. 542 (May 18, 1867): 312–13, 318. Eckel Collection, Princeton University Library.

THEIR VOCATION.

WASH ROOM.

EVENING SCHOOL.

HOW THEY SLEEP.

RK—Sketched by Charles G. Bush.—[See Page 318.]

included a dining room, schoolroom, gymnasium, staff quarters, and washrooms with hot and cold running water. The two top-floor dormitories held 260 iron bunk beds.[91]

In 1872 the state legislature allocated $30,000 to the CAS to refurbish the old Shakespeare Hotel, a seven-story red and gray building on Duane and Chambers Streets near City Hall Park, which served as a second Newsboys' Lodging House for the next seventy years. Longtime supporters Mrs. John Jacob Astor and Mrs. William B. Astor commissioned Central Park co-designer Calvert Vaux to design another lodging house on Seventh Avenue and 32nd Street, which was nicknamed the "Newsboys' Astor House." A third Newsboys' Lodging House was erected at 287 East Broadway and Gouverneur Street, near the tip of Manhattan, in May 1880 with a bequest from Miss Catharine L. Wolfe—"the richest young lady in the United States." In 1886 the CAS opened another Vaux-designed lodging house opposite Tompkins Square, and dedicated another purpose-built facility on 44th Street and Second Avenue in 1889.[92]

To finance such expansion, the society maintained a high profile in New York newspapers. "Having, fortunately, an early connection with the press," said Brace, "I made it a point, from the beginning, to keep our movements, and the evils we sought to cure, continually before the public in the columns of the daily journals." In the 1850s he wrote columns for the *New York Times* and the *New York Independent*, an influential Congregationalist weekly, and he now contributed sketches to *Harper's Weekly* and *St. Nicholas*. He gained his largest audience with the serial publication of his memoir, *The Dangerous Classes of New York and Twenty Years' Work Among Them*, in *Appleton's Journal* in 1870 and then as a book in 1872. Superintendents contributed to publicity efforts by conducting tours of the premises and keeping the press informed of its banquets, concerts, spelling bees, and declamation contests.[93]

Soliciting aid, or "going begging," as he called it, helped Brace and the CAS open a Sick Children's Mission in 1872 and win passage of New York's Children's Law of 1875, which mandated the removal of all children, except the mentally or physically ill, from almshouses to institutions expressly for children. The society drummed up support for its causes by printing thousands of handbills depicting a homeless waif on one side and seeking donations on the other. Johnny Morrow's autobiography, reprinted in 1870, also inspired sympathy and support. Several novels of the period functioned similarly; Madeline Leslie's *Never Give Up* (1863) and Alger's *Mark, the Match Boy* (1869) include scenes set in the Newsboys' Lodging House. A frequent visitor, Alger appealed directly for donations in the *Liberal Christian*: "Perhaps some of the boys who, I hope, will read this article may have an old cap or other garment which they would like to bestow on some one of these poor boys in the lodging-house, who, without parents, is sturdily fighting the battle of life on his own account." Donations poured in.[94]

Many others gave their time. In addition to salaried personnel, volunteers ranging from poor divinity students to Gotham's elite staffed the lodging houses. One of the society's best friends was Theodore Roosevelt Sr., father of the future president. A regular Sunday visitor to the Lodging House, he also attended Christmas and Thanksgiving dinners there, often with his sickly son and namesake in tow. In 1868 he helped establish a second lodging house on West 18th Street and in 1875 supported a CAS night school for Italian immigrants. "At a very early age," recalled the younger Roosevelt, "we children were taken with him and required to help." Teddy taught a mission class during his own school years and spoke at newsboy meetings and dinners throughout his life. When his father lay dying in the winter of 1878, ragged newsboys stood vigil for several nights in the rain outside the family's brownstone on East 20th Street.[95]

CAS lodging houses became models for institutions throughout North America. In addition to the one in Washington, newsboys' homes opened in Chicago (1865);[96] Brooklyn, Detroit, and Cincinnati (1866);[97] Baltimore (1867);[98] Newark (1868);[99] New Orleans (1869);[100] Toronto and St. Louis (1870);[101] Louisville (1872);[102] Cleveland and Philadelphia (1875);[103] Boston and Indianapolis (1879);[104] Denver (1882);[105] Pittsburgh and Buffalo (1885);[106] Kansas City and Minneapolis (1886);[107] Duluth (1887);[108] Hartford (1888);[109] Los Angeles (1890);[110] Salt Lake City (1897);[111] Butte, Montana (1899);[112] Omaha (1902);[113] and Houston (1910).[114] Many of these homes were founded by "prominent ladies" such as Elizabeth Hutter of Philadelphia, who had organized sanitary fairs, orphans' schools, and other projects during the Civil War, and Sara Farr of Minneapolis, whose efforts on behalf of newsboys and bootblacks began in 1880 with weekly meetings and a savings club. Newsboys' homes offered such women a sphere for continued social and political influence.[115]

By 1910, the US Census Bureau counted thirty homes for "newsboys and other working boys and girls." Besides the CAS, sponsors included the YMCA, the Catholic Church, and many ad hoc charities. Whatever their affiliation, the homes were usually located near newspaper offices and received some support from them.[116]

The Brooklyn Newsboys' Lodging House, founded by the Children's Aid Society in February 1866, had all the amenities of its Manhattan precursors. Located in a three-story brownstone at 69 Poplar Street, the house featured a large dining room on the first floor, dormitories and classrooms on the second floor, and a gymnasium on the third floor. It began admitting boys each evening at 6:00 p.m., allowed them to bathe, and fed them dinner at 7:00 p.m. "The meals furnished are of course plain," reported the *Brooklyn Eagle*, "but the boarders are not restricted as to quantity. They can eat their fill, and one would be astonished to see the amount it takes to fill them." According to Superintendent William Kirkby, evenings were devoted to play in the gymnasium, a half-hour of class-room work, and then "to bed." The house could sleep thirty-two boys when it first opened. "The hour of breakfast is 5½ A.M.," noted the *Eagle*, "—rather early, some of us might think, but the boys have to be out in time to sell the morning papers." Lodgers were charged 5¢, plus 2¢ for breakfast, "merely to get the boys in the habit of paying their own way," said Kirkby, but no one was ever turned away. The boys themselves rebelled against the admittance of a Negro boy in 1869, but police quelled the disturbance. From the outset, *Union* pub-lisher Chittenden treated the boys to a Thanksgiving banquet. "Probably many of these juvenile paper dealers will look back to this as their first Thanksgiving day," said the *New York Tribune*.[117]

The Brooklyn home received much praise during its first nine months of operation, but in October the *Eagle* ran a scathing letter from a lodger who complained that they were treated brutally, fed poorly, and ejected if they dared complain. "There might as well be no Lodge," he said, "for they are trying to rob and starve the newsboys." The *Eagle* looked into the matter and dismissed the charges. "The discipline, we are assured, is of the most paternal character," said the *Eagle*. It attributed the misunderstanding to the fact that the house, despite its name, aimed not just to lodge newsboys but also to reclaim young vagrants. "The newsboy is an Arab in disposition, free as the air, scorning all restraint. He is not legitimately a subject for charity." The vagrant "castaways," by contrast, re-gard food and lodging as a "Godsend" and are "sufficiently grateful." Both were in need of rescue, said the *Eagle*, "but different means may be required." The editorial was a triumph of diplomacy, simultaneously supporting the influential Brooklynites who founded the home and the aggrieved lodgers whose labor the *Eagle* needed.[118]

Similar controversies erupted elsewhere. In 1872 lodgers at the newsboys' home in Philadelphia told guardians to either "set up knobbier grub or close the caboose." The caboose was closed. Four years later several older boys at the Quince Street home in Chicago complained to the *Tribune* about the bad food, hard beds, and inhumane rules that forced them out before dawn. When another lodger sat down to write a letter defending the home, the malcontents roughed him up. The board of directors then banned all boys over 16 years old. "The excitement was prodigious," reported the *Tribune*. The bounced boys, ten in number, resolved themselves into an indignation mass-meeting and appointed committees, one of which visited the *Tribune* to demand "reparation through the public prints." Some thirty lodgers appeared in court the following year to testify on behalf of a boy who was beaten with a loaded cane by the janitor.[119]

The Chicago home, which accommodated about seventy boys, suffered an-other black eye in 1881 when 10-year-old Thomas Weaver was hauled off for disorderly conduct. The home's aged janitor testified against him. "You see, judge," he said, "kind words and Christian treatment ain't no good in such a place, and the only way to do is to go through the crowd with a club and hit first this way and then that."

Weaver interrupted: "Yes, but if you did the right thing by the boys you wouldn't have to beat 'em that way. Your Honor, he uses a revolver, and threatens to shoot us if we don't behave."

"So I do," admitted the janitor, "and I tell them if they ain't quick I'll give them the contents of it, too."

"And he uses a broom-stick to beat the boys when they make fun getting up in the morning," said the accused.

"No, it's not a stick, your honor; it's a rawhide, and I lay it about, too, you bet."

The judge cut off the exchange and fined young Weaver $5. Afterward, a director of the home assured the public that the janitor's bark "was worse than his bite."[120] The home did function as a refuge for victims of domestic violence; its matron, Mrs. Forsythe, took in many a beaten boy, filed complaints against their parents, and in one instance took legal custody of a child. The home also published the *Newsboys' Appeal*, an illustrated paper given to destitute boys to sell. Its first editor, Miss Flora A. Brewster, ran the night school on Friedrich Froebel's song-, story-, and play-oriented kindergarten plan before becoming a physician and surgeon.[121]

By far the biggest critic—and imitator—of the Children's Aid Society was the Catholic Church. Its clergy saw the CAS as perpetrators of a plot to rip Catholic children from their parents and place them in Protestant homes. Priests in the Midwest reported that children were being sold into slavery, and raised fears that separated siblings might unknowingly marry each other when they grew up. Brace railed against such "rumors" and denounced the "prejudiced Priests." Catholics developed their own placing-out system in the 1850s and established homes for working boys in several cities. In New York, the Society of St. Vincent de Paul, a lay organization, established St. Vincent's Home for Homeless Boys of All Occupations in 1870. Located in a converted warehouse at 53 Warren Street, the operation floundered but was revitalized the following year by Father John C. Drumgoole, an Irish-born priest who was himself a product of the slums of New York. Drumgoole shortened the name to St. Vincent's Newsboys Home and incorporated a gym, night classes, and other features pioneered by Brace. Funded primarily by lotteries, it formed the nucleus of what would become the largest orphanage in the United States.[122]

Though nearly forgotten, Father Drumgoole's achievements in child welfare work rivaled those of Brace. The differences between the two men are striking. Brace was a Yale-educated child of privilege, while Drumgoole, his senior by sixteen years, was a poor immigrant who struggled into adulthood to attain an education. Not a gifted writer like Brace, Drumgoole nevertheless became a tireless institution builder. He moved into the home to exert a greater influence on the boys. Their daily schedule began with early morning prayers followed by Mass with brief sermons tailored to the boys. Like Brace, he tried to instill self-reliance by charging them 5¢ for lodging and 5¢ for meals, yet he housed and fed many who could not pay. Also like Brace, he expanded constantly, first renting the adjoining building and remodeling it to include a chapel, gymnasium, lecture hall, schoolroom, and sleeping quarters for two hundred boys. He held day classes for the tykes and night classes for the older boys. The curriculum included courses in business, Latin, and Greek. St. Vincent's was open to boys of all faiths and races. Reporting on the home's Thanksgiving banquet in 1873, the New York Sun remarked, "Colored boys also, that other places will not take, here find a dormitory and table, several feasting on turkey and pudding yesterday among their white friends. The white boys bring them in, and Father Drumgoole encourages the generous spirit of fellowship."[123]

Drumgoole raised money by holding bazaars and concerts, several of which took place at Tammany Hall. Thousands of ticket-holders would gather for the drawings. Police cracked down on the drawings, however, for violating state anti-lottery laws. But Drumgoole continued to solicit donations in innovative ways; he started The Homeless Child magazine and sold 25¢ subscriptions worldwide. He distributed cards with short prayers on the back that could be recited for long indulgences. And he received public support from the city's excise fund for taking in boys committed by city magistrates. After six years Drumgoole reported that five thousand boys had been sheltered and more than a thousand prepared for the sacraments.[124]

In 1879 Drumgoole began construction on an impressive ten-story Home for Boys on Lafayette Place and Great Jones Street at a cost of $69,000, paid in cash. When completed in 1881 it housed four hundred boys, many in single rooms. Drumgoole turned over management of the home to Franciscan nuns and embarked on other projects. The desire to give his charges a country experience led him to found the Mission of the Immaculate Virgin and St. Elizabeth's orphanage on Staten Island six months later. By the mid-1880s it housed fifteen hundred children, more than any other institution in the country.[125]

One of the most illustrious supporters of the home was the Earl of Rosebery, future prime minister of England. Lord Rosebery made regular donations and took a special, perhaps carnal, interest in one of its regulars, a bootblack named Patrick Shea who had approached him in City Hall Park. Rosebery agreed to underwrite Pat's education after a Brevoort House detective questioned the propriety of the boy's visit. Rosebery, age twenty-six, first toured St. Vincent's in November 1873. He found it "very clean and comfortable" and praised its little gymnasium and theater. "Most of the boys are Irish," he noted in his diary, "and so was the kind hearted zealous Superintending Priest. It is through such men that the Catholic Church obtains its hold over the poorer classes of the community." Rosebery later told Drumgoole, "You have a theater to capture the little fellows' bodies, and then you have your chapel to capture their souls." Rosebery always visited when in New York. Whenever a boy complained about the hash, he would be told, "It was good enough for Lord Rosebery."[126]

"We Ain't No Rothschilds"

Newsboys were not just passive recipients of philanthropy; they were also generous givers to charities and active defenders of their own economic interests. Residents of the New York Newsboys' Lodging House contributed to many causes over the years—from the relief of families in Bleeding Kansas to the restoration of Mount Vernon. Cincinnati's "big-hearted" newsboys were known to donate a day's earnings to yellow-fever sufferers. Inspired by workers' campaign for the eight-hour day, newsboys also formed unions, mounted strikes, and engaged in other forms of collective action—including attempted arson at the new St. Vincent's Home on Poplar Street. Their organizations and uprisings were usually crushed or co-opted, but a propensity to protest endured. There is no telling how many confrontations occurred in the 1870s and early 1880s without mention in the press, but disputes in ten cities garnered enough attention to demonstrate that newsboys possessed levels of class consciousness and labor militancy that Alger and Brown never imagined.[127]

One of the first clashes took place on May Day 1871, when an "immense crowd of the craft" met in front of the office of the *Cincinnati Weekly Times*, newly consolidated with the *Daily Chronicle*, and yelled themselves hoarse, crying, "Five papers for ten cents or we won't buy!" The "arabs" threatened would-be purchasers and delayed distribution by thirty minutes, until a group of strikebreakers rushed the building and secured copies at the new price of four for a dime. "It remains to be seen whether the guild will take any further hostile steps," said the *Cincinnati Enquirer*, "lung power having proven ineffectual." The boys organized a union the following year with the help of Judge A. G. W. Carter and Col. Robert Moore, a Mexican War and Civil War veteran who, with the union's support, would be elected mayor in 1877. "The Cincinnati newsboys are becoming so dignified, and assuming such a lofty tone that it will soon be the style to raise your hat when you buy a newspaper," observed a Chicago paper. The boys were not just seeking respectability; after marching in a victory parade for the mayor-elect and shaking his hand, one little fellow broke the silence by saying, "We want to eat."[128]

Unlike in Cincinnati, newspaper publishers in Chicago responded to recalcitrant hawkers with an iron fist. In March 1875 a strike by Milwaukee newsboys who sold the Chicago morning papers resulted in the importation of thirty Chicago toughs. A "smart fight between the gamins" ensued and the strike collapsed.[129]

In August, St. Louis newsboys formed their own "protective organization." One member characterized it as "a mutual admiration society same as big guns." The *Chicago Times* told of an incident in which a dispute at the window of the *Evening Republican* led the aggrieved "urchin" to repair to the alley where he "caucused" with his "pals," who appointed a delegation to meet with the managing editor. They refused to deal with any of his underlings. On reaching the manager's fifth-floor office, they informed him that if he failed to "come to scratch," he would most assuredly "hear from them in a way that would make it unhealthy for even him."[130]

The following year newsboys waged a nine-day strike against the *St. Louis Evening Dispatch* over the price of the paper. The paper charged the boys 30¢ a dozen, while the rival *Republican* charged only 20¢. The boys refused to yield even after they were offered a compromise of 24¢, or 2¢ apiece for the 3¢ paper. "Every newsboy in the city is in the strike," reported out-of-town papers, "and, so far, they have prevented the *Dispatch* being sold on the street." They "hallooed and cursed and maltreated" every carrier and train boy who tried to sell it, prompting the *Dispatch*'s manager to ask the mayor for protection from the "pestiferous gamins." The *Cincinnati Enquirer* viewed the situation with alarm, saying that the St. Louis boys wanted nothing less than "to conduct the newspaper business of that city." What's more, Cincinnati's union newsboys "may yet hold the circulation of newspapers in their right hands." The strikers ultimately took the paper at the old rate, but strike leader Dutch Hiney (real name William Henry Oertel) vowed revenge.[131]

Meantime, newsboys in Nashville, Tennessee, held an indignation meeting on top of a pile of cottonseed down at the levee in which "Little Mike," the elected chairman, gave a rousing speech in language unsuitable for publication. And Philadelphia's heavily Irish newsboys and bootblacks took advantage of the 1876 Centennial International Exhibition to form a "beneficial society" that adopted by-laws, elected officers, and held regular meetings conducted under parliamentary procedures. Their stated aim was mutual protection from frostbite, starvation, and the police during the coming winter.[132]

Newsboys in Chicago next struck the *Post* in February 1877, reportedly "becoming riotous and abusive toward the proprietor and policemen." They paraded the streets with banners declaring, "We want cake and pie or blood." The *Post* charged that the boys had been hired to cause unrest by recently discharged union printers, victims of a failed strike. They had in fact aided striking compositors at the *Evening Mail* in their 1871 protest against the hiring of women—their sense of male solidarity heightened by cash payments. In any event, the *Post* appealed to the superintendent of police, a frequent target of the *Post*, who promptly "squelched the row." According to the *Chicago Tribune*, he "scattered the strikers and mobocrats" and "chucked" five boys into Bridewell prison for thirty days. Meanwhile, the *Post* instructed its carriers to sell papers on the street and hired a "sufficient number" of new men to do the same.[133]

In still another case, two hundred newsboys struck the *Detroit Evening News* on July 20, 1877, seeking a cut in the wholesale price from 1¼¢ to an even penny, which meant a difference of 3¢ on the sale of a dozen papers. "You see, fellows, we ain't got no fair show," a lad named Carrot-top told his comrades. "A cent apiece is all we orter pay for them papers, and if we buck together that's all they kin git. We ain't no Rothschilds." Publisher James E. Scripps noted the disturbance in his diary: "A great crowd gathers and some violence toward news boys and carriers is attempted. Several boys arrested and excitement over at 5 o'clock." But that was not the end of it. "The newsboys riot continues today with more serious assaults," he wrote on July 21. "Stone thrown windows broken, boys hurt policemans head cut open etc Convoyed myself a lot of carriers away from the office and narrowly escaped being hit by stones." The next day Scripps called on the mayor to "warn him of the danger of letting the news boy strikes proceed too far." They discussed arrangements for clearing the streets, and on the 23rd Scripps reported: "All quiet with the newsboys today." The strike's collapse merited comment in the *Brooklyn Eagle*, which said that the boys' failure to "stick" meant that many "will have to wear shoes next Winter in place of boots, and will have to abjure cigars and tobacco in addition to their other woes."[134]

Hardly an isolated incident, the Detroit conflict coincided with a national rail strike that shocked the nation with its violence. A virtual insurrection left scores dead and millions of dollars in property damage. Trouble flared after a pool of railroad companies imposed a third consecutive pay cuts on employees. The men walked off the job rather than accept this indignity, and they won support from workers in all regions and industries who endorsed their demands for a living wage, the eight-hour day, and an end to child labor. The walkout began in Wheeling, West Virginia, on July 14, and spread to Pittsburgh, Chicago, Philadelphia, Baltimore, and St. Louis, where newsboys voted to join the work stoppage. Up to that point, the boys had "found a three-story bonanza in the strike," with train boys commanding from 10¢ to 50¢ per copy.[135]

Chicago newsboys also dispensed papers hand over fist: the *Tribune* issued its first Sunday extra since the Civil War and the circulation of the *Daily News* rose from 14,000 to almost 70,000 during the forty-five-day insurrection. Other dailies saw similar gains as the violence spread and casualties mounted. President Rutherford B. Hayes ultimately crushed the strike by calling out federal troops fresh from the Indian campaign on the plains. "These fellers ain't got no bouquets in their muskets," remarked a Chicago newsboy. Soldiers shot down at least thirteen men and boys in Chicago and twenty-six in Philadelphia. State militiamen killed ten in Baltimore, including Willie Hourand, a 15-year-old newsboy shot in the head while standing with other newsboys at the corner of Baltimore and Halliday Streets (Figure 5.18). A hero to his comrades, Hourand was treated to a lavish funeral in which fellow newsboys sent wreaths, served as pallbearers, and led the funeral procession. Like workers everywhere, they viewed the strike as the birth pangs of a resurgent labor movement that would resist starvation wages and protected capitalists. Employers, on the other hand, feared that the strike presaged a revolution akin to the Paris Commune.[136]

To the degree that striking newsboys represented a law-and-order problem, newspaper publishers made common cause with city officials. Publishers endorsed rather than resisted municipal ordinances requiring newsboys and other juvenile street peddlers to obtain licenses as a way to control their number and behavior. Newsboys and bootblacks "are useful exponents of American enterprise," said the *Minneapolis Tribune* in 1874, "but they are apt to run wild, and certainly need restraint. If these gamins were required to qualify and wear some badge of their public office, the lives they are leading and circumstances

Firing into a Mob on Baltimore Street.

Figure 5.18. Baltimore newsboy Willie Hourand was killed by militia in the Great Railroad Strike of 1877, but he appears here as a victim of mob violence. Earlie and Beale, "Firing into a Mob on Baltimore Street," in Allan Pinkerton, *Strikers, Communists, Tramps and Detectives* (New York: G. W. Carleton, 1878), 181.

could be better watched, and more done to ameliorate their condition." Grown-up vendors and their professional associations also supported licensing as a way to limit competition.[137]

Boston was probably the first city to license—and educate—newsboys. "City Fathers" issued licenses to forty of the neediest boys (only one of which had American parents) in 1855 in an effort to force the others into school.[138] Officials raised the number of newsboy licenses to four hundred in 1868 and established a pair of day schools for licensed minors so that their comings and goings would not disrupt regular students. The school located on North Margin Street enrolled between twenty and thirty "two-hour pupils," most of whom were Irish, while the other, larger school on East-street Place served mainly Italians. Miss Sarah Brackett ran the former and Miss M. Taylor the latter. Newsboys attended from nine to eleven in the morning, and bootblacks from two to four in the afternoon. Their curriculums included Christian training and lessons in reading, writing, and ciphering. Visitors were struck by the sonorous tones with which the children read aloud. "It sounded just as if they were crying out, 'Journal,' 'Herald,'" said one guest. "This was not owing to any training of teachers, but to habit." City officials also enrolled working boys in night schools; indeed, the Harrison Avenue Evening School, under the direction of Gettysburg battle veteran Sylvanus T. Rugg, was "devoted almost entirely to newsboys."[139]

Cincinnati's Board of Aldermen proposed a street trade ordinance in 1873 that was roundly denounced by the local newsboys' union on the grounds that it was able to secure the good conduct of members without the aid of the "tyrannical and oppressive" measure. "As to the proposed badge," wrote union secretary John King, "it is a badge of dishonor—a regular 'leather medal' concern—which its projector wouldn't wear a bit sooner than he would a ball and chain." In the end, the union won the right to issue the badges and purge all "scalawags" and "till tappers" from the rolls. It claimed as many as 112 members out of a pool of 800. They included Irish, German, and Jewish boys and at least one black youth on crutches. "Blood's a kind of a smoked Italian from old Virginny," said Executive Committee member Moses Doyle, "but he's just as white inside as George Washington." The officers tended to be older teens who owned profitable stands and corners. Ex-mayor Robert Moore outfitted half of the members in gray uniforms with red trimming and caps bearing the initials N.B.U.[140]

Passed in November 1877, Detroit's badge system came in response to newsboys' "unruly character" during the national rail strike. The ordinance required each boy to obtain a yearly license and badge for 10¢ from the police sanitary division. An amendment stipulated that the badges were to be issued "only on satisfactory assurance of good conduct." But the law did not regulate the age or hours children could work, and it was only enforced twice a year, when the police were ordered to send all boys who had no badges to the Juvenile Home to secure them. Some 4,200 boys passed through the system in its first four years, which theoretically improved their behavior and self-respect since they felt "the eyes of the city are upon them." City fathers in nearby Jackson, Michigan, instituted a similar license scheme the next year, as did officials in Covington, Kentucky, across the river from Cincinnati, but only after members of the Newsboys' Union agreed to wear numbered German silver shields supplied by a local newsdealer.[141]

None of these measures squelched labor unrest in the wake of the 1877 riots. Newsboys in Baltimore won a major price concession (⅓¢) from the *Evening News* in November 1879 after they marched through the streets two hundred strong, bearing transparencies reading "Bread or Blood," "Darn the News," and "Boys, Stand Up for Your Rights."[142] Newsboys in St. Louis, however, met stiff resistance six months earlier from the newly merged *Post-Dispatch*, a feisty nickel paper owned by 32-year-old Hungarian immigrant and American Civil War veteran Joseph Pulitzer. Scraping by with a circulation of just over of 3,000, Pulitzer raised the wholesale price from 2½¢ to 3¢ a copy. According to the rival *Missouri Republican*, the strikers "took charge of things" within a two-block radius of the paper: "They gathered in a swarm about the office, making it pretty lively for any boy or man, even, that undertook to carry out papers. One stout fellow, that looked like he ought to be a match for a score of boys, was placed *hors du combat* before he got a square from the office, and his papers were quickly torn and trampled in the mud. . . . Even the carriers, except under the protection of the police, were not permitted to take out their papers." Union treasurer Dutch Hiney vowed, "We will paralyze them." Yet on further reflection he admitted they could probably hold out only a day or two, as their mothers did not like to see them idle. The newsboys lost the strike, but ultimately prevailed when the paper reinstated the original price.[143]

The newsboys' union demanded even better terms in August 1880 after Scripps weakened Pulitzer's hold on the market by introducing a 2¢ paper, the *Evening Chronicle*, overseen by his half brother Edward Willis Scripps. To promote street sales, E. W. gave free copies to newsboys, many of whom were following a new fad—getting their arms tattooed with stars, doves, mottos, and trade emblems, in red or blue, for 25¢ apiece. Recognizing their new bargaining power—and perhaps egged on by Scripps—the boys declared themselves "out on strike." Hiney and a boy named Hoppie headed a deputation of newsboys, many flourishing sticks, who gathered outside the *Post-Dispatch* office to chant, "Three for a nickel." Though friendly to labor and an advocate of the poor, Pulitzer felt no sympathy for the boys' "shabby showing." "Their demand is for three copies of the paper for five cents," said the *Post-Dispatch*. "They now get two, but a hundred per cent profit does not strike these merchants as quite enough. . . . The newsboys make as much on each copy of the *Post-Dispatch* sold as we do, and we furnish the white paper, ink, presswork, type-setting and just enough brain to keep the thing going."[144]

Inexperience and lack of organization brought a quick collapse to the protest, but as the depression receded, newsboys—including those who distributed the nation's eight hundred ethnic newspapers—felt entitled to a fairer share of the wealth they helped create. "Editor Byron of the *Arbeiter Zeitung* is having a heap of trouble with his paper carriers," sympathized a fellow Milwaukee editor in 1880. "During the past week he has builetined [served notice of dismissal] several of the boys." That same year Italian newsboys in Cleveland hired a lawyer to challenge the constitutionality of the city's street trading ordinance after the mayor had refused them licenses for allegedly driving smaller boys from their corners. Then in the spring of 1881, newsboys of the *Cleveland Leader* joined tailors, coopers, mill workers, boilermakers, and longshoremen in what the *Washington Post* termed "a season of strikes." The *Leader*, a thrice-weekly nickel paper that wholesaled for 3¢, accused the *Cleveland Herald*, which was sold to the boys at half price, with instigating the strike. The "little newsboys" nightly paraded the street of Cleveland with a banner inscribed with the word "BLOOD" in large red letters. While the *Herald* praised them as "manly and courageous," the *Leader* warned that they were learning dangerous lessons: "Is it desired by the men who paid for this banner, and told them to carry it, that they should grow up to be red-handed communists and raise the cry of pillage and bloodshed whenever their whims are not gratified?"[145]

Newsboys who came of age amid the flash and soot of America's second industrial revolution were clearly products of their own working-class experiences, not just the overripe imaginations of middle-class writers, artists, and composers. The boys' understanding of industrial capitalism was far more complex and critical than that depicted in juvenile novels, genre paintings, popular songs, and the pictorial press. The relationship between these children and the newspapers they sold was fundamentally an economic one fraught with conflict. The social ascent of some members of this postwar cohort seems to validate the vision of Horatio Alger and J. G. Brown, who claimed that one of his urchin models grew up to become a millionaire. George Appo and Owen Kildare, two illiterate delinquents, sought, and to some degree achieved, moral regeneration in writing their life stories; Chuck Connors and Steve Brodie, two inheritors of the b'hoy tradition, became living legends in the world of sport and entertainment; and James Hudson Maurer, William Lorimer, and Bill Sullivan parlayed their street smarts into extraordinary political careers—Maurer served six years as Pennsylvania's first Socialist legislator, Lorimer dominated Illinois politics at every level, and Sullivan held seats for over twenty years in New York's Assembly and Senate and in the US House of Representatives.

Yet newsboys' utterances and actions expose the real poverty of imagination behind storybook narratives of individual success. Real newsboys took part in political campaigns, aligned with striking workers, and banded together to defend their own economic interests. They denounced the interference of officials who would bar them from selling on streetcars or bathing in public, resisted the mistreatment of benefactors who would house and feed them badly, and alternately barred and defended African Americans in the trade.

Newsboys' solidarity sometimes extended beyond death, as demonstrated by the funeral Baltimore newsboys gave to Willie Hourand in 1877 and St. Louis lads gave to strike leader Dutch Hiney in May 1886. According to the *Post-Dispatch*, "A large number of newsboys of all ages and descriptions attended Hiney's funeral service and followed the body to its last resting place." One of the wreaths on display featured newspapers bordered by half-opened white rosebuds. Placed diagonally across the arrangement were the words "Latest Edition" in purple immortelles surrounded by white carnations.[146]

Such expressions of sorrow and solidarity were not anomalies. Newsboys everywhere would continue to mourn their own and demand better terms and treatment from publishers, politicians, and philanthropists. This quest put them in the path of the most powerful economic force in industrial America: the railroad.

6

Riding the Wanderlust Express

Railroads reigned supreme in industrial America. They were the engines that drove the postwar economy, stimulated western expansion, and imposed their corporate time zones on the nation. Local, state, and transcontinental railways employed thousands of workers, carried millions of passengers, and brought a cornucopia of goods—including newspapers—to distant markets. By 1869, one out of three daily papers crossed state lines via wholesale firms reliant on rail service and boy labor.[1]

Three types of newsboys emerged from this transportation network: salaried news agency employees, who rode and met trains to ship and receive local and out-of-town papers; uniformed "news butchers," who plied passengers with reading material and sundry items; and footloose "tramp newsboys," who hitched rides on freight and passenger cars in search of work or adventure. Each of these types occupied a separate niche in the distribution process and a different rung on the social ladder, but they shared a dependence on railroads and newspapers for their daily bread. Their experiences offer a unique bottom-up perspective on the spread of print capitalism and its connection to the industry that defined America's machine age.

Vital Links

Of the three, news agency hands enjoyed the safest and steadiest employment. They piloted papers through channels first formed in the antebellum era by independent firms, most of which were absorbed by the Union News Company and Sinclair Tousey's American News Company. By 1888 Tousey's firm employed a thousand men and boys on board trains connecting thirty-three thousand towns from Maine to California. The total number and average age, wage, and working conditions of agency personnel are not known, but the daily routine of those employed by Detroit news dealer William E. Tunis in the 1850s sheds light on the workings of the industry. Tunis relied on "five or six smart young lads" to rush newspapers to distribution points throughout Michigan. They worked round the clock, sleeping six nights a week in the back of his office. They began their day at 9:00 a.m. when they caught a ferry across the river to Windsor, Canada, to await the arrival of the Great Western, which carried day-old papers from New York. Each of the boys brought wrappers on which they had written the names and addresses of Michigan newsdealers. When the train arrived at 10:00 a.m., the boys dashed for the express car. They loaded bundles of the *Herald, Tribune,* and *Times* onto the ferry and began counting them out and tying them in bundles for the dealers. Passengers marveled at the boys' "lightning speed." On reaching the Detroit side of the river, they threw the bundles onto special express trains and carried the remaining papers to Tunis's shop, where customers would call for them. The crew rested until 3:00 p.m., and then commenced writing up wrappers for the next day's delivery. They stopped for supper at 6:00 p.m. and were free until 11:00 p.m., when they returned to sort the weekly papers, magazines, and dime novels that arrived on the night train from New York. These periodicals were delivered to Tunis's office by American Express wagons. At 3:00 a.m. came the Detroit morning papers, which the boys prepared for shipment on the early trains. They then slept until 9:00 a.m., when the routine started all over again.[2]

Variations of this process occurred all across the country. In Harrisburg, Pennsylvania, newsboys and depot agents had to contend with large crowds that "swayed and fought and pushed and shouted and grabbed and yelled and clamored" for Philadelphia newspapers. The greatest activity was on Sunday, when the papers were larger. In the 1870s and 1880s, several New York newspapers relied on express trains and distribution cars to transport their papers to the nation's capital or up to Newport, Saratoga, and other resorts. Early risers routinely saw men "staggering along through the ghostly, snow clad, gaslit streets, with regular Pisa towers of newspapers on their shoulders, to board the newspaper train with them."[3]

The Long Island Rail Road introduced Sunday newspaper trains in 1877 that sped breakfast copies of New York City papers to readers all the way to the North Fork village of Greenport, three hours and one hundred miles away. Union News Company employees carried five thousand papers from boat to train at the Hunters Point station at 4:30 a.m., folded and sorted them in the smoking car, and delivered them "on the fly" to waiting carriers at depots and junctions (Figure 6.1). Carriers waiting along the line in wagons or on horseback had to take care not to be hit, as the sacks came flying out the windows of trains traveling up to fifty miles per hour. (Nine-year-old Hugh Bradley of Mineral Wells, Texas, suffered a broken leg when struck by a sack; some boys trained their dogs to fetch the papers after they landed.) On the Sag Harbor branch for Moriches and the Hamptons, "an army of newsboys left the main line to enlighten the people

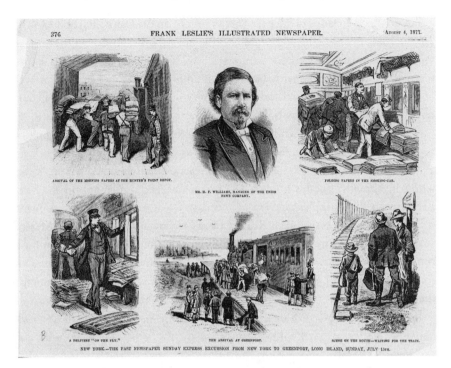

Figure 6.1. "New York.—The Fast Newspaper Sunday Express Excursion from New York to Greenport, Long Island, Sunday, July 15th. Arrival of the morning papers at the Hunter's Point Depot; Mr. H. F. Williams, manager of the Union News Company; Folding papers in the smoking-car; A Delivery 'On the Fly'; The Arrival at Greenport; Scene on the Route—waiting for the train," *Frank Leslie's Illustrated Newspaper*, Aug. 4, 1877, 376. Eckel Collection, Princeton University Library.

of those villages." Circulation on the North Shore of Long Island nearly doubled the next year, and by 1881 the system was extended to the South Shore. It killed the local pony express service but created more than two hundred jobs. To maximize profits, the LIRR added passenger cars to the news train and promoted excursions to hotels, beaches, and fishing grounds.[4]

Sunday newspaper trains leaving Grand Central Station soon provided the same early morning service to all the hotels and hamlets around Lake George in upstate New York, and to shore towns extending to Newport, Rhode Island. Such coverage yielded the *New York Herald* headline "Summer Resorts Melodious with the Cry of the Newsboy."[5]

Newspaper publishers and dealers made similar inroads into the Deep South. In November 1876, the *Atlanta Constitution* recruited a hundred boys—"first come, first served"—to sell the paper exclusively in the one hundred towns on the railroad lines radiating out from Atlanta for a hundred miles. It promised them "a little winter bonanza." In 1888 the *St. Louis Republic* used thoroughbred horses to speed editions to the depot for shipment on the Cairo Short Line to Du Quoin, Illinois, and transfer to the Illinois Central's Chicago–New Orleans fast mail train. Readers in Kentucky, Tennessee, Mississippi, Louisiana, and Alabama received copies within twelve to twenty-four hours. The weekly *Birmingham Age-Herald* made a similar assault on Montgomery in 1899 by dispatching a dozen boys on the "Age-Herald Special."[6]

There seems to have been real opportunity for advancement with the news agencies that made these feats possible. Frederick P. Morris started out as a "butch" on the LIRR in 1869 at age 16, carried on when the Union News Company bought out his boss in 1876, and five years later outbid the firm and formed the Long Island News Company. Most of Tunis's lads also went on to become successful news dealers or railway agents. One, Joseph Marsh, succeeded Tunis as manager in 1876, opened a branch in Toronto, and joined the board of directors of the American News Company. Tunis himself gained a seat on the New York Stock Exchange. But beyond individual accomplishment, the more profound cumulative effect of the boys' labor was to link America's "island communities" with its urban centers. These youths supplied the news and information needed for widespread civic engagement and commercial exchange.[7]

To Stick or Quit

Trains were not just vehicles for the wholesale distribution of print; they were important retail sites as well. Big-city and small-town stations leased space for newsstands and, to varying degrees, tolerated ambulatory vendors, some of whom acted as "runners" for hotels and boardinghouses. Most railroad lines permitted newsboys on their cars as well, but the news agencies that employed them had to pay for the privilege. These agencies increasingly fell under the sway of regional or national conglomerates. In 1874 Tunis's Railroad News Agency employed and supplied 150 train boys, who worked nine different roads. The company paid $8,000 a year for the privilege and kept 80 percent of what the boys took in. By 1892 there were six major railroad news companies in the country—three in New York, one in Louisville, one in New Orleans, and one in Chicago—plus a half dozen smaller firms in the Far West. Their vendors had to post bonds, buy uniforms, and conform to strict codes of conduct. Yet like street newsboys, they cried their wares and survived on tips, tricks, and profits rather than wages. In so doing, they became both minor comforts and major afflictions to rail travelers, and helped revolutionize the reading habits of the nation. They also encountered unique risks, notably train wrecks. Lawsuits arising from these accidents helped rewrite liability law in the United States. More than any other child laborers, train boys forced judges and legislators to decide who, if anyone, was responsible when young workers were killed or injured on the job.[8]

Denied a steady wage, news butchers held the "poorest job" on passenger trains, but they represented a kind of aristocracy among newsboys. Dapper in their uniforms and seasoned by travel, they tended to regard regular newsies as scruffy stay-at-homes. Train boys ranged in age from 12 to 18 until the 1890s, when many agencies established 16 as the minimum. Yet poverty gave them a good incentive to lie about their age, as most came from needy families. "The men and boys who sell these goods are characters recruited from a hundred different occupations," observed the *St. Louis Republic.* "Elderly men, who have failed in salesmanship or clerical positions, former jockeys, boys from the farms, former street fakers whose original graft has worn out, and once in a while a broken down university man who is trying to make a stake." One of the oldest news butchers was 82-year-old Henry Warren, a retired country schoolteacher who peddled on the New Haven and Derby Railroad in Connecticut into the 1890s. One of the youngest was 9-year-old Harry Vest, a conductor's son who worked the Kansas and Missouri Railroad's hundred-mile run from Gauley to Point Pleasant, West Virginia, in 1901.[9]

Many train boys were children of railway workers, whose employment was erratic and dangerous; they, too, became news butchers if injured on the job. Middle-class boys attracted by the romance of the road generally did not last. Nor did girls; 17-year-old Margaret Patrick worked the Lake Shore trains from Toledo in 1910 dressed as a boy but was dismissed when she was found out. Among the collegians was Leo Stanley, who withdrew from Stanford University his sophomore year in 1906 when his money ran out and peddled on the Southern Pacific Railroad from Portland to New Orleans. "I believe that that one year as peanut butcher was better than a whole at Stanford," he recalled. "I learned to know people, I learned to merchandise, to sell; I really think it was a wonderful experience." Stanley returned to graduate and put himself through medical school by working the Del Monte Express to Monterey on weekends.[10]

Earnings varied widely; some boys made fortunes while others quit in debt and disgust. Irish-born Patrick Farrelly, as we saw, served as a newsboy on the Canandaigua and Elmira Railroad in the 1850s before becoming a wholesale newsdealer and an official of the American News Company. Hugh Chisholm went to work on the Grand Trunk Railroad around 1860 at age 13 when his father died. He and his brothers soon acquired rights to sell newspapers aboard all Grand Trunk trains running between Chicago and Halifax, Nova Scotia, as well as on board most of the steamboats that plied the St. Lawrence River. One of their innovations was the uniform soon worn by all train boys. By age 20 Chisholm employed two hundred boys on routes covering more than five thousand miles. He also established a publishing company that produced the first railroad tourist guides. Chisholm served as a model for Fred Fenton, hero of Horatio Alger's 1890 novel *The Erie Train Boy*. A "resolute and manly boy of seventeen," Fred supports his widowed mother and brother and outsmarts his uncle to retain their inheritance.[11]

Also successful was William A. Brady, a news butcher on the immigrant trains of the Central Pacific and Union Pacific Railroads in the 1870s. He built up his run until it grossed $400 a week, of which 20 percent was his commission. He was a "walking general store" who carried books, magazines, newspapers, groceries, hardware, bedding, and souvenir mineral specimens. "You could work off an awful lot of that kind of junk on prosperous drunks," Brady recalled, "and the prices charged were as much as you dared to ask over and above the news company's bookkeeping prices. The difference went into your own pocket." Brady later utilized these skills as a boxing promoter and theater producer.[12]

At the other end of the spectrum was Charles P. Brown, aka "Brownie the Boomer." He began his lifelong career with railroads in 1895 at age 16 selling papers on the Peoria & Eastern line of the Big Four, running between Indianapolis and Springfield, Ohio. He got the job after talking with a Union News Company boy during a layover in Indianapolis. The boy introduced him to his boss, who offered Brown employment if he bought his uniform and put up $10 security for his stock. Brown talked it over with his mother and stepfather, but it was a formality; they all knew it was time for him to fend for himself. Brown worked on commission but soon learned to supplement his income. "The news butcher that don't sell nothing but straight company stock all of the time," he said, "is a dumbbell, and I think that I am safe in saying that all train news butchers, after they have been in the game for a while, gets wise to themselves and carry a side line of their own." Brown's most lucrative items were penny cigars, which he sold for a nickel apiece. They were so bad that the men in the smoking car called them "old cabbage ropes." "But the wise cracks from those guys did not mean anything," said Brown, "for I was out to get the jack and that was just one of my ways of getting it." Brown quit the job after nine months, saying it provided only "a kid living."[13]

Most news butchers earned from $6 to $15 a week, or "about $60 a month to the right man." However, some bragged that they made $15 to $30 a week, or more than the conductors. Those with low averages usually quit. Walter Elliott, 15, of Fort Madison, South Carolina, lasted only four months in 1902. "I lost money every trip I made," he said. "I kept getting further and further behind with my cash and I decided it was about time to throw up the sponge." He said the 20 percent sales commission (some earned 15 percent) was inadequate, especially when he was given poor stock. Percy Martin found himself in a similar situation after working two months on the run between Atlanta and Savannah in 1901. He was charged for the wormy fruit and other items he couldn't sell, and quit when his debt reached $50. The company had him arrested on his way home.[14]

Agencies took pains to ensure that newsboys didn't jump out on their debts. The Harrisburg, Pennsylvania, firm of Riley & Sargent employed 190 boys on various railroads and required that they settle up at the end of each day. Superintendents kept a record of the boys' "height, build, complexion, eyes, hair, and general habits" and any "impediment in speech, blemish or cast in the eye, irregularity or loss of teeth, scars, lameness, missing finger or anything of the kind" that would aid in identification. They would search the pockets of boys who came in short; one manager in Omaha was known to threaten his crew with a hatchet.[15]

At the height of the system in the 1880s railroads earned from $10,000 to $15,000 a year by granting selling privileges, while news companies cleared $20,000 to $25,000. Except for a brief, successful strike by news butchers on the Erie Railway in 1874, and inclusion in Eugene Debs's American Railway Union in the 1890s, no separate union or brotherhood of train boys seems to have emerged during this period of labor upsurge. Their merchant status and isolation from each other on different trains and lines hindered organization, and indeed sometimes compelled them to couple cars and do other "rough work" during walkouts. Quitting remained the most common response to intolerable conditions.[16]

Fifteen-year-old Walt Disney faced this decision after replacing his brother Roy on the Santa Fe Railroad in 1917. Like most train boys, the Disneys came from a needy family; their father had just lost his newspaper delivery service in Kansas City. Roy put up the necessary $15 bond and secured the required blue serge uniform with a badge on the lapel and gold buttons marked "Van Noyes Interstate." Walt was proud of the uniform and enjoyed seeing the countryside as the train chugged through six states, but he couldn't make any money. Passengers would hurl empty bottles from the train, depriving him of the deposit. Brakemen would pilfer candy and cigars from his unguarded hampers, leaving him owing the company. He quit, forfeiting his brother's bond.[17]

In addition to newspapers, tobacco, and edibles, train boys also sold pillows, postcards, spectacles, and seasonal fare. R. R. Burke vended oysters aboard a New Jersey train, but was arrested for having no license. World's Fairs and exhibitions provided a "golden harvest" for train boys. Fair-goers spent money more freely than other passengers and indulged in souvenir books, puzzle rings, and other novelties. During the 1876 Centennial Exhibition in Philadelphia, many news companies offered butchers a 25¢ specialty book, *Going to the Centennial*, but the sharpest boys bought copies at wholesale for 15¢ and "worked off their own stock." Others distributed souvenir programs or cartes de visite. In a stroke of marketing genius, the Waterbury Watch Company recruited train boys to peddle its line of products, thereby associating the company with the regularity of the railroad and helping convert the public to the novel notion of standard time, which railroads introduced in 1883, dividing the continent into Pacific, Mountain, Central, and Eastern time zones.[18]

The most enterprising train boy was Thomas Edison (Figure 6.2). His use of the telegraph to attract customers on the Grand Trunk line after the Battle of Shiloh was just one instance of his budding genius. Edison was a master of business efficiency and diversification. He began in the tradition of Benjamin Franklin by making the most efficient use of his time. Possessing little education beyond home schooling, Edison started selling papers on the Grand Trunk in 1859 at age 12. He worked the 7:00 a.m. run to Detroit and the 6:00 p.m. return train. The layover allowed him to read eight hours a day in the Detroit Free Library.

Edison received no wages, just profits. His first challenge was to solve what business theorists call the "blind newsboy problem," which confronts all dealers in perishables: What is the optimal amount of stock to buy to avoid selling out while demand is high or getting stuck after demand dries up? Scholars

Figure 6.2. Thomas Alva Edison, age 14 in 1861, with a white carnation. Edison National Historic Site, National Park Service, U.S. Department of the Interior (14.910/2).

still devise formulas (profit = $2\mu/\Sigma/x = 1 \, \varnothing x \times \mu\{\max [0, \text{price} - \max (0, \mu \times c \; (\mu/x - 1))] - \text{cost}\}$) and publish papers on the problem. With his livelihood at stake, Edison found his own way "to hit the happy mean": "I made a friend of one of the compositors in the *Free Press* office, and persuaded him to show me every day a 'galley proof' of the most important news article. From a study of its head lines I soon learned to gauge the value of the day's news and its selling capacity, so that I could form a tolerably correct estimate of the number of papers I should need. As a rule, I could dispose of about 200; but if there was any special news from the seat of war, the sale ran up to 300 or more."[19]

Edison soon started buying butter and vegetables along the line and selling them in Detroit and Port Huron. When the Grand Trunk added an express train and then a slow, third-class "immigrant train," he secured the concessions and employed four boys to work for him. He also went into publishing. With a small hand press and donated type, he produced the *Weekly Herald* from the baggage car. "My news was so purely local that outside the cars and the shops I don't suppose it interested a solitary human being," he recalled. "But I was very proud of my bantling, and looked upon myself as a simon-pure newspaper man. My items used to run about like this: 'John Robinson, baggage-master at James's Creek station, fell off the platform yesterday and hurt his leg. The boys are sorry for John.'" Edison's circulation averaged 300 copies a week and sometimes reached 800, and at 3¢ a copy he netted $45 a month. He thus earned about $500 a year, out of which he gave his mother $1 a day.[20]

Edison's empire collapsed after he set up a chemistry laboratory in his compartment to conduct experiments between rounds. All went well until the train derailed, tipping over his chemicals and causing a fire. The conductor stomped out the flames and threw Edison and his lab off the train. Another incident in which a trainman pulled him aboard a moving car by his ear contributed to his deafness. Edison ended up selling his news business to his friend Chisholm and became a telegraph operator. But his idea of an onboard newspaper caught on with the appearance of the *Great Pacific Line Gazette* and the *Trans-Continental*.[21]

Prurience and Politics

Because they affected a more worldly air than most boys their age, news butchers were subject to the adulation of their peers. "He smoked cigarettes before the rest of us had got through the cubeb period," explained one lifelong admirer. "He read the *Police Gazette*, which he also sold, and he was thought to know all about Sex." Many train boys fancied themselves ladies' men. Taking their cues from the "drummers," or traveling salesmen, who were their regular customers, they flirted with women passengers and waved at the farm girls who stood forlornly

beside barns. A lothario on the New York Central in 1885 claimed he kept a regular Saturday night date with a girl near Syracuse by stepping from an express to
a local train, with his basket in his hand, at fifty miles per hour. Eugene Vandrin,
who worked on the Minneapolis and St. Louis Railway, eloped with a girl of 16
in 1903, inspiring "Newsboys Sweetheart," a song about a train boy who woos
an otherwise overprotected girl when her father sends her on the coach alone:

> There I met my Dolly
> Became her loving swain
> And now I'm always wishing
> For Dolly on the train.[22]

News butchers who passed through dry states in the early 1900s also
purveyed half-pint bottles of liquor. But the most common sideline was peddling "marriage guides" and other risqué material. This was a firing offense.
Company detectives, or "spotters," mingled with passengers to ferret out the
traffic. Butchers took extra precautions; they spoke in hushed tones and ambig-
uous slang when pitching "something snappy." They would pass the forbidden
item, be it a book of "French Secrets" or a set of postcards known as the "Paris
Package," in plain sealed envelopes with grave instructions that it not be opened
on the train, for if caught they would both be sent to prison for life. Such subter-
fuge provided half the thrill for buyer and seller alike.[23]

Forrest O. Hayes, who worked on the Buffalo, Rochester & Pittsburgh
Railroad (aka the "Bums, Robbers, and Pickpockets") in the 1890s, was one such
trafficker in smut. He counted among the bestsellers of this class Boccaccio's
Decameron, a fake edition of *Fanny Hill*, and Albert Ross's *His Private Character*.
"For these supposedly off-color books we charged $2.50 to $3," said Hayes, "and
butchers were pretty good at holding the market that high. We unloaded them
largely on lumberjacks up around Mt. Jewett, Pennsylvania." In so doing, Hayes
was not just supplementing his income but subverting the censorship laws of
Anthony Comstock and other self-appointed guardians of public morality. Like
Comstock's nemesis, birth control crusader Margaret Sanger, Hayes realized
that access to information about sex or any other subject was a class issue, since
poverty kept people in the dark even more effectively than censorship. "The
Swedes who worked in the tanneries bought almost nothing from us butchers,"
he recalled. "Nor did the coal miners who were Welsh, English and Irish, and
were pretty hard up in the Nineties, being unorganized and exploited."[24]

But the revolution in reading wrought by steam presses and steam trains extended far beyond the prurient. These inventions spawned a new kind of book,
the pamphlet novel—a cheap, pocket-sized paperback set in columns of small
type between crimson or yellow covers. Most cost a nickel or a dime and were

marketed to railroad travelers. British publisher George Routledge began his Railway Library series in 1848, and opened a New York office to distribute them in the United States in 1854. The American firm G. P. Putnam & Co. followed with its Railway Classics series, which could be obtained at railway bookstalls or from news butchers on board. By 1890, publishers sold $500,000 worth of these paperbacks each year on Western railroads alone. They were so popular that some health advocates feared they would cause widespread ocular damage to young readers.[25]

Among the bestselling authors in this form were William Thackeray and Edward Bulwer-Lytton, both of whom were accosted by news butchers pushing their own works. Horace Greeley and Ulysses Grant endured similar encounters when their memoirs appeared in print. "Who is this about," feigned Grant, now a civilian. "You must be a darned greeny not to know who General Grant is," replied the boy. Grant "surrendered" and bought the book.[26]

Like their counterparts on the street, train boys played an active role in political affairs. During the elections of 1868, George Snyder, a butcher on the Baltimore and Ohio line between Washington and Philadelphia, reportedly took "every occasion to insult Republican passengers" and once "in collusion with ruffians" went around the cars identifying passengers who were on their way to vote for the Republican ticket, some of whom were assaulted in the Baltimore depot. Snyder won a libel suit against the paper that published the accusation that led to his firing, but newsboys, agencies, and even railroads clearly tried to sway voters. During the 1872 campaign no newspaper endorsing Grant could be had on the Pennsylvania Railroad between Chicago and Philadelphia. The hucksters replied they had "none left" or "no demand," but one boy admitted he "was not allowed to carry them." The *St. Louis Times* tried to combat a similar freeze-out by the *Globe Democrat* by offering passengers a two-month subscription for reporting perennially out-of-stock newsboys. In 1889 the *Omaha World-Herald* "fed" thirteen news agency train boys $10 every six months to push its paper over the *Omaha Bee*. When the *Bee's* manager got suspicious, he was offered a similar deal.[27]

News butchers later aided the anti-monopoly, populist, anti-lynching, and progressive movements. They were alternately credited and blamed for converting passengers to Henry George's single-tax theory through the sale of his 1883 book *Social Problems* and for promoting state ownership of industry by pushing Edward Bellamy's 1888 utopian novel *Looking Backward*. They fostered critique of the gold standard as a curse to farmers and workers, and they promoted bimetallism (backing the dollar with gold *and* silver)—ideas put forward in the illustrated bestseller *Coin's Financial School*. A Mississippi congressman informed Grover Cleveland's administration in 1895 that the tract, which held that 2 percent of the population owned 50 percent of the nation's wealth, was "being sold on every railroad train by the newsboys." Street newsboys in Chicago who endorsed the movement called themselves "bimets," as in "Say Jakey, I'm a bimet."[28]

News butchers on the Chicago and Eastern Illinois Railroad pushed *Riddle of the Sphinx* by National Farmer's Alliance lecturer N. B. Ashley. Among the panaceas decocted in the book, ridiculed the *Chicago Tribune*, was "the idea that a turnip is a dollar . . . and that the railroads should be wrested from the men who engineered and now operate them." One boy discounted the book from $1.50 to 35¢, said the *Tribune*, and "would plunk himself down beside a man, and, with an elucidating air, attempt to expound the principles found in the flat rot of the author." The paper charged that train boys employed by the Union News Company sold only "Anarchist sheets" that "patted the backs" of the men who had destroyed railroad property and tied up its wheels during the national rail strike of 1894. The GOP countered in the 1896 election pitting William McKinley against William Jennings Bryan by issuing an anti-Bryan pin featuring a newsboy thumbing his nose under the letters "NIT" for "Not in Trust." Republic newspapers also spread rumors that newsboys and bootblacks in Canada were boycotting American silver for fear of Bryan's election.[29]

Train boys also raised awareness of racial violence in the South by carrying the *Memphis Free Speech and Headlight*, co-owned and edited by anti-lynching crusader Ida B. Wells. The boys rarely carried African American newspapers, but demand for Wells's weekly was such that they circulated it throughout the Mississippi delta, Tennessee, and Arkansas from 1890 to 1892, when a mob attacked the office, destroyed the press, and forced Wells to flee North.[30] Clearly, as sellers and symbols, railroad newsboys stimulated the era's debate over what constituted a just and moral economy.

Indispensable Nuisance

Wherever they stood on the social and political questions of their day, railroad news sellers employed many of the same tricks as street newsboys, such as carrying only pennies and being slow to make change. They chalked the edges of soiled books to make them look new, and they "purged" discarded newspapers from the seats to resell or return for credit. Edison admitted he sold figs in boxes with bottoms an inch thick. Many boys came up with signature sales pitches. William Brady always entered a coach for the first time on a run, spouting lines from Shakespeare at the top of his lungs. When put in charge of platform sales in Buffalo, 16-year-old Sam Golden assumed the title of "Conductor of Literature" and "would make a little speech in each car to the effect that nothing would be sold after the train left the station." He said this dodge always "tickled the old time traveling men, who came to wait for my lecture."[31]

Some train boys liked to entertain passengers with gags, prize packages, and other games of chance. Smitty, a news butcher on the Minnesota and St. Louis line in the early 1900s, was an amateur ventriloquist who carried on conversations through the vents with "free riders" on the roof. Charles Crawford, another Minnesota train boy, used to amuse (some said swindle) passengers with card tricks using a marked deck. Yet newsboys who fancied themselves card sharks were sometimes fleeced by superior talents. Some boys could be coaxed into parting with a newspaper for a mere kiss from a pretty girl.[32]

Train boys also had to watch out for marauders. Some butchers served as "ammunition boys" who cared for weapons to repel Indian attacks or robberies. More than a few outlaws made a special point of relieving newsboys of their earnings. Frank Lombard, a butcher on the Rock Island road outside Independence, Missouri, in 1881, had the presence of mind to hide his money under a cushion when he realized a robbery was in progress. But when the desperado pointed a revolver at him and ordered him to "fork over," he fetched the money as fast as he could. Train boys sometimes got revenge by identifying suspects. Rail banditry declined after 1890 due to the use of steel mail cars, better policing, and the fading romance of the crime. The intrepid Bert Walker of the Union News Company nevertheless foiled a holdup his second day on the job in the 1896 juvenile novel *The Fast Mail: Story of a Train Boy*.[33]

Dealing with drunk and disorderly passengers was a more common occurrence. Train boys had to break up card games and enforce other unpopular rules at their own risk. While traveling in Dakota Territory in 1883, young Theodore Roosevelt heard about a "lunatic" who shot the newsboy on his train. The other passengers threw the culprit off the train. In 1890 another Dakota train boy was murdered in cold blood in a quarrel over the price of an orange, only this time the shooter faced a murder charge. Conversely, newsboy Charles Bartlett, 18, stood trial in West Virginia in 1893 after fatally striking a traveling salesman who had been annoying him. Train boys were vulnerable to passenger violence in the Jim Crow South, where railroads required that they store their goods on a bench in the colored car. Rowdy whites who liked to pass the time drinking tended to congregate in these cars, and when trouble started, it usually started there.[34]

Of course, some train boys asked for trouble. A hustler named Hamlet who worked the line between Asheville, North Carolina, and Spartanburg, South Carolina, in 1892 routinely claimed to be out of change and would hand departing customers an extra paper instead. Passengers got so upset that the conductor had to lock the boy in the baggage car for his own safety. Train boys who failed to turn in forgotten items or spot counterfeit money were fired or worse. Ben Lane, who worked the Beaumont-to-Dallas line of the Texas & New

Orleans Railroad in 1911, served two years in the state penitentiary for keeping the $393.15 he found in a handbag left on board.[35]

Felonious behavior aside, train boys grated on passengers' nerves due to their shameless price gouging and obnoxious sales methods. If they had a chance to sell a 10¢ magazine for 50¢, it was done; a wreck or delay on the road sent sandwich prices through the roof. "The drummers liked to kid us old-time train butchers," said Hayes, "calling us Train Robbers, naming us Jesse, Frank, and Cole [after the notorious James gang], and we enjoyed it too."[36]

Passengers also objected to their constant banging of doors and crying of wares up and down the aisle. Indeed, some riders believed that the boys were "selected for their vocal capacity to compete with the locomotive whistle." Train boys might walk ten miles a day on the job, making separate trips with their book stock, monthly magazines, and then the daily papers. "I sell my things the way I do," explained one butcher to an irate woman, "because if a man's got a penny evening paper to read he won't be half so likely to buy a 25 or 30 cent magazine." Women travelers also complained about the boys' sexist presumptions in offering only ladies' magazines to women. An avid newspaper reader, Woman's Christian Temperance Union founder Frances Willard, lashed back: "I clutch his sleeve with a vim and buy one of every variety he has, and ask him what he is thinking about to lose patronage in that way."[37]

Foreigners found news butchers to be a distinctly American annoyance; many remarked on their habit of strewing periodicals over the seats and passengers, and then returning to collect payment for the unwanted merchandise. One Englishman described dozing off on a journey only to "awake covered with a heavy snow of handbills." Thomas Nast depicted one such "patient railroad traveler" (Figure 6.3). "The conduct of the train boy would infallibly lead to assault and battery in England," grumbled a British tourist, "but hardly elicits an objurgation in America."[38]

In truth, Americans also railed against the newsboy practice of "lapping" their wares; the *Boston Globe* suggested that they could do less damage to people's bodies and clothing by tossing anvils or sacks of flour at them. A letter writer to the *Newark Advertiser* threatened to lead a boycott against the Pennsylvania Railroad unless the "train boy nuisance" was rectified. "If the peddlers are to be masters," he said, "let the passengers either retire to other modes of conveyance or unite firmly for resistance to the repressive tyranny of the fellow who throws his wares into their laps and then stands ready to revile them and their ancestors if they fail to govern themselves according to his convenience and pleasure." A reader of *Appleton's Journal* voiced similar complaints in 1876: "Because one has purchased a seat in a public vehicle is that any reason why a vast army of small boys must be turned loose upon him?" One rider proposed replacing "ear-lacerating" train boys with girls, whose gentle voices would fall "like music on

Figure 6.3. Thomas Nast, "A Patient Railroad Traveler," *Harper's Weekly* 18, no. 898 (Mar. 14, 1874): 244. Eckel Collection, Princeton University Library.

the traveling car," though others warned that their voices would soon be sharper and more piercing than the boys'. Long Island Rail Road conductors put a homeless deaf-mute child to work as a newsboy in the 1860s, but more for his own relief than that of the passengers.[39]

Playwrights exploited the train boys' renowned impudence in two 1879 productions, *The Tourists* and *Go West!; or, The Emigrant Car*, which debuted in Washington and New York, respectively. The scenes in which the newsboy entered the car with an armful of books and pitched them at the heads of passengers were "true to life and to nature," noted a review of *The Tourists*. A similar entrance by wisecracking Dan the newsboy in *Go West!* culminated in an elaborate song-and dance-number. Lapping produced mixed results in real life;

out of fifty books thrown, three to ten would find purchasers, said one practitioner. The Hudson River Railroad banned the practice in 1875, and most gave it up by the 1890s due to heavy losses from theft.[40]

Scottish author Robert Louis Stevenson offered the most balanced view of train boys after taking the transcontinental railroad from New York to San Francisco in August 1879. He testified to what a "great personage on an American train is the newsboy. He sells books (such books!), papers, fruit, lollipops, and cigars; and on emigrant journeys, soap, towels, tin washing-dishes, tin coffee pitchers, coffee, tea, sugar, and tinned eatables, most hash or beans or bacon." Stevenson said a great deal of an emigrant's comfort depended on the character of these youths. "The newsboy with whom we started from the Transfer was a dark, bullying, contemptuous, insolent scoundrel, who treated us like dogs," he said, but "the lad who rode with us in this capacity from Ogden to Sacramento made himself the friend of all, and helped us with information, attention, assistance, and a kind countenance."[41]

Railroad officials defended the boys, saying they heard more complaints when the vendors could not be found than when they could be. Nevertheless, many companies developed detailed work rules intended to improve their deportment. In 1873 the Pennsylvania Railroad issued a circular reminding conductors of their authority to discipline newsboys who offered goods "in such a manner, or with such frequency, as to discommode or annoy the passengers." The railroad also urged vigilance against the sale of "immoral or obscene" publications, lotteries, and other games of chance. In 1883 the Chicago & Alton Railroad issued six rules stipulating that newsboys must not "importune passengers, nor force sales, nor annoy passengers in any way," and must announce their wares "in a low and respectful tone at intervals." It set a maximum price for papers and forbade boys from soliciting business for hotels or restaurants, distributing flyers, circulating "immoral, improper, vicious, obscene, or vulgar" material, selling prize packages, or engaging in any activity intended to swindle passengers. The Big Four Railway announced similar rules in 1905, but such practices continued anyway.[42]

While technically in charge of newsboys, conductors sometimes colluded with them to scalp tickets or otherwise circumvent regulations and enhance their earnings. "Any tricks a conductor needs assistance in he will look for a newsboy to help him," said an 1890 manual for railroad detectives. Yet newsboys were adept at spotting the spotters. Conductors, in turn, protected the train boy's turf by driving off local newsboys who tried to board cars during station stops or even while the train was moving.[43]

Despite their sullied reputations, railroad newsboys distinguished themselves by saving innocent girls from seduction, aiding injured passengers, or preventing collisions. A train boy on the Louisville and Nashville Railroad averted a disaster one night in 1884 by rushing to the rear platform of his stalled train and lighting his entire bundle of papers on fire as a warning to the engineer of an oncoming train.[44]

A Question of Liability

Sadly, train boys were more often victims than heroes of train accidents. Rare is the news report of a railroad accident that does not list a newsboy among the casualties. They died or were injured in collisions, explosions, derailments, bridge collapses, and missteps. Many of these reports were no more than an inch long and served as handy column fillers:

> One of the newsboys employed by J. D. Sawyer, of Galveston, on the Galveston, Harrisburg and San Antonio Railroad, accidently [sic] fell between the cars on train No. 8 to-day, about two miles west of East Bernard, and was instantly killed. Both his legs were cut off. No blame is attached to the Railroad Company. —*Galveston Daily News*, June 8, 1876
>
> James Hutton, railroad newsboy, was found twenty feet from the track, near Allaire's Corners, [NJ] this morning. Hutton was missed from his train last night, and it is supposed he was blown from the platform while passing from the baggage to the smoking car during last night's heavy gale. —*New York Tribune*, March 26, 1880
>
> Joseph Warner, the newsboy who was scalded in the wreck on the Union Pacific near Umatilla, is now in the hospital at Walla Walla. He is in a very critical condition. His lungs being injured, besides being horribly burned about the head and limbs, and his chances for recovery are very small. His family lives in Chicago. —*Salt Lake Tribune*, February 4, 1892

Accidents were the most serious occupational hazard confronting rail-riding newsboys. Rail accidents killed six thousand people a year and injured another forty thousand by 1890. Fatalities neared twelve thousand annually by 1907, generating lawsuits on behalf of employees, passengers, and newsboys. In 1911 alone fifty-seven newsboys, express or mail clerks, and Pullman employees were killed in accidents for which railways were not held responsible. The number injured in this category totaled 1,391. Some judges and juries upheld newsboys' right to collect damages, but most sided with railway lawyers, who argued that passengers traveled at their own risk. Newsboys constituted a distinct set of claimants, since they were neither railroad employees nor customers. Those who hitched rides or hawked without permission were classified as trespassers. News butchers rode on passes exempting the railroad from any liability for losses or injuries. The newsboy's pass issued to J. Loupton in 1881 stipulated "that the Delaware, Lackawanna & Western Railroad Company shall not be liable under any circumstances, whether of negligence by their agents or otherwise, for any injury to the person, or for any loss or injury to the property of the passenger using this Pass" (Figure 6.4). News agencies agreed to similar indemnity clauses in exchange for exclusive rights to sell on railroads. These agreements left their young employees unprotected when collisions or derailments occurred. Newsboys and their survivors nevertheless tried to collect damages under the doctrine of *respondeat superior*, which held companies responsible for the negligent actions of their employees.[45]

Legal scholars disagree on the historical pattern of railroad liability cases in the nineteenth century. Some argue that judges limited liability for personal injury to preserve the profitability of these heavily capitalized enterprises. Others maintain that tort law was used to reduce injuries and safeguard community standards. Still others hold that fault was the only legitimate basis for imposing liability.[46] The experience of railroad newsboys in court was a mixed bag, providing ample evidence to support any one of these generalizations. Most of

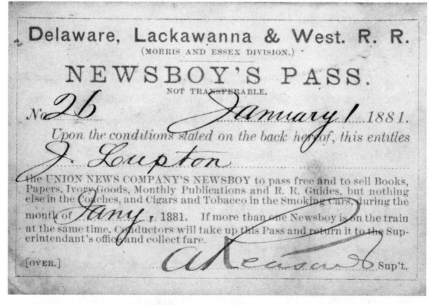

Figure 6.4. Newsboy's pass issued January 1, 1881 to J. Lupton on the Morris & Essex Division of the Delaware, Lackawanna & Western Railroad. The back of the card states that under no circumstances shall the bearer hold the railroad liable for any loss or injury. Eckel Collection, Princeton University Library.

their cases were litigated at the state level, since national laws governing railroad safety and liability issues began only with the Safety Appliance Act of 1893 and developed slowly. A Lexis-Nexis survey of some forty cases decided in seventeen states between 1882 and 1937 suggests that courts were as likely to rule for newsboys as against them. Judges and juries generally upheld newsboys' right to work in a safe environment without abuse and to collect damages when accidents occurred. Some lawyers appealed to jurors' resentment of these big corporations and reminded them of their deep pockets. But courts in New York (as well as in Canada and England) often sided with railroad lawyers, who argued that companies should not be liable under any circumstances, even in cases of gross or willful negligence by their employees.

By the turn of the century the *New York Times* was calling news butchers a "curious survival in the transportation system" and asking why some railroads tolerated them. The newsboys' impertinence, said the *Times*, provided "an object lesson in what Herbert Spencer justly denounced as the criminal good nature of the Americans." Several railroads—the Erie, Lehigh, Burlington, New York Central, and Chicago and Alton—had recently banned them as nuisances, forcing travelers to rely on station newsstands. The same agencies that owned these stands employed the train boys, and so claimed disinterest. "It rests entirely with the railroads whether or not the news butcher should be abolished," said a Union News Company official in 1900. "We understand that the public has come to look on the butcher as a nuisance, and I would not be at all surprised if he disappeared within two or three years." The company also faced legal challenges from independent newsboys who objected to its monopoly on sales in and around stations.[47] News butchers would continue to ply their trade into the early 1920s, particularly in the West, though their numbers waned as dining cars, library cars, and station kiosks multiplied. Adult competition—not irate passengers, personal injury lawyers, or child labor crusaders—finally ended the career of America's train boys, the attentive and aggravating alike.

Tramps in the Making

Economic slumps, political conventions, state fairs, title fights, and circulation wars spanned the railway era and created yet another breed of news sellers: tramp or hobo newsboys. "Troupin'" alone or in gangs, often perched on the underside of freight cars (aka the "possum's belly"), or atop the caboose, with heads wrapped in a towel to protect against flying cinders, these boys hit the road whenever prospects looked better elsewhere. On arriving in a new place they tried to earn a stake by begging or selling some "cheap trifle"—sometimes matches, laces, berries, or poems, but most of all newspapers, the possession of which did not preclude using their best hard-luck stories.[48]

One of the first sightings of this type occurred in the new railroad hub of Omaha, Nebraska, in 1869 when a local paper reported the arrival of one who was "quite a curiosity as a specimen of young America. He is but ten years old and has made his way through eleven states already. He travels, according to his own words, on his cheek. He rides on railroads for nothing, and eats at restaurants ordering his meals first and looking for his money afterwards. He now rejoices over the completion of the Pacific Railroad, and proposes to strike for the Pacific."[49]

The proliferation of Atlas-inspired nicknames attests to the mobility of newsboys. Among those who worked in New York in the 1870s were "Rockaway," "Kalamazoo," and "Country." Two newcomers to Philadelphia in 1880 were simply dubbed "Fresh" and "Recently." The fraternity of St. Louis newsboys and bootblacks in 1881 included "Memphis Kid," "Texas Kid," "Big Jersey," "Jersey Slim," "Cincinnati Fat," "Saratoga Bill," "Canada Jimmie," "Boston Jimmie," and "Jimmie Runaway." Between the ages of 8 and 16, John "Clinkers" Wallace of St. Louis bummed across the country on freight cars, selling papers in Chicago, Toronto, Detroit, and Memphis. His nickname may refer to the practice of bedding down in jails, or "clinks." Like hobo road names, newsboy monikers ensured anonymity while permitting a kind of fellowship within the trade. "Dey ain't wot yer mouf call nice names; but den, yer know, dey all means somethin' wot a feller is or does," explained a New Orleans boy named "Seven Colors" on account of his hair.[50]

Disabled newsboys, some with nicknames like "Leggy," "Army," or "Handy," were also great travelers and would steal rides all over the country; railroad employees tended to overlook their trespass. Walter B. Evans, a mute teen-ager from Wilkes-Barre, Pennsylvania, worked his way from the Atlantic to the Pacific, selling papers and shining shoes. Starting out from New York in 1901, he visited scores of cities and towns, staying for weeks or months. Unable to shout, he compensated by wearing a hat emblazoned with the words "The Dumb News Boy" (Figure 6.5). He carried a notepad to communicate with people, and told different stories about his past. According to press reports, he was run out of Tampa, Florida, for begging and sleeping on private property. He was accused of enticing a boy to run away from home in Portland, Oregon, and of stealing a bike in Ontario, but mostly he stayed out of trouble and paid his own way.[51]

Tramp newsboys were particularly attracted to fairs, conventions, and other seasonal venues where sales looked promising. In June 1880, nearly all inmates at the newsboys' lodging house in St. Louis took off for the Republican National

Figure 6.5. Walter B. Evans, 19, wearing a cap identifying him as "The Dumb News Boy," works a corner in Salt Lake City in 1904. Mute and probably deaf, he hit the road at age 15, selling papers throughout the country. Harry Shipler Collection, 5 × 7 #021. Used by permission, Utah State Historical Society.

Convention in Chicago to exploit the many news-hungry reporters, lobbyists, and delegates who thronged the city during the weeklong conclave. Their successors kept up the tradition. The party's 1888 convention, also in Chicago, attracted what one paper called "an army of juvenile laborers looking for honest nickels. They are the traveling bootblacks and newsboys. There are fully 2,000 of the little stranger vagrants in the city up to this time, and every empty box-car brings in an additional bunch of them."[52]

Typical of this type was a New York youth who, for half a dollar and a chance to warm himself at a fire, told his story to a reporter in Milwaukee on New Year's Day 1883. The "little talkative vagabond" didn't give his name and said he didn't know his age or anything about his parents, but revealed much about the hobo newsboy lingo and lifestyle. He said he grew up in a place where he "used to get a licking most every day" until he ran away and fell in with an older fellow named Joe Grubbs who taught him the ropes. "Oh, he's the boss chap he is. He can beat any of us selling papers or telling a whopper." Huddled against the January cold, the boy fondly recalled the summer fair season:

A fair's the place to make money. That's what I went to Minneapolis
for. The show lasted two months and I scooped in dead oodles of swag.
Oh, no, I didn't go there alone. There was a big crowd of us, and a lot of
Chicago roosters. The way we do is to catch on to the trains on the back
of the sleeper. Sometimes the porter is a bully sort of a chap and don't
care, but most of 'em are mean. . . . Well, when he makes us git off we
have to get in under the cars and catch on to the trucks. Risky kind of
business, too. First time I tried it I got scared nearly to death. The train
went so fast that I got dizzy seeing the ground fly away back so fast right
under me, but I held on, bet your bottom dollar. Didn't try it again for
a long time, neither, but I am used to it now and kinder like it to see the
rocks and the stones and the ties fly back like a streak o' lightning and
cross over a river and see the water a rushing one way and me a going
another way. It ain't so much fun though, when the conductor gets on
to the racket. One time there was forty of us kids under a train and the
porter got on to it. Well you ought to have seen us get out in a jiffy. It
looked like a lot of rats let loose out of a trap. The porter caught one
of the bootblacks and made him black all the boots in the sleeper for
nothing. Darn mean cuss, he was.[53]

The fair-goers usually camped out together and passed the time gambling.
"I'm honest, but some of the boys don't mind cheating," he said, holding his
bluish hands over the flames. "At night we get together and they'll play cards for
all they're worth. One feller had to 'truck' it back 'cause he lost all his boodle that
way. I had hard luck up there the second night. One of the bootblacks stole all
I had while I was snoozing. I knew who it was, but that didn't do any good 'cause
he was bigger than me. Made lots of wealth, though, before I got through." The
boy lauded "Little Crickett," the Kentucky racehorse that came through for him,
but denounced the crooks in his circle. "Some of the kids use the paper bizness
for a blind," he admitted, "and rake in the cash by stealing. There's a lot of those
fellers, and they give us a bad reputation."[54]

Another cadet in this unwashed army was 12-year-old John Mason, who traveled from his home in Beardstown, Illinois, to New York City in 1884 "to see
something of the world." Riding mainly on freight cars, he made his way through
Cincinnati, Pittsburgh, and Philadelphia before arriving at his destination. He
came to the attention of the New York Society for the Prevention of Cruelty to
Children on his second day in the city after tussling with a local newsboy over a
dime. A judge dismissed the case but held Mason on charges of vagrancy, as preferred by the SPCC, and arranged for his return to Illinois.[55]

Newsboys did not restrict themselves to domestic travel but also went
abroad, taking the working-class equivalent of the Grand Tour. Jimmie "de

Globe Trotter" Sullivan, a Bowery newsboy, claimed to have circled the globe twice and crossed the Atlantic seventeen times, mostly as a stowaway, by age 14. He regaled reporters with tales of travels to Sydney, Ceylon, Bombay, Cape Town, Alexandria, Malta, London, and Greenland. These were the days before passports or visas were required. Likewise, muckraker Ernest Poole told of a 16-year-old newsboy named Mike who, after traveling across America, got the urge "to do Europe." He sailed to England as a cabin boy and from habit stole a ride on the underside of a train from Southampton to London. He found the accommodations "stingier" than those on American trains because of the narrower-gauge tracks. Once in London, he and an English acquaintance invested in a lantern and earned money guiding people home through the fog. Then they saw the town in high style. Jimmie and Mike may have been inveterate liars, but theirs were the kind of "highly colored yarns" that Poole said helped beguile "the raw recruits of the newsboys."[56]

Prushuns and Jockers

Given the dangers of hopping freights, no boy ever said goodbye, as they considered the word a "Jonah." Nevertheless, the most effective way for reformers to overcome the public's apathy was to stress the "moral dangers" of the road, specifically children's sexual vulnerability. In his magazine articles, sociologist Josiah Flynt told of tramps who lured newsboys from home with enthralling "ghost stories" about life on the road. But in an essay written for Havelock Ellis's multivolume *Studies in the Psychology of Sex*, Flynt shed all Victorian reticence and described with clinical precision the seduction ritual and sexual practices of adolescent and adult tramps, or "prushuns" and "jockers," as they were known in hobo lingo.* "The tramps gain possession of these boys in various ways," said Flynt. "A common method is to stop for awhile in some town, and gain acquaintance with the slum children. They tell these children all sort of stories about life 'on the road,' how they can ride on the railways for nothing, shoot Indians, and be 'perfeshunnels' (professionals), and they choose some boy who specially pleases them. By smiles and flattering caresses they let him know that the stories are meant for him alone, and before long, if the boy is a suitable subject, he smiles back just as slyly."[57]

Flynt estimated that there were seven thousand boy tramps in the United States in 1899, and about five hundred spent each winter in New York City.

---

* The etymology of *prushun* is unclear; some say it is a corruption of *impressionable* or *protégé*, though another possibility is that it owes its origin to the famed horsemen of the 1870–71 Franco-Prussian War.

Their average age was 14, but some were as young as 9 or as old as 17. They were distinguishable by their "shambling gait, rounded shoulders, harsh voices and exaggerated 'tough manner.'" Each was compelled by "hobo law" to beg for his jocker and gratify the jocker's sexual desires. Some did so under compulsion, he said, but most learned to enjoy it. He said the usual method of intercourse was "'leg-work' (intercrural), but sometimes *immissio penis in anum*, the boy, in either case, lying on his stomach."[58]*

Flynt went on to describe brutal gang rapes and tender partings between men and their boy lovers. Like other tramp memoirists, he acknowledged that many youths enjoyed platonic, even fatherly relationships with older tramps. St. Louis newsboy Robert Saunders, who made three long rail trips in the early 1910s, credited experienced hobos with teaching him vital lessons about hopping freights, begging meals, and finding jobs.[59] Sometimes the young preyed on the old; Chicago newsboys Nels Anderson, Philip Marcus, and Clifford Shaw admitted to having "jackrolled" (befriended and robbed) drunks and homosexuals in the "main stem" or transient district. "It was bloody work," said Shaw, "but necessity demanded it—we had to live."[60]

Tramp newsboys could be equally ruthless on behalf of the newspapers that hired them. Many of them were "toughs" in their late teens or twenties who could be called in to break strikes or win circulation wars. As outsiders, they ignored turf rights and picked fights with local boys. Tramp newsboys usually worked only long enough to earn a few dollars for food or to replenish their traveling stake. Publishers let them sleep on the premises or put them up in flophouses, and paid them cash bonuses and commissions.[61]

Many people considered tramp newsboys the most corrupted and corrupting of all news peddlers, as they encouraged younger boys to steal by acting as fences for stolen goods, enticed them into their poker and dice games, cheated them, stole their money, knocked them around, introduced them to prostitutes, and used the "younger newsboys for immoral purposes." The Los Angeles police concluded in 1895 that "vicious newsboys from abroad" were one of the "gravest problems" that confront the city. They came from all parts of the country—San Francisco, Portland, Denver, Chicago, New York—and even from London. "They are adept liars and thieves and frequently quarrel and fight to the verge of bloodshed," said the *Los Angeles Times*. "Several stabbing affrays are instances. They also learn to gamble and cheat, drink, smoke and swear viciously and they have a painfully amusing system of blackmail with which the detectives are all familiar. Their regard for purity of course is nil." The proposed solution was an

---

* Not solely the practice of vagrants, intercrural sex was also known as the "Princeton First Year" because of its role in college initiation rites.

ordinance requiring newsboys and bootblack to take out licenses, thus excluding the rovers.[62]

Newspaper executives had a higher opinion of this class of newsboy. Sidney Long, who ran the Wichita *Eagle* and headed the International Circulation Managers Association, preferred to call them "professional hustlers" or "wandering newsboys." The country was "full of them," he said in his 1928 memoir. "They used to ride the freight trains and the bumpers on the passenger trains. Now they either ride on the cushions or they have their own little car or they start out and walk and catch rides wherever they can. Sometimes they go clear across the continent." Whenever one of these hustlers would show up in a new town he would seek out the man in charge of street circulation and tell him about his experience, which was obvious the moment he opened his mouth. "His very language is his card," said Long. They were especially valuable in starting up a paper: "All you have to do is to send out a few wires to the street circulators within three or four hundred miles of your town and in these fellows will flock. When you are through with them, they are gone. You don't know from where they come and you don't know where they go but they put the deal over for you mighty good and pretty straight."[63]

Two Minneapolitans who fit this description were James A. Garfield Dunn, 14, and Francis "Foghorn" O'Meara, who logged more than four thousand train miles, alone and together, from May to June 1895, selling papers and earning reputations in Wisconsin, Illinois, Missouri, and Iowa. "Glib of tongue and unafraid of dirt," Dunn made a beeline to the sports editor on arriving in Duluth, and presented him letters of recommendation from others in the "biz." On a subsequent trip to Buffalo, Dunn kept a diary telling how he survived on the road. Some editors turned him away, but then he'd steal apples from orchards, cut wood, or do other jobs for food. And "there is never any trouble in battering a house for a handout," he wrote. Foghorn's stentorian voice put him in high demand in Kansas City. He was arrested and fined for setting fire to a float full of newsboys, but mended his ways and became "chief newsboy" of the city.[64]

While most tramp newsboys rode the rails in search of work or adventure, Jack Ross was on a mission to find his parents. He traveled the country for twelve years, from 1898 to 1910, looking for the couple that had abandoned him in the care of an aunt when he was a child. "As soon as he was old enough," reported the *Rochester Herald*, "Ross took a bundle of newspapers and started to pay his own way. He drifted around the country, traveling on the bumpers of freight trains and the head ends of baggage trains. He became well known in many newspaper offices throughout the country where he found employment." Editors ran stories about his Telemachus-like quest and helped him to locate his father, a fire captain in Elizabeth, New Jersey, and his mother and sister. A photograph of Ross circa 1910 shows a strapping, big-eared youth framed against the looming office

Figure 6.6. Jack Ross, "The Wandering Newsboy," ca. 1910, in Rochester, NY. Acc. No. sct01998. From the Albert R. Stone Negative Collection, Rochester Museum & Science Center, Rochester, NY.

buildings of Rochester, New York (Figure 6.6). The pin on his lapel marks him as a bona fide vendor registered with the city.[65]

Dunn's diary, Long's memoir, and Ross's saga reveal two unexpected truths about tramp newsboys. First, they were not lone drifters who blew in and out of town like tumbleweeds but members of a reliable labor force that could be mobilized through established networks. Second, some young men felt little compunction about betraying their brothers in trade. Hobos in the 1880s and 1890s were widely seen as radical agitators who traveled from strike to strike to stir up trouble. Those who belonged to the anarcho-syndicalist Industrial Workers of the World in the early 1900s reinforced their reputation as rabble-rousers. Many hobos were indeed class-conscious critics of industrial capitalism, yet the accounts of tramp newsies remind us that some sided with management over labor; these drifters may have flouted bourgeois customs of settled domesticity, but when bosses called they came running.

Whatever the economic or psychological forces behind it, newsboys' wanderlust sometimes proved fatal. According to newspaper clippings found on his body, Harry Blanche of New York "beat his way" across the country selling papers in quest of the title "King of the Newsboys." His journey began with a trip to Reno, Nevada, in 1910 for the "fight of the century" between Jack Johnson and Jim Jeffries. Blanche, age 19, set out from Grand Central Station on June 1 disguised in workman's overalls and reached Reno in time for the Fourth of July fight. He peddled papers and lemonade at ringside, and cut a souvenir square from the canvas ring before pushing on. He preferred to steal rides on passenger trains because they moved faster than freights and were rarely checked for stowaways. It was risky business, but he became expert at riding in coal boxes and engine tenders, on brake beams and underslung dining car refrigerators. He traveled in this fashion to the West Coast, back to Denver, south through Texas and Louisiana, northward to Winnipeg, and then down to Jacksonville, Florida, and up to St. Louis. Along the way he sold papers, gave lectures, and collected badges from newsboys' clubs and unions. On returning to New York in mid-October, Blanche proclaimed himself "King of the Newsboys" by virtue of having logged twenty thousand miles and visited 250 cities. He made the Newsboys' Home his headquarters and enjoyed his celebrity among the boys. Blanche got the travel bug again the next summer, but this time his luck ran out. He slipped from a perch on the Barnum and Bailey circus train and was found dead on the Delaware and Hudson tracks near Saratoga. In addition to the clippings, the coroner found in Blanche's bundle of possessions forty-six newsboy badges wrapped in a square of canvas.[66]

Conspicuously absent from the history of American labor, journalism, and railroads, young men and boys played prime roles in expanding the nation's information economy. They worked for wages and profits, risked life and limb, and hurled words across great distances. News agency boys facilitated greater public dialogue by shipping papers to previously unreachable areas. Train boys contributed to a veritable revolution in reading by providing passengers with a range of news and opinion—including their own. And tramp newsboys rode the rails driven by a mix of want and wanderlust. While newsboys symbolized enterprise and tramps epitomized laziness in popular culture, they both filled out the ranks of a wandering proletariat that raised their voices and banners high throughout the industrial era.

Those who lit out for the territories or otherwise came of age in the West would leave their mark on that region as well.

7

Rumblings in the West

At first glance, the streetwise, strike-prone newsboys and worldly train boys who worked the eastern half of the United States would seem to have had little in common with their country cousins out west. Largely of immigrant stock, big-city distributors usually flogged ad-rich dailies with large circulations. Frontier newsboys, by contrast, supposed native sons of alkali and sagebrush, served small, often struggling concerns grateful for a few hundred paying customers. The boys wandered along dusty streets, clambered over plank sidewalks, and covered their routes on mule or horseback, all apparently immune to the militant trade unionism that infected their counterparts in the East.

In truth, however, western states and territories were just as profoundly affected by the surge of immigration, industrialization, and urbanization that transformed the eastern and midwestern states in the nineteenth century. The West was in fact the most ethnically diverse region in the nation; by 1880 not a single Pacific Coast, Rocky Mountain, or southwestern town had a working class in which native-stock whites made up more than a quarter of male wage earners. Workers of all races and nations toiled in fields, factories, mines, and streets, constituting a veritable industrial frontier from the Yukon to the Rio Grande. It was also an urban frontier, as western cities swelled at a faster clip and claimed a greater proportion (30 percent) of the population than did eastern cities.[1]

Nor was the region barren of newspapers. By 1900 more than seven hundred dailies and weeklies were published west of the Mississippi, raising the number of American cities with dailies from 389 in 1880 to 915. Westerners were particularly amendable to socialist, labor, and woman's suffrage papers, as well as German, Spanish, Cherokee, Chinese, and other non-English or bilingual publications. These papers circulated through the mail but also via hawkers and carriers of every age and ethnicity. "They are as numerous and as urgent here as farther East," reported a visitor to Denver in 1879. The local news alley, said the *Rocky Mountain News*, was the unrestricted province of "Americans, Europeans, Chinamen, Mulattos, and one Mexican."[2]

These young men and boys were part of a burgeoning labor movement that formed unions, waged strikes, and protested abuses in dozens of western cities and towns in the last quarter of the nineteenth century. Their unions received charters from local labor councils, the Knights of Labor, and the American Federation of Labor. Others became vehicles for rival publishers to wage circulation wars or for clubwomen to mount reform efforts. Most left few traces and go unmentioned in histories of the West, the press, and the labor movement. But a dusty trail of sources—news articles, court reports, photographs, and memoirs—reveals that western newsboys shared many of the same traits, conditions, and discontents as those in the East, and, if anything, were the more militant of the two.

Hazards of Occupation

While fewer in number compared to the East, the children who distributed newspapers in the mining, lumber, trail, and cow towns of the West were no less important to their families, publishers, or communities. Indeed, children's work was more valued in the labor-hungry states and territories of the West than in the East. Young people constituted a larger proportion of the population, according to the 1880 US Census, and they were needed to raise crops, tend livestock, gather fuel, and market produce. Western youths took on adult responsibilities early, working as teamsters, stonemasons, teachers, and in other occupations that would have been closed to them in the East. They also engaged in traditional boy work such as distributing newspapers, yet here, too, they often competed against grown men who held the most lucrative routes and corners, especially in isolated boomtowns where papers sold for exorbitant sums.[3]

Newspapers were as essential as railroads to western expansion. Both stimulated the flow of people, products, and capital that made settlement and the extraction of natural resources possible. The primary purpose of frontier papers was not so much to serve a reading public as to create one—to attract settlers and investors who could transform isolated forts and farmsteads into thriving communities. A publisher in Fargo, North Dakota, in the 1880s used to "boom" the town by sending newsboys to meet the trains and distribute papers free to passengers. No town could hope to grow without a newspaper or two. Elko, Nevada, with a population of 752 in 1880, was the smallest town in America with a daily paper. Tombstone, Arizona, with 973 residents, had two dailies. And Eureka, California, population 2,639, had three. Developers in Boise, Los Angeles, and other backwaters tried to lure printers with offers of rent-free office space and stipends of $500 to $1,500.[4]

Frontier publishers set up shop in a motley array of shelters: tents, barns, adobes, sod huts, and log cabins (Figure 7.1). Some even worked out of railroad cars, giving new meaning to the term *rolling press*. Most of these papers were printed on old Washington hand presses, rugged Ramage screw presses, or portable army presses originally used to issue field orders. Many publishers combined journalism with job printing and devoted a corner of their premises to serve as general store, assay office, or barbershop. Some papers occupied the back room of a saloon or pool hall. Wherever situated, newspaper offices became gathering spots for children and adults interested in the latest news or rumor of the next great bonanza.[5]

Nothing could hasten a territory's development more swiftly than the discovery of some precious or heavy metal. In 1853, five years after the gold strike in Sutter's Mill, San Francisco was home to a dozen daily papers. By 1870 it was the tenth-largest city in the United States with 170,000 residents and still about a dozen dailies but with much greater circulation. One of them, the *San Francisco Daily Evening Bulletin*, fielded a "newsboy brigade" of forty-five carriers and forty hawkers who were reputedly younger and more respectable than Eastern newsboys. The *Bulletin* said its boys ranged in age from 9 to 16, compared to 16 to 20 in the East. Four out of ten attended school, and none were vagrants. In 1877 *Harper's Weekly* artist Paul Frenzeny sketched local carriers engaged in the

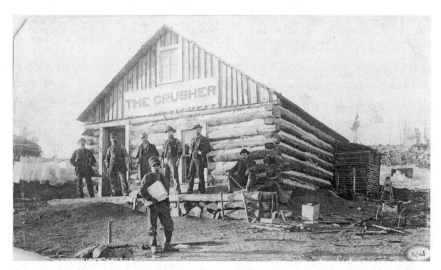

Figure 7.1. Newsboy Oakley Spell and the staff of the weekly *Crusher* mark the opening of their log cabin office in Fremont, Colorado, ca. 1893, prior to the town's incorporation as Cripple Creek. The paper previously shared space with a laundry and a lunch counter. William Henry Jackson, *Cripple Creek Crusher*, Denver Public Library, Western History Collection, WHJ-788.

twice-daily routine of packing damp sheets into their saddlebags and galloping off on their mustangs to all parts of the city (Figure 7.2).[6]

Newspaper publishers and peddlers also joined the thousands who flocked to the Black Hills of South Dakota after the gold strike of 1875. Some mining camps had as many as four papers going at once, and there were no fewer than a dozen around Deadwood.[7] Why so many? Because mining gold on an Indian reservation closed by treaty to whites required political allies. Stakes included not just land and mineral rights but statehood and the location of rail lines or a capital. A political faction without a newspaper was no faction at all. Newspapers were weapons in the struggles between natives and newcomers, railroaders and farmers, mine owners and mine workers. Newsboy did not just witness these struggles but took sides.

Western conquest was as much a product of federal policy as pioneer spirit. Land, survey, timber, and townsite legislation provided tangible incentives to those who dreamed of new lives in the West. These laws stimulated the growth of newspapers as well. The 1862 Homestead Act, for example, stipulated that those willing to pay $1.25 an acre could obtain title to their land after six months'

Figure 7.2. "The moment a carrier gets his supply, he thrusts the damp sheets into the pouches, springs upon his mustang, and dashes off at break-neck speed.... When several start at once, ... the race becomes quite exciting." Paul Frenzeny, "San Francisco Newsboys Distributing the Evening Papers," *Harper's Weekly* 21, no. 1059 (Apr. 14, 1877): 292, 294. Author's collection.

residence as opposed to getting it free after five years. Homesteaders had to place "proving up" notices in local newspapers, some of which carried up to two hundred notices per issue at $5 to $6 apiece. Newsboys in these towns literally did a land-office business.[8]

One of the largest scrambles of settlers was the Oklahoma land rush of April 22, 1889, in which 50,000 people lined up to stake claims to two million acres appropriated from the Cherokee. Walter Brady, 15, of St. Louis, claimed to be the first newsboy to set foot on the "promised land" and was thereafter nicknamed "Oklahoma." The rush made news everywhere: in Concordia, Kansas, population 2,000, one newsboy peddled the *Kansas City Times*, shouting, "All about the Opening of Oklahoma! Twenty miles of boomers stuck in the mud."[9]

Some two hundred Kansas City boys made their living selling papers and blacking boots in the mid-1880s. They ranged in age from 7 to 15. In April 1884 an unknown number of whites and blacks clubbed together to bar outside competition. They elected officers, levied a 5¢ tax on members, and resolved to "lick" anyone who worked the streets without affiliation. "They were fast organizing a reign of terror in the city," said the *Kansas City Star*. Bruised and beaten, outsiders sought protection from police, who in turn confiscated the badges of the "midget mercuries." The crackdown destroyed the union and set off a free-for-all in the news and boot trades.[10]

Many Kansas City newsboys lived on the streets or squatted in the basement of the Board of Trade Building, "huddling about the steam heater to keep from freezing to death." But others had homes or rented rooms for 75¢ a week. The most successful of them built savings accounts and acquired Indian ponies to distribute their papers. "They ride as if they were built on horseback," marveled a visiting New Yorker, "and very frequently do the hurdle act over the citizen who is endeavoring to pull himself, by the hair, out of the mud." These boys sold the *Star, News*, and *Traveler* for a nickel, and often threw in an "overripe" *Times* or *Journal* to seal the deal. Their competitors on foot could not cover as much ground but made up for it by combining news peddling with boot blacking. Mud for them was a source of income.[11]

The boys revived their union in November 1898 with 186 members dedicated to "giving Kansas City the best newsboys in the country." They passed bylaws against gambling, overcharging, and other "ungentlemanly conduct" but granted no courtesies to nonmembers. When "little" Nathan Miller, an African American, was arraigned in police court for interfering with a nonunion boy at the Junction, he explained to the judge, "The boss of de union tole us to do dis." "Well you'll make a black Debbs [*sic*] some day if you keep on," replied the judge, "but you must stop. Tell your boss that it will cost his boys $3 apiece every time that they get funny with other boys who do not wear a union badge." Soon after, the cigar makers union welcomed the newsboys into the labor movement by presenting them with their own union banner and five hundred hats bearing the cigar makers union label and motto: "Smoke Home Cigars."[12]

Western publishers and carriers encountered the same business and health risks as their eastern equivalents, including nonpaying subscribers, paper shortages, and reckless drivers. But mountain lions, bears, prairie fires, flash floods, and gunfighters also plagued them.[13] Payment for ads and subscriptions took forms unfathomable in the East. Vital commodities such as chickens, eggs, wheat, potatoes, and firewood were solicited: "Good wood—four foot or stove length—received as welcome as cash," wrote the *Dakota Republican*. A Nebraska publisher once accepted a bronco from a subscriber and turned it over to his typesetter in lieu of back wages. Others took lard, tallow, beeswax, gold dust, and mink skins in exchange for subscriptions. Even rags were appreciated when paper was scarce. The first copies of the *Frontier Index*, published in Julesberg in the Colorado Territory in 1867, were printed on grocers' wrapping paper and had to be picked up by subscribers at the post office because "the boys are too negligent to be trusted as carriers." Indeed, carriers, printers, and editors would run off at the first rumor of gold.[14]

Violence was another occupational hazard on the frontier. Readers who felt themselves, their party, or their associates libeled were more likely to tar and feather an editor than to sue him. Those injured by a damaging news story or jackass editorial sometimes resorted to press-napping: the aggrieved would ransack the newspaper office and haul off the mechanical offender, which might turn up in a creek or in the office of a more agreeable printer. Newsboys sometimes exacerbated these rivalries. In Galveston, Texas, hawkers of the *Daily News* regularly attacked carriers of the *German Post* in the winter of 1877–78. The two papers did not compete directly for readers, since one was an English-language daily and the other a German weekly, but *News* carriers resented the *Post*'s presence. As one of its more pugnacious hawkers, 18-year-old Billy Rowan, explained after his arrest, "All the d———d Dutch papers live off the News anyhow, and it was only right such papers should be tore up."[15]

Frontier journalism was a young man's game, which, according to historian Robert Karolevitz, "took physical stamina, a minimum of family responsibilities, and, in many instances, a little foolhardiness." Collecting for ads and subscriptions was the most dangerous part of the job. An editor in Oregon told readers it was "worse than painful dentistry, and when I tried to collect bills, I invited getting shot, or at least half-shot. So I got scared . . . joined the army and went scouting through three Indian wars, thus getting into the safety zone." Delegating such jobs to kids made sense, which is what Tombstone, Arizona, mayor and postmaster John P. Clum, founder of the *Tombstone Epitaph*, did in the 1880s during the political feud that climaxed with the infamous gunfight at the OK Corral. It was difficult to get out an edition, he said, "without the death of a compositor or an

adventurous newsboy." Publishers in New Mexico complained that eight, sometimes nine, out of ten subscribers were delinquent. Some papers published their
names, which could result in a duel as easily as a payment. Others auctioned off
their debts to gunslingers, who had their own ways of dealing with deadbeats.[16]

Newsboys sometimes contributed to the violence meted out by the state.
In 1890 one overzealous hawker in Helena, Montana, found a way to sell papers to an impaneled jury in a capital murder trial. For two days in a row, jurors
procured copies of the *Helena Journal*, which contained stories prejudicial to the
defendant. "Evidence Given that is likely to Hang Jackson," read one headline.
"The halter draws," opined another. One witness was quoted as saying she would
commit suicide if the accused was not convicted. The newsboy's and the jurors'
contempt for the law formed the basis of an appeal, but the state Supreme Court
denied the motion, leaving the defendant to swing on the gallows.[17]

Prodigies and Provocateurs

Independence and advancement were the central promises of the West, as
conveyed in Horace Greeley's dictum: "Go West, young man, and grow up
with the country." Charles Loring Brace saw western settlement as a solution to the social problems of the East, and his orphan train boys became
leading proponents of the idea. One of them addressed his old colleagues
from atop a chair at the Newsboys' Lodging House in New York on the eve
of his departure:

> Boys, gintlmen, chummies: P'raps you'd like to hear summit about the
> West, the great West . . . where so many of our old friends are settled
> down and growin' up to be great men, maybe the greatest men in the
> great Republic. Boys, that's the place for growin' Congressmen, and
> Governors, and Presidents. Do you want to be newsboys always, and
> shoe-blacks, and timber-merchants in a small way by sellin' matches? If
> ye do, you'll stay in New York, but if you don't, you'll go West and begin
> to be farmers, for the beginning of a farmer, my boys, is the making of a
> Congressman and a President.[18]

The experience of orphan train riders and territorial governors Andrew Burke
and John Brady gave credence to the promise, however remote their posts. But
another orphan train boy, "Kansas Charley" Miller, confirmed westerners' worst
fears that the Children's Aid Society was using the region as a dumping ground
for incorrigibles. Miller reaped a harvest of shame in 1890 when he murdered
two men in a boxcar in Wyoming. He was hanged for the crime two years later.

Between these extremes lay the vast majority of orphan train riders who strove to improve their lot, achieving neither greatness nor infamy.[19]

In addition to the emigrants, the West produced homegrown successes such as Frank Burr and Charles Curtis. Burr was stolen by the Chippewa Indians in 1847 at the age of 3 and remained with them until he was 9, when they left him behind on a trip to the small trading post of Detroit. He survived as a newsboy until 1861 when, at age 17, he joined the army and rose to the rank of colonel. He gained prominence later as a journalist and biographer.[20] Born in the territory of Kansas in 1860, Curtis was a mixed-race child descended from Kaw and Osage chiefs. He was raised by his maternal grandmother on a Kaw reservation and then moved in with his white grandparents for high school in Topeka, where he earned his keep as a newsboy, bootblack, and jockey. He read law while working as a hack driver and was admitted to the bar in 1881. He served in both the House and Senate and was Herbert Hoover's vice president.[21]

Eleven-year-old Theodore De Harport served a prairie route on the outskirts of Denver in 1870. "More than once, herds of antelope sped out of my way as I rode out," he recalled. De Harport carried seventy-five papers in bags slung over the saddle horn. "I went out on plenty of blustery days when both my pony and I would far rather have stayed at home," he said. "But that was good training for me, because, a few years later, I was riding for my father on the cattle drives from Texas to Kansas."[22]

San Francisco–born Robert Frost peddled papers downtown as a 10-year-old in the 1880s. He loved the grown-up feeling of independence it gave him, but the long hours, small profits, and rival gangs took their toll. Farther west, in Honolulu, Hiram Bingham III, a descendent of missionaries, serviced the city's longest route—more than twenty miles—on horseback in the 1880s. "Daily I arose at 4:30 a.m. and rode two miles to get the papers. . . . By the time the last paper was left at its destination the sun was well up and it was a tired youngster who reined his horse in at the home gate. For this service I received fifty cents per day." Bingham was forced to surrender his route after his horse took a fall. But the money he saved helped pay for his studies at Phillips Academy in Andover, Massachusetts. He went on to Yale, where he became a professor of archeology. He discovered the Inca citadel of Machu Picchu in 1911, trained aviators during World War I, and served as Connecticut's governor and US senator. Meantime, newsboys, chiefly Portuguese but also Chinese, Hawaiians, and whites, had become a recognized institution in his hometown of Honolulu, numbering around sixty.[23]

The boomtowns of Colorado also offered opportunity. Harry Ruffner, at age 15, became the first newsboy of Leadville in 1878 by peddling the *San Juan Prospector*, issued in Del Norte. Leadville's population jumped from 300 to 10,000 that year due to the silver rush, and reached 50,000 the next year, making it the second-largest city in the state and one of the wickedest in the world. The rush spawned several dailies (the morning *Herald, Reville,* and *Eclipse News,* and the afternoon *Chronicle*), as well as four dealers who also handled Denver papers. "His admirable corps of well-trained newsboys penetrate every section of the city ten minutes after The News is place in his hands," said the *Rocky Mountain News* of one dealer. When the *Herald* appeared in the fall of 1878, boys lined up at the office door to get their twenty copies maximum. It retailed for a nickel, but demand drove the price up to a quarter.[24]

Leadville also attracted homeless little "rustlers" and bands of newsboy pickpockets. "Some of the language used by them would knock an eastern newsboy blind," commented one paper. In June 1882 civic-minded adults founded the Bootblacks' and Newsboys' Association of Leadville and rented two rooms in the Nye Building on West Chestnut Street to serve as its headquarters. Charter members paid 50¢ initiation and 50¢ for the first month's dues, each receiving a uniform cap in return. "Nineteen have signed a constitution which has all the formality of that under which the United States exists," said the *Rocky Mountain News.* The organizers envisioned a character-building institution but quickly learned what they were in for. At the association's first dinner the presiding minister asked O. J. Owens, a "deformed" 23-year-old member and known versifier, to give the blessing. Owens stood on his chair and, after securing silence, bowed his head, and prayed:

> May Leadville ever prosper.
> May she forever grow.
> And all her common preachers
> Go where they belong, below.

There would be no more banquets until Owens left town. Moreover, in March 1885 association newsboys struck the *Chronicle,* seeking to pay 2½¢ instead of 3¢ a copy.[25]

Will Irwin and his older brother Wally joined the ranks of Leadville's newsboys around this time. Will rose by 4:00 a.m. to carry the renamed *Herald Democrat* on pony back, sometimes traveling through blizzards, to California Gulch and over Carbonate Hill, while Wally got to sleep in and peddle the evening *Chronicle,* doing a lucrative business among the brothels and gambling houses. Their father was a successful lumber salesman and dairy manager, but he still expected the boys to work. One morning on his route, 14-year-old Will saw a woman suffering from an accidental poisoning. He reported it to the editor, who instructed him to write up the story. The result was Irwin's first published piece. He went on to become a celebrated muckraker, war correspondent, and biographer, publishing more than thirty books.[26]

Lowell Thomas began delivering the *Victor Daily Record* in Colorado in 1902 at age 10. Victor had a population of 12,000 and supported forty-eight saloons, fifteen restaurants, twelve unions, eight pharmacies, six churches, two banks, and two newspapers. Thomas joined the local union, Victor Newsboys No. 32, which had thirty-five dues-paying members. He also hawked the *Denver Post* in the saloons, brothels, and gambling halls of Victor and Cripple Creek, but kept up his studies. He became editor of the *Record* when he turned 19. It was a one-man operation, and he covered everything from crime to opera. Thomas later edited the rival *Victor News,* worked as a reporter for the *Chicago Evening Journal,* and earned degrees from Valparaiso College, the University of Denver, Kent College of Law, and Princeton University. Street-smart, book-wise, and blessed with a resonant voice, he became a pioneer broadcaster. He covered both world wars and published fifty-two books.[27]

Frontier newsboys did not just peddle papers; they also published them. J. Allen Hosmer was 15 when he started the *Beaver Head News* in Virginia City, Montana, in 1867; Lee Travis was 14 when he issued the *News Letter* in Helena, Montana, in 1875; and the Olcovich brothers, Isaac and Selig, were 9 and 11, respectively, when they launched the *Sun,* a semiweekly "story paper" in Carson City, Nevada, in 1888 (Figure 7.3). These were real newspapers that circulated throughout their communities, not the amateur papers that middle-class youths in the Northeast were then producing on mail-order novelty

Figure 7.3. The staff of the *Carson Weekly* in Nevada, May 3, 1892. From left: George T. Davis, Charles Piper, publishers Selig and Isaac Olcovich, and Isador A. Jacobs. Jacobs taught the boys how to set type and operate the press, which is visible inside the doorway. Courtesy Nevada State Museum, Carson City, Nevada Department of Cultural Affairs.

presses. Two economic facts underlay the western boys' accomplishments. First, start-up costs were small on the frontier. A castoff press, a "shirttail full o' worn type," a keg of ink, and a bundle of paper were all anyone with a little know-how needed to commence printing. Henry George started the *San Francisco Evening Post*, the first penny paper west of the Rockies, in 1871 with capital raised by selling delivery routes in advance; he even managed to put his newsboys in uniforms. Second, frontier families considered their children capable of handling heavy workloads and adult responsibilities. Boys and girls cleared fields, built cabins, and tended livestock. Juvenile newspaper publishers were clearly precocious, but the Old West was a time and a place that required and rewarded precocity.[28]

Such opportunities made the West home to some of the richest newsboys in the country. In 1877, after four years in business, 14-year-old James Handley of San Francisco had amassed $6,000, including lots on Telegraph Hill. Handley handled only the *Bulletin*, paid a small boy to help him, and stayed in school. Even wealthier was William J. "Mike" Mykins of Denver. In 1882 the young man was worth $50,000, most of it invested in real estate. He owned a shoeshine stand and a newsstand. An assistant handled the shine business, but Mykins worked from dawn to midnight crying papers from Boston, New York, Philadelphia, Chicago, Cincinnati, St. Louis, and Kansas City. He claimed he could tell at a glance what part of the country a stranger came from. He died in 1920 leaving an estate worth $400,000.[29]

Not all western news sellers aspired to be capitalists. Some, like "Father" Levi Elphick, Native American Elijah Brown, and writer Jack London, rejected the system as unfair and unhealthy. Elphick, an original Forty-Niner, never struck pay dirt and supported himself in old age by selling papers at Lotta's Fountain in downtown San Francisco. A gift to the city from entertainer Lotta Crabtree in 1875, the fountain served as the epicenter of the retail news trade. Elphick cut a striking figure in the 1880s with his bronzed skin, leonine mane, and youthful vigor. A socialist and naturist, he set forth his philosophy in a pamphlet called *Conversations or Street Dialogues with Father Elphick*, in which he advised eating only raw fruits and vegetables and wearing no hats or heavy clothes. Elphick joined a commune in the Sierras, where he died in 1891 at age 86 while tending his pea patch.[30]

Elijah Brown was an 1899 graduate of the Indian Normal School in Lawrence, Kansas, one of 157 Indian boarding schools operating in the United States, with a combined attendance of more than 15,000. Brown set out to prove that education was beneficial to Indians, but he couldn't find steady work after graduation and had to peddle papers to survive. "It is such times as these that try the young man's soul, whether he be red or white," Brown told the *San Francisco Call*. "As I walked up and down the streets with an empty stomach, I formed my first opinion of civilization, and that opinion was unfavorable. Never in the midst of my own people did I need food or shelter."[31]

When 11-year-old Jack London started selling papers in Oakland, California, in 1886, doubling his capital "with a turn of the wrist," he thought he had found his true calling: "The business ladder was the ladder for me, and I had a vision of myself becoming a baldheaded and successful merchant prince." But the trade was brutal. Fights with his 13-year-old nemesis "Cheese-Face," as named in his autobiographical novel *Martin Eden*, occurred daily, without rounds, for twenty to thirty minutes, fed by the bloodlust of the news alley crowd. The feud ended only when Cheese-Face's father had the temerity to die and require his son's presence at the funeral. London then became an oyster pirate, exploiting his crew and stealing from other fishermen. "It was robbery, I grant, but it was precisely in the spirit of capitalism." Yet after working other jobs for less than the full worth of his muscle power, he, too, became a socialist.[32]

Frontier Philanthropy

Compared to the East, newsboys in the West could count on relatively few charitable institutions. One exception was the Newsboys' and Bootblacks' Home on Larimer Street in Denver. Opened in January 1882 and operated by the local Humane Society, it came equipped with gaslight, steam heat, and twenty cots. The first boy admitted was Frank Smart, a frontier waif who had taken the wrong train from Cheyenne and gotten stranded and frostbitten. The home housed six boys its first night, then fourteen, then sixteen. It offered meals and eventually night classes. Its governor, Edward J. Benninger, had run the Sea Boys Home in Liverpool and the Street Boys Home in St Louis. The Denver home closed after six months as costs mounted, but other efforts followed. The most successful was the Haymarket Mission and Newsboys' and Boot Black's Home, opened in 1893 by the Woman's Christian Temperance Union. Housed in an old theater on Arapahoe Street, it could accommodate three hundred lodgers, plus Sunday school students.[33]

One of the biggest spurs to newsboy philanthropy was newsboy unionism. In 1874 twenty-three boys formed the Newsboys' Union of Denver and instituted a badge system to reduce competition from outsiders. In 1883, their successors threatened to strike the *Denver Times* over the "wholesale fraud" of having to pay a nickel for two papers. Their protest failed, but some sixty newsboys mounted a boycott the next year in support of striking pressmen and in hopes of winning their old demand of "three for a nick." Rallying the troops was O. J. Owens, poet laureate of the newsboy fraternity. Denver newsies affiliated with the State Federation of Labor in 1896, but clubwomen, newly emboldened by the right to vote in Colorado, attacked the newsboys' local as an abusive institution. They charged that the older boys intimidated the younger ones, spent their dues money on beer and cigarettes, and devoted their meetings to gambling and dissipation. The women got the union's charter withdrawn and the city's curfew and compulsory education laws toughened, but the hundred or so members refused to disband.[34]

Denver, "Queen City of the Rockies," was a thriving metropolis of more than 100,000 people in the early 1890s. It boasted the finest architecture of any city between Chicago and San Francisco, the most perfect streetcar system in the country, and an abundance of crystal-clear air and mountain scenery. Visitors remarked on the magnificent working dogs—mastiffs, Newfies, and St. Bernards—that sauntered along the boulevards. Less well behaved were its newsboys, who struck the *Denver Evening Times* in February 1894 to clip its wholesale price from 2¢ to 1¢, in line with the other papers in town. The newsboys destroyed the stock of any man or boy they caught selling the *Times* without the benefit of police protection. A similar protest erupted in July against the *Times* and *News* in Colorado Springs, where fifteen newsboys were arrested for rioting. Some, such as Denver union president "Face" Murphy, paid a heavy price for their defiance. With two arrests already on his record, the 11-year-old was convicted of filching a newspaper from a porch in 1895 and sentenced to reform school until he turned 18. His successor, Francis Norton, was also hauled before a judge while in office and fined for deterring boys from selling the *Times*. The *Post* accused police of acting as cat's-paw for the *Times*, calling it a "corporation organ." Undeterred, 160 members of the Newsboys' Union No. 1, including Owens after a brief desertion, struck the *Times* again in February 1896, the same month the newsboys union joined the Trades and Labor Assembly and gained its AFL charter.[35] A versatile advertising force, they mounted torchlight parades to publicize union lectures, distributed circulars during the 1896 election, and promoted pro-silver fundraising stunts, including a staged train smash-up in nearby Elyria. Their occasional arrest by Republican opponents only generated more publicity.[36]

Newsboy militancy spread throughout the state. In March 1896 twenty-six newsboys in Colorado Springs formed a union and struck twice before the year was over, once to protest increased rates during times of sensational news. In May newsboys in Pueblo boycotted the distributor who handled the Denver *News* and *Republican*, and insisted on dealing with the publishers. And in October newsboys in Cripple Creek, organized since 1894, struck in sympathy with their union brothers in Denver, who were at it again. The Denver boys went on to wage a dozen strikes in 1897 and 1898.[37]

Partly because of the agitation, Denver charities formed a civic federation in 1897 that turned the city into a national leader of juvenile justice reform.

From his appointment in 1901, Judge Ben Lindsey introduced a system of probation, sealed records, and other innovations intended to reform rather than punish youthful offenders. He headed the Juvenile Improvement Association of Denver, which in 1905 opened a Newsboys' Club in a basement on Arapahoe Street to provide an alternative to the Newsboys and Workingboys Protective Union No. 7. Though dark and dingy, the club served 167 registered members, all of whom peddled papers. Three out of four were Jewish, reflecting the influx of immigrants who were "chasing the cure" for tuberculosis, a leading cause of death in the East. The club's matron kept the doors open from 9:00 a.m. until 8:00 p.m. and operated a lunch counter that served soup and sandwiches for 2¢ each and coffee for a penny. The club also sponsored a ball team and a band that gained a large following after the *Denver Post* assumed sponsorship. The paper agreed to pay the conductor, provide "first-class" uniforms, and defray all other expenses if the club renamed the band in its honor.[38]

As the number of poor, sometime homeless newsboys grew throughout the West, community leaders emerged to aid and instruct them. Their efforts took many forms. In 1890 a citizen of Salt Lake City, Utah, promised all newsboys $25 apiece on the next Thanksgiving Day if they could produce satisfactory evidence that they had not used profanity, drunk intoxicants, or consumed tobacco during the year. In 1892 the "ladies of Dallas" organized the Newsboys' Relief Corps and founded a home for thirty boys on Elm Street. This was the period in which the US Census declared the frontier "closed" due to sustained population growth, triggering anxieties about the loss of a character-defining aspect of the American experience.[39]

More by custom than by law, few girls peddled papers on the urban frontier. But there were exceptions. The first "newsboy" of the *Deseret News*, founded in 1850 by the Mormon Church in Salt Lake City, was 18-year-old Hannah Jones, adopted daughter of the editor. She retailed its initial circulation of 220 copies at 15¢ apiece. In 1882 10-year-old Maggie peddled a Denver daily and thrived for two years among the "tough citizens" of news alley before some "charitable ladies" packed her off to school. Following in her footsteps in 1886 was Nathaniel Belle Fulton. She carried a boy's name but wore dresses, acted demurely, and won many loyal customers, all of which helped ward off charity workers. Girls also distributed the many suffrage newspapers that cropped up in the West, although some women's clubs preferred to hire experienced newsboys to do the job.[40]

Though primarily self-employed, news sellers and carriers on the wage workers' frontier identified more with the interests of labor than those of capital. This preference can be seen in the many strikes and boycotts they mounted, in the language they used to articulate their demands, and in their tendency to affiliate with labor organizations to advance their social and political agendas.

While newsboy strikes in the West were generally spontaneous protests sparked by pay cuts or other perceived slights, they were also part of a regional upsurge in working-class activism that differed markedly by city and state.

Pacific Eruptions

San Francisco was probably the strongest union town in the West, as friendly to organized labor as Los Angeles was hostile to it. The local newsboy union organized during the Great Upheaval of 1886 disappeared with the decline of the Knights of Labor, but it reemerged in 1892 when a thousand San Francisco hawkers and carriers mounted a successful two-day strike against the *Daily Report* and the *Evening Post* over a rate hike that excluded newsstands and bookstores. The boys got subscribers to boycott the paper and persuaded two clothing stores to withdraw their advertising. The newspaper reinstated the old rates. The boys followed up their victory by organizing another union that marched "200 strong" in uniform caps, coats, and short pants in the city's massive Labor Day parade.[41]

The great strikes and other dramatic events of the period brought many newcomers into the field and reduced profits, prompting the boys to reorganize in August 1894 under new leaders who instituted a badge system. The San Francisco Newsboys' Union showed its strength in October 1896 when its members boycotted three afternoon dailies, the *Post*, *Bulletin*, and *Report*, for discontinuing their "check system" of exchanging old papers for new editions. At an indignation meeting on the second day of the strike, Eugene "Happy" Dougherty mounted a carriage step at the corner of Geary and Grant Avenue, near Union Square, and addressed several hundred fellow strikers in what the *Chronicle* called "true newsboy eloquence:"

> Say, it's just like this, fellers. Der punks wot runs der papers wants ter put us up der flume. Now we're out here ter express our free feelin's, and we ain't a going to propose to take no such guff. Say, didn't we pick up der Bulletin a while ago and advertise der bloomin' sheet and help it out of a hole? An' before that we built up the Report. An' what would der Post be widout us? We made der papers and now dey want ter do us dirt. All we want you blokes ter do is ter take yer ads out and buy der Oakland papers.[42]

As in the 1892 strike, two clothiers withdrew their ads in support of the strike. The union also got help from across the bay in Oakland, where 150 Newsboys' Union members paraded up Broadway in solidarity and a sympathetic publisher supplied the strikers with two wagonloads of papers to sell. The story faded from the headlines after five days with no settlement reported. The Scripps-McRae syndicate acquired the *Report* in 1898 and turned it into the city's first penny daily, but the hostility of the newsboys proved fatal to the enterprise after two years.[43]

San Francisco's union newsboys, now numbering three hundred, struck all the afternoon papers again for seven weeks in the summer of 1903 over a price increase. The anti-union *Los Angeles Times* took perverse delight in reporting that the union of "toughs" organized by William Randolph Hearst's *Examiner* to injure the *Bulletin* had now turned on their masters. It alleged that the union was a school for crime and that the "king bee" had embezzled enough funds to open a saloon.[44] Two years later, with a membership of one thousand, the newsboys' union launched its most raucous and politically charged strike. It targeted the *Bulletin*, a newspaper hostile to the corrupt Union Labor Party regime of Mayor Eugene Schmitz, the newsboys' biggest ally. "We recognize in him our sincere friend," resolved the union during the previous election, "and we will use all the influence we possess to assist him to a second term." Schmitz and political boss Abe Ruef instigated the strike to silence the *Bulletin's* crusading editor, Fremont Older. The commissioner of public works had earlier denied permits to *Bulletin* and *Chronicle* newsboys and targeted them for obstructing sidewalks. On the eve of the 1905 strike Mayor Schmitz addressed a mass meeting of newsboys in a rented hall on O'Farrell Street and urged them to hawk a pro-administration daily on the exceptional terms of four copies for a nickel. He also distributed badges designating them union newsboys. "Our relations with the newsboys was entirely pleasant until the Mayor addressed them," *Bulletin* owner R. A. Crothers complained. "We have not even been requested by the boys—there is no 'union' by the way—to change our rate."[45]

For several days, newsboys, aided by miscellaneous "roughs," cut the tugs of *Bulletin* delivery wagons, stoned shops that displayed the paper, slugged and clubbed its reporters, carriers, and vendors, and snatched copies from the hands of purchasers. These "outrages" occurred with so little police interference that the sheriff was asked to preserve order. His men arrested nine boys between the ages of 10 and 15, including Irish, Italian, and African Americans. Mayor Schmitz eventually published a letter in a friendly newspaper asking the strikers to refrain from violence but assuring them of his sympathy for their cause. To show their support, he and Boss Ruef supplied fireworks and a brass band for 350 striking newsboys to parade down Market Street. The *Bulletin* withstood the violence and hoopla, a rash of boycotts and libel suits, and even the kidnapping of Older, eventually seeing the administration brought down on charges of graft after the 1906 earthquake.[46]

That disaster proved a boon to newsboys everywhere. Joseph Wilder made a killing in Winnipeg, Manitoba, crying, "San Francisco on fire—everybody dead—read all about it." Newsboys in Oakland cleared $30 a day. The line in front of the *Tribune* stretched two blocks long for weeks and was so rambunctious that two militiamen were posted there to keep order. Some boys made money by selling their place in line. The burned-out San Francisco papers were also printed in Oakland; a combined edition of the *Call*, *Chronicle*, and *Examiner* was loaded into an automobile and distributed free through city parks. "No bread wagon, no supply of blankets, has caused so much stir as did the arrival of the news," reported Will Irwin. Among the casualties of the quake were four newsboys in Santa Rosa who died when the wall of the *Press Democrat* building collapsed on them and caught fire.[47]

Los Angeles, meanwhile, had swelled from a city of 11,000 in 1880 to more than 50,000 in 1890, during which the *Times*, under the control of Colonel Harrison Gray Otis, grew from a four-sheet country paper to an influential eight-page daily with a circulation of 6,000. Independent contractors handled the distribution, hiring their own delivery crews, usually schoolboys. One of these contractors, Harry Chandler, was a Dartmouth dropout who had come to Southern California to cure his tuberculosis. He hauled tomatoes to market when he first arrived, thus learning the demands of handling perishables. Chandler regained his health and acquired distribution routes for the *Herald*, *Evening Express*, and *San Diego Union*. He also worked as a circulation clerk and then manager of the *Times*, where he oversaw fifty "ragtag newsboys." They started work at 4 a.m. The boys paid 2½¢ per copy, which they hawked or delivered for 5¢ apiece. They earned up to $1.50 a week, while Chandler made between $50 and $100 a week. He worked sixteen hours a days, and if a boy failed to show up, he would mount a horse, ride a bike, or row a boat down the Los Angeles River to get papers to customers.[48]

When Los Angeles newsboys unionized and struck the *Times* in November 1887, Chandler blamed rival newspapers: "When a paper gets so hard up as to try to put up combinations with street urchins against a more successful contemporary, it is laughable indeed." He named the *Tribune* and *Herald* as co-conspirators who had long sabotaged its deliveries and were now "egging on" the Newsboys' Union, which had, in fact, first met in the *Tribune's* office. *Tribune* managers offered the newsboys ten free copies of their paper if they refused to carry the *Times*. "The newsboys are pretty sensible little youngsters, as a rule, and never would have thought of such a silly trick if the vicious *Tribune* gang hadn't cajoled, begged, bribed and bulldozed them into it," said the *Times*. It predicted the newsboys union would "die a natural death *poco* shortly." Chandler felt he was doing the boys and their families a favor by hiring them. He liked to quote an immigrant rancher who had sought jobs for his two sons because they needed breaking, like young colts who would otherwise be "no tam goot."[49]

Chandler's value to the *Times* and his skills as a businessman became apparent during this circulation war. Having secretly bought up the *Herald's* routes, he hired a big tallyho and shipped off the entire circulation and carrier crew to the San Bernardino Mountains for a five-day holiday, during which time he appealed to the irate subscribers to switch to the *Times*. About half of them did so. He then steered customers to either the *Times* or *Herald*, but never the *Tribune*, forcing its sale. Chandler, still in his twenties, was the buyer. A year after the strike Chandler and Otis treated their newsboys to the first of many Christmas banquets. "There is no disgrace in being a newsboy," Otis told them, "and you can all rise to any position you need if you'll only be honest, hardworking and faithful." After his death in 1917, Otis's heirs honored him with a set of sculptures in Westlake (now MacArthur) Park featuring a newsboy in cap and knickers crying his wares.[50]

Clashes in Cascadia

Newsboy protests also flared in the Pacific Northwest. Boys in Portland, Oregon, struck in 1892 and 1900 over pricing and return policies. The first dispute affected a hundred boys who demanded that the *Oregonian* offer them the same wholesale rate and return privileges as newsdealers. The paper claimed the boys were mistaken and admonished them to cease their attacks on those who were content with the terms. These were probably Italians because the union instituted a "no dagoes" policy. The union endured and in 1896 started an afternoon paper that was edited and printed by the boys. In January 1900, 150 Portland newsboys struck the *Evening Telegram* when it refused to allow them to return unsold papers. The strikers made up a large portion of the 300 to 400 boys, mostly Jews and Italians, who distributed the city's four dailies: the *Telegraph, Journal, News,* and *Oregonian*. "All carriers were stopped and several thousand copies of the paper were destroyed by the boys," reported the Associated Press. "Every person seen with a Telegram was given rough usage, and many were knocked down on the street." Police arrested several of these "newsboycotters" and the protest fizzled.[51]

Seattle, with four daily newspapers and a population of about 50,000, was also a hotbed of newsboy discontent. By the early 1890s it was the economic and cultural capital of the Pacific Northwest, the terminus of the nearly completed Great Northern Railway and the heart of the region's extractive industries. Fishermen, lumberjacks, miners, and longshoremen flocked to the area and established a vital trade union movement.[52] Newsboys were part of this movement. They waged a vigorous strike in April 1891 against the *Press-Times* after it refused to accept the return of unsold copies. The business manager hired messenger boys to distribute the paper, but the newsboys, led by "Pud" Leckie, destroyed the papers and beat the messengers until the effort was abandoned. The newsboys formalized their alliance in November 1892 by forming Seattle Newsboys Union Local 15834 and receiving a charter from the American Federation of Labor. The local averaged thirty members over the next ten years, but then grew to eighty members in 1902. These boys, some of whom earned $2.50 a day, represent a fraction of Seattle's newsboys. The city had four dailies in 1895, six in 1900, and thirteen by 1916. Union membership in that period grew to 402, including two females.[53]

A photograph taken shortly after the local's founding shows thirty-seven young men and boys posing with their union banner (Figure 7.4). They are all well groomed and well shod. Some sport ties, and all wear hats—traditional newsboy caps, but also homburgs, porkpies, and the new trilbies. Their posture is perfect, their expressions serious, and the ribbons pinned to their lapels mark them as bona fide union newsboys. The union flexed its muscle in 1899 by refusing to sell the new Seattle *Star* when publisher E. W. Scripps insisted

Figure 7.4. Chartered in 1892, the Seattle Newsboys Union offered its members job protection, medical benefits, and recreation, including the 1903 outing to Bainbridge Island that occasioned this picture. Asahel Curtis, *Seattle Newsboys Union.* Courtesy Washington State Historical Society.

on cash up front and no returns. The boys relented, but they launched another, more successful strike against the *Seattle Times* in 1901 when that paper tried to force them to sell only the *Times*.[54]

Union newsboys in Boise, Idaho; Rossland, British Columbia; and Spokane, Washington, also engaged in collective action. The Boise boys formed a union in October 1892, two years after Idaho became a state, by declaring that any non-union "kid" who presumed to sell papers would be thumped and his stock in trade destroyed; the organization was still going strong ten years later when it brought up the rear of the city's Labor Day parade. The Canadian lads struck the *Daily Miner* during a mining strike in 1901 but were promptly replaced.[55]

Spokane newsboys first declared their dissatisfaction with the *Daily News* in August 1892 over its price hike and no-return policy. They presented the proprietor with a piece of paper on which they had scrawled the word "Stricke," followed by their names or initials. The newspaper treated the uprising as a joke, quoting the banter between strikers and non-strikers:

> "You're a regular Andrew Carnejee."
> "I ain't no Carnejee a'tall."
> "Betcher are. Didn't Carnejee go back on de strikers?"
> "Haven't yu gone back on us?"

The strike collapsed, but twenty-two boys became charter members of the union. Their first order of business was to declare: "No dagoes allowed to sell." Apparently, no Chinese dared vend a newspaper in the West, though they peddled cigars and other items and were subject to baiting by newsboys. Here, too, they followed the lead of union men.[56]

The Spokane boys next boycotted the *Daily Chronicle* in January 1895 over its refusal to take back unsold papers at cost. They struck again in August 1896. "As yet the state militia has not been called out," quipped the *Oregonian*.[57]

The Pacific Northwest was the jumping-off point for the Klondike gold rush in 1896. Every paper in Seattle published guides to the Yukon Territory, complete with maps, travelers' information, and lists of what the well-appointed gold seeker should bring.[58] More than a few sourdoughs thought to lug a sack full of old newspapers from Skagway up the treacherous Chilkoot Pass, confident that the law of supply and demand would render them worth their weight in gold once they reached the tent cities billowing along the Klondike River some five hundred miles away. Seventeen-year-old Chicago newsboy John Carmody made this trip seven times during the summer of 1899, selling papers in Juneau, Skagway, and Dyea for 10¢ to 25¢ each and in distant Dawson for $1 to $1.50 apiece. Yet even here other boys with fresher papers soon showed up, forcing him to lower prices.

Skagway's population swelled to 10,000 during the gold rush, not counting the thousand or so miners who passed through each week. The town possessed two papers, *Skagway News* and the *Daily Alaskan*. Newsboys circulated both of them, sometimes by dog sled or wagon (Figure 7.5). They were treated to an annual banquet by saloonkeeper Pat Renwick, who entertained the boys with his pet bear. The town's notorious lawlessness extended to the news trade. A gang of twenty-five newsboys once tried to steal Carmody's stock of 1,600 papers, but he fended them off. He said he made $4,000 in two months, yet spent the money almost as fast as he made it. He returned home at the end of July, his pockets bulging with gold dust and nuggets worth $2,000, more than enough to show his Chicago chums a good time.[59]

The most successful newsboy in Dawson was a one-legged youth named Ring who had sold papers outside the Seattle Athletic Club. He, too, trekked over the Chilkoot Pass in 1898 and saw the demand for newspapers, which he begged or bought from incoming prospectors. Situated at the confluence of the Yukon and Klondike Rivers, Dawson so abounded in mud and boredom that an ancient newspaper soaked in bacon grease once sold for $15. When the

Figure 7.5. H. C. Barley, "Taking a Rest After a Hard Drive." A newsboy returns with his team to the Skagway News Depot at the corner of Broadway and 4th Ave., June 1899. Yukon Archives, White Horse, Yukon, Canada. H. C. Barley fonds, # 5068.

Spanish-American War broke out, five hundred men paid a dollar each to enter a hall to hear a man read the latest news from the *Seattle Times*.

By the summer of 1898, stampeders had swelled Dawson's population to 30,000, and the town claimed two newspapers of its own, the *Klondike Nugget* and the *Yukon Midnight Sun*, and plenty of disillusioned ex-miners to peddle them. A year's subscription sold for $24 or an ounce and a half of gold dust. The rival papers supplied readers with rumors of new gold strikes, reports of murders and accidents, ribald stories, classified ads, and a smattering of poems and jokes. Great bales of out-of-town papers continued to arrive by boat, and Ring got the job of delivering them. He ordered newspapers and magazines on his own account and acquired dog teams to distribute them among the claims out on the creeks. He also opened a circulating library in Dawson, charging $2 a month for the loan of a book.[60]

Lines in the Sand

Some of the most committed union newsboys plied their trade in the Southwest. Salt Lake City newsies, Mormon and non-Mormon, united in February 1890 when a contingent took part in a Federated Labor and Trades Council parade for the eight-hour day. Newsboys' Union members marched in Fourth of July parades throughout the decade. They faced a stiff challenge in 1900 when four women preempted the best corners on East Temple Street. The union signed a protocol that admitted them as full members. It formalized its alliance with the trades council and elected a slate of officers who presided over an annual Thanksgiving dinner, arranged free baths, and provided gallery seats at the theater.[61]

One of the union members, William John Gilbert Gould, was the Mormon son of a railroad section boss. His recollections provide a rare glimpse of the political maturation of a working-class boy on the industrial frontier. Gould started selling the *Deseret Evening News* in 1898 at age 10 when his friends told him he could get two papers for 5¢ and sell them for a nickel each. Gould couldn't understand why anyone would pay twice what an item cost. "The whole idea of profit didn't make sense to me," he said. But he was so excited when he doubled his money that he ran home to tell his mother rather than continue selling. Gould's mother had no objections to this new pursuit: she woke him every morning by five, fixed him a hot breakfast, bundled him up, and sent him on his way.[62]

Gould rarely made more than a quarter hawking afternoon papers, but in the morning he earned as much or more than his father. He handled the *Tribune* and the *Herald* and received most of the papers free in return for carrying papers from the pressroom to the streetcars for suburban delivery. The *Tribune* supplyman paid him four papers for his work, "but the guy at the *Herald* just reached over and grabbed a handful, maybe fifteen or twenty, and passed them through to me. So on my first round everything I sold was clear profit." There were few boys on the street early in the morning and Gould had the market mostly to himself; he met the streetcars as they came out of the car barns and sold many papers to the streetcar men.[63]

Gould's education continued when he was called a scab. There was no union or strike at the time; the epithet simply meant he was an outsider cutting in on the trade. Gould soon helped organize a union and was elected sergeant at arms to keep order at the weekly meetings in the Federation of Labor Hall. The union balked when another evening paper, the *Telegram*, required kids to show a handful of pennies before they were supplied. The *Telegram* set its price at 3¢ to undercut the 5¢ *Deseret News*, but boys usually got a nickel for it by claiming to be out of change. Hence the new rule. "We boycotted the *Telegram*," recalled Gould. "If any kid showed up on the street with those papers, he had them taken away and torn to pieces by the goon squad. After a few days of this the *Telegram* changed its advertised price to five cents a copy."[64]

Another victory came in June 1902 when union newsboys applied for membership into the Utah Federation of Labor. They demanded a "closed shop"—that only union members be allowed to sell the *Telegram*. The paper agreed. When some nonunion lads pushed in a few weeks later, the members bombarded the office windows with eggs and destroyed newspapers. Police arrived with their "hurry-up" wagon and arrested "ringleader" Ferdinand Desky. The *Telegram's* manager apologized, saying that he did not know the union boys from the nonunion ones, and resolved to do better.[65]

Two months later in Bisbee, Arizona, members of the Amalgamated Association of the Independent Order of Newspaper Carriers, whose ages ranged from 9 to 16, struck the *Miner* in a dispute over wages, fines, and other grievances. "We don't work no more for that *Miner* until we gets our rights," said one boy. "We don't want to suppress the freedom of the press, and are willing to submit to arbitration, but the strike is on."[66]

The frontier myth of rugged individualism and the newsboy myth of plucky enterprise coexisted uneasily in places such as Kansas City, Tombstone, San Francisco, Salt Lake City, and Bisbee. Frontier newsboys were indeed the advance guard of boomerism, helping to build communities and their economies. Yet they both aided and resisted the local businessmen and distant corporations that sought to extract the region's mineral wealth and exploit those who had come to work on their own terms. Like their counterparts in the East, immigrant and native newsboys on the industrial frontier enjoyed much independence but withstood the harsh realities of life. They knew poverty and hardship as well as wealth and achievement, and acquired the skills and values that would shape their adult lives. Some developed an easy acceptance of violence and an exploitative frame of mind, while others opted for cooperation over conflict. Frontier newsboys, like frontier newspapers, were catalysts of social change who reflected the tensions in their communities. Would those tensions be resolved peacefully or violently, with carrots or sticks? That was the question of the hour in nineteenth-century America. It would continue to be asked and answered by newsboys east and west in the twentieth century, particularly with the arrival of a new group on the scene: the Industrial Workers of the World.

8

Press Philanthropy and the Politics of Want

On Christmas Day 1885, the Rev. Dr. W. W. Boyd happened to pass the Market Street office of the *St. Louis Post-Dispatch* and was shocked to see more than 150 children being led inside. He asked what was happening and was told that they were newsboys going to an annual dinner given by publisher Joseph Pulitzer. Boyd frowned. He had just compiled an immense Christmas register of all the charitable institutions in the city, reported the *Post-Dispatch*, "and was annoyed to think that there was one he had overlooked."[1]

Boyd's oversight is understandable. Despite constant self-promotion, newspapers were hardly viewed as philanthropies. Yet their range of charitable giving, particularly on behalf of children, was extraordinary. Publishers set up coal and ice funds to help poor families keep warm in the winter and cool in the summer. They established milk depots, distributed vaccines, built hospitals, aided disaster victims, and supported myriad other good causes. Indeed, even as the St. Louis lads were filing in for their holiday meal, Pulitzer's recent acquisition, the *New York World*, was winning praise for having raised the money to build the pedestal for the Statue of Liberty. Donations had poured in from more than 120,000 readers including the *World*'s own newsboys, all of whom got their names in the paper.[2]

Newsboys were by far the main recipients of publishers' largesse. Hawkers and carriers had long relied on their favors, but this rich tradition of giving flourished most spectacularly in the 1880s and 1890s, especially in the boom-and-bust cities of the Midwest. The volatile industrial economy and surging labor movement created great need among the masses and great trepidation among employers, who generally preferred to reward valued workers with gold coins and holiday turkeys rather than grant union recognition and higher wages. Grand gestures of benevolence also helped employers repair damaged reputations. Pulitzer's Christmas banquet, for instance, came after the St. Louis Trade Union Assemblies had labeled the *Post-Dispatch* a "rat" paper for mistreating printers and maligning unions. To combat the charge, the *Post-Dispatch* reported that the newsboys presented Pulitzer with a gold-headed cane on New Year's Day as a token of their esteem. It was a welcome tribute for a man who saw himself as a champion of working folk, who were, after all, his chief customers.[3]

Pulitzer's *Post-Dispatch* exemplified the new breed of feisty and frugal dailies cropping up in the region. "New" or "Western Journalism," as it was called, sought to expose wrongdoing, support the legitimate demands of labor (though not necessarily unions), and amuse readers with short, lively features, humor columns, and fiction, all while keeping a close eye on the bottom line. Priced at a penny or two, these four-to-six-page dailies devoted more space to advertising, which made up a growing proportion of all newspaper revenue, rising from 44 percent in 1880 to 55 percent by 1900. With ad rates tied to circulation, innovative publishers like Pulitzer were not content to leave distribution to that proverbial "man in the basement." In keeping with the era's increased reliance on the "visible hand" of middle managers, newspaper publishers sought specialists to build street sales and subscriptions, coordinate routes and schedules, oversee rail, mail, and wagon deliveries, and counter the growing power of dealers, distributors, and do-gooders.[4]

All newspaper owners and managers needed to recruit and supervise a steady supply (ideally an oversupply) of hawkers and carriers who could cheaply disseminate their product. The most successful executives were experts in newsboy management and their initiatives revolutionized commercial journalism. They lavished gifts on "newsies"—a new term of the period—at Christmas and hosted banquets and excursions throughout the year. They sponsored newsboy sports teams and marching bands long before most public schools. Some papers established their own reading rooms, scholarships, and schools for newsboys, or helped others to do so. A few erected palatial office buildings complete with newsboy entrances, auditoriums, gymnasiums, and swimming pools. Commenting on the profusion of these "not altogether philanthropic" benefits, the *New York Commercial Advertiser* observed in 1887 that the newsboy "bids fair to become one of the most pampered members of society. Newspaper publishers are beginning to appreciate the value of his influence in building up circulations, and are therefore making much of him." If such coddling continued, said the paper, "we may expect to see free excursions to Europe provided for newsboys, and find them selling their papers from coupes." Both of these absurd predictions would of course come true.[5]

What combination of altruism and self-interest underlay these charitable schemes? How did they change in response to business cycles, reform movements, and labor trouble? And what did they mean to the children who took advantage of them? A key to understanding this golden age of newsboy welfare is to recognize that it coincided with a resurgence of trade unionism and industrial conflict. Due to deteriorating wages and job conditions, nearly 23,000 strikes broke out in more than 117,000 workplaces between 1881 and 1900. Newsboys joined this march of labor, rattling the windows and nerves of what some called the "fleecing classes." The boys asserted their rights as citizens and workers by taking part in political debates and campaigns, joining in riots and rallies, and organizing their own unions and strikes. These activities were neither exceptional nor precocious, and suggest that working-class youth in general and newsboys in particular—despite the sometimes quelling effects of a holiday meal—played a much larger and louder role in Gilded Age civic and industrial affairs than has been acknowledged.[6]

Oysters and Outings

Press philanthropy took many forms in industrial America, the oldest of which were carriers' addresses. Publishers still produced these "screeds in rhyme" for boys to distribute on New Year's Day, much as they had in the eighteenth century. But their charm began to fade as newspapers procured boilerplate poems and merely printed their names at the top. Some papers, beginning with the *Utica Herald* in 1869, gave boys advertisement-filled almanacs to pass out to subscribers, or supplied them with city maps or calendars. Others, such as the *Providence Journal* and *Kansas City Star*, forbade addresses of all kinds, calling them a form of begging that tempted carriers to slight stingy subscribers. The *New York Herald* and *Journal of Commerce* also banned the practice, pledging to raise carriers' incomes instead. Trade unionists agreed that raises would foster a "more intelligent manhood."[7]

Unlike most other occupations, news peddling itself could be a kind of charity. People of all ranks regarded the purchase of a paper from a poor waif, widow, or "defective" as an act of benevolence. Anyone could play the philanthropist by letting peddlers keep the change or, if really generous, by purchasing their entire stock and sending them home. Woeful little hawkers sometimes received gifts of clothes, shoes, or meals from strangers, while carriers delighted in the odd ministration of coffee or rolls from kindly subscribers. Whatever form they took, tips were not simply handouts but part of the surplus value that newsboys created and counted on—a little too assuredly at times. Novelist William Dean Howells worried that he was demoralizing the boys by failing to demand his change: "These small wretches sometimes winked to their friends, in the belief that they had cheated me; and now I let them offer to get the change before I let them keep it."[8]

If tipping a newsboy could be regarded as a compassionate act, then setting him up in business was an even greater kindness. Friends and relatives would secure routes and corners for boys whose father had died, thus reinforcing the link between paper buying and almsgiving. Fraternal societies and trade unions made similar provisions for widows and orphans. Even state legislatures treated news selling as a form of public assistance: in 1879 Massachusetts granted a free peddler's license to any bona fide Civil War veteran, wounded or not.[9]

Of the many newsboy charities devised, holiday dinners and summer excursions proved most popular. The first regularly held newsboy banquet took place January 1, 1859, when 16-year-old Pittsburgh stationer and news dealer John W. Pittock invited a group of boys to dine at his expense. The dinner became a yearly event, which expanded after Pittock founded the *Sunday Leader* in 1864 and the *Evening Leader* in 1870. Some of the banquets were held in City Hall with five hundred boys present. Pittock also rallied support for a newsboys' home that opened in 1880, the year before his death at age 38.[10]

Even more influential were the Fourth of July feasts given to newsboys—and the odd newsgirl—by *Philadelphia Public Ledger* publisher George W. Childs, beginning in 1867. The dinners fit with a vision of labor patronage and civic improvement that made Childs the most admired employer of his day. Born poor in Baltimore in 1829 and soon orphaned, he started out as a bookshop errand boy at age 11, earning $2 a week. After a stint in the navy at age 13, he settled in Philadelphia, where five years later he opened his own shop in the *Public Ledger* building. He acquired the ailing newspaper in 1864 and turned it around by doubling the price to 2¢, raising advertising rates, and editing it as a family paper unsullied by scandal or sensation. Ten profitable years later he endowed the Philadelphia Zoo (America's first) and backed countless other causes, including the Newsboys' Aid Society and its newsboys' home.[11]

Like Pittock, Childs was the archetypal self-made man, but he didn't see himself in those terms. Nor did he expect others to advance through individual effort alone. He believed in trade unions, especially the International Typographical Union, to which his printers belonged. He paid ITU members above scale and subscribed his employees to labor newspapers, the possession of which got men fired elsewhere. He introduced pensions and paid vacations, donated ground for a printer's cemetery, and contributed to the ITU's building fund. Members across the country set a thousand ems and donated their pay to the fund every year on his birthday. Such amity was unheard of in the conflict-ridden newspaper industry. *Harper's Weekly* called Childs the "Santa Claus of the newspaper world" because of his gifts to his workers. Yet he called it profit sharing, not philanthropy. Economist Richard T. Ely termed Childs's approach "preventative philanthropy" because it lessened the need for almshouses, soup kitchens, and the like.[12]

Pittock and Childs's aid to newsboys inspired others to action just as the plunging economy made such help essential. In 1873 the *Detroit Free Press* treated 150 newsboys to the first of many New Year's dinners at a local restaurant. That same year James Gordon Bennett Jr.'s *New York Herald* established eight soup kitchens overseen by the chef of Delmonico's. In 1875 Bennett treated twelve hundred newsboys and newsgirls to Christmas dinner at Moquin's on Ann Street. The children were divided into squads of two hundred and admitted at different hours according to the color of their tickets. An Italian street band accompanied the children as they sang and drew lots for new clothes. It was a publicity stunt, to be sure, but one that filled empty stomachs during a winter in which nine hundred New Yorkers starved to death.[13]

Endowments to newsboys' homes also expanded during this period in which great fortunes were made and lost; the Pittsburgh home, for example, received steady infusions of cash from land heiress Mary Schenley, financier Andrew Mellon, and industrialist Henry Clay Frick. Philanthropists in New York vied for the privilege of sponsoring holiday banquets at the Children's Aid Society's lodging houses. Liquor merchant William Fleiss and his wife laid an early family claim to Christmas in 1860 and held it for about sixty years (though J. P. Morgan also pitched in); Mrs. William Waldorf Astor elbowed out all rivals at Thanksgiving; Wall Street lawyer Randolph Guggenheimer—"Guggy" to the boys—and his wife, Eliza, captured Washington's Birthday (though one busy year they observed Thomas Jefferson's nativity instead); fellow attorney F. Delano Weekes held the monopoly on Lincoln's Birthday; and artist Richard Wittman made do with Valentine's Day. February, it seems, was overpacked with charity dinners, but CAS founder Charles Loring Brace considered it "the most pinching time of the year for the poor."[14]

Newsboys' banquets inverted class hierarchies as professional men and society women waited on the boys, who were notoriously unruly. E. L. Godkin, founding editor of *The Nation*, visited the Thanksgiving dinner at Brace's lodging house in 1870 and was appalled at how "piggy" the boys were when they ate. Table manners aside, sponsors used the banquets to reinforce bourgeois values. The dinners invariably began or ended with a motivational speech. In 1872 former president Millard Fillmore presided over the Thanksgiving dinner for newsboys and bootblacks in Buffalo, while editor J. G. Pangborn did the honors at Christmas in Jersey City. "Sell all the *Journals* you can," he told the newsboys. "Don't cheat, don't lie, don't swear and don't fight." In March 1880, the editor of Washington's *Evening Critic* advised two hundred newsboys "to be good and true and learn their Sunday-school lessons" before letting them tear into the first course of stewed oysters.[15]

Contrary to such advice, newsboys sometimes disrupted the dinners by throwing food, stealing pies, lighting firecrackers, or asserting union sympathies. On New Year's Day 1890, five hundred Pittsburgh newsboys rioted on Fifth Avenue after an annual dinner hosted by the *Leader*. According to wire reports,

"They first attacked a crowd of Italians and Hebrews, and then turned their attention to the nonunion gripmen and conductors on the Pittsburgh traction road. The boys began calling them 'scabs,' and then made an assault upon the cars. Sticks, stones, and mud were thrown and a general fight followed." Rioting also marred an 1892 Christmas dinner in Toledo hosted by railroad ticket agent John Gunckel, who aimed to displace the militant, strike-born Toledo Bootblacks' and Newsboys' Union with his benevolent, industry-backed Boyville Newsboys' Association. A series of brawls led police to remove 50 of the 152 newsboys in attendance. Rather than feeling sated and grateful, some boys left the banquets feeling ill and resentful, a point not missed by cartoonists of the era: "First Newsboy—Wot did you git at de noosboy's Christmas dinner? Second Newsboy—De cramp colic."[16]

Yet on the whole, newsboy banquets generated such good publicity— including the 1893 parlor song "The Newsboys' Christmas Dinner"—that businessmen clamored to underwrite them and to donate the shoes, gloves, scarves, suspenders, and peacoats that were often distributed as parting gifts (Figure 8.1). Chicago clothier Isaac Woolf, an erstwhile London news hawker, began hosting Thanksgiving dinners for newsboys in 1882 when he fed a hundred "ragged and hungry little guests" at his store. In 1895, ten thousand of the city's poor sat at his table in the First Regiment Armory and consumed a

Figure 8.1. Newsboys enjoy Christmas dinner and celebrate winning tickets for peacoats donated by the *New York Herald. Once a Week* 6, no. 13 (Jan. 18, 1891): 4. Eckel Collection, Princeton University Library.

"monster menu" requiring 520 turkeys, 10 barrels of mashed potatoes, and 1,800 pies. The repast cost Woolf $5,000. The tradition ended with his death and the store's bankruptcy in 1906.[17]

In addition to hosting dinners, newspaper publishers and distributors also organized outings for their slum-dwelling subordinates. They took them to beaches, ball games, circuses, rodeos, and Wild West shows. The *New York Times* transported 900 boys on a barge to Oriental Grove, Long Island, in 1872. The *Herald* sent 1,346 newsboys there in 1875. The trips began with noisy parades from City Hall Park and ended just in time for the evening editions, with copies delivered to the pier to avoid delays. Newsboys in Boston, Philadelphia, Baltimore, Chicago, and Milwaukee enjoyed similar excursions at this early date. Some trips were underwritten by the YMCA or businessmen. In 1876 New York banker, congressman, and steamship magnate John H. Starin began treating hundreds of newsboys and bootblacks to a day at his amusement park on Glen Island in Long Island Sound and then at Alpine Grove, nineteen miles up the Hudson River (Figure 8.2). Starin touted the decorum of his visitors, but chaos prevailed whenever the newsboys descended: they got into rock fights, destroyed fruit trees, stole beer, and once set fire to a barn. Discipline broke

Figure 8.2. "New York City.—Annual Excursion of the Newsboys to Alpine Grove, July 1st, 1880," July 24, 1880, n.p. Eckel Collection, Princeton University Library.

down as soon as they boarded the barges; some boys would jump overboard on a dare or throw off benches, grates, and other heavy objects just to watch them sink. Starin placed two policemen with bullwhips on the barges and hired a crewman to ride in a towboat and retrieve any jumpers. A passing yachtsman once shouted, "Are you going to take those boys out to sea and dump 'em? Thank God!"[18]

Because the public relations value of these excursions was paramount, even the most tragic outings received praise. In 1878 a Starin-sponsored picnic for three thousand newsboys resulted in the drowning of 10-year-old Willie Brooks, who was pushed overboard while crossing from barge to barge. The boys fell silent as Willie's older brother Frank sobbed inconsolably. But they "were soon as uproarious and happy as usual over their continuous lunch and lemonade," reported the *National Police Gazette*. Tragedy also spoiled the homecoming of five hundred Chicago newsboys and girls after picnicking at Jackson Park in 1886. Harry Burreson, 11, fell under the wheels while trying to board the moving train and lost both legs. The *Chicago Tribune* nevertheless headlined its story "Happy Newsboys."[19]

These one-day excursions soon blossomed into overnight trips and the founding of the Fresh Air Fund. The Rev. Willard Parsons of Sherman, Pennsylvania, started it with a visit to New York in the summer of 1877 to gather a company of tenement children to stay as guests of his congregation. The *New York Evening Post* began funding the program the next year. The *New York Tribune* took it over in 1882, and eventually the *New York Times*. The newspapers publicized the program with accounts of "pathetic little street waifs" adjusting to country life. "This is a hell of a place, with no street to play in!" lamented one newsie after arriving at a Hudson River campground. Cartoonist Michael Angelo Woolf specialized in these fish-out-of-water gags, thus becoming "the greatest asset the Fresh Air Fund ever had." By 1897 seventeen American cities had organized Fresh Air Relief. Groups in England and France also took up the cause, all of which spread the idea of summer camps for middle-class children.[20]

Discipline and Publish

Like all forms of welfare capitalism, newspaper charities blended good works with good business. One of the first to recognize their economic value was James E. Scripps, who founded the *Detroit Evening News* in 1873. The paper was a four-page tabloid that sold for 2¢ when most dailies were bigger and cost a nickel. The reduced price appealed to workingmen who earned about a dollar a day. The paper also carried free want ads and won the contract to publish city council proceedings. Scripps started out with a bare-bones staff of ten and personally delivered papers to hawkers, carriers, and agents. He treated them all as subcontractors to avoid incurring distribution costs. His indispensable factotum in this work was Charles A. Worthington, a devout Christian bachelor who became "a sort of daddy" to the boys. Worthington is said to have kept his pockets filled with peanuts, licorice, and cheap candy, which he dispensed liberally, along with oranges or watermelon on Saturdays. Yet the *Evening News's* most successful agent was James's 19-year-old half-brother, Edward Willis Scripps, who serviced almost half of the paper's 4,000 subscribers. He cleared $50 a week, earning more than either the city editor or his publisher brother. Edward later leased out his routes and taught boys to build similar ones in neighboring towns, which nearly doubled the paper's circulation. "More than half of my success depends on getting the right boy to carry the route," he explained in an unpublished memoir. "The best type of boy would be ten- or twelve-years-old, the son of a widow, who was known to be worthy, a hard-worker; in fact, had the sympathy of the community."[21]

By 1876 the *Evening News's* circulation reached 10,000, equaling all other Detroit papers combined. The partners began to think about exporting their formula. They invested in a failing penny paper in Cincinnati in 1881 and persuaded Worthington to become business manager. They also hired 24-year-old Milton McRae away from the *Detroit Evening Sun* to secure advertising. McRae had been circulation manager at the *Sun* since 1874 and may be the first person to hold that title. When Edward Scripps took sole control of the Cincinnati paper in 1883, he renamed it the *Penny Post* (later the *Evening Post*) and, with Worthington's departure, promoted McRae to business manager. McRae raised advertising rates and circulation by raising the number of newsboys from seventy-five to fifteen hundred in five years. He inaugurated night classes to teach them the principles of business: efficiency, salesmanship, and the profit system. When attendance fell, he organized a newsboy band, sports teams, and Sunday socials at a cost of about $2,000 a year. During a circulation war in 1885 he treated all fifteen hundred newsboys to the theater, parading them through the streets with banners and a brass band. He capped the year with a Christmas benefit for ten thousand guests and a gift for every newsboy. He also experimented with contests, games, and posters to boost sales. Together, Scripps and McRae formed the first newspaper "league," or chain, in America. Its letterhead insignia was a running, hollering newsboy. By 1907 their empire comprised twenty-four newspapers, a national wire service, and an illustrated news feature syndicate.[22]

Another expert in newsboy management was Victor Lawson of Chicago. Born to immigrant parents in 1850, Lawson started working on his family's Norwegian-language newspaper, the *Skandinaven*. Cofounder John Anderson was himself a newsboy who had prospered after taking over distribution of Chicago's *Commercial Advertiser*. Anderson made extensive use of newsboys when the *Skandinaven* began in 1866, a fact not lost on Lawson. He had been bound for Harvard when the Chicago fire wiped out his family's fortune and sent his father to an early grave. Lawson took over his real estate holdings, which included the premises of the feisty but struggling *Daily News*. Lawson bailed out the paper in 1876 and at age 26 became its publisher. The *Daily News* was a penny paper with a circulation of 10,000, but it generated little revenue. Lawson sought advice from George Childs and then instituted a series of reforms; he revamped the advertising policy and, after riding with drivers, reorganized the distribution system. He contracted all newsstand deliveries to John R. Walsh's Western News Company, recruited downtown hawkers "of the street gamin class" and carrier boys in the residential districts, and sent circulation agents into Iowa and Nebraska. Lawson also published circulation figures, hastening their industry-wide transition from trade secrets to commodities that could be marketed to advertisers.[23]

Lawson promoted many benevolent institutions, including an employment agency, public baths, a fresh-air sanitarium for slum children, and shelters for fallen women and homeless youths. He devoted most of the second story of his four-story building to the use of newsboys. One regular visitor, future sociologist Nels Anderson, said it was a place "where the boys could buy at cost price pop, hot dogs, ice cream or they could sit reading dime novels, or indulge in penny pitching." The *Daily News* sent newsboys on picnics and organized them into a marching band and drill team, providing instructors, instruments, and Zouave uniforms. James Petrillo, future president of the American Federation of Musicians, learned to play trumpet in the band.[24]

Lawson further assisted newsboys by promoting his product in novel ways. He advertised the *Daily News* on posters, handbills, calendars, clocks, fans, and letter openers, many of which depicted newsboys. He ran contests, games, and true crime mysteries to spark interest. At the same time, he was not afraid to stir up trouble between newsboys and his competitors. In March 1886 he organized a mass meeting of newsboys to instigate a boycott against the *Chicago Tribune*, which had sweetened the profit margin to authorized carriers while cutting off independent, or "guerrilla," carriers who handled various papers. Lawson's chief newsboy blasted the *Tribune* for "its hypocrisy to its carriers, subscribers, and advertisers." One rabble-rouser advocated lynching everyone connected with the *Tribune* except the elevator boy. Ultimately, however, the city's leading publishers were able to accomplish more through cooperation than confrontation, effectively controlling distribution and advertising via the auspices of the Daily Newspaper Association of Chicago.[25]

What Pulitzer, Scripps, McRae, and Lawson realized was that the key to success in the news business was not content or even capital, but "kids"—another neologism of the day. The trade journal *Printer's Ink* stated unequivocally in 1894

that publishers owed much of their success to the recruitment and discipline of
boy labor. Those who neglected this aspect of the business did so at their own
peril. *New York Sun* reporter Julian Ralph, for example, founded *Chatter*, a promising weekly distinguished by yellow paper and big-name contributors such as
Thomas Hardy and Arthur Conan Doyle. But as returns started to pile up in
Ralph's office he made a pact with members of the Ann Street gang, who offered
to sell the returns in Newark and Paterson, New Jersey. "If they goes good, we'll
buy all y' got. Savvy? Y' got ter trust us for the first ones. Cash for all the rest."
Ralph agreed, even though he considered newsboys to be feral creatures. The
gang hawked the *Chatter* on local streets for a penny apiece, which killed the
paper and sent Ralph crawling back to the *Sun*.[26]

The savviest publishers, by contrast, strove to increase their control of
newsboys and enhance their image as benefactors by instituting publicity and
welfare programs. Pulitzer's genius for promotion led him to offer $50 to the man
on his staff who came up with the best idea for launching the *Evening World* in
1887. The winning scheme was to offer Bowery Theatre tickets to every newsboy
who bought twenty copies. "For a block around the World office that afternoon,"
said one admirer, "the streets were full of unwashed Arabs yelling for twenty
copies of the World." Pulitzer and other publishers increasingly tried to steer
newsies away from their usual haunts of cheap theaters, low saloons, nickel pool
halls, and dime museums by exploiting their twin passion for sports and music.[27]

Playing for Keeps

Boxing was king in this post-bare-knuckle era and newspapers were its biggest
promoters. They staged "smokers" in their mailrooms in which fat-gloved
newsboys squared off for the betting pleasure of pressmen and other workers.
Some newspapers erected regulation rings in their alleys and promoted public
exhibitions of newsboy boxers. In September 1892, twelve New Orleans
newsboys known as "Duffy's Kids," after trainer-saloonkeeper John Duffy, took
part in well-publicized bouts at the Academy of Music, despite the objections
of the Society for the Prevention of Cruelty to Children, which claimed that
such events contributed to the upsurge of "ruffianism and hoodlumism" in the
city. New Orleans had recently become the first major city to permit prizefights
staged by athletic clubs. The newsboy bouts opened a three-day carnival of
contusions that climaxed with Gentlemen Jim Corbett's defeat of heavyweight
champion John L. Sullivan. The title fight was refereed by Duffy and reported
blow-by-blow by the national press. "Duffy's Kids" were in the best bad company of their day. Some newsboy pugs turned pro and rose to the top of the
lightweight ranks, among them Tim Callahan of Philadelphia, Benny Yanger of

New York, and "Kid Ashe" (Albert Laurey) of Cincinnati. They were billed not as Irish, Jewish, or Negro fighters but as newsboy fighters.[28]

In addition to boxing, newspapers also promoted youth baseball. Managers had long encouraged pickup games outside their offices or in nearby parks to keep boys busy until their papers were ready. *Detroit Journal* publisher William H. Brearley, past advertising manager of Scripps's *Evening News*, recognized the publicity potential of these contests. In the spring of 1887 he formed the *Detroit Journal* Newsboys' Baseball Club and arranged a five-game series against Cincinnati newsboys for $1,000 in prize money. Detroit won, but Cincinnati demanded a rematch. Brearley next challenged a team of *Chicago Mail* newsboys. He hired a sleeping car to bring them to Detroit, boarded them at the city's best hotel, and gave each of his newsboys a fistful of tickets to sell or keep. Detroit won 14–13. These games proved so popular with readers, advertisers, and spectators that the following spring Brearley issued a blanket challenge for teams to contend for the newsboys' championship of the United States. Eleven other newspapers agreed to field teams: the *Buffalo News, Rochester Post-Express, Syracuse Herald, Albany Press, Boston Globe, New York World, Philadelphia Call, Baltimore Sun, Pittsburgh Leader, Cincinnati Post,* and *Cleveland Plain Dealer.* Thus was born the Newsboys' Base Ball Club (NBBC).[29]

More than just a random good idea, Brearley's league was a response to labor conflict and management collaboration. In January 1888, *Detroit Evening News* hawkers protested the firing of a mailroom boy by refusing to sell the paper until he was reinstated. Brearley gave a staffer, A. G. Crane, the task of recruiting replacements, but the strikers skirmished with the recruits for several hours in front of the office and won their demand. The industry was rife with such conflicts.[30] To address them, Brearley organized the American Newspapers Publishers Association (ANPA). He presided over its founding meeting in February 1887 in Rochester, New York, where forty-six publishers, including Scripps, Lawson, and McRae, agreed to combine to advance their business and advertising interests and repel what they called the "strange and oppressive" demands of labor. All the newspapers fielding teams were charter members of the ANPA except Pulitzer's *World*, which joined later. Ultimately, Pulitzer took up Brearley's challenge with the most gusto, forming teams in Manhattan and Brooklyn. He hired managers, held tryouts, and kept the progress of the squads before the public in a barrage of front-page stories. The *Plain Dealer* installed electric lights so its boys could practice in the evenings.[31]

Over the summer of 1888, the thirteen "redoubtable" NBBC teams barnstormed the country playing each other and teams of reporters, jockeys, soldiers, and collegians. When *Syracuse Herald* newsboys trounced the Syracuse University team 19 to 6, some called it "an argument against college education." Although touted as an "upright" game, newsboy baseball could be rough, with beanballs and thrown bats. Ringers were another problem; by rule, all players had to be under 18 years old and genuine newsboys. Yet ages and occupations were hotly disputed. "The battery of the Syracuse nine were bearded men," complained the Detroit manager while on a four-city tour. Teams played under National League rules in big stadiums such as the Polo Grounds in Manhattan. Newsboys' games in Detroit attracted 12,000 spectators, while those in Chicago drew 20,000. Newsboys watched for free, but others paid 25¢ admission. A quarter of the proceeds went to newsboy charities and a quarter to the league. The other half was split by the players: 75 percent to the winners and 25 percent to the losers.[32]

Further emulating the big leagues, star players appeared in a set of forty-four Newsboys League cards issued by the Hess Tobacco Company in Rochester (Figure 8.3). Photographed in portrait and action poses, the athletes (all white) display serious, manly expressions and appear in uniform with the names of their city or paper emblazoned across their chests. Measuring 1½ by 3 inches, these little cards did big work promoting the league, the newspapers, and the tobacco.[33]

After logging many miles, innings, and protests, the *Detroit Journal* took home the league trophy. The NBBC faded with the summer, but local leagues carried on in New York, Brooklyn, Jersey City, and Washington, DC, while papers from Boston to Honolulu fielded teams for decades to come. Advertisers often provided the uniforms, refreshments, and other swag. The *Cincinnati Post* outfitted its ballplayers in pink uniforms and paid them a dollar a game, but only if they won. Circulation managers liked to pit downtown newsboys against those from the suburbs, or "whites" against "coloreds," as these games generated the most interest and heaviest betting. Reformers denounced them as a spur to racism and a cloak for gambling.[34]

Whether newsboy baseball fostered racial prejudice, deepened company loyalties, or promoted working-class solidarity is debatable. It probably did all these things, as newsboys were forever adapting company perks to their own ends. In the summer of 1892, for example, Pulitzer distributed 2,500 white *Evening World* baseball caps to newsboys throughout the metropolitan area. Some boys recognized their advertising value and took extra papers as urged. But others pinned the crown to the visor in the fashion of lawn-tennis champions, thus hiding the newspaper's name. It was a small subversion, but bigger ones followed. Indeed, when New York and Brooklyn newsboys united to strike the *World* and *Journal* in 1899, they were building on years of contact on the ball field.[35]

The roller-skating and football crazes also presented newspapers with opportunities to generate publicity. Pulitzer's *St. Louis Post-Dispatch* sponsored a newsboy skating tournament in 1885 that offered $10 in gold to winners of a mile

Figure 8.3. Newsboy League Baseball Cards, S. F. Hess & Co. Syracuse, NY, 1888. Berg Collection, Metropolitan Museum of Art, New York.

race and a barrel race. Washington, DC, newsies took advantage of its asphalted streets to tie on skates and race uptown with their papers. "They will all come to the skate before long," the *Star* wrongly predicted. Football was a leather-helmeted college game scandalized by crippling injuries and cash payoffs, but newspapers in Salt Lake City and Colorado Springs sponsored newsboy football squads in the late 1890s.[36]

Newsboys' bands were even more popular than sports teams. The first ones arose in New Orleans in 1887 when hawker Billy Norton, 16, and pressman George Queen, 22, both products of the all-white Catholic newsboys' home, organized a fourteen-member Newsboys' Brass Band that played at banquets, fundraisers, and parades, gaining national attention for its novelty. Individual newsboys such as Emile "Stale Bread" Lacoume, a resident of the home, also sang and played music to attract customers. In 1895 the 10-year-old formed his pals "Monk," "Whiskey," "Warm Gravy," "Cajun," and "Family Haircut" into a string band in which all the instruments were homemade, including a soapbox banjo, half-barrel bass fiddle, and tin tray mandolin (Figure 8.4). Stale Bread's Spasm Band played barefoot on street corners for nickels, improvising the ragtime tunes they heard in bars. The band was noisy, crude, and full of comic antics, especially when headlining at the newsboys' home. "Wise with the wisdom of the streets, axiomatic in gamin lingo, generous to his friends, reckless as the winds that blow his tattered clothes hither and thither, the more one knows of 'Stale Bread,' the more one wants to know," said one critic in 1897. Stale Bread lost his sight three years later, but continued to play the "hot style" that would become jazz. His banjo now rests in the New Orleans Jazz Museum, and the entire band can be seen in the city's wax museum.[37]

Figure 8.4. Founded in New Orleans in 1894, Stale Bread's Newsboys Spasm Band played barefoot on the streets of Storyville with homemade instruments. Shown here are Frank "Monk" Bussey on tambourine, Emile "Stale Bread" Lacoume seated with zither, and Willie "Cajun" Bussey on harmonica. The band also included Emile "Whiskey" Benrod, Harry Gregson, "Warm Gravy," "Sluefoot Pete," and vocalist "Family Haircut." All those pictured display copies of the *New Orleans Telegram*'s racing edition. Photo by Chas T. Yenni, Mar. 1899. Courtesy of Hogan Jazz Archive, Tulane University. Gift of Maurice Ries, Apr. 25, 1979.

Following New Orleans's lead, newsboys' homes and associations in Detroit, Toledo, Cincinnati, and Louisville formed bands in the 1890s, as did several dailies. Like many employers, publishers sponsored bands to enliven community events, boost workplace morale, and generate publicity. McRae's *Cincinnati Post*, Lawson's *Chicago Daily News*, and dailies in St. Louis, Milwaukee, Grand Rapids, and Minneapolis all jumped on the bandwagon, while a Kansas City paper opted to field a newsboy drill team and "pickaninny band." Newspapers bore all expenses; they supplied the instruments, hired the bandleaders (usually a military man known for strict discipline), and secured the uniforms, sometimes in trade with advertisers. Donning the uniform was enough to change newsboys "from so many scattered personalities into an entity," said the *St. Paul Globe*. "The brass buttons are something to live up to." Resplendent in their uniforms and perfect in their harmonies, newsboy bands stood before audiences as living proof that ragged, barefoot urchins could be forged into proud and productive citizens. From a business standpoint, the bands also raised the profile of the newspapers and marked them as institutions committed to improving the welfare of their youth and the future of their communities.[38]

Newsboys' bands rehearsed two or three nights a week; some gave their first concerts just months after forming, even if their members had never before touched an instrument. Ages ranged from 6 to 16 in some bands, 9 to 20 in others. Many newspapers formed junior bands for boys who aspired to make the senior unit, and some, including the *Milwaukee Journal*, established a "cadet band" for members who had passed acceptable newsboy age. The bands played at dances, fairs, parades, ball games, beer gardens, and election night galas. Some embarked on statewide "serenading tours" and a few performed at world's fairs and presidential inaugurations. The Detroit newsboys' band made a splash at the World's Columbian Exposition in Chicago in 1893, and the *Minneapolis Journal* Newsboys' Band (Figure 8.5) got rave reviews at the Pan-American Exposition in Buffalo in 1901. "The discipline has been greatly to their advantage," commented the *Buffalo Enquirer*. "Their bearing and conduct is excellent." The Indianapolis Newsboys Band took first prize for juveniles at the 1904 Louisiana Purchase Exposition in St. Louis.[39]

Newsboys' bands played patriotic songs and newly popular newspaper marches. Marine Corps bandleader John Philip Sousa started the fad in 1889 with "The Washington Post March," commissioned for a student essay contest award ceremony. Soon more than a hundred papers had marches composed in their honor. A distinct subgenre emerged with the "News Boy March" (1904) and the "Newsboy Galop" (1905). The titles indicate just how idealized newsboys were compared to other child laborers: a "Breaker-Boy March" or "Mill Girl Galop" was inconceivable.[40]

Figure 8.5. Resplendent in their scarlet and gold braid coats, the Minneapolis Journal Newsboy Band was a hit at the Buffalo Exposition in 1901. A. D. Roth, photographer, Hennepin County Library, No. R008.

Schooling the Streetwise

Even more than their bands and ball teams, newspaper educational programs offered lasting benefits to newsboys and valuable publicity for publishers. News peddling had long been praised as a "good school for boys," and this sentiment gained currency in the period. Publishers argued that the work taught valuable business skills and work habits. They noted that it encouraged, even demanded, basic numeracy and literacy. Some educators agreed. Chicago superintendent of schools Albert Grannis Lane, who started hawking at age 7 and became a principal at 17, liked to credit the *Chicago Tribune* for his success. "I did not forget to read it myself," he said. "Indeed, I believe I could not even have carried so much political and civic wisdom under my arm without absorbing some of it." Yet few doubted that newsboys also needed formal educations; penologists warned that illiterates were ten times more likely to be incarcerated than those who could read and write, and were responsible for a third of all crime. Thus the many newsboys' schools, classes, reading rooms, and clubs that flourished in the last quarter of the nineteenth century were more than benevolent institutions; they were law and order measures.[41]

Urban missionaries such as Brace in New York, Henry Morgan in Boston, and Dwight Moody in Chicago made the earliest efforts to educate America's newsboys in the 1850s. They founded night, industrial, and Sabbath schools under the aegis of the CAS, Methodist Church, and YMCA, respectively. Municipalities soon joined in. Cincinnati established a public school for more than twenty newsboys in 1862. Boston opened two schools for licensed minors in 1868. Louisville followed suit in 1873 when it introduced a special curriculum for newsboys at public expense. Classes met at the newsboys' home weeknights from 7:00 to 9:00. "The newsboys think what is recommended to them as good English, is singularly thin and lacking in vigor," remarked a visitor. The Wilkes-Barre *Plain Dealer*, one of three Sunday papers in this heavily immigrant Pennsylvania coal town, opened a Sabbath school for newsboys in its sanctum in 1878. In 1880 the Cleveland Board of Education began staffing and equipping the Newsboys' and Bootblack's Home Association night school, as did the St. Louis's school board in 1886.[42]

Opinions differed on the value of these schools. Chicago settlement house founder Jane Addams disparaged them as places where boys came only to "doze in the warmth, or torture the teacher with the gamin tricks acquired by day." But reporter Jacob Riis praised them as "a kind of latch-key to knowledge for belated travelers on the road." Riis visited the evening history class at the Newsboys' Lodging House on Duane Street in New York in 1891 and declared the pupils "surprisingly proficient." A photograph from that evening (Figure 8.6) shows sixteen teenage scholars, most of serious mien. (One clowns for the camera by peeking through his fingers.) Cleveland's efforts to educate newsboys netted good results, according to Julian Ralph. "Truants are so strictly looked after in Cleveland," he wrote in 1895, "that the city's streets seem to me more free from the general American newsboy and *gamin* curse than the streets of any other city I have ever visited."[43]

Newsboy night classes multiplied with the emergence of reading rooms tailored to their needs. Women's clubs founded the first ones in Hartford and New Haven, Connecticut, in 1873. A similar institution opened in Boston on Christmas Day 1879. Located at 35 Bromfield Street, near the newspaper district, it shelved three hundred well-chosen volumes. The reading room drew about twenty boys a night and provided evening classes, including drawing lessons. Good behavior was the only condition of admittance. The institution soon moved to more spacious quarters at 16 Howard Street, next door to the newsboys' burlesque haunts. It offered two billiard tables, gym equipment, baths, board games, and twice as many books. Novelist Louisa May Alcott donated a hundred herself. The *Globe* and *Herald* sent free subscriptions, as did

Figure 8.6. Jacob Riis, "Newsboys' Lodging House (Duane Street) night class in history—called the 'Soup House Gang' by the other boys," 1892. Museum of the City of New York, 90.13.1.176.

Century, Scribner's, St. Nicholas, and *Youth's Companion.* "But we spent enough of the day with paper and print," recalled Isaac Goldberg. "This was, for us, no reading-room, but a billiard parlor." He nevertheless obtained three degrees from Harvard.[44]

Inspired by the success of these experiments, citizens founded newsboys' reading rooms in Washington, DC, Baltimore, Chicago, and elsewhere. Though not initiated or run by newspapers, the rooms received support from them in the form of cash, clothing, dinners and entertainments, and the occasional box of oranges. Like newsboys' lodging houses, the reading rooms gave publishers a reliable source of labor whenever extras were issued or circulation wars flared. However, the Baltimore reading room also hosted a strike meeting in 1896.[45]

Newsboys were notoriously avid readers even before the establishment of reading rooms. Brace reported in 1870 that more than half of his 8,655 lodgers could read and write, and a quarter more could read only. Newsboys were spotted on the street and under lampposts at night reading books and newspapers to themselves or aloud to each other. Journalists praised them as "colporteurs

Color Plate 1. The arrival of the mail coach in rural Pennsylvania is portrayed as a democratic moment in John Lewis Krimmel's *Village Tavern*, 1813–14, oil on canvas, 16 ⅞ × 22 ½ in. Toledo Museum of Art, Toledo, OH. Purchased with funds from the Florence Scott Libbey Bequest in Memory of Her Father, Maurice A. Scott, 1954.13. Photo Credit: Photography Incorporated, Toledo.

Color Plate 2. Foot soldiers in America's market revolution, newsboys traversed a changing world of print and commerce. *No. 7½ Bowery, N.Y.C.,* ca. 1837–39, oil on panel, 20 × 24¾ in. Andrew B. Smith Collection, 1936.799. New-York Historical Society.

Color Plate 3. A humble winter stand made of salvaged material suffices to sell the *Sun* and *Whip* in Old New York. Nicolino Calyo, *The Newspaper Stand* (1840–44), watercolor on paper, 12 × 9½ in. Collection of the New-York Historical Society.

Color Plate 4. Joe, a "fine specimen of the newsboy race." Henry Inman, *The Newsboy,* 1841, oil on canvas, 30 × 25 in. 1955.14, Addison Gallery of American Art, Phillips Academy, Andover, MA.

Color Plate 5. Quibbling curb merchants reflect the tensions between nativists and immigrants in early industrial Pittsburgh. Credit: David Gilmour Blythe, *The News Boys*, ca. 1846–52, oil on canvas mounted on academy board, 29¾ × 25¾ in. Carnegie Museum of Art, Pittsburgh, PA. Gift of Haugh and Keenan Galleries, 1956.

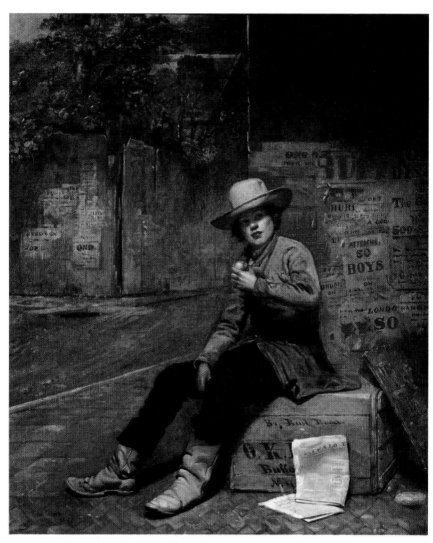

Color Plate 6. Optimism suffuses the westward-looking Buffalo newsboy. Thomas Le Clear's *Buffalo Newsboy*, 1853, oil on canvas, 24 × 20 in. Albright-Knox Art Gallery, Buffalo, NY, Charlotte A. Watson Fund, 1942.

Color Plate 7. Profiting from panic. James Henry Cafferty, *Panic of 1857, Wall Street, Half Past 2 o'Clock, October 13, 1857,* in collaboration with Charles G. Rosenberg, 1858, oil on canvas, 50 × 39½ in. Museum of the City of New York, Gift of the Honorable Irwin Untermyer 40.54.

Color Plate 8. Urchins filled the streets and sketchpads of Young America. John Mackie Falconer, *New York Life: The Newsboy.* Watercolor on paper. 10¼ × 7 in. dated "Jany. 27/ 1860." Albert Stackman Collection, 1944. New-York Historical Society, 1944.364.

Color Plate 9. Moses Small, one of the "monuments" of the city. James Henry Cafferty, *Baltimore News Vendor*, 1860, after a painting by Thomas Waterman Wood. Oil on canvas, 24⅛ × 15⅛ in., New-York Historical Society. The Robert L. Stuart Collection, the gift of his widow Mrs. Mary Stuart.

Color Plate 10. A newsboy leads New York's Seventh Regiment down Broadway en route to its defense of Washington, DC. Thomas Nast, preliminary sketch for *The Departure of the Seventh Regiment for the War, April 19, 1861* (1869), oil on canvas, 54½ × 109 in. Collection of the New-York Historical Society.

Color Plate 11. In a rush to sell their extras, two boys stumble amid the panoramic tumult of a regiment's return. Louis Lang, *Return of the 69th (Irish) Regiment, N.Y.S.M., from the Seat of the War, N.Y.,* 1862–63, oil on canvas, 87 × 140 in. Gift of the artist, 1886.3. Collection of the New-York Historical Society.

Color Plate 12. "I want people a hundred years from now to know how the children I painted looked." J. G. Brown, *"Extra!"* ca 1889, oil on canvas, 30 × 35 in., private collection.

Color Plate 13. African American painter Edward Mitchell Bannister challenged racial stereotypes with his artistry and choice of subjects. *Newspaper Boy,* 1869, oil on canvas. 30⅛ × 25 in. Archive of American Art, Washington, DC, gift of Frederick Weingeroff 1983.95.85.

Color Plate 14. The arrival of the *Daily Evening News* wagon inspired German-born genre painter William Hahn to contrast the child-rearing practices of working- and middle-class New Yorkers. The steeple in the background belongs to All Souls Unitarian Church. To the left is the Everett House Hotel. William Hahn, *Union Square, New York City*, 1878, oil on canvas, 25½ × 40½ in. Hudson River Museum, Yonkers, NY.

Color Plate 15. Undaunted and unmittened, a *Louisville Courier Journal* seller carries on in a blizzard. Aurelius O. Revenaugh, *Newsboy*, ca. 1889, oil on canvas, 43 × 27 in. Collection of The Speed Art Museum, Louisville, Kentucky. Gift of Mrs. Silas Starr, 1939.22.7. Conservation funded by The Courier Journal/Gannett Foundation.

Color Plate 16. Hopeful yet leery, this African American newsgirl stands ready to make a sell in turn-of-the-century New York. J. G. Brown, *Morning Papers*, 1899, oil on canvas. Formerly Copley Newspapers, Inc., The James S. Copley Library, La Jolla, CA.

Color Plate 17. Neat and courteous newsboys enhanced the quality of life in the ideal City Beautiful, just as ragged and pesky children undermined it. Childe Hassam, *The Manhattan Club*, ca. 1891, oil on canvas, 18¼ × 22⅛ in. Santa Barbara Museum of Art, Gift of Mrs. Sterling Morton to the Preston Morton Collection.

The present method of delivery is too quiet — if you want
to succeed, you must make a noise.

Color Plate 18. Modern antinoise crusaders believed newsboys' cries were not just a nuisance but a health hazard. F. Opper, "The 'Hustling' Style of Journalism. What It Will Probably Come to Very Shortly," *Puck* 31 (Apr. 20, 1892): 144. Author's collection.

THE NEWSBOY.

Color Plate 19. The creator of this advertising print would change the name of the paper to match that of his various clients. Karl Witkowski, *The Newsboy*, 1897. 10½ × 13 in. Eckel Collection, Princeton University Library.

Color Plate 20. The ups and downs of newspaper peddling could also be experienced vicariously in board games. The News Boy Game, Parker Brothers, ca. 1895. Cardboard, paper, wood, metal, ⅞ × 7½ × 7½. Collection of the New-York Historical Society.

Color Plate 21. Tobacco companies found newsboys to be ready consumers and appealing promoters of their products. Newsboy Cigars, manufactured by Brown Brothers, Detroit. Calvert Lithograph Co., 1894. Library of Congress, Washington, DC.

Color Plate 22. Originating in the *New York World* and syndicated nationally in 1905–6, George McManus's comic strip was dedicated to whimsy, not reform. *Nibsy the Newsboy in Funny Fairyland*, in *San Francisco Bulletin*, 1906. Author's collection.

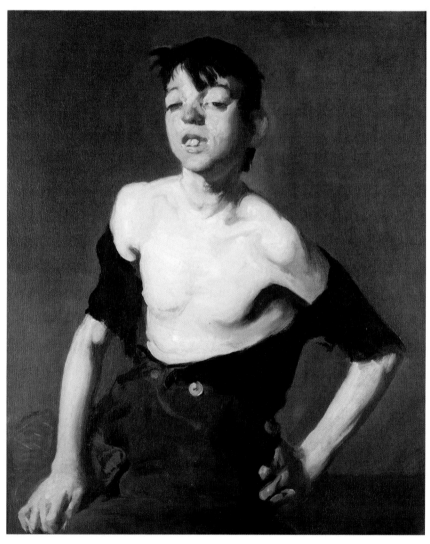

Color Plate 23. An ashcan artist's study of pugnacity. George Wesley Bellows, *Paddy Flannigan*, 1908, oil on canvas, 30 ¼ × 25 in. (76.8 × 63.5 cm). Erving and Joyce Wolf.

Color Plate 24. "A type that reflects our problems." Robert Henri, *Portrait of Willie Gee*, 1904, oil on canvas, 31¼ × 26¼ in. Collection of The Newark Museum, Anonymous Gift, 1925, 25.111, reproduced in *Harper's Weekly* 58, no. 2983 (Feb. 21, 1914): 2.

Color Plate 25. World War I ratcheted up the patriotic utility of America's newsboys. Emmett Olafson, *Join the American Red Cross*, color lithograph, 74 × 50 cm, Washington, DC, Potomac Litho. Mfg. Co., ca. 1917. Library of Congress, Washington, DC.

SCOTTY AND HIS BELOVED SHO-SHO GUN: From a Painting by Gayle Porter Hoskins

Color Plate 26. More than a few underage newsies answered the call to arms. "Scotty and His Beloved Sho-Sho Gun," from a painting by Gayle Porter Hoskins. *The Ladies' Home Journal* 3 (Jun. 1919): 22. Delaware Art Museum.

Impossible interviews—no. 16

Walter Lippmann vs. Walter Winchell

WINCHELL: Of all things, Lippy, you and me ankling together down the Main Stem. ... Is my face red? ... As Techs Guinan would hand it to me, "It's a small world, but there's still pah-lenty of suckers to go around." LIPPMANN: The world, Mr. Winchell, is in a position where only confidence in the ability of its leaders and the conviction that a comprehensive program for recovery is to be resolutely pursued can avert international catastrophe—WINCHELL: That's the trouble with you, Lippy, you take the world too serious. As one Park Rowgue to another, you and the cosmos ought to have the handcuffs melted ... or get things Reno-vated. ... LIPPMANN: When the country is bewildered by conflicting testimony and contradictory voices concerning the present economic order, it is not Utopian to hold that it is the mission of every public-spirited citizen to view the cosmos as a whole and achieve the international outlook, even in a daily newspaper column. WINCHELL: But can't you jazz up your colm just a little, old kid? ... F'r instance: As pah-lenty of the cinemoguls from Rawleywood tell us, China and Japan have pfff-f-ft. ... A scallion to France for rendering on her Blessed Expense. ... Now Franklin D. ("Old Potato") Roosevelt and Congress are posting. ... What stout ex-President with a large celluloid collar is That Way about 1936? ... Recommended to diversion seekers: The Congressional Record, "Hooey" Long, and Ogden Mills Budget figures. LIPPMANN: The execrable prose-style which you suggest, Mr. Winchell, is not suited to the international character of my daily opinions. When I write, I feel that posterity is just around the corner. WINCHELL: After all, Lipp, maybe we're just a couple of Walters under the skin. You see the world through a telescope, and I see it through a keyhole—but it's the same world after all. O.K., Walter? LIPPMANN: O-ha-a-ay ... Walter!

Color Plate 27. Respected pundits and notorious gossip columnists both relied on street sales in the Tabloid Twenties. "Of all things, Lippy, you and me ankling together down the Main Stem." Miguel Covarrubias, *Impossible Interviews—No. 16, Walter Lippmann vs. Walter Winchell. Vanity Fair*, April 1933, 33. Courtesy Estate of Miguel Covarrubias.

Color Plate 28. West Coast fruit growers and shippers prospered in the 1920s by introducing newsboy-themed brands and labels to a national market. Author's collection.

Color Plate 29. Proletarian newsboy heroes abounded in the popular culture of the 1930s. Here Jackie Cooper stars as "Rifle" Edwards in Universal Studio's *Newsboys' Home*, 1938. Everett Collection, Inc.

Color Plate 30. New Deal murals portrayed newsboys' labor as integral to their industry. Detail, Suzanne Scheuer and Hebe Daum, *Newsgathering*, Coit Tower, San Francisco. Public Works of Art Project, 1934. By Diderot, Creative Commons.

Color Plate 31. Members of DC Comics' crimefighting Newsboy Legion are stunned by news of their own gangland murder. Nov. 1946. Author's collection.

Color Plate 32. " 'Hot' off the wires . . ." Pinup artist Earl Moran drafted this newsgirl into patriotic service in 1941. She adorned electrical supply company calendars and ink blotters throughout the war. "Special Extra," mutoscope card, 5 × 7 in. Author's collection.

Color Plate 33. First day cover, U.S. stamp commemorating National Newspaperboy Day, October 4, 1952.

of intelligence—humble ministers at the shrine of knowledge," and told of instances in which they expounded on the classics, corrected the grammar of their betters, or refused to sell a paper until they had read it. The newsboys and girls in these anecdotes functioned as democratic figures who challenged presumptions about the low intelligence of people in low occupations. British scholar Matthew Arnold contributed to his effort in 1883 when he saw a barefoot newsboy reading the *Life of Washington* undisturbed in one of the finest chairs in the Boston Public Library. "You would never see such a sight as that in Europe," he said.[46]

There was a wide range of literacy among newsboys. The most literate tended to acquire nicknames inspired by their favorite authors. Such was the case with "All Carlisle" in 1890s New Orleans. While this kind of razzing was acceptable, it was unwise to tease an abecedarian as it would likely lead to a fight and ostracism of the teaser. A New York newsboy explained in 1884 that most of his peers preferred cheap story papers and five-cent novels. "They buy 'em and they read 'em in the day," said the 12-year-old. "Some of the stories are funny, about niggers and Irishmen getting into scrapes; some stories are about Injuns, some about murders, and a good many of 'em are about detectives. I like the detective stories the best, and I guess the rest of 'em does too. I can't read very good—a good many of the words in the paper I can't call right, and I don't know what they mean, but I skip along and I allus know what the story is about."[47]

While most newsboys could read the papers they sold, they didn't read them like other people. "No man of business scans the morning daily more thoughtfully, seated at his luxurious breakfast table," said the *New York Tribune*, "than these would-be merchants." Newsboys looked first for the best story to cry, sometimes ignoring the ones that circulation managers posted on chalkboards. Experienced hawkers knew that a buried item about a two-headed calf might generate more sales than the lead story on a Senate vote. Yet there was other valuable information to be gleaned as well; the arrival of a canal boat or a fruit schooner suggested opportunities to scrub a deck or gather oranges, and notice of an uptown fire boded well for a job clearing debris. If read correctly, the entire issue was a want ad.[48]

The most voracious reader in the trade was John King, secretary of Cincinnati's Newsboys' Union (Figure 8.7). A disabled adult who had vended papers since his teen years, King built up the union's library. In 1879 he donated 2,500 volumes from his own collection to the public library, including works of history, philosophy, science, and literature. His only condition was that his marginalia be erased before the books went into circulation. We will never know what these penciled jottings might have revealed about King's intellect, but their existence shows that he was not just a collector but a reader.[49]

HARPER'S WEEKLY.

JOHN KING, THE CINCINNATI NEWSBOY.—Photographed by Landy.

Figure 8.7. He amassed a library of more than 2,500 books. "John King, The Cincinnati Newsboy—Photographed by Landy," *Harper's Weekly* 23, no. 1180 (Aug. 9, 1879): 632. Author's collection.

The literary tastes of newsboys and their benefactors can also be ascertained from the acquisition policies and circulation records of their libraries and reading rooms. In 1894, the youth-run Cleveland newsboys' union resolved to build a library in which "novels and works of fiction shall have no place." Adult-run newsboys' reading rooms also endeavored to shelve only edifying works, but they allowed novels to avoid protests. The authors and titles most popular with Grand Rapids newsboys in 1897 were Thomas Bailey Aldrich's *The Story of a Bad Boy*, Thomas Bullfinch's *Mythology*, James Fenimore Cooper's Leatherstocking Tales series, and the works of Charles Dickens, George Eliot, and Benjamin Franklin. Newsies also patronized public libraries and lyceums. "In that way I've picked up a good deal," explained 13-year-old James Murphy of Rochester. "Murph the Newsboy" told a reporter that he had read almost all of Dickens, Dumas's *Three Guardsmen* and *Twenty Years After*, Hugo's *Les Misérables*, and the novels of Charles Anderson Read. He said American literature wasn't high on his list, and he offered an astute critique of Mark Twain: "He tries to be funny but makes it all a tragedy." Shakespeare was too heavy for him, he admitted, but vowed to tackle Charles Lamb's work on him and then try Thackeray's *Vanity*

Fair. Murphy had but one year of school before quitting at age 8 to support his family. He said he aspired to be a great man but wanted to do it on his own, without school. Twelve-year-old Chicago newsboy Charles Winter Wood gladly accepted help in 1882 when one of his customers, an elocution teacher, heard him reciting soliloquies from *Hamlet, Othello,* and the other Shakespearean dramas imbibed at local theaters. The teacher helped Wood, an African American, finish school, attend Beloit College, and become an elocutionist himself.[50]

Among those who stepped forward to assist boys like Murphy and Wood were Frances Willard and members of the Woman's Christian Temperance Union (WCTU). They saw newsboys as sons of struggling mothers and drunkard fathers. Founded in the depression winter of 1874, the WCTU adopted the motto "Do Everything" and addressed a broad range of issues, including child labor. It did not try to stamp out news peddling, but rather encouraged the boys to be virtuous, continue their educations, and rise above their circumstances. Beginning in the 1880s, WCTU chapters in St. Louis, Cleveland, Kansas City, Baltimore, Denver, and Leadville, Colorado, sponsored newsboys' reading rooms, night schools, Sunday schools, and homes. Members in Minneapolis and St. Paul founded newsboy and bootblack clubs so highly regarded that when the state required a $2 newsboy license fee in 1888 it allocated all the revenue to the WCTU as a nucleus for a newsboys' home. The organization ran its own home in Indianapolis and carried on other "newsboy work" in Chicago, Brooklyn, Milwaukee, and Louisville; Camden, New Jersey; Canton, Ohio; and the noxious mining town of Butte, Montana, where it also campaigned for playgrounds. Delegations of flower-bearing newsboys appeared at several WCTU conventions to show their thanks. In 1888 they peddled two hundred thousand New Testaments outside the meeting in New York. "The Gospel's good news of brotherhood was for the first time in history cried by newsboys upon city streets," exclaimed Willard.[51]

Also devoted to serving the moral and intellectual needs of newsboys was Col. Alexander Hogeland, a Civil War veteran with the 7th Tennessee Volunteers (Figure 8.8). Hogeland settled in Kentucky after the war and became superintendent of news carriers for the *Louisville Commercial.* In 1873 he joined the *Courier-Journal's* editor in founding the Newsboys' Home and Night School. Hogeland later published a memoir, *Ten Years Among the Newsboys of Louisville,* which he peddled throughout the country. Easily recognized by his derby hat and brush mustache, Hogeland would spend weeks in a city investigating newsboy conditions and addressing civic groups on how to rescue the boys. He advocated curfew laws that would bar children under 15 from public places after 9:00 p.m., as signaled by fire bells or factory whistles. His first success came in Omaha, Nebraska, in 1880. He claimed that more than three thousand cities and towns, mostly in the Midwest, had instituted curfews by the turn of the century.[52]

Figure 8.8. "A Group of Louisville Newsboys and Their Friend." Frontispiece of Col.
Alexander Hogeland, *Ten Years Among the Newsboys* (Louisville: John F. Morton,
1884), 4.

Hogeland was a master of publicity. On the death of Ulysses Grant in July
1885, he led several hundred Chicago newsboys on a march to city hall, where
they presented the police chief with a resolution of sympathy for the Grant
family. He once addressed President Benjamin Harrison, and ended some
talks by asking homeless newsboys to give testimony and placing them with
families that promised to raise them as farmers or tradesmen. Anticipating the
magic lantern lectures of Jacob Riis, Hogeland displayed canvasses illustrating
the hardships of itinerant newsboys. Louisville artist Aurelius O. Revenaugh,
a Union army veteran whose studio was in the *Courier-Journal* building, probably painted the pictures; his portrait of an unmittened youth stoically selling
Courier-Journals in the snow circulated widely as a print (Plate 15).[53]

To further promote newsboys' health, welfare, and education, several cities
passed ordinances in the mid-1880s that required peddlers to obtain permits

and wear badges. These laws regulated the hours, ages, number, and behavior of children in the street trades. Most required parental consent and proof of school attendance, and forbid working at night or during school hours. Although enforcement was lax, licenses could be revoked for truancy, gambling, cheating, cruelty, or drunkenness. Such laws implicitly recognized newsboys as "industrial beings" whose rights demanded protection, noted Cornell undergraduate Florence Kelley in her 1882 senior thesis.[54] Newsboys were divided on the subject. St. Louis "gamins" objected to licensing in March 1884, but young street merchants in Chicago accepted regulation as a way to protect their turf. In April 1884 newsboys and bootblacks in Chicago marched in a torchlight parade and held a mass meeting at the Newsboys' Home in support of a proposed license law. It required that they pay a dollar every year for their badges, which most felt would keep out the "pikers." Their placards read "Protect the boys," "No distinction of color, race, or nationality," and "Hurrah for the license." Arthur Johnson, the first speaker, asserted that they were not vagabonds or urchins, as one paper called them, and proposed that they unionize. Others suggested they assess themselves a dime a week from their "cigaret money" for a mutual protection fund and keep small boys out of the trade.[55] Newsboys in Minneapolis likewise endorsed a badge and license ordinance in April 1885 "'cos there's a lot o' bums comes up here from Chicago and knocks us out on our trade." The Knights of Labor said the $2 fee represented an unfair tax on labor that reduced the newsboys' ranks by a hundred, or 40 percent: "They can't sell papers without a license; and they can't pay for a license without first selling papers."[56]

Adult newsdealers welcomed licensing schemes as a way to reduce competition from children. "When the cry of 'Extra' sounds in front of my door at night," said one Brooklyn shopkeeper in 1890, "that ends the sale of my Brooklyn papers." The Protective and Benevolent Association to which he belonged couched its concern in the welfare of the boys: "Is there a more sickening and degrading sight than children of the age of 9, 10 and 11 years, peddling papers in the streets?" asked the president. "They can be seen at the ferries, the bridge, and in all public places, practically serving their apprenticeship in crime. And how can it be otherwise, when they are allowed to roam the streets at all hours of the day and night, constantly commingling with the vile characters, listening to the grossest obscenity, witnesses of examples on all sides of the greatest depravity? What can the future of such children be?"[57]

In response to such criticism newspapers began organizing newsboys clubs to inculcate good habits in the boys, improve their prospects, and deflect charges of exploitation. The clubs often started out modestly but grew to rival those sponsored by churches and charities. The *Minneapolis Journal*, for example, founded a club in 1882 and publicized its existence with a photograph showing twenty ragtag boys and two dogs lined up in front of a woodpile (Figure 8.9). The

Figure 8.9. Hats, but not shoes, were de rigueur for members of the *Minneapolis Journal's* first newsboy club in 1882. Dogs were welcomed too. Minnesota Historical Society. HC1.17r3.

club apparently disbanded, allowing St. Mark's Episcopal Church to start a more ambitious newsboys club in 1892. It attracted thirty boys a night to its basement reading room, debating society, music classes, carpentry shop, gymnasium, and baths. But in 1898 the *Journal* outfitted meeting rooms on its third floor and reasserted control of the unoccupied time of its newsboys. Newspapers in many cities offered similar programs to stay ahead of the competition presented by other papers and an independent Boys' Club movement.[58]

River City Magic

No newspaper demonstrated a greater commitment to newsboy welfare than the *Grand Rapids Evening Press*, first under the direction of owner George G. Booth and later his brother Edmund, who joined the paper after heading the YMCA in New York. "Boy work," as it came to be known, was integral to their business plan, but it was circulation building more than character building that first spurred them into philanthropic action.

The *Press* was one of six dailies in town in 1892 when George Booth acquired it with the help of his father-in-law, James Scripps. Within the year Booth bought up and killed one of the competing papers and moved into the evening field, which entailed attracting more newsboys with footraces, sleigh rides, and strawberry-picking parties. A thriving furniture-making center, Grand Rapids was the second-biggest city in the state, with a population of 60,000; its population reached almost twice that number by 1910 due to an influx of immigrants. Newsboys sold about 30 percent of the *Evening Press*'s 12,000-plus daily circulation, and they were integral to its success. Embroiled in a circulation war with the *Grand Rapids Eagle* in the spring of 1894 and threatened by the formation of an independent Newsboys' Association, the *Evening Press* girded for battle. "It is very evident that we have got a fight before us that will challenge our strictest attention," wrote circulation manager Willis H. Turner to Booth in March. "I have no fears as to the outcome but at the same time it is not safe to underestimate the strength of our enemy."[59]

The "enemy" was A. G. Crane, who had managed the Detroit *Evening News*' newsboy baseball club in 1888 and organized a newsboy association that would reach eight hundred members, black and white. He established similar associations in Cleveland, Cincinnati, Columbus, and St. Louis. These were mutual aid societies that provided sick pay and funeral benefits, but in February 1893 a price hike by Scripps's *Evening News* (still under Booth's management) led association members in Detroit to mount a two-day strike in which fifteen newsboys were arrested for acts of violence. Crane was accused of engineering the revolt and dismissed by the association's board of directors. Unrepentant, he moved to Grand Rapids and began to organize newsboys there. Turner corresponded with Booth during the crisis and in one letter asked him if he should try to run Crane out of town or buy him off. A week later he reassured Booth of victory, and, in a juvenile touch, drew a skull and crossbones to convey his fighting spirit. Turner was up to the challenge. Two months later he reported to Booth: "Everything is OK now. Crane killed Newsboy's Asso last Eve. We get all the boys *and the band.* Think of it a band of 50 pieces in our hands! Ye Gads!" Crane, in turn, accepted a cash payoff and a full-time job as superintendent of newsboys at the *Detroit Evening News.* He administered the paper's Newsboys' Aid Fund, which covered more than a thousand boys, and oversaw an elaborate music program featuring band, choir, jubilee singers, and bugle corp.[60]

Back in Grand Rapids, the *Evening Press* made the newsboys' band the centerpiece of its welfare work. Led by Professor Frank Wurzburg and a "sprightly little drum major," they marched in parades and gave concerts throughout the state. "It is something remarkable that, in so short a time three dozen untutored newsboys could be made to play so well," remarked John Philip Sousa. "As a rule I abhor juvenile bands, but these little chaps delight me."[61]

Booth discontinued the Sunday edition and introduced Sunday afternoon Happy Hours for boys as young as 6. They met in an 800-seat auditorium called Newsboys' Hall. Patterned after the Pleasant Sunday Afternoon movement in England, meetings began with a prayer and included music, singing, readings, guest speakers, and discussions. Discipline was not a problem, as troublemakers were promptly ejected. Patriotic songs and flag ceremonies abounded, for Booth believed that citizenship training was the best remedy for juvenile delinquency.[62]

Other programs soon followed. The *Evening Press* set up its own aid fund and job placement service. To comply with a new compulsory education law in 1895, Booth took the unprecedented step of opening a school next to the counting room (Figure 8.10). It enrolled forty-five students who took either morning or evening classes, which enabled them to sell all three editions. The scholars sat in two paired rows of bolted-down desks in a long, high-windowed room lined with chalkboards, coat pegs, and portraits depicting George Washington and other worthies. A modest library of a hundred volumes filled the shelves behind the teacher's elevated desk. The newspaper also built a playground, complete with a ten-foot-high hoop for the newly invented game of basketball, and served hot meals in its basement café to spare all newsboys the trouble of going home for supper. "The objects of the school are worthy and its ambitions high," announced the *Evening Press*. "The little fellows whose few cents a day count for so much in the aggregate, are forced to attend school under pain of the law. It is for the benefit of those that the Evening Press Newsboys' school was established." The school was ungraded and covered a first- through eighth-grade curriculum of reading, writing, geography, manual arts, and cooking. "To be sure there is a drone or two among them," remarked the teacher, Clark L. Brown, "but on average they are by far the brightest crowd of boys whose education I have

Figure 8.10. "Evening Press Newsboy School," *The Newsboy Year, 1898, Grand Rapids Evening Press,* 1899. Grand Rapids Public Museum. Accession No. 155801.

ever undertaken to accomplish." Discipline was maintained by seating mischievous boys far from the door so they were the last to receive their noon papers.[63]

In December 1897 the *Evening Press* added a school of dancing and deportment to prepare boys for the social realm as well as the business world. Shy at first, they and their sisters soon mastered the basic steps and rules of etiquette, which they displayed at annual fancy dress balls. In 1898, the newspaper acquired a houseboat, *The Newsboys' Rest*, to take boys on cruises and swimming parties up the Grand River. A picture of the craft graced the newspaper's letterhead. Correspondence between the Booths and their managers indicates that they took genuine pride in their newsboy welfare schemes—the concerts, races, outings, and "man-to-man talks" with the boys. They welcomed the compliments received from parents, and basked in the "glory" bestowed on their enterprise. "Charity is a magic word," said Turner.[64]

Yet management insisted that the programs be coordinated by *Evening Press* employees rather than volunteers "to accomplish definite business ends." Their costs totaled $3,200 in 1899 (around $37,000 in today's money), and less than $2,000 in later years, some of which was recouped from income generated by the band. The expense exceeded that of ink, and accounted for less than 2 percent of the paper's operating budget, which was typical of corporate welfare schemes. The newspaper likened the expense to that of a manufacturer who lays aside a fixed sum annually for the repair of machinery. "Whether all this pays the *Evening Press* in a financial way is something that has not been, and cannot be, computed," said an editorial. "The owners feel that in the highest and best sense it does pay."[65]

One celebrated example of the value of Grand Rapids newsboys occurred on July 2, 1900, when Burt Botsford noticed a leak in the city's largest reservoir while carrying his 5:00 a.m. route. Sensing the threat to the hundred factory cottages below, the "newsboy Paul Revere" ran from house to house arousing residents and aiding their escape minutes before the deluge wrecked their homes, resulting in one death rather than many. The *Evening Press* Newsboy Association rewarded Botsford with a summer job at the US Census Bureau in Washington.[66]

The paper's pragmatic paternalism took its most tangible form in 1905 when the Booths built a four-story Doric-columned building designed by Detroit's fast-rising industrial architect Albert Kahn. This purpose-built "temple of enterprise" housed the *Evening Press*'s editorial offices, printing plant, and allied activities, including the newsboy school, club, and band rooms, and a 100-by-60-foot auditorium occupying most of the third and fourth floors. The newsboys' lobby faced the pressroom, which was accessible via doors and windows thrown open at press time. "When we have an extra," said the manager, "I just press a button and the teacher empties the school; so we can put an extra on considerably ahead of our competitors." Down in the basement were the lunch counter, manual training workshop, and the largest swimming pool in the state, complete with showers and locker rooms. Instead of using towels, the boys dried off by running through an eighty-foot long blow-drying hall.[67]

The *Evening Press*'s newsboys' school "kept on par" with the city's public schools, and had a lower dropout rate. It was also cheaper for the students because it they did not have to buy paper, pencils, or other supplies. Jacob Riis paid an approving visit in 1908. Several prominent publishers came to study the school with the idea of replicating it, but none followed through. The school operated well into the 1920s, accepting both white and black students.[68]

Newsboys' schools represent a rare exception to the main objective of public education in industrial America, which was to simultaneously prepare and withhold working-class youth from the labor market. School officials in Boston, Louisville, Cleveland, and Grand Rapids knowingly granted children's labor to newspapers to combat poverty and truancy. It wasn't a perfect solution, but for a time it served the interests of both the industry and its children.

Politics of the Pave

Historically, the main reasons for supporting public schools and protecting press freedom were political, knowledge being necessary to good government. Whether in or out of the classroom, children who came of age during this period of astonishing political violence and corruption could hardly avoid developing lifelong attitudes and opinions about public affairs. But where exactly did Gilded Age newsboys stand on the major issues of their day? Their mailroom discussions and curbstone debates rarely found their way into print, so it is hard to know. But their voices can be heard in letters to the editor and other sources. In July 1876, for example, a newsboy wrote to the editor of the *Daily National Republican* in Washington, saying, "Why don't you buy a Winchester rifle and shoot a few Democrats!"[69]

Though prone to bellicosity, the keenest newsboys held more sophisticated views stemming from a realization that their incomes depended not just on the quality of the news or the force of their own exertions but also on federal policies. Patrick O'Toole, a homeless hawker on New York's Printing House Square, showed his grasp of current affairs in February 1878 when a *New York Times* reporter posed the age-old question: "How's business?" "It's werry good, werry good indeed," he said. "You mightn't think it, but I sell more papers now than I ever sold in my life. You see, with those old fellers getting married to young wives and then hiding away, and the Turkeys fighting over in Africa, and Congress meeting, and the Exercise Commissioners running away, and the preachers all talking about hell, everybody's bound to have his paper."[70]

Despite the upturn, O'Toole averaged only a dollar a day and slept on steam grates most nights. Yet he opposed the populist-backed Bland-Allison Act authorizing the free and unlimited coinage of silver. "We're afraid of them Westerners," he explained. "They keep us in a flutter. If Congress can make a silver dollar worth only 92 cents, why wot's to stop 'em from makin' one that's worth only 60 cents! That's wot bothers us. You see, most all our money comes in in silver, and we have to take it at par. If a man buys a Times of us for 4 cents, and hands us a 5 cent piece, we can't pocket the whole and say, 'That's all right, silver's gone down.' He wouldn't stand it. 'Spose we sell a dollar's worth in a day, and we have to work hard to do it, too, why then we only have 92 cents. A good soft bed in the lodging-house only costs 6 cents. So Congress beats us out of a bed and two doughnuts every day."[71]

Asked if his customers had changed to cheaper papers during the depression, O'Toole became indignant: "Changed! I guess not. My customers are all solid men. I know nearly every one of 'em. If I was to offer one of 'em a cheap paper, he wouldn't have nothing more to do with me. . . . My customers all goes out to dine—none of your sandwich and glass of beer kind—and four of 'em comes down town every morning in their carriages." O'Toole clearly felt that the status of his clientele reflected his status as a merchant. Their politics—and those of the Republican *New York Times*—were his politics.[72]

A greater diversity of newsboy opinion can be heard in a carriers' address issued by the *Salem Gazette* in 1882. Most addresses reflect the views of adult editors, but this one documents a meeting of six Massachusetts carrier boys trying to decide the content of the annual message. They discussed temperance, women's rights, the "Irish question," jobs, politics, and the environment (i.e., their polluted swimming hole). There was much disagreement. On temperance, "one wanted prohibition, one license, and one 'free rum.'"[73] The boys agreed that each would make a minute-long speech on any subject, and their statements would constitute the year's address.

"We boys think we ought to have a better chance," said the first speaker. "We don't think a boy ought to have to go away from Salem to learn a trade or earn a living." The next boy said he didn't believe in running down the place you live in, and called Salem "a good healthy place" and the most enterprising city in the state. "Oh! oh!" Where's the Public Library? Free Baths?" interrupted the others. The third boy suggested licensing liquor and quoted his father as saying that "politics makes all the trouble." He said the city ought to look out for the boys. "There's plenty of rich people who could give everybody good wages if they wanted to, and the city government ought to make 'em. If they don't want us to drink and loaf round they ought to do something about it."[74]

The fourth carrier called for a public library or reading room, saying he knew a lot of fellows who went to rum shops just to get out of the cold. But he added,

"I don't ask any favors beyond a good start and a fair chance. . . . I wish what was said about politics could be left out of the Address. I don't want people to think we are such confounded fools. ['Order, order.'] Well, I've said it and I'll stick to it. I should like to know what would become of this country if it wasn't for politics. We boys have to go take hold of this thing and make politics mean something. ['Oh, ain't you green?'] Well I should like to find a greener looking boy than Garfield was when he was sixteen years old."[75]

The fifth speaker liked the idea of mentioning the slain president and onetime newsboy James A. Garfield in the address. He said he cried when his funeral train passed through Salem. (Newsboys elsewhere draped their arms in mourning.) "I think every poor boy in the country feels more sure that a poor boy can have a chance if he wants one, since knowing about him." The final speaker summed up: "We want good air to work in and to sleep in. We've got good water to drink; now we want clean water to swim in. We want less rum and more books; we want fewer rum-holes and a Public Library. We want the men who have got money to do business right here in Salem so that we boys won't have to go to Springfield or Worcester to learn a trade." Such were the sentiments of Salem's carriers circa 1882.[76]

Future New York governor Al Smith traced his political awakenings and associations to his own newsboy days. Born in the melting pot of the Lower East Side, Smith quit school in 1886 at age 13 after his father died, and started delivering papers in the Fourth Ward. He handled a variety of dailies, including the *New York Leader*, a small campaign paper that supported single-tax theorist Henry George for mayor. George narrowly lost the election and Smith went on to align himself with Tammany Hall Democrats by attending their chowders and shoe-giveaways, and running errands for their chiefs or "sachems." Smith became an effective and incorruptible office holder at a time when slum-bred machine politicians were being maligned by middle-class reformers for their crass "I seen my opportunities and I took 'em" morality.[77]

In an era when presidential candidates did not campaign on their own behalf, some newsboys parlayed their skills into careers as stump speakers. Most notable were Joseph Murray and "Fighting Joe" Merrick of New York and Sam Hillier of Toledo. Republican strategists sought their support not so much to gain votes, since most newsies were minors, but to demonstrate their standard-bearer's popularity among the working class. Known throughout the state as "the Depew of the Newsboys," Murray styled himself after the silver-tongued senator Chauncey Depew and formed a newsboys' Republican Club of two hundred members, ages 5 to 20. The 18-year-old Merrick chaired a raucous meeting of about ninety newsboys and bootblacks in New York's Pearl Hall in September 1892 in which he told them, "Down with free trade and foreign labor." Hecklers shouted, "Wot did yer get fer dat?" and "Send us in an ice cream."[78]

Hillier emerged as the most mellifluous "newsboy orator" earlier that year when the Grand Old Party recruited him to work the hustings for several candidates, including President Benjamin Harrison. Hillier also took the stage in Pearl Hall, which was decorated with pictures of Harrison and his running mate, *New York Tribune* editor Whitelaw Reid, under a sign reading: "These Are Our Candidates. And We Are the Hustlers." A "long, gawky, yellow haired youth, with a wheedling voice," Hillier proceeded to put the tariff issue into terms the boys—and newspaper readers—could easily grasp. "In England," he said, "where they have free trade, the bootblacks only get half a cent a shine, while in our country, where we have protection, the kids get a nickel and sometimes a dime for a shine. . . . Here some of the kids who used to snipe and hustle papers now own a 'brownstone' on Fifth Avenue. Would they have done this in a free trade country and where everybody is poor but a few dukes and lords? No."[79]

Hillier urged the older boys to vote for Harrison and asked the younger ones to persuade their fathers and friends to do so. The assembly then passed a "Newsboys and Bootblacks' Supplement to the Platform of the Republican Party": "*Resolved.* That we indorse and support every word and sentence in the bully, daisy, and dead-right platform of the Republican Party, and kind of feel sorry that it ain't a little stronger; but still, as we can afford to be charitable, we'll give the 'Demmies' a little show, so that they won't have to go too far down the salty and Farmers' Alliance river, just for old acquaintance sake." Before adjourning, the meeting agreed to hold a "monster parade" in October and extend invitations to "Toledo Abe," champion newsboy of the United States; "Whistling Jack," president of the Buffalo Newsboys; "Chicago Eddy"; and "Missouri Pacific," the champion newsboy of the West. The final resolution of the night, passed unanimously in a ringing voice vote, stated: "*Resolved.* That who ain't with us is against us, and whoever is against us in the coming campaign might just as well consider himself newsboycotted and bootblacklisted."[80]

Murray, Merrick, and Hillier certainly contributed to the theater of the campaign, as intended by party chairman Thomas Henry Carter of Montana. He enlisted their aid to help Republicans beat back the Populist insurgency in the South and West and drum up urban working-class support for their pro-business incumbent. Their efforts fell short as Harrison lost the rematch to ex-newsboy Grover Cleveland by 365,000 votes, or 3 percentage points. Yet the strategy paid off in the 1894 midterm elections, when workingmen shifted en masse to the Republican camp, giving the GOP a record 117-seat gain in the House of Representatives. The newsboys' message finally got through.[81]

While these accounts attest to the active political lives of just a handful of Gilded Age newsboys, they were not alone. Newsies everywhere appreciated the material aid provided by party-backed charities, the increased sales generated by campaign hoopla and high voter turnout, and the excitement of election-night bacchanals. Mostly it was good fun, but not in the case of Patrick Eugene Prendergast. The 26-year-old Irish-born news carrier fatally shot Chicago mayor Carter Harrison, publisher of the *Chicago Times*, in October 1893 after not receiving a patronage job. So incredible was the news that the line of hawkers at the *Tribune* the next morning curled and twisted about the counting room, wiggled out the door, and squirmed down Dearborn Street past the Saratoga Hotel and beyond Monroe Street to the Adams Express Building. Prendergast's trial broke new ground in the use of insanity pleas and expert witnesses, including two news alley beat cops who attested to Prendergast's "unlovely traits." "Attorney for the damned" Clarence Darrow defended the accused and made a memorable appeal to the jury for his life, but even he could not save the "mad newsboy" from the gallows.[82]

Upheavals Great and Small

For all their generosity toward newsboys, publishers clearly did not win their undivided loyalty. Newsboy activism surged during this period of economic revival and labor protest. In 1883, as we saw, newsboys mobilized against the *Denver Times* over a price hike and boycotted the paper in 1884 in support of striking pressmen. In July 1883, thirty-five Milwaukee boys refused to sell the *Evening Wisconsin* after it reduced its retail price. One lad who tried to cash in on the lack of competition received "quite a shaking up" from the other boys. Only then did he agree to "stand out with the 'Brotherhood.'" The newspaper had strike leader Ed Howe arrested, but he was released after fellow strikers followed him "in bulk" to the police station and paid his bail.[83]

In August newsboys in Washington, DC, targeted the Sunday papers, objecting to a new quarter-cent surcharge if they bought their papers Sunday morning instead of Saturday night. "An attempt was made at the *Herald* and *Capital* offices to prevent non-strikers buying checks," reported the *Washington Post*, "but the police put a stop to the foolishness."[84]

Then in October hundreds of newsboys joined the newsdealers' boycott against the *New York Herald*, which had cut its retail price from 3¢ to 2¢, reducing their profit margin from a penny per copy to ⅓ of a penny. The boys marched in their torchlight parades and attended mass meetings in which the vendors denied claims that they all wore diamond stickpins, and asserted their rights as workingmen entitled to "fair wages for faithful work." One transparency displayed outside their meeting hall in Brooklyn (Figure 8.11) showed publisher James Gordon Bennett Jr. as a donkey-eared newsboy trudging through the snow with his two-cent *Heralds*, beset by a barking dog representing "the public." In the background a woeful woman and child tend a table for the "⅓

Figure 8.11. New York Herald publisher James Gordon Bennett Jr. endured much ridicule when newsboys and vendors boycotted his paper over a wholesale price hike. "What He's Coming To," 1883, New York Public Library. Image ID: 1109487.

ct. profit" in front of a fence depicting the *Herald*'s ill-fated publicity stunts and Bennett's high lifestyle. The *Herald* building looms above, topped by a "To Lease" sign and the ghost of his father, James Gordon Bennett Sr., saying "Wat a dom'd fule!" Bennett responded to the boycott by recruiting hawkers from flophouses and the Newsboys' Lodging House. *Judge* magazine mocked his efforts in a cartoon (Figure 8.12) showing flush-nosed, stubble-chinned men rushing from the newspaper office crying their papers as Bennett peers out a window beside a sign reading: "Notice—Tramps Wanted—Orphans Wanted—Widows Wanted— Cripples Wanted—To Sell the Herald at 2 cts."[85]

Figure 8.12. Bennett responded to the boycott by recruiting vagrants to hawk his paper. Grant E. Hamilton, "A Suggestion to J. G. B.—How to Utilize Tramps," *Judge* 4, no. 104 (Oct. 20, 1883): 16. Library of Congress, Washington, DC.

A year later, in Pottsville, Pennsylvania, all seventy-five newsboys in town boycotted the *Evening Chronicle* after failing to win a price cut. Four boys broke ranks and were set upon by the strikers, one of whom was stabbed, reported the *New York Times*. A coal town on the Schuylkill River, Pottsville hadn't made national news since the late 1870s when the Molly Maguires, a secret society of Irish American miners, made it a hotbed of labor resistance. Nineteen members were hanged, nine of them in Pottsville. The community regarded them as martyrs, and their legacy lived on in song and story.[86]

Yet the most shocking action involving newsboys was not a strike but an insurrection in the "Queen City," Cincinnati, renowned for its art, culture, and upstanding German population. In March 1884, a mob outraged at the light manslaughter conviction of a man who had robbed and killed his employer, marched to the city jail and courthouse. Their ire had been raised by graphic accounts of the killing in flash papers and dime novels, coupled with allegations about corrupt officials and high-priced lawyers. A three-day riot ensued in which fifty-six people were killed and two hundred wounded. On the second night ten thousand men and boys laid siege to the courthouse. They built a bonfire inside, feeding it with furniture and county records. Standing on the portico above the flames, newsboy Johnnie Schneider held a mock auction, calling for bids on the "temple of justice." The scene, illustrated in *Harper's Weekly* (Figure 8.13), dramatized the protesters' main grievance: that justice was for sale. The propertied classes, on the other hand, saw it as a sign that aliens who had no respect for democratic institutions were overrunning the country. They pressed for curbing immigration, restricting suffrage via literacy and residency requirements, passing curfew and vagrancy laws, suppressing flash literature, building armories, and

Figure 8.13. Cincinnati newsboy Johnnie Schneider and pals put justice on trial after a disputed verdict. F. H. Farny, "The Cincinnati Riots—Destruction of the court-house—Street arabs burning the court records, and calling for bids on 'The Temple of Justice,'" *Harper's Weekly* 28, no. 1425 (Apr. 12, 1884): 236. Author's collection.

strengthening the militia, but such measures could not stem the rising tide of discontent.[87]

In January 1886 a hundred newsboys in Lynn, Massachusetts, organized a union for "self-protection" and demanded 8¢ a dozen for all penny dailies. In March, two hundred newsboys mounted a one-day strike against a dealer in Natick, Massachusetts, winning a ⅓¢ price cut. Chicago newsboys under Lawson's influence rose up against the *Tribune* the same month, followed by *Brooklyn Times* newsboys in Williamsburg, who objected to the price favoritism shown to boys in other districts. More than a hundred newsies armed with sticks and stones tried to overturn a *Times* delivery wagon and block the entire fleet. The driver used his whip liberally and held off the mob until police arrived, but publisher William Cullen Bryant Jr. immediately reinstated the old price for all, saying the discount to other boys was just temporary.[88]

Then in April the Washington Newsboys' Union, representing 175 members, won a price cut from the *National Republican* and the *Post*. Meanwhile, 1,300 Detroit newsboys dug in for a protracted battle against Scripps's *Evening News*, demanding two papers for a cent instead of one. The strike lasted two weeks, caused many clashes, and threatened to spread to Jackson, Michigan, eighty miles to the east, but ended in defeat on May 1 after a brawl between strikers and salaried distributing boys. May Day 1886 also saw the culmination of a three-day strike by newsboys against the *Evening Times* in San Antonio, Texas. The region was steeped in labor solidarity due to railroad workers' struggle against Jay Gould's Southwestern System. The boys joined striking printers and demanded three papers for a nickel instead of two, with the right to return unsold copies. They blockaded the office doors so that no "guilty" boys could escape with papers. Management capitulated, giving the strikers their usual number gratis. There followed an open-air meeting in which the boys formed an organization called the Kids of Labor. They elected one of their own as Grand Master Workman and chose a three-member executive board, but stopped short of picking a treasurer, saying it was unwise to trust a newsboy with money.[89]

These confrontations coincided with the rise of the Noble and Holy Order of the Knights of Labor, whose 750,000 members included small proprietors as well as wage earners, skilled and unskilled. They all identified as part of the "producing classes" who "were suffering under the same general causes." Blacks, women, and children also were welcomed into the fold.[90] On May 2, 1886, just one day after the Knights mounted peaceful nationwide demonstrations for the eight-hour day, about a hundred "youngsters" between the ages of 15 and 21 met secretly in Boston to form the Juvenile Knights of Labor. The founding members included newsboys and bootblacks, clerks and factory hands. They numbered 3,365 in fourteen states and one territory, with the majority in New York, Brooklyn, and Boston. It was intended to be an independent organization that would support the adult Knights, who would in turn help them win recognition and concessions from employers. Strikes were not to be countenanced, as disputes would be referred to the nearest assembly of the Knights of Labor for settlement. The founders elected a slate of officers and agreed to form local assemblies, but events overtook them.[91]

The entire trade union movement suffered a devastating blow on May 4 when a bomb exploded in the ranks of the police during a labor rally in Chicago's Haymarket Square. The blast left eight policemen and at least four civilians dead, and scores wounded by police fire. Eight prominent radicals were arrested, tried, and convicted of the murders, although no evidence linked them to the bombing. Four of the men were hanged, including 39-year-old Albert Parsons, a carrier at age 12 of the *Galveston News* in Texas. The only fact proven at the trial, he said, "was that we held opinions and preached a doctrine that is considered dangerous to the rascality and infamies of the privileged, law-creating class, known as monopolists." The Knights were henceforth associated with anarchists and bomb-throwers, and their influence waned. One Detroit paper ridiculed working people's understanding of the affair by calling attention to newsboys' mispronunciation of the word *anarchists*: "Paper, sir? All about the narkemists hung!" "Extra 'dition? Ankermus hung!" "Annerkiss hung! 2¢!"[92]

Agitation continued nonetheless with newsboy strikes and boycotts in Lowell, Massachusetts, in May and November, and the formation of newsboy unions in San Francisco, Sacramento, Brooklyn, New York, and several New Jersey cities in June, and in Springfield, Ohio, in September.[93] The San Francisco group was a product of labor solidarity and social uplift. It began with a meeting of 120 boys, ages 6 to 17, in Silver Star Hall on Sansome Street. Federated Trades Council men helped them elect officers and form a Committee on Constitution and By-laws, while WCTU members urged good conduct. The boys agreed not to favor or boycott any paper, and set dues at $1 for founders and $5 for others. All would receive badges identifying them as union members. Days later a splinter group of ferry newsboys formed their own union.[94]

On July 2 newsboys in Buffalo boycotted the *Commercial* after management raised the wholesale price from 1¢ to 1¼¢ on account of putting in a folding machine. Meanwhile, their counterparts downstate formed the Brooklyn Newsboys' League, one of five such leagues in New York and New Jersey, and agreed to back the action of the adult Newsdealers' Association in "cutting" (boycotting) Pulitzer's *Evening World*. The dealers planned an Independence Day parade in Manhattan to win support for their cause. They distributed flags, fireworks, money, and cigarettes to ensure a turnout of 600 to 700 boys. Only a fraction of that number showed up, however, as several mysterious characters appeared at ferry terminals on the morning of the Fourth handing out free tickets to Coney Island to any newsboy or bootblack who wanted them. Pulitzer had outsmarted the dealers. New York newsboys pledged solidarity again later that month when the Third Avenue Streetcar Company started enforcing its ban on peddlers under 16 years old. Young and old vowed to boycott the road "until doomsday."[95]

These were just three of the 186 labor boycotts recorded by the state that year. The number grew to 242 in 1887, beginning in January when more than fifty newsboys in Manhattan's Yorkville district refused to buy the *Daily News* in opposition to the 10 percent commission charged by delivery wagon drivers. Boys in Greenpoint, Brooklyn, also boycotted the paper for several days demanding better terms.[96] That same month newsboys struck the New York *Leader*, now a Knights of Labor paper, over a price hike and the firing of a friendly circulator. Enemies of labor were tickled when newsboys picketed the William Street office and attacked its news wagons, crying, "We are de Knights of Labor" and "De *Leader* is getting a dose of its own soup." The paper rescinded the order.[97] The New York boys, whose numbers had tripled with the advent of the one-cent evening newspapers, according to labor journalist John Swinton, formed a union in May and boycotted all "rat" papers, the *Tribune, Mail,* and *Express* among them. A similar effort was made in strike-torn Paterson, New Jersey, and Omaha, where striking newsboys and union bootblacks took part in the Knights of Labor's Fourth of July festivities.[98]

In August newsies in Los Angeles boycotted the second edition of the *Express* because the entire first edition had been sold to one boy. The "little strikers" gathered around the chalkboard, reported the *Los Angeles Times*, and amused themselves by writing "The newsboys have gone on strike." It took the whole *Express* staff and two policemen to keep the board clean. Three months later it was the *Times's* turn to face a strike by the newly formed Newsboys' Union, which signed up thirty of the city's eighty-five newsboys. The *Times* dismissed it as the weak invention of a "tricky and gopher-like gang" egged on by the rival *Tribune* and *Herald*.[99]

Newsboys in Washington, DC, Pittsburgh, Rochester, and Milwaukee also struck. The Washington boys targeted the *Capital* and the Sunday *Herald* in August, calling for a wholesale price cut from 3¢ to 2½¢ per nickel paper. They marched two hundred strong up Pennsylvania Avenue, shouting, singing, and cheering to the amusement of evening strollers. Strike leaders "Sheeny Mike" and "English Bill" presented demands to management, backed by committee members "Limpy," "Pug Nose Jack," and "Gouger." Pittsburgh newsies boycotted the *Chronicle-Telegraph* in October and thrashed those who sold it. Rochester's nearly one hundred newsboys boycotted the *Union and Advertiser* in August because the company reneged on a picnic. They stopped selling it again, along with the *Democrat, Herald,* and *Post-Express,* in November in support of striking compositors. And Milwaukee carriers struck the *Evening Wisconsin* in December, seeking a 50 percent discount on the 3¢ paper.[100]

The conflict in Milwaukee, where the militia had killed five Polish marchers and injured a dozen more during the eight-hour-day demonstrations in May, had repercussions beyond the city limits. Violence threatened as the *Evening Wisconsin* imported strikebreakers from St. Louis, yet the Milwaukee boys promised to organize them within days. Chicago newsboys, meanwhile, assured the strikers that no carriers would come from their city. The dispute lasted two weeks, during which the newsboys elected officers and adopted a constitution. They enrolled sixty-nine members—nearly every newsboy in the city. Each member received a silver diamond-shaped badge engraved "Milwaukee Newsboy's Union No. 1."[101]

Chicago's *Arbeiter-Zeitung*, the German-language radical newspaper formerly edited by Haymarket martyr August Spies, praised newsboys' esprit de corps and characterized their struggle as part of the class struggle: "The products of the capitalistic press would not yield such big profits, some even could not exist without those little children who are forced to sacrifice their youth and health while their more lucky contemporaries have a chance to go to school and prepare for a better future as well as enjoy their life while studying."[102]

Schoolchildren also got into the act. From March 1886 to May 1887, thousands of students at dozens of schools used the strike weapon to win shorter hours, longer recesses, lower fees, and better books. They issued demands and organized walkouts in Brooklyn, Troy, and Newburg, New York; in Columbus and Cleveland, Ohio; in Vandalia, Salem, Rockford, Clinton, and East St. Louis, Illinois; in Indianapolis and Elkhart, Indiana; as well as in Detroit, St. Louis, Baltimore, Boston, and Philadelphia. The strikers, mostly boys, made "incendiary and anarchic speeches," called non-striking classmates "scabs," and likened their principals to slave drivers or the capitalist villains Jay Gould and Andrew Carnegie. Strikers in Baltimore nailed shut the gates of their school with six-inch nails while those in Troy filled the keyholes with mud. Some school boards capitulated to demands, but most had the leaders flogged and expelled. The upsurge nevertheless inspired choirboys in New Haven to strike.[103]

The next two years found newsboys embroiled in a spate of work disputes. In July 1888 hawkers in Dallas struck the *Morning News* because a circulator refused to drop the price from 3¢ to 2½¢ per copy. They wouldn't sell the paper and forcibly prevented other boys from doing so. Their counterparts in Cleveland struck the *Sunday World* in September over a price hike and tried to form a "trust" with bootblacks to protect their earnings. Then in June 1889, forty St. Louis boys brazenly defied Pulitzer's policy of not selling the *Post-Dispatch* to anyone who sold other papers. The boys acquired papers anyway, and Joe Barr, a "dago" with a "sky scraping voice," had the audacity to cry them outside the *Post-Dispatch* office, offering free copies of Pulitzer's paper as a premium to anyone who bought the *Chronicle* or *Star Sayings*. He and a comrade were arrested for disturbing the peace. They charged police abuse and considered boycotting the *Post-Dispatch* but said there wasn't enough business in it as it was.[104]

In August about five hundred newsboys in Manhattan and Brooklyn struck the *New York Evening Sun* and *Evening World* after the papers raised wholesale prices from 50¢ to 60¢ per hundred. The strikers "roughly handled" some boys who bought papers after being told the price hike didn't affect them. Arrested were two 11-year-olds: Joseph Baldi, an Italian who had torn up a boy's papers, and Arthur Luft, a Pole who had assaulted the policeman who was marching him to jail. They were also accused of throwing mud at *Evening Telegraph* cartoonist R. H. Mohr. Hostility spread to Brooklyn, where a crowd burned a bundle of five hundred papers. Both the *Sun* and the *World* went back to their old price. "One newsboy is not a very formidable fellow," said the *Washington Post*, "but several thousand of him at one time going in the same direction can make it uncomfortable for whatever comes in his way."[105]

In yet another display of collective action in October 1889, Chicago newsboys waged a multifront "war" against traction magnate Charles Yerkes's order banning news peddling on his cable car line. The nine hundred boys affected by the edict held mass meetings, wrote letters to editors, and tried to parley with Yerkes. They also waged a campaign of civil disobedience that wore down conductors and resulted in an "embargo" that permitted older boys to sell on board.[106]

Finally, four East St. Louis boys left the Union News Company in December because they felt underpaid, and, with the benefit of police protection, they started distributing papers on their own behalf at the depot and on trains.

And so it went into the nineties. A particularly telling clash occurred in January 1895 when St. Louis lads launched a "newsboycott" against three dailies over price cuts that had reduced their profits. "A howling mob of boys" gathered in front of the *Post-Dispatch* office to interfere with business. Fifty of them chased the business manager down an alley, knocked him down, tore off his clothes, and were trying to kick him out from under a wagon when police arrived. Nine years had passed since the Rev. Boyd noticed the children lining up outside the *Post-Dispatch* for their Christmas dinner. Pulitzer still prized the gold-headed cane they gave him, but the goodwill it represented had clearly vanished.[107]

For all the claptrap about newsboys being rugged individualists, publishers, philanthropists, women's groups, party bosses, and trade unionists did their utmost to instill in them the benefits of association—of uniting to advance their collective interests. These adults formed newsboy clubs, leagues, societies, associations, and unions throughout the 1880s and beyond. Most of these groups offered social, recreational, and educational programs that improved the lives and life chances of their members. The boys got to pick club officers, passwords, and yells. They chose the sites and menus for their annual picnics. And they sometimes got their pictures in the paper. But most of these organizations wielded no economic power and tolerated no dissent. They served as company unions that sought to preempt or replace real newsboys unions affiliated with local trade councils or national bodies such as the Knights of Labor or, later, the American Federation of Labor, also a product of the Great Upheaval of 1886. But the character of these organizations was always subject to change. As A. G. Crane's checkered career shows, a paternalistic adult-run newsboy association could morph overnight into a militant youth-led newsboy union, and vice versa.

Despite the risks, newsboy clubs were an industry imperative by 1890. A newspaper that failed to form one was, in effect, handing over its valuable labor and advertising force to competitors or charitable societies unsympathetic to their business interests. Press philanthropy coexisted with the efforts of those outside the industry, notably the WCTU, to minister to the needs of America's newsboys. Few reformers in the 1880s were calling for an end to child news peddling. Most felt that newspapers' best philanthropy was providing work for poor boys; they simply wanted to take better care of them.

Like most employee benefit programs, newsboy welfare schemes were primarily designed to help management recruit and retain workers, instill company loyalty, stifle labor militancy, and generate good publicity. Their efforts paid off handsomely; it is no coincidence that the pioneers of newsboy management—Pulitzer, Scripps, McRae, Lawson, and the Booth brothers—founded the first newspaper chains and amassed fortunes by persuading the public that building the circulation of newspapers and the character of newsboys was one and the same project. Their success spawned imitation as employers in other industries began to offer adult workers the same kinds of sports, music, and educational programs developed for newsboys.

Yet the rash of newsboy strikes and boycotts also reflects the pronounced class consciousness of Gilded Age workers. The violence associated with their walkouts may be explained as products of youthful exuberance and indiscretion, or rationalized as evidence of righteous conviction and trade union influence. It may also reflect the violence unleashed on them by managers and strikebreakers. At minimum, these clashes speak to the limits of paternalism. If the many gay accounts and illustrations of newsboy dinners and excursions are any indication, the boys enjoyed these events and took advantage of the bands, clubs, and reading rooms founded on their behalf. Yet these offerings did not prevent them from organizing for self-protection against slashed profits and punitive work rules. They sought justice not charity in their strikes and boycotts, and would continue to do so throughout the 1890s, when the economy tanked, class tensions peaked, and the capitalist press turned a nasty shade of yellow.

9

Yelling the Yellows

About fifty newsboys and their long afternoon shadows were milling around New York's Union Square on May 1, 1898, when a newspaper wagon pulled by a huge white horse came clattering along. The boys—most still in knee pants—rushed to meet the van. Among the stragglers were a one-legged boy on a crutch, a penny-pitcher who had to gather his winnings, and a man in a vest who already held an armful of papers. One boy skipped as he shouted back at the man. Two others bumped into each other and fell. The swarm then reversed direction and ran alongside the wagon. Some boys came perilously close to the rumbling wheels and clomping hooves. The vehicle circled as it slowed, exposing on its side the name and globe insignia of the *New York World*. Before the driver came to a stop, a helper raised the tailgate and threw out a bundle of papers to the tall supplyman who had cut to the front of the throng. Two other white men in derbies and shirtsleeves pushed through and caught the next bundles. As they hurried off, the boys pressed closer to the van, bouncing up and down and waving their arms. Next served was a husky African American who waded swiftly out of the sea of children. Wagons and streetcars passed in the background as the smaller boys now scrambled for papers with much pushing and shoving. Two boys wearing long pants and clutching the same bundle wrestled furiously out of the crowd; the white-shirted one put his dark-clad opponent in a headlock and punched him repeatedly in the stomach. The recipient tried to wrest free but was hindered by the papers under his arm. Once he let them drop, the pair fought full force—punching, spinning, and crashing like a top into the other boys, many of whom had gotten their papers but wanted to see the fight's finish before racing off to make their sales.

This scene, captured in a grainy fifty-three-second single-edit silent film by Thomas Edison's American Mutoscope and Biograph Company, represents one of the earliest motion picture appearances of newsboys. Many artists and illustrators had depicted similar deliveries, including W. R. Leigh, whose drawing in *Scribner's* months earlier showed a medley of ages, races, and sexes fetching papers from a Union Square wagon (Figure 9.1).

Figure 9.1. The carnival of labor required to distribute newspapers provided city folk with a daily spectacle. W. R. Leigh, "Wagons Distributing Evening Papers at Union Square, New York," *Scribner's Magazine* 23, no. 4 (Oct. 1897): 455. Author's collection.

But never had anyone been able to unfreeze time the way cinematographers Billy Bitzer and Arthur Marvin did in documenting this ordinary yet picturesque event.[1]

The news that day was anything but ordinary. In the most decisive battle of the Spanish-American War, Commodore George Dewey had sunk Spain's entire fleet in Manila Bay. Word had reached the *World* ahead of the other newspapers, but after its morning edition had been put to bed. The editor rallied enough workers to issue an extra, but too few men or wagons were on hand to give it much play. The *World* sold only 20,000 penny copies, mostly around Union Square and the Brooklyn Bridge, netting just $120 on the scoop. The newsboys would have collectively earned $80 plus tips, not to mention the cuts, bruises, and bloody noses that also figured into the cost of doing business.[2]

The war, the camera, and the fierce competition were just part of what made the 1890s an extraordinary time for America's newsboys. Even while they and their families endured a devastating economic crisis, 657 new daily papers emerged, making a total of 2,179. New York City began the decade with 55 dailies; the number dropped to 29 by 1899, but their combined circulation rose by almost a million.[3] Newspapers of every size and opinion used marvelous new technologies of production and distribution, but they still relied on legions of children as hawkers and carriers. It was largely a foreign legion, as a flood tide of European immigrants provided publishers with an abundance of cheap labor.

One segment of this labor pool, African Americans, suffered the sting of segregation, now sanctioned by the highest court in the land. Hard times forced girls and women to peddle papers in disturbing numbers; many haunted the streets after dark, blurring the line between business and beggary, virtue and vice. Their presence and the widening gap between rich and poor heightened concerns among reformers of various faiths and agendas. A small but jumpy set of do-gooders tried not to save newsboys but to shush them, condemning their cries as part of the enervating racket of modern life. In 1890 reporter Jacob Riis introduced a new tool of social inquiry, flash photography, that opened the eyes and hearts of the comfortable classes to the plight of the "other half."

Yet as purveyors of a vital commodity, newsboys of the nineties were impossible to eradicate. As ubiquitous in popular culture as they were on city streets, they became versatile symbols of enterprise and exploitation in songs, stories, sculptures, and the sassy color comic strip that gave "yellow journalism" its name. Newsboys' cries stoked the jingoism that sparked America's "splendid little war" abroad and rekindled the acrimony that fueled labor unrest at home. They expressed their own discontent in dozens of strikes, climaxing in 1899 with a two-week tussle with those two "great octopuses" of New York journalism, Joseph Pulitzer's *Evening World* and William Randolph Hearst's *Evening Journal*, all of which helped to remake and reawaken the American working class.[4]

Other than that, it was business as usual.

Crucible of Crisis

The peculiar blend of progress and poverty that sent newsboys careening through the decade was already evident during the 1893 World's Columbian Exposition in Chicago. Held to mark the four hundredth anniversary of Columbus's arrival in the Americas, the exposition became a dream destination for newsies of every stripe. Publishers rewarded circulation contest winners with free trips and dispatched newsboys' bands to generate publicity. Clubwomen and millionaires also sent trainloads of newsboys to the fair. Lumber baron and former Michigan governor Russell Alger (a distant relation of Horatio) treated six hundred Detroit hawkers to a one-day romp on the mile-long Midway, where they savored such novelties as hamburgers, Cracker Jacks, and soda water. Tramp newsboys also rode the rails to Chicago hoping to join the fun and cash in on the crowds. Among the top attractions were George Ferris's giant observation wheel and the log cabin where Abraham Lincoln was born. A cavalcade of entertainers passed through, including illusionist Harry Houdini and frontiersman Buffalo Bill, who set up his Wild West show across the street and burnished his reputation by admitting Chicago's newsboys and bootblacks—all freshly bathed and barbered—free of charge.[5]

City mayors and missionaries from throughout North America met at the fair to discuss the welfare of newsboys, the management of their homes, and other "waif problems." Attendees apparently did not object to the uniformed newsboys who cried the fair's own newspaper, the *Daily Columbian*, issued from Printing Press Row in Machinery Hall. Its circulation manager, 18-year-old Max Annenberg, was a scrappy Prussian immigrant who had spent half his life in the trade. The youths in his employ were just a fraction of the two thousand newsboys and bootblacks under 15 who worked the streets of Chicago during the exposition, some making $8 to $10 a day. Adult hawkers also vied for sales, including the long-haired, Bible-thumping "Willie the Apostle" and 84-year-old Orasmus Page, a white-bearded rustic who ambled about on a wooden leg. They stood out as curiosities, but both took pride in earning their own living.[6]

Yet the flush times didn't last. The fair's opening coincided with a stock market panic that set off the worst economic depression of the century. Over the next five years, more than 150 railroads, 500 banks, and 16,000 businesses failed, casting three million people—roughly 20 percent of the labor force—out of work. Pressured by industrialist Philip Armour, Chicago's chief of police cracked down on newsboys' "pernicious" cries of bank failures. But the boys wouldn't be stilled. "I'll cry what I want to," said one. With a hundred thousand unemployed in Chicago alone, news peddling kept many families from starvation. Fourteen-year-old Andrew Snell of Avondale supported six relatives; his idled father set a quota of a hundred copies a day—or else![7]

The homeless also multiplied. New York accommodated a hundred thousand displaced youths under 18, reported the *Commercial Advertiser*, displaying more alarm than evidence. Yet the problem was undeniable. Broadway cafés were besieged by hungry boys who leaned through windows to beg patrons for bread or their old newspapers to resell. One diner complained that eight to ten newsboys, "usually ill-bred and dirty," ruined his modest sirloin with their solicitations. Another objected to the "syndicates" of older boys who sent news-carrying tots into cafés to wheedle change from customers. Such cheats, he said, were destined for the "electrocution chair," another invention on display at the Columbian Exposition.[8]

As ever, the destitute valued newspapers not just as commodities but also as insulation. In Chicago, the homeless huddled nightly around City Hall, where police distributed newspapers for them to sleep on. When they ran short, "Little Joe" Robertson collected unsold copies from his pals and passed them out. Editors still let newsboys curl up on delivery-room floors (Figure 9.2), but the practice led to an outbreak of typhus at the *Sun*, *World*, and *Staats-Zeitung*. The disease spread to the Newsboys' Lodging House on Duane Street, which sheltered four hundred boys a night. Superintendent Rudolph Heig said his charges were refused admittance to the nearby Hudson Street hospital, with fatal results. Ironically, epidemics boosted street sales, allowing healthy boys to capitalize on the misfortune of others, and tempting some to falsely announce the arrival of cholera-infected "pest ships."[9]

According to Heig, New York newsboys made 75¢ to $1 a day if they sold morning and afternoon papers. Their earnings compared well to those of

Figure 9.2. Jacob A. Riis, *2 A.M. in the Delivery Room in the "Sun" Office*, ca. 1890. Gelatin dry plate negative. Museum of the City of New York, 90.13.1.131.

bootblacks, telegraph messengers, and shopboys. Lodgers could live comfortably on 18¢ a day, he said, and were less wretched than boys who lived at home because their money was not drunk up by dissolute parents. Nevertheless, homelessness was a detriment to advancement, as employers spurned boys who did not live with their parents.[10]*

However much they suffered from poverty, disease, or neglect, newsboys of the nineties were frequent subjects of heartwarming human-interest stories. Reporters took note of the kindnesses they showed each other, their willingness to return lost wallets, and their clever methods of harvesting coins from grates and fountains. These stories alleviated the public's fear of them as rabid strays, yet also functioned as parables of political economy that illuminated children's class consciousness. An item in the *New York Times*, for instance, described a streetcar transaction between a ragged newsie and a dandy in kid gloves. Everyone could read on the newsboy's face what he was thinking, said the paper, as he counted the change into the palm of the kid glove: "'Things don't seem to be very well evened up in this world.'"[11]

Economic disparities—and occasionally political disputes—led newsboys to mount strikes and join demonstrations throughout the decade. The first was the January 1890 strike against three penny papers in Buffalo, New York, after they raised their prices from 50¢ to 60¢ per hundred. Two hundred newsboys "made things lively" by attacking anyone who peddled the *Times, News,* or *Commercial.* "Cries of 'scabs' were heard all day and sticks and bricks were used freely as weapons," reported out-of-town papers. Across the continent, the *Sacramento Daily Record Union*'s headline read, "Newsboys Claim the Great American Privilege of Striking." The Buffalo boys reclaimed that privilege in August 1892, again demanding the old price from the *Evening News.* The result was eight arrests and no price cut.[12]

A similar row broke out in Brooklyn in July 1890 when the *New York World* raised its wholesale price 20 percent. A rumor spread that Pulitzer imposed the hike because he saw three of his newsboys wearing new shoes. *World* newsies had in fact reaped a harvest earlier that year by selling "Nellie Bly extras" detailing the intrepid girl reporter's race around the world. But they now paraded outside City Hall carrying placards and shouting, "Boycott, boycott, boycott the Evening World." Striker Denis Iago was arrested for "soaking a scab," but released when no one would testify against him.[13]

---

* In their desperation, several daredevils sought relief by replicating Steve Brodie's jump off the Brooklyn Bridge. James Duffy of Ireland drowned in the attempt, but Buffalo newsboy Thomas J. Tremain (aka "Toronto Red") survived to collect on a $700 bet. See "Jumped to a Watery Grave," *Omaha World-Herald*, Apr. 14, 1895, 2; "Jumped from the Bridge," *New York World*, May 16, 1895, 5; and "Imitation Bridge Jumping," *New York Sun*, May 17, 1895, 1.

Newsboys in Texas rose up in December 1890 when the *Dallas Times-Herald* raised prices from 2¢ to 2½¢ a copy. The paper's circulator tried to protect the boys who were willing to stand out on Main Street, but a platoon of thirty strikers showered one with dirt clods. Police arrested several of his assailants. Some furnished bonds, but most remained behind bars. In Waco, Texas, politics prompted all the town's hawkers and carriers to strike the *Evening News* eighteen months later after it endorsed the sitting governor over the People's Party candidate.[14]

In Duluth, Minnesota, newsboys struck in May 1891 when sellers of the *News-Tribune* stopped work in support of striking compositors and affiliated with the American Federation of Labor. AFL president Samuel Gompers personally welcomed them into the fold. "Look at that little banner," he said after it was unfurled at a meeting. The words "Newsboys' Union" stood out in large gold letters against a white background. "Look at their president," he went on, turning to the young clerk who had helped organize them. "Why the very children take up our cause. Crush out unionism! No, not till you pluck out the human heart."[15]

Labor news dominated the headlines. The deadliest showdown occurred in July 1892 when Carnegie Steel locked out the nation's strongest union in Homestead, Pennsylvania, and imported three hundred armed guards to restart the plant. The ensuing clashes led to sixteen deaths on both sides and the deployment of eight thousand militiamen. Newsboys in Pittsburgh cried extras about the "Homestead war" with an avidity unmatched since the Civil War. When anarchist Alexander Berkman tried to kill Carnegie's managing partner, Henry Clay Frick, in his office, Frick himself heard newsboys crying "All about the assassination" as he was being taken home to recover.[16]

Newsboys struck repeatedly over the next two years. In May 1893 Brooklyn newsies attacked an *Evening World* wagon and boycotted the paper until it repealed a new policy that allowed only two new papers for every five old ones returned. Their counterparts supported striking compositors in Boston in October, threw off "the foot of monopoly" in Omaha in November, and won an arbitration the following year. They struck papers in Denver and Cripple Creek, Colorado, in February 1894 and in Duluth in May.[17]

Newsboys also joined the ranks of Coxey's Army. Led by Ohio quarry owner Jacob Coxey, thousands of unemployed men and boys set out for Washington, DC, in March 1894 to demand work or relief. Printer and ex-newsboy Charles T. Kelley organized a West Coast contingent. A resident of the Chicago Newsboys' Home during the last depression, he had been radicalized by the national rail strike of 1877. Barely scraping by in San Francisco sixteen years later, he and six hundred men signed on to Coxey's "petition in boots." Traveling by foot and freight train, and subsisting on blackberries and handouts, their numbers swelled to two thousand, including a brash 18-year-old news alley kid from

Oakland, California, named Jack London. Kelley's unit got bogged down in Iowa, and London got "vagged" (arrested for vagrancy) in Buffalo, but Coxey reached the capital with a weary force of five hundred. Newsboys heralded their arrival by peddling *Christ and Coxey*, a 3¢ pamphlet. The movement gained sympathy across class lines, but police routed the men before they could present their petition to Congress.[18]

Then in May, a strike at the Pullman Palace Car factory outside Chicago widened into another national rail strike affecting newsboys. Members of the American Railway Union (ARU), led by Eugene V. Debs, refused to work any train carrying Pullman cars. Railroad owners secured injunctions outlawing the ARU strike and pressured officials to call out state and federal troops to confront demonstrators. Violence erupted in twenty-six states, causing thirty-four deaths and millions of dollars in property damage. Newsboys sold papers hand over fist, and the Chicago police chief blamed them for inciting violence with their "exaggerated accounts of the trouble."[19]

Two months later a thousand Chicago newsboys and many in St. Paul, Minnesota, and Sioux City, Iowa, answered Debs's call for a general strike by refusing to handle all "capitalist papers" in Chicago that denounced the strike. The targeted newspapers included the morning *Herald, Tribune,* and *Inter Ocean,* and the evening *Mail, Post,* and *Journal,* which jointly controlled distribution through an association. The boys, some wearing strikers' ribbons, gathered in Printing House Square and other spots to vote up the measure. They then paraded to the newspaper offices and dumped the "anti-union" sheets into the sewers. The only daily they would handle was the pro-union *Chicago Times.* Heartened by their solidarity, Debs wired a friend: "Newsboys have struck and boycotted the subsidized press. Let none return to work until the General Managers' Association agrees in writing to reinstate every man the country over. Good men will win this strike." Gompers and the AFL opposed the general strike, however, and it lasted just a day. The *Tribune* ridiculed the boycott as a "boomerang of the worst description," but journalist John Swinton considered it "one of the mightiest protests that has gone forth this century." He told a convention of news dealers in September: "Those hundred boys made life a burden for the Chicago millionaire newspaper proprietor. They demoralized the monopoly papers, and in three days nearly doubled the circulation of the Times."[20]

Meanwhile, newsboys out West boycotted the *Spokane Daily Chronicle* over the right to return papers, and struck the *Los Angeles Times* in response to "Debs's Rebellion" and the paper's use of scab printers. Anyone who asked a newsboy for a copy of the *Times* risked verbal damnation. Rogue hawkers received worse. "There were men and boys whose ears were torn off," charged the *Times,* "and who suffered other assaults and mutilations in the struggle for the right to maintain free speech and the right to work without special permission from the unions."[21]

Newsboys also struck in Cleveland, Toledo, and Massillon, Ohio (Coxey's hometown) over retail price cuts that would reduce their earnings. Charles Washington, Cleveland's "first colored news kid," joined two Jewish boys, Dave "Piggy" Friedman and Morris Hertz, to lead the protest against the *Leader* and the *Plain Dealer*. The strikers upset a news wagon and attacked boys who failed to honor the strike. Piggy and three others were arrested and fined $5 each, plus costs, for the disturbances. The newsboys took up a collection for the "patriots." The strike failed, but the boys formed a union to carry on. Plunking down a dollar, mostly in pennies, they rented a hall on Scovill Avenue that had hosted Republican, Democratic, and Populist conventions. They elected officers and passed resolutions "to conserve the best interests of the great republic and their God." They vowed to establish a newsboys' home, library, and sick fund, and to follow the coffins of members "to their last resting place." Like the other eighty-two industrial conflicts in the city between 1893 and 1898, the Cleveland newsboys' strike led to a new politics of reform and the progressive mayoralty of ex-newsboy Tom L. Johnson.[22]

One alternative to reform was revolution—the inevitable result, said Karl Marx, of a system in which the labor of many created wealth for a few. "Orphans and pauper children" were part of this "industrial reserve army," he explained in *Das Kapital*, that dwelled in poverty during hard times and joined the active ranks of laborers in prosperous times. Steeped in these writings, Lucian Sanial, the leader of the Socialist Labor Party in New York, argued in the slumping fall of 1894 that no one exemplified capitalist exploitation better than newsboys: "It is upon their puny shoulders that have been reared the magnificent piles of brass dome journalism." Despite a reputation for rabble-rousing, Sanial's solution to income inequality was not strikes and riots but compulsory education and the ballot box.[23]

Wheels of Commerce

The proliferation of newspapers, newsboys, and the class tensions that bound them stemmed in part from new technology. On the production end, the introduction of linotype machines and the enhanced use of wood pulp cut composition and newsprint costs by 75 percent. "Lightning" web presses churned out more copies in less time than the old presses, enabling publishers to move from four-page papers to eight pages. Thanks to a newsboy's suggestion, most American dailies reduced the page size for ease of handling. Sunday papers kept growing in bulk, however. The *Boston Globe*'s standard eight-page Sunday offering swelled to forty pages in 1895, and sixty pages soon after. The *New York World* issued a record-breaking hundred-pager in 1893 to celebrate its tenth anniversary under Pulitzer's ownership. "It was tough on the newsboys," remarked an observer. Foreshadowing their rivalry in New York, Hearst's *San Francisco Examiner* topped Pulitzer the next year with a 120-page edition extolling the virtues of California's Midwinter Exposition in Golden Gate Park.[24]

Long anathema to pious Christians, Sunday papers were wickeder than ever in the 1890s. In addition to lurid accounts of crime, scandal, and suicide, they carried ads for brothels and abortionists, and blatantly catered to gamblers in covering sports. Known as "cheap," "nasty," and eventually "yellow" or "yellow kid" journalism, this style of newspapering valued sensation over truth, speed over accuracy, and sales over all else. New York set the pace, but big-city dailies across the country adopted their business and editorial practices. Emulating Pulitzer's *World*, the *Philadelphia Inquirer* dropped its price to 1¢ and recruited boys to shout such ghastly headlines as "Killed Herself by Her Own Hair" and "He Held Dynamite Between His Teeth." Its circulation soared from 5,000 to 70,000 in the early 1890s.[25]

In addition to their attention-grabbing news columns, Sunday editors introduced women's pages that offered beauty tips, sewing patterns, and club news; they launched children's pages featuring puzzles, paper dolls, and paint-by-number pictures; and they enticed all ages and reading levels with contests, coupons, and color art and comic supplements. The *Chicago Tribune's* art section was so prized that 13-year-old Jakey Klein got 85¢ for every hundred he swiped from the pressroom for dealers who would frame them for resale.[26]

The number and circulation of Sunday papers soared throughout the period, generating important earnings for working-class families. Newsboys called them "breadwinners" because they made a penny on each nickel copy sold. Some 250 dailies published Sunday editions in 1890, climbing to 700 by 1900. Their success eventually drove independent Sunday papers—those not affiliated with dailies—out of business. Even when attached to dailies, Sunday papers usually had their own staffs, schedules, and distributors. In 1890 the *Los Angeles Times* relied on fifty newsboys who sold an average of 560 copies during the week, but a hundred boys who disposed of 1,200 copies on Sundays. New York's twenty-nine dailies issued 2.7 million copies a day in the mid-nineties, while its thirty-four Sunday papers turned out 2.1 million.[27]

For all their proclaimed devotion to the truth, newspaper executives could not be trusted to accurately report the number of copies they sold. Circulation managers (aka "circulation liars") routinely inflated street sales, falsified post office receipts, and padded subscription lists to secure higher advertising rates. Some stole their competitors' carriers' lists to expose such lies. Cleveland private detective Jake Mintz got his start sleuthing as a newsboy when the circulation man of the *Cleveland Leader* asked him to find out the print run of the *Herald*. Mintz hid under a pile of mailbags and counted the revolutions of the press, earning free copies of the *Leader* for days. Even more effective than espionage was double-talk; the industry redefined the word *circulation* to mean the number of copies printed or sent to dealers, ignoring the percentage that were returned or recycled, unsold and unread. Nevertheless, the best estimates suggest that between 1890 and 1900 the combined circulation of American dailies nearly doubled from 8 million to 15 million, while Sunday circulation increased from 63 million to 75 million.[28]

The number of hands needed rose accordingly. In greater New York and Jersey City, there were nearly 7,000 news dealers in 1898, every one of whom employed from two to ten boys, sometimes even fifteen, to deliver papers. On a "very conservative average" of four helpers to each dealer, estimated one trade journal, "this makes a total of twenty-eight thousand people, at least, engaged for an hour or two every morning delivering papers in this vicinity, besides the wholesale dealers and the American News Company." The job entailed inserting advertising circulars into the papers—sometimes as many as three or four, for which the dealer received 25¢ to 50¢ per hundred, depending on the quality of the neighborhood.[29]

Improvements in office and transportation technology simultaneously quickened the distribution process. The ringing of telephones, clattering of typewriters, and soft, smokeless glowing of Edison's electric lights transformed Victorian newsrooms into modern workspaces. Dispatches no longer came over the wire but arrived through the air with the invention of wireless telegraphy. Photographs supplemented illustrations with the perfection of halftone printing. Most dailies now used cash registers to issue brass checks to the boys indicating the number of papers they bought. Papers acquired metal-topped tables so that bundles could be easily slid from one side to the other, or installed electric conveyer belts to move them from pressroom to loading dock. News agencies routinely appropriated electric trolleys, steam trains, and cable cars to serve readers, especially commuters, in distant suburbs and cities. Beginning in 1889, newsboys wearing crimson *Brooklyn Eagle* hatbands cried the paper on Sunday afternoons in Washington, DC. By 1896 the *New York Times*, recently acquired by former Chattanooga, Tennessee, newsie Adolph Ochs, sped breakfast copies the same distance to delegates at the state Democratic Party convention in Syracuse.[30]

News carriers were by necessity early risers. Those who handled "rooster editions" had to set out at 2:30 a.m., when only the poorest people went to work. Judging from news reports, they were forever stumbling over foundlings, "crapes" (corpses), and other casualties of the night. Some boys still bedded down in pressroom gunnysacks to avoid commuting, but even they were prone to oversleeping. Most carriers depended on their mothers to shake them awake. "Business is business," said one, "and the boy cannot sell papers lying in bed." Tim Kelley of New York spared his parents the task by placing a caged sparrow near a window to cheep at first light. A more common trick was to drink lots of water before retiring. The introduction of inexpensive wind-up alarm clocks in the late 1880s also helped. Whatever their method, the most reliable carriers earned extra money "knocking up" customers, serving, in effect, as human alarm clocks.[31]

The most appealing invention to newsboys was the bicycle. London dailies introduced the technology in 1884 when the *Evening Standard* adapted a Singer tricycle to make deliveries. Telegraph companies led the way in the United States, but by the early nineties many newspapers, including the Salvation Army's *War Cry*, promoted the bicycle as a cost-effective means of distribution. Some acquired fleets for their carriers to use or buy. The *Cincinnati Times Star* soon relied on an elite corps of African American "scorchers" to distribute its "Base Ball Extra" (Figure 9.3). Many papers offered bicycles as prizes in circulation contests. One such promotion by the *Rochester Post-Express* in 1890 split the ranks of the newsboys, as carriers pitched subscriptions to the hawkers' regular downtown customers. The hawkers—dubbed "Powderly's Partisans" because they belonged to the Knights of Labor, headed by Terence Powderly—struck

Figure 9.3. "Speedy Travelers with Cincinnati Papers," No. 2195 in series, Kraemer Art Co., ca. 1907–1913. Cincinnati Post Card Collection, Rare Books and Special Collections Department. From the Collection of The Public Library of Cincinnati and Hamilton County.

in protest. The *Post-Express* responded by recruiting bootblacks to sell down-town, but the strikers seized their papers; they felt honor-bound to reimburse the shine boys, but threatened full vengeance if they dared peddle any more pa-pers. The strike ended after two days when the newsboys' parents demanded that they bring home their earnings, reduced or not.[32]

Circulation managers also dangled bicycles in front of youngsters, asserting in ads and speeches that there was no better way to earn money for a new wheel than by delivering papers. In 1891 the Curtis Company, publisher of the *Ladies' Home Journal* and several dailies, issued *Jim Preston's Bicycle*, an illustrated novel-ette about a newsboy who overcomes all obstacles to pay for his bike. The firm, founded by ex-newsboy Cyrus Curtis of Portland, Maine, mailed the book free to anyone who sent in the names and addresses of five prospective carriers.[33]

Some publishers soured on the cycling craze, blaming it for a decline in the sale of Sunday papers. But the industry as a whole did much to promote it. Newspapers employed cycling editors, publicized the latest models and champions, and even sponsored races. In the summer of 1896, Hearst and the E. C. Stearns Bicycle Company held a transcontinental relay in which contestants, outfitted in yellow from head to toe, rode Stearns bikes from the offices of the *San Francisco Examiner* to the *New York Evening Journal*. More than four hundred riders took part in the lavishly reported two-week circulation stunt. One in seven Americans then owned bicycles, their average price having dropped from $100 to $40. Secondhand bikes were even cheaper, but newsboys had to consider the cost of repairs and risk of theft or injury. Indeed, by 1912, stealing bicycles and selling parts was "probably the largest trade among the newsboys of Los Angeles," said one probation officer. Twenty years later, almost half of California newsboys injured on the job were hurt in bicycle accidents.[34]

Disabled newsboys also took advantage of new assistive technology such as "invalid chairs" equipped with spoke wheels and push rims. New York pho-tographer Alice Austen captured one such boy, Charlie Hardell, sitting in a wheelchair at the corner of 23rd Street and 5th Avenue (Figure 9.4). He was so absorbed in reading that he paid her no mind.[35] Newsboys who could not af-ford wheelchairs (about $18 new, $10 used) sometimes received them as gifts. Harry Johnson of Minneapolis acquired a three-wheeled velocipede from local businessmen in 1895, a year after losing both feet in a streetcar accident. Until then, he had sold papers and shined shoes from a low red "Express" wagon. Lacking even a wagon, Patsy Lavelle dragged himself around Cleveland on his stumps, eliciting both pity and disgust until the director of outdoor relief sur-prised him with a rolling chair. Dick Bicknell of Salt Lake City dispensed with his crutches after fellow newsies "chipped in" for a chair. The gifts reportedly increased the boys' earnings, as it alerted the public to their desire to better themselves.[36]

Figure 9.4. Charles Hardell is more absorbed in reading his papers than in selling them. His regular spot was on 23rd Street and Fifth Avenue in New York. Fellow newsies helped him set up in the morning, brought him water on hot days, and included him in the banquets, excursions, and clothing raffles that brightened their year. Alice Austen, 1896. Gelatin silver print, 3⅝ × 4 in. New York Public Library. Image ID: 79826.

Technology could reduce as well as raise newsboys' income. The invention of newspaper vending machines by some "soulless genius" threatened to make real vendors obsolete. Called "silent" or "mechanical" newsboys, the first models marketed in America in 1892 came from a Seattle firm founded by owners of the *Seattle Telegraph* and *Victoria News.* It was a six-foot-high cabinet made of polished oak with nickel-plated fittings. Customers dropped a coin into a slot next to the desired paper, opened the door, and grabbed the paper as it shot out. "It is absolutely honest," assured the manufacturer, "it never fails to deliver the goods." The company made an iron version that could be placed in remote areas "where a newsstand does not pay and which the ubiquitous newsboy does not penetrate." The machines proved successful in Washington, DC, which had no shortage of newsboys. New manufacturers sprang up in Chicago, New York, and St. Louis, raising speculation that newsboys' days were numbered.[37]

But the dispensers failed dramatically in San Francisco when *Chronicle* publisher Michael de Young put one in front of his building. The newsboys "made it so hot for him" with their boycott and banners that he removed it after a day. A prospective candidate for the US Senate, de Young received "a most unmerciful roasting" from opposition newspapers. The *San Francisco Call* tagged him "nickel-in-the-slot De Young." The *Lake County Avalanche* labeled him a Judas for betraying the boys who had made him his fortune. And the *Bakersfield Echo* accused him of taking bread from the mouths of hungry mothers and sisters. De Young's hopes of nomination vanished overnight. Circulation managers continued to try new models that rented for pennies a day, but no machine could match the pathos, persistence, and productivity of real newsboys. Nor could they stand up to the vandalism of the little Luddites who had no qualms about thrashing flesh-and-blood rivals, let alone mechanical ones.[38]

One result of the mass production of newspapers was increased wastage from unsold copies and an industry-wide effort to make newsboys absorb the losses. The *New York World*'s weekly returns totaled fourteen tons for its daily and twenty-one tons for its Sunday edition, which business manager Don Seitz called "one of the greatest pilferers of newspaper earnings." The *World* allowed boys and dealers to return 5 to 15 percent of their stock, costing $20,000 and 500 tons of newsprint a day—or "the needless sacrifice of the spruce trees on fifty acres of land!" Others complained that "sturdy beggars, male and female," abused the system by gathering newspapers from commuters and ironing them in basement shops for resale or return. Junkmen bought returns for $5 to $8 a ton to be recycled into cardboard. But publishers tried to shift the remaining costs onto distributors by abolishing return privileges or paying only half price for returned papers. These policies provoked newsboy strikes in San Diego and Seattle in 1891, Portland, Oregon, in 1892, Brooklyn in 1893, and New Orleans in 1895, where managers rustled up replacements. "There were lots of black eyes and torn clothes," reported the sympathetic *New Orleans States*, "but it is safe to say that the little newsboys who were defending what they believed to be their prerogative, have not many of them."[39]

Little Aliens

Immigration transformed the news trade even more than technology. The arrival of eight million foreigners in the closing decades of the nineteenth century, followed by another thirteen million between 1901 and 1914, profoundly altered the demographic profile of America's newsboys, the accents of their cries, and the meanings attributed to their work. New arrivals still came in large numbers from Germany, England, Ireland, and Scandinavia, but the majority now hailed from southern and eastern Europe. With no bars to entry, the street trades absorbed them by the boatload. In 1882 fully 80 percent of Cleveland's licensed newsboys and bootblacks were Hungarian Jews. "The Irish street boy goes before him as does the snow before the Spring sun," lamented the *Cleveland Herald*. The same trend held in Boston, where at one time 75 percent of licensed newsboys had been of Irish descent. By 1889 they accounted for 40 percent of the workforce due to the influx of Jews, who represented 15 percent, and Italians, 7 percent. The number of Jewish newsboys also skyrocketed in New York and Chicago. "Some of them are smart, smarter than most of their Gentile rivals," said the *New York Sun*. Among the sharpest were the two Annenberg brothers, whose families fled pogroms in East Prussia in 1885. Steaming past the unfinished Statue of Liberty, they made their way to Chicago, where 9-year-old Max, one of eleven children, began peddling papers before he could pronounce their names. He and his brother Moe grew up to dominate the city's news trade and build major media empires.[40]

Italians in the trade garnered more scorn than praise. The *National Police Gazette* disparaged those in Baltimore in 1882 as " 'Tony' newsboys" who affected a ridiculous "aristocratic style." The *Catholic World* distinguished between the steady northern Italians and voluble southerners, but said both were obsessed with "money-getting." No wonder they thought one could "pick up gold in the streets" of America, said the author, an Irish Catholic priest. "This is literally the case with those who are rag-pickers and bootblacks, and whose children are newsboys." As a result of these "youthful recruits from the Italian and Jewish quarters," the average age of the city's newsboys "greatly decreased" in the early nineties, said writer Edward W. Townsend.[41] Commentators invoked stereotype more than social science to explain the newcomers' rapid rise in the trade. "The Italian boys are more wide awake, and they stick more faithfully to their post," said a Chicago reporter. Muckraker William Hard later theorized that the Italian was almost as good a bargainer as the Jewish boy and almost as good a fighter as the Irish boy, but the two qualities rendered him "almost irresistible, especially when combined with his marvelous power of persistence."[42]

If Jews and Italians distinguished themselves as the smartest, toughest, and most tireless traders, it was partly because they were also the hungriest. Immigrants from these two groups arrived in the United States with an average of $8 in cash per person, compared to $13 for the Irish, $25 for the English, and $48 for the Germans. Their children's income became even more important after passage of an 1891 law that allowed families to be deported if they became public charges within a year of arrival. The loss of a newsboy's earning power deepened such worries, as in the case of 13-year-old Giuseppe Magalto of New York, who died in February 1891 in a fire at the City Hall Post Office, where he had crawled into a ventilation shaft to escape the cold. The *Press* reported that his death "would be a severe loss to his mother and father [as] he was the eldest of six children and made $7 to $8 a week." Five months later, 15-year-old

Abraham Frank, son of a Jewish tailor, died of smoke inhalation in a news agency fire on nearby Spruce Street, leaving a similar void.[43]

Such tragedies led middle-class observers to cast aspersions on immigrant child-rearing practices. "What kind of mother could it be that possessed so hard a heart," asked a Seattle paper, "as to [send] mere babies . . . to the newspaper office to sleep, that she might be spared the annoyance of getting them out in the morning?" "You will find that newsboys and bootblacks always come from large families," explained a birth control advocate. "The large family is the basis of child labor. The Italians are just like animals. They produce as freely and naturally and they expect their children to look out for themselves almost as early as animals do." The shrinking size of middle-class families due to late marriage and improved contraception heightened such anxieties.[44]

Many newspapers contributed to anti-Italian prejudice with their biased reporting. In New York, a whole colony of Italians thrived amid "mud, microbes, and macaroni," said the *Washington Post* in 1895. "The fat brown, ragged imps romp in the gutters and play at being organ-grinders and rag-pickers . . . or stay in the gutter and develop into cutthroats, newsboys, or bootblacks, or get run over." Nativists took issue with the children's Catholicism, saying that their "blind obedience" to the Church made them poor clay for citizenship. The anti-Catholic American Protective Association (APA) saw Italian emigration as part of a papal plot to flood the country with ignorant peasants who undercut wages, sparked strikes, and set off bank runs. That "Romish" ruffians harassed vendors of APA weeklies in Chicago, said its allies, further attested to their barbarism and disregard for press freedom.[45]

Critics also charged that immigrant children fell under the sway of Fagin-like padrones who taught them to beg and cheat. Italian labor contractors mainly provided their countrymen with jobs in industry, agriculture, or construction, but some did supply children for the street trades. "How many children have been sent here, particularly from Southern Italy, for the mere sake of gain!" railed Father Pietro Bandini in New York in 1892, the year Ellis Island greeted its first immigrants. "Laws have been made and penalties threatened, but this barbarous treatment of children still exists. Immediately after their arrival they are set to work as bootblacks, newsboys or the like. They are driven out of the house early in the morning and woe to them if they do not return at night with the money exacted from them by their inhuman masters. Some streets are overrun by these children growing up without any education of heart or mind."[46]

News reports suggest that the padrone system operated among newsboys in Jersey City, Rochester, Cleveland, Chicago, and Los Angeles. "The 'Dagos,' or Italian boys, with cunning and avarice written all over their faces, are among the largest purchasers, and usually earn the most money," observed the *Los Angeles Times*.[47] A reporter who followed a group of them home to a row of squalid adobe shanties in the riverbed near Boyle Heights found several "brutes" who he said lived off the boys' earnings and beat those who dared return without sufficient change. As a ruse, the reporter tried to hire the boys to pick fruit, but the padrone would not agree to anything less than a dollar a day, which the boys could make selling papers. News peddling, in effect, set the local minimum wage for child labor.[48]

Concerns about "slave-dealing" padrones verged on a moral panic in the early nineties when wire stories circulated nationwide about Bertie Kearney, a missing child from Montreal who turned up seven years later as a newsboy in New York with tales of having been "stolen by a Dago" organ grinder and forced to beg and sell papers. The claim was never substantiated, but it reinforced anti-Italian prejudice. Newspapers characterized any Italian youth who sold papers to younger boys as "a sort of newsboy padrone" and accused the publishers of Italian-language newspapers of practicing padronism when they recruited child sellers—even though these practices were common among publishers of all nationalities. In truth, ethnic newspapers such as *L'Italia* in Chicago led the community's effort to win passage and enforcement of compulsory education laws and anti-begging and rag-picking ordinances, and to support the efforts of Jane Addams's Hull House. Nevertheless, a double standard prevailed. Whereas native newsboys gained praise for their energy and acumen, immigrants who demonstrated comparable traits aroused suspicion. An 1897 study by the Department of Labor concluded that Italians gravitated to the trade because it required little skill or muscular effort and only a low-grade intelligence.[49]

The odd child padrone notwithstanding, news selling was primarily a family business for immigrants and nonimmigrants alike. Mothers in particular took an active interest in their children's work life. They not only got them up in the morning but extended them the capital to start, helped them obtain licenses, rescued them from beatings, and invested in the purchase of routes, corners, and newsstands that provided income for the entire family. Catholic or Jewish, many immigrant parents felt they had no choice but to send their children out to work rather than to school until their family achieved some economic security. This was especially true of boys over the age of 10. Shortly after arriving from Ukraine in 1891, John Cournos's penniless mother took him aside and explained their great want. "What can I do?" asked the 10-year-old. "Why not try selling pa-pers?" she urged. "After school, I mean. Abie does it. Why not you?" Cournos, who would become a celebrated writer and translator, was horrified by the sug-gestion. He felt himself much younger than the boy upstairs, who had been brought up in the city. "I was literally afraid," he admitted in his autobiography. "Yet what was to be done?"[50]

Immigrants and natives alike disagreed as to whether street peddling provided boys with a positive means of assimilation. Journalist Hutchins

Hapgood considered it the most important influence in the Americanization of Jewish boys, even more effective than public schools: "Insensibly—at the beginning—from his playmates in the streets, from his older brother or sister, he picks up a little English, a little American slang, hears older boys boast of prize-fighter Bernstein, and learns vaguely to feel that there is a strange and fascinating life on the street. At this tender age he may even begin to black boots, gamble in pennies, and be filled with a 'wild surmise' about American dollars."[51]

Newsboys' exposure to American popular culture, combined with a measure of economic independence, often led to generational conflicts. Some boys contributed more to their family's support than did their fathers, whose authority diminished accordingly. Growing up in Milwaukee in the early 1880s, go-getter Erich Weiss (Harry Houdini) replaced his impecunious rabbi father in his mother's affections. Erich peddled his papers even during blizzards, leading his mother to call him *tata* or *tateleh*, Yiddish for "little papa" or "little provider." After she died, the world-famous escape artist hired several mediums to contact her. To test the authenticity of the summoned spirit, Houdini always asked the pet name his mother gave him. None ever knew it.[52]

Jewish newsboys also aided their families and communities by supporting strikes of Jewish workers. In the summer of 1895, when fifteen thousand tailors and garment workers on New York's Lower East Side walked out to protest sweatshop conditions, newsboys hawked their strike papers, pamphlets, and songsters. When the protest spread to Brooklyn, Newark, and Boston, newsboys in these cities could be heard crying the same material in Yiddish, concluding with "Extry, extry."[53]

Whatever their ethnic background or economic circumstance, immigrant newsboys were soon heard to speak a common dialect, both on and off the job. Irish, Italian, and Jewish boys in New York cried "Rextry" or "Nextry" when hawking extras, and "swipe de base" or "chase de rub" when playing ball. Immigrant newsboys never hollered headlines in clear English, said the *Washington Star*. "Instead they shriek the names of the newspapers they purvey in a weird patois, partly Yiddish, partly German; of south European a modicum, of English hardly any. 'Woil!' 'Choinal!' 'Hoil!' "[54]

Italians made their mark on the trade in other ways as well. They introduced a new game, *morra*, while waiting for their papers. Passersby marveled at the excitement the boys generated throwing their hands at each other, crying out the number of fingers extended, and then swatting the loser with a rolled-up newspaper. Italian newsies in Los Angeles liked to amuse their friends by singing opera or doing folk dances. Raphael Gurriero of Chicago made charcoal sketches on the pavement. His "war pictures" of Admiral Dewey, President McKinley, and the sinking of the *Maine* attracted large crowds and donations.[55]

Ethnic differences sometimes spawned rivalries in the trade. Native-born newsies in Portland, Oregon, and many other cities adopted organized labor's hostility toward Italians and barred them from their unions. Such campaigns inspired James Otis's 1894 novel, *The Boys Revolt: A Story of the Street Arabs of New York.*[56] Even among the native born, newsboy gangs tended to be ethnically based and fiercely protective of their turf. More than a few Jewish newsies in New York learned what it meant to be "cockalized." "The enemy kids threw the Jew to the ground," explained victim Harry Golden, "opened his pants, and spat and urinated on his circumcised penis while they shouted 'Christ killer.' " To avoid such bullying from the Irish toughs on his route, young David Sarnoff crossed from tenement to tenement via the rooftops.[57]

Working the Color Line

African American newsboys faced even more adversity than immigrant newsboys. As a low-skilled subsistence occupation, news peddling had long attracted a mix of races. Barred from many jobs and schools, black adults and youths had made niches in the street trades since before the Civil War, but there they remained. "Very few colored apprentices can be seen anywhere except as bootblacks or newsboys," wrote National Colored Labor Union founder Isaac Myers to a Philadelphia editor in 1881, "and this makes us apprehensive of the future."[58]

The situation improved little over the next two decades. The most prominent African American news vendor in the city was a one-armed youth who operated a stand on the Chestnut Street Bridge. Always dressed in black broadcloth, he employed several boys to sell for him and took in $6 to $8 a day. In 1896 another African American, W. S. Johnson, operated a news and tobacco stand from a decommissioned streetcar on 44th Street. In his pioneering survey of Philadelphia's largely black Seventh Ward, W. E. B. Du Bois, who had distributed the militant "Afro-American" *New York Globe* while in high school in Great Barrington, Massachusetts, found only five newsboys, six bootblacks, and four peddlers. They accounted for less than 20 percent of regularly employed black males between the ages of 10 and 20. The others were porters, errand boys, servants, and laborers. Aside from helping around the house, concluded Du Bois, "there is really very little that Negro children may do."[59]

Blacks in the 1890s made up 15 percent of the nation's population under age 20. Most lived in the rural South. The city dwellers had to fight their way into the street trades. "Since Emancipation-day colored boys have wanted to sell papers and black boots," wrote Col. Alexander Hogeland, founder of the Newsboy Night School in Louisville, Kentucky, "but whenever they appear they are run off the street." Their arrival at his school one night set off a brawl that brought out the riot police. Embarrassed by the bad publicity, Hogeland preached tolerance, telling his charges about a black youth he knew who once saved a white man from drowning. Someday their own livelihood might be in jeopardy, he told them, and they would need the help of Negroes. The boys voted to let blacks sell papers and shine shoes unmolested.[60]

Louisville was exceptional in this regard, as discrimination rose steadily in the trade throughout the South. In 1881 white newsboys in Memphis organized a union to keep blacks out of the trade and restrict them to the shoeshine business. In 1887 white boys in San Antonio, Texas, boycotted the *Times* and clubbed all violators because blacks were allowed to sell it. That same year Birmingham, Alabama, codified its biases by licensing bootblacks, who were colored, but not newsboys, all of whom were white. In 1888 newsboys in Atlanta demanded that the *Constitution* bar black newsboys or face a strike after one of their own was shot by a black youth on election night. And in 1891 a mob of white newsies in Dallas stripped and beat a 13-year-old African American who dared apply for papers at the offices of the *Times-Herald*.[61]

Continuing this backlash, arch-segregationist Hoke Smith, publisher of the *Atlanta Journal* and future governor of Georgia, discharged all black carriers in 1897 and refused to sell papers to black hawkers, claiming that they spread smallpox by refusing to be vaccinated. Backed by their churches, the banned newsboys held a "monster mass meeting" to protest their ouster. Smith's diktat stood nonetheless and produced similar measures elsewhere. A prohibition against "colored newsboys" in Manchaca, Texas, in 1903 proved to be the last straw for 16-year-old William King; he packed his bags and headed north to Chicago.[62]

Racial slurs contributed to discrimination in the trade. African American newsboys were usually identified in the press by nicknames like "Lily," "Snowball," and "Cottonhead." New York was home to "Daylight," "Midnight," and "Fleece." Chicago papers reported the affairs of "Kinkey Sam," "Mokey Mame," and "Coon Charlie," who was known for his "Sullivanic proclivities." (He liked to fight.) White ethnics acquired similar tags, such as "Dago," "Sheeny," and "Dutchy," which attest to the fraternity as well as the bigotry of newsboys.[63]

Images of black newsboys were even more insidious than their nicknames. *Harper's Weekly* illustrator Charles Stanley Reinhart made a blatant visual argument for white supremacy in his 1892 drawing of a black newsboy accosting a dapper white gentleman in Washington, DC (Figure 9.5). Looking more like a field hand than a street merchant, the straw-hatted ragamuffin cries, "Read me sumpin to holler, Boss," simultaneously asserting his ignorance and deference. "All this shouting, eager life scrambles along on two bare black legs," says the text, "with gaping shirts and ruptured hats, with eager laughing

ON CONNECTICUT AVENUE, WASHINGTON.—Drawn by C. S. Reinhart.—[See Page 654.]
Colored Newsboy: "Read me sumpin to holler, Boss."
665

Figure 9.5. "Read me sumpin to holler, Boss." Charles Stanley Reinhart, "On Connecticut Avenue, Washington," *Harper's Weekly* 39, no. 1855 (July 9, 1892): 665. Eckel Collection, Princeton University Library.

face and shining teeth, with big black eyes and innate tendency to small peculations, but with the utmost confidence in the sympathy of the white people." The writer insists that blacks are "kindly treated at the capital, treated as we treat irresponsible children" who "afford amusement and add to the pleasures of life."[64]

Once known as "the colored man's paradise," Washington had been home to hundreds of "black mercuries" who worked beside white boys, played "sweat" and other games of chance with them, and benefited from the same charities. In 1888 the Newsboys' and Children's Aid Society paid the tuition of twenty-eight black newsies to learn trades at Howard University. But in 1899 the CAS barred blacks from staying at its Maulsby House on Third and C Streets. It separated evening students by race, arguing that it would not be "elevating" for white newsboys to rub shoulders with "colored children." The *Washington Bee*, an African American weekly, acquiesced to the segregation. Advocating less reliance on white philanthropists, it asked, "Why not some of our worthy colored friends take a little more interest in the newsboys?" Mrs. Frederick Douglass denounced the practice in which "white and colored are separated as sheep from goats" as a victory of aristocracy over democracy.[65]

Other signs of deteriorating race relations in the District were the draconian penalties imposed on black youths who fell afoul of the law. In 1891 14-year-old West Dent was stoned by a white boy for selling papers at the corner of 15th Street and New York Avenue, and then arrested because the rock ricocheted off his head and broke a plate-glass window. In 1895, the year Tuskegee Institute founder Booker T. Washington urged African Americans to "cast down your bucket where you are," that is, to strive for economic self-sufficiency rather than aspire to social and political equality, ten "pickaninnies," ages 12 to 15, were jailed for disorderly assembly in the alley behind the *Evening News*. The boys insisted that they had done nothing wrong, said the *Post*, "and made the walls of the Twelfth Street jail fairly ring with negro ballads and plantation melodies."[66]

Photographers employed the same pictorial codes put forward by artists to perpetuate racial prejudice. Chicago's Sigmund Krausz included two studio portraits of black newsboys in his 1891 book *Street Types of Great American Cities*. Expanded and reissued in 1896, when the US Supreme Court's *Plessy v. Ferguson* decision upheld the segregation of public facilities, the book contains photogravure images of peddlers of all ages and ethnicities, accompanied by dopey captions. One picture shows a "mighty 'culiah newsboy" screaming, "Extry! All About the West Side Murder!!":

> His ha'r is so't o' crinky,
> En dar's tatters in 'is dress.
> Ole Africa is in 'is face,
> De chalk is in 'is eye,
> Yet far above all other waifs
> I hear 'is plaintive cry.[67]

Krausz showed black and white newsboys shaking their fists at each other to "typify the feud of the races" (Figure 9.6). "The black may struggle," he wrote, "but in the end he shall fail. Land of Goshen shall be taken from him." Similar images also circulated on a new medium—postcards.[68]

Figure 9.6. Sigmund Krausz, *Competitors*, Chicago, ca. 1891, Library of Congress, Washington, DC. LC-USZ62-42628. Published in *Street Types of Great American Cities* (Chicago: Werner Company, 1896), 54.

Minor scraps between black and white newsies occasionally escalated into major confrontations. In 1890 a "plucky" white newsboy in Marietta, Georgia, horsewhipped a black boy for insulting him, and then thrashed a Yankee who dared to intervene. Friends of the newsboy hung his whip in a saloon under a sign saying "This settles the race question." In November 1896, authorities in Winchester, Kentucky, exchanged fire with a "squad of negroes" who protested the arrest of a black youth for snatching papers from a white newsboy and trampling them underfoot. Ten people, including three policemen, were wounded in the battle. Three of the blacks died of their wounds.[69]

Clashes in northern cities revealed similar tensions. When violence flared in October 1897 in the alley behind several Indianapolis dailies, the press reported it as a "Race War Among Newsboys." An Irish gang called the Bungalows formed near the Park Theater at dusk, while the blacks assembled north of the State House. Police sent patrol wagons to disperse the two groups, but succeeded only in creating roving bands of skirmishers. Casualties on both sides included cracked skulls, broken limbs, and stab wounds.[70]

Figure 9.7. Newsboys, Ann Arbor, 1892. University of Michigan Bentley Historical Library.

Despite such violence, black and white newsboys worked closely in many cities, posed for hand-on-shoulder photographs (Figure 9.7), and sometimes united in common cause. In 1883, for example, the "colored newsboys" of Richmond refused to sell the weekly *Democratic Campaign* and persuaded their "white news brother" to do the same. Blacks and whites led the Cleveland newsboys' strike of 1894 and mounted a protest the same year in response to a mayoral edict barring all newsboys from the Junction area downtown. The boys chose Frank Powers, "a short, jolly-faced colored lad of perhaps a dozen summers," as their spokesman: "Dey says we gits in people's way and breaks their laigs, and shoots craps and mashes de girls and dat's why dey gives us de run," quoted the *Star*. "It ain't no truf in it." The youths staged a sit-in on the tracks, circulated a petition, and demanded meetings with the chief of police and the mayor, who ultimately rescinded the order. "Dot felly Powers 'as got er good pipe on 'im an' 'e makes er good spiel," acknowledged one of the white newsies. In a dispute two years later, a new union leader emerged: Henry Porter, aka "Black Snow Ball."[71]

Newsboys in New York showed interracial solidarity in February 1899 after Aaron "the Slave" Charity caught pneumonia and died. The orphaned son of former slaves, Charity had fled South Carolina two years earlier at age 17 amid mounting tension that culminated in the 1898 Wilmington riot, a coup d'état against the duly elected black mayor that left eleven blacks dead and dozens wounded. As Charity lay dying in the Hudson Street Hospital, he revealed his dread of potter's field. The *World* and celebrity newsboy Steve Brodie spared him this fate by treating him to a "first class funeral." Charity's body lay in state at the Newsboys' Lodging House, where scores of colleagues filed past to pay their respects. A minister gave a funeral oration on "The Value of Manliness" and a newsboy chorus sang "Nearer, My God, to Thee." Two hired carriages carried a delegation of boys to Mount Olivet Cemetery in Queens, where Charity's body was interred in a private plot. If nothing else, his funeral suggests that staged pictures of fist-shaking newsies do not begin to capture the relationship of black and white children who self-consciously shared the same trade, class, and mortal condition.[72]

Few white portrayals of black children countered the virulent racism of the day, but those that did did important work. Albert Leslie Smith's 1889 oil painting *The News Boy* sensitively depicts an African American youth eating an orange on a street corner.[73] J. G. Brown also saw black children's humanity and fellowship. His oft-reproduced 1888–89 oil painting *Give Us a Light* profiles a white shoeshine boy cheerfully lighting the cigarette of a black newsboy. Brown's subject "is always a good republican-democrat," noted one critic. "He knows no classes in society, rich or poor, white or black, bond or free; all the 'fellers' he knows in his busy little world are judged on their merits." While overstated, the assessment suggests that Brown recognized real camaraderie among the boys he met. Maulsby House notwithstanding, most newsboys' homes were integrated. "I've had as many as thirty-nine different nationalities in this lodging house in one night," said Rudolph Heig, superintendent of the home on New Chambers Street in New York between 1875 and 1910, "including Chinese, negroes, Arabs and Egyptians, and never once has there been a fight between the boys while they were inside the building."[74]

Brown cast a compassionate eye on black girls, too. His 1899 painting *Morning Papers* portrays an African American, about 13 years old, hawking papers alone on a street (Plate 16). She wears heavy boots and a muslin change-apron over her drab skirt and once fancy pink blouse. Her hair has been pulled into knots. She tentatively holds out a paper and warily eyes someone approaching from off canvas. It is one of Brown's most naturalistic works; the girl exhibits none of the exaggerated dash and spirit of his newsboys. Nor does she possess the coy femininity he gave his white flower peddlers. Instead, *Morning Papers* is a study of everyday courage. One could hardly have hoped for more at a time when "the problem of the color-line," in Du Bois's prescient phrase, was emerging as "the problem of the Twentieth Century."[75]

The Midnight Newsgirl Evil

Newsgirls presented Victorian America with one of its most vexing problems. Their increasing number, indigence, and brashness raised concerns over the dangers of street work. "Girls who begin with selling newspapers usually end with selling themselves," said New York police captain Edward Tynan. Buffalo mayor Grover Cleveland, a onetime newsboy, agreed. "No pretext should be permitted to excuse allowing young girls to be on the streets at improper hours," he told his city council, "since the result must necessarily be their destruction."[76] Elbridge Gerry, founder of the Society for the Prevention of Cruelty to Children in 1874, enforced the law to the letter with girls, who, he said, "fell into bad company [and] tread the downward path almost before they are women." Indeed, by 1886 news peddling and prostitution were so firmly equated that a New York police court released a man who had tried to assault two newsgirls, Minnie and Ida Brink, ages 10 and 11, because their occupation alone was proof of their "bad character." The sisters were committed to the Juvenile Asylum, where Ida died five months later of pleuropneumonia.[77]

Sexual predators and SPCC officers targeted newsgirls without recrimination throughout the 1890s. One well-to-do merchant who pleaded guilty to abducting a 13-year-old vendor on the Battery was allowed to remain anonymous and pay a $1,000 fine in lieu of jail. The SPCC's solution was to remove potential victims from the streets, even girls like Maggie O'Connell, who worked at her mother's newsstand. Officers kept her under surveillance and reported that by age 16 she had developed into a "bold, 'tough' young girl." They finally arrested her in December 1899 for trying to sell a pair of stolen shoes while on her rounds.[78]

Newspaper publishers responded variously to reformers' interest in newsgirls. Victor Lawson of the *Chicago Daily News* applauded their efforts. "I do not believe that selling newspapers is demoralizing to boys," he said. "But [it] is the ruin of girls." He had ordered his staff to stop selling papers to girls in 1883, but found that they simply paid boys to buy papers for them. *Hartford Times* publisher A. E. Burr objected to the indiscriminate mixing of the sexes. He set up separate entrances, waiting rooms, and counters for girls, and hired staff to supervise them on the premises.[79]

Other publishers defended newsgirls' honor and their right to work. In 1896 the *New York Journal* depicted in words and pictures the Gerry Society's "capture" of sobbing newsgirls who called for their mothers in Italian, German, Hebrew, and English. Two years later it played up the arrest of "pretty" 13-year-old Lillian Hadley of Hoboken, New Jersey, for "the crime of being a little girl and selling newspapers long after dark." The family had fallen on hard times after

Lillian's father was injured on the job at the Fulton Fish Market. Her mother took in washing and her older brother worked as a peddler's helper. "I sell papers because Emma and Irene are too small to do anything," Lillian explained to a reporter. "I go to school at St. Mary's. When school is out mother gives me 10 cents and I come to New York and sell papers. Lots of people buy papers from me. Some of 'em give me 5 cents for a one-cent paper and won't take any change. I stay till the theatres are out and then I go home. I 'most always have more'n a dollar." When told that she was better off with the SPCC than at home, Lillian replied, "Excuse me for contradicting, but I don't think I am."[80]

Girls like Lillian fought back in many ways. They stood up verbally and physically to newsboys who tried to drive them off. They peddled in groups and developed a lacerating pertness to parry indecent proposals. They resisted arrest by lying on the ground, forcing police to carry them bodily, kicking and screaming, to stationhouses. And they crashed newsboy banquets and excursions. In sum, America's newsgirls demanded not just protection but equality.

Newsgirls of the nineties fell into three recognized age categories: prepubescent girls up to 13 years old, sexually maturing girls in their teens, and grown women in their twenties or older. The youngest girls usually worked with parents or siblings, as exemplified by 3-year-old Annetta in Chicago. Praised in 1888 as the "smallest newsvendor in the world," she toddled around beside her elder sister in a coarse, stuffed petticoat and oversized boots. Annetta gave her papers away but took in tips hand over dimpled fist. Also in this class is the squinting newsgirl photographed by Alice Austen in 1896, one of five girls who sold in New York's City Hall Park during the four o'clock rush (Figure 9.8). "Each one is surrounded by a phalanx of small boys, who make it their duty to look after their gentle competitor in a fatherly and superior way," reported the New York Sun.[81]

Another strategy of girls in this and the elder cohort was to pass themselves off as boys. Fourteen-year-old runaway Lily Thompson Brown, alias Harry O'Brien, did this successfully for three weeks in the early 1880s. Twenty years later, eight or ten "rather delicate looking specimens" were caught among the 2,000 boys filing in for the Thanksgiving dinner at the Newsboys' Lodging House in New York. They were all under 10 years old and dressed in boys' clothes. They told Heig that they wanted to partake of the feast, as they sold papers too. It violated house rules for girls to enter, but he made an exception and had the girls fed separately. While transgressing gender boundaries can arouse erotic pleasure, newsgirls' masquerade seems to have been economically motivated: the pleasures they sought were those of fair treatment and a full stomach.[82]

Unlike their male counterparts, preadolescent newsgirls were usually characterized as beggars rather than merchants. Girls merely "pretend" to offer their newspapers for sale to passersby, said the Chicago Tribune in 1890. "They add tears and pitiful appeals to their suffering and bedraggled appearance,

Figure 9.8. Alice Austen, *City Hall Park, New York, April 13, 1896*. New York Public Library.

and no stranger is able to resist them." Even their raggedness took on different meanings; it connoted poverty and neglect in boys but nakedness and sexual exposure for girls.[83]

The middle group of newsgirls, those "just starting to put up their hair," attracted the most attention due to their budding sexuality. Indeed, the specter of prostitution led reformers to focus more attention on prohibiting these girls from peddling papers than the younger ones. Authorities at the turn of the century believed that delinquency in girls coincided with sexual maturity (then common at age 14) but preceded it in the case of boys. Physicians concurred that puberty weakened the constitution and confidence of girls through the "illness" of menstruation but brought strength and vigor to boys.[84] Hence news peddling was widely regarded as a crime of precocious sexuality for adolescent girls. Those who peddled after dark constituted what came to be known in Chicago as "the midnight newsgirl evil."

The number of newsgirls in the Windy City doubled from fifty in the early 1880s to a hundred in the early 1890s. Three out of four were Italian, with Danes, Irish, Jews, and African Americans filling out the ranks. They made up 5 percent of the newsboy population. The proliferation of these "frizzle-haired damsels" reflected not just the surge in immigration, but also the commercial nightlife that came to define the Gay Nineties. Modest increases in wages and decreases in work hours, coupled with the untaxed incomes of the "society set," meant that more people could frequent neighborhood bars and dancehalls, downtown theaters and concert saloons, and the new storefront nickelodeons. Newsboys and newsgirls were drawn to these bright lights as hawkers and consumers.[85]

Newsgirls' parents did not think that the streets were devoid of danger, only that their daughters could take care of themselves. Elgar Jacobson and Nellie O'Meara in Chicago were known to thrash four boys at a time, but they also relied on policemen to protect them from the bigger boys and, for a fee, save them a place at the head of the line at one of the newspaper offices. Illustrations in the *National Police Gazette* showed how one "Amazonian Slogger" used her fists to rescue an abused comrade, and depicted a mixed-sex gang of snowball-throwers subduing "the newsgirl masher of City Hall Park."[86]

"Girl newsboys" also faced harassment from boys. The boys subjected them to a "most vicious kind of persecution," observed the *Brooklyn Eagle*, and chased them "from the most profitable places." "We don't get the same chances as the boys, and they don't treat us fairly," one "swarthy faced" 12-year-old told the *New York Sun*. "We don't make a dollar a day, or anything near it. The boys may do that, and better, but we can't. Some of the boys sleep around the newspaper offices all night to get the early morning papers. We mustn't do that, you know. Then, the boys save money, at least the big ones do, those that live in the Newsboys' Home. There is no News-girls' Home. . . . I wish I was a beauty. I'd get along well enough then."[87]

Some newsgirls did trade on their sex appeal. Reporters observed them flirting with men, slapping them on the arm in overly familiar ways or holding their fingers while coaxing them to buy. "A newsgirl has little hope of success if she is not pretty," commented the *Sun* in 1886. Recognizing the rewards of pulchritude, rival vendors under the Chauncey Street platform in Brooklyn employed their prettiest daughters and nieces to attract customers. A "merry war" broke out among the girls in the summer of 1890 that escalated from threats and slaps to overturned tables and arrests.[88]

The most famous newsgirls in fin de siècle New York were the Horn sisters, Winnie, 22, and Sadie, 16, who vended papers at the bottom of the El at Sixth Avenue and 23rd Street (Figure 9.9). With their plumed hats, tapered shirtwaists, and billowing skirts, the sisters were as fashionable as any shopgirl, exemplars of the stylish "New Woman" of the nineties. "Winsome Winnie" liked to write bits of scripture or hymn verses on the margins of the papers she sold. Dubbed "Queen of the Newsgirls," she was celebrated in photographs, illustrations, and human-interest stories that circulated nationally. So complete was her fame that actress Theresa Vaughn immortalized her in a production at the Olympia Theatre

Figure 9.9. Alice Austen, *Newsgirl, Twenty-third Street El Station, Sixth Avenue.* (Probably one of the Horn sisters.) 1896. New York Public Library.

and the Eden Musée exhibited her form in wax. Some upper-class women nevertheless disapproved of their vocation. "Haven't you any home or any parents?" they would ask. They did indeed; their father was a disabled Civil War veteran, and he was as proud of them as their mother was. "My two gals there earn all we eat and pay for our clothes and supplies," said Mrs. Horn. "They're smart— they're smart!" [89]

However pretty or smart, most girls worked the streets as part of a family plan to pay rent and put food on the table. Jennie Reimers, the first newsgirl in St. Paul, Minnesota, started peddling papers at 7th and Wabasha in 1885 at age 11 after her father took sick. The family had recently arrived from Germany, and Jennie was the eldest of five children. Her sister Minnie joined her a few years later, along with a half-dozen other girls, ages 5 to 13. The local humane society pressured police to shoo them off the streets for their own good. Mrs. Reimers, a midwife, resented their interference. "Vhat you vhants mit mein girls?" she roared. "I am te mutter of mein own children." Jennie saw ulterior motives. "What these women wanted," she said, "was me to do housework for them." Her male competitors thought it only fair. "Ha! he!" they taunted. "Yeze 'll have to go to washin' dishes, where yeze belong."[90]

Jennie and the boys had assessed the situation correctly. Middle-class women in many cities contrasted the moral domestic space of the home with the immoral commercial space of the street. They viewed their recruitment of servants as a kind of missionary work. In Cleveland, they supported a city ordinance barring girls from the news trade and steering them into jobs minding children or doing housework, ignorant of the fact that more prostitutes came out of domestic service than out of other occupations.[91]

The newsgirl problem sparked a particularly heated debate in Hartford, Connecticut, where fifty girls regularly sold papers downtown after dark in the mid-1890s. Clubwomen and teachers complained in letters to the editor of the *Hartford Courant* that the girls ran in and out of saloons, where they encountered "low" men and—judging from the vulgarities hurled at those who declined to buy their papers—became coarse. A member of the local working girls' club said these girls "noticeably trade upon their sex, begging for patronage and playing the piteous, as girls." Whatever blows they received at home, she said, were far less injurious than the flirtatious taps under the chin they received from the men who bought their papers. Several city councilmen, urban missionaries, and newspaper publishers disagreed, insisting that the girls had as much right to peddle as the boys.[92]

To settle the question, Trinity College sociologist and Episcopal minister John J. McCook visited the homes of some thirty Hartford newsgirls, nearly all of whom were from poor Jewish families. His handwritten field notes provide a rare glimpse into the economic and emotional realities that underlay parents' decision to let their children peddle papers. The girls, McCook found, came from large families and ranged from age 7 to 14, with 12 the median. Both parents usually worked, and three families admitted to having received public aid. Most of the girls peddled papers on their own, but some worked with siblings. Their parents approved of their efforts. "We would all have died if it hadn't been for the children selling papers this winter," Yetta Rogers's mother told McCook. She said Yetta made $2 to $3 a week, while her husband sent $1 a week from Boston. She earned $6 a week taking in washing, for a total of $10. Their rent was $8 a week, minus the $3 the town provided. The mother of Rosa Rosenfeld echoed Mrs. Rogers's sentiments: "If they stop her from selling we shall starve." Two other mothers pointed out that news peddling enabled their daughters to stay in school, as they otherwise would have had to find regular employment. Still, parents were often torn over the issue. "I am ashamed to have my children sell papers but had to make them do it," said Mrs. Sedlesky. "I and my husband cried the first time they went out."[93]

McCook concluded that the girls should be allowed to peddle so long as their hours were regulated. The Hartford Common Council agreed; in January 1896 it prohibited all street sales by girls or boys under 14 during school hours and after 8 p.m., but otherwise let them be. McCook and the council acknowledged that news peddling made the girls "tougher" than normal, but unlike the SPCC, they saw this toughness as an acquired defense against moral corruption, not evidence of corruption itself.

The mature women who formed the oldest cohort of "newsgirls" usually outnumbered the younger ones and faced different challenges. Mothers sometimes peddled with babes in arms or toddlers tethered to stands. The elderly worked from stools and acquired honorifics like "Grandma" or "Aunty." "Aunt" Jane Syron of Elizabeth, New Jersey, for instance, started peddling papers in 1850 as a 12-year-old and stayed on the job for more than seventy years. Her only concession to age was using a baby carriage to transport her papers.[94]

The women's age afforded them little protection from the predations of boys and men, especially if they failed to support their strikes, placate local merchants, or dress conventionally. Fifty-nine-year-old "Aunty" Mary Kennedy, who sold papers for fifteen years in front of the *New York Herald* building on Ann Street and Broadway, kept a whip on hand to repel boys who would pilfer her stock. Exceedingly devout after her newsboy son was run over by a fire engine, she often sat reading a prayer book, saying her rosary, or singing hymns to herself. Her presence grew to annoy the manager of a nearby drugstore. On Thanksgiving Day 1891, Officer John J. Gallagher accused Kennedy of bothering pedestrians. He threw her stool into the street, tossed her papers into the gutter, and flung her by the neck onto the sidewalk. He then kicked and cursed her until she fled. When she returned for her belongings, the officer struck her several times more in the face and marched her to the Tombs. Witnesses lodged complaints against Gallagher. He testified that Kennedy was drunk and disorderly, but the court didn't believe him. He served six months in jail and was dismissed from the force.[95]

Kennedy's ordeal was not unique; some newswomen endured years of harassment. Anna Perkins of Cleveland withstood a torrent of abuse between 1886 and 1900 for daring to wear men's clothes and speak her mind. A small woman who liked to write poetry and talk politics, Perkins became a fixture on the southeast corner of Cleveland's Public Square. An admirer of dress reformer Dr. Mary Walker, she wore white duck knee pants or brown denim bloomers and an assortment of headgear, from jockey caps to sombreros. The *Cleveland Leader* called her the "pantalooned poetess" and teased her about carrying on a romance with the police superintendent to whom she complained. The *Cleveland Plain Dealer* questioned her sanity. Both papers ran anonymous letters criticizing her outfits as affronts to decency. Perkins usually challenged her critics to debate, but none ever accepted. Her lack of "beauty show" looks led sponsors of a Thanksgiving Day raffle to name one of the turkeys after her.[96]

Such ridicule emboldened newsboys to insult her as well. "They abuse me foully and say the nastiest things," she said. "The policemen who hang about the corners look on and laugh. The boys hired this big fellow, who came up and grabbed me by the throat, knocking my head against the lamppost. I screamed, but no help came. A lot of nicely dressed women stood near and grinned, as if it was a good joke." Boys followed her home and threw firecrackers through her window; once they tossed in a dead cat. Perkins withstood the bullying and spurned every offer of charity when she fell ill or lost her lodgings. Hospitalized with typhoid fever in her early fifties, she would call out her papers in her delirium. Anna Perkins died on February 1, 1900, having left $15 for her burial. Her bloomers, trousers, and white linen jacket somehow found their way into the Western Reserve Historical Society, where they remain.[97]

Such was the fate of America's newsgirls; however old, attractive, or accommodating, they met with abuse from their patrons, peers, and would-be protectors.

Gospels of Reform

An array of solutions emerged in the late 1880s and early 1890s to address the news peddler problem in all its guises: the annoying beggar, bellicose striker, unsightly cripple, treacherous alien, ignorant Negro, brazen she-devil, and eccentric old crone. Behind most of these efforts stood middle-class Protestants infused with the spirit of the gospels. Their loosely organized Anglo-American movement reflected dissatisfaction with laissez -faire capitalism and the dog-eat-dog ethos of social Darwinism. Adherents felt that it was their Christian duty to build God's kingdom on earth by eradicating poverty, vice, and other social evils, particularly in cities. In 1886 the Rev. Charles Goss of Chicago backed a law prohibiting girls from peddling papers by saying, "God holds cities responsible, just as he does individuals." His Brooklyn colleague the Rev. Thomas De Witt Talmage turned CAS founder Charles Loring Brace's warning on its head and preached that the most dangerous classes were not poor street children but the idle rich. Nor did the capitalist press's use of child labor escape criticism. English Social Gospeler W. T. Stead blasted newspapers for abdicating their God-given role as moral guardians. In his 1894 diatribe *If Christ Came to Chicago!* Stead singled out the *Evening Dispatch* as "the drunken helot of journalism" for defiling its columns with ads for brothels and feigning ignorance of the "mere lads" who sold papers there.[98]

Catholic social action simultaneously accelerated with Pope Leo XIII's 1891 encyclical *Rerum Novarum* (Of Revolutionary Change), which called for greater attention by the Church to the problems of the industrial working class. "In regards to children," he wrote, "just as very rough weather destroys the buds of spring, so does too early an experience of life's hard toil blight the young promise of a child's faculties, and render any true education impossible." Catholic clergy and laity established newsboys' homes, shoe drives, and orphan trains. The pope specifically recognized America's newsboys and their guardians in a benediction read at the 1894 unveiling of a statue honoring Father Drumgoole, the late chaplain of St. Vincent's Newsboys' Home. Located in front of Drumgoole's ten-story Mission of the Immaculate Virgin, at the corner of Lafayette Place and Great Jones Street in New York, the ten-foot-high bronze tableau showed the priest turning from his breviary to comfort a little newsboy who has thrown down his papers and clings to Drumgoole's cassock for protection. Opposite sits the same boy, no longer ragged, reading his lessons.[99]

Jewish community leaders also unfurled the banner of reform. Following the "Deed, not Creed" motto of Dr. Felix Adler's nonsectarian New York Society for Ethical Culture, and suspending their suspicion of proselytizing perfectionists, prominent Jews throughout the United States joined local charity organizations, sanitary unions, and playground societies in building newsboys' homes, reading rooms, and other facilities. They also established their own Hebrew schools, hospitals, and orphan asylums. Such work sometimes led to vocations. New Haven produced both a priest and a rabbi from the ranks of its newsboys. Once a "wild lad" of the street, John C. Collins was ordained in 1886 after completing seminary and doing volunteer work with boys, while Russian immigrant Bernard Liebowitz hawked and delivered papers for years before entering rabbinical school in 1888.[100]

This interfaith fervor for social justice took many practical forms, including a newsboy washroom in Louisville, a proposed newsboys' college at the Brooklyn Tabernacle, and a string of cheap coffee stands in New York that exposed fissures in the reform front. The first of six St. Andrew's One Cent Coffee Stands opened near the office of the *New York Herald* in 1887. It was the brainchild of Mrs. Clementine Lamadrid ("Mrs. St. Andrew" to the boys). The stands served food and drink to more than two thousand people a day, but irritated the powerful Charity Organization Society (COS). "We are convinced," said the head of the COS in 1890, "that they are patronized principally by tramps, who thus find an added facility for living without labor, and by newsboys, who thus have more money to gamble by policy-making, and to attend the theaters." The stands nevertheless served the poor for forty years.[101]

The most effective response to social and economic disparities was the settlement house movement inspired by London reformers and the Knights of Labor, which, in 1886, enlisted women of all ranks to investigate the working conditions of their sex. Settlement workers lived communally in poor, heavily immigrant districts and offered their neighbors a range of services, such as well-baby clinics, day nurseries, kindergartens, and newsboys' clubs. Two of the most active settlements on newsboy issues were Chicago's Hull-House, founded in 1889 by Jane Addams and Ellen Gates Starr, and the Henry Street Settlement, founded in New York in 1893 by public health nurse Lillian Wald. Hull House was the donated mansion of real estate developer Charles J. Hull, a friend and mentor to many newsboys and an early supporter of the city's newsboys' home.[102]

By the turn of the century there were over a hundred settlement houses in the United States, including some staffed exclusively by Catholic nuns or Jewish social workers. They became sites of mounting opposition to child labor, especially street labor. In 1895 Hull House resident and Illinois state factory inspector Florence Kelley likened street work to "white child slavery" and lobbied for stronger compulsory education laws. "There is no body of self-supporting children more in need of effective care than these newsboys and bootblacks," she said. "They are ill-fed, ill-housed, ill-clothed, illiterate, and wholly untrained and unfitted for any occupation. The only useful thing they learn at their work is the rapid calculation of small sums in making change; and this does not go far enough to be of any practical value."[103]

A committed socialist and licensed attorney, Kelley was well ahead of the public and her sister reformers on this issue. The only speaker to address the subject at the National Conference on Charities and Corrections in New York in 1898 was Mrs. Emily Williamson of the New Jersey Board of Children's Guardians. She paid tribute to the "street Arab" of New York, Chicago, Baltimore, and Boston, calling them "our best and noblest citizens." "I have made a close study of them," she said, "and have made up my mind that they are not only honest, honorable, and industrious, but that they are chivalrous." She offered several anecdotes in which newsboys refused handouts and extended aid to strangers or consociates. She urged conference-goers to help these children in their natural habitat rather than remove them from their families. This was a dig at the Children's Aid Society's orphan trains and the SPCC's institutionalization of young peddlers. No one challenged Williamson's remarks, yet within a few years, largely through Kelley's efforts, any such idealization of the "street Arab" in reform circles would get a speaker booed off the stage.[104]

Newsboys' biggest advocates during the decade were not the settlement women who wished to abolish their trade, nor evangelical reformers like Brace or his son, Charles Loring Brace Jr., but public-spirited "boy workers"—adults who believed in guiding their efforts to earn a living. Chief among these was John Gunckel, a Toledo ticket agent for the Lake Shore Railroad. Shocked at the swearing and fighting among the scores of newsboys who waited at the station for their papers, he began to "weave" himself among them. He gathered over a hundred for a Christmas dinner in 1892, which marked the founding of the Boyville Newsboys' Association. Membership was at first restricted to news peddlers and bootblacks, but the boys decided to let carriers in. The club was "self-governing," a philosophy born of necessity when a local clothier offered to give fifty coats to the neediest boys. With twice that many members, there was only one solution: "Let the boys do it." Adult control remained strong nonetheless; Gunckel held on to the reins as president and the club's trustees were chosen from newspaper men and other "leading citizens." Club rules prohibited swearing, lying, stealing, gambling, drinking, and smoking, and its Sunday afternoon meetings were scheduled to conflict with Sunday theater matinees.[105]

Newsboys also came under the scrutiny of reformers, architects, and urban planners associated with the City Beautiful movement. Repulsed by squalid tenements and disorderly downtowns, and stimulated by the pristine "White City" of the Columbian Exposition, city beautifiers sought to raise the moral and aesthetic standards of their communities. Those in Chicago, Detroit, Hartford, and Washington, DC, saw the children who blocked sidewalks and pestered pedestrians with their papers as an urban blight in need of removal.[106] Yet other citizens felt that neat, courteous, and accommodating newsboys enhanced the quality of city life. Newspaper publishers certainly thought so, as did many newsboys' parents and customers. This more sympathetic view found expression in the impressionist paintings of Frederick Childe Hassam. He placed a lone newsboy in several of his Boston and New York street scenes (Plate 17). These little dabs of humanity complemented the clean streets, stately buildings, and lush parklands of Gilded Age cities on the cusp of modernity.[107]

Yet one of the main objections to real newsboys was their incessant shouting. Their cries generated opposition from resurgent sabbatarians and secular "scientific" anti-noise crusaders. Sabbatarians failed in their petition for a federal Sunday rest law in 1889, but forced city officials in both North and South, and the entire state of Kentucky, to ban "halloaing in public" and to resurrect ancient blue laws (Philadelphia's dated back to 1794) that forbade the "worldly employment of business on the Lord's Day." "There are 200,000 newsboys in this country selling Sunday papers," evangelist Dwight L. Moody declared in an 1896 sermon at the Cooper Union in New York. "I would not touch a Sunday paper any more than I would touch tar. They have done more to demoralize the Church of God than anything else."[108]

Jack "Speedy" Moxley, onetime "king" of the newsboys in Dallas, inadvertently confirmed Moody's charge with a little ditty published in the *Dallas Morning News*:

> Wots de use uv filling pews,
> Where ders so much Sunday News,
> Latest bout de poison case.

Prize fight and suburban race;
Latest scandal in high life.
Chuck McCarty kills his wife . . .
Wots de use uv fillin pews,
Stay at home an git de News.[109]

Citing medical rather than biblical texts, scientific anti-noise advocates agitated for the passage of "shush laws," claiming that the cacophony of city life constituted a health hazard. Neurologist George M. Beard argued that the din of traffic, factories, and peddlers, exacerbated by the yowl of the yellow press, left city dwellers in a perpetual state of alarm, causing pulses to race, mouths to dry, and muscles of the digestive tract to tense involuntarily. These nervous disorders led to fatigue, accidents, and loss of production that took as big a toll on business as fire. Because they equated noise with youth, savagery, and "the raucous taint of the lower classes," both secular and religious noise reformers made newsboys prime targets.[110]

But the boys proved impossible to shush. A group in Pittsburgh resolved in 1892 that it is "no more sinful to sell newspapers on Sunday than it is to stew hash for a preacher's breakfast on the same day."[111] Citing their inalienable right to petition against grievances, Washington, DC, newsies, both black and white, met in Willard Hall in January 1897 to denounce the district's new Sabbath law. William Sabbs, "a big colored newsboy," told how he supported his widowed mother selling Sunday papers, while other newsboys enabled their siblings to attend school. W. H. Washington got a laugh when he noted that one of his subscribers was a minister who scolded him when he missed a Sunday delivery due to illness. The boys passed a resolution calling for the ruling to be rescinded. The city's Secular League promised to post bail for all violators. The brouhaha was resolved by the adoption of an industry-backed "newsboy clause" which allowed hawkers to cry their papers between 7 a.m. and 8 p.m. on "secular days of the week," between 8 a.m. and 10:30 a.m. on Sundays, and whenever extras were issued.[112] Newsboys in Michigan, Colorado, Indiana, and other states won similar exemptions from curfew laws.[113]

Hollered headlines were music to the ears of publishers. Pulitzer once complained that he couldn't sleep when "a big loud-mouthed boy" was yelling other papers under his window, but slept like a baby when a strong-lunged *World* newsboy replaced him. Circulation managers augmented the noisiness of their sales force by issuing whistles to carriers and bells to hawkers. They sponsored yelling contests and deployed newsboy bands to drum up readers. A *Puck* cartoon hardly exaggerated by depicting an elephant carrying a brass band on its back and holding a sign in its trunk saying "Buy the Daily Cyclone" while a man dispenses copies to newsboys from a booth strapped to its side (Plate 18). "The present method of delivery is too quiet," reads the caption. "If you want to suc-ceed, you must make a noise."[114]

A distinctive cry or voice functioned in the marketplace like a trademark. "Their voices are the[ir] fortune," observed the *Omaha Herald* about two transients from Chicago, "Pinafore" and "Waffles." Many hawkers earned col-orful nicknames with their hullabalooing. Chicago's press chorus included a whooper known as "Indian," a howler dubbed "Big Mouth Jane," and a crower called "Rooster." Salt Lake City claimed "Squeak," Omaha had "Foghorn," and New York was home to Eddie Carroll, aka "De Goat" because of the hoarse-ness of his yell.[115] Newsboys' cries "burned themselves like odors into my brain," wrote poet John Hall Wheelock, "Sharp and yet sweet." Other auditors likened them to Gregorian chants and called their creators "undeveloped Mozarts." One composer was inspired to write a "Newsboy Rondo," while another penned the operetta *Jimmy the Newsboy*.[116]

Newsboys also distinguished themselves by their tricks and patter. Peddling papers doubled as a kind of performance art, with the most talented vendors using the sidewalk as a stage. In 1893 13-year-old runaway "Whitey" Dukenfield juggled folded newspapers and concocted ridiculous news stories to attract atten-tion on the streets of Philadelphia: "Bronislaw Gimp acquires license for three-legged sheepdog. Details on page 26," he called, or "Amos Stump Discovered Living in Eagle's Nest." When a customer complained that his paper contained no such story, Dukenfield acted as if the injured party had won the lottery. "My dear sir, you were the victim of a printer's error. Due to a mechanical imperfec-tion, three papers out of thousands failed to carry the item." Dukenfield grew up to be comedian W. C. Fields, whose motto was "Never give a sucker an even break."[117]

Flattery was perhaps the most effective stratagem of the street seller, and no compliment paid so well as simply calling a customer by name. For instance, when the multi-talented lawyer and educator James Weldon Johnson came to New York in the late 1890s he gained a reputation as a prolific songwriter and "physician for ailing musicals." He was walking up Broadway one evening with an out-of-town guest when "a little newsboy ran up to me shouting, 'Mr. Johnson, you want the latest edition?' I didn't want it," he said, "but I bought it."[118]

Dash and panache netted cash in the news trade. Given the public's insa-tiable demand for amusement, some hawkers leaped onto the legitimate stage. In 1895 a sketch called "Urchins of New York" featuring real buskers trained up to professional standards debuted at the Union Square Theater. It opened with a gang of newsboys and bootblacks playing street games, only to be set wheeling with the arrival of an Italian organ grinder. In comes his dark-eyed wife with a tambourine, followed by four colorfully costumed newsgirls. They dance, skip rope, and join in singing "The East Side Girl" and "Sally in Our Alley." "One of the newsboys—a little colored chap—dances with such enthusiasm," said a reviewer, "that his legs seem like snare drumsticks in active play." The scene ended with a mad scramble for coins tossed onto the stage. Audiences regarded these newcomers not as exploited victims but as evidence of the vitality of the American dream. Child labor reformers clearly had more work to do.[119]

In the Camera's Eye

New reforms require new stories, and some of the period's most effective storytellers used cameras. Photography was primarily a city hobby that boomed in the 1890s with improved technology and the spectacle of urbanization. The introduction of compact handheld "detective" cameras and roll film meant that amateurs and professionals alike could dispense with large-format cameras, plates, and tripods. "The camera never traveled so well as it has since losing its legs," quipped hobbyist Alexander Black in the children's magazine St. Nicholas. Children and buildings proved to be the most popular subjects; slum kids were as obliging as they were abundant, sometimes mobbing photographers and demanding to be "taken." Boys who sold papers could be found in all parts of the city. In New York, Black snapped them huddled around a news wagon, while the commercial father-son team of Joseph and Percy Byron caught them standing against the human tide at rush hour or patronizing pushcarts during slack times. These camera buffs were driven by no greater social agenda than a desire to document their growing city, and to do it, as modernist photographer and artist Edward Steichen later said, "without opinion, comment, slant or emotion."[120]

Other photographers consciously exploited newsboys' comic, sentimental, or aesthetic appeal. In 1895 Demorest's Family Magazine published a flipbook-like sequence showing newsboys lounging in a park, relieving a man of his roller skates, shooting craps, accosting passersby, and driving off a rival. The series makes no effort to critique their behavior, only to present it as an amusing slice of city life, much like the "actualities" coming out of Edison's studio and playing in vaudeville theaters and kinetoscope parlors. More cloying specimens could be found among the winners of Overland Monthly's 1898 photo contest, including "The Good Samaritan," a staged depiction of a San Francisco Examiner newsboy bandaging a dog's paw.[121]

Pictorialists—those who practiced photography as a fine art—also set their sights on newsboys, but usually to portray them as embodiments of truth and beauty. Boston pictorialist and settlement house volunteer F. Holland Day selected so many models from the city's urchin class in the late nineties that he was known as "the Pied Piper of the South End." He soon treated his favorites, the six Constanza brothers—all Boston Herald newsboys—and their bootblack cousin Nicola Giancola, to vacations at his summer home in Maine, where, in the spirit of the old masters, he produced gauzy photographs of them in the nude as nymphs, fauns, and saints.[122]

It thus fell to the seemingly artless photography of *New York Tribune* (and later *Evening Sun*) reporter Jacob Riis to alter the way Americans saw street kids. Newsboys figured prominently in his decade-long "battle with the slum" because, for him, they epitomized both the problem of the working poor and the solutions: wise charity and individual initiative. Riis portrayed children on the Lower East Side as victims of what he called the "tenement-house problem."[123] Unlike most of his contemporaries, he traced the roots of social misery not to alcohol, low wages, or innate character flaws but to overcrowding in squalid apartments that bred vice, crime, and disease. Riis pierced the darkness of these "rookeries" and awed their inhabitants with a new invention from Germany— magnesium *Blitzlichtpulver*, or flash powder—that allowed him and his raiding party to provide irrefutable evidence of the appalling conditions that had only previously been sketched by the subjective pencils of artists and writers.

To Riis, the least culpable slum-dwellers were the children, and the most admirable of these were newsboys. "Down on Nassau Street and Printing-house Square is the place to find them after midnight," he wrote, "when the big newspaper presses have begun to rattle and spin. The boys there are not all homeless, but little shivering groups of real street Arabs will be found bunched together on the grated openings in the pavement that let out the heat and noise of the underground press-rooms." Riis backed up his description with candid and posed photographs that tended to reduce his human subjects to frozen tableaus of suffering. Riis projected these images in lantern-slide lectures he delivered throughout the country in his peculiar, rasping, slightly accented voice. He leavened these "lay sermons" with humor and music: when the picture of the sleep-outs went up during a Brooklyn engagement, two cornetists in the wings of the stage played "Where Is My Wandering Boy To-night?"[124]

Riis used his photos to equally good effect as line drawings or halftones in his magazine articles, his 1890 shocker *How the Other Half Lives*, and its 1892 sequel *Children of the Poor*. Whether in print or onstage, his aim was to spur the public into action. "What are you going to do about it?" he would ask. Thirty-two-year-old Theodore Roosevelt responded in 1890 by leaving a card on Riis's desk saying, "I have read your book and I have come to help." Five years later, as New York City police commissioner, Roosevelt joined Riis's "midnight rambles" to root out vice, crime, and police misconduct.[125]

Riis distrusted the schemes of government and labor, but not practical philanthropy like that of the Children's Aid Society, which also began using photographs to illustrate its annual reports. Like Brace, but unlike the emerging generation of reformers, Riis saw news peddling by children as a way to allay urban poverty and stave off social unrest. Although once a friendless immigrant himself, Riis, too, was prone to pigeonhole his subjects. Referring to New York newsboys, he spoke of the "jovial Irish," "sunny Italian," and "sharp-witted Jew." Yet this stereotyping never approached the bigotry of Chicago's Sigmund Krausz. Riis believed that environment exerted a much greater influence on the development of character than ethnicity, and that "it all comes down to character in the end."[126] He praised Brace's efforts to "set a little chap up in business with a capital of five cents to buy papers." The effect, he said, "is to avoid the trap of charity or dependence, and to encourage in the boys their strong quality of self-help." Riis also lauded the CAS's orphan trains, industrial schools, and six newsboys' lodging houses. He photographed lodgers at the Duane Street home attending night classes, washing up, and horsing around:

> "If they would only behave, sir!" one of the boys said to Riis, "you could make a good picture."
> "Yes," he agreed, "but it isn't in them, I suppose."
> "No, b'gosh!" said the boy, "them kids ain't got no sense, no-how!"[127]

Riis's lodging house photos presented the boys as high-spirited citizens-in-the-making, worthy of all the efforts undertaken on their behalf. The interior scenes, in conjunction with his street photos, also helped him create his own before-and-after narrative intended to win friends for Brace's charity. There were other possible narratives. Brooklyn photographer Julius Wilcox suggests one of uninhibited bonhomie in his 1892 series on the Duane Street home: he shows the boys using the gymnasium and receiving post-workout rubdowns in the buff (Figure 9.10). Riis offered no hint of this intimate, perhaps homoerotic, side of life in the home. Nor did he ever mention the fights and occasional stabbings that occurred there.[128]

Though uncredited, Riis's pictures and anecdotes found their way into the 1892 bestseller *Darkness and Daylight: or Lights and Shadows of New York Life*, a 740-page tour of the city's underclass. "How," asked coauthor Helen Campbell, "shall one condense into one chapter the story of an army of newsboys in which each individual represents a case not only of 'survival of the fittest,' but of an experience that would fill a volume?" She did so by drawing heavily on the blend of romance, reportage, and religion found in Riis's study, Brace's 1872 memoir *The Dangerous Classes*, and evangelist George Needham's 1884 tract *Street Arabs and Guttersnipes*. Like them, she described newsboys as fatalists despite their propensity to protest. "He is every inch a philosopher," she said, "for he accepts bad fortune with stoical indifference."[129]

A respected home economist, Campbell linked the glut of newsboys to the industry in which they worked, saying, "Only the modern newspaper and its

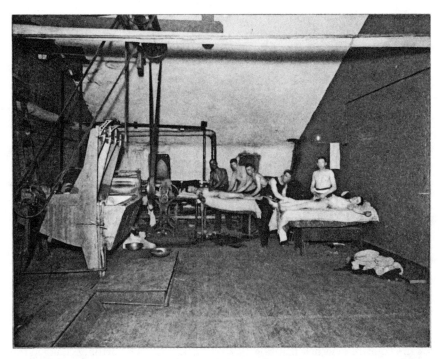

Figure 9.10. Young men give each other rubdowns after working out in the gym of the Newsboys' Lodging House on Duane Street in New York, 1892. Julius Wilcox, black and white canotype, 5 × 6 in. Brooklyn Collection, Brooklyn Public Library, Wilcox 1. Call No. WLC 0012.

needs could require the services of this numberless host." Her previous studies had taught her that some families relied on newsboy sons for "half at least of their future dependence," and she roundly criticized "the present system" in which ruthless and unregulated competition pauperized women and children and made class conflict inevitable. The antidote, she believed, was industrial education and cooperation. In 1891 she, Riis, Kelley, and others founded the Consumers' League of New York City to investigate and remedy the long hours and deplorable working conditions in shops, factories, and eventually the street trades.[130]

Riis abandoned the camera in 1898 but continued his campaign for slum clearance, housing codes, neighborhood parks, open schoolyards, boys' clubs, kindergartens, summer schools, and truant schools. He also helped close police lodging cellars, expose the padrone system, publicize the *Tribune*'s Fresh Air Fund, and launch the Scouting movement. While his blunt photographs, martial rhetoric, and manifold reforms may be criticized as mechanisms of social control, they required extraordinary moral and physical courage on Riis's part in standing up to police and landlords, and they materially improved the lives of

America's newsboys. Moreover, they led to a new form of exposure journalism—muckraking—that would carry the campaign against child street labor into the next century.[131]

The Gamin Fad

In the meantime, Riis's harrowing depictions of street children contributed to a veritable "gamin fad" that did more to retard than advance the abolition of child news peddling. Newspaper owners and managers began using photos and other images of newsboys to serve their own ends. Newsboy dinners and outings were now routinely photographed and used for advertising. The *Saginaw Evening News* stood more than four hundred carriers before the camera en route to Buffalo Bill's Wild West Show in July 1897, and then projected the image every night via a stereopticon lamp at Riverside Park to draw crowds to the park's amusements. The *Daily American* in Waterbury, Connecticut, commissioned a lithotype composed of nineteen photos of newsboys arranged across its front page (Figure 9.11). Several metropolitan dailies promoted themselves by distributing prints of an exquisite newsboy painting by Karl Witkowski, who artfully changed the banner of the boy's paper to match the client's (Plate 19).[132]

America's first comic-strip character, the Yellow Kid, also became a pitchman in 1896, shortly after Hearst lured his creator from Pulitzer's *World* to the *Evening Journal* (Figure 9.12). A native midwesterner, R. F. Outcault spotted the Kid's prototype during forays into the tenement wards, where he saw many little boys who wore their sisters' smocks and had their heads shaved to combat lice. In Hearst's employ, the big-eared, bald-headed, slang-spewing, shanty-Irish slum dweller recruited hawkers for the *Journal* by pointing to an enormous diamond stickpin on his nightshirt and saying: "Git onto me dimund!, I made it in one week sellin New York Evening Journals See!" But Pulitzer still owned the strip, so he hired George Luks to draw it for the *World*. Both papers paid gangs of boys to put up Yellow Kid posters and tear down those of the opposition. The Kid's toothy grin appeared on billboards, lampposts, newsstands, and streetcars—with gangs often clashing in the vicinity.[133]

Newspapers also produced a plethora of newsboy signs, sculptures, and objects to attract attention. The *Pawtucket Record*'s hand-carved trade sign of a running newsboy personified the paper's commercial vigor and became a recognizable symbol to passersby (Figure 9.13). The *Boston Herald* turned a colorful cartoon newsboy into its logo and placed his scampering likeness on trays, placards, and buildings. Newsboys were molded into kerosene lamps, penny banks, cigar cutters (Figure 9.14), and a host of other items marketed to the general public.

Figure 9.11. Newspapers used all their design and technical expertise to multiply newsboys' appeal. Lithotype Printing and Publishing Co., *Newspaper Boys of the Waterbury Daily American*, 1890, David A. Hanson Collection of the History of Photomechanical Reproduction, Sterling and Francine Clark Art Institute Library, Williamstown, MA.

A few former newsies erected life-sized monuments to the boys. In 1895 Colonel William Lee Brown, co-owner of the *New York Daily News*, built a fountain near his estate in Great Barrington, Massachusetts, featuring a bronze newsboy atop a ten-foot granite column. Two years later, *Detroit Evening News* founder James Scripps presented the city with *Partners*, a granite fountain on Belle Isle surmounted by a bronze newsboy and his dog. Five thousand Michigan newsies and three newsboy bands took part in the unveiling ceremony. These monuments paid solid if silent tribute to the "strive and succeed" legacy of the newsboy just as a small group of reformers was starting to chip away at it.[134]

At the same time, New England game manufacturers R. Bliss and Parker Brothers introduced newsboy board games in 1890 and 1895, respectively, to foster the character-building benefits of street peddling among those luckless lads born into middle-class families (Plate 20). In the safety of their own homes, players of the Parker Brothers' game used a spinner to advance wooden pieces along a winding path from the Newsboys Home to the Books and Stationery

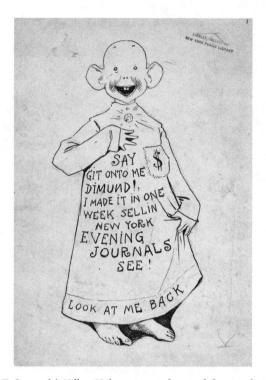

Figure 9.12. R. F. Outcault's *Yellow Kid* comic strip boosted the circulation of Hearst's *New York Evening Journal* by the thousands in 1896. Ink over pencil on paper, 10 11/16 × 7 9/16 in. Print Collection, Miriam and Ira D. Wallach Division of Art, Prints and Photographs, The New York Public Library; Astor, Lenox and Tilden Foundations.

store. Strictly a game of chance, contestants skipped ahead if they landed on blue circles marked Enterprise, Honesty, or Bright Manner, and fell back or went to Lock Up if they alighted on ones marked Dishonesty, Poor Trade, or Impudence.[135]

Newspapers were not the only firms that used real and metaphorical newsboys to push their products. Beginning in the 1880s, the nascent advertising industry put newsboys on trade cards promoting everything from tonics and tea to stoves and sewing machines. Manufacturers produced millions of these cards and had them placed in packages, distributed door-to-door, and circulated by merchants. Trade cards became so popular with young collectors that shopkeepers complained they were constantly pestered for new ones. In terms of dress and demeanor, most of the children depicted on the cards belonged to the same middle-class families that companies sought as customers. Newsboys—and stereotyped black children—were conspicuous exceptions, as they possessed the rascally charm that appealed to all classes.[136]

Figure 9.13. The Newsboy, 1888. Carved, assembled, and painted wood with folded tin, 4 × 20 × 11 in. (106.68 × 50.8 × 27.94 cm). The Michael and Julie Hall Collection of American Folk Art, Milwaukee Art Museum. M1989.125. Photo by John Nienhuis.

Advertising spending multiplied tenfold in the last quarter of the century with the growth of department stores and mass circulation magazines. Grown-ups were the primary focus of these ads, but businessmen quickly recognized young people as consumers who also influenced their parents' spending. Newsies now appeared in ads and on calendars flogging national brands including Colgate soap and Lippincott's Cough Syrup. Quaker Oats began a marketing campaign that entailed hiring hundreds of newsboys to hand out samples of the cereal in towns along the two-thousand-mile rail line from Cedar Rapids, Iowa, to Portland, Oregon.[137]

Newsies also lent their personas to tobacco-related products such as Daily Cry matches, Newsboy Plug Tobacco ("Fit for a king to chew"), and Newsboy Cigars (Plate 21). In 1899 Kansas City newsies tried to capitalize on their own image when the local newsboys' union introduced a line of cigars known as Newsboy Specials (10¢) and Newsboy Juniors (5¢). Each box bore the union's seal and a picture of its president, pool hall proprietor Barney Harvey. Proceeds went to the newsboys' home building fund. These boys stood before the public as unionized workers, marketing devices, and charity solicitors all at once.[138]

Figure 9.14. Retail display and cigar cutter: Extra Fine Cut Chewing Tobacco, by John Anderson & Co., ca. 1890–1910. Bronze colored metal, 5¾ × 16 × 5½ in. Collection of the New-York Historical Society.

The gamin fad extended to the performing arts as well. Music publishers issued newsboy songs year after year—tunes like "The Orphan Newsboy" (1891), "I've Not Sold a Paper Today" (1893), "The Newsboys of Chicago" (1895), and "Pity the Newsboy" (1897). Even Hearst's recruiting slogan urging boys to sell the *Journal*—"Den Yer Don't Get Stuck, See?"—was set to music and performed in theaters.[139] News gamins also cavorted onstage in solo acts such as the Newsboy Tenor, ensembles like Gus Edwards's Newsboys' Quintet, and plays in the mold of *The Newsboy Witness* and *The War of Wealth*, an 1895 melodrama ripped from the headlines in which newsies spark a climactic bank run.[140]

Meanwhile, a young cohort of journalists infiltrated the ranks of established juvenile novelists such as Horatio Alger and James Otis to transform newsboys into unwashed literary lions. Writing for both adult and juvenile markets, this new generation mixed fact and fiction, humor and pathos, and words and pictures to create a genre known as the slang story. Their protagonists are more complicated and authentic than the one-dimensional strivers in Alger's still popular Luck and Pluck series. Even Riis turned to fiction in two short-story collections, *Nisby's Christmas* (1893) and *Out of Mulberry Street* (1898). Critics praised them as straightforward tales, as artless as his photographs, but all the more true to life because of it. Riis's fiction was steeped in sentiment as well as fact. The eponymous Nisby, for example, burns to death in a pressroom fire, much like Giuseppe Magalto and Abraham Frank in 1891, only Nisby dies on Christmas Eve, after being driven from home for not selling enough papers and spending his last pennies on honey cakes for two boys who had doubted the existence of Santa Claus.[141]

Stephen Crane's stories and poems convey a harder-edged reality unrelieved by Santas and sentiment. His novellas *Maggie, a Girl of the Streets* (1893) and *George's Mother* (1896) chart the descent of working-class youths into prostitution and criminality. *Godey's* magazine warned readers that the language in *Maggie* might "give a shock to spasmodic prudishness, but there is nothing to harm a healthy mind." Seeking to really shock, Crane started a novel called *Flowers of Asphalt* about a boy prostitute, but tossed it aside on the advice of a friend who said it would ruin his career.[142]

Fiction writers also exploited—and perhaps stimulated—the practice in which police used newsboys as detectives, or "fly cops," to shadow suspects and gather intelligence. The boys were usually paid in streetcar tickets or theater passes, but sometimes in cash. One example is the Newsboy Detective Agency, formed in 1897 by *Chicago Daily News* alley cop Owen Doherty. He and his two protégés, "Sleep-Out Louis" and "The Brute," aka "Bulldog," reputedly captured more runaways than any six child-saving agencies combined. Their literary predecessors were the Baker Street Irregulars, London urchins who assisted Sherlock Holmes. Their US equivalents appeared in the dime novel *Newsboy Ned, Detective* (1888), Richard Harding Davis's Gallegher stories (1891), *The Ex-Newsboy Detective's Apprentice* (1895), and George Ade's *Chicago Reader* columns about "Eddie Parks, the Newsboy Detective." Ade's 9-year-old hero was a master of disguise who smoked cigars, carried a revolver, and helped Chicago police crack their toughest cases with his uncanny ability to see what adults overlooked.[143]

The most popular newsboy character of the nineties was Edward Townsend's Chimmie Fadden, a case-hardened Bowery hustler with a soft heart: "Here, kid, you'se take diss, an' go eat; I'll earn some more to-night somehow, I guess." As a type, Chimmie resembled the Irish American b'hoys of Young America and Bowery legends Brodie and Kildare. Like them, he was the quintessential New Yorker: "I expected to cross de Harlem river and run right into de Pacific ocean." Townsend stumbled on a real Chimmie and Miss Fannie, a slum worker, while covering a newsboys' dinner at the Brace Memorial Home for the *New York Sun*. Thus began the vogue for all things Chimmie. Townsend's stories were syndicated in newspapers, serialized in magazines, and published in books. In 1896 Hearst hired him to write copy to accompany the Yellow Kid comic strip. Chimmie and the Kid soon appeared together in books and plays—and later movies—that delighted audiences by poking fun at upper- and lower-class pretensions.[144]

Newsboys enjoyed the gamins as much as anybody, especially when their popularity increased sales. Baltimore was an exception, however. The evening *World* and *Journal* retailed there for 2¢, but dealers kept raising the wholesale price, from 60¢ to 75¢ and then to $1.25 per hundred. Moreover, the papers sometimes arrived late, and the boys were allowed no rebate for unsold copies. Fed up, the Baltimore boys struck in December 1896. About fifty of them paraded outside the post office displaying banners saying, "Don't grind down the newsboys." Another bore a picture of the Yellow Kid torn from a Sunday edition. Hand-lettered below were the words: "This don't cut no ice with us." The boys protested for three days with the aid of a drum and a load of sticks good for pounding on ashcans, wagons, and trolleys.[145]

Generally speaking, newsboy ads, comics, statues, games, songs, and stories did not raise concerns about poverty and exploitation. If so, they would have been useless to their sponsors. Instead, the images reinforced the consensus that news peddling was a harmless, even beneficial, childhood activity. Ultimately, their effect muted whatever objections Social Gospelers, settlement house workers, city beautifiers, sabbatarians, noise reformers, photojournalists, and fiction writers tried to mount. And with the yellow press now beating its own war drum, there was little hope for change.

War—One Cent!

"Havana Shelled!" yelled New York newsboys at the top of their lungs. "Havana Shelled!" announced their headlines in letters fifteen-inches long that could be read a block away. "Thousands of people rushed hither and thither to buy them," said reporter Elizabeth L. Banks; "timid women gasped and almost fainted at the sight of the scare-heads." Yet even after reading their papers many failed to notice the words "to be," printed in minute type between the two principal words. The headline wasn't a hoax but a daily occurrence for the yellows. With the outbreak of the Spanish-American War in April 1898, the *New York World* and *Evening Journal*, the largest-circulation dailies on the planet, routinely issued thirty to forty editions a day, fresh news or not. Newspaper wagons bearing placards announcing "Latest War News!" raced about town, clearing the streets like fire engines, dropping their bundles on corners, and servicing the more than five thousand newsstands of greater New York. Many operators hired extra boys, put them in uniforms, and paid them $4.50 a week to tend stands or work the sidewalks. Some toiled twelve hours a day, from 7:00 a.m. to 7:00 p.m.[146]

Children flooded the trade and stretched the truth. Newsboys in Sioux City, Iowa, established a union and badge system in May 1898 to ward off "one day sellers." Boston, by contrast, had to suspend enforcement of its license law until war's end. San Francisco newsies made "small fortunes" peddling sheets that falsely reported the discovery of torpedoes under the wreckage of the *Maine*, bloody massacres in Havana, and imminent declarations of war. The boys knew they were trafficking in falsehoods. "Here's yer latest extra," cried one New York boy. "Fake extra! All the fakes. Exclusive fakes! Extra! Extra! Fake extra!!" Customers snatched up the papers quicker than ever, and soon all the boys were singing the fakes in unison. A cartoon in *Puck* showed a bewildered pedestrian being accosted by two newsboys, one shouting, "Extree! Spanish is sailin' fer New York!" and the other hollering, "Extree! They ain't doin' no such thing!" Illustrator J. Campbell Cory documented the absurdity in a caricature of Pulitzer as an old woman selling copies of the *World* with the headline "War—One Cent!" (Figure 9.15).[147]

As in the Civil War, many newsboys specialized in serving military personnel. Hawkers in Brooklyn had full access to the Navy Yard until sailors circulated a petition criticizing McKinley's delay in avenging the sinking of the *Maine*. Officers

Figure 9.15. J. Campbell Cory, "Joseph Pulitzer (War One Cent) New York World," The Bee's Gallery of Notables, Journalistic Series, *The Bee*, New York, 1898.

blamed the yellow press and banned newsboys. Long Island youths supplied papers to soldiers at Camp Black in Hempstead Plains and Camp Wykoff in Montauk, where they were caught tramping through the hospital's quarantine wards. Artie Douglas sold papers exclusively to the Third Wisconsin at Camp Harvey in Milwaukee. He followed the unit to a training camp in Georgia, which soldiers feared was at the mercy of "indolent Southern newsboys." The 10-year-old had his own bunk in the cook tent and expected to ship out with the regiment to Puerto Rico, but was turned away.[148]

Newsboys in Florida also cashed in on war news. Key West newsies routinely rowed out to the warships to dispose of their papers; some of their dinghy races erupted into oar-swinging brawls that were said to be the first naval engagements of the war. Hawkers in Jacksonville boasted peak earnings of $4 a day, but those in Tampa, an army embarkation point, said such crumbs would be cause for suicide, as boys there cleared up to $7 a day selling copies to citizens and soldiers, the latter numbering almost forty thousand. "While the troops were here, even the gutters of the streets ran silver," recalled one old hand.[149]

Chicago Record newsboy George J. Kavanaugh made it all the way to Cuba, and he regaled reporters with the story for years to come. On assignment from his newspaper, the 18-year-old reputedly took a train to Tampa, chartered a boat to Cuba, and loaded it with papers. Once there, he "confiscated" a mule and made his way to the front, where he sold papers to American soldiers on the second day of the Battle of Santiago. As they were the first American papers seen on the island since the outbreak of war, Kavanaugh "was cheered time and again by the soldiers" and warmly received by the top brass.[150]

Back in Chicago, the "little shavers" reportedly saw profits jump a hundredfold, from $3 to $300 a day. Everything from a handbill to a little suburban sheet sold for a dime, and thousands of them were snatched from the boys' hands for a quarter apiece. This business lasted from morning to night, often without recourse to hollering. In addition to their usual wares, Chicago newsboys peddled out-of-town newspapers shipped in by speculators hoping to profit from the insatiable demand and, in early July, take advantage of a six-day strike by Chicago stereotypers. Papers came pouring into the breach from nearby Evanston, Aurora, and Joliet, and far-off Rockford, Milwaukee, and Cincinnati. Two-day-old New York papers fetched up to 50¢ a copy, as the strike coincided with the US Navy's defeat of the Spanish flotilla in Santiago de Cuba and the sinking of the French liner *Bourgogne* off Nova Scotia with the loss of 549 lives.[151]

While never known as sticklers for the truth, yellow-era newsboys were constantly chided for their lack of honesty. The manager of the Newsboys' Home in St. Paul said their entire morality was contained in two mottos: "Stick to your friends and get even with your enemies" and "The only crime in breaking the commandments is in being found out." Newsboys easily rationalized their actions. Pedestrians "stole" looks at their headlines or thumbed through copies for up to fifteen minutes, they said, and suppliers sometimes slipped them old editions. Besides, unembellished street cries brought ruin: "Ah, youse blokes give me a pain!" 12-year-old Park Row hawker Johnny Dacey told a passing scold. "Why, if yer tells de trut' yer gets nothin', but if yer gives a good song an' dance yer gets der dust, see?"[152]

Another Manhattan sharpie caught foisting an old edition on financier Russell Sage justified himself by saying that Sage, a notorious skinflint, always pressed a penny down hard in his hand, making it feel like a nickel or dime. "T'aint cheatin' t' 'do' a man wot does dat to yuse, is it?" he asked. Such retorts were good for a laugh, but also provoked serious discussion about journalism ethics and claims that newsboys' dishonesty simply reflected the norms of the industry. Besides fabricating news, editors invented bogus "newspaper laws" to threaten delinquent subscribers with arrest for fraud.[153]

Even more deplorable to some was running a business composed chiefly of children. The public's hunger for war news presented school-age children with great temptation to play hooky. Mrs. M. K. R. Alger of New York, the nation's first female truant officer, went on the offensive, personally descending on the boys, confiscating their papers and escorting them to school. "One boy had been making a dollar a day for several days and thought himself in clover," reported the *New York Sun*. "I was sorry to have to do it," said Mrs. Alger, "but they can get plenty of time to sell papers before school and in the afternoon. These extras have completely demoralized some of them and they stay up till 12 and 1 o'clock selling them."[154]

The *New York Journal* set up a billboard outside its headquarters near City Hall Park and hired an artist and orchestra to keep the assemblage entertained when news slackened.[155] All the big dailies used special trains to transport copies up to Buffalo or down to Washington, DC, where commissioners lifted the ban against news crying after 8:00 p.m. The law had aimed to stop boys from invading the uptown quarters with yellow extras from New York, but its repeal allowed them to resume the practice with impunity. The papers arrived in Washington around 5:00 p.m., after the local afternoon editions had had their sale; their news was six hours old, but still they sold. After several weeks, authorities in Washington cracked down on those who sold the New York papers, on the grounds that they carried no new news. The first arrested was Walter Brown, "a colored newsboy" who claimed ignorance of the law.[156]

Many could not figure out how the publishers managed to turn a profit on the 1¢ papers. The truth is that many didn't. All the dailies in New York lost money during the war. Those that had revenues from $400,000 to $750,000 a year were spending at least $625,000 chartering boats, paying cable tolls, and hiring celebrity writers and artists like Crane and Frederic Remington. In addition, the price of paper rose due to government restrictions on sulfur, an ingredient in gunpowder and newsprint. According to *New York Journal* Sunday editor Arthur Brisbane, the only ones who made any money were "the little newsboys [who] sold their bundles of newspapers as fast as they could scatter them through the crowds." Indeed, 10-year-old Izzy Baline (later Irving Berlin) discovered while hawking the equally jingoistic *New York Evening Herald* at the Brooklyn Bridge that people would toss coins at him if he sang.[157]

No longer were newsboys the only ones who worked on piece rates. Most advertising agents in the 1890s earned commission only, and many reporters were paid by the inch instead of the hour. Some newspapers let compositors go home early after setting a specific number of ems. Even Brisbane worked for an incentive; in 1897 Hearst granted him an extra dollar a week for every thousand increase in the *Evening Journal's* circulation. With the outbreak of war, this bonus pushed his $10,000 starting salary to $40,000 a year.[158]

Despite their own windfall profits, newsboys organized strikes and boycotts against newspapers in Los Angeles, Denver, Omaha, Spokane, and a half dozen other cities when publishers and distributors adjusted prices or suspended return privileges to offset their increased expenses.[159] The *Omaha World-Herald* reduced the retail price of its daily from a nickel to 2¢, and castigated hawkers in nearby Sioux City and Council Bluffs, Iowa, as "dictators" when they refused to comply.[160] In New York the *World* and *Evening Journal* raised prices to newsboys from 50¢ to 60¢ per hundred papers in May 1898. The boys mounted a boycott that involved five hundred hawkers in Manhattan, Brooklyn, and Jersey City, and featured parades, skirmishes, and arrests. Some trade unions publicly endorsed the boycott, but the Central Labor Union refused to intervene, saying a dispute over a tenth of a cent was "too small a matter." Hearst didn't think so; he got a large quantity of dimes and quarters, rode to their meeting place in a hansom cab, and showered them with coins. He refused to budge on the price, however, and the newsboycott fizzled after a week due to the bull market for war news.[161]

Newsies in Rhode Island and Connecticut picked up the banner. "We's goin' ter strike and won't sell enny more New York extras until dey coughs up dat extra ten cents an' quits playing de hog act," said a boy in Pawtucket. Meanwhile, more than a hundred New Haven newsboys paraded in the streets for two days carrying placards and singing, to the tune of "John Brown's Body," "We won't read the Journal and we won't read the World . . . As we go marching on." Hearst and Pulitzer held firm on the rate hike, but the *World* agreed to take back all unsold papers, which split the ranks of the New Haven boys and ended the strike. The publishers tried another tactic in Hartford—importing scabs from Philadelphia—young toughs in their twenties who enjoyed police protection. The strikers ran them off, but failed to win concessions.[162]

The jingoism of the press, coupled with the potential for profit, led many newsboys to support US intervention. In January 1897, after the widely reported execution of Cuban rebel Adolfo Rodríguez by a Spanish firing squad, the Newsboys' Union in Kansas City offered the use of its hall as a headquarters for the rebel cause.[163] The sinking of the battleship *Maine* in February 1898 gave vent to a crescendo of newsboy bellicosity. In Grand Rapids, Michigan, it took the form of a fight song:

> The Evening Press Association
> Twelve hundred Newsboys Strong
> stand pat for the soldiers of the nation
> To fight and revenge The wrong
> Down with The foe who Kill our Heroes
> Down with the spies of Treacherous Spain
> Down with Their ships with shell and fire
> Let's avenge our gallant Maine.[164]

A "yellow kid" paper in Dallas expressed similar sentiments in a March cartoon depicting a tattered newsboy in pants with two apertures resembling portholes in a man-of-war. Wielding a nail-studded barrel stave, he beckons to a gang of boys similarly armed and attired. "Come on, fellers," he cries. "I knows where dere is a Spanish kid!" On April 2, 800 Milwaukee newsboys waving American flags and led by a newsboys' band paraded to the dock to salute the captain and crew of the US revenue cutter *Greshem* before its departure for the Atlantic. When the vessel sank in the St. Lawrence River six weeks later, Spanish perfidy was alleged. On April 8, with the Yellow Kid temporarily missing in action, possibly because his nightshirt was the same color as the hated Spanish flag, Outcault launched a new series in the *New York Evening Journal* about a troop of kid soldiers called "The Hucklberry Volunteers." Led by an arch-coon figure, and armed with rakes, axes, and pitchforks, the rowdy unit included a "News Boys Battalion" that marched under a crate sign saying "Watch us fire de extras at em—say."[165]

Many young hustlers longed to ship out with the troops. "If you wish to send a newsboy I am ready to go," wrote Andrew Szymanski of Frankfort, Kentucky. "I am 16 years old, and I will fight for my country." Members of the Newsboys' Band of Louisville enlisted en masse. Most were orphans between 15 and 18 years old and residents of the newsboys' home. They were rejected because of their age or height, but the band received permission to join the First Kentucky Volunteers in Ponce, Puerto Rico, where it gave two concerts a week. Thirteen-year-old Arthur Gluckman of San Francisco caught "martial fever" so bad in the spring of 1899 that he boarded a troop transport on the pretext of selling papers and stowed away to Manila. The 20th Infantry adopted him as a mascot and fitted him out with a uniform. He was wounded when insurgents stormed his trench, and returned home with dreams of entering West Point.[166]

All wars have unintended consequences, and one result of the Spanish-American War was the creation of hundreds of thousands of orphans and a cohort of politically active newsboys in Cuba and the Philippines. Boys in Havana formed the Newsboys' Protective Association in 1899 and honored their pledge to boycott any newspaper that did not support the cause of Cuba Libre. Two hundred members refused to sell *El Diario de Marina* after it published an editorial favoring a long American occupation. Meanwhile, the English-language *Manila Freedom* took credit for introducing newsboys to the Philippines: "They are a cosmopolitan lot—Filipino, Chinese, Japs, Hindus and representatives of races from all the Islands—but quite like the newsboy wherever found." The boys cried headlines, acquired English phrases, and sang popular tunes like "Hot Time in the Old Town To-Night." "We are amused and laugh at the ragged, yes, here the almost naked, newsboy," said the *Freedom*, but acknowledged that most of the "urchins" would benefit from the training in business and public affairs. The boys did learn some valuable lessons. In November 1905 Manila newsies led by walking delegates Pedros Cantino, age 8, Resurrection de Santo Tomas, 11, and Tomas Quinsomboy, 12, waged a month-long strike for lower prices from the *Manila Cable News*. The US Constitution may not have followed the flag to these new American possessions, but a belief in its rights and freedoms certainly did.[167]

Carrying the Banner

After the war with Spain, newsboys waged a war of their own against the New York *World* and *Evening Journal*. It started on July 18, 1899, coincidentally the day Horatio Alger died, when boys in Long Island City, Queens, caught the *Journal* deliveryman selling them short bundles. They tipped over his wagon, chased him up the street, and triumphantly carried off armloads of papers. No cameraman was on hand to film the incident, but word spread quickly, inspiring what nearly became a children's general strike. Over the next two weeks boys in all five boroughs, and in cities and towns throughout the region, boycotted the two papers. Their actions emboldened newsboys as far away as Cincinnati, Lexington, Kentucky, and Nashville, Tennessee—and bootblacks and messengers in other cities—to stop work and demand better terms from their own bosses. Far from aberrations, these strikes capped a decade of discontent in the street trades.[168]

The time was ripe for a showdown. The revolt in Queens rekindled the boys' ire over price hikes imposed on them by Pulitzer and Hearst at the start of the

war. It also coincided with a national strike wave, a local heat wave, and a militant protest by streetcar motormen in Brooklyn and Manhattan that kept police
tied up. Many children—boys and girls—blocked tracks with debris and threw
stones at nonunion drivers. Redressing grievances about paying wartime prices
for peacetime papers gave newsies the chance to mobilize on their own behalf.
Three hundred of them met in City Hall Park on July 19 and agreed to strike
if their demands weren't met. "Go ahead and strike," said the *World*'s circulation manager. Following the example of adult trade unionists, the boys elected
officers, formed a discipline committee, and sent envoys to spread the word: "Ye
don't sell no more *World* 'r *Joinal* 'r ye git yer face punched in—see?"[169]

Most of the boys thus approached "saw." Newsboys refused to handle the
"yellow kid" dailies from Wall Street to Harlem, Brooklyn to the Bronx, and
in the Westchester County towns of Yonkers, Mount Vernon, New Rochelle,
Mamaroneck, and White Plains. They also honored the strike upstate in Troy,
Saratoga, and Rochester, and on Staten Island in Tomkinsville, Stapleton,
and Clifton.[170] Garden State newsboys joined in as well, starting with Jersey
City, Hoboken, Newark, and Plainfield, then spreading to Bayonne, Trenton,
Paterson, Elizabeth, and Asbury Park.[171] New Englanders extended the boycott
to New Haven, Norwalk, Danbury, and Hartford, Connecticut, and to Fall River,
Massachusetts, and Providence, Rhode Island.[172]

Management couldn't help but take notice. In a July 22 memo to Pulitzer,
World business manager Don Seitz reported that the strike "has grown into an
extensive and menacing affair, encouraged by the other newspapers and backed
by street railway people. Practically all the boys in New York and many of the
adjacent towns have quit selling. Incendiary circulars are being distributed and
the boys so far have sent two Journal men to the Manhattan Hospital and have
scared three World men so that they have disappeared from their posts. A call
is out for a Mass Meeting of the boys in front of the Pulitzer Building and we
have just been compelled to ask the police for assistance."[173] Police ran off five
hundred demonstrators that afternoon and arrested two "ringleaders," Cornelius
"Grin" Boyle, age 14, and Albert Smith, 15. A large contingent followed them to
the Oak Street station house, resulting in the arrest of five more boys, ages 13 to
17. To divide the strikers, the *World* feigned acceptance of their two-for-a-cent
demand. The *Evening Journal* offered them papers for free. Strike leaders had to
physically dissuade boys from taking the bait without assurance that the price
cuts would be permanent.[174]

The strikers represented the full range of ages, ethnicities, and physical
imperfections found in the news trade. Kid Blink (legal name Louis Balletti),
the red-haired spokesman for most of the strike, was a charismatic 18-year-old
Italian American with a bum eye. Dave Simons, also 18, was a Jewish boxing
champion in the 105-pound class. Arbitration committee member Jack Sullivan,

21, also had ring experience and Jewish roots. Brooklyn's brain trust included the Gaelic duo of "Race Track" Higgins and "Spot" Conlon, 14.[175] African American "Black" Diamond was elected to the Manhattan strike committee, William "Coon" Reese was chosen sergeant-at-arms, and "Black Wonder" held strikers spellbound with his oratory at the Brooklyn Post Office.[176] Disabilities didn't matter either; in addition to Kid Blink, "Crutch" Morris served on the executive committee in New York and "Blind" Huber cochaired the "consultation of war" held outside the ferry building in Hoboken. Courage, conviction, and eloquence were the only requirements for leadership.

Sex did matter, though. Newsgirls and women played only peripheral roles in the strike. However, one little Park Row "Joan of Arc" was credited with driving off two big strikebreakers whom the boys had failed to subdue. Among the women vendors who backed the boys were "Auntie" Corcoran, the "awful rich" Mrs. Shea, Hannah Kleff, and "Brooklyn Bridge" Annie Kelly. "Course, I'm helpin' the boys out," said Kelly. "Two for a cent's little enough to make. Ef you sell a hundred papers you only make 40 cents, an' ef you git stuck on twenty, you don't make only 20 cents after all day's work." One newsboy paid Kelly and Kleff the ultimate compliment: "Dey is union men for fair, but some of de udder has got money to burn, but are scabs just de same." The women were indeed divided. "Naw, I ain't strikin'," Eliza Myers told a reporter. "All these boys out o' school, they don't gi' me a chance." An "ancient lady" known only as "The Squealer" said the only strike she'd support was one "to make all the young women who are able to wash and scrub leave the Row to us old uns." She sold the proscribed dailies from under her apron, and clobbered a boy who harassed her for doing so. Some thirty strikers retaliated by stripping off her blouse and skirt. They hoisted the garments on a stick and waved them around like a captured flag. Fearing that such behavior would hurt the union's cause, Kid Blink urged restraint. "A feller can't soak a lady," he told the boys.[177]

The *World* and *Evening Journal* reported not a word about the strike, but the other New York papers ran long, widely reprinted articles detailing the skirmishes, mass meetings, and negotiations, always quoting the newsboys in their signature slang. The *Tribune* published a photo essay on the strike in its Sunday supplement. The morning *Herald* and *Evening Telegram* captured the action in a series of cartoons as if the strike were a comic strip episode (Figure 9.16). These papers benefited financially from the strike, as dealers tripled and quadrupled their usual orders; one estimated that the two struck papers were losing a hundred thousand sales a day. Seitz admitted to a 20 percent drop and much lost advertising. The *Telegram* materially aided the strikers by printing up circulars and a four-page "special extra" urging the public to help the boys by buying the *Telegram*. The newsboys sought support themselves by writing letters

THE EVENING TELEGRAM—NEW YORK, THURSDAY, JULY 27, 1899.

IN THE ENEMY'S COUNTRY.

Figure 9.16. "In the Enemy's Country," *New York Evening Telegram,* July 27, 1899, 8. Author's collection.

to editors and chalking sidewalks with messages such as "World & Journal. Scab Papers for Scabs."[178]

Even if exaggerated in tortuously misspelled Chimmie Fadden slang, working-class solidarity and anti-monopoly sentiment surfaced as common themes of the strike. "Wot 'ell should wese fellers run de legs of 'n ourselves ter make forty cents on 100 papers for?" asked a newsboy named Billy, co-chair of the strike committee in Jersey City. "Talk about yer trusts, wot 'ell! Dey isn't in it wid dem papers, dey isn't. Wese uns has got ter stand by one another dese times, 'cause if we don't sure's hell we'll git it in de neck from dem capitalists." This was music to the ears of Socialist Labor Party members who met at the Cooper Union on July 24. "The capitalist class may well look to their defenses," said the party's candidate for governor, "when five and ten year old boys go out on strike against their infernal system." Even pillars of society like Bishop James Augustine McFaul of Trenton urged the strikers to stick up for their rights and pull together.[179]

Although portrayed by the press in comic fashion, strike violence was no joke. Some scabs wielded table legs and carried revolvers; one forced a loaded gun down Kid Blink's throat. The strikers played rough, too. They armed themselves with horseshoes, baseball bats, barrel staves, and wheel spokes. "Yer clubs ain't meant for toot'picks," "Spot" Conlon reminded the other newsboys. They forced scabs to literally eat their papers, pushed them off moving streetcars, and raided stands, shops, and wagons that dared disseminate the *World* or *Journal*. Those arrested were brought before a magistrate and either fined and released, remanded to the custody of the Gerry Society, or, if they had a record, committed to the Juvenile Asylum for up to six months.[180]

While the chronically ill, 52-year-old Pulitzer received regular reports on the strike at his summer retreat in Bar Harbor, Maine, the 36-year-old Hearst remained in the city and dealt personally with the strikers. On Saturday, July 22, "a great mob of boys" spotted him buying a paper in Herald Square. "They hooted him and for a while it looked as if they might attack him," reported the *San Francisco Call*. "He finally made his escape, followed by the howling strikers."[181] That same day, a "small army" of newsboys, tired of fooling with the "cellar bosses," waited for Hearst in front of the *Journal* office. When his cab pulled up, the smallest boy touched him on the arm and said:

> "We're the strikers, Mr. Hearst."
> "Well, boys, what can I do for you?" he said.
> "Well, we want 100 papers for 50 cents. We get it from the other papers
>   except the World."
> "Come in and talk it over," said the publisher.

Kid Blink, Dave Simons, and two other boys formed themselves into a committee and went in. When they returned, Blink gave the strikers a full report: "He wanted to know what the World was goin' to do. I told him that we was dealing with the Journal now, and that if he cut the World would cut quick enough. He says he had to talk it over with some other guys before he gives an answer, and I then asked him if he would arbitrate like his papers says. He laughed and said he'd give us an answer Monday right here." The boys got their answer on Monday the twenty-fourth, when Hearst and Pulitzer rounded up scores of men at Bowery flophouses to sell papers for $2 a day. The strikers ran off many of them. "A man wot'll take a job like dat is worse 'en a Spaniard," said Kid Blink. Hearst later told him that he'd go out of business before giving in to the union.[182]

That night, after a day of running battles, the newsboys held a mass meeting at the New Irving Hall on Broome Street. A capacity crowd of two thousand packed the place, while another three thousand boys remained outside. The East Side politicians and news veterans present shared memories of past struggles. Assemblyman Philip Wissig told about selling papers in the 1860s and counseled moderation: "Don't use dynamite, and you will win." "Warhorse" Brennan talked about his twenty years in the trade. Kid Blink reminded them of their victory in 1893 against the *Evening World*'s no-return policy, and urged them to "stick together like plaster. Ain't that 10 cents worth as much to us as it is to Hearst and Pulitzer, who are millionaires? Well, I guess it is. If they can't spare it, how can we?" Blink won a floral horseshoe sent by an ex-alderman as prize for the best speech and was photographed wearing it. The heads of two newsdealer associations also pledged support at the meeting. Some boys suspected that the adults' real motive was to form a United Newsboys' Protective Party or a Park Row Association of Affiliated Newsboys' Clubs.[183]

Civic leaders did see the strike as an opportunity to organize the boys. A group of eighteen men and women, including city missionaries, teachers, and an alderman, met in a Broadway hotel the next day to discuss the situation. One proposed that newsboys be licensed, badged, and uniformed, and that boys under 10 be forbidden from selling after 9:00 p.m. Another suggested that the Gerry Society oversee the street trades. They stressed that scores of cities were waiting to follow New York's lead. The group went on to form the New-York Child Workers' Protective Association, which tried to establish shelters where newsboys and bootblacks could find rest, warmth, free lockers, and cheap meals.[184]

The city's most prominent reformer, Jacob Riis, doesn't appear to have taken a side or a photograph during the strike. Nor did his onetime crime-fighting partner, Theodore Roosevelt, who had become governor of New York after winning renown with the Rough Riders in Cuba. TR visited the city during the strike and no doubt read about it in the papers. His affinity for newsboys and loathing for Hearst's and Pulitzer's Democratic scandal sheets suggest that he might have been rooting for the boys. Then again, he once said that rifle fire was the only proper response to strikers who riot.[185]

Still unable to break the strike, Hearst and Pulitzer asked Salvation Army lasses to sell their papers, but the girls refused to break the boycott. The publishers then tried to buy off strike leaders for $300 to $600 apiece. They appeared to succeed when Kid Blink and Dave Simons showed up on Park Row on July 26 with bundles of *World*s and *Journal*s, saying they had negotiated a settlement. Kid Blink sported a new suit of clothes, complete with straw hat and russet shoes, and unwisely flashed a roll of bills. The strike committee put the pair on trial for high treason and low bribery. Kid Blink eloquently maintained their innocence. Both escaped conviction but were removed from office. A mob of newsboys chased Blink through the streets that night. He escaped only by getting himself arrested.[186]

On July 27 the *World* and *Evening Journal* offered to sell papers to the boys at 55¢ per hundred, but the union rejected the compromise. Defections increased, however, and two days later, when the papers offered to accept the return of all unsold copies, the New York boys saw victory as imminent. The strike lasted longer in New Jersey but limped to a close in New York on August 1 without meeting or vote. They might have gotten more, one newsie explained to a customer, but "de leaders was bought off."[187]

Still, the strike had lasting consequences. Hearst felt betrayed by his fellow publishers and withdrew from their association. He and Pulitzer entered into a five-year covenant to fix the price of their daily and Sunday offerings and mutually establish their return policies.[188] The newsboys union did not disband but continued under an adult president who advocated wearing union badges and affiliating with other labor organizations. Their first action, decided August 13 at a mass meeting of two thousand Brooklyn and Manhattan newsies in Teutonia Hall on the Lower East Side, was a pledge not to sell copies of their former ally, the *New York Sun*, until the paper took back its locked-out printers. A few days later two hundred newsboys brought up the rear of a solidarity parade. The boys waved flags and carried banners affirming their boycott. "War is a lamentable business," said *Life* magazine, "but if newspapers must have it, it is far more satisfactory to have them wage it on their own account, and at their own cost, than to stir it up between nations."[189]

To be a newsboy in the 1890s was to be part of the epic changes fracturing America at the close of the century. It was to bring home table money for families impoverished by a pitiless depression and to generate millions in a technologically advanced industry led by the richest and most powerful men in the country. To be a newsboy in the 1890s was to become American, learn English, and partake of a dizzying array of commercial amusements. It offered boys a taste of independence and girls an introduction to inequality.

To be a newsboy in the 1890s was to be an object of charity and coercion by a disparate community of reformers who heard your cries as sinful, noxious, or plaintive. It was to be stereotyped by all manner of artists, writers, and photographers—to be portrayed as a little alien of a beaten race, a grinning imp from Africa, an incorrigible hoyden, or a cantankerous old crone. It was to realize that newspapers were commodities, and so were your labor and your image, the latter staring back at you from billboards, cigar boxes, and postcards.

To be a newsboy in the 1890s was to share in the clamor and profits of war, to spread falsehood as well as truth, and to provide a running account of the glories and horrors of empire. It was also to cry news of the bloodiest labor conflicts ever visited on a nation, and to be embroiled in innumerable strikes and boycotts of your own. It was to discover firsthand the limits of individual effort and the possibilities of collective action. In short, it was to make history as well as to shout it.

PART THREE

CHILDREN OF THE STATE, 1900–1940

10

Bitter Cry of Progress

Speaking at the Pan-American Exposition in Buffalo on September 5, 1901, President William McKinley praised the peaceful pursuit of trade as the chief stimulus to progress and the bridging of political and geographical divides. With telegraph and cable, "isolation is no longer possible or desirable," he told the huge outdoor audience dotted with the colorful costumes of foreign dignitaries. "The same important news is read, though in different languages, the same day in all Christendom." The truth of this statement was demonstrated the next day when shots rang out in the exposition's Temple of Music at 4:07 p.m. The local press association notified an editor by phone in New York City at 4:29. Five minutes later hawkers were crying the news. "McKinley Shot!" screamed their headlines in blood-red ink. "The newsboys, scenting prosperity from afar, were out in countless swarms," said the *New York Times*, their voices "blending into one continuous ear-splitting screech." Some papers issued six extras before midnight using telegraphic updates that flashed around the world. The torrent of news raged for eight more days as McKinley hovered between life and death.[1]

Newsboys rode this information storm like little Argonauts. Vendors everywhere tangled with paper-grabbing, coin-foisting customers, few of whom expected or received change back. "Any boy who did not make at least $5 was regarded as a dismal failure," said the *Washington Star*, whose regular newsies purchased fifty copies twice a day. When the news reached the Rockies, the *Denver Post* rang its gong every thirty seconds, summoning sellers and buyers alike. Hawkers cleared up to $15 a day, and carriers on horseback sped the paper overland to remote mining camps. Back on the exposition grounds in Buffalo, 31-year-old Jack Lloyd sold 12,000 copies in twenty-four hours while his fourteen helpers dispensed 124,000 copies, earning Lloyd lifelong renown as the city's "King of the Newsboys."[2]

The demand for news attracted amateurs and opportunists. A bricklayer in Washington, DC, filled his long-handled hod with a stack of *Stars* to peddle on his way home. A New Jersey constable carted three hundred copies of the *Trenton Times* to sell in nearby Lambertville. Boys who tried to unload stale editions by crying that the president was dead received kicks and curses once their deception was discovered. Vendors of Hearst papers also suffered beatings in retaliation for the chain's relentless attack on the Republican president, including an April editorial that said his killing would be justified. Repulsed by the effects of such rhetoric, Joseph Pulitzer renounced yellow journalism forever.[3]

Like other tradesmen, newsies expressed their sympathy collectively. Some 250 members of the newly formed Boston Newsboys' Protective Union met three days after the shooting to issue a letter of condolence to McKinley and family. When the president died of infection the following week, hawkers in Trenton's news alley hanged the accused in effigy. Stirred by the oratory of newsboy William Brown, they hurled stones at the stuffed-feedbag figure, dragged the remains around town, and then dumped it into the Delaware River.[4]

The assassin, 28-year-old Leon Czolgosz, was the American-born son of Polish Catholic immigrants. He grew up in Detroit shining shoes and peddling papers, but the press described him as an idle and effeminate Pole whose crime could be traced to his unmitigated foreignness and half-baked anarchist beliefs. Emma Goldman, the infamous "anarchist queen" whom Czolgosz idolized, was arrested in Chicago on suspicion of conspiring with him. Newspapers said her failure to buy a paper from the first boy she heard crying the news proved her guilt, but authorities released her after two weeks of torture for lack of better evidence. Czolgosz, meanwhile, was declared sane by alienists and swiftly tried, convicted, and electrocuted, which generated another flurry of street sales. Twelve-year-old Mike "Barto" Bartoni of Omaha, Nebraska, made $50 flogging execution extras. Few news criers anywhere could pronounce the assassin's name correctly; most settled on "Selgus." When pressed for clarification, a boy in Springfield, Illinois, snapped, "Why the Dago what killed McKinley."[5]

The assassination was a turning point for America and its newsboys. McKinley's murder brought to a head the long-festering fears of unassimilable aliens—including "dagoes" (Italians)—washing up on America's shores and undermining democratic institutions. Nativists advocated stanching the flow of almost a million immigrants a year, while their defenders recommended ameliorating the intolerable living and working conditions that made radical ideas so appealing to the masses. No longer could despotic trusts and corrupt politicians be tolerated, they said. No longer could social evils and personal vices be overlooked. The need for change was urgent, for crony capitalism, highest-bidder democracy, and class violence threatened to bring down the entire system.[6]

Leading this charge was McKinley's vice president, Theodore Roosevelt, who, at age 42, became America's youngest chief executive. He was also a recognized friend to newsboys, who said he once carried a route himself. Growing up in Manhattan, he accompanied his philanthropist father to Christmas banquets at the Newsboys' Lodging House, taught Sunday school there while on break from Harvard, and, in the winter of 1878, watched with heartfelt gratitude as newsboys stood vigil outside the family brownstone on East 20th Street, where his father lay dying. Twelve years later, as US civil service commissioner, Roosevelt lectured capital newsboys on the joys of ranch life. As police commissioner in New York, he once bought dinner for a hungry boy who offered him a paper in a restaurant, then accompanied him home and made provisions for his sick mother and siblings. As vice president, he waited tables at a newsboys' banquet sponsored by his sister Corinne, and in 1905 invited the Toledo newsboys' band to march in his inaugural parade. Roosevelt saw newsies as exemplars of the "strenuous life" he famously advocated—youngsters who possessed the stern, manly qualities so vital to the nation, but who still needed a helping hand. He also recognized the boys' publicity value in winning support for his reform agenda (Figure 10.1).[7]

Roosevelt's presidency coincided with an era of prosperity that was conducive to reform. Progressives from every class and party—women and socialists among them—stepped forward to remedy the social, political, and economic ills that made life precarious for those whom TR called "the plain people."[8] Newsboys were as plain as porridge, and they soon found themselves the subject of national debates about child labor, delinquency, truancy, and a host of related issues. Clad in their manly caps and boyish knickers, newsboys stood at the

Figure 10.1. Newsboy Howard Cunningham joins the welcoming committee for Theodore Roosevelt at Milwaukee's North Western station on September 7, 1910. J. Robert Taylor Collection, Wisconsin Historical Society, WHS 2096.

center of the epochal changes set off by McKinley's murder. Pushed and pulled by the economic needs of their families, the commercial interests of publishers, and the social agendas of reformers, this generation of newsies rose up to assert their own vision of progress.

Economies of Scale and Speed

The early twentieth century was, in many respects, the heyday of America's newsboys. From McKinley's assassination to the sinking of the *Titanic*, the era was a prodigious producer of headlines and hawkers. And if news lagged, the boys would declare war on Japan or invent some other lucrative crisis. With a third of the population under 15, "the streets boiled over with children," observed journalist John Reed in New York. Half were immigrants, or the offspring of immigrants. All were eager for income and excitement.[9]

Estimates of newsboys' number in the early 1900s ranged from 500 to 700 in Buffalo, Los Angeles, and Kansas City;[10] 1,200 to 2,000 in Grand Rapids, St. Louis, and Cincinnati;[11] 4,000 to 8,000 in Cleveland, Chicago, and Boston;[12] and between 15,000 and 30,000 in New York.[13] Their ethnicity reflected the immigration patterns of their cities, with the newest arrivals growing fastest due to the trade's ease of entry. Half the newsboys in Kansas City in 1914, for instance, were Jews, and a third were Italian.[14]

Girls remained a small minority in the trade. Indeed, the Society for the Prevention of Cruelty to Children declared in 1902 that newsgirls under 16 were no longer seen on the streets of New York due to its vigilance. But the visual record suggests otherwise. Lewis Hine photographed bevies of newsgirls in New York, Hartford, Wilmington, Hoboken, Providence, and Los Angeles. Progressives strategically focused on girls, seeing them not just as victims but also vehicles by which to alert the public to the larger problem of boy street labor. A delegate to a child labor conference in 1910 told how this wedge strategy worked in St. Louis, where she found two sisters selling papers after dark. "I spoke in public twice and told the same story," she said, "and the fact that it was girls and not boys selling papers won a hearing, and the press took it up and backed the charity workers and social workers in their efforts to get these little girls off the streets. Before that they have been trying and trying, but had been unsuccessful."[15]

Women vendors were also numerous. Mothers and sisters sometimes minded their stands with babes in arms or toddlers at play under the counter (Figure 10.2), while older women drew sympathy with their age and infirmities. "Poor, beshawled, and elderly," they belonged to any one of a dozen nationalities and operated a quarter of the 677 stands in New York City in 1908. Many women made more than a subsistence living, which fueled

Figure 10.2. A Yiddish newspaper stand in New York doubles as a playpen, ca. 1903.
New York Child Labor Committee Papers, box 42, folder 1a [3636.2 Newsboys].
New York State Library, Manuscripts and Special Collections, Albany, NY.

resentment in some circles. Brooklyn Bridge vendor Joe Rosenthal, president of the Downtown Newsboys Club, a dubious organization "with offices
wherever he happened to be," denounced their incursion as contrary to
history and nature: "If you take and read way back the books what the old
highbrows used to turn out you will find that women was female always, and
it ain't never mentioned as where they sells papers. Not once. Why do they do
it now, then?" A self-styled street philosopher given space in the *New York Sun*,
Rosenthal blamed the suffrage movement for pushing women beyond their
proper sphere: "Why don't she stop this 'Woman's Suffering' business? It don't
go." Some boys agreed that news peddling robbed girls of their femininity. "I
can't do anything with them," complained a St. Louis newsie. "They are so
pert, and they are getting worse every day." Artist J. R. Shaver depicted these
frustrations in a 1912 cartoon showing a newsgirl making a sale while four
newsboys look on enviously (Figure 10.3).[16]

    The number and standing of African Americans in the trade varied by city
and fluctuated with the news. They constituted 2 percent of hawkers in Syracuse
but 10 percent in St. Louis and 20 percent in Cincinnati, as reflected in a 1908

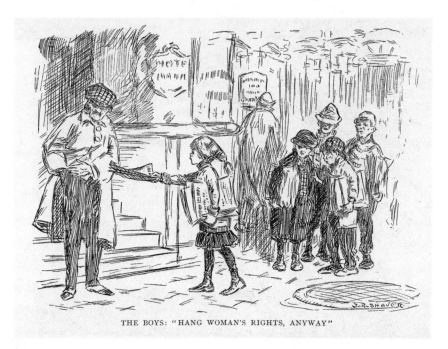

THE BOYS: "HANG WOMAN'S RIGHTS, ANYWAY"

Figure 10.3. J. H. Shaver, "The Boys: 'Hang Woman's Rights, Anyway,'" in Jacob
A. Riis, "The New York Newsboy," *Century Magazine* 85, no. 2 (Dec. 1912): 248. Eckel
Collection, Princeton University Library.

photograph by Hine (Figure 10.4). In Richmond, Virginia, the *Times Dispatch*
printed special editions for distribution by Negroes in Negro wards. Yet in
Chicago blacks had trouble cracking the better-paying downtown districts, except as strikebreakers.[17] Beyond the usual tensions, violence flared whenever
Jack Johnson, the first African American heavyweight champion, defended his
title. Such was the case on July 4, 1910, when he defeated former champ Jim
Jeffries, the "Great White Hope," in Reno, Nevada. The news sparked race riots
nationwide: whites attacked blacks for announcing the result too vociferously
or for simply buying a paper, and blacks in Louisville, Kentucky, attacked white
newsboys for inciting violence with their cries of Negro rioting. A flamboyant
celebrity, Johnson liked to tell assembled newsies that he had peddled papers
himself as a boy in Galveston, Texas. Sports editors usually weaved laurels from
such facts, but in this case they used it only to demean the champ. "Jack Johnson
and Caesar Both Got Start as Newsies," joked a *Wilkes-Barre Times* headline.[18]

America's newsboys still included truants, orphans, "skip-outs" (runaways),
and the disabled, but most attended school, lived at home, earned family money,
and avoided injury. Despite accusations of neglect, many of their parents—
mothers in particular—managed and monitored their children's labor according

Figure 10.4. Most of the dozen African Americans photographed by Lewis Hine outside the *Cincinnati Post* are older than the whites, illustrating the difficulty blacks had in escaping traditional forms of boy labor, especially during the brief but hobbling Panic of 1907–8. Hine's caption suggests he saw them oppressors more than oppressed: *Newsboys and Supply Men Waiting at Newspaper Office for Base-ball Edition, 5 P.M. The boys got rough treatment from the Negro supply men. The short negro without a hat is a pugilist. (Cincinnati, Ohio, August 1908).* Gelatin silver print, 5 × 7 in. Courtesy of the Lewis Hine Collection, University of Maryland–Baltimore County Library.

their ages, abilities, and family needs. The mother of 11-year-old Raphael Starr in New York gave him money every day to buy papers, with orders to return with exactly 23¢. She sent out his 9-year-old brother a few times a week when she needed an extra 10¢. He could sell as he wished on other days, but if she furnished the stake he had to bring home the money. Parents also intervened if their children's safety or earnings were jeopardized. Mrs. Horn in New York became her son's bodyguard after he was robbed, and soon began selling alongside her daughters. Some parents insisted that their children work in pairs, avoid busy streets, or stay out of unfamiliar saloons. One Italian-born mother allowed her son to sell only in City Hall Park, where there was no traffic and lots of police and office workers, "not dirty people to spoil a boy and teach him bad things to know." Her precaution backfired when park newsboys threatened to kill her son if he didn't beat it.[19]

The constant turnover of children in the trade reflected not just its dangers or the lure of better jobs but also the shifting fortunes of working-class families.

When rent was due or a parent was laid off or ill, mothers would encourage their children to peddle papers. When income was steady and a little money could be put away, they might decide that their children were better off at home or in school.[20]

Progressive Era newsboys, even more than their forerunners, kept step with an industry undergoing rapid expansion and modernization. Nationally, they helped distribute an all-time high of 2,600 daily newspapers whose combined circulation in 1909 exceeded 24 million, plus 520 Sunday papers good for another 13 million copies. As in other industries, consolidation altered the corporate landscape. In 1900 ten chains owned 32 dailies; in 1910 thirteen chains operated 62 dailies; and by 1920 thirty-one chains controlled 153 dailies. In addition, hundreds of newspapers subscribed to national wire services for news, features, and comics. They also forged cooperative purchasing, advertising, and distribution agreements.[21] "In every city the papers may appear to fight one another upon the surface," St. Louis Mirror editor William Marion Reedy told fellow newsmen in 1908, "but in every case they have a business combination to shut out the newcomer." Big dailies and the Associated Press were as much monopolies as Standard Oil, he said, and whoever could amass the capital necessary to challenge their "controlling and owning carriers, newsboys, and newsdealers absolutely" was unlikely to side with the interests of labor over capital.[22]

Other press critics agreed. Muckraker Lincoln Steffens called the Associated Press a "newspaper trust," albeit a benign one. Radical labor organizer "Mother" Jones accused Pennsylvania mill owners of acquiring stock in newspapers to stifle the child labor debate. And journalist Will Irwin denounced the "unhealthy alliance" between publishers and advertisers, which he said corrupted the press's advocacy of the public's interest, which caused editors to bury stories, ignore wrongdoing, and otherwise favor those they recognized as "our kind of people."[23]

The shrewdest media mogul of the era was William Randolph Hearst. With his eye on the White House, the yellow-press lord expanded his empire between San Francisco and New York. He started the Chicago American as a Democratic, pro-labor evening sheet in July 1900 and introduced the morning American in 1902, when he was elected to Congress. He founded the Los Angeles Examiner in 1903 and the Boston American in 1904. By the late 1920s his holdings included twenty-six papers in eighteen cities, plus magazines, wire services, and movie and newsreel companies. His modus operandi was everywhere the same. He offered distribution, production, and editorial staff above-average splits and salaries to get a foothold in the market. Once established, he raised prices, cut wages, and eliminated returns, all of which guaranteed labor trouble, including the bloodiest newsboy strike in Chicago history.[24]

To be fair, Hearst encountered opposition wherever he set up shop. Established dailies in Chicago hired sluggers to wreck his news wagons and terrorize any man or boy who carried his papers. Hearst retaliated in kind, bringing in New York muscle to protect his interests. In a tactical masterstroke, he hired away *Chicago Tribune* circulation manager Max Annenberg, a seasoned circulation warrior at age 25, and his equally hard-bitten brother Moe, 22, whose "education committees" ensured that Hearst's deliveries weren't spurned or sabotaged. The market for brawny "educators" boomed, averaging $3.50 a day, plus doctor's bills, and $15 a week for hospital time. Legal counsel could be had from the *American*'s lawyer, Clarence Darrow.[25]

Flourishing alongside these big-city dailies were a host of ethnic, radical, and woman's suffrage papers that sought to reach and create their own communities while challenging the images and values of the mainstream press. In addition to mail delivery, many developed their own sales and distribution forces. More than 1,100 ethnic papers served readers in twenty-three languages at the turn of the century, representing 6 percent of the nation's circulation.[26] The Yiddish *Tageblatt* in New York had a daily circulation of 100,000 in 1900. "Not to take a paper was to confess you were a barbarian," explained a subscriber. Competition could be fierce: when the *Jewish Daily Forward* gained ground, the *Tageblatt* threatened to cut off any boy who sold it. The *Forward* nonetheless surpassed the *Tageblatt* in circulation and influence. Meanwhile, Italian readers, who numbered more than half a million in New York, could choose from a dozen dailies and weeklies. A visitor to Little Italy in 1901 almost felt himself in a foreign city when newsboys cried their papers "at the top of their voices in Italian or Arabic, with an extra loud shriek of 'Wuxtra!' added for the sake of deference to American custom."[27]

Many of New York's ethnic journals enjoyed nationwide distribution. "We sold more Jewish newspapers than we did English newspapers—probably twenty-five to one," recalled Ben Brochin of Milwaukee. "There was *Der Tog*, and the *Forward*, and *Morning Journal*, and *Tageblatt* and the *Courier* and *Freiheit* and the *Barheit*, and there were two weekly magazines. One was a satire magazine, the *Kundes*, and then there was the *Americaner*." Brochin was around 10 years old when he and his brother started to ride the streetcars to the depot and pick up the papers. "I would hop right into the boxcar and find our bundles and throw them off. There was at least two of us went down to get the papers, and they weighed more than we did at the time." The boys would load the papers onto a streetcar with the help of passengers, who would also throw them off when they reached their father's grocery store. Waiting customers would help carry them across the street. "Boy, they went like hot cakes, one-two-three!" said Brochin. "People could hardly wait, not only for the political news and happenings of the day, but also for the features called the 'roman,' the romances in serial form."[28]

The children who peddled ethnic newspapers usually belonged to the same groups that consumed them, but not always. Harry Golden sold all the major English and Yiddish dailies in New York, plus *Mong Gee*, a Chinese-language weekly. "It was a profitable sideline," he said. "*Mong Gee* cost a nickel, and I kept three cents." When in Chinatown, Golden fantasized that he was in "the wicked and exotic East, not knowing it was the most law-abiding and decent neighborhood in all New York."[29]

The rare appearance of Asian news peddlers in eastern cities made news itself. Ki-Ko cried the *Chinese Weekly Herald* at the corner of Pell and Dover Streets in New York in 1901, yelling "Extra!" and summarizing contents like other newsboys. Thirty-year-old Ung Hou Chee, by contrast, stood quietly with the local dailies at Niagara and Vermont Streets in Buffalo in 1904. Dressed in his native garb, the onetime Seattle laundryman was razzed by his competitors. Detroit's first Chinese American news peddler, 10-year-old Sacramento-born Horace Way, "nattily attired in a suit of the most approved cut" circa 1908, encountered no such abuse.[30]

African American newspapers numbered 260 in the early 1900s; a hundred emerged in 1901 alone. They thrived despite low literacy rates perpetuated by segregated schools and white-only libraries. Most black papers started out as shoestring operations, the proprietor serving as writer, printer, and circulator. *Chicago Defender* publisher Robert Abbott hand-peddled the 300 copies of his first issues in 1905. Ten years later, with a circulation of 16,000, the *Defender* drew scores of schoolchildren every Friday afternoon to its 39th Street office, where they bought copies at 6¢ apiece and sold them for 10¢, rarely receiving tips. Likewise, the weekly *Pittsburgh Courier*, unwelcomed at white-owned newsstands, found distributors within its own community in needy high school students and elderly, race-conscious men. In 1907 Kansas City's *Rising Son* reached every Negro hamlet in the region via thirty newsboys, and aspired to 10,000 subscribers. The *Dallas Express* attained that goal using three hundred child and adult "newsboys" who distributed the paper every Saturday over a five-hundred-mile radius extending north to Kansas City, south to Galveston, east to Meridian, Mississippi, and west to El Paso.[31]

Three hundred socialist newspapers, including thirteen dailies, also circulated hand to hand between 1902 and 1912. They made strategic use of child labor for distribution and editorial purposes. The *Daily People*, founded in New York in 1900, recruited members and their sons to peddle copies "at the Brooklyn Bridge, the ferries, at factory gates and such other places where workingmen can be reached in large numbers." The term *newsboy* was not to be taken literally, said the paper: "Grown men can take a hand in the work as well." Innocence had its advantages, however. In January 1902, several of its boys were smuggled into a Brooklyn shoe factory during a labor dispute. Sales were brisk until a

foreman shooed them off, yelling, "Get out of here with that damned paper."
The *People's* use of minors did not prevent it from criticizing their exploitation
by the capitalist press; it once printed a Christmas appeal from the Newsboys'
Lodging House under the headline "Wants Cast-Off Clothes for Child Slaves
of Press to Fall Back Upon." Nor did its opposition to newsboy slavery mitigate
the paper's outrage when vending machines threatened their livelihoods. Since
their introduction in the early 1890s coin boxes had become part of the street
furniture of many cities, including Los Angeles, where they were also placed
on streetcars. In 1908, when a firm announced plans to install a thousand such
machines throughout the city and more across the state, the *People* bid farewell
to America's newsboys, saying, "The Newspaper Bosses, with Your Welfare Only
at Heart, Are to Knock Your Jobs to Pieces So That You Can Suffer Some More
of the Glories of Capitalism."[32]

In Milwaukee, the four-page, trilingual newspaper *Voice of the People* was
disseminated by its famed "Bundle Brigade," which could place copies behind
nearly every doorknob in the city in forty-eight hours. Two thousand strong,
the brigade consisted of workingmen and their wives and children, who would
get up at 5:00 a.m. to cover their districts before going to work or school. The
brigade also circulated strike notices and campaign literature in languages suited
to the neighborhood, thus helping to elect socialist mayor Emil Seidel in 1910
and twenty-one socialist aldermen. Similarly, during the 1909 "Uprising of the
20,000" in New York, striking shirtwaist makers, primarily Jewish and Italian
women, aided by Vassar students, raised money and sympathy by selling 45,000
copies of a special edition of the year-old socialist *New York Call*, printed in
Italian, Yiddish, and English. When the strike spread to Chicago, "strike newsies"
likewise distributed special editions of the *Chicago Daily Socialist*, securing more
than $3,000 for the relief fund.[33]

Following their lead were newspapers of the woman's suffrage movement,
which also advanced the cause of child labor reform. Made up of socialists
and trade unionists, immigrants and African Americans, shop girls and society
women, the movement met newsboys and newsgirls on their own terms when
they abandoned the genteel tactics of the parlor for the boisterous politics of
the street. The *Women's Journal* organized a street sales force in 1909 and issued
its hawkers yellow-and-black canvas "newsy bags." Other movement papers
equipped their peddlers with leather megaphones. When traditionalists charged
that street hawking undermined women's dignity, *Women's Journal* business
manager Agnes Ryan asked, "What is dignity? Of what value is it in itself? And
how does it compare in value with getting Votes for Women? At best are we not
in an undignified position before the world as long as we are disfranchised?" In
1910 the Equality League of Self-Supporting Women opened the first suffragist newsstand outside its office on East 22nd Street in New York. The "staff"

included Nora Stanton Blatch Barney, granddaughter of Elizabeth Cady Stanton, and socialist agitator Leonora O'Reilly, cofounder of the Women's Trade Union League. More than the vote, these suffragists wanted to eliminate the economic inequities that kept women out of skilled occupations and in perpetual poverty. Indeed, many became feminists through charitable and political work to improve the conditions of newsboys and other poor children.[34]

Whatever their size, market, or ideology, newspaper publishers and distributors quickly adapted to emerging modes of transport. Electric trolleys replaced horsecars at a rapid clip at the turn of the century, and a few cities introduced underground travel. At the opening of Boston's electric subway system in 1897 some boys tried to boost street sales with false cries of a fatal accident on the line. Bostonians would not be deterred. Stations became prized territory where adult vendors stomped on the feet of newsboys they caught selling in their vicinity—until the mayor granted the boys special permits.[35] Platform stands and street-level kiosks also sprouted up in and around New York's new subway in 1904 and Philadelphia's in 1906, attracting bands of children who worked either for or against their operators in pursuit of the commuter trade. Sixteen-year-old girls staffed many of the station stands in New York, working from 7:00 a.m. to 7:00 p.m., with a few hours off before noon. They earned $6 a week, but they threatened to walk out in the spring of 1905 when their bosses demanded a continuous twelve-hour shift and began hiring boys at $8 a week. "Will I stand for a twelve hour day?" replied one uptown newsgirl. "Well, I guess not. What do you think I'm made of?" Florence Kelley's National Consumers' League soon championed their right to a forty-five-minute lunch break.[36]

Also propelling newspapers into the new century were automobiles. Pulitzer purchased several steam cars in 1901 and put them into service on Long Island. They worked so well he bought sixteen more. His business manager calculated that twenty "machines" at $1,800 each offered better value than the sixty horses and forty wagons that would otherwise be needed. Newspapers as far west as San Francisco and Honolulu used automobiles to distribute hawkers around the city after elections or title fights (Figure 10.5). America's most prosperous carriers soon acquired cars of their own. In 1912 Walter Gee of West Haven, Connecticut, traded his horse-drawn rigs for a Model T that enabled him to cut more than two hours off his morning deliveries to fifteen hundred customers. "Now," reported a motoring magazine, "with eight boys on the running board of the single machine, he seldom is later than 5:50 in finishing his route."[37]

Efficient as they were, automobiles presented newsboys with a new occupational hazard. Seventeen-year-old Aaron Snodk of Boston fell off a running board in September 1901 and was hit by a car going the opposite direction. Nine-year-old Sandy Fowler of Salt Lake City was run over in June 1904 while being chased by a gang; somehow unscathed, he retrieved his papers to work the

Figure 10.5. Salt Lake City news sellers use a new Buick to distribute extras describing Jack Johnson's "fight of the century" in 1910. Used by permission, Utah State Historical Society.

sympathetic crowd that had gathered. These buggies traveled no more than ten miles an hour, but as speeds and traffic increased so, too, did the number and severity of accidents. In December 1905 14-year-old newsboy George Lawrence was struck and killed by a touring car in downtown Cleveland. In August 1906 10-year-old Archibald Attell was fatally hit selling papers at the corner of Van Ness and Eddy in San Francisco. And four Cleveland newsies, ages 8 to 12, were injured by vehicles on a single day in August 1909—two by autos, one by a streetcar, and one by a newspaper delivery wagon—which led the city to install the world's first electric traffic signal. Newsgirls were also victims; 9-year-old Eva Brach of Detroit suffered two broken legs in a hit-and-run in 1911. Though not counted as such, these were industrial accidents. Circulation managers vigilantly opposed ordinances penalizing fast drivers. Any such proposal, said one insider, "induces them to rush upstairs to see the editors, downtown to see lawyers, and across town to see politicians." Speeders sometimes had to pay damages for running over people ($300 was standard), but newspapers rarely bore any liability. A few produced handbooks to promote traffic awareness among their boys.[38]

The Imperatives of Pep

The status and income of circulation managers rose in the early 1900s along with two business trends: professionalization and scientific management. Following the example of doctors, lawyers, historians, and other occupations, thirty-five circulation bosses met in Detroit in 1898 to draw up a code of ethics, select a motto ("Honesty First"), start a newsletter, and schedule annual meetings. By 1910 the International Circulation Managers Association (ICMA) represented four hundred members in the United States and Canada. "Circulation is the life blood of the newspaper organism," explained C. M. Welch of the *Syracuse Journal*, "and just so surely as impoverished blood or impaired circulation shows itself in the countenance of the physician's patient, so will a weak, restricted or limited street sale mar the complexion of a newspaper."[39]

Welch and his associates were also influenced by efficiency expert Frederick Winslow Taylor, whose time-motion studies helped employers improve work-flow and create reward systems. Circulation managers had been streamlining distribution and incentivizing their distributors for decades, but their efforts gained new currency. Those at big dailies were soon pulling down $100 a week, or $5,000 a year, compared to $500 a year for the average laborer. The position sometimes served as a stepping-stone to the managing editor's desk or even to newspaper ownership, as it required mastery of all aspects of the business.[40]

The Annenberg brothers dominated the field in Chicago. Max kept a close eye on content so he could say with conviction how many copies his vendors should buy. "You'll want 100—or 200 or 1,500—extra copies this morning," he'd advise. "Such and such is in the paper." ("Such and such" was usually a juicy murder or scandal.) He also oversaw advertising space, which doubled industry-wide from 30 to 60 percent of total space in the first two decades of the century, with department store ads occupying a third of it. When Marshall Field's withdrew its ads from the *Evening American*, Max marched sixty newsboys and drivers into the store chanting, "Marshall Field's closed!" Shoppers fled and the store resumed its ads. Later, when the City Railway Company barred boys from selling on streetcars, he led fifty newsies on board the cars in defiance of the order. They created havoc in the Loop for hours and won the public's sympathy with coverage of policemen clubbing and cuffing the boys. Moe also became a field general in the newspaper circulation wars. He not only joined in brawls on behalf of his employers but devised a successful circulation-building scheme whereby newspapers offered subscribers silver teaspoons imprinted with the official seal of each state.[41]

Raising the number, loyalty, and productivity of newsboys was a topic of every ICMA newsletter and convention, culminating in the formation of its

Newsboys Welfare Committee in 1915. Many managers eased boys into the trade by giving them papers for free or at a heavy discount, and lavishing them with attention. "Mingle with the boys you want to win over to your paper," advised Welch. "Learn their names, fix their identity in your mind and greet them as Heinie, Issie, Nate, Abe, Tom, John, etc., with a cheery word for each. The boy will soon begin to prize your friendship and will be proud of his familiarity with you." He noted that in some areas street sales were in the hands of one nationality. "Don't antagonize them by bringing in rank outsiders," he said, as they would only be driven off. Rather, "induce the old boys to bring in more of their own set."[42] Publishers of ethnic newspapers offered their boys benefits as well, including meals and coats. Proprietors of the Italian-language *Bolletino della Sera* in New York began hosting banquets for them in 1899 that included "nearly a dozen courses," plus wine. Many foreign-language newspapers took group portraits of their newsboys outside their offices, dressed in their best to epitomize ethnic pride and accomplishment (Figure 10.6).[43]

One thing all circulation managers shared was the need to "ginger up" the enthusiasm of their hawkers. Some held mass sales meetings featuring demonstrations by self-styled "newsboy kings" such as Jack Lloyd of Buffalo, Harry "The Human Megaphone" Schatz of Denver, and Chimmie "De Big

Figure 10.6. Newsboys and staff of New York's Greek daily *Atlantis*, ca. 1904. Albumen photograph, 27 × 22.5 cm. Historical Society of Pennsylvania, No. 1063.

Noise" McFadden of New York. These charismatic hucksters were arguably the first motivational speakers in corporate America.[44] Most effective was Clint "Noodles" Fagan (Figure 10.7), a grown-up Bowery urchin with a skyscraper voice who earned his nickname fetching noodles for Tammany boss Richard Croker. By 1904 Fagan claimed to have represented 2,900 dailies. He displayed his vocal talents outside the new Flatiron Building and other world landmarks. His sales were legendary—and he created the legend himself in speeches, interviews, and an illustrated training manual: "During the Harwick disaster at Pittsburgh, Pa., I sold 19,000 copies of the *Press* in three hours. At the time of the

"NOODLES" CLINT FAGAN, CHAMPION NEWSBOY OF THE WORLD

Figure 10.7. Newspapers across the country hired famous ex-newsies to "ginger up" their sales force. Clint "Noodles" Fagan, Champion Newsboy of the World, in *The Life of Noodles Fagan, by Himself,* 4th ed. (Buffalo: Buffalo Evening News, 1904). Eckel Collection, Princeton University Library.

Chicago Theatre fire I sold at the Chicago Stock Yards, to employees and union strikers 27,000 copies of the *Chicago American*. At the Atlantic City Jubilee, the day of the Slocum disaster, I sold 32,000 New York and Philadelphia papers— a whole baggage car load." Fagan's manual was chock-full of pithy maxims, including "You can sell papers with a clean face as well as a dirty one," and tips for advancement: "Be prompt. Be courteous. Be thoughtful. Do as you are told." His presentations evolved into an elaborate vaudeville act featuring songs, skits, movies, and athletic contests.[45]

Newspaper executives also modernized their product and facilities with newsboys in mind. Rejecting the featureless mass of gray text that characterized the layout of nineteenth-century newspapers, publishers now offered eye-catching front pages with big headlines, photographs, and illustrations favorable to street sales. They expanded readership by starting children's pages containing serial fiction, puzzles, and handicraft projects. In 1902 the *New York Sunday Journal* kept twenty-five clerks busy answering children's letters.[46] Publishers also added comic supplements, which appealed to all ages and could increase a paper's circulation by 50,000 copies. Following in *The Yellow Kid*'s footsteps, many comic strips featured child characters, including Richard Outcault's *Buster Brown* (1902), Winsor McCay's *Little Nemo in Slumberland* (1905), and George McManus's *Nibsy the Newsboy in Funny Fairyland* (1906) (Plate 22). *Nibsy* originated in the *New York World* and was syndicated nationwide for fourteen months. Though ostensibly inspired by Jacob Riis's tenement tale "Nisby's Christmas," the strip was a source of anarchic comedy, not humanitarian concern.[47]

To further attract youngsters, newspapers tried to make their offices child friendly. The *Los Angeles Record* installed swings and exercise bars in its alley and placed punching bags and medicine balls in its distribution room. Following the *Grand Rapids Press*, the *Detroit News* hired architect Albert Kahn to design a medieval-style office that featured a grand Newsboy Entrance, glistening new lavatory, and 1,600-square-foot Newsboy Room adorned with a terrazzo floor and Kittanning brick wainscoting. Next door was the office of the Newsboys' Sales Clerk, who sold tokens through a little wicket. The tokens could be exchanged for papers over at the Sales Counter, behind which were the presses, mail room, and shipping platform, all linked by conveyor belts. Upstairs were the editorial offices, which the circulation manager could reach via his own elevator, another sign of the profession's growing prestige.[48]

To address concerns that news peddling contributed to truancy, some papers hired social workers, primarily young women who got to know the boys and made home visits if necessary. Newspapers in Louisville and Grand Rapids continued to support newsboy homes and schools founded in the 1890s. Attendance at the Louisville school peaked in 1906–7, when 114 boys and 8

girls attended classes five nights a week. The newsboy school was a public institution staffed and equipped by the school board. Its students were mainly the
children of immigrants, and one year the student body represented fourteen
nationalities. Before its closure in 1917 the school had taught 3,600 students
and graduated 1,000.[49]

Newsboys also figured in newspaper circulation campaigns. They competed in
sales tournaments and posed for pictures with chorus girls and other celebrities.
Dailies from Philly to Frisco hired the vaudeville elephant Little Hip to sell papers on the street beside their boys (Figure 10.8). The *Denver Post* extended the
joke by enrolling him in the local newsboys union.[50]

The most incredible circulation stunt began in May 1901 when three newsies
took off on a Hearst-sponsored race around the world. The boys, supposedly selected after rigorous testing, were William Clark Crittenden of the *San
Francisco Examiner*, Charles Cecil Fitzmorris of the *Chicago American*, and Louis
St. Clair Eunson of the *New York Evening Journal*, all 17 years old. Two adult
journalists representing *Le Journal* and *Le Matin* of Paris also competed. All left
their cities at the same moment. Two of the Americans went west by rail and
ship to Yokohama, Vladivostok, Moscow, London, and Dublin, and one went
east. The racers posted daily accounts of their progress, setbacks, and greetings

Figure 10.8. Vaudeville veteran "Little Hip" shows off his sales skills on the streets of
Denver, 1909. Newspapers across the country employed him to entertain their newsboys
and boost street sales. Denver Public Library, Western History Collection, X28840.

by heads of state, including President McKinley. A $1,000 prize was offered to the reader who picked the winner and came closest to guessing his finishing time. The victor, Fitzmorris of Chicago, completed the journey in 60 days, 13 hours, 29 minutes, and 42⅘ seconds. He received a hero's welcome and grew up to become the city's youngest chief of police. But the race was fixed. The boys were selected without the expense of a real contest, and it was arranged in advance that Fitzmorris would win because the year-old *Chicago American* needed the publicity more than the other papers and the politically ambitious Hearst wanted to woo Irish American voters.[51]

Newspaper contests and charities invariably sought to increase publishers' profits, sometimes at newsboys' expense. In 1901 the *New York Evening Telegram* gave its newsies the Christmas day edition for free and treated them to a banquet. But on New Year's Day it raised the wholesale price of ten copies from 4¢ to 5¢. "In other words," said the *Daily People*, "the 'Evening Telegram,' owned by the luxurious James Gordon Bennett, has invested in one edition and a dinner, so that it might dazzle the boys sufficiently to allow their being squeezed of a little additional profit." That, said the paper, is "capitalist charity."[52]

Some publishers sought to deflect criticism and win allegiance by producing newspapers especially for the boys. Known as "junior publications," these four-page monthlies bore clever names such as *Pep, Live Wire,* and *Times Junior.* Intended to edify and motivate their young sales force, the papers contained human-interest stories, profiles of contest winners, and "shop talk" columns such as "Carrier Boys' Ten Commandments" or tips on "porching every paper." Circulation managers oversaw the publications but trained boys to edit them. *The Newsboy,* founded by the *New York Evening World* in 1898, named Louis Feinberg, 14, and Samuel Cantor, 16, its editors after a month-long sales contest that promised entrants a chance to learn the trade "from the cellar to the dome."[53]

Newsboys also produced amateur trade publications for their peers. In 1899 three boys in Jackson, Michigan, founded *Newsboy Magazine,* which won praise as a "bright little publication" containing "some very commendable writings." Its "worldly affairs" editor, Holmes S. Kimball, 20, went on to a long reporting career in Detroit. In 1906 B. E. Winningham of Red Sulphur Springs, Tennessee, started *The Newsboy* with type he cut with a bowie knife. These publications were printed in newspaper job rooms or on small "novelty presses."[54]

Better-financed adult-run serials included the *American Newspaper Boy,* founded in Winston-Salem, North Carolina, in 1900; *Our Boys,* originating in Pittsburgh in 1902; and *The American Newsboys Magazine,* first published in New York in 1903. These were commercial/philanthropic ventures that sought to instill thrift in the boys who sold them. The 1903 effort, launched by journalist William F. Gilchrist and poet Kate Thyson Marr, wholesaled for 2¢ a copy and retailed for 10¢. Sellers had to deposit half the profit into a savings account; 20 percent could be withdrawn before Christmas, with the balance payable on the boy's sixteenth birthday.[55] When told of the publication, Pi Alley newsboy Benjamin Galp in Boston offered sage advice: "Why, the magazine will make a hit right away if they know what's what and give it to us on the level. If they go and stick a lot of hot air in it and don't give us the real goods, why it will go up, that's all there is to it."[56] The magazine failed in 1905 after promoters were accused of using Theodore Roosevelt's endorsement to bilk investors. "Watch your checkbook," advised the *New York Sun*. To counter the bad publicity, the magazine treated 3,500 New York newsies to a day at Rockaway Beach, during which the boys wearied police by climbing the windmill, turning on fire hydrants, and bombarding everything along the rail line with chunks of coal.[57]

Other periodicals followed. *The Newsboy*, a Pittsburgh monthly founded by railroad baron Milton Hays in 1909, featured inspirational poems and articles ("Have Faith in Yourself") before its demise in 1910. Former carriers in Cleveland, Des Moines, and Pittsburgh mounted similar ventures in the years before World War I, but no one found the right formula for success in this golden age of magazines. For all their charm and chicanery, the publications never met newsboys' needs as sellers or readers.[58]

Laying Down the Law

Despite the best efforts of management to make news peddling appealing to children in the early 1900s, newsboys became objects of intense scrutiny by a coalition of reformers united to expose the "evils" of child labor in all sectors of the economy. Their attention to "juvenile street trading"—a new term in reform circles that encompassed the work of newsboys, bootblacks, messengers, and others—struck a chord. Newsboys, in particular, served a smorgasbord of progressive interests, attracting not just child labor foes but also advocates of birth control, immigration restriction, sanitary housing, supervised playgrounds, educational uplift, Sunday rest, juvenile justice, social hygiene, temperance, good government, Americanization, and woman's suffrage. Newsboys clearly needed the motherly embrace of the state from head to toe. And because they plied their trade throughout the country, they became valuable assets in building a national, multi-pronged child welfare movement.

By the turn of the century twenty-eight of forty-five states had passed child labor laws. They applied mainly to children in factories. Another ten states regulated their work in mines as well. Most of these laws set a minimum age of 12, fixed their maximum daily hours at ten, required basic literacy or school attendance, and provided no funds for enforcement. With southern textile states largely unregulated, the number of working children ages 10 to 14 reached 1.75 million nationally, or 18 percent of children in that age group. Muckraker John Spargo put the number at 2.25 million. Children's premature labor, he argued, meant lower wages for adults, immoral profits for owners, dishonorable savings for consumers, and higher taxes to support the growing number of delinquent, disabled, and truant children in prisons and asylums. If the twentieth century was to be realized as "The Century of the Child," wrote Swedish sociologist Ellen Key in her international bestseller of 1900, then the "industrial and street work of children will be everywhere forbidden."[59]

Without meaning to exaggerate, Key, Spargo, and their ilk referred to juvenile street traders as "slaves" and "outlaws"—slaves because they were forced to work by callous parents, and outlaws because they fell outside the protection of existing laws. Few children, in fact, peddled papers against their will or beyond the reach of local vagrancy and compulsory education laws. Cincinnati, Detroit, and Boston had permit systems for newsboys and bootblacks, yet their effect was slight. Boston's 1892 licensing scheme fell victim to the news bonanza of the Spanish-American War, which made enforcement impossible and, according to one school principal, provoked an upsurge in theft, burglary, and pickpocketing.[60]

Statewide regulation of child street labor began in June 1902 when the Massachusetts Civic League pushed through legislation that transferred licensing authority from Boston's aldermen to its school board, effective January 1, 1903. The board issued 3,500 permits on approval of the children's teachers or principals, but enforcement remained in the reluctant hands of the police. After six months, a special officer was assigned to the task. He made sixty-five arrests the first year, but children—primarily Jews in the North End and downtown, and Irish in the South End and suburbs—continued to flout the law in droves. When asked to show their badge, they told him, "It is broken" or "Another boy swiped it." Though weak, the law was extended to all interested cities of the commonwealth in 1906. Only ten chose to implement it (Cambridge, Chelsea, Newton, Fall River, Medford, Somerville, Fitchburg, Worcester, Quincy, and Salem). School boards still lacked the authority to enforce their rules, especially after school hours. Defenders of child labor in the state's textile mills liked to say, "The spinners are better off than the newsboys!"[61]

In New York, the first call for newsboy restriction came from adults in the trade, not the reform community. In September 1901 the National Association of Newsdealers, Booksellers and Stationers passed a resolution seeking to improve the condition and education of an estimated 3,000 child news peddlers in that city. Many children were beyond their parents' control, said the association president. They peddled papers as a ruse to pick pockets or cut school, thus bringing the whole profession into disrepute. The dealers recommended a small license fee of 50¢ to drive off "illegitimate sellers" and allow others to make a fair living. They offered to pay the fee for worthy boys unable to do so.[62]

Nothing came of the idea until the state Department of Labor issued its first report in March 1902. This massive survey of labor conditions devoted just twelve pages to women and children but noted, "The evils of child labor are much greater outside than inside our factories, wherein relatively few children are employed." Of the estimated 450,000 truants, said the report, at most 50,000 worked in factories, while the majority toiled in homes, offices, and streets. It recommended stricter enforcement of compulsory education laws.[63]

Seeking stronger medicine, the New York Association of Neighborhood Workers, a group formed fifteen months earlier by Florence Kelley and Lillian Wald to coordinate the efforts of the city's thirty-one settlement houses, organized a child labor committee and persuaded University Settlement House director Robert Hunter to head it. Hunter, 28, a past Hull House resident and author of the highly regarded *Tenement Conditions in Chicago*, raised $1,000 to hire research librarian Helen Marot to investigate conditions in the state, including the home and street trades. Marot had recently completed a detailed study of the needle trades in Philadelphia. In New York, she oversaw a team of settlement and trade union volunteers who compiled data on a thousand child labor cases via interviews with teachers, parents, children, factory inspectors, and newsboys' lodging house superintendents.[64]

Early on, the committee sought the counsel of Jacob Riis. "If it was the last service I could render New York," he replied, "I could think of nothing of greater importance." Riis lent his name to the campaign and kept attention on the issue with *Children of the Tenements*, a collection of older writings, and "Children of the People," a magazine piece lauding the child-saving efforts of the SPCC, Children's Aid Society, and Fresh Air Fund.[65] Riis had retired his camera, so a young volunteer from Harvard photographed East Side newsboys and bootblacks on the streets at night, playing craps on the steps of City Hall and at the Mulberry Street police station, and sleeping in boxes and on gratings. The committee used the pictures to lobby legislators in Albany and raise public awareness. "Their life grows to be a life of dishonesty, of tearing away from their home influence," said Kelley, who raised the subject in speeches before women's clubs and civic groups. Hunter and Felix Adler of the New York Ethical Culture Society also spoke widely, published articles, and met with reporters to summarize the group's findings on what was called the "newsboy problem."[66]

Much of what is known about newsboys during this period grew out of Marot's investigation. The "newsboy cards" she compiled in 1902 have gone missing, but an unpublished typescript summarizing the committee's study of 220 newsboys reveals that three-quarters were 12 or under. According to this record, most began selling by age 9 or 10 and attended school "more or less" regularly. Peak hours of selling were from 4:00 p.m. to 7:00 p.m., but some stayed out until ten o'clock or later if sales were good. Many of the boys worked with their brothers. They seldom ate dinner at home, subsisting on coffee, candy, and sandwiches procured at stands or saloons. Few boys got enough sleep to concentrate well in school. They earned on average $1.60 a week, and gambled much of it away. Their incomes were hardly necessary to family survival, concluded investigators, as 80 percent of their fathers worked.[67]

The committee disseminated its findings in periodicals and pamphlets that ushered in the muckraking era. Many young activists cut their teeth on this campaign. During a Saturday work session with Marot, Florence Kelley turned to her unpaid assistant, 25-year-old Bryn Mawr graduate Josephine Goldmark, and handed her a sheaf of questionnaires completed during staff visits to the homes of lawbreaking newsboys confined at the New York Juvenile Asylum and Catholic Protectory. Kelley asked Goldmark to analyze the material for evidence about the relationship between street peddling and delinquency. The result was Goldmark's first article, "Evils of Newsboy Life," published in the *New York Evening Post* in February 1903. It took a broad inventory of the "sinister realities" of child street labor and then focused on the lives of Abraham S., Bennie R., and Ignatius G.—real boys who, Goldmark concluded, were robbed of their childhoods by needless toil. She elaborated on her findings the next year in an essay in *Political Science Quarterly* that urged strengthening street trade regulations.[68]

Ernest Poole, another of Marot's volunteers, took on the task of producing a pamphlet on street traders for the University Settlement House, where he lived and helped organize basketball games for neighborhood youth. A recent Princeton graduate who revered Jacob Riis, Poole threw himself into the assignment. He chummed around with newsboys, messengers, and bootblacks for weeks, plying them with suppers, stage shows, and cigarettes. "By such bribes I got the facts and stories I wanted about their jobs and lives," Poole said in his autobiography. "In true reformer fashion then I centered on the worst ones, the toughest and the wildest, the hundreds down by City Hall near what was then still Newspaper Row. For these were the real street Arabs who slept at night in doorways or under Brooklyn Bridge close by."[69]

These "newsboy wanderers" were the focus of Poole's debut article in the *Evening Post* and an expanded version in *McClure's Magazine*, illustrated by 25-year-old Frank E. Schoonover, a specialist in outdoor adventure stories. "The newsboy is forever restless," wrote Poole. "He works only when the crowds are thickest; he shapes all his habits to suit the changing, irregular, life of the metropolis; and its life makes the life of his boyhood." Poole described his 1:00 a.m. encounter with "Nick," a little "Guiney" (Italian) who had been selling papers since the age of 8 and had become a "degenerate crapshooter." He told of the group who "beat it" by train to "Philly" and earned enough working on a news wagon "for a two nights' tour of 'the town.' " "Us kids ain't built fer de home an' mudder racket," one of the "worse ones" told him. Other boys boasted of adventures in Buffalo, Chicago, St. Louis, Texas, Cuba, and London, their descriptions "too accurate for falsehood." These were "tramps in the making," said Poole, ruined forever for steady, disciplined labor.[70]

Reformers documented corrupting conditions in other cities as well. H. Brewster Adams, a divinity student at the University Settlement House, returned home to Buffalo in March 1903 to help his brother Myron prepare a report on its newsboys. They hoped to refute claims that juvenile street traders in smaller cities did not need protection. In two days, the brothers interviewed 328 newsboys, representing almost half of the hawkers in the city. Eight out of ten were under 14, more than a quarter were under 10, and a "considerable number" were 5 or 6. The younger boys were, with few exceptions, Italians; three were orphans. The danger of their work was evident, said Adams, in the fact that two-thirds of the inmates at the Rochester State Industrial School had been newsboys. Adams blamed the children's parents, whom he described as greedy, slothful, and violent. He also scolded the public: "If you buy of such a boy you only increase his slavery." Newspaper owners and managers somehow escaped rebuke.[71]

These reports, with their accompanying charts and tables, attest to the committee's faith in the power of facts. The consensus was clear: street trading contributed to truancy and delinquency, netted "pauperizing" tips rather than honest wages, and exposed children to vices that killed their self-respect.[72] The committee sought better enforcement of existing labor and education laws, and the passage of new laws modeled on those recently passed in Great Britain, where Parliamentary inquiries characterized news peddling as "blind alley" employment that curtailed children's education and ruined them for adult wage labor. Six cities—London, Liverpool, Manchester, Bradford, Edinburgh, and Dublin—set up license schemes that prescribed the hours, ages, and conditions in which children could work on the streets.[73]

New York Child Labor Committee (NYCLC) members pushed several bills through the state legislature that mandated school attendance and age verification for children in factories and department stores. They then turned their attention to the newsboy problem, backing a bill sponsored by Senator Henry Hill of Buffalo and Assemblyman Edward Ridley Finch of New York to prohibit the sale of papers by children under 10, and permit those between 10 and 14 to sell out of school hours, up to 9:00 p.m., if they registered with school authorities and secured a badge. Testifying on behalf of the bill before the Senate Judiciary Committee in Albany, Adler urged the senators to "think of your own children . . . waiting at 4 o'clock in the morning for the early newspapers. What kind of school is that for children?" American Federation of Labor president Samuel Gompers pressed lawmakers to "remove the blot from the State and the shame from its business life of compelling babies to fight for their living in the streets." Robert Hunter simply pleaded, "Give the kids a chance."[74]

The press's response ranged from mild derision to qualified support. "As yet," teased the *New York Tribune*, "the newsboys have not even talked of sending an opposing lobby to Albany." Pulitzer's *World* lauded the bill as "one of the most desirable measures ever introduced" but raised the "perplexing question" of the newsboy's rights in the matter. "There is no doubt that he would be better off morally if kept from the streets," said the paper. "Whether there would be a corresponding mental and physical improvement is not so certain. The battle of wits in which he engages daily is a hard one, but it is a first skirmish in the great battle of life."[75]

Opposition arose from an unlikely source, the Society for the Prevention of Cruelty to Children. Founder Elbridge Gerry, now 66, had spent thirty years rescuing children from neglect and abuse, but he felt there was nothing intrinsically harmful about peddling papers and that existing law could deal with those who used it as a cover for beggary or vagrancy. "The bill would render the unhappy boy's life even more miserable than it is at present," he said. "He is first to be dosed with education, then to be branded with a license." Gerry argued that newsboys were less prone to the temptations of the street than idle children of the same class, and expressed disappointment that the law overlooked girls between the ages of 14 and 16. Other SPCC officials noted that Boston's ten-year-old permit system was hardly a model of success, and reported that some judges feared the law would double their workload.[76]

Any newsboy following the dispute would have recognized it for what it was: a turf war. Differences between the SPCC and the NYCLC were generational but also philosophical. Society officials felt that it was the conditions of work, not the work itself, that endangered children, whereas committee members objected to all forms of paid labor for minors, regardless of the conditions. Also, while Gerry subscribed—and testified—to the belief that many fine men had been newsboys, Adler called them exceptions to the rule.

Popular culture sided with Gerry on this point. The publication of Horatio Alger's posthumous novel, *Adrift in New York*, in 1900 and the reissue of his *Ben Bruce: Scenes from the Life of a Bowery Newsboy* and *Nelson the Newsboy* affirmed the durability of the rags-to-riches myth. A similar nostalgia sugared plays such as *Grit the Newsboy* (1902), *A Boy of the Streets* (1903), *Nettie the Newsgirl* (1904), and *The Bowery Newsgirl* (1905). These shows filled playhouses from Baltimore to Kalamazoo and, like other representations, infused the work of real boys and girls with an unattainable romance. Illustrator Jessie Willcox Smith exploited this trend with her 1906 drawing in *Collier's Weekly* of a sad-eyed, tousle-haired

A Tempered Wind
JESSIE WILLCOX SMITH

Figure 10.9. Jessie Willcox Smith, "A Tempered Wind," *Collier's Weekly*, April 26, 1906. Eckel Collection, Princeton University Library.

gamin looking seductively forlorn with her oversized papers and one lost shoe (Figure 10.9).[77]

Newsboys' masculine virtues, meanwhile, were celebrated in pulp novels and self-improvement magazines such as *Ambition* and *Success* (Figure 10.10). Newspapers hammered home the same message. "Don't Pity This Boy—He Will Become a Self Made Man," assured the *Denver Sunday Post* over a full-page cartoon newsboy. Former Bowery urchin Owen Kildare offered living proof of the possibility of advancement in his 1903 memoir *My Mamie Rose: The Story of My Regeneration*, later adapted for the screen. If any doubt remained, Cleveland oil tycoon John D. Rockefeller assured readers of *Cosmopolitan* magazine that opportunities were greater than ever: "No boy, howsoever lowly—the barefoot country boy, the humble newsboy, the child of the tenement—need despair. I see in each of them infinite possibilities. They have but to master the knack of economy, thrift, honesty, and perseverance, and success is theirs."[78]

Ironically, it took the intervention of financier J. P. Morgan to move the bills along. According to Hunter's unpublished autobiography, legislators in Albany were unreceptive to the committee's agenda until Morgan pulled some strings.

Figure 10.10. "Distinguished Americans Who Once Sold Papers for a Living," *Success,* July 15, 1899. Eckel Collection, Princeton University Library.

The street trades bill passed on April 8 and was signed into law the next day by Governor Benjamin Odell, effective September 1, 1903. The result was a watered-down version of the original bill. It applied only to the state's two largest—or "first-class"—cities, greater New York and Buffalo. Boys under 10 and girls under 16 were prohibited from selling papers. Boys 10 to 14 had to obtain a badge, but they were not required to provide proof of age. They could sell until 10:00 p.m., and parents could not be penalized for their children's violations. Messengers were exempt due to opposition from the telegraph and telephone companies, and all other forms of street trading were left unregulated. Nevertheless, the bill was touted as a model for other states, and its sponsors received hearty congratulations from President Roosevelt.[79]

Implementation was not left to chance. Letters were sent to all public and private schools asking principals to explain the provisions of the law to their pupils and estimate the number of students who expected to sell papers. Nearly ten thousand boys filled out applications. Thinking that half were not serious, officials ordered six thousand nickel-plated badges bearing the Board of Education's seal (Figure 10.11). To prevent the unauthorized transfer of badges, as was common in Boston, each badge had a space for the holder's name and number on the front and signature on the back. The licenses were free but had to be renewed annually or surrendered.[80]

Parents complied with the law. The day before it took effect, "anxious crowds of mothers," some carrying babies, accompanied their children to public schools throughout the city to secure licenses for them. Lines formed at daybreak. Some families waited hours for the required health examination. The crush was greatest on the Lower East Side, where police were called in to maintain order. Many of these mothers "told wild and fantastic tales of the ages of their offspring," reported the *New York Tribune*. A thousand licenses were issued that day, and five thousand more in the weeks that followed, leaving little doubt that parents approved their children's peddling and valued their income.[81] The same pattern held in Buffalo, where the Board of Education granted licenses to fifteen hundred boys while turning away more than three hundred underage applicants.[82]

Yet timid enforcement limited the law's effectiveness. Truant officers in New York City devoted just two evenings a week to chasing delinquent newsies, and police took their "newsboy duty" lightly. Overcrowded conditions in public

Figure 10.11. Newsboy Badge of Dominic Danza. Six thousand nickel-plated badges were issued after passage of the 1903 Newsboy Law in New York. Eckel Collection, Princeton University Library.

schools required half-day schedules, which made it hard for police to identify truants. Newspapers badgered the police with headlines such as "Tiny
Breadwinner for Sick Mother Arrested." Many boys dispensed with their badges
or let them out to underage boys for 5¢ to 10¢ a day. Few felt any worries about
staying out past 10:00 p.m. Newsboys also hampered enforcement by refusing
to display their badges, as required by law. Boys who were influenced by detective stories sewed their badges inside their coats so they could flash them with
a dramatic flair if challenged. Others did so to prevent older boys from stealing
them so as to drive them out of the trade. A year after its passage, Kelley declared
the newsboy law a "dead letter," saying, "No uniformed officer has ever yet been
found who was willing to run after such an urchin." A brawny sergeant admitted
as much after being reprimanded by the superintendent of schools: "Ar, wot d'ye
t'ink av me pullin' in a kid thot ain't t'ree feet high? De whole station w'u'd be a
laughin' at me!"[83]

In May 1905 New York's police commissioner appointed a squad of four
plainclothes officers to enforce the law. They made five hundred arrests in eight
months, but newsboys learned to spot them. The men worked in pairs to reduce the likelihood of being mobbed by passersby who saw their duty as harassment. Police also encountered opposition from magistrates, some of whom
dismissed newsboy cases and scolded the officers for wasting taxpayers' money.
The squad's arrest rate dwindled to two a day.[84]

To increase compliance with the law, the committee started a scholarship
fund to aid the estimated one in four families that might be distressed by the
loss of their children's income. It also wished to alleviate officers' fears that their
diligence would cause hardship. In the first four months of the experiment, the
committee investigated 117 applicants and made thirteen awards of $1 to $3 a
month. Lillian Wald of the Henry Street Settlement admitted that it was a labo-
rious and inadequate solution. Her ally Kelley objected on principle, citing the
example of Angelo, a promising singer who had accepted a subsidy from a settlement house vocal instructor but could not resist selling election extras. "The
greedy peasant family had not withstood the temptation to get both the music
teacher's gift and the newsboys' earnings," she said. "Weariness, cold and wet
did their work; pneumonia followed the election night and Angelo never sang
again."[85]

Amendments improved the law's effectiveness. In 1905 its provisions were extended to the "second-class" cities (population 50,000 to 250,000) of Rochester,
Syracuse, Albany, and Troy. Girls under 16 were forbidden to sell papers. Kelley
said the law represented "a distinct ethical gain," but she called for raising the
legal age and lowering the permissible hours of street work, noting that "it was
still possible for a lad of fourteen to perish of privation and exhaustion while
striving to support himself on the streets of New York." She was referring to

Abraham Koudos, a newsboy who had starved to death while supporting his widowed mother and sister.[86] A 1907 study of the law's effectiveness by Cornell graduate student Carol Aronovici warned that the vices acquired on the street by underage sellers were not just "physically, mentally, and morally injurious to the boys" but threatened to "infect the schools" and endanger the healthy development of nonworking children as well.[87] That year legislators banned the sale of magazines to rid the streets of small fries hustling the *Saturday Evening Post*, and they charged school officials with enforcement. In 1910 violations were reduced from misdemeanors to infractions. A 1913 amendment extended the law to "third-class" cities (under 50,000 population) and raised the minimum age to 13.[88]

Newark, Hartford, Portland (Maine), Detroit, and the state of Wisconsin followed suit. But the wording and enforcement of their street trades laws left much to be desired. Newark's ordinance banned only newsboys under 8 and omitted bootblacks. Hartford's was repealed due to opposition from the *Hartford Times*.[89] And in 1908 Washington, DC, issued badges to fifteen hundred juvenile street traders, fourteen hundred of whom were newsboys, only to exempt them the next year on the grounds that newspapers weren't merchandise. This reversal occurred even though Roosevelt's labor commissioner, Charles P. Neill, singled out street trading as "particularly dangerous to the morals of children." Street traders made up only a quarter of the capital's child laborers, he said, but two-thirds of those sent to reform schools. A former Austin, Texas, newsboy, Neill rejected the idea that peddling papers built character, saying it was "a training in either knavery or mendicancy." But his words went unheeded.[90]

Chicago pols and publishers were equally adept at fending off reform. In the fall of 1903, the Federation of Chicago Settlements recruited Myron Adams, fresh from his exertions in Buffalo, to conduct a study of newsboys and newsgirls (chiefly Italian) in their city. A team of twenty investigators surveyed a thousand hawkers, mainly in the Loop, in just twenty-eight hours. "We found exactly what made them leave school, the circumstances of their family, how much their earnings were needed, their truancy record and all the rest," said Jane Addams. With report in hand, she met with leaders of the publishers' association, hoping to gain support for an ordinance. But the men closed ranks. Two attributed their own success to having once peddled papers. One kept a bronze statue of a newsboy on his desk. Moreover, a Chicago judge ruled in April 1904 that the state's anti-peddling law didn't apply to newsboys because they performed a public service in the distribution of information.[91]

Kelley never conceded the point. "There is no essential difference between selling information, selling papers and selling chewing gum," she told a convention in 1909. "The trouble is we are afraid of the newspapers. We are not afraid of the chewing gum manufacturer . . . and so we have worked out a combination that a newsboy is a merchant, which is simply ridiculous." University of Chicago Settlement founder Mary McDowell rose to object: "We gave the matter up, not because we were afraid of the newspapers, but because we could not proceed without the help of the newspapers."[92]

Reformers redoubled their efforts. On April 15, 1904, a week after the Chicago ruling, Kelley, Wald, Hunter, Adler, and Addams met in New York's Carnegie Hall with activists from across the country to form the National Child Labor Committee. They pledged to investigate workplace conditions in all regions and industries, publicize their findings, and promote "wise" legislation. Among its thirty charter members were former president Grover Cleveland and *New York Times* publisher Adolph Ochs, who had just moved his paper uptown from its cramped Park Row headquarters into a stunning Gothic tower on Longacre Square, renamed Times Square. Ochs owned three dailies that relied on newsboy labor, but this apparent conflict of interest troubled no one. Press support was imperative and progress imminent.[93]

Vanguard of Change

One notable aspect of Progressive Era reformers drawn to the newsboy problem is the extent to which they were socialists. From Kelley, Marot, Hunter, and Poole to muckrakers John Spargo, Scott Nearing, Upton Sinclair, and Jack London, ardent socialists provided much of the intellectual energy and documentary evidence that drove the crusade. They took aim at outdated notions of newsboys as repositories of Franklinian virtue, poor souls in need of salvation, or feral cubs engaged in a Darwinian struggle for existence. Socialists saw them in a new light—as members of an exploited class entitled to the full protection of the state.

Kelley blazed this ideological trail, putting socialist thought into progressive action. The daughter of an abolitionist congressman from Philadelphia whose favorite aunt was an antislavery Quaker, Kelley embraced socialism as a graduate student in Zurich in the 1880s. She translated Friedrich Engels's *The Condition of the Working-Class in England* and on returning to the United States joined the German-dominated Socialist Labor Party. Although expelled from the party, along with her husband, in a factional dispute, she never doubted the utility of a Marxian class analysis, the need to expose the structural causes of poverty, and the benefits of reforms that aided the downtrodden and ensured what she called "the right to childhood."[94]

Like Kelley, Helen Marot also had Quaker roots in Philadelphia and drew inspiration from abroad. She and her partner Caroline Pratt opened the Free

Library of Economic and Political Science in 1897 to advance the cause of Fabian socialism, then emerging at the London School of Economics. The Fabian commitment to gradualist, democratic social change underlay Marot's work with the New York Child Labor Committee and her subsequent leadership of the Women's Trade Union League.[95]

Robert Hunter's conversion came in the wake of his marriage to mining and railroad heiress Caroline Phelps Stokes and the publication of his bestseller *Poverty* in 1904. The couple joined the Socialist Party of America the next year and were henceforth saddled with the title "millionaire socialists." Hunter argued in his book that despite unprecedented prosperity, ten to twenty million people in the United States lived in dire want—their idleness and misery not, in most cases, the result of bad habits but a product of larger forces over which they had no control, such as industrial depressions, manipulative trusts, labor-saving machinery, workplace accidents, and excessive immigration. In the book's most provocative chapter, "The Child," Hunter pointed out that children made up the majority of the nation's poor. "The lowest," he said, "is the street Arab, the waif, or gamin,—the child who is stunted in body and crooked in mind." However blameless for their poverty, newsboys, he assured readers, were on the road to ruin.[96]

Hunter's comrade John Spargo, an English socialist, sounded the same note in his 1906 call to arms, *The Bitter Cry of the Children*. "Nor is it only in factories that these grosser forms of immorality flourish," he said. "They are even more prevalent among the children of the street trades. . . . The proportion of newsboys who suffer from venereal diseases is alarmingly great." Those who attended school, he said, were on average one-third below the ordinary standard of physical development due to their "irregular habits, scant feeding, sexual excesses, secret vices, sleeping in hallways, basements, stables, and quiet corners."[97]

Despite their reverence for facts, fiction was an equally powerful weapon in the socialist muckrakers' arsenal. In 1904 a 26-year-old City College of New York graduate, Upton Sinclair, set off for Chicago to expose the exploitation of immigrant families in the meatpacking industry. On assignment from the socialist weekly *Appeal to Reason*, and with four published novels under his belt, he announced to Ernest Poole, "I've come here to write the *Uncle Tom's Cabin* of the Labor Movement." Poole, two years his junior, was there with journalist William Hard to cover a packinghouse strike for *Outlook* magazine. He offered Sinclair some tips and contacts. Sinclair would in turn influence Poole's own shift leftward and toward fiction. The immediate result of this encounter was *The Jungle*—unquestionably one of the most influential social novels in America since Harriet Beecher Stowe's antebellum classic.[98]

Famous as an exposé of Chicago's meatpacking industry and a clarion call to socialism, *The Jungle* also dramatizes news peddling's role in working-class family economies. The protagonist, Jurgis Rudkus, possesses all the determination an immigrant needs to succeed in America, yet his family's fortunes decline after he is injured on the job. Two of his relatives, Nikalojus and Vilimar Lukoszas, ages 10 and 11, quit school to sell papers. Each is given 25¢ and told to walk several miles to the city center, where they are cheated of their money. On returning home, they are whipped for their incompetence, but the next day they are sent out again. This time they procure their stock and make sales but are roughed up for encroaching on someone's turf. After a week of such hard lessons, they manage to earn about 40¢ a day. They also learn how to steal rides on streetcars, swear in English, smoke discarded cigar butts, gamble away their earnings, steer customers to brothels, and stay out all night. Jurgis sends the boys back to school once he recovers, only to find out that his wife, who had taken a factory job, was abused by her foreman. Jurgis beats the villain and is jailed. The boys resume peddling, now accompanied by their older sister, who must repel sexual advances, too, and the interference of "severe old lady" reformers. Unable to find a job after his release, and distraught over his wife's death, Jurgis turns to drink whenever he can get his hands on his children's money. Hunger drives a third brother, Juozapos, to scavenge for stale bread and potato peelings at the local dump, while Jurgis's neglected baby drowns in a mud puddle outside their wretched home.[99]

Sinclair plagued the Rudkuses and Lukoszases with every misfortune that could befall poor immigrant families. His account reflects his familiarity with the recent newsboy studies, as well as his reading of local papers, which, during his weeks of research, told of 5-year-olds who made their way downtown every morning at three o'clock to fetch their weight in newspapers. Other reports identified newsboys as victims and perpetrators of robberies, kidnappings, and murder. These items ran beside happier accounts of newsboy banquets and excursions, which didn't interest Sinclair. The Chicago press denounced him as the "slaughterhouse novelist" whose book was "95 percent lies." Libraries banned it as "unfit to be read." Sinclair stood by every word and was vindicated by US Senate hearings on the meatpacking industry and passage of the Meat Inspection and Pure Food and Drug Acts of 1906. The novel had no equivalent impact on the street trades.[100]

Pennsylvania, with its unregulated coal mines, textile mills, and glass factories, earned a reputation as the nation's worst exploiter of children. Improving conditions in the Keystone State was the task of radical economist Scott Nearing, who after graduation from the Wharton School of

Business in 1905 served as secretary of the Pennsylvania Child Labor Committee. Though there were many industries requiring attention, Nearing did not overlook the street trades. He inspected conditions in downtown Philadelphia one Saturday night in November 1906 and found a gang who smoked, gambled, fought, and swore while waiting for their Sunday papers. One 10-year-old directed him to a Chinatown brothel. Writing in the reform journal *Survey*, Nearing coined the term "newsboyism" to describe the trade's deleterious effects. "The professional newsboy is the embryo criminal," he concluded."[101]

Accompanying Nearing was 31-year-old Lewis Wickes Hine, whose photos heightened the impact of his reportage. The boys' reaction to Hine's camera became the focus of the article. Most of them were glad to "have their faces pulled," wrote Nearing, but some feared that the pictures would find their way into a "rogue's gallery" where they could be identified and "pinched." "Me face? Not on yer life. You don't git me face." Hine was a teacher who, even more than Riis, saw the camera as a lever for social uplift. The NCLC hired him in 1908 to raise awareness of the inherent evils of child labor. The following year he produced an album of fifty photographs documenting violations of the New York newsboy law.[102] Hine worked with Nearing, Spargo, and Kelley, and his photos appeared in socialist publications, but his was an "aesthetic socialism" inspired by his mentors, educator Frank Manny, philosopher and former Vermont paperboy John Dewey, and nineteenth-century artist and reformer William Morris, founder of the Anglo-American Arts and Crafts movement.[103]

For ten years, from 1908 to 1917, Hine traveled the country taking pictures for the committee's reports, lectures, and exhibitions. Sometimes he worked alone. At other times his wife or his colleague Edward Clopper acted as official witness. Hine often went undercover, posing as a tramp or Bible salesman to gain entry into factories. He would hide his box camera under his coat and surreptitiously gather visual and oral evidence for his reports. During these years Hine took more than 5,000 photographs, or "human documents," as he called them, including some 550 of newsboys in forty cities. The photos include action shots, worksite scenes, and portraits. Some captions simply state where and when the picture was taken. Others describe the action in straightforward terms: "Newsboy asleep on subway stair" or "Little newsboy in front of saloon." Other Hine photos record the boys' environment: the street corners, storefronts, and neighborhoods where they worked. Some of these images call attention to the children's smallness by showing them standing beside lampposts or holding giant newspapers (Figure 10.12). Hine often engaged his

Figure 10.12. Lewis Hine, *Young Newsie Working, Pathetic Story,* 1908. Gelatin silver print, 16.9 × 12.3 cm. Gift of the Photo League Lewis Hine Memorial Committee. George Eastman Museum, 1977.0178.0015.

subjects in conversation and put what he learned into captions that give the photographs a cinematic quality: "Late at night these boys 8 & 10 years old had been pitching pennies all evening. After 9 p.m. I saw the little one going into a saloon with a bunch of papers and a pitiful tale. Been selling 2 years. Bridgeport, Conn." Here Hine's narration strives for objectivity, but he also employed sarcasm; under a picture of a newsgirl and an aloof cop, he writes, "Against the law but 'who cares'" (Figure 10.13).[104] Hine identified most of his subjects by name. They posed for him alone and in groups. The resulting head-and-shoulders shots taken at eye level call attention to the expression on their faces. Many have dark eyes, olive skin, and surnames that suggest southern

Figure 10.13. Lewis Hine, *Newsgirl, Park Row. Against the Law, but "Who Cares."*
New York, July 1910. Library of Congress, LOT 7480, v. 2, no. 1641 [P&P].

or eastern European origin. Others have lighter complexions and Anglo-Saxon
names. Few offer smiles; they look impassive, quizzical, cocky, or tired. Some
boys appear appallingly young and vulnerable.

Many Hine photos document the specific moral or physical hazards his
colleagues noted in their tracts and testimonies. We see the boys shooting dice,
entering saloons, "flipping" streetcars, and sparring in alleys. These photos serve
as character studies, more objective than not, saying plainly: *These are the children who peddle papers in your city.* Seeing, Hine believed, was necessary for true
understanding. Sometimes his shadow intruded on the scene (Figure 10.14),
calling attention to the fact that he was there with his camera, a living witness
who was more concerned with the plight of the children than with the aesthetic
judgment of posterity.[105]

Yet despite his reform agenda, Hine provided an appealing visual ethnog-
raphy of newsboy life. He illuminated their social interactions and work routines.
He showed them horsing around and going about their business as if it were the
most natural thing in the world, unconscious of being a problem. Hine believed
the work was harmful, and said so in his captions and essays. But his photos
are more ambivalent; they allow us to see newsboys and newsgirls as exploited
victims *and* autonomous individuals. This duality is what makes the images so
captivating long after they served their immediate legislative, not to say socialist,
purpose.

Figure 10.14. Indianapolis newsboy John Howell pauses warily for a stranger's camera. Lewis W. Hine, *Self-Portrait with Newsboy*, 1908, Gelatin silver print, 5 × 4 ⅝ in. (13.8 × 11.8 cm). The J. Paul Getty Museum, Los Angeles.

In the revolving door of history, Hine's arrival on the reform scene coincided with Roosevelt's temporary departure, as he had vowed in 1904 not to seek reelection. Progressivism continued apace under the administration of William Howard Taft, and newsboys remained prime objects of reform. Indeed, their labor and leisure habits came under such scrutiny in the 1910s that it provoked a backlash by parents, publishers, and the children themselves.

11

Sidewalks of Struggle

Long at issue, the moral legitimacy of juvenile street trading became a major concern in the Progressive Era. Parents, publishers, and reformers all asserted their right to define news peddling as a social good or evil and control children's labor power. In a sense, each party was simply trying to make do without wages—without earning a sufficient amount of them, in the case of newsboys' parents; without paying them at all to youngsters, in the case of publishers; and without accepting any economic rationale for children's exploitation, in the case of reformers. Yet the alliances shifted constantly: parents sometimes sided with publishers, to protect their children's right to work, and sometimes backed reformers' efforts, to curb their children's independence. Such switches characterized the campaigns to abolish newsboys' night work and stop their fighting, gambling, smoking, spitting, drinking, swearing, and sexual precocity. Investigators amassed damning evidence of these rife practices, but their findings also reveal the industrial pressures, parental logic, and working-class customs that underlay them. These mitigating factors weakened the case for abolition and stimulated the founding of newsboy unions, clubs, courts, and "republics" that aimed to lessen the moral and physical dangers of street work. However, the success of these efforts depended entirely on the boys' cooperation, making them agents rather than mere targets of progressive reform.

The Virtues of Vice

Conflicts of interests in the news trade flared most fiercely over the issue of night hawking. Pennsylvania child labor foe Scott Nearing called it indefensible in 1907, given that route men effectively distributed most of Philadelphia's morning papers. Yet newspapers encouraged children's night work with their late editions, all-night lunchrooms, and self-serving praise. Speaking of newsboys and their sisters, the *Philadelphia Inquirer* said in 1900, "Neither feel the pillows under their heads until the night is well spent, and many crawl into their beds after midnight has passed. What a storehouse of energy are their small bodies." Most publishers defended juvenile night work as necessary if they were to get out late-breaking sports or election news. Those who had qualms said they were help-less to stop the practice unless their competitors did. In New York, the *Evening Telegram, World, and Journal* printed editions every hour or so until 11:00 p.m., and the *Morning Telegram* followed soon after midnight (Figure 11.1). Chicago papers kept a similar schedule. The early morning "glory" edition of William Randolph Hearst's *Journal* required graveyard shifts, for which he paid experi-enced hawkers 50¢ a night until the competition withdrew. In 1915, forty of these "bootjackers," most in their teens, organized the Midnight Newsboys' Association, demanding $3 a week and the right to return unsold papers.[1]

Figure 11.1. Lewis Hine, *3 A.M. Sunday, February 23rd, 1908. Newsboys selling on Brooklyn Bridge. Harry Ahrenpreiss, 30 Willet Street. (Said was 13 years old). Abe Gramus. 37 Division Street. Witness Fred McMurray.* Library of Congress, Washington, DC.

Sunday editions stole the most sleep from newsboys. The papers appeared around midnight and even earlier in outlying areas, albeit with older news. Children in Louisville, Kentucky, sold Chicago Sunday papers to the after-theater crowd on Saturday night. In Cleveland, dozens of "bedless" boys slept on the same stairway to ensure an early start on Sunday. Such routines reflected not just the demands of the news cycle but also the needs of families. The Consumers' League of Syracuse identified a boy who "scarcely spent a night at home" between the ages of 7 and 14. With his mother's permission, he slept in the city's news alley, waiting for the early edition. Only a disabling accident ended his streak.[2]

As the story suggests, reformers and their allies used the night-work issue much as they did the topic of "girl newsboys"—as a wedge to pry open the conscience of an apathetic public and win protective legislation. Every documentary form and literary technique was put to the wheel. In their 1908 article "The Boy Wot Works at Night," William Hard and photographer Emmett V. O'Neil combined personification, slang dialogue, and chiaroscuro images to interrogate "Mother Night" and her brood of "mischievous children." In "State Street at Night," Chicago poet Harriet Monroe appealed directly to her subjects:

> You tiny newsboy, calling extras there,
> Pitiful burden-bearer, born for blight,
> What of the night?[3]

But night peddling wasn't just a long slog toward dawn. In New York and other cities, weekend crowds filled the streets, packed the streetcars, and patronized the restaurants and food stalls well into the night. The smell of frankfurters, sauerkraut and kerosene wafted through the air as ragtime tunes poured out of clubs and dancehalls. The streets quieted around 2:00 a.m., but then bakers, milkmen, and postmen appeared. Long before sunup, news wagons and vans tore down the streets at breakneck speed, the drivers lashing their horses or yanking their throttles, and their helpers rolling bundles onto sidewalks for waiting carriers.[4] Artist Everett Shinn, a member of the Ashcan School, caught this predawn scene in *Park Row, Morning Papers*, an impressionistic mixed media work in grays and yellows. Shinn's Park Row thrums with wagons and workers toting and stacking newspapers under lamplight. In *Newspaper Stand*, another Shinn painting circa 1900, an old woman occupies a well-lit stand as two silhouetted figures lean familiarly against her counter. Their sociability glows like a beacon in a sea of darkness. An aficionado of the night, Shinn saw the nocturnal news trade not as a social problem in need of fixing, but as a marvelous spectacle worthy of notice. From this perspective, New York's "night hawks" were part of a tight-knit occupational community, not some sordid juvenile demimonde.[5]

Which is not to say that the hazards of night work were mere figments of the progressive imagination. The failure of a son or brother to come home at night raised legitimate fears. Things happened. Boys had to fend off the depredations of muggers, pedophiles, and worse. Newsboys were occasionally kidnapped and murdered. In December, 1902, the body of 10-year-old Michael Kruck was discovered lying on his papers along a remote bridle path in New York's Central Park. An autopsy determined that he was strangled to death. He had not been molested or robbed of the 21¢ and three streetcar transfers found in his pockets. Kruck lived with his parents and brother in a dumbbell apartment on Columbus Avenue. He sold papers at the park's entrance on 86th Street. His father was a tailor who had emigrated with his family from France six years earlier. The press followed the story for days, characterizing it as a "Newsboy Murder Mystery." Clues pointed to a Greek flower peddler who had clashed with newsboys and to members of the 93rd Street gang who had tried to drive Kruck from his corner. Police cleared them all, and the case remained unsolved until 1912 when a serial killer in Buffalo confessed to the murder.[6] Six months after Kruck's death the mutilated body of 7-year-old Richard Tibbitts was found a mile and a half from his Rockford, Illinois, home. Beside him lay his unsold papers, a bag of candy and some pennies. No one was ever convicted of that crime.[7]

While such killings were rare, physical assaults were not. The kick, the shove, and the poke in the back with a nightstick were common occurrences for newsboys, the blows often dispensed as needed discipline rather than gratuitous bullying. And fighting among themselves was unavoidable. Ernie Fliegel, who immigrated from Romania to Milwaukee in 1910 at the age of 6, fought every day on the way to school and at recess to protect himself or his brother. "Joe was a fat little kid and they'd say, "C'mere, you greenhorn! And bam! they'd whack him . . . And they'd whack me too . . . And then I started selling papers, and when we bought the papers there was a fight, and on the corner—we'd call 'em the Polacks—they'd come through. So I thought this was a way of life . . . that in America, you're supposed to fight."[8]

Many observers considered toughness to be the newsboy's most laudable trait. "The little lad has in his nature the twin germs of combativeness and commercialism" that flourishes in the "strenuous life of the street," asserted philanthropist Randolph Guggenheimer. "Your newsboy does not disdain to fight, nor flee from it. He gives or takes a drubbing with about equal satisfaction. It is part of the day's work."[9] These pugnacious fellows filled the canvases of George Bellows, another member of the Ashcan School who moved to New York in 1904 and began painting the "kids" he saw playing in vacant lots, diving from old piers, and brawling in the streets. Two newsboys, probably brothers, posed for portraits in 1908. In *The Newsboy*, Jimmy Flannigan grins impishly as he sits wearing a dark coat and white shirt. His hands are folded prayer-like in his lap, but his cocked eyebrow suggests he is no angel. In *Paddy Flannigan* (Plate 23), the buck-toothed adolescent thrusts his bare chest forward, hand on hip, thumb in belt loop, his cauliflower ear ever sensitive to insult. His impudent, heavy-lidded expression almost dares the viewer to say something smart and see what happens. These paintings affirmed the widely held beliefs expressed by Guggenheimer, and found prime wall space in the mansions of Bellows's patrons, many of whom saw themselves as self-made men who took on all comers in their struggle to succeed.[10]

Robert Henri, the leader of this artistic circle, urged his friends and students, including Bellows, to paint city life as they found it, ashcans and all, unconcerned about genteel tastes or academic norms. A sensitive portraitist, he spoke fondly of his working-class subjects, calling them "my people." In 1908 he produced an oil painting of his own newsboy, Willie Gee, "a full-blooded black, son of a Virginia slave woman" (Plate 24). Holding an apple instead of newspapers, and spared a clichéd pose, Willie transcends his type. His eyes are averted from the viewer's gaze in contemplation, not deference. Identified by name, he demands consideration as a real person. *Harper's Weekly* reproduced the image in 1914 as "a type that reflects our problems"—a reference not just to Jim Crow segregation but to the propensity of blacks to defy prejudice and compete with whites. Later that year Henri painted several studies of Sylvester, an African American youth who sold papers at the La Jolla train depot in California. Rather than criticizing these sympathetic portrayals of newsboys and newsboy labor, Jane Addams, the nation's preeminent child labor reformer, complimented the Ashcan School when she asked, "Is it only the artists who really see these young creatures as they are—the artists who are themselves endowed with immortal youth?"[11]

Street gambling also divided the ranks of child savers. Journalists had long winked at the activity, calling newsies "skinners," "speculators," and "gamesters by nature." They noted that the boys risked their capital daily in choosing how many papers to buy, what to cry, and whether it was safe to dart through traffic or jump on a streetcar to make a sale. "It must be conceded," said the *New York Tribune*, "that the little chaps take chances. In that they are not so far from the broadcloth coated gentleman who takes his chance on the floor of the Stock Exchange."[12]

In truth, the boys more closely resembled the shabby-coated men of their own class. Gambling was pervasive among the poor, and its appeal was not lost on their children, especially the newsboys whose idle moments and disposable incomes gave them more opportunity to pitch pennies, shoot dice, and play cards than other boys. "Money talks with the newsboy," continued the *Tribune*, "and you never see any of them fooling away valuable time on marbles or other ordinary schoolboy games. They are seeking an increase of visible capital at all times."[13]

Their most popular game was craps. Newsies in all regions were said to be addicted to it. Having originated in the South, it was particularly popular among African Americans. "Most all of the kids sit up shooting craps till two or three in the morning," said one Detroit newsie. "The officers never bother 'em. I bet you can't find one newsboy in 20 that ain't got a pair of real dice or sugar lumps in his pockets." Boston newsboys indulged mostly on weekends, according to truant officer Philip Davis, but not without immunity. "Sunday is truthfully 'crap day,' " he said, which meant that Monday was " 'crap day' in court." A 1908 study by the New York Association of Neighborhood Workers found 8,455 craps players, ranging in age from 6 to 30, engaged in 437 games on a single Sunday in Manhattan, Brooklyn, and the Bronx (Figure 11.2). On the Lower East Side alone, investigators counted 1,448 players, two-thirds of whom were under 15.[14]

Such findings led to crackdowns. Police seemed to time their raids to pinch the biggest pots. "You can jes bet they do," said one New York newsie; "they can scoop in a pot slickern anything you ever see." Big pots ranged from $4 to $12; more typical were the 10¢ to 40¢ variety. When the heat was on, newsboys abandoned dice altogether and "matched" coins instead. Even the blind could detect

Figure 11.2. Lewis Hine, *A Crap Game in the Paper Alley*, Rochester, NY, Feb., 1910. Library of Congress, Washington, DC.

heads or tails, as demonstrated nightly by two boys, one black and one white, who sold "bulldog" editions at 13th and Market Streets in Philadelphia.[15]

Reformers objected to street betting on several grounds. New York Society for the Suppression of Vice founder Anthony Comstock, influential until his death in 1915, saw it as the promise of getting something for nothing—the "gnawing worm at the root of honest industry." Milwaukee investigator Alexander Fleisher said gambling taught newsboys to lie to their parents when they came home broke, cheat their friends if they could get away with it, and fear the law. It also provoked violence, notably in 1896 when 21-year-old Tom Johnson fatally shot 18-year-old William "Chronicle Red" Amend after a craps game in the distribution depot of the *St. Louis Star.* Johnson went to the gallows, but the incident inspired a group of society women to form the Newsboys' Home Association and establish a lodging house and social center for the boys.[16]

Working-class parents did not worry much about their children's gambling. Many in fact resented prosecuting an activity that met no opposition when practiced by those who could afford to do it in private. Writer Paul Laurence Dunbar, the son of former slaves, addressed this double standard in his migrant story "An Old-Time Christmas," in which young Jimmy Lewis is arrested on Christmas Eve in New York for "t'rowin' de bones" with his chums. "The crime of gambling among the news-boys was a growing evil," rationalizes the arresting officer, and "the dignity of the law must be upheld." The judge wanted to release the boy with a reprimand but decided it was "high time to make an example of one of the offenders." Jimmy's mother pays the fine with money she had saved to make him an old-time southern Christmas dinner.[17]

Compounding this hypocrisy is the fact that newspapers catered to all kinds of speculators—not just high-rolling investors who scanned the stock tables, but also low rollers who entered newspaper lotteries or relied on sports-page betting odds. Newsstands also carried racing forms and tip sheets. Some of their publishers hired youths to circulate them directly, which led to a strike by eighty Chicago newsboys in 1905. "We've got to have more money," explained "Tiny" Moore, the leader. Newsboys' own contests attracted wagers. Before racetracks were wired, the *New Orleans States* and *Item* recruited their fastest runners to get the results to their office first. Rival squads raced along Canal and Camp Streets, handing off their dispatches like batons. The relays attracted large crowds and lively betting.[18]

Like gambling, smoking had long been endemic among newsboys, but tobacco use rose at the turn of the century due to falling prices and aggressive advertising. The formation of a tobacco trust that gobbled up competitors and invested in labor-saving Bonsack rolling machines made cigarettes affordable to even the poorest guttersnipe. Children in Chicago could buy one or two a penny at stands that sprang up outside their schools. During the 1896 price war, when independents challenged the trust, a pack of twenty cigarettes sold for a nickel. Mass marketing heightened demand. Tobacco companies spent millions on print and wall ads, gave free smokes to disembarking immigrants, and placed baseball cards in the packages to entice youngsters.[19]

Newspapers aided this effort. Most promoted smoking as a harmless, even healthy habit: "a preventer of malaria, a safeguard against colds in the head, and sure cure for nervousness." The *Chicago Tribune* gave boys plugs of sweet Cavendish tobacco in the early morning hours as an incentive to buy more copies. A cartoon in the *Omaha World-Herald* mocked busybodies who dared to intervene: "Old Lady—You don't chew tobacco, do you, little boy? Newsboy—No, 'm, but I kin give yer a cigarette."[20]

The cartoon was a jab at Woman's Christian Temperance Union activist Lucy Page Gaston, who organized the Chicago Anti-Cigarette League in 1899. The group focused first on local newsboys; Gaston estimated that five out of six were addicted to "the noxious little rolls"—themselves the product of child labor in fields and factories. She addressed newsboy clubs and sponsored anti-smoking conventions, track meets, and essay contests. In the summer of 1900, the league sent Chicago newsboy Ralph Reynolds on a regional speaking tour to establish newsboys' branches to help each other quit smoking. The branches secured local ordinances against underage smoking and deployed newsboy detectives to build cases against shopkeepers who persisted in selling tobacco to minors.[21]

Temperance crusader Carrie Nation also joined the fight against underage smoking. A national celebrity after being arrested thirty-two times for breaking up saloons, she attracted a retinue of newsboys whenever she arrived in a city. "Carrie Nation! See Carrie Nation. Real live Carrie Nation. Where's your hatchet, Carrie?" shouted Cleveland newsies in August 1901. A large woman, she was not afraid to snatch cigarettes from the mouths of newsboys and lecture them if they objected. She, too, addressed newsboy assemblies about the dangers of smoking.[22]

Lewis Hine pitched in by photographing newsboys puffing on cigarettes as clouds of smoke swirled around their prematurely wizened faces (Figure 11.3). Boys struck these poses whether cameras were present or not. "One of the main things a boy has to do to keep his corner," explained a Chicago teen, "is be tough, have a cigarette in his mouth, or be chewing tobacco, to show the other boys that he is a tough guy and [they] can't beat him up or take his money." Smoking was an assertion of manhood at a time when even adult factory workers couldn't light up on the job.[23]

A gateway vice, smoking led to spitting, said reformers, which in turn spread consumption. Clubwomen joined public health advocates in urging passage of anti-spitting ordinances and targeted newsies as the worst offenders. The first person prosecuted under a resurrected anti-spitting law in Portland, Oregon,

Figure 11.3. Lewis Hine, *11:00 A.M. Monday, May 9th, 1910. Newsies at Skeeter's Branch, Jefferson near Franklin. They were all smoking. Location: St. Louis, Missouri.* Library of Congress, Washington, DC.

in 1912 was 18-year-old newsboy Joe Parnas. One newspaper insisted that newsboys were in fact no more egregious expectorators than judges, lawyers, and policemen.[24]

Drinking posed another occupational hazard. Reformers felt that even if newsboys' lips never touched a glass, they could be corrupted simply by fraternizing with saloon-goers. Jack London agreed: "In saloons I saw reporters, editors, lawyers, judges, whose names and faces I knew. They put the seal of social approval on the saloon." Ordinances in Cleveland, Kalamazoo, and other cities barred minors from entering any place that served liquor. Carriers routinely flouted these laws; they would leave a paper for the house and circulate among the customers for extra sales. A kidder might offer them a swig of beer or a shot of whiskey, but more often they were treated to ginger ale. "The only reason I did not drink was because I didn't like the stuff," said London. One proprietor would pour him a glass of wine when he came in to collect. "I was ashamed to refuse, so I drank it. But after that I watched the chance when she wasn't around so as to collect from her barkeeper." A carrier might also be allowed to snatch a sandwich or dig into a pile of clams from the free lunch counter. They were welcome to use the restroom or even sleep in the backroom.[25]

Chicago had hundreds of hospitable saloons. Most famous was the Workingman's Exchange on Haymarket Square, owned by alderman Michael "Hinky Dink" Kenna. An old newsboy who peaked at five feet one, Kenna loomed large in city politics. He fed thousands of indigent men and boys and urged them to peddle papers and vote Democratic. "There was about twenty-five of us used to eat out of the Hinky Dink," recalled Bob Hall, a 13-year-old runaway from Indiana who peddled the *Tribune* from 1908 to 1909. "And them wuz some pretty tough winters." Hall and his gang partook of the free lunches at the saloon or finished the meals of customers who had passed out; the bartenders would push the plate to the side or set it close to the door. "Oh yes. All the bartenders wuz helpin' the newspaper kids," said Hall. "I'm not lying. That's the way they lived." Ordinances barring newsboys from saloons thus represented a loss of nourishment, revenue, and comfort.[26]

Swearing likewise led to antisocial activity, said reformers. Newsboys had long shown a keen capacity to cuss, wielding threats and insults like "some sabre-stroke of Saxon speech." Yet blasphemy and obscenity were more often markers of belonging than signs of degeneracy. "Irreverent language" also functioned as a defense against competitors and tormenters. Newsgirls were notoriously foul-mouthed, which helped them navigate the masculine world of the street where sexual taunts and propositions abounded.[27]

More troubling to reformers than all other vices was the propensity of news peddlers to become prematurely wise about sex. Hawkers had displayed this tendency since the 1840s, when they helped circulate the flash press, but the new social hygiene movement refocused attention on the subject by promoting sex education and the suppression of commercialized vice. Modern cities were rife with penny arcades, peep shows, dance halls, burlesque houses, nickelodeons, and brothels, none of which discriminated against children. The "spicy" and "rich" fare of peep shows featured flickering images of girls undressing for bed or dancing the hootchie-kootchie. These hand-cranked contraptions may have been designated "MEN ONLY," but some arcades provided step stools for boys who were too small to reach the peephole.[28]

Movie and burlesque houses supposedly exerted even more sordid influences. "Their main function," said Philip Davis, "is to make 'vice attractive' at the matinee and 'virtue abominable' in the evening." Reformers believed that darkened theaters provided youths with opportunities to do more than just watch sin and seduction on screen, as the darkness encouraged boys to commit "indecent assaults upon girls, often with their acquiescence," and allowed "depraved adults" to "beguile children with candy and pennies." One 9-year-old newsgirl in Baltimore told an interviewer in 1912, "Yes, lot o' times mens want me to go to the movin' picture shows with 'em, but I never go 'cause I gotta hustle."[29]

While always a factor in the news trade, sexual bartering drew the spotlight of reform in the Progressive Era. Myron Adams's 1903 Chicago study described newsboys as easy victims. "Although the city is full of unscrupulous men," he wrote, "it is toward the newsboy that such a man may most easily hold the advantage of an employer of boys under fourteen." Adams cited the case of a prosperous Chicago dealer who required the eight boys in his employ to pick up their pay in his room, where he "committed violence" on each of them: "Instances of this kind are of frequent occurrence although they are seldom made public." One consequence was the spread of disease. The superintendent of an Illinois reformatory said that a third of the onetime newsboys in his care had contracted venereal infections, and that 10 percent of those at a similar institution were infected "due to unnatural relationships with men." "The newsboy," he said, "is in a class by himself in this respect."[30]

Growing up in Los Angeles, Frank Capra endured similar assaults selling morning, evening, and Sunday papers through his grammar school years. Born in Sicily in 1897, he was one of seven children in a family that couldn't read or write any language. They came to America in 1903 with no objections to child labor. Capra gave every penny he earned to his mother. "I hated being poor," he said. "Hated being a peasant. Hated being a scrounging newskid trapped in the sleazy Sicilian ghetto of Los Angeles." Capra rode the trolley downtown at 3:00 a.m.: "Oh boy, it was no time for kids to be out. If you met anybody he'd be a man and he'd be drunk and he'd make a grab for you and try to screw you. I'd fight like hell."[31]

In 1911 the newly created Chicago Vice Commission targeted newsboys in an effort to clean up the streets. Made up of the city's business, religious, and professional elite, the commission linked street trading to the spread of pornography, prostitution, underage drinking, cocaine use, violent crime, and venereal disease. Newsboys, bootblacks, and messengers "have an intimate knowledge of the ways of the underworld," said the commission. "Their moral sense is so blunted as to be absolutely blind to the degradation of women and the vile influence of vicious men." It described the custom whereby prostitutes gave boys free sex on Christmas day for good luck, or because they thought they could cure venereal disease by transferring it to a virgin. In just over two years Cook County Hospital treated six hundred children under 12 for venereal diseases; 15 percent had syphilis and 85 percent had gonorrhea. The commission's report included several studio portraits of boys found selling papers in vice districts after midnight, their faces kindly but ghoulishly whited out to protect their anonymity (Figure 11.4).[32]

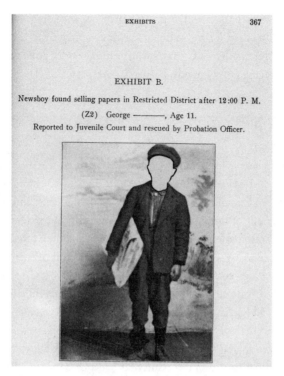

EXHIBITS 367

EXHIBIT B.

Newsboy found selling papers in Restricted District after 12:00 P. M.

(Z2)　George ————, Age 11.

Reported to Juvenile Court and rescued by Probation Officer.

Figure 11.4. "EXHIBIT B. Newsboy found selling papers in Restricted District after 12:00 P. M. (Z2) George _____, Age 11. Reported to Juvenile Court and rescued by Probation Officer." *The Social Evil in Chicago: A Study of Existing Conditions with Recommendations by the Vice Commission of Chicago* (Chicago: Gunthorp-Warren, 1911), 367.

Given these dangers, many parents forbade their children to peddle papers no matter how great their need for income or how liberal the laws. Such decisions divided families. The mother and aunts of Christopher Zarce in New York had a "little family squall over the question" of news selling after officers brought the boy home saying that a man had solicited him for sex. In another case, the wife of a Hungarian machinist was terrified that her husband would find out that their son had forged his signature and obtained a street trading license. "I am so nervous that I want to scream out," she told investigators. "I know my husband will turn crazy when he knows it. He has such great anger and is such a strict man." Licensing schemes made little difference to parents who were unwilling to hand over their authority to the state. "I am only an old fool Italiano mans," said a laborer in New York, "but I know more what is good for the kids than the smart mens who maka the laws in the country. No badge could make it good for my Tony to sell the pape'—it was that bad business . . . that maka all the Italiano kids bums."[33]

Perhaps these parents were lying, strategically concealing their "peasant" acceptance of child labor. It's more likely that they spoke from the heart, and that their words reflect the diversity of opinion among immigrants, a diversity ever in flux due to changing family needs, industry practices, and class awareness.

Injuries to One and All

Parents and reformers were not the only ones to protest the problems associated with street work. Between 1900 and 1914, thousands of newsboys across the United States and Canada engaged in strikes to defend their interests. With and without the benefit of unions, disgruntled hawkers and carriers of all ages rose up against the newspapers and news agencies that aided, feted, and squeezed them. These conflicts varied in scale, circumstance, and outcome, but together demonstrate that newsboys of the era possessed their own vision of progress.

One early confrontation occurred in Baltimore on July 30, 1900, after the arrest of 17-year-old Richard Vaughan for playing craps in the *Sun*'s news alley. He was fined $1 and then jailed when he couldn't pay. Fellow newsboys demanded that the business manager pay the fine. When he refused, they threatened to strike. Boys tore up copies of the issue that had just come off the press. A small riot ensued, and the police were called.[34]

A week later, fifty to sixty newsboys in Brooklyn struck two evening papers that had raised wholesale prices from 50¢ to 60¢ a hundred. Grown men showed up with bundles at the ferry entrance, but they were knocked down and their papers ripped to shreds. One of the six strikers arrested for assault and disorderly conduct was 8-year-old Harry Sackman.[35]

That same evening, seven newsboys met on the platform of Track 17 at Union Station in St. Louis ("Muggs' Landing," they called it) and agreed to strike. They had been making $1.75 a week selling for the Union News Company but felt that they deserved $2.50, or a 20 percent commission on sales. When Jimmy Connelly presented the demand earlier that day, the manager told him to get lost. After voting, the boys marched back to the office, threw their uniform hats and coats onto the floor, and announced: "We've struck." The next night a hundred newsboys gathered in front of the station to "wreake vengeance" on the replacements. The protesters brandished clubs and canes, and their pockets bulged with chunks of brick. Police dispersed them easily, however, and the strikers never got their jobs back.[36]

In September newsboys in Milwaukee formed a union to combat "hustlers" sent in to boom the Chicago papers. Members approached an organizer from the American Federation of Labor, but he said they were too young to help. The boys continued the struggle on their own. The AFL apparently regretted this snub and voted to lower the tax on local unions whose members were less than 18-years-old, mainly newsboys, messengers, and cash girls.[37]

To some degree, these boys were just doing what they saw their elders—and sisters—doing. In the winter of 1901, during a three-month strike by young women in the silk mills of Scranton, Pennsylvania, local newsboys and bootblacks organized a union with the help of the United Mine Workers (UMW) and waged a successful boycott over their grievances against the *New York Journal*. UMW firebrand Mother Jones addressed the fledgling unionists at a mass meeting April 28 at St. Thomas College (later University of Scranton). Some 350 boys filled the hall, drawn in part by the free lunch. In her customary black bonnet and floor-length gown, the 64-year-old Jones assured them of the benefits that would accrue from organizing, such as reading rooms and a band. When the mill girls won their strike, 125 members of the newsboys' union marched with them, two abreast, through the streets of Scranton, with Mother Jones leading the way.[38]

Similarly, on May Day 1901, a group of teenagers in Boston who could no longer abide publishers' preferential discounts and refusal to accept returns formed Boston Newsboys' Protective Union (NPU) No. 9077. They affiliated with the American Federation of Labor and mounted a successful boycott against the *Boston Globe* that secured refunds for 10 percent of all unsold papers. The NPU then called for increasing the legal minimum age of newsboys to 14 to reduce competition from smaller boys and to eliminate the need for state regulation.[39]

Across the border in Toronto, three hundred newsboys formed a union in March 1903 to protect themselves against price hikes and rate cuts. They resolved to wear a union button and informed all local papers that boys who could not produce the button must not be served.[40] Five months later, boys in New Britain, Connecticut, struck over the higher price of New York papers. Johnny Griffin was arrested for breach of peace, and Joe Cotter and Jimmy Callahan for assault. Each was fined $10, but judgment was suspended for a week to see how they behaved. The walkout ended when strikers agreed to pass on the higher prices to their customers.[41]

The year 1904 saw more newsboy militancy in small town and cities. Boys in Hoosick Falls, New York, struck a dealer in March who required them to carry out-of-town papers from the railroad depot to his newsroom without extra pay. The boys demanded a half cent more for every five papers sold. They slugged those who wouldn't go along with the strike and tore papers from the hands of buyers. "By night a large and violent mob of over twenty small boys had gathered in front of the news room," reported the *Bennington Daily Banner*. "Speeches, mostly short and pointed, were made and for a time it was undecided whether to destroy the monopoly, the monopolist, or the building." Newsies in Sioux City, Iowa, next formed a union in July to fight the Chicago Newspaper Trust. And twenty-five men and boys in Fremont, Nebraska, population 8,000, unionized in December to limit competition from "rich kids."[42]

Most newsboy labor disputes were responses to the industrialized mass production and distribution of newspapers in which proprietors strove to lower costs and raise profits. With trade unionism on the rise and strike rhetoric in the air, newsboys became increasingly aware that their labor was essential to the industry. As the peripatetic "newsboy king" Chimmie McFadden said, "The newsboys are the ones who make the paper, for without street sales a paper would not live." McFadden claimed to have organized seventeen of the largest newsboys' unions in the country and to have settled more than a few of their strikes.[43]

This surge in newsboy militancy occurred although the boys and their unions lacked the negotiating leverage of skilled workers and the unifying employee status of common laborers. Still, they learned from both groups how to call meetings, articulate demands, and exert their will on the shop floor—in their case, the street. Newsboys' status as minors and merchants made their unions more ephemeral than adult unions because members usually aged out of the trade or stayed in and became employers. Their organizations were also vulnerable to take over by grown-ups—philanthropists, circulation managers, adult vendors, rival unions, and gangsters. Many newsboys also had to answer to their parents, some of whom forbid their participation in strikes. These youths nevertheless helped redefine and redress the newsboy problem.

The most successful newsboy union in the country was the NPU in Boston, due to its forthright entry into local politics, firm ties to the labor movement, and unmatched educational programs. The union campaigned to lift the 8:00 p.m. vending curfew for boys over 14 and protested police harassment of its members. In 1902 its Lithuanian-born, 16-year-old president, Nathan Sodekson, arranged with former congressman John Fitzgerald, who had just acquired the *Republic*, a small struggling weekly, to post boys outside every Catholic church on Sunday to peddle the paper to parishioners between masses. The *Republic* thrived and helped Fitzgerald become mayor in 1905. The newsboys lobbied him afterward to build parks, ball fields, and bathhouses.[44*]

Boston's Central Labor Union welcomed the newsboys' delegates from the beginning, and the AFL, convening in Boston in 1903, passed a resolution

---

* Mayor Fitzgerald also sponsored a newsboy essay contest in 1911 that offered the winner, Alexander Brin, a job as office boy at the *Boston Herald*. It paid less than he was earning selling papers, but he took it and rose to staff reporter within three years. He covered the 1915 trial and lynching of Leo Frank in Atlanta. He published the *Jewish Advocate* in Boston at age 22 and remained there for more than sixty years. See "Old Times Newsies, Now Making Good, to Recall Early Struggles," *Boston Post*, May 21, 1921, 75.

stating that attendees should buy papers only from boys wearing the NPU button. The newsboys in turn assessed themselves 10¢ a week to aid striking messenger boys. In 1904 the union felt emboldened to ask all Boston papers to stop publishing evening editions on holidays so that they might enjoy the day like other people.[45] By 1906 the Newsboys Protective Union claimed 600 dues-paying (5¢ a month) members—none under age 13. Its rolls included not just newsboys, but also supply men and truck drivers. The union beat back a takeover bid by the Teamsters that year and got publishers to consider members for apprenticeships in their mechanical departments. "You know that newsboys used to be looked upon as objects of pity," said Sodekson. "Well, nobody thinks of pitying them now. They are comparatively well off and as much respected as any body of business men in the city. The Union has done what the police were never able to accomplish."[46]

Headquartered in the newsboys' old gambling den overlooking Pi Alley, the union banned gambling among its members, sponsored an annual ball, and hosted a series of speakers. Democratic Party standard-bearer William Jennings Bryan denounced trusts as blights on the industrial landscape, AFL president Samuel Gompers espoused the principles of trade unionism, and Harvard president Charles William Elliott proclaimed the advantages of poor men's sons, due to their superior work habits. Sodekson later approached Elliott about starting a scholarship for union members who passed the college's entrance exam. Established in 1906 with an endowment of $2,700, the fund provided the first year's tuition for Myron Heller, Harvard class of 1910. More than thirty newsboy scholars followed in his footsteps over the next forty years.[47]

However much it strove for respectability, the NPU remained a militant labor union. It struck Hearst's *Boston American* in January 1908 after the paper raised its wholesale price from 1¢ to 2¢ a copy. Hearst hired nonunion labor, which led to clashes when two hundred union newsboys gathered at North Station and attacked the arriving newspaper wagons and those who tried to take possession of their stock. The strikers tore up thousands of copies and clashed with police, stripping them of their hats and badges. Three strikers were arrested for rioting, but hundreds of their union brothers followed them to the police station, demanding their release. In a show of solidarity, the Hebrew bakers' union refused Hearst's $100-a-week donation to its bread distribution charity because of his attempt to break the newsboys' union.[48]

The Boston Newsboys' Protective Union served as a model for newsboys unions throughout the country, including those founded in Chicago and Salt Lake City in 1902;[49] Toronto in 1903;[50] New York City, Worcester, Massachusetts, and Sioux City, Iowa, in 1904;[51] Berlin, New Hampshire, in 1905;[52] and Peoria and Galesburg, Illinois, in 1906.[53] The Peoria local claimed fifty of the city's eighty newsboys as charter members. It, too, affiliated with the AFL and demanded that the *Peoria Star* grant return privileges, like the other dailies in town. Despite its long-standing bias against low-skilled immigrant workers, the AFL passed a resolution at its next convention asking state and local labor bodies "to make a special endeavor during the coming year to organize the newsboys throughout the country."[54]

Southern newsboys also stood up for their rights as workers and citizens. Politics provoked a "hot fight" among newsies in Memphis, Tennessee, in October 1908. With elections approaching, many boys agreed (for a dollar) to give customers a free copy of the *Evening Press* whenever they bought a *News-Scimitar*. The *Press* backed the incumbent Democratic machine, while the *News-Scimitar* supported the progressive Republican ticket, which advocated a commission form of government. The *News-Scimitar's* circulation manager raised a fuss when he got wind of the arrangement, but the boys would not be dictated to. They struck instead, tearing up every copy of the paper that appeared on the street and sending their sellers scurrying home. Newsboys also struck in Mobile, Alabama, in August 1911, but progressives there had pushed through a three-person commission government that successfully arbitrated the strike.[55]

Newsboys in New Orleans erupted earlier that summer when the *States* and *Item* raised the wholesale price of their 2¢ papers from 1¢ to 1½¢. "A howl of indignation went up from one end of newspaper row to the other," reported the *Times-Picayune*. Some 250 boys marched to Lafayette Square and organized pickets to protect against "scabs." Circulation managers sent out several "over-bold" boys, but they were pounced on at once despite police protection. Strikers tore the boycotted papers to shreds, leaving Gravier, Common, and Camp Streets looking like "the proverbial snow storm in July" had passed through. The strikers paraded that night. Their placards read "To the Public—No Gentleman Would Buy a Paper from a Scab" and "Help Us in Our Rights." Seven boys, ages 12 to 15, were arrested for disturbing the peace, among them policeman's son Daniel Riley, the disabled Arthur Sherlock, and several residents of the Newsboys' Home. Nine more strikers were hauled in the next day. The papers then raised their retail price to 3¢, thus preserving the boys' half-price discount.[56]

Newsboy unions also took root in the Mountain West, where a hodgepodge of industrial workers struggled to reap the fruits of their own labor. In November 1907, for example, forty union newsies in Colorado Springs, Colorado, protested a fractional increase in the wholesale price of the Sunday *Denver Post* by laying siege to an express wagon as it arrived at the Santa Fe Depot. They cut the strings of the bundles and scattered the papers along Pikes Peak Avenue, engaging in a free-for-all with the special delivery boys and others who were on hand to receive the papers. Police put down the "miniature riot" around Tejon Street and arrested ringleader Howard "Red" Bell and his two lieutenants, "Slim" Solass and Mike Brennika.[57]

Other western showdowns bore the signature of the Industrial Workers of the World (IWW), known colloquially as Wobblies, the most militant labor organization in the country. Founded in Chicago in 1905, the Wobblies organized loggers, miners, longshoremen, and other western migrants. Their members included men, women, and children; blacks, Mexicans, and Chinese. The IWW sought improved pay and conditions but ultimately hoped to overthrow the capitalist order through job actions and replace it with a "workers' commonwealth."[58]

Newsboys in Montana were ripe for organization after waging noisy strikes in Butte and Anaconda in 1899 and 1901, respectively. The Woman's Christian Temperance Union started a newsboys club in Butte in March 1903 that met monthly in the Carpenter's Union hall. The club claimed 135 members, including girls. Its musical and literary offerings won favorable notice. But members struck the *Butte Evening News* in June 1907 after it started giving them two papers instead of three for a nickel. A hundred strikers created a "lively time" on Broadway and stopped sales for two days. It is unclear how the dispute ended, but ten months later "prominent men" in the city formed an auxiliary to the Butte Newsboys Club that offered edifying lectures and concerts and allowed the boys to elect their own "mayor." Membership cards stated that the holder disapproved of swearing, lying, stealing, gambling, drinking, and smoking cigarettes, and was "therefore entitled to the respect and esteem of the public."[59]

Torn by adult labor unrest, Butte saw newsboy strikes again in 1913 when carriers of the *Evening Post* went out in sympathy with the hawkers. The two factions split after the paper cut subscriptions below the agreed upon wholesale rate. Carriers refused to support the hawkers' demand for parity. Fighting broke out on January 5, 1914, outside the paper's West Granite Street office and throughout the business district. "The police came down in what they called the 'Black Mariahs,'" reminisced striker John Sheehy. "We all crowded around . . . and said, 'Take us all.' And they gave up . . . They didn't take anybody because they couldn't figure out who to take." The *Evening Post* halted street sales altogether the next day, and the boys marched through town with IWW banners stating "Direct action gets the goods" and "An injury to one is an injury to all." Management refused to negotiate. The club's adult leaders called an emergency meeting that night to urge an end to the strike and the violence, which they blamed on radical nonmembers. After several speeches, newsboys voted 58 to 30 to end the strike. Some walked out in protest. There was talk that the IWW would continue the strike, but the *Evening Post* resumed distribution the next day without incident. At the club's next meeting a Presbyterian minister lectured the boys on how to lead orderly lives.[60]

The IWW's dream of "one big union" briefly became a reality in Goldfield, Nevada, where virtually every worker in town was a member, including the newsboys. Prior to the discovery of gold in 1902, Goldfield was a windswept patch of desert studded with Joshua trees. But it attracted twenty thousand people overnight, making it the second-largest city in Nevada. Goldfield supported several daily and weekly newspapers, plus miscellaneous advertising, mining, sports, and gossip bulletins. It was home to fifteen hundred children, half of whom attended school sporadically, developing instead, said some observers, an aptitude for petty thievery, animal torture, and saloon gambling. Most newsboys were children of miners or other industrial workers, and all belonged to IWW Newsboys' Union Local 45, formed in February 1906 in a drive led by IWW stalwart Vincent St. John to organize all unorganized workers in the city.

One of the local's first actions was to donate money for the defense of three mine union officials who had been kidnapped in Denver and spirited away to Boise, Idaho, to face charges for the assassination of Idaho's anti-union governor during a strike in Coeur d'Alene. The newsies ponied up $25 for the defense of Charles Moyer, George Pettibone, and "Big Bill" Haywood, which they sent along with a note saying, "We, the boys of Newsboys' local No. 45, I.W.W., realize that an injury to one is an injury to all and stand ready to give our all for the cause if necessary." The defendants were eventually cleared of all charges.[61]

In May IWW messenger boys struck Goldfield's Western Union office for higher pay and won a favorable contract in negotiations presided over by the governor and state attorney general. Hoping to build on this success, newsboys launched a sympathy boycott of the anti-union *Goldfield Daily Sun* after its sister local in nearby Tonopah declared the *Tonopah Daily Sun* unfair. Publisher Lindley C. Branson later sued Local 45, charging that it drove him out of business "by means of boycotts, threats, intimidation, and violence." He said he could not abide the union's demand for a closed shop requiring all employees to join the IWW. In September, 1906, the union "procured" a strike of the newsboys, he said, all of whom refused to sell or deliver the *Sun* and prevented others from doing so as well.[62]

The strike had certainly been violent. Scabs enjoyed the protection of "Diamondfield Jack" Davis, a gunslinger who operated a brokerage firm that imported strikebreakers. Witnesses said he once drove off a gang that had cornered an out-of-town newsboy in his office. "Get the ——— out of here, you ———," he roared, waving pistols, "or I'll blow ye all to hell!" After the gang dispersed, Davis strode up and down the street calling for them to come back and get killed. Bob Brown, a retired Wild West showman, served as Goldfield's deputy sheriff during the strike; he busted up union meetings and sold the struck paper himself. The newsboys' third adversary was gambling house proprietor George Wingfield, who once pistol-whipped a miner for harassing nonunion newsboys and vowed to kill anyone who bothered them.[63]

Despite such formidable allies, Branson caved to the IWW. According to his lawsuit, IWW members visited the *Sun's* advertisers and threatened boycotts if they continued to run ads. They photographed purchasers of the paper and posted the pictures on a billboard along with the names of offending businesses. They pressured all the vendors in Goldfield, Tonopah, and nearby Manhattan to stop handling the *Sun*, and enlisted fellow IWW members on the Tonopah-Goldfield Railroad to stop handling freight going to or from the newspapers. They passed a resolution urging members to cancel their subscriptions, and authorized a $15 fine for those caught reading it. And they established $1.50-a-day strike fund for the newsboys. Branson further alleged that the IWW plotted to blow up his plant in Tonopah, but he offered no evidence to back up the charge.

The IWW's real source of power was not dynamite but solidarity. Community support led union leaders to insist that Branson publish an apology to the union, run a column devoted to the IWW, and promise to sell his Goldfield plant only to union vendors. To Branson, the demands and tactics constituted a criminal conspiracy for which he sought $25,000 in damages. A Nye County court dismissed his complaint, but the Nevada Supreme Court reversed the decision, allowing Branson to pursue his case. Instead, he sold the two papers for $15,000 to buyers who were friendly to the IWW. They merged the papers under a new name, the *Goldfield Daily Tribune*, and reinstated all striking employees, including the newsboys.[64]

Rarely insulated from the news they peddled, western newsboys could hardly avoid taking sides in the labor disputes that split their communities, even if their own livelihoods weren't at stake. In the coalfields of Colorado, for example, during a fifteen-month strike by ten thousand miners against John D. Rockefeller's Colorado Fuel and Iron Company and other firms in 1913–14, their sons hawked the *Trinidad Free Press*, a pro-labor weekly that became a daily to counter what they called the "kept," "prostitute," or "capitalist" press controlled by the mining firms (Figure 11.5). Tensions peaked on April 20, 1914, when company guards sworn in as state militia opened fire with machine guns on the strikers' camp in nearby Ludlow, killing eighteen strikers, including twelve children. Outraged at the massacre, union newsboys in Denver raised funds for the "Ludlow sufferers." The survivors had fled to Trinidad, where the lines were drawn as in a civil war. "The newsboys on the street were divided into two armies," observed correspondent Max Eastman, "and it was only by pressure of special friendship that a *Free Press* newsboy would call an *Advertiser* newsboy if it happened to be the *Advertiser* you asked for."[65]

Wielding the Club

As demonstrated in Butte, the best way to neutralize a newsboys' union was not to smash it but to supervise, subsidize, and separate it from the labor movement.

Figure 11.5. Newsboys, many of them miners' sons, display copies of the *Trinidad Free Press* in front of the Trades' Assembly Hall. The paper was published daily during the fourteen-month strike against John D. Rockefeller's Colorado Iron and Fuel Co., which culminated in the Ludlow Massacre on April 20, 1914. Their headlines offer a rebuttal to the "subsidized organs" controlled by the company: "Owners Stole Public Lands from Colorado"; "Charges Hatched by the Military Officers"; "Messer Says Union Men Are Not to Blame"; "Mother Jones Sent to Denver During Night." United Mine Workers organizer Mary Harris "Mother" Jones liked to address newsboy banquets and ride with the boys in Labor Day parades, as they always received the biggest cheers. *Trinidad Newsboys*, Western History Collection, Denver Public Library.

At the annual convention of circulation managers in 1903, R. S. Grable of the *St. Louis Star* advised members to support newsboys' unions and turn them to their advantage.[66] To this end, the managers welcomed John Gunckel, founder of the Toledo Newsboy Association, to their next meeting, which was held at the St. Louis World's Fair. Gunckel's association had itself supplanted a strike-prone newsboy and bootblack union in 1892. He now announced the formation of the National Newsboy Association and his appointment as president for life, which the circulation managers enthusiastically endorsed. Gunckel's employer, the Lake Shore Railroad, named him general inspector so he could recruit boys along the line from Toledo to Chicago. He soon claimed ten thousand card-carrying members, who pledged not to swear, steal, lie, gamble, or smoke (Figure 11.6). "Your work in teaching boys to be better men means you have saved the railroads thousands of dollars' worth of property," a railroad detective told him. In 1908

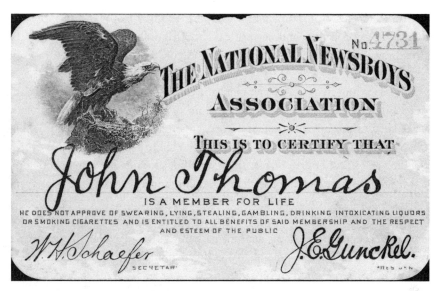

Figure 11.6. National Newsboys Association membership card no. 4731, issued to John Thomas, ca. 1908. Eckel Collection, Princeton University Library.

Gunckel raised $100,000 to break ground on a three-story clubhouse located on Superior Street, around the corner from the *Toledo Blade*. The handsome brick edifice became a symbol of practical philanthropy. Postcards proclaimed it the "first Newsboys Building erected in the World."[67]

Gunckel's scheme did not go unnoticed. A renowned tipper of newsboys, Rockefeller stepped up his giving in 1905, when he donated $150,000 to build a home for them in Cleveland and underwrote a newsboys' Sunday school at his Euclid Avenue Baptist Church. Opening day attracted two thousand boys "of almost every race and color, many still carrying news bags over their shoulders." A congregant tried to interest Rockefeller in a scheme to shelter all homeless newsboys in New York under one roof as the nucleus of a national organization. "If he were to scatter newsboys' homes or newsboys' clubs about the country with the same free hand that Mr. Carnegie has scattered libraries," opined an editor in Oklahoma, "even the most cynical critic would be able to dig up very little objection." But Rockefeller declined to expand his newsboy holdings.[68]

Others leaped into the breach. In December 1905 Jack Sullivan, yet another "King of the Newsboys," founded the Newsboys' Home Club of New York, purportedly with just 18¢ capital. Sullivan was inspired by the success of Gunckel's association and the Newsboys' Protective Union in Boston, whose headquarters he visited before launching his venture. Also known as the Newsboys' Athletic Club, Sullivan's club attracted the backing of publishers William Randolph Hearst (*Evening Journal*), Ralph Pulitzer (*World*), Ogden M. Reid (*Tribune*),

Victor F. Ridder (*Staats-Zeitung*), Herbert F. Gunnison (*Brooklyn Eagle*), and other civic leaders and celebrities. Early fundraisers featured the best of Broadway—George Cohan, Al Jolson, and Victor Moore. (President Roosevelt sent his regrets.)[69]

With two hundred charter members, the club aimed to encourage good conduct and domestic habits, aid the sick and needy, offer sports and amusements, teach citizenship, and secure steady employment. Sullivan's club was located in the old Krywaczy's Hall (renamed McKinley Hall in 1901), a four-story brick building at 74 East Fourth Street. There were beds for fifty boys on its top floor, but it was more of a clubhouse than a lodging house. "De newsboys in every town in de U.S. has organized," Sullivan told the *New York Times* after receiving the club's charter. "De New York boys was out in de cold till I woke 'em up, 'cos dere was certain parties as was out ter smash any gittin' togedder. Every time we held a meetin' de police come in an' did de great lid stunt. Dey said as how we was gittin' togedder for de purpose o' strikin'—but we ain't! All de boys wants is a place where dey can enjoy demselves an' get a bath."[70]

Sullivan, 28, had been peddling papers and palaver for most of his life. Born Jacob Abraham Reich, he started selling "under the bridge" at age 6 and later operated a booth on Frankfort Street. He gained a following as an amateur boxer and put his skills to work in the 1899 strike. He negotiated return rights with the major dailies, who empowered him to buy back unsold copies from the boys. Sullivan also moonlighted as a bookie and bail bondsman, but he assured the public that "the bad element don't belong in our club."[71]

The club was dogged by scandal from the outset, beginning with a "riot" that erupted at its first Christmas dinner when one of Sullivan's ex-newsie pals threw $100 in coins down the tables. Another crony, gambler Herman "Beansie" Rosenthal (no relation to Brooklyn Bridge pundit Joe Rosenthal), promised Sullivan's boys a supper on New Year's Day, but he reneged on the offer. Six months later a club solicitor was arrested for pocketing a $5,000 check from Randolph Guggenheimer, sponsor of the Christmas fiasco, and of keeping more than the 25 percent commission. Sullivan raised eyebrows himself when NYCLC investigator Carol Aronovici discovered that he was using club furnishings as collateral to bail out women arrested for loitering, that is, prostitution. Sullivan responded by hiring Richard S. Crummey, an experienced "boy worker" from Boston, as superintendent. "Wot he says goes," said one member, "for he's de goods." Despite this spotty record, Sullivan opened a newsboy summer camp on Staten Island in 1909 (Figure 11.7) and planned to establish newsboys clubs around the country. With publishers and philanthropists who were eager to kick in, it looked like a good racket.[72]

Sullivan's notoriety veered toward infamy in July 1912, when he was implicated in Rosenthal's murder and the biggest police corruption scandal of

Figure 11.7. A visitor inspects Jack Sullivan's Newsboys Summer Camp near Midland Beach, Staten Island, New York, ca. 1909. Bain Collection, Library of Congress, Washington, DC.

the era. Jack and Beansie had sold papers together as boys; Rosenthal helped him get his club off the ground and was the best man at his wedding. Rosenthal ran a gambling joint under the patronage of flyboy turned newsdealer turned pol "Big Tim" Sullivan (no relation to Jack) and the protection of police lieutenant Charles Becker, a brazen abuser of newsboys and streetwalkers. Upset after a vice raid, Rosenthal blabbed that Becker was a silent partner. Two days later Rosenthal was shot dead outside a Tenderloin hotel by four thugs in a Packard. Sullivan was present, allegedly to identify Rosenthal to the gunmen. He and Becker were indicted as accomplices. In an admiring profile of New York newsboys, Jacob Riis told readers of *Century Magazine*: "Jack Sullivan, 'the King of the Newsboys,' lies in the Tombs at this writing, mired in the infamy that bred the Rosenthal murder. His was the choice of the gutter that is always handy to the street, but it was not typical." Sullivan escaped prosecution but stayed in the spotlight by testifying on Becker's behalf in two trials. Becker was found guilty and executed at Sing Sing in 1915.[73]

These doings did little to enhance the reputation of the Newsboys' Home Club. A committee of newspaper publishers' wives had secured the club's move to the vacated home of the New-York Historical Society at Second Avenue and 11th Street in 1911, but reform women were not impressed. National Child Labor Committee investigator Helen Dwight inspected the club in March

1915 and found it "inexpressibly dirty" and staffed by "real Bowery bums." Her guide said that fifty to seventy-five boys visited each night. However, Brooklyn Bridge newsies told her that no decent fellows went there. Compounding the club's problems was its continued victimization by fundraisers who obtained donations that never found their way into club coffers.* The NCLC urged publishers to support regular Boys' Clubs and cease glorifying news peddling as a route to success. "It is not enough to form Newsboys' Clubs and Homes in the hope of lessening the moral contamination of the boys," said Dwight. "The evil cannot be mitigated; it must be stopped."[74]

Yet mitigation remained the order of the day, as a new kind of club emerged that aimed to instill civic virtue and ensure compliance with local street trading ordinances. Called Newsboy Republics, these municipally sponsored, industry-backed, boy-run organizations cropped up in Boston, Milwaukee, and Birmingham between 1908 and 1914. They were inspired in part by the George Junior Republic, an association of communal farms for wayward children founded by New York businessman William R. "Daddy" George in the 1890s. Unashamedly paternalistic, George adhered to the principle of self-governance, allowing his young "citizens" to set the rules by which they lived and worked. He advocated the same system for newsboys.[75]

Underscoring the need for early lessons in applied democracy were revelations of municipal corruption by Lincoln Steffens in *The Shame of the City* and William Riordan in *Plunkitt of Tammany Hall*, in which the impenitent "boodler" (and wholesale news dealer) George Washington Plunkitt rationalized his chicanery as "honest graft." More than a few crooked politicians were former newsboys, including "Boss" Cox of Cincinnati and James McGuire, the "boy mayor" of Syracuse. On the positive side of the ledger were reform mayors Tom L. Johnson of Cleveland and Mark Fagan of Jersey City, both of whom burnished the myth of their newsboy origins. Johnson noted in his memoirs that he began selling papers as an 11-year-old in Staunton, Virginia, after the Civil War. A train conductor offered to supply him exclusively so he could charge whatever he wanted. He retailed the Richmond and Petersburg dailies for 15¢ each and picture papers for 25¢. "The lesson of privilege taught me by that brief experience was one I never forgot," said the traction magnate, "for in all my subsequent arrangements

---

* Such scams plagued many newsboy charities. In 1909 juvenile con artists in Los Angeles printed up "Remember the Newsboys" cards seeking aid for a newsboys' home, shoe drive, and other bogus causes. This didn't qualify as stealing or begging, one of the scammers explained, "only mooching." "Dodge of Newsboys to Hold Up Pedestrian Is a Public Nuisance," *Los Angeles Herald*, July 10, 1909, 1. See also "Swindles the Charitable," *San Francisco Chronicle*, Nov. 28, 1901, 12; "Child Beggars Called to Halt," *Chicago Tribune*, Dec. 21, 1904, 7; "This Man Is an Impostor," *Chicago Examiner*, Feb. 15, 1911, 6; and *Oregonian*, Dec. 14, 1911, 11.

I sought enterprises in which there was little or no competition. In short, I was always on the lookout for somebody, or something which should stand in the same relation to me that my friend, the conductor, had." Yet after reading Henry George's *Social Problems* at the recommendation of another train boy, Johnson became an enemy of privilege and served as progressive mayor of Cleveland from 1901 to 1909. A similar apprenticeship molded the sterling character of Jimmy Devlin, protagonist of the 1901 novel *J. Devlin—Boss: A Romance of American Politics*. It follows a newsboy's rise to ward boss and his love since age 14 for Kate Mayne, a long-legged, sharp-tongued, quick-with-her-fists newsgirl.[76]

Founders of the Newsboys' Republic were further influenced by psychologist G. Stanley Hall's seminal study *Adolescence*, which defined the period between ages 13 and 18 as a "savage" stage of life mirroring the human race's own evolution from a primitive to a civilized state. It was a time of emotional storm and stress, he said, requiring both the freedom to act out (for boys at least, not girls) and the supervision of age-specific institutions such as high schools, sports teams, and youth clubs. Hall's ideas resonated with child labor reformers, who intuitively believed that children prematurely forced into the workplace with adults would grow up morally, physically, and mentally stunted. Hall disseminated his ideas in reform journals and women's magazines. As president of Clark University in Worchester, Massachusetts, he hosted a groundbreaking five-day conference on child welfare in July 1909 that brought together scholars and social activists from around the world.[77]

Another factor in the rise of newsboy republics was the growing clout of newsboy unions. It's no coincidence that the Boston newsboys' republic emerged in the wake of the NPU's boisterous strike against Hearst's *American* in January 1908. The Boston School Committee promoted truant officer Philip Davis to supervisor of licensed minors at its February meeting. Four months later, on Bunker Hill Day, June 17, he established the Boston School Newsboys' Association in a mass meeting of newsboys at Keith's Theatre. In January, the school committee sent him on a whirlwind tour of newsboy clubs and conditions in New York, Philadelphia, Washington, Chicago, St. Louis, Detroit, and Toledo. He was most impressed with Gunckel's operation and Toledo's strict laws. Davis persuaded school officials to raise the minimum age for newsboy licenses from 10 to 11 (later 12), but his proposal to impose a $200 fine on parents and employers of underage peddlers got no traction.[78]

Born Feivel Chemerinsky in a Russian shtetl, Davis came to America alone in 1890 at age 14. He knew sweatshops and street peddling, yet got his own Harvard education by way of Hull House and returned to the slums as a social worker. Steeped in the socialism of the Yiddish press, labor schools, and debating circles, and the pragmatism of William James at Harvard, Davis aimed to put his idealism into action. In 1909 the newsboys' association opened a clubhouse in the old Children's Mission on Tremont Street, newly renovated with a $30,000 bequest from the estate of Frederick Gray Frothingham, an early supporter of the newsboys' reading room. The following year the club welcomed the Newsboys' Trial Board, in which newsboy judges heard cases and rendered decisions. None of their rulings had any legal standing, but they spared parents the shame of accompanying their children to regular courts and cleared city dockets of the most trivial infractions, which numbered three hundred per year. Police recognized the trial board, and Davis was empowered to bring complaints before it instead of the juvenile court. Nine out of ten cases concerned boys working without a license, in proscribed hours, or in a disorderly manner. Charges were rarely contested, and penalties ranged from a warning to a two-week suspension. The Newsboys' Protective Union generally cooperated, but it balked in 1911 over Davis's frequent revocation of its members' badges.[79]

Boston's newsboys' club thus morphed into a republic whose overarching aim was to foster respect for the law. It soon claimed four thousand citizens between the ages of 11 and 14 (later raised to 12 to 16), led by one hundred captains and lieutenants. They sang the club song, "The Newsboys of Boston," to the tune of "Marching Through Georgia." Legally barred from the street trades, girls did not qualify for membership. Taking a page from the NPU, the club secured scholarships to four local institutions: the YMCA (later Northeastern College), Burdett College, Berkeley Prep, and, with a donation from Thomas Edison, the Massachusetts Institute of Technology. Davis soon moved on, but the court met until the early 1920s when its boy judges were replaced by adults and the Newsboys' Republic was absorbed into a municipal federation of Boys' Clubs whose membership was not restricted to newsboys.[80]

The Milwaukee Newsboys' Republic, established in November 1912 under the auspices of the state industrial commission and street trades commissioner P. O. Powell, sought to curb juvenile delinquency and uplift the city's four thousand licensed newsboys. Its constitution was based on that of the United States, with three branches of government. Newspaper circulation men served in the Senate, while boys occupied the House. The city was divided into six "states" or congressional districts, and a mechanism was set up for the election of officers. Candidates representing two parties addressed the electorate at twenty-four meetings held across the city with great hoopla. "They are now convinced that the Street Trades Law is a benefit to them instead of a menace, as some had anticipated," said Powell. The 124 elected congressmen were given star-shaped badges that entitled them to "arrest" violators in their district. Unlike the Boston Republic, Milwaukee's citizens came from the city's approximately sixty Lutheran and Catholic schools as well as public schools. "When one considers the cosmopolitan character of Milwaukee's population," said Outlook magazine, "this little democracy, with its American Chief Justice, its German President, and its Russian-Jew Vice-President, becomes an important agent for the assimilation of our second and third generations of foreigners."[81]

By 1916, Milwaukee's Newsboy Republic had overseen the activities of nearly ten thousand street peddlers between the ages of 10 and 16. It was credited with reducing the flow through the newsboy pipeline to the state reform school to a trickle. That same year authority over the republic was transferred from the industrial commission to the school board, with Powell still in charge. The republic sponsored track meets, a summer baseball league, and other playground activities. It also launched a subgroup, Knights of the Canvas Bag, for carriers, and gave them their own grip, sign, motto, song, and yell. The republic published its own newspaper, *Newsboys' World*. One editor, 12-year-old Sol Tax, gained skills and interests he would use his whole life. "I was a Walter Mitty," he said, "and had constant dreams of glory . . . somehow or other saving the troubled world." Outraged at adult domination of the Republic, Tax transformed it into a genuine union, winning bargaining rights—all before he was 15. He went on to major in anthropology at the University of Wisconsin and earn his PhD at the University of Chicago, where he edited the leading journals in his field and became an expert on Native American culture and the small-scale economic practices he termed "penny capitalism."[82]

Founded in 1915, the same year Alabama regulated juvenile street trading, Birmingham's Newsboys' Republic was a product of the city's changing demographics. Birmingham's population rose from 38,000 in 1900 to 133,000 in 1910. Many of the newcomers were southern and eastern European immigrants drawn by the city's iron and steel plants. They typically earned half the pay of their Scottish, American, or African American coworkers—hence the greater need for their children's earnings. The republic's court met every Saturday before three judges, all newsboys duly elected by their peers. The only adult present was the president of the Boys' Club. Good humor and kindliness reigned in the court, according to one report, along with an atmosphere of dignity, straight and keen questioning, prompt decisions, and "no fooling." In addition to the usual violations, Birmingham boys were charged with poaching another boy's territory, stealing from fruit stands, gambling, misbehaving in school, and truancy. Sentences ranged from reprimands to three-day suspensions. Like the other republics, Birmingham's was an agent of Americanization that simultaneously sought to instill civic virtue and exert social control without depriving boys of their work or newspapers of their boys.[83]

The same forces that spawned newsboy clubs and republics set newsboys' home and lodging houses on the path to extinction. New homes were established in Omaha in 1902, Toronto in 1903, St. Louis in 1906, Houston in 1910, and Portland, Oregon in 1912, yet they encountered mounting opposition from reformers who saw them as remnants of an outdated philanthropy that

tacitly encouraged boys to abandon their families. Lillian Wald rejoiced when
the newsboys' home on East Broadway, near her Henry Street settlement, shut
down. She praised mothers in the neighborhood for removing this "hang out."
Newsboys' homes in Baltimore, Boston, Chicago, Cleveland, Indianapolis, and
Louisville also came under attack for garrisoning idle, delinquent, and unkempt
youths, many of the "transient foreign element," and few actual paper sellers. In
deference to such criticism, superintendents hung signs in their foyers reading,
"Boys having homes not received here."[84]

A 1910 survey of benevolent institutions by the US Census lists thirty
homes for working children, including three identified specifically as newsboys'
homes—in New York, New Orleans, and Pittsburgh (founded in 1854, 1879,
and 1884, respectively). This was an incomplete listing, but the "newsboy" designation was clearly in decline.[85] Newspapers continued to support the homes
with publicity and donations. In April 1904, the New-York Tribune featured a
photo essay showing boys depositing money in the home's savings bank and bedding down in the "Waldorf Room"—the eight-bed, 15¢-a-night, top-floor dormitory to which all the residents supposedly aspired. "We'd rather be the main
guys here," one of them explained, "than be an under dog at a cheap boarding
house." Superintendent Rudolph Heig, who lived on the premises for thirty-five
years with his wife, four children, and their shaggy dog Leo, told a reporter in
1910 that past lodgers included two US congressmen, four state legislators, eight
postmasters, fifteen journalists, seventeen physicians, twenty-one clergymen,
twenty-two merchants, twenty-seven bankers, thirty-four lawyers, eighty-one
teachers, and more than a thousand soldiers and sailors.[86]

Though challenged by progressives, newsboys' homes remained viable and
versatile institutions in the early 1900s as reform journals continued to run
want-ads for superintendents who could do probation work in juvenile courts.[87]
One who possessed the requisite skills and believed in the regenerative power of
newsboys' homes was Father Peter Joseph Dunne, who founded Father Dunne's
Newsboys Home in St. Louis in 1906, two years after the city's previous home
closed. It started out at 1013 Selby Place, but neighbors blamed every act of vandalism or mischief on the boys. By May Father Dunne moved to a larger house
at 2737 Locust Street, where thirty-five boys took up residence. He attended
sessions of the juvenile court as a probation officer. He fed and clothed the boys
in his care, sending the younger ones to school, finding jobs for the older ones,
and supervising those who sold papers. His efforts were so effective that other
newsboys came to resent Father Dunne's boys as a kind of "aristocracy" of the
trade. "They were organized," recalled one competitor. "By sheer weight of numbers they took the best corners, and left us fighting over what was left."[88]

Dunne's counterpart in Omaha was Moses "Mogy" Bernstein, who founded
a home for newsboys in 1902 in the basement of his Farnham Street shoeshine

parlor. "Yes, if I should sit up in my office and leave the work to attendants, the boys probably would abuse the privileges and the home might work more injury than good," he conceded. "But, instead, I get right in among the boys every evening and know every one of them personally. I know where they live and the condition of their parents. No gambling of any kind is permitted. My boys exercise in their gymnasium, play games, go to their own night school, and in time will become useful members of business life."[89]

Mogy had traveled to New York to study the operation of the Newsboys' Lodging House, but he brought a lifetime of experience to the venture. Born with a clubfoot in Lexington, Kentucky, in 1875, he started peddling papers at age 5. His family moved to St. Paul, Minnesota, and then to Omaha, where he was elected treasurer of the local newsboys union, established with sixty charter members on April 20, 1898, the day President McKinley signed Congress's joint resolution for war with Spain. The boys hoped to organize the many newcomers who were hawking war extras, and increase their bargaining power with local dailies and the incoming Chicago papers. Their first victory was a city ordinance, passed in May over the mayor's veto, which required all newsboys to purchase a $2 license, thereby limiting competition from transients. The law was repealed five months later, however, and the payees reimbursed.[90]

Mogy made news again in 1902 when he led a strike by seventy-five unionized Sunday newsboys against the half-cent price hike imposed by distributors of Hearst's *Chicago American* and Joseph Pulitzer's *St. Louis Post-Dispatch*. "This left the newsies but a penny margin on a ten-pound paper," explained the *Omaha World-Herald*, "and they concluded not to stand for it." F. C. Smith, the 23-year-old distributor, hired "a motley crew of swaggering buccaneers" for $3 apiece to sell the paper in the streets, but the union boys responded with placards and shinny sticks. When Smith pushed one of the little boys, Mogy, now union president, attacked him. Everyone scrammed when the patrol wagon arrived except the two men, both of whom were arrested and ordered to pay bonds of $100 each. Smith and the *Post-Dispatch* came to terms with the union a few days later, but the boycott of Hearst's *American* continued.[91]

Recognized as Omaha's "King of the Newsboys" not just by virtue of his physical courage but also due to the annual newsboy dinners, picnics, and masquerade balls he sponsored, Mogy transformed himself into a proper "boy worker." He was always on hand to bail out boys who got into trouble with the law. He visited Denver to observe Judge Ben Lindsey's juvenile court in action, and in 1905 became Omaha's first probation officer. He soon oversaw six assistants, and by 1910 he was a recognized expert in the field. "It is all in knowing your ground," he told the *Journal of Education*. "I have known the bad boys of Omaha for a great many years, ever since I was a bad boy among them, and there is very little that takes place in the city that I cannot get a line on, through the boys whom I have always known."[92]

Through it all, Mogy never stopped selling papers. He also owned a café, secured the city's confetti concession, and opened one of its first car dealerships. In August 1919, he was found dead in his café from a gunshot wound, apparently self-inflicted, having fallen into debt. Omaha's mayor eulogized him as a true friend and role model for newsboys. "How many of you will be a 'Mogy'?" he asked?[93]

Postlude: 1912

The conjunction of forces that shaped the experience of Progressive Era newsboys came to a head in 1912. The year was packed with momentous events—most notably the sinking of the *Titanic*—that riveted the reading public, strained the industry's distributive capacities, and kept newsboys' pockets jingling with coins. That year also featured a hotly contested presidential race in which newsboy labor (sometimes coerced) lubricated the democratic process. Workplace clashes filled the papers, too, including bloody strikes by newsboys in Kansas City and Chicago. Child welfare reformers scored a major victory with the founding of the US Children's Bureau. This success, coupled with the spread of newsboy clubs and republics, roused a chorus of voices lamenting the passing of the wily, ragged news gamin of old and his replacement by a tamer, tidier schoolboy version.

One might think that news sellers in this period were accustomed to retailing disaster, having cried headlines about the Great Galveston Hurricane that left 8,000 Texans dead in 1900, the Iroquois Theatre blaze in Chicago that killed 600 matinée-goers in 1903, the Harwick Mine explosion that buried 181 Pennsylvania coal miners in January 1904, the *General Slocum* steamboat fire in New York that took the lives of 1,021 excursionists five months later, and the San Francisco earthquake that killed 3,000 people in 1906. But the *Titanic* disaster, with more than 1,500 casualties, eclipsed them all as "the biggest story ever reported." One difference was the greater number and circulation of newspapers and their access to wireless telegraphy—the same technology that proved so ineffectual in rescue efforts. Not surprisingly, it was an ex-newsboy, Marconi Company telegrapher David Sarnoff, who heard the initial wire reports from the *Carpathia* as it rushed to pick up survivors. He stayed at his post atop the Wanamaker department store in New York for three days, getting the names of the rescued, relaying information to Hearst's *New York American*, and making the reputation that would catapult him to the pinnacle of power in network radio and television.[94]

Newsboys everywhere caught *Titanic* fever. They worked round the clock as new editions flew off the nation's presses every hour, the pace barely subsiding for weeks. Lewis Hine, who was on assignment in Washington, DC, said, "Night after night hundreds of boys and men hung around the newspaper offices, fought their way to the distributing counters and out into the streets." Many stayed out until one or two in the morning in their quest for sales. In Massachusetts, the *Springfield Union's* 135 newsboys sold fifteen thousand copies of the *Boston Herald*, a record that stood until the kidnapping of the Lindbergh baby twenty years later.[95] Despite having treated hundreds of newsies to holiday meals every year, the *Richmond Times-Dispatch* couldn't round up enough boys to hustle its *Titanic* extras and had to send out its printers. Some people objected to the obscene profits hawkers reaped from the disaster. The *Winston-Salem Journal* criticized a boy who bought four hundred penny extras at 60¢ per hundred and hired four boys to peddle them for a nickel apiece. He paid them 60¢ each while netting almost $15 profit. "Wouldn't that money have smelt too much of the 'loan shark,' the note shaver, and the Scrooge?" asked the *Journal*, failing to disclose its own profit margin.[96]

To their credit, newsies near and far donated to *Titanic* relief funds. Merrel Alte of Indianapolis gave to New York mayor William Gaynor's Red Cross fund: "I am a newsboy 9 years old and I want to help those poor people who were saved from the Titanic. I am sending one dollar. That is all I have. I pray for them every night. Goodby." Jack Sullivan, as yet unsullied by serious scandal, teamed up with George Cohan to sell Hearst's *New York American* at clubs and the Polo Grounds, collecting $6,500 in *Titanic* donations.[97]

Theodore Roosevelt was back on the scene in 1912, trying to regain the presidency from his old friend and secretary of war William Taft and defeat Democrat Woodrow Wilson and Socialist Eugene Debs. Newsboys shadowed Roosevelt, the Progressive "Bull Moose" Party nominee, all along the campaign trail; strikers in Chicago appealed to him for relief from the near constant slugging, while admirers in Milwaukee saw him take a bullet in the chest and go on to give an eighty-minute speech before seeking medical attention.[98]

Reliance on newsboy labor during the campaign led an Alabama newspaper to cross the line between recruitment and kidnapping. The case occurred in June when Republican delegates in Chicago were deadlocked between Taft and Roosevelt for the nomination. Looking to issue an extra the moment the results came over the wire, the *Birmingham Ledger* put out an early call for hawkers. The boys paid for their papers, received their slips, and entered a waiting area enclosed by wire. Between fifty and a hundred boys, including 10-year-old Alfred Buchanan, soon packed the cage. Managers locked the door when agents from another daily trolled the block looking for boys. Hours passed and still no extras. Alfred and some of the younger ones began to cry, only to be knocked around by the older boys. *Ledger* men brought in sandwiches and ice cream, but kept the exit blocked. A teen who tried to push his way out was beaten. The extras finally appeared at 9:00 p.m. and the boys were released to trumpet Taft's victory. Alfred's mother was so outraged when she heard about his detention that she sued the *Ledger* and won "liberal damages."[99]

Nineteen twelve was also a watershed year in terms of newsboy labor activism. In February, the Newsboys' Protective Union in Boston sent a "large donation" to striking mill workers in Lawrence, Massachusetts.[100] Kansas City newsboys waged their own week-long campaign that month against the *Star* after its bumptious publisher, William Rockhill Nelson, cut the retail price of its daily from 2¢ to 1¢ and its Sunday edition from 5¢ to 2¢, simultaneously shrinking the boys' profit margins. With a combined circulation of 630,000, the Republican-leaning *Star* was one of the largest papers in the country, making Nelson a political force in the state. But competition from the *Kansas City Post*, a Democratic yellow sheet, had reduced its street sales to less than a thousand a day.[101] The city's latest newsboys union, now four years old with more than two hundred members, represented nearly every paper crier in town. Strikers were arrested "by the dozen" on charges of assault or blocking sidewalks, the boys arraigned in juvenile court and the young men in municipal court.[102]

Among those caught up in the sweep were minor league ball player Casey Stengel and Sam "Jew" Miller, the 17-year-old president of the newsboys union. Miller was arrested and released five times in three days.[103] Pro bono attorneys obtained an injunction to stop police from interfering with the strikers' lawful activities, but the chief ignored the order. "Mounted policemen herded them as a rancher would herd cattle into the patrol wagon," said the *Post*, whose sports editor put up a $10,000 bail bond for the strikers. Its coverage included triple banner headlines, front-page photo collages, and cartoons of Nelson whipping or clubbing newsboys (Figure 11.8).[104] The *Star* hired down-and-outers and sent staff and reporters out to hawk. The dispute ended, according to one account, when the paper agreed to pay four hundred newsboys' salaries for a year and let them keep half the take on street sales. Union president Miller resumed selling papers at 10th and Main. He caught the movie bug while on vacation in California and cowrote a screenplay, *The Life of a Newsboy*, in which he hoped to play the lead.[105]

If the Kansas City strike was a brawl, Chicago's was a slaughter. Always a tough newspaper town, Chicago outdid itself in savagery between 1910 and 1912 when, by one count, twenty-seven newspaper dealers, newsboys or others were killed in a circulation war that involved nearly every newspaper and newspaper union in town. "This was the beginning of gangsterism and racketeering in Chicago," said Burton Rascoe, a cub reporter for the *Chicago Tribune* at the time.[106] Mired in the violence was Chicago's Newsboys' Protective Association,

Figure 11.8. "Let's stop this modern Simon Legree." *Kansas City Star* publisher William Rockhill Nelson is likened to the sadistic overseer in *Uncle Tom's Cabin* by a rival daily during the newsboy strike of 1912. *Kansas City Post,* Feb. 19, 1912, 1.

an adult organization "born in Bedlam," according to one headline, in 1902 when the city barred all sellers from erecting stands or setting their wares on the street. Its first meetings resounded with raucous debate in English and Italian. The association defeated the ordinance and continued to provide aid and advice to its two hundred members. These "whiskered capitalists" made up only 5 percent of the city's news sellers; many employed sons, daughters, and neighbor kids, who in turn supplied papers or sublet sidewalks to other children. Their stands changed hands for anywhere from $500 to $2,000, the prices reflecting the value not of the humble pinewood boxes but of their exclusive right to receive papers at that location, a right recognized by cards issued by the circulation managers of the city's newspapers.[107]

These arrangements broke down after Hearst arrived. Early casualties included 20-year-old *Daily News* circulation department worker Morris F. Clark, an African American who was shot to death on a contested corner by 22-year-old Lawrence Finn in March 1901. The Higgins brothers, William, 21, and Richard, 23, employees of the *Chicago Journal* and *Daily News*, met similar fates at the hands of Hearst killers in November 1905. In each case the accused were acquitted on grounds of self-defense.[108]

Publishers of the Chicago *Examiner, American, Daily News,* and *Record-Herald* soon consolidated their cutthroat tactics by ganging up against the *Tribune* and dictating prices and terms to dealers.[109] Reeling from this collusion, the *Tribune,* now managed by cousins Robert "the Colonel" McCormick and Joseph Patterson, lured former *Tribune* circulation manager Max Annenberg away from Hearst with the princely salary of $20,000 a year, plus a place on the payroll for his best plug-uglies. Newspaper circulation became a no-holds-barred contest with rival papers employing career criminals to do their bidding, such as torching stands and wagons, blowing up delivery trucks, and beating, stabbing, or shooting anyone who got in their way. Enraged that trolley riders were not reading the *Examiner,* one Hearst gunmen emptied his revolver into the car's ceiling. Conveniently deputized by the chief of police, Max Annenberg opened fire on Hearst men on several occasions, while his brother Moe, still in Hearst's employ, engaged in shootouts with *Tribune* deliverymen.[110]

This sibling rivalry became deadly in 1910 when Hearst joined the trust to form a united front against organized labor. The violence escalated throughout 1911. Stray bullets cut down innocent bystanders, but the major papers stayed mum, muffling public outrage. Then came the strike. On May 1, 1912, Hearst unilaterally reduced the number of men needed to run the presses and locked out those who objected. The seven other trust publishers fell in line. Printers stayed on the job citywide, but union stereotypers, mailers, drivers, venders, and newsboys struck in sympathy, correctly surmising that the publishers' ultimate goal was a union-free industry.[111]

By 1912 the Newsboys' Protective Association of Chicago had grown to 432 members ranging in age from 20 to 65. They and the boys who hawked or delivered papers for them were routinely caught in the crossfire or recruited as saboteurs. According to press reports, paid sluggers smashed 8-year-old Tim Gento in the nose and crippled 12-year-old James McGilligen by taking a club to his kneecap. With several thousand men gathered at West Madison and Halsted Street on May 6 to prevent distribution of a wagonload of *Examiners* under police escort, an unnamed 6-year-old was induced to hold a lighted match to the bundles. A New York motion picture company filmed the confrontation. City officials charged that it was staged for the camera to ruin Chicago's reputation, and passed an ordinance denying permits for any recording or exhibition of a "riotous, disorderly, or unlawful scene."[112]

While pulled into the fray in solidarity with the pressmen, newsboys young and old had their own grievances as well. The trust had advanced the price of the weekday paper from 50¢ to 60¢ per 100 and the Sunday paper from 3¢ to 4¢ per copy, revoked return privileges, and compelled them to take and pay for a set number of papers, whether they wanted them or not. In addition, the *Examiner* stretched out their workday—already sixteen hours, from 4:00 a.m. to

8:00 p.m.—by introducing an obligatory bulldog edition, forcing every vendor to stay open at least two more hours. With local politicians in their pocket, publishers secured passage of an ordinance forbidding any stand on public property to change hands without the trust's approval and receipt of a fee. Vendors who operated stands on the elevated train stations were threatened with revocation of their leases unless they sold trust newspapers. To win sympathy after these affronts, trust papers published stories about vendors who earned $20,000 a year or otherwise deserved public scorn.[113]

True to their word, police ousted owners who refused to carry trust newspapers. Arrests and punch ups followed. The city also required carriers to take out a $25 permit to deliver papers, and restricted them to handling certain papers, thereby allowing the trust, through the police, to control every news seller in Chicago. Cops further intimidated strikers by showing up at their union meetings, questioning all who arrived, and turning away some. "The war of the publishers, and the mayor, and the police, upon the newsboys would be ridiculous," said the *Day Book*, "were it not so deadly serious." The "war" dragged on until mid-November, when members voted to return to their stands and sell trust papers if they wanted. In seven and a half months, four strikers and sympathizers had been killed by gunfire, several more seriously wounded, hundreds beaten, and almost fifteen hundred arrested by baton-wielding patrolmen. The lesson of the strike was unmistakable: in the raging debate over child labor, press freedom, and crony capitalism, clubs had the last word.[114]

Child labor reformers had reason to weep and rejoice. After ten years of agitation, only nine states, four cities, and the District of Columbia regulated child street trading.* Yet on April 9, 1912, President Taft created the first federal agency devoted to the welfare of minors. Headed by Hull House veteran Julia Lathrop, the Children's Bureau was charged with investigating the working and health conditions of America's children and publicizing its findings. Though poorly funded, the bureau promised to make the "Century of the Child" a reality.[115]

The struggle continued. Lewis Hine photographed underage newsboys and newsgirls on city streets in New York, New Jersey, Rhode Island, Virginia, and Washington, DC, including ironic images of boys unlawfully selling papers in front of the Capitol dome (Figure 11.9). His colleague Edward Clopper

---

* The states were Massachusetts (1902), New York (1903), Oklahoma and Wisconsin (1909), and Colorado, Missouri, Nevada, New Hampshire, and Utah (1911); the cities Boston (1902), Newark, New Jersey (1904), Washington, DC (1908), Cincinnati (1909), and Hartford (1910). Kentucky exempted news peddlers from regulation and Oklahoma only barred girls from the trade. See Edward N. Clopper, *Child Labor in City Streets* (New York: Macmillan, 1913), 194–96, and US Dept. of Commerce and Labor, "Labor Laws and Factory Conditions," 19, *Report on Conditions of Woman and Child Wage Earners in the United States* (Washington, DC: Government Printing Office, 1912), App. A, 655–856, 922.

Figure 11.9. Lewis W. Hine, *Group of Newsies Selling on Capitol Steps, April 11, 1912.*
Tony Passaro (8 yrs. old). Dan Mercurio (9 yrs. old). Joseph Tucci (10 years old). Peter Peper
(10 yrs. old). John Carlino (11 yrs. old). LOT 7480, v. 3, no. 2905 [P&P] LC-H5- 2905,
Library of Congress, Washington, DC.

published *Child Labor in City Streets*, the first book-length treatment of the subject. "Street workers have always been far more conspicuous than any other child laborers, and it seems that this very proximity has been their misfortune," he explained. "If we could have focused our attention upon them as we did upon children in factories, they would have been banished from the streets long ago. But they were too close to us." Clopper called this myopic condition the "illusion of the near," a phrase coined by pioneer sociologist Lester Ward. Like most progressives, Clopper believed that only by amassing a wealth of information about his subjects—their ages, hours, earnings, conditions, health, and hazards—could he cut through contemporary prejudices and lay bare the truth about the dangers facing newsboys, bootblacks, and messengers.[116] Yet his reference to the illusion of the near acknowledges the movement's failure to effectively regulate, let alone abolish, child street labor. Clopper blamed parents, publishers, and the public that patronized these children. His findings inspired many approving sermons and editorials, but responsibility for the lack of progress also belonged to the boys and girls themselves, who refused to leave the trade no matter the costs.

While always contested, ideas about what constituted a legitimate newsboy charity changed dramatically during the period. Not only were lodging houses accused of perpetuating the problems they were intended to eradicate, but the Children's Aid Society's "wooden leg" fund also came under fire. Florence Kelley said it exemplified the backwardness of newsboy philanthropy, not just because it supplied children with wooden limbs when modern prosthetic devices were available but also because it didn't go to the crux of the problem. "Instead of seeing that the little boys keep their legs," said Kelley, "we still let them lose their legs and then give them legs that are of no use to them."[117]

Making matters worse, the muckraking mood was tapering off. Most of the magazines that had investigated newsboy conditions had either changed hands or direction. Bucking this trend was *The Masses*, a new socialist monthly based in Greenwich Village that supported progressive causes, writers, and artists, including Ashcan School member John Sloan, who hawked seventy-eight copies of the first issue one brisk evening and claimed the staff record.[118]

All the while, idealized depictions of newsboys kept cropping up in the marketplace of ideas to provide a counternarrative to reformers' diminishing but still dire warnings. Newsboys triumphed in juvenile fiction by James Otis and Alma Woodward, and shared their earnings with Santa on the cover of the *Saturday Evening Post*.[119] But the most heroic "newsboy" of 1912 was 41-year-old Billy Rugh, a vendor in Gary, Indiana, who had his withered leg amputated to provide a skin graft for a girl he had never met. Rugh caught pneumonia and died. Twenty-five thousand people attended his funeral. His last words—"It's all right if the girl's all right!"—inspired sermons, editorials, and a popular ballad called "His Sacrifice."[120] Sentimental songs about newsboys circulated throughout the era.[121] The much-ballyhooed discovery of Ziegfeld Follies star Fanny Brice in 1910 while tending a newsstand at the corner of Bergen Street and Vanderbilt Avenue in Brooklyn perpetuated the allure of the trade, even though the story was mostly the product of Florenz Ziegfeld's press agentry.[122]

Movies offered another way to idealize news criers, albeit silently. They were the striving protagonists of melodramas such as *A Newsboy's Luck* (1911) and archetypal waifs in reform tracts like *The Land Beyond the Sunset* (1912). Newsboy characters also helped establish the comedy, horror, and biopics genres in *Mutt and Jeff and the Newsboys* (1911), *The Newsboy's Christmas Dream* (1913), and *The Life of Big Tim Sullivan; or, From Newsboy to Senator* (1914). While some of the films put a human face on statistics, most emphasized the unusual circumstances and singular qualities of the boys, thus lessening their propaganda value.[123]

Still, child welfare reformers had made enough gains by 1912 that many people looked back wistfully on the passing of the genuine article. "The newsboy of old," observed Jacob Riis, "who foraged for himself, . . . who curled up by the steam-pipes or on the manhole-covers in the small hours of the morning for a 'hot-pipe nap' 'til the clatter of the great presses began below, and was rounded up there by the 'Cruelty man' in zero weather, is a rare bird nowadays. In his place has come the commercial little chap who lives at home and sells papers after school-hours, sometimes on his own account, but oftener to eke out the family earnings with what maybe the difference between comparative comfort and abject poverty.... He has surrendered some of his picturesqueness to become a cog in the industrial wheel, small but indispensable."[124]

The 81-year-old J. G. Brown was even more nostalgic at the end of his life. "My boys are all gone," he lamented. "It has been four years since I have seen a newsboy who had even any trace of the picturesqueness and quaintness that once characterized them. It's a great pity, too. But they had belonged to the old order, and it was only natural that they had to go." Brown blamed compulsory education, which not only removed children from the streets during the day but also crushed their independent spirit. "They are just ordinary school children," he said.[125] In other words, the newsboys immortalized by Brown and Riis had fallen victim to the very progress meant to save them from lives of toil and want. Brown died in 1913, followed by Riis in May 1914, neither suspecting that the progressive commitment to newsboy reform—indeed, all reform—would wane as the world drifted inexorably toward war.

12

Call to Service

The lead story on the front pages of America's newspapers on June 29, 1914, bore an unusual dateline: Sarajevo. Wire reports said a Serbian youth had jumped onto the motorcar of Austrian archduke Franz Ferdinand II and his wife as it wound its way through the Bosnian capital and shot them to death to avenge Austria's seizure of his homeland. News of the assassination initiated brisk newspaper sales in the United States and heightened interest in the troubled region, long known as the "chessboard of Europe." But no one imagined that it would spark a four-year conflagration that would kill ten million people and maim twice that number. "Another Balkan incident was what we newsboys thought of World War I," said Harry Golden.[1]

Golden was one of 2,835 licensed newsboys in New York City. Born Herschel Goldhirsch in a Jewish ghetto in Ukraine, the 11-year-old had once been a cipher in the Austro-Hungarian Empire. His family had moved to the Lower East Side in 1905 when he was 2 years old, and in due time he was hawking papers at the corner of Delancey and Norfolk Streets every day after school. "I sold the *Journal, World, Mail, Telegram, Sun, Globe,* the *Jewish Daily Forward,* and the *Post,*" he said. "Each of them was deposited on the corner in a bundle of 20, and I opened them, spread them out, and started off with the one with the most lurid headline." Golden bought his papers on credit for a penny apiece and retailed them for 2¢. He sold a hundred copies a day (two hundred on good days), mainly to garment workers heading home on the subway. "A little after six in the evening the distributor would come around to collect," he said. "First he had a horse-drawn cart, but before I moved on, he was driving an electric truck."[2]

The Great War, from 1914 to 1918, hastened many changes in the American news trade that transformed both the meaning and experience of child street peddling. The war redefined the role of children in civic affairs and enhanced newsboys' reputation for patriotism. The public came to regard news peddling less as a demoralizing form of labor and more as a branch of national service. Child labor reformers, many of whom opposed the war, lost much of their clout, while publishers gained stature and profit mobilizing newsboys to sell war bonds and form Scout troops. Thousands of former newsboys became part of the American Expeditionary Force (AEF) and dozens won distinction for heroism. Those too young to bear arms sometimes showed their mettle by harassing "slackers" or German Americans. Yet boys who cried false news or mounted strikes faced their own charges of disloyalty. Whether as soldiers, sailors, strikers, or street sellers, America's newsboys now entered the world's stage.

Fruits of War

America had stood on the sidelines for almost three years as the Central Powers pushed France, England, and Russia to the brink of defeat. President Woodrow Wilson insisted on remaining neutral while banks and businesses traded with belligerents on both sides. This policy became less tenable after May 7, 1915, when a German U-boat torpedoed the British luxury liner *Lusitania* off the coast of Ireland, killing almost 1,200 people, including 128 Americans.* Not since the sinking of the *Titanic* did newsboys yell so loudly and reap such rewards. Most newspapers abandoned neutrality overnight and threw their support to the Allies. Wilson navigated a middle course: aiming to win reelection in 1916, he named progressives to important posts, backed bills favoring the interests of farmers and workers, and, to the great if fleeting jubilation of reformers, signed the Keating-Owen Child Labor Act, which barred the interstate commerce of goods produced by children. National Child Labor Committee secretary Edward Clopper called the act a "national ratification" of the many state laws regulating child labor, and credited the war with its passage. Even so, it applied to only 15 percent of the children employed in "gainful occupations." Among those untouched were the 20,450 newsboys and newsgirls enumerated in the 1910 US Census—and the thousands more who went uncounted. These limitations became moot in 1918 when the US Supreme Court overturned the law in a 5–4 decision in the case of *Hammer v. Dagenhart*, ruling that only states, not the federal government, could regulate commerce.[3]

Regulating newsboys had never been high on Wilson's reform agenda. He received his own four dailies from Sam and Israel April, brothers who had secured sole rights to the White House during the Taft administration. Lewis Hine photographed 9-year-old Izzy at work in 1912 and found him "quite a pugnacious little chap" who regularly worked past midnight (Figure 12.1).

* Among them was former *New York Daily Graphic* newsboy and Broadway producer Charles Frohman, carrying the play that was to be his masterpiece.

Figure 12.1. Lewis Hine, *Israel April, 314 I St., S.W., Washington, DC.* Hine's caption: "'I serves the President.' 9 yr. old newsboy with no badge selling near Willard Hotel, Sunday PM. 4.14.12. Been selling for several years. I found him selling after midnight April 17th and 18th. Quite a pugnacious little chap. He and his brother are said to have a large clientele among ambassadors and senators." Library of Congress, Washington, DC.

"I serves the President," he told Hine. Wearing his usual suit, tie, and pocket handkerchief, Izzy also served the F Street offices of the Congressional Union for Woman Suffrage, delivering papers free twenty-five days a month in lieu of the 25¢ dues. Wilson, by contrast, was slow to support the suffrage movement but quick to curry favor with newsboys. In 1915 he sent a "goodwill letter" to an assembly of Baltimore newsies, reminding them, "The right road is the straight road." They in turn presented him with a badge entitling him to sell papers in the city. While he never used his direct line to Congress, in 1916 Wilson spoke to 120 New York newsboys sharing sixty telephones in the Avenue A Boys' Club.[4]

Wooing progressives, maintaining good press relations, and staying out of the war paid off, as Wilson narrowly won reelection. The race was so close that *New York Times* newsboys hawked early editions proclaiming victory for Republican Charles Evans Hughes. Pacifists had little time to rejoice. Even before the inauguration, Germany resumed its submarine attacks on American vessels and solicited the aid of Mexico should the United States enter the war. On April 2, 1917, Wilson asked Congress to declare war on the Central Powers to make the world "safe for democracy." Newsboys raked in the dough selling extras that week. As a bonus, *Washington Post* newsboys received thousands of free copies.[5]

Unlike in previous wars, more newsboys left the trade than entered it. In Buffalo the number of licensed newsies fell 26 percent (from 1,067 to 790), even though circulation soared. In Louisville the number of juvenile street traders dropped 66 percent (from 712 to 244). And in Baltimore newsboys' ranks thinned 69 percent (from 1,965 to 612). Most boys went on to better-paying jobs vacated by army recruits or found work in the war industries. In Baltimore two out of every five newsies who surrendered their badges in 1917 took full-time jobs paying $4.50 to $9 a week. Elementary and high school attendance also fell due to the allurements of the job market. More than one-third of Boston's schoolchildren who turned 14 in 1914 took out employment papers, and the number of working children increased threefold through 1918. In Washington, DC, the superintendent of schools attributed a 41 percent drop in enrollment to school leavers' ability to command $12.50 to $25 a week working in government or private offices. Harry Golden, who graduated from high school in 1917, gave up his corner to become a telegraph messenger, which paid better than news selling. The *Rochester Herald* resorted to a self-service scheme in which it placed sacks of newspapers on poles or tree branches in outlying districts with instructions to "take paper and deposit coin." Newspapers from New York City to Cheyenne, Wyoming tried to bolster their dwindling sales force by running ads asking parents to make sure each boy would "do his bit." Some papers played down the defections, insisting that they preferred newsracks to newsboys.[6]

Such claims ring false given the press's unflagging reliance on, investment in, and defense of boy labor. In 1915 the *Indianapolis News*, a 2¢ evening paper with a circulation of 105,000, used more than 6,000 distributors. They included 300 newsboys, 1,600 carriers (average age 11), 800 adult agents, 4,000 boys under these agents, and 160 helpers in the main circulation department. The "vast majority" of this workforce handled only the *News*, which claimed 65 percent of total newspaper sales in the city and suburbs. If this ratio holds, then the other newspapers sharing the remaining 35 percent of the market required another 2,000 boys. Altogether, Indianapolis, the twenty-first-largest city in the country, with a population of 275,000, relied on 8,000 youths to disseminate the news. Child labor still greased the gears of mass circulation journalism.[7]

The average age of newsboys fell during the war in all parts of the country. Most newsboys in Des Moines, Iowa, a city of 100,000, were 12 and under in 1916, while the number of teenagers dwindled. Minimum-age laws remained in place in many cities, but authorities relaxed enforcement because of labor shortages. Prosecuted violations of New York's newsboy law dropped 73 percent, from 5,764 in 1916–17 to 1,557 in 1918. Truant officer E. H. Sullivan said his office remained vigilant but there was a "free masonry" among the boys to get badges through forged signatures and aliases. Such fraud declined the next year as the Board of Education reduced the number of officers on "newsboy duty" from eight to two.[8]

Kentucky and Oklahoma also reported decreases in the ages of newsboys. Those in Louisville formerly had to be at least 14 to get a street-trading license, but during the war 10- and 11-year-olds were routinely permitted to sell papers. In 1917 Lewis Hine counted several hundred newsboys 5 years old and up in Oklahoma City. He asked one truant, 9-year-old Charlie Scott, why he wasn't in school, and the boy answered, "I dunno where the school is."[9]

War production itself stimulated newspaper sales. The opening of army cantonments and government nitrate plants in Anniston and Florence, Alabama, for example, doubled the population and created a demand for out-of-town papers. "In Anniston, boys of 8 and 10 get up at 4 in the morning, get their papers at the station and go out to the camp with them," reported the NCLC in 1918. "They come back to town between 8 and 9 and many do not go to school but remain on the streets selling during school hours." The problem in Florence was "almost as acute," but little could be done since Alabama's street trading law applied only to cities with populations greater than 25,000. As a result, fewer than half of Anniston's newsboys would be promoted in subsequent school years. Truancy was also rife in the capital; public schools in Montgomery now served as adjuncts, not impediments, to news peddling. Circulation managers would phone up principals to inform them that a noon extra was coming out, and all the newsboys would be dismissed. Such arrangements were not unique to Alabama or the news trade, as many states relaxed compulsory education laws to allow the hiring of students on farms and in munitions factories to meet wartime emergencies.[10]

Night work remained a common if officially proscribed practice among newsboys. In January 1914, New York City truant officers rounded up more than eighty boys selling papers after hours and fined their parents. New York was one of thirty states that regulated child street trading by 1915, but only one of twelve that prohibited children from peddling after 8:00 or 9:00 p.m. Illinois law was silent on the subject, but Chicago assigned policewomen to keep kids off the streets at night. Washington, DC, had a 10:00 p.m. curfew for young hawkers, as did East St. Louis, Illinois, yet enforcement was sporadic. Ultimately, even nighttime bowed to the god of war, as the most effective curb on night work was the adoption of Daylight Saving Time as an energy-saving measure in April 1918. Newsboys could be heard over the next seven months crying their final editions while the sun was still shining.[11]

Children of immigrants continued to dominate the trade. They accounted for 75 to 80 percent of newsboys in New York; Kansas City; Seattle; Cincinnati; Omaha; Newark and Paterson, New Jersey; Wilkes-Barre, Pennsylvania; and all

Connecticut cities. The largest ethnic groups were Italians or Russians. Many newsboys were but a generation removed from the belligerent nations. Yet the war reinforced their identity as Americans first and ethnics second. Hartford newsboy Joseph Mirman, a Russian immigrant, told the *Courant* in 1918 that he joined the army out of a sense of duty to the country that gave him freedom, citizenship, and an education.[12]

Ironically, when the war broke out many schools forbade mention of it or the teaching of European geography, for fear of offending immigrant children. Newsboys learned more about the war on the street than in school. Even after the United States entered the war, the press took a leading role in educating youth and instilling patriotism. In 1918 the *Pasadena Star News* published "The Great War," a lesson plan for city high schools, while New York newspapers used National Anthem Day (September 14) to teach newsboys "The Star-Spangled Banner."[13]

African American newsboys were also children of migration. In 1917 blacks numbered 30,000 in Cincinnati, or about 8 percent of the population, and 325 (or 8 percent) of its 2,600 newsboys. Their representation among newsboys would be even greater, said one community leader, if not for better-paying jobs. Another explained that Negroes were "not in the whirl of things" compared to whites. In Baltimore, by contrast, 250 blacks accounted for 12 percent of the city's newsboys. They were considered the worst violators of Maryland's street trading laws because many were new to the state and unfamiliar with its laws. Most came from rural Virginia and North Carolina, part of the Great Migration, in which half a million southern blacks moved north beginning in 1915–16 in search of greater opportunity. Many boys helped their families make this transition by peddling papers.[14]

Labor was in such short supply during the war that girls were welcomed into the news trade, especially in smaller cities. Newsgirls were hardly more visible in Baltimore, but they were 17 percent of carriers in western Maryland. Restrictions remained formidable in many places; street trading laws allowed 10-, 12-, or 14-year-old boys to obtain permits but required girls to be 16 or 18. Lewis Hine found no newsgirls in Oklahoma in 1917, but he attributed their absence to custom rather than law enforcement, which was nonexistent. Some newspapermen preferred girls to boys. The editor of the *Burlington Banner* in Vermont told Hine he wished he had more girls on the streets, as "they are more honest than the boys generally." Circulators at the *Seattle Star* praised the dependability of their "beskirted delivery girls," while a reporter on the *Lexington Herald* in Kentucky defended carrier work as "a healthful and invigorating practice" for girls. As in other industries disrupted by the war, some workers resented the incursion of females in a traditionally male-dominated occupation. "It ain't right for girls to sell papers," railed a newsboy in Covington, Kentucky. "They get tough and heaps o' things." The *Syracuse Herald*'s circulation manager assured the public that after the war "the girls will go back to home life where they belong by temperament, by nature, and by physique."[15]*

Junior Breadwinners

While wages increased steadily in many industries because of the revived economy, newsboys' incomes spiked but then flattened out. In 1914, the year Henry Ford introduced the Five Dollar Day to reduce worker turnover and prevent unionization, the typical newsboy earned from 25¢ to 30¢ a day for a few hours' work, or about $2 a week, according to sociologist George B. Mangold, while a rare few earned as much as $10 a week. Baltimore newsboys fit this average; many reported their customers bought two or three editions when they had previously bought one. "This has increased their earnings and has decreased begging and gambling among newsboys," reported a state inspector. "Industrious boys attending strictly to business," she said, earned from $2.50 to $5 a week selling papers out of school hours, Saturdays and holidays. Those selling full-time earned from $6 to $9 per week. Grown-up criers such as Mike Barto of Omaha tended to do much better. "A good one would average $40 and up every week until the time America got in," he said. "From our entry into the fray the hustler that didn't clear $50 a week and better was the exception."[16]

Nine-year-old Nick Zades of Springfield, Massachusetts, registered at the low end of the scale, averaging 35¢ a day or $2.45 a week in 1917. But he supplemented his income by shining shoes, mopping floors, selling peanuts, and toting bags. "The extra money at the railroad station was hard earned," he recalled, "since the Red Caps, employed by the railroad companies, would 'shoo' me off the property. However, there were some days when they seemed to understand the problems some of the newsboys had—that of being the main support of our families—and allowed us to carry luggage at the railroad main entrance." Zades's father, an immigrant from Smyrna, was a sign painter who had injured his back in a fall and had trouble earning grocery money, paying the $8 weekly rent, and keeping the gas meter supplied with quarters. Nick was the eldest son, and his earnings were critical to the family's survival. His father

* Labor shortages also hampered the news trade in England, causing "a regular famine in boys" by spring 1915. The railway news stall giant W. H. Smith replaced them with girls, who achieved near parity with the boys and forced a name change of its employee publication to *The Newsgirl and Newsboy*. Smith and many English papers organized "round servers" into uniformed Boy Scout and Girl Guide troops. *The Newsboy*, No. 5, Mar. 1915; Edgar Wallace, "Smith's," *Town Topics*, Aug. 7, 1915; folios 87 and 88 of scrapbook, W. H. Smith Archives, University of Reading.

closely monitored his activities, advising him to "keep it simple, focus on school and one job, be honest, do not be greedy." Nick never changed jobs without consulting his father.[17]

The Zades family's reliance on Nick's earnings was not unusual: working children accounted for 23 percent of total family income in 1917–19, according to a Department of Labor survey. This average rose considerably in households like the Zadeses', where a father was absent or out of work. Another such family was the Meyners of Paterson, New Jersey. Bob Meyner was 10 years old in 1918 when his father, a labor organizer, was blacklisted from the silk mills. Meyner became what he called the "junior breadwinner," delivering morning and evening newspapers for 75¢ a week. His boss promoted him to a $3-a-week downtown route, which Meyner later bought for $25. He also paid $10 for the right to sell papers on a downtown corner. Together, the route and corner netted him $20 a week. When his family left Paterson in 1922, Meyner, the future governor of New Jersey, sold the two "properties" for $96.[18]

Newsboys also took advantage of a wartime sales tax and penny shortage by selling their coppers to stores and theaters at the rate of ninety-five for a dollar. On the downside, the proliferation of coin-operated newsracks from Connecticut to Colorado cut into their earnings. One newsagent-inventor promoted his model as a surefire way to overcome boy labor shortages during the school year and to frustrate the cheats who read from the old-style "honor racks" without paying. The new machines displayed part of the front page, accommodated papers of different prices, and automatically returned slugs. They worked in all kinds of weather and could be moved where needed. "One boy can attend from fifteen to twenty machines and the papers are delivered clean and with edges unworn," reported the *Wall Street Journal*.[19]

As in the 1890s, real newsboys resisted such progress. In Hartford a hundred members of the Newsboys' Protective Association met in June 1917 and voted to strike if the *Hartford Times* did not cease its experiment with "automatic paper-selling boxes." The main speaker was a "man-sized 'newsboy'" who insisted that the boxes promised to increase publishers' profits, not customers' convenience. He pointed out that they accepted nickels for the 3¢ paper but did not give change, and warned that they would spread throughout the city if the boys did not act now. He was right. One manufacturer advertised his product as "an understudy for the newsboy . . . that will take his place when sick or when drastic laws prohibit his further employment."[20]

Most newspaper owners and managers still knew that boys could do things that machines couldn't, including contribute to war-related charities, promote Liberty Loan drives, and generate heaps of good publicity (Plate 25). Newsboys in Pittsburgh, who won their own strike over a price hike in December 1916, donated a day's earnings to the Red Cross War Fund in 1917 and 1918 when

East End, West Side, and downtown hawkers vied for bragging rights as the city's most generous givers. Likewise, railroad newsboys from Sausalito, California, to Montclair, New Jersey, did their bit by organizing Liberty Loan parades or letting "society girls" sell papers for a day to benefit the Red Cross. The girls at the Lackawanna station in Montclair handled all the New York papers except William Randolph Hearst's antiwar *New York American* and raised $270. Meantime, newsboy bands in Toledo and Indianapolis added George M. Cohan's "Over There" to their repertoires and played benefits for the Red Cross. Several Indianapolis alumni became regimental bandleaders in the army. One of the busiest newsboy bands was the Grand Rapids News Jackies Drum and Bugle Corp, so called because their uniforms resembled those of sailors, or Jack Tars (Figure 12.2). Sponsored by the *Grand Rapids News*, the band consisted of eighty-six musicians between the ages of 8 and 13. They toured the state in a special train to aid naval recruitment and Liberty Loan sales.[21]

Newsboys also joined movie stars Douglas Fairbanks and Mary Pickford in urging the public to buy war bonds. The boys usually made their pitches in movie theaters before the show. Speaking on behalf of his pals, one youngster who had "not yet shed his milk teeth" told an audience in New York, "Every man of us

Figure 12.2. Members of the Grand Rapids News Jackies Drum and Bugle Corps, ca. 1918, directed by 10-year-old drum major Eugene Fisher (far left) and bandleader Andy Mouw (far right). Courtesy of Grand Rapids Public Museum. Accession No. 1986.38.4.

engaged in selling these bonds in this theater tonight has himself bought a bond. We are paying for them at a dollar a month. We are asking you to do the same." In Baltimore, some boys declared that their main reason for applying for street trading licenses was to buy Liberty Bonds or Thrift Stamps. Other newsboys regularly carried flags or offered special terms to servicemen; one Hartford boy placed a large sign over his pile of papers announcing free copies for all men in uniform.[22]

"Noodles" Fagan, "King of the Newsboys," also devoted himself to war work. He put on shows in army camps and cantonments throughout the United States under the auspices of the Red Cross, and raised hundreds of thousands of dollars in Liberty Loan and War Savings Stamp drives. He addressed about three million newsboys a year and was recognized by President Wilson as "an evangelist to the newsboys in patriotic appeals."[23]

While individual newsboys contributed liberally to bond drives, their campaigns enjoyed the support of newspapers bent on improving their image and escaping government regulation. Boston circulation managers organized the Liberty Loan Newsboys' Association in 1917 to coordinate their collection efforts. With office space and staff provided by the *Boston Transcript* and $5,000 in seed money from the *Boston Record*, the association held rallies that raised more than $800,000 in donations during the war. The group later changed its name to the Roosevelt Newsboys' Association as a tribute to the former president, who died unexpectedly at his Long Island home in January 1919 at the age of 60.* The association held regular meetings and issued a monthly magazine, *Newsboy World*, loaded with motivational stories. Yet the group's chief accomplishment, said founder Edward Keevin, was defeating a Massachusetts bill that would have prevented boys from distributing papers after 6:30 p.m.[24]

In the Trenches of Reform

World War I represented a continuation of progressivism in its idealistic aims and efficient marshaling of the nation's human and industrial resources. It created a climate favorable to the US Children's Bureau's efforts to improve the health of mothers and children, especially after almost one-third of potential selectees were found unfit for military service. Wisconsin's "crippled newsboy legislator," Thomas Mahon, introduced a pioneer minimum wage bill in 1918

---

* As letters of condolences came pouring in from around the world and heads of state assembled for his funeral in Oyster Bay, two New York newsboys were heard to say, "Well, he is dead, and now I can never vote for him." "Naw," replied the other, "but you can be like him, can't you." "Eminent Men In All Walks Praise Roosevelt," *New York Times*, Oct. 26, 1919, 31.

developed with labor economist John R. Commons. "I am pretty sure it will be good enough to serve as a model for every state in the Union," said Mahon. But the war ultimately weakened the resolve and influence of those committed to protecting workers and ending child labor.[25]

The first to stray from the cause was Denver journalist George Creel, coauthor of the 1914 exposé *Children in Bondage*. In their book, Creel, poet Edwin Markham, and judge Ben Lindsey denounced child news peddling as an "infernal training for crime" in the "black-letter college of the street." Once the war broke out Creel transferred his considerable talents as a propagandist to President Wilson's Committee on Public Information (CPI). Creel recruited artists, photographers, and advertising men he knew from his newspaper and reform days to serve gratis in the CPI's Division of Pictorial Publicity. The committee used newspapers, movies, billboards, celebrities, and fast-talking "Four-Minute Men" to drum up support for the Allies. It also planted false stories about German atrocities, U-boat attacks, and spy rings, and quashed accurate stories as threats to national security. The day Congress declared war, for example, censors ordered the *Milwaukee Free Press* to kill an article outlining the plan for conscription. Editors took a chisel to the stereotype plate since there was no time to remake it. Newsboys waved copies that day containing a half column of meaningless hieroglyphics on the front page.[26]

Creel had been preparing the ground for a military draft since May 1916, when he argued in *Century Magazine* that compulsory military service would strengthen the moral fiber of American youth and develop their sense of nationalism over individualism. The onetime foe of child labor urged readers to think of conscription as an extension of compulsory education. Wilson instituted a draft three weeks after declaring war. It required the registration of all men between 21 and 30 years old (later expanded to those between 18 and 45) and provided a big payday for newsboys whose papers carried the registration numbers of those selected by lottery. Wall Street hawkers sold a record number of lottery extras; no sooner would a boy appear with papers containing the first thousand numbers than another would show up with an edition proclaiming 1,500 numbers. Newsboys commanded premium prices for these papers. When the 1¢ *New York Times* printed the names of all conscripts in the city, boys sold copies for a nickel in the morning and not less than 2¢ in the afternoon.[27]

Meanwhile, many of Creel's old comrades in the child labor reform movement were silenced. Muckrakers William Hard and Scott Nearing denounced the war, suffered censorship, and were imprisoned under the Espionage Act. Judge Lindsey supported the war, as did John Spargo and Upton Sinclair, who later regretted it. Settlement house founders Jane Addams, Florence Kelley, Grace Abbott, and Lillian Wald formed the Woman's Peace Party in 1915 and were stalked by charges of disloyalty. Wald led a march of twelve hundred women down New York's Fifth Avenue in August 1914 and hosted a peace conference, but once the United States entered the war she offered her house as headquarters for the draft board. "Many of our boys became officers, and were reported to have done good work," she said. But the Henry Street Settlement never regained its prewar prominence in national politics. Addams assisted with relief efforts in Europe but continued to agitate for peace, winning the Nobel Peace Prize in 1931.[28]

Even Lewis Hine suspended his ten-year campaign against child news peddling. Between 1914 and 1917 he documented newsboy conditions all across the country on behalf of the National Child Labor Committee, but failure to secure a lasting federal child labor law, coupled with a pay cut, undermined his faith in reform work. "I have to sit down, every so often and give myself a spiritual antiseptic," he confided to a friend. "Sometimes I still have grave doubts about it all. There is need for this kind of detective work and it is a good cause, but it is not always easy to be sure that it is all necessary." The war soon stirred Hine's creative juices. He captured the camaraderie of young recruits in a military training camp in a photo essay for *Everybody's Magazine*, and in May 1918 shipped out himself, at age 44, in full uniform as a captain in the American Red Cross. His assignment was to document relief efforts in Europe. Unable to shake old habits, he photographed several *crieurs des journaux* in France and Belgium, but he depicted them as resilient survivors, not exploited victims.[29]

Progressives continued to fight the good fight in California. In 1917 state senator Henry Lyon of East Los Angeles introduced an amendment to prohibit boys under 14 and girls under 18 from street trading in cities with populations over 23,000. The proposal enjoyed support from the Juvenile Protection Association of San Francisco, the California State Federation of Labor, and scores of women's clubs, but opposition from the *Los Angeles Times*. The *Times* denounced the bill as "aristocratic legislation" whose "lady proponents" did not appreciate what it was like to lack money for food, fuel, and medicine. It said the law would take bread out of the mouths of babes, interfere with parental authority, violate children's right to work, and lead them to "idleness or worse." Harry Chandler's anti-labor organ insisted that it had no financial interest in the question since adults distributed most of its copies. Yet the paper sent newsboy lobbyists to Sacramento and sponsored mass meetings where newsboys and their mothers tearfully testified to the importance of their earnings. Such a bill might be needed in the urban jungles of New York or Chicago, said one, but not in the "great open-air State of California." The bill lost by a vote of 21 to 16 two days before Congress declared war.[30]*

---

* Organized labor and the "moral uplift lobby" reunited in 1919 to back the "antinewsboys' bill." Sponsored by Alameda County assemblyman Edgar S. Hurley, the bill banned the sale or delivery of

Juvenile delinquency emerged as the most pressing child welfare issue of the war. Offenses by kids shot up not just in the United States but also in Canada, England, France, Italy, Germany, Hungary, and Russia, with officials reporting 34 to 56 percent increases. Social workers in these countries attributed the breakdown to the sudden release of thousands of children from school discipline to the relative freedom of wage earning. They cited the absence of fathers (who were at the front) and mothers (who were in the workforce), the depletion of the ranks of police officers and settlement workers, and children's vulnerability to the aggressive "war spirit" in the air.[31] Their American counterparts also observed greater "excitement and restlessness" among boys but were baffled by the uptick in delinquency because job opportunities, Scout troops, and other youth groups were abundant, and most delinquents came from families not fractured by the war.[32] Stanford University psychologist Lewis M. Terman theorized that young people had more energy as a result of better wages and nourishment and more opportunities to misuse that energy. He said their misconduct might also reflect the "psychical contagion" of the moral chaos in Europe. As one minister put it, "The frequent accounts and vivid enactments of scenes of carnage, destruction of property, life and a disregard for individual rights has had a tendency to inflame juvenile minds to acts of destruction and violence bordering on criminality."[33]

America's newsboys were more familiar with the reported horrors of war than most other boys. Child labor reformers argued that news peddling was a primary cause of delinquency. Such claims were not new. A 1911 US Department of Labor survey of juvenile courts and reform schools indicated that more than half of all boys between 6 and 16 years old who were brought before the courts were engaged in some form of street work, and most of them were newsboys. Their offense ranged from trivial to serious, with recidivists outnumbering first-time offenders.[34] This pattern persisted as the war raged and worsened after the United States entered the war. Juvenile delinquency shot up 13 percent in New York, 21 percent in Cincinnati, and 54 percent in Chicago, as measured by probation records. A National Child Labor Committee study of the links between child labor and juvenile delinquency in Manhattan in 1917 found that working children contributed *"four times their share* to the ranks of juvenile delinquency" compared with nonworking children, and that newsboys alone accounted for 24 percent of delinquent activity. Newsboys in Cincinnati were 12 percent of all 10- to 16-year-old boys in the city, but 28 percent of its delinquents. In most cases newsboys' only crime was selling papers after hours or without a license or defending themselves against imported thugs during a 1916 circulation war

newspapers by boys under 14 during the day and under 18 at night. All twenty-eight ex-newsboys in the state assembly opposed the bill. See "Theory and Practice Clash over Newsboys," *Los Angeles Times*, Mar. 18, 1919, 17.

between the *Post* and the *Times-Star*. More than half of the adult circulators on
the two papers had extensive criminal records. Other common newsboy offenses
were begging, gambling, disorderly conduct, and incorrigibility. Less common
were arson, assault, drug selling, drunkenness, forgery, sexual activity, and theft.
Backing up these local studies, the US Children's Bureau found increases in juvenile crime in twenty cities in 1918.[35]

Was news peddling a stepping-stone to the penitentiary? Those closest to
the boys had no doubt. New York City truant officer Owen Martin said street
hawking threw boys into contact with unsavory characters insofar as their work
led them to frequent saloons, dance halls, and poolrooms where prostitutes
worked. Writing confidentially to his superiors in 1917, Martin said many pool
hall proprietors became newsagents on the side, employing boys between 12
and 20 years old, "usually a type which belongs to street gangs." Many of these
boys worked without permits. "Hence such individuals have little respect for
law . . . and are a source of contamination to the younger boys."[36] In addition,
the news trade led boys to hang around on street corners and subways stations,
awaiting an opportunity to pick pockets and ply other trades of the underworld.
Martin acknowledged that they often received protection from the adults who
owned or worked in these places and acted as lookouts or took care of "swag."
"In the course of a few years," he said, "many of our newsboys become members
of the long fingered fraternity." Street gambling was also a problem in that bigger
boys fleeced smaller ones by enticing them to pitch pennies and shoot craps.
"Then he is told he must make enough money 'to cash in for his stock.' As a result
he either stays out late or takes to begging—very often both."[37]*

On the contrary, the war may have done more to instill patriotism than encourage delinquency among newsboys. Those in Chicago, for example, proudly
marched in the city's colossal Labor Day parade in 1918, in which labor unions
"dedicated themselves anew to the job of winning the war." Like all schoolchildren,
newsboys responded to the United States Food Administration's propaganda
campaign to conserve meat, wheat, and other food for the Allies; many children
signed pledges to clean their plates and not snack between meals.[38]

---

* News peddling was the most common juvenile street trade, but junk dealing took off during the
war due to increased demand for paper, rags, bottles, and scrap metal. "It is a stepping-stone to burglary," said a Chicago reform school official, who estimated that 90 percent of the delinquents in his
charge had dealt in junk. Investigators found that nearly nine out of ten scavengers were between 14
and 16 years old, mainly "colored" boys and those of the "foreign type," especially Poles, Irish, Italian,
Germans, and Bohemians. Many cities prohibited the purchase of junk from minors without parental
permission and banned junk shops within four hundred feet of schools, but the traffic in castoff and
claimed items continued to bolster a $2 billion a year industry. See Albert E. Webster, *Junk Dealing
and Juvenile Delinquency* (Chicago: Juvenile Protective Association, 1920), 5–6, 10, 12–13, 24–25.

Yet the public's tolerance for juvenile misbehavior lessened during the war. Newsboys now got into serious trouble for the once trivial scam of hawking fake extras. Los Angeles newsies faced fines and arrest for crying their 6:00 p.m. editions at 10:00 p.m., causing people to come out onto their porches in their nightclothes and buy up papers that had nothing new in them. A Denver paper perpetrated a similar scam in Cheyenne, sending boys across state lines to hawk old extras with a new cry: "German Army Wiped Out!" The *New York Herald* could print "British Navy Sunk!" or "Tourist Saw Soldier with Bagful of Ears!" but those who cried such headlines faced charges of petty larceny or disturbing the peace. In Philadelphia, Abraham Krup, 23, was jailed for ten days for selling papers that purportedly described the sinking of an American battleship. The magistrate said the sentence was the beginning of a "crusade" against anyone who dared "mulct and terrify people with fake reports of disasters in the army and navy." A Justice Department investigator in Cleveland warned that in extreme cases lying newsboys might be prosecuted under the Espionage Act.[39]

Wartime newsboys in Chicago and Ogden, Utah, also came before authorities for counterfeiting coins and blowing newspaper-issued whistles early in the morning. To stem the tide of newsboy delinquency, women's groups and fraternal organizations started to work more closely with law enforcement and newspaper personnel. In the summer of 1918, the Consumers' League of Ohio and the Cleveland Committee on Women and Children in Industry of the Council of National Defense hired a policewoman to enforce the local street trading ordinance. Her duties were to issue warnings, make arrests, take second offenders to the juvenile court, and cooperate with the truancy department of the Board of Education. The Consumers' League justified this intervention by saying each newsboy was a "respectable citizen of the commonwealth" whose "spiritual, mental, and physical welfare" had to be conserved. In Fort Wayne, Indiana, the local Rotary Club "adopted" the city's eighty newsboys to "keep the little fellows constantly in sight to help make them better men than they could otherwise hope to be." And in St. Paul, Minnesota, the Women's Welfare League revived the local newsboys' club, saying that its dissolution had increased delinquency.[40]

On the national front, the Children's Bureau succeeded in having 1918 declared the "Year of the Child." President Wilson allocated $150,000 from a special wartime defense fund to launch back-to-school, recreation, and hygiene drives. The bureau also supported legislation to extend aid to the families of servicemen and strengthen enforcement of child labor laws.[41]

While officials across the country struggled to find the appropriate means to deal with delinquent street traders, newsboys in Detroit policed themselves. In 1914 the American Federation of Labor urged all newsboys to organize unions, and the Detroit boys were among the first to respond. They formed a union recognized by the Detroit Federation of Labor and waged a successful strike

over the right to return unsold papers. The Newsboys Union then passed a resolution to keep all boys under 16 off the streets after 9:00 p.m. Its aim was not
so much to safeguard their moral welfare as to eliminate competition. Union
officials asked the police commissioner for help but were put off until the next
election. They pleaded with local newspapers to stop selling papers to underage
boys at night but were told to mind their own business. So the union organized a
"free-lance squad" to enforce the resolution. In one night they cleared the streets
of most of the younger boys, though it took "a good many small fights to do it."
The Newsboys Union later approved a street trades law drafted by the National
Child Labor Committee for Detroit, but the city failed to pass it.[42]

Memphis newsboys became pioneers of organized labor in Tennessee by
forming a union in November 1916 that included more than half the newsies in
the city. But underage peddlers continued to be a problem. In 1918 investigators
in Memphis, Chattanooga, Nashville, and Knoxville found "large numbers" of
boys under 14—"many as young as 10, 9, and often 6 years—employed in selling newspapers." Reformers attributed the influx to child labor laws that forced
youngsters out of factories.[43]

At the same time a subtle semantic shift was taking place that weakened all
efforts to curtail child street peddling. The newspaper industry and even some
academics began to refer to the sale and distribution of newspapers by children
not as work or commerce but as service or duty. One reflection of this trend is
the 1917 book *Newsboy Service: A Study in Educational and Vocational Guidance*
by Anna Y. Reed, PhD. Based on interviews with more than thirteen hundred
Seattle newsboys, surveys of their teachers, and direct observation of the boys
at work, *Newsboy Service* sought an objective picture of the trade unwarped
by the biased pronouncements of the industry and "moral propaganda" of
reformers. Reed found that Seattle newsboys attended school more regularly
than other boys. Although they were slightly "retarded" in their studies, this
condition was not necessarily attributable to their jobs. Reed rejected the idea
that news peddling was a "blind alley" occupation, mentioning several boys
who had used the work as a stepping-stone to permanent jobs in the industry.
Most prominent was Arthur Heymanson, "Seattle's Newsboy Capitalist," who
started selling papers in 1905 at age 7. By 1917 he "owned" the intersection
of Madison Street and 2nd Avenue—each corner worth between $750 and
$1,000. He netted $50 to $150 a week and acquired a "handsome limousine"
that he operated as a taxi. Even if Heymanson's success was extraordinary, said
Reed, "there is always a future, provided there be ability to see it and perseverance to pursue it."[44]

Seattle had no street trading law in 1917. Reed acknowledged that some regulation was needed to keep boys under 14 off the streets at night. But overall she
endorsed the value of "newsboy service" and recommended that schools use it

as vocational training. She said newspaper work could play an important role in "continuation schools," which allowed youths more flexibility to work while earning their high school diplomas. Reed's recommendations disappointed progressives who had hoped to see child street trading abolished.[45]

The expansion of newsboy welfare and charity schemes contributed to the rehabilitation of news peddling during the war years. Employers in many industries responded to labor shortages by establishing personnel departments and programs, but newspaper publishers led the way. They had to halt newsboy periodicals such as *The Hustler* in Portland, Oregon, due to the government's call for the elimination of nonessential publications, but they continued to sponsor banquets, excursions, and summer camps and to promote the distribution of milk, ice, and medicine in poor neighborhoods. The *Baltimore Sun* established a social department headed by Miss Hulda Lael Beurriere, who became known as the "Big Sister of the Newsboys." She supervised a library and helped the boys improve their manners, morals, and safety. "The law is your friend," she would say, and "it doesn't pay to get killed." A circulation manager in Richmond, Virginia, visited the homes of his carriers to praise parents for their children's good upbringing and strong sense of responsibility.[46]

The most successful child welfare organization to emerge during the war was Father Flanagan's Boys Town, founded in Omaha, Nebraska, in 1917. Two homeless newsboys and three wards of the court were the first residents. Flanagan received no aid from the Catholic Church, but he solicited private donations and sent his charges out to sell papers—his own *Boys Home Journal* as well as the *Omaha Bee, World Herald*, and *Daily News*. Boys Town became one of the largest newspaper delivery depots in the city and the subject of an Academy Award–winning movie in 1938.[47]

Another group, the Old Newsboys' Foundation, got its start in the miserable recession winter of 1914–15 when *Detroit News* artist Burt Thomas drew a cartoon to promote its annual Christmas giveaway. Entitled "The Boy He Used to Be" (Figure 12.3), it pictured the ghost of a ragged newsboy walking hand in hand with a gentleman carrying a basket of gifts. Detroit banker and US customs collector James J. Brady, a former newsboy, was so touched that he organized his old newsboy buddies and members of the Detroit Newsboys Association to peddle papers for a day to raise money for poor children in the city. Seventy-eight businessmen took part in the event and raised more than $400. The oldest was 82-year-old hardware merchant W. K. Bartholomew. "I'm going to sell at Fort and Griswold," he informed the others. "That's my old corner, and I'd like to see any of you fellows get it away from me." Chicago mayor Carter Harrison Jr., another grown-up newsie, then organized Old Newsboys' Day. One of the participants was Judge Kenesaw Mountain Landis, the first commissioner of baseball. From there, the charity spread to St. Louis, Toledo, Lansing, and other

THE BOY HE USED TO BE

Figure 12.3. Burt Thomas, "The Boy He Used to Be," *Detroit News*, Dec. 10, 1914. Author's collection.

midwestern cities. Intentionally or not, it reinforced the notion that peddling papers was a path to success.[48]

The Valor Roll

As with previous conflicts, World War I presented new opportunities to honor newsboys, particularly those who joined the armed forces. The *Boston Globe* made a minor celebrity of Fifekey Bernstein, the first Boston newsboy to enlist in the war. The *Chicago Tribune* placed former Loop news crier Joe Bagnuola on its "valor roll" after he distinguished himself as a battlefield messenger. And the *Hartford Courant* lauded the fighting spirit of Nat Fierberg, who joined the army to avenge the death of his brother Sam, a former Main Street hawker. Sam had enlisted at age 14 and died at Seicheprey, the first major action involving US ground troops. The *Courant* commended the boys who joined up "to make news instead of sell it." Newspapers also applauded newsboys who demanded to see the draft cards of suspected "slackers," who taunted those who drove on gasless days as "Hun lovers," or, in the case of a 10-year-old in New York, who gut-punched a suspected German spy as he was being led through Penn Station under armed guard.[49]

Newsboys were anything but slackers. At least a dozen *Fort Worth Star-Telegram* newsies became soldiers and corresponded with the women who doled out their papers. Newsboys' homes also supplied raw recruits. Father Dunne's home in St. Louis sent 126 residents into the armed forces, five of whom were killed in action. The Brace Memorial Home in New York contributed 2,890 current or past residents to the military. Its superintendent signed enlistment papers for 1,600 boys. Fifteen were killed in action and twenty were wounded. The first to fall, at Château-Thierry, was George "Blackie" Kammers. Others included "Libby" Labenthal, a pitcher on the home's baseball team, and Peter Cawley and Jackie Levine, who starred in the home's minstrel shows. Their inch-long obituaries mention their affiliation with the Newsboys' Lodging House, just as those of Ivy Leaguers mention their association with Harvard, Princeton, or Dartmouth. A service flag with 2,520 stars representing the number of past residents then in service was unfurled in front of the home in November 1917. Ex-newsboy Al Smith, president of the Board of Aldermen, told the assembly, "There are only two classes of people in the country today—the man who is with his country and the man who is against it. There will be two classes of people in this country after the war—the man who did his bit and the man who did not."[50]

Eighteen was the minimum age for induction into the army, yet boys like Sam Fierberg sometimes lied their way into service. The foremost example is Albert Edward Scott, a newsboy from Brookline, Massachusetts, who enlisted in July 1917 at age 15 and became a machine gunner in the 101st Regiment. The youngest American casualty of the war, "Scotty" died defending a road near Eipedes, killing thirty "boches" before a sniper got him. He received a hero's burial in France and posthumous honors at home. An oil painting by Gayle Porter Hoskins showing four soldiers gathered around Scotty's body in the woods was one of the *Ladies' Home Journal*'s "souvenir pictures of the Great War" (Plate 26). The Roosevelt Newsboys' Association raised funds to install a bronze tablet and bas-relief sculpture of the painting in Brookline's town hall. Vice President Calvin Coolidge ordered two navy destroyers to convey a three-hundred-piece newsboy band from New York for the dedication ceremony, attended by former secretary of state William Jennings Bryan. Scotty was eulogized as a "steady, self-reliant, manly American boy" who "did his duty in war and in peace, in France and in Brookline." On a visit to Boston, Marshal Ferdinand Foch, supreme commander of the Allied armies, left a wreath of roses bearing the French tricolor to be placed on Scotty's tablet. The next year the corner of Chambers and Spring Streets in Boston was renamed Benjamin Rutstein Square after a popular West End newsboy killed in the Argonne in 1918. Thus did newsboys participate in the culture of commemoration that followed the war. Plaques, parades, paintings, wreath layings, and street dedications helped give meaning to the slaughter and replenish the wellsprings of nationalism.[51]

By far the most celebrated ex-newsboy war hero was Eddie Rickenbacker, America's "ace of aces," with twenty-six kills. Born in Columbus, Ohio, in 1890, he delivered the *Columbus Dispatch* as a child and attributed his later success to this work. "This first job was as important as any I ever had," he said in a ghostwritten autobiography. "It was my initiation into a man's world. Being a newsboy taught me the meaning of duty, and without a sense of duty a man is nothing. Like the other newsboys, in Columbus and all over the world, I delivered my papers in the dark, in the cold, in the rain, in the snow." As a role model, Rickenbacker felt obliged to sugarcoat his childhood. He actually started hawking the *Dispatch* at age 5, not 10, as claimed in the book, and spent his money on Bull Durham tobacco for cigarettes he learned to roll by hand. Leaving school at 13 after his father was murdered, he went to work in a glass factory to support his family. He held many jobs, often quitting for lower pay to work on automobiles. He was a champion racecar driver when the United States declared war on Germany. He enlisted in the army as a sergeant after arranging to become General George Pershing's chauffeur, but left that job, too, to fly. It is hard to overstate the romance of aviation during the war. Many boys who read about Rickenbacker's exploits imagined themselves as pilots. His celebrity, along with the production of toy planes and dogfight fiction, contributed to what one historian has called "the moral and intellectual mobilization of children." The spread of doughboy slang such as *pigsticker* (bayonet), *plaster* (bombard), and *newsboys* (planes that dropped propaganda leaflets) also brought kids closer to the action.[52]

Movies and songs about newsboy proliferated during the period, and some directly addressed the theme of making the world safe for democracy. The silent film *Ginger, the Bride of Chateau Thierry,* follows two tenement sweethearts who are separated when Ginger is adopted by a judge. She befriends his son Bobby but stays true to newsboy Tim Mooney. Once grown up, the two men vie for her hand, but they call a truce when war is declared; they ship out to France, and Ginger follows with the Red Cross. When Tim is wounded, Bobby risks his life to carry him to a hospital where he dies in Ginger's arms, freeing her to marry Bobby. The movie, which includes actual scenes of trench combat, portrays the war as a great crusade unifying the classes. Striking the same note musically was the 1919 Tin Pan Alley flag-waver "I'd Rather Be a Newsboy in the USA than a Ruler in a Foreign Land" (Figure 12.4). One critic called it "pathetic patriotic piffle," but it got a smile from AEF commander Pershing when sung for him by a wounded Yank at Walter Reed Hospital.[53]

While British troops had access to the *Daily Mail* and other London papers distributed free at the back of the front, American soldiers in 1917 could obtain the "Army Edition" of the *Chicago Tribune*, which was published in Paris, airlifted to the trenches, and sold by French newsboys. The US Army paper, *Stars and Stripes*, appeared in February 1918. Printed on borrowed presses in Paris, the

Figure 12.4. Starmer, "I'd Rather Be a Newsboy in the U.S.A. than a Ruler in a Foreign Land," sheet music to Charles Kuhn, Jeff Branen, and Robert Kuhn's hit song of 1919. Author's collection.

eight-page weekly sold for 50 centimes. Its peak wartime circulation was 526,000. Newsboy-soldiers distributed it via trains, cars, and motorcycles. Its first carrier, "Li'l Dan'l" Sowers, overcame the icy blasts of the Haute-Marne region to sell a thousand copies of the first issue in the great quadrangle at Chaumont, France, headquarters of the AEF. He solicited corporals and generals alike, and was rewarded for his enterprise with free staff rations whenever he was in Paris. Another *Stars and Stripes* peddler, Corporal Pat Ryan, an ex-newsboy from Des Moines, sold a record twenty thousand copies one day in Paris and became the paper's circulation manager. He won the Croix de Guerre by braving German barrages and machine-gun fire to deliver orders. After the war, Ryan returned home like a modern-day Cincinnatus and resumed work at his old stand.[54]

A salty breed of newsboys specialized in serving naval personnel. Nearly every ship in the Pacific Fleet had its own newsboy who followed it from port to port, providing local and hometown papers to officers and enlisted men. Most of these youths were New Yorkers who had attached themselves to units stationed in Hampton Roads, Virginia, and then traveled west by train when the ships set out for San Diego. "These 'newsies' become the genuine friends of the sailors," reported the *San Francisco Chronicle*, and "familiar with affairs aboard ship." In addition to plying the gobs with newspapers, the boys posted letters, delivered messages, and acted as their agents ashore. In return, the seamen patronized them liberally, enabling the boys to make more money than ordinary newsies. The chief newsboy of the fleet was a disabled ex-sailor named "Pegg" Brown who had served the dreadnaught *Mississippi* since its launch in 1915.[55]

Best known was "Abe the Newsboy" Hollandersky. Born in Russia in 1887, he grew up in New London, Connecticut, where he supported his mother and blind father by peddling papers to sailors, and boxing on the side. He was named "Newsboy of the Navy" in 1906 after he sold a paper and took a playful poke at Theodore Roosevelt on board the presidential yacht. The title allowed him to supply naval vessels with papers. He "bumboated" around the world for years, staging sailor bouts and challenging local champs. He once wrestled a muzzled bear for $5 a minute. Although he weighed only 150 pounds, Abe became heavyweight champion of Central and South America in 1913. He claimed 1,309 bouts over a nineteen-year career, a record that appeared in the syndicated newspaper comic *Ripley's Believe It or Not*. A voyage through the Panama Canal in 1914 made him the first person to sell papers on two oceans the same day.[56]

One of the most devastating effects of the war was the influenza pandemic of 1918, which killed 650,000 Americans and 50 million people worldwide. The scourge pushed war news off the front pages and took its toll on many of the children and elderly who sold those papers. One casualty, "Mullen the newsboy," was a Chicago Loop vendor who gained notoriety after passage of the Seventeenth Amendment by vowing to run for the Senate and introduce legislation allowing indigent newsboys to live in old-soldiers' homes. Chicago newsies came under scrutiny as carriers of the disease because of their habit of spitting for good luck on every nickel earned. Newsies in Norwood, Massachusetts, had to put their money on a table for the manager to spray with a disinfectant before he'd touch it. In Harrisonburg, Virginia, the *Daily Independent* suspended publication after its entire workforce fell ill. Newspapers from Pueblo, Colorado, to Winnipeg, Manitoba, outfitted carriers with gauze masks to protect their health and alleviate subscribers' fears (Figure 12.5). The *Wichita Eagle* went further, offering its newsboys mittens, health insurance, and the services of a physician.[57]

To recruit more boys to their ranks and to profit from the vogue for all things military, newspaper publishers also began sponsoring Boy Scout troops. They printed membership coupons in their pages and urged boys over 12 to fill them out and return them to the paper's circulation manager. "The newsboys are just the kind of boys the scout movement should reach," explained an organizer for the *Cleveland Plain Dealer*. "These little fellows are ambitious. They are quick to grasp opportunities, and the training they would receive in the scout ranks would make better boys of them. Manliness, fairness in dealing with customers

Figure 12.5. "Business as usual for newsboys in Winnipeg, Manitoba." *Winnipeg Free Press* newsboys don germ masks during the 1918–19 influenza pandemic, which killed 824 people in the city and millions worldwide. Author's collection.

and more consideration for one another in the daily struggle for business in the city's streets would be taught these boys if they become scouts." Such appeals helped pushed Scout membership from 128,000 in 1914 to 462,000 in 1919. Newspaper sponsorship also made Scouting more accessible to working-class boys who could not afford uniforms.[58]

American newspaper publishers had taken a keen interest in the Scouting movement when it first arrived from England in 1910. Among its earliest proponents were William Boyce, Milton McRae, and William Randolph Hearst. Boyce was a charismatic entrepreneur and outdoorsman who owned two national weeklies, the *Saturday Blade* and the *Chicago Ledger*. He used 20,000 to 30,000 boys to sell them, and his training manual took the form of a comic book (Figure 12.6). Modeled after Pulitzer's *World* and the *New York Ledger*, Boyce boosted the appeal of his papers by running matrimonial ads and classifieds offering "baths and massage." Boyce said he met his first Boy Scout while lost in a London fog and was so impressed by him that he sought out the movement's founder, Sir Robert Baden-Powell, and received permission to establish a branch in the United States. Boyce did so in grand fashion, stopping in Washington to seek a congressional charter for the organization. In 1912, as one of four vice presidents of the Boy Scouts of America (BSA) and a member of its executive board, he agreed to underwrite its official magazine, *Boy's Life*, for three years. In 1915 he was permitted to organize isolated rural boys into the Lone Scouts

The best call is whatever interests the prospect most.

Figure 12.6. "The best call is whatever interests the prospect most." W. D. Boyce, *Secret of Selling Papers: A Moving Picture Book of How to Make Money Selling the Blade and Ledger* (Chicago, 1913), 18. Eckel Collection, Princeton University Library.

of America. He soon added *Lone Scout* magazine to his list of publications. The twenty-four-page weekly originally sold for 1¢ and contained articles, short stories, war news, and a coupon in every issue. Five coupons qualified readers for membership, but only one coupon was required if they agreed to become an "agent" and sell Boyce's papers. Boyce claimed 225,000 Lone Scout agents in 1918, and offered "War Work" medals for those who planted gardens, wrote to servicemen, and otherwise contributed to the war effort. His commercial exploitation of the Scouts led to strained relations with the BSA leadership. Revenue and recruitment plummeted in the postwar years, and in 1924 the now white-only Lone Scouts of America, with an actual membership of 65,000, merged with the Boy Scouts. Boyce ended his involvement with both organizations.[59]*

McRae, co-founder of the Cincinnati-based Scripps-McRae League of Newspapers and the United Press Associations, was one of the original vice presidents of the Boy Scouts in 1910 and served as its third national president in 1926. His support for scouting was genuine. Hearst, on the other hand, recognized the movement's usefulness to his business and political interests. In 1910 his chain launched the rival American Boy Scouts, which emphasized militarism over wood lore. Its members drilled with real rifles, and its leaders tried to instill anti-union beliefs, all of which worried YMCA officials and others trying to consolidate the various scouting movements. These leaders reached out to Boyce and Hearst. While Boyce saw the wisdom of joining forces, Hearst rebuffed all overtures. By the end of the year he cut all ties with the American Boy Scouts when it was embroiled in a financial scandal. He changed his group's name to the United States Boy Scouts and then, in 1917, to the American Cadets after the BSA finally secured a federal charter and exclusive use of the term "Scout." The reborn Cadets, along with such groups as the Boy Spies of America, was little more than a nativist organization devoted to harassing German Americans and others whom they deemed disloyal.[60]

The Cost of Dissent

While most newsboys tacitly participated in the manufacture of consent, some opposed the war or sided with the Central Powers. Opponents included native-born Quakers and pacifists who rejected all war on principle, and radicals who decried the war as a capitalist slaughterfest. Among those who advocated neutrality were German Americans, some of whom sympathized with the kaiser's

---

* In 1992 Boyce's grandson, William Boyce Mueller, co-founded Forgotten Scouts, a group devoted to ending the BSA's exclusion of gays. See Jay Mechling, *On My Honor: Boy Scouts and the Making of American Youth* (Chicago: University of Chicago Press, 2001), 211.

imperial aims; Irish Americans, who could not stomach an alliance with their English oppressors; and Jews, who felt the same way about tsarist Russia. Harry Golden could always unload copies of the *Jewish Daily Forward* by shouting "Russians retreat again!" even when they advanced. Golden got away with this ruse, but three boys in San Diego were arrested in February 1916 for crying the contents of the *American Independent*, a propaganda sheet founded by German American and Irish American isolationists.[61]

The war wasn't the only issue that polarized readers of ethnic newspapers. A strike by hawkers of the beloved *Forward* incited a riot in April 1916 at a mass meeting in New York organized by Emma Goldman in support of the McNamara brothers, who had been convicted of dynamiting the *Los Angeles Times* building in 1910. Some 2,500 people from eighty radical groups filled the Star Casino and listened to speeches for two hours in five languages, applauding and passing resolutions with extraordinary unanimity. But "brotherly love vanished," reported the *New York Times*, when Goldman introduced some of the striking newsboys. "The radicals, who had been basking in one another's friendship the minute before and calling one another 'comrade,' sprang to their feet and began to bark recriminations in the faces of belligerent neighbors," said the *Times*. Goldman cried for order, but the boys headed for the doors. Someone cut the lights, creating even more chaos. When the lights came back on, the strikers were brought back to the platform to state their grievances. Pandemonium broke out anew, however, when a husky voice demand that "the heads of the brats be bumped together."[62]

Though notoriously jingoistic, the most strident antiwar newspapers in the country were the seven dailies owned by Hearst. In 1914 he denounced the hostilities as a "war of kings" with no benefit to Americans. His news columns and editorials bore an anti-British, pro-German bias. That he published the German-language *New Yorker Deutsches Journal* raised further doubts about his loyalty. He was forced to shut down that paper in April 1918. Rival publishers continued to attack his positions, expose his ties to German businesses, and urge his prosecution under the Espionage Act, but the government could find no evidence of disloyalty.[63]

Defense clubs across the country urged readers, advertisers, and distributors to boycott the *American* and *Evening Journal* "on patriotic grounds." In August, twelve hundred Brooklyn dealers refused to sell the papers, followed by vendors in Manhattan, Queens, and Long Island; some also boycotted the Hearst magazines *Cosmopolitan*, *Good Housekeeping*, and *Harper's Bazaar*. Scores of local unions and trade councils endorsed the boycott. City councils from Mount Vernon, New York, to Berkeley, California, passed resolutions banning Hearst publications. In some towns, mobs burned "Wilhelm" Hearst in effigy and fed his papers into bonfires.[64]

Yet Hearst had his defenders, particularly among immigrants and pacifists. As one of Harry Golden's customers liked to say, "Hearst, Hearst. Hearst ain't the worst." Hearst's staunchest ally was the American News Company, which ignored cancellations and delivered his publications as usual. When bundles piled up, dealers complained to the War Industries Board about the waste of paper. Meanwhile, Hearst built his own distribution system; he outfitted men and boys in Brooklyn with American flag armbands and dispatched them to sell papers in the outlying areas. He also bribed boycotting newsagents to share their subscription lists.[65]

The crackdown on dissidents intensified in June 1917 with the passage of the Espionage Act, which made it a crime to "make or convey false reports or false statements with intent to interfere with the operation or success of the military or naval forces of the United States, or to promote the success of its enemies." Former Chicago newsboy Ralph Chaplin, editor of the IWW's *Solidarity*, served more than four years of a twenty-year sentence for violating the law. Later that year, the Trading with the Enemy Act empowered postal officials to secure translations of any foreign-language paper it deemed suspicious, which further burdened publishers and heightened the importance of street sales. The Sedition Act, passed the following year, made it illegal to "willfully utter, print, write, or publish any disloyal, profane, scurrilous or abusive language" about the American government, its flag, or military. Seventy-five papers either lost their mailing privileges or kept them by agreeing to print nothing more on the war. Hardest hit were radical dailies, such as the *New York Call* and the *Milwaukee Leader*, and German American newspapers, even though most rallied to the American cause. African American periodicals were also kept under surveillance. At the local level, town councils banned "enemy language" papers, including the venerable *New Yorker Staats-Zeitung* and Milwaukee's *Der Sonntagsbote*. In all, 225 of America's 1,350 foreign-language newspapers succumbed during the war.[66]

Despite the widespread equation of labor strife with treason, American workers engaged in more than six thousand strikes during the nineteen months of war. Newsboys in Butte, Montana, and Miami, Arizona, struck in June and July 1917, followed by their counterparts in New York, Minneapolis, and Seattle the next year. On January 26, 1918, the National Association of News Dealers and Stationers called a strike of all dealers and newsboys in greater New York to protest wartime austerity measures. "They left everything to the so-called circulation managers," said association president Jerry Lyons, "but they never consulted us. The newsboy is just as much a part of the newspaper outfit as the printers, the pressmen, the mailers or the stereotypers. They recognize these trades because they are organized, but they do not recognize us because we are not organized." Most newspapers in the city had doubled their retail price to 2¢, raised wholesale prices from 60¢ to $1.40 per hundred, and banned returns.

Dealers demanded the old wholesale rate of 60 percent and reinstitution of the return privilege. They replaced their usual cry of "Wha-d'ya'read?" with "Help the newsboys win their strike!" Strikers and "buckers"—transients hired to sell or give away the boycotted papers—clashed throughout the week. Strikers overturned delivery wagons and set fire to their papers or dumped them into the East River. Some four hundred messengers joined the strike on February 2 and talked of forming a union with the newsboys.[67]

During the first week of the strike, few New Yorkers could get their hands on any paper except the *Brooklyn Eagle* and the socialist *Call*, both of which continued to sell to retailers at half price. Public opinion favored the strikers against the "Plutes," or plutocrats, but it wasn't enough, as the *Times, Sun, World, Herald, American*, and *Evening Mail* formed the United Newspaper Delivery Company and instituted a carrier zone system to distribute their papers.[68]

After two weeks Mayor John Hylan, a Hearst ally, intervened. He notified dealers who operated stands near public parks and buildings that they did so as a public convenience and would have their licenses pulled unless they resumed selling. Meanwhile, the papers extended return privileges for sixty days, which split the ranks of the dealers and led to pitched battles. As the strike collapsed, New York's police commissioner instructed his men to keep two squads in reserve to make sure the strikers did not interfere with the non-striking dealers. The mayor's threat to revoke licenses was no bluff. Six months later, when dealers resisted pressure to accept more Hearst papers than they could sell, Brooklyn Borough Hall newsstand operator John Williamson lost his license. Contributions poured into the Newsboys Union legal defense fund, culminating in his reinstatement by the state Supreme Court.[69]

Minneapolis authorities led by socialist mayor Thomas Van Lear showed much more sympathy to striking members of the Newsboys Union in the summer of 1918. Theirs was a weeklong struggle involving three newspapers and hundreds of sellers. The dispute started on July 1 when the *Minneapolis Journal, Tribune*, and *Daily News* raised prices, claiming that they had long sold their daily and Sunday papers below cost but could no longer do so because of federally imposed price increases on paper and postage. The papers raised the retail price of their dailies from 1¢ to 2¢ and the wholesale price from ½¢ to 1¼¢. They argued that the changes would boost sellers' profits, but hawkers, carriers, and vendors united in protest. "We'd only make ten cents more and we'd have almost three times as much invested," recalled newsie Ernie Fliegel, who was 14 years old that summer. "But the worst part of it was, there was no returns. Before, if we were stuck with some papers, if there was a storm, say, we could return 'em and get credit for 'em. But now if there was a storm, we would be out of luck."[70]

The strikers tipped over trucks or let air out of the tires so they couldn't move the papers. Newspapers blamed "professional agitators" and socialists and criticized police for standing idle. "Citizens who entered newspaper offices to purchase papers were attacked on the streets," reported the *Journal*. "Even women and girls were manhandled and their clothing torn." It said most of those "mauled" were businessmen, attorneys, and advertisers. Strikers blocked Newspaper Alley with a ladder and attacked trucks that tried to break through the blockade. They also carried their campaign into the residential areas, following delivery trucks, confiscating bundles, and either burning them or throwing them into the Mississippi River.[71]

The *Journal* referred to the strikers as "thugs," "roughs," "bullies," "gangsters," and "agitators" and called their activities "a reign of terror." Members of the city's Home Guard, who used to demand military registration cards from older, immigrant newsboys, now tried to intimidate some into signing affidavits that Mayor Van Lear had incited the strike. Most of boys arrested for strike violence were Jewish. Jacob Jacobson, Harry Truppman, and Harry Weisman, all age 18, were sentenced to twenty days in the workhouse, but each had his sentence reduced to six months' probation except Weisman, a Russian immigrant. Other judges showed leniency by ruling that strikers who took papers from pedestrians were guilty of disorderly conduct rather than the higher crime of robbery. Police also aided strikers by discouraging regular employees from selling papers on the street, saying it would incite riot. Some refused to protect those who did sell or to disperse the roving bands of youths that scoured the business district for "scabs."[72]

Another patriot group, the Minnesota Motor Reserve, also got involved. Seventy-five cars under the command of Major J. R. Histed patrolled the city to monitor police response to any strike violence that occurred during distribution of the Sunday papers. They reported several incidents in which "wrecking crews" scared off carriers and destroyed papers at key distribution points. Not to be outdone, fifty newsboys met at police headquarters Saturday night, ostensibly to help guard the papers. "We want to carry out the mayor's orders," explained one. Several of the bundles they were guarding soon disappeared, as did the boys. The anti-union Citizens Alliance tried to bait newsboys by planting a scab vendor on the corner of Fourth and Nicollet and setting up a movie camera in the window of the Palace Building to capture his thrashing. But the savvy strikers merely bawled out the scab and thumbed their noses at the cameraman.[73]

The reluctance of city officials to back the publishers and crack down on the boys had real political repercussions. A local minister delivered a "pulpit editorial" holding the city government responsible for the strike violence and accusing officials of conducting a "school for anarchy." The newsboys, said the Rev. Charles W. Burns of the Hennepin Avenue Methodist Church, "have had stamped on their minds a lack of reverence for law and for individual and property rights that never will be erased from their minds. All the teachings of our public school system have been nullified." He said the strike had unmasked socialism as a destructive, antisocial force, and he vowed defeat at the polls for Van Lear, a former mechanic, and his Public Ownership Party. Van Lear was defeated by a conservative in 1919, but his defeat had more to do with the split among socialists over the war than with his role in the strike.[74]

Striking vendors had recruited boys to destroy papers, but they changed their tactics in the last week of the strike, jeering vendors and swarming around customers rather than attacking them. Minnesota governor J. A. A. Burnquist warned the mayor and chief of police that if they did not maintain order in the city he would have them removed from office. Van Lear replied: "There are no disorderly conditions except in the minds of the three great newspapers of this city. They lie from morning until night, and may deceive the governor, who is in St. Paul, but I doubt if they can put it over on the people of Minneapolis."[75]

The strike ended two days later after the publishers, a committee of newsboys, and local businessmen hashed out a compromise. All sellers accepted the new $1.25 price scale for morning papers, but downtown newsboys won the right to pay less ($1.10) for afternoon and evening papers through September. After the agreement had been reached, the *Journal* published a conciliatory statement by Harry Dickerman, treasurer of the Newsboys' Club. "We have found the publishers open-minded and fair in the negotiations," he said. "We ask those who have shown interest in us the last week to continue to show their interest by liberal buying of newspapers at the new retail price, which we believe is justified by war conditions."[76]

Lastly, Seattle newsboys extended their tradition of labor activism with a successful strike against four city dailies. Founded back in 1892, the local newsboys union had fallen under the control of a handful of newsstand owners and circulation managers who hired boys to sell for them, retaining half their profits. George Ault, editor of the *Union Record*, the weekly organ of the county's Central Labor Council, likened the system to peonage. A committed socialist who had peddled the *Kentucky Post* at age 5, Ault identified with the newsboys' plight. He and labor council agent Nathan P. Birch instigated a revolt of three hundred newsies in September 1918. The resulting contract limited members to control of just one intersection and issued pins to union members now affiliated with the American Federation of Labor. The labor council urged Seattleites to "demand the button" when buying a paper. Marring the victory was Birch's conviction for violating the Selective Service law by misstating his age. He claimed that publishers instigated the prosecution because of his union activity.[77]

Two months later the war was over, or so Americans thought. On the afternoon of November 7, newsboys throughout the United States cried extras headlined "Germany Surrenders" (Figure 12.7). Their voices rose above the din of church bells, factory whistles, and car horns. "I can still hear the newsboys in 1918 yelling through the streets at night: 'Extra, extra, the war is over, the armistice has been signed,'" recalled a Chicago woman eighty years later. "People poured out of their homes, laughing and crying, embracing each other." But the wire service got the story wrong. German officials hadn't yet signed the armistice. Some papers issued corrected editions, but jubilant throngs stripped them from their sellers. Snowy drifts of newsprint and tickertape wafted through the canyons of New York as soldiers, sailors, secretaries, and students snaked down the streets in impromptu parades. When office workers headed home they were replaced by exultant youths from the outer boroughs who hadn't heard that the news was false. Their response was, "Well, they're going to sign it pretty soon, and I'll just keep on celebrating until they do." When the armistice was signed four days

Figure 12.7. False Armistice Day, New York, 1918. New York Public Library.

later, newsboys hit the streets again with their extras, and folks rejoiced with even more gusto. "Nobody wanted to buy a paper that day," said Fred Witte of Omaha. "All they wanted was something that would make a lot of noise."[78]

Fearing that the flush times were over, Dean Collins of Portland, Oregon, eulogized:

> How can I jar the people loose to buy the sheet and read,
> If I start yelling 'bout the rise in price of clover seed?
> When they are used to war and smoke and sulphur burning blue,
> Will they warm up to read about the W.C.T.U.?
> O, Maybe Sherman had it right on war—but wars must cease—
> And Sherman never tried to peddle papers after peace.[79]

Fortunately, the postwar years would prove far from quiet for America's newsboys.

13

Roar of the Tabloids

No decade has been slapped with so many aural metaphors as the 1920s. Even before it was over, it was known as the Roaring Twenties, the Jazz Age, and the Ballyhoo Years. Writer Herbert Asbury dubbed 1927 alone the "Year of the Big Shriek" because of its astounding news stories: Lindbergh's transatlantic flight, Sacco and Vanzetti's execution, Babe Ruth's sixty home runs, Jack Dempsey's title fights, and a host of epic floods, fires, and hurricanes—all of which were bellowed by newsboys. Add two inventions to the mix—radio and talking movies—and the decade's legendary loudness seems hardly exaggerated. Former Washington, DC, newsie Asa Yoelson (Al Jolson) wasn't kidding when he ad-libbed in *The Jazz Singer*, "Wait a minute, wait a minute. You ain't heard nothing yet."[1]

Newsboys personified this new era of automobiles, skyscrapers, and celebrities. Their cries punctuated the urban air along with the blare of taxicab horns, the pounding of jackhammers, and the syncopated rhythms pouring out of nightclubs and cabarets. Their trademark slang spiked the already heady brew of Broadway plays, tabloid gossip columns, and radio broadcasts, raising their profile as little smart-alecks who epitomized the freewheeling spirit of the age. They were sidewalk speculators in an age of speculation, media entrepreneurs in the midst of a media revolution, and rugged individualists in a society that extolled individualism. In a world seething with communists, socialists, and anarchists, newsboys seemed to offer living proof that democracy and capitalism provided more opportunity than any other system. Profit-making quickly supplanted patriotism as the newsboy's most laudable trait. "The chief business of the American people is business," Vice President Calvin Coolidge told a convention of newspaper editors in 1925. His Midas-like treasury secretary, Andrew Mellon, agreed, singling out "the newsboy of today, as America's leading citizen of tomorrow."[2]

Rapid change and real conflict underlay the din. The 1920s contained a cacophony of feuding factions pitting guardians of tradition against the forces of modernity. Small-town America detested the vice and depravity of the metropolis. White supremacists resented the black and immigrant hordes invading their neighborhoods and workplaces. Fundamentalists felt bullied by godless advocates of evolution. Businessmen touted the harmony of interests between capital and labor but tried to bust unions with their flag-waving American Plan. Republicans took out a twelve-year lease on the White House and returned to a rapacious "normalcy" the likes of which hadn't been seen since the Gilded Age. After winning the vote, suffragists splintered into factions that could agree on little except the need to drain the nation's casks of demon rum. And America's "flaming youth" turned their backs on their parents' prim styles and staid values as they shimmied their way into the future. Such tensions sold a lot of papers, but newsboys were not mere merchants of discord; they were also its agents. As predominantly immigrant, sexually precocious city kids from non-teetotaler, non-Protestant, working-class families, they represented the troubling symptoms of modernity over tradition.[3]

An Unquiet Peace

Change came fast after the armistice. A sharp economic downturn led to mass unemployment and a retreat from progressivism. Newsboys felt the full force of these reverses. In Maryland, street trade violations jumped from 772 to 964 between 1920 and 1921. The most common offense was selling without a license, usually to offset reduced family incomes. In many cases, said the state labor board, "the only money the parents had coming in was what the children earned in selling papers and other articles." Some boys cracked under the pressure: 13-year-old Raphael Annese of Boston shot himself after his father berated him for not selling enough papers.[4]

These were especially lean years for farmers, two-thirds of whom fell into debt even with the aid of their children's unpaid labor. Many lost their farms and hit the road. A 1921 study of newsboys in Dallas found a "more or less shiftless" class of children "from families that pick cotton in the summer and fall, drift to Dallas for three months in the winter and are in Arkansas, Oklahoma or South Texas in the spring." These migrant attest to the links between urban and rural labor markets in which children sowed and reaped both printed and plantation goods.[5]

At the federal level, the recession muted the impact of the US Children's Bureau's 1918–19 "Children's Year" campaign intended to improve the health and welfare of mothers and minors. Congress passed the Sheppard-Towner Act in 1921, which funded infant and child health programs and routinized the issuance of birth certificates. Child mortality rates dropped, but the medical establishment opposed the act as socialistic, guaranteeing that it would be allowed to lapse in 1929.[6]

The hard times led some newsboys to traffic in drugs, alcohol, and sundry items. In 1919 several Georgia newsboys were arrested for dealing dope at Fort Gordon near Atlanta. Three New York City teens were suspected of the same when military police at Camp Mills in Mineola, Long Island, found $2,000 in cash on them, more than most families made in a year. The boys said the money represented three days' earnings selling newspapers, mirrors, "tidies," and embroidered pillowcases. Complaints by mothers led police to crack down on the newsstand heroin trade in Manhattan's theater district. Many boys branched out into the liquor business upon passage of state or federal prohibition laws. Denver newskids distributed cases of hooch at $8 a pint from *Rocky Mountain News* vehicles. Cheston Knight, 15, of Atlanta, was arrested in 1920 after offering pints of whiskey from his newsbag to two detectives and the police commissioner. Anthony Morelos Brown, also 15, scored big in suds. The Salt Lake City newsboy sold a merchant 1,800 copies of a nickel newspaper containing a coupon good for a 25¢ box of soap powder. "I made forty-five dollars on them," said Brown. "Mother thought I had robbed a bank."[7]

Newsboys also spread the music that gave the Jazz Age its name. In Chicago, African American youths peddled "race records" along with newspapers. Issued weekly by Paramount and Vocalian Records, the disks sold for $1 and netted 25¢ profit. "You'd go to one customer," said a newsboy, "and she'd get all excited over a new blues and start in to telling you all about her girl friend or some relative who was sure to buy one, too." Meanwhile, 12-year-old Mario Palarosa of San Leandro, California, learned to play "Blue Heaven" and "My Baby's Ankles" on the harmonica to entice the flappers to buy papers.[8]

Newspapers hustled to stay afloat during the postwar slump and cope with an inflation rate that doubled the cost of living in five years. Newsprint and other production costs skyrocketed, causing scores of dailies and hundreds of weeklies to be merged, acquired by chains, or laid to rest. Circulation plummeted, and it would take four years to regain the 1918 level of 28.6 million copies. Contributing to the drop in readership was the public's disgust with baseball after the "Black Sox" scandal in which Chicago White Sox players took bribes from gamblers to throw the World Series to the Cincinnati Reds. In a story that is perhaps apocryphal, a newsboy expressed the nation's disbelief when he confronted Chicago star "Shoeless Joe" Jackson and pleaded, "Say it ain't so, Joe." It was so. The Boston Newsboys' Club passed a resolution calling the White Sox "the Benedict Arnolds of Baseball." Then along came slugger Babe Ruth, an incorrigible reform school product from Baltimore who would revitalize the national pastime with the Yankees and become known as the "Idol of the Urchins."[9]

The return of 204,000 disabled soldiers created competition for newsboys. With unemployment topping 11 percent, a clamor arose for the men to have priority in obtaining street vending licenses. "The crippled veterans from our armies in France and Italy should be given a monopoly of the newspaper selling business," said charity worker and ex-newsboy Maurice Hexter in Cincinnati, "and boys under sixteen should be eliminated entirely from such work." Businessmen in Akron formed a nonprofit company to erect newsstands for the blind. Others exploited the veterans. Hearst dailies specialized in the "sympathy racket," hiring ex-servicemen still in khakis to sell subscriptions on the promise that a portion of the fee would aid needy vets. The nation's highest-ranking officers called the practice "disgraceful."[10] The veterans wanted better, too. Former cavalryman Boyd "Gimpe" McNutt hawked papers in Chicago in the winter of 1918–19 but then formed the "crutch gang," which specialized in stealing cars from garages. When arrested, he said he was going to use the loot to fix his leg, but he wanted no pity: "I know how to stand the gaff, and I'll plead guilty and take my medicine like a soldier."[11]

While some men turned to crime, the most common response to worsening conditions was to protest, or, in the vernacular of the day, to "roar." More than four million Americans—almost a quarter of private-sector employees—struck in 1919. Some veterans picketed in uniform and likened their bosses to the kaiser. Newsboys first turned out in January when the *Atlanta Constitution*, following the advice of War Industry Board chairman Bernard Baruch, extended its rationing and no-return policies despite the rescinding of federal mandates. Six months later city officials made all news sellers over 16 obtain badges or face arrest.[12]

In February, newsboys in Butte, Montana, struck in sympathy with miners organized by the Industrial Workers of the World (IWW). Hundreds of boys between the ages of 10 and 12 attacked those who persisted in selling the *Miner* and *Daily Post*, two dailies aligned with the Anaconda Copper Mining Company. The *Anaconda Standard* deplored their "Bolshevist methods," but the socialist *Butte Daily Bulletin* said the boys had realized that mine owners who made millions during the war while workers sacrificed should now pay a fair wage. The *Bulletin* called their action a "Fight for Democracy."[13]

Other confrontations followed. In August, carriers in Mount Vernon, New York, boycotted all twenty-four dealers in the city for a 25 percent wage hike. And in September, boys in Manistee, Michigan, threatened violence if anyone dared deliver papers during their strike.[14] Newsboys also took part in the Seattle General Strike, which began when a walkout by 25,000 shipyard workers in February 1919 led 35,000 other trade unionists to lay down their tools in sympathy. Members of Newsboys Local 15834 kicked off the revolt when they stilled their voices and dumped their papers precisely at the 10:00 a.m. strike call. Strike leaders banned the distribution of Seattle's major newspapers, which had joined in the postwar attack on socialists and unionists. Silencing these "capitalist mouthpieces" symbolized working-class solidarity to the strikers but a breakdown of law and order to the business community. The *Seattle News-Tribune* ignored the ban and ran a seven-column headline: "Troops in Seattle." Those troops guarded delivery trucks and handed out the paper in the business district. Newsboys nevertheless seized copies and tore them up. Mayor Ole Hanson, a former Chicago hawker, bristled. "This is not a strike but a revolution," he declared as he beefed up the police force. The strike committee called off the strike after five days and declared a moral victory, but the newsies knew better. "I thought we were going to get the industries," lamented one.[15]

Reds and Revivals

America's newsboys and newsgirls continued to agitate for better terms, fueling the anti-Red frenzy of the twenties. In September 1920, 150 women vendors at Boston's elevated and subway stations formed the News Stand Girls' Union to secure shorter hours and better pay. They received help from the Women's Trade Union League but had to elude Burns detectives and hold midnight meetings. Their employer, the Hotel and Railroad News Co., split their ranks by firing forty-seven members, securing an injunction against the union, and raising the wages of those who remained.[16]

In 1920–21 Montana high school senior Henry Stanley got a lesson in power when he organized thirty-five carriers of the *Butte Daily Post* to strike for pay equal to that of other carriers in town. The *Post* enlisted a scoutmaster to offer the boys a bonus plan instead of the $2 raise they wanted. It had a truant officer threaten Stanley with a beating if he went near the newspaper office, and it secured militia to oversee distribution. "This was pure tactic to teach children not to grow up and become striking miners," said Stanley. After two weeks of street clashes, the boys won their raise.[17]

Few of their comrades were so fortunate. In February 1921, newsboys in San Francisco and Oakland rioted when the morning nickel papers raised their wholesale price from 2½¢ to 3¢. In September thirty boys, ages 5 to 15, struck a newsagent in the California oil town of Taft. Fed up with getting 2¢ for the sale of a 10¢ paper, they futilely demanded a fairer split.[18]

Four other disputes followed in 1922. In February, hawkers and carriers of the *Des Moines Capital* struck to increase earnings by raising the price of the paper from 1¢ to 2¢. In April, New Yorkers witnessed yet another riotous newsboy strike when Joseph Medill Patterson's *Daily News* and William Randolph Hearst's *American* raised the wholesale price of their bulldog editions to $3 a hundred.

Vendors had previously paid $1.40 per hundred for the *Daily News* and $2.10 for the *American*. Since these papers retailed for 2¢ and 3¢ apiece, there looked to be little profit on the former and none on the latter. Management justified the hike by saying dealers were "profiteers" who had been "getting away with murder" by charging 4¢ and 5¢ per paper. "We thought we would give them something to think about," said the *Daily News* circulation manager. For days newsboys of all ages boycotted the two sheets, and a "lively disorder" erupted around Park Row, City Hall Park, the Brooklyn Bridge, and Times Square when circulation managers imported vendors from nearby Newark and far-off Chicago, a Hearst and Patterson stronghold.[19]

In May, newsboys in Kansas City refused to sell the penny *Star* for less than 2¢ and dealt harshly with the "foreigners" sent out to vend the paper at the published price. And in July, newsboys in Decatur, Illinois, voted unanimously to strike rather than submit to an order to keep their hands, faces, and clothes clean. But strikes in all sectors of the economy then dropped to an all-time low due to the sapped strength of unions. The IWW was crushed in California by the firing or arrest of anyone who peddled a Wobbly paper. They were charged with violating the state syndicalism law, which banned advocating any change in industrial ownership or control. Fred Thompson, age 22, was among those arrested for distributing papers in Marysville in April 1923. He served three years in San Quentin for the offense. The first trial ended in a hung jury. "At the second trial," he recalled, "the prosecutor didn't make the long-winded speech he had at the first. Instead he said, 'It's a hot day. Let's let the jury go out and get some refreshments.' I was told that when they went outside, newsboys, who didn't usually sell their papers there, were hollering, 'IWW sets fire to the rice fields of California!' The jury came back rather quickly and convicted us. And there had been no rice field fires."[20]

Some boys bucked the no-strike trend in the second half of the decade. Carriers of the *Harvard Crimson* threatened a walkout in 1926 because their wages had not kept up with the cost of living. Drivers and carriers struck in Newark, New Jersey, in 1928, as did hawkers in Oakland in response to cost-cutting measures by a big news agency. The firm laid off many corner boys, halved their weekly guarantee to $3, and dropped commissions to a penny a paper. Strikers petitioned the American Federation of Labor for a charter, but it showed no interest in representing them. They then turned to the Trade Union Education League (TUEL), the labor-organizing wing of the Communist Party, which had just won a strike of fifteen thousand textile workers in Passaic, New Jersey. One of the boldest hawkers, 17-year-old Archie Brown, snuck TUEL literature into copies of the *San Francisco Chronicle*. Such antics got him arrested and fired, but he went on to join the Young Communist League, organize migrant farm workers and Bay Area longshoremen, and fight fascism in Spain with the Abraham Lincoln Brigade.[21]

Fear of radicals peaked after the Russian Revolution. Most employers saw Reds and unionist as cut from the same cloth. The capitalist press joined the witch hunt, partly as a substitute for war news. Newsboys in 1919 and 1920 cried headlines about the rash of bombs mailed to prominent officials and financiers. They publicized Attorney General A. Mitchell Palmer's skull-cracking raids on suspected subversives. And they retailed reports of the Wall Street bombing that left 38 people dead and 143 injured. The *Chicago Socialist* greeted these events as the rumblings of a welcome revolution, saying, "The Earthquake is here." Congress introduced legislation providing up to twenty years' imprisonment and $10,000 in fines for anyone who produced *or circulated* material advocating changing the government or defying its laws. To further combat the appeal of radicalism among America's youth, the Rotary Club established Boy's Week, featuring an all-boy parade up New York's Fifth Avenue on May Day 1921, renamed Loyalty Day. "This parade will call attention to the fact that the future of America lies not in red uprisings," said an organizer, "but in the boys growing up in school and shop and office." Contingents of newsboys filled out the ranks of marchers for the next several years. The *Chicago Daily News* asserted the "100 percent Americanism" of its boys in 1926 by outfitting them in military-style uniforms complete with jackboots and peaked caps (Figure 13.1).[22]

Whatever their sympathies, newsboys earned steady incomes shouting about the trial of anarchists Nicola Sacco and Bartolomeo Vanzetti. From their arrest for the murder and robbery of two payroll guards in South Braintree, Massachusetts, in 1920 to their execution in 1927, news about the accused—and the many rallies and work stoppages their case inspired—spiked sales of both radical and capitalist papers. One newsboy, 14-year-old Maynard Freeman Shaw, offered dubious testimony linking Vanzetti to an earlier holdup, when he got a "fleeting glance" at the gunman, about 150 feet away. "The way he ran I could tell he was a foreigner," swore Shaw. The anarchists were found guilty and sentenced to death. Their execution sparked protests worldwide and led to the arrest of six Boston newsboys who were charged with hawking material critical of the state on the day of Sacco and Vanzetti's funeral.[23]

"Banned in Boston" became a badge of honor in some circles. Suppression of the *American Mercury* by local censors in 1926 over a Herbert Asbury story about small-town prostitution prompted editor H. L. Mencken and American Civil Liberties Union lawyer Arthur Garfield Hays (a Sacco and Vanzetti attorney) to peddle the issue in hopes of being arrested and making a test case. Another rumpus occurred in 1929 when Boston newsies agreed to distribute the *Harvard Progressive*, a journal started by socialist undergraduates. Carriers were threatened with dismissal if they touched the Red sheet. The *Crimson* rose in defense of the boys, saying "Every true upholder of American liberty must

Figure 13.1. Newsboys drill on the roof of the *Chicago Daily News,* 1926. DN-0081069, Chicago Daily News negatives collection, Chicago History Museum.

hope that the Harvard Progressive will emerge the victor, even if its editors have to carry out their promise to peddle the copies themselves."[24]

California hosted a free speech free-for-all in August 1926 when four grown-up vendors in Los Angeles were arrested on obscenity charges for selling a San Diego weekly that claimed that evangelist Aimee Semple McPherson had been holed up in a Carmel "love nest" during the weeks she said she was kidnapped. "The failure—or perhaps innate inability—of some women to keep their legs crossed has been the cause of more wars, murders and general crime than all the other reasons in the catalog," said the offending editorial. Bootlegged copies sold for up to $2. The vendors were fined, but Sister Aimee's disciples weren't satisfied; Anthony Latell, 28, was shot in the back while crying extras about the scandal at Fourth and Bixel, not far from McPherson's Angeles Temple. The shooter escaped and Latell lived to cry another day.[25]

Other evangelists enjoyed more cordial relations with the press. Former major league ball player Billy Sunday spent lavishly on newspaper advertising for his traveling revivals, preaching to an estimated hundred million people by 1930. Newsboy clubs would send out squads to assist attendees; the reformed base-stealer reciprocated by sponsoring kosher banquets and galas for the newsies. Yet even he encountered opposition in 1918 when eight newsies were arrested for disorderly conduct outside his tabernacle in Chicago. They had been crying a paper with a front-page cartoon showing him wearing a sweater covered with dollar signs. The Rev. Andrew Jenkins of Atlanta was himself a vendor. Partially blind since infancy, he earned his living selling papers, singing, and preaching outside city hall. Billed as "the blind newsboy evangelist," Jenkins and family started performing gospel music in 1922 on the *Atlanta Journal*'s powerful radio station, WSB. He composed hundreds of songs, including "news ballads" such as "The Death of Floyd Collins," based on the sensational 1925 effort to rescue a man trapped in a Kentucky cave.[26]

Meantime, newsboys throughout the country faced down a third wave of sabbatarianism. Protestant clergy mobilized the Lord's Day Alliance in 1920 to limit Sunday streetcar service to churchgoers and ban Sunday movies, ball games, and newspaper sales. "The hawking of newspapers on the streets on Sunday," said alliance secretary Harry Bowlby, "is an insult to the decent, intelligent, Christian observers of the Sabbath." If such practices continued, he vowed, "we will have no alternative but to ask for an amendment to the Constitution of the United States." The alliance backed a Sunday rest bill for the District of Columbia in 1927, but it led to a filibuster and mini-brawl in Congress (a "fistibuster," *Time* magazine called it) in which the Rev. Bowlby threw an errant punch.[27]

Muscle Journalism

Moralists had good reason to worry. Newspapers were wickeder than ever in the 1920s. While the number of dailies fell from 2,300 to 2,100 during the decade, their circulation rose to an all-time high of 43 million by 1929. The sale of Sunday papers shot up by 10 million. Population increases aided the rise in readership, but it stemmed mainly from the advent of racy tabloids, a national obsession with celebrity, and the mass production of desire for radios, refrigerators, and roadsters—a whole cornucopia of commodities advertised on the installment plan. Although few of their families could afford such items, newsboys stirred these desires with every paper sold. It was a good racket while it lasted.[28]

The crass materialism of this "sordid decade," as *Emporia Gazette* editor William Allen White called it, emboldened the *Wall Street Journal* to shed all pretense about serving the public. "A newspaper is a private enterprise, owing nothing whatever to the public, which grants it no franchise," declaimed a frontpage editorial in 1925. "It is therefore 'effected' with no public interest. It is emphatically the property of its owner, who is selling a manufactured product at his own risk." The editorial reveals just how far the pendulum had swung since the war, when nationalism was the highest journalistic virtue. Indeed, the 1922 federal court decision by Judge Kenesaw Mountain Landis in *Journal of Commerce v. Chicago Tribune* held that newspapers were not public service corporations and could sell their product to whomever they chose. The ruling upheld newspapers' right to forbid dealers from carrying competing papers.[29]

In their quest for readership, tabloids employed gossip columnists who kept their ears to the gutter, eyes to the keyhole, and tables at the Stork Club or Brown Derby. They dispatched flying squads of photographers who wielded bulky Speed Graphic cameras, wore press-card-plumed fedoras, and stunned their prey with blinding flashes. Neither minded fudging the facts. The *New York Evening Graphic* (aka "Porno-Graphic") hyped its contrived photos as "composographs." Tabloids turned murder and divorce trials into titillating morality tales that saddled their subjects with lasting infamy. They started Lady Luck lotteries, Most Beautiful Secretary contests, and a new craze: crossword puzzles. Polite society deplored the "tabs," along with jazz, as vulgar, primitive, and obscene. One wit suggested that newsboys might well cry their scandal sheets as "sextras!" Yet one of the biggest stories of this modern era turned people's attention back three millennia: the discovery of King Tut's tomb in 1922 set off a vogue for all things Egyptian. The demand for papers made 8-year-old Chicago newsboy "Red" Pruett feel as rich as the boy pharaoh himself. "It sold good," he said.[30]

The movie business, now based in Hollywood, also produced stars and street sales. Heartthrob Rudolph Valentino served as headline fodder up to his death and beyond. As the Italian-born actor lay sick in a New York hospital after an operation for appendicitis and a gastric ulcer, "leather lunged" newsboys caused a flurry of excitement outside crying a tabloid's two-word headline: "Rudy Dead!" Below in much smaller type was the line: "Cry Startles Film World as Sheik Rallies." But the Sheik did die four days later, and the *Evening Graphic* splashed a composograph across its front page depicting his celestial welcome by his recently deceased *paisan*, opera singer Enrico Caruso. The issue sold 100,000 extra copies.[31]

As their circulations soared, the tabs forced even respectable dailies to jazz up their style and push street sales. *Vanity Fair* illustrator Miguel Covarrubias caricatured their sordid influence by showing the natty newshound Walter Winchell escorting a gimlet-eyed Walter Lippmann, esteemed opinion-maker of the New York *World*, past the tawdry dance halls and burlesque houses of Broadway (Plate 27). Shocked at seeing this journalistic odd couple in the neighborhood is the one character they both relied on—the newsboy.

Winchell had the biggest name and the largest readership of any journalist in America. Once a newsboy, he epitomized the brash, streetwise style of the era. He virtually invented the gossip column for Bernarr Macfadden's *Evening Graphic* and Hearst's *Daily Mirror*. Winchell styled himself "your newsboy" in print, and offered a pithy definition: "A newsboy is a citizen immature in everything but nerve, who posts himself conspicuously in a public place and shrills so relentlessly as to menace the stoutest eardrums for a radius of several blocks."

Winchell's syndicated column reached thirty million readers a day and informed his Sunday radio show, which debuted in 1929. His columns and broadcasts were a barrage of celebrity gossip ("She's been on more laps than a napkin"), political scoops, and flash bulletins, all delivered in a torrent of Broadway slang backed, at least on radio, by the clacking of a telegraph machine.[32]

Winchell made his first foray into journalism in 1905 at age 8 hawking the *New York Journal* and *Harlem Home News* outside the subway kiosk on 116th Street and Madison Avenue. "I met the world and all comers as catchweights on the Harlem and other New York Streets as a newsboy," he said. "The only thing in my corner (when I was 12) was the corner lamp post. . . . Any tenderness I may have developed is entirely due to the cold iron and steel in that lamp post." A talented kid who craved attention, Winchell gravitated to vaudeville. He left school in the sixth grade, at age 13, and toured the country for three years as the lead singer in Gus Edwards's expanded Newsboys Sextet, which included future stars Georgie Jessel, Eddie Cantor, and Irene Martin as "Jennie, the news girl" (Figure 13.2). Wearing soft caps and wide, gaudy ties, the boys opened the act shooting dice and singing "Why Can't I Be a Millionaire?" Thus motivated, Winchell acquired a Broadway gossip sheet, which led to his glory years as a columnist. But his newsboy instincts never dulled. "Get me a good murder or a train wreck," he'd say to his staff as he strode into the studio. "I want to hit my audience tonight." As his fame grew, more writing offers came in than he could complete. In true hustler fashion, Winchell farmed out the work to his pals, pocketing the money and repaying them with mentions in his column.[33]

Winchell's counterpart in Los Angeles was Hedda Hopper, a silent screen star turned gossip columnist who also evinced an image-enhancing fondness for newsboys. A divorced mother of a 9-year-old in 1924, she would swoop down Hollywood Boulevard in her limousine, pick up half a dozen newsies, and take them to her Fairfax Avenue mansion for a home-cooked meal and a romp with her son.[34]

Jazz journalism was also called "muscle journalism" because in reporting and distributing the news, city editors and circulation managers resorted to strong-arm tactics including wiretapping, burglary, bribery, kidnapping, and even murder. No town saw more of this rough stuff—and more newsboy violence—than Chicago. The running circulation war in the early 1900s laid the foundation for the organized crime spree of the Prohibition era. Many bootleggers cut their teeth as newspaper sluggers who helped draw the original battle lines in the distribution of beer and liquor. News sellers in Chicago ranged in age from 12 to 80, and neither youth nor age afforded them protection from suppliers and sluggers. Newspaper deliverymen were both salesmen and collectors who pressured vendors and carriers to take more papers than they could sell and to pay for them in advance, making each delivery a kind of shakedown. A staff of inspectors and division men in turn leaned on the drivers. Without the benefit

Figure 13.2. Will D. Cobb and Gus Edwards, "If I Was a Millionaire" (New York: Gus Edwards, Inc. (1910). Gus Edwards (standing), Georgie Jessel (first from right), Walter Winchell (second from right), Eddie Cantor (fourth from right). Library of Congress, Washington, DC.

of returning unsold papers, vendors would have to put in longer hours or absorb the losses. It was a hard system, mitigated only by the papers' selective dispensing of subsidies, bonuses, premiums, and loans.[35]

Violence in the trade rose due to the erosion of workers' rights. Like businesses everywhere, newspapers in Chicago reneged on wartime agreements with organized labor and took advantage of court injunctions that outlawed strikes, boycotts, picket lines, and other legitimate union practices. The hostile climate left unions vulnerable to the extralegal activities of racketeers, who used their coercive methods against employers and workers alike. By 1927 organized crime had its mitts on more than ninety industries and unions in the city, including newspaper distribution. Under the direction of circulation managers Max and Moe Annenberg, Chicago's biggest papers and their counterparts in New York relied on gangsters Dion O'Banion, Al Capone, and Lucky Luciano to win corners, avert strikes, and eliminate opponents. Cutthroat competition was not just a metaphor in the trade. "Them circulation fights was murder," Capone told a warden. "They knifed each other like hell and they didn't give a damn what happened. And who do you think settled all them strikes and fights? Me!" Hardly an impartial mediator, Capone's crony Daniel Serritella was president of the newsboys union, and Capone himself became reliant on newsboy labor in 1923 when he moved his operation to the working-class suburb of Cicero and bought out the crusading editor of the *Cicero Tribune*.[36]

Even tougher, smarter, and richer than "Scarface" were the Annenberg brothers. As circulation manager of the *Chicago Tribune* in 1921, Max oversaw the distribution of 3.5 million newspapers a week, the largest morning circulation in America. It required a staff of six hundred people just to get the paper out the door each day; they worked in the pressroom, on the loading docks, and in garages, gas stations, wagon shops, and stables. Max also directed the circulation of other McCormick-Patterson properties: the New York *Daily News*, the *New York Picture Paper, Liberty Magazine*, and the European edition of the *Chicago Tribune*, while Moe oversaw the circulation of all Hearst newspapers and magazines, operated his own Milwaukee newspaper agency, acquired the *Elizabeth Journal*, the *Daily Racing Form*, the General News Bureau (a mobbed-up racing news wire service), the *New York Morning Telegraph*, the *Miami Tribune*, and the *Philadelphia Inquirer*. "If we lads who grew up at the stands and had at most only our two or three years grammar school, can manage to swing a proposition like that," Max told a group of Northwestern University journalism students in 1921, "what cannot you young people, with the technical school and expert counsel at your command, do with it! We were—and are—newsboys, and proud of it."[37]

New technology also helped revolutionize the trade. Big dailies now used counting devices and stuffing machines to insert supplements, thereby relieving boys of that burden. Other machines addressed papers for the mail, bagged them, and kicked the bags onto conveyor belts. Motorized vehicles began to outnumber horse-drawn wagons in most circulation departments. Wagons still made up 60 percent of the *Chicago Tribune*'s vehicles in 1922, but the *Boston Globe*'s delivery fleet was completely motorized. Newspapers originally adapted the Model T and other cars to their needs, but International Harvester made light trucks designed specially for newspaper work. Trucks enabled newspapers to reach further into the hinterland; they boosted the *New York Times* rural circulation to 75,000 a day by 1925 and extended the *Chicago Tribune's* reach to more than 3,000 towns in five states. Trucks allowed the *Portland Oregonian* to serve 320 city carriers, 200 suburban carriers covering a forty-mile radius, and 15 rural carriers serving routes up to 260 miles long.* The *Baltimore Sun* relied on 95 independent route owners who supplied their own vehicles and employed 500 sub-carriers, some of whom used motorcycles with sidecars.[38]

More spectacularly, the decade saw the rise of "flying newsboys." Whenever Calvin Coolidge was aboard the presidential yacht *Mayflower*, he had fresh papers flown in by Chief Mate E. Dietrich. Ordinary citizens received such service as early as 1911 when French aviator Didier Masson delivered copies of the *Los Angeles Times* to San Bernardino, sixty miles away, in a Curtiss-Farman biplane. He, Paul Peck, and ex-newsboy Glenn Martin repeated similar stunts the following year to raise funds for their endeavors (Figure 13.3).[39] By 1919 the *Denver Post* and *Schenectady Union-Star* were experimenting with air delivery, and by 1921 the *Daily Sun* in Corsicana, Texas, was making regular air deliveries to oil field workers thirty miles away. In 1928 the *Los Angeles Times* chartered a tri-motor Fokker monoplane to deliver its morning edition to northern California. The trip covered five hundred miles and took four hours. The plane touched down at daybreak in Oakland, where newsboys transferred the papers to trucks for delivery via ferry to San Francisco and throughout the San Joaquin Valley. The *New York Times, World*, and *Evening Journal* introduced air delivery the next year, followed by the *Chicago Daily News* and *Boston Transcript*.[40]

Small-town publisher Harry D. Strunk of the *McCook Daily Gazette* also looked to the skies to build circulation. In 1929 he bought a Curtiss Robin to serve subscribers in thirty-three isolated communities in Nebraska and Kansas. Christened *The Newsboy*, the plane came equipped with a chute that allowed canvas bags full of papers to be dropped from the air at five hundred feet. Strunk drafted an 18-year-old carrier, Leopold "Bus" Bahl, to assist the pilot. Boys aground collected the bags and delivered the papers. Accidents inevitably occurred, as when 17-year-old Herbert Downey, a newsboy-pilot from South Bend, Indiana, died in a crash in 1934. These experiments in air distribution nevertheless represent a quantum leap in the industry's efforts to conquer space

---

* Because the *Oregonian* didn't reach Roseburg, 180 miles to the south, until 9:10 a.m., schoolboys couldn't distribute the paper. Their places were taken by two men and 5-year-old Roy Nash. See *Oregonian*, May 15, 1921, 15.

Figure 13.3. Pioneer aviator Glenn Martin, 25, delivering copies of the *Fresno Republican* to Madera, California, twenty-four miles away, in an open-framework pusher biplane, April 13, 1912. It was a publicity stunt to raise funds for his first airplane plant, but air delivery caught on in the twenties. Library of Congress, Washington, DC.

and time. Yet they also show that however advanced the technology, boy labor remained integral to the process.[41]

The Hardest Sell

Except for the news trade, child labor was on the wane in 1920s America. According to the US Census, the number of 10- to 15-year-olds in the workplace fell 38 percent, from just over 1 million in 1920 to 667,000 in 1930. Yet the proportion of newsboys rose slightly, from 20,513 to 21,700, representing 9 percent of all boys in non-agricultural occupations. The US Children's Bureau insisted that the census figures on newsboys would be more accurate if multiplied by at least two and bumped an additional 10 to 20 percent to account for the presence of children under 10, putting the total closer to 50,000. The National Child Labor Committee felt that even this figure fell short of reality; it claimed in 1922 that between 200,000 and 300,000 children under 16 worked the streets, mostly as news peddlers. All agreed that the number of newsboys dropped to about 100,000 before the end of the decade, yet their labor remained indispensable to the industry. In 1928 circulation expert Sidney Long said America's newsboys handled 7.5 million papers a day or 2.5 billion a year.[42]

Local surveys confirmed the boys' importance. Cleveland counted an incredible 10,000 newsboys in 1924. Buffalo reported a near tripling of licensed newsboys from 790 in 1919 to 2,061 in 1925. Denver identified 228 newsboys in 1924; most were between 12 and 15 years old, but a quarter were between 9 and 11, and 8 percent (nineteen boys) were between 5 and 9. They rejoiced in 1925 when a judge overturned a local ordinance preventing them from crying their wares. Toledo relied on 2,000 newsies in 1923, while Trenton made do with 500. Investigators in other cities found newsstand "helpers" of 6, 7, and 8 years old, and peddlers as young as 2 or 3 "with the technique of the professional." In sum, after two decades of concerted reform, child news selling was still firmly entrenched.[43]

Enough was enough. Marginalized during the Great War, reformers took up their task with renewed vigor and raised expectations. "The War has enhanced the national consciousness," proclaimed the National Child Labor Committee in 1919. "Those evils that are national evils must be attacked by national, or nation-wide action." Inspired by the gains of the temperance and woman's suffrage movements, the NCLC put its energy into a constitutional amendment to grant Congress the power to "limit, regulate, and prohibit the labor of persons under eighteen." The campaign took on new urgency in May 1922 when the US Supreme Court decision in *Bailey v. Drexel Furniture Co.* overturned a 1919 law taxing the profits of firms that used child labor.[44]

Endorsed by sixty newspapers, the child labor amendment sailed through Congress in 1924, but popular support evaporated during the ratification process. Opposition came from farmers and manufacturers who feared they would lose their supply of cheap labor. Southern textile producers saw the proposal as a Yankee plot to sabotage their industry and undermine states' rights. Catholic priests blasted the amendment from their pulpits as an infringement of parental rights, reminding parishioners that the boy Jesus worked as a carpenter. Others equated the measure with Prussianism, Bolshevism, or "white collarism" (contempt for manual labor).[45]

Children's Bureau chief Grace Abbott, who succeeded Julia Lathrop in 1921, defended the broad language of the amendment as giving Congress needed flexibility in setting age and hour standards for different occupations. But voters objected to categorizing older teens as children and feared that the reference to *labor* instead of *employment* would bar young people from doing chores around the house or farm and traditional jobs such as delivering newspapers. Vocational education advocates worried that the amendment, like some state laws, would disallow training programs. One by one, northern newspapers abandoned the cause. By 1930, only five states—Arkansas, Arizona, California, Wisconsin, and Montana—had ratified the amendment. But the reeling economy would soon pump new life into the campaign.[46]

Meantime, reformers tried to build on gains made at the state and local levels. In 1924 fourteen states and the District of Columbia had laws regulating child street trading. Seven more joined the club by 1928. (They included Alabama, Arizona, California, Colorado, Delaware, Florida, Iowa, Kentucky, Maryland, Massachusetts, Minnesota, New Hampshire, New Jersey, New York, North Carolina, Oklahoma, Pennsylvania, Rhode Island, Utah, Virginia, and Wisconsin.) Up until then, newspapers in these states ran ads seeking newsboys as young as 9 years old. Nine other states (Arkansas, Connecticut, Georgia, Illinois, Maine, Michigan, Ohio, Oregon, and Washington) relied on municipal ordinances to regulate newsboys in their largest cities. That left eighteen states, primarily in the South and West, with no applicable street trade laws.[47] Children certainly distributed newspapers in these states. In North Dakota, street trading was the most common work for boys under 15; 38 percent of the children in Fargo, Grand Forks, and Minot held jobs in 1923, and 57 percent of those peddled or delivered newspapers. Almost one in three were under 10 years of age. Most worked several hours a day year-round, selling not just local sheets but also Minneapolis and St. Paul papers on Saturdays.[48]

Ironically, enforcement was laxest in states with the toughest laws. In 1921 New York magistrate Francis X. McQuade let off many newsboys charged with "inconveniencing" pedestrians and subway passengers. "Newsboys are not a nuisance," he told the patrolman who arrested 17-year-old Irving Slown on Broadway and 34th Street. "The public enjoys them." Four months later McQuade released Carmen Pasquale, who was detained for similar reasons in the Canal Street station. "Inconveniencing passengers!" said the incredulous Tammany stalwart. "I know I find it convenient to be able to get my newspapers in the subway late at night or early in the morning and I don't see where the inconveniencing comes in. Discharged."[49]

New York Supreme Court justice John Ford also dealt reformers a blow in 1920 when he found photographer Lewis Hine and the Russell Sage Foundation, publisher of *Boyhood and Lawlessness*, guilty of libeling William McCue, an 11-year-old labeled the "Toughest Kid" in Hell's Kitchen. Ford awarded the former altar boy $3,500 in damages, saying there was "not a scintilla of evidence that he was a tough at all." Editorialists in both North and South used the case to bash righteous "uplifters" whose careless claims denigrated poor people and regions.[50]

Signs of issue fatigue were evident throughout the Empire State. In 1926 thirty-two of fifty-nine cities did not issue a single badge to juvenile street traders. Scores of boys and girls under 16 still sold papers late at night in Buffalo, despite a state law banning the practice. When complaints forced truant officers in Manhattan to crack down on night hawkers in 1927, two hundred officers raided a distribution center on Cortlandt Street and Broadway in which about 1,000 boys were milling about. They caught 350 of them, ages 8 to 14, whose parents received summonses. But sporadic sweeps offered little deterrence.[51]

Code revisions in this era of laissez-faire usually weakened rather than strengthened existing laws. In 1928 circulation managers in Washington, DC, persuaded Congress to lower the legal age of news peddling from 14 to 12, drop the minimum age of carriers from 12 to 10, and allow 14-year-olds to work until 7:00 p.m. instead of 6:00 p.m. Amendments also absolved newspapers of liability for children hurt on the job. While these changes reflect the pro-business drift of the 1920s, they run counter to the cultural trend in which children's sentimental value waxed while their economic value waned. Clearly, newspapers still valued newsboys' labor and depicted them as happy, healthy, industrious little chaps (Figure 13.4). Plagued by double-digit unemployment through much of this supposedly prosperous era, many blue-collar families also relied on child labor to stay afloat. From 35 to 40 percent of non-farm families fell into poverty nonetheless.[52]

Child labor reformers did not defer to these economic realities but continued to document the hazards of juvenile street trading. They deplored old-fashioned tales of dutiful children supporting widowed mothers, relying instead on sociological and epidemiological studies—even if those studies sometimes undermined the reformers' objectives. Surveys of newsboys in Boston, New Haven, Philadelphia, Cincinnati, Cleveland, Toledo, St. Louis, Chicago, Des Moines, Mobile, Dallas, and Denver found that most lived with both parents but rarely gave them money; they attended school as regularly as other boys and were "more agile in number computations" but usually fell behind their classmates; and they invariably gambled, occasionally tramped, and had a higher (one in four) chance of coming before a juvenile court.[53]

Findings about the effects of heavy loads and inclement weather on newsboys were also worrying. Despite the trimmer dimensions of tabloids, the overall size and weight of newspapers swelled in the twenties. The *Chicago Sunday Tribune* averaged 150 pages and weighed in at two and a half pounds. Even heftier was the ad-packed *Miami Daily News*, which ran to 500 pages during the Florida real estate boom. Such ballooning hadn't been seen since the mammoth weeklies of the 1840s, and it raised fresh concerns about the danger of hernias, back strain, and curvature of the spine among the boys. The weight of ordinary evening papers also added up; a Toledo study found that two-thirds of the city's newsboys

Figure 13.4. *Detroit News* hawkers promote the Old Newsboys Goodfellow Fund drive. *Detroit News*, Rotogravure Section, Dec. 16, 1923. 1. Author's collection.

started out with twenty-five to a hundred copies, weighing between eleven and forty-four pounds. A Cincinnati study found that 11 percent of newsboys had orthopedic problems, compared with 5 percent of non-newsboys; 38 percent had throat trouble, compared with 17 percent of others; and 14 percent had heart disease, compared with 4 percent. Street traders in Buffalo showed a slightly higher incidence of heart disease (6 percent compared with 4 percent), but a 1925 study sponsored by the New York Tuberculosis and Health Association, under the direction of future New Dealer Harry Hopkins, determined that aside from a greater propensity for flat feet, newsboys were as hale and hearty as boys who didn't sell papers. Life out of doors, said the experts, built up a resistance to disease that offset the strains of the job. Circulation managers concurred, pointing out that their sports programs contributed to the boys' health and made them the envy of their peers.[54]

Little Sluggers

Even more than scandal or aviation, athletics engrossed tabloid journalists. The 1920s became the golden age of sports due to the power of the press and a mad hankering for heroes. Newspapers—and increasingly radio—transformed local prizefights and ball games into national events. Newsstands sometimes exhibited hand-made scoreboards to keep pedestrians informed round by round or inning by inning. From April to October, thousands of newsboys sold "baseball extras" containing the day's scores and highlights. These late editions were printed and sold with breathtaking speed. At the first "Colored World Series" in 1924, newsboys at Baker Field in Philadelphia hawked papers describing the game before the stands had even emptied.[55]

Ballpark newsboys scalped tickets on opening day and at other big games. Some took part in an illegal nationwide baseball lottery that surfaced in 1922. Centered in Cleveland, the ring paid $1,000 daily, based on the total runs of six selected teams in four leagues (the National, American, International, and American Association). Newsboys were avid buyers and sellers of the tickets, which could be had for anywhere from a dime to a dollar at cigar stores, candy shops, coffeehouses, and newsstands. A St. Louis newsie brought down the ring when he told police that his supplier had cut him off when he refused to sell the tickets.[56]

Newspapers, clubs, and municipalities continued to sponsor newsboy baseball. In San Francisco, the Playgrounds Commission formed a special newsboy league in 1922 for boys who could only play on Sundays. Likewise in Louisiana, street circulators and dealers organized teams under the banner of the *Shreveport Journal*, but boys who got hurt on the field learned that the paper assumed no liability.[57]

Boxing flourished in both the amateur and professional ranks during the twenties. In the 1910s, when many states permitted only non-judged exhibitions of the manly art, sportswriters determined the winners as a service to gamblers. In some cases, no bettor knew the outcome of a fight until newsboys showed up with their extras. Circulation managers continued to host newsboy bouts to amuse and expand their distribution force. Until state officials intervened in 1923, some newsies in Troy, New York, boxed two or three nights a week, often traveling to nearby cities and receiving "fabulous" sums. The bouts served business interests. The day the *Milwaukee Journal* launched its Saturday sporting green (on greenish paper) in 1927, for example, the rival *Milwaukee News* treated all newsboys in town to a free movie. The *Journal* countered by arranging a boxing match in its mailroom, which attracted enough boys to circulate the issue. From such backroom bouts grew the prestigious Golden Gloves boxing tournament. The *Chicago Tribune* sponsored the first citywide amateur meet in 1923. Its sister sheet, the New York *Daily News*, took charge in 1927. Scores of other big-city dailies joined in, with winners meeting in regional and national championships.[58]

Ex-newsboy Jack Dempsey dominated the professional heavyweight division during these years. One of eleven children, he grew up in dusty poverty in Manassa and Montrose, Colorado, selling papers, shining shoes, washing dishes, and boxing. He tramped the country during his teen years, fighting for small purses in rough towns such as Goldfield, Victor, and Salt Lake City, where his kid brother sold papers in 1917 and was stabbed to death in a "war argument." Dubbed the "Manassa Mauler," Dempsey, at age 24, won the heavyweight title on July 4, 1919, before twenty thousand spectators in Toledo. Although outweighed by seventy pounds, he crushed his opponent's cheekbone with a "whirl-powered shovel hook." The next day around 4:00 a.m. the champ woke from a nightmare in which he had lost the fight. He threw on some clothes and found a newsboy outside the hotel still selling extras. "Who won the fight, son?" Dempsey asked. The newsboy gaped. "You did, ya big jerk. Look at the paper." The champ bought one for a buck and went back to bed.[59]

Dempsey defended his title twenty-four times over the next seven years and became the most popular sports figure of his time. In the midst of his reign he bemoaned all the schemers and sycophants who glommed on to him. The only consolation, he said, were the kids. He attended newsboy banquets in Salt Lake City and refereed newsboy charity bouts in Los Angeles. "I'm never so happy," he said, "as when I get into a gymnasium with a lot of newsboys and other kids and box with about a dozen of them. Gee! Kids like that!"[60]

Newsies liked it most when Dempsey boxed for real. His title fights set circulation records across the country. His famous 1927 "long count" rematch with Gene Tunney at Soldier Field in Chicago boosted sales of the *Oregonian* by 30,000, *New York Times* by 40,000, *Buffalo Courier Express* by 50,000, *New York Tribune* by 60,000, *Pittsburgh Post* by 75,000, *Cleveland Plain Dealer* by 100,000, and *Chicago Tribune* by 250,000. Using trucks, wagons, and speedboats, the Chicago paper had extras in newsboys' hands sixteen minutes after the referee raised Tunney's hand in victory.[61]

Other prominent pugilists of the period who got their start in newsboy clubs and alleys were three-time world welterweight champion Jack Britton, who began boxing while selling papers "back of the yards" in Chicago; Fidel LaBarba, a Los Angeles slugger who won the gold medal as a flyweight in the 1924 Olympic

Games in Paris and went on to become the world title holder; and "Rocky Kansas" (Rocco Tozzo) of Buffalo, who won the lightweight title in 1925 after fourteen years in the cauliflower trade. The list also includes "Newsboy Brown," aka Dave Montrose (originally Montrochevski), a Russian-born scrapper from Sioux City, Iowa, who became a flyweight and bantamweight title holder; world junior welterweight champ "Mushy Callahan" (Moshe Scheer) of New York; and featherweight Eddie Curley, "Champion Newsboy Fighter of New England" (Figure 13.5). Like Dempsey, these "sensational newsboy battlers" offered working-class youths hope that they just might be able to slip some of life's punches and finish on top.[62]

But newspapers had more than a sporting interest in developing newsboys' punching power. A kid who couldn't defend his corner was a dead loss. Mail room boxing matches enabled circulation managers to spot and nurture fistic talent. The diminutive LaBarba credited his early success in the ring to his on-the-job training. "I learned to fight here as a newsboy," he explained. "I used to fight in all those newsboy smokers. I worked for the *Los Angeles Express*, which was a tough paper to sell, so they had to pay you to hustle them. They carried me

Figure 13.5. Featherweight Eddie Curley, "champion newsboy fighter of New England," ca. 1929. After retiring from the ring, Curley worked in the circulation department of the *Boston Record American*. Eckel Collection, Princeton University Library.

around in the truck till they found a corner where they were having trouble, the guy wouldn't handle the *Express*, and it was always some big, tall guy. . . . When a customer walked up, I would rush in with my paper, pushing the other guy back. The pushing match ended with me 'Bingo!' knocking him down. After that, the guy would leave us alone. This went on and on. They gave me $3 a week, plus the money I received from the papers."[63]

Street violence peaked in the City of Angels in 1923 when Cornelius Vanderbilt Jr. launched the short-lived *Illustrated Daily News* as a respectable tabloid to compete with Hearst's *Examiner*. Hearst sluggers responded with threats and bribes, then fists and clubs. "Our hospital bills became exceedingly heavy," said Vanderbilt; "from fifty to one hundred boys had to be treated weekly for serious bruises, lacerations, etc." In lieu of legal action, Vanderbilt published pictures of his battered newsboys over a caption reading: "Is Los Angeles going to stand for such jungle methods of competition?" The warfare ceased only after an *Examiner* truck was firebombed, leaving the driver, a disabled vet, severely burned. While newspaper owners publicly bemoaned such thuggery, most accepted it as the price of doing business. They knew that peddling papers and pummeling the competition went together hand in glove.[64]

Alleys of Evil

Frustrated at their failure to raise concern over the "social evils" of street trading, reformers in the 1920s refocused attention on the corrupting habits that some newsboys acquired on the job, such as drinking, gambling, smoking, swearing, and whoring. Reformers had been documenting and denouncing these activities for years through the auspices of vice commissions, but they now sought to shine a spotlight on one source of the problem: news alleys. These were the busy back entrances and loading docks of newspaper offices, where children, adults, and vehicles converged at all hours of the day and night.[65]

One of the first to call attention to the moral danger of these alleys was Elsa Wertheim of Chicago's Juvenile Protective Association (JPA), a coalition of reform groups associated with Jane Addams's Hull House. Speaking at the National Child Labor Committee's thirteenth annual conference in Baltimore in 1917, Wertheim described Hearst Alley in Chicago as a depraved "club" or "hotel" for the down-and-out: "There are men from every part of the country and they find here shelter, bed and board, and a free lunch of coffee and rolls. They drink, gamble and swear the time away." She said the men trained the boys to be thieves and made dates with streetwalkers for them. "One boy accused another of attacking him and committing a pervert act upon him," she told the conference. "The younger boy is now in the hospital being treated for venereal disease and the older boy who is 16 is in the county jail and later will be sent to the home for the feeble-minded."[66]

Before the war, JPA members, accompanied by juvenile court officials and Boy Scout leaders, rounded up scores of boys from the alley and escorted them home or institutionalized them. This campaign ended after newspapers agreed to ban boys under 17 from their alleys, prohibit overnight sleeping, and allow police to patrol the premises. When management's commitment waned, the JPA resumed its investigations. Undercover agents revisited Hearst Alley in December 1923 and March 1924 and gathered evidence of rampant depravity. According to their field notes, a sordid, carnivlesque atmosphere prevailed. Hearst Alley was not a narrow dead end but a large courtyard with four or five gated entrances, which, when opened, formed a recess fifty feet deep into the distribution rooms. The concrete floor was strewn with old papers and fouled from spitting. An open trench served as a lavatory. Its walls were covered with graffiti—phrases such as "Cinci is a punk / Cinci eats cunt" and crude pictures of genitalia.[67]

Up to a hundred men and boys were milling about waiting for the night edition, which came off the press around seven-thirty. A vendor equipped with a gas stove sold hot dogs and hamburger for 5¢ or 10¢ apiece. Men sat around drinking from hip flasks and playing the harmonica. Boys sang dirty songs, teased each other, and smoked. Ten-year-old Isadore Weisman, a fifth-grader, finished off a twelve-pack of Lucky Strikes he had opened an hour before. Sex was the main topic of conversation. The men told about their "manly experiences" to interested groups of all ages. Older boys offered to make dates with prostitutes for the younger ones. All the new arrivals were asked "debauching questions" about their sisters. Laughter and foul language filled the air ("You can't shit me," "Fuck you!"). One boy told his friends he knew a good man to sleep with who paid two dollars. "Damn! I'll fuck him all night for that," replied another. Two boys then began wrestling; bystanders egged them on rather than breaking them up. A long line of boys danced behind a harmonica player of "subnormal" intelligence.[68]

A half dozen small craps games were in progress throughout the alley, and one big one made up of men and boys was under way on the thirty-foot-long iron counter of the mailroom. Dozens of spectators cheered and taunted the gamblers, who were known to lose a day's earnings in a single throw. A policeman passed by on his rounds and separated two fighting boys but paid no attention to the gamblers. Jake, a Polish kid, bragged that policemen frequented his parents' saloon and gambling den. A 10-year-old snuck up behind the patrolman, threw his arms around his waist, and cried in a shrill voice, "Officer, officer, call a cop!"[69]

The games and horseplay ceased as soon as the papers appeared. Drivers and their helpers loaded up while the hawkers elbowed their way to the counters. Those who wanted a batch on credit wrote their names and the quantity on a wall. Murder threats followed the slightest shove or disagreement until everyone had been served and the alley emptied.[70]

Newsboys started trickling back a few hours later to pay for their papers or get out the bulldog edition between midnight and 4:00 a.m. Jimmy C., age 15, hopped rides on news trucks "jes fer fun," but the steady helpers got a dollar a night and sometimes breakfast. Some drivers offered to take the boys home to sleep with them, whether out of kindness or lust. Those who remained in the alley sat around drinking or talking and eventually found a quiet corner, table, or cart on which to sleep. Many stuck close to a buddy to keep from being robbed or molested. A watchman kept an eye on things, and the janitors began cleaning up before the morning edition was ready and the next group of boys arrived.[71]

Far from exaggerating conditions, the JPA reports are substantiated by recollections of boys who worked in Chicago's news alleys. Among them was Clifford Shaw, who described in his autobiography how he started drinking, gambling, and "jack-rolling" drunks while a newsboy. "We sometimes stunned the drunks by 'giving them the club' in a dark place near a lonely alley," said Shaw. "It was bloody work, but necessity demanded it—we had to live."[72]

Likewise, Philip Marcus, who began selling papers in Chicago as an 8-year-old runaway, took pride in his intimate knowledge of the streets. "You could find out from us almost anything you wanted to know," he recalled in a 1939 interview, "the location of the gambling joints, the whorehouses, almost anything.... We was always on the make. We had to be."[73]

Then there was Nels Anderson, who hustled the *Daily News* and *Journal* up and down Madison Street. He routinely shortchanged customers, stole from peddlers, ran errands for prostitutes, and lied to his parents. He subjected his actions to a strict moral calculus, "always weighing rewards against punishements."[74]

These accounts suggest that news alleys could be vile places indeed. Reformers who tried to expose their darker side wanted to shame publishers into upholding the same standards of decency that they advocated in their editorial columns. JPA director F. Zeta Youmans said that newspapers possessed the power but not the will to clean up the alleys: "Business cares so much more about itself than anybody cares about the city's children."[75]

Some papers bowed to the pressure. Hearst's *American* and *Herald and Examiner* pledged to monitor their employees' treatment of newsboys, build restrooms for them, and enforce rules against sleeping in the alleys or mailrooms. But *Tribune* publisher Robert McCormick got fed up with the JPA's snooping and sniping. He informed the association that "any stranger trespassing on our property after midnight and hiding in some room takes on the guise of a burglar" and would be treated accordingly. Newsies, too, got wise to the investigators, one of whom earned the nickname "John D.," after John D. Rockefeller, because he tipped big but was never seen working.[76]

Chicago was by no means an anomaly. Philip Davis, supervisor of licensed minors in Boston, said he broke up many "questionable associations" in their earlier stages. Survey takers in Salt Lake City found that its hundred or so newsboys, who ranged in age from 8 to 16, encountered "all forms of unwholesomeness," from drinking, gambling, and prostitution to "exploitation by degenerates." And Tulane University sociologist Ben Kaplan attested to the key role of New Orleans newsboys in the city's underground sex economy. To research his 1929 master's thesis, Kaplan donned old clothes, mingled with the boys, and sold newspapers himself. He said many boys peddled the weekly *Sun*, "house organ for the red-light district," and escorted prostitutes to prevent their arrest under an ordinance regulating women's movements after dark. Despite the vigilance of patrolman Fred Mischler, the city's longtime supervisor of newsboys, the children also passed out advertising cards for brothels and served them as "runners," "look outs," or "watchboys."[77]

Many newsies patronized brothels as well. "No mister, tain't nothing wrong wid dat," one boy explained to Kaplan. "If God didn't want dat He never woulda made it." Another newsboy spotted leaving a house of prostitution told Kaplan he had been in there with a mulatto girl whom he had paid 40¢ and two newspapers. "Dat ain't nothing Mister," clarified Kaplan's young guide, "sometimes the boys goes to nigger gals and pays dem only two bits." And for those who couldn't afford that price, there was a dance hall on Iberville Street where 10¢ could buy a waltz with a girl "wot ain't had on very much clothes." Kaplan photographed "typical" newsboys riding streetcars, shooting dice, and hanging out. Many are black or Italian. One photo with the caption "A newsboy resort on Liberty Street" shows a smiling white girl in a sleeveless dress standing barefoot in a doorway. One of Kaplan's informants told him, "Sho man—dey gets kids in there and takes their money away from dem—sure." The phrasing positions the youths as innocent victims of wicked women. Yet the girl in the picture looks to be in her early teens, no older than many of the newsboys in Kaplan's photographs.[78]

While these exposés of news alley life paint a dark picture of the occupational subculture of newsboys, they also offer evidence that newsboys were not necessarily corrupted by the streets. Rather, they acquired necessary survival skills and a genuine moral outlook there. In January 1925, for instance, a JPA investigator overheard a group of fifteen boys in Hearst Alley discussing a front-page item about the "expectant condition" of Mrs. Nicholas Longworth, the daughter of Theodore Roosevelt and wife of an Ohio congressman. "One after another gave opinions on why wealthy people so often went childless while the poor people were over-burdened," reported the investigator. "Several aired their knowledge of prevention used in families where there was plenty of money for expensive douches and medical treatment. A debate then followed as to whether or not such persons were actual murderers."[79] To eavesdrop on this conversation is to gain a greater appreciation of the rich and varied sex education acquired in news alleys. These little "Hearstlings," as they were called, not only discussed birth control and abortion but understood them as class issues with profound moral implications.

Capitalists in Embryo

Despite their propensity for vice and violence, newsboys' reputations rose in the twenties with every uptick of the Dow. As purveyors of a consumer good that advertised other consumer goods in a culture that exalted consumerism, carrier and holler boys became paragons of commerce and achievement. Long a staple in American newspapers, stories about ex-newsies who made good now glutted the market. The tag "Once a Newsboy" sat atop so many profiles and obituaries that news peddling seemed a prerequisite for success. Among the tycoons whose humble newsboy origins merited frequent mention in the press were theater chain owner Marcus Loew, RCA executive David Sarnoff, Yellow Cab founder John Hertz, Ford Motor Company magnate and Michigan senator James Couzens, Chicago Cubs president William Veeck Sr., and American Express vice president Howard K. Brooks, inventor of the traveler's check.[80]

Other prominent figures who enhanced newsies' value as "diamonds in the rough" were the 28-year-old president of the University of California, Berkeley, Robert Gordon Sproul; Chicago bishop Bernard James Shell; and Florida real estate developer D. P. Davis, who got his start hawking papers to soldiers during the Spanish-American War. More than biographical facts, such details proclaimed the virtues of laissez-faire capitalism. The inventive genius of Thomas Edison never would have developed, argued *Living Age* magazine, if he had been born in Germany, where the state would have prevented him from selling newspapers until he was 25 years old, then charged him 150 marks for the privilege and prohibited him from crying his papers aloud.[81]

The popular or "lively" arts reinforced the image of newsboys as capitalists, not "criminals in embryo," as muckraker Scott Nearing had called them back in 1907. Cartoonists showed them banking their earnings and paying their "income tax" to elderly lady vendors. *Life* magazine illustrator J. R. Shaver depicted a gang of awed street kids ogling the headline "Newsboy Leaves Millions." The caption asks, "Why Not?" (Figure 13.6). Dime novelists writing for the *Fame and Fortune Weekly* inspired similar hopes with serials such as "Dick, the Wall Street

Figure 13.6. J. R. Shaver, "Why Not?" *Life*, May 19, 1921, 715. Eckel Collection, Princeton University Library.

Waif; or, From Newsboy to Stock Broker. By A Self Made Man." Newspapers lent credence to such dreams with stories about vendors like 94-year-old Francis Gurks of Portland, Oregon, who wore burlap on his feet in lieu of shoes but left a $50,000 estate to the US Bureau of Education.[82]

Following in his footsteps was 11-year-old Bernard Green of the Bronx. He earned $1.75 a day in the early 1920s selling the *Daily News* at subway stations. He passed up high school so he could continue selling papers on ferries and trains and in hotels and office towers, building an empire of 120 newsstands in dozens of cities. Not counting those who got their start in the 1920s, a record number of millionaires were minted during the decade; this once-exclusive club swelled from 8,600 Americans in 1923 to almost 40,000 in 1928, reported the US Treasury.[83]

Public attitudes toward the rich simultaneously swung away from the gospel teaching that they had little chance of salvation to the modern notion that most deserved their wealth. The newsboy figure shouldered these shifting beliefs along with his papers. He managed the feat, in part, through the power of advertising. He graced the labels of Newsboy Oranges, Headline Peaches, Hustler Pears, and Scoop Melons (Plate 28) and appeared in ads for General Electric, Dodge Trucks, Trans World Airlines, and Cream of Wheat cereal. Cream of Wheat's signature artist, Edward Brewer, made the black chef Rastus and his little white newsboy pal into national icons, a pairing reminiscent of antebellum minstrel shows. These firms portrayed news peddling as a noble pursuit rather than a regrettable hardship. One company, Prudential, deviated from the norm with a 1927 ad showing a thinly clad youth hawking papers on a snowy street over a caption reading, "His Father Let His Life Insurance Lapse."[84]

Newsboys became insurance salesmen themselves when *Terre Haute Post* publisher R. H. Gore began offering accident insurance to subscribers. He formed his own underwriting company, which acquired 130 client newspapers that sold 60,000 penny-a-week policies, earning him a fortune. To help recruit and motivate salesmen-carriers, Gore launched the Newspaper Boys' Series of juvenile novels in 1921 featuring Renfro Horn, a tireless suburban paperboy from a well-to-do family. In *The Mystery of the Missing Eyebrows*, the first (and last) of twelve planned stories, Gore, writing under a pseudonym, tells how the boy builds up the town's most difficult route ("Old Grief") while gathering clues that expose a ring of jewel thieves, counterfeiters, and kidnappers. "The newspaper training is valuable," says the preface, "as much so as school, but you must be a go-getter like Renfro Horn."[85]

Rather than leave success to chance, several businessmen established savings-and-loan schemes to encourage newsboys to follow in their footsteps. Los Angeles clothier F. B. Silverwood opened thousands of $1 savings accounts for local newsies and encouraged their own deposits. Another thrift plan devised by James Milford Place of Washington, DC, and popularized by Civil War–era newsboy and mining engineer John Hays Hammond called on newspapers to form groups of fifty boys who would each deposit $1 a month for five years. Local philanthropists would add $100 a year to the account, earning each boy 19 percent interest, or $100 on his $60 investment. Hammond's plan won endorsements from President Coolidge, Chief Justice Taft, and cabinet secretaries Hoover and Mellon.[86]

Newsboy scholarship funds also took on new life in the twenties. The Boston Newsboys' Protective Union revived its annual award to the member who scored highest on the Harvard entrance exam. Joseph Schneider, 19, of Roxbury, took top honors in 1920, followed by Israel Kopp, 17, of the West End, in 1921. Dozens of others gained admittance, perhaps contributing to the college's 1926 decision to cut Jewish enrollment from 30 to 15 percent of the student body. In addition, the Harry E. Burroughs Newsboys' Foundation in Boston offered scholarships shortly after opening its doors on Beacon Hill in 1927. Burroughs (originally Hersh Baraznik) began selling papers the day he arrived alone in this country in 1903 at age 12. He wore a fur coat that smelled of Mother Russia and spoke no English except the names of the newspapers he cried. Four years later he won a scholarship from the *Boston Traveler* and went on to Suffolk Law School and a lucrative legal practice. Over the next forty years his foundation awarded interest-free loans of $200 to more than three hundred college-bound newsboys.[87]

Despite the exclusion of women from many schools and professions, gender was ostensibly no barrier to success in the news trade. The 1921 novel *Youth Triumphant* told the story of Patsy, a girl of the slums who disguises her sex in a newsboy's tattered garb and fights to regain her rightful station in life. Runaway rich girls passed as newsboys during the twenties, and poor girls such as San Francisco assistant city attorney Mary Rantz Schwab used the trade to achieve their goals.[88]

Another role model was Little Orphan Annie, star of the era's most popular comic strip. Always self-reliant, Annie discovered the virtues of news peddling in a two-month-long series that ran in the winter of 1927 and 1928. Strapped for rent and tired of taking in washing, she starts selling the *Daily Reflector* on a neglected corner. She fends off crooks and competitors by wielding her lucky horseshoe, and builds up her business until a "wrecking crew" of toughs runs her off the corner (Figure 13.7). She retaliates by forcing a motorist to swerve into her stand and then clobbering the villains as they give chase. "Huh! Think they can ruin my business an' get by with it, eh?" she says. "An' they tell yuh to forgive an' forget—huh! Not while I've got my health—If yer too proud, or scared, to fight for what's yours yuh don't d'serve to have anything." Creator Harold Gray

Figure 13.7. Harold Gray, *Little Orphan Annie,* "The Horseshoe Trick," *Chicago Tribune,* Jan. 4, 1928, 18. Courtesy Tribune Content Agency.

received a call from circulation boss Max Annenberg, saying, "That's exactly the way it operates, that's real. How did you know about it?"[89]

Some African Americans realized and perpetuated a color-blind myth of success in the twenties. Playwright Garland Anderson, a former San Francisco newsie, won acclaim with the 1925 production of *Appearances*, the first full-length Broadway play written by a Negro and starring an interracial cast. Backed by Al Jolson, it was a serious courtroom drama about a black bellboy falsely accused of raping a white woman. Anderson, with just four years of schooling, also self-published a memoir, *From Newsboy and Bellhop to Playwright*, in 1925. Subtitled *The Hows and Whys of Your Success*, it helped launch his next career as a motivational speaker. He saw no contradiction in his dual role as critic and defender of American society and values.[90]

Another black newsboy, 17-year-old Harry F. Liscomb, enjoyed fleeting fame in 1925 as author of *The Prince of Washington Square*. The Harlem-born prodigy wrote the novel in three months. "Of course it might have been finished long before then had I not had so many brothers and sisters around me," he explained. The son of a street cleaner, Liscomb wrote amid the hubbub of six siblings. The story, in which a brave newsboy rescues a young heiress, owes much to Horatio Alger but is told in a torrent of words fashioned from pulp romances, stage and screen melodramas, and the latest slang. A publisher's note attests to its authenticity, "undisturbed by editorial blue pencil." The novel received good reviews amid the swirl of the Harlem Renaissance, only to be slapped by a cheeky new magazine, the *New Yorker*, as "just the story that would be written by a clever kid with the kind of head big words stick wrongside-up in, after his consuming bales of magazine and newspaper trash and acres of movie captions."[91]

Intrepid newsboys and insidious racial stereotypes did populate the silent movies of the era; the boys overcame disabilities, reformed traffic laws, and defeated all foes. The 1920 hit *Dinty* follows a fighting Frisco newsie, the sole support of his Irish mum, whose intimate knowledge of Chinatown enables him and his two associates (a black boy and a Chinese boy) to outwit Wong Tai, a sinister opium dealer who has kidnapped a judge's daughter. Played by Wesley Barry, "the freckle-faced kid," *Dinty* shows that Good can triumph over Evil as long as Good knows his way around town. Given the appeal of such plots and protagonists, Richard Harding Davis's fictional newsboy-detective leaped onto the screen in the 1928 six-reeler *Let 'Er Go Gallegher*, starring 12-year-old Junior Coghlan. The thrilling climax placed him behind the wheel of a car wedged between two speeding fire engines.[92]

Challenging these fanciful tales was the lone voice of novelist Thomas Wolfe. *Look Homeward, Angel*, his autobiographical first novel of 1929, plumbed the psychological depths of several brothers who support their family by selling newspapers and magazines in a town like Wolfe's native Asheville, North

Carolina. The youngest, 8-year-old Eugene Gant, tries to affect the kind of "insane extraversion" of his older brother Luke, whose wide grin and ready wit distinguish him as one who will "make his mark." Yet Luke's "hungry gregariousness" is fueled by a deep-seated need for affection that gives rise to stammering and bedwetting. The shy, bookish Eugene, by contrast, feels humiliated "making such a wretched little nuisance of himself that riddance was purchased only at the price of the magazine." Ultimately, his embittered eldest brother, Ben, who had to leave school in the eighth grade to work full-time as a carrier, rebukes his parents for exploiting Eugene and ruining all their children with their "cant and twaddle" about independence, self-reliance, and success.[93]

Road to the White House

Complicating the myth of success was the newsboy's real and rhetorical participation in Republican-era politics. Newsboys asserted their presence in the field early on when pundits billed the 1920 presidential race between GOP senator Warren Harding and Democratic governor James Cox, both newspaper publishers, as a "Competition Between Two Ohio Newsies." There was some truth to the claim. After college in the early 1880s, Harding wrote editorials, set type, solicited ads, and delivered copies of the weekly *Mirror* in Marion, Ohio. As a low-paid teacher in the late 1880s, Cox delivered the entire run of his brother-in-law's *Middletown Weekly Signal*. Thus did the pair earn the right to run for the nation's top job.[94]

The conservative Harding campaigned from his front porch, while the moderate Cox stumped the country. Both played up their newsboy credentials. A hundred of Harding's newsboys celebrated his nomination by pounding the walls of his *Marion Daily Star* with sticks until the plaster fell down on their heads. He attributed their usual good behavior to Mrs. Harding, who ran a "business kindergarten" for the boys. "This good wife marshaled the newsies into the little army that carried The Star to our homes," he told reporters. "Her guiding influence . . . were such that they have almost without exception developed into the leading business men of Marion." One who went astray, little Norman Thomas, grew up to bear the standard for the Socialist Party of America. "No pennies ever escaped her," recalled Thomas.[95]

Cox, meanwhile, enjoyed the showy support of his own newsboys in Dayton and Springfield. Five hundred of them marched in a parade, shouting "Hurrah for the boss!" and carrying banners depicting Cox as one of their own. "We deliver the goods. So does Cox," read one banner. "No kicks on Jimmie's route," assured another. Cox even posed for a film tracing his rise from small-town newsboy to presidential nominee. He was incensed, however, by a cartoon that appeared in the *Saturday Evening Post* on the eve of the election portraying him as an excitable, scandal-mongering newsboy in short pants, in contrast to the dignified Harding tending a Safe & Sane News Stand (Figure 13.8). "The impression is sought . . . that I am irresponsible. Senator Harding grave and reliable," seethed Cox, who called the drawing "disloyal propaganda" from a magazine that claimed to be objective.[96]

The cartoon had little bearing on Harding's victory given the country's disillusionment with Wilsonian internationalism, but the Cox character was right: Harding's administration would be plagued by scandal. The president appoined his wife's favorite newsboy, Ora Baldinger, as a military aide, and his cronies looted the nation's oil reserves, health care budgets, and other assets. Harding died unexpectedly in 1923, and accusations of incompetence melted into declarations of affection. Members of the Boston Newsboys' Club wore black badges inscribed "In Memory of President Harding" and raised funds to complete a bronze statue of his Airedale, Laddie Boy, which they donated to the Smithsonian. The club rarely missed a chance to extract a civics lesson or wring publicity from the headlines. The boys next started a nickel drive to erect a tablet honoring Lindbergh. And when in January 1929 the US Senate approved the Kellogg-Briand Pact, intended to outlaw war, they decorated their headquarters with flags of the fifteen signatory nations and read the pact in unison.[97]

The politician who best exemplified the urban, ethnic, working-class ethos of the newsboy was New York governor Al Smith. Adopting "The Sidewalks of New York" as his campaign song, the "onetime 'wuxtry' shouter" won

Figure 13.8. Herbert Johnson, "Safe & Sane News Stand." Published a month before the 1920 presidential election, the cartoon favored Republican Warren Harding over Democrat James Cox, both of whom were ex-newsboys. Cox felt it cost him the race. *Saturday Evening Post* 93, no. 14 (Oct. 2, 1920): 7. Library of Congress, Washington, DC.

Figure 13.9. New York governor Al Smith at the annual Washington Birthday's banquet at the Newsboys' Lodging House, 1920. Eckel Collection, Princeton University Library.

four terms between 1918 and 1926. He attended the Washington's Birthday banquet at the Newsboys' Lodging House, where he would talk about his days on the street and encourage the boys to make something of themselves (Figure 13.9). "Here in America men succeed only through their own labor," he told them in 1921. "It makes no difference where you come from or what sort of start you have." When he won the Democratic nomination for president in 1928, New York newsies pledged a dollar each for his war chest. But the country wasn't ready for an Irish Catholic "wet" in the White House, let alone the Socialist Party's ex-newsboy ticket of Norman Thomas and James Hudson Maurer. Instead it elected Herbert Hoover, a temperate Quaker whose record of public service included a stint in the news trade, having started a campus paper route while a student at Stanford University. Also on the ticket was the Native American newsboy from Kansas, Senator Charles Curtis.[98]

Hyphenated Americans with bona fide newsboy credentials gained real power in the 1920s as members of Congress. They include Adolph Sabath of Chicago, Peter Tague of Boston, Meyer Jacobstein of Rochester, and Robert F. Wagner of New York—all progressive Democrats who defended worker and immigrant rights and opposed Prohibition and the Ku Klux Klan. Jacobstein

Figure 13.10. Congressman Meyer Jacobstein, a former Rochester newsie, takes part in a newsboys' theater party sponsored by three local papers in December 1927. Glass negative, Acc. No. 40.332.487. From the Albert R. Stone Negative Collection, Rochester Museum & Science Center, Rochester, NY.

(Figure 13.10) dropped out of grammar school in the 1890s to sell papers and shine shoes on the streets of Rochester, but he managed to become an economics professor and serve three terms in the House of Representatives, from 1923 to 1929. He denounced on principle the Immigration Act of 1924, which excluded Asians and cut the flow of southern and eastern Europeans to a trickle. "Nothing is more un-American," the freshman congressman told his colleagues, "nothing could be more dangerous, in a land the Constitution of which says that all men are created equal, than to write into our law a theory which puts one race above another, which stamps one group of people as superior and another as inferior."[99]

Wagner, the German-born son of a janitor, reached the Senate in 1927. He started selling papers at age 9, shortly after his family arrived in steerage. He soon acquired a route that got him up every day at 3:00 a.m., and by 13 he occupied a choice location in City Hall Park, all while excelling in school. As the youngest of seven children, he was afforded the privilege of going to City College and then law school. As state senator, he cut his teeth investigating and eliminating the conditions that led to the Triangle Shirtwaist Fire in 1911. In Washington he introduced bills calling for job insurance and old-age pensions while Hoover was still in office, and he went on to push through landmark New Deal legislation on health, housing, and labor. If someone suggested that his early struggles and later successes were arguments in favor of child labor and slum poverty, Wagner, eyes blazing, would snap, "That is the most god-awful bunk. I came through it, yes. That was luck, luck, luck! Think of the others."[100]

Defenders of Justice

Newsboys both challenged and contributed to the rising tide of xenophobia that swept 1920s America. Some defied the intolerance of Henry Ford and the Ku Klux Klan, while others shouted hateful headlines that set off a spate of race riots. With his eye on the White House, Ford acquired the *Dearborn Independent* in 1919 and began peddling a virulent brand of anti-Semitism. The sixteen-page weekly contained shrill diatribes against Jews, immigrants, and unions. "A union is a neat trick for a Jew to have in hand when he wants to get a clutch on an industry," declared one editorial. The paper also charged (not altogether inaccurately) that the American stage was under the control of "a group of former bootblacks, newsboys, ticket speculators, prize ring habitués and Bowery characters." Ford foisted the ad-free *Independent* on his dealers, who in turn forced subscriptions on customers. Some dealers hired vendors to peddle the nickel sheet on street corners. They met mounting opposition in 1921. In Chicago, newsboys selling the Jewish weekly *Sentinel* took up posts opposite *Independent* newsboys and tried to outshout them, which led to scuffles and a police order banning the *Independent* as a menace. In Columbus, newsboys who were imported from Philadelphia sold the anti-Ford paper *Fact* on the same corners as the *Independent* vendors, which again caused clashes and the barring of both parties from crying their wares. Mayors and police chiefs in Toledo, Cleveland, St. Louis, Pittsburgh, Boston, and Detroit issued similar bans, which were overturned on First Amendment grounds. But the bad publicity, coupled with dwindling auto sales, a damaging libel suit, and fear of a Jewish boycott of his new Model A, led Ford to issue an apology and stop the paper in 1927.[101]

Newsboys played a similar role in the backlash against the resurgent Klan, its hate now directed not just at blacks but also at Jews, Catholics, Bolsheviks, and bootleggers. The "Invisible Empire" claimed more than three million members in the 1920s, including hundreds of thousands in the North. Members from all social ranks found common ground in blaming ethnic and religious minorities for the postwar recession, job losses, and crime sprees. Also troubling was the fact that these "undesirables" were reproducing at a much faster clip than old-stock Americans. The reborn Klan used the latest media and marketing techniques to trumpet its message; it hired public relations experts and produced movies, records, and radio shows. Yet it did not forswear time-honored methods of recruitment and intimidation, such as newspapers, cross burnings, parades (including marches down Pennsylvania Avenue in Washington, DC, in 1925 and 1926), and assaults. During a 1922 Klan campaign against a hostile newspaper in central California, Hammonton newsboy Emil Raets was beaten on his route by young "night riders" dressed in white robes and hoods. Klan parents inculcated their beliefs in their children and inducted those under 14 as Junior Klansmen, who patrolled the periphery of rallies and peddled Klan papers. They distributed such organs of hate as the *Searchlight* in Georgia, the *Kluxer* in Tennessee, the *Western American* in Oregon, and the *Fiery Cross* throughout the Midwest.[102]

Klan newsboys not only espoused violence in their papers but also tasted a bit of it. Catholic newsboys chased them off the streets of Indianapolis, Bloomington, and Hammond, Indiana, and destroyed their papers in two towns in Ohio. The hooded order in Steubenville appealed to the governor in 1923 for protection from the "mostly foreign" newsboys. In nearby Niles, clashes broke out in 1924 between Klansmen and members of a predominantly Italian American anti-Klan group, the Knights of the Flaming Circle. A cross burning outside a Catholic church led the group to retaliate by blowing up the front porch of the pro-Klan mayor. The National Guard was called in, and the commander's first order was to eject all Youngstown newsboys who had shown up to sell papers touting the Grand Titan's threat to parade in Niles "no matter what."[103]

Anti-Klan newsboys in the Midwest did not just disrupt the sale of Klan papers but also sold their own papers, such as *Our Neighbor, Toleration*, and *Tolerance*, put out by the Catholic-led American Unity League. The paper sometimes unmasked Klan members, thereby placing vendors in jeopardy. In Racine, Wisconsin, newsboys sold issues of *Tolerance* that identified a candidate for sheriff as a Klansmen, despite threats of arrest and physical retribution. Newsboys in Washington, DC, meanwhile, boycotted a newspaper that carried false accusations against the Catholic Church.[104]

Moreover, newsboys played a central role in the impeachment trial that helped bring down the Klan in Indiana and dash its efforts to build a national political machine. Their involvement began in February 1927 when a judge in Muncie— the era's prototypical "Middletown"—ordered the arrest of forty newsboys for selling a weekly paper that claimed Klan domination of local government. The *Muncie Post-Democrat* reported that Judge Clarence Dearth had close ties to the Klan and "fixed" juries in his crusade against bootleggers. Judge Dearth, who taught the largest adult Bible class in the city, charged editor George Dale with libel and contempt of court. Dale fled the state, but his wife put out the paper and kept up the editorial attacks.[105]

A month later Judge Dearth faced the Indiana Senate on impeachment charges. Three newsboys bore witness against him. Johnny Raines, clad in knee breeches and a red sweater, told how he and his pals had been brought into Dearth's court and robbed of their papers. "The judge said there was a piece in the paper that slandered him and the mayor," testified Raines. "He told us not to sell the paper again until he saw what was in it." Raines sold the paper anyway, earning good money until a policeman spotted him and chased him up an alley. "I stopped when he put his hand on his gun," said Raines. "He said: 'You'd feel funny if I shot your hind end off, wouldn't you?' He slapped me and took me to court again." Undaunted, Raines sold 415 copies of the proscribed paper the next week, but said he was still owed for the fourteen copies confiscated by the judge.[106]

Despite evidence of jury packing and verdict fixing, Judge Dearth retained his office. Dale was arrested on his return to the state, convicted of trumped-up liquor violations, and sentenced to eighteen months in prison. While free on appeal, the crusading editor was elected mayor of Muncie. Franklin Roosevelt pardoned him in 1933, by which time the Klan was a spent force in Indiana.[107]

For African Americans, the 1920s were a decade of pride and possibility, of rights fairly won and fiercely denied. The race was on the move—literally, from south to north as the Great Migration hit its stride, and politically, from caution to militancy through the efforts of the National Association for the Advancement of Colored People, Marcus Garvey's Universal Improvement Association, and a thriving ethnic press. Some two hundred African American dailies and almost five hundred weeklies, including Garvey's *Negro World*, flourished in the 1920s. As readers, merchants, and vendors, black families relied on them as they built new lives in what poet Langston Hughes called the "cities of hope." As a 12-year-old in Lawrence, Kansas, Hughes hawked the socialist *Appeal to Reason*, along with the *Saturday Evening Post* and the *Lawrence Democrat* until the latter's editor warned him that the *Appeal* would "get colored folks in trouble."[108]

These cities of hope exploded during the "Red Summer" of 1919, when 76 blacks were lynched and another 250 killed in race riots throughout the country.

Some of the worst violence occurred in Chicago, where the fatal stoning of a black youth, 14-year-old Eugene Williams, in a whites-only swimming area of Lake Michigan led to a five-day rampage that left 38 men and boys dead and 500 injured. Amidst the mayhem, African American newsboys handed out 30,000 *Chicago Defender* handbill "extras" urging readers to stay indoors. Order was restored only with the arrival of the National Guard.[109]

White newsboys, by contrast, found race riots exciting and profitable. Omaha vendor Fred Witte's "best day" in a fifty-seven-year career was September 29, 1919, when he sold 5,200 papers hours after the courthouse riot and spectacle lynching of Will Brown, an African American accused of a rape. Witte made $46 on that day of shame. Newsboys actually sparked two subsequent riots. In 1921 Baltimore, the cheating and slapping of a black newsboy by a crowd of whites escalated into a night of armed clashes between the races. And in Tulsa, white newsboys shouting "Negro Assaults a White Girl" preceded a riot that killed 300 people and destroyed the black section of town, leaving thousands homeless. Six-year-old John Hope Franklin, the future historian, would never forget those inflammatory cries.[110]

Coming of age amid such mayhem also left a lasting impression on future novelist Richard Wright. He started selling two Chicago weeklies in 1919 as a sixth-grader in Jackson, Mississippi, to earn spending money and gain access to the Zane Grey westerns that were serialized in the papers. Wright built up a string of customers, and his grandmother, a former slave, thought that her troublesome charge was at last "becoming a serious, right-thinking boy." Then a neighbor pointed out that the papers—W. D. Boyce's *Saturday Blade* and *Chicago Ledger*—were filled with Ku Klux Klan propaganda that advocated lynching. "If you sell 'em, you're just helping white people to kill you," the man explained. On his way home Wright threw the papers into a ditch. What had looked to him like opportunity was exploitation; what had seemed like free enterprise was race suicide. In dumping his papers, Wright rejected the acquisitive individualism inherent in the American ideology of success. The black boy repudiated the newsboy.[111]

Black youths nevertheless continued to peddle papers throughout the twenties as a means of personal advancement, family support, and even community uplift. They accounted for 3 percent of newsboys in Omaha, 8 percent in Atlanta, and 10 percent in Columbus, Ohio, and Newark, New Jersey. Lewis Hine's 1924 portrait of Roland, a smiling 11-year-old newsboy from Newark, evokes the "joy in work" theme he started to recognize in his subjects (Figure 13.11). In Washington, DC, almost half (46 percent) of the newsboys were black; two out of three were hawkers rather than carriers, while the reverse was true of whites. According to a survey by the US Children's Bureau, most were the sons of factory and construction workers, though a higher percentage of blacks

Figure 13.11. Lewis Hine, *Roland, Eleven-Year-Old Negro Newsboy, Newark, N.J.—August 1st, 1924.* Library of Congress, Washington, DC.

than whites had mothers who were the chief breadwinner, usually working as maids.[112]

News peddling enabled African American youths such as Ralph Bunche in Southern California to buy necessities including food and clothing and to afford luxuries like movies and candy. The future United Nations ambassador delivered the *Los Angeles Times* until his senior year in high school in 1922, which alleviated his grandmother's financial burdens and enhanced his status in the family. African American news sellers took pride in their work: adult dealers in Cincinnati hosted the annual Colored Newsboys' Ball in the city's grandest hotel, and the black press routinely praised the work ethic of its young distributors.[113]

The most influential African American newspaper was the *Chicago Defender,* founded in 1905 by Robert Abbott of Georgia (Figure 13.12). He had learned the printing trade at Hampton Institute in Virginia and been inspired by visitors who included Frederick Douglass and Ida B. Wells. Like most of his readers, Abbott arrived in Chicago nearly penniless. He started the paper as a weekly and built a national circulation that peaked at 250,000..[114]

The paper's reputation and circulation reached the remotest hamlets of the Deep South, where it was distributed by local agents, theatrical troupes, and Pullman porters, who formed the race-proud Brotherhood of Sleeping Car

Figure 13.12. Chicago Defender newspaper publisher Robert Sengstacke Abbott and some of the paper's more than 500 newsboys in the 1920s. Courtesy of the Chicago Defender Charities, Inc.

Porters in 1925. "Along the road, where a whole lot of people couldn't get to town, we used to roll up the papers and tie a string around 'em," recalled porter E. D. Nixon of Alabama. "We'd throw these papers off to these people." The *Defender* infuriated southern whites with its fearless coverage of lynching and its forceful editorials and cartoons urging blacks to leave the fields for factory jobs up north. Communities tried to ban the paper. When that failed they resorted to violence. A dozen agent-correspondents were driven from their homes and two were killed while distributing the *Defender*.[115]

During the postwar years Abbott and circulation manager Phil Jones, the *Defender's* first newsboy at age 6, supervised more than five hundred paperboys and launched contests to recruit sellers nationwide. Young men in Harlem received their papers from a shiny *Defender* truck and distributed them dressed in their Sunday best. Children could join the *Defender* Newsies' Club, founded in New York in 1921. The paper launched a children's column that year edited by 10-year-old Chicago newsboy Robert Watkins, who adopted the pen name Bud Billiken, after a popular papier-mâché doll. Taken over by 13-year-old Willard Motley two years later, the column grew to a full page featuring a Bud Billiken comic strip about a mischievous *Defender* newsboy that spawned a network of Bud Billiken Clubs, whose membership of boys and girls reached 250,000 by 1927. In 1929 Abbott sponsored a parade and picnic for his Chicago boys, with appearances by Duke Ellington, Amos 'n' Andy, and other celebrities. Known as the Bud Billiken Parade, it remains the largest annual African American parade in the United States.[116]

Aiming to step up its youth work and improve sales, Abbott founded the *Defender*'s Newsboys' Band in 1923. Newsboy bands had remained popular since the 1880s, and new ones were still being created. The *Baltimore Evening Sun* started its high-profile newsboy band in 1922 with a series of guest conductors, including John Philip Sousa and Babe Ruth, who led them in an original tune, "Battering Babe." The white-owned *New Orleans Item* started a colored newsboy band in 1924 with forty members. But Abbott aimed to top them all. He hired Major Nathaniel Clark Smith, an army bandmaster during the Spanish-American War and former music director of Booker T. Washington's Tuskegee Institute. Abbott supplied the uniforms and instruments, and Smith provided the lessons. From the ranks of its newsboys, the *Defender* formed a seventy-five-piece marching band that, in its brief two-year existence, gained national renown. Some of the world's greatest jazzmen passed through its ranks, including percussionist Lionel Hampton, bassist Milt Hinton, tenor sax virtuoso David A. Young, and tubist Bill Oldham. Hampton said he sold the *Defender* just to get into the band.[117]

An old-fashioned form of advertising in a new media age, newsboy bands became expendable as more schools began to sponsor orchestras. Junior highs proliferated and high school attendance doubled during the decade, surpassing five million nationally. Music programs flourished as a form of vocational education that raised school spirit and public interest in education. School bands began performing at the same venues that newsies once had to themselves. Then tragedy struck. On July 5, 1924, a steamer carrying the *Baltimore Evening Sun*'s newsboy band home from a concert burst into flames on the Chesapeake. The musicians helped wake the other passengers and get the women and children into lifeboats, but ten people died, including five band members: Walter Millikin, Thomas Pilker, Vernon Jefferson, Alfred Lester Seligman, and Nelson Miles. Their bodies were interred together in Loudon Park Cemetery, with band members serving as pallbearers and honor guard. A memorial went up the next year. The band carried on until 1932, but under a shadow that never lifted. Cornetist Melvin Otter recited a rosary at the gravesite every week for the rest of his life.[118]

However costly or rewarding, the experiences of newsboys in the 1920s lingered in their minds like an old alley blues tune. The unforgettable fights, friendships, and frustrations helped shape who they became as adults. The streets taught many lessons, such as how to beat back bigotry, outfox reformers, and negotiate the sexual advances of bosses, coworkers, and customers. Becoming wise to these threats constituted an important occupational skill. The news trade was a school for vice, violence, and working-class masculinity, but the education newsboys received was not that of a depraved class. Rather, it reflected the ascendant get-ahead values of modern America. Newsboys of the 1920s were nothing if not children of their era—a crass, commercial era of excess and energy, breakthrough and backlash, scandal and speculation. Little did they know it would all come crashing down on October 24, 1929, otherwise known as Black Thursday.

14

Son of the Forgotten Man

Despite many warning signs, the stock market crash of 1929 took the nation by surprise. One Oklahoma teenager was so baffled when he heard newsboys shouting "Extra! Extra! Stock Market Collapses" that he thought it referred to a disaster at a cattle auction barn. The boys who cried the headlines knew better, of course, and cashed in on the panic. Nine-year-old Dempsey Travis hustled the *Chicago Defender* right up to October 24, Black Thursday, but then sales plunged. "Before the year's end," he said, "my customers were more concerned about feeding their stomachs than feeding their minds."[1]

Few people were left untouched by the falling economy, and certainly not America's newsboys. If it didn't drive them from the trade, it stretched out their news careers longer than most would have liked. The proportion of newsboys between 16 and 19 years old rose during the decade, according to the US Census, and they had to contend with an influx of adults into their ranks. Chicago artist John Groth observed this trend in 1931 when he sketched a burly vendor bellowing a tiny rival off the street (Figure 14.1).[2]

In Detroit, automobile production ground to a halt and half the adult population lost their jobs. City officials converted factories into homeless shelters and issued the unemployed licenses to sell apples in lieu of relief. Four thousand hungry schoolchildren stood daily in bread lines while seventeen thousand worked the streets, almost half of whom either sold or delivered newspapers. With so much competition, one newsboy gang formed a "vengeance squad" to protect its turf. In December 1931, four of the boys went looking for 15-year-old Joe Przystas for beating up a pal. They found him at home carrying a scuttle of coal upstairs. One of the boys pulled a rifle from his pant leg and fired at the scuttle to frighten Przystas but drilled him in the heart instead. The killing drew national attention as symptomatic of the moral breakdown accompanying the city's economic collapse.[3]

The most devastating financial crisis in American history, the Great Depression exposed newsboys to the vicissitudes of the market and the power of the state in unprecedented ways. The crisis sparked renewed debate at the highest levels of

"EXTRY!"

Figure 14.1. John Groth, *Extry* (1931), dry point, 8 × 6⅞ in. (20.3 × 17.5 cm). Smithsonian American Art Museum, Gift of Chicago Society of Etchers. 1935.13.129.

government about the social costs of child street labor. Newsboys came under federal protection for the first time with the passage of New Deal legislation, but publishers resisted such "meddling" as threats to press freedom. Rising discontent and a surging labor movement led newsies to mount strikes and support those of other workers. Caught up in this tug-of-war between a paternalistic capitalist press and an expansive welfare state, the newsboy became a contested figure in popular culture, appearing more often as a symbol of working-class resentment than as an icon of bourgeois virtue. He was the shrill, restless son of the Forgotten Man, and in this capacity helped America reassess the merits of laissez-faire capitalism and recalibrate government's responsibility to citizens young and old.

Feeling the Pinch

There were more than half a million juvenile news sellers and carriers at work in the early 1930s, according to the US Children's Bureau, and their numbers climbed throughout the decade, with carriers outnumbering sellers four to one. Circulation managers put the number of newsboys under age 18 at 570,000 and said they handled eight out of every ten papers sold. Sales dipped 12 percent, however, and advertising revenue dropped almost in half, causing papers to fail in record numbers. Of the 2,086 dailies in the United States on the eve of the crash, 206 died or were absorbed by 1940. One of three salaried news workers lost their jobs, and 108 clamorous cities became relatively quiescent one-newspaper towns. Three trends helped sustain the other papers: the public's heightened need for cheap diversions and fresh want ads, the era's unflagging eventfulness, and the industry's benevolent squeezing of its juvenile labor force.[4]

Reading newspapers remained the most common leisure activity, ahead of radio listening and movie-going. All ages craved the new comics—*Tarzan, Buck Rogers, Dick Tracy*, and *Popeye*—and the unemployed desperately sought relief in the job ads. Crowds gathered daily outside newspaper offices, "snapping up the papers when newsboys appeared with them and then breaking in all directions with the Help Wanted sections flying in their hands." Director Lee Strasberg staged such a scene in the Group Theatre's stunning Broadway production *1931* to dramatize the degradation resulting from unemployment.[5]

Meanwhile, a steady stream of must-read stories rolled off the presses and into the hands of newsboys. They did a "thriving business" in February 1933 after the attempted assassination of president-elect Franklin D. Roosevelt and mortal wounding of Chicago mayor Anton Cermak in Miami. Theodore White of Boston posted record sales in March when FDR ordered a "bank holiday" to restructure the nation's financial institutions. "Roosevelt closes the banks!" shouted the aspiring journalist. "Read all about it!" The shutdown lasted eight days and left merchants without enough cash to make change. Some sent clerks to buy coins from newsies. Towns and newspapers in thirty states issued scrip, including the proverbial wooden nickel. Brothers Frank and Mario DeMarco, who hawked papers outside the Waldorf Hotel in New York, chalked up a string of record-breaking sales days following the kidnapping of the Lindbergh baby, the repeal of Prohibition, the plane crash that killed humorist Will Rogers and aviator Wiley Post, and the historic boxing matches between Joe Louis and

German heavyweight Max Schmeling. Depression or no, the boys could always sell a few hundred extras after a World Series game.[6]

Crime news also generated big paydays. Newsies worshipped outlaws such as John Dillinger and Bonnie and Clyde and bolstered their reputations as sagebrush Robin Hoods who robbed from the rich to give to the poor. Dillinger—public enemy number one—slipped in their estimation after his capture in Tucson, Arizona. If he hadn't been too cheap to buy an extra, they said, he would have known that his gang had already been nabbed there. The symbiotic relationship between newsmakers and news sellers was not lost on Bonnie Parker, who wrote in one of the many poems she sent to editors while on the lam:

> A newsboy once said to his buddy:
> "I wish old Clyde would get jumped;
> In these awful hard times
> We'd make a few dimes
> If five or six cops would get bumped."

Dallas newsboys sold half a million extras describing the police ambush that ended the couple's crime spree. They paid their respects by sending the largest wreath to her funeral.[7]

"Big play" stories alone couldn't offset waning sales. To save their own shaky jobs, circulation managers set quotas or "crowded" newsboys, making them take more papers than they wanted. They persuaded the most desperate to stand in traffic and solicit motorists (Figure 14.2). (To boost safety and sales, the *Los Angeles Times* and *Philadelphia Inquirer* supplied their nighthawks with battery-operated neon signs that flashed the paper's name across their chests.) Managers stopped paying bonuses to top sellers and increased prices to those who didn't take papers six days a week. Some required cash bonds and instituted fines for minor infractions. They made carriers pay for route books, wire cutters, and New Year's greetings. Bosses charged vendors at the busiest corners full price for their papers, forcing them to profit from tips alone, which naturally fell off during these hard times. One Detroit paper billed carriers for the life insurance it offered subscribers, whether they collected the weekly premiums or not. Nationally, hawkers made about 50¢ less per week than in the 1920s. Their median weekly income in 1934 was $1.41, according to the Children's Bureau. Carriers earned slightly more, $1.86, but that too represented a loss. Some carriers made as little as $1 for a thirty-hour week, while others wound up owing money to their suppliers. Yet in some cases the pennies added up. Robert Ross of Detroit claimed he earned $100 a week at age 15 delivering four hundred papers a day. Boston philanthropist Harry Burroughs put the annual income of newsies

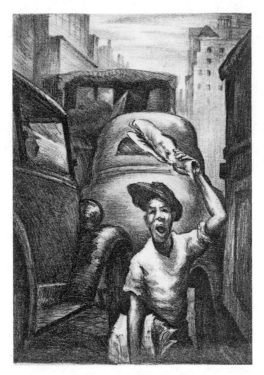

Figure 14.2. Carl G. Hill, *Newsboy, 1938*, lithograph, 11½ × 8⅛ in. (29.2 × 20.6 cm).
Metropolitan Museum of Art. Gift of Reba and Dave Williams, 1999. Acc. No.
1999.529.65.

in 1934 at $175 million. Carriers alone brought home $85 million in 1939, according to another estimate.[8]

The most common solution to slumping sales was the establishment of newspaper carrier schools. In 1930 circulation managers launched a national campaign to cut costs and raise subscriptions by firing adult solicitors and organizing
sales classes for carrier boys. The sharpest circulation men had been coaching
boys for decades, but the trend now swept the industry like an Oklahoma dust
storm. The highlight of the International Circulation Managers Association's
1930 convention was a carrier sales talk contest among four regional championship teams. The winning pair, Albert Sostilo, 14, and Joseph Milford, 15, of the
Boston Herald-Traveler, edged out boys from Toledo, Toronto, and Yonkers to
take home the trophy, a sixteen-inch statuette of a newsboy.[9]

By 1936, more than three hundred newspapers had started carrier schools
on their premises or in rented halls. Carriers had to memorize fact sheets and
perfect sales pitches. Boys practiced their spiels amid the "good-natured cat-
calls and Bronx cheers of fellow carriers." Yet classes organized by the *Decatur
Herald and Review* were part of a rigorous six-week program capped by a written

exam. Boys who scored below 75 percent had to retake the course; those who fell below 50 percent were let go. Management also applied the latest psychological theories to motivate boys. The circulation boss at the *Santa Barbara Press* urged colleagues to "strike at the subconscious mind" to develop the "habit part of the carrier brain."[10]

Insecure about their own status, circulation managers portrayed themselves as teachers who had nothing in common with the "slave bosses" of bygone days. Yet like them, they hosted banquets, outings, and athletic events, and issued carriers' addresses to recruit and retain their staff. The *Grand Rapids Herald*'s address for 1933 offered a historical perspective to keep the boys upbeat:

> Speaking of Depressions
> Let's Give a Smile and a Cheer
> It was Lots Tougher for Early Grand Rapids Pioneers.[11]

Newspapers continued to hold circulation contests that offered traditional prizes like bikes and baseball gloves and new ones like radios, airplane rides, and even trips to Europe. Some papers offered coupons that boys could redeem for merchandise in specialty catalogs (Figure 14.3). In 1933 the *Dayton Daily News* sponsored a soapbox derby for newsboys and other youths as a promotional stunt. Within a year more than thirty newspapers were holding races and sending their winners to Dayton for the national championship. These activities presented news selling more as a game than as a job and helped the industry fend off regulation. In 1935, when New York State raised the age at which compulsory schooling ended from 14 to 16 and reduced the maximum work week for minors from fifty-four to forty-eight hours, the American Newspaper Publishers Association (ANPA) cried foul, saying, "The newspapers of the State are doing a real job in the training of their newsboys for futures positions in the business world."[12]

Educators came down on both sides of the question. Studies of newsboys in Philadelphia high schools found that they attended more regularly, lost fewer days due to illness, and were promoted at a higher rate than non-newsboys. They averaged 48¢ an hour, more than most of their peers who worked part-time. The study concluded that a paper route was "a good moral substitute for chores." But University of Southern California sociologist George B. Mangold disagreed. He disparaged carrier schools as offering "courses in dishonesty" in which boys learned to tell "hard luck" stories to obtain subscriptions. "Is there any wonder that America is suffering from dishonest business practices throughout its economic structure!" he said. A scholar who surveyed teen carriers in Phoenix found that most earned better grades and were more active in student government before they acquired their routes or after they dropped them. Theodore

Figure 14.3. Chicago Evening American, Junior Carrier Coupon Catalog, Mar. 25, 1930. Eckel Collection, Princeton University Library.

White dropped out of Boston Latin to peddle full-time when his parents could no longer afford the tuition. "I could sell almost as many papers," he said, "if I put emotion into the call by shrieking, '*Quo usque, O Catilina, tandem abutere patentia nostra, quem ad finem eludet iste furor tuus . . .*' as I could by shrieking anything else."* White liked to greet his old classmates in Latin when they passed by on the trolley, but they soon shunned him.[13]

With so few jobs available, America's teenagers stayed in school longer than ever during the Depression. Newspapers tried to tap this labor pool by promoting newsboy clubs and vocational programs. The industry-backed Newsboys' Republic in Milwaukee started clubs in eleven high schools and urged principals to set up clubs under the guidance of an interested teacher. Meanwhile, the city's street trades director experimented with a new tool—the public opinion poll—by asking newsboys in the fifth and sixth grades how they might become good workers and develop healthy habits. Given that one in five schoolchildren was not getting enough to eat and that most schools were operating on slashed budgets and shortened semesters, many educators favored closer ties to industry. In Omaha, *World-Herald* trucks transported child sellers to school in the morning and then back to their corners after the final bell. "Newspaper personnel should be allowed to call on schools in their search for hawkers or carriers," urged street trades supervisor George W. Zorsch of Rochester, "as this will place on the street a better class of boys that the principal of that particular school will have jurisdiction over."[14]

To link these clubs, the *Indianapolis Star*'s Maurice G. Lipson founded the Newspaper Boys of America (NBA). Its pledge resonated with the same themes and cadences as the Boy Scout pledge: "As a newspaper boy, I pledge upon my honor, to do my duty to God, my country, my family, my friends and my newspaper." NBA members had to have regular routes or corners. They accumulated merit badges for appearance, punctuality, courtesy, scholarship, salesmanship, and "reporting" (gathering names and addresses of new neighbors). There were no uniforms, but senior members got to wear NBA buckles and badges. On Christmas Day 1930, a group made the First Annual Patriotic Pilgrimage to Washington to meet President Herbert Hoover.[15]

Gents and Nomads

America's newsboys were still a diverse bunch. Carriers tended to come from better-off Americanized families, but most hawkers were children of recent

---

* From Cicero's oration against Catiline: "How long, O Catiline, will you abuse our patience; to what limit will this your madness make playthings of us?"

immigrants. A 1931 survey of 119 newsboys in downtown Omaha found 45 Italians, 29 Jews, 11 "white Americans," 10 Irish, 6 Negroes, 4 Bohemians, 3 Germans, and 11 of other nationalities. Most said they worked because they needed the money. One musical expression of these demographic and financial realities is the 1934 Yiddish song "The Newsboy ('Koift a Paper')," which is the plea of a ragged little *boytchikl* who is the sole provider for his family after his father loses his job. One verse ends "*Di brider meine un di schvester, Geien ois in noit der grester* [My brothers and my sister are perishing in utmost poverty]—Buy a paper mister, please!"[16]

African Americans constituted a small minority of newsboys in northern cities but a large proportion (along with Italians) of shoeshine boys. They came from the poorest families and suffered the highest rates of joblessness: 43 percent for black youths between 16 and 24, compared to 33 percent for whites the same age. In this context, struggling African American newspapers such as the *Cleveland Call & Post* provided important income and pride to their newsboys (Figure 14.4). Yet black newsboys also had to contend with racism. The *Oregonian*, for instance, refused to hire 11-year old William Hilliard in 1938 as a

Figure 14.4. Proud distributors of the *Cleveland Call and Post*. The popularity of aviation is evident in the strapped leather helmets and goggles worn by many of the boys. Allen Cole Collection, The Western Reserve Historical Society, Cleveland, Ohio.

carrier on the belief that white subscribers would not want their paper touched by a Negro. Southerners were usually more accepting, but not always. When Joe Louis, the "Brown Bomber," beat James Braddock, an Irish American, to win the world heavyweight title in 1936, two black newsboys in New Orleans went down the street yelling, "Louis K.O.s Braddock." A white man came out and told them to shut up. "I say what I want with my papers," answered Chester, the braver one. The man called to his wife on the porch, "Honey, give me my gun." He took it, put it to the boys' backs, and marched them four blocks out of the neighborhood. This was not the kind of character-building adversity that white newsboys faced.[17]

The number of girls in the news trade was still "negligible," according to the Children's Bureau, which counted 2,530 in 1934, not including those who helped their brothers fold and deliver papers. Many northern cities set a higher minimum age for newsgirls than newsboys—usually 18 or 21. But Paterson, New Jersey, and New Haven, Connecticut, had no such minimum and allowed 10-year-olds of either sex to peddle. Charleston, South Carolina's newsgirls were reportedly "quite as business-like as their male competitors." The *Iola Register* in Kansas built an entire staff of "girl 'newsboys.'" "Well, all the boys I tried were no good," said the manager. The first girl he hired, 12-year-old Carrie Barber, came recommended by her mother. She did well, and when complaints, or kicks, about the boys continued, he replaced them all with girls.[18]

Parents and guardians had few qualms about letting children peddle papers during the Depression. Mothers in particular expected their kids to "pitch in," "pull their own weight," and "work for their keep." Russell Baker's widowed mother found him his first job selling the *Saturday Evening Post* in Belleville, New Jersey, at age 8. After they moved to Baltimore she got him a newspaper route for his twelfth birthday. Growing up in Minneapolis, Samuel Hynes found many jobs through his stepmother; he sold magazines door-to-door, distributed handbills, delivered groceries, and then landed a *Star-Journal* paper route.[19] Bounced between relatives, orphanages, and foster homes, Lawrence Ferlinghetti did similar work throughout his grammar school years in Bronxville, New York. In his poem "Autobiography," he wrote:

> I am an American.
> I was an American boy
> I read the American Boy Magazine. . . .
> I had a baseball mit
> and an American Flyer bike
> I delivered the Woman's Home Companion
> at five in the afternoon
> or the Herald Trib

at five in the morning.
I still can hear the paper thump
on lost porches.[20]

The experiences of Baker, Hynes, Ferlinghetti, and 570,000 other boys suggest that the Great Depression challenged the pervasive bourgeois notion that children's real value to their parents was emotional rather than economic. Scholars have identified the tendency of children to contribute to family incomes in the nineteenth century and drain them in the twentieth as a major historical shift, but the seemingly endless Depression interrupted this trend.[21]

Authorities enforced street trading laws with a gentle hand in the 1930s. At least a third of the newsboys in Boston had no badges. Likewise in Rochester, supervisor Zorsch noticed more boys selling papers even though the number of permits issued stayed the same. He figured they either dug up their old badges or risked selling without them. "He feels he is justified in violating the law for the sake of food and clothing," explained Zorsch, "as in many cases he is and has been the main support of the family." Despite their poverty, newsboys of the thirties appeared no scruffier than those in the twenties. Investigators in New York reported a "scarcity of ragamuffins" and categorized only one in five as poorly clad or dirty. Shoes might be provided by charities or stuffed with cardboard, but most newsboys had them. A neat appearance was essential, explained Zorsch. "The public has no sympathy today with the loafer. A newsboy today must be clean, neat, and as much of a little gentleman as possible." One such figure darts across the bas-relief street scene sculpted by Lee Lawrie over the entrance to St. Paul, Minnesota's new city hall and county courthouse, dedicated in 1932.[22]

In addition to local boys in the trade, many communities saw the arrival of thousands of itinerant youths seeking work. These "Wild Boys of the Road" numbered 250,000 in the early 1930s; one in ten was a girl. They walked, hitchhiked, and hopped freight cars heading in all directions. On reaching a city, many gravitated to newspaper offices to earn a stake. From downtown Omaha to midtown Manhattan, adult vagrants were equally conspicuous among the newsboys. According to one observer, the five hundred hawkers who gathered nightly in the distribution room of the New York Daily News comprised "seedy old men clutching at the respectability of derby hats, seedier young fellows in dirty shirts and suits who look as though they had been sleeping in the parks recently, ragged youngsters, athletic-looking older boys in jerseys, occasional bright-looking older boys of high school age, a handful of girls and older women, a sprinkling of negro lads, an occasional cripple, and a few obvious mental defectives."[23]

Young transients posed real challenges for cities; many received several thousand a year. New York put up more than five thousand boys in 1932. Far from being the habitual "hobo" type, said Children's Bureau chief Grace Abbott, many of them had left decent but struggling families rather than burden them. Former governor Al Smith felt they were cause for concern, not condemnation. "If the country is to have any future, these boys must have a future," he said. Smith recommended increased federal aid to distressed families, a media campaign to keep boys at home, and the creation of newsboys' lodging houses in every city.[24]

The Children's Aid Society, which sent its last orphan train west in 1929, expanded services to accommodate this flood tide of "nomad youth." Its 250-bed Brace Memorial Home was filled to the rafters with boys between the ages of 16 and 21. In 1932 the CAS aided three thousand boys from forty-two states, a 77 percent increase in one year. Overcrowding prompted lodgers to picket the home in October 1934. They complained about poor food, mandatory chores, midnight curfews, and 7:30 a.m. wake-up calls. Part of the radical unemployed workers movement, the picketers demanded $2 a week spending money. Police arrested the lot of them.[25]

Preachers and publishers tried to alleviate the dire need and rippling discontent by stepping up their charitable work. Just as Father Divine in New York and Aimee Semple McPherson in Los Angeles attracted thousands of followers with their sermons and soup kitchens, so, too, did the Missouri-born evangelist Harry Black. Known as the "Converted Newsboy," he held marathon revival meetings and put his autobiographical tract, *From Newsboy to Preacher*, into the hands of boys throughout the western states. "What a glorious thing it would be," he mused, "to have a newsboys' church not only in Los Angeles, but in every large city of our nation." Black's vision of the juvenilization of Christianity would be realized with the establishment of youth ministries in denominations throughout Depression-era America. A Catholic church in Baltimore supported its congregation by offering a 4:00 a.m. "newsboys Mass" on Sundays.[26]

Meanwhile, William Randolph Hearst sponsored the biggest soup kitchen in Manhattan and used *Journal* delivery trucks to dispense soup and bread in all five boroughs. Yip Harburg, a down-on-his-luck songwriter, saw it as shameless self-promotion and wrote a skit satirizing the false philanthropy of press barons. The song he wrote for it—"Brother, Can You Spare a Dime?" —became the anthem of the era.[27]

A Code of Their Own

As unemployment ran rampant, a chorus of voices called for removing children from all sectors of the economy. "The use of child labor in the sale and distribution of newspapers is indefensible during normal times," declared the New York Child Labor Committee in 1932, "and is doubly so during periods of economic depression and widespread unemployment." The journal *Publishers Service* advocated converting the nation's youth carrier force into adult labor even though it would raise subscription rates. "The public would gladly pay this increase in price," it said, as "the tens of thousands of carrier jobs given to men will help the nation as a whole."[28]

The issue gained government attention early on. In November 1930, President Hoover convened the White House Conference on Child Health and Protection, which produced a 10,511-page report and a nineteen-point Children's Charter affirming children's right to attend good schools, live in safe environments, and receive proper medical care. About the street trades, the report said more kids were engaged in news peddling and delivery than any other type of work. It urged that no one under 16 be permitted to leave school for work except 14- and 15-year-old boys, who could peddle papers if they obtained a permit attesting to their age, health, school attendance, and parental permission. A believer in voluntarism, Hoover neither allocated funds nor sought legislation to achieve these ends. Far from grateful, New York newsboys blamed him for their troubles when they recited their new favorite street rhyme:

> Hoover blew the whistle
> Mellon rang the bell
> Wall Street gave the signal
> And the country went to Hell! [29]

Roosevelt's election in 1932 transformed the state's relationship with children in general and newsboys in particular. New Deal programs established the first federal day care centers, introduced subsidized school lunches, and built playgrounds, swimming pools, and athletic fields. The National Youth Administration granted students financial aid and put graduates to work in hospitals, schools, and public agencies. And the Civilian Conservation Corps (CCC) provided paid forestry work for 300,000 unmarried males between the ages of 18 and 25 whose families were on relief. Created in March 1933, the CCC eased the problem of the young nomads. Disabled himself, Roosevelt showed uncommon consideration for people with special needs. Shortly after his inauguration, Helen Keller wrote him urging support for a proposal to employ blind people at newsstands in federal buildings. "Work," she said, "is the only way for the blind to forget the dark and the obstacles in their path." FDR complied by signing the Randolph-Sheppard Act in 1936.[30]

At the same time the administration stimulated a spate of workplace reforms—the National Industrial Recovery Act (NIRA), a proposed child labor amendment, Social Security Act, and Fair Labor Standards Act—that challenged newspapers' right to use children as they pleased. The first of these measures authorized the National Recovery Administration (NRA) to hammer out voluntary industrial agreements to promote fair competition, or, as its administrator General Hugh S. Johnson, a former newsboy, put it, "to cut out such rough stuff as sweating labor, exploiting the public, [and] working children." Developed with input from business and labor, these agreements, or codes, regulated 562 industries ranging from auto manufacturing to zinc mining. To show compliance, workplaces across the country displayed the NRA Blue Eagle insignia and its motto, "We Do Our Part."[31]

Testifying at a newspaper code hearing in September 1933 in Washington, DC, Howard W. Stodghill, business manager of the *Louisville Courier-Journal* and chairman of the ICMA's Newspaperboy Welfare Committee, presented himself as the voice of the boys, not of the publishers. He said he favored a code that protected boys from working during school hours and prevented the employment of girls, but he objected to banning boys' part-time work because it was not really child labor, since each was a merchant engaged in healthful outdoor work that taught good citizenship. Elisha Hanson of the ANPA complained that the proposed code applied only to newspapers and not distributors, failed to distinguish between big and little papers, and violated the First Amendment's guarantee of a free press.[32]

Publishers took their case to the public, insinuating in speeches and editorials that the NIRA gave the president power to license newspapers as well as newsboys. They likened it to a Nazi edict abolishing free speech in Germany. "Many a high school boy with a good paper route is contributing more to his family than his older brother is able to send home from a C.C.C. camp," said one editorial. It was pure hyperbole: the three million young men in the CCC earned $30 a month, or double the income of the average newsboy.[33]

Acting on their own, or at the instigation of their circulation managers, many carriers appealed directly to General Johnson and FDR for fair treatment. "I am a strong, healthy newsboy," wrote 12-year-old Jimmy Macios of Hattiesburg, Mississippi. "I need this exercise to keep me strong and healthy as well as make my spending money. Will you please allow me to sell newspapers?" "Most of your N.R.A. laws are what the country needs," wrote 12-year-old Leonard Frumoutz of Chicago, "but this law about no child labor should not have been used for I think I am old enough to work my papers and earn my weekly allowance." Others boys sought NRA help in boosting their earnings. "Things are costing more including shoeleather," wrote two newsies in a postcard to Johnson. "Look into this matter at once. Thank you." Adult vendors also sent letters, mainly seeking relief from juvenile competition.[34]

Adopted in February 1934, the National Newspaper Code prohibited the hiring of news sellers or carriers under 16 years of age "except those who are able, without impairment of health, or interference with hours of day school."

Also exempt were minors who sold papers for newsagents or distributors. In signing the code, Roosevelt rebutted the charge that it infringed on the First Amendment: "The freedom guaranteed by the Constitution is freedom of expression, and that will be scrupulously respected—but it is not freedom to work children or do business in a fire trap or violate the laws against obscenity, libel and lewdness." He said he was not satisfied with the provisions applying to minors and ordered a special report on newsboy labor, due on his desk in sixty days. The Children's Bureau took up the task, surveying more than four thousand juvenile news sellers and carriers in seventeen cities about their ages, hours, earnings, and conditions. The upshot was a proposed amendment prohibiting boys under 14 and girls under 18 as sellers or carriers (except boys over 12 who already had routes), and barring carriers from working before 6:00 a.m. or after 7:00 p.m. in winter, 8:00 p.m. in summer. In addition, all newsboys were required to carry a permit or badge authorized by the secretary of labor.[35]

Newspapers fought the changes tooth and nail. Fifty publishers testified at a second round of NRA hearings in June 1934, and only one recommended toughening the code's child labor provisions. Sing Sing Prison warden Lewis E. Lawes weighed in on the debate with a telegram stating that 69 percent of his inmates had peddled papers in their youth. Only the strongest characters could be expected to "withstand the hard knocks, the temptations, and the bad associations that are a definite part of the life of the newsboy," he said. A Chicago circulation man took umbrage as the telegram was read aloud, shouting, "Loeb and Leopold never sold papers!" His counterpart at the *Los Angeles Herald-Express* warned that code amendments would "result in an outbreak of crime due to enforced idleness that would exceed any crime wave this country has ever seen." Edward Keevin, head of the Roosevelt Newsboys' Association in Massachusetts (named in honor of Theodore), agreed. Stripping boys of their routes, he said, "would constitute a national menace and drive them into the Devil's Workshop." Keevin asked juvenile justice pioneer Judge Ben Lindsey to refute the link between news selling and crime. Lindsey said it was "very rare, if ever," that a newsboy passed through his court. "Indeed, I am confident that the occupation of newsboy does far more to prevent delinquency than it ever does to cause it."[36]

Newsboys also piped up. Eleven-year-old Graydon Tolson of Bethesda, Maryland, his voice still weak from a tonsillectomy, testified: "I make seven to eight dollars a month. I have a savings account. I have bought myself a bicycle, a lot of good books and other things and I intend to enroll in Maryland University when I finish high school. I have always had high marks in school and I will appreciate it if you will let me keep my job." After similar testimony by two other carriers, newly crowned sales-pitch champions Sostilo and Milford demonstrated their winning routine.[37]

The result of all this theater was the gutting of the code's child labor provisions. In May 1935 the Code Authority accepted the publishers' entire slate of modifications, which kept the minimum age of 14 for boy peddlers in cities with populations of 50,000 or more but lowered it to 12 for those in smaller cities. It also allowed 12-year-old boys to work as carriers, and grandfathered in 10-year-old boys who already had routes in small cities. Girls still had to be 18 to sell papers. Hawkers and carriers could now begin work as early as 5:00 a.m. on school days but were limited to four and three hours, respectively. All had to submit a certificate signed by a parent or guardian and school official, but no badge system was set up.[38]

Shortly before the modified code was to take effect, the US Supreme Court struck down all codes, ruling unanimously in *Schechter v. United States* that Congress had unconstitutionally delegated its lawmaking authority to the NRA. The decision knocked the stuffing out of the Blue Eagle and threatened the regulatory power of all New Deal agencies. Publishers pledged to honor the terms of the stricken code, but without enforcement the use of child labor rose in all industries, including newspaper distribution.[39]

Taking It to the Courts

One way around the ruling was to amend the Constitution. Efforts to pass a child labor amendment, begun in 1924 but abandoned short of ratification, were revived in 1933 under impetus from FDR, who wanted to reinforce the temporary provisions of the codes. Eleanor Roosevelt was the campaign's leading supporter. Newspaper publishers set their heels against the so-called youth control amendment. Sixty papers, including those belonging to the Scripps-Howard and Hearst chains, which had endorsed the amendment in 1924, reversed their positions. Many papers misrepresented the amendment's scope and purpose, suggesting, said *Survey Graphic*, that it would "make it a crime for mothers to send Johnny out to the shed for a basket of cobs." The Associated Press showed bias by failing to report FDR's endorsement of the amendment while his home state legislators debated ratification.[40]

Mistrust of newspapers was widespread in the thirties. Two out of three papers opposed Roosevelt in 1932 and 1936, and the ANPA challenged nearly all New Deal reforms, especially those that threatened newspaper revenues (Figure 14.5). Yet *Editor & Publisher* and several prominent papers broke ranks and supported the child labor amendment. The liberal *Christian Century* charged publishers with blocking ratification to seize the "blood-encrusted pennies of profit which they squeeze out of the children whom they employ to peddle their product." Such rhetoric proved unpersuasive. By 1937 only twenty-eight states

Figure 14.5. A hawker for the Democratic *Buffalo Times* helps generate excitement over FDR's campaign visit. *Newsboy—1936.* © Western New York Heritage Press, Inc. Used by permission.

had passed the amendment, eight short of the three-fourths needed for ratification. The press's opposition was key: if not for their vested interest in using newsboy labor, more newspapers would have likely thrown their collective weight behind the campaign, making child labor reform, not presidential term limits, the focus of the Twenty-second Amendment.[41]

Meanwhile, the Social Security Act of 1935 addressed the needs of minors as well as elders. In addition to its core pension plan, which reduced the perennial need of the elderly to peddle papers as a hedge against destitution, the act established Aid to Families with Dependent Children—those under 16 (later 18) living in homes without a breadwinner. It also provided needy mothers with maternal and child health care, and it extended benefits to parentless, abandoned, and disabled children. For the first time, the prototypical orphaned, homeless, or crippled newsboy had access to federal funds. Yet newsboys under 18 were exempt from paying into and collecting the old age and unemployment benefits of the act.[42]

Not surprisingly, the legal status of newsboys as independent contractors met stiff challenge in the courts. Newsboys or their survivors filed claims under the new workmen's compensation laws for injuries or deaths on the job. At first, courts throughout the country ruled that child hawkers and carriers were not compensable because they either were illegally employed, had no dependents, or were non-payroll personnel, in which case newspapers had no right to control the time, place, or manner of their work, even if they did exercise such control in practice. This logic, applauded by the industry-backed Newspaper Boys of America, prevailed in the oft-cited case of John Sturgeon, who was killed by a car while peddling the *Birmingham Post* in 1933. His parents argued that their son was a de facto employee, as the *Post* required him to call for papers at stated times, sell at prescribed prices in defined areas, cry specific headlines, shun other papers, and wear straps and bags blazoned with the paper's name. But the court disagreed, ruling that it was impossible to control this "numerous army of more or less irresponsible persons of immature years, of physical infirmities, and of failures in other vocations."[43]

Nonetheless, by the end of the decade newsboys started to win such cases. Seventeen jurisdictions provided additional compensation in the case of injury to minors who were working illegally. The penalties ranged from an extra 10 percent of damages in Pennsylvania to 300 percent in Wisconsin. In Berkeley, California, the League of Women Voters pushed publishers to insure hawkers and carriers against accidents.[44]

In June 1938 President Roosevelt hoped to eradicate child labor by signing the Fair Labor Standards Act, the first law regulating juvenile employment nationally. It made 16 the legal working age, established a minimum wage of 25¢ per hour, and banned the interstate commerce of goods made by children. This last piece of New Deal legislation initially decimated the ranks of news carriers, but in December Mac Myers, a 13-year-old carrier from Ithaca, Michigan, sued the *Lansing State Journal* for unfair dismissal under the act. The judge, a former paperboy, ruled that Myers was an independent contractor who did not work "in or about" the newspaper plant and was thus exempt from the law. The *Los Angeles Times* praised the judge's decision and pointed to onetime newsboy William O. Douglas's recent appointment to the US Supreme Court as further proof of the merits of newspaper selling and delivery.[45]

Hitting the Bricks

Paperboys everywhere returned to work, yet not all accepted the legal fiction that they were independent contractors. Even before passage of the NIRA or the 1935 Wagner Act, in which ex-newsboy Robert F. Wagner secured workers' right to organize, news sellers formed unions and waged strikes to win better pay and conditions. They did so in Baltimore in 1930; Pittsburgh and the Bronx in 1933; Cleveland in 1934; Holyoke, Massachusetts, in 1934; Seattle in 1936; Chicago and Oakland in 1937; Pittsfield, Massachusetts, in 1939; and Cleveland again in 1940.

Each strike was different. Baltimore's downtown newsboys took a one-day "holiday" in October to protest the *Sun's* new evening distribution system. The paper likened the walkout to "high-school boys playing 'hooky' from class." The Pittsburgh strike was sparked by a 25 percent cut on commissions that led roving bands of strikers to upset trucks, destroy papers, and harass newsstand operators. "Newsies Strike—Dailies Rob 'Em," read the *National Labor Tribune's* banner headline. Police guarded the plants of the city's three newspapers and arrested about twenty strikers, including 21-year-old George Bailey, an organizer for the Communist Party–backed Unemployment Council, which sought to boost relief payments. The labor press insisted that the "daily chain newspaper vultures" brought the Communists into the strike and that the fifteen thousand striking sellers, deliverers, and carriers in the newly formed Pittsburgh Newsboys' Protective Association were all loyal Americans opposed to the un-American "sweatshop practices" of the Scripps-Howard and Hearst chains. Strikers said they were forced to work twelve- to fourteen-hour days, "stuff" papers for nothing, and sell extras at all hours of the day or night.[46]

The Bronx strike started in June 1933 when members of a recently formed carriers union refused to deliver the *Bronx Home News* because of its punitive work rules. The paper's eight hundred carriers—all boys over 16—worked seven days a week, for a weekly total of at least twenty-five hours. They earned about $4 a week in summer and $5 in winter but had to pay 50¢ fines if they arrived fifteen minutes early or late, made noise, or smoked. Carriers also had to canvass for new subscribers, collect payments, and distribute samples and circulars without extra pay. If a customer cancelled, the newsboy had to keep paying for the paper or find a new subscriber. The *News* had signed the 1933 Newspaper Code, but when the boys appealed to the NRA for help, officials said they were not employees and thus not eligible to bring their case before the board. Union lawyers successfully argued that the boys were employees since the paper hired and fired them, assigned them territory, set their hours, determined their pay, and subjected them to fines and assessments. Two months later the *Home News* fired the leaders and weeded out a hundred union members and sympathizers, mostly Jews, on the grounds that they had failed to canvass on the eve of Rosh Hashanah and were spreading communism among the ranks. The boys also faced a reign of terror: Leon Felderman, 17, was beaten and hospitalized with a concussion; Benjamin Gura was visited at home by his boss and a "bunch of thugs" who pressured him to surrender his route; and two organizers were jailed on trumped-up charges of petty larceny. Circulation managers often bragged about the practical business training carriers received on the job, but they rarely mentioned that it included lessons in head-busting and Red-baiting.[47]

Newsboys in Cleveland protested three dailies in May 1934 after the *Press* and *News* eliminated some editions and the *Plain Dealer* pushed its bulldog edition past midnight, thereby reducing the number of boys needed to distribute it. Instead of accepting management's authority, the boys refused to handle any of the papers. They destroyed bundles of *Plain Dealers*, attacked those who persisted in selling them, and withstood clubbing by police. About a hundred strikers were held without charge. The boys sent a delegation to the mayor, who was already beleaguered by striking taxi drivers and gas station attendants. The boys then took their case to the public via sidewalk placards stating "We Can Not Starve; We Must Strike" and "Newsboys are ashamed to tell their mothers what they earn." The newspapers relented after four days and signed a pact with the United Brotherhood of Newspaper Carriers, Sellers, and Handlers. The bosses refused to reinstate the old editions or allow a closed shop but did agree to lower wholesale prices, accept returns, and guarantee $15 a week to boys who sold all day at downtown corners. The union won a closed shop guarantee the next year for its twelve hundred members, ages 8 to 82.[48]

Street clashes also occurred in a strike by newsboys in Holyoke, Massachusetts, in September 1934 after a unilateral price hike. The issue was settled in the boys' favor through the mediation of a probation officer and a Catholic priest.[49]

Seattle street newsboys won small raises and union recognition in arbitration with the Seattle *Times* and *Post-Intelligencer* in 1936 and, in affiliation with the American Federation of Labor, set out to organize the entire city. Yet the newsboys union met a wall of resistance from publishers, the Teamsters Union, and the increasingly conservative AFL the following year when it sought a fifty-fifty profit split and an end to the ban on selling left-wing publications. Teamster leader Dave Beck, a former newsboy, typically used goon squads in jurisdictional disputes with other unions and did so again. The newsboys won police protection and in 1937 left the AFL for the more progressive Committee for Industrial Organization (later the Congress of Industrial Organizations, CIO).[50]

In April 1937, members of the newly organized Wayne County Newsboys' Association in Chicago's Loop district refused to sell Detroit newspapers, while newsboys in Oakland, California, struck local papers through the summer, forcing die-hard baseball fans to procure bootleg copies in dark alleys. In August 1939, the predominantly Italian American hawkers and carriers of the *Berkshire Eagle* in western Massachusetts waged a two-day strike, with suspected CIO assistance, to win a full penny profit per paper sold.[51]

The labor peace achieved in Cleveland fell apart in June when the now four-hundred-member newsboys union tried to bring the area's ten thousand home carriers under contract. The publishers association stood firm: "They are for the most part, schoolboys," said its secretary. "Each year there is a 65 per cent turnover. . . . Every boy has an individual contract signed and approved by his parents." The union called this arrangement "involuntary servitude" and demanded that the city's three dailies, all of which sold for 3¢, raise carriers' profit from the prevailing ⅞¢ to an even penny. After nine days of picketing, which included exuberant paper-trashing parties (Figure 14.6) and the arrest of sixty strikers, the papers abolished street sales, confining deliveries to stores and homes. The union filed a complaint with the NLRB, affiliated with the AFL, and staged sit-ins at lunch counters that sold papers—all to no avail.[52]

When not agitating on their own behalf, newsboys aided other embattled workers, including projectionists, butchers, autoworkers, longshoremen, truck drivers, and reporters. In December 1930, a business agent for the Los Angeles Projectionists' Union tried to get around an anti-picketing ordinance by recruiting newsboys to hawk special editions of the *Los Angeles Citizen*, a labor paper, outside the Rialto Theater, which had locked out union employees. Ernest Apac, Joe Hough, and James Doyle worked the sidewalk for weeks, crying, "Rialto Unfair to Labor." They were repeatedly arrested. The boys said they were

Figure 14.6. Cleveland Press newsboys stand in piles of destroyed newspapers on June 12, 1940. The sign in the background reads "Newsboys forced out of their job." Fred Bottomer, The Cleveland Press Collection, Michael Schwartz Library, Cleveland State University.

simply exercising their First Amendment right to free speech, but a jury found them guilty of loitering and picketing, resulting in fines of $25 each. A local meatcutters union employed the same tactic in 1937 and met the same results.[53]

Michigan newsies joined several dangerous protests, including a hunger march in Dearborn on March 7, 1932, that resulted in the death of "Joe the Newsboy" Bussell and three others. Some four thousand laid-off autoworkers and their allies had marched to Ford's River Rouge plant to demand work, relief, and the right to organize when police fired on them. Bussell, 16, sold papers near the plant and was a Communist Party member slated to go to Russia for training. Instead, he and the other victims were laid to rest in four red coffins banked by red wreaths. The funeral service at Workers Hall featured revolutionary songs and speeches instead of prayers, and ended with a train of fifteen thousand people escorting the hearse to Woodmere Cemetery. Undaunted, local youths continued to distribute papers at rallies and marches, leading to the union's victory in 1937 (Figure 14.7).[54]

Likewise, many West Coast newsboys got caught up in the labor battles that rocked the waterfront in the early 1930s. Some youths began by vending the

Figure 14.7. In a historic organizing drive beset by violence, union activists hand out copies of the United Auto Workers paper while newsboys push the anti-union *Detroit Free Press* outside Ford's River Rouge plant in Dearborn, Michigan, Aug. 11, 1937. From the Collections of The Henry Ford, Dearborn, MI, No. 833.69368.

Western Worker, a Communist paper in Los Angeles, in 1932 despite police efforts to sweep them off the streets. Rank-and-file longshoremen in San Francisco issued a mimeographed sheet in December 1932 called the *Waterfront Worker* to expose conditions on the docks—"speedups, chiseling, forcing payoffs, and things like that," explained future union president Harry Bridges. "We had young guys from Skid Row that would come down and sell the paper. At first it was a penny—then the price was raised a 100 percent to two cents. The guys'd get about 50 cents for the job. They'd sell the paper during the shape-up and then around the docks." The *Waterfront Worker* soon reached other ports and helped spark a coastwise strike in 1934. During the struggle, Bill Ward, son of a San Pedro dockworker, used his cover as a newsboy to spy on strikebreakers. "I used to sell papers at the scab compound," he said, "hear things the scabs were talkin' about, and tell my father where I thought these people were gonna be the next day. This allowed the union to know where to demonstrate with a great amount of vigor. One day the scabs or the Pinkertons started giving me false information. So my cover was blown. Finally they wouldn't let me back in there anymore." The strike climaxed on July 5, "Bloody Thursday," when clashes with police in San Francisco left two workers dead. Newsboys rejected the contents of their papers, which accused strikers of fomenting the riot, and instead shouted, "Read all about it! They're murdering pickets on the waterfront! Read how they slaughter strikers!"[55]

Newsboys risked their lives at other labor conflicts that year. During the so-called Battle of Toledo at the Electric Auto-Lite plant in May 1934, young Orville Fuller, a *Toledo News-Bee* carrier, waved a white handkerchief to signify his neutrality and strode into the danger zone between strikers and the National Guard. Meanwhile, in Minneapolis, members of the local newsboys' union supported the three-month-long truckers' strike by distributing copies of a labor paper, the *Organizer,* "to counteract the lies and propaganda [of the] united boss press." Priced at a penny, the paper sold for up to $3, providing a sympathetic public with an easy way to aid the truckers. The employer-dominated Citizens Alliance called for the arrest of the vendors on charges of criminal syndicalism, but authorities demurred.[56]

Later, in October 1938, newsboys in Wilkes-Barre, Pennsylvania, and its suburbs refused to deliver papers during a strike by editorial workers belonging to the newly formed American Newspaper Guild. The strike, which concerned wages and hours, involved a hundred reporters, desk men, circulators, clerks, and correspondents at the city's four newspapers—the morning *Record, Evening News, Times Leader,* and Sunday *Independent*—all of which suspended publication for five and half months before conceding to union demands.[57]

Whatever their outcomes, the strikes illustrate how America's newsboys contributed to the labor upsurge of the 1930s. In word and deed, they showed more affinity with the militant working class than with the discredited titans of business who were their supposed role models. A survey conducted in the late thirties confirmed news sellers' low status; it ranked them ninety-third out of a hundred in terms of occupational prestige, just below janitors and longshoremen but above scrubwomen and garbage collectors.[58]

On the Culture Front

Artists, writers, and performers also saw newsboys as part of the proletariat, and they effectively turned the "little merchant" stereotype on its cloth-capped head. Depression-era newsies were cultural symbols par excellence. They could personify the capitalist system and its discontents simultaneously. They did so in plays, comics, movies, music, radio shows, murals, drawings, photographs, and fiction, some of it funded by the federal government and much of it arising from the pro-labor, anti-fascist Popular Front. Newsboys took center stage, for instance, in the Federal Theatre Project's 1937 play *Morning Paper*, which dramatized the efforts of the National Youth Administration (NYA) to break up the crooked newspaper rackets in Boston and establish a legitimate Street Trade Boys Club:

SLIM: Sounds like another crowd musclin' in.
CHARLEY: Don't be a wise guy, Slim—Dis is on da level. Dis guy is from da NYA. Dey're gonna organize da newsies.[59]

Slim's suspicions were not unwarranted given the ideological aims of the NYA, which sought not just to remove young people from the workforce, like a junior WPA, but also to bolster the New Deal coalition by providing citizenship training to idle youth who might otherwise fall under the spell of right-wing demagogues or left-wing revolutionists.[60]

From the left came *Newsboy*, a playlet created by the Workers' Laboratory Theatre in New York in 1933 and staged by workers' theater groups nationwide and abroad. Adapted from a poem by Communist Party cultural apparatchik V. J. Jerome, this dramatic montage blended modern dance, mass chants, and snappy dialogue to expose the class struggle behind the day's headlines. As a newsboy cries his papers about follies girls, love nests, and ball games, a crowd gathers to remind him of Sacco and Vanzetti, the Scottsboro Boys, and seventeen million unemployed. Hungry and cross, the newsboy fends off their intrusions, but by the final curtain he recognizes his complicity in duping the masses and begins selling the *Daily Worker*. "Climb to the top of the Empire State Building," a man tells him, "and blare out the news—Time to revolt! Black man, white man, field man, shop man—Time to revolt!"[61]

The radical press used newsboys to foment reform more than revolution. In 1931 the *New Masses* ran a William Gropper cartoon in which a newsie shouts "Extry! Corrupt Judge in Hiding" as the shifty jurist sidles by under a low-pulled fedora.[62] Soon after, the *Daily Worker* introduced *Red Builder Tales*, a comic strip about a *Daily Worker* newsboy who routinely outwitted antagonists and broke sales records. "Compare its news with the distortions of the capitalist press!" he advised. The strip's main function was to recruit vendors among the unemployed. Dust Bowl balladeer and *People's World* columnist Woody Guthrie also wakened readers to the malarkey masquerading as objective journalism. He called Hearst's strident anti-communism "Randolphism" and said it aimed to keep people "ignernt" of their exploitation. "He's got more slaves than Mr. Lincoln turned a loose," wrote Guthrie. "White collar slaves. Limosene slaves. Movie Star Slaves. News boy slaves." Press critic George Seldes and historian Alfred McClung Lee likewise brought a materialist moral analysis to their writings in the 1930s. Seldes blasted the press's use of children as anti-labor and anti-democratic, while Lee wielded an "ethical measuring stick" to investigate how newspapers traveled "From Press to People."[63]

Hollywood movies offered yet another view of the newsboy type. Celluloid newsies were "little tough guys" from poor, ethnic neighborhoods who suspended all rules of morality to survive. The system bred poverty, and poverty bred them. The quintessential "dead-end kid" aimed not to destroy the system but only to turn it upside down and shake it until he got his. Child star Jackie Cooper specialized in such roles. In Universal's *Newsboys' Home* of 1938, he plays Rifle Edwards, a gang leader fighting a circulation war on behalf of a naive newspaper heiress (Plate 29). That same year Republic Pictures released *King of the Newsboys*, starring Lew Ayres as a scrappy vendor who becomes a ruthless distribution mogul determined to ruin the suave gangster husband of his childhood sweetheart. Metro-Goldwyn-Mayer's *Boys Town*, starring Spencer Tracy as Father Flanagan and Mickey Rooney as his toughest egg, won two Oscars that year. Such movies combined comedy, action, and romance to affirm the potency of the "American dream" (a common phrase of the period) and the essential goodness of the nation's hard-boiled newsboys. It was as if the future of capitalism required rehabilitating their reputations no less than rehabilitating the economy.[64]

The iconoclastic hobo composer Harry Partch contributed to this project in 1933 when he dashed off "A Modern Parable I," which juxtaposed the harsh barkings and streetwise banter of a newsboy with a university president's pompous valedictory speech. The vocal piece climaxes with the boy telling his boss what he can do with his corner—and coincidentally answering the president's rhetorical question to his scholars: "What shall we do with this magnificent learning?" "You can stick it up their ass!" replies the newsboy.[65]

Radio amplified newsboys' cries throughout the thirties and exerted a lasting impact on their trade. Eight-year-old Mel Tormé became a star in 1934 playing Jimmy the Newsboy on the Chicago soap opera *Song of the City*. Jimmy Donnelly provided the voice of Matey the Newsboy on the *Popeye* radio show. And each episode of the syndicated serial *The Green Hornet* ended with a newsboy crying, "Read all about it! Green Hornet still at large!" *The Chase and Sanborn Hour*, the most popular radio show of 1937, featured ventriloquist Edgar Bergen and his wisecracking dummy Charlie McCarthy, whom Bergen modeled after a "rascally" Irish newsboy in his old neighborhood. The medium's impact on real boys was much less positive, as radio reduced newspapers' share of national advertising by 28 percent and hurt circulation. Radio news flashes stimulated street sales at first, but in the long run they lessened the demand for extras, multiple editions, and the children who sold them.[66]

The most distinctive art form of the era was the mural. Beginning in 1933, the Civil Works Administration and its successor, the Works Progress Administration (WPA), commissioned hundreds of wall paintings in schools, post offices, and other public buildings to put artists back to work. Several of these frescos, such as Suzanne Scheuer's panels in San Francisco's Coit Tower, executed during the 1934 West Coast maritime strike, feature newsboys as working-class figures (Plate 30). Mischa Richter's fifty-foot mural installed in the Burroughs Newsboys' Foundation building in Boston was, by contrast, a paean to paternalism: until demolished by a wrecking ball, it showed a newsboy working his way up the ranks with the help of his superiors.[67]

Aiding the advance of civilization is the newsboy pictured in Edward Laning's *The Story of the Recorded Word*, on the walls of the New York Public Library in 1938. Laning, who earned $21.90 a week working for the WPA, traces the history of print from Moses's tablets to Ottmar Mergenthaler's linotype machine in 1886. In the last of four panels, *New York Tribune* editor Whitelaw Reid inspects the first mechanically typeset page proof while the inventor sits at his keyboard eyeing the fruits of his labor—a newsboy crying cheap extras under the looming towers of that other marvel of the age, the Brooklyn Bridge.[68]

Most New Deal–era artists worked on a smaller scale, and many of them found newsboys to be worthy subjects. San Francisco artist Pauline Vinson produced a series of lithographs for the WPA that included a portrait of a Chinese American newsie. New Yorker Winifred Milius executed a woodcut that captures the whirl of activity around a busy Union Square newsboy. And illustrator Don Freeman, a member of the WPA graphics program in Manhattan, documented the rambunctious camaraderie of black and white boys receiving a delivery on a wintry night in Times Square (Figure 14.8). Freeman's jolly scene corroborates the findings of child labor investigators who staked out eleven nighttime newspaper distribution centers in Manhattan and Brooklyn in 1932. They found 450 illegal child

Figure 14.8. Work and play roll into one in Don Freeman's *Late Editions*, black and white print, 12¾ × 15 in. Public Works of Art Project, 1934. New York Public Library.

sellers who began gathering around 7:30 for the 8:00 p.m. delivery. "The time is passed standing around and talking, participating in general rough-house, or in games of various sorts," they wrote, as if captioning Freeman's drawing. "Serious fighting is not often seen."[69]

Newsboys in small-town America came in for documentary treatment in the latter years of the Depression by "photographer investigators" of the Farm Security Administration (FSA). Their task was to show the faces behind the statistics and make a complete record of this "agonizing interlude in American life." They produced more than 270,000 photographs but were peculiar propagandists in that they focused more on the need for federal intervention than on its results. They were less interested in extreme cases of privation than in the crucial everyday; hence the focus on newsboys. Theodor Jung followed three peddlers of the *Columbus Dispatch* in Jackson, Ohio, in 1936 as they loitered around town and peered longingly into a shop window (Figure 14.9). Ben Shahn, Russell Lee, John Vachon, Arthur Rothstein, and other FSA photographers snapped pictures of newsboys in towns and cities across the country, never bothering to ask their

Figure 14.9. Theodor Jung, *Newsboys Admiring Sporting Goods, Jackson, Ohio,* April 1936. Library of Congress, Washington, DC.

names or solicit their stories. Their newsboy pictures appeared in government reports and exhibitions, academic journals and art annuals, general circulation newspapers and magazines. The images took on different meanings in each of these contexts, but were part of an unsentimental public construction of poverty and childhood. Then as now, the rhetorical power of the photos lay in their directness and authenticity.[70]

While some Depression-era novelists depicted newsboys as heralds of class struggle or critics of class oppression, others tried to portray them in more complex ways. Drawing on memories of peddling papers in Fresno, California, during World War I, William Saroyan wrote "Resurrection of Life," a 1935 short story that offers a stream-of-consciousness critique of American culture and society. Saroyan's newsboy "used to go through the city like an alley cat, prowling all over the place, into saloons, upstairs into whore houses, into gambling joints, to see: their faces, the faces of those who were alive with him on the earth." The boy sees the ignorant rich eating in high-toned restaurants and bloated drunks dozing in saloons. He recognizes the falsity of Hollywood movies, the shallowness of school lessons, and the indignity of having to buy stale bread meant for chicken feed. He tries to reconcile the hypnotic hymns and pie-in-the-sky sermons he hears in church with the mad, godless headlines he cries to giddy customers—"Ten thousand huns killed." Caught up in all its ugliness and glory, the grown-up 10-year-old narrator can do little but rejoice in the endless, fleeting mystery of the human condition.[71]

Less fatalistic is Upton Sinclair's *The Flivver King—A Story of Ford-America*, published in 1937, three years after his failed End Poverty in California (EPIC) campaign for governor. Intended as an organizing tool for the United Auto Workers, the lunch-pail-size novella exposes industrial capitalism's false ideology of success via the intersecting lives of Henry Ford and his luckless admirer Abner Shutt: "It was the fate of little Abner to be fourteen years old in a time of 'trade depression,' so he did not get quite enough to eat, and his growth was stunted, and he had to leave school and go out on the streets to earn a few pennies selling newspapers." In addition to being chased and beaten by other boys, Abner loses a finger to frostbite, giving him "a souvenir of the 'hard times' to carry through life."[72]

James T. Farrell's vision was even darker. His story, "The Scoop," also published in 1937, recounts the murder and mayhem perpetrated by a Chicago supplyman, or swamper. Once a newsboy, Dennis McDermott worked his way up the ranks to become the one who cheats and terrorizes the new generation of corner kids. He is a company goon bereft of humanity, let alone class feeling. He no sooner slits the throat of an honest vendor than he is back on the truck distributing extras with the headline "NEWSBOY MURDERED; SLAYER UNAPPREHENDED."[73] The circle is complete: The victim has become the victimizer.

The jaded, maimed, and psychotic newsboys of 1930s fiction represent the antithesis of the striving Horatio Alger hero. McDermott would just as soon stick a shiv in Ragged Dick as look at him. The popularity of Alger's "onward and upward" school of fiction crashed along with the stock market. Despite the fanfare accompanying the author's centenary in 1832, Alger's formulaic plots and didactic themes held little appeal to youths reeling from an economic crisis that could not be overcome by hard work and frugality alone. A survey taken at the Brace Memorial Home and at the CAS's nine boys' clubs revealed that the older a boy got the more he objected to Alger's urban fairy tales. "Success may be gotten by starting at the bottom," said one boy, "but it's not as easy as Alger says." Boys did not turn to proletarian fiction or radical tracts. On the contrary, they preferred dime novels featuring Yale's Frank Merriwell, whose athletic and academic exploits were recycled in comics, radio plays, and movies. And the bestseller of the so-called Red Decade was Dale Carnegie's *How to Win Friends and Influence People*, which held that success could be attained by adjusting one's personality, not the social order.[74]

The Great Depression was as much a psychological condition as an economic one, and it struck young and old alike. Children no less than parents often blamed themselves for their plight. Joblessness isolated people from family and friends, resulting in despair and even suicide. To the degree that news peddling required daily contact with people, it inoculated youths against the despondency born of idleness and dependence. If nothing else, being a newsboy could make one a familiar face on the street and a member of a fraternity. Bringing home money for food and rent also boosted children's sense of self-worth. On his first day selling papers Mario DeMarco netted 15¢, which he said enabled his mother to buy a loaf of bread and a quart of milk with a few cents to spare. The ability to earn not only filled kids with pride but stirred sensual pleasures as well. Frank Russo of Brooklyn liked to empty his pockets onto his bed and roll around on the coins before handing them over to his mother.[75]

Newsboys in the thirties also took pride in their command of world affairs. After winning an award from the Burroughs Newsboys' Foundation to attend Harvard, Theodore White became a war correspondent in China and a Pulitzer Prize winner. Despite the strain of early rising, Russell Baker of Baltimore felt that "it was always exciting to rip open the bundles of fresh newspapers and be the first in the neighborhood to know tomorrow's news." Likewise, future black power leader Robert F. Williams became a valued interpreter in his Monroe, North Carolina, community. "The *Charlotte News* gave me status and some money to boot," he recalled. After finishing his route he would linger at the downtown store where the railroad men and other workers gathered to talk, joke, and play checkers. "Most of them could read and write but some couldn't," he said, "and the ones that could didn't know very much about the news. . . . Each day I would go and explain who Hitler was and Mussolini and what was taking place."[76]

News sellers in Italy, Spain, and Germany, by contrast, were jailed if they cried papers critical of the fascists. They were among the first casualties of a totalitarian model of mass communication devoted to extending the power of the state. By 1935 every newsboy in Germany had to submit proof of his "Aryanism" back to 1800.[77] America's newsboys escaped such tyranny, but the Depression left a lasting mark on them just the same. It shaped the attitudes and values they carried with them into adulthood, such as a fear of quitting jobs or incurring debts. Some observers say it left children psychologically scarred, while others argue that it forged them into the "greatest generation," capable of overcoming all subsequent adversities, including another world war.[78] Ferlinghetti refused to romanticize either the hardships or the heroism:

> I had an unhappy childhood.
> I saw Lindbergh land.
> I looked homeward
> and saw no angel. . . .
> I chopped trees for the CCC
> And sat on them.

I landed in Normandy
in a rowboat that turned over.[79]

Newsboys were both scarred and steeled by the hard times. Yet their stories suggest an even more common outcome: the Depression politicized them. It made them see their family's hardships and their own struggles to realize the American dream not as products of bad luck or bad habits but as the result of something bigger that needed fixing. Like many of their counterparts in 1930s popular culture, real Depression-era newsboys paid precocious attention to the ways in which ordinary people and their elected leaders could, if they only would, use the tools of a liberal democratic government to better their lives. In so doing, they helped save the capitalist system they had so long epitomized.

Conclusion

The Thump on Lost Porches

From their humble beginnings in the 1830s to their strapped maturity in the 1930s, newsboys came of age with the country. They cried its news, embodied its myths, and influenced its destiny. For all their individual lack of power and prestige, they developed into important historical figures—members of a constantly regenerating army of hawkers and carriers whose long, noisy march across time gave shape, substance, and timbre to their times. They did not just careen from decade to decade, banner headline to banner headline, but made their presence felt in chord-like fashion as workers, children, and symbols.

They arose with the founding of cheap dailies for the masses in an age of expanding democracy and chattel slavery. Members of an essentially new occupational group with links to the colonial and revolutionary eras, these children of the penny witnessed and hastened fundamental shifts in American social, economic, and political affairs. From poor, predominantly Irish immigrant families, this generation served as shock troops in newspaper circulation wars and organized strikes and boycotts on their own behalf. With their distinctive dress, slang, and sauciness, newsboys formed one of America's early youth subcultures, capturing the attention of artists, writers, and performers. Some depicted them as poor waifs who implicitly critiqued the society that produced them, while others cast them as mock symbols of Whigs, Democrats, or Young America itself. These youths trumpeted war with Mexico and contributed to the major reform movements of their day, including temperance, abolition, nativism, spiritualism, and anti-sabbatarianism. A savvy few consolidated their routes into giant distribution firms, but most barely eked out a living. Philanthropists in New York shipped thousands west on orphan trains and founded lodging houses and night schools for those who would not leave the city. During the Civil War, newsboys served both Union and Confederate causes, hiking prices and swaying the morale of soldiers and civilians alike.

Newsboys in the last third of the nineteenth century emerged as a major social problem due to their growing numbers and naked exposure to the upheavals of industrialization. Now primarily from southern and eastern Europe, these children of the breach grew up amid the titanic struggle between capital and labor, forcing them to take sides early in life. Novelists and genre painters romanticized their hardships, while Social Gospelers exposed their neglect and exploitation. Newsgirls came under special scrutiny for their presumed moral vulnerability. Railroad news butchers expanded the nation's burgeoning information economy, while tramp newsies rode the rails in search of opportunity and adventure. Newsboys in western boomtowns displayed a precocious ability to get ahead, yet also challenged the economic inequities of the industrial frontier. They tried to lift themselves collectively, not just individually, by their bootstraps. In all regions newsboys organized unions and affiliated with labor federations, alternately broadening and bridging the racial divides drawn by their elders. To maintain control of the distribution process, circulation managers in the Midwest introduced paternalistic newsboy welfare schemes that soon spread to other areas and industries. Newsboys were also complicit in the rise of yellow journalism and the cacophony of headline cries that characterized metropolitan life and advanced imperialist aims in the 1890s.

Newsies in the early decades of the twentieth century encountered all the adversities of their predecessors, which attracted the attention of muckraking journalists and progressive reformers who sought to regulate their hours, ages, and school attendance. Issued badges and licenses, these children of the state complied with the laws at first, but increasingly flouted them to aid their families or afford the candy, cigarettes, and theater tickets they desired. Youths in some cities formed unions or took part in industry-backed, municipally sponsored newsboy clubs, courts, and republics that encouraged self-regulation. World War I undermined the influence of child savers and bolstered the clout of publishers, many of whom recruited newsboys to sell war bonds and form Scout troops. Nostalgia-prone pundits of the 1920s obfuscated newsboys' unwaged labor by celebrating them as little merchants whose entrepreneurial spirit mirrored that of Wall Street speculators. The boys expressed a wider range of convictions by battling union-busters, Red-baiters, prohibitionists, fundamentalists, mobsters, and the Ku Klux Klan. The Great Depression increased competition from adult news vendors and effectively tore holes in newsboys' pockets, leading many to join Unemployed Councils and support the resurgent labor movement. No longer idealized as future captains of industry, they became icons of discontent in proletarian art, literature, and theater.

Root Notes

Thus did the reality and representation of news peddlers change over time. Their experiences varied as the economy revved or faltered, as rival papers warred or merged, as child labor markets expanded or contracted, and as social workers and circulation managers professionalized. America's newsboys also had to adapt to a perpetual information technology revolution. Their numbers and sales grew as innovative paper-making, printing, and folding machinery created larger, cheaper, and more appealing products. Newsroom telegraphy stimulated the circulation of multiple editions, which enabled hawkers to put distant events into people's ears minutes after they occurred. Moreover, every generation had to learn to use—and dodge—new forms of transportation, including streetcars, bicycles, and automobiles. The deployment of trains, trucks, and planes widened distribution zones, leading boys in far-flung locales to distribute metropolitan dailies along with their hometown gazettes.

Attitudes about child news peddling fluctuated, too, as modern ideas took hold about the nature of childhood and adolescence, the causes of poverty and delinquency, and the uses of philanthropy and reform. These ideas met and grappled in a raucous marketplace of ideas that was itself continually transformed by a deluge of print and pictures representing various literary, journalistic, and artistic forms and styles, which in turn influenced public thinking, debate, and legislation that materially affected newsboys' lives.

Despite these relentless changes, newsboys from all eras shared common traits and experiences. The first similarity is their demographic diversity. From the beginning, news peddling was an unrestricted occupation that attracted people of all ages, backgrounds, and abilities. Newspaper proprietors required thousands of people to meet—and stoke—the demand for their product, and they weren't particular about who did the job or in what dialect. Conflicts between blacks and white, women and boys, natives and newcomers routinely occurred, but the trade usually remained open to anyone willing to invest a few coins.

For all their diversity, news peddlers overwhelmingly belonged to the working class. Aside from the occasional displaced German prince, Russian aristocrat, or Oak Park, Illinois, runaway, they shared similar incomes, identities, and outlooks as members of a non-wage-earning proletariat.[1] Their evolving identification with the working poor was as evident in the 1830s as in the 1930s, and varied little among boys whose families fled the poverty of Ireland and Italy or the pogroms of the Russian pale and the Deep South. Indeed, the history of newsboys is the history of the working class writ small.

Fraternizing with these fellows over time, as closely as the sources allow, offers myriad rewards. First and foremost, it expands the roster of recognized historical actors. Many of the children named herein have never before appeared in the pages of a book. They obviously caught the attention of some contemporary chronicler who recognized their singular charms, needs, or newsworthiness, but that attention was usually short-lived and inattentive to the larger story of how ordinary people lived big changes such as industrialization, urbanization, and mass migration. A study of news peddlers in America demands consideration of the most marginalized members of society—the young, old, disabled, indigent, and outcast of every race and ethnicity. It also highlights the differential socialization of boys and girls in places that did not welcome them equally, even when they shouldered similar economic responsibilities.

A residual benefit to entering the social world of newsboys is that it expands our appreciation of the common spaces of childhood, which must rightly include news alleys and press rooms, all-night cafés and boxing gyms, lodging houses and reading rooms, brothels and jail cells, theater pits and bandwagons, immigrant trains and union halls. Shining a light in these places illuminates not just children's daytime exertions and enjoyments but also their nocturnal doings. Whatever the case for the middling sorts, working-class children and adults clearly did not occupy separate spheres.

It should also be apparent that the hawkers and carriers who numbered among America's poorest children were serious economic actors whose labor helped sustain themselves, their families, and their industry. To the thousands of vagrant children who struggled for survival, selling a few papers could mean the difference between eating and not eating on a given day, or sleeping inside or outside at night. To the majority of newsboys who lived with their families, news peddling helped their parents or guardians make ends meet, especially when the primary breadwinner was sick, injured, out of work, or on strike, which were not uncommon occurrences among the working class. Progressive reformers challenged the necessity of children's earnings to family economies and tried to document newsboys' prodigal spending, arguing that the fraction of their income that made it into their mothers' aprons could not offset the costs in terms of vices acquired and educations lost. Some newsboys' parents agreed, but most expected that their children would contribute to their upkeep and look out for each other.

Newsboys' economic importance clearly extended to the newspaper industry. Their labor was integral to the development of an affordable, mass circulation, capitalist press. Children and advertisers formed the basis of an economic model that enabled a highly perishable product to reach consumers in a cheap and timely fashion. The model made sense given the abundance of poor children and the paucity of public relief, and the state's reluctance to regulate children's street labor or adequately enforce the regulations it did pass. For better or worse, lawmakers allowed shoeless tykes and boys on bikes to subsidize American journalism for much of its existence.

Newsboys were also political actors who played multiple roles in local, state, and national elections. Too young to vote, they peddled partisan papers, speeches, and campaign biographies throughout the nineteenth and early twentieth centuries. They physically and metaphorically entered the fray between Whigs and Democrats in the early republic, backed and attacked antislavery Republican papers in the antebellum and Civil War years, and promoted populist candidates and writings in the 1890s, socialists in the 1900s, and woman's suffragists in the 1910s. They could be hired to paper their cities with a candidate's posters and tear down those of his opponents. They filled out crowds at political meetings, torchlight parades, and election night bonfires. They held their own rallies, which generated "newsboy orators" whose vernacular appeal won them jobs as traveling stump speakers. This work influenced their own political development and led some to enter politics as shoulder-hitters, ward heelers, aldermen, mayors, governors, congressmen, and, yes, presidents.

Newsboys' cries and lies also wreaked the kind of havoc that led to war. They stimulated the spread-eagleism that provoked the Mexican-American War, stirred the sectional animus that led to the Civil War, fueled the jingoism that underlay the Spanish-American War, and ginned up the 100 percent Americanism that preceded—and followed—World War I. Newsboys weren't responsible for these conflicts, but they clearly helped build popular support for them, earning money all the while. Theirs is a story of opportunity *and* exploitation, profit *and* loss, agency *and* victimization.

Home Front Heroes

And their story continued. Newsboys did not disappear after the Great Depression, nor find sanctuary from the historical forces that shaped the work and representation of their forebears. But they did become younger and less militant as World War II transformed their lives and trade. The global rise of fascism dominated the headlines in the early forties, which spurred military production and revitalized the economy. Men and women marched into factories to produce armaments and uniforms. Full employment was soon followed by labor shortages, which were filled by teenagers: one million students dropped out of high school to enter the workforce between 1940 and 1944.[2] The War Manpower Commission facilitated their exit by relaxing minimum age requirements. In New York State alone, the number of work permits granted to boys and girls under 18 jumped sevenfold, from 71,000 to 478,000, during the first three years of the war. At the same time, the number of street trading badges issued dropped

50 percent. Twelve- and 13-year-olds now accounted for two-thirds of the state's news sellers and carriers.[3] Newspapers maintained access to their labor via innovative lobbying and public relations campaigns that, in effect, rewrote their history, implicitly arguing that character, not class, exerted a greater influence in shaping individual and national destinies.

Nationally, newsboys numbered 350,000 at the start of the war and soon reached 500,000, nine out of ten of whom were carriers, according to industry estimates.[4] The attack on Pearl Harbor altered their schedules and spiels overnight. Most people heard about the attack on the radio, but newspapers from Hawaii to Florida called boys in to hawk Sunday extras and the next day's regular editions. "Gotta whip those Japs!" bawled a strong-lunged Kansas City newsboy on December 8 after Congress declared war on the Japanese Empire. Every battle thereafter generated brisk sales, especially around the sprawling shipyards and military bases that hummed with activity day and night (Figure 15.1).

"When the soldiers were in town I sold a thousand papers every Sunday," recalled George Coston of St. Petersburg, Florida. He retailed copies of the local

Figure 15.1. With 79,000 shipyard employees working round the clock in Richmond, California, the change of shift generated huge sales for local newsboys. Dorothea Lange, Richmond general scenes, *Planes Devastate Reich*, 1944. The Dorothea Lange Collection, the Oakland Museum of California, Gift of Paul S. Taylor.

Times for a nickel and made 2¢ off each one. He and his pals also sold "Invasion Extras" on D-Day in 1944 and broke all sales records when Roosevelt died in 1945 and on VE Day (victory in Europe) and VJ Day (victory in Japan). Only the wartime shortage of newsprint limited newsboys' sales potential; hawkers sold out their allotments in half the normal time and carriers weren't allowed to accept new customers unless old ones cancelled or died. Newsboys and their friends recycled newspapers and other scrap material to aid the war effort and supplement their incomes.[5]

The war was not so rewarding for Japanese American youths, most of whom lost their jobs and their freedom. Ben Tonooka, for example, was 17 in 1941 and the only Nisei newsboy in Fresno, California. He earned 40¢ a day delivering papers by bike to his customers, all of whom were white. He worked seven days a week and brought home $12 a month—less if he was fined for complaints or late with his collection. It wasn't much, and no one ever thought to tip him, but every penny counted to his widowed mother and four siblings. Like most Americans, Tonooka had never heard of Pearl Harbor until it was attacked, but that didn't stop a shopkeeper from taunting him when he came around to collect. Instead of cash, the man handed him a news magazine with Japanese prime minister Tojo on the cover. "I just froze," recalled Tonooka. "I didn't know what to do or say." A few weeks later Tonooka's supplier called him into his office and said, "People don't want Japanese delivering papers so I have to let you go." Tonooka said okay and went home. "I would have had to quit anyway because the martial law came in right after that." The Tonookas spent the next several years in relocation camps in Jerome, Arkansas, and Gila Bend, Arizona. They were among the 110,000 Japanese Americans, including 30,000 youths, who were locked behind barbed wire by order of the president. To keep up their spirits, the internees started camp papers such as the *Jerome Communiqué* and the *Gila News-Courier*, which they circulated throughout the blocks.[6]

Meanwhile, to ensure unfettered access to children's labor, the International Circulation Managers Association lobbied to block or weaken child labor laws in Michigan, Indiana, Connecticut, and California, and launched two campaigns to burnish the image of newsboys as model citizens. The ICMA laid the semantic foundation by introducing the term *newspaperboy* to replace the more familiar *newsboy* or *newsie*. "These words automatically called to mind a ragged uncared for street urchin," said one member, "a picture not helping the newspaper business in any way." The association secured endorsements from President Roosevelt and several governors to declare October 4, 1941, National Newspaperboy Day. Pollster George Gallup conveniently reported the following year that nine out of ten Americans would permit their sons to sell papers at age 14. FDR praised newsboys on the third anniversary of the holiday. "They are doing two important war jobs at once," he said, "first in studying to prepare themselves for good

citizenship in tomorrow's world, and second, in serving as a vital link in the process of news gathering and reporting that makes our people the best informed
people in the world." Building on this success, the ICMA secured federal author-
ization in 1943 for its Newspaperboys for Victory program, in which carriers
raised $180 million selling War Savings Stamps (Figure 15.2).[7]

Girls were shut out of this patriotic program, as many cities and states still required them to be 18 years old to peddle papers, while boys could lawfully do so
at 12 or 14. In a historic challenge to these restrictions, 9-year-old Betty Simmons
and her aunt thrice refused to stop selling Jehovah's Witness publications,
Watchtower and *Consolation*, on the streets of Brockton, Massachusetts. They
said the law violated their freedom of religion, as both of them were ordained
ministers who believed that the street was their church and the dissemination

Figure 15.2. Office for Emergency Management, Office of War Information, Domestic
Operations Branch, Bureau of Special Services. 3/9/1943–9/15/1945. National Archives
and Records Administration, College Park, MD.

of tracts a form of worship. The case, *Prince v. Massachusetts*, culminated in a 1944 US Supreme Court decision against Simmons and her guardian. Citing the 1838 doctrine of *parens patrie*, the justices ruled 7–2 that a state may limit parental authority, including in matters of conscience and religious conviction, if a child's welfare was in jeopardy.[8] The presumption that boys outgrew their jeopardy earlier than girls went unchallenged.

The mobilization of newsboys for an Allied victory also occurred in the popular arts. In February 1940 *Whiz Comics* introduced the character of Captain Marvel, the alter ego of newsboy Billy Batson, who had only to shout "SHAZAM!" to become "the world's mightiest man—powerful champion of justice—relentless enemy of evil." Captain Marvel rivaled Superman in popularity and beat him to the screen in 1941. His nemesis, Captain Nazi, was a genetically altered "perfect specimen" sent over by Hitler to crush America's superheroes. Also patrolling the home front was the Newsboy Legion—a gang of crime-fighting slum kids created by ex-newsboy Jack Kirby and introduced by DC Comics in 1942 (Plate 31). Made up of Tommy Tomkins, Anthony "Big Words" Rodriguez, Patrick "Scrapper" MacGuire, and "Gabby" Gabrielli, the group subdued every Axis agent and gangland villain who crossed their path until decommissioned in 1947.[9]

Other industries also harnessed the versatile cultural power of newsboys and newsgirls. Turner Supply Company of Mobile, Alabama, exploited the vogue for pinups by circulating calendars and ink blotters featuring a long-legged, ruby-lipped newsgirl in high heels and hot pants offering news from the front (Plate 32). And Republic Steel, one of the most fiercely anti-union companies of the Depression era, whose reliance on hired guns culminated in the 1937 Memorial Day massacre in Chicago, launched an advertising campaign in 1944 that portrayed a big-eared newsboy as the epitome of "American-style capitalism" (Figure 15.3):

> He's in business for himself, this kid.
> He invests his own money in his newspapers because he has confidence in his own ability to sell them at a profit.
> He has learned by experience that business grows through hard work, salesmanship and thrift.
> He gets plenty of hard knocks—but profits by them.
> He knows what competition means—and has learned to meet it.
> He uses his wits.
> He gets ahead.
> He is capitalist, laborer and consumer combined.
> He is typically American.
> Multiply this boy by millions—and you'll see what makes America tick.[10]

Figure 15.3. "We're all capitalists in America," declared the anti-union Republic Steel. *Saturday Evening Post,* Oct. 7, 1944, 73.

Underlying this ringing tribute was Republic Steel chairman Tom Girdler's unbending resistance to government regulation, workers' rights, and consumer protection. The company and its hired pens ignored the newsboy's history of collective action and political dissent to turn him into a symbol of acquisitive individualism. Its efforts were reinforced by the reappearance of Horatio Alger's "strive and succeed" stories in comic books issued by Street & Smith, and the bestowing of the first Horatio Alger Award, introduced by the American Schools and Colleges Association in 1948 to honor successful men and women in business, politics, and the arts. RKO Pictures did no harm to the newsboy myth with the release of *Fighting Father Dunne,* starring Pat O'Brien as the founder of the St. Louis Newsboys' Home. However trivial by themselves, to-gether these terms, days, polls, stamps, comics, ads, awards, and films ensured publishers continued access to children's labor by characterizing it as patriotic and entrepreneurial.[11]

Cold Warriors

Newspaper publishers maintained a united front after the war to define carriers and sellers of all ages as independent merchants rather than employees. During the strike wave of 1945–46, three papers in St. Louis beat back the efforts of two hundred adult carriers to shed their merchant status and gain collec-tive bargaining rights. A similar number of adult carriers of the *Kansas City Star* lost their battle for union recognition in 1947 after a sixteen-day strike.[12] Fearing new restrictions on child labor, the American Newspaper Publishers Association persuaded the Republican-dominated Congress to alter the Fair Labor Standards Act so that it "shall not apply to any child engaged in the de-livery or sale of newspapers and periodicals outside of school hours."[13]

The industry had failed to win such protection in the 1944 case of *National Labor Relations Board v. Hearst Publications*, when the US Supreme Court upheld the employee status and bargaining rights of the mostly adult, full-time vendors represented by Los Angeles Newsboys Local Industrial Union No. 75, CIO. In 1948, however, the California Senate's Committee on Un-American Activities, with the full-throated support of the daily press, declared Local 75 to be a com-munist front, mainly because it refused to cooperate with its investigation. The committee also accused union leaders of forcing members to handle Soviet propaganda. Most of the 150 periodicals alleged to be "in the Stalin solar system" were published by labor, Jewish, African American, and civil rights groups.[14]

No one's loyalty was above suspicion in this political climate. Bill Mauldin, the Pulitzer Prize–winning "kid cartoonist" of World War II, whose Willie and Joe characters captured the foxhole humor of ordinary GIs, derided the postwar resurgence of racism and Red-baiting in his syndicated column. He did so by introducing a new character, a spunky newsboy who resembled himself as a child. A cartoon published in June 1946 shows the boy peddling papers with the headline "The Classes vs. the Masses" as a large man holds him up by the scruff of the neck (Figure 15.4). "I hear yer tryin' to overthrow th' gover'ment," he says. FBI director J. Edgar Hoover placed Mauldin under surveillance, and in 1948 United Features dropped him from syndication.[15]

The 1950s brought full employment and economic security to many Americans. More families entered the middle class, which meant they could afford nonessentials such as appliances and automobiles. Home ownership

Figure 15.4. "I hear yer tryin' to overthrow th' gover'ment." Bill Mauldin, United Feature Syndicate, June 18, 1946. Prints and Photographs Division, Library of Congress, DLC/PP-1975:078.1335.

rates soared as growing families flocked to the suburbs, mainly for the sake of their children. To better serve commuters, newspapers in New York introduced sophisticated "robot newsboys" (vending machines) in subway stations, while those in Minneapolis and St. Paul, Minnesota, installed news racks on streetcars.[16] Relatively few children hawked papers anymore or worked in any capacity; the US Census determined that only 2 percent of youths between ages 10 and 15 were gainfully employed, while 78 to 88 percent stayed in school up to age 19. Newspapers in New York City, Boston, Chicago, St. Louis, and Kansas City largely relied on adult carriers, but 97 percent of the remaining 1,739 dailies still depended on boys for home delivery. Despite declining circulation due to competition from radio and television, half a million youths spent several hours a day delivering papers in the early 1950s.[17]

These boys received a signal honor in 1952 when the US Postal Service acceded to lobbying by the International Circulation Managers Association and issued a violet-colored 3¢ stamp honoring the newspaperboys of America (Plate 33). (Newspapergirls went unmentioned, as publishers had advocated their elimination since 1950.) The stamp features an engraving of a carrier in cuffed jeans toting a bag labeled "Busy Boys . . . Better Boys." He is shown walking in a leafy suburban neighborhood toward a giant hand gripping a torch marked "Free Enterprise." First-day-sale ceremonies were held at the base of the Benjamin Franklin statue in Philadelphia. Comedians Abbott and Costello headlined the ICMA's publicity campaign, which included movie trailers depicting the newspaperboy as the "Leader of Tomorrow." The still vigilant National Child Labor Committee refused to get on board: "Until the newspapers are ready to accept for their carrier boys the legal regulations that apply to other forms of part-time employment and until they assume responsibility for injured workers and the financial risk of uncollectible accounts, we cannot accept the commemorative stamp's symbolization of the newspaper boy as an appropriate example of our American system of free enterprise."[18]

Into this debate walked 14-year-old *Brooklyn Eagle* carrier Jimmy Bozart, who enhanced the reputation of America's paperboys by initiating what came to be known as the Hollow Nickel Case. In June 1953, Bozart noticed that a nickel given to him by a customer in an East Flatbush apartment house was lighter than normal. And when he dropped it, it split in two, exposing a piece of microfilm. Bozart showed the coin to a classmate's father who was a police detective. The detective passed it on to the FBI, whose four-year investigation led to the arrest and conviction of Rudolph Ivanovich Abel, a Soviet spy later exchanged for American U2 pilot Francis Gary Powers. When the FBI revealed Bozart's role in the case, the press celebrated him as an all-American hero.[19]

The newspaper industry gave all carriers a chance to be heroes in these years by recruiting them to collect "truth dollars" for Radio Free Europe, the anticommunist network that broadcast news and information to seventy-nine million "captive people" behind the Iron Curtain. "Will your grandchildren grow up under communism?" asked the *Trenton Times*. "Nikita Khrushchev says 'Yes!' Your newspaperboys say '<u>No!</u>' "[20]

To further immortalize newsboys and advance their economic and political interests, newspaper publishers emulated professional baseball and college football entrepreneurs to establish the Newsboys Hall of Fame. It took the form of a book in 1953, an industry-sponsored program in 1960, and a modest exhibition in ANPA headquarters in Reston, Virginia, in 1974. The forty-four charter members included president Harry Truman, FBI director J. Edgar Hoover, boxer

Figure 15.5. "John Wayne," Hubert Bushey's Newsboy Hall of Fame Member Panel, ca. 1975.

Figure 15.6. Emory, "All Power to the People," *The Black Panther*, Berkeley, CA, Mar. 9, 1969, 20.

Jack Dempsey, and actor John Wayne (Figure 15.5). The induction of a new class every year guaranteed continued press coverage, which, in contrast to the free speech and antiwar protests disrupting college campuses, gave editorial writers and cartoonists a chance to praise newspaper delivery as "A 'Youth Movement' to Be Proud Of."[21]

Yet sixties radicals were loath to relinquish such a versatile symbol and useful worker to the establishment. The March 1969 issue of the Black Panther Party newspaper contained a bold graphic of an African American boy with a carbine slung across his shoulder crying the paper's headline: "ALL POWER TO THE PEOPLE." (Figure 15.6). The next issue featured an article denouncing black capitalism as a "quest for the scraps from the master's table," yet also included an ad recruiting hawkers and carriers. The photograph shows a boy on a bicycle. The caption reads: "The young man in the picture earned enough money in 3 weeks to buy the bike on which he is sitting. You can do the same or better."[22]

A Vanishing Breed

The decline of newsboys over the next thirty years mirrored the end of the "American Century," a term coined by magazine publisher Henry Luce in 1941 in anticipation of an Allied victory. By the 1970s the spread of newspaper stands, racks, and home deliveries rendered corner news sellers obsolete. A handful of

9- to 13-year-olds in Coos Bay, Oregon, and other cities sold afternoon papers, but most of those who remained were well past retirement age. Even carriers were in short supply. Circulation managers offered more incentives—trips, bikes, cameras, and premiums for signing up new subscribers—but fewer kids could be cajoled. When told about all the millionaires who had carried papers as boys, a disgruntled carrier in Kurt Vonnegut's 1969 novel *Slaughterhouse-Five* replied, "Yeah—but I bet they quit after a week, it's *such* a royal screwing." Among the gripes listed by 14-year-old Terry Pickens of Newburgh, Indiana, were long hours, low pay, deadbeat customers, and aggressive German shepherds. "If anybody told me being a newsboy builds character," he told Studs Terkel, "I'd know he was a liar." Such attitudes and conditions were widespread. A 1970s study found that paperboys in Utah earned $42.56 a month for 50.7 hours of work, well below the federal minimum wage of $1.60 per hour.[23]

As fewer boys could be found to carry routes, newspapers turned to girls even though many states still barred them from street work. In 1974, 13-year-old Lynn Warshafsky challenged a Wisconsin statute that prohibited the employment of girls under 18 in "street trade" occupations but allowed boys as young as 12 to do the work. Her lawyer father argued that the law violated Title VII of the 1964 Civil Rights Act and the equal protection clause of the Fourteenth Amendment. The Wisconsin Supreme Court ruled against her, holding that Title VII did not apply to minors and that the state had a right to protect girl carriers, who would be more vulnerable to sexual assault than boy carriers.[24]

Yet the threat of violence was no less real for men and boys than for girls. The urban crisis of the 1970s jeopardized carriers, who faced increased threats of assault and robbery. Weighing the risks, several dailies abandoned home delivery altogether in high-crime minority neighborhoods, leading to charges of racism. But violence against white paperboys in small-town America generated greater concern, beginning with the abduction and killing of 15-year-old Joseph Didier in March 1975 while he was delivering the *Rockford Register Star* in Rockford, Illinois.[25]

These dangers worsened over the next two decades. At least seven children were kidnapped, raped, or murdered on their routes in the early 1980s, which led to a national panic over child abduction. Indeed, the first kidnap victims pictured on milk cartons to aid in their recovery were carriers of the *Des Moines Register*: 12-year-old Johnny Gorsch, who went missing in 1982, and 13-year-old Eugene Wade Martin, who disappeared in 1984. To law-and-order conservatives, child abduction was the by-product of permissive laws and attitudes toward drug use, pornography, and homosexuality. The cases drew comment from President Ronald Reagan during a campaign stop in Cedar Rapids, Iowa. "Nancy and I join all of you, I'm sure, in praying for the safe return of Johnny and Eugene," he told the crowd. "And I pledge to you that none of us will rest until the streets in Iowa and throughout this nation are once again safe, particularly for our children." The boys were never found.[26]

The other paperboy murder victims were Brian Bleyl, 12, who went missing in February 1981 while collecting for the *Phoenix Gazette* in Phoenix, Arizona; Christopher Gruhn, 14, killed in March 1983 while delivering *Newsday* in Rockville Centre, New York; Danny Joe Eberle, 13, killed in September 1983 while delivering the *Omaha World-Herald* in Bellevue, Nebraska; Cheri Lindsey, 12, killed in March 1984 while collecting for the *Evening Press* in Binghamton, New York; and Christy Ann Fornoff, 13, killed in May 1984 while collecting for the *Phoenix Gazette* in Tempe, Arizona. Their cases contributed to a steep drop in the number and proportion of carriers under 18; the number fell from 823,746, or 90 percent of all carriers, in 1980 to 362,470, or 66 percent, in 1990. Parental fears also led to the mass fingerprinting of schoolchildren and the establishment of the private National Center for Missing and Exploited Children in Washington, DC, in 1984.[27]

Despite these safeguards, more children disappeared from their routes in the 1990s. Eleven youth and ninety-nine adult carriers died "in the line of duty" in that decade. They were kidnapped, shot as burglars, or struck by vehicles. Among the murder victims were Katie Clarey, 11, killed in May 1991 while delivering the *Argus Leader* in Sioux Falls, South Dakota; Charlotte Schmoyer, 15, killed in June 1993 while delivering the *Morning Call* in Allentown, Pennsylvania; Jeralee Underwood, 11, killed weeks later while collecting for the *Idaho State Journal* in Pocatello, Idaho; Joel Trinidad, 14, killed in September 1995 while collecting for the *Chicago Sun-Times* in Chicago; and Angelica Padilla, 11, killed in August 1998 while delivering the *Willimantic Chronicle* in Willimantic, Connecticut.[28]

The industry responded feebly. Some newspapers gave their carriers whistles to blow if they felt threatened. Others had them watch safety videos or identify safe houses along their routes. Registering the public's alarm over the crisis, the TV series *The Untouchables* featured back-to-back episodes in February 1993 in which treasury agent Elliot Ness and bootlegger Al Capone join forces to catch a serial killer who preys on Chicago street children.[29]

Insurance companies also took note, charging almost double to cover newspaper carriers compared to workers in other industries. In New York, where newspaper delivery was the leading cause of child labor injuries and deaths, the state required newspapers to provide carriers of all ages with workers' compensation coverage to help pay medical bills, lost wages, or death benefits. So, too, did Wisconsin, Nevada, Kentucky, and Maryland, but no other states mandated coverage for minors. Nor did they require firms to provide unemployment insurance, social security benefits, or the minimum wage to independent contractors. This exemption represented a savings of hundreds of millions of dollars in payroll taxes for the industry.[30] Newspaper revenues soared all the while, with profit margins topping 20 percent in 1997.

Safety concerns were just one factor in the decline of youth carriers. The "baby bust" that followed the post–World War II baby boom shrank the pool of potential paperboys just as the expanding fast food industry gave them other job options. Beginning in 1980, the number of carriers under 18 declined at a rate of ten thousand a year. They were replaced by retirees who needed to supplement fixed incomes and adult immigrants who, in time-honored fashion, saw the news trade as a way up. Newspaper owners and managers realized that a corps of grown-up, nonunion, independent carriers with their own cars and insurance was cheaper and more efficient than uninsured adolescents on foot or bicycles.[31]

The boys did not go quietly. In 1987, when the *Santa Rosa Press Democrat* dismissed its entire youth carrier force of 550 boys and replaced them with half that many adults, children and parents protested by picketing, signing petitions, and pressuring subscribers and advertisers to cut ties with the paper. "It's a sad day in American history," said one parent, "if it is a trend in the newspaper industry to eliminate paperboys and papergirls. This job has been a tradition in our country—like baseball, apple pie and Mom. What will happen to our kids if we phase this out? This great learning experience will be lost forever." The publisher regretted the end of the tradition but insisted that the switch was overdue.

Although free to use children without employing them, several newspapers and distribution companies still managed to violate child labor laws in the early nineties. They were fined for using underage boys—some as young as 8—in "crewing" operations to solicit newspaper and magazine subscriptions far from home, after dark, or for excessive hours. Among the newspapers promoted in this fashion were the *Knoxville News-Sentinel, Boston Globe,* and *Dallas Times Herald.* The *Providence Journal* also faced allegations of child labor abuses lodged by seventeen youths who formed the Rhode Island Carriers Association to secure higher profits and an expanded college tuition program. The *Journal* refused to recognize the group, just as Hearst and Pulitzer had refused to negotiate with the strikers of 1899.[32]

In some respects, being a newsboy in the 1990s was less appealing than in days of Kid Blink, especially for those who still hawked papers. The *St. Louis Post-Dispatch* used a hundred "live sellers" in the early nineties, mostly sixth- and seventh-graders who set up outside churches on Sundays and sold to congregants as they exited. Whereas hawkers in the 1890s received 50 to 60 percent of their newspaper's retail price and could return unsold papers, their counterparts in the 1990s received 20 to 30 percent on a nonreturnable basis.[33]

One similarity of the two eras—rising levels of homelessness—led to the revival of a nineteenth-century remedy: newspapers produced specifically for homeless people to sell. Beginning in 1989 with *Street News* in New York and

Street Sheet in San Francisco, these publications offered young and old an alternative to panhandling and gave readers a compassionate look at the causes of poverty and the realities of food and housing insecurity. Over the next ten years, street newspapers appeared in Boston, Chicago, Cleveland, Seattle, and Portland, Oregon.[34]

In hindsight, the most devastating trend affecting newspapers and carriers in the 1990s was expanded public access to the World Wide Web. By 2005, classified ads had migrated to Craigslist and display ads drifted to other internet sites, taking huge revenues from newspapers. The free fall continued between 2010 and 2015, when newspaper advertising income fell from $60 billion to about $20 billion. Readership also declined, especially among young people, leading to layoffs and other cutbacks by media corporations that had come to expect profits of 20 percent or more.[35]

Among the venerable dailies that succumbed to internet competition in recent years are the *Seattle Post-Intelligencer* (1863–2009), *Rocky Mountain News* (1859–2009), *Ann Arbor News* (1835–2009), and *Honolulu Advertiser* (1856–2010). Additionally, the *Washington Post, Boston Herald,* and *Los Angeles Times* found themselves on the brink of bankruptcy until rescued in Alger-like fashion by self-made tech billionaires. The internet's ability to circulate news and information more quickly than traditional newspapers and without the expense of physically transporting a product poses an ongoing threat to print journalism.

Despite their virtual absence from the media landscape, newsboys can still be seen waving their papers from atop fountains and pedestals in parks and squares around the country. Many of these statues went up at the turn of the twentieth century to remind passersby of the spirit of youth, the dignity of labor, or the value of a free press. In 1973, the Smithsonian Institution—then known as the "Nation's Attic"—paid further tribute to the industry by installing a life-size replica of Bernard Flaherty, America's "first" newsboy, at the entrance of the Henry R. Luce Hall of Reporting in the Museum of History and Technology. Displayed alongside period prints and photos and an authentic newsboy wagon, this corporate-sponsored storytelling embellishment silently welcomed visitors throughout the 1980s.[36] Oddly, newsboy statues multiplied just as the industry began to decline. New ones were unveiled outside newspaper offices, libraries, and on malls in St. Joseph, Missouri (1992); White Plains, New York (1995); Cary, North Carolina (c. 1995); Helena, Montana (1999); Champaign-Urbana, Illinois (2002); Golden, Colorado (2002); Austin, Texas (2005); and Tucson, Arizona (2009). They all look backward, monuments to a bygone era.

None of them call attention to the plight of today's newspaper carriers—the men and women who drive through residential neighborhoods before sunrise flinging papers from their car windows. Subscribers hardly ever see them and only sometimes hear the thump on their porches. But a visit to any newspaper distribution depot around 3:00 a.m. will reveal adults of all ages and nationalities unloading bundles from trucks, double-bagging papers one by one on long tables and running them out to their cars in grocery carts. Immigrants dominate the trade, with eight out of ten foreign-born; they come from Brazil, Haiti, Guatemala, and elsewhere around the globe. Most are legal residents, but no one looks too closely, as their labor is vital to the industry.[37] Their ranks are filled out by American-born senior citizens, war veterans, and expectant mothers. They work for distribution firms rather than the newspapers themselves, but they are independent contractors, which means they have no company health plans, paid sick days, or benefits of any kind. Most earn a few hundred dollars a week, minus gas, repairs, towing, insurance, and fines for traffic violations and customer complaints. Like their forerunners, today's "little merchants" still rely on tips to bring their earnings up to par. Raises are rare, turnover is constant. There is little banter or camaraderie around the tables; most carriers bag and load their papers in silence. Dare to ask what a guy thinks he's earning per hour and you're likely to get a testy response: "You can't think like that! You'll go crazy. We're just putting food on the table." No one talks union. Many go off afterward to second or third jobs in other low-paying service industries. They are inheritors of a forgotten past, a faded myth, and a living dream.

NOTES

Introduction

1. Charles Coleman Sellers, *Charles Willson Peale: Early Life, 1741–1790* (Philadelphia: American Philosophical Society, 1947), 1:136; "Bogus Despatches," *Boston Courier*, in *Alexandria Gazette*, Apr. 2, 1861, 1; "Lillian Sold Papers After Dark," *New York Sun*, May 16, 1898, 5; Allison Davis and John Dollard, *Children of Bondage: The Personality Development of Negro Youth in the Urban South* (Washington, DC: American Council on Education, 1940), 122.

2. Frankl Luther Mott, *American Journalism: A History of Newspapers in the United States Through 250 Years, 1690–1940* (New York: Macmillan, 1947), 314. While preoccupied mainly with great men and institutions, some media historians have turned their attention to workers and young people. See David Nasaw, *Children of the City: At Work and at Play* (New York: Oxford University Press, 1985); Jon Bekken, "Newsboys: The Exploitation of 'Little Merchants' by the Newspaper Industry," in *Newsworkers: Toward a History of the Rank and File*, ed. Hanno Hardt and Bonnie Brennen (Minneapolis: University of Minnesota Press, 1995), 190–225; and Gregory J. Downey, *Telegraph Messenger Boys: Labor, Technology, and Geography, 1850–1950* (London: Routledge, 2002).

3. See Karen F. Beall, *Kaufrufe und Strassenhandler: Eine Bibliographie* [*Cries and Itinerant Trades: A Bibliography*], trans. into German by Sabine Solf (Hamburg: Dr. Ernst Hauswedell, 1975); Robert Darnton, "The Forgotten Middlemen of Literature," in *The Kiss of Lamourette: Reflections in Cultural History* (New York: W. W. Norton, 1990), 136–153; Laurence Fontaine, *History of Pedlars in Europe* (Cambridge: Polity Press, 1996), 150, 195–196; Robert Munter, *The History of the Irish Newspaper, 1685–1760* (Cambridge: Cambridge University Press, 1967), 79–81; and Anthony Smith, *The Newspaper: An International History* (London: Thames and Hudson, 1979), 56–58.

4. George C. Needham, *Street Arabs and Guttersnipes: The Pathetic and Humorous Side of Young Vagabond Life in the Great Cities, with Records of Work for Their Reclamation* (Boston: D. L. Guernsey, 1884).

5. "New-York Newsboys," *New York Tribune Illustrated Supplement*, July 30, 1899, 2.

6. "The Newsboys and the Penny Press," *New York Herald*, Oct. 7, 1839, 1; "The News-Boy," *Child's Paper* 3, no. 10 (Oct. 1854), 37; Mary Wager-Fisher, "The Philadelphia Newsboys," *Wide Awake* 11, no. 1 (July 1880), 16–18; "Feasts and Addresses in Buffalo," *New York Herald*, Nov. 29, 1872, 7; "Sidewalk Notes," *Atlanta Constitution*, Oct. 12, 1878, 4; Paul Ward, "Street Arabs, Bootblacks and Newsboys," *Oliver Optic's Magazine* 18, no. 269 (Dec. 1875), 949; Thomas S. Sprague, *Sprague's Visitors Guide and Dictionary of Detroit and Vicinity* (Detroit: Author, 1883), 48.

7. "Statistics of Laboring Classes," *Chicago Tribune*, Sept. 9, 1893, 8; Bishop Joseph F. Berry, "Waifdom," quoted in Leonard Benedict, *Waifs of the Slums and Their Way Out* (New York: F. H. Revell, ca. 1907), 228; "Newsboys in Gotham," *True Republic*, June 1904, 122; Mrs. E. J.

Bissell, *The Child Workers of the Nation: Proceedings of the Fifth Annual Conference*, Chicago, *Jan. 21–23* (New York: American Academy of Political and Social Science, [Mar. 1909]), 33 Supplement, 231; William Byron Forbush, "A Western Newspaper and Its Newsboys," *Charities and the Commons* 19 (Oct. 5, 1907), 798; Edward N. Clopper, "Children on the Streets of Cincinnati," *Annals of the American Academy of Political and Social Science* 32 (July 1908), 113; Bruce Watson, "Street Trades in Pennsylvania," *American Child* 4, no. 2 (Aug. 1922), 125; R. F. Woodbury, Fred R. Davis, and Julia E. Chadwick, "Street Traders of Buffalo, New York, 1925: A Study Made by the Juvenile Protective Department, Children's Aid and Society for the Prevention of Cruelty to Children of Erie County, New York," *Foundation Forum* 52 (Aug. 1926), 13; Charles Gibbons, *Child Workers in Oklahoma: A Study of Children Employed in Enid, Oklahoma City, and Lawton*, NCLC Pub. No. 351 (1929), 10, 32–33; "Extra, Extra!," *Survey*, July 1934, 222.

8. Edward N. Clopper, *Child Labor in City Streets* (Norwood, MA: Macmillan, 1912), v.

9. On the power of the myth, see Sid Marks and Alban Emley, *The Newspaperboy's Hall of Fame* (Hollywood, CA: House-Warven, 1953); Irvin G. Wyllie, *The Self-Made Man in America: The Myth of Rags to Riches* (New Brunswick, NJ: Rutgers University Press, 1954); R. Richard Wohl, "The 'Country Boy' Myth and Its Place in American Urban Culture: The Nineteenth-Century Contribution," *Perspectives in American History* 3 (1969): 77–156; David E. Whisnant, "Selling the Gospel News, or: The Strange Careers of Jimmy Brown the Newsboy," *Journal of Social History* 5, no. 3 (1971–72): 269–309; Richard Weiss, *The American Myth of Success: From Horatio Alger to Norman Vincent Peale* (Urbana: University of Illinois Press, 1988); and Rollo May, *The Cry for Myth* (New York: W. W. Norton, 1991).

10. Doris Kearns Goodwin, *The Fitzgeralds and the Kennedys* (New York: Simon & Schuster, 1987), 41; Mervyn LeRoy, *Take One* (New York: Hawthorne Books, 1974), 93–94.

11. Christopher Lasch, *The True and Only Heaven: Progress and Its Critics* (New York: W. W. Norton, 1991), 82–83.

12. E. L. Doctorow, *The Waterworks* (New York: Random House, 1994), 26–27.

13. "The Police Court. Local Rights," *Chicago Tribune*, Mar. 21, 1869, 3.

14. Benjamin Franklin, *Autobiography* (1793; Harmondsworth, UK: Penguin Books, 1986), 20, 14; Carl Bridenbaugh, *Cities in Revolt: Urban Life in America, 1743–1776* (New York: Knopf, 1955), 186.

15. "The Boston News-Letter," *New York Times*, Jan. 12, 1896, 29.

16. See John Benson, *The Penny Capitalists: A Study of 19th Century Working-Class Entrepreneurs* (Dublin: Gill and Macmillan, 1983).

17. Patrick Clark, "Counting America's Freelance, Ahem, 'Self-Employed' Workers," *Bloomberg Businessweek*, Sept. 10, 2013; "Intuit 2020 Report: Twenty Trends That Will Shape the Next Decade," 20–21, accessed Oct. 30, 2016, http://about.intuit.com/futureofsmallbusiness.

18. On the informal economy, see Louis A. Ferman, Stuart Henry, and Michele Hoyman, eds., "The Informal Economy," special issue, *Annals of the American Academy of Political and Social Science* 493 (Sept. 1987); Alejandro Portes, Manuel Castells, and Lauren A. Benton, eds., *The Informal Economy: Studies in Advanced and Less Developed Countries* (Baltimore: Johns Hopkins University Press, 1989); and J. J. Thomas, *Informal Economic Activity* (Ann Arbor: University of Michigan Press, 1992). For critiques of the concept, see Philip Harding and Richard Jenkins, *The Myth of the Hidden Economy: Towards a New Understanding of Informal Economic Activity* (Milton Keynes: Open University Press, 1989), and Michael Denning, "Wageless Life," *New Left Review* 6 (Nov.–Dec. 2010), 79–97.

19. For two comprehensive overviews of the field, see Paula S. Fass, ed., *Encyclopedia of Children and Childhood in History and Society* (New York: Macmillan Reference, 2004), and her edited volume *The Routledge History of Childhood in the Western World* (London: Routledge, 2013). On the history of childhood in America, see Steven Mintz, *Huck's Raft: A History of American Childhood* (Cambridge, MA: Harvard University Press, 2004), and E. Anthony Rotundo, *American Manhood: Transformations in Masculinity from the Revolution to the Modern Era* (New York: Basic Books, 1993).

20. Robert Park, "Natural History of the Newspaper," *American Journal of Sociology* 29 (Nov. 1923): 273–289.

21. *Incidents and Sketches Among the Newsboys*, pt. 5 (1856), 17, 76–77, 132, New York Children's Aid Society Archive, now at New-York Historical Society.
22. Lawrence Ferlinghetti, "#1 Everything Changes and Nothing Changes," in *A Far Rockaway of the Heart* (New York: New Directions, 1997), 1.

Chapter 1

1. *New York Sun*, Sept. 4, 1833, 1.
2. Isaiah Thomas, *The History of Printing in America* (New York: Weathervane Books, 1970), 399–400; Clarence S. Brigham, ed., "William McCulloch's Additions to Thomas's History of Printing," *Proceedings of the American Antiquarian Society* 31, pt. 1 (Apr. 1921): 103.
3. Joseph C. Neal, "The News-Boy," *U.S. Magazine and Democratic Review* 13, no. 61 (July 1843), 90. On the period's momentous changes, see George Rogers Taylor, *The Transportation Revolution: 1815–1860* (New York: Harper & Row, 1951); Daniel Walker Howe, *What Hath God Wrought: The Transformation of America, 1815–1848* (New York: Oxford University Press, 2007); Charles Coleman Sellers, *The Market Revolution: Jacksonian America, 1815–1846* (New York: Oxford University Press, 1991); and Sean Wilentz, *The Rise of American Democracy: Jefferson to Lincoln* (New York: W. W. Norton, 2005).
4. David A. Copeland, *Colonial American Newspapers: Character and Content* (Newark: University of Delaware Press, 1997), 275; Clarence S. Bingham, *Journals and Journeymen* (Philadelphia: University of Pennsylvania Press, 1950), 20–21; Anna J. DeArmond, *Andrew Bradford, Colonial Journalist* (Newark: University of Delaware Press, 1949), 21; James Grant, *The Newspaper Press: Its Origin—Progress—And Present Position* (London: Tinsley Brothers, 1871), 2:167; Milton Hamilton, *The Country Printer* (New York: Columbia University Press, 1936), 31–32.
5. Benjamin Franklin, *Autobiography* (1793; Harmondsworth, UK: Penguin Books, 1986), 20; Sidney Kobre, *The Development of the Colonial Newspaper* (Gloucester, MA: Peter Smith, 1960), 43.
6. Alfred McClung Lee, *The Daily Newspaper in America: The Evolution of a Social Instrument* (New York: Macmillan, 1937), 25–26; James Melvin Lee, *History of American Journalism* (Boston: Houghton Mifflin, 1917), 87.
7. *Des Herumtragers des Staatsboten Neujahrs-Wunsch, bey seine resp. Geehrten Kunkleuten abgelegt den 3ten Jenner, 1769*, cited in Willi Paul Adams, "The Colonial German-Language Press and the American Revolution," in *The Press and the American Revolution*, ed. Bernard Bailyn and John B. Hench (Worcester, MA: American Antiquarian Society, 1980), 197–198; Gerald D. McDonald, Stuart C. Sherman, and Mary T. Russo, comps., *A Checklist of American Newspaper Carriers' Addresses, 1720–1820* (Worcester, MA: American Antiquarian Society, 2000), nos. 76 and 84, pp. 10–12; Karen F. Beall, *Kaufrufe und Strassenhandler: Eine Bibliographie (Cries and Itinerant Trades: A Bibliography*, trans. into German by Sabine Solf) (Hamburg: Hanswedell, [1975]); Dwight Miller, *Street Criers and Itinerant Tradesmen in European Prints* (Katalog der Ausstellung Exhibition) (Palo Alto, CA: Stanford University Press, 1970).
8. Aquila Rose, *Poems on Several Occasions* (Philadelphia: Joseph Rose, 1740), 32.
9. On carriers' addresses, see Ola Elizabeth Winslow, *American Broadside Verse: From Imprints of the 17th and 18th Centuries* (New Haven, CT: Yale University Press, 1930); Gerald McDonald, "New Year's Address of American Newsboys," in *Bookmen's Holiday: Notes and Studies Written and Gathered in Tribute to Harry Miller Lydenberg* (New York: New York Public Library, 1943), 57–69; Clarence S. Brigham, "Carriers' Addresses," in *Journals and Journeymen: A Contribution to the History of Early American Newspapers* (Philadelphia: University of Pennsylvania Press, 1950), 84–98; John Lent, "Newsboys Begging Broadsides in Pennsylvania," *Media History Digest* 2 (1982): 45–49; Francis O. Mattson, *Another New Year: Nineteenth-Century American Newspaper Carriers' Addresses from the Berg Collection of English and American Literature* (New York: New York Public Library, 1987), and "Carried Away: The Story of an Ephemeral Phenomenon," *American Book Collector* 8, no. 3 (Mar. 1987): 3–9; Russo, ntroduction to *Checklist*,vii–xii; and Leon Jackson, "We Won't Leave Until We Get Some: Reading the Newsboy's New Year's Address," *Common-Place* 8, no. 2 (Jan. 2008), www.common-place.org/vol-08/no-02/reading.

10. McDonald et al., *Checklist*, nos. 476 and 73, pp. 68, 10; Winslow, *American Broadside Verse*, 211; Howard P. Chudacoff, *How Old Are You? Age Consciousness in American Culture* (Princeton, NJ: Princeton University Press, 1989), 9–28; Nancy F. Cott, "Eighteenth-Century Family and Social Life Revealed in Massachusetts Divorce Records," *Journal of Social History* 10, no. 1 (1976): 29–30.

11. "Address of the Carrier of the American Telegraphe to Its Patrons" (Jan. 1, 1799), in McDonald et al., *Checklist*, no. 369, pp. 51, viii. With the magnetic telegraph not yet invented, the Newfield paper took its name from the semaphore systems then in vogue.

12. "The News-Boy's Verses at the Conclusion of the Year 1757," American Antiquarian Society (henceforth AAS), Broadsides Collection (henceforth BDSDS) 1757. See also Harvey J. Graff, "Literacy," in *Oxford Companion to United States History*, ed. Paul S. Boyer (New York: Oxford University Press, 2001), 450–451, and Jill Lepore, *Book of Ages: The Life and Opinions of Jane Franklin* (New York: Vintage, 2013).

13. Frederic Hudson, *Journalism in the United States, from 1690 to 1872* (New York: Harper and Brothers, 1873), xxxiii; Anthony Smith, *The Newspaper: An International History* (London: Thames & Hudson, 1979), 56–58.

14. Thomas, *History of Printing in America*, 524; Carl Bridenbaugh, *Cities in Revolt: Urban Life in America, 1743–1776* (New York: Knopf, 1955), 186.

15. Robert L. Berthelson, "An Alarm from Lexington," Connecticut Society of the Sons of the American Revolution, accessed Jan. 16, 2007, www.connecticutsar.org/articles/lexington_alarm.htm; Copeland, *Colonial American Newspapers*, 350 n. 11. On the origins of the term *extra*, see James B. McMillan, "Historical Notes on American Words," *American Speech* 21, no. 3 (Oct. 1946): 179.

16. Arthur M. Schlesinger, *Prelude to Independence: The Newspaper War on Britain, 1764–1776* (New York: Knopf, 1958), 190–195; "Our Post-Office," *New Englander and Yale Review* 6, no. 23 (July 1848): 403; Lee, *Daily Newspaper in America*, 27; United States Continental Congress, *In Congress* (May 12, 1777); Richard R. John, *Spreading the News: The American Postal System from Franklin to Morse* (Cambridge, MA: Harvard University Press, 1995), 27.

17. Hamilton, *Country Printer*, 222; E. S. Thomas, *Reminiscences of the Last Sixty-Five Years* (Hartford, CT: Case, Tiffany, and Burnham, 1840), 2:4–5.

18. Charles E. Clark, "Early American Journalism: News and Opinions in the Popular Press," in *A History of the Book in America*, vol. 1, *The Colonial Book in the Atlantic World*, ed. Hugh Amory and David D. Hall (Cambridge: Cambridge University Press and the American Antiquarian Society, 2000), 361; Lee, *Daily Newspaper in America*, 711; Carol Sue Humphrey, *The Press of the Young Republic, 1783–1833* (Westport, CT: Greenwood, 1994), 135; Edwin Emery, *The Press and America: An Interpretive History of the Mass Media*, 5th ed. (Englewood Cliffs, NJ: Prentice Hall, 1972), 135; Robert A. Gross, "The Print Revolution," in *Encyclopedia of American Cultural and Intellectual History*, ed., Mary Kupiec Cayton and Peter W. Williams (New York: Scribner, 2001), 1:274. Collector R. J. Brown counts 582 newspapers in 1820 and asserts that between 1704 and 1820 1,634 newspapers "came to life and died," which suggests that news carrying was not so uncommon. See R. J. Brown, "Colonial American Newspapers," accessed Apr. 4, 2004, www.historybuff.com/library/refcolonial.html.

19. John Lambert, *Travels in Lower Canada, and the United States of North America, in the Years 1806, 1807, & 1808*, 2nd ed. (London: C. Cradock and W. Joy, 1814), 2:498–499.

20. Eber D. Howe, *Autobiography and Recollections of a Pioneer Printer* (Painesville, OH, 1878), 378. See also Joyce Appleby, *Inheriting the Revolution: The First Generation of Americans* (Cambridge, MA: Harvard University Press, 2000), 99–102.

21. "Charles O'Conor," *New York Herald*, Oct. 24, 1869, 4.

22. Richard R. John and Thomas C. Leonard, "The Illusion of the Ordinary: John Lewis Krimmel's *Village Tavern* and the Democratization of Public Life in the Early Republic," *Pennsylvania History* 65, no. 1 (Winter 1998): 87–96.

23. Brigham, *Journals and Journeymen*, 57; Allan R. Pred, *Urban Growth and the Circulation of Information: The United States System of Cities, 1790–1840* (Cambridge, MA: Harvard University Press, 1973), 12–17.

24. *The Complete Poetical Works of John Greenleaf Whittier* (Boston: Houghton, Mifflin, 1894), 293.

25. The richest monographic study of the dissemination of printed material in America is William J. Gilmore, *Reading Becomes a Necessity of Life: Material and Cultural Life in Rural New England, 1750–1835* (Knoxville: University of Tennessee Press, 1989). See also Richard D. Brown, *The Strength of a People: The Idea of an Informed Citizenry in America, 1650–1870* (Chapel Hill: University of North Carolina Press, 1996), and *Knowledge Is Power: The Diffusion of Information in Early America* (New York: Oxford University Press, 1989); Vincent DiGirolamo, "'Heralds of a Noisy World': Carrier Boys, Post Riders, and the Print Revolution in Early America," in *The Worlds of Children*, 2002 Annual Proceedings of Dublin Seminar for New England Folklife (Boston: Boston University Press, 2004), 171–184; Vincent DiGirolamo, "In Franklin's Footsteps: News Carriers and Post Boys in the Revolution and Early Republic" and introduction to "Boys' Lives in the Early Republic: Selections from Joseph T. Buckingham, Personal Memoirs and Recollections of Editorial Life" (1852), in *Children and Youth in a New Nation*, ed. James Marten (New York: New York University Press, 2008), 48–66, 229–241; David Jaffee, "Peddlers of Progress and the Transformation of the Rural North, 1760–1860," *Journal of American History* 78, no. 2 (Sept. 1991): 511–535; Ned C. Landsman, *From Colonials to Provincials: American Thought and Culture, 1680–1760* (New York: Twayne, 1997); Rosalind Remer, "Preachers, Peddlers, and Publishers: Philadelphia's Backcountry Book Trade, 1800–1830," *Journal of the Early Republic* 14 (Winter 1994): 351–362; David S. Shields, "Eighteenth-Century Literary Culture," in *A History of the Book in America*, vol. 1, *The Colonial Book in the Atlantic World*, ed. Hugh Amory and David D. Hall (Cambridge: Cambridge University Press and the American Antiquarian Society, 2000), 438–442; and Ronald J. Zboray, *A Fictive People: Antebellum Economic Development and the American Reading Public* (New York: Oxford University Press, 1993).

26. Nathan Kantrowitz, "Population," in *The Encyclopedia of New York City*, ed. Kenneth Jackson (New Haven, CT: Yale University Press, 1995), 923; Lee, *Daily Newspaper in America*, 718, 730.

27. Hudson, *Journalism in the United States*, 431; "Newsboys Celebrate Fourth Anniversary," *Boston Globe*, May 1, 1905, 2; J. Alexander Patten, "The Eagle's Early Days," *Brooklyn Eagle*, May 19, 1895, 8.

28. Lee, *History of American Journalism*, 186–187; Don C. Seitz, *The James Gordon Bennetts: Father and Son* (Indianapolis, IN: Bobbs-Merrill, 1928), 31–33; Philip Hone, *The Diary of Philip Hone, 1828–1851*, ed. Bayard Tuckerman (New York: Dodd, Mead, 1889), Jan. 20, 1836, 1:193; Isaac Clark Pray, *Memoirs of James Gordon Bennett and His Times* (New York: Stringer and Townes, 1855), 178; Jason Rogers, "The One-Cent Idea," *Printers' Ink* 16, no. 5 (July 29, 1896), 22–23; "An Old Journalist Dead," *New York Times*, Feb. 26, 1879, 5.

29. Sean Wilentz, *Chants Democratic: New York City and the Rise of the American Working Class, 1788–1850* (New York: Oxford University Press, 1984), 21; Alexander Saxton, "Problems of Class and Race in the Origins of the Mass Circulation Press," *American Quarterly* 36 (Summer 1984): 221.

30. *New-York American*, June 19, 1832, 2; Edwin G. Burrows and Mike Wallace, *Gotham: A History of New York City to 1898* (New York: Oxford University Press, 1999), 590; Harry W. Baehr Jr., *The New York Tribune Since the Civil War* (New York: Dodd, Mead, 1936), 4.

31. L. Stebbins, *Eighty Years' Progress of the United States* (Hartford, CT: L. Stebbins, 1867), 305; "Census of 1830. Taken from the Marshal's Returns," in *Miller's New York as It Is* (New York: Miller, 1833), 162.

32. Alexander Keyssar, *Out of Work: The First Century of Unemployment in Massachusetts* (Cambridge, MA: Cambridge University Press, 1986), 91; Allan S. Kullen, comp., *The Peopling of America*, 3rd ed. (Beltsville, MD: Portfolio Project, 1994), 187; Frank M. O'Brien, *The Story of the Sun* (New York: D. Appleton, 1928), 18, 73.

33. "New York's First Newsboy," *Book and Newsdealer* 12, no. 150 (May 1902), 27; "Henry L. Gassert Was New York's First Newsboy," *Brooklyn Eagle*, Sept. 8, 1901, 39; "Oldest Tobacco Dealer Is Dying on Park Slope," *Brooklyn Eagle*, Dec. 7, 1902, 41.

34. O'Brien, *Story of the Sun*, 19. See also *Longworth's American Almanac New York Register and City Directory* (New York: T. Longworth, 1832–33), 480, and the 1837–38 edition, 433.

35. Pray, *Memoirs of James Gordon Bennett*, 181; Seitz, *James Gordon Bennetts*, 69; Lee, *Daily Newspaper in America*, 261; William J. Thorn with Mary Pat Pfeil, *Newspaper*

Circulation: Marketing the News (New York: Longman, 1987), 45–47; W. J. Rorabaugh, *The Craft Apprentice: From Franklin to the Machine Age in America* (New York: Oxford University Press, 1986), 152.

36. Pray, *Memoirs of James Gordon Bennett*, 180–184; *Longworth's New York City Directory*, 1829–39. The directory identifies Southwick as a shoemaker from 1829 to 1831, a paper carrier from 1831 to 1835, and then again as a shoemaker. "The Story of the Sun for Its First 100 Years," *New York Sun*, Sept. 2, 1933, 1.

37. John C. Nerone, "The Mythology of the Penny Press," *Critical Studies in Mass Communications* 4, no. 4 (Dec. 1987): 384.

38. Thorin Richard Tritter, "Paper Profits in Public Service: Money Making in the New York Newspaper Industry, 1830–1930," PhD diss., Columbia University, 2000, 55–61; Hone, *Diary*, May 22, 1837, 1:260.

39. Richard J. Koke et al., comp., *American Landscape and Genre Paintings in the New-York Historical Society: A Catalog of the Collection, Including Historical, Narrative, and Marine Art* (New York: New-York Historical Society, 1982), 3:331–332. See also Joyce Appleby, *Capitalism and a New Social Order: The Republican Vision of the 1790s* (New York: New York University Press, 1984), and David Henkin, *City Reading: Written Words and Public Spaces in Antebellum New York* (New York: Columbia University Press, 1998).

40. Cornelius Mathews, *A Pen-and-Ink Panorama of New-York City* (New York: John S. Taylor, 1853), 194; "Mark Maguire," *National Police Gazette* 41, no. 288 (Mar. 31, 1883), 12; "Obituary. Mark Maguire," *New York Times*, Apr. 26, 1889, 5; "The Death of Police Captain Walsh," *National Police Gazette* 39, no. 222 (Dec. 24, 1881), 4; "Superintendent Jourdan," *New York Times*, Oct. 10, 1870, 5; "The Turf," *New York Times*, July 18, 1854, 1; *New York Clipper*, July 22, 1854, n.p.; Lloyd Morris, *Incredible New York: High Life and Low Life of the Last Hundred Years* (New York: Random House, 1951), 32; George G. Foster, *New York by Gas-Light: With Here and There a Streak of Sunshine*, ed. Stuart Blumin (1850; Berkeley: University of California Press, 1990), 115–116.

41. "A Real Alger Hero," *New York Mail*, June 4, 1868, reprinted in *Dime Novel Round-Up* 60, no. 1 (Feb. 1991): 8–10.

42. Hudson, *Journalism in the United States*, 425; Alfred McClung Lee, "Fifty Years of Daily Newspapers," *Editor & Publisher* 67, no. 20 (July 21, 1934): 294; Eugene H. Munday, "The Press of Philadelphia in 1870," *Proof-Sheet* 3, no. 17 (Mar. 1870) to 6, nos. 31, 32 (July–Sept. 1872); Thorn and Pfeil, *Newspaper Circulation*, 46.

43. Lee, *Daily Newspaper in America*, 98–100; Thorn and Pfeil, *Newspaper Circulation*, 43–44; Virginia Penny, *The Employment of Women: A Cyclopaedia of Woman's Work* (Boston: Walker, Wise, 1863), 466–468; "Our Rag Pickers," *Daily Graphic*, Mar. 11, 1873, 3; Lyman Horace Weeks, *A History of Paper Manufacturing in the United States, 1690–1916* (New York: Lockwood, 1916), 297; W. Eric Gustafson, "Printing and Publishing," in *Made in New York: Case Studies in Metropolitan Manufacturing*, ed. Max Hall (Cambridge, MA: Harvard University Press, 1959), 142.

44. Howe, *What Hath God Wrought*, 627; Pray, *Memoirs of James Gordon Bennett*, 198–199.

45. See also H. R. Robinson's 1838 lithograph *Loco Foco Persecution, or Custom House, Versus Caricatures*, in which Robinson thumbs his nose at an irate Democrat in defense of two newsboys who demand more Whig caricatures to peddle. AAS, Polit Cart. L791.

46. Hudson, *Journalism in the United States*, 437–438; "From a Newsboy to a Millionaire," *Troy Times*, in *Galveston Daily News*, Jan. 5, 1878, n.p.

47. *Covering a Continent: A Story of Newsstand Distribution and Sales* (New York: American News Company, 1930), 48; "American Sleeping Cars," *All the Year Round* 4, no. 90 (Jan. 12, 1861), 328.

48. "The First Train Boy," *Omaha Railway News*, in *St. Louis Globe-Democrat*, Aug. 17, 1886, 5. Another contender, L. N. Spear, monopolized train butchering on the New York Central & Hudson River Railroad, but his dates are vague. See Stewart H. Holbrook, *The Story of American Railroads* (New York: Crown, 1947), 410.

49. Holbrook, *Story of American Railroads*, 399; "A Friend Indeed," *Book and News Dealer* 12, no. 144 (Nov. 1901), 4; Stebbins, *Eighty Years' Progress of the United States*, 307; *Covering a Continent*, 48; "The New York News Company," *Brooklyn Union*, Feb. 2, 1867, 1.

50. *New York Tribune*, Oct. 1, 1857, 4; "A Female Newsboy," *Cairo Times*, in *New York Herald*, Feb. 23, 1858, 5.

51. Stephen Vail, "The First Telegraphic Message," *Baltimore Sun*, Jan. 29, 1900, 6; "The Last Newsboy," *Yankee Doodle* 1, no. 6 (Nov. 14, 1846), 72.

52. *Memoirs of Matthias the Prophet, with a Full Exposure of His Atrocious Impositions, and of the Degrading Delusions of His Followers* (New York: New York Sun, 1835); Paul E. Johnson and Sean Wilentz, *The Kingdom of Matthias: A Story of Sex and Salvation in 19th-Century America* (New York: Oxford University Press, 1994); Nell Irvin Painter, *Sojourner Truth: A Life, a Symbol* (New York: W. W. Norton, 1996), 48–61; Matthew Goodman, *The Sun and the Moon: The Remarkable True Account of Hoaxers, Showmen, Dueling Journalists, and Lunar Man-Bats in Nineteenth-Century New York* (New York: Basic Books, 2008), 75.

53. Richard Adams Locke, *The Celebrated "Moon Story": Its Origin and Incidents: With a Memoir of the Author and an Appendix*, ed. William N. Griggs (New York: Bunnell & Price, 1852), 23; Asa Greene, *A Glance at New York* (New York: A. Greene, 1837), 246–247; O'Brien, *Story of the Sun*, 37–57: Neil Harris, *Humbug: The Art of P.T. Barnum* (Chicago: University of Chicago Press, 1973), 68–70, 72; Pray, *Memoirs of James Gordon Bennett*, 180–184. See also Goodman, *Sun and the Moon*.

54. Hudson, *Journalism in the United States*, 459; "The Penny Press Versus the Sixpenny," *New York Herald*, July 14, 1836, 1.

55. Patricia Cline Cohen, *The Murder of Helen Jewett: The Life and Death of a Prostitute in Nineteenth-Century New York* (New York: Knopf, 1998), 30–31, 309, 415 n. 6; David Anthony, "The Helen Jewett Panic: Tabloids, Men, and the Sensational Public Sphere in Antebellum New York," *American Literature* 69, no. 3 (Sept. 1997): 489; Greene, *Glance at New York*, 131.

56. "Sketches of Life in New York," *Spirit of the Times*, July 22, 1837, 182; "Daily Buffalonian," *Milwaukee Sentinel*, July 3, 1838, 3; Frank H. Severance, comp., "Bibliography: The Periodical Press of Buffalo, 1811–1915," *Publications of the Buffalo Historical Society* 19 (1915): 278; "Our News Boys *Versus* Those of London and New York," *New Orleans Times-Picayune*, Sept. 29, 1839, 2; "The Model Newsboy," *New Orleans Daily Delta* (Oct. 14, 1849), 1.

57. Hone, *Diary*, Jan. 20, 1836, 1:193; "New York's First Newsboy," *Book and Newsdealer* 12, no. 150 (May 1902), 27; Richard Gooch, *America and the Americans—in 1833–4: By an Emigrant*, ed. Richard T. Widdicombe (New York: Fordham University Press, 1994), 53–54; Joseph Kett, *Rites of Passage: Adolescence in America, 1790 to the Present* (New York: Basic Books, 1977), 89.

58. Wilentz, *Chants Democratic*, 294; Edward Pessen, *Jacksonian America: Society, Personality, and Politics* (Urbana: University of Illinois Press, 1985), 147; Michael Schudson, *Discovering the News: A Social History of American Newspapers* (New York: Basic Books, 1978), 56; Herbert G. Gutman, *Work, Culture, and Society* (New York: Vintage, 1977), 60–61.

59. Edwin Emery, *The Press and America: An Interpretive History of the Mass Media*, 3rd ed. (Englewood Cliffs, NJ: Prentice-Hall, 1972), 174; Paul Starr, *The Creation of the Media: Political Origins of Modern Communication* (New York: Basic Books, 2004), 131; O'Brien, *Story of the Sun*, 79.

60. Charles Quill [James Alexander], "The Mechanic's Children," *Newark Daily Advertiser*, July 6, 1837, 2; Burrows and Wallace, *Gotham*, 509.

61. See Steven Mintz, *Huck's Raft: A History of American Childhood* (Cambridge, MA: Harvard University Press, 2004), 163; David J. Rothman, *The Discovery of Asylum: Social Order and Disorder in the New Republic* (Boston: Little, Brown, 1971); Walter I. Trattner, *From Poor Law to Welfare State: A History of Social Welfare in America* (New York: Free Press, 1994); and Michael B. Katz, *The Undeserving Poor: From the War on Poverty to the War on Welfare* (New York: Pantheon Books, 1990).

62. Sellers, *Market Revolution*, 365–366. See also Lee Soltow and Edward Stevens, *The Rise of Literacy and the Common School in the United States: A Socioeconomic Analysis to 1870* (Chicago: University of Chicago Press, 1981), 34, 50–53, 155, and Walt Whitman, "The Penny Press," *Aurora*, Mar. 26, 1842, in Walt Whitman, *The Journalism: 1834–1846*, ed. Herbert Bergman, Douglas A. Noverr, and Edward J. Recchia (New York: Peter Lang, 1998), 1:74.

63. Charles Lanham, *Letters from a Landscape Painter* (Boston: James Munroe, 1845), 240, cited in Nichols B. Clark, *Francis W. Edmonds: American Master in the Dutch Tradition* (Washington, DC: Smithsonian Institution Press, 1988), 49; Maybelle Mann, "Humor and Philosophy in the Paintings of Francis William Edmonds," *Antiques* 106 (Nov. 1974): 862–870; Henry Tuckerman, *Book of the Artists* (New York: G. P. Putnam, 1870), 411–412; Benedict Anderson, *Imagined Communities: Reflections on the Origin and Spread of Nationalism* (London: Verso, 1991).

64. On movement newspapers, see John Nerone, "Newspapers and the Public Sphere," in *A History of the Book in America*, vol. 3, *The Industrial Book, 1840–1880*, ed. Scott Casper, Jeffrey D. Groves, Stephen W. Nissenbaum, and Michael Winship (Chapel Hill: University of North Carolina Press, 2007), 235–237; Henry Mayer, *All On Fire: William Lloyd Garrison and the Abolition of Slavery* (New York: St. Martin's Griffin, 1998), 317–321; and Sean Wilentz, introduction to *David Walker's Appeal* (1829; New York: Hill and Wang, 1995), xix.

65. Mayer, *All On Fire*, 316, 112; "Lewis H. Latimer, Edison's Assistant, Dies at Age of 81," *New York Amsterdam News*, Dec. 19, 1928, 1.

66. "The News-boys and the Penny Press," *New York Morning Herald*, Oct. 7, 1839, 2.

67. "Excitement over Amistad Increases Newspaper Sales," *New York Morning Herald*, Sept. 4, 1839; "The News-boys and the Penny Press," *New York Morning Herald*, Oct. 7, 1839, 2.

68. "La Petite Guerre," *New York Morning Herald*, Oct. 8, 1839, 2; "The Progress of the War," *New York Morning Herald*, Oct. 9, 1839, 2.

69. "Great Moral Movement—The Newsboys Turned Reformers," *New York Morning Herald*, Mar. 11, 1840, 2. On the moral war, see also Schudson, *Discovering the News*, 55, and Daniel Schiller, *Objectivity and the News: The Public and the Rise of Commercial Journalism* (Philadelphia: University of Pennsylvania Press, 1981), 53.

70. Hudson, *Journalism in the United States*, 459; Pray, *Memoirs of James Gordon Bennett*, 267; Seitz, *James Gordon Bennetts*, 83.

71. Isabelle Lehuu, *Carnival on the Page: Popular Print Media in Antebellum America* (Chapel Hill: University of North Carolina Press, 2000), 48; Alan R. Pred, *Urban Growth and the Circulation of Information: The American System of Cities, 1790–1840* (Cambridge, MA: Harvard University Press, 1973), 23; "The Progress of the Revolution in the Newspaper Press," *New York Weekly Herald*, Nov. 27, 1841, n.p.

72. The New York *American*, for example, reduced its price to 2¢ a copy in April 1843, stating, "Newsboys will be supplied at the usual rate." See Lee, *Daily Newspaper in America*, 263–264; James L. Crouthamel, *Bennett's New York Herald and the Rise of the Popular Press* (Syracuse, NY: Syracuse University Press, 1989), 34–38; and "To the Public—Progress of the Herald—The Future," *New York Weekly Herald*, Aug. 21, 1841, 399.

73. "Golden Wedding in Stratford," *New York Tribune*, Aug. 16, 1896, 7; "The Tribune: 1841–1890," *New York Tribune*, Apr. 10, 1890, 6.

74. Pray, *Memoirs of James Gordon Bennett*, 197; Don C. Seitz, *Horace Greeley: Founder of the New York Tribune* (Indianapolis, IN: Bobbs, 1926), 88; Francis N. Zabriskie, *Horace Greeley, the Editor* (New York: Funk & Wagnalls, 1890), 81; "Conspiracy," *New York Tribune*, May 4, 1841, 4, and May 5, 1841, 2; James Parton, *The Life of Horace Greeley* (Boston: Houghton Mifflin, 1889), 159–160, 247; Augustus Maverick, *Henry J. Raymond and the New York Press* (Hartford, CT: A. S. Hale, 1870), 92.

75. "Poetry in New Orleans," *Philadelphia Public Ledger*, Jan. 16, 1840, 2.

76. "Bill Lovell Dead," *New York Sun*, Feb. 5, 1900, 5; "Obituary. Barney Williams," *New York Times*, Apr. 26, 1876, 5; "Barney Williams," *New York Tribune*, Apr. 26, 1876, 5; Joseph N. Ireland, *Records of the New York Stage from 1750–1860* (New York: T. H. Morrell, 1867), vol. 2, pt. 7, pp. 331–332; *Boston Herald*, Apr. 24, 1854, 3.

77. "New York's First Newsboy," *Book and Newsdealer* 12, no. 150 (May 1902), 27; "Henry L. Gassert Was New York's First Newsboy," *Brooklyn Eagle*, Sept. 8, 1901, 39; "Oldest Tobacco Dealer Is Dying on Park Slope," *Brooklyn Eagle*, Dec. 7, 1902, 41.

78. O'Brien, *Story of the Sun*, 19; A. L. Stimson, "The History of the Express Business," *Bankers Magazine* 12, no. 4 (Oct. 1857), 306.

79. "A 'Penn Paper,'" *Philadelphia Public Ledger*, Sept. 5, 1843, 2; Neal, "News-Boy," 89.

Chapter 2

1. "The News Boy," *Sunday Morning Atlas*, Sept. 6, 1840, 1.
2. George D. Strong, "Limnings in the Thoroughfares: The News-Man and the News-Boy," *Knickerbocker* 15, no. 2 (Feb. 1840): 143; *Elephant* 1, no. 2 (Jan. 29, 1848): 12.
3. "The News Boy," *Sunday Morning Atlas*, Sept. 6, 1840, 1.
4. Ibid.
5. Don C. Seitz, *Horace Greeley* (Indianapolis, IN: Bobbs-Merrill, 1926), 88–89. The other Sunday papers in New York were the *Times, Mercury, News,* and *Sunday Herald,* with a combined circulation of 17,500. See Frederic Hudson, *Journalism in the United States, from 1690 to 1872* (New York: Harper & Brothers, 1873), 337–341.
6. "The News Boy," *Sunday Morning Atlas*, Sept. 6, 1840, 1. The *Atlas* was conducted by John Herrick, Frederick West, and Peter Ropes. See "New Sunday Paper—Morality of the Sabbath Day—Caution to Newsboys," *New York Weekly Herald*, Dec. 4, 1841, 84.
7. "'The News Boy.' The Atlas Picture Gallery . . . 1840," *Sunday Morning Atlas*, Jan. 24, 1841, 1.
8. Gerald Baldasty, "The Press and Politics in the Age of Jackson," *Journalism Monographs* 89 (1984): 1–28; Jeffrey L. Pasley, *The Tyranny of Printers: Newspaper Politics in the Early American Republic* (Charlottesville: University Press of Virginia, 2001), 13–17; "The Newsboy," *Literary World*, Dec. 2, 1848, 879.
9. On the Young America movement, see Glenn Wallach, *Obedient Sons: The Discourse of Youth and Generations in American Culture, 1630–1860* (Amherst: University of Massachusetts Press, 1996); Edward L. Widmer, *Young America: The Flowering of Democracy in New York City* (New York: Oxford University Press, 2000); Perry Miller, *The Raven and the Whale: The War of Words and Wits in the Age of Poe and Melville* (New York: Harcourt, Brace, 1956); and Claire Perry, *Young America: Childhood in Nineteenth Century Art and Culture* (New Haven, CT: Yale University Press, 2006).
10. David S. Reynolds, *Beneath the American Renaissance: The Subversive Imagination in the Age of Emerson and Melville* (Cambridge, MA: Harvard University Press, 1988), 442. See also John William Ward, *Andrew Jackson: Symbol for an Age* (New York: Oxford University Press, 1955); Carroll Smith-Rosenberg, "Davy Crockett as Trickster: Pornography, Liminality, and Symbolic Inversion in Victorian America," in *Disorderly Conduct: Visions of Gender in Victorian America* (New York: Knopf, 1985), 90–108; and Winifred Morgan, *An American Icon: Brother Jonathan and American Identity* (Newark: University of Delaware Press, 1988).
11. "The News Boy," *Sunday Morning Atlas*, Sept. 6, 1840, 1.
12. US Bureau of the Census, *Historical Statistics of the United States, Colonial Times to 1970* (Washington, DC: Government Printing Office, 1975), 1:15–17.
13. Alfred McClung Lee, *The Daily Newspaper in America: The Evolution of a Social Instrument* (New York: Macmillan, 1937), 731; Hudson, *Journalism*, 654; "Newspaper Facts," *New York Clipper*, Apr. 10, 1858, 401.
14. "The News Boys," *Flash* 1, no. 9 (Aug. 14, 1842): 2; "To the American Public," *Carlisle Herald and Expositor*, Aug. 17, 1842, 2; "American Newspaper Enterprise," *New York Herald*, Sept. 11, 1848, 2; "Retail News-Dealers of New York," *New York Clipper*, Oct. 15, 1853, n.p.; "The News-Boys," *Independent*, in *Pittsfield Sun*, May 18, 1854, 1; *Child's Paper* 3, no. 10 (Oct. 1854): 37; "The News' Boy's [sic] Lodging House," *Five Points Monthly Record*, Aug. 1854, 98; Robert Ernst, *Immigrant Life in New York City, 1825–1863* (Syracuse, NY: Syracuse University Press, 1994), 85, 212, 217.
15. "Sketches of the Publishers. The American News Company," *Round Table*, Apr. 7, 1866, 218; George Foster, *New York by Gaslight, with Here and There a Streak of Sunshine*, ed. Stuart Blumin (1850; Berkeley: University of California Press, 1990), 117. See also *The Great Metropolis; or Guide to New York for 1846* (New York: John Doggett Jr., 1845), 133–134; Henry Collins Brown, ed., *Valentine's Manual of Old New York* (New York: Valentine's Manual, 1920), 285–303; Joanne Reitano, *The Restless City: A Short History of New York from Colonial Times to the Present* (New York: Routledge, 2006), 56; and Cornelius Mathews, *A Pen-and-Ink Panorama of New-York City* (New York: John S. Taylor, 1853), 132–133.
16. Charles Mackay, *Life and Liberty in America; or Sketches of a Tour in the United States, in 1857–1858* (New York: Smith, Elder, 1859), 21.

17. Lydia Maria Child, *Letters from New-York* (New York: C. S. Francis, 1845), 1:95; "Charity Versus Ice Cream," *Brother Jonathan*, Sept. 30, 1843, 126.
18. "Retail News-Dealers of New York," *New York Clipper*, Oct. 15, 1853, n.p.; Joseph C. Neal, "The News-Boy," *U.S. Magazine and Democratic Review* 13, no. 61 (July 1843): 88–96, reprinted in Neal, *Peter Ploddy, and Other Oddities* (Philadelphia: Cary and Hart, 1844), 62–81; "The Streets of Gotham," *Boston Herald*, Nov. 2, 1848, 2.
19. Strong, "Limnings," 140–141, 144; "How Illustrated Newspapers Are Made," *Frank Leslie's Illustrated Newspaper*, Aug. 2, 1856, 124; "The News Boy," *Sunday Morning Atlas*, Sept. 6, 1840, 1.
20. "The News Boys," *Flash* 1, no. 9 (Aug. 14, 1842): 2; George Foster, *New York in Slices: By an Experienced Carver* (New York: William H. Graham, 1849), 106; "Death of Timothy Madden," *National Police Gazette* 2, no. 13 (Dec. 5, 1846): 100.
21. "The Newsboys," *Flash* 1, no. 7 (July 31, 1842): 1; "The News Boys," *Flash* 1, no. 9 (Aug. 14, 1842): 2.
22. "News-Boys," *New York Times*, Aug. 31, 1853, 1; Foster, *New York by Gaslight*, 113–119; Foster, *New York in Slices*, 103; "The News-Boys," *Independent*, in *Pittsfield Sun*, May 18, 1854, 1.
23. "The News Boys," *Flash* 1, no. 9 (Aug. 14, 1842): 2; "The News Boy," *Sunday Morning Atlas*, Sept. 6, 1840, 1; "The News Boys of New York," *National Aegis*, Feb. 1, 1849, 1.
24. "A Nuisance," *American Masonic Register and Literary Companion* 2, no. 11 (Nov. 14, 1840): 87; "Old Times in New-York," *New Mirror*, June 3, 1843, 132; "Morals of the Town," *Subterranean*, May 24, 1845, n.p.; "Killed on the Harlem Railroad," *Brother Jonathan*, Oct. 28, 1843, 246.
25. William Chambers, *Things as They Are in America* (London: Chambers, 1854), 203; "A Financial Operation," *Boston Courier*, Jan. 2, 1845, 4.
26. Eyre Crowe, *With Thackeray in America* (New York: Scribner's, 1893), 22; William Makepeace Thackeray, *Memoirs of a Victorian Gentleman*, ed. Margaret Forster (London: Secker & Warburg, 1978), 218.
27. Edwin G. Burrows and Mike Wallace, *Gotham: A History of New York City to 1898* (New York: Oxford University Press, 1999), 671–672.
28. "The Navy Department Foreignized," *Brooklyn Eagle*, Sept. 3, 1845, 2. See H. G. Cantzler, "On the Waterfront," Sketchbook, 1849–50, Print Collection, New York Public Library.
29. Greenfield, "'Westward Ho!' July 28, '45," *Brooklyn Eagle*, Aug. 7, 1845, 2; N. P. Willis, "The Four Rivers," *New-Yorker* 3, no. 25 (Sept. 9, 1837): 389.
30. "The News Boys," *Flash* 1, no. 9 (Aug. 14, 1842): 2; James T. Lloyd, *Lloyds Steamer Directory* (Cincinnati, OH: James T. Lloyd, 1856), 229.
31. "A Half-Century's Growth," *New York Times*, May 5, 1890, 8; Charles Dickens, *American Notes* (London: Chapman and Hall, 1842), 79; Dickens, *The Life and Adventures of Martin Chuzzlewit*, ed. Margaret Cardwell (1844; New York: Oxford University Press, 1982), 254–255.
32. James J. Barnes, *Authors, Publishers and Politicians: The Quest for an Anglo-American Copyright Agreement, 1815–1854* (Columbus: Ohio State University Press, 1974), 11–12; "Dickens' Work on America," *Brooklyn Eagle*, Nov. 9, 1842, 2; "Copyright," *Literary Gazette* 1349 (Nov. 26, 1842): 802; Frankl Luther Mott, *A History of American Magazines* (Cambridge, MA: Harvard University Press, 1957), 1:360.
33. "Newspaper Quackery," *Brother Jonathan*, Mar. 26, 1842, 353. See also Helen Lefkowitz Horowitz, *Rereading Sex: Battles over Sexual Knowledge and Suppression in Nineteenth Century America* (New York: Knopf, 2002), 159, 173; Lefkowitz Horowitz, *Attitudes Toward Sex in Antebellum America: A Brief History with Documents* (Boston: Bedford/St. Martin's, 2006), 24–27, 130–141; and Patricia Cline Cohen, Helen Lefkowitz Horowitz, and Timothy J. Gilfoyle, *The Flash Press: Sporting Male Weeklies in 1840s New York* (Chicago: University of Chicago Press, 2008).
34. "Some Passages in the Life of G. W. Dixon, the American Coco La Cour, Negro Dancer and Buffalo Singer," *Flash* 1, no. 16 (Dec. 11, 1841): 1, *Flash* 1, no. 17 (Dec. 18, 1841): 1.
35. *Morning Courier & New-York Enquirer*, Jan. 18, 1842, 2; "Obituary," *Flash* 1, no. 18 (Jan. 22, 1842): 2; "General Sessions," *New York Herald*, Sept. 29, 1842, 1.
36. *American Masonic Register and Literary Companion*, Sept. 3, 1842, 6; "Religious Intelligence," *New York Evening Post*, Mar. 21, 1846, 2; Foster, *New York in Slices*, 106–107.

37. "Newsboys in Trouble," *New York Herald*, Jan. 31, 1855, 8; William Sanger, *The History of Prostitution: Its Extent, Causes, and Effects Throughout the World* (New York: Harper, 1858), 521–522; C. L. B., "The Street-Boys," *New York Times*, Sept. 28, 1853, 2; Walt Whitman, "Song of Myself," sec. 8, *Leaves of Grass* (1855; New York: Signet Classics, 1955), 55; William Sloane Kennedy, *Reminiscences of Walt Whitman* (London: A. Gardner, 1896), 3:73–74; "The Newsboy," *Broadway Belle* 1, no. 5 (Jan. 29, 1855): 4; "The News Boy. From the Broadway Belle," Ballads N558b 01, AAS.

38. Donald Yannella, "Cornelius Mathews," *Dictionary of Literary Biography* (Detroit: Bruccoli, Clark, Layman, 1988), 64:180.

39. Foster, *New York in Slices*, 104; "'The News Boy.' The Atlas Picture Gallery . . . 1840," *Sunday Morning Atlas*, Jan. 24, 1841, 1.

40. Frances Osgood, *Cries of New-York with Fifteen Illustrations*, by Nicolino Calyo, engraved by Harrison (New York: John Doggett Jr., 1846); William Croome, *City Cries; or, A Peep at Scenes in Town* (Philadelphia: George S. Appleton, 1850), 3. On city cries, see Michael Joseph, "The Cries of Pearl Street," *American Book Collector* 8, no. 4 (Apr. 1987): 3–8; Margaret Sloane Patterson's unfinished study of Calyo in the Patterson Papers, Museum of the City of New York; and Sean Shesgreen, *Images of the Outcast: The Urban Poor in the Cries of London* (New Brunswick, NJ: Rutgers University Press, 2002).

41. Foster, *New York in Slices*, 106; Mathews, *Pen-and-Ink Panorama*, 183, 190.

42. "Steamship Atlantic," *Brooklyn Eagle*, Feb. 15, 1851, 2; "City Items," *New York Tribune*, Feb. 17, 1851, 4; "The Newsboys," appendix, *Second Annual Report of the Children's Aid Society* (1855; New York: Arno Press, 1970), 24; Alexander Crosby Brown, *Women and Children Last: The Loss of the Steamship "Arctic"* (New York: G. P. Putnam's Sons, 1961).

43. J. D. Borthwick, "Three Years in California," *Blackwood's Edinburgh Magazine* 81, no. 498 (Apr. 1857): 483; Richard Henry Dana, "Twenty Four Years After" (1859), in *Two Years Before the Mast*, 2nd ed. (1869; New York: P. F. Collier and Son, 1909), 465; *Young America or, The New York Newsboy!*, Metropolitan Theatre, San Francisco, May 5, 1854, BDSDS, 1854 F, AAS; "City Intelligence," *Alta California*, Mar. 1, 1852, 5; "Valuable Donation," *Sacramento Union*, Sept. 13, 1855, 2.

44. *Marysville Herald*, Mar. 13, 1851, 3; "The Newsboys," *Democratic State Journal* (Sacramento, CA), June 12, 1855, 2; *New Orleans Crescent*, July 9, 1855, 2; H. Willis Baxley, *What I Saw on the West Coast of South and North America, and at the Hawaiian Islands* (New York: D. Appleton, 1865), 412; "From Australia," *Boston Courier*, Feb. 13, 1854, 3.

45. "The First Newsboy," *San Francisco Chronicle*, Feb. 11, 1892, 5.

46. *Norfolk Advertiser*, July 14, 1838, 2; Strong, "Limnings," 140; Charles Mackay, *Memoirs of Extraordinary Popular Delusions* (London: Richard Bentley, 1841), 619–631; *Young America* 2, no. 11 (June 7, 1845): 3; "The Dialect of Railway Employees," *Journal of American Folklore* 4, no. 13 (Apr.–June 1891): 175.

47. Foster, *New York in Slices*, 104; Strong, "Limnings," 142, 140.

48. Strong, "Limnings," 140; Q. K. Philander Doesticks, *What He Says* (New York: Edward Livermore, 1855), 235; Neal, "News-Boy," 65.

49. Strong, "Limnings," 140; Foster, *New York in Slices*, 104; "The Newsboy on Bonaparte," *Harper's New Monthly Magazine* 9, no. 53 (Oct. 1854): 701.

50. Richard Dorson, "Mose the Far Famed and World Renowned," *American Literature* 15, no. 3 (Nov. 1943): 288–300; Christine Stansell, *City of Women: Sex and Class in New York, 1789–1860* (New York: Knopf, 1982), 90–96; Sean Wilentz, *Chants Democratic: New York City and the Rise of the American Working Class, 1788–1850* (New York: Oxford University Press, 1984), 300–301; Michael Kaplan, "The World of the B'hoys: Urban Violence and the Political Culture of Antebellum New York City, 1825–1860," PhD diss., New York University, 1996; Peter Adams, *The Bowery Boys: Street Corner Radicals and the Politics of Rebellion* (New York: Praeger, 2005).

51. Strong, "Limnings," 140–142.

52. Mary Mapes Dodge, "The Artist and the Newsboy," *Independent*, Nov. 19, 1863, reprinted in *The Irvington Stories*, illus. F. O. C. Darley (New York: James O'Kane, 1865), 247–248. A similar account is related in "Editor's Table," *Knickerbocker* 60 (July 1862): 91. See William H. Gerdts, catalogue by Carrie Rebora, *The Art of Henry Inman* (Washington, DC: National

Portrait Gallery and Smithsonian Institution, 1987), 131; and Susan R. Gannon and Ruth Anne Thompson, *Mary Mapes Dodge* (New York: Twayne, 1992), 43–44.

53. *New-York Mirror*, May 22, 1841, 167; *Arcturus*, June 1841, 61; *Knickerbocker* 60, no. 1 (July 1862): 91; "The Great Decade in American Writing," American Academy of Arts and Letters, Dec. 3–30, 1954, exhibition catalogue, 23, cited in William H. Gerdts, "Henry Inman: Genre Painter," *American Art Journal* 9, no. 1 (May 1977): 39–41; "Artists' Fund Exhibition," *Philadelphia Public Ledger*, May 17, 1842, 1; Seba Smith, "Billy Snub, the Newsboy," *The Gift: A Christmas and New Year's Present*, illus. Henry Inman, engraved by Richard W. Dodson (Philadelphia: Carey and Hart, 1843), 58–84. The story appeared earlier in the *Inquirer and National Gazette* 102 (Oct. 31, 1842): n.p., and *Ladies' Garland and Family Wreath* 6, no. 6 (Dec. 1842): 173–181. It was reprinted in Smith's *'Way Down East; or, Portraitures of Yankee Life* (New York: Derby and Jackson, 1856), 280–318; Mr. Chapman, "The Newsboy," Thayer & Co. Lith. (Boston: Henry Prentiss, 1844).

54. Gerdts, "Henry Inman: Genre Painter," 39–41; Elizabeth Johns, *American Genre Painting: The Politics of Everyday Life* (New Haven, CT: Yale University Press, 1991), 184–186; Lisa N. Peters, "Images of the Homeless in American Art, 1860–1910," in *On Being Homeless: Historical Perspectives*, ed. Rick Beard (New York: Museum of the City of New York, 1987), 43–67.

55. Strong, "Limnings," 141.

56. Tyler Anbinder, *Five Points: The 19th-Century New York City Neighborhood That Invented Tap Dance, Stole Elections, and Became the World's Most Notorious Slum* (New York: Plume, 2001), 21, 27; Kaplan, "World of the B'hoys," 66–67.

57. Neal, "News-Boy," 65, 64, 67, 69.

58. R. H. Stoddard, "Felix O. C. Darley," *National Magazine* 9, no. 15 (Sept. 1856): 195–197; William Russell and John Goldsbury, *Introduction to the American Common-School Reader and Speaker* (Boston: Tappan, Whittemore & Mason, 1845), 74–76; Neal, "News-Boy," 73, 79.

59. *Spirit of the Times*, June 10, 1843, 171; *Brooklyn Eagle*, Oct. 17, 1851, 4.

60. "*New York Tribune*, Apr. 20, 1848, 2; "Caution to Newsboy Rioters, Fire Engine Rowdies, &c.," *New York Herald*, July 10, 1844, n.p.; "Fracas Among the News Boys," *Brooklyn Eagle*, May 12, 1851, 3.

61. "The Great Fight," *Evening Tattler*, in *Spirit of the Times* 13, no. 5 (Apr. 1, 1843): 58; "Muss Among the Newsboys," *New York Clipper*, June 4, 1853, n.p.; "The Clipper and the Newsboys," *New York Clipper*, May 7, 1853, n.p.

62. "A New's [*sic*] Boy Victorious," *Whip and Satirist*, Feb. 19, 1842, 3; "Heroic Attack upon a Newsboy," *Subterranean*, Sept. 2, 1843, 61; "A Queer Feat and Funny Challenge," *New York Sporting Whip*, Feb. 11, 1843, 7; "Curious Challenge," *New York Clipper*, Mar. 25, 1854, n.p.; "Counting Newspapers," *New York Clipper*, Jan. 9, 1858, n.p.

63. "Two Murders in New York," *Baltimore Sun*, Jan. 13, 1849, 4; "Affray and Death of a Newsboy," *New York Evangelist*, Jan. 18, 1849, 11; "Intemperance and Homicide," *Christian Advocate*, Jan. 18, 1849, 11; "Justifiable Homicide," *New Orleans Times-Picayune*, Jan. 23, 1849, 5. On tavern culture, see Michael Kaplan, "New York City Tavern Violence and the Creation of a Working-Class Male Identity," *Journal of the Early Republic* 15 (1995): 591–617; and Richard Stott, *Jolly Fellows: Male Milieus in Nineteenth-Century America* (Baltimore: Johns Hopkins University Press, 2009), 97–128.

64. "The News Boy," *Sunday Morning Atlas*, Sept. 6, 1840, 1; Bruce W. Chambers, *The World of David Gilmour Blythe, 1815–1865* (Washington, DC: Smithsonian Institution Press, 1980), 37. See also Chambers, *David Gilmour Blythe's Pittsburgh, 1850–65* (Pittsburgh: Museum of Art, Carnegie Institution, 1981); Johns, *American Genre Painting*, 190–196; and Dorothy Miller, *The Life and Work of David G. Blythe* (Pittsburgh: University of Pittsburgh Press, 1950).

65. "Interesting Sketch of a Herald Newsboy in Philadelphia," *New York Weekly Herald*, July 23, 1853, 238.

66. "Notice to Our Carriers," *New York Herald*, Oct. 10, 1840, 2; "Demand for Newspapers," *Brooklyn Eagle*, Jan. 19, 1857, 3; N. P. Willis, "Why Don't You Take the Papers," *Rural Repository* 22, no. 19 (May 23, 1846): 152; "The Newsboys' Day," *Chambers' Edinburgh Journal* 489 (May 14, 1853): 306.

67. "The Newsboys," *New-York Mirror*, Jan. 27, 1838, 247; "Reported Arrest of Another Express Robber," *New York Morning Express*, Apr. 8, 1846, 2; *Subterranean*, June 7, 1845, n.p.;

"Singular," *Whip*, Oct. 22, 1842, 2; "Stealing Newspapers," *Baltimore Sun*, Apr. 25, 1839, 2; *Milwaukee Sentinel*, Feb. 20, 1849, 3; *Milwaukee Sentinel*, June 11, 1849, 2; *Milwaukee Sentinel*, June 14, 1849, 2; *Milwaukee Sentinel*, Dec. 24, 1857, 1.

68. "A Hoax," *Philadelphia Ledger*, Mar. 9, 1841, 2; M. R. Werner, "The 'Feejee Mermaid,'" *Los Angeles Times*, Aug. 12, 1923, X19; Edgar Allan Poe, "Doings of Gotham—Letter II," *Columbia Spy*, May 25, 1844, n.p. See also Fred Fedler, *Media Hoaxes* (Ames: Iowa State University Press, 1989), 24–28.

69. George Lippard, "Jake Heydigger, the Newsboy of the Ledger Corner," *Lady's Wreath* 5, no. 6 (Dec. 1845): 139–152.

70. "Mean Men," *Brooklyn Eagle*, Mar. 29, 1856, 2; "An Incident," *Boston Transcript*, July 24, 1861, 2.

71. *New York Clipper*, Oct. 15, 1853, n.p.; "The Newsboys," *Independent*, in *Pittsfield Sun*, May 18, 1854, 1; "Great Economy in Literature," *New York Clipper*, Dec. 12, 1856, 268.

72. "Demand for Newspapers," *Brooklyn Eagle*, Jan. 19, 1857, 3; Osgood, *Cries of New-York*, 19; Joseph Holt Ingraham, *Jemmy Daily: or, the Little News Vendor* (Boston: Brainard, 1843), 27; "The Little Lame Boy," *Broadway Belle* 1, no. 7 (Feb. 12, 1855): 2; Mathews, *Pen-and-Ink Panorama*, 190; "Truant and Vagrant Children," *Christian Register* 28, no. 12 (Mar. 24, 1849): 46.

73. "Imposition by Newsboys," *New York Tribune*, Mar. 1, 1848, 2; *Pittsfield Sun*, Mar. 6, 1856, 1; "The Heat and Its Incidents," *New York Times*, June 18, 1852, 2; "The Eclipse," *New York Evangelist*, Aug. 12, 1869, 8; F. Ratchford Starr, *Didley Dumps or John Ellard, the Newsboy* (Philadelphia: William S. and Alfred Martien, 1860), 5th ed. (Philadelphia: American Sunday-School Union, 1884), 37; *New Orleans Times*, Feb. 1, 1870, 3.

74. "The News Boy," *Sunday Morning Atlas*, Sept. 6, 1840, 1; "Record of Minnesota's Governor," *Chicago Tribune*, Oct. 14, 1893, 9; Foster, *New York in Slices*, 106.

75. Mathews, *Pen-and-Ink Panorama*, 186–187.

76. Doesticks, *What He Says*, 49; "Popular Amusements in New York," *National Era*, Apr. 15, 1847, 3; *New York Sporting Whip*, Feb. 18, 1843, cited in Dale Cockrell, *Demons of Disorder: Early Blackface Minstrels and Their World* (Cambridge: Cambridge University Press, 1997), 25; "The News-Boy, in the Pit of the Chatham Theatre," *Rural Repository* 23, no. 19 (May 23, 1846): 145–146.

77. "New Movements in Theatricals—The Rival Theaters—Bombast and Anti-Bombast," *New York Herald*, Jan. 30, 1840; Allston T. Brown, *A History of the New York Stage: From the First Performance in 1732 to 1901* (New York: Dodd, Mead, 1903), 301. On theater prices, see Richard Butsch, *The Making of American Audiences: From Stage to Television, 1750–1990* (Cambridge: Cambridge University Press, 2000), 51; John W. Frick, "Theater," in *The Encyclopedia of New York City*, ed. Kenneth T. Jackson (New Haven, CT: Yale University Press, 1995), 1167; and Bruce McConachie, "'The Theatre of the Mob': Apocalyptic Melodrama and Preindustrial Riots in Antebellum New York," in *Theatre for Working-Class Audiences in the United States, 1830–1980*, ed. Daniel Friedman and Bruce McConachie (Westport, CT: Greenwood Press, 1985), 43 n. 14.

78. "The News Boy," *Sunday Morning Atlas*, Sept. 6, 1840, 1; "The News-Boy, in the Pit of the Chatham Theatre," *Rural Repository* 23, no. 19 (May 23, 1846): 145–146.

79. George C. D. Odell, *Annals of the New York Stage* (New York: Columbia University Press, 1927–49), 3:402, illus. opposite p. 414; "The News Boy," *Sunday Morning Atlas*, Sept. 6, 1840, 1; John D. Vose, *Seven Nights in Gotham* (New York: Bunnell & Price, 1852), 50; Mathews, *Pen-and-Ink Panorama*, 187–188; "The Newsboy," *Literary World*, Dec. 2, 1848, 879. See Allen F. Stein, *Cornelius Mathews* (New York: Twayne, 1974), 84–86; *Spirit of the Times*, Dec. 1, 1832, and *New York Herald*, Oct. 13, 1840, cited in Cockrell, *Demons of Disorder*, 31, 67.

80. *New York Herald*, Dec. 26, 1844, quoted in Stephen Nissenbaum, *The Battle for Christmas* (New York: Knopf, 1996), 124; Doesticks, *What He Says*, 236.

81. *Philadelphia Public Ledger*, Dec. 27, 1843, Dec. 25, 1844, Dec. 24–25, 1845, in Nissenbaum, *Battle for Christmas*, 335; "New Movements in Theatricals—The Rival Theaters—Bombast and Anti-Bombast," *New York Herald*, Jan. 30, 1840; *The Boys of the Bowery Pit. By W. C. Tune—The Newsboys. Andrews, Printer, 38 Chatham St., NY*, Library of Congress, accessed May 29, 2017, https://www.loc.gov/item/amss.sb10039a.

82. "Street Arabs," *Cincinnati Enquirer*, Sept. 18, 1870, 1; "The News-Boy's Medley," *The New Negro Forget-Me-Not Songster* (Cincinnati, OH: Stratton and Barnard, 1848), 41–43. See also Cockrell, *Demons of Disorder*, 17; Alexander Saxton, "Blackface Minstrelsy," in *The Rise and Fall of the White Republic: Class Politics and Mass Culture in Nineteenth-Century America* (London: Routledge, 1990), 165–182; and W. T. Lhamon Jr., *Raising Cain: Blackface Performance from Jim Crow to Hip Hop* (Cambridge, MA: Harvard University Press, 1998), 43.

83. Samuel D. Johnson, *The Fireman* (New York: Samuel French, 1856), 25–26.

84. *Young America or, the New York Newsboy!*, Metropolitan Theatre, San Francisco, May 5, 1854, AAS; Odell, *Annals*, 6:380; "Amusements," *New York Tribune*, July 13, 1857, 7; *New York Herald*, June 14, 1867, 12.

85. *North American*, July 29, 1844, 2; "A Hint for the News-Boys," *New York Herald*, Nov. 18, 1844, 2.

86. "A Two-Penny Strike," *Brooklyn Eagle*, Nov. 13, 1844, 2.

87. Wilentz, *Chants Democratic*, 349–356; "The Case of 'The Mirror vs. The Express,'" *Brooklyn Eagle*, Aug. 13, 1845, 2.

88. "The Newsboys in Their Majesty," *New York Tribune*, Apr. 6, 1846, 2; "Newsboys Strike," *New York Sunday Times and Messenger*, Apr. 5, 1846, 2.

89. *New-York Mirror*, May 23, 1835, 375, in Mott, *History of American Magazines*, 1:466, 360–361; "Newspaper Quackery," *Brother Jonathan*, Mar. 26, 1842, 353, Dec. 25–Jan. 1, 1844, 4.

90. Mathews, *Pen-and-Ink Panorama*, 12; Cornelius Mathews, *The Career of Puffer Hopkins* (New York: D. Appleton, 1842), 140–141; *New York Express*, in *Aberdeen Journal*, Jan. 26, 1848.

91. "A Millerism," *Literary Gazette* 1349 (Nov. 26, 1842), 802; "Spirit of Romanism," *New York Evangelist*, Nov. 26, 1841, 178; "A Portrait and a Question," *New York Tribune*, Nov. 21, 1850, 4; "Special Correspondence," *Alta California*, Jan. 4, 1851, 2; "The Creole and the Newsboys," *New Orleans Daily Creole*, Aug. 4, 1856, 2.

92. "The News Boys," *Flash* 1, no. 9 (Aug. 14, 1842): 2; "The Newsboys," *Trumpet and Universalist Magazine* 19, no. 4 (July 11, 1846): 15; "Newsboys Association," *Hartford Courant*, Oct. 22, 1850, 2; *Sacramento Transcript*, Jan. 6, 1851, 2; "The Difficulty Settled," *Democratic Advocate* (Baton Rouge, LA), May 17, 1855, 6.

93. "Humanity of the Newsboy," *Mirror of Saturday*, in *Brooklyn Eagle*, Feb. 23, 1846, 2. See also Vincent DiGirolamo, "Newsboy Funerals: Tales of Sorrow and Solidarity in Urban America," *Journal of Social History* 36, no. 1 (Sept. 2002): 5–30.

94. Wilentz, *Chants Democratic*, 524; Hudson, *Journalism*, 495; John C. Nerone, "The Press and Popular Culture in the Early Republic: Cincinnati, 1793–1848," PhD diss., University of Notre Dame, 1982, 80, 15, 58; Alexander Mackay, *The Western World, or, Travels in the United States in 1846–47* (Philadelphia: Lea & Blanchard, 1849), 3:238; "The War News," *New York Herald*, May 15, 1846, 1.

95. The *Newsboy* cost the partners $20,000 a year to operate, mainly cruising off Sandy Hook; it was let go in May 1849. *New Bedford Mercury*, May 25, 1849, 1; "The European News—to the Public," *Associated Press*, Jan. 24, 1850, www.littletechshoppe.com/ns1625/craig02.html; "A Promising Swindle," *New York Times*, Feb. 25, 1853, 4; Robert Sobel, *Machines and Morality: The 1850s* (New York: Crowell, 1973), 153.

96. Eugene H. Munday, "The Press of Philadelphia in 1870," *Proof-Sheet* 5, no. 28 (Jan. 1872): 51; "Newspapers in 1846," *New York Tribune*, Feb. 16, 1876, 2; George Martin, "The News-Boy," in *Marguerite, or, The Isle of Demons and Other Poems* (Montreal: Dawson Brothers, 1887), 215–218; Robert W. Johannsen, *To the Halls of the Montezumas: The Mexican War in the American Imagination* (New York: Oxford University Press, 1988), 224, 325 n. 44.

97. *The New Negro Forget-Me-Not Songster*, 28–29, 41–43.

98. Gail E. Husch, *Something Coming: Apocalyptic Expectation and Mid-Nineteenth-Century American Painting* (Hanover, NH: University Press of New England, 2000), 44–45; Johannsen, *To the Halls of the Montezumas*, 226.

99. Johannsen, *To the Halls of the Montezumas*, 302–304; "New York Gossip," *New Orleans Times-Picayune*, Sept. 14, 1847, 2; "The Newsboy," *Literary World* 3, no. 96 (Dec. 2, 1848), 879.

100. "Great Times Among the Codfish Aristocracy!," *John-Donkey*, May 6, 1848, 19; "The Fate of Kings," *John-Donkey*, May 13, 1848, 308.

101. "The Newsboys," *Young America*, Aug. 30, 1845, 2; N. P. Willis, *Home Journal*, May 12, 1849, n.p., in Peter George Buckley, "To the Opera House: Culture and Society in New York City, 1820–1860," PhD diss., Stony Brook University, 1984, 335.

102. "National Academy of Design," *New York Times*, June 22, 1850, 1; *Brooklyn Eagle*, Dec. 16, 1852, 2; Mary Bartlett Cowdrey, *American Academy of Fine Arts and American Art Union Exhibition Record, 1816–1852*, 77 (New York: New-York Historical Society, 1953), 334–335; Joan Murray, "Rags to Riches," *Canadian Collector*, Sept./Oct. 1982, 27; Husch, *Something Coming*, 47.

103. William H. Gerdts, *Art Across America: Two Centuries of Regional Painting, 1710–1920* (New York: Abbeville Press, 1990), 1:208; Chase Viele, "Four Artists of Mid-Nineteenth Century Buffalo," *New York History* 43 (Jan. 1962): 49–78; Herman Warner Williams Jr., *Mirror to the American Past: A Survey of American Genre Painting, 1750–1900* (Greenwich, CT: New York Graphic Society, 1973), 129; Susan Krane, with William H. Gerdts and Helen Raye, *The Wayward Muse: A Historical Survey of Painting in Buffalo* (Buffalo, NY: Albright-Knox Art Gallery, 1987); Karen Sanchez-Eppler, *Dependent States: The Child's Part in Nineteenth-Century American Culture* (Chicago: University of Chicago Press, 2005), 157–162.

Chapter 3

1. Famine Irish Entry Project, 1846–1851, National Archives and Records Administration, Washington, DC; Johnny Morrow, *A Voice from the Newsboys* (New York: A. S. Barnes, 1860), 26–60.

2. *Second Annual Report of the Children's Aid Society* (New York: M. B. Wynkoop, 1855), 15; *Third Annual Report*, 1856, 19; *Fourth Annual Report*, 1857, 17; *Fifth Annual Report*, 1858, 24; *Sixth Annual Report*, 1859, 19; *Seventh Annual Report*, 1860, 10.

3. "Our Newspapers," *Nassau Literary Magazine* 18, no. 5 (Feb. 1858): 219; Elizabeth Oakes Smith, "The Newsboys of New York," *Great Republic Monthly*, Feb. 1859, 243, 247; *First Annual Report of the Children's Aid Society* (1854), 13.

4. Morrow, *Voice from the Newsboys*, 126–127.

5. Christine Stansell, *City of Women: Sex and Class in New York, 1789–1860* (Urbana: University of Illinois Press, 1986), 199; *Third Annual Report of the Children's Aid Society* (1856), 43; David Rothman, "Discovering Asylum," in *On Being Homeless: Historical Perspectives*, ed. Rick Beard (New York: Museum of the City of New York, 1987), 198–199; Julie Miller, *Abandoned: Foundlings in Nineteenth-Century New York City* (New York: New York University Press, 2008), 47.

6. "A Curbstone Hero," *New York Tribune*, Oct. 5, 1857, 7; "The Financial Crash," *New York Tribune*, Oct. 14, 1857, 5; "The Crisis," *New York Clipper*, Oct. 24, 1857, 216; *Hartford Courant*, Oct. 16, 1857, 2.

7. David Stewart Hull, *James Henry Cafferty, N.A.* (New York: New-York Historical Society, 1986), 33–34; *Crayon* 5 (June 1858): 177. See also Cafferty's *Newsboy Selling New-York Herald* (1857), oil on canvas, 16 × 12 in., Lucille and Walter Rubin Collection.

8. On "rag money," see *Eighty Years' Progress of the United States* (Hartford, CT: L. Stebbins, 1867), 333, and David Henkin, *City Reading: Written Words and Public Spaces in Antebellum New York* (New York: Columbia University Press, 1998), 137–165.

9. David Tatham, "A Drawing by Winslow Homer: Corner of Winter, Washington and Summer Streets," *American Art Journal* 18, no. 3 (1986): 40–50; "Art Gossip," *Cosmopolitan Art Journal* 4 (1860): 127; *Young America* 1, no. 2 (1856): 168; *Aegis & Transcript*, Sept. 7, 1861, 1.

10. See George Henry Yewell, *The Bootblack (Doing Nothing)* (1851), oil on canvas, 14 × 12 in., New-York Historical Society; William Winner, *Newsboy* (Feb. 26, 1853), Library of Congress; Moses Wight, *The Newsboy* (1857), in *Catalogue of the Thirteenth Exhibition of Paintings and Statuary, at the Atheneum Gallery, Beacon-Street, Boston, 1857* (Boston: J. H. Eastburn's Press, 1857), 15; John McRae McLenan, *Newsboy* (1858), watercolor on cardboard, 9¾ × 6¾ in., Hood Museum of Art, Dartmouth College, Hanover, NH; Charles Blauvelt, *The Newsboy*, in "The Artists' Reception," *New York Evening Post*, Mar. 23, 1859, 2; James Johnson, *Newsboy Eating an Apple* (1860), oil, 12 × 8 in.; William Penn Morgan, *New York Newsboy* (1860), oil

on canvas, 9½ × 7⅜ in., location unknown, and *Politics Among Newsboys* (1860), also location unknown.

11. S. N. D. North, *History and Present Condition of the Newspaper and Periodical Press of the United States* (Washington, DC: Government Printing Office, 1884), 8:159; Edgar W. Martin, *The Standard of Living in 1860: American Consumption Levels on the Eve of the Civil War* (Chicago: University of Chicago Press, 2007), 316–317; "Progress of the Age—New-York Newspapers in the Country," *New York Times*, Apr. 5, 1858, 1.

12. Alfred McClung Lee, *The Daily Newspaper in America: The Evolution of a Social Instrument* (New York: Macmillan, 1937), 718, 725; J. R. Oertel, *A Vision Realized: A Life Story of Rev. J. A. Oertel, D.D., Artist, Priest, Missionary* (Milwaukee, WI: Young Churchman, 1917), 33–34.

13. Elizabeth Oakes Smith, "The Newsboys of New York," *Great Republic Monthly*, Feb. 1859, 243; "The Ocean Telegraph," *New York Evening Post*, Aug. 17, 1858, 3.

14. "Then and Now, Newspaper Distributing in Detroit in the '50s," n.p., May 26, 1896, Friend Palmer Scrapbook, 13:70, Detroit Public Library; "John B. Walsh, News Agent," *Chicago Tribune*, Mar. 23, 1890, 25; "Sketches of the Publishers," *Round Table*, Apr. 14, 1866, 234; Mary Noel, *Villains Galore: The Heyday of the Popular Story Weekly* (New York: Macmillan, 1954), 66–67; "The 'Ledger' Day," *Frank Leslie's Illustrated Newspaper*, Sept. 3, 1859, 210–211; Edward Everett, "The New York Ledger," in *The Mount Vernon Papers* (New York: D. Appleton, 1860), 480–490; *Covering a Continent: A Story of Newsstand Distribution and Sales* (New York: American News Company, 1930), 12.

15. "Letter from a Newsboy," *New York Tribune*, Jan. 11, 1856, 6; Morrow, *Voice from the Newsboys*, 131, 43; Allen Hampden, *Hartley Norman: A Tale of the Times* (New York: Rudd and Carleton, 1859), 40.

16. *Chicago Tribune*, Mar. 4, 1872, 4; William Colopy Desmond, Sept. 17, 1855, *Incidents and Sketches Among the Newsboys*, pt. 3, 22, New York Children's Aid Society Archive, now at New-York Historical Society.

17. Morrow, *Voice from the Newsboys*, 131, 43, 129; "'The Professor's' Account of His Travels," Sept. 11, 1855, *Third Annual Report of the Children's Aid Society* (1856), 42.

18. "The Model Newsboy," *Philadelphia Bulletin*, Sept. 15, 1857, n.p.; "The Buffalo Newsboys—Their Numbers, Manners and Habits," *Buffalo Morning Express*, Nov. 7, 1868, 4; Henry Collins Brown, *Valentine's Manual of Old New York* (New York: Valentine's Manual, 1926), 301; *Scientific American* 2, no. 43 (July 17, 1847): 338; "The Boot-Black's Story," *Saturday Evening Post* 55, no. 22 (Dec. 25, 1875), 5; Charles Dawson Shanly, "The Small Arabs of New York," *Atlantic Monthly* 23, no. 137 (Mar. 1869), 284; "More of the News-Boys," *Five Points Monthly Record*, Oct. 1854, 137.

19. *New York Herald*, Oct. 25, 1844, 2; "Little Broken Nose," n.p., Oct. 1, 1855, in *Third Annual Report of the Children's Aid Society* (1856), 43.

20. "Another Painful Rumor," *New York Times*, Nov. 1, 1854, 3; "News-Boys," *New York Times*, Aug. 31, 1853, 1; Jared Benedict Graham, *Handset Reminiscences* (Salt Lake City, UT: Century, 1915), 112; "Brevities," *Hartford Daily Courant*, July 1, 1868, 2.

21. "The News-Boy," *Child's Paper* 3, no. 10 (Oct. 1854): 37; Charles Loring Brace, *Short Sermons to Newsboys* (New York: Scribner's, 1866), 222; "The Newsboys," *Atlanta Constitution*, Oct. 28, 1888, 14.

22. F. Ratchford Starr, *Didley Dumps; or, John Ellard, the Newsboy* (1860; Philadelphia: American Sunday-School Union, 1884), 26; Frank St. Clair, *Six Days in the Metropolis, or Phases of Life in Town* (Boston: Redding, 1851), 49.

23. Bruce W. Chambers, *The World of David Gilmour Blythe, 1815–1865* (Washington, DC: Smithsonian Institution Press, 1980), 37. See also Chambers, *David Gilmour Blythe's Pittsburgh, 1850–65* (Pittsburgh, PA: Museum of Art, Carnegie Institution, 1981); Elizabeth Johns, *American Genre Painting: The Politics of Everyday Life* (New Haven, CT: Yale University Press, 1991), 190–196; Dorothy Miller, *The Life and Work of David G. Blythe* (Pittsburgh, PA: University of Pittsburgh Press, 1950); and Sarah Burns, *Painting the Dark Side: Art and the Gothic Imagination in Nineteenth-Century America* (Berkeley: University of California Press, 2004), 44–74.

24. Morrow, *Voice from the Newsboys*, 38–40; Stansell, *City of Women*, 206–207. See also Lewis Aptekar, "Family Structure in Colombia: Its Impact on Understanding Street Children," *Journal of Ethnic Studies* 17, no. 1 (Spring 1989): 104.

25. *New York Dispatch*, May 28, 1854, in *Newsboy* 14, no. 4 (Nov. 1975): 5; Oakes Smith, "Newsboys of New York," 247, 243; Horatio Alger, "The Gold Piece; or, The Newsboy's Temptation," *Gleason's Weekly Line-of-Battle Ship* 1, no. 9 (Feb. 26, 1859): 3–4; "The Newsboy," *New York Times*, Mar. 10, 1854, 4; C. L. B., "The News-Boys," *New York Times*, Mar. 12, 1853, 3.

26. Walt Whitman, "Playing in the Park" and "About Children," *Aurora*, Apr. 12, 16, 1842, in Walt Whitman, *The Journalism: 1834–1846*, ed. Herbert Bergman, Douglas A. Noverr, and Edward J. Recchia (New York: Peter Lang, 1998), 1:112, 122; George Foster, *New York in Slices: By an Experienced Carver* (New York: William H. Graham, 1849), 104.

27. Charles Loring Brace, *The Dangerous Classes of New York and Twenty Years' Work Among Them* (New York: Wynkook & Hallenbeck, 1872), 228, 100; Oliver Dyer, "The New York Sun," *American Agriculturalist*, Dec. 1869: 463–467; Stansell, *City of Women*, 206.

28. "The South," *New York Times*, Sept. 28, 1852, 2; "Mayor's Black Book," *New York Times*, Feb. 8, 1855, 3; "Sketches of City Life: The Newsboy," *Frank Leslie's Illustrated Newspaper*, Oct. 18, 1856, 304.

29. "A Business Street at Evening," *New York Times*, Oct. 20, 1853, 4; *Third Annual Report of the Children's Aid Society* (1856), 43.

30. "People in the Parks," *Appleton's Journal* 6, no. 123 (Aug. 5, 1871), 155. See Marilyn Thornton Williams, *Washing "The Great Unwashed": Public Baths in Urban America, 1840–1920* (Columbus: Ohio State University Press, 1991).

31. Morrow, *Voice from the Newsboys*, 49; "River Bathing," *New York Times*, July 2, 1876, 5; C. L. B., "White Washing an Ethiopian," *Sketches and Incidents in the Office of the Children's Aid Society*, part 1 (Jan. 1, 1857–Feb. 1, 1859), 175; *Columbian Register*, Feb. 18, 1860, 2.

32. Samuel Byram Halliday, *Little Street Sweeper* (New York: Blakeman & Mason, 1860), 49 (orig. pub. as *The Lost and Found; or, Life Among the Poor*, 1859).

33. Joseph M. Hawes, *Children in Urban Society: Juvenile Delinquency in Nineteenth-Century America* (New York: Oxford University Press, 1971), 108, 132–133; Jeremy P. Felt, *Hostages of Fortune: Child Labor Reform in New York State* (Syracuse, NY: Syracuse University Press, 1965), 5; Paul Boyer, *Urban Masses and Moral Order in America, 1820–1920* (Cambridge, MA: Harvard University Press, 1978), 96; Brace, *Dangerous Classes*, 236, 381; Edwin Burrows and Mike Wallace, *Gotham: A History of New York City to 1898* (New York: Oxford University Press, 1999), 780.

34. See Charles Loring Brace, *The Life of Charles Loring Brace, 1826–1890*, ed. Emma Brace (1894; New York: Arno Press, 1976), and Charles Loring Brace, *The Best Method of Disposing of Our Pauper & Vagrant Children* (New York: Wynkoop, Hallenbeck & Thomas, Printers, 1859).

35. Brace, *Dangerous Classes*, 29.

36. Ibid., 110; Catherine J. Ross, "Society's Children: The Care of Indigent Youngsters in New York City, 1875–1903," PhD diss., Yale University, 1977, 130; Viviana Zelizer, *Pricing the Priceless Child: The Changing Social Value of Children* (New York: Basic Books, 1985), 173; Miriam Z. Langsam, *Children West: A History of the Placing-Out System of the New York Children's Aid Society, 1853–1890* (Madison: University of Wisconsin Press, 1964), 64. See also Annette Riley Fry, "The Children's Migration," *American Heritage* 26, no. 1 (Dec. 1974): 4–10, 79–81, and Lori Askeland, "'The Means of Draining the City of These Children': Domesticity and Romantic Individualism in Charles Loring Brace's Emigration Plan, 1853–1861," *American Transcendental Quarterly* 12, no. 2 (1998): 145–162.

37. *Five Points Monthly Record*, July 1854, 91, 306–307; *Sketches and Incidents in the Office of the Children's Aid Society, by WCD* (Dec. 5, 1855), 31–32; (Mar. 24, 1856), 111; "The News-Boys' Home," *New York Times*, Jan. 16, 1856, 4; Hawes, *Children in Urban Society*, 102–103. See also Bruce Bellingham, "'Little Wanderers': A Socio-Historical Study of the Nineteenth Century Origins of Child Fostering and Adoption Reform, Based on Early Records of the Children's Aid Society," PhD diss., University of Pennsylvania, 1984, and Clay Gish, "Rescuing the 'Waifs and Strays' of the City: The Western Emigration Program of the Children's Aid Society," *Journal of Social History* 33, no. 1 (Fall 1999): 121–141.

38. Donald Dale Jackson, "It Took Trains to Put Street Kids on the Right Track out of the Slums," *Smithsonian Magazine* 17, no. 5 (Aug. 1986): 99. On Burke and Brady, see Stephen O'Connor, *Orphan Trains: The Story of Charles Loring Brace and the Children He Saved and Failed* (Boston: Houghton Mifflin, 2001), 177–202.

39. See Jack Bales, "A History of the Newsboys' Lodging House," *Newsboy* 14, no. 4 (Nov. 1975): 2–10; and Bales, "The Newsboys' Lodging House: Impetus for an Immortal," 1–8, undated typescript in author's possession.

40. On the Philadelphia home on Pear and then Spruce Street, see *New York Times*, Feb. 8, 1858, 8; Mar. 20, 1858, 1; J. Thomas Scharf and Thompson Westcott, *History of Philadelphia, 1609–1884* (Philadelphia: L. H. Everts, 1884), 2:1478, and clippings in Charles Augustus Poulson, *Illustrations of Philadelphia Scrapbook, 1850–1860*, 1:40, 8:50, 10:65, Library Company of Philadelphia. On the Chicago home at 1421 Wabash Avenue, see *Chicago: An Instructive and Entertaining History of a Wonderful City* (Chicago: Rhodes & McClure, 1888), 193.

41. "The Lodging House and School for the Newsboys," *New York Tribune*, Mar. 25, 1854, 7; *New York Times*, Mar. 10, 1854, 4; *New York Times*, June 6, 1855, 4.

42. "Homeless Children," *New York Times*, May 4, 1854, 6; "A Newsboys' Lodging-House," *New York Tribune*, Apr. 11, 1880, 2; Charles Loring Brace, "Wolf-Reared Children," *St. Nicholas* 9, no. 36 (May 1882): 551. On lodging houses, see Kenneth A. Scherzer, *The Unbounded Community: Neighborhood Life and Social Structure in New York City, 1830–1875* (Durham, NC: Duke University Press, 1992), 97–134; and Wendy Gamber, *The Boardinghouse in Nineteenth Century America* (Baltimore: Johns Hopkins University Press, 2007), 157–164.

43. C. L. B., "Boys from the Children's Aid Society," *Incidents and Sketches Among the Newsboys*, pt. 3 (Nov. 19, 1855), 126; Gish, "Rescuing the 'Waifs and Strays,'" 124, 127.

44. *Five Points Monthly Record*, Aug. 1854, 98; Oct. 1854, 139; Harry D. Jones, "Weapons the Boys Carry," *New York Sunday News*, n.d., in Rudolph Heig Scrapbook (henceforth Heig Scrapbook), 3, Peter J. Eckel Newsboy Collection, Department of Rare Books and Special Collections, Firestone Library, Princeton University; Ednah D. Cheney, ed., *Louisa May Alcott: Her Life, Letters, and Journals* (Boston: Roberts Brothers, 1889), 283; C. L. B., "Homeless Children," *New York Times*, May 4, 1854, 6; "The Children's Aid Society," *New York Times*, Apr. 7, 1860, 2.

45. "The Children's Aid Society," *New York Times*, Apr. 7, 1860, 2; *Fifth Annual Report of the Children's Aid Society* (1858), 24; *Incidents and Sketches Among the Newsboys*, pt. 5, 17, 76–77, 132, New York Children's Aid Society Archive (henceforth NYCAS Archive).

46. *Eighth Annual Report of the Children's Aid Society* (1861), 14; "An Item for the Newsboys," *Independent*, May 2, 1861, n.p.; "Making Rum Take Care of the Children," *Jersey Journal*, May 15, 1868, 2; Brace, *Dangerous Classes*, 282–283.

47. George S. Boutwell, *Thoughts on Educational Topics and Institutions* (Boston: Phillips, Sampson, 1859), 117; "'Jayhawker,'" *Los Angeles Times*, Mar. 20, 1887, 3; *Third Annual Report of the Children's Aid Society* (1856), 41, 43; W. C. D., "Visit from the 'Newsboy Professor,' Returned from Boston," in *Sketches and Incidents in the Office of the Children's Aid Society*, part 1 (Dec. 2, 1857), 130, NYCAS Archive. Morrow calls him O'Sullivan or "English."

48. *Second Annual Report of the Children's Aid Society* (1855), 24; *Third Annual Report of the Children's Aid Society* (1856), 40; "David Johnson the Coloured Orphan Boy," *Incidents and Sketches Among the Newsboys*, pt. 5 (Feb. 21, 1856), 63, NYCAS Archive.

49. Brace, *Dangerous Classes*, 104–105; "Smallest Savings Bank in the World," *New York Journal*, Feb. 16, 1896, 19; "The News-Boys," *Frank Leslie's Illustrated Newspaper*, Dec. 29, 1855, 44; Henry Howe, "Philanthropic Enterprises," in *Adventures and Achievements of Americans* (Cincinnati, OH: Henry Howe; New York: Geo. F. Tuttle, 1858), 589.

50. "The Children's Aid Society," *New York Times*, Apr. 7, 1860, 2; "Death Among the News-Boys," in *Fifth Annual Report of the Children's Aid Society* (1858), 36–37; Brace, *Short Sermons*, 234–236. A clipping in Brace's personal scrapbook circa May 1855 names the boy as Pickety. See also "The Newsboy's Funeral," *New York Times*, Feb. 26, 1859, 5, and *New York Observer and Chronicle*, Mar. 10, 1859, 10.

51. Brace, *Short Sermons*, 234–236; Brace, *Dangerous Classes*, 103–104, 244, 269; *New York Tribune*, May 15, 1856, 7.

52. W. Colopy Desmond, "Office-Journal," in *Sixth Annual Report of the Children's Aid Society* (1859), 57; *Eighth* (1861), 17; *Tenth* (1863), 12–14.

53. C. L. B., "Incidents Among the Newsboys. An Extempore Speech," *Independent*, July 12, 1855, 1. Fatty's real name was Matt Coleman.

54. "The News-Boys," *New York Times*, Mar. 12, 1853, 3; St. Clair, *Six Days in the Metropolis*, 49; *Incidents and Sketches Among the Newsboys*, pt. 5, 134–135, NYCAS Archive.

55. Brace, *Dangerous Classes*, 65.

56. "Meeting of the Police Commissioners," *New York Herald*, June 12, 1858, 2; "Hurrah for the Newsboys," *Alta California*, Jan. 3, 1857, 7; "Obscene Publications—Caution to Newsboys," *San Francisco Bulletin*, Nov. 21, 1857, 2; "The Rough Newsboys of the 50s," *New York Times*, Sept. 19, 1926, AN54. See also Richard R. John, "Taking Sabbatarianism Seriously: The Postal System, the Sabbath, and the Transformation of American Political Culture," *Journal of the Early Republic* 10 (Winter 1990): 517–567.

57. I. Edwards Clark, "A Great Advocate. James T. Brady," *Galaxy* 7, no. 5 (May 1869): 718; James D. McCabe Jr., *Great Fortunes, and How They Were Made* (Philadelphia: Maclean, 1871), 435–447; Philip Hone, ed., *The Diary of Philip Hone, 1828–1851*, ed. Allan Nevins (New York: Dodd, Mead, 1936), 335.

58. Henri Herz, *My Travels in America*, trans. Henry Bertrain Hill (Ann Arbor: University of Michigan Press, 1963), 65; *Brooklyn Eagle*, Feb. 8, 1849, 2; "Selections," *Frederick Douglass' Paper*, Apr. 6, 1849, 1; Lee, *Daily Newspaper in America*, 393; "Newsboys on Sunday," *New York Clipper*, Nov. 12, 1853, n.p.; "Cold Weather," *Baltimore Sun*, Feb. 28, 1855, 4.

59. "Grand Meeting of Newsboys," *New York Tribune*, in *Hudson River Chronicle*, Feb. 19, 1850, 2; "Mass Meeting of Newsboys," *Baltimore Sun*, Feb. 16, 1850, 1; Moness, "The News Boys' Procession," *Hartford Courant*, Feb. 15, 1850, 2; "Review of the Past Week," *Hartford Courant*, Feb. 18, 1850, 2.

60. "The Alderman and the Newsboy," *Brooklyn Eagle*, June 24, 1850, 3; Brace, *Short Sermons*, 121–122; "Sunday Dinner for the Newsboys," *New York Observer and Chronicle*, Aug. 11, 1859, 254.

61. "A Great Reform at Last," *New York Herald*, May 25, 1858, 4; "Meeting of the Police Commissioners," *New York Herald*, June 12, 1858, 2; *Sunday Atlas*, June 13, 1858, in *First Five Years of the Sabbath Reform, 1857–62* (New York: Edward O. Jenkins, 1862), 16.

62. *Topics of the Times: A New Comic Song Written by J. F. Poole for Jerry Merrifield* (New York: J. Andrews, ca. 1858).

63. *New York Clipper*, June 5, 1858, 50; "War upon the Newsboys!," *New York Clipper*, June 25, 1858, 80.

64. "The Recorder on Sunday Laws," *New York Times*, Oct. 7, 1858, 4; "Terrible Fight in a Lager-Bier Garden," *New York Times*, Oct. 5, 1858, 1.

65. "Newsboys," *Newark Daily Advertiser*, Sept. 9, 1854, 2.

66. Augustine J. H. Duganne, *The Tenant-House, or Embers from Poverty's Hearth Stone* (New York: Robert DeWitt, 1857), 21.

67. "Is This Mr. Casey?," *Baltimore Sun*, July 12, 1922, 8; "Crickets of Journalism," *Washington Post*, Jan. 19, 1902, 11; "Writing for the Newsboys," *New Orleans Times-Picayune*, Nov. 29, 1853, 2; "The Newsboy," *New York Times*, Mar. 10, 1854, 4; "The News Boys' Lodging-House," *New York Dispatch*, May 28, 1854, in Brace, *Short Sermons*, 224; George Douglas Brewerton, *The War in Kansas* (New York: Derby & Jackson, 1856), 14; *Young America* 1, no. 2 (1856): 27; William Standish Hayes, "Began Life as Newsboys," *Breckenridge News* (*Cloverport, KY*), Oct. 4, 1893, 1.

68. Ralph Waldo Emerson, "The Fugitive Slave Law" (1854), in *Emerson's Complete Works* (Boston: Houghton, Mifflin, 1886), 206.

69. "'Uncle Tom' Among the Bowery Boys," *New York Times*, July 27, 1853, 1; Dyer, "New York Sun," 463–467.

70. "Popular Sovereignty," *Liberator* 24, no. 40 (Oct. 6, 1854): 159.

71. "'Communipaw,' the Black News-Vendor," *Frederick Douglass' Paper*, Mar. 25, 1852, n.p.

72. Ibid.

73. Ibid.

74. On Smith, see Benjamin Quarles, *Frederick Douglass* (Washington, DC: Associated Publishers, 1948), 85, 156–157; and Bruce Dain, *A Hideous Monster of the Mind: American Race Theory in the Early Republic* (Cambridge, MA: Harvard University Press, 2002), 229–263. On the *Tuscarora*, see "Mysterious Affair," *New-Bedford Mercury*, May 16, 1851, 1.

75. "Moses Small," *Baltimore Sun*, Sept. 7, 1860, 1; J. Thomas Scharf, *The Chronicles of Baltimore* (Baltimore: Turnbull Brothers, 1874), 586–587; James W. Palmer, "The City of Monuments," *Lippincott's Magazine* 8, no. 4 (Oct. 1871): 371–372.

76. See *Harry Wilson, the Newsboy* (Philadelphia: American Sunday-School Union, 1851); *John, the Outcast, The Homeless Heir; or, Life in Bedford Street: A Mystery of Philadelphia* (Philadelphia: J. H. C. Whiting, 1856); and Philip Wallys, *About New York: An Account of What a Boy Saw in His Visit to the City* (New York: Dix, Edwards, 1857).

77. Howard C. Hopkins, *History of the YMCA in America* (New York: Association Press, 1951), 16, 26–27, 203; "Editorial Melange," *Ballou's Pictorial*, Feb. 13, 1858, 111; Elizabeth Oakes Smith, *Selections from the Autobiography of Elizabeth Oakes Smith*, ed. Mary Alice Wyman (Lewiston, ME: Lewiston Journal and Columbia University Press, 1924), 149–150; Wyman, *Two American Pioneers: Seba Smith and Elizabeth Oakes Smith* (New York: Columbia University Press, 1927), 187–189; *Autobiography of Elizabeth Oakes Smith*, unpublished MS, Portland Collection, S-164, box 5/17b, 181–182, Maine Historical Society, Portland, ME.

78. Elizabeth Oakes Smith, *The Newsboy* (New York: J. C. Derby, 1853), 28, 21, 24.

79. J. C. Derby, *Fifty Years Among Authors, Books and Publishers* (New York: G. W. Carleton, 1884), 546; *Putnam's Weekly* 5, no. 26 (Feb. 1855): 216.

80. Ann Douglas, *The Feminization of American Culture* (New York: Doubleday, 1988), 6. See also Daniel Rodgers, "Socializing Middle-Class Children: Institutions, Fables, and Work Values in Nineteenth-Century America," in *Growing Up in America: Children in Historical Perspective*, ed. N. Ray Hiner and Joseph M. Hawes (Urbana: University of Illinois Press, 1985), 125; Anne Scott MacLeod, "Children's Literature and American Culture, 1820–1860," in *Society and Children's Literature*, ed. James H. Fraser (Boston: Godine, 1978), 11–31; and Diana Loercher Pazicky, *Cultural Orphans in America* (Jackson: University Press of Mississippi, 1998), 170–173.

81. "Philip Mortimer! The Boston Newsboy!, or, The Intellect of Rags!," *Boston Herald*, Feb. 10–28, 1857; F. Ratchford Starr, *Didley Dumps, or John Ellard, the Newsboy* (Philadelphia: William S. and Alfred Martien, 1860), 36; "Local Intelligence," *Philadelphia Inquirer*, Dec. 17, 1859, 1; Morrow, *Voice from the Newsboys*, xiv.

82. "Communication from a Newsboy Who Died of Cholera Last Fourth of July, to Hon. John W. Edmonds," *Chicago Tribune*, Sept. 18, 1854, 1. See also *The Newsboy*, Spiritual Tracts No. 3 (New York: S. T. Munson, 1858), 10.

83. Q. K. Philander Doesticks, *What He Says* (New York: Edward Livermore, 1855), 260. See also "Judge Edmonds on Spiritualism," *Putnam's Monthly* 2, no. 12 (Dec. 1853): 680–681; John W. Edmonds and George T. Dexter, *Spiritualism* (New York: Partridge & Brittan, 1855), 2:120, 132; Bret E. Carroll, *Spiritualism in Antebellum America* (Bloomington: Indiana University Press, 1997), 52, 72–74, 83, 118; and Barbara Weisberg, *Talking to the Dead: Kate and Maggie Fox and the Rise of Spiritualism* (San Francisco: HarperCollins, 2004), 129–132, 176–177.

84. Joanne Dobson, introduction to E. D. E. N. Southworth, *The Hidden Hand or, Capitola the Madcap* (New Brunswick, NJ: Rutgers University Press, 1988), xxxi, xxvi–xxvii, 41, 44; Dobson, "The Hidden Hand: Subversion of Cultural Ideology in Three Mid-Nineteenth-Century American Women's Novels," *American Quarterly* 38, no. 2 (Summer 1986): 223–242; Michele Ann Abate, "Launching a Gender B(l)acklash: E. D. E. N. Southworth's *The Hidden Hand* and the Emergence of (Racialized)White Tomboyism," *Children's Literature Association Quarterly* 34, no. 1 (Spring 2006): 41.

85. Anna Hope, "The Boy Who Confessed His Sin," *Independent* (ca. 1854–55), in *Newsboy* 16, no. 1 (Aug. 1977): 21–22; C. L. B., "The Little Theologue," in *Fifth Annual Report of the Children's Aid Society* (1858), 38; C. L. B., "The Lame Boy," *Independent*, Nov. 15, 1855, 366; *Youth's Companion*, Oct. 22, 1857, n.p.; *Seventh Annual Report of the Children's Aid Society* (1860), 96.

86. Morrow, *Voice from the Newsboys*, 122, xiii; Eliot, "Johnny Morrow, the Newsboy," *New York Evangelist*, June 6, 1861, 2; J. A. Humphrey, *Englewood: Its Annals and Reminiscences* (New York: J. S. Ogilvie, 1899), 48, 58–59, 66, 96–97.

87. "Literary Notices," *Godey's Lady's Book* 62 (May 1861): 466; Eliot, "Johnny Morrow, the Newsboy," 2; "Johnny Morrow in Town," *Philadelphia Inquirer*, Feb. 20, 1861, 2; *Brooklyn Eagle*, Dec. 1, 1860, 3.

88. Eliot, "Johnny Morrow, the Newsboy," 2; "A Bright Spark Suddenly Extinguished," *Brooklyn Eagle*, May 25, 1861, 3; "Give Me a Motive," *Christian Recorder*, June 29, 1861, n.p.; C. L. B., "A Newsboy's Funeral," *Independent*, June 6, 1861, in *Ninth Annual Report of the Children's Aid Society* (1862), 34–37; "A Newsboy's Funeral," *New York World*, May 28, 1861, 6.

89. "An Old Newsboy," *National Intelligencer*, in *United States Magazine* 1, no. 4 (Aug. 15, 1854): 126. See also Freeman Hunt, *Worth and Wealth: A Collection of Maxims, Morals and Miscellanies for Merchants and Men of Business* (New York: Stringer & Townsend, 1856), 445–446, and "Perseverance—Its Value," in *Merry's Gems*, ed. Uncle Merry [John Newton Stearns] (New York: H. Dayton, 1860), 139–141.

90. "The Newsboy," *New York Times*, Mar. 10, 1854, 4; "Charles Loring Brace. A Statue of the Philanthropist Asked For," *New York Times*, Nov. 28, 1890, 2.

91. Lee, *Daily Newspaper in America*, 395; Frankl Luther Mott, *American Journalism: A History of Newspapers in the United States through 250 Years, 1690–1940* (New York: Macmillan, 1947), 373, 480.

Chapter 4

1. Walt Whitman, *Specimen Days* (Glasgow: Wilson & McCormick, 1883), 21; "A Bold Imposture," *New York Times*, Feb. 14, 1861, 8.

2. "Effects of the News in the North," *New York Herald*, Apr. 14, 1861, 8; Abby Howland Woolsey to Eliza Newton Howland, Apr. 14, 1861, in *Letters of a Family During the War for the Union 1861–1865* (privately printed, 1899), 1:37; "The Newsboy," *New York Ledger*, Nov. 15, 1862, 4; Oliver Wendell Holmes, "Bread and the Newspaper," Sept. 1861, in *Pages from an Old Volume of Life: A Collection of Essays, 1857–1881* (Boston: Houghton, Mifflin, 1883), 1.

3. "Canvassers Wanted," *Chicago Press and Tribune*, July 17, 1860, 1; O. Coe, "One of Nature's Nobility," *Milwaukee Sentinel*, Apr. 17, 1861, 1.

4. Alfred McClung Lee, *The Daily Newspaper in America: The Evolution of a Social Instrument* (New York: Macmillan, 1937), 731; James Crouthamel, *Bennett's New York Herald and the Rise of the Popular Press* (Syracuse, NY: Syracuse University Press, 1989), 117; Frankl Luther Mott, *American Journalism: A History, 1690–1960* (New York: Macmillan, 1962), 403; "Wendell Phillips on the War," *Liberator* 31, no. 19 (May 10, 1861): 76.

5. Lee, *Daily Newspaper in America*, 263, 278, 731; "Sketches of the Publishers, No. 3. The American News Company," *Round Table* 3, no. 33 (Apr. 21, 1866): 250; "The New York Newsboys," *Leisure Hours*, Nov. 1, 1869, 716; Edward Dicey, *Six Months in the Federal States* (London: Macmillan, 1863), 1:45–46.

6. "Then and Now, Newspaper Distributing in Detroit in the '50s," May 26, 1896, in Friend Palmer Scrapbook, 13:70, Detroit Public Library; Silas Farmer, *The History of Detroit and Michigan* (Detroit: Silas Farmer, 1889), 693; *Ladies' Repository* 22, no. 5 (May 1862): 317; "The Newsboys," *Chicago Tribune*, Jan. 23, 1865, 4; "Licensed News Boys," *Chicago Tribune*, Jan. 29, 1862, 4; "Licensing Newsboys," *Chicago Tribune*, Jan. 31, 1862, 4; "Newsboys' Licenses," *Chicago Tribune*, Feb. 10, 1862, 4; "The Newsboys," *Chicago Tribune*, Sept. 26, 1864, 4; "New York Newsboys," *Leisure Hours*, Nov. 1, 1869, 717; Helen Campbell et al., *Darkness and Daylight: Lights and Shadows of New York Life* (Hartford, CT: A. D. Worthington, 1892), 112; "The Weekly Standard," *Brooklyn Eagle*, Apr. 19, 1862, 3; "The Way the News Was Received," *Brooklyn Eagle*, May, 9, 1864, 2.

7. "Something About the Newsboys," *National Republican*, Sept. 21, 1861, 3; Ida M. Tarbell, "Lincoln Gathering an Army," *McClure's Magazine* 12, no. 4 (Feb. 1899), 328; "Washington Correspondence," *Chicago Tribune*, May 19, 1863, 2, quoted in J. Cutler Andrews, *The North Reports the Civil War* (Pittsburgh, PA: University of Pittsburgh Press, 1955), 27, 50.

8. Allen C. Clark, "Abraham Lincoln in the National Capital," *Records of the Columbia Historical Society*, Washington, DC, 1925, 27:39; William Simmons, *Men of Mark: Eminent, Progressive and Rising* (Cleveland, OH: Geo. M. Rewell, 1887), 118–121; Hal S. Chase, "'Shelling the Citadel of Race Prejudice': William Calvin Chase and the *Washington Bee*, 1882–1921," *Records of the Columbia Historical Society*, 49:371.

9. Bennett's *Herald* netted annual profits of $100,000 to $150,000 during the 1860s. Dicey, *Six Months in the Federal States*, 1:34; James Parton, *The Life of Horace Greeley* (Boston: Houghton, Mifflin, 1889), 376; "A New Dodge of the New York Beggars," *Saturday Evening Post*, Aug. 5, 1865, 7; "The Newsboy," *New York Ledger*, Nov. 15, 1862, 4; "The Newsboys of New-York," *New York Weekly Tribune*, Nov. 11, 1868, n.p.; A. P., "The Street-Arabs of New York," *Appleton's Journal 9*, no. 198 (Jan. 4, 1873): 47.

10. "Fire Extraordinary," *Boston Transcript*, Oct. 30, 1861, 2; Harry W. Baehr Jr., *The New York Tribune Since the Civil War* (New York: Dodd, Mead, 1936), 1.

11. "A Quiet Sabbath," *Boston Post*, June 3, 1861, 2; "The Newsboys," *Milwaukee Sentinel*, Mar. 28, 1861, 1; "In Times Gone By," *Milwaukee Sentinel*, Apr. 12, 1885, 9; Herman Bleyer, "Milwaukee's Civil War Newsboys," *Once a Year* (1905), in *Milwaukee History 14*, no. 2 (1991): 70–71; "Sarah Butler Wister's Civil War Diary," *Pennsylvania Magazine of History and Biography 102*, no. 3 (July 1978): 308; "Local Affairs," *Philadelphia Public Ledger*, May 2, 1862, 1.

12. "A Newsboy Drowned," *New York Evening Post*, Dec. 20, 1861, 3; "Sold Papers in Civil War," *Kansas City Star*, Aug. 26, 1917, 8; *Chicago Tribune*, Apr. 21, 1862, 2.

13. Thomas Edison, *The Papers of Thomas A. Edison: The Making of an Inventor, February 1847–June 1873*, ed. Reese V. Jenkins et al. (Baltimore: Johns Hopkins University Press, 1989), 1:629–630; "Edison as a Newsdealer," *Newsdealer 1*, no. 2 (Apr. 1890): 39.

14. *Detroit Free Press*, July 19, 1864, 1; "A Strike and What Came of It," *Cleveland Herald*, July 20, 1864, 2; *New-York Daily Reformer*, Aug. 12, 1864, 2.

15. "Forgery of Newspaper Extras—An Atrocious Fraud," *San Francisco Evening Bulletin*, Dec. 26, 1864, 3; "Gustavus De Young Dead," *San Francisco Call*, Oct. 13, 1906, 2; J. B. Graham, *Handset Reminiscences: Recollections of an Old-Time Printer and Journalist* (Salt Lake City, UT: Century, 1915), 109–111.

16. Percy F. Smith, *Memory's Milestones: Reminiscences of Seventy Years of a Busy Life in Pittsburgh* (Pittsburgh, PA: Murdock-Kerr, 1918), 8; "In Times Gone By," *Milwaukee Sentinel*, Apr. 12, 1885, 9.

17. Frederick Hudson, *Journalism in the United States, from 1690 to 1872* (New York: Macmillan, 1873), 99; Robert Bremner, *The Public Good: Philanthropy and Welfare in the Civil War Era* (New York: Knopf, 1980), 207; Catherine J. Ross, "Society's Children: The Care of Indigent Youngsters in New York City, 1875–1903," PhD diss., Yale University, 1977, 17, 8; Charles Loring Brace, *The Dangerous Classes of New York and Twenty Years' Work Among Them* (New York: Wynkook & Hallenbeck, 1872), 302–309; Charles Loring Brace, *Life and Letters of Charles Loring Brace, 1826–1890*, ed. Emma Brace (New York: Scribners, 1894), 251–255.

18. "Local Matters," *Baltimore Sun*, May 10, 1861, 1; "Suppression of Treasonable Newspapers," *Boston Traveler*, Aug. 24, 1861, 2; United States War Dept., Record and Pension Office, *The War of the Rebellion: A Compilation of the Official Records of the Union and Confederate Armies*, ser. 2, vol. 2 (Washington, DC: Government Printing Office, 1897), 787–788; Joe Skidmore, "The Copperhead Press and the Civil War," *Journalism Quarterly 16* (1939): 345–355; John Nerone, *Violence Against the Press: Policing the Public Sphere in U.S. History* (New York: Oxford University Press, 1994), 117; "Stirring Times," *Brooklyn Eagle*, Aug. 30, 1885, 1.

19. Rick Bell, "'Oh Yes!' The Cry of Louisville's Legendary Newsboy, Pat Murphy," *Main Street*, Sept. 1982, 5–6.

20. *War of the Rebellion*, ser. 2, vol. 2 (1897), 73.

21. Ibid., 776; Clement L. Vallandigham, "The Conscription Bill.—Arbitrary Arrests. Speech delivered in the House of Representatives, February 23, 1863," in *Speeches, Arguments, Addresses, and Letters of Clement L. Vallandigham* (New York: J. Walter, 1864), 472.

22. *War of the Rebellion*, ser. 1, vol. 23, pt. 2, 381; E. W. T. Nichols, *Oppression!! Suppressing the Press*, lithograph on woven paper, 24.1 × 31.5 cm (Boston: 1863).

23. "News Boy Telegraph," *Chicago Tribune*, May 25, 1864, 4; James Brooks, "Hold Fast to the Constitution," speech before the Union Democratic Association, New York, Dec. 30, 1862; "News for the Newsboys," *New York Times*, May 27, 1864, 4; Henry J. Raymond, *The Life and Public Services of Abraham Lincoln* (New York: Darby and Miller, 1865), 568. See also Mark Neely, *The Fate of Liberty: Abraham Lincoln and Civil Liberties* (New York: Oxford University Press, 1991).

24. "Fine Arts," *New York Evening Post*, Mar. 16, 1863, 1, in Martha Hoppin, *The World of J. G. Brown* (Chesterfield, MA: Chameleon Books, 2010), 66.

25. Ernest A. McKay, *The Civil War and New York City* (Syracuse: Syracuse University Press, 1990), 96; Edwin G. Burrows and Mike Wallace, *Gotham: A History of New York City to 1898* (New York: Oxford University Press, 1999), 895; Ross, "Society's Children," 8–9; *Harper's Weekly* 7, no. 343 (July 25, 1863): 466; "Our Foreign Population," *Round Table* 1, no. 24 (May 28, 1864): 371. See also Iver Bernstein, *The New York City Draft Riots: Their Significance for American Society and Politics in the Age of the Civil War* (New York: Oxford University Press, 1990), and Nerone, *Violence Against the Press*, 120–122.

26. Parton, *Life of Horace Greeley*, 485; William M. Bobo, *Glimpses of New-York City* (Charleston, SC: J. J. McCarter, 1853), 66; Armond Fields, *Eddie Foy: A Biography of the Early Popular Stage Comedian* (Jefferson, NC: McFarland, 1999), 13.

27. Sinclair Tousey, *Papers from Over the Water* (New York: American News Company, 1869); *Indices of Public Opinion, 1860–1870* (New York: printed for private circulation, 1871); Abel C. Thomas, *An Antislavery Alphabet* (New York: T. W. Strong and American News Company, 1864); Charles Loring Brace, "A Statement to the Public of a Portion of the Work of the Children's Aid Society" (1863), 1–2, quoted in Stephen O'Connor, *Orphan Trains: The Story of Charles Loring Brace and the Children He Saved and Failed* (New York: Houghton Mifflin, 2001), 167; Brace, *Life of Charles Loring Brace*, 257–258.

28. W. R. Rose, "Early Day Newspaper Carriers," *Cleveland Plain Dealer*, July 15, 1926, 10, in "Cleveland–Newsboys" clipping file, Cleveland Public Library.

29. Mutual Life Insurance Co. of New York Annual Report, 1889, 18–19; *Baltimore Sun*, Feb. 16, 1863, 4; Nettie P. McGill, *Child Workers on City Streets*, Children's Bureau, Pub. No. 188 (Washington, DC: Government Printing Office, 1928), 1; C. C. Darwin, "The Newsboys Lodging House," *Christian Weekly*, Mar. 16, 1872, 124.

30. "A Man with a History," *Worcester Spy*, May 16, 1895, 8; O'Connor, *Orphan Trains*, 195; C. L. Brace, *Dangerous Classes*, 242; "Charities in War-Time," *New York Times*, Mar. 16, 1865, 6; McGill, "Child Workers on City Streets," 1; F. Ratchford Starr, *Didley Dumps or John Ellard, the Newsboy*, 5th ed. (Philadelphia: American Sunday School Union, 1884), 21. On boys in the armed forces, see Peter W. Bardaglio, "On the Border: White Children and the Politics of War in Maryland," in *The War Was You and Me: Civilians in the American Civil War*, ed. Joan E. Cashin (Princeton, NJ: Princeton University Press, 2002), 316, 329 n. 11; James Marten, *The Children's Civil War* (Chapel Hill: University of North Carolina Press, 1998), 244 n. 6; Jim Murphy, *The Boys' War: Confederate and Union Soldiers Talk About the Civil War* (New York: Clarion Books, 1990), 2; Emmy E. Werner, *Reluctant Witnesses: Children's Voices from the Civil War Era* (Boulder, CO: Westview Press, 1998), 9; Bell I. Wiley, *The Life of Johnny Reb: The Common Soldier of the Confederacy* (1943; repr., Baton Rouge: Louisiana State University Press, 1971), 331; and Robert Bremner, *Children and Youth in America: A Documentary History*, vol. 2, *1866–1932* (Cambridge, MA: Harvard University Press, 1971), 94–96.

31. Henry Morgan, *Ned Nevins the Newsboy; or, Street Life in Boston* (Boston: Lee & Shepard, 1866), 64–65.

32. Ibid., 223–224. See also "Gen. Mitchel and the Newsboys," *Independent*, Feb. 6, 1863, n.p.

33. G. B. P. Ringwault to Young, July 26, 1861, in Louis M. Starr, *Bohemian Brigade: Civil War Newsmen in Action* (New York: Knopf, 1954), 49–50.

34. Thomas W. Knox, *Camp-Fire and Cotton-Field: Southern Adventure in Time of War* (New York: Blelock, 1865), 119.

35. Noah Brooks, "Washington in Lincoln's Time," *Century Magazine* 49, no. 1 (Nov. 1894): 141; Frazar Kirkland, *The Pictorial Book of Anecdotes and Incidents of the War of the Rebellion* (Hartford, CT: Hartford Publishing, 1867), 482.

36. "Company of Newsboys," *New Orleans Times-Picayune*, Feb. 23, 1862, 4; Benjamin F. Butler, "Some Experiences with Yellow Fever and Its Prevention," *North American Review* 147, no. 384 (Nov. 1888): 529.

37. C. N., "How the South Gathered News During the Civil War," *Collectible Newspapers* 4, no. 2 (Apr. 1987): 10; J. Cutler Andrews, *The South Reports the Civil War* (Princeton, NJ: Princeton University Press, 1970), 44–45; E. Merton Coulter, *The Confederate States of America, 1861–1865: A History of the South* (Baton Rouge: Louisiana State University Press, 1950), 7:493.

38. Thomas Nast, "Richmond Newsboy Announcing the Rebel Success!," *Harper's Weekly* 7, no. 290 (July 19, 1862): 464; "Richmond and Washington During the War," *Cornhill Magazine* 7 (Jan. 1863), 93, 102, reprinted in *Richmond Record* 1, no. 5 (July 16, 1863), 42–43.

39. J. T. Trowbridge, *The South: A Tour of Its Battle-Fields and Ruined Cities* (Hartford, CT: L. Stebbins, 1866), 408; T. B. G., "The Enmity to Gen. Butler by Wealthy Classes," Dec. 27, 1862, *New York Tribune*, n.d., in Thomas Butler Gunn Diaries, 20:123, Missouri History Museum Archive, St. Louis, MO; "The Brooklyn Boys South," *Brooklyn Eagle*, Oct. 17, 1863, 2; "Romantic Story of a 'Girl' Newsboy," *Utica News*, Jan. 6, 1871, 1.

40. "Civil War: Atlanta Home Front," *New Georgia Encyclopedia*, accessed Aug. 9, 2004, www.georgiaencyclopedia.org/nge/Article.jsp?path=/HistoryArchaeology/CivilWarandReconstruction/Topics-12&id=h-824; "The Last Atlanta Newsboy," *Atlanta Constitution*, June 1, 1892, 4.

41. Andrews, *South Reports the Civil War*, 39, 41; "The Rebel's Triumph," *Atlanta Constitution*, May 13, 1877, 3; Hope, "Our Chattanooga Correspondent," *Charleston Mercury*, July 19, 1861, n.p.

42. John Beauchamp Jones, "Diary," Oct. 1862, in *A Rebel War Clerk's Diary at the Confederate States Capital* (New York: Old Hickory Bookshop, 1935), 1:161; Fred William Allsopp, *Twenty Years in a Newspaper Office* (Little Rock, AR: Central Printing, 1907), 106–107.

43. Clarence S. Brigham, "Wall-Paper Newspapers of the Civil War," in *Bibliographical Essays: A Tribute to Wilberforce Eames*, ed. George Parker Winship and Lawrence C. Wroth (Cambridge, MA: Harvard University Press, 1924), 203–209; Lee, *Daily Newspaper in America*, 270; *Athens Southern Watchman*, May 3, 1865, quoted in Coulter, *Confederate States of America*, 7:494–495; Andrews, *South Reports the Civil War*, 42–43; "The Price of Our Paper and the News Boys," (Vicksburg) *Citizen*, June 18, 1863, in James Melvin Lee, *History of American Journalism* (Boston: Houghton Mifflin, 1917), 307.

44. Hermes, "War Gossip in Richmond," *Charleston Mercury*, July 26, 1862, n.p.; Andrews, *South Reports the Civil War*, 47–48; Michael B. Chesson, "Harlots or Heroines? A New Look at the Richmond Bread Riot," *Virginia Magazine of History and Biography* 92, no. 2 (Apr. 1984): 165.

45. "Recorder's Court," *Nashville Dispatch*, Mar. 17, 1863, 2.

46. David Q. Bowers, *The History of United States Coinage: As Illustrated by the Garrett Collection* (Wolfeboro, NH: Bowers and Merena Galleries, 1979), 242–245; A. N. K., 2nd Wisconsin Regiment, letter from camp near Fredericksburg, VA, Apr. 27, 1862, www.secondwi.com/fromthefront/april%201862.htm.

47. "Sixty Years as a New Orleans Newsboy," *Fourth Estate* 27, no. 1397 (Dec. 4, 1920): 13. "Memphis," *Frank Leslie's Illustrated Newspaper*, July 5, 1862, 3; Jenkin Lloyd Jones, "Diary of Jenkin Lloyd Jones, May, 1865," in *An Artilleryman's Diary* (Wisconsin History Commission, 1914), 395; "Sold Papers in Civil War," *Kansas City Star*, Aug. 26, 1917, 8; "A Strange Story," *Atlanta Constitution*, Mar. 6, 1879, 1; "Counterfeit Confederate Money," *New Orleans True Delta*, Apr. 29, 1862, 2; "Southern News," *Frank Leslie's Illustrated Newspaper*, May 17, 1862, 24.

48. "Miller on the New College," *Columbia State*, Apr. 9, 1896, 8; Francis P. Weisenburger, "William Sanders Scarborough: Early Life and Years at Wilberforce," *Ohio History* 71 (1962): 205–208; *The Autobiography of William Sanders Scarborough: An American Journey from Slavery to Scholarship*, ed. Michele Valerie Ronnick (Detroit, MI: Wayne State University Press, 2005), 27–36.

49. William Gilmore Beymer, *On Hazardous Service: Scouts and Spies of the North and South* (New York: Harper and Brothers, 1912), 157; *Richmond Daily Whig*, Nov. 11, 1863, 1.

50. Edward W. Bok, *A Man from Maine* (New York: Scribner's, 1923), 8–10; *Ninth Annual Report of the Children's Aid Society* (1862), 37; Eugene H. Munday, "The Press of Philadelphia in

1870," *Proof-Sheet* 3, no. 18 (May 1870): 83; "A Trip to Antietam," *Continental Monthly* 3, no. 2 (Feb. 1863): 149.

51. George F. Williams, "Lights and Shadows of Army Life," *Century Magazine* 28, no. 6 (Oct. 1884): 806; *New York Herald*, Mar. 13, 1862, n.p.

52. Lewis O. Saum, *The Popular Mood of America, 1860–1890* (Lincoln: University of Nebraska Press, 1990), 211–212; "Our Fifth Army Corp Correspondence," *New York Herald*, Jan. 21, 1863, 1; Osborn Hamiline Oldroyd, *A Soldier's Story of the Siege of Vicksburg: From the Diary of Osborn H. Oldroyd* (Springfield, IL: H. W. Rokker, 1885), 43.

53. Edwin Forbes, *Thirty Years After: An Artist's Memoir of the Civil War* (1890; repr., Baton Rouge: Louisiana State University Press, 1993), 133–134.

54. General Fitz John Porter, "The Battle of Gaines's Mill and Its Preliminaries," *Century Magazine* 30, no. 2 (June 1885): 322; Charles Wright Wills, Aug. 29, 1864, in *Army Life of an Illinois Soldier*, comp. Mary E. Kellogg (Washington, DC: Globe Printing, 1906), 293.

55. "Enterprising Newsboys," *Cleveland Herald*, Oct. 11, 1861, 2.

56. "Old Newspapers That Improve with Age," *Kansas City Times*, Mar. 9, 1885, 4; Wendell Philips Dodge, "A Fortune in Old Papers," *Technical World Magazine* 20, no. 1 (Sept. 1913): 113–114; Ellen Gruber Garvey, *Writing with Scissors: American Scrapbooks from the Civil War to the Harlem Renaissance* (New York: Oxford University Press, 2012), 230–235.

57. Doc Aubery, *Recollections of a Newsboy in the Army of the Potomac, 1861–1865* (Milwaukee, WI, n.p., 1902), 10, 14.

58. Ibid., 17, 69–70; William Cullen Bryant, Sydney Howard Gay, and Noah Brooks, *Scribner's Popular History of the United States* (New York: Charles Scribner's Sons, 1898), 374.

59. Aubery, *Recollections*, 138–139.

60. George Augustus Sala, *My Diary in America in the Midst of War* (London: Tinsley Brothers, 1865), 1:290; William Wilson Chamberlaine, *Memoirs of the Civil War Between the Northern and Southern Sections* (Washington, DC: B. S. Adams, 1912), 10–11.

61. Warren H. Cudworth, *History of the First Regiment (Massachusetts Infantry)* (Boston: Walker, Fuller, 1866), 541; *War of the Rebellion*, ser. 1, vol. 36, pt. 1 (1891), 791; "Late Southern News," *Chicago Tribune*, Apr. 23, 1862, 3; David Evans, *Sherman's Horsemen: Union Cavalry Operations in the Atlanta Campaign* (Bloomington: University of Indiana Press, 1996), 86.

62. Rufus Robinson Dawes, *Memoir of Rufus Dawes, 1890, in Service with the Sixth Wisconsin Volunteers* (Marietta, OH: E. R. Alderman & Sons, 1890), 188; *War of the Rebellion*, ser. 1, vol. 15, p. 860; vol. 25, pp. 548, 554–555, 745; vol. 31, pt. 3, pp. 93, 123, 134; vol. 45, pt. 2, pp. 52, 443; vol. 49, pt. 1, p. 871, pt. 2, p. 892; *The American Annual Cyclopaedia and Register of Important Events of the Year 1863* (New York: D. Appleton, 1864), 3:70.

63. "Something About the Newsboys," *National Republican*, Sept. 21, 1861, 3.

64. Williams, "Lights and Shadows of Army Life," 807.

65. James Joseph Williamson, *Mosby's Rangers: A Record of the Operations of the Forty-Third Battalion Virginia Cavalry, from Its Organization to the Surrender, from the Diary of a Private, Supplemented and Verified with Official Reports of Federal Officers and Also of Mosby* (New York: Ralph B. Kenyon, 1896), 291–294; John H. Alexander, *Mosby's Men* (1907), 147, in William E. Boyle Jr., "Under the Black Flag: Execution and Retaliation in Mosby's Confederacy," *Military Law Review* 144 (Spring 1994): 148; and Jeffry D. Wert, *Mosby's Rangers* (New York: Simon & Schuster, 1990), 246–247.

66. D. P. Coningham, "Meade's Army," *New York Herald*, Sept. 16, 1863; *Hartford Courant*, Oct. 3, 1864, 2; Philip H. Sheridan, *Personal Memoirs* (New York: Charles L. Webster, 1888), 1:385.

67. Captain J. McEntee to Major-General Humphreys, Office of the Provost-Marshal-General, Armies Operating Against Richmond, VA, Nov. 1, 1864; Jno. C. Babcock to Major-General Humphreys, Headquarters Army of the Potomac, Office of the Provost-Marshal-General, Nov. 5, 1864, *War of the Rebellion*, ser. 1, vol. 42, pt. 3, pp. 472, 517.

68. "James Kellan, A Confederate Spy," *McAlester Capital*, Apr. 4, 1895, n.p., www.usgennet.org/usa/ok/topic/veterans/wars/civilwar/clippings/jkellan.htm.

69. Beymer, *On Hazardous Service*, 158, 167. Charlie was in his sixties when he told Beymer his story and its accuracy is disputed. It was first published as "The Phillipses—Father and Son," *Harpers Monthly*, Oct. 1911, and excerpted in the *Washington Post*, Jan. 5, 1913, MT1. Their names were aliases; the father was William S. Rowley and Charlie was Merritt A. Rowley.

See Meriwether Stuart, "Of Spies and Borrowed Names: The Identity of Union Operatives in Richmond Known as 'the Phillipses' Discovered," *Virginia Magazine of History and Biography* 89, no. 3 (July 1981): 317.

70. M. S. Schroyer, *History of Company "G" 147th Regiment, Pennsylvania Volunteer Infantry* (Selinsgrove, PA: Penn Valley, n.d. [ca. 1912]), www.skyenet.net/~larrya/cw.htm; "Hanging of a Rebel Spy," *Washington Union*, July 7, 1863, 4; *Boston Herald*, July 9, 1863, 2; *New York Tribune*, July 13, 1863, 1; *Portland Argus*, July 28, 1863, 4; "Richardson the Spy," *New York Post*, Aug. 12, 1863, 1.

71. *New York Herald*, June 20, 1862; "Arrest of a Rebel Newsboy," *Philadelphia Press*, June 21, 1862, 1; Joel Cook, *The Siege of Richmond: A Narrative of the Military Operations of Major-General George B. McClellan During the Months of May and June, 1862* (Philadelphia: George W. Childs, 1862), 286.

72. *Brother to the Eagle: The Civil War Journal of Sgt. Ambrose Armitage, 8th Wisconsin Infantry*, ed. Alden R. Carter (Bradenton, FL: Booklocker.com, 2006), 249.

73. "The Newsboys," *Arithmetic*, Jan. 22, 1865, 4; "The Newsboys," *Chicago Tribune*, Jan. 23, 1865, 4; "Our Entrance into Richmond," *Beadle's Monthly*, June 1866, 515; Theodore C. Wilson, "The Herald in Richmond," *New York Herald*, Apr. 13, 1865, 5.

74. "Treatment of Prisoners at Camp Morton: 1. A Reply to 'Cold Cheer at Camp Morton,'" by W. R. Holloway, "2. Rejoinder by Dr. Wyeth," *Century Magazine* 42, no. 5 (Sept. 1891): 770–771; "Camp Douglas Matters," *Chicago Tribune*, Oct. 5, 1863, 4.

75. David Kaser, *Books and Libraries in Camp and Battle: The Civil War Experience* (Westport, CT: Greenwood Press, 1984), 66; "Late News in Brief," *Chicago Tribune*, Jan. 22, 1862, 2; Willard W. Glazier, *The Capture, the Prison Pen, and the Escape* (Albany, NY: J. Munsell, 1866), 45, 54, 62–63, 170; Alfred Ely, "Memoir of Alfred Ely," in *Journal of Alfred Ely, a Prisoner of War in Richmond*, ed. Charles Lanman (New York: D. Appleton, 1862), 359, 33; *Charleston Courier*, Aug. 22, 1861, 1.

76. Aubery, *Recollections*, 149–150; "A Newsboy's Romance," *Los Angeles Times*, Nov. 2, 1884, 4; "Mistaken for a Spy," *Washington Post*, Feb. 23, 1896, 23.

77. Tom Brice, *The News-Boy; or, Honesty Rewarded* (New York: T. W. Strong, 1862); Oliver Optic, *The Little Merchant: A Story for Little Folks* (Boston: Lee & Shepard, 1862); Ann S. Stephens, "The Soldier's Orphans," *Peterson's Magazine* 49, no. 6 (Jan.–Dec. 1866); Wm. Cook, M.D., "Robert and the Newsboys: A True Story for Children," *Ladies' Repository* 23, no. 10 (Oct. 1863), 634–635; Rebecca, *Tramps in New York* (New York: American Tract Society, ca. 1863), 39. See also M. A. Hall, *Lizzie's Visit to New York* (New York: Protestant Episcopal Society for the Promotion of Evangelical Knowledge, ca. 1862); Madeline Leslie, *Never Give Up; or, The News-Boys* (Boston: Graves & Young, 1863); James Barton Lomgacere, *Willie Wilson: The Newsboy* (New York: William Wood, 1865); Alice Warren, "Paddy Lyons the Newsboy," in *Horace Welford, and Other Stories* (Boston: Graves & Young, 1866), 19–28; and William O. Stoddard, *The Battle of New-York* (New York: D. Appleton, 1892).

78. Mantle Fielding, *Dictionary of American Painters, Sculptors, and Engravers* (1926; repr., New York: J. F. Carr, 1965), 413; Lisa N. Peters, "Images of the Homeless in American Art, 1860–1910," in *On Being Homeless: Historical Perspectives*, ed. Rick Beard (New York: Museum of the City of New York, 1987), 47; *PMA Bulletin* 35, no. 186 (May 1940), illus. no. 68: 39; Darrel L. Sewell, "William Winner," in *Philadelphia: Three Centuries of American Art* (Philadelphia: Philadelphia Museum of Art, 1976), 376–377; John F. Watson, ed., *Annals of Philadelphia, and Pennsylvania, in the Olden Times*, rev. ed. by Willis. P. Hazard (Philadelphia: Edwin S. Stuart, 1887), 3:452; Herman Warner Williams Jr., *Mirror to the American Past: A Survey of American Genre Painting, 1750–1900* (Greenwich, CT: New York Graphic Society, 1973), 168, 170; Teresa A. Carbone and Patricia Hills, eds., *Eastman Johnson: Painting America* (New York: Brooklyn Museum of Art/Rizzoli, 1999), 59, 260.

79. "The Artists' Fund Exhibition," *New York Evening Post*, Nov. 6, 1866, 2; Albert Boime, "Burgoo and Bourgeois: Thomas Noble's Images of Black People," in *Thomas Satterwhite Noble, 1835–1907* (Lexington: University of Kentucky Art Museum, 1988), 40, www.albertboime.com/Articles/66.pdf.

80. Dominique C. Fabronius, untitled lithograph, designed by R. Thayer, Louis Prang Co. (Boston: Thayer, ca. 1861), 50 × 41 cm. (19.5 × 16 in.), Library Company of Philadelphia.

81. Forbes, *Thirty Years After*, 133–134.

82. *War of the Rebellion*, ser. 1, vol. 25, pt. 2 (1889), 58; vol. 21 (1888), 806; "A Strike Among the Newspaper Venders," *New York Times*, Feb. 20, 1863, 8; *New York Tribune*, Feb. 20, 1863, 1; "Mutiny of Newsboys," *New York Times*, Feb. 21, 1863, 4; "Newsboys from the Army," *New York Times*, Mar. 22, 1863, 4.

83. "Newspapers in the Army," *New York Times*, June 15, 1863, 1; Provost-Marshal-General M. R. Patrick to Maj. Gen. George Meade, Aug. 10, 1863, *War of the Rebellion*, ser. 1, vol. 29, pt. 2 (1890), 26–27; "News of the Week," *Harrisburg Weekly Patriot and Union*, Feb. 26, 1863, 1; *New York Herald*, May 20, 1863; June 6, 1863; July 2, 1863.

84. *Baltimore Sun*, Nov. 4, 1863, 4; "New Items," *Saturday Evening Post*, Dec. 20, 1862, 7; Charles L. Brace, "The Street-Boy," *Independent*, Oct. 16, 1862, 6; "A Romantic Story of a Newsboy," *Hartford Courant*, Mar. 22, 1870, 1.

85. Letter from F. Glackmeyer to Col. G. W. Lee, Montgomery, AL, Aug. 1, 1863. Gilder Lehman Collection, New-York Historical Society; "Sketches," *Round Table*, Apr. 21, 1866, 250; Nathaniel H. Puffer, "Sinclair Tousey," in *Publishers for Mass Entertainment in Nineteenth Century America*, ed. Madeline B. Stern (Boston: G. K. Hall, 1980), 303–305; Donna Nance, "American News Company," *Dictionary of Literary Biography* 49, pt. 1 (Detroit: Gale, 1986), 10–11; Alice Fahs, "A Thrilling Northern War," in *An Uncommon Time: The Civil War and the Northern Home Front*, ed. Paul A. Cimbala and Randall M. Miller (New York: Fordham University Press, 2002), 32–35; George C. Jenks, "Dime Novel Makers," *Bookman* 20 (Oct. 1904): 109–110; "John R. Walsh, News Agent," *Chicago Tribune*, Mar. 23, 1890, 25.

86. *War of the Rebellion*, ser. 1, vol. 29, pt. 2 (1890), 26–27; Williams, "Lights and Shadows of Army Life," 807; W. T. Sherman to General Webster, in the field near Atlanta, Aug. 12, 1864, *War of the Rebellion*, ser. 1, vol. 38, pt. 5 (1891), 351.

87. "'Tween Decks After Action—News from Home," *Harper's Weekly* 9, no. 422 (Jan. 28, 1865): 52; "The War in the Southwest," *Brooklyn Eagle*, Dec. 18, 1862, 2.

88. Williams, "Lights and Shadows of Army Life," 807.

89. James McPherson, *Ordeal by Fire: The Civil War and Reconstruction*, 3rd ed. (New York: McGraw Hill, 2001), 440–442, 492–494.

90. National Archives, pension claims No. 100, 129 by Harriet M. Himes on behalf of veteran Alfred E. Himes, can 61, bundle 7.

91. Bleyer, "Milwaukee's Civil War Newsboys," 70–72.

92. Johnson Brigham, "Memory Pictures of Lincoln," *Youth's Companion* 90, no. 6 (Feb. 10, 1916): 76; Julia Truitt Bishop, "Newspaper Carrier Fifty-Seven Years," *New Orleans Times-Picayune*, Mar. 10, 1918, 53; *Rockford Republic*, Oct. 9, 1929, 1.

93. John L. McLaurin, *Sketches in Crude Oil* (Harrisburg, PA: published by the author, 1896), 396; "Diary of Annie Adams Fields, May, 1865," 198, in *Memories of a Hostess: A Chronicle of Eminent Friendships*, ed. Mark A. de Wolfe Howe (Boston: Atlantic Monthly Press, 1922), 312.

94. Graham, *Handset Reminiscences*, 176; Toby Edward Rosenthal, "A Newsboy in Early San Francisco," in *Memoirs of American Jews, 1775–1865*, ed. Jacob Rader Marcus (Philadelphia: Jewish Publication Society of America, 1955), 2:146, 152–153; *Sacramento Union*, Aug. 10, 1868, 2.

95. Ben Maryniak, "The Soldiers & Sailors Monument in Lafayette Square Buffalo, New York," accessed July 29, 2012, www.buffaloah.com/a/lafsq.

96. Philips joined the force on Mar. 20, 1875, not as Merritt Rowley but under his wartime alias. Augustine Costello, *Our Police Protectors* (New York: published by the author, 1885), 550, in Stuart, "Of Spies and Borrowed Names," 316; Bell, "'Oh Yes!,'" *Main Street*, Sept. 1982, 5–6.

97. Morgan, *Ned Nevins*, 385; Junius Henri Browne, *The Great Metropolis: A Mirror of New York* (Hartford, NJ: American Publishing, 1869), 432–433.

98. Whitman, *Specimen Days*, 80.

Chapter 5

1. Charles Dawson Shanly, "The Small Arabs of New York," *Atlantic Monthly* 23, no. 137 (Mar. 1869): 279.

2. "Sketches of the Publishers," *Round Table* 3, no. 32 (Apr. 14, 1866): 234; "The New York News Company," *Brooklyn Union*, Feb. 2, 1867, 1; *Manufacturer and Builder* 8, no. 5 (May 1876): 102–103; 9, no. 5 (May 1877): 118; S. N. D. North, *History and Present Condition of the Newspaper and Periodical Press of the United States* (Washington, DC: Government Printing Office, 1884), 8:159; *Covering a Continent: A Story of Newsstand Distribution and Sales* (New York: American News Company, 1930), 13–18; Alfred McClung Lee, *The Daily Newspaper in America: The Evolution of a Social Instrument* (New York: Macmillan, 1937), 263; *Serving the Reading Public* (New York: American News Company, 1944), 4; Mary Noel, *Villains Galore: The Heyday of the Popular Story Weekly* (New York: Macmillan, 1954), 141–142; Donna Nance, "American News Company," *Dictionary of Literary Biography* 49, pt. 1 (Detroit: Bruccol Clark, 1986), 10–11; Nathaniel H. Puffer, "Sinclair Tousey," in *Publishers for Mass Entertainment in Nineteenth Century America*, ed. Madeline B. Stern (Boston: G. K. Hall, 1980), 303–305; "Distribution of Current Literature," *Current Literature* 1, no. 4 (Oct. 1888): 284; *Book and News Dealer* 10, no. 115 (Sept. 1898): 90. See also Laura J. Miller, *Reluctant Capitalists: Bookselling and the Culture of Consumption* (Chicago: University of Chicago Press, 2006).

3. *New York Evening Post*, June 3, 1872, 2; "Horace Greeley," *New York Tribune*, Dec. 5, 1872, 5; *Hartford Courant*, Nov. 4, 1869, 2; Frederic Hudson, *Journalism in the United States, from 1690 to 1872* (New York: Harper & Brothers, 1873), 687.

4. Don C. Seitz, *The Dreadful Decade, 1869–1879* (Indianapolis, IN: Bobbs-Merrill, 1926); "Life in Chicago," *Pomeroy's Democrat*, July 7, 1877, 4; "A Newsboy's Rhyme," *Chicago Herald*, Aug. 8, 1873, 4.

5. Thomas Kessner, *Capital City: New York City and the Men Behind America's Rise to Economic Dominance, 1860–1900* (New York: Simon & Schuster, 2003), 161; Sean Dennis Cashman, *America in the Gilded Age: From the Death of Lincoln to the Rise of Theodore Roosevelt* (New York: New York University Press, 1993), 29; "Brevities," *Atlanta Constitution*, Oct. 9, 1873, 2; Ted Curtis Smythe, *The Gilded Age Press, 1865–1900* (Westport, CT: Praeger, 2003), 24–26; Joshua Brown, *Beyond the Lines: Pictorial Reporting, Everyday Life, and the Crisis of Gilded Age America* (Berkeley: University of California Press, 2002), 67.

6. Samuel Fletcher, *The Bloody Footprint, or, The Adventures of a Newsboy* (New York: George Munro, 1867); James D. McCabe, *Lights and Shadows of New York Life* (Philadelphia: National, 1872), 739; Edward Crapsey, "The Nether Side of New York," *Galaxy* 12, no. 3 (Sept. 1871): 356.

7. Dewitt Talmage, "Mills of Death," *Stark County* (OH) *Democrat*, Nov. 14, 1878, 1, reprinted in *Night Scenes of City Life* (Chicago: Donohue, Henneberry, 1891), 91–92.

8. Louisa May Alcott, "Our Little Newsboy," in *Youth's Companion*, June 18, 1868; A. O. Halsey, "Joe Willis, the Newsboy's Story," *Oliver Optic's Magazine* (Nov. 16–Dec. 7, 1867), 623–625, 640–641, 655–656, 671–672; Mrs. C. A. Merighi, "My Little News-Boy," *Harper's New Monthly Magazine* 42, no. 247 (Dec. 1870): 271–277; L. G. M., "Pete," *St. Nicholas* 1, no. 3 (Jan. 1874): 117–120; and "Chubby Ruff's Dream. A Christmas Story," *Commoner* 1, no. 4 (Nov. 27, 1875): n.p.

9. Maggie Lute Sullivan Burke, "Only a Newsboy," *Ballou's Monthly* 26, no. 4 (Apr. 1869): 359. Other poems of this ilk are E. C. Stedman, "Pan in Wall Street," *Atlantic Monthly* 19, no. 111 (Jan. 1867):119; H. R. Hudson, "The Newsboy," *Flag of Our Union*, Apr. 2, 1870, 222; "My Little Newsboy," *Harper's Monthly* 42, no. 248 (Jan. 1871): 271–176; Miss H. R. Hudson, "The Newsboy's Debt," *Harper's Monthly* 46, no. 276 (May 1873): 876–877; Francis Shubael Smith, "Rat, the Newsboy," *The Young Magdalen; and Other Poems* (Philadelphia: T. B. Peterson & Bros., 1874), 268–270; Alice and Phoebe Cary, "Nobody's Child," *The Poetical Works of Alice and Phoebe Cary* (New York: Hurd and Houghton, 1877), 341; and "A Newsboy's Gift," *Harper's Weekly* 23, no. 1180 (Aug. 9, 1879): 632.

10. *Luke Darrell, the Chicago Newsboy* (Chicago: Tomlinson Bros., 1866); Henry Morgan, *Ned Nevins, the Newsboy; or, Street Life in Boston* (Boston: Lee & Shepard, 1866); Thomas March Clark, *John Whopper the Newsboy* (Boston: Roberts Bros., 1871). See also Jane G. Austin, "Lawless Lives; or, The Boston Newsboy," *Boston Daily Evening Transcript*, May 25, 1869, 1; *Jim the Newsboy, and His Friends* (Boston: Congregational Publishing Society, c. 1871); and Caroline E. Kelly Davis, *Benny the Newsboy* (Boston: D. Lothrop, 1878). On Morgan, see *A Trip Through Morgan Memorial and a Biographical Sketch of Rev. Henry Morgan*

(Boston: Morgan Memorial, ca. 1917); Ivan D. Steen, "Cleansing the Puritan City: The Reverend Henry Morgan's Antivice Crusade in Boston," *New England Quarterly* 54, no. 3 (Sept. 1981): 385–411; and *New Hampshire Sentinel*, May 9, 1867, 2.

11. "A Real Alger Hero. Personal Sketches. Sinclair Tousey, The Newsman," *New York Mail*, June 4, 1868, in *Dime Novel Round-Up* 60, no. 1 (Feb. 1991): 8–9; J. G. Brown, *The Beggars* (1863), oil on canvas, 15⅙ × 12⅛ in., Wichita Art Museum, Wichita, KS; Pierce Rice, "J. G. Brown: The Bootblack Raphael," *American Art & Antique* 2, no. 3 (May–June 1979): 90–97; Martha Hoppin, *The World of J. G. Brown* (Chesterfield, MA, Chameleon Books, 2010), 168–170; *Country Paths and City Sidewalks: The Art of J. G. Brown* (Springfield, MA: George Walter Vincent Smith Art Museum, 1989), 18; and "The 'Little White Slaves' of New York: Paintings of Child Street Musicians by J. G. Brown," *American Art Journal* 26, nos. 1–2 (1994): 5–43.

12. J. G. Brown, "The Painter of the Street Arab," *The Art Amateur* 31, no. 6 (Nov. 1894): 125; Horatio Alger Jr., "Are My Boys Real?," *Ladies' Home Journal* 7, no. 12 (Nov. 1890), in *Newsboy* 13, Nos. 6–7 (Jan.–Feb. 1975): 15–16; J. G. Brown, "Street Arabs I Have Painted," *Harper's Young People* 11 (June 24, 1890): 530; Ishmael, "Through the New York Studios," *Illustrated American* 6, no. 65 (May 16, 1891): 624.

13. "Bold Bank Robbery," *Chicago Tribune*, Aug. 2, 1868, 1; *Chicago Tribune*, Nov. 19, 1871, 2; "How a Hero Lost His Shoes," *New York Times*, Sept. 29, 1878, 9; W. H. Bishop, "Nan, the Newsboy," *St. Nicholas* 6, no. 10 (Aug. 1879): 677; "Telegraphic Tales," *Washington Post*, Aug. 6, 1879, 1; "'Steve' Brodie Dead," *New York Times*, Feb. 1, 1901, 6.

14. *Brooklyn Eagle*, Mar. 27, 1868, 1; "Fine Arts," *New York Herald*, Feb. 21, 1876, 10; Herbert Spencer, "Specialized Administration," *Fortnightly Review* 10, no. 6 (Dec. 1871): 647–648. See also Carol Nackenoff, *The Fictional Republic: Horatio Alger and American Political Discourse* (New York: Oxford University Press, 1994).

15. Jack R. Hart, "Horatio Alger in the Newsroom: Social Origins of American Editors," *Journalism Quarterly* 53, no. 1 (Spring 1976): 20; "Modern Slang," *Evansville Courier & Press*, Apr. 13, 1903, 4; James H. Maurer, "How I Became a Rebel," *Labor Herald*, July 1922, 24; *It Can Be Done: An Autobiography* (New York: Rand School Press, 1938), 9–11.

16. Augustus Maverick, *Henry J. Raymond and the New York Press* (Hartford, CT: A. S. Hale; Chicago: Geo. W. Rogers, 1870), 330; "Matrimonial Advertisements," *Brooklyn Eagle*, Nov. 26, 1870, 1; *Luke Darrell*, 91.

17. Walter Blair, "Mark Twain, New York Correspondent," *American Literature* 11, no. 3 (Nov. 1939): 255–256; Minnie M. Brashear, *Mark Twain: Son of Missouri* (Chapel Hill: University of North Carolina Press, 1934), 109, 116; Mark Twain, *A Connecticut Yankee in King Arthur's Court* (1889; New York: Signet Classics, 1963), 186.

18. *Brooklyn Eagle*, June 18, 1867, 3, and July 11, 1867, 2; Quigley, "Journalism in New York," *Chicago Tribune*, Aug. 30, 1867, 2; "James Gordon Bennett," *Brooklyn Eagle*, Sept. 30, 1867, 4.

19. Quigley, "Journalism in New York," *Chicago Tribune*, Aug. 30, 1867, 2; Frank Luther Mott, *American Journalism: A History of Newspapers in the United States Through 250 Years, 1690 to 1940* (New York: Macmillan, 1947), 352–354; "How Bennett's Evening Paper, Was Started," *New York Tribune*, in *San Diego Sun*, May 27, 1885, 1; David, "Spice in Original Packages," *Hartford Courant*, Aug. 7, 1872, 1.

20. "Frohman Was a Newsie," *Washington Post*, May 14, 1915, 6; Isaac Marcosson and Daniel Frohman, *Charles Frohman: Manager and Man* (New York: Harper & Brothers, 1916), 18; "Brevities," *Atlanta Constitution*, Sept. 5, 1875, 4.

21. Alan J. Lee, *The Origins of the Popular Press, 1855–1914* (London: Croom Helm, 1976), 65; "Editorial and Other Items," *New Orleans Times-Picayune*, Oct. 14, 1866, 3; "Newspaporial," *Elevator* (San Francisco), Dec. 24, 1869, 2; "Major Jack Stratman," *American Newsman* 11, no. 11 (Nov. 1894): 39; "Uniforms for Newsboys," *Chicago Tribune*, Aug. 15, 1873, 2; *New York Daily Graphic*, Dec. 19, 1876, 2; "Les Griefs des Newsboys," *Courrier des Etats-Unis*, Jan. 29, 1880, 2.

22. *Brooklyn Eagle*, Aug. 29, 1868, 1; "Homes for the Peddling and Poorest Classes," *Boston Daily Advertiser*, May 22, 1866, 2; "Boot Blacks and Newsboys," *Boston Daily Evening Traveler*, Mar. 5, 1868, 2; Paul Ward, "Street Arabs," *Oliver Optic's Magazine* 18 (Dec. 1875): 949; *Hartford Courant*, Mar. 9, 1868, 2; *Boston Globe*, Apr. 22, 1873, 8; "The Newsboys," *Philadelphia Inquirer*, July 29, 1868, 8; "New Movement," *Philadelphia Public Ledger*, Nov. 6, 1865, 1; "The

'Press Gang,'" *Indianapolis Sentinel*, Nov. 16, 1873, 3; "Reporter Interviews Some Newsboys," *St. Louis Republican*, Nov. 5, 1873, 8; "The Buffalo Newsboys," *Buffalo Morning Express*, Nov. 7, 1868, 4; "Local Affairs," *Cheyenne Daily Leader*, Mar. 21, 1868, 4; "Over the Mountain," *San Francisco Bulletin*, July 19, 1870, 3.

23. *Laws and Ordinances Governing the City of Chicago, Jan. 1, 1866* (Chicago: E. B. Myers & Chandler, 1866), 289, 448; "The Newsboys' and Bootblacks' Sabbath-School," *Chicago Inter Ocean*, Mar. 21, 1867, 3; "The Bedouins of Our Streets," *Chicago Tribune*, Mar. 29, 1867, 4; *Baltimore Sun*, Jan. 2, 1867, 4; "Our Street Arabs," *Chicago Tribune*, Jan. 25, 1868, 4; "The Industries of the Street," *Hartford Courant*, Jan. 23, 1869, 1.

24. "The Common Council," *Chicago Tribune*, Apr. 26, 1870, 3; "The Chicago Newsboys," *Chicago Tribune*, Nov. 20, 1870, 2; *Brooklyn Eagle*, May 22, 1871, 2; *Harper's Bazar* 4, no. 23 (June 10, 1871): 363; "Bailiff, Newsie in 1870, to Yell 'Extry' Again," *Chicago Examiner*, Dec. 31, 1914, 5; "The Tax on Newsboys and Bootblacks," *Chicago Tribune*, Dec. 24, 1868, 3; "The Arab Concert," *Chicago Tribune*, Jan. 16, 1869, 4.

25. "Ere's Yer Paper-e-e!," *Chicago Sunday Times*, Aug. 29, 1875, 5.

26. Crapsey, "Nether Side of New York," 357, 359–360; Ben Cary, "Child-Life. Waifs of New York," *New York Evening Telegram*, Dec. 24, 1872, 5.

27. Francis A. Walker, *Remarks on the Statistics of Pauperism and Crime in the United States Census Office: Ninth Census, 1870* (Washington, DC: Government Printing Office, 1872), 1:565; Frederick H. Wines, *Report on the Defective, Dependent and Delinquent Classes of the United States as Returned at the Tenth Census, 1880* (Washington, DC: Government Printing Office, 1888), 28, 443, 465.

28. Walker, *Remarks*, 565; F. J. Ottarson, "New York and Its People," *Galaxy* 4 (1867): 61; An American Consul, "The New York Newsboy," *Leisure Hour*, Nov. 1, 1869, 717.

29. "Easy as Drinkin'," *New York Herald*, Jan. 22, 1888, 11; Herbert Asbury, *The Gangs of New York: An Informal History of the Underworld* (New York: Knopf, 1928), 238–239; Timothy J. Gilfoyle, *A Pickpocket's Tale: The Underworld of Nineteenth Century New York* (New York: W. W. Norton, 2006), 22.

30. Gilfoyle, *Picketpocket's Tale*, 22; C. L. B., "The School-Ship," *New York Times*, July 17, 1871, 4; "A Study in Crime—With a Moral," *New York Journal*, July 26, 1896, 18.

31. Emerson Ellick Sterns, "The Street-Venders of New York," *Scribner's Monthly* 1, no. 2 (Dec. 1870), 115; "All Sorts of Items," *San Francisco Bulletin*, May 7, 1870, 5; *Cincinnati Daily Star*, May 20, 1879, 3; "'Virginia in the Union!'" *Richmond Whig*, Jan. 25, 1870, 3; "The New South," *New York Tribune*, June 9, 1870, 2; "The Street Arabs of Charleston," *Charleston News and Courier*, June 9, 1874, 1.

32. August P. Trovaioli and Toledano B. Roulhac, *William Aiken Walker: Southern Genre Painter* (Baton Rouge: Louisiana State University Press, 1972), 7; Bruce W. Chambers, *Art and Artists of the South* (Columbia: University of South Carolina Press, 1984), 46–47; Cynthia Seibels, *The Sunny South: The Life and Art of William Aiken Walker* (Spartanburg, SC: Saraland Press, 1995), 10, 108. See also Timothy A. Eaton, *William Aiken Walker: In Florida* (West Palm Beach, FL: Eaton Fine Art, 2003).

33. Leon F. Litwack, *Been in the Storm So Long: The Aftermath of Slavery* (New York: Vintage, 1979), 29, 367; "Outrages in Missouri," *Memphis Avalanche*, Dec. 29, 1866, 2; "Communication," *New Orleans Tribune*, Apr. 28, 1867, 4; "The Case of Mayor Horton, of Mobile—The Biter Bitten," *Chicago Tribune*, Jan. 4, 1868, 1.

34. "Negro Equality in Kentucky," *Brooklyn Eagle*, May 13, 1871, 3; "A War of Races Among the Newsboys," *Minneapolis Tribune*, June 4, 1874, 6.

35. "General Notes," *New York Herald-Tribune*, Mar. 18, 1878, 4.

36. Lynda Roscoe Hartigan, *Sharing Traditions: Five Black Artists in Nineteenth Century America* (Washington, DC: Smithsonian Institution Press, 1985), 69–84; Roberta Smith, "A Forgotten Black Painter Is Saved from Obscurity," *New York Times*, June 12, 1992, C18.

37. *New Orleans Times*, Sept. 6, 1865, 4; Virginia Penny, *The Employments of Women: A Cyclopaedia of Woman's Work* (Boston: Walker, Wise, 1863), 421, 9–10, 290, 372, vii.

38. *The Revolution* 1, no. 5 (Feb. 5, 1868): 76; *Illinois State Journal*, Feb. 13, 1868, 2; Carol S. Lomicky, "Frontier Feminism and the Woman's Tribune: The Journalism of Clara Bewick Colby," *Journalism History* 28, no. 3 (Fall 2002): 107; "The Police Court," *Chicago Tribune*, Mar. 21, 1869, 3.

39. *Cincinnati Gazette*, Feb. 28, 1880, 8; *St. Louis Republic*, Dec. 25, 1894, 11; *Daily Illinois State Register*, Feb. 12, 1896, 5; Diane Winston, *Red Hot and Righteous: The Urban Religion of the Salvation Army* (Cambridge, MA: Harvard University Press, 1999), 78.

40. "Squatters in the Streets," *New York Tribune*, May 31, 1878, 3; *The People vs. John Butler, a Newsboy, et al.*, Court of Oyer and Terminer, First Dept. (New York: Martin B. Brown, 1878).

41. "Mrs. Tom-Ri-Jon," *National Police Gazette* 32, no. 39 (June 22, 1878): 5, 14.

42. "Squatters in the Streets," *New York Tribune*, May 31, 1878, 3; "'Kids,'" *Pomeroy's Democrat*, June 2, 1869, 3; "The Gamin World," *Pomeroy's Democrat*, July 28, 1869, 3; "Something New Under a Cincinnati Sun," *Cincinnati Enquirer*, Mar. 18, 1872, 8; "'Our Katie'—The Newsgirl," *Washington Critic-Record*, Mar. 20, 1874, 4; "New York News Girls," *New York Star*, in *Cleveland Leader*, May 29, 1871, 3. See also *Lowell Daily Citizen and News*, July 19, 1867, 1; "How Newspapers Are Made," *Scientific American* 19, no. 17 (Oct. 21, 1868): 258; "The News Girls," *St. Paul Daily Press*, Apr. 12, 1868, 2; and Nathan D. Urner, "News Children of New York," *Packard's Monthly* 3, no. 3 (Mar. 1870): 102–108.

43. John B. Gough, *Sunlight and Shadow: or, Gleanings from My Life Work* (Hartford, CT: A. D. Worthington, 1881), 68; *Detroit Free Press*, Nov. 17, 1874, 1, and Apr. 16, 1875, 1; Shanly, "Small Arabs of New York," 283; Sterns, "The Street-Venders of New York," *Scribner's Monthly* 1, no. 2 (Dec. 1870): 114.

44. George C. D. Odell, *Annals of the New York Stage* (New York: Columbia University Press, 1928–31), 8:641; Horatio Alger, *Tattered Tom; or, The Story of a Street Arab* (Boston: Loring, 1871); Michele Ann Abate, "Launching a Gender B(l)acklash: E. D. E. N. Southworth's *The Hidden Hand* and the Emergence of (Radicalized) White Tomboyism," *Children's Literature Association Quarterly* 31, no. 1 (Spring 2006): 40–64; Robert Jones, *The Hidden Hand. A Drama, in Five Acts*, ca. 1889; Mary Noel, *Villains Galore: The Heyday of the Popular Story Weekly* (New York: Macmillan, 1954), 289.

45. *Thirteenth Annual Report of the New York Society for the Prevention of Cruelty to Children* (1887), 31; Linda Gordon, *Heroes of Their Own Lives* (Harmondsworth, UK: Penguin 1988), 27; *Oxford English Dictionary*, 2nd ed.; "A Little Common Sense for the Society for the Prevention of Cruelty to Children," *Puck* 5, no. 113 (May 7, 1879): 144; "Taking Care of the Children," *New York Times*, Jan. 7, 1881, 3; Anthony Comstock, *Traps for the Young* (New York: Funk & Wagnalls, 1883), 19; "Flash Literature," *Chicago Tribune*, Nov. 8, 1884, 4; "Comstock in New Business," *New York Evening World*, Nov. 17, 1887, 1.

46. "The Baxter Street Varieties," *New York Herald*, Feb. 20, 1874, 5; *New York Daily Graphic*, Mar. 3, 1874, 3; *Indianapolis Sentinel*, May 10, 1874, 4; *Columbian* (CT) *Register*, Nov. 14, 1874, 1; *New York Daily Graphic*, Jan. 30, 1877, 7; R. D., "The Grand Duke's Opera House," *New York Spirit of the Times*, Mar. 31, 1877, 204–205; "The Visiting Governors," *New York Herald*, Sept. 6, 1877, 3; "An Old Times Theater," *Columbus* (GA) *Daily Enquirer*, Jan. 24, 1892, 10; Max R. Shohet, "A Duke Went Slumming," *New York Times*, Oct. 10, 1937, 2X. See also Tyler Anbinder, *Five Points: The 19th Century New York City Neighborhood That Invented Tap Dance, Stole Elections, and Became the World's Most Notorious Slum* (New York: Plume, 2001), 190–191, and Michelle Granshaw, "The Mysterious Victory of the Newsboys: The Grand Duke Theatre's 1874 Challenge to the Theatre Licensing Law," *Theatre Survey* 55, no. 1 (Jan. 2014): 48–80.

47. Oliver Dyer, "The New York Sun;—Its Rise, Progress, Character, and Condition," *American Agriculturalist*, Dec. 1869, 467.

48. Miss Jennie Collins, *Nature's Aristocracy; or, Battles and Wounds in Time of Peace—A Plea for the Oppressed* (Boston: Lee & Shepard, 1871), 61–63.

49. "Education for All," *New York Times*, Feb. 4, 1877, 6; "Truants," *New York Times*, Sept. 30, 1877, 6; "In the City Hall Tower," *New York Times*, Aug. 18, 1878, 2.

50. Owen Kildare, *My Mamie Rose: The Story of My Regeneration* (New York: Baker & Taylor, 1903), 47–48. Kildare's real name was Tom Carroll.

51. "Homes for the Peddling and Poorest Classes," *Boston Daily Advertiser*, May 22, 1866, 2; Kildare, *My Mamie Rose*, 47–48; "The Bowery Mourns for Owen Kildare," *New York Times*, Feb. 12, 1911, 16.

52. "Senator Lorimer: A Veritable 'Ragged Dick' Hero," *Current Literature* 49, no. 1 (July 1910): 33–34; Joel Tarr, *A Study in Boss Politics: William Lorimer of Chicago* (Urbana: University of Illinois Press, 1971).

53. Dyer, "The New York Sun," *American Agriculturalist*, Dec. 1869, 463–467.

54. "The Newsboy," *Hearth and Home* 4, no. 31 (Aug. 3, 1872): 605; "Senator Sullivan Makes Maiden Speech," *New York Times*, Oct. 16, 1902, 3. See also Daniel Czitrom, "Underworlds and Underdogs: Big Tim Sullivan and Metropolitan Politics in New York, 1889–1913," *Journal of American History* 78, no. 2 (Sept. 1991): 536–558.

55. "Patent Newspaper Folder," *Boston Evening Transcript*, May 30, 1861, 4; "Newspaper Folding Match," *American Newspaper Reporter* 5, no. 31 (July 31, 1871): 781; Lee, *Daily Newspaper in America*, 119.

56. "Scene at the Office of the *New York Daily News*," *Frank Leslie's Illustrated Newspaper*, Dec. 28, 1867, 233; "The Newsboys," *Brooklyn Eagle*, Dec. 5, 1868, 2.

57. "Sinclair Tousey's Feeling Relieved," *New York Times*, Nov. 20, 1878, 8; "Base-Ball," *Chicago Tribune*, Jan. 14, 1877, 2; "A Newsboys' Game," *Chicago Herald*, June 21, 1890, 9; "The Perilous Game 'of Cat.'" *National Police Gazette* 23, no. 1156 (Oct. 26, 1867), 1, 6; "All Fools' Day," *New York Herald*, Apr. 2, 1875, 10; *New York Times*, July 20, 1867, 4; Rebecca, *Tramps in New York* (New York: American Tract Society, ca. 1863), 42.

58. "A Mischievous Newsboy," *Brooklyn Eagle*, Dec. 2, 1863, 3; "Carriers," *Cincinnati Enquirer*, Sept. 27, 1874, 1.

59. Fred William Allsopp, *Twenty Years in a Newspaper Office* (Little Rock, AR: Central Printing, 1907), 70; "Reminiscences of Edward Speich," *Buffalo Times*, Mar. 1928, www.newspaperabstracts.com/link.php?id=2746; William Stanley Braithwaite, "The House Under Arcturus: An Autobiography," *Phylon* 2, no. 2 (1941): 127; "Billy, the Scrapper," *Philadelphia Record*, in *Kansas City Star*, Oct. 25, 1884, 5; Justin McCarthy, "Lady Judith: A Tale of Two Continents," *Galaxy* 11, no. 5 (May 1871), 633; Jacob Riis, *The Making of an American* (New York: Macmillan, 1901), 133.

60. "'The Sun,' New York," *Centennial Newspaper Exhibition* (New York: Rowell, 1876), 201; "A Tricky Newsboy," *New York Times*, Apr. 6, 1855, 8; *Brooklyn Eagle*, Nov. 11, 1867, 11; "The Newsboy," *Chicago Tribune*, Jan. 14, 1877, 8.

61. *Pomeroy's Democrat*, July 28, 1869, 5; "The Democrat Pony Express Wagons," *Frank Leslie's Illustrated Newspaper*, Apr. 16, 1870, 75.

62. Augustus Maverick, *Henry J. Raymond and the New York Press for Thirty Years* (Hartford, CT: A. S. Hale, 1870), 347–348; Junius Henri Browne, *The Great Metropolis. A Mirror of New York* (Hartford, NJ: American Publishing, 1869), 663–665; "Charles P. Sykes," *Phrenological Journal and Science of Health* 50, no. 5 (May 1870): 321; *New York Times*, Aug. 28, 1867, 4; "Excerpts from Samuel Gompers' Testimony Before the Education and Labor Committee of the US Senate, New York," Aug. 16, 1883, in *The Samuel Gompers Papers. The Making of a Union Leader, 1850–86*, ed. Stuart B. Kaufman (Urbana: University of Illinois Press, 1986), 1:308; "Witnesses Before the Senate Subcommittee," *New York Herald*, Aug. 17, 1883, 6.

63. "The New York Herald," *North American Review* 102, no. 211 (Apr. 1866): 377–378; Louis M. Lyons, *Newspaper Story: One Hundred Years of the Boston Globe* (Cambridge, MA: Harvard University Press, 1971), 97–98; Ralph Frasca, *The Rise and Fall of the Saturday Globe* (Selinsgrove, PA: Susquehanna University Press, 1992), 22.

64. Edward Winslow Martin, *The Secrets of the Great City* (Philadelphia: Jones, Brothers, 1868), 261–262; Jennie Brownscombe, "A City Railroad Car," *Harper's Bazar* 6, no. 19 (May 10, 1873): 1–2; "The Newsboy," *New York Daily Graphic*, Dec. 8, 1872, 5.

65. *Harper's Weekly* 11, no. 554 (Aug. 10, 1867): 510; "The Railroad Tragedy," *National Police Gazette* 23, no. 1144, Aug. 3, 1867, 3; *New York Times*, July 23, 1867, 7; "The Newsboy Tragedy," *New York Times*, July 28 and 29, 1867), 8; "News at Retail in the Streets," *New York Times*, July 30, 1867, 4.

66. *Brooklyn Eagle*, Nov. 9, 1869, 2; "From a Newsboy," *New York Times*, Feb. 28, 1874, 4.

67. "Newsboys' Troubles," *Cincinnati Enquirer*, Aug. 6, 1871, 4; "Let the Boys Alone," *Chicago Tribune*, June 28, 1876, 8.

68. "Wants a Rest," *New Orleans Times*, Dec. 21, 1877, 6.

69. "The Price of a Newsboy's Leg," *Chicago Tribune*, Dec. 19, 1888, 6; *Washington Post*, Mar. 25, 1883, 4.

70. Martin, *Secrets of the Great City*, 262; "The Newsboys of New-York," *New York Weekly Tribune*, Nov. 11, 1868, n.p.; A. P., "The Street-Arabs of New York," *Appleton's Journal* 9, no. 198 (Jan. 4, 1873), 48; Crapsey, "Nether Side of New York," 360; "Personal," *Cincinnati Enquirer*, Mar. 4, 1870, 2.

71. "The Buffalo Newsboys," *Buffalo Morning Express*, Nov. 7, 1868, 4; "The 'Press Gang,'" *Indianapolis Sentinel*, Nov. 16, 1873, 3; "What the Daily News Is Doing," *Chicago Daily News*, ca. Apr. 14, 1877, cited in Charles H. Dennis, *Victor Lawson: His Time and His Work* (1935; repr., New York: Greenwood, 1968), 39.

72. Melville Elijah Stone, *Fifty Years a Journalist* (Garden City, NY: Doubleday, 1921), 60; "Melville E. Stone Dies in 81st Year at His Home," *New York Times*, Feb. 16, 1929, 1, 7; Henry L. Smith, "Recalling Some Old Time Cleveland Newsboys," *Cleveland Plain Dealer*, July 1, 1934, 6; "A California Newsboy," *Deseret News*, Dec. 1, 1869, 9; "Pennies in the South," *Concordia Eagle*, Oct. 2, 1875, 1.

73. A. P., "The Street-Arabs of New York," *Appleton's Journal* 9, no. 198 (Jan. 4, 1873), 48–49; "How the Impeachment News Was Received," *Brooklyn Eagle*, May 18, 1868, 2; Walter Blair, "Mark Twain, New York Correspondent," *American Literature* 11, no. 3 (Nov. 1939): 255; Eugene H. Munday, *Proof Sheet* 5, no. 27 (Nov. 1871), 35; Richard Grant White, "Popular Pie," *Galaxy* 18, no. 4 (Oct. 1974), 536–537; "To the Newsboys," *Daily Critic*, Nov. 5, 1872, n.p.

74. "New York and Vicinity," *Independent*, Jan. 28, 1869, 4; "Advice from Horace Greeley," *New York Evangelist*, Mar. 11, 1869, 6; "Horace Greeley. The Closing Ceremonies," *New York Herald-Tribune*, Dec. 8, 1872, 1; "A Tribune Newsboy," *New-York Tribune*, May 30, 1886, 11.

75. Robert D. Armstrong, *Nevada Printing: A Bibliography of Imprints and Publications, 1858–1880* (Carson City: University of Nevada Press, 1981), 195; *Proof-Sheet* 6, no. 33 (Nov. 1872), 29; *Milwaukee Sentinel*, Aug. 6, 1870, 1.

76. "The Mississippi Race," *New York Times*, July 6, 1870, 5; *Brooklyn Daily Eagle*, Aug. 27, 1867, 2; Munday, "The Press of Philadelphia in 1870," *Proof-Sheet* 4, no. 20 (Sept. 1870), 23–24; *Philadelphia Patriot*, Aug. 25, 1876, 8, and Sept. 1, 1876, 8; *Charleston Daily News*, Aug. 27, 1869, 3.

77. Robert Neilson Stephens, *The Life and Adventures of Steve Brodie, B.J., of the Bowery, New York* (New York, 1897), 5–12; "Brodie's Leap," *St. Louis Globe-Democrat*, July 29, 1886, 3; "Steve Brodie Dead," *New York Times*, Feb. 1, 1901, 6; "Out Among the Newsboys," *New York Times*, Aug. 17, 1879, 5; Lyons, *Newspaper Story*, 25; "The Crusaders," *Forest and Stream* 12, no. 3 (Feb. 20, 1879), 58; *N Y Star Almanac for 1880* (New York: National Printing Co., 1879), 44.

78. "Chuck Connors Dies on Bowery," *New York Times*, May 11, 1913, 3; "Chuck Connors Is Buried," *New York Times*, May 14, 1913, 20; Art Young, *Art Young—His Life and Times* (New York: Sheridan House, 1939), 209–210; B. A. Botkin, ed., *Sidewalks of America: Folklore, Legends, Sagas, Traditions, Customs, Songs, Stories and Sayings of Cityfolk* (Indianapolis, IN: Bobbs-Merrill, 1954), 70–73; Luc Sante, *Low Life: Lures and Snares of Old New York* (New York: Farrar, Straus, Giroux, 1991), 125–127; "Out Among the Newsboys," *New York Times*, Aug. 17, 1879, 5; "Brodie's Leap," *St. Louis Globe-Democrat*, July 29, 1886, 3; Neal Gabler, *Winchell: Gossip, Power and the Culture of Celebrity* (New York: Knopf, 1994), 34.

79. "'Swipes, the Newsboy,' Released," *Brooklyn Eagle*, Jan. 25, 1888, 2; "A Monster Benefit," *Brooklyn Eagle*, Feb. 9, 1888, 2; "Swipes, the Newsboy, Defeated," *Brooklyn Eagle*, June 9, 1888, 6; "'Swipes' Again Beaten," *Brooklyn Eagle*, July 26, 1888, 1; "Devlin Put to Sleep," *Brooklyn Eagle*, Mar. 23, 1889, 6; "For the Johnstown Sufferers," *Brooklyn Eagle*, June 7, 1889, 1; "A Pugilistic Couple," *Utica Observer*, Feb. 19, 1892, n.p.; "Whipped by a Bantam," *Los Angeles Times*, Dec. 29, 1890, 4; "Coney Island Divertisement," *Brooklyn Eagle*, July 23, 1894, 5; "'Swipes, Newsboy,' Dead," *New York Times*, Jan. 28, 1926, 23; "And They Do Such Things in the Bowery," *Los Angeles Times*, Oct. 8, 1933, A2.

80. "Street Cries," *Round Table* 3, no. 39 (June 1866), 337; *Hartford Courant*, Aug. 20, 1869, 2; "Letter from Washington," *Baltimore Sun*, Oct. 26, 1870, 4; Grace Abbott, "Child Labor," *Proceedings*, National Conference on Social Work (Washington, DC: Government Printing Office, 1923), 109–110; Raymond G. Fuller, *Child Labor and the Constitution* (New York: Crowell, 1923), 236.

81. Martin, *Secrets of the Great City*, 261–262; T. De Witt Talmage, *T. De Witt Talmage As I Knew Him* (New York: E. P. Dutton, 1912), n.p., www.gutenberg.org/files/15693/15693-h/15693-h.htm.

82. "Philadelvings," *Punchinello* 1, no. 13 (June 25, 1870), 200; Munday, "The Press of Philadelphia in 1870," *Proof-Sheet* 4, no. 19 (July 1870), 6–7; *Proof-Sheet* 6, nos. 31–32 (July–Sept. 1872), 4; H. C. S., "Sketches of Philadelphia," *Lippincott's Magazine* 9 (May 1872), 507; William J. Thorn, with Mary Pat Pfeil, *Newspaper Circulation, Marketing the News* (New York: Longman, 1987), 46; "Broadway, New York," *Harper's Bazar* 6, no. 5 (Feb. 1, 1873): 74.

83. "The Northern Mind," *Vanity Fair*, June 21, 1862, 303; J. E. P Doyle, comp., *Plymouth Church and Its Pastors, or Henry Ward Beecher and His Accusers* (Hartford, CT: Park Publishing, 1874), 480; "New York," *Minneapolis Tribune*, June 25, 1873, 1; "Telegraph News," *Baltimore Sun*, July 28, 1874, 4; "Brevities," *Atlanta Constitution*, Sept. 17, 1874, 2; "Rev. Henry Ward Beecher Purchasing Extras from the Newsboys," *Frank Leslie's Illustrated Newspaper*, Aug. 8, 1874, n.p.

84. "A Newsboy Arrested for Trickery," *New York Times*, Mar. 30, 1877, 3; Pinto, "Newsaporial," *Hartford Courant*, May 9, 1868, 1; "Hartford and Vicinity," *Hartford Courant*, Feb. 16, 1869, 2; "False Alarms," *New York Times*, Apr. 5, 1872, 4; "Awful Calamity," *New York Herald*, Nov. 9, 1874, 3; "A Serious Joke," *Cleveland Leader*, Nov. 12, 1874, 4.

85. "Nebulae," *Galaxy* 21, no. 3 (Mar. 1876), 435–436; "Mail Day in the West," *All the Year Round* 6, no. 153 (Nov. 4, 1871), 539; "An Evening Paper," *San Francisco Daily Evening Bulletin*, June 10, 1870, n.p.

86. Rodman Gilder, *The Battery* (Boston: Houghton Mifflin, 1936), 210. One hero of the day was 12-year-old newsboy James Connors, who dove in "like a water rat" to rescue more than ten people. "One of the Boys," *Watertown Times*, Aug. 4, 1871, 4.

87. "A Friend of the Newsboys," *Chicago Tribune*, Nov. 13, 1871, 6.

88. Alfred L. Sewell, *"The Great Calamity!": Scenes, Incidents, and Lessons of the Great Chicago Fire of the 8th and 9th of October 1871* (Chicago: Alfred L. Sewell, 1871), 56–57; "No Extortion," *Chicago Tribune*, Oct. 13, 1871, 2; "A Little History," *Skandinaven*, May 6, 1899; "Tells of Days When He Was Young, 90 Years Ago," *Chicago Tribune*, Aug. 6, 1924, 19; John F. Cowan, *Will Waffles; or, The Freaks and Fortunes of a Newsboy*, Ornum & Co.'s Fifteen Cent Romances, no. 2 (New York: American News Company, 1871).

89. Carl Smith, *Urban Disorder and the Shape of Belief: The Great Chicago Fire, the Haymarket Bomb, and the Model Town of Pullman* (Chicago: University of Chicago Press, 1995), 22; "The Chicago Fire," *Cincinnati Gazette*, Oct. 12, 1871, 4; John J. Pauly, "The Great Chicago Fire as a National Event," *American Quarterly* 36, no. 5 (Winter 1984): 668–683; *Brooklyn Eagle*, Oct. 17, 1871, 8; Edgar Johnson Goodspeed, *History of the Great Fires in Chicago and the West* (New York: H. S. Goodspeed, 1871), 440–443; "Chicago Newsboys in New York," *Chicago Tribune*, Oct. 25, 1871, 1.

90. Goodspeed, *History of the Great Fires*, 440–443; "Chicago Newsboys in New York," *Chicago Tribune*, Oct. 25, 1871, 1.

91. Michael B. Katz, *In the Shadow of the Poorhouse: A Social History of Welfare in America* (New York: Basic Books, 1986), 107; Charles Loring Brace, *The Dangerous Classes of New York and Twenty Years' Work Among Them* (New York: Wynkook & Hallenbeck, 1872), 105, 107; "The New York Newsboys," *Hartford Courant*, Apr. 16, 1868, 1.

92. "A Newsboys' Lodging House," *New York Tribune*, Apr. 11, 1880, 2; "In General," *Atlanta Constitution*, Sept. 2, 1880, 2; "Newsboys' Lodging House, Eighth Street and Avenue B, New York," *Harper's Weekly* 30, no. 1524 (Mar. 6, 1886): 156; "Newsboys' Lodging House," *Washington Post*, Jan. 16, 1889, 1.

93. Brace, *Dangerous Classes*, 282; Charles Loring Brace, "Wolf-Reared Children," *St. Nicholas* 9, no. 36 (May 1882): 553; Charles Loring Brace, "The Poor Boy's 'Astor House,'" *St. Nicholas* 3, no. 25 (Apr. 1876), 360. For a critical assessment of Brace's writings, see Kenneth B. Kidd, *Making American Boys: Boyology and the Feral Tale* (Minneapolis: University of Minnesota Press, 2004), 93–99.

94. Paul J. Ramsey, "Wrestling with Modernity: Philanthropy and the Children's Aid Society in Progressive-Era New York City," *New York History* 88, no. 2 (Spring 2007): 166; David Dudley

Field, "The Child and the State," *Forum* 1, Apr., 1886, 8; Horatio Alger Jr., "The Newsboys' Lodging-House," *Liberal Christian*, Apr. 20, 1867, 6, in *Newsboy* 20, no. 5 (Dec. 1981), 9–10.

95. Brace, *Dangerous Classes*, 88, 455–457; Catherine J. Ross, "Society's Children: The Care of Indigent Youngsters in New York City, 1875–1903," PhD diss., Yale University, 1977, 124–125; Theodore Roosevelt, *An Autobiography* (New York: Macmillan, 1913), 13; Joseph Lash, *Eleanor and Franklin* (New York: Norton, 1971), 30; David McCullough, *Mornings on Horseback* (New York: Simon & Schuster, 1981), 28–30, 102, 183, 232; "Theodore Roosevelt," *Dictionary of American Biography / under the auspices of the American Council of Learned Societies* (New York: Scribner, 1928–1936 16:135–136; Ray Stannard Baker, "Theodore Roosevelt: A Character Sketch," *McClure's Magazine* 12, no. 1 (Nov. 1898), 23.

96. "The Newsboys," *Chicago Tribune*, Feb. 7, 1865, 4.

97. "Brooklyn. The Newsboys' Lodging House," *New York Tribune*, Nov. 29, 1866, 8; "The News Boys' Home," *Detroit Advertiser-Tribune*, Aug. 23, 1866, 3; George E. Stevens, *The City of Cincinnati* (Cincinnati: Geo. S. Blanchard, 1869), 125, 128.

98. "The Boys' Home of Baltimore," *Baltimore Sun*, Feb. 27, 1867, 1.

99. *Boston Herald*, June 9, 1868, 4.

100. *New Orleans Picayune*, Sept. 12, 1874; *New Orleans Times*, July 31, 1878, 3; *New Orleans Picayune*, Dec. 26, 1883; *New Orleans States*, Nov. 8, 1885.

101. C. S. Clark, *Of Toronto the Good: The Queen City of Canada as It Is* (Montreal: Toronto Publishing, 1898), 81–85; "The Courts," *Missouri Democrat*, Jan. 12, 1870, 4. See also William Greenleaf Eliot, "Newsboys Home Lecture," Jan. 29, 1871, Eliot Papers, A0444, Missouri Historical Society and Research Center.

102. "Newsboys and Bootblacks of Louisville," *Louisville Commerce*, May 19, 1872, 4.

103. Newsboys and Bootblacks Home Association, *Constitution, By-laws, and Annual Report* (Cleveland: Leader Printing, 1880).

104. Genevieve C. Weeks, "Oscar C. McCulloch: Leader in Organized Charity," *Social Service Review* 39, no. 2 (June 1965): 217.

105. Dorothy Hutchison, "History of Colorado's Private Child Placing Agencies," MA thesis, University of Denver, 1944, Appendix A, "The Newsboys and Bootblacks Home," in Colorado Historical Society.

106. George Thornton Fleming, *History of Pittsburgh* (New York: American Historical Society, 1922), 3:573–574; *Proceedings at the Opening of the Newsboys and Bootblacks Home, 29 Franklin St., Buffalo, NY* (Buffalo: Press of the Courier Company, 1885).

107. "Running Over with Schemes," *Chicago Tribune*, Jan. 24, 1886, 18; *Second Annual Report of the Newsboys' Home Association of St. Paul* (St. Paul, MN: The Association, 1888).

108. "Newsboys Home Association," *Duluth Weekly Tribune*, Feb. 18, 1887, 4.

109. *Hartford Weekly Times*, Jan. 19, 1888, 4.

110. "Newsboys' Home," *Los Angeles Times*, Dec. 1, 8, 1890, 3.

111. "Local Chronology," *Salt Lake Tribune*, Jan. 1, 1897, 2.

112. "Newsboys and Bootblacks' Home," *Anaconda Standard*, Feb. 28, 1899, 7; "Will Ask Contributions," *Anaconda Standard*, Jan. 23, 1900, 5.

113. "Newboys' Home Opens with Amusement Galore," *Omaha World-Herald*, Dec. 21, 1902, 11.

114. Kate Sayen Kirkland, *The Hogg Family and Houston: Philanthropy and the Civic Ideal* (Houston: University of Texas, 2009), 89–90.

115. J. Thomas Scharf and Thompson Westcott, *History of Philadelphia, 1609–1884* (Philadelphia: L. H. Everts, 1884), 1456–1457, 1478, 1702; "A Friend of the Boys," *St. Paul Daily Globe* (Dec. 5, 1886), 10.

116. Department of Commerce, Bureau of the Census, *Benevolent Institutions*, 1910 (Washington, DC: Government Printing Office, 1913), esp. 158–173, cited in LeRoy Ashby, *Saving the Waifs: Reformers and Dependent Children, 1890–1917* (Philadelphia: Temple University Press, 1984), 13–14, 226.

117. "Newsboys Lodging House—A 'Home for the Homeless,'" *Brooklyn Eagle*, Sept. 3, 1866, 4; "Brooklyn. The Newsboys' Lodging House," *New York Tribune*, Nov. 29, 1866, 8. "Aristocratic Newsboys," *Minneapolis Tribune*, Mar. 24, 1869, 1.

118. "A Complaint Against the Newsboys' Lodge," *Brooklyn Eagle*, Oct. 22, 1866, 2; "The Newsboys and Their Friends," *Brooklyn Eagle*, Oct. 23, 1866, 2.

119. *Springfield Republican*, Dec. 20, 1872, 6; "Conflicting Accounts," *Chicago Tribune*, July 20, 1876, 8; "A Newsboy's Gore," *Chicago Inter Ocean*, Oct. 30, 1877, 8.

120. "Mornin' Paper, Sir?," *Chicago Inter Ocean*, Dec. 26, 1878, 8; "Rule of the Rod," *Chicago Tribune*, Mar. 18, 1881, 8; "Newsboys' Home," *Chicago Tribune*, Mar. 24, 1881, 8.

121. "Child-Beating," *Chicago Tribune*, July 11, 1880, 6; Frances E. Willard and Mary A. Livermore, eds., *A Woman of the Century* (Buffalo: Charles Wells Moulton, 1893), 119.

122. Jay P. Dolan, *The Immigrant Church: New York's Irish and German Catholics, 1815–1865* (Baltimore: Johns Hopkins University Press, 1975), 137–138; *Fr. John C. Drumgoole: Mount Loretto* (New York: St. Anthony's Guild, 1981), 13–15; Brace, *Dangerous Classes*, 265, 425; "A New Charity in Behalf of the Newsboys," *New York Tribune*, Sept. 5, 1870, 8; "New York Charity," *Springfield Republican*, Apr. 9, 1874, 3. See also Catherine Burton, *Children's Shepard: The Story of John Christopher Drumgoole, Father of the Homeless and Founder of the Mission of the Immaculate Virgin* (New York: P. J. Kennedy & Sons, 1954); George Paul Jacoby, *Catholic Child Care in Nineteenth Century New York* (Washington, DC: Catholic University of America, 1941), 158–175; and Marguerite Elizabeth Mahoney, "A History of the Mission of the Immaculate Virgin, Staten Island: 1870–1945," MS thesis, Fordham University School of Social Service, 1945.

123. "Thanksgiving in Earnest," *New York Sun*, Nov. 28, 1873, 1.

124. "A Check to Church Lotteries," *New York Times*, Dec. 1, 1875, 1; Jacoby, *Catholic Child Care in Nineteenth Century New York*, 162–163.

125. "A Ceremony Postponed," *New York Times*, Dec. 15, 1879, 8; "The Care of Dependent Children," Jan. 16, 1887, 6; *Father Drumgoole*, Mission of the Immaculate Virgin for the Protection of Homeless and Destitute Children circular, Mar. 1, 1885.

126. A. R. C. Grant, with Caroline Combe, eds., *Rosebery's North American Journal—1873* (London: Sidgwick & Jackson, 1967), 87, 145; William P. Letchworth, *Homes of Homeless Children: A Report on the Orphan Asylum and Other Institutions for the Care of Children*, Annual Report, New York State Board of Charities, 1876 (New York: Ayer, 1974), 24; "Earl of Rosebery and the Newsboys," *New York Times*, Apr. 8, 1894, 21.

127. *Eighth Annual Report of the Children's Aid Society* (1861), cited in Robert H. Bremner, *The Public Good: Philanthropy and Welfare in the Civil War Era* (New York: Knopf, 1980), 21–22; "Cincinnati's Big-Hearted Newsboys," *Memphis Daily Appeal*, Sept. 26, 1878, 1; *New York Evening Post*, Aug. 23, 1875, 4.

128. "Newsboys' Strike," *Cincinnati Enquirer*, May 2, 1871, 4; "Newsboys' and Bootblacks' Picnic," *Cincinnati Times*, Sept. 5, 1872, 1; "The Arabs," *Cincinnati Enquirer*, Sept. 9, 1872, 8; "The Newsboys Want Col. Moore for Mayor," *Cincinnati Gazette*, Apr. 2, 1877, 3; "Death of R. M. Moore," *Cincinnati Gazette*, Feb. 24, 1880, 6; *Chicago Inter Ocean*, Mar. 20, 1874, 4; "The Newsboys' Reception," *Tiffin Tribune*, Apr. 9, 1877, 1.

129. *New York Commercial Advertiser*, Mar. 10, 1875, 1.

130. "Ere's Yer Paper-e-e!," *Chicago Sunday Times*, Aug. 29, 1875, 5.

131. "St. Louis Newsboys," *Chicago Tribune*, Aug. 11, 1876, 5; *Brooklyn Eagle*, Aug. 18, 1876, 2; *Cincinnati Gazette*, Aug. 11, 1876, 1; "Newsboys on the War Path," *Boston Globe*, Aug. 15, 1875, 2; *Boston Globe*, Aug. 18, 1876, 1; *Cincinnati Enquirer*, Aug. 13, 1876, 4; "The Newsboys and the Strike," *St. Louis Globe-Democrat*, Aug. 19, 1876, 8.

132. *Memphis Public Ledger*, Nov. 8, 1875, 3; "The Shine 'Em-Ups," *Augusta Chronicle*, Aug. 17, 1876, 1.

133. "Chicago. The Strike," *Cleveland Plain Dealer*, Feb. 8, 1877, 1; *Chicago Tribune*, Feb. 14, 1877, 4; *Lowell Citizen and News*, May 16, 1871, 2; "False Weights in Luxuries," *Chicago Tribune*, Sept. 12, 1905, 8.

134. "Failure of a Newsboys' Strike," *New Orleans Times-Picayune*, Aug. 4, 1877, 7; James E. Scripps, Diary, July 20–21, 23–24, 1877, 112–115, Scripps Papers, box 1, Bentley Historical Library, University of Michigan; *Brooklyn Eagle*, July 24, 1877, 2.

135. "The Situation at St. Louis on Monday," *New Orleans Picayune*, July 27, 1877, 2; *Stark County Democrat*, July 26, 1877, 5.

136. Smythe, *Gilded Age Press*, 78–79; Charles King, "After Chief Joseph," *Cleveland Leader*, Apr. 21, 1889, 14; Bessie Louise Pierce, *A History of Chicago: The Rise of a Modern City, 1871–1893* (Chicago: University of Chicago Press, 1957), 3:251; "Maryland. The Dead and

Wounded," *Chicago Tribune*, July 22, 1877, 2; "Civil War," *Chicago Tribune*, July 23, 1877, 5; "The Labor Revolt," *Huntingdon Journal*, July 27, 1877, 2; Robert V. Bruce, *1877: Year of Violence* (Indianapolis, IN: Bobbs-Merrill, 1959), 108; "Funerals of Victims of the Riot," *Baltimore Sun*, July 23, 1877, 4.

137. "Our Vagrants," *Minneapolis Tribune*, Nov. 19, 1874, 2.

138. "Newsboys to Be Extinguished," *Boston Herald*, Mar. 14, 1855, 2; "Newsboy Regulation," *Boston Evening Transcript*, Apr. 30, 1855, 1; "Licensing the Newsboys of Boston," *New York Evening Post*, May 4, 1855, 1.

139. "Samuel Eliot Fraser's Report on the Common-School System," *North American Review* 106, no. 218 (Jan. 1868), 145; "Items," *Minneapolis Tribune*, May 4, 1870, 2; "The Street Trades of Children," *Cincinnati Commercial Tribune*, Mar. 29, 1873, 6; Ward, "Street Arabs," 949; Emma Brown, *Child Toilers of Boston Streets* (Boston: D. Lothrop, 1879), 20–23; *The Boston Directory* (Boston: Sampson & Murdock, 1870, 1872, 1875), n.p.; "Reading," *Massachusetts Teacher and Journal of Home and School Education* 22, no. 5 (May 1869), 171; "Our Evening Schools," *Boston Globe*, Dec. 2, 1872, 8.

140. "The Newsboys' Estimate of the Board of Aldermen," *Cincinnati Gazette*, Feb. 18, 1873, 5; "The Newsboys' Protest," *Cincinnati Times*, Feb. 18, 1873, 1; "Newsboys' Union," *Cincinnati Times*, May 22, 1873, 4; "N.B.U.," *Cincinnati Commercial Tribune*, July 11, 1873, 2; "Our Progressive Newsboys," *Cincinnati Gazette*, Dec. 16, 1873, 4; "The Newsboys' Picnic," *Cincinnati Gazette*, Aug. 25, 1882, 3.

141. "The Sanitary Police," *Detroit Advertiser and Tribune*, Apr. 13, 1876, n.p.; "A Newsboys' Riot," *Detroit Evening News*, July 21, 1877, 4; Silas Farmer, *The History of Detroit and Michigan* (Detroit: Silas Farmer, 1889), 693; "Detroit Newsboys," *Youth's Companion* 58, no. 1 (Jan. 1, 1885), 6; *Sprague's Visitors Guide and Dictionary of Detroit and Vicinity* (Detroit: Author, 1883), 48; Herschel H. Jones, "Unregulated Street Trading in a Typical City," NCLC Pamphlet No. 264 (July 1916), 4; *Muskegon Chronicle*, Jan. 4, 1878, 3; *Cincinnati Gazette*, Oct. 7, 1878, 3.

142. *North American*, Nov. 18, 1879, 1; *Stark Democrat*, Nov. 20, 1879, 1.

143. "Striking Newsboys," *Missouri Republican*, May 24, 1879, 4.

144. "The Tattoo Artists," *St. Louis Post-Dispatch*, in *Washington Post*, Apr. 15, 1883, 2; Julian S. Rammelkamp, *Pulitzer's Post-Dispatch, 1878–1883* (Princeton, NJ: Princeton University Press, 1967), 59–60, 111; "The Newsboys' Strike," *St. Louis Post-Dispatch*, Aug. 3, 1880, 5; *St. Louis Post-Dispatch*, Aug. 4, 1880, 4.

145. Lee, *Daily Newspaper in America*, 735; *Milwaukee Sentinel*, Feb. 22, 1880, 8; "City Hall Affairs," *Cleveland Leader*, Apr. 8, 1880, 5; "A Season of Strikes," *Washington Post*, Apr. 26, 1881, 4; "A Business Matter" and "Bloody Instructions," *Cleveland Leader*, May 2, 1881, 2.

146. "'Dutch Hiney's Funeral," *St. Louis Post-Dispatch*, May 3, 1886, 7; Vincent DiGirolamo, "Newsboy Funerals: Tales of Sorrow and Solidarity in Urban America," *Journal of Social History* 36, no. 1 (Fall 2002), 5–30.

Chapter 6

1. "Newspapers," *Eight Years' Progress of the United States* (Hartford, CT: L. Stebbins, 1867), 304; Howard Barger, *Distribution's Place in the American Economy Since 1869* (Princeton, NJ: Princeton University Press, 1955), 142.

2. "Distribution of Current Literature," *Current Literature* 1, no. 4 (Oct. 1888): 284; Sigmund Diamond, *The Nation Transformed: The Creation of an Industrial Society* (New York: George Braziller, 1963), 7; "Then and Now, Newspaper Distributing in Detroit in the '50s," n.p., May 26, 1896, Friend Palmer Scrapbook 13, 70, Burton Historical Collection, Detroit Public Library.

3. "On the Fast News Train," *Lancaster Daily Intelligencer*, Nov. 1, 1881, 2; "The Herald Express," *New York Herald*, July 3, 1877, 4; "Tribune Expresses," *New York Tribune*, Aug. 13, 1883, 5; "Lightning Journalism," *New York Herald*, Dec. 7, 1886, 5; "Sunday Morning Paper Trains," *New York Herald*, June 11, 1893, 28.

4. "A Fast Newspaper Train," *New York Herald*, June 18, 1877, 5; "The Fast Sunday Train," *Brooklyn Eagle*, June 22, 1877, 4; "The Sunday Newspaper Train on Long Island," *Frank*

Leslie's Illustrated Newspaper, Aug. 4, 1877, 376; "Rapid Newspapers," *Brooklyn Eagle*, July 8, 1878, 3; *Dallas Morning News*, Oct. 19, 1912, 14; "Faithful Canine Paper-Carriers," *New Haven Morning News*, in *Kansas City Times*, Jan. 25, 1885, 8; "Dogs as Newspaper Carriers," *American Naturalist* 19, no. 2 (Feb. 1885): 204–205.

5. "Sunday Suns at Lake George," *New York Sun*, Aug. 2, 1886, 3; "The Sunday Herald," *New York Herald*, Aug. 18, 1884, 5.

6. "One Hundred Boys Wanted," *Atlanta Constitution*, Nov. 28, 1876, 2; "Grand Success," *St. Louis Republic*, May 4, 1890, n.p.; "The Age-Herald Always First," *Birmingham Age-Herald*, May 2, 1899, 1.

7. "Mr. Morris' Silver Jubilee," *Brooklyn Eagle*, Dec. 22, 1895, 12; Robert H. Wiebe, *The Search for Order, 1877–1920* (New York: Hill & Wang, 1967), xiii.

8. "Affairs of the City," *San Diego Union*, May 18, 1899, 3; "On the Road," *Chicago Tribune*, Sept. 6, 1874, 2; George J. Manson, "Modern Travel," *Christian Union* 45, no. 23 (June 4, 1892): 1080.

9. Raymond Sinclair, "How News Butchers Make Money," *Chicago Tribune*, Aug. 11, 1912, E2; "Tricks of the News Butcher," *St. Louis Republican*, in *Washington Post*, Aug. 29, 1909, M1; "Smart Old Stagers," *New York Herald*, Mar. 10, 1889, 9; "A Newsboy at Eighty-Two," *New York Times*, Apr. 30, 1890, 3; "Youngest Railway Newsboy," *New York Times*, June 24, 1901, 7.

10. "Men Who Have Seen Better Days," *St. Louis Republic*, Feb. 16, 1896, 22; "Clothed as a Boy, Girl Won a Husband," *Atlanta Constitution* Nov. 3, 1910, 11; Leo L. Stanley, interview with Carla Ehat and Anne T. Kent, Aug. 7, 1974, Oral History Project of the Marin County Free Library.

11. "Death of Patrick Farrelly," *New York Times*, Apr. 24, 1904, 7; "Death of Patrick Farrelly," *Book and News-Dealer* 15, no. 174 (May 1904): 42; G. R. Clarke, "Rich Men Had No Childhood," *Chicago Tribune*, May 27, 1906, E3; "Hugh Joseph Chisholm," *American National Biography*, accessed Oct. 11, 2001, www.anb.org/articles/10/10-00280.html; Horatio Alger, *The Erie Train Boy* (New York: US Book, 1890), 13, 201.

12. Stewart H. Holbrook, *The Story of American Railroads* (New York: Crown, 1947), 402.

13. Charles P. Brown, *Brownie the Boomer: The Life of Charles P. Brown, an American Railroader*, ed. H. Roger Grant (DeKalb: Northern Illinois University Press, 1991), 14–15; *Cigar Makers Official Journal* 24, no. 7 (Apr. 1899): 5; 24, no. 9 (June 1899): 7.

14. R. R. Burke, *"Keep the Change": A Sketch of the Life of a News Agent with Details of Many Experiences On and Off the Cars* (Pittsburgh: Commercial Printing and Publishing, 1895), 169; "How to Make Good Peddler," *San Francisco Chronicle*, Dec. 10, 1905, 38; "A Defaulting Newsboy," *Chicago Tribune*, June 24, 1867, 4; "On the Road," *Chicago Tribune*, Sept. 6, 1874, 2; "No Money Working as Newsbutcher," *Atlanta Constitution*, Dec. 1, 1902, 5; "News Butcher in the Toils," *Atlanta Constitution*, Apr. 15, 1901, 5.

15. "Newsboys on Railroad Trains," *Harrisburg Patriot*, Dec. 4, 1873, 1; Ralph B. Mayo, "News Butchers on Western Railroads," *1949 Brand Book* (Denver: Denver Posse Brand, 1949), 218–219.

16. "Passing of the Train Peddler," *People*, Dec. 21, 1900, 2; *Boston Journal*, Mar. 2, 1874, 4; *Jersey City Evening Journal*, Mar. 4, 1874, 4; "Gompers's Appeal," *Boston Journal*, July 23, 1894, 2; "Third Day of the Big Strike," *Watertown Times*, Aug. 11, 1890, 1.

17. Bob Thomas, *Walt Disney: An American Original* (New York: Simon & Schuster, 1976), 40–41.

18. Burke, *"Keep the Change,"* 70–74, 114; Holbrook, *Story of American Railroads*, 408; Michael O'Malley, *Keeping Watch: A History of American Time* (Washington, DC: Smithsonian Institution Press, 1990), 175–183; "A Glimpse of Mormonism," *Appleton's Journal* 6, no. 125 (Aug. 19, 1871): 214; "Travelling, Then and Now," *True Flag* 4 (Sept. 22, 1855): 3; "Full and Running Over," *Springfield Republican*, Aug. 8, 1885, 4.

19. Rommert J. Casimir, "Strategies for a Blind Newsboy," *Omega* 27 (1999): 133; George Parsons Lathrop, "Talks with Edison," *Harper's New Monthly* 80, no. 477 (Feb. 1890): 428.

20. Lathrop, "Talks with Edison," 427, 429; Holbrook, *Story of American Railroads*, 401; Matthew Josephson, *Edison: A Biography* (New York: McGraw Hill, 1959), 28.

21. John A. Lent, "News Butches, Presses on Wheels, and Reading Travelers," *Antiques & Collecting Hobbies* 93 (May 1988): 56–57, 77–78.

22. Holbrook, *Story of American Railroads*, 400; "A Fly Newsboy," *Utica Observer*, in *Galveston Daily News*, June 4, 1885, 6; "Pretty Girl Elopes with Railroad Newsboy," *St. Paul Globe*, Mar. 8, 1903, 1; Maude Anita Hart, *The Newsboys Sweetheart* (Chicago: McKinley Music, 1905).

23. "Why Newsboys Must Go," *Scranton Tribune*, Aug. 27, 1900, 8; Holbrook, *Story of American Railroads*, 400, 411.

24. Holbrook, *Story of American Railroads*, 406–407.

25. Kevin J. Hayes, "Railway Reading," *Proceedings of the American Antiquarian Society* 106, pt. 2 (1997): 301–326; Manson, "Modern Travel," 1080.

26. Frank Weitenkampf, "Social History of the United States in Caricature," unpublished type-script, New York, 1954, 44–45, AAS; Jeter Allen Isley, *Horace Greeley and the Republican Party, 1853–1861* (Princeton, NJ: Princeton University Press, 1947), 124; Colonel Nicholas Smith, *Grant, the Man of Mystery* (Milwaukee: Young Churchman, 1909), 348.

27. "Newsboys Who Have Risen," *Boston Herald*, Sept. 24, 1893, 30; *George Snyder vs. Charles C. Fulton and Albert K. Fulton*, Court of Appeals of Maryland, 34 Md. 128; 1871 Md. Lexis 43, Feb. 21, 1871; "Suppressing Papers on Railroads," *New York Times*, Aug. 5, 1872, 4; *St. Louis Globe-Democrat*, Dec. 11, 1876, 4; "A News Boys' 'Combine,'" *Omaha Bee*, Oct. 19, 1889, 4.

28. Tom L. Johnson, *My Story*, ed. Elizabeth J. Hauser (New York: Huebsch, 1911), 49; Lawrence Goodwyn, *The Populist Revolt: A Short History of the Agrarian Revolt in America* (New York: Oxford University Press, 1978), 246; "Better Mouse Trap?," *Cleveland Plain Dealer*, Jan. 23, 1950, 6; W. H. Harvey, *Coin's Financial School Up to Date* (Chicago: Coin Publishing, 1895), 67.

29. "Union News Scheme," *Chicago Tribune*, Sept. 15, 1894, 8; "The American News Company and the News Business," *Newsdealer* 1, no. 5 (July 1890): 114; "American Silver," *Minneapolis Journal*, Aug. 12, 1896, 1.

30. Ida B. Wells-Barnett, "Lynch Law in All Its Phases," *New York Age*, June 25, 1892, n.p.; Arna Botemps and Jack Conroy, *They Seek a City* (New York: Doubleday, 1945), 77.

31. John W. Moore, comp., *Moore's Historical, Biographical, and Miscellaneous Gatherings* (Concord, NH: Republican Press Assoc., 1886), 138–138; Charles Lyell, *A Second Visit to the United States of North America* (New York: Harper, 1850), 2:41; Josephson, *Edison*, 27; Holbrook, *Story of American Railroads*, 402–404.

32. Frank P. Donovan Jr., "Passenger Trains of Yesteryear on the Minneapolis and St. Louis," *Minnesota History* 30 (Sept. 1949): 238; Manson, "Modern Travel," 1080; *State v. Charles Crawford*, Nos. 14,414-(26), Supreme Court of Minnesota, 95 Minn. 467; 104 N.W. 295; 1905 Minn. Lexis 717, July 14, 1905, Decided; Henry Collins Brown, ed., *Valentine's Manual of Old New York, 1926* (New York: Chauncey Holt, 1925), 164; "Popular Currency," *Gallipolis* (OH) *Journal*, Dec. 23, 1876, 1.

33. Burke, *"Keep the Change,"* 58; "Extensive Railway Robberies," *New York Tribune*, Jan. 25, 1866, 11; "Another Train Robbery," *Winona Daily Republican*, Sept. 8, 1881, 2; "Daring Train Robbers," *Winona Daily Republican*, May 18, 1887, 1; "The Express Messenger Attacked," *Los Angeles Times*, June 19, 1887, 5; John F. Stover, *American Railroads* (Chicago: University of Chicago Press, 1960), 170; William Drysdale, *The Fast Mail: The Story of a Train Boy* (Boston: W. A. Wilde), 1896.

34. Theodore Roosevelt, *An Autobiography* (New York: Charles Scribner's Sons, 1913), 116; "Murdered for an Orange," *Tacoma Daily News*, Dec. 29, 1890, 1; "May Be Murder," *Wheeling Register*, Nov. 30, 1893, 3; "Butchering a 'Butcher,'" *State* (Columbia, SC), Sept. 28, 1894, 2; "What Southern Railroad Should Furnish Race," *Chicago Defender*, May 23, 1914, 1.

35. "A Disgusting Outrage," *State* (Columbia, SC), Sept. 12, 1892, 8; "A Riot of Roughs Over Five Cents," *Charleston News and Courier*, Sept. 12, 1892, 2; "Counterfeit Coin," *Birmingham Age-Herald*, Jan. 15, 1899, 5; *Ben Lane v. State*. No. 2138. Court of Criminal Appeals of Texas. 69 Tex. Crim. 65; 152 S.W. 897; 1913 Tex. Crim. App. Lexis 43. Jan. 8, 1913, Decided.

36. "Modern 'News Butcher' Discards the Old Name and Old Method," *Duluth News-Tribune*, Oct. 2, 1921, 1; Holbrook, *Story of American Railroads*, 407.

37. "How to Make Good Peddlers," *San Francisco Chronicle*, Dec. 10, 1905, 38; "Railroad Miseries," *Round Table* 4, no. 56, Sept. 29, 1866: 132–133; "The Cute Railroad Newsboy," *Winona Daily*

Republican, Dec. 13, 1893, 6; Frank L. Packard, *The Night Operator* (New York: George H. Doran, 1919), 2; Emily Huntington Miller, "Along the Road, No. 1," *Ladies' Repository* 27, no. 6 (June 1867): 342; *New York Sun*, Feb. 22, 1891, 24.

38. Walter Thornbury, "American Sleeping Cars," *All the Year* Round 90 (Jan. 12, 1861): 329; Thomas Nast, "A Patient Railroad Traveler," *Harper's Weekly* 18, no. 898 (Mar. 14, 1874): 244; Weitenkampf, "Social History of the United States in Caricature," 44–45.

39. "Restricting the Privileges of Newsboys," *Baltimore Sun*, Oct. 21, 1875, 4; "The Train Boy Nuisance," *Railroad Gazette*, Nov. 1, 1873, 441, cited in Sarah H. Gordon, *Passage to Union: How the Railroads Transformed American Life, 1829–1929* (Chicago: Ivan R. Dee, 1996), 257; *Appleton's Journal* 15, no. 359 (Feb. 5, 1876): 183–184; "Train-Girls," *Jackson Citizen Patriot*, June 1, 1883, 1; "Deaf and Dumb Child," *Stark County* (OH) *Democrat*, June 7, 1877, 3.

40. "Amusements," *Washington Post*, Oct. 25, 1879, 4; Susan Kattwinkel, *Tony Pastor Presents: Afterpieces from the Vaudeville Stage* (Westport, CT: Greenwood Press, 1998), 171; "On the Road," *Chicago Tribune*, Sept. 6, 1874, 2; "Restricting the Privileges of Newsboys," *Baltimore Sun*, Oct. 21, 1875, 4; "A Railroad Newsboy Talks," *Cleveland Plain Dealer*, Sept. 28, 1890, 14.

41. Robert Louis Stevenson, "Across the Plains," *Longman's Magazine* 2, no. 9 (July 1883): 298–301.

42. *Boston Globe*, Sept. 10, 1875, 4; "News Agents and Train Boys," *Railroad Gazette*, June 7, 1873, 234; "Rules for News Agents," *Railroad Gazette*, Aug. 24, 1883, 364–365; "An Order for 'Newsies,'" *Urbana Daily Courier*, Nov. 15, 1905, 9; L. E. T., "The O. F. News Butcher," *Chicago Tribune*, Sept. 15, 1911, 8.

43. William J. Lee, *The Spotter: Simplified Instructions* (New York: Williams, 1910), 64; Sunshine, *Judas Exposed, or, The Spotter Nuisance* (Chicago: Utility Book and Novelty, 1889), 44.

44. "Villain All Over," *Chicago Tribune*, Apr. 25, 1873, 5; Virginia F. Townsend, *The Boy from Bramley* (Boston: Loring, 1868), 54–55; "Presence of Mind," *Chicago Tribune*, Sept. 19, 1884, 11.

45. James W. Ely Jr., *Railroads and American Law* (Lawrence: University Press of Kansas, 2001), 211; Mark Aldrich, *Death Rode the Rails: American Railroad Accidents and Safety, 1828–1965* (Baltimore: Johns Hopkins University Press, 2006), 2; *Railway World*, Nov. 24, 1911, 980; Newsboy's Pass, Peter J. Eckel Newsboy Collection, box 10, Firestone Library, Princeton University.

46. Ely, *Railroads and American Law*, 212. See also Barbara Young Welke, *Recasting American Liberty: Gender, Race, Law, and the Railroad Revolution, 1865–1920* (Cambridge: Cambridge University Press, 2001), and John Fabian Witt, *The Accidental Republic: Crippled Workingmen, Destitute Widows, and the Remaking of American Law* (Cambridge, MA: Harvard Univeristy Press, 2004).

47. "The Train Boy," *New York Times*, June 12, 1900, 6; "'Train Butcher' Abolished," *New York Times*, July 16, 1901, 1; *Akron Weekly Pioneer Press*, Sept. 7, 1900, 7; "Newsboy Plan Test Case," *Daily Illinois State Journal*, Nov. 29, 1903, 3.

48. "Modern Slang," *Evansville Courier & Press*, Apr. 13, 1903, 4; Will Branan, "The Ubiquitous and Unaccountable Newsboy," *New Orleans Times-Picayune*, Apr. 24, 1910, 3; Wiebe, *Search for Order*, 204; "City Briefs," *Los Angeles Times*, May 9, 1890, 8; W. H. Davies, *The Autobiography of a Super-Tramp* (1918; Brooklyn: Melville House, 2011), 215. See also Vincent DiGirolamo, "'Tramps in the Making': The Troubling Itinerancy of America's News Peddlers," in A. L. Beier and Paul Ocobock, eds., *Cast Out: A History of Vagrancy in Global Perspective* (Athens: Ohio State University Press, 2008), 209–249.

49. *New York Tribune*, Mar. 3, 1869, 2.

50. Josephine C. Goldmark, "Street Labor and Juvenile Delinquency," *Political Science Quarterly* 29 (Sept. 1904): 426; "The Boot-Black's Story," *Saturday Evening Post* 55, no. 22 (Dec. 25, 1875): 5; Mary Wager-Fisher, "The Philadelphia Newsboys; and Their Annual Fourth of July Dinner," *Wide Awake* 11, no. 1 (July 1880): 16–23, in *Newsboy* 14, no. 1 (Aug. 1975): 18; "Odd Names," *Columbus Enquirer*, Dec. 31, 1881, 4; "Our Boys," *St. Louis Republic*, Jan. 19, 1890, 1; Will Branan, "The Ubiquitous and Unaccountable Newsboy," *New Orleans Times-Picayune*, Apr. 24, 1910, 3.

51. "Deaf and Dumb Newsboy Must Seek New Fields," *Tampa Tribune*, Dec. 19, 1901, 15; "Dumb Newsboy Is in Denver," *Denver Post*, Jan. 26, 1903, 2; "'Dumb Newsboy' Visits Salt Lake," *Salt Lake Telegram*, July 8, 1904, 3; "Runs Away with Tramp," *Oregonian*, Nov. 2, 1904, 9; "Dumb Newsboy Wanted in Ontario," *San Diego Union*, Sept. 10, 1906, 2.

52. "Newsboys Lodgings and Vagrancy," *Boston Daily Advertiser*, Sept. 16, 1880, n.p.; "Rush of Bootblacks to Chicago," *New York Tribune*, June 21, 1888, 7.

53. "Newsboys," *Milwaukee Sentinel*, Jan. 2, 1883, 2.

54. Ibid.

55. New York Society for the Prevention of Cruelty to Children, *Tenth Annual Report* (1884), 54.

56. "'Jimmie de Globe Trotter,'" *Cleveland Plain Dealer*, Dec. 5, 1894, 1; "Trots the Globe," *Omaha World-Herald*, Dec. 22, 1894, 2; "Easy for Him," *Cleveland Leader*, Feb. 28, 1896, 12; "'Jimmie the Devil,'" *New York Journal* (n.d.), Heig Scrapbook, and *Newsboy* 19, no. 3 (Oct. 1980): 10; Ernest Poole, "Waifs of the Street," *McClure's Magazine* 21 (May 1903): 42.

57. "Something About Newsboys," *Chicago Times*, in *Arizona Silver Belt*, Aug. 29, 1891, 1; Josiah Flynt, "Tramp Boys," *Independent* 51, no. 2623 (Mar. 9, 1899): 673.

58. Josiah Flynt, "Homosexuality Among Tramps," in Havelock Ellis, *Studies in the Psychology of Sex*, vol. 2, *Sexual Inversion* (1913), appendix A, www.psyplexus.com/ellis/25.htm.

59. Tobias Higbie, *Indispensable Outcasts: Hobo Workers and Community in the American Midwest, 1880–1930* (Urbana: University of Illinois Press, 2003), 181–182; Robert S. Saunders, "A Montage of the River," ca. 1966, 60, and "The Road," 7–8, 71–72, Robert S. Saunders Papers, Western Historical Manuscripts Collection, University of Missouri–St. Louis.

60. Nels Anderson, "The Mission Mill," *American Mercury* 8 (Aug. 1926): 489–491; Nels Anderson, *The Hobo: The Sociology of a Homeless Man* (Chicago: University of Chicago Press, 1923); Nels Anderson, *The American Hobo: An Autobiography* (Leiden: E. J. Brill, 1975); Philip Marcus, "Newsboys. When Papers Was a Penny Apiece," WPA-LC Writers' Unit, Chicago, May 18, 1939, iv, Library of Congress; Clifford R. Shaw, *The Jack-Roller: A Delinquent Boy's Own Story* (1930; Chicago: University of Chicago Press, 1994).

61. *Children Engaged in Newspaper and Magazine Selling and Delivering*, Children's Bureau, Pub. No. 227 (Washington, DC: Government Printing Office, 1935), 50–51.

62. Nettie P. McGill, *Children in Street Work*, Children's Bureau, Pub. No. 183 (Washington, DC: Government Printing Office, 1928), 18, 75, 177–180; "Tough Youngsters," *Los Angeles Times*, Jan. 25, 1895, 8.

63. Sidney D. Long, *The Cry of the News Boy* (Kansas City, MO: Burton, 1928), 46–47.

64. "A Boy Who 'Bums,'" *Duluth News-Tribune*, July 14, 1895, 6; "Bumming a Fine Art," *Minneapolis Journal*, July 7, 1895, 2; "'Foghorn' in Trouble," *Minneapolis Journal*, Sept. 30, 1895, 2.

65. *Rochester Herald*, May 15, 1910.

66. "Champion Newsboy Is in Chicago," *Chicago Examiner*, Sept. 13, 1910, 7; "Back in New York," *Richmond Times-Dispatch*, Oct. 17, 1910, 1; "Newsboy Works His Way Thirty Thousand Miles," *Los Angeles Times*, Oct. 30, 1910, V12; "Rides on the Brake Beam," *New Orleans Herald*, June 15, 1911, 5; "King of Newsies Falls to Death Under a Train," *New York World*, Aug. 10, 1911, 9; "'King of Newsboys' Killed," *Washington Post*, Aug. 10, 1911, 1; "Traveling Newsboy Killed," *New York Times*, Aug. 10, 1911, 16.

Chapter 7

1. Herbert G. Gutman, with Ira Berlin, "Class Composition and the Development of the American Working Class, 1840–1890," in *Power and Culture: Essays on the American Working Class* (New York: Pantheon, 1987), 386; Carlos A. Schwantes, *The Pacific Northwest: An Interpretive History* (Lincoln: University of Nebraska Press, 1984), 96; Lawrence H. Larson, *The Urban West at the End of the Frontier* (Lawrence: Regents Press of Kansas, 1978); Carl Abbott, "Western Cities," in *Encyclopedia of Urban America: The Cities and Suburbs*, ed. Neil Larry Shumsky (Denver, CO: ABC-CLIO, 1998), 871.

2. William David Sloan, "The Frontier Press, 1800–1900: Personal Journalism or Paltry Business?," in *Perspectives on Mass Communication History* (Hillsdale, NJ: L. Erlbaum, 1991), 104; Edwin Emery, *The Press and America: An Interpretive History of the Mass Media*, 3rd

ed. (Englewood Cliffs, NJ: Prentice-Hall, 1972), 443; "Our Colorado Letter," *Indianapolis Sentinel*, Apr. 7, 1879, 2; "Street Scenes," *Rocky Mountain News*, Mar. 17, 1881, 3.

3. On children's work in the West, see Elliott Robert Barkan, *From All Points: America's Immigrant West, 1870s–1952* (Bloomington: Indiana University Press, 2007); Marilyn Irvin Holt, *Children of the Western Plains: The Nineteenth Century Experience* (Chicago: Ivan R. Dee, 2003), 106–127, and Elliott West, *Growing Up with the Country: Childhood on the Far Western Frontier* (Albuquerque: University of New Mexico Press, 1989), 73–98.

4. "Fargo's Fatty Fraud," *Grand Forks Herald*, Oct. 30, 1883, 1; James Melvin Lee, *History of American Journalism* (Garden City, NY: Garden City Publishing, 1923), 348, 351; Robert Karolevitz, *Newspapering in the Old West: A Pictorial History of Journalism and Printing on the Frontier* (New York: Bonanza Books, 1965), 76, 93; David Fridtjof Halaas, *Boom Town Newspapers: Journalism on the Rocky Mountain Mining Frontier, 1859–1881* (Albuquerque: University of New Mexico Press, 1981), 40–42; Henry W. Splitter, "Newspapers of Los Angeles: The First Fifty Years, 1851–1900," *Journal of the West* 2, no. 4 (Oct. 1963): 436.

5. Karolevitz, *Newspapering in the Old West*, 136; John A. Lent, "The Press on Wheels: A History of *The Frontier Index*," *Journal of the West* 10, no. 4 (Oct. 1971): 674.

6. "An Evening Newspaper," *San Francisco Daily Evening Bulletin*, June 10, 1870, 3; S. N. D. North, *History and Present Condition of the Newspaper and Periodical Press of the United States, with a Catalogue of the Publications of the Census Year, Tenth Census, 1880* (Washington, DC: Government Printing Office, 1884), 8:207; "Printing Business in San Francisco," *San Francisco Bulletin*, Feb. 4, 1870, 3; "San Francisco Newsboys," *Harper's Weekly* 21, no. 1059 (Apr. 14, 1877): 292, 294. See also Robert Taft, "The Pictorial Record of the Old West, I. Frenzeny and Tavernier," *Kansas Historical Quarterly* 14, No. 1 (Feb. 1946): 1–35.

7. Karolevitz, *Newspapering in the Old West*, 79.

8. Ibid., 72–73.

9. "Our Boys," *St. Louis Republic*, Jan. 19, 1890, 2; Steve Wilson, "Documenting Our Heritage: Manuscript Collections of the Museum of the Great Plains," *Great Plains Journal* 17 (1978): 10.

10. "In the City by the Kaw," *Chicago Tribune*, Apr. 22, 1888, 4; "Boycotting Newsboys," *Kansas City Star*, Apr. 29, 1884, 4; "Midget Mercuries," *Kansas City Star*, May 3, 1884, 1.

11. "Arabs of the Street," *Kansas City Times*, Jan. 18, 1885, 9; "Home for Bootblacks," *Kansas City Star*, Apr. 17, 1885, 2; "In the City by the Kaw," *Chicago Tribune*, Apr. 22, 1888, 4.

12. "Newsboys in a Riot," *Kansas City Star*, Oct. 3, 1896, 1; "News and Notes," *Literary World* 29, no. 23 (Nov. 12, 1898): 376; *Topeka Colored Citizen*, Nov. 11, 1898, 3; *Cigar Makers Official Journal* 24, no. 7 (Apr. 1899): 6.

13. "Trodden Down," *Rocky Mountain News*, Jan. 4, 1882, 8; "Scared by a Mountain Lion. A Newsboy's Adventure in the Black Hills in '76," *Washington Post*, Dec. 17, 1893, 19; "Newsboy Has a Fight with a Bear," *Chicago Tribune*, Feb. 28, 1895, 7.

14. Ted Curtis Smyth, *The Gilded Age Press, 1865–1900* (Westport, CT: Praeger, 2003), 33–36; Monte McLaws, "The Mormon *Deseret News*: Unique Frontier Newspaper," *Journal of the West* 19, no. 2 (Apr. 1980), 35; Karolevitz, *Newspapering in the Old West*, 12, 21, 31, 110, 143, 148; Lent, "Press on Wheels," 670; Barbara Cloud, *The Business of Newspapers on the Western Frontier* (Reno: University of Nevada Press, 1992), 134.

15. "Casus Belli," *Galveston Daily News*, Oct. 25, 1877, n.p.

16. Karolevitz, *Newspapering in the Old West*, 12, 137; "An Editor's Hardships," *Washington Post*, Oct. 30, 1882, 1; Porter A. Stratton, *The Territorial Press of New Mexico, 1834–1912* (Albuquerque: University of New Mexico Press, 1969), 19; Cloud, *Business of Newspapers*, 45–46.

17. *State v. Jackson*, Supreme Court of Montana, 9 Mont. 508; 24 P. 213; 1890 Mont. Lexis 39, 1.

18. Charles Loring Brace, *The Dangerous Classes of New York and Twenty Years' Work Among Them* (New York: Wynkook & Hallenbeck, 1872), 111–112.

19. Stephen O'Connor, *Orphan Trains: The Story of Charles Loring Brace and the Children He Saved and Failed* (New York: Houghton Mifflin, 2001), 258–283, 177–202; Joan Jacobs Brumberg, *Kansas Charley: The Boy Murderer* (New York: Viking, 2003).

20. "Col. Frank A. Burr Dead," *New York Times*, Jan. 16, 1894, 2.

21. Dexter Marshall, "New Timber in Senate," *Dallas Morning News*, Jan. 26, 1908, 7; "Charles Curtis," *Kansapedia* (Kansas Historical Society), accessed June 24, 2012, www.kshs.org/kansapedia/charles-curtis/12029.

22. "Three Newsboys of 1870 Are Still Living Near Here," *Rocky Mountain News*, Apr. 22, 1934, D3.

23. Lawrance Thompson, *Robert Frost: The Early Years, 1874–1915* (New York: Holt, Rinehart & Winston, 1966), 29; Stephen H. Anderson, *Newspaper Circulation Manual for Carrier-Salesmen Coaches and District Supervisors* (Seattle: Pigott-Washington Printing, 1937), 99; "Honolulu's Newsboys," *Pacific Commercial Advertiser*, Aug. 7, 1904, 2.

24. Wilbur Fiske Stone, *History of Colorado* (Chicago: S. J. Clarke, 1919), 4:182; *Chicago Tribune*, Dec. 18, 1890, 9; Marshall Conant Graff, "A History of Leadville, Colorado," master's thesis, University of Wisconsin, 1920, 93–99.

25. "The News in Leadville," *Leadville Chronicle*, in *Rocky Mountain News*, Aug. 20, 1879, 8; "Pity the Poor," *Leadville Herald*, Dec. 17, 1880, 4; "Stuffed Goods," *Leadville Democrat*, May 18, 1881, 8; "Scenes Among Newsboys," *Leadville Chronicle*, Dec. 14, 1887, 4; *Leadville Herald*, June 9, 1882, 1; *Rocky Mountain News*, June 13, 1882, 2; *Leadville Herald*, June 16, 1882, 4; *Rocky Mountain News*, June 17, 1882, 2; "A Jolly Time," *Rocky Mountain News*, Dec. 27, 1887, 5; *Rocky Mountain News*, Mar. 12, 1885, 7.

26. Robert Hudson, *The Writing Game: A Biography of Will Irwin* (Ames: Iowa State University Press, 1982), 7.

27. Lowell Thomas, *Good Evening Everybody: From Cripple Creek to Samarkand* (New York: Morrow, 1976), 35–40; "Who Is Lowell Thomas?," Victor Lowell Thomas Museum, accessed Mar. 9, 2014, www.victorcolorado.com/lowellthomas.htm.

28. Karolevitz, *Newspapering in the Old West*, 96, 100, 117; Robert L. Housman, "Boy Editors of Frontier Montana," *Pacific Northwest Quarterly* 27 (July 1936): 219; Henry George Jr., *The Life of Henry George* (Garden City, NY: Doubleday, Page, 1911), 237; "The Despised Cent," *Evansville Courier & Express*, Oct. 31, 1895, 3; Elliott West, "Heathens and Angels: Childhood in the Rocky Mountain Mining Towns," in *Growing Up in America: Historical Experiences*, ed. Harvey J. Graff (Detroit: Wayne State University Press, 1987), 369–384.

29. "What a Newsboy Can Do," *Perrysburg Journal*, Apr. 6, 1877, 1; "A Wealthy Newsboy," *Washington Post*, June 30, 1882, 2; "A Rich Newsboy," *Frank Leslie's Illustrated Newspaper* 54, no. 1401 (July 29, 1882): 366; "The Day in Denver," *Los Angeles Times*, Jan. 24, 1920, 13.

30. "Publications Received," *Phrenological Journal of Science and Health* 84, no. 2 (Aug. 1887): 115; "Father Elphick," *San Francisco Chronicle*, July 28, 1891, 10l; "Elphick's Death," *San Francisco Chronicle*, July 31, 1891, 3; "Street Characters of San Francisco," *Overland Monthly and Out West Magazine* 19, no. 113 (May 1892): 9, 12–13; Paul Kagan, *New World Utopias: A Photographic History of the Search for Community* (New York: Penguin Books, 1975), 93–94.

31. "An Indian Talks of Civilization as It Appears to Him, a Newsboy," *San Francisco Call*, Mar. 25, 1900, 8; Rebecca Edwards, *New Spirits: Americans in the Gilded Age, 1865–1905* (New York: Oxford University Press, 2006), 113.

32. Jack London, "What Life Means to Me," *Cosmopolitan* 40, no. 5 (Mar. 1906): 526–530; Jack London, *Martin Eden* (1909; New York: Penguin Books, 1993), 174–183.

33. "Aid for the Arabs," *Rocky Mountain News*, Jan. 17, 1882, 10; "The Newsboy's Home Opened," *Rocky Mountain News*, Jan. 20, 1882, 4; *Denver Republican*, Jan. 23, 1882; "Home for the Friendless," *Rocky Mountain News*, July 11, 1882, 5; "Law and Order," *Rocky Mountain News*, Feb. 4, 1885, 8; "A Permanent Newsboys' Home," *Rocky Mountain News*, Jan. 2, 1893, 8; Dorothy Hutchison, "History of Colorado's Private Child Placing Agencies," master's thesis, University of Denver, 1944, Appendix A, "The Newsboys and Bootblacks Home," in Colorado Historical Society.

34. "The Newsboys Are Going to Protect Themselves," *Rocky Mountain News*, Mar. 15, 1874, 4; "A Newsboy's Strike," *Rocky Mountain News*, May 24, 1883, 8; "A Strike Among Small Boys on the Price of a Small Paper," *Rocky Mountain News*, Sept. 5, 1884, 4; "Still Striking," *Rocky Mountain News*, Sept. 6, 1884, 8; "The Newsboys' Strike," *Rocky Mountain News*, Sept. 7, 1884, 1; "Newsboys' Union a Mistake," *Rocky Mountain News*, June 3, 1898, 4; Margaret Hamilton Welch, "The Woman's Club of Denver," *Harper's Bazar* 32, no. 7 (Feb. 18, 1899): 147.

35. H. S. Bunting, "Denver Described," *Atlanta Constitution*, Apr. 30, 1893, 8; "Strike of Denver Newsboys," *Chicago Tribune*, Feb. 18, 1894, 11; "The Newsboy's King," *Denver Post*, July 8, 1895, 1; "Happy Newsboys," *Denver Post*, Feb. 6, 1896, 2; "Senator Wolcott Scored," *Denver Post*, Feb. 10, 1896, 5; "So That the People May Know," *Denver Post*, Feb. 29, 1896, 1; "Was Without Pull," *Denver Post*, Feb. 29, 1896, 2; "A Boycott," *Denver Post*, May 19, 1896, 2.

36. "Brave Union Newsboys," *Denver Post*, Feb. 8, 1896, 6; "'Post' Boys Parade," *Denver Post*, Sept. 29, 1896, 2; "Newsboys in Jail," *Denver Post*, Sept. 29, 1896, 2; "Newsboys Advertising," *Rocky Mountain News*, Sept. 30, 1896, 9; "Newsboys on Trial," *Denver Post*, Nov. 22, 1896, 3.

37. "Colorado Springs Newsboys," *Denver Post*, Mar. 17, 1896, 1; "Newsboys on Strike," *Denver Post*, Sept. 25, 1897, 1; "A Boycott," *Denver Post*, May 19, 1896, 2; "Newsboys' Strike in Cripple Creek," *Denver Post*, Oct. 22, 1896, 2.

38. Lilburn Merrill, *Annual Statement*, Juvenile Improvement Association of Denver, 1905, n.p. See also Charles Larsen, *The Good Fight: The Life and Times of Ben B. Lindsey* (Chicago: Quadrangle Books, 1972), and Jeanne E. Abrams, *Jewish Women Pioneering the Frontier Trail: A History in the American West* (New York: New York University Press, 2006), 59–60.

39. *Boston Journal*, Dec. 6, 1890, 2; "The Dallas Newsboys," *Dallas Morning News*, Nov. 13, 1892, 12. See Frederick Jackson Turner, "The Significance of the Frontier in American History," *Proceedings of the 41st Annual Meeting of the State Historical Society of Wisconsin* (Madison, WI, 1894), 79–112.

40. Karolevitz, *Newspapering in the Old West*, 176–177; McLaws, "The Mormon *Deseret News*," 32; Claire Noall, *Intimate Disciple: A Portrait of Willard Richards* (Salt Lake City: University of Utah Press, 1957), 553, 619; "A Newsgirl," *Rocky Mountain News*, Mar. 26, 1884, 3; "Denver's Newsgirl," *Rocky Mountain News*, Aug. 19, 1886, 8; Carol S. Lomicky, "Frontier Feminism and the Woman's Tribune: The Journalism of Clara Bewick Colby," *Journalism History* 28, no. 3 (Fall 2002): 107. See also Maria DeCenzo, "Gutter Politics: Women Newsies and the Suffrage Press," *Women's History Review* 12, no. 1 (2003): 15–33.

41. "Paper, Sir?," *Los Angeles Times*, Nov. 7, 1885, 5; "The Newsboys' Union," *Alta California*, June 2, 1886), 1; "Newsboys Are Triumphant," *San Francisco Call*, Aug. 10, 1892, 8; "The Newsboys' Union," *San Francisco Call*, Aug. 13, 1892, 2; "Labor's Great Day," *San Francisco Call*, Sept. 6, 1892, 3.

42. "Newsboys' Union," *San Francisco Evening News*, Aug. 11, 1894, 4; "Newsboys Plead for Their Cause," *San Francisco Chronicle*, Oct. 17, 1896, 7.

43. "City Newsboys on Strike," *San Francisco Call*, Oct. 16, 1896, 9; "Went to the Council," *San Francisco Call*, Oct. 17, 1896, 11; "Newsboys Are Sanguine," *San Francisco Call*, Oct. 18, 1896, 9; "The Newsboys' Strike," *Los Angeles Times*, Oct. 18, 1896, 3; "Are Still on Strike," *San Francisco Call*, Oct. 20, 1896, 5; "Natives in Parade," *San Francisco Call*, Apr. 24, 1895, 9; John P. Young, *Journalism in California* (San Francisco: Chronicle Publishing, 1915), 145.

44. "Union Circus," *Los Angeles Times*, July 24, 1903, A23; "Newsboys' Strike Settled," *Los Angeles Times*, Aug. 29, 1903, 2; "Unions Reek with Crime," *Los Angeles Times*, Aug. 29, 1903, A3.

45. "The Newsboys' Union," *San Francisco Call*, Oct. 18, 1903, 35; Mrs. Fremont Older, "The Story of a Reformer's Wife," *McClure's Magazine* 33, no. 3 (July 1909): 278; "Newsboys Hold Large Meeting," *San Francisco Chronicle*, June 28, 1905, 5; "Riot and Outrage Permitted by Police," *San Francisco Chronicle*, June 30, 1905, 18.

46. "Boys Start Rioting in the Streets," *San Francisco Call*, June 30, 1905, 2; "Strike Now Dying Out," *San Francisco Chronicle*, July 1, 1905, 14; "Newsboys on Parade Amuse Market Street," *San Francisco Chronicle*, July 2, 1905, 30; "Ex-Sergeant Ellis Is Severely Beaten," *San Francisco Call*, July 25, 1905, 9; "Badly Beaten by Newsboys," *San Francisco Chronicle*, July 25, 1905, 16; Franklin Hichborn, *"The System" as Uncovered by the San Francisco Graft Prosecution* (San Francisco: James H. Barry, 1915), 73.

47. Joseph E. Wilder, *Read All About It: Reminiscences of an Immigrant Newsboy*, ed. Fred C. Dawkins and Micheline C. Brodeur (Winnipeg, MB: Peguis, 1978), 26; "Oakland Aids Businessmen," *New York Times*, Apr. 24, 1906, 2; Will Irwin, "The American Newspaper: A Study of Journalism in Its Relations to the Public. V. What Is News?," *Collier's* 46, no. 2 (Mar. 18, 1911): 16; repr., ed. Clifford F. Weigle and David G. Clark (Ames: Iowa State University Press, 1969), 30; Neal Thompson, *A Curious Man: The Strange and Brilliant Life of Robert "Believe It or Not" Ripley* (New York: Three Rivers Press, 2014), 19.

48. Charles F. Lummis, "Across Country to His Job," *Los Angeles Times*, Dec. 4, 1921, VIII2; George Seldes, *Lords of the Press* (New York: Julian Messner, 1938), 71–72; "Harry Chandler, 'Oldest Employee, Has Seen This City Transformed," *Los Angeles Times*, Dec. 4, 1941, 21, 25; Splitter, "Newspapers of Los Angeles," 441–443.

49. Splitter, "Newspapers of Los Angeles," 441–443; "Hard Up," *Los Angeles Times*, Nov. 27, 1887, 8; *Los Angeles Times*, Nov. 29, 1887, 4.

50. "Times Newsboys," *Los Angeles Times*, Dec. 26, 1888, 2; "Serving the 'Times,'" *Los Angeles Times*, Apr. 6, 1890, 9; "Soon to Unveil Otis Memorial," *Los Angeles Times*, July 25, 1920, II9.

51. "Strike of Newsboys," *Oregonian*, Aug. 17, 1892, 8; "They Object to Paying Big Prices for the Oregonian," *Morning Olympian*, Aug. 17, 1892, 1; "A Newsboys' Union," *Oregonian*, Aug. 21, 1892, 3; "General Labor News," *Minneapolis Journal*, Nov. 7, 1896, 9; "News Boycotters," *Los Angeles Times*, Jan. 17, 1900, 12; *Deseret Evening News*, Jan. 17, 1900, 3.

52. Ross Anderson, "Pinpoints, Plots, Plats and Panorama," *Seattle Times*, Sept. 16, 2001.

53. "The Season of Strikes," *Los Angeles Times*, Apr. 5, 1891, 5; "How 'Pud' Leckie Lost a Finger," *Anaconda Standard*, Mar. 16, 1893, 7; *Third Biennial Report of the Bureau of Labor of the State of Washington, 1901–1902* (Seattle: Metropolitan Press, 1903), 97; *Eleventh Biennial Report of the Bureau of Labor of the State of Washington, 1917–1918* (Olympia, WA: Frank M. Lamborn, 1918), 86.

54. *Third Biennial Report of the Bureau of Labor of the State of Washington, 1901–1902*, 105; *Sixth Biennial Report of the Bureau of Labor Statistics and Factory Inspection of the State of Washington, 1907–1908* (Olympia: C. W. Gorham, 1908), 146; Gerald J. Baldasty, *E. W. Scripps and the Business of Newspapers* (Urbana: University of Illinois Press, 1999), 33; Roger Simpson, "Seattle Newsboys: How Hustler Democracy Lost to the Power of Property," *Journalism History* 18 (1992): 18–25.

55. "Local Brevities," *Idaho Statesman*, Oct. 11, 1892, 5; "Great Labor Day," *Idaho Statesman*, Sept. 2, 1902, 5; "The Rossland Strike," *Anaconda Standard*, July 17, 1901, 6.

56. "The Newsboys' Union," *Tacoma Daily News*, Aug. 30, 1892, 1; "The Humanitarians," *Rocky Mountain News*, Mar. 14, 1882, 8; "Baiting a Chinaman," *Sacramento Record Union*, Mar. 5, 1897, 5.

57. "Miscellaneous Mites," *Salt Lake Tribune*, Jan. 21, 1895, 7; *Oregonian*, Aug. 22, 1896, 18.

58. Sharon A. Boswell and Lorraine McConaghy, *Raise Hell and Sell Newspapers: Alden J. Blethen and the Seattle Times* (Pullman, WA: Washington State University Press, 1996), 109.

59. "Chicago Boy Makes Small Fortune in the Klondike," *Chicago Tribune*, July 25, 1898, 1; "Newsboy Has Luck in Alaska," *New York Times*, July 31, 1898, 2; "Newsboy Luck," *Oregonian*, Aug. 31, 1898, 3.

60. "Dawson's Lame Newsboy," *New York Sun*, Dec. 10, 1899, 2; "Klondike Children," *Canton Repository*, Aug. 22, 1897, 19; Pierre Berton, *The Klondike Quest: A Photographic Essay, 1897–99* (Boston: Little, Brown, 1983), 63, 124–125; Charlotte Gray, *Gold Diggers: Striking It Rich in the Klondike* (Berkeley, CA: Counterpoint, 2010), 208, 221–222.

61. "The Federated Trades and Labor Council Parade," *Salt Lake Herald*, Feb. 23, 1890, 5; "A Glorious Celebration," *Salt Lake Tribune*, July 10, 1890, 5; "The Ups and Downs of a Newsboy's Life in Salt Lake," *Deseret Evening News*, Jan. 17, 1903, 9.

62. William John Gilbert Gould, *My Life on Mountain Railroads*, ed. William R. Gould (Logan: Utah State University Press, 1995), 29.

63. Ibid., 30.

64. Ibid., 30.

65. "Local Briefs," *Deseret Evening News*, June 30, 1902, 10; "Newsboys on a Strike," *Salt Lake Herald*, July 22, 1902, 8.

66. "Newsboys on Strike," *Bisbee Daily Review*, Sept. 18, 1902, 8.

Chapter 8

1. "The Arab Appetite," *St. Louis Post-Dispatch*, Dec. 26, 1885, 3.

2. Alfred McClung Lee, *The Daily Newspaper in America: The Evolution of a Social Instrument* (New York: Macmillan, 1937), 633; James McGrath Morris, *Pulitzer: A Life in Politics, Print, and Power* (New York: HarperCollins, 2010), 238.

3. "Notice to Workingmen," 1885, and "New Years, 1886," Pulitzer Papers, Columbia University; W. A. Swanberg, *Pulitzer* (New York: Scribner, 1967), 131.

4. J. J. B., "Our New York Letter," *Saulte Ste. Marie News*, Mar. 1, 1890, 5; William S. Rossiter, "Printing and Publishing," in 12th US Census, 1900 (Washington, DC: Government Printing Office, 1902), 1041–1042; Ted Curtis Smythe, *The Gilded Age Press, 1865–1900* (Westport, CT: Praeger, 2003), 71–104; Alfred D. Chandler Jr., *The Visible Hand: The Managerial Revolution in American Business* (Cambridge, MA: Harvard University Press, 1977).

5. "Courting the Newsboys," *New York Commercial Advertiser*, in *Daily Yellowstone Journal*, Dec. 17, 1887, 2. On press philanthropy, see James Melvin Lee, *History of American Journalism* (Garden City, NY: Garden City Publishing, 1923), 357–360; and Jon Bekken, "Newsboys: The Exploitation of 'Little Merchants' by the Newspaper Industry," in *Newsworkers: Toward a History of the Rank and File*, ed. Hanno Hardt and Bonnie Brennen (Minneapolis: University of Minnesota Press, 1995), 190–225. Also helpful is Robert H. Bremner, *American Philanthropy* (Chicago: University of Chicago Press, 1960, rev. ed. 1988); Robert L. Payton, *Philanthropy: Voluntary Action for the Public Good* (New York: American Council on Education and Macmillan, 1988); Lawrence Friedman and Mark D. McGarvie, eds., *Charity, Philanthropy, and Civility in American History* (Cambridge: Cambridge University Press, 2003); Stuart D. Brandes, *American Welfare Capitalism, 1880–1940* (Chicago: University of Chicago Press, 1970); Sanford M. Jacoby, *Modern Manors: Welfare Capitalism Since the New Deal* (Princeton, NJ: Princeton University Press, 1997); and Andrea Tone, *The Business of Benevolence: Industrial Paternalism in Progressive America* (Ithaca, NY: Cornell University Press, 1997).

6. G. W. W. Hanger, "Strikes and Lockouts in the United States," *Bulletin of the Bureau of Labor* 9, pt. 2, no. 54 (Sept. 1904): 1099.

7. "North Revels in Figures," *Washington Post*, June 25, 1905, E2; Lee, *Daily Newspaper in America*, 288–289; Henry R. Davis, *Half a Century with the Providence Journal* (Providence: Journal, 1904), 175–176; William J. Thorn, with Mary Pat Pfeil, *Newspaper Circulation, Marketing the News* (New York: Longman, 1987), 37; *Paper Makers Journal* 9, no. 1 (Dec. 1909): 13.

8. William Stanley Braithwaite, "The House Under Arcturus: An Autobiography," *Phylon* 2, no. 2 (1941): 126–128; William Dean Howells, "Tribulations of a Cheerful Giver," *Century Magazine* 50, no. 2 (June 1895): 181–185.

9. "Only a Newsboy," *Newsvendor* No. 155 (Apr. 11, 1877): 5; E. W. Townsend, "Boys and Girls of New York Streets," *Harper's Young People* 16, no. 792 (Jan. 1, 1895): 163; *Amended Manual of Laws of Massachusetts Concerning Children* (Boston: Massachusetts Society for the Prevention of Cruelty to Children, 1890), 123–124.

10. Lee, *Daily Newspaper in America*, 288; "The Black Days of Circulation Management," *Pollak's Circulation News*, Aug. 1963, 10; "High Times for the Newsboys and Boot Blacks," *Chicago Tribune*, Jan. 4, 1869, 1; George H. Thurston, *Allegheny County's Hundred Years* (Pittsburgh, PA: A. A. Anderson & Sons, 1888), 302; Percy Frazer Smith, *Memory's Milestones: Reminiscences of Seventy Years of a Busy Life in Pittsburgh* (Pittsburgh, PA: Murdock-Kerr Press, 1918), 91; Abraham Oseroff, *Report on Subsidized Institutions for the Care of Dependent, Delinquent, and Crippled Children* (Pittsburgh, PA: Public Charities Association of Pennsylvania, 1915), 35; *Cleveland Leader*, Mar. 10, 1881, 1.

11. "Fourth of July at the New Ledger Building," *Columbia Spy*, July 13, 1867, 1; *New York Evangelist* 39, no. 30 (July 23, 1868): 4; "Pennsylvania," *Hartford Courant*, Dec. 26, 1868, 3; "The Newsboys' Jubilee," *Frank Leslie's Illustrated Newspaper*, July 21, 1877, 337; "Philadelphia Newsboys," *Harper's Weekly* 21, no. 1073 (July 21, 1877): 570; Mary Wager-Fisher, "The Philadelphia Newsboys; and Their Annual Fourth of July Dinner," *Wide Awake* 11, no. 1 (July 1880): 16–23.

12. *The Public Ledger Building* (Philadelphia: G. W. Childs, 1867), 103–105, 116–117; "Personal," *Harper's Weekly* 34, no. 1725 (Jan. 11, 1890): 19; Richard T. Ely, "George W. Childs in His Relations to His Employees," in George W. Childs, *Recollections* (Philadelphia: J. B. Lippincott, 1890), 319–340; J; Thomas Scharf and Thompson Westcott, *History of Philadelphia* (Philadelphia: L. H. Everts, 1884), 2:1478; Jacqueline Steck, "George W. Childs," *Dictionary of Literary Biography* (Ann Arbor: University of Michigan Press, 1983), 23:26–30.

13. "Newsboys' New Year," *Detroit Free Press*, Jan. 5, 1873, 1; "The Newsboys," *Detroit Free Press*, Jan. 4, 1874, 1; "For the Boys," *Detroit Free Press*, Feb. 28, 1875, 1; "The Labor of Charity,"

New York Times, Dec. 26, 1875, 1; Michael Angelo Woolf, "A Christmas Dinner," *Harper's Weekly* 20, no. 994 (Jan. 15, 1876): 53.

14. "Newsboys with Appetites," *New York Times*, Dec. 26, 1891, 8; "Feast for Newsboys at Lodging House," *New York Times*, Dec. 26, 1909, 6; "A Banquet to Newsboys," *New York Times*, Apr. 14, 1902, 6; "Newsboys' Dinner," n.p., Feb. 22, 1904; "Newsboys Dined by Mrs. Guggenheimer," *New York Sun*, Feb. 28, 1918, 14; "Randolph Guggenheimer's Dinner to the Newsboys," *Commercial Advertiser*, Mar. 14, 1903, 15; "Newsboys Enjoy a Feast," Heig Scrapbook; "Hard Times in Society," *Chicago Tribune*, Jan. 5, 1891, 7; "The Poor—A Suggestion," *New York Times*, Jan. 29, 1874, 4.

15. E. L. Godkin, *The Gilded Age Letters of E. L. Godkin*, ed. William Armstrong (Albany, NY: SUNY Press, 1974), 164; Irene Beale, *William P. Letchworth: A Man for Others* (Geneseo, NY: Chestnut Hill Press, 1982), 56; "Annual Christmas Dinner," *Frank Leslie's Illustrated Newspaper*, Jan. 11, 1873, 287; "A Dinner for the Newsboys," *Washington Post*, Mar. 16, 1880, 1.

16. "Dining with the Waifs," *Chicago Tribune* Oct. 28, 1889, 6; "Some Roosevelt Anecdotes," *New York Times*, Nov. 25, 1901, 7; J. A. Edgerton, "Christmas with the Newsboys," *Pensacola Journal*, Dec. 16, 1906, 10; "Newsboys Capture the Town," *Chicago Tribune*, Jan. 2, 1890, 3; *Toledo News-Bee*, Apr. 14, 1923, 3; LeRoy Ashby, *Saving the Waifs: Reformers and Dependent Children, 1890–1917* (Philadelphia: Temple University Press, 1984), 108; "The Natural Result," *Wheeling Intelligence*, Jan. 22, 1898, 6.

17. Theo. H. Northrup, *The Newsboys' Christmas Dinner* (Chicago: National Music Co., 1893); "Services and Entertainments," *Chicago Tribune*, Nov. 27, 1895, 7; "The Newsboys' Dinner: A Thanksgiving Tradition," *Chicago History Journal*, Nov. 2008, accessed Oct. 13, 2010, www.chicagohistoryjournal.com/2008/11/newsboys-dinner-thanksgiving-tradition.html (no longer available online); "Isaac Woolf's Newsboy Dinner," *New York Tribune*, Nov. 27, 1904, 2; "Child Beggars Called to Halt," *Chicago Tribune*, Dec. 21, 1904, 7; Anne Shannon Monroe, "Isaac Woolf and His Thanksgiving Day Guests," *Common-Sense* 4, no. 11 (Nov. 1904): 8–9.

18. "What a Little Money Can Do," *New York Times*, July 31, 1872, 4; "The Poor Children's Excursion Fund," *New York Times*, Sept. 1, 1875, 2; "The Newsboys' Excursion," *Harper's Weekly* 19, no. 979 (Oct. 2, 1875): 803; "Profligate Peck," *Chicago Tribune*, June 11, 1883, 3; "A Parade by Chicago Newsboys," *New York Tribune*, Sept. 5, 1883, 1; "Newsboys Let Loose," *Quincy Daily Whig*, ca. 1886, 7; "Tenth Free Excursion," *New York Times*, July 13, 1886, 8; "Six Hundred Imps on a Flatboat," *New York Tribune*, June 19, 1888, 4; "Lots of Fun Afloat," *New York Herald*, June 19, 1886, 5.

19. C. S. Reinhart, "The Newsboys' Picnic—Tumbling into the Water," *Harper's Weekly* 17, no. 870 (Aug. 30, 1873): 757, 766; "Six Hundred Imps on a Flatboat," *New York Tribune*, June 19, 1888, 4; "A Holiday for the Newsbogys [*sic*]," *New York Times*, Oct. 11, 1878, 8; "The Newsboys' Picnic," *National Police Gazette* 33, no. 57 (Oct. 26, 1878): 5; "Happy Newsboys," *Chicago Tribune*, Aug. 6, 1886, 3.

20. I. N. Ford, "Fresh Air Fund," *St. Nicholas* 10 (June 1883): 616–626; Mrs. Hamilton Mott, "Mr. Woolf and His Waifs," *Ladies' Home Journal* 13, no. 7 (June 1896): 13; W. G. Vinal, "Nature Study as a Form of Play," *Playground and Community Recreation Statistics for 1924* 19, no. 1 (Apr. 1925): 558; W. A. Rogers, *A World Worth While: A Record of "Auld Acquaintance"* (New York: Harper and Brothers, 1922), 9; Julia Guarneri, "Changing Strategies for Child Welfare, Enduring Beliefs About Childhood: The Fresh Air Fund, 1877–1926," *Journal of the Gilded Age and Progressive Era* 11, no. 1 (Jan. 2012): 27–70.

21. Cyril Arthur Player, "The Story of James Edmund Scripps," typescript, n.d., 1:137–138, 146, James E. Scripps Papers, Bentley Historical Library, University of Michigan; Richard Kaplan, "The Economics of Popular Journalism in the Gilded Age," *Journalism History* 21, no. 2 (Summer 1995): 66–69; E. W. Scripps, "History of Scripps League," typescript, 1899, 32–33, cited in Vance H. Trimble, *The Astonishing Mr. Scripps: The Turbulent Life of America's Penny Press Lord* (Ames: Iowa State University Press, 1992), 26; Charles R. McCabe, ed., *Damned Old Crank: A Self-Portrait of E. W. Scripps, Drawn from His Unpublished Writings* (New York: Harper & Brothers 1951), 159–160; Gilson Gardner, *Lusty Scripps: The Life of E. W. Scripps* (New York: Vanguard Press, 1932).

22. Lee, *Daily Newspaper in America*, 264, 289; Trimble, *Astonishing Mr. Scripps*, 124–125, 137; Milton A. McRae, *Forty Years in Newspaperdom* (New York: Brentano's, 1924), 78–79; George E. Stevens, "From Penny Paper to *Post* and *Times-Star*: Mr. Scripps' First Link," *Cincinnati Historical Society Bulletin* 27 (Fall 1969): 206–222; "An Editor as Santa Claus," *Washington Post*, Dec. 25, 1885, 1; "He Is One of 'Em," *Cincinnati Post*, Feb. 28, 1889, 4; Kaplan, "Economics of Popular Journalism," 65–78; Gerald J. Baldasty, *E. W. Scripps and the Business of Newspapers* (Urbana: University of Illinois Press, 1999), 44.

23. Agnes M. Larson, "The Editorial Policy of Skandinaven, 1900–1903," *Norwegian American Studies* 8 (1934): 112–135. www.stolaf.edu/naha/pubs/nas/volume08/vol08_8.htm; Charles H. Dennis, *Victor Lawson: His Time and His Work* (Chicago: University of Chicago Press, 1935), 51; David Paul Nord, "Victor F. Lawson," *Dictionary of Literary Biography* (Ann Arbor: University of Michigan Press, 1983), 24:161–169; Smythe, *Gilded Age Press*, 78, 100 n. 30; Charles O. Bennett, *Facts Without Opinion: First Fifty Years of the Audit Bureau of Circulation* (Chicago: ABC, 1965), 11.

24. Cynthia Mathews, "This Haven of Rest and Health: The *Chicago Daily News* Sanitarium," *Chicago History* 83, no. 3 (Spring 2000): 20–39; Nels Anderson, *The American Hobo: An Autobiography* (Leiden: E. J. Brill, 1975), 26; "Parade on Labor Day," *Chicago Tribune*, Sept. 8, 1896, 2; Wayne Klatt, *Chicago Journalism: A History* (Jefferson, NC: McFarland, 2009), 202.

25. "The Hit Bird Flutters," *Chicago Tribune*, Mar. 25, 1886, 1. See also Jon Bekken, "'The Most Vindictive and Most Vengeful Power': Labor Confronts the Chicago Newspaper Trust," *Journalism History* 18 (1992): 11–17.

26. *Printers' Ink* 10, no. 13 (Mar. 28, 1894): 371; W. A. Rogers, *A World Worth While: A Record of "Auld Acquaintance"* (New York: Harper & Bros., 1922), 264–266; Julian Ralph, "Scene on the Bowery," *San Diego Union*, Feb. 17, 1888, 7.

27. "Advertising Dodge," *Charleston News and Courier*, Nov. 11, 1887, 5.

28. "Arrested at the Prize Ring," *Chicago Tribune*, Nov. 9, 1895, 5; "Protest Against Boy Prize Fighting," *New York Times*, Sept. 4, 1892, 3; Steven A. Riess, *Sport in Industrial America, 1850–1920* (Wheeling, IL: Harland Ellison, 1995), 146–147; Melissa Haley, "Storm of Blows," *Common-Place* 3, no. 2 (Jan. 2003), www.common-place.org/vol-03/no-02/haley/haley-2.shtml; "Before Entering the Ring," *Washington Post*, July 1, 1906, S4; David L. Calkins, "Chronological Highlights of Cincinnati's Black Community," *Cincinnati Historical Society Bulletin* 28 (Winter 1970): 28.

29. *New York Sun*, Sept. 2, 1887, 3; "Courting the Newsboys," *New York Commercial Advertiser*, in *Daily Yellowstone Journal*, Dec. 17, 1887, 2; "Six Games This Week," *Washington Post*, Apr. 16, 1888, 2; "The Newsboys' Base Ball Club," *Detroit Journal Year-Book for 1889* (Detroit: Journal, 1888), 142; Silas Farmer, *The History of Detroit and Michigan* (Detroit: Silas Farmer, 1889), 1078–1081.

30. "General State News," *Jackson Citizen*, Jan. 18, 1888, 2; "Newsboys Organizing a Trust," *Cleveland Plain Dealer*, Sept. 9, 1888, 8.

31. "A Newspaper Combine," *Philadelphia Record*, Apr. 20, 1886, n.p., in *Fort Worth Gazette*, Apr. 28, 1886, 6; Edwin Emery, *History of the American Newspaper Publishers Association* (Minneapolis: University of Minnesota Press, 1950), 22–24; Lee, *Daily Newspaper in America*, 232; "Newsboys to Play," *New York World*, Apr. 11, 1888, 1; "Yesterday's Base Ball Games," *Brooklyn Eagle*, Apr. 14, 1888, 1; "Six Games This Week," *Washington Post*, Apr. 16, 1888, 2; "Notes," *Washington Post*, May 10, 1888, 2; "The Newsboy Teams," *Cleveland Plain Dealer*, May 1, 1888, 5.

32. "Baseball Notes," *Cleveland Plain Dealer*, Apr. 28, 1888, 5; "Newsboys at the Play," *New York World*, May 15, 1888, 1; "Hear the Wail of Detroit," *New York World*, May 12, 1888, 2; "Those Detroit Newsboys," *New York World*, May 26, 1888, 1; "The Date Here Changed," *New York World*, May 23, 1888, 4; "Victorious Newsboys," *New York World*, May 24, 1888, 1; "A Great Game," *New York World*, June 7, 1888, 2; "Newsboy Baseball," *New York World*, Apr. 27, 1888, 1; "Monday and the Newsboys," *New York World*, May 18, 1888, 1; "Newsboys to Play," *New York World*, Apr. 11, 1888, 1.

33. *American Card Catalog* (US Tobacco Inserts, 1960), 21; Bob Lemke, ed., *1997 Standard Catalog of Baseball Cards*, 6th ed. (Iola, WI: Krause Publications, 1996), 1119, 1434.

34. *Detroit Journal Year-Book for 1889*, 142; "Newsdealers Enjoy Themselves," *Brooklyn Eagle*, June 2, 1886, 4; "Amateur Baseball," *Washington Post*, Aug. 11, 1889, 3; "Yer Out!," *Cincinnati Post*, July 20, 1894, 1; "First Game Is Won by White Newsboys," *Washington Times*, May 1, 1909, 3; Maurice B. Hexter, "The Newsboys of Cincinnati," *Studies from the Helen S. Trounstine Foundation* 1, no. 4 (Jan. 15, 1919): 148–149.

35. "White Caps, Indeed!," *New York World*, July 29, 1892, 5.

36. "Newsboys on Rollers," *St. Louis Post-Dispatch*, Dec. 11, 1885, 7; "Newsboys on Skates," *Brooklyn Eagle*, May 14, 1899, 18; *Salt Lake Tribune*, Nov. 20, 1897, 5; "Newsboys vs. the Garfield," *Colorado Spring Gazette*, Sept. 24, 1899, 5.

37. "A Newsboy Brass Band," *Los Angeles Times*, Aug. 14, 1887, 12; "George Queen's Death," *New Orleans Times-Picayune*, Sept. 1, 1905, 10; "Billy Norton Back," *New Orleans Times-Picayune*, Jan. 27, 1914, 12; *New Orleans Times-Democrat*, in *Dallas Morning News*, Sept. 5, 1897, 18; Orin Blackstone, "'Hot' Music Born Here, Says Blind Musician Who Played with the Band That Started It," *New Orleans Times-Picayune*, Nov. 3, 1935, sec. 2, 2; Elizabeth Bennett, "Jazz, Man, Real Jazz!," *New Orleans Times-Picayune*, Nov. 5, 1961, 8; "Changes," *Mobile Register*, July 15, 1975, 4.

38. "Newsboys' Band," *Daily Kentuckian*, May 25, 1898, 2. "Brass Buttons," *St. Paul Globe*, July 21, 1903, 4.

39. "Newsboys' Band a Great Attraction," *Marion* (OH) *Daily Mirror*, Oct. 1, 1909, 3; "The Journal's Big Band of Little Men," *Minneapolis Journal*, Apr. 29, 1902, 10; "World's Fair Notes," *Chicago Tribune*, Oct. 15, 1893, 3; "Some Press Tributes to the Little Red Coats," *Minneapolis Journal*, Aug. 17, 1901, 12; John Gunckel, *Boyville: A History of Fifteen Years' Work Among Newsboys* (Toledo, OH: Toledo Newsboys' Association, 1905), 55–58; "Capital All Ready for Taft Inaugural," *Washington Post*, Mar. 4, 1909, 1; Martha F. Bellinger, "Music in Indianapolis, 1900–1944," *Indiana Magazine of History* 42, no. 1 (Mar. 1946): 60.

40. "Resurrecting the Lost Tradition of Newspaper Marches," *Chronicle of Higher Education*, June 14, 1996, B5; D. W. Crist, *News Boy March* (Moultrie, OH, 1904); C. W. Crist, *Newsboy Galop* (Moultrie, OH, 1905); O. E. Sutton, *The Newsboys March* (Cincinnati: Sutton Music Co., 1905).

41. "A Good School for Boys," *Urbana Daily Courier*, Sept. 6, 1903, 2; "Once a Carrier for the Tribune," *Chicago Tribune*, Dec. 1, 1895, 7. See also E. C. Wines, *The Science of Prison Reform: The State of Prisons and of Child-Saving Institutions in the Civilized World* (Cambridge, MA: John Wilson & Sons, 1880), 80–81, 125–132, and Amos G. Warner, *American Charities: A Study in Philanthropy and Economics* (New York: Crowell, 1894), 237.

42. "Domestic Gossip," *New York Evening Post*, Mar. 15, 1862, 1; "Samuel Eliot Fraser's Report on the Common-School System," *North American Review* 106, no. 218 (Jan. 1868): 145; "Matters and Things," *Minneapolis Tribune*, Oct. 26, 1873, 2; *Washington Critic*, Oct. 30, 1873, 1; Peggy Lovvo, "Society for the Protection of Newsboys and Waifs: The Newsboys Home," unpublished paper, Aug. 26, 1985, 4–5. Filson Club; C. C. Ousley, *A Newsboys' Club House or Where Boys Are Made Men* (Louisville: Hugh & Ousley, 1903), 36–38; *Wilkes-Barre Leader*, Sept. 19, 26, 1878, 3; "Board of Education," *Cleveland Leader*, Nov. 30, 1880, 6; *Cleveland Plain Dealer*, Oct. 16, 1883, 4, Feb. 5, 1884, 2; "The Newsboys' Night School," *St. Louis Post-Dispatch*, Jan. 18, 1886, 7.

43. J. W. Skinner, "How May We Rescue Street Children," *Proceedings of the Ninth Annual Conference on Charities and Corrections*, Aug. 7–12, 1882 (Springfield, IL: H. W. Rokker, 1883), 123; Florence Kelley and Alzine P. Stevens, "Wage-Earning Children," in *Hull-House Maps and Papers* (New York: Crowell, 1895), 54–55; Jacob Riis, *Children of the Poor* (New York: Charles Scribner's Sons, 1892), 267; Julian Ralph, "A Recent Journey Through the West," *Harper's Weekly* 8, no. 31 (1895): 829–830.

44. *Washington Critic*, Jan. 7, 1873, 4; *New York Commercial Advertiser*, Jan. 13, 1874, 1; "Newsboys' Reading-Room," *Boston Advertiser*, Oct. 10, 1879, 4; Emma Brown, *Child Toilers of Boston Streets* (Boston: D. Lothrop, 1879), 20–23; "About People," *Cleveland Plain Dealer*, Jan. 13, 1880, 2; *Newsboys' Reading Room of Boston* (Boston: Alfred Mudge & Son, 1890); Louis M. Lyons, *Newspaper Story: One Hundred Years of the Boston Globe* (Cambridge, MA: Belknap Press of Harvard University Press, 1971), 163; Isaac Goldberg, "A Boston Boyhood,"

American Mercury 17, no. 67 (July 1929): 360. See also Lewis Hine, "Newsboy Reading Room, Boston," n.d. George Eastman House Collection 77:178:30 GEH Neg. 30083.

45. "The Newsboys," *Baltimore Sun*, Dec. 17, 1885, 4; "The Newsboys' Aid Society," *Washington Post*, Jan. 13, 1886, 2; "For a Bootblack's Reading Room," *Chicago Tribune*, June 10, 1890, 3; "The Newsboys' War," *Baltimore News*, in *Omaha World-Herald*, Dec. 30, 1896, 5.

46. *Eighteenth Annual Report of the Children's Aid Society* (New York: Wynkoop and Ballenbeck,1870), 18; "Boston Street Characters," *Ballou's Pictorial* 8, no. 4 (Jan. 27, 1855): 59; "Mr. Mathew Arnold and the Barefooted Newsboy," *Rocky Mountain News*, Nov. 6, 1887, 6. For images of newsboys and bootblacks reading in public, see Thomas Westerman Wood, *Spelling It Out*, 1879 (20 × 14¼ in., location unknown); J. G. Brown, *The Latest Novel*, in *Harper's Young People* 10, no. 489 (Apr. 2, 1889): 329; and Frederick Dielman, *Newsboy Reading the Paper*, in Alfred Trumble, "A Painter of the Beautiful," *Monthly Illustrator* 5, no. 16 (Aug. 1895): 136. Journalistic references include "Pursuit of Knowledge," *New York Times*, Aug. 27, 1853, 6; "The Newsboy on Bonaparte," *Harper's New Monthly Magazine* 9, no. 53 (Oct. 1854): 701; "A Young Grammarian," *Ballou's Pictorial* 13, no. 23 (Dec. 5, 1857): 365; *New York Tribune*, Oct. 30, 1871, 8; *Figaro*, in *Winona Republican*, Sept. 16, 1887, 2; "The Learned Newsboy," *Philadelphia Inquirer*, Nov. 26, 1889, 5; and James Parton, *The Life of Horace Greeley* (Boston: Houghton Mifflin, 1889), 111–112.

47. "How Some Folks Spent Christmas," *New Orleans Times-Picayune*, Dec. 26, 1897, 3; George J. Manson, "Walks and Talks with the Working Classes," *Christian Union*, May 8, 1884, 440.

48. Smythe, *Gilded Age Press*, 40; "Young Trade Adventurers," *New York Tribune*, Dec. 22, 1895, 18; "Boy Peddlers," *Philadelphia Inquirer*, Dec. 29, 1895, sup. 25.

49. "A Poor Newsboy's Gift," *Cincinnati Commercial*, June 3, 1879, in *New York Times*, June 5, 1879, 2; "Personal," *Washington Post*, June 10, 1879, 2; "The Book-Collecting Newsboy," *New York Times*, July 12, 1879, 3; "A Newsboy's Gift," *Harper's Weekly* 23, no. 1180 (Aug. 9, 1879): 632–633; *Cincinnati Gazette*, May 4, 1880, 8; "Literary Cincinnati," *Literary World* 13, no. 15 (July 29, 1882): 249; "An Accumulative Newsboy," *Chicago Tribune*, Feb. 26, 1886, 3; "The Newsboys' Union," *Cincinnati Daily Times*, Dec. 15, 1872, 4.

50. "Newsboys' Union," *Cleveland Plain Dealer*, July 31, 1894, 1; "The Evening Press Newsboys' Library," *Grand Rapids Evening Press*, Jan. 2, 1897, 6; "'Murph' Wants to Be Great," *New York Times*, July 9, 1893, 9; "Charles W. Wood Dramatic Reader Rare Genius," *Chicago Defender*, Apr. 17, 1915, 4; J. Shirley Shadrach, "Charles Winter Wood; or, From Bootblack to Professor," in *Daughter of the Revolution: The Major Nonfiction Works of Pauline E. Hopkins*, ed. Ira Dworkin (New Brunswick, NJ: Rutgers University Press, 2007), 259–262.

51. *Minutes of the Eleventh Annual Meeting of the National Woman's Christian Temperance Union*, St. Louis, 1884 (Chicago: WCTU, 1884), cxvii–cxix, cxxiii–cxxiv, xxxv; *Minutes of the Eighth Annual Meeting of the National Woman's Christian Temperance Union*, Washington, DC, 1881 (Brooklyn: Union-Argus, 1881), cxv–cxvi; *Minutes of the Fourteenth Annual Meeting of the National Woman's Christian Temperance Union*, Nashville, 1887 (Chicago: WCTU, 1888), xcviii; *Minutes of the Thirteenth Annual Meeting of the National Woman's Christian Temperance Union*, Minneapolis, 1886 (Chicago: WCTU, 1886), cixvii–cixviii, 46–47, 93; "W.C.T.U.," *Chicago Inter Ocean*, May 20, 1890, 9; "Events in Camden," *Philadelphia Inquirer*, Feb. 20, 1891, 2; "Newsboys," *Canton Evening Repository*, Apr. 23, 1891, 1; "The Original Crusaders," *Cincinnati Commercial Tribune*, Oct. 28, 1882, 1; *Minutes of the Ninth Annual Meeting of the National Woman's Christian Temperance Union*, Louisville, 1882 (Brooklyn: Martin, Carpenter, 1882), 23; *Leadville Herald*, Mar. 20, 1884, 3; "Playgrounds, or Bust," *Anaconda Standard*, May 23, 1905, 11; *Minutes of the Fifteenth Annual Meeting of the National Woman's Christian Temperance Union*, New York, 1888, 16.

52. "Newsboys and Bootblacks of Louisville," *Louisville Commercial*, May 19, 1872, 4; Alexander Hogeland, *Ten Years Among the Newsboys of Louisville* (Louisville: John P. Morton, 1883); Alexander Hogeland, *Boys and Girls of 100 Cities* (Louisville, 1886); "60,000 Boy Tramps," *Chicago Inter Ocean*, Oct. 18, 1889, 7; "Differ as to Curfew," *Baltimore Sun*, Dec. 16, 1900, 12; *Interior Journal (Stanford, KY)*, June 21, 1907, 1. See also Peter C. Baldwin, "'Nocturnal Habits and Dark Wisdom': The American Response to Children in the Streets at Night, 1880–1930," *Journal of Social History* 35, no. 3 (2002): 602–605. Baldwin sees Hogeland as a huckster whose first curfew win came in Omaha, Nebraska, in 1896, well after Waterloo, Ontario,

introduced an ordinance in the late 1880s. Yet Hogeland won earlier victories in Nebraska, Kansas, and Missouri. "Col. Hogeland's Curfew," *Sioux City Journal*, May 1, 1895, 5.

53. "Newsboys Sympathy," *Minneapolis Tribune*, July 31, 1885, 1; Among the Newsboys," *Washington Post*, Nov. 4, 1889, 2; "A Youthful Audience," *Kansas City Star*, Feb. 8, 1886, 2; "Lecture To-night," *Kansas City Star*, Feb. 10, 1886, 1; "The Newsboy's Friend," *Rockford Gazette*, June 4, 1887, 4.

54. Florence Kelley, "On Some Changes in the Legal Status of the Child Since Blackstone," *International Review* 13 (Aug. 1882): 96.

55. "Everybody's Column," *Leadville Herald*, Mar. 15, 1884, 2; "In General," *Chicago Tribune*, Apr. 22, 1884, 8; "A Night for Newsboys," *Chicago Tribune*, Apr. 29, 1884, 8; "A Licensed Guild," *Chicago Tribune*, May 9, 1884, 8.

56. "The Newsboys and Bootblacks," *St. Paul Daily Globe*, May 7, 1885, 3; "The Newsboys' License," *Minneapolis Tribune*, May 13, 1885, 4.

57. "To Care for the Newsboys," *New York Times*, May 7, 1886, 3; *Baltimore Sun*, Dec. 18, 1888, 4; "License for Newsdealers," *Brooklyn Eagle*, Oct. 15, 1890, 4.

58. "Practical Philanthropy," *Minneapolis Journal*, Sept. 8, 1896, 5; "Work for the Boys," *Minneapolis Journal*, Jan. 19, 1898, 8; "Club Is 'Hot Stuff,'" *Minneapolis Journal*, Dec. 5, 1898, 7; William Byron Forbush, "A Sketch of the History of the Street Boys' Club Movement in America," *Work with Boys* 6, no. 1 (Jan. 1906), 2–25.

59. "Scripps Gets a Grip," *Saginaw News*, May 11, 1892, 3; "Newsboys and Carriers," *Grand Rapids Evening Press*, Jan. 13, 1893, 1; "Happy Newsboys," *Grand Rapids Evening Press*, Jan. 15, 1893, 1; "To the Newsboys," *Grand Rapids Evening Press*, June 27, 1893, 1; Turner to Booth, Mar. 28, 1893, Apr. 6, 1893, Mar. 14, 1893, George G. Booth Papers, Correspondence, 1892–1893, Bentley Historical Library, University of Michigan (henceforth Booth Papers).

60. "A Challenge from the Straits," *Grand Rapids Telegram-Herald*, June 12, 1888, 3; "Organizing the Newsboys," *Cleveland Plain Dealer*, May 19, 1891, 8; "Newsboys' Aid Association," *Cleveland Plain Dealer*, May 21, 1891, 8; "Newsboys' Benefit Association," *Chicago Tribune*, Feb. 15, 1892, 3; "The Newsboys' Association," *Detroit Plaindealer*, May 27, 1892, 5; "Newsboys Strike," *Grand Rapids Press*, Feb. 15, 1893, 1; "A News Boys' Strike," *Bay City Times*, Feb. 16, 1893, 1; "Detroit Newsboys Strike," *Rockford (IL) Morning Star*, Feb. 17, 1893, 6; "The Newsboys' Strike," *Grand Rapids Press*, Feb. 17, 1893, 1; "An Undesirable Immigrant," *Grand Rapids Press*, Feb. 24, 1893, 1; Turner to Booth, Spring 1894, Booth Papers; George W. Stark, "Newsboys of '91," *Detroit News*, Dec. 10, 1940, n.p., D / Newsboys—1931–40 (envelope of clippings), Detroit Public Library.

61. Anita Wallgren, "The Grand Rapids Press Newsboys at the Turn of the Twentieth Century," 5, unpublished paper, 1975, University of Michigan Department of Journalism, Bentley Historical Library, box 2, folder 105; "Grand Rapids Newsboys," *Jackson Patriot*, Sept. 26, 1896, n.p.; *Ludington Mail*, July 3, 1896, n.p., Scrapbook, Grand Rapids Press Collection, Grand Rapids History & Special Collections Center, Grand Rapids Public Library, box 5, folder 30, pp. 25, 9.

62. Mary Willcox Brown, "The Evening Press Newsboys' Association: A Business Enterprise," *Charities Review* 8, no. 5 (July 1898): 237; John Ihlder, "The Press and Its Newsboys," *World To-day* 13 (July 1907): 737–739; William Byron Forbush, "A Western Newspaper and Its Newsboys," *Charities and the Commons* 19, no. 1 (Oct. 5, 1907): 798–802; Arthur Pound, *The Only Thing Worth Finding: The Life and Legacies of George Gough Booth* (Detroit: Wayne State University Press, 1964), 461–467.

63. "Newsboys' School," *Grand Rapids Evening Press*, Dec. 14, 1895, 4.

64. William Orr to George G. Booth, July 22, 1892; W. H. Turner to Booth, Mar. 14, 1894; Turner to Booth, Mar. 20, 1893; Turner to Booth, May 1894; "Competition," *Grand Rapids Eagle*, May 8, 1894, n.p.; "Newspapers and Competition," *Grand Rapids Eagle*, May 10, 1894, n.p.; C. S. Burch to Booth, Oct. 25, 1897, Booth Papers, Correspondence, box 1; Mary Ann Wellman, "Examination of Selected Letters from the George Booth Papers," unpublished paper, 1974, University of Michigan Department of Journalism, box 1, Bentley Historical Library, Ann Arbor, Michigan.

65. Willcox Brown, "Evening Press Newsboys' Association," *Charities Review* 8, no. 5 (1898): 236–241; Grand Rapids Press Collection, box 1.5, ledger No. 4, 155–156, Grand Rapids Public

Library; George W. Stark, "Newsboys of '91," *Detroit News*, Dec. 10, 1940, n.p.; "The 'Evening Press' of Grand Rapids," *Inland Printer* 39, no. 2 (May 1907): 229–230; Wallgren, "The Grand Rapids Press Newsboys," 11; Forbush, "A Western Newspaper and Its Newsboys," 801.

66. "Hundreds Saved by a Newsboy," *Chicago Tribune*, July 3, 1900, 6; "Off for Washington," *Grand Rapids Evening Press*, July 7, 1900, 1. Botsford returned to clerk for the railroad, but died soon after in a rail accident. "A Tree on the Track," *Jackson Citizen Patriot*, Nov. 13, 1902, 2.

67. "Half Building Is for Newsboys," *Saginaw Evening News*, Apr. 7, 1905, 12; Arthur W. Stace, "The Evening Press," *Grand Rapids Evening Press*, Jan. 1, 1907, sup. 1–5; "Greatest of New Year Calls," *Grand Rapids Evening Press*, Jan. 2, 1907, 1; *Minutes of the Ninth Annual Convention of the National Association of Managers of Newspaper Circulation* (Milwaukee, WI, 1907), 39–40.

68. Forbush, "A Western Newspaper and Its Newsboys," 801; Norman J. Radder, *Newspapers in Community Service* (New York: McGraw Hill, 1926), 190–191; Tom Rademacher, "He still recalls days at Newsboy School," *Newsboy* 30, no. 1 (Jan.–Feb. 1992): 14.

69. *National Republican*, July 29, 1876, 2. Six years later an angry reader would shoot the news editor in his office.

70. "The State of Business," *New York Times*, Feb. 3, 1878, 8.

71. Ibid.

72. Ibid.

73. "Carrier's Address," *Salem Gazette*, Jan. 1, 1882, Peter J. Eckel Newsboy Collection, Firestone Library, Princeton University.

74. Ibid.

75. Ibid.

76. Ibid.; *Charleston News and Courier*, Oct. 22, 1877, 1; *Memphis Public Ledger*, Sept. 22, 1881, 4.

77. Alfred E. Smith, *Up to Now: An Autobiography* (New York: Viking, 1929), 8–9; Henry Moskowitz, *Alfred E. Smith: An American Career* (New York: Thomas Seltzer, 1924), 11; Christopher M. Finan, *Alfred E. Smith: The Happy Warrior* (New York: Hill & Wang, 2002), 24; William L. Riordan, *Plunkitt of Tammany Hall* (1905; Boston: Bedford Books, 1994), 49; Francis Churchill Williams, *J. Devlin—Boss: A Romance of American Politics* (Boston: Lothrop, 1901).

78. "Fighting Joe in the Chair," "Depew of the Newsboys," and "Newsboys in the Fray," Heig Scrapbook, 12, 17; "Bootblacks Howl for Both Candidates," *New York Herald*, Sept. 23, 1892, 9.

79. "Sam Hilliar [*sic*] Returns," *Washington Post*, Nov. 27, 1891, 4; "Sam Hillier Gets a Place," *Washington Post*, Feb. 10, 1892, 5; "A Call on the Bootblacks," *New York Times*, Sept. 20, 1892, 4; "Bootblacks Howl for Both Candidates," *New York Herald*, Sept. 23, 1892, 9; "Boys Do the Dirty Work," *New York Herald*, Sept. 24, 1892, 8; "A Campaign of Humbug," *New York Times*, Oct. 23, 1892, 16.

80. "All Over but the Shouting," *New York Times*, Sept. 23, 1892, 5.

81. Morton Keller, *Affairs of State: Public Life in Late Nineteenth Century America* (New York: Oxford University Press, 1977), 568–571.

82. "Prendergast Was from Omaha," *Kansas City Times*, Oct. 31, 1893, 2; "Testimony for the Defense," *Chicago Tribune*, Dec. 30, 1893, 3; "In re Prendergast Address to the Jury," July 1894, 1050, University of Minnesota Law Library, http://darrow.law.umn.edu/trials.php?tid=9; "The Tribune Newsboys," *Chicago Tribune*, Nov. 11, 1894, 25; John A. Farrell, *Clarence Darrow: Attorney for the Damned* (New York: Random House, 2012), 55–62.

83. "A Newsboy's Strike," *Rocky Mountain News*, May 24, 1883, 8; "A Strike Among Small Boys on the Price of a Small Paper," *Rocky Mountain News*, Sept. 5, 1884, 4; "Terrorized by the Union," *Milwaukee Sentinel*, July 19, 1883, 5; "Newsboys' Strike," *Milwaukee Sentinel*, July 21, 1883, 5; "Notes," *Chicago Tribune*, July 22, 1883, 3.

84. "Newsboys on a Strike," *Washington Post*, Aug. 12, 1883, 8.

85. "What the Newsdealers Are Doing," *New York Tribune*, Oct. 2, 1883, 5; "Newsdealers Protest," *New York Tribune*, Oct. 3, 1883, 5; "Newsdealers in Mass Meeting," *New York Tribune*, Oct. 13, 1883, 5.

86. "Newsboys Strike," *New York Times*, Oct. 14, 1884, 1.

87. F. H. Farny, "Destruction of the Court-House—Street Arabs Burning the Court Records, and Calling for Bids on the 'Temple of Justice,'" *Harper's Weekly* 28, no. 1425 (Apr. 12, 1884): 236; Charles T. Greve, *Centennial History of Cincinnati* (Chicago: Biographical Publishing, 1904), 1:1002; Samuel Haber, *The Quest for Authority and Honor in the Professions* (Chicago: University of Chicago Press, 1991), 189–190; Stephen W. Plattner, "Days of Dread," *Queen City Heritage* 42 (Spring 1984): 26, 29; *Cleveland Plain Dealer*, Jan. 3, 1884, 2.

88. Selig Perlman, *A History of Trade Unionism in the United States* (New York: Macmillan, 1922), 81–105; "Brief Locals," *Boston Evening Transcript*, Jan. 30 1886, 1, Feb. 6, 1886, 1; "Striking Newsboys Pummel a Scab," *Boston Globe*, Mar. 16, 1886, 2; "Needn't 'Boycott Johnnie' Now," *Boston Globe*, Mar. 17, 1886, 2; "The Hit Bird Flutters," *Chicago Tribune*, Mar. 25, 1886, 1; "And Now the Newsboys Strike," *Brooklyn Eagle*, Mar. 30, 1886, 6; "Newsboys Indulge in a Strike," *New York Times*, Mar. 30, 1886, 5; "Eastern District Newsboys," *Brooklyn Eagle*, Mar. 31, 1886, 4; "Boys Tired of Striking," *Brooklyn Eagle*, Apr. 1, 1886, 4; "The Newsboys; Strike Ended," *Brooklyn Eagle*, Apr. 2, 1886, 6; "Removing a Boycott," *New York Times*, Apr. 2, 1886, 2.

89. "Octavia," *National Republican*, Apr. 24, 1886, 8; *Richmond Labor Herald*, Apr. 24, 1886, 3; "News and School Boys," *Boston Globe*, Apr. 20, 1886, 5; "Newsboys Strike," *Jackson Citizen Patriot*, Apr. 19, 1886, 1, Apr. 29, 1886, 4; "The Strike Ended," *Jackson Citizen Patriot*, May 3, 1886, 4; "The 'Kids of Labor' Win a Strike," *Kansas City Star*, May 1, 1886, 1; "Newsboys Force a Paper to Yield," *Kalamazoo* (MI) *Gazette*, May 2, 1886, 3.

90. "Self Employed and Unemployed Forgotten People," *Dallas Morning News*, Apr. 16, 1886, 4. See also Victoria C. Hattam, *Labor Visions and State Power: The Origins of Business Unionism in the United States* (Princeton, NJ: Princeton University Press, 1993).

91. "Juvenile Knights of Labor," *Boston Herald*, May 2, 1886, 4.

92. Paul Avrich, *The Haymarket Tragedy* (Princeton, NJ: Princeton University Press, 1984), 5, 283; "Couldn't Say 'Anarchists,'" *Detroit Tribune*, in *Kansas City Times*, Dec. 11, 1887, 18.

93. "Occurrence of a Newsboys' Strike in Lowell, Mass.," *Zion's Herald*, May 9, 1886, 160; "Newsboys Strike," *Boston Herald*, Nov. 30, 1886, 2; *San Francisco Bulletin*, May 25, 1886, 3; *Sacramento Union*, June 12, 1886, 1; "Organized Newsboys," *Springfield Globe-Republic*, Sept. 29, 1886, 1.

94. "The Newsboys' Union," *Alta California*, June 2, 1886, 1; "Labor Organizations," *San Francisco Bulletin*, June 3, 1886, 2; *San Francisco Bulletin*, June 15, 1886, 1; "The Little Newsboys," *San Francisco Bulletin*, July 21, 1886, 1; "Newsboy Badges," *San Francisco Bulletin*, Aug. 13, 1886, 2.

95. "The Knights of Labor," *Chicago Inter Ocean*, July 3, 1886, 2; "Boys on the Boycott," *Brooklyn Eagle*, June 17, 1886, 2; "The Newsboys' Parade," *Brooklyn Eagle*, July 6, 1886, 2; "Newsboys Must Keep Off," *New York Sun*, July 22, 1886, 1.

96. Michael A. Gordon, "The Labor Boycott in New York City, 1880–1886," *Labor History* 16, no. 2 (Spring 1975): 184; "Angry Newsboys Gain Their Point," *New York Herald*, Jan. 18, 1887, 5; "Failure of a 'Capitalistic' Design," *New York Tribune*, Jan. 18, 1887, 2; *New York Herald-Tribune*, Jan. 19, 1887, 4.

97. "Current Events," *Brooklyn Eagle*, Jan. 29, 1887, 2; "A Newspapers' Strike," *Brooklyn Eagle*, Jan. 29, 1887, 4; "Strike of Newsboys," *New York Times*, Jan. 29, 1887, 8; *Detroit Free Press*, Jan. 29, 1887, 4.

98. "Labor Items," *Kansas City Star*, May 18, 1887, 2; "The New York Press," *Arkansas Gazette*, Oct. 22, 1887, 6; "Central Labor Union Topics," *New York Sun*, Apr. 4, 1887, 3; "Next Month's Fourth," *Omaha Bee*, June 21, 1887, 2; "Newsboys' Strike," *Omaha Bee*, July 3, 1887, 8.

99. "A Small Strike," *Los Angeles Times*, Aug. 10, 1887, 1; "Hard Up," *Los Angeles Times*, Nov. 27, 1887, 8; "The Managers," *Los Angeles Times*, Nov. 29, 1887, 4.

100. "Washington Newsboys on Strike," *New York Sun*, Aug. 28, 1887, 1; *Saginaw News*, Oct. 26, 1887, 4; "Newsboys Boycott a Paper," *Maysville Daily Evening Bulletin*, Aug. 6, 1887, 1; "Printers on Strike," *San Diego Union*, Nov. 8, 1887, 1; "Newsboys on Strike," *Milwaukee Sentinel*, Dec. 1, 1887, 3.

101. "The Striking Newsboys," *Milwaukee Sentinel*, Dec. 7, 1887, 2; *Milwaukee Sentinel*, Dec. 9, 1887, 2; "Seeking Information," *Milwaukee Sentinel*, Dec. 13, 1887, 3.

102. "The Business of Being a Newsboy," *Chicago Arbeiter Zeitung*, June 1, 1888, http://flps.newberry.org/article/5418474_6_0182.

103. A history of this juvenile strike wave remains to be written. See "A Burlesque on Strikes," *New York Times*, Mar. 18, 1886, 8; "Mr. Richardson on Strikes," *New York Times*, Apr. 2, 1886, 5; "School Children Attempt to Strike," *Washington Post*, Apr. 2, 1886, 2; "The Scholars Attempted to Strike," *Washington Post*, Apr. 3, 1886, 2; "Another Strike by Schoolboys," *Washington Post*, Apr. 13, 1886, 1; "Schoolboys on Strike," *New York Times*, Apr. 13, 1886, 2; Schoolboys Go on Strike," *Washington Post*, Apr. 13, 1886, 1; "The Schoolboys' Strike," *Baltimore Sun*, Apr. 14, 1886, 1; "Another Schoolboys' Strike," *New York Times*, Apr. 16, 1886, 2; *Washington Post*, Apr. 16, 1886, 2; *Elkhart Daily Review*, Apr. 16, 1886, 3; "Striking School-Children," *Chicago Tribune*, Apr. 17, 1886, 6; "Refractory Schoolboys," *New York Times*, Apr. 17, 1886, 5; "The School-Boys' Strike," *Chicago Tribune*, Apr. 18, 1886, 9; "News and School Boys," *Boston Globe*, Apr. 20, 1886, 5; "A Strike of School Boys," *Washington Post*, June 20, 1886, 6; "Colored Pupils on Strike," *New York Times*, Oct. 20, 1886, 2; "More School Boys Strike," *Washington Post*, Apr. 21, 1886, 1; "Boston Schoolboys on Strike," *New York Times*, Apr. 21, 1886, 3; "Striking Schoolboys," *New York Times*, Apr. 22, 1886, 3; "A Successful Strike," *Chicago Tribune*, Apr. 23, 1886, 3; "More Schoolboys to Strike," *Washington Post*, Apr. 24, 1886, 1; "Silly School-Children," *Chicago Tribune*, Apr. 24, 1886, 1; "A School on Strike," *New York Times*, Jan. 26, 1887, 5; "Striking Schoolboys," *New York Times*, May 7, 1887, 5; "Baseball May Cause Strike," *Washington Post*, May 7, 1887, 1; and "The Strike at Trinity," *New Haven Register*, May 3, 1886, 1.

104. "Telegraphic Brevities," *St. Louis Republic*, July 25, 1888, 3; "Newsboys Organizing a Trust," *Cleveland Plain Dealer*, Sept. 26, 1888, 8; "Arresting Newsboys," *St. Louis Republic*, June 22, 1889, 7.

105. "An Infantile Boycott," *Brooklyn Eagle*, Aug. 12, 1889, 4; "Newsboys on Strike," *New York Times*, Aug. 13, 1889, 8; "A Howling Crowd of Young Tigers," *New York Tribune*, Aug. 13, 1889, 4; "Newsboys on Strike," *Boston Globe*, Aug. 13, 1889, 4; "Newsboys Win the Day," *Chicago Tribune*, Aug. 13, 1889, 5; "Topics in New York," *Baltimore Sun*, Aug. 13, 1889, 4; Aug. 14, 1889, 1; *Washington Post*, Aug. 14, 1889, 4.

106. "The New Yerkes Outrage," *Chicago Daily News*, Oct. 29, 1889; "Yerkes Great Scheme," *Chicago Daily News*, Oct. 30, 1889; "Bound to Sell Papers," *Chicago Tribune*, Oct. 31, 1889, 6; "They Defy Baron Yerkes," *Chicago Daily News*, Oct. 31, 1889; "Newsboys in Battle Array," *Chicago Tribune*, Nov. 1, 1889, 6; "Yerkes and the Newsboys," *Chicago Daily News*, Nov. 1, 1889 (3 p.m. ed.), n.p.; "The Newsboys' War," *Chicago Daily News*, Nov. 1, 1889 (5 p.m. ed.), n.p., all in *Newsboy* 25, no. 2 (Sept.–Oct. 1986): 3–18; "The Embargo on the Newsboys," *Chicago Tribune*, Nov. 2, 1889, 6.

107. "The Newsboys' Strike," *St. Louis Republic*, Dec. 21, 1889, 8; "Beaten by a Mob of Newsboys," *New York Times*, Jan. 4, 1895, 5; "Beaten by Newsboys," *Atlanta Constitution*, Jan. 4, 1895, 1.

Chapter 9

1. *Distributing a War Extra*, May 1, 1898, American Mutoscope & Biograph Co., 1903, Library of Congress, H30745. Among the company's first offerings in 1896 was *Newsboys Scrambling for Pennies*, by James White.

2. Charles E. Chapin, *Charles Chapin's Story: Written in Sing Sing Prison* (New York: G. P. Putnam's Sons, 1920), 182–184.

3. Alfred McClung Lee, *The Daily Newspaper in America: The Evolution of a Social Instrument* (New York: Macmillan, 1937), 722, 731.

4. *Fort Worth Morning Register*, July 30, 1899, 4.

5. "All After the Prize," *Chicago Tribune*, Apr. 15, 1893, 7; "For Newsboys and Bootblacks," *Chicago Inter Ocean*, Oct. 8, 1893, 2; "Newsboys at the Fair," *Atlanta Constitution*, Nov. 4, 1893, 1; Kimberly Louagie, "The Bonds He Did Not Break: Harry Houdini and Wisconsin," *Wisconsin Magazine of History* 85, no. 3 (Spring 2002): 6; "Waifs Take a Bath," *Chicago Tribune*, July 26, 1893, 1.

6. "To Hold a Waif Problem Congress," *Chicago Tribune*, Sept. 2, 1893, 3; *The Care of Dependent, Neglected and Wayward Children: Being a Report of the Second Section of the International Congress of Charities, Correction and Philanthropy, Chicago, June, 1893* (Baltimore: Johns Hopkins University Press, 1894); "Printing Press Row," *Duluth News-Tribune*, May 24, 1893, 1; "Would Amaze Gutenberg," *Chicago Inter Ocean*, May 24, 1893, 5; Richard Norton Smith,

The Colonel: The Life and Legend of Robert R. McCormick, 1880–1955 (Boston: Houghton Mifflin, 1997), 137; "Statistics of Laboring Classes," *Chicago Tribune*, Sept. 9, 1893, 8; "Chicago's Newsboys," *Perrysville Journal*, June 17, 1899, 3; "Chicago's Apostolic Newsboy," *Evansville Courier and Press*, Apr. 5, 1895, 4; "Oldest Newsboy; Chipper, Too," *New York American*, Mar. 7, 1898, 10.

7. American Social History Project, *Who Built America?* (Boston: Bedford/St. Martin's, 2000), 2:122–123; "All Runs Seem Ended," *Chicago Tribune*, June 7, 1893, 10; "Passed the Crisis," *Chicago Inter Ocean*, June 7, 1893, 2; "Little Newsboy Afraid to Go Home," *Chicago Tribune*, Jan. 13, 1894, 1.

8. "The Homeless Boy," *New York Commercial Advertiser*, in *Idaho Statesman*, Feb. 11, 1893, 3; "Begging Through Windows," *Washington Post*, Nov. 7, 1894, 12; "Concerning Needed Reforms," *New York Times*, Apr. 29, 1894, 21; "A Small Newsboy Decoy," *New York Herald*, Mar. 19, 1893, 16.

9. "He Has a Kind Heart," *Chicago Inter Ocean*, Dec. 12, 1893, 7; "Typhus Fever Spreading," *Atlanta Constitution*, Jan. 5, 1893, 1; "Typhus Fever in Prison," *New York Tribune*, Jan. 5, 1893, 1; "He Slept in a Police Station," *New York Times*, Jan. 19, 1893, 8; "Plague Boy Turned Loose," *New York World*, Jan. 23, 1897, n.p., in Heig Scrapbook, 23; see also 20, 35; "The Cholera and the Newspaper Fool," *New York Times*, Sept. 7, 1892, 4.

10. "Boy Workers," *Cleveland Plain Dealer*, Mar. 8, 1891, 16.

11. "The Newsboy's Kindness," *New York Herald*, in *Duluth News-Tribune*, Aug. 31, 1892, 3; "Mrs. Johnson's Diamonds Found," *New York Times*, May 20, 1893, 1; "Newsboys Dive for Dimes," *New York Evening World*, June 24, 1893, 5; "Fought for Stored Treasure," *New York Times*, Oct. 17, 1893, 8; "Slings and Arrows," *New York Times*, June 28, 1893, 4.

12. "A Newsboy Strike," *Salt Lake Tribune*, Jan. 15, 1890, 1; "On a Strike. Newsboys Claim the Great American Privilege of Striking," *Sacramento Daily Record Union*, Jan. 15, 1890, 4; "Dots and Dashes," *Watertown* (NY) *Daily Times*, Aug. 13, 1892, 7; Charles F. Marlak, "A Labor History of the Niagara Frontier (1846–1917), Containing an Introduction Consisting of Conditions Prior to 1846," PhD diss., University of Ottawa, 1947, 103.

13. "Nellie Bly's Ride," *New York Evening World*, Jan. 25, 1890, 1; "Newsboys on a Boycott," *Brooklyn Eagle*, July 29, 1890, 6; "Boycotting the 'World,'" *Brooklyn Eagle*, Aug. 2, 1890, 5.

14. "Newsboys Strike," *Dallas Morning Herald*, Dec. 30, 1890, 8; "Well, Well," *New Orleans Item*, Aug. 22, 1892, 4.

15. "Duluth's Newsboys," *Duluth News-Tribune*, Apr. 1, 1891, 4; "Clement's Capture," *Duluth News-Tribune*, Apr. 1, 1891, 2; "Gompers' Gumption," *Duluth News-Tribune*, Apr. 2, 1891, 2; "The Newsboy Muddle," *Duluth News-Tribune*, Apr. 2, 1891, 4; "A Newsboy Assaulted," *Duluth News-Tribune*, Apr. 3, 1891, 2; "Union and Violence," *Duluth News-Tribune*, Apr. 3, 1891, 4; "Newsboys Organize," *Minneapolis Tribune*, Apr. 5, 1891, 1; George B. Engberg, "The Knights of Labor in Minnesota," *Minnesota History* 22, no. 4 (Dec. 1941): 385; "Arrival of Mascot," *New York Tribune*, May 1, 1891, 20.

16. "Riot Is the End," *Chicago Inter Ocean*, July 7, 1892, 1; "Out on Bail," *Boston Journal*, July 25 1892, 1.

17. "Boycotted with Brickbats," *Brooklyn Eagle*, May 24, 1893, 1; "Their Services Appreciated," *Boston Herald*, Oct. 23, 1893, 2; "Newsboys' Strike," *Omaha World-Herald*, Nov. 4, 1893, 8; "Newsboys Strike," *Hickman* (KY) *Courier*, Oct. 5, 1894, 1; "Strike of Denver Newsboys," *Chicago Times*, Feb. 18, 1894, 11; *Duluth News-Tribune*, May 16, 1894, 2.

18. Henry Vincent, *The Story of the Commonweal* (Chicago: W. B. Conkey, 1894; repr., New York: Arno Press, 1969), 125–162; Jack London, *The Road* (New York: Macmillan, 1907), 57, 175–195; "Coxey Is Coming," *Washington Times*, May 1, 1894, 2.

19. "His Men Are Heroes," *Chicago Tribune*, Mar. 22, 1895, 1; Bruce C. Johnson, "Taking Care of Labor: The Police in American Politics," *Theory and Society* 3, no. 1 (Spring 1976): 99.

20. "A Labor Leader Arrested," *Brooklyn Eagle*, July 10, 1894, 1; "Gleaned from the Dispatches," *Elkhart Daily Review*, July 10, 1894, 1; "Newsboys Catch the Fever," *Omaha Bee*, July 11, 1894, 1; "Newsboys Boycott Chicago Papers," *New York Times*, July 11, 1894, 3; Willis J. Abbot, "Chicago Newspapers and Their Makers," *Review of Reviews* 11, no. 6 (June 1895): 647; "Debs Arrested," *Atlanta Constitution*, July 11, 1894, 1; "Practical Joke on Sympathizers," *Chicago Tribune*, July 15, 1894, 12; *Daily People*, July 22, 1894, 1; "Debs's Telegram Read in Court," *New York Times*, Sept. 7, 1894, 2; *American Newsman* 11, no. 11 (Sept. 1894): 15–16.

21. *Salt Lake Tribune*, Jan. 21, 1895, 7; "Petty Business," *Los Angeles Times*, July 7, 1894, 5; "The 'Times' Boycott," *San Diego Union*, July 7, 1894, 2; "Disorderly Newsboys," *Los Angeles Times*, July 12, 1894, 6; Amelia Wells, "Manufacturing Anarchists," *Los Angeles Times*, July 13, 1894, 8; "Times in Midchannel," *Los Angeles Times*, Dec. 4, 1921, Sec. 8, 1.

22. "A Newsboys' Strike," *The State* (Columbia, SC), July 17, 1894, 5; "Tells of Experience of Newsboys in Nineties," n.d., in "Cleveland—Newsboys" clipping file, Cleveland Public Library; "A Strike," *Cleveland Plain Dealer*, July 17, 1894, 8; *Cleveland Gazette*, July 21, 1894, 3; "Youthful Penitents," *Cleveland Plain Dealer*, July 18, 1894, 2; "Newsboys' Union," *Cleveland Plain Dealer*, July 31, 1894, 1; "Newsboy's Union," *Cleveland Plain Dealer*, Aug. 5, 1894, 2; Shelton Stromquist, "The Crucible of Class: Cleveland Politics and the Origins of Municipal Reform in the Progressive Era," in *Who Were the Progressives?*, ed. Glenda Elizabeth Gilmore (Boston: Bedford/St. Martin's, 2002), 145–147. See also Robert D. Johnston, *The Radical Middle Class: Populist Democracy and the Question of Capitalism in Progressive Era Portland, Oregon* (Princeton, NJ: Princeton University Press, 2003).

23. Karl Marx, *Capital: A Critique of Political Economy*, trans. Samuel Moore, ed. Edward Aveling, rev. Frederick Engels (New York: Modern Library, 1906), 706; "Lucian Sanial," *Baltimore Sun*, July 31, 1894, 8; Lucian Sanial, "The Hartford Debate," *Daily People*, Oct. 14, 1894, 2.

24. Louis M. Lyons, *Newspaper Story: One Hundred Years of the Boston Globe* (Cambridge, MA: Belknap Press of Harvard University Press, 1971), 113; Hy B. Turner, *When Giants Ruled: The Story of Park Row, New York's Great Newspaper Street* (New York: Fordham University Press, 1999), 121; *Elkhart Daily Review*, May 8, 1893, 1; Eugene M. Camp, "Conscience in Journalism," *Century Magazine* 42, no. 3 (July 1891): 473.

25. "Cheap and Nasty Journalism," *Cleveland Plain Dealer*, Apr. 16, 1883, 1; "A Journalistic Scavenger," *San Diego Evening Tribune*, Apr. 29, 1897, 2; *Philadelphia Inquirer*, June 1, 1892, 1, and July 21, 1894, 1. See also David R. Spencer, *The Yellow Journalism: The Press and America's Emergency as a World Power* (Evanston, IL: Northwestern University Press, 2007).

26. "For Buying Stolen Pictures," *Chicago Tribune*, Jan. 4, 1895, 8.

27. "Sunday Papers," *Printers' Ink* 25, no. 11 (June 10, 1896): 8; Hartley Davis, "The Journalism of New York," *Munsey's Magazine* 24, no. 2 (Nov. 1900): 228; "Serving the Times," *Los Angeles Times*, Apr. 6, 1890, 9; Lee, *Daily Newspaper in America*, 731.

28. "Trenton Newpapers," *Trenton Times*, July 8, 1898, 5; *Cincinnati Enquirer*, Apr. 2, 1872, 4; Charles E. Kennedy, *Fifty Years of Cleveland, 1875–1925* (Cleveland: Weidenthal, 1925), 45; Donald J. Wood, *Newspaper Circulation Management—A Profession* (Oakland, CA: Newspaper Research Bureau, 1952), 5; Gerald J. Baldasty, *The Commercialization of News in the Nineteenth Century* (Madison: University of Wisconsin Press, 1992), 63.

29. "Inserting Circulars in Newspapers," *Book and News-Dealer* 10, no. 116 (Oct. 1898): 114–115.

30. Bush to Booth, Aug. 23, 1899, Booth Papers; "Edward J. Nieuwland, Sr.," *American Newsman* 11, no. 11 (Nov. 1894): 32; "Getting the Spy to the Newsdealers and Home of Its Thousands of Readers in City and Country," *Worcester Spy*, Aug. 24, 1902, 7; "Trolley Car Used for Early Delivery of 'The Tribune,'" *Chicago Tribune*, July 3, 1902, 4; "The Brooklyn Eagle to Washington," *Brooklyn Eagle*, Mar. 4, 1889, 9; "Syracuse Astonished," *New York Times*, Sept. 24, 1896, 1.

31. *Cleveland Plain Dealer*, Nov. 6, 1882, 5; "The Newsboy's Girl-Baby," *Atlanta Constitution*, Jan. 28, 1881, 1; "Mystery of Newsboy's Baby," *Denver Post*, May 11, 1903, 4; "Modern Slang," *Evansville Courier & Press*, Apr. 13, 1903, 4; "Tried to Drown the Sound," *Kalamazoo* (MI) *Gazette*, Aug. 23, 1890, 8; "A Day in a Newsboy's Life," *New York Times*, July 6, 1890, 6; "Tim Kelley's Sparrow Dies, Victim of Drink," *New York Times*, Apr. 9, 1905, 9.

32. *Washington Bee*, May 3, 1884, 4; R. Ponsonby Staples, "A Novel Feature in London Life: The Distribution of Newspapers by Bicycle Boys," *Graphic*, Apr. 9, 1898, n.p.; Michael Taylor, "Rapid Transit to Salvation: American Protestants and the Bicycle in the Era of the Cycling Craze," *Journal of the Gilded Age and Progressive Era* 9, no. 3 (July 1910): 356; "The Value of Bicycles to Newspaper Men," *Fourth Estate*, Jan. 10, 1895, 4; "More of Powderly's Partisans," *New York Times*, Aug. 28, 1890, 2.

33. Ellen Le Garde, *Jim Preston's Bicycle. A Story for Boys* (Philadelphia: Curtis Publishing, 1891).

34. Lyons, *Newspaper Story*, 83; E. S. Martin, "This Busy World," *Harper's Weekly* 43, no. 2222 (July 29, 1899): 733; Bill Blackbeard, *R. F. Outcault's* The Yellow Kid: *A Centennial Celebration*

of the Kid Who Started the Comics (Northampton, MA: Kitchen Sink Press, 1995), 56–61; W. Joseph Campbell, *Yellow Journalism: Puncturing the Myths, Defining the Legacies* (Westport, CT: Praeger, 2001), 27–29; Ruth Margaret Iliff Nordahl, "A Social Study of the Newsboys' Trade in Los Angeles," master's thesis, University of Southern California, 1912, 10, 13; Marian Faas Stone, "Industrial Accidents to Employed Minors in California in 1932," *Monthly Labor Review* 39 (Nov. 1934): 1078.

35. On Hardell, see "Shouted with Joy," *New York Evening World*, Aug. 18, 1890, 2; "Gotham's Heart Warms for Those Peajackets," *New York Herald*, Dec. 23, 1890, 4; *Boston Herald*, Aug. 21, 1892, 23; and Brander Matthews, "In the Midst of Life," *Harper's Weekly* 37, no. 1930 (Dec. 16, 1893): 1199, 1206.

36. "Almost as Good as Legs," *Minneapolis Journal*, July 15, 1895, 6; "Patsy Proud of His Chair," *Cleveland Plain Dealer*, June 18, 1901, 10; "Newsies Buy a Crippled Brother a Wheeled Chair," *Salt Lake Telegram*, May 17, 1907, 6.

37. "In Labor's Field," *Minneapolis Journal*, Dec. 26, 1896, 9; "The Silent Newsboy," *San Francisco Chronicle*, May 12, 1892, 12; "A Mechanical Newsboy," *Book and Newsdealer* 14, no. 165 (Aug. 1903): 34; Lee, *Daily Newspaper in America*, 300; *Sacramento Record Union*, July 21, 1892, 1; *American Newsman* 11, no. 11 (Nov. 1894): 21; *Publisher's Weekly* 50, no. 25/1299 (Dec. 19, 1896): 1190; *Cleveland Leader*, July 27, 1897, 4.

38. "Roasted to a Turn," *San Francisco Call*, May 22, 1892, 8.

39. Don C. Seitz, *Training for the Newspaper Trade* (Philadelphia: J. B. Lippincott, 1916), 84–85, 149–150; "Where 'Returns' Go To," *Book and News-Dealer* 10, no. 114 (Aug. 1898): 41; "As to Returns," *Book and News-Dealer* 12, no. 153 (Aug. 1902): 20; "The 'Union' and the Newsboys," *San Diego Union*, Apr. 3, 1891, 4; "Newsboys on Strike," *Daily Alta California*, Apr. 5, 1891, 1; "Boycotted with Brickbats," *Brooklyn Eagle*, May 24, 1893, 1; *New Orleans States*, Dec. 3, 1895, cited in John Wilds, *Afternoon Story: A Century of the New Orleans States-Item* (Baton Rouge: Louisiana State University, 1976), 180.

40. Paul Spickard, *Almost All Aliens: Immigration, Race, and Colonialism in American History and Identity* (New York: Routledge, 2007), Tables B.6–B.15, 485–494; Roger Daniels, *Not Like Us: Immigrants and Minorities in America, 1890–1924* (Chicago: Ivan R. Dee, 1997), 58; "Facts About the Street Gamins," *Cleveland Herald*, in *New York Times*, Aug. 27, 1882, 9; "Jerusalem to the Front," *Boston Herald*, May 6, 1889, 5; "Notes of the Jews," *New York Sun*, Nov. 11, 1894, 3; Christopher Ogden, *Legacy: A Biography of Moses and Walter Annenberg* (New York: 1999), 18.

41. "Five 'Tony' Newsboys," *National Police Gazette* 40, no. 262 (Sept. 30, 1882): 9; "The Italians in New York," *Catholic World* 47, no. 277 (Apr. 1, 1888): 67; Edward W. Townsend, "Newsboys of City Hall Park," *Harper's Young People* 15, no. 768 (July 17, 1894): 638.

42. "Italian Newsboys are the Best," *Chicago Tribune*, Oct. 9, 1903, 15; Myron E. Adams, "Children in American Street Trades," *Annals of the American Academy of Political and Social Science* 25 (May 1905): 439, reprinted as NCLC Pamphlet No. 14 (1905), 5; William Hard, "De Kid Wot Works at Night," *Everybody's* 18 (Jan. 1908), 30–32.

43. *New Orleans Times-Picayune*, Aug. 23, 1897, 4; Daniels, *Not Like Us*, 45; "Two Hours of Fire in the Post Office," *New York Herald*, Feb. 15, 1891, 17; "Mails Escape Harm," *New York Press*, Feb. 16, 1891, n.p.; "Fatal Work of the Flames," *New York Tribune*, July 6, 1891, 1.

44. "A Fool's Diary," *Seattle Mail and Herald*, Mar. 22, 1902, 2; Lydia Kingsmill Commander, "Why Do Americans Prefer Small Families," *Independent*, Oct. 13, 1904, 848.

45. "An Unknown Italian Quarter," *Washington Post*, Feb. 10, 1895, 7; Frances A. Walker, "Restriction of Immigration," *Atlantic Monthly* 77, no. 646 (June 1896): 828; Thomas J. Archdeacon, *Becoming American: An Ethnic History* (New York: Free Press, 1983), 150; "A Chicago Incident," *Northern Christian Advocate*, Apr. 25, 1894, 1.

46. Murat Halstead, "Waifs of New York," *Trenton Times*, Nov. 8, 1884, 2; "A Good Work," *Irish World*, Dec. 3, 1892, 4.

47. "Five 'Tony' Newsboys," *National Police Gazette*, 9; "The Italians in New York," *Catholic World* 47, no. 277 (Apr. 1, 1888): 67; "The Newsboy," *Los Angeles Times*, Oct. 13, 1889, 9.

48. "The Padrone System," *Los Angeles Times*, Sept. 16, 1889, 2; "The Newsboy. How He Works and Lives, Struggles and Endures," *Los Angeles Times*, Oct. 13, 1889, 9. On indentured or captive newsboys in Rochester and Montreal, see "Facts in re Street Trades Bill," n.d., 2, box 31,

folder 9, New York Child Labor Committee Papers, New York State Library, Albany (hence-forth NYCLC Papers), and "Found His Stolen Brother," *New York Journal*, in *Galveston Daily News*, Jan. 8, 1893, 11. On the padrone system, see Robert H. Bremner, "The Children with the Organ Man," *American Quarterly* 8, no. 3 (Autumn 1956): 277–282; John Zucchi, *The Little Slaves of the Harp: Italian Child Street Musicians in Nineteenth-Century Paris, London, and New York* (Montreal: McGill-Queen's University Press, 1992); Martha J. Hoppin, "The 'Little White Slaves' of New York: Paintings of Child Street Musicians by J. G. Brown," *American Art Journal* 26, nos. 1–2 (1994): 4–43; and Carl Ipsen, *Italy in the Age of Pinocchio: Children and Danger in the Liberal Era* (New York: Palgrave Macmillan, 2006).

49. "The Mayor Studying Italian," *Cleveland Plain Dealer*, Mar. 9, 1890, 1; "Stolen by a Dago," *New Orleans Times-Picayune*, Nov. 27, 1892, 16; "To the Inter-Ocean. the Italians Have Done Their Duty," *L'Italia*, July 21, 1894, http://flps.newberry.org/article/5425702_1_0810; "Chicago Italians Viewed by Experts," *New Orleans Times-Picayune*, Jan. 9, 1898, 27.

50. John Cournos, *Autobiography* (New York: G. P. Putnam's Sons, 1935), 71–72; Roger Daniels, *Not Like Us: Immigrants and Minorities in America, 1890–1924* (Chicago: Ivan R. Dee, 1997), 45.

51. Hutchins Hapgood, *Spirit of the Ghetto* (New York: Funk and Wagnell, 1902), 23.

52. Manny Weltman, *Houdini: Escape into Legend, the Early Years: 1862–1900* (Van Nuys, CA: Finders/Seekers Enterprises, 1993), 11.

53. "In and About the Metropolis," *New York Sun*, Aug. 20, 1895, 7.

54. "New York Newsboys," *Harper's Young People*, in *Washington Post*, Aug. 26, 1894, 12; "About the Newsboy," *Washington Star*, Jan. 16, 1897, 16.

55. "The Newsboys' New Game," *New York World*, Aug. 17, 1892, 2; "Newsboys Play Morra," *New York Globe*, in *Olympia Recorder*, Jan. 27, 1906, 3; "And Now the Boys," *Los Angeles Times*, Apr. 6, 1890, 9; "Pavement Artists," *San Jose Evening News*, Sept. 15, 1898, 2.

56. "New York Newsboys," *Harper's Young People*, in *Washington Post*, Aug. 26, 1894, 12; "A Newsboys' Union," *Oregonian*, Aug. 21, 1892, 3; James Otis, *The Boys' Revolt: A Story of the Street Arabs of New York* (Boston: Estes & Lauriat, 1894).

57. Harry Golden, *The Right Time: An Autobiography* (New York: G. P. Putnam's Sons, 1969), 49; Carl Dreher, *Sarnoff: An American Success* (Chicago: Quadrangle, 1977), 19.

58. Zane L. Miller, "The Black Experience in the Modern American City," in *The Urban Experience: Themes in American History*, ed. Raymond A. Mohl and James F. Richardson (Belmont, CA: Wadsworth, 1973), 47–48.

59. Mary Wager-Fisher, "The Philadelphia Newsboys," *Wide Awake* 11, no. 1 (July 1880): 16–23; "A Home Built on City Dumps," *Philadelphia Inquirer*, Jan. 24, 1897, 13; W. E. B. Du Bois, *The Philadelphia Negro: A Social Study* (New York: Lippincott, 1899), 111; Floyd J. Calvin, "'Press Holds Domininat Place in Negro Life'—T. T. Fortune," *Pittsburgh Courier*, Nov. 13, 1926, A1.

60. David I. Macleod, *The Age of the Child: Children in America, 1890–1920* (New York: Twayne, 1998), 5; Alexander Hogeland, *Ten Years Among the Newsboys* (Louisville, KY: John P. Morton, 1883), 6.

61. *Memphis Daily Appeal*, July 8, 1881, 4; *Memphis Public Ledger*, July 8, 1881, 4; "San Antonio Siftings," *Dallas Morning News*, Feb. 18, 1887, 2; *New York Freeman*, Mar. 5, 1887, 2; "Trouble Among the Newsboys," *Augusta Chronicle*, Nov. 10, 1888, 5; "The Newsboys," *Atlanta Constitution*, Dec. 25, 1890, 2; "Ketch That Nigger," *Dallas Morning News*, Feb. 18, 1891, 5.

62. "A Boycott in Atlanta," *New York Times*, Nov. 30, 1897, 1; "Finds Chicago Harsh as Texas," *Chicago Tribune*, May 7, 1903, 3.

63. J. W. Alexander, "Excursion of Newsboys and Boot-Blacks," *Harper's Weekly* 25, no. 1289 (Sept. 3, 1881): 596, 603; Helen Campbell et al., *Darkness and Daylight: Lights and Shadows of New York Life* (Hartford, CT: A. D. Worthington, 1891), 124; "Life of a Gamin," *New York Evening World*, Dec. 22, 1893, 9; "Newsboys' Christmas," *Dallas Morning News*, Dec. 28, 1892, 6; Heig Scrapbook, 36; *Chicago Tribune*, 1889; Noodles Fagan, *The Life of Noodles Fagan, by Himself*, 4th ed. (Buffalo: Buffalo Evening News, 1904), 44; box 31, folder 22, NYCLC Papers.

64. Henry L. Nelson, "The Washington Negro," *Harper's Weekly* 36, no. 1855 (July 9, 1892): 665, 654.

65. Constance McLaughlin Green, *The Rise of Urban America* (New York: Harper & Row, 1965), 131; "The Colored Press Convention in Washington," *Independent*, Aug. 10, 1882, 6; "City Talk and Chatter," *Washington Post*, Mar. 24, 1881, 4; "The Newsboys' Aid Society," *Washington Post*, Jan. 11, 1888, 3; "District of Columbia," *Baltimore Sun*, Sept. 6, 1899, 2; "A Good Work," *Washington Bee*, Sept. 16, 1899, 4; "Status of the Negro," *Washington Post*, Mar. 11, 1900, 28.

66. "The Color Line Drawn," *Washington Post*, July 25, 1891, 2; "Sang Ballads in a Cell," *Washington Post*, Jan. 20, 1895, 8.

67. Ben King, "Extry! All About the West Side Murder!!," in Sigmund Krausz, *Street Types of Great American Cities* (Chicago: Werner, 1896), 14. On Krausz, see Peter B. Hales, *Silver Cities: The Photography of American Urbanization, 1839–1915* (Philadelphia: Temple University Press, 1984), 225–233.

68. Le Roy Armstrong, "Competitors," in Krausz, *Street Types of Great American Cities*, 54.

69. "The Newsboy was Plucky," *Atlanta Constitution*, Apr. 22, 1890, 2; "Winchester War," *Lexington Morning Herald*, Nov. 5, 1896, 5; "Fifty Shots Fired," *Winona Daily Republican*, Nov. 5, 1896, 1; "Battle in the Streets," *Philadelphia Inquirer*, Nov. 6, 1896, 1.

70. "Race War Among Newsboys," *Washington Post*, Oct. 15, 1897, 11.

71. "The Old Dominion," *New York Globe*, Oct. 20 1883, 4; "Dey Give Us De Run," *Kansas City Star*, Sept. 14, 1894, 2; "Big Business for His Honor," *Kansas City Times*, Sept. 15, 1894, 2; "And His Honor Crawled," *Kansas City Times*, Sept. 18, 1894, 8; "Newsboys in a Riot," *Kansas City Star*, Oct. 3, 1896, 1.

72. "Brodie Will Bury Aaron 'The Slave,'" *New York Evening Journal*, Feb. 6, 1899, n.p.; "Evening World Buries a Boy," *New York Evening World*, Feb. 8, 1899, n.p., in Heig Scrapbook, n.p.

73. Albert Leslie Smith, *The News Boy* (1889), oil on canvas, 76.2 × 127 cm., Granite Club Limited, Toronto.

74. J. G. Brown, *Give Us a Light*, oil on canvas, 25 in. × 20 in., ca. 1888–89. Private Collection, n.p., 1901, 93. Peter J. Eckel Newsboy Collection, Firestone Library, Princeton University; "39 Nations Sit Down at Newsboys' Feast," *New York Times*, Feb. 3, 1909, 5; "'Foster Father' of 100,000 Newsboys Tells How Many Fought Their Way to Fame," *New York Evening Telegram*, June 27, 1910, 14.

75. J. G. Brown, *Morning Papers* (1899), oil on canvas, Copley Newspapers, Inc., Courtesy James S. Copley Library, La Jolla, CA. This same model and outfit appear in Brown's *The New Puppy*, oil on canvas, 25¼ in. × 20 in., location unknown. See W. E. B. Du Bois, *The Souls of Black Folk* (1903; repr., Boston: Bedford/St. Martin's, 1997), 61.

76. "Miseries of News-Girls," *New York Tribune*, Feb. 20, 1881, 12; Grover Cleveland, "Message to the Buffalo Common Council, June 5, 1882," in *The Writings and Speeches of Grover Cleveland*, ed. George F. Parker (New York: Cassell, 1892), 180. Kathleen Mathew, "New York Newsboy," *Leslie's Illustrated Monthly*, Apr. 1895, 455.

77. NYSPCC, *13th Annual Report* (New York, 1887), 31; NYSPCC, *12th Annual Report* (New York, 1886), 21–23; "A Little News Girl's Death," *New York Herald*, Oct. 1, 1886, 9; "Deputy Mothers," *New York Sun*, Dec. 10, 1886, 4; "Little Ida's Last Sleep," *New York Herald*, Dec. 10, 1886, 9; "Mr. Levy Thinks the Verdict Uncalled For," *New York Tribune*, Dec. 10, 1886, 5.

78. "A Very Bad Citizen," *North American*, Nov. 25, 1890, 5; NYSPCC, *24th Annual Report* (New York, 1899), 55–56.

79. "Waifs of the Midnight," *Chicago Tribune*, Dec. 19, 1890, 9; "Newsgirls in Connecticut," *Springfield Republican*, Feb. 12, 1905, 3.

80. "Seven Little Girls Plead to Go Free," *New York Journal*, Apr. 18, 1896, 3; "Young Girl's Crime; Selling Papers," *New York Journal*, May 16, 1898, 5; "Lillian Sold Papers After Dark," *New York Sun*, May 16, 1898, 5, in Clippings on Charity, vol. 12, Gift of Prudential Insurnce Company to Princeton University, 65, Firestone Library, Princeton University.

81. "A Mite of a Newsgirl," *Chicago Tribune*, Oct. 6, 1888, 2; "Newsgirls About Town," *New York Sun*, Apr. 26, 1896, 5; Ann Novotny, *Alice's World: Life and Photography of an American Original: Alice Austen, 1866–1952* (Old Greenwich, CT: Chatham Press, 1976), 91–93.

82. "The Girl in Boy's Clothes," *New York Times*, July 8, 1882, 8; "Fire Alarm at Newsboys' Dinner," *New York Tribune*, Nov. 28, 1902, 2; "Boy Started Fire Panic at Newsboys' Feast" and

"One Lad Almost Causes Panic," n.d., in Heig Scrapbook, n.p. See Marjorie Garber, *Vested Interests: Cross-Dressing and Cultural Anxiety* (New York: Routledge, 1992), 4.

83. "Waifs of the Midnight," *Chicago Tribune*, Dec. 19, 1890, 9; "Miseries of News-Girls," *New York Tribune*, Feb. 20, 1881, 12.

84. Carroll Smith-Rosenberg, "Puberty to Menopause: The Cycle of Femininity in Nineteenth-Century America," in *Disorderly Conduct: Visions of Gender in Victorian America* (New York: Knopf, 1985), 182–196. On female delinquency, see Steven L. Schlossman, *Love and the American Delinquent: The Theory and Practice of "Progressive" Juvenile Justice, 1825–1920* (Chicago: University of Chicago Press, 1977); Steven L. Schlossman and Stephanie Wallach, "The Crime of Precocious Sexuality," *Harvard Educational Review* 48, no. 1 (Apr. 1978): 65–94, and Ruth M. Alexander, *The "Girl Problem": Female Sexual Delinquency in New York, 1900–1930* (Ithaca, NY: Cornell University Press, 1994).

85. *Chicago Inter Ocean*, Aug. 2, 1881, 8; "Newsgirls," *Chicago Tribune*, May 3, 1884, 15; *St. Paul Globe*, May 17, 1898, 4. See also Peter C. Baldwin, "'Nocturnal Habits and Dark Wisdom': The American Response to Children in the Streets at Night, 1880–1930," *Journal of Social History* 35, no. 3 (Spring 2002): 595.

86. *Chicago Inter Ocean*, Aug. 2, 1881, 8; "Newsgirls," *Chicago Tribune*, May 3, 1884, 15; "An Amazonian Slogger," *National Police Gazette* 41, no. 287 (Mar. 24, 1883): 13; "Cooling His Ardor," *National Police Gazette* 43, no. 335 (Feb. 23, 1884): 3, 16.

87. "Walks About the City," *Brooklyn Eagle*, Aug. 11, 1889, 10; "Must Be Pretty," *New York Sun*, in *Daily Morning Astoria*, Dec. 27, 1885, 1.

88. "Voice of the People," *Cleveland Leader*, Jan. 8, 1885, 6; "Life of the Newsgirls," *New York Sun*, Nov. 1, 1885, 6; "Newsboys and Newsgirls," *New York Sun*, July 25, 1886, 6; "Affairs in Brooklyn," *New York Tribune*, Aug. 21, 1890, 12.

89. "The Soubrette Newsgirl," *New York World*, Jan. 19, 1896, 22; "Misplaced Quotations," *Washington Post*, Oct. 28, 1894, 22; "The Soubrette News Girl and a Diamond in the Rough," *Cleveland Plain Dealer*, May 24, 1896, 7; "New York Street Scenes," *New York Times*, Sept. 4, 1898, SM10.

90. "She Was St. Paul Newsie in 1885," *St. Paul Dispatch*, Oct. 6, 1955, 1; "Not All She Devils," *St. Paul Daily Globe*, Apr. 22, 1888, 13.

91. "Not All She Devils," *St. Paul Daily Globe*, Apr. 22, 1888, 13; "Voice of the People," *Cleveland Leader*, Jan. 8, 1885, 6; Alice Kessler-Harris, *Out to Work: A History of Wage-Earning Women in the United States* (New York: Oxford University Press, 1982), 103.

92. "The Bore and the Enthusiast," *Springfield Republican*, Mar. 17, 1895, 7; "The 'News'-Girls," *Hartford Courant*, Mar. 11, 1895, 6; "The News-Girls. A Protest from Young Women Who See Facts," *Hartford Courant*, Mar. 15, 1895, 6; "Letters from the People. Protest the Little Girls," *Hartford Courant*, Mar. 11, 1895, 6; Peter C. Baldwin, *Domesticating the Street: The Reform of Public Space in Hartford, 1850–1930* (Columbus: Ohio State University Press, 1999), 105.

93. The Social Reform Papers of John James McCook, 1890–1926, Antiquarian and Landmarks Society, Inc. of Connecticut (Trinity College), reel 7, folder B, Feb. 6, 1894–Dec. 20, 1895; materials related to the working conditions of newspaper girls in Hartford.

94. "In New Jersey," *New York Times*, May 26, 1915, 22; "Oldest 'Newsgirl,' Jane Syron, Dies," *New York Herald*, Feb. 20, 1923, 11; "Seventy Years a News Girl," *New York Herald*, Feb. 21, 1923, 10.

95. "Attack on a Half-Demented Woman," *New York Tribune*, Nov. 27, 1891, 1; "Kicked and Cuffed Poor Old 'Aunty,'" *New York Herald*, Nov. 28, 1891, 4; "Gallagher on Trial for Beating 'Aunty,'" *New York Herald*, Dec. 16, 1891, 4; "Gallagher in Trouble Again," *New York Times*, Nov. 29, 1892, 10.

96. "The Pantalooned Poetess," *Cleveland Leader*, Sept. 1885, 8; "Poverty and Poetry," *Cleveland Leader*, Feb. 6, 1886, 8; "Colonel Lipps' Picture," *Cleveland Leader*, Oct. 3, 1885, 5; "Ruffianism," *Cleveland Plain Dealer*, Sept. 8, 1887, 8; "Three Cleveland Cranks," *St. Louis Republic*, July 13, 1889, 10; "Annie's Accident," *Cleveland Plain Dealer*, July 4, 1890, 8; "Annie Will Enjoin," *Cleveland Plain Dealer*, Aug. 29, 1890, 6; "Presented on a Platter," *Cleveland Leader*, Nov. 27, 1890, 8; "Ana Perkins Is Chided," *Cleveland Leader*, Sept. 8, 1894, 2; "A Foggy Critic," *Cleveland Leader*, Sept. 15, 1894, 3.

97. "Ana Perkin's [sic] Life Work Done," Cleveland Plain Dealer, Feb. 2, 1900, 1, 8; John E. Vacha, "Flashback, 100 Years: Newspaper Annie," Cleveland Plain Dealer Magazine, Jan. 20, 1985, 6, 7, 27; "Anna Perkins Dress, 1900," Permanent Collection, 822, Western Reserve Historical Society.

98. "Chicago Churches," Chicago Tribune, Apr. 5, 1886, 5; Rev. T. DeWitt Talmage, "Dangerous Classes," Duluth News-Tribune, Apr. 13, 1891, 4; William T. Stead, If Christ Came to Chicago! (Chicago: Laird & Lee, 1894), 327–328, 386.

99. "Rerum Novarum: On Capital and Labor," Encyclical of Pope Leo XIII, May 15, 1891, Papal Encyclicals Online, www.papalencyclicals.net/Leo13/l13rerum.htm; "Religious Notes," New York Herald, Dec. 1, 1889, 24; "Shoes for Newsboys," Kansas City Star, Dec. 21, 1898, 4; "The Drumgoole Memorial," Irish American Weekly, Apr. 16, 1894, 1; "An Uncanonized Saint," New York Sun, Apr. 16, 1894, 2. See Ilia Delio, "The First Catholic Social Gospelers: Women Religious in the Nineteenth Century" and Elizabeth McKeown and Dorothy M. Brown, "Saving New York's Children," both in U.S. Catholic Historian 13, no. 3 (Summer 1995): 1–22, 77–95.

100. Moses Riscin, The Promised City: New York's Jews, 1870–1914 (New York: Harper Torchbooks, 1970), 195–220; Irving Howe, World of Our Fathers: The Journey of the East European Jews to America and the Life They Found and Made (New York: Touchstone, 1976), 398–401; "Mr. Heymann Back from the Meeting," New Orleans Times-Picayune, July 23, 1897, 3; "A Newsboy's Career," Rocky Mountain News, June 27, 1886, 9; "A Self-Made Man in Formation," Kansas City Times, Apr. 23, 1888, 2.

101. Cincinnati Gazette, Mar. 16, 1882, 4; "Louisville Night Schools," New York Freeman, Jan. 23, 1886, 1; "College for Newsboys," Brooklyn Eagle, Jan. 14, 1894, 20; "Newsboys' Home and School," New York Times, Jan. 15, 1894, 9; Standard 1 (Jan. 22, 1887), 4; Charles Force Deems, "The St. Andrew Coffee-House Charity," Frank Leslie's Sunday Magazine 21, no. 6 (June 1887): 561; Charles D. Kellogg, "Blundering Charity," Independent, Dec. 11, 1890, 2.

102. Robert A. Woods and Albert J. Kennedy, The Settlement Horizon: A National Estimate (New York: Russell Sage Foundation, 1922), 178; Robert A. Woods, "Settlements 25 Years Old," Illinois State Register, Sept. 24, 1911, 3. On Hull, see Guy C. Sampson, Charles J. Hull, Esquire (Chicago: Jameson & Morse, 1867), 12; "Miss Culver's Fortune," Chicago Tribune, Feb. 21, 1889, 1; and "Chicago Pioneers: Charles Jerold Hull," Magazine of Western History 14, no. 6 (Oct. 1891): 641.

103. "White Child Slavery—A Symposium," Arena 1 (Apr. 1890): 594–595; A. Sinclair Holbrook, Florence Kelley, and Alzine P. Stevens, "Wage-Earning Children," in Hull-House Maps and Papers (New York: Thomas Y. Crowell, 1895), 54–55; "To Stop Child Labor," Chicago Tribune, Dec. 10, 1895, 7; Florence Kelley, "Principles and Aims of the Consumers' League," American Journal of Sociology 5, no. 3 (Nov. 1899): 289. On Catholic settlement houses, see Margaret M. McGuinness, "Body and Soul: Catholic Social Settlements and Immigration," U.S. Catholic Historian 13, no. 3 (Summer 1995): 63–75.

104. Mrs. E. E. Williamson, "The Street Arab," Proceedings of the National Conference of Charities and Correction at the Twenty-Fourth Annual Session, Toronto, Ontario, July 7–14, 1897, ed. Isabel C. Barrows (Boston: Geo. H. Ellis, 1898), 358–361. See also Emily E. Williamson, "Our Little Street Merchants," How to Help Boys 3, no. 1 (Jan. 1903): 40–43.

105. John Gunckel, Boyville: A History of Fifteen Years' Work Among Newsboys (Toledo: Toledo Newsboys' Association, 1905), 26, 32.

106. William H. Wilson, The City Beautiful Movement (Baltimore: Johns Hopkins University Press, 1989); Baldwin, Domesticating the Street, 59–60, 93–115.

107. See also Hassam's Clearing Sunset (1890) and Spring Morning in the Heart of the City (1890, reworked 1895–99). H. Barbara Weinberg, Childe Hassam, American Impressionist (New York: Metropolitan Museum of Art, New Haven, CT: Yale University Press, 2004), 87–117.

108. "Against Sunday Papers," New York Times, Dec. 10, 1896, 6.

109. Speedy, "Here You Git De Sunday News," Dallas Morning News, Mar. 18, 1899, 6.

110. George M. Beard, American Nervousness: Its Causes and Consequences (New York: G. P. Putnam's Sons, 1881), 98–116; Hiram P. Maxim, "Noise Costs More than Fire," Outlook 153 (Dec. 18, 1929): 609–911, cited in Raymond W. Smilor, "Cacophony at

34th and Sixth: The Noise Problem in America, 1900–1930," *American Studies* 18, no. 1 (Spring 1976): 27; "A Question of Street Noises," *New York Times*, June 12, 1898, 13. On Beard, see Charles E. Rosenberg, *No Other Gods: On Science and American Social Thought* (Baltimore: Johns Hopkins University Press, 1997), 98–108.

111. "No More Sinful than Making Hash," *Pittsburgh Dispatch*, Jan. 17, 1892, 4.

112. Lee, *Daily Newspaper in America*, Table 13, 725–726; "Little Newsboy Arabs of the Street and How They Live," *Washington Times*, Mar. 29, 1903, 5; "Protest of Newsboys," *Washington Post*, Jan. 8, 1897, 4; "Counsel for the Newsboys," *Washington Post*, Feb. 9, 1897, 3.

113. "The Curfew Law Opposed," *Kansas City Star*, May 7, 1896, 8; "State Curfew Law for Michigan," *Elkhart Daily Review*, Apr. 2, 1897, 1; "New Curfew Rule Causes Trouble at Goldfield," *Rocky Mountain News*, Dec. 9, 1906, 3; *Oregonian*, July 9, 1912, 4.

114. Sidney D. Long, *The Cry of the Newsboy* (Kansas City, MO: Burton, 1928), 25; Katherine Fiske Berry, *Diary*, Oct. 29, 1890, 94, in *North American Women's Letters and Diaries, Colonial to 1950*, accessed Nov. 3, 2016, http://www.alexanderstreet.com/products/nwld.htm; F. Opper, "The 'Hustling' Style of Journalism," *Puck* 31 (Apr. 20, 1892), 144.

115. "'Pinafore' and 'Waffles,'" *Omaha Herald*, Jan. 20, 1889, 7; "A Mite of a Newsgirl," *Chicago Tribune*, Oct. 6, 1888, 2; Chicago Boys' Club, *Darkest Chicago and Her Waifs* (Chicago: 1909), 1; Fagan, *Life of Noodles Fagan*, 44; "Now in Possession," *Kansas City Journal*, Jan. 29, 1899, 9; "New York's Newsboy and How He Lives," *New York Herald*, Dec. 21, 1890, 27; Daniel T. Rodgers, *Atlantic Crossings: Social Politics in a Progressive Age* (Cambridge, MA: Harvard University Press, 1998), 397.

116. John Hall Wheelock, "Whistles at Night," in *The Human Fantasy* (Boston: Sherman, French, 1911), 108–9; Frank Norris, *The Pit: A Story of Chicago*, ed. Joseph R. McElrath Jr. and Gwendolyn Jones (1902; repr., Harmondsworth, UK: Penguin Books, 1994), 356; "About the Newsboy," *Washington Star*, Jan. 16, 1897, 16; "Some Queer Street Cries," July 28, 1887, n.p., Street Vendors Folder, Library Company of Philadelphia; W. C. Parker, *Jimmy the Newsboy* (Boston: White-Smith, ca. 1893).

117. Carlotta Monti, with Cy Rice, *W. C. Fields & Me* (Englewood Cliffs, NJ: Prentice Hall, 1971), 34; Robert Lewis Taylor, *W. C. Fields: His Follies and His Fortunes* (New York: Doubleday, 1949), 32.

118. James Weldon Johnson, *Along This Way: The Autobiography of James Weldon Johnson* (New York: Viking Press, 1933), 191–192.

119. *New York Sun*, May 22, 1895, 7.

120. Alexander Black, "Through a Detective Camera," *St. Nicholas* 17, no. 12 (Oct. 1890): 1024, 1026; Colin Westerbeck and Joel Meyerowitz, *Bystander: A History of Street Photography* (Boston: Little, Brown, 1993), 83–88; Grace Mayer, *Once Upon a City: New York, 1890–1910* (New York: Macmillan, 1958), ix.

121. J. Carter Beard, "The Newsboys of New York. A Study from Life," *Demorest's Family Magazine* 31 (May 1895), 377–382; "Overland Prize Photographic Contest—X," *Overland Monthly and Out West Magazine* 32, no. 187 (July 1898), 115, no. 188 (Aug. 1898), 124, and no. 189 (Sept. 1898), 216.

122. Patricia G. Berman, "F. Holland Day and His 'Classical' Models: Summer Camp," *History of Photography* 18 (1994): 353, 365 n. 42; Pam Roberts, ed., *F. Holland Day* (Amsterdam: Waanders/Van Gogh Museum, 2000), 88.

123. Jacob A. Riis, *How the Other Half Lives: Authoritative Text, Contexts, Criticism*, ed. Hasia R. Diner (New York: Norton, 2010), 151.

124. Jacob A. Riis, "Homeless Waifs of the City," *Harper's Young People* 10, no. 482 (Jan. 22, 1889): 204; James B. Lane, *Jacob A. Riis and the American City* (Port Washington, NY: Kennikat Press, 1964), in Riis, *How the Other Half Lives*, ed. Diner, 441; Maren Stange, *Symbols of Ideal Life: Social Documentary Photography in America, 1890–1950* (Cambridge: Cambridge University Press, 1989), in Riis, *How the Other Half Lives*, ed. Diner, 486.

125. Riis, *How The Other Half Lives*, 6; Alexander Alland, *Jacob A. Riis: Photographer and Citizen* (New York: Aperture, 1993), in Riis, *How the Other Half Lives*, ed. Diner, 422–423. See also Richard Zack, *Island of Vice: Theodore Roosevelt's Doomed Quest to Clean Up Sin-Loving New York* (New York: Doubleday, 2012), 94–107.

126. Jacob A. Riis, "The New York Newsboy," *Century Magazine* 85, no. 2 (Dec. 1912): 247–255. On this point, see Richard Tuerk, "Jacob Riis and the Jews," *New-York Historical Quarterly* 63, no. 3 (1979), in Riis, *How the Other Half Lives*, ed. Diner, 463–477.

127. Jacob A. Riis, "Homeless Waifs of the City," *Harper's Young People* 10, no. 482 (Jan. 22, 1889): 205; Riis, *How the Other Half Lives*, 116. See also Jacob A. Riis, "A Christmas Reminder of the Noblest Work in the World," *Forum* 16 (Jan. 1894), 624–633.

128. Julius Wilcox, black and white canotype, 5 × 6 in., Brooklyn Public Library, Brooklyn Collection, Wilcox 1, Call No. WLC 0012; "One Newsboy Stabbed by Another," *New York Tribune*, Jan. 2, 1897, 1.

129. Campbell et al., *Darkness and Daylight*, 111, 116. The quotation can also be found in "New York's Newsboy and How He Lives," *New York Herald*, Dec. 21, 1890, 27.

130. Campbell et al., *Darkness and Daylight*, 111; Helen Campbell, *Prisoners of Poverty: Women Wage-Workers, Their Trades and Their Lives* (Boston: Roberts Bros., 1889), 21, 249. See also Robert M. Dowling, *Slumming in New York: From the Waterfront to Mythic Harlem* (Urbana: University of Illinois Press, 2007), 21–34, and Susan Henry, "Reporting 'Deeply and at First Hand': Helen Campbell in the 19th-Century Slums," *Journalism History* 11, no. 2 (Spring–Summer 1984): 18–25, 145.

131. For valuable critiques of Riis's work, see Sally Stein, "Making Connections with the Camera: Photography and Social Mobility in the Career of Jacob Riis," *Afterimage* 11, no. 10 (May 1983), 9–16; Maren Stange, *Symbols of Ideal Life: Social Documentary Photography in America, 1890–1950* (Cambridge: Cambridge University Press, 1989); and Susan M. Ryan, "'Rough Ways and Rough Work': Jacob Riis, Social Reform, and the Rhetoric of Benevolent Violence," *American Transcendental Quarterly* 11, no. 3 (1997): 191–212. For more positive assessments, see Peter Bacon Hales, *Silver Cities: The Photography of American Urbanization, 1839–1915* (Philadelphia: Temple University Press, 1984), 162–217; David Leviatin, "Framing the Poor: The Irresistibility of How the Other Half Lives," in Jacob Riis, *How the Other Half Lives: Studies Among the Tenements of New York* (Boston: Bedford/St. Martin's, 1996), 1–50; and Bonnie Yochelson and Daniel Czitrom, *Rediscovering Jacob Riis: Exposure Journalism and Photography in Turn-of-the Century New York* (New York: New Press, 2007).

132. "The Surprising Popularity of the Gamin," *Munsey's Magazine* 16, no. 3 (Dec. 1896): 379; "Saginaw Pictures," *Saginaw Evening News*, July 26, 1898, 3; "Local Artist's Illness Fatal," *Newark Evening News*, May 18, 1910.

133. R. F. Outcault, "How the Yellow Kid Was Born," in Blackbeard, *Outcault's* The Yellow Kid, 146; Joyce Milton, *The Yellow Kids: Foreign Correspondents in the Heyday of Yellow Journalism* (New York: Harper & Row, 1989), 43.

134. Barrie J. Hughes, *The World Honors the News Carrier* (Watertown, NY, 1975), 16, 19; Gary T. Leveille, "The Newsboy Statue—11 Decades of Mystery," *Advocate*, Dec. 8, 2005, 38–40; Will M. Clemens, The Man who Carves Ships' Figure-Heads," *Harper's Weekly* 36, no. 1837, Mar. 5, 1892, 235.

135. Game of the Newsboy, R. Bliss, Pawtucket, RI, 1890, in Rick Tucker, ed., *The Game Catalog: U.S. Games Through 1950*, 8th ed. (Drescher, PA: American Game Collectors Association, 1998), 21; The News Boy Game, Parker Brothers, Salem, MA, 1895, New-York Historical Society, Liman Collection, 2000.336.

136. Susan Strasser, *Satisfaction Guaranteed: The Making of the American Mass Market* (New York: Pantheon Books, 1989), 163–165; Henry Collins Brown, ed., *Valentine's Manual of Old New York* (Hastings-on-Hudson, NY: Valentine's Manual, 1926), 312–313; Robert Jay, *The Trade Card in Nineteenth-Century America* (Columbia: University of Missouri Press, 1987), 39–40, 99–100.

137. Alan Trachtenberg, *The Incorporation of America: Culture and Society in the Gilded Age* (New York: Hill & Wang, 1982), 136; Frank Lee Farnell, "Advertising in Juvenile Magazines," *Printers' Ink* 13, no. 25 (Dec. 18, 1895): 65; Strasser, *Satisfaction Guaranteed*, 163–165.

138. "The Newsboys' Cigars," *Kansas City Star*, Mar. 5, 1899, 1.

139. F. J. Hamill, *The Orphan Newsboy* (Chicago: National Music Co., 1891); Eugene Banks and Carl Carlton, *I've Not Sold a Paper Today* (Chicago: National Music Co., 1893); Reginald Mowbray and Lutie St. Clair, *The News Boys of Chicago* (Chicago: Temple Music Co., 1895);

Abbie A. Ford, *Pity the Newsboy* (Chicago: National Music Co., 1897); *Denver Times*, Sept. 28, 1896, 4.

140. "Notes," *Cleveland Plain Dealer*, May 18, 1899, 7; "Amusements," *Omaha World-Herald*, Dec. 9, 1898, 5; program, *The Newsboy Witness*, 1895, New York Public Library for the Performing Arts; "The War of Wealth," *Minneapolis Journal*, Mar. 27, 1895, 4; *Idaho Falls Times*, Nov. 21, 1895, 3.

141. Jacob Riis, *Nisby's Christmas* (New York: Scribner's, 1893; Jacob Riis, *Out of Mulberry Street* (New York: Century, 1898). See also David M. Fine, *The City, the Immigrant, and American Fiction, 1880–1920* (Metuchen, NJ: Scarecrow Press, 1977), and Richard Tuerk, "The Short Stories of Jacob A. Riis," *American Literary Realism* 13, no. 2 (Autumn 1980): 259–265.

142. "Chelifer" [Rupert Hughes], "The Justification of Slum Stories," *Godey's* 131, no. 784 (Oct. 1895): 430–432; Thomas A. Gullason, *Stephen Crane's Career: Perspectives and Evaluations* (New York: New York University Press, 1972), 492.

143. "Gamins as 'Fly Cops,'" *Chicago Tribune*, July 29, 1897, 7; "Boy Detectives Work for City," *Chicago Tribune*, Apr. 21, 1901, 54; Arthur Conan Doyle, *A Study in Scarlet* (London: Ward Locke, 1887); Charles Morris, "Newsboy Ned, Detective; or, Two Philadelphia Gamins," *Beadle's Pocket Library* 19, no. 237 (July 25, 1888); Richard Harding Davis, *Gallegher and Other Stories* (New York: Scribner's, 1891); J. C. Cowdrick, "The Ex-Newsboy Detective's Apprentice; or, Bob Buckle's Big Inning," *Beadle's Half-Dime Library*, No. 35 (June 25, 1895); George Ade, *Bang! Bang!* (New York: J. H. Sears, 1928).

144. "Chimmy and de Kid," *Current Literature* 7, no. 4 (Aug. 1891): 547; "Queer Ideas of Gotham Youths," *Cleveland Plain Dealer*, Mar. 9, 1900, 5. See also Laura Hapke, *Labor's Text: The Worker in American Fiction* (New Brunswick, NJ: Rutgers University Press, 2001), 98–102.

145. "Newsboys on a Strike," *Baltimore Sun*, Dec. 16, 1896, 10; "Newsboy Strike Still On," *Baltimore Sun*, Dec. 17, 1896, 10; "Newsboy Strikers," *Baltimore Sun*, Dec. 18, 1896, 10; "The Newsboys' War," *Baltimore News*, in *Omaha World-Herald*, Dec. 30, 1896, 5.

146. Elizabeth L. Banks, "American 'Yellow Journalism,'" *Living Age* 218, no. 2826 (Sept. 3, 1898): 649; "Humors of Yellow Journalism," *Saturday Evening Post* 178, no. 42 (Apr. 14, 1906): 2; E. Idell Zeisloft, *The New Metropolis* (New York: D. Appleton, 1899), 193; *Congregationalist* 83, no. 13 (Mar. 31, 1898): 449–450.

147. "Newsboy's Union," *Sioux City Journal*, May 15, 1898, 3; "Matters of Interest," *Pawtucket Times*, May 11, 1899, 10; "Gossip in San Francisco," *New York Times*, Feb. 27, 1898, 7; *Fourth Estate*, Apr. 14, 1898, n.p.; "News to Suit," *Puck*, in *Outlook* 59, no. 9 (July 2, 1898): 698; B. O. Flower, "J. Campbell Cory: Cartoonist," *Arena* 35, no. 194 (Jan. 1906): 49–52.

148. "They Are Spoiling for a Fight," *New York Tribune*, Apr. 6, 1898, 3; "New York Boys in Camp," *New York Times*, June 12, 1898, 22; "The Fly Pest at Montauk," *Brooklyn Eagle*, Nov. 20, 1898, 1; "Newsboy in the War," *Milwaukee Sentinel*, Dec. 18, 1898, 3.

149. "First Naval Battle in the Waters of the Gulf," *Cincinnati Post*, June 3, 1898, 6; *Tampa Tribune*, June 11, 1898, 2; July 7, 1898, 2; July 12, 1898, 2; Aug. 14, 1898, 3.

150. "New Book About Hawaii," *Hawaiian Star*, Sept. 13, 1898, 1; "Famous Newsboy Recounts Experiences in Many Wars," *Daily Oklahoman*, Oct. 31, 1909, 18.

151. "Millionaire Newsboys," *Boston Transcript*, in *Salt Lake Tribune*, Aug. 4, 1898, 3; *The W.G.N.: A Handbook of Newspaper Administration* (Chicago: Tribune Co., 1922), 57; "Chicago's News Hunger," *Birmingham Age-Herald*, July 6, 1898, 4; "A City Without Newspapers," *Springfield Republican*, July 22, 1898, 2; "The Lack of Newspapers," *New Haven Register*, Aug. 5, 1898, 6.

152. Grace Johnston, *Report of the Newsboys' Home Association of St. Paul*, Sept., 1888, 10; "A Newsboy's Philosophy," *Los Angeles Times*, Apr. 23, 1893, 2.

153. "Mr. Sage and the Newsboy," *New York Tribune*, Mar. 30, 1900, 1; "A Warning to Newspaper Publishers," *New York Tribune*, Mar. 6, 1895, 5; Alexander Saxby, "Ethics of the Newsboy," *Westminster* 158 (Nov. 1902), 575.

154. "Taming the Truant Boys," *New York Sun*, May 29, 1898, 3.

155. Grace M. Mayer, *Once upon a City* (New York: Macmillan, 1958), 480–481; Raymond A. Schroth, *The Eagle and Brooklyn: A Community Newspaper, 1841–1955* (Westport, CT: Greenwood Press, 1974), 113–114; Arthur Brisbane, "The Modern Newspaper in War Time," *Cosmopolitan* 25, no. 5 (Sept. 1898): 547.

156. "A Question of Street Noises," *New York Times*, June 12, 1898, 13; "Yellow Extras from New York," *New York Times*, May 1, 1898, 24; "Against the Newsboys," *Washington Post*, May 23, 1898, 10.

157. *Tit-Bits* 11, no. 129 (Jan. 1900): 6; "War Affects Price of Paper," *Publisher's Weekly* 53, no. 18/1370 (Apr. 30, 1898): 740; William S. Rossiter, "The American Newspaper," *Publisher's Weekly* 62, no. 7/1594 (Aug. 16, 1902): 248; Arthur Brisbane, "The Modern Newspaper in War Time," *Cosmopolitan* 25, no. 5 (Sept. 1898): 552–553; Philip Furia, with Graham Wood, *Irving Berlin: A Life in Song* (New York: Schirmer Books, 1998), 10–11.

158. Baldasty, *Commercialization of News*, 89; Ted Curtis Smythe, *The Gilded Age Press, 1865–1900* (Westport, CT: Praeger, 2003), 128; George Murray, *The Madhouse on Madison Street* (Chicago: Follett, 1965), 31.

159. *San Francisco Call*, Jan. 14, 1898, 5; "Brave Cops," *Denver Post*, May 30, 1898, 7; "Central Labor Union Meets," *Omaha Bee*, June 18, 1898, 8; "Spokane Newsboys on a Strike," *Tacoma Daily News*, Oct. 28, 1898, 8.

160. "Newsboys Boycott the News," *Sioux City Journal*, Aug. 9, 1898, 2; "Newsboy Dictators," *Omaha World-Herald*, Aug. 10, 1898, 3.

161. "Boycott by Newsboys," *Brooklyn Eagle*, May 9, 1898, 16; "War Rates," *Cincinnati Post*, May 10, 1898, 4; *Irish World*, May 14, 1898, 6; "The Central Labor Union," *New York Times*, May 16, 1898, 3; "A New Hero," *New York American*, May 16, 1898, 10; "Newsboys Strike for Better Terms," *New York Herald*, July 21, 1899, 7.

162. "Newsboys Angry," *Pawtucket Times*, May 18, 1898, 9; "Newsboys on a Strike," *New Haven Register*, July 11, 1898, 2; "Newsboys' Strike Rages," *New Haven Register*, July 12, 1898, 1; "Newsboys' Strike Over," *New Haven Register*, July 13, 1898, 1; "The Striking Newsboys," *Hartford Courant*, Aug. 2, 1899, 5.

163. *Salt Lake Tribune*, Jan. 18, 1897, 3.

164. "The Evening Press Newsboys Song in 1898," Grand Rapids Press Collection, #2012.2, Grand Rapids Public Museum. *Evening Press* newsboy James Huso memorized the song and shared it with readers during the 1962 Cuban Missile Crisis.

165. "The War Feeling in Dallas," *Dallas Morning News*, Mar. 31, 1898, 12; *New York Times*, Apr. 3, 1898, 3; "Sunk by Spaniards," *Wisconsin Weekly Advocate*, May 21, 1898, 2; Blackbeard, *Outcault's* The Yellow Kid, 116.

166. "Boy Patriot," *Cincinnati Post*, Apr. 19, 1898, 6; "Newsboys' Band," *Daily Kentuckian*, May 25, 1898, 2; *St. Paul Globe*, Dec. 14, 1898, 4; "Newsboy Who Went to War," *Pratt City* (AL) *Herald*, Mar. 11, 1899, 2; "Drummer Ends 30 Years in U.S Army," *Washington Post*, Aug. 18, 1928, 7; "A Newsboy Hero," *Atchison* (KS) *Daily Globe*, May 10, 1899, 1.

167. "In Aid of Cuban Orphans," *New York Times*, Feb. 25, 1900, 6; "The Cuban Leaders May Make Trouble," *San Francisco Call*, Mar. 17, 1899, 1; "Manila's Cosmopolitan Newsboys," *Los Angeles Times*, July 9, 1899, 9; "Manila Newsboys Strike," *Washington Post*, Nov. 14, 1905, 5.

168. "Newsboys' Strike Becomes General," *New York Herald*, July 26, 1899, 7; "Kentucky Newsboys Win" and "Nashville Strike Over," *Fourth Estate*, July 27, 1899, 2. See also David Nasaw, *Children of the City: At Work and at Play* (New York: Oxford University Press, 1985), 177, and Susan Campbell Bartoletti, *Kids on Strike!* (Boston: Houghton Mifflin, 1999), 44–61.

169. "Newsboys Start a Strike," *Brooklyn Eagle*, July 20, 1899, 2; "Newsboys Go on Strike," *New York Tribune*, July 21, 1899, 5; "Newsboys 'Go Out,'" *New York Sun*, July 20, 1899, 3.

170. "The Strike of the Newsboys," *New York Times*, July 22, 1899, 4; "Strike That Is a Strike," *New York Sun*, July 22, 1899, 3; "Newsboys Riot in Mount Vernon," *New York Tribune*, July 25, 1899, 1; "Yonkers Boys to Parade," *New York Tribune*, July 31, 1899, 2; "Troy Newsboys in the Fight," *New York Sun*, July 25, 1899, 2; "Great Meet of Newsboys," *New York Sun*, July 25, 1899, 2.

171. "The Newsboys Strike," *Jersey City Evening Journal*, July 20, 1899, 1; "Strike? Yes, Rather," *Jersey City Evening Journal*, July 21, 1899, 3; "Strike That Is a Strike," *New York Sun*, July 22, 1899, 3; "Strike Hits Bayonne," *Jersey City Evening Journal*, July 26, 1899, 3; "The Strike of the Newsboys," *Trenton Times*, July 26, 1899, 1, 8; "Newsboys Strike in Paterson," *New York*

Tribune, July 26, 1899, 2; "Great Meet of Newsboys," *New York Sun*, July 25, 1899, 2; "Newsboys' Strike Becomes General," *New York Herald*, July 26, 1899, 7.

172. "New Haven Newsboys Join," *New Haven Register*, July 24, 1899, 1; "Norwalk," *New York Sun*, July 26, 1899, 2; "Dealers Boycott to Aid Newsboys," *New York Herald*, July 28, 1899, 6; "The Striking Newsboys," *Hartford Courant*, Aug. 2, 1899, 5; "Fall River," *New York Sun*, July 24, 1899, 3; "Providence Boys Join the Strike," *New York Tribune*, July 28, 1899, 6.

173. Don Seitz, "Memo for Mr. Pulitzer on the Newsboys' Strike," July 22, 1899, Pulitzer Papers, Columbia University, New York.

174. "Newsboys' Strike Swells," *New York Sun*, July 23, 1899, 2; "Striking Newsboys Are Firm," *New York Times*, July 23, 1899, 3; "Newsboys' Strike Promises Success," *New York Herald*, July 23, 1899, 6.

175. On Kid Blink's real name, see "Noisy New York Newsboys," *Washington Times*, July 28, 1899, 4; "Fourth Arrest for Murder," *New York World*, June 1, 1905, 10; and "One More Eat-'Em-Up Boaster," *New York Sun*, June 2, 1905, 4.

176. "Parade To-Night, Sure," *New York Sun*, July 27, 1899, 3.

177. "Newsboys Go on Strike," *New York Tribune*, July 21, 1899, 10; "New-York Newsboys," *New York Tribune Illustrated Supplement*, July 30, 1899, 2; "Policy of 'Newswomen,'" *New York Tribune*, July 21, 1899, 5; "The Only Tie Up in Town," *New York Sun*, July 21, 1899, 2; "Newsboys' Strike Swells," *New York Sun*, July 23, 1899, 2.

178. "Spread of Strike Fever Among Lads," *New York Herald*, July 22, 1899, 7; "Strike That Is a Strike," *New York Sun*, July 22, 1899, 3; Nasaw, *Children of the City*, 167; "Newsboys' Strike Promises Success," *New York Herald*, July 23, 1899, 6; "Boy Strikers Sweep the City," *New York Evening Telegram*, July 22, 1899, 3.

179. "The Newsboys Strike," *Jersey City Evening Journal*, July 20, 1899, 1; "Labor Leaders Hissed," *New York Times*, July 25, 1899, 2; "Bishop McFaul and the Newsboys," *Trenton Times*, July 27, 1899, 1.

180. "Newsboys' Strike Goes On," *New York Tribune*, July 22, 1899, 3; "Strike That Is a Strike," *New York Sun*, July 22, 1899, 3; "Newsboys Start a Strike," *Brooklyn Eagle*, July 20, 1899, 2.

181. "Hooted by Newsboys," *San Francisco Call*, July 23, 1899, 2.

182. "Newsboys' Strike Swells," *New York Sun*, July 23, 1899, 2; "Newsboys' Word Stands," *New York Tribune*, July 23, 1899, 3; "Plan to Down Newsboys," *New York Sun*, July 24, 1899, 3; "Newsies Standing Fast," *New York Tribune*, July 26, 1899, 2.

183. "Great Meet of Newsboys," *New York Sun*, July 25, 1899, 2; "Newsboys Act and Talk," *New York Times*, July 25, 1899, 3; "A Newsboys' Meeting," *New York Tribune*, July 24, 1899, 1.

184. "Newsboys in Uniforms," *New York Times*, June 21, 1899, 14; "Seek to Help the Newsboys," *New York Times*, July 26, 1899, 3; E. S. Martin, "This Busy World," *Harper's Weekly* 43, no. 2227 (Aug. 26, 1899): 833; "For Newsboys' Shelters," *New York Tribune*, Feb. 4, 1901, A5.

185. Doris Kearns Goodwin, *The Bully Pulpit: Theodore Roosevelt, William Howard Taft, and the Golden Age of Journalism* (New York: Simon & Schuster, 2013), 159.

186. "Salvation Lassies Wouldn't Sell Them," *New York Evening Telegram*, July 27, 1899, 8; "'Kid' Blink Arrested," *New York Tribune*, July 28, 1899, 2; "Newsboys Get New Leaders," *New York Sun*, July 28, 1899, 2; "Dealers Boycott to Aid Newsboys," *New York Herald*, July 28, 1899, 6; "Noisy New York Newsboys," *Washington Times*, July 28, 1899, 4; "Newsboys' New Leaders," *New York Sun*, July 29, 1899, 2; "Little Bayards of the Street," *New York Commercial Advertiser*, in *Wasatch Wave* (Heber, UT), Aug. 12, 1899, 8.

187. "'World' Jails Newsboys," *New York Sun*, Aug. 1, 1899, 3; "Newsboys Up for Blackmail," "Declare Newsboys' Strike a Failure," *New York Times*, Aug. 1, 1899, 3; "Newsboys Plan Another Meeting," *New York Tribune*, Aug. 1, 1899, 3; "Little Bayards of the Street," *New York Commercial Advertiser*, in *Wasatch Wave* (Heber, UT), Aug. 12, 1899, 8.

188. "Newsboys' Boycott," *Fourth Estate*, Aug. 3, 1899, 2; Don C. Seitz, "Memorandum of Agreement as discussed by Mr. Seitz and Mr. Carvalho," Columbia University Libraries Online Exhibitions, accessed July 18, 2014, https://exhibitions.cul.columbia.edu/items/show/2958.

189. "Newsboys Form a New Union," *New York Times*, July 31, 1899, 4; "Newsboys Join in Boycott," *Baltimore Sun*, Aug. 14, 1899, 7; "Striking Printers Parade," *New York Times*, Aug. 20, 1899, 3; *Life* 34, no. 875 (Aug. 31, 1899): 174.

Chapter 10

1. William McKinley, *President McKinley's Last Speech: Delivered September 5, 1901, President's Day at the Pan-American Exposition, Buffalo, New York* (New York: Henry Malkan, 1901), 8; "A 'News' Drama," *Newspaper Owner and Modern Printer*, Sept. 25, 1901, 11; "How the News Was Received in New York," *New York Times*, Sept. 7, 1901, 2; "How the News Was Received by Citizens of Omaha," *Omaha World-Herald*, Sept. 7, 1901, 5; "Whole City Horrified," *Muskegon Chronicle*, Sept. 7, 1901, 4.

2. "Tremendous Shock," *Washington Star*, Sept. 7, 1901, 8; "The Newsboys Reaped a Rich Harvest Selling the Post Extras Yesterday," *Denver Post*, Sept. 7, 1901, 2; "'Newsy,' 54 Years Old, Demonstrates Art to R-G Street Carrier Boys Today," *Rockford* (IL) *Register Gazette*, July 9, 1924, 1.

3. "Tremendous Shock," *Washington Star*, Sept. 7, 1901, 8; "Those Two Times Extras," *Trenton Times*, Sept. 7, 1901, 1; "How the News Was Received Here," *Jersey Journal*, Sept. 7, 1901, 3; David Nasaw, *The Chief: The Life of William Randolph Hearst* (Boston: Houghton Mifflin, 2000), 156–158; Eric Rauchway, *Murdering McKinley: The Making of Theodore Roosevelt's America* (New York: Hill and Wang, 2003), 171.

4. "Newsboys Take Action," *Boston Herald*, Sept. 9, 1901, 5; "Tried to Mob Editor Jones," *Cleveland Plain Dealer*, Sept. 15, 1901, 13; "Czolgosz Was Hanged in Effigy," *Jersey Journal*, Sept. 20, 1901, 5.

5. "Assassin's Early Days," *Kalamazoo* (MI) *Gazette*, Sept. 10, 1901, 2; *Boston Herald*, Sept. 8, 1901, 5; "Story of Arrest of Anarchist Queen," *New York World*, Sept. 11, 1901, 1; "Wolves of Anarchy," *Idaho Statesman*, Sept. 17, 1901, 4; Emma Goldman, *Living My Life* (New York: Knopf, 1931), 1:355; "Selling Papers on the Street," *Omaha World-Herald*, June 23, 1929, 7; "Stumped by the Name," *Daily Illinois State Journal*, Oct. 30, 1901, 5.

6. On the Progressive Era, see John Whiteclay Chambers, *Tyranny of Change: America in the Progressive Era, 1890–1920* (New York: St. Martin's Press, 2000); John Milton Cooper, *Pivotal Decades: The United States, 1900–1920* (New York: Norton, 1990); Steven J. Diner, *A Very Different Age: Americans of the Progressive Era* (New York: Hill and Wang, 1998); Maureen A. Flanagan, *America Reformed: Progressives and Progressivism, 1890s–1920s* (New York: Oxford University Press, 2007); Richard Hofstadter, *The Age of Reform* (New York: Vintage, 1960); Michael McGerr, *A Fierce Discontent: The Rise and Fall of the Progressive Movement in America* (New York: Oxford University Press, 2003); Walter Nugent, *Progressivism: A Very Short Introduction* (Oxford University Press, 2009); Nell Irvin Painter, *Standing at Armageddon: A Grassroots History of the Progressive Era* (New York: Norton, 2008); Daniel T. Rodgers, *Atlantic Crossings: Social Politics in a Progressive Age* (Cambridge, MA: Belknap Press of Harvard University Press, 1998); and Robert H. Wiebe, *The Search for Order, 1877–1920* (New York: Hill and Wang, 1966).

7. Theodore Roosevelt, *An Autobiography* (New York: Macmillan, 1913), 13; David McCullough, *Mornings on Horseback* (New York: Simon & Schuster, 1981), 28–30, 102, 183, 232; Ray Stannard Baker, "Theodore Roosevelt: A Character Sketch," *McClure's Magazine* 12, no. 1 (Nov. 1898): 23; "Talking for Newsboys," *Washington Post*, Apr. 30, 1890, 4; "In Little Hungary," *Washington Star*, Feb. 4, 1905, 27; "The Newsboy's Candidate," *Cleveland Leader*, Jan. 11, 1902, 4; "Roosevelt Waits on Newsboys," *New York Tribune*, Apr. 19, 1901, 5; John Gunckel, *Boyville: A History of Fifteen Years' Work Among Newsboys* (Toledo, OH: Toledo Newsboys' Association, 1905), 49.

8. Theodore Roosevelt, "State of the Union Address," Dec. 2, 1902.

9. "Newsies, Enterprising, Have President Shot," *Cleveland Plain Dealer*, Nov. 28, 1907, 2; "Out for Business," *Morning Astorian*, Jan. 21, 1908, 1; John Reed, "Seeing Is Believing" (1913), in *Adventures of a Young Man: Short Stories from Life* (San Francisco: City Lights, 1975), 45; Frank Hobbs and Nicole Stoops, *Demographic Trends in the Twentieth Century: Census 2000 Special Reports* (Washington, DC: US Census Bureau, 2002), 56; Conrad Taeuber and Irene B. Taeuber, *The Changing Population of the United States* (New York: John Wiley & Sons, 1958), 82.

10. E. Myron Adams, "What of the Newsboy of the Second Cities?," *Survey* 10, no. 15 (Apr. 11, 1903): 368–371; Ruth Margaret Iliff Nordahl, "A Social Study of the Newsboys' Trade in

Los Angeles," master's thesis, University of Southern California, 1912, 2; Eva M. Marquis, "A Survey of Working Children in Kansas City," Kansas City, Mo., Board of Public Welfare, *Annual Report* (1914–15), 121.

11. William Byron Forbush, "A Western Newspaper and Its Newsboys," *Charities and the Commons* 19, no. 1 (Oct. 5, 1907): 798; George B. Mangold, "Child Welfare and Street Trades in the United States of America," *The Child* 1 (Aug. 1911): 956; Edward N. Clopper, "Children on the Streets of Cincinnati," *Annals of the American Academy of Political and Social Science* 32 (July 1908): 113–123; NCLC Pamphlet No. 82, 113.

12. "Seeking Aid of Other Creeds," *Cleveland Plain Dealer*, Dec. 11, 1905, 15; Bishop Joseph F. Berry, "Waifdom," quoted in Leonard Benedict, *Waifs of the Slums and Their Way Out* (New York: F. H. Revell, ca. 1907), 228; "Making Citizens," *First Annual Report*, Boston Newsboys Club, 1911, 3.

13. David Willard, "Studies of Boy Life in New York," *Ethical Record* 1, no. 4 (June 1900): 110; Haryot H. Cahoon, "Children in Factory and Commercial Life," *New England Magazine* 25, no. 4 (Dec. 1901): 505; Robert Hunter, *Poverty* (New York: Macmillan, 1904), 238–240.

14. Marquis, "A Survey of Working Children in Kansas City," 123.

15. "'Glorified Gang' System," *New York Tribune*, Feb. 19, 1902, 7; *Proceedings, Sixth Annual Conference, National Child Labor Committee, Boston, Jan. 13–16, 1910* (New York: American Academy of Political and Social Science, 1910), 228.

16. C. L. C., "Make Good Livings," *Washington Post*, Sept. 22, 1900, 18; "The Little Magnates of Street Corners," *New York Times*, June 21, 1908, 8; "Interviews with the Rank and File," *Book and News-Dealer* 14, no. 161 (Apr. 1903): 47–48; "The Newsgirl," *New York Sun*, Jan. 18, 1909, 9; *Proceedings, Sixth Annual Conference, National Child Labor Committee*, 228; J. H. Shaver, "The Boys: 'Hang Woman's Rights, Anyway,'" in Jacob A. Riis, "The New York Newsboy," *Century Magazine* 85, no. 2 (Dec. 1912): 248.

17. "Facts in re Street Trades Bill," NCLC Papers, box 31, folder 9, 2, New York State Library, Albany; Ina Tyler, *The Newsboy of Saint Louis* (1910; St. Louis, MO: Washington University School of Social Economy Alumni Association, 1913), 5; Clopper, "Children on the Streets of Cincinnati," 113; Henry Lewis Suggs, ed., *The Black Press in the South, 1865–1979* (Westport, CT: Greenwood Press, 1983), ix–x. Moses Koenigsberg, *King News: An Autobiography* (Philadelphia: F. A. Stokes, 1941), 289.

18. "Fight Result Leads Blacks to Riot," *Gulfport Herald*, July 5, 1910, 5; "Summary of Race Riots," *Tacoma Times*, July 5, 1910, 1; *Wilkes-Barre Times*, Aug. 23, 1910, 11.

19. "18. The Newsboys," ca. 1903, 18, NYCLC Papers, box 31, folder 12; "The Soubrette Newsgirl," *New York World*, Jan. 19, 1896, 22; "The Dirty Business," NYCLC Papers, box 31, folder 9.

20. On the strategic use of children's labor, see Stephen Lassonde, "Learning and Earning: Schooling Juvenile Employment, and the Early Life Course in Late Nineteenth-Century New Haven," *Journal of Social History* 29 no. 4 (Summer 1996): 840.

21. Alfred McClung Lee, *The Daily Newspaper in America: The Evolution of a Social Instrument* (New York: Macmillan, 1937), 215; John C. Busterna, "Trends in Daily Newspaper Ownership," *Journalism Quarterly* 65, no. 4 (Winter 1988): 833.

22. William Marion Reedy, "The Myth of a Free Press," *St. Louis Mirror*, 1908, in *Catholic Fortnightly Review* 16, no. 5 (Mar. 1909): 139.

23. Lincoln J. Steffens, "The Business of a Newspaper," *Scribner's* 22, no. 4 (Oct. 1897): 455; Mother Jones, *The Autobiography of Mother Jones* (Chicago: Charles H. Kerr, 1925), 71; Will Irwin, *The American Newspaper: A Series First Appearing in Colliers, January–July, 1911*, with comments by Clifford F. Weigle and David G. Clark (Ames: Iowa State University Press, 1969), 57, 65.

24. Nasaw, *The Chief*, 233–237; Kenneth Whyte, *The Uncrowned King: The Sensational Rise of William Randolph Hearst* (Berkeley, CA: Counterpoint, 2009), 463; James Sullivan, "How Hearst Beat the Newsboys," Affidavit, Oct. 20, 1905, in *The Story of Two Scab Jobs: Also an Affidavit—Read It and Get Wise* (New York, 1905), 10–11.

25. "Thugs to Wallop Newsboys," *Chicago Dispatch*, July 13, 1900, in *Charlotte Observer*, July 17, 1900, 7; "Bloody Plot Is Exposed," *Los Angeles Times*, Apr. 16, 1906, I11; "Carriers

Balk," *Los Angeles Times*, Oct. 5, 1906, I1; George Murray, *The Madhouse on Madison Street* (Chicago: Follett, 1965), 41–54.

26. Gunther Barth, *City People: The Rise of Modern City Culture in Nineteenth-Century America* (New York: Oxford University Press, 1980), 64. See also Leara D. Rhodes, *The Ethnic Press: Shaping the American Dream* (New York: Peter Lang, 2010); Peter Conolly-Smith, *Translating America: An Ethnic Press and Popular Culture, 1890–1920* (Washington, DC: Smithsonian Books, 2010); and Sally M. Miller, introduction to *The Ethnic Press in the United States: A Historical Analysis and Handbook*, ed. Sally M. Miller (Westport, CT: Greenwood Press, 1987), xvii–xviii.

27. Goldman, *Living My Life*, 1:156; Irving Howe, *World of Our Fathers: The Journey of the East European Jews to America and the Life They Found There* (New York: Simon & Schuster, 1976), 518, 528; Ehud Manor, *Forward: The Jewish Daily Forward (Forverts) Newspaper: Immigrants, Socialism, and Jewish Politics in New York, 1890–1917* (Brighton, UK: Sussex Academic Press, 2009), 17; Peter G. Vellon, *A Great Conspiracy Against Our Race: Italian Immigrant Newspapers and the Construction of Whiteness in the Early Twentieth Century* (New York: New York University Press, 2014), 22–23; M. W. Harvey, "Little Italy's Dormitory in Mulberry Park Is Being Improved," *Brooklyn Eagle*, July 28, 1901, 2.

28. Ben Brochin interview, June 17, 1979, Jews in Minneapolis Oral History Project, Minnesota Historical Society.

29. Harry Golden, *The Right Time: An Autobiography* (New York: G. P. Putnam's Sons, 1969), 54–55. For a fictional account of an Irish immigrant who tries to pass as a Jew by selling the Yiddish papers in New York, see E. R. Lipsett, "Denny—The Jew from Ballintemple," *Everybody's* 29 (July 1913): 87–96.

30. "A Chinese Newsboy," *Washington Star*, July 20, 1901, 18; "Chinaman Tries Selling Papers," *Boston Journal*, Sept. 20, 1904, 2; "Detroit's First Chinese Newsboy," *Detroit Free Press*, Aug. 30, 1908, n.p.

31. *New York Amsterdam News*, Nov. 23, 1927, 5; Charles A. Simmons, *The African American Press: A History of News Coverage During National Crises, with Special Reference to Four Black Newspapers, 1827–1965* (Jefferson, NC: McFarland, 1998), 21; Patrick S. Washburn, *The African American Newspaper: Voice of Freedom* (Evanston, IL: Northwestern University Press, 2006), 49; Andrew Buni, *Robert L. Vann of the Pittsburgh Courier: Politics and Black Journalism* (Pittsburgh, PA: University of Pittsburgh Press, 1974), 44–49; *Rising Son*, Nov. 15, 1906, 1, and June 15, 1907, 1; *Dallas Morning News*, Mar. 18, 1901, 6; "Dallas Express," *Chronicling America*, accessed Aug. 17, 2016, http://chroniclingamerica.loc.gov/essays/478. See also Roland E. Wolseley, *The Black Press: USA*, 2nd ed. (Ames: Iowa State University Press, 1990), and Christopher B. Daly, *Covering America: A Narrative of a Nation's Journalism* (Amherst: University of Massachusetts Press, 2012), 158–159.

32. Daniel Bell, "Marxian Socialism in the United States," in *Socialism and American Life*, ed. Donald Drew Egbert and Stow Persons (Princeton, NJ: Princeton University Press, 1952), I:283–284; "Attention!," *Daily People*, July 21, 1900, 4; "Shoe Strikers' Score," *Daily People*, Jan. 3, 1902, 1; *Daily People*, Dec. 20, 1910, 3; "Goodbye, Newsboy," *Daily People*, May 23, 1908, 1.

33. Charles Willis Thompson, "'Catholicism Our Final Foe,' Says Socialist Chief," *New York Times*, June 5, 1910, SM4; A. W. Mance, *History of the Milwaukee Social-Democratic Victories* (Milwaukee: Milwaukee Social-Democratic Publishing, 1911), 15; Mari Jo Buhle, *Women and American Socialism, 1870–1920* (Urbana: University of Illinois Press, 1981), 193–196.

34. Margaret Finnegan, *Selling Suffrage: Consumer Culture and Votes for Women* (New York: Columbia University Press, 1999), 63–67, 148, 204 n. 38; "To Help the Suffragists," *New York Times*, July 14, 1910, 6; "Open Their Own Newsstand," *New York Tribune*, July 21, 1910, 9.

35. "Our Boston Letter," *Caledonian*, Sept. 10, 1897, 2; "He Assaulted Newsboys," *Boston Advertiser*, Oct. 21, 1899, 6; "Newsboys Happy on Anniversary," *Boston Herald*, May 1, 1905, 4.

36. "Subway Newsgirls May Strike," *New York Tribune*, Feb. 26, 1905, 5; "A 12 Hour Working Day Unbroken Underground," *Charities* 14, no. 9 (May 27, 1905): 769–770; "Subway Girls' Noon Hour," *New York Tribune*, Dec. 15, 1905, 4.

37. Don Seitz to Joseph Pulitzer, Jan. 8, Apr. 26, Aug. 17, 1900, folder Jan.–Dec. 1900 letterbook, box 1900 General, *World* Papers, Rare Books and Manuscripts, Columbia University; John L. Given, *Making a Newspaper* (New York: Henry Holt, 1907), 318; "Newsboys Cover City in Autos," *Hawaiian Star*, Nov. 4, 1908, 5; "'Newsboy' Delivers by Automobile," *Automobile Topics*, Sept. 7, 1912, 264.

38. "Electric Car Accidents," *Boston Herald*, Sept. 11, 1901, 4; "Newsboy Run Over by an Automobile," *Salt Lake Tribune*, June 23, 1904, 12; "Not Told of Boy's Death," *Cleveland Plain Dealer*, Dec. 6, 1905, 11; "Crushed to Death Beneath Wheels," *San Francisco Chronicle*, Aug. 30, 1906, 3; "Vehicles Injure Four Newsboys," *Cleveland Plain Dealer*, Aug. 4, 1909, 12; "Struck by an Auto," *Grand Rapids Press*, Oct. 12, 1911, 10; Given, *Making a Newspaper*, 317; "The Price of a Newsboy," *Norwich Bulletin*, Feb. 3, 1910, 4; "Newsies Sell Handbooks," *Harrisburg Telegraph*, Aug. 5, 1915, 9.

39. William R. Scott, *Scientific Circulation Management for Newspapers* (New York: Ronald Press, 1915), vi, 19–20. See also Edwin Emery, *History of the American Newspaper Publishers Association* (Minneapolis: University of Minnesota Press, 1950), and William J. Thorn, with Mary Pat Pfeil, *Newspaper Circulation: Marketing the News* (New York: Longman, 1987), 52–53.

40. Scott, *Scientific Circulation Management*, 19–20; Frederick Winslow Taylor, *The Principles of Scientific Management* (1911; repr., New York: W. W. Norton, 1967), 94.

41. John Cooney, *The Annenbergs: The Salvaging of a Tainted Dynasty* (New York: Simon & Schuster, 1982), 32, 45; "Club Newsboys from Spot Cash Cars; Police Aid City Railway Stalwarts," *Chicago Examiner*, Mar. 18, 1908, 2; "Arrest of 5 Newsboys as Result of Riot Lasting 2 Hours," *Chicago Examiner*, Mar. 19, 1908, 2; "Newsboys Assail Cars on Wabash," *Chicago Tribune*, Mar. 19, 1908, 1.

42. *Minutes of the Ninth Annual Convention of the National Association of Managers of Newspaper Circulation* (Milwaukee, WI, 1907), 130, 133. See also Michael Schudson, *Discovering the News: A Social History of American Newspapers* (New York: Basic Books, 1978), 93, and Si Sheppard, *The Partisan Press: A History of Media Bias in the United States* (Jefferson, NC: McFarland, 2008), 196.

43. "Italian Newsboys Dined," *New York Times*, Jan. 1, 1899, 7.

44. *Springfield Republican*, Sept. 11, 1912, 4; "Chimmie Fadden [sic] Makes Good with School Kids of Omaha," *Omaha Evening World*, May 29, 1914, 1; "Newsboy King Gives Journal Boys Big Time," *Flint Journal*, Apr. 30, 1915, 6.

45. US Bureau of the Census, *Historical Statistics of the United States, Colonial Times to 1970* (Washington, DC, 1975), 2:810; Noodles Fagan, *The Life of Noodles Fagan, by Himself*, 4th ed. (Buffalo: Buffalo Evening News, 1904), 17, 22; "'Noodles' Fagan, King of Newsboys, in Town," *Salt Lake City Evening Telegram*, May 19, 1910, 1.

46. "Children's Pages," *Newspaper Owner and Modern Printer*, Apr. 16, 1902: 22.

47. Hartley Davis, "The Journalism of New York," *Munsey's Magazine* 24, no. 2 (Nov. 1900): 228; George McManus and Henry La Cossitt, "Jiggs and I," *Collier's* 129 (Jan. 19, 1952): 10; Bill Blackbeard in Maurice Horn, *The World Encyclopedia of Comics* (New York: Chelsea House, 1976), 517–518; Maurice Horn, *100 Years of American Newspaper Comics: An Illustrated Encyclopedia* (New York: Random House, 1996), 223–224.

48. On the design of turn-of-the-century newspapers, see John Henry Hepp IV, *The Middle-Class City: Transforming Space and Time in Philadelphia, 1876–1926* (Philadelphia: University of Pennsylvania Press, 2003), 102–109; "Building for the Detroit News, Detroit, Mich.," *American Architect* 109, no. 2100 (Mar. 22, 1916): 197.

49. C. C. Ousley, *A Newsboys' Club House or Where Boys are Made Men* (Louisville: Hugh & Ousley, 1903), 8, 36–38; Peggy Lovvo, "Society for the Protection of Newsboys and Waifs: The Newsboys Home," Aug. 26, 1985, 4–5, unpublished paper, Filson Historical Society, Louisville, Kentucky.

50. *Philadelphia Inquirer*, July 14, 1907, 3; *San Francisco Call*, Feb. 7, 1913, 12; *Denver Post*, June 2, 1909, 14.

51. "A Newspaper Race," *Newspaper Owner and Modern Printer*, Sept. 11, 1901: 14; Ben Proctor, *William Randolph Hearst: The Early Years, 1863–1910* (New York: Oxford

University Press, 1998), 165–166; Ferdinand Lundberg, *Imperial Hearst: A Social Biography* (New York: Random House, 1936), 141–142.

52. "A Very Happy New Year," *Daily People*, Jan. 1, 1902, 2.

53. International Circulation Managers' Association, *Official Bulletin* 15, no. 2 (Sept. 1919): 10, 17; *Minutes of the Ninth Annual Convention of the National Association of Managers of Newspaper Circulation* (Milwaukee, WI, 1907), 135; *Newsboy* 19, no. 4 (Nov. 1980): 5; "'The Newsboy,'" *Boston Herald*, Apr. 18, 1899, 12.

54. John Marshall, "Amateur Journalism," *Atlanta Constitution*, Feb. 19, 1899, A4A; David Kimball, interview by author, Oct. 25, 2010; *The Newsboy*, Broadside Collection, 1900–1919, Hargrett Library, University of Georgia. On novelty presses, see Paula Petrik, "The Youngest Fourth Estate: The Novelty Toy Printing Press and Adolescence, 1870–1886," in *Small Worlds: Children and Adolescents in America, 1850–1950*, ed., Elliott West and Paula Petrik (Lawrence: University of Kansas Press, 1992), 125–142.

55. *American Newspaper Boy*, Winston-Salem, NC, 1900, Library of Congress; "Newsboys Own a Paper," *Dallas Morning News*, July 13, 1902, 13; "'The Newsboys' Magazine,'" *New York Tribune*, Mar. 3, 1903, 6; "The 'Newsboys' Magazine,'" *Book and News-Dealer* 14, no. 161 (Apr. 1903): 41.

56. "Newsboys Will Have a Magazine," *Boston Herald*, Oct. 14, 1904, 4; "How Pi Alley Boys Would Edit a Magazine," *Boston Journal*, Oct. 15, 1904, 2; "Murat Halstead's New Post," *New York Times*, Oct. 27, 1904; "President Roosevelt Believes in American Newsboy," *Newsdealer* 10, no. 1 (Dec. 1904): 9.

57. "T R Withdraws Name from American Newsboy Magazine," *New York Times*, Jan. 1, 1905, in *Newsdealer* 10, no. 3 (Feb. 1905): 5; "Mr. Roosevelt Displeased with 'Newsboys' Magazine' Methods," *New York Tribune*, Jan. 11, 1905, 2; "Police Informed Roosevelt," *New York Times*, Jan. 12, 1905, 5; *Reporters' Association of America v. Sun Printing and Publishing Association*, Court of Appeals of New York, 186 NY 437, 79 N.E. 710, 1906 NY Lexis 1133; Donald Walter Curl, "Murat Halstead, Editor and Politician," PhD diss., Ohio State University, 1964, 401–2; *Writer* 17, no. 8 (June 1905): 128; "3,500 Newsboys Descend upon Rockaway Beach," *New York Times*, June 5, 1905, 9.

58. *Newsboy* (Pittsburgh) 1, no. 1 (Mar. 1909), to 2, no. 3 (Apr. 1910); "National Paper for Newsboys," *Fourth Estate*, May 1, 1915, 7; "Newsboys Start a Magazine," *Editor & Publisher and the Journalist* 48, no. 29 (Dec. 25, 1915): 807; "Newsboys' Magazines," *Publishers' Mail* no. 9 (Jan. 1916): 2.

59. Elizabeth Sands Johnson, "Child Labor Legislation," *History of Labor in the United States, 1896–1932*, ed. John R. Commons et al. (New York: Macmillan, 1935), 3:404–405. See also Walter I. Trattner, "The First Federal Child Labor Law (1916)," *Social Science Quarterly* 50, no. 3 (Dec. 1969): 507–508; John Spargo, *The Bitter Cry of the Children* (New York: Macmillan, 1906), 145; and Ellen Key, *The Century of the Child* (1900; repr., New York: G. P. Putnam's Sons, 1909), 327.

60. "Child Slavery," *Daily People*, Jan. 13, 1903, 2; "The Newsboys' Estimate of the Board of Aldermen," *Cincinnati Gazette*, Feb. 18, 1873, 5; Silas Farmer, *The History of Detroit and Michigan* (Detroit: Silas Farmer, 1889), 693; Pauline Goldmark, "What Boston Has Done in Regulating the Street Trades for Children," *Charities* 10, no. 6 (Feb. 14, 1903): 159–160.

61. "Habits of Boston Newsboys," *Boston Herald*, Mar. 4, 1901, 6; "The Newsboys," *Boston Journal*, Mar. 5, 1901, 4; "Looking After Newsboys," *Boston Herald*, May 9, 1902, 6; Everett W. Goodhue, "Boston Newsboys, How They Live and Work," *Charities* 8, no. 23 (June 7, 1902): 527–532; "Newsboys Committee," *Annual Report of the Massachusetts Civic League for the Year Ending November 30, 1903* (Boston: Geo. H. Ellis, 1904), 44–45, *1904*, 18–19, *1905*, 22–23, *1906*, 15–18; Grace W. Ward, "Weakness of the Massachusetts Child Labor Law," in *Labor Laws and Their Enforcement, with Special Reference to Massachusetts*, ed. Charles Edward Person et al. (New York: Longman, Green, 1911), 2:213; Mrs. John Van Vorst, *The Cry of the Children: A Study of Child-Labor* (New York: Moffat, Yard, 1908), 244.

62. "To License Newsboys," *New York Tribune*, Sept. 3, 1901, 9.

63. New York State Department of Labor, *First Annual Report of the Commissioner of Labor and the Sixteenth Annual Report on Factory Inspection, 1901* (Albany: J. B. Lyon, 1902), 141.

64. C. L. Stewart, "Child Labor in This City," *New York Tribune*, May 18, 1902, 9; "United Neighborhood Houses," in *American Settlement Houses and Progressive Social Reform: An Encyclopedia of the American Settlement Movement*, ed. Domenica M. Barbuto (Phoenix, AZ: Oryx Press, 1999), 211–212; Kathleen Banks Nutter, "Marot, Helen," *American National Biography Online* (New York: Oxford University Press, 2000), http://www.anb. org/articles/15/15-00840.html; Jeroen Staring and Jerry Aldridge, "Helen Marot's Life and Socio-Political Works from 1900–1920," *Case Studies Journal* 4, no. 2 (2015), http://www. casestudiesjournal.com/volume-4-issue-2.

65. Riis to New York Child Labor Committee, 1903, cited in Forest Chester Ensign, *Compulsory School Attendance and Child Labor* (Iowa City, IA: Athens Press, 1921), 135; Jacob A. Riis, "The Newsboy Bill; Some of Its Endorsers" (NY 1903), 2 1; "Child Labor Evil," *New York Times*, Jan. 12, 1902, 3; Jacob A. Riis, *Children of the Tenements* (New York: Macmillan, 1903); Jacob A. Riis, "Children of the People," *Century Magazine* 67, no. 2 (Dec. 1903): 227–229. See also Moses Stambler, "The Effect of Compulsory Education and Child Labor Laws on High School Attendance in New York City, 1898–1917," *History of Education Quarterly* 18, no. 2 (Summer 1968): 189–214.

66. "Newsboys Gamble, Messengers Cheat," *Pawtucket Times*, Jan. 23, 1903, 4; "To Albany in Children's Interests," *New York Tribune*, Feb. 24, 1903, 8; "Child Labor at Night," *Washington Post*, May 7, 1903, 3.

67. "Miss Watson's Newsboy Report," memo by Fred Hall, July 28, 1911, 3, NCLC Papers, box 3, folder 4; "The Newsboys," typescript (ca. 1902–3), 1–20, NYCLC Papers, box 31, folder 12.

68. Josephine Goldmark, *Impatient Crusader: Florence Kelley's Life Story* (Urbana: University of Illinois Press, 1953), 80–83, "Evils of Newsboy Life," *New York Evening Post*, Feb. 21, 1903, 3, Josephine C. Goldmark, "Street Labor and Juvenile Delinquency," *Political Science Quarterly* 19 (Sept. 1904): 417–438.

69. Ernest Poole, *The Bridge: My Own Story* (New York: Macmillan, 1940), 68.

70. "Newsboy Wanderers," *New York Evening Post*, Jan. 26, 1903, 6; reprinted in *Charities* 10, no. 6 (Feb. 14, 1903): 160–162; Ernest Poole, "Waifs of the Street," *McClure's Magazine* 21, no. 1 (May 1903): 40–48.

71. Myron E. Adams, "Municipal Regulations of Street Trades," in *Proceedings, National Conference of Charities and Correction, 1904*, 296; Myron E. Adams, *The Buffalo Newsboy and the Street Trades Bill, Prepared for the Charity Organization Society of Buffalo, in Mar. 1903* (Buffalo: H. Brewster Adams, University Settlement, 1903), 1–12; Myron Adams, "What of the Newsboy of the Second Cities?," *Survey* 10, no. 15 (Apr. 11, 1903): 368–371; "New York's Newsboys Licensed," *Survey* 11 (Sept. 5, 1903): 189.

72. "Those Wicked Messengers," *New York Sun*, Feb. 6, 1903, 12.

73. "Child Street Traders in London," *Charities* 10, no. 6 (Feb. 14, 1903): 149–150. See also Parliamentary Papers, *Education (England and Wales)* 75, *Elementary Schools (Children Working for Wages)*, 1899: 433–632; *Report of the Inter-Departmental Committee on the Employment of School Children*, 1901; *Report of the Inter-Departmental Committee on the Employment of Children During School Age, Especially in Street Trading in the Large Centres of Population in Ireland*, 1902 [Cd.1144] XLIX, 209–412; J. G. Cloete, "The Boy and His Work," in *Studies of Boy Life in Our Cities*, ed. E. J. Urwick (London: J. M. Dent, 1904), 131–132; and Stephanie Rains, "City Streets and the City Edition: Newsboys and Newspapers in Early Twentieth-Century Ireland," *Irish Studies Review*, 24, no. 2 (Feb. 2016): 142–158.

74. "Child Labor Legislation in Five States," *Literary Digest* 26, no. 10 (Mar. 7, 1903): 332; "Plea for Tiny Workers," *New York Times*, Mar. 5, 1903, 7; "The Child Toilers," *New York Evening World*, Mar. 6, 1903, 14.

75. "Consternation Among Newsboys," *New York Tribune*, Feb. 10, 1903, 9; "The Child Toilers," *New York Evening World*, Mar. 6, 1903, 14.

76. "Plea for Tiny Workers," *New York Times*, Mar. 5, 1903, 7; "S.P.C.C. and Child Labor Laws," *New York Tribune*, Mar. 8, 1903, 6; Fred S. Hall, "Selling Papers Under Ten. Is It Necessary, Is It Right?," open letter from secretary of the Child Labor Committee, Mar. 9, 1903, New York Public Library TDV p.v. 5, no. 25; "Child Labor Bill Attacked," *New York Times*, Mar. 10, 1903, 8; "Newsboy Temptations," *New York Evening World*, Mar. 11, 1903, 10; Robert Hunter, Felix Adler, William H. Maxwell, and Mornay Williams, "Where We Disagree with the New York

Society for the Prevention of Cruelty to Children," Mar. 1903, NYCLC Papers, box 32, folder 2; E. Fellows Jenkins, "Newsboys, Bootblacks, and Youthful Vendors," *Charities* 8, no. 8 (Feb. 22, 1902): 186–188; and Jeremy P. Felt, *Hostage of Fortune: Child Labor Reform in New York State* (Syracuse, NY: Syracuse University Press, 1965), 58–59.

77. Horatio Alger, *Adrift in New York: Tom and Florence Braving the World* (New York: A. L. Burt, 1900), Horatio Alger, *Ben Bruce: The Life of a Bowery Newsboy* (New York: A. L. Burt, 1901); Horatio Alger, *Nelson the Newsboy* (New York: Mershon, 1901); *Muskegon Chronicle*, Mar. 7, 1902, 4; "People's—A Boy of the Streets," *Philadelphia Inquirer*, Feb. 22, 1903, 12; "Newsgirl at the Orpheum," *Harrisburg Patriot*, Apr. 14, 1910, 8.

78. "The Bradys and the Newsboy; or, Saved from the State Prison, by a New-York Detective," Secret Service No. 534, Apr. 16, 1909; Rosebud Folsom, "Whistlin' Joe, 'the Best Feller t' Ever Live,'" *Success*, Jan. 1900, 15; *Ambition: A Journal of Inspiration and Self Help*, Sept. 1913; "Don't Pity This Boy," *Denver Sunday Post*, Oct. 21, 1900, 13; Owen Frawley Kildare, *My Mamie Rose: The Story of My Regeneration* (New York: Baker & Taylor, 1903); *Regeneration* (Fox Film Corp., 1915); "John D. Rockefeller on Opportunity in America," *Cosmopolitan* 43, no. 4 (Aug. 1907): 372. On the success industry, see Judy Hilkey, *Character Is Capital: Success Manuals and Manhood in Gilded Age America* (Chapel Hill: University of North Carolina Press, 1997) and Scott A. Sandage, *Born Losers: A History of Failure in America* (Cambridge, MA: Harvard University Press, 2005).

79. Robert Hunter, "Memoirs," Robert Hunter Papers, Lilly Library, Indiana University, Bloomington, IN, cited in Edward Allan Brawley, *Speaking Out for America's Poor: A Millionaire Socialist in the Progressive Era* (Amherst, NY: Humanity Books, 2007), 97; "Newsboy Bill Amended," *New York Tribune*, Mar. 18, 1903, 4. Hunter also mentioned the influence of "rather powerful persons" in gutting the street trades bill when he spoke at the NCLC's second annual conference in 1905. See *Child Labor: A Menace to Industry, Education, and Good Citizenship* (Philadelphia: American Academy of Political and Social Science, 1906), 124.

80. "Laws of New York.—By Authority," 1903, 1–3, Lillian Wald Papers, Columbia University, New York, box 41, folder 1.1; "Newsboys Badges Ready," *New York Tribune*, Aug. 31, 1903, 4; "Newsboy Law Operative," *New York Times*, Aug. 31, 1903, 10.

81. "Newsboys' Badge Rush," *New York Tribune*, Sept. 1, 1903, 4; "New York's Newsboys Licensed," *Survey* 11, no. 10 (Sept. 5, 1903): 189.

82. Myron E. Adams, *The Buffalo Newsboy and the Street Trades Bill, Prepared for the Charity Organization Society of Buffalo, in Mar. 1903* (Buffalo: H. Brewster Adams, University Settlement, 1903), 1–12; Myron E. Adams, "What of the Newsboy of the Second Cities?," *Survey* 10, no. 15 (Apr. 11, 1903): 368–371; Myron E. Adams, "Municipal Regulations of Street Trades," in *Proceedings, National Conference of Charities and Correction, 1904*, 296; "Municipal Regulations of Street Trades," *Charities* 12, no. 26 (June 25, 1904): 666.

83. "The Newsboy Breadwinner Story," *Charities* 11, no. 21 (Nov. 28, 1903): 482; "Newsies Break Many Rules," *New York Times*, Sept. 7, 1904, 3; *Proceedings, Thirty-first Annual Conference on Charities and Corrections, Portland, Maine, 1904*, 516; letter, Edward B. Shallow to Fred S. Hall, Jan. 28, 1909, NYCLC Papers, cited in Ensign, *Compulsory School Attendance and Child Labor*, 145 n. 116.

84. *Child Labor: A Menace to Industry, Education, and Good Citizenship* (Philadelphia: American Academy of Political and Social Science, 1906), 124; James K. Paulding, "Enforcing the Newsboy Law in New York and Newark," *Charities* 14 (June 10, 1905): 836–837; "Bad Boys Can't Work," *Washington Star*, Aug. 23, 1908, 12; "Children in Street Trades," in *Proceedings, Fifth Annual Conference on Child Labor, Chicago, Jan. 21–23, 1909*, NCLC Pamphlet No. 114, 2; Ensign, *Compulsory School Attendance and Child Labor*, 145.

85. Robert Hunter and Lillian Wald, "Reports from State Committees," in "Proceedings, Second Annual Meeting of the National Child Labor Committee," *Annals of the American Academy of Political and Social Science* 27, no. 2 (Mar. 1906), reprinted as *Child Labor: A Menace to Industry, Education, and Good Citizenship* (Philadelphia: American Academy of Political and Social Science, 1906): 124–126; Florence Kelley, "Boy Labor," *How to Help Boys* 3, no. 1 (Jan. 1903): 29–30; Florence Kelley, "The Sordid Waste of Genius," *Charities* 12, no. 18 (May 7, 1904): 453–454. On the question of families' need for children's income, see

Selwyn K. Troen, "The Discovery of the Adolescent by American Educational Reformers, 1900–1920: An Economic Perspective," in *Growing Up in America: Historical Experiences*, ed. Harvey J. Graf (Detroit: Wayne State University Press, 1987), 420.

86. Florence Kelley, "Child Labor Legislation and Enforcement in New England and the Middle States," *Annals of the American Academy of Political and Social Science* 25 (May 1905): 69–70; "Boy Starved Aiding Mother," *New York Evening World*, Feb. 14, 1905, 3; "Boy Dies of Want," *New York Sun*, Feb. 15, 1905, 5; "Hungry a Month: Full Meal Kills," *Chicago Tribune*, Feb. 15, 1905, 4.

87. *University Settlement Studies* 2, no. 3 (Oct. 1906): 5–6; Carol Aronovici, "Digest of an Investigation into the Newsboy Problem in New York City," *Kindergarten Magazine and Pedagogical Digest* 19, no. 7 (Mar. 1907): 483–484; "New York State in the Lead," *Woman's Home Companion* 34, no. 8 (Aug. 1907): 22.

88. "Newsboy Law," *Annals of the American Academy of Political and Social Science* 31, suppl. 21 (May 1908): 63–64; Mary Stevenson Callcott, *Child Labor Legislation in New York* (New York: Macmillan, 1931), 34–38; "The Child Workers of the Nation," in *Proceedings, Fifth Annual Meeting of the National Child Labor Committee, Chicago, Jan. 21–23, 1909* (Philadelphia: American Academy of Political and Social Science, 1909), 256; Owen Lovejoy, "The Year's Progress in Child Labor Legislation," *Survey* 24 (July 2, 1910): 570–572. See also Moses Stambler, "The Effect of Compulsory Education and Child Labor Laws on High School Attendance in New York City, 1898–1917," *History of Education Quarterly* 18, no. 2 (Summer 1968): 198, 201–202, 207.

89. "Enforcing the Newsboy Law," May 1905, NYCLC Papers, box 31, folder 5; James K. Paulding, "Enforcing the Newsboy Law in New York and Newark," *Charities* 14 (June 10, 1905): 836–837; Josephine C. Goldmark, "Child Labor Legislation," *Annals of the American Academy of Political and Social Science* 29, suppl.18 (Jan. 1907): 51; E. W. Lord, "Child Labor in New England," *Annals of the American Academy of Political and Social Science* 32, suppl. 22, "Child Labor and Social Progress," *Proceedings, Fourth Annual Meeting of the New York Child Labor Committee, July 1908*, 35; George Hall, "The Newsboy," *Annals of the American Academy of Political and Social Science* 37–38 (Jan.–Sept. 1911), 100; Elizabeth B. Butler, "New Jersey Children in the Street Trades," *Charities and the Commons* 17, no. 24 (Mar. 16, 1917): 1062–1064.

90. "Bad Boys Can't Work," *Washington Star*, June 20, 1908, 1; Arthur I. Street, ed., *Street's Pandex of the News: 1908 Annual Edition* (Chicago: Pandex, 1909), 216; Charles P. Neill, "Child Labor at the National Capital," *Annals of the American Academy of Political and Social Science* 27, no. 2 (Mar. 1906), 17–18.

91. Newsboy *Conditions in Chicago* (Chicago: Federation of Chicago Settlements, 1903), 1–28; Myron E. Adams, "Children in American Street Trades," *Annals of the American Academy of Political and Social Science* 25 (May 1905): 437–458, reprinted as NCLC Pamphlet No. 14; "Children in Street Trades," in *Proceedings, Fifth Annual Conference on Child Labor, Chicago, Jan. 21–23, 1909*, reprinted as NCLC Pamphlet No. 114, 8; Edward N. Clopper, "Children in Street Trades," in *Proceedings, Sixth Annual Conference of the NCLC, Boston, Jan. 13–16, 1910, Annals of the American Academy of Political and Social Science*, 35, suppl. "Child Employing Industries" (Mar. 1910): 229; "Newsboys Are Not Peddlers," *Chicago Tribune*, Apr. 9, 1904, 1.

92. NCLC Pamphlet No. 114, 1909, 9–10.

93. "A National Child-Labor Committee," *Charities* 12, no. 16 (Apr. 23, 1904): 409–411; Elizabeth Sands Johnson, "Child Labor Legislation," in John R. Commons et al., *History of Labor in the United States* (New York: Macmillan, 1918–35), 3:408; Dale Cressman, "From Newspaper Row to Times Square: The Dispersal and Contested Identity of an Imagined Journalistic Community," *Journalism History* 34, no. 4 (Winter 2009): 182–193.

94. Florence Kelley, *Some Ethical Gains Through Legislation* (New York: Macmillan, 1905), 3. See also Kathryn Kish Sklar, *Florence Kelley and the Nation's Work: The Rise of Women's Political Culture, 1830–1900* (New Haven, CT: Yale University Press, 1995), 93–139.

95. Staring and Aldridge, "Helen Marot's Life," 3.

96. Hunter, *Poverty*, 28, 241.

97. Spargo, *Bitter Cry of the Children*, 184–185.

98. Poole, *The Bridge*, 95–96; Anthony Arthur, *Radical Innocence: Upton Sinclair* (New York: Random House, 2006), 48; Truman Frederick Keeper, *Ernest Poole* (New York: Twayne, 1966), 31–32.

99. Upton Sinclair, *The Jungle: The Uncensored Original Edition* (1906; repr., Tucson, AZ: Sharp, 2003), 111–112, 122, 184.

100. John Callan O'Laughlin, "Find 'The Jungle' 95 Per Cent Lies," *Chicago Tribune*, May 5, 1906, 7; *Chicago Tribune*, June 30, 1906, 1.

101. Scott Nearing, "The Newsboy at Night in Philadelphia," *Survey* 17, no. 18 (Feb. 2, 1907): 778–784.

102. Ibid.; Scott Nearing, "The City Newsboy," *Woman's Home Companion* 34 (Oct. 1907), 13; Lewis Hine, Newsboys Album, PR 188, Department of Prints, Photographs, and Architectural Collections, New-York Historical Society; Bonnie Yochelson, "Lewis Hine's New York City 'Newsies,'" *New-York Journal of American History* (Fall 2003): 94–106.

103. Lewis Hine, "Social Photography, How the Camera May Help in the Social Uplift," in *Classic Essays on Photography*, ed. Alan Trachtenberg (New Haven, CT: Leete's Island Books, 1980), 111. On Hine's uncredited work with Nearing, see Daile Kaplan, ed., *Photo Story: Selected Letters and Photographs of Lewis W. Hine* (Washington, DC: Smithsonian Institution Press, 1992), xxvii. On his "aesthetic socialism," see Kate Sampsell-Willmann, *Lewis Hine as Social Critic* (Jackson: University Press of Mississippi, 2012), 140; Alexander Nemerov, *Soulmaker: The Times of Lewis Hine* (Princeton, NJ: Princeton University Press, 2016); and Max Eastman, "The Hero as Teacher: The Life Story of John Dewey," in *Heroes I Have Known: Twelve Who Lived Great Lives* (New York: Simon and Schuster, 1942), 278.

104. Robert Macieski, *Picturing Class: Lewis W. Hine Photographs Child Labor in New England* (Amherst: University of Massachusetts Press, 2015), 18.

105. Kaplan, *Photo Story*, 23–34. See also Daile Kaplan, *Lewis Hine in Europe: The Lost Photographs* (New York: Abbeville Press, 1988); Alan Trachtenberg, *Reading American Photographs: Images as History, Matthew Brady to Walker Evans* (New York: Hill & Wang, Noonday Press, 1989), 164–230; John R. Kemp, ed., *Lewis Hine: Photographs of Child Labor in the New South* (Jackson: University Press of Mississippi, 1986); Judith Mara Gutman, *Lewis Hine and the American Social Conscience* (New York: Walker, 1967); Cornell Capa, Judith Mara Gutman, and Bhupendra Karia, eds., *Lewis W. Hine, 1874–1940: Two Perspectives* (London: Studio Vista, 1974); Judith Mara Gutman, "The Worker and the Machine: Lewis Hine's National Research Project Photographs," *Afterimage* 17, no. 2 (Sept. 1989), 13–15; and Alison Devine Nordström, *Lewis Hine, from the Collections of George Eastman House International Museum of Photography and Film* (New York: Distribute Art Publishers, 2012), 12–35.

Chapter 11

1. Scott Nearing, "The City Newsboy," *Woman's Home Companion* 34 (Oct. 1907): 13; "The Child Merchants of Philadelphia," *Philadelphia Inquirer*, Sept. 9, 1900, 8; Ferdinand Lundberg, *Imperial Hearst: A Social Biography* (New York: Random House, 1936), 140; Harry Beardsley, n.d., Heig Scrapbook, 69; George Murray, *The Madhouse on Madison Street* (Chicago: Follett, 1965), 93; *Chicago Day Book*, Apr. 22, 1915, 3.

2. William R Scott, *Scientific Circulation Management for Newspapers* (New York: Ronald Press, 1915), 201; "Public Makes Sweatshops," *Cleveland Plain Dealer*, May 17, 1904, 7; Maud Nathan, *The Story of an Epoch-Making Movement* (Garden City, NY: Doubleday, Page, 1926), 190.

3. William Hard, "De Kid Wot Works at Night," *Everybody's* 18, no. 1 (Jan. 1908): 25–37; Harriet Monroe, "State Street at Night," *Twentieth Century* 5, no. 1 (Nov. 1911): 36. See also Florence Cross Kitchelt, "To Those Asleep," *Twentieth Century* 6, no. 5 (Sept. 1912), in *Survey* 29, no. 4 (Oct. 26, 1912): 100.

4. "New York at Night," *Evening Post*, in *Current Literature* 30 (Mar. 1901): 324–325.

5. On Shinn, see Edith DeShazo with Richard Shaw, *Everett Shinn, 1876–1953: A Figure in His Time* (New York: C. N. Potter, 1974), 154, 208; Sylvia L. Young, "Consuming Drama: Everett Shinn and the Spectacular City," *American Art* 6, no. 4 (Fall 1992): 87–109; Janay Wong,

Everett Shinn: The Spectacle of Life (New York: Berry-Hill Galleries, 2000), 20–22; and Rebecca Zurrier, *Picturing the City: Urban Vision and the Ashcan School* (Berkeley: University of California Press, 2006), 170–176. On children's night work, see Peter C. Baldwin, *In the Watches of the Night: Life in the Nocturnal City, 1820–1930* (Chicago: University of Chicago Press, 2012), ch. 8.

6. "Newsboy Murdered in Central Park," *New York Times*, Dec. 12, 1902, 16; "Kruck Boy's Death," *New York Times*, Dec. 13, 1902, 2; "Newsboy Murder Mystery," *New York Times*, Dec. 14, 1902, 12; "Mystery of Boy's Death May Be Cleared Up," *New York Times*, Dec. 15, 1902, 3; "The Michael Kruck Mystery," *New York Times*, Dec. 16, 1902, 16; *Jewish Daily Forward*, Dec. 20, 1902; "Hickey Slew N.Y. Boy?," *Watertown Herald*, Nov. 30, 1912, 4; "Hickey Killed Man and Murdered Boys," *New York Times*, Nov. 30, 1912, 7.

7. "Newsboy Found Where He Was Killed," *Richmond Times-Dispatch*, July 1, 1903, 3.

8. Ernie Fliegel interview, May 7, 1976, Jews in Minneapolis Oral History Project, Minnesota Historical Society.

9. "Plea for the Newsboy," *Daily Oklahoman*, Jan. 16, 1910, 5; Randolph Guggenheimer, "Newsboys' Chance for the Presidency," *Daily State* (Baton Rouge, LA), Dec. 6, 1906, 2.

10. Zurrier, *Picturing the City*, 218–226, 237–238.

11. Robert Henri, "My People," *The Craftsman*, 1915, reprinted in Henri, *The Art Spirit* (1923; repr., Boulder, CO: Westview Press, 1984), 143–152; Jane Addams, *The Spirit of Youth and the City Streets* (New York: Macmillan, 1910), 9. See also Bennard B. Perlman, *Robert Henri: His Life and Art* (New York: Dover, 1991), 61; Bruce Weber, *Ashcan Kids: Children in the Art of Henri, Luks, Glackens, Bellows & Sloan* (New York: Berry-Hill Galleries, 1998), 10–11, 32–33; and Vincent DiGirolamo, "The Negro Newsboy: Black Child in a White Myth," *Columbia Journal of American Studies* 4 (2000): 63–92.

12. "Darkies and the Dice," *Chicago Herald*, Sept. 28, 1890, 25; "Newsboys and Their Games," *New York Tribune*, Oct. 27, 1895, 28.

13. New York Society for the Prevention of Cruelty to Children, 22nd Annual Report, Dec. 31, 1896, 56; 24th Annual Report, 1898, 56; 30th Annual Report, 1904, 27–28; "Newsboys and Their Games," *New York Tribune*, Oct. 27, 1895, 28.

14. "Uses for Cherry Pits," *Washington Post*, June 26, 1897, 9; Philip Davis, "Child Life on the Street," in *Proceedings, Conference on Charities and Corrections, Buffalo, 1909*, 252; "'Oliver Twists' of the East Side," *New York Times*, Aug. 2, 1908, SM3; Anna Y. Reed, *Newsboy Service: A Study in Educational and Vocational Guidance* (Yonkers-on-Hudson, NY: World Book Company, 1917), 104.

15. "Life in the Metropolis," *New York Weekly Sun*, July 24, 1889, n.p.; "Life of a Gamin," *New York World*, Dec. 22, 1893, n.p., in Heig Scrapbook; Alexander Fleisher, "The Newsboys of Milwaukee," Milwaukee Bureau of Economy and Efficiency, *Bulletin* 8 (Nov. 15, 1911): 68; "Blind Boys Match Pennies," *Colorado Springs Gazette*, Feb. 11, 1915, 2.

16. Anthony Comstock, *Traps for the Young*, ed. Robert Bremner (1883; repr., Cambridge, MA: Belknap Press of Harvard University Press, 1967), 57–59, 93; Fleisher, "Newsboys of Milwaukee," 68–69; Bonnie Stepenoff, "Child Savers and St. Louis Newsboys, 1896–1948," *Missouri Historical Review* 104, no. 3 (2010): 128–129.

17. "Darkies and the Dice," *Chicago Herald*, Sept. 28, 1890, 25; "The Game of Craps," *Fort Worth Morning Register*, Aug. 22, 1897, 3; Paul Laurence Dunbar, "An Old-Time Christmas," in *The Complete Stories of Paul Laurence Dunbar*, ed. Gene Andrew Jarrett and Thomas Lewis Morgan (Athens: Ohio University Press, 2005), 160–162.

18. "'Tiny' Leads Kids' Strike," *Chicago Tribune*, Jan. 20, 1905, 3; John Wilds, *Afternoon Story: A Century of the New Orleans States-Item* (Baton Rouge: Louisiana State University Press, 1976), 181.

19. Allan M. Brandt, *The Cigarette Century: The Rise, Fall, and Deadly Persistence of the Product That Defined America* (New York: Basic Books, 2007), 25–43, 59; "Suicide Made Easy," *Idaho Statesman*, Jan. 30, 1896, 2.

20. *Owyhee Avalanche*, June 26, 1880, 4; "Willing to Oblige," *Omaha World-Herald*, Oct. 15, 1902, 11.

21. "Field Full of Athletes," *Chicago Tribune*, June 28, 1903, 11; "Cigaret War Is Revived with Boy Detectives Used," *Chicago Tribune*, Apr. 7, 1904, 14.

22. "In Wrong Place," *Kansas Semi-Weekly Capital*, Mar. 19, 1901, 6; "After Indecent Pictures," *Adrian Daily Telegram*, Mar. 22, 1901, 2; "Carrie's New Crusade," *Daily Illinois State Register*, Mar. 23, 1901, 1; "Newsboys Were Carrie's Retinue," *Cleveland Plain Dealer*, Aug. 23, 1901, 2; "Carrie Nation of Saloon Smashing Fame Is in the City," *New Orleans Times-Picayune*, Dec. 20, 1907, 11; "Mrs. Nation Gives Third of Lectures," *Anaconda Standard*, Jan. 28, 1910, 7; "Saloon-Smasher Is Nervous Wreck," *Oregonian*, Jan. 31, 1911, 1.

23. Pauline V. and Erle F. Young, "Getting at the Boy Himself: Through the Personal Interview," *Social Forces* 6, no. 3 (Mar. 1928): 410; Brandt, *Cigarette Century*, 25–43, 59.

24. "Rep Keefe Speaks," *Boston Globe*, Mar. 11, 1907, 2; "Anti-Spitting Law Revived," *Oregonian*, May 14, 1912, 11; "Who Are the Spitters?," *Kalamazoo* (MI) *Gazette*, Sept. 25, 1914, 4.

25. "Bar Boys from Saloons," *Cleveland Plain Dealer*, Jan. 19, 1906, 4; "Salvation and News Will Be Barred from Saloons by Measure," *Kalamazoo* (MI) *Gazette*, Dec. 7, 1911, 7; NCLC Papers, box 4, folder: NY—Newsboys—1913; Jack London, *John Barleycorn* (1913; repr., New York: The Modern Library, 2001), 27–28.

26. "'Hinky Dink' Kenna to Give Up Office," *Baltimore Sun*, Jan. 18, 1923, 1; "Illinois: Decline of Hinky Dink," *Time*, July 13, 1944; Oral History Interview with R. H. (Bob) Hall, Nov. 28, 1965, Archives of American Art, Washington, DC, http://www.aaa.si.edu/collections/interviews/oral-history-interview-r-hbob-hall-13043.

27. "Private Life of the Gamin," *New York Daily Graphic*, Mar. 11, 1873, 3.

28. David Nasaw, "Children and Commercial Culture: Moving Pictures in the Early Twentieth Century," in *Small Worlds: Children and Adolescents in America, 1850–1950*, ed. Elliott West and Paula Petrik (Lawrence: University of Kansas Press, 1992), 20.

29. Philip Davis, *Street-Land: Its Little People and Big Problems*, with Grace Kroll (Boston: Small, Maynard, 1915), 246, 80; New York Society for the Prevention of Cruelty to Children, *34th Annual Report*, 1909, 22–23, in Nasaw, "Children and Commercial Culture," 15; M. S. Hanaw, "A Street Corner Interview," *Survey* 27 (Feb. 24, 1912): 1797.

30. *Newsboy Conditions in Chicago*, 7.

31. Frank Capra, *The Name Above the Title* (New York: Macmillan, 1971), xi; Joseph McBride, *Frank Capra: The Catastrophe of Success* (New York: Simon & Schuster, 1992), 53.

32. Chicago Vice Commission, *The Social Evil in Chicago: A Study of Existing Conditions, with Recommendations* (Chicago: Gunthorp-Warren, 1911), 35–36, 240–241.

33. "The Mother Who Is Afraid," in "True Stories of Newsboys" (c. 1913–16), NYCLC Papers, box 31, folder 9.

34. "Small Riot of Newsboys," *Baltimore Sun*, July 31, 1900, 10.

35. "Newsboys Are on a Strike," *Brooklyn Eagle*, Aug. 8, 1900, 2.

36. "Union Newsboys Dispersed," *St. Louis Republican*, Aug. 9, 1900, 9; "Modern Slang," *Evansville Courier & Press*, Apr. 13, 1903, 4.

37. *Springfield Republican*, Sept. 13, 1900, 12; *Baltimore Sun*, Dec. 13, 1900, 9.

38. *Freeland Tribune*, Apr. 24, 1901, 1; "The Young Unionists," *Scranton Tribune*, Apr. 29, 1901, 5; "Mill Girls Resume Work," *Scranton Tribune*, Apr. 30, 1901, 10; William Mailly, "In Scranton," *New York Worker*, May 5, 1901, 1; "Boys Held a Meeting," *Scranton Tribune*, May 6, 1901, 8. See also Bonnie Stepenoff, "Keeping It in the Family: Mother Jones and the Pennsylvania Silk Strike of 1900–1901," *Labor History* 38, no. 4 (1997): 432–449, and Bonnie Stepenoff, "Family Ties and Labour Activism Among Silk Workers in Northeastern Pennsylvania, U.S.A., 1900–1920," in *Rebellious Families: Household Strategies and Collective Action in the Nineteenth and Twentieth Centuries*, ed. Jan Kok (New York: Berghahn Books, 2002), 125–139.

39. "A Newsboys' Union," *Birmingham Labor Advocate*, July 6, 1901, 1.

40. "The World of Work," *Baltimore Sun*, Mar. 22, 1903, 10.

41. "Newsboys' Strike Is Over," *Hartford Courant*, Aug. 10, 1903, 12.

42. "Newsboys on Strike," *New York Times*, Mar. 16, 1904, 2; "Newsboys on Strike," *Bennington Evening Banner*, Mar. 21, 1904, 1; *Urbana Daily Courier*, July 29, 1904, 6; "Fremont Newsies Form a Trust," *Omaha Bee*, Dec. 25, 1904, 3.

43. "'Chimmie' M'Fadden, King of the Newsboys, Visits Ogden," *Ogden Standard*, Aug. 1, 1914, 5.

44. *Omaha Bee*, Nov. 10, 1903, 3; "Indorse Newsboys' Stand," *Boston Globe*, Apr. 13, 1904, 5; "Newsboys Up in Arms," *Boston Globe*, Apr. 25, 1904, 8; "Editor Fitzgerald," *Boston Herald*, Feb. 7, 1902, 6; "Republic's New Editor," *Boston Herald*, Feb. 15, 1902, 3; Jack Henry Cutler,

"He Bought Newspaper to Boost Career," *Boston Advertiser*, Jan. 20, 1963, 15; John Henry Cutler, *"Honey Fitz": Three Steps to the White House—The Life and Times of John F. (Honey-Fitz) Fitzgerald* (Indianapolis, IN: Bobbs-Merrill, 1962), 79–81.

45. "Local Labor Notes," *Boston Globe*, July 8, 1903, 5; "Newsboys Have New Button," *Boston Globe*, Sept. 16, 1903, 2; *Proceedings*, Twenty-Third Annual Convention, American Federation of Labor, Boston, Nov. 9–23, 1903 (Washington, DC: Law Reporter, 1903), 11; *Chicago Tribune*, Nov. 10, 1903, 4; "Girl Messengers Attacked," *Washington Post*, Oct. 26, 1903, 1; "Want Their Holidays," *Boston Globe*, Apr. 11, 1904, 4.

46. "Retired Globe Circulation Man Political Sage in Early Days," *Boston Globe*, May 12, 1957, A11; *Minnesota Labor Review*, Nov. 14, 1907, 15; "Lads File Complaint," *Washington Star*, Sept. 19, 1906, 13; "Boston Newsboys Win in Their Controversy with the Teamsters," *Washington Times*, Sept. 21, 1906, 5; Bruère, "Industrial Democracy," *Outlook* 84, no. 15 (Dec. 8, 1906): 880–881.

47. "Bryan to Newsboys," *Boston Herald*, July 25, 1902, 5; "The Bulletin," *Harvard Crimson*, Feb. 4, 1903, n.p; O. M. Boyd, "News of the Labor World," *San Francisco Call*, Oct. 18, 1906, 9; "Newsboy College Boy," *Washington Post*, Nov. 4, 1906, 2. See also Elizabeth Powell Bond, "The Youth Founder of the News Boys' Protective Union," *Friend's Intelligencer* 64, no. 3 (Jan. 19, 1907): 33; "Lads File Complaint," *Washington Star*, Sept. 19, 1906, 13; "Sends 25 Youths Through Harvard," *Charleston News & Courier*, Mar. 9, 1941, 13; *Harvard Gazette*, May 28, 1951, n.p.; and *Boston Herald*, May 28, 1951, 1, 4.

48. "200 Boys Fight Policemen," *Washington Post*, Jan. 12, 1908, 1; "Newsboys Beat Policemen," *New York Times*, Jan. 12, 1908, 1; *Washington Star*, Apr. 1, 1908, 19.

49. *Washington Post*, Mar. 9, 1902, 29; "The Ups and Downs of a Newsboy's Life in Salt Lake," *Deseret Evening News*, Jan. 17, 1903, 9.

50. "The World of Work," *Baltimore Sun*, Mar. 22, 1903, 10.

51. *Urbana Daily Courier*, July 29, 1904, 6.

52. "The World of Work," *Baltimore Sun*, Mar. 5, 1905, 14.

53. "Peoria News Boys Organize," *Quincy Daily Whig*, Mar. 18, 1906, 2; "Shumway as Candidate," *True Republican*, July 11, 1908, 7.

54. *Proceedings*, Twenty-Fifth Annual Convention, American Federation of Labor, Minneapolis, Nov. 12–24, 1906 (Washington, DC: Graphic Arts Printing, 1906), 175.

55. "Memphis Newsboys Strike," *New Orleans Times-Picayune*, Oct. 31, 1908, 15; *Tampa Tribune*, Aug. 31, 1911, 4.

56. "A Striker Grown Can Be Fought Outright," *New Orleans Times-Picayune*, July 18, 1911, 4; "Gloom at Midnight," *New Orleans Times-Picayune*, July 19, 1911, 2; "Evening Papers Raise Their Price; Newsboys Still Refuse to Sell," *New Orleans Times-Picayune*, July 19, 1911, 4; "Newsboys Selling Evening Papers; Net Strike Result, Raised Prices," *New Orleans Times-Picayune*, July 20, 1911, 6; "Facts About the Newsboys' Strike," *New Orleans Item*, July 20, 1911, 1; "A Strike Lesson," *New Orleans Item*, July 26, 1911, 6.

57. "Free-for-All Fight," *Colorado Springs Gazette*, Nov. 4, 1907, 5.

58. See Melvyn Dubofsky, *We Shall Be All: A History of the IWW, the Industrial Workers of the World* (New York: Quadrangle, 1969); Philip S. Foner, *The Industrial Workers of the World, 1905–1917*, vol. 4, *History of the Labor Movement in the United States* (New York: International Publishers, 1965); and Joyce L. Kornbluh et al., *Rebel Voices: An IWW Anthology* (Oakland, CA: PM Press, 2011).

59. "Newsboys on a Strike," *Anaconda Standard*, Nov. 22, 1899, 10; "Newsboys on a Strike," *Anaconda Standard*, July 27, 1901, 4; Dale Martin, "School for Struggle: The Butte Newsboys Strikes of 1914 and 1919," *Speculator* 2, no. 2 (Summer 1985): 9–11; Newsboys' Club membership card, box/folder 2/9, Russell H. Meinhart Papers, Montana Historical Society Research Center Archives; "Newsboys on Strike Create a Commotion," *Anaconda Standard*, June 29, 1907, 7; "Newsboys on Strike," *Salt Lake Herald*, June 29, 1907, 8.

60. "Strike of Newsboys Starts Small Riot," *Anaconda Standard*, June 21, 1913, 7; "Newsboys on Strike Ask Cheaper Rate," *Anaconda Standard*, Jan. 6, 1914, 2; "Newsboys Vote to End Their Strike," *Anaconda Standard*, Jan. 7, 1914, 11; "Newsboys Back on the Job at the Butte Post," *Anaconda Standard*, Jan. 8, 1914, 2; "Newsboys All Back," *Anaconda Standard*, Jan. 9, 1914, 7; "Riot of the Butte Newsboys," *First Biennial Report of the Montana Dept. of Labor and Industry*,

1913–1914, 22; Martin, "School for Struggle," 9–11; Janet Finn, *Mining Childhood: Growing Up in Butte, 1900–1960* (Helena: Montana Historical Society Press, 2012), 220–222.

61. Philip S. Foner, ed., *Fellow Workers and Friends: IWW Free Speech Fight as Told by Participants* (Westport, CT: Greenwood Press, 1981), 216 n. 57; Fred Thompson and Patrick Murfin, *The IWW: Its First Seventy Years (1905–1975)* (Chicago: Industrial Workers of the World, 1976), 31; "Goldfield Newsboys Give to Defense Fund," *Denver Post*, Mar. 13, 1906, 3.

62. "How the West Dealt with One Labor Union," *Colorado Springs Gazette*, July 11, 1907, 4; *L. C. Branson, Appellant, v. the Industrial Workers of the World et al.*, No. 1736, Supreme Court of Nevada, 30 Nev. 270; 95 P. 354; 1908 Nev. Lexis 17.

63. "America's Brand-New Millionaire Is a Deadly Expert in Gun Plays," *Washington Post*, Dec. 23, 1906, A10l; "How Goldfield Picked a Site for a Cemetery," *Washington Post*, Dec. 30, 1906, A5; "The Goldfield and Bullfrog Anarchy," *Los Angeles Times*, Mar. 16, 1907, II4; "Gun Fighter's Behind Bars," *Los Angeles Times*, Jan. 17, 1908, III1; "Famous Gambler and Gun Man," *Washington Post*, June 23, 1912, M3; C. Elizabeth Raymond, *George Wingfield: Owner and Operator of Nevada* (Reno: University of Nevada Press, 1992), 65–67.

64. Renshaw, *The Wobblies*, 109; James W. Byrkit, "Lindley C. Branson and the Jerome *Sun*," *Journal of the West* 10, No. 4 (Oct. 1971): 51–63.

65. *Rocky Mountain News*, May 25, 1914, 9; Max Eastman, "Class Lines in Colorado," *New Review* 2, no. 7 (July 1914): 383–385. See also Thomas G. Andrews, *Killing for Coal: America's Deadliest Labor War* (Cambridge, MA: Harvard University Press, 2008).

66. "Circulation Men Adjourn," *Boston Herald*, June 11, 1903, 6; William Byron Forbush, "Clubs for Street Boys," *Charities and the Commons* 16, no. 5 (May 5, 1906): 213–215; "Reading Clubs and Boys' Gangs," *Survey* 23 (Mar. 5, 1910): 859.

67. C. L. Van Cleve, "John Gunckel and His Work in Behalf of the Boys," *Journal of Education* 68, no. 8 (Sept. 3, 1908): 220–221; "Lake Shore Endorses Work for Newsboys," *Elkhart Truth*, Aug. 4, 1905, 6; Gunckel, *Boyville*; A. E. Winship, "John E. Gunckel as I Knew Him," *Journal of Education* 82, no. 14 (Oct. 21, 1915): 373. For a kindlier view of Gunckel's boy work, see Patrick Joseph Ryan, "Shaping Modern Youth: Social Policies and Growing Up Working-Class in Industrial America, 1890–1945," PhD diss., Case Western Reserve University, 1998, 86–131.

68. "Seeks Aid for Waifs," *Urbana Courier*, Nov. 22, 1905, 1; "Rockefeller Will Help Build Newsboys' Home," *Trenton Times*, Dec. 1, 1905, 16; "A Rockefeller Philanthropy," *Guthrie Daily Leader*, Dec. 7, 1905, 4; and J. E. Randall, "A Church's Unique Plan to Benefit Newsboys," *Leslie's Weekly*, Jan. 4, 1906, 6.

69. "Roosevelt's Greetings to Athletic Newsboys," *New York Times*, Dec. 15, 1905, 10; "$5,000 Obtained for 'Newsies' Club," *New York Times*, Mar. 4, 1907, 9.

70. "Newsboys Meet Again," *New York Times*, Apr. 4, 1904, 9; "Athletic Newsboys Have Their Own Club," *New York Times*, Dec. 5, 1905, 11; "Kelly Defeats Murphy," *New York Sun*, Sept. 22, 1898, 4; "Newsboys Go on Strike," *New York Tribune*, July 21, 1899, 10; "'Noosies' to Have Their Own Fireside," *New York Times*, Mar. 30, 1904, 9.

71. "Newsboys Clubs and a Leader," *New York Evening World*, Dec. 14, 1905, 14.

72. "Coins Wreck Dinner," *New York Tribune*, Dec. 26, 1905, 2; "Club Solicitor Held," *New York Tribune*, July 27, 1906, 4; "Robbed Newsboys' Club," *New York Sun*, Dec. 13, 1906, 11; "Newsboy Club Trouble," *New York Tribune*, Oct. 21, 1906, 12; "The World's Oldest Club," *Kansas City Star*, Feb. 24, 1908, 9; "Newsboys' Summer Camp Ready," *New York Tribune*, June 20, 1909, 7; "Newsboys' Camp Reopens To-Day," *New-York Tribune*, July 1, 1909, 3; "Country Estate of the 'Newsies,'" *New York Sunday Tribune*, June 21, 1914, Sup. 3, 28.

73. "Becker, Terror of the Tenderloin," *New York Journal*, June 12, 1897, 2; "Paul Lent a Newsboy $150 to Buy Diamonds," *New York Tribune*, July 23, 1912, 2; "Sullivan There When Rosenthal Was Shot Down," *New York Times*, July 27, 1912, 1; "An Eruption from New York's Underworld," *Current Literature* 53, no. 3 (Sept. 1912): 15–19; Jacob A. Riis, "The New York Newsboy," *Century Magazine* 85, no. 2 (Dec. 1912): 253; Meyer Berger, "The Becker Case—View of 'The System,'" *New York Times*, Nov. 11, 1951, SM8.

74. Helen C. Dwight, "The Newsboys' Home Club (Visited, March 26, 1915). STR NY n3," NCLC papers, box 4, Library of Congress, Washington, DC; "Fraud Solicitors," *Fourth Estate*,

May 1, 1915, 7; Helen C. Dwight, "The Menace of Street Trading by Children," *American City* 12 (Jan. 1915): 24.

75. Thomas M. Osborne, "The George Junior Republic," *Journal of Social Science* 36 (Dec. 1898): 134–138; Lyman Abbott, "A Republic in the Republic," *Outlook* 88, no. 7 (Feb. 15, 1908): 351–354; O. F. Lewis "The Junior Republic," *Survey* 23 (Feb. 12, 1910): 734–736; William R. George, *The Junior Republic: Its History and Ideals* (New York: D. Appleton, 1910); "Newsboys Want Their Own Court," *Boston Journal*, June 18, 1910, 8.

76. See Lincoln Steffens, *The Shame of the Cities* (New York: McClure, Philips, 1904); William R. Riordan, *Plunkitt of Tammany Hall* (New York: McClure, Phillips, 1905); Tom L. Johnson, "My Memoirs," *Cleveland Plain Dealer* (June 18, 1911), 17; Louis Leonard Tucker, ed., "The Life of the 'Boss of Cincinnati,'" *Cincinnati Historical Society Bulletin* 26 (Apr. 1968): 150; Joseph E. Fahey, *James K. McGuire: Boy Mayor and Irish Nationalist* (Syracuse: Syracuse University Press, 2014), 17; Lincoln Steffens, "A Servant of God and the People: The Story of Mark Fagan, Mayor of Jersey City," *McClure's Magazine* 26, no. 3 (Jan. 1906): 297; and Francis Churchill Williams, *J. Devlin—Boss: A Romance of American Politics* (Boston: Lothrop, 1901).

77. G. Stanley Hall, *Adolescence: Its Psychology and Its Relations to Physiology, Anthropology, Sociology, Sex, Crime, Religion, and Education* (New York: D. Appleton, 1904). See also Joseph F. Kett, *Rites of Passage: Adolescence in America: 1790 to the Present* (New York: Basic Books, 1977); Elizabeth Lunbeck, *The Psychiatric Persuasion: Knowledge, Gender, and Power in Modern America* (Princeton, NJ: Princeton University Press, 1994), 188–89, 232; Kent Baxter, *The Modern Age: Turn of the Century American Culture and the Invention of Adolescence* (Tuscaloosa: University of Alabama Press, 2008); and Sarah E. Chinn, *Inventing Modern Adolescence: The Children of Immigrants in Turn-of-the-Century America* (New Brunswick, NJ: Rutgers University Press, 2009).

78. *Boston Herald*, Feb. 4, 1908, 3; *Boston Herald*, Jan. 5, 1909, 7; "Care of Newsboys," *Boston Globe*, Feb. 7, 1909, 26; "New Rules for Street Trades," *Common Welfare*, Feb. 13, 1909, 953; *Annual Report of the School Committee, City of Boston, 1909, School Document No. 15–1909* (City of Boston Printing Department, 1909), 34–37; Philip Davis, "Appendix D. Fourth Annual Report of the Supervisor of Licensed Minors," in *Annual Report of the School Committee, City of Boston, 1910, School Document No. 14–1910* (City of Boston Printing Department, 1910), 132–138; Davis, *Street-Land*, 221.

79. Philip Davis, *And Crown Thy Good* (New York: Philosophical Library, 1952); "Newsboys Elect Judges to Preside over Court," *Christian Science Monitor*, Nov. 8, 1910, 12; "Newsboys Elect Their Own Judge," *Survey* 25 (Nov. 26, 1910): 312; "A Newsboy Trial Board," *Law Notes*, Jan. 1911, 188–189; "Many Injured Stealing Rides," *Boston Journal*, Jan. 10, 1911, 3; Thomas D. Lavell, "Some Impressions of the Newsboys Court," *Hustler* 1, nos. 3&4 (Apr.–May, 1911): 1–2; Lewis E. Palmer, "Horatio Alger, Then and Now," *Survey* 27 (Dec. 2, 1911), 1276; Rheta Childe Dorr, "The Child Who Toils at Home," *Hampton Magazine* 28, no. 3 (Apr. 1912): 222; Livingston Wright, "The Boston Newsboys' Trial Board," *Case and Comment* 19, no. 9 (Feb. 1913): 586–589.

80. Palmer, "Horatio Alger, Then and Now," 1276; "The Court with Juvenile Judges, Where Other Boys Are Instructed in the Moral Art of 'Bracing Up,'" *Boston Sunday Herald*, Nov. 9, 1916, 2; Denis A. McCarthy, "The Newsboys of Boston, Written for the Little 'Merchants of the Street,'" in "Making Citizens," *First Annual Report*, Boston Newsboys Club, 1911, 25; "Four Scholarships," *Boston Globe*, Feb. 12, 1911, 8; "227,201 Enrolled in 276 Boys' Clubs," *New York Times*, Jan. 15, 1928, 31.

81. "Milwaukee's Newsboys' Republic," *Outlook*, Apr. 5, 1913: 743–744; *52nd Annual Report of the Board of School Directors of the City of Milwaukee, 1911* (Milwaukee: Radtke Bros. & Korsch, 1911), 192; "The Milwaukee 'Newsies,'" *Youth's Companion* 87, no. 28 (July 10, 1913): 358; P. O. Powell, "Getting Hold of Milwaukee's Newsboys," *Playground* 10, no. 1 (Apr. 1916): 296–299; Jennifer S. Light, "Building Virtual Cities, 1895–1945," *Journal of Urban History* 38, no. 2 (2012) 349–350.

82. Powell, "Getting Hold of Milwaukee's Newsboys," 296–299; George W. Stocking Jr., "Sol Tax, 1907–1995," *University of Chicago Record* 30, no. 5 (May 23, 1996): 22–23; Sol Tax, "Pride and Puzzlement: A Retro-Introspective Record of 60 Years of Anthropology," *Annual Review of Anthropology* 17 (1988): 2, 6; John W. Bennett, "Applied and Action

Anthropology: Ideological and Conceptual Aspects," *Current Anthropology*, 37, no. 1, supp., "Special Issue: Anthropology in Public" (Feb. 1996): S33–S34.

83. William Paul Dillingham, US Senate Committee on Immigration, *Reports of the Immigration Commission, Immigrants in Industries, 1907–10* (Washington, DC: Government Printing Office, 1911), pt. 2, 2:159–166; Lee McCrae, "The Newsboys' Court of Birmingham, Alabama," *Boys' World* 13, no. 41 (Oct. 10, 1914): 2; "The Birmingham Boys," *Work with Boys* 15, no. 2 (Feb. 1915): 67–73.

84. Lillian D. Wald, *Windows on Henry Street* (Boston: Little, Brown, 1934), 34; "Police Watch Newsboys' Home," *Cleveland Plain Dealer*, Nov. 21, 1900, 4; "Child Labor at Night," *Washington Post*, May 7, 1903, 3; Kathleen Mathew, "New York Newsboy," *Frank Leslie's Popular Monthly* 39, no. 4 (Apr. 1895): 458.

85. US Department of Commerce, Bureau of the Census, *Benevolent Institutions, 1910* (Washington, DC: Government Printing Office, 1913), 158–173.

86. "Waldorf Room at the Newsboys' Lodging House," *New-York Tribune Illustrated Supplement*, Apr. 17, 1904, 5–6; "Famous Newsboys," *Canton Repository*, June 6, 1906, 8; "Newsboys' 'Foster Father' Tells How They Won Fame," *New York Evening Telegram*, June 27, 1910, 3.

87. *Charities* 14, no. 8 (May 20, 1905): 768, and 14, no. 10 (June 3, 1905): 780.

88. Stepenoff, "Child Savers and St. Louis Newsboys," 130–131; Rev. J. W. Gormley, *History of Father Dunne's News Boys' Home and Protectorate* (St. Louis: Father Dunne's Newsboys, 1927); "A Montage of the River," Robert S. Saunders Papers, Western Historical Manuscript Collection, University of Missouri–St. Louis, 60.

89. "Sticks Up for His Home," *Minneapolis Journal*, Mar. 3, 1903, 6.

90. "Form Newsboys' Union," *Omaha World-Herald*, Apr. 21, 1898, 3; *Omaha Bee*, Oct. 18, 1898, 8; *Omaha World-Herald*, Jan. 1, 1899, 23.

91. "Newsboys Declare Strike," *Omaha Bee*, Jan. 19, 1902, 5; "Newsboys Strike and Fight," *Omaha Bee*, Jan. 20, 1902; "'Newsies' Wage War and Shed Much Blood," *Omaha World-Herald*, Jan. 20, 1902, 8; "Newsboys' Riot in Omaha Leads to Broken Heads," *Chicago Tribune*, Jan. 20, 1902, 9; "Newsboys Win in Fight with One," *Omaha World-Herald*, Jan. 23, 1902, 6.

92. "Probation Officer's View," *Journal of Education* 71, no. 2 (Jan. 13, 1910): 38.

93. "Doing a Grand Work," *Minneapolis Labor Review*, Jan. 25, 1908, 4; "Mogy Bernstein Found Dead with Gun by His Side," *Omaha Morning World-Herald*, Aug. 16, 1919, 1, 10; "Mogy Was Boys' Friend; Helped Many to Success," *Omaha Evening World-Herald*, Aug. 16, 1919, 1–2; "Newsboys Honor Memory of 'Mogy' Their Friend," *Omaha Morning World-Herald*, Aug. 19, 1919, 1; "'Mogy' Bernstein—The Story of a Newsboy Who Made Good," *Jewish Daily News*, Nov. 20, 1919, 2.

94. Kenneth Bilby, *The General: David Sarnoff and the Rise of the Communications Industry* (New York: HaperCollins, 1986), 32.

95. Hine is quoted in McKelway, *Child Labor at the National Capital*, NCLC Pamphlet No. 264 (1916), 10–11; Nick Zades, *"Those Days": Newspaper Newsboy Stories* (Chicopee, MA: Pond-Ekberg, 1992), 22–24; "Police to Keep Order Among Fellows," *North Platte Semi-Weekly Tribune*, Dec. 17, 1912, 3.

96. "Printers Take a Look Back on 100 Years," *Richmond Times-Dispatch*, Oct. 22, 1950, 11; "Crowds Seize Herald Extras," *Boston Herald*, Apr. 19, 1912, 3; "A Little Deal in High Finance," *Winston-Salem Journal*, May 12, 1912, 10.

97. *New York Times*, Apr. 22, 1912, 5; *Springfield Daily News*, Apr. 24, 1912, 8.

98. "T.R. Jumps in with a Bang," *San Francisco Call*, July 16, 1912, 1; *Milwaukee Journal*, Sept. 16, 1943, 1.

99. *Birmingham Ledger Co. v. Buchanan*, Court of Appeals of Alabama, 10 Ala. App. 527; 65 So. 667; 1914 Ala. App. Lexis 233. May 19, 1914, decided; "False Imprisonment," *American Law Review*, Mar. 16, 1915, 288–289.

100. "Newsboys' Meeting," *Boston Journal*, Feb. 26, 1912, 11.

101. "So the People May Know," *Kansas City Post*, Feb. 12, 1912, 1; "Newsboys' Strike," *Day Book*, Feb. 12, 1912, 27; "The Underpaid Newsboys Strike on the Star," *Kansas City Post*, Feb. 14, 1912, 1; *Printers' Ink* 41, no. 4 (Apr. 22, 1915): 56.

102. "Newsboys Have a Real Union," *Kansas City Star*, June 10, 1908, 6; "Newsboys' Club Reorganized," *Kansas City Star*, Nov. 18, 1911, 13; "Throws Newsies into Cells," *Kansas City*

Post, Feb. 15, 1912, 1; "Paper Sellers Herded to Jail Freed by Court," *Kansas City Post*, Feb. 15, 1912, 1; "Fines in Newsboy 'Strike,'" *Kansas City Star*, Feb. 16, 1912, 1; "Judge Lucas Enjoins the Police," *Kansas City Star*, Feb. 16, 1912, 1; "The 'War' Goes On," *Topeka State Journal*, Feb. 17, 1912, 4; *Topeka State Journal*, Feb. 19, 1912, 4. See also Eva M. Marquis, "A Survey of Working Children in Kansas City," Kansas City, Mo., Board of Public Welfare, *Annual Report* (1914–15), 108–160.

103. "Change Was His Hoodoo," *Kansas City Star*, Apr. 29, 1910, 7; "Paper Sellers Herded to Jail Freed by Court," *Kansas City Star*, Feb. 15, 1912, 1; "King of Newsies, Held 17 Hours Without Cause, Freed by Judge Burney," *Kansas City Post*, Feb. 16, 1912, 9; "Was It Because He Was a Jew?," *Kansas City Post*, Feb. 16, 1912, 9; "King of the Newsboys Is Held Without Bail," *Kansas City Post*, Feb. 16, 1912, 15; "King of Newsies Freed the Fifth Time in Three Days by Judge Burney," *Kansas City Post*, Feb. 17, 1912, 1.

104. Ed. A. Goewey, "The Charge of the Cop Brigade at Petticoat Lane," *Kansas City Post*, Feb. 16, 1912, 2.

105. "Two Reporters Arrested," *Kansas City Post*, Feb. 16, 1912, 15; "The 'War' Goes On," *Topeka State Journal*, Feb. 17, 1912, 4; *Topeka State Journal*, Feb. 19, 1912, 4; "Nelson's Abuse of Boys Is Rebuked," *Denver Post*, Feb. 20, 1912, 1; "King of Newsboys," *Jackson Citizen Patriot*, May 6, 1915, 3.

106. Burton Rascoe, *Before I Forget* (New York: Doubleday, Doran, 1937), 269. Rascoe's account provoked a $250,000 libel suit from Max Annenberg that was finally dropped in 1939 when the publisher agreed to delete the offending pages from remaining copies. See also "The Press: Men & Ink," *Time*, Aug. 2, 1937; "Press: Rascoe's Annenberg," *Time*, Dec. 13, 1937; Thomas Forbes, "Mean Street Sales," *Newsinc.*, Feb. 1991, 48; and Donald M. Hensley, *Burton Rascoe* (New York: Twayne, 1970), 33–34.

107. "Newsboys Union Born in Bedlam," *Chicago Tribune*, Feb. 28, 1902, 5; "Downtown Newsboys Are Now Whiskered Capitalists," *Chicago Tribune*, Dec. 4, 1904, F1–2; *Newsboy Conditions in Chicago* (Chicago: Federation of Chicago Settlements, 1903), 7; Myron E. Adams, "Children in American Street Trades," *Annals of the American Academy of Political and Social Science* 25 (May 1905): 440–442.

108. "Slain by Rival in Trade," *Chicago Tribune*, Mar. 9, 1901, 1; "Two Acquitted of Murder," *Chicago Tribune*, Mar. 12, 1902, 9; "Brothers Die in Same Hour," *Chicago Tribune*, Nov. 29, 1905, 3; "Hearst Sluggers," *Los Angeles Times*, Nov. 30, 1905, I1; Hard, "De Kid Wot Works at Night," 33.

109. "Find Publishers in a Conspiracy," *Chicago Tribune*, June 2, 1907, 1; "News Trust Plan Exposed in Court," *Chicago Tribune*, June 29, 1907, 2.

110. Rascoe, *Before I Forget*, 269–270; Wayne Andrews, *Battle for Chicago* (New York: Harcourt, Brace, 1946), 32–37; Jay Robert Nash, "Heyday! Chicago's Golden Era of Journalism," *Mankind* 31, no. 9 (1972): 12–18, 52–53; Joseph Gies, *The Colonel of Chicago* (New York: Dutton, 1979); Thomas Forbes, "Mean Street Sales," *Newsinc.*, Feb. 1991, 48; Richard Norton Smith, *The Colonel: The Life and Legend of Robert R. McCormick; 1880–1955* (Boston: Houghton Mifflin, 1997); Steve Mills, "Vending Violence in a '.38-Caliber Circulation Drive," *Chicago Tribune*, June 8, 1997; Rose Keefe, *Guns and Roses: The Untold Story of Dean O'Banion, Chicago's Big Shot Before Al Capone* (Nashville, TN: Cumberland House, 2003), 67–79.

111. On the Chicago circulation wars, see Philip Taft, "The Limits of Labor Unity: The Chicago Newspaper Strike of 1912," *Labor History* 19, no. 1 (1978): 100–129; Jon Bekken, "'The Most Vindictive and Most Vengeful Power': Labor Confronts the Chicago Newspaper Trust," *Journalism History* 18 (1992): 11–17, and Jon Bekken, "Crumbs from the Publishers' Golden Tables: The Plight of the Chicago Newsboy," *Media History* 6, no. 1 (2000): 45–57. For a fictional account, see James T. Ferrell, "The Scoop," in *Can All This Grandeur Perish? And Other Stories* (New York: Vanguard, 1937), 130–135.

112. "Strike Sluggers Beat Children and Threaten Women," *Chicago Tribune*, May 5, 1912, 1; "Violence Attends Efforts of Newsboys and Women to Sell Their Papers," *Chicago Examiner*, May 5, 1912, 2; "Violence Done in Newspaper Strike," *Twice-a-Week Plain Dealer*, May 7, 1912, 4; "Moving Pictures of Strike Riots Banned," *Chicago Examiner*, May 7, 1912, 2; "Stop Picture Men," *Flint Journal*, May 7, 1912, 1.

113. *Chicago Day Book*, May, 11, 1912, 31; May 22, 1912, 9; June 1, 1912, 9.

114. *Chicago Day Book*, May 20, 1912, 4; "Attempt to Force Newsboys to Give In Fails," *Chicago Day Book*, July 27, 1912, 1–2; "Newsboys' Statement," *Chicago Day Book*, Sept. 19, 1912, 21; *Chicago Evening World*, June 17, July 5, 1912, cited in Taft, "The Limits of Labor Unity," 111.

115. Florence Kelley, "Standards of Life and Labor," *Twentieth Century* 5 (Nov.– Dec. 1911): 31.

116. Edward Clopper, *Child Labor in City Streets* (Norwood, MA: Macmillan, 1912), v; Lester Frank Ward, *Pure Sociology: A Treatise on the Origin and Spontaneous Development of Society* (New York: Macmillan, 1903), 49–51, 297, 554. On Ward, see Henry Steele Commager, ed., *Lester Ward and the Welfare State* (Indianapolis, IN: Bobbs-Merrill, 1967), 390, and Dorothy Ross, *The Origins of American Social Science* (Cambridge: Cambridge University Press, 1992), 88–97.

117. Riis, *How the Other Half Lives*, 157; Florence Kelley, "The Street Trader Under Illinois Law," *The Child in the City* (Chicago: Department of Social Investigation, Chicago School of Civics and Philanthropy, 1912), 297–298.

118. John Loughery, *John Sloan: Painter and Rebel* (New York: Henry Holt, 1995), 179.

119. James Otis, *Wanted* (New York: Harper & Bros., 1912); Alma Woodward, *A Midas of the Street* (New York: Frank A. Munsey, 1912); J. C. Leyendecker, "Newsboy and Santa," *Saturday Evening Post* Dec. 7, 1912, cover.

120. "City Honors a Newsboy," *New York Times*, Oct. 21, 1912, 5; Captain W. Purdue, "Billy Rugh, a Newsboy Hero," *The War Cry*, Dec. 7, 1912, 10; Washington Gladden, *The Interpreter* (Boston: Pilgrim Press, 1918), 145–147; Mark Skertic, *A Native's Guide to Northwest Indiana* (Chicago: Lake Claremont Press, 2003), 86–87; Earl Franklin, *His Sacrifice, Being a Story in Song of Billy Rugh, Newsboy* (Chicago: National Music, 1914).

121. See, for example, Oliver Collins and John May, *Newsboy's Helper* (Chicago: National Music, 1901); Maude Anita Hart, *The Newsboy's Sweetheart* (Chicago: McKinley Music, 1905; and Mary Ruth Meyer and Paul Shannon, *Everybody's Loved by Someone* (Brunswick, GA: Glover Bros., 1916).

122. "Newsgirl Now Stage Star," *Oregonian*, Sept. 14, 1910, 4; "From Newsgirl to Singing Comedian," *Cleveland Plain Dealer*, Nov. 6, 1910, 40; Barbara W. Grossman, *Funny Woman: The Life and Times of Fanny Brice* (Bloomington: Indiana University Press, 1991), 3, 10; Norman Kartov, *The Fabulous Fanny* (New York: Knopf, 1953); Fanny Brice as told to Palma Wayne, "Fanny of the Follies," pt. 1, *Cosmopolitan*, Feb. 1936, 4, 20.

123. *Pensacola Journal*, Sept. 28, 1911, 8. See Kay Sloan, *The Loud Silents: Origins of the Social Problem Film* (Urbana: University of Illinois Press, 1988), 74.

124. Jacob Riis, "The New York Newsboy," *Century Magazine* 85, no. 2 (Dec. 1912): 248.

125. "The Street Gamin Has Vanished from New York," *New York Times*, Nov. 17, 1912, SM9; Clopper, *Child Labor in City Streets*, 36, 83–92; "The Greek Boy Who Shines Shoes," *Survey* 26 (July 22, 1911): 591; Leola Benedict Terhune, "The Greek Bootblack," *Survey* 36 (Sept. 26, 1911): 852–854.

Chapter 12

1. Henry Norman, "In the Balkans—The Chessboard of Europe," *Scribner's Monthly* 19, no. 6 (June 1896): 663; Harry Golden, *The Right Time: An Autobiography* (New York: G. P. Putnam, 1969), 54.

2. New York City Department of Education, *Sixteenth Annual Report of the City Superintendent of Schools for the Year Ending July 31, 1914*, table 15, 367; Golden, *Right Time*, 54.

3. Neil MacNeil, "American Newspapers Through Two World Wars," *American Journal of Economics and Society* 6, no. 2 (Jan. 1947): 245–260; Edward N. Clopper, "The Federal Child Labor Law," *Elementary School Journal* 17, no. 5 (Jan. 1917): 326–327; Florence I. Taylor, *Child Labor in Your State: A Study Outline*, NCLC Pamphlet No. 267, 1916, 3; Hugh Hindman, *Child Labor: An American History* (Armonk, NY: Sharpe, 2002), 70.

4. "Sam April Got the Place of President's Newsboy," *Christian Science Monitor*, Mar. 22, 1913, 23; "Sammy April Is 'Official Presidential Newsboy,'" *Vernal Express*, Mar. 5, 1915, 7; Lewis Hine, *Israel April, 314 I St., S.W., Washington, DC*, Acc. No. 2930. Special Collections, Albion O. Kuhn Museum and Gallery, University of Maryland, Baltimore County; "Newsboy a Suffragist," *Washington Post*, July 24, 1914, 4; "Wilson's Advice to Boys," *New York Times*, Apr. 9, 1915, 6; "Wilson Is Newsboy," *Salt Lake Telegram*, Apr. 16, 1915, 3; "Wilson over Phone Talks to Newsboys," *New York Times*, Jan. 18, 1916, 6.

5. Jean Edward Smith, *FDR* (New York: Random House, 2007), 134; Woodrow Wilson, "Address to Congress Requesting a Declaration of War," Apr. 2, 1917; "Extras, Legitimate and Deliberate," *Washington Post*, Apr. 4, 1917, 1.

6. R. F. Woodbury, Fred R. Davis, and Julia E. Chadwick, "Street Traders of Buffalo, New York, 1925: A Study Made by the Juvenile Protective Department, Children's Aid and Society for the Prevention of Cruelty to Children of Erie County, New York," *Foundation Forum* 52 (Aug. 1926): 13–14; Loraine B. Bush, *Child Welfare in Kentucky* (New York: NCLC, 1919), 183, 186; *Annual Report of the Maryland State Board of Labor and Statistics* (1916), 125; (1917), 48, 51, 59; (1918), 51; (1919), 76; Helen Sumner Woodbury, "Working Children of Boston," *Monthly Labor Review*, Jan. 1921: 45–59; "No Newsboys Required," *Wall Street Journal*, Jan. 22, 1917, 2; New York City, Board of Education, *Twenty-Seventh Annual Report of the City Superintendent of Schools for the Year Ending July 31, 1925* (New York, 1925), 519, in Moses Stambler, "The Effect of Compulsory Education and Child Labor Laws on High School Attendance in New York City, 1898–1917," *History of Education Quarterly* 8, no. 2 (Summer 1968): 200; Mabel Brown Ellis, "Child Labor and Juvenile Delinquency in Manhattan," *Child Labor Bulletin* 6, no. 3 (Nov. 1917): 5; "Wanted, Waiting List of Local Newsboys," *Wyoming Tribune*, Sept. 17, 1918, 5; Edward N. Clopper, "Street Trades Regulations," *Child Labor Bulletin* 5, no. 2 (Aug. 1916): 98.

7. William R. Scott, *Scientific Circulation Management for Newspapers* (New York: Ronald Press, 1915), 90–96.

8. Anna L. Burdick, *Vocational Guidance Bulletin* 2 (1916), in Sara A. Brown, "Juvenile Street Work in Iowa," *American Child* 4, no. 2 (Aug. 1922): 140–141; "Section 11—Street Trades," 8, box 3, folder 8; "IV. View of Situation—2/13/17—E. H. Sullivan," box 31, folder 32, NYCLC Collection, New York State Library, Albany.

9. Bush, "Child Welfare in Kentucky," 183, 186; Lewis Hine, "Child Labor," in *Child Welfare in Oklahoma: An Inquiry by the National Child Labor Committee for the University of Oklahoma*, ed. Edward N. Clopper (New York Child Labor Committee, 1918), 107.

10. Loraine B. Bush, "Street Trades in Alabama," *American Child* 4, no. 2 (Aug. 1922): 107; Helen Dwight Fisher, "Recent Child Welfare Report," *American Child* 2, no. 4 (Feb. 1921): 305; Edward N. Clopper, *Child Welfare in Alabama* (New York: NCLC, 1918), 141; Ellis, "Child Labor and Juvenile Delinquency in Manhattan," 4.

11. George A. Hall, "The Newsboy Law," *New York Times*, Jan. 21, 1914, 8; Helen L. Sumner and Ella A. Merritt, *Child Labor Legislation in the United States*, Children's Bureau, Pub. No. 10 (Washington, DC: Government Printing Office, 1915), 382–417. See also Peter C. Baldwin, "'Nocturnal Habits and Dark Wisdom': The American Response to Children in the Streets at Night, 1880–1930," *Journal of Social History* 35, no. 2 (2002): 593–611; "Curfew Bans Newsboys," *Christian Science Monitor*, June 20, 1914, 20; and "Report Big Success in Daylight Saving," *New York Times*, Apr. 2, 1918, 13.

12. "The Newsboys Stood the Test," *New York Herald*, Nov. 14, 1920, 2; Eva M. Marquis, "A Survey of Working Children in Kansas City," Kansas City, Mo., Board of Public Welfare, *Annual Report* (1914–15), 123; Maurice B. Hexter, "The Newsboys of Cincinnati," *Studies from the Helen S. Trounstine Foundation* 1, no. 4 (Jan. 15, 1919): 131–132; Nettie P. McGill, *Children in Street Work*, Children's Bureau, Pub. No. 183 (Washington, DC: Government Printing Office, 1928), 25; Herbert Maynard Diamond, "Street Trading Among Connecticut Grammar School Children," *Report of the Commission on Child Welfare to the Governor* (Hartford, CT, 1921), 10–12, 45; "Newsboy Few Years Ago, Now Lieutenant," *Hartford Courant*, Sept. 5, 1918, 16; Christopher M. Sterba, *Good Americans: Italian and Jewish Immigrants During the First World War* (New York: Oxford University Press, 2003).

13. New York City Department of Education, *Sixteenth Annual Report of the City Superintendent of Schools for the Year Ending July 31, 1914*, 177–179; Vincent Tompkins, *American Decades, 1910–1919* (Detroit: Gale Cengage, 1996), 5:129; "New York City Newsboys Learning 'The Star-Spangled Banner,'" *Outlook*, Oct. 2, 1918: 176.

14. Hexter, "Newsboys of Cincinnati," 122, 132; *Twenty-sixth Annual Report of the Maryland State Board of Labor and Statistics* (1917), 48; "An Alarming Migration of Negro Labor," *New York Tribune*, Oct. 22, 1916, 5.

15. "Third Newsgirl Added to Staff of Herald," *Lexington Herald*, July 10, 1918, 1; "Richmond Girls Discover Cure-All; Recipe Is Simple: Be a Newsgirl," *Lexington Herald*, Jan. 12, 1919,

1; *Twenty-seventh Annual Report of Maryland State Board of Labor and Statistics* (1918), 75; Lewis Hine, "Child Labor," in *Child Welfare in Oklahoma*, 109; Hine, "Conditions in Vermont Street Trades," NCLC (Dec. 1916), in David Nasaw, *Children of the City: At Work and at Play* (New York: Oxford University Press, 1985), 103; "Of Interest to Circulators," *Editor & Publisher* 51, no. 7 (July 27, 1918): 37; Bush, "Child Welfare in Kentucky," 185; "Newsboy Problem Not Serious," *Editor & Publisher* 51, no. 24 (July 23, 1918): 24.

16. George B. Mangold, *Problems of Child Welfare* (New York: Macmillan, 1914), 294–295; *Twenty-sixth Annual Report of Maryland State Board of Labor and Statistics* (1917), 53; "Selling Papers on the Street," *Omaha World Herald*, June 23, 1929, 7.

17. Nick Zades, *"Those Days": Newspaper Newsboy Stories* (Chicopee, MA: Pond-Ekberg, 1992), 27–29. Zades became press foreman and superintendent of newspapers in Springfield.

18. Robert Whaples, "Child Labor in the United States," *EH.Net Encyclopedia*, edited by Robert Whaples, Oct. 7, 2005, http://www.eh.net/encyclopedia/article/whaples.childlabor; "Bob Meyner: From Newsboy to Governor," *Democratic Digest*, Oct. 1957, 11.

19. "Pennies Sell at a Premium," *Kansas City Star*, Nov. 5, 1917, 8; "Automatic Newsboy," *Wall Street Journal*, Feb. 16, 1917, 2.

20. *Editor & Publisher* 51, no. 1 (June 15, 1918): vi; Donald J. Wood, *Newspaper Circulation Management—A Profession* (Oakland, CA: Newspaper Research Bureau, 1952), 88; "Newsboys Protest Against Automatic Paper-Selling Box," *Hartford Courant*, June 26, 1917, 10; "An Understudy to the Newsboy," *Fourth Estate* 20, no. 1377 (July 17, 1920): 9.

21. "Pittsburgh Newsboys Are Out on Strike," *Atlanta Constitution*, Dec. 3, 1916, 9; "Newsboys Strike Off," *Baltimore Sun*, Dec. 8, 1916, 1; *The Pittsburgh Chapter, American Red Cross* (Pittsburgh: American Red Cross, 1922), 267; "Newsboys Will Parade at Sausalito Tonight," *San Francisco Chronicle*, Apr. 26, 1918, 9; "Society Girls as 'Newsies,'" *New York Times*, May 28, 1918, 8; *Hancock County Kaleidoscope, 1917–1919* (Hancock County Historical Society, 1976), 8; Karl F. Ahrendt, "Memoirs," 1987, www.karlahrendt.com/IN_THE_BEGINNING.htm; Norman J. Radder, *Newspapers in Community Service* (New York: McGraw-Hill, 1926), 192; "40 Boys in Drum and Bugle Corps Boosting Bonds," *Bay City Times*, Apr. 21, 1919, 2; Mouw Family Papers, Grand Rapids History and Special Collections, Grand Rapids Public Library.

22. Isa C. Cabell, "Drinking the Iron Tonic," *Hartford Courant*, Apr. 21, 1918, 8; "Offenders Fined," *Christian Science Monitor*, Mar. 4, 1918, 6; "War Relief Work," *Hartford Courant*, Nov. 1, 1918, 15.

23. "Noodles Fagan's in Town," *Salt Lake Telegram*, July 31, 1918, 5.

24. "F. A. Russell Heads 'Scotty' Committee," *Boston Globe*, May 12, 1920, 11; "Newsboys Organize for Mutual Uplift," *Hartford Courant*, Sept. 13, 1925, A8.

25. Alice Boardman Smuts, *Science in the Service of Children, 1893–1935* (New Haven, CT: Yale University Press, 2006), 95; "Seeks to Provide Living Wage by Law," *Grand Rapids Press*, Mar. 18, 1918, 2.

26. Edwin Markham, Benjamin B. Lindsay, and George Creel, *Children in Bondage* (New York: Hearst's International Library, 1914), 225–226; "Attack on Creel Cheered in House," *New York Times*, July 11, 1917, 3; James Melvin Lee, *History of American Journalism* (Garden City, NY: Garden City Publishing, 1923), 425; James R. Mock and Cedric Larson, *Words That Won the War: The Story of the Committee on Public Information, 1917–1919* (Princeton, NJ: Princeton University Press, 1939); Minna Lewinson and Henry B. Hough, *A History of the Services Rendered to the Public by the American Press During the Year 1917* (New York: Columbia University Press, 1918), 6.

27. George Creel, "Military Training for Our Youth," *Century Magazine* 92 (May 1916): 20–22; "Wall Street Absorbed in Numbers," *New York Times*, July 21, 1917, 12; "Times List at Premium," *New York Times*, July 31, 1917, 9.

28. James R. Mock, *Censorship 1917* (Princeton, NJ: Princeton University Press, 1941), 140, 146; Lillian Wald, *Windows on Henry Street* (Boston: Little, Brown, 1934), 7.

29. Daile Kaplan, *Lewis Hine in Europe: The Lost Photographs* (New York: Abbeville Press, 1988), 44, 79, 89, 133; Judith Mara Gutman, *Lewis D. Hine and the American Social Conscience* (New York: Walker, 1967), 26–27.

30. "Unfair to the Boys," *Los Angeles Times*, Mar. 20, 1917, II4; Oscar Lawler, "Decry Plan to Abridge the Newsboy's Rights," *Los Angeles Times*, Mar. 20, 1917, 17; "Newsboys Launch

Fight for Their Livelihood," *Los Angeles Times*, Mar. 21, 1917, II1; "Newsboys to Send Lobby," Mar. 22, 1917, 17; T. L. O'Brien, "A Word for the Newsboy," *Los Angeles Times*, Mar. 31, 1917, II3; Lyle Eveland, "Justice for the Newsie," *Los Angeles Times*, Apr. 2, 1917, 18; "Happenings on the Pacific Slope," *Los Angeles Times*, Apr. 5, 1917, 14.

31. Owen R. Lovejoy, "Safeguarding Childhood in Peace and War," Thirteenth Annual Conference on Child Labor, Baltimore, 1917, 5–6; Anna Rochester, *Juvenile Delinquency in Certain Countries at War*, Children's Bureau, Pub. No. 39 (Washington, DC: Government Printing Office, 1918).

32. Joel D. Hunter, "Juvenile Delinquency," *Journal of American Institute of Criminal Law and Criminology* 8 (May 1917–Mar. 1918), 287–289. Between 1914 and 1919 in Hartford, Connecticut, the number of Boy Scouts rose from 230 to 1,300, Scout troops from 18 to 64, and troop leaders from 30 to 130. See *Annual Report of the Juvenile Commission to the Mayor and Court of Common Council of the City of Hartford, Conn.* (1916), 27–29; (1919), 29.

33. Betty B. Rosenbaum, "The Relationship Between War and Crime in the United States," *Journal of Criminal Law and Criminology* 30, no. 5 (Jan.–Feb. 1940): 735–736.

34. US Department of Labor, "Juvenile Delinquency and Its Relation to Employment," *Report on Conditions of Woman and Child Wage Earners in the United States* (Washington, DC, 1911), 8:89–93, cited by Edward N. Clopper in "Why Overlook Street Worker?," *Child Labor Bulletin* 3, no. 1 (May 1914): 57–58 and "Street Work and Juvenile Delinquency," NCLC Pamphlet No. 221 (1914), 5.

35. Helen C. Dwight, "Menace of Street Trading by Children," *American City* 2 (Jan. 1915): 24; "Child Delinquency and the War," *Survey* 40 (May 4, 1918): 131–132; Leon Charles Faulkenor, "Effect of the War on Juvenile Delinquency," *American Prison Association Proceedings*, 1919, 156; Rosenbaum, 737; Ellis, "Child Labor and Delinquency in Manhattan," 16–20, 36; Hexter, "Newsboys in Cincinnati," 1919, 138, 144–147; "Motz Answers for the Times-Star," *Cincinnati Labor Advocate*, June 30, 1917, 4.

36. Owen Martin, "What a Member of the Newsboy Law Enforcing Squad Thinks About Newspaper Selling for Young Boys," ca. 1917, box 33, folder 20, NYCLC Collection, New York State Library, Albany.

37. Ibid.

38. George H. Nash, *The Life of Herbert Hoover: Masters of Emergencies, 1917–1918* (New York: Norton, 1996), 3:158.

39. "Labor Attention," *Chicago Tribune*, Sept. 1, 1918, 7; "Hundreds Buncoed by Paid Newsboys from Denver with Fake News Extras," *Wyoming State Tribune*, Sept. 3, 1917, 1, 2; "Legions March in Biggest City Labor Parade," *Chicago Tribune*, Sept. 3, 1918, 3; "Nothing Extra," *Los Angeles Times*, Feb. 19, 1914, II7; "Puts Check on Newsboys," *Kansas City Star*, Feb. 6, 1917, 1; "Selling Fake 'Extras' Larceny in New York," *Chicago Tribune*, May 29, 1918, 15; Theodore H. Price, "The Commercial By-Product of the War," *Outlook*, Aug. 29, 1914, 1068; "The Newsboy of To-Day," *New York Sun*, Jan. 11, 1909, 5; Byron Farwell, *Over There: The United States in the Great War, 1917–1918* (New York: W. W. Norton, 1999), 23; "Police Move to Stop Noise of Newsboys," *New York Times*, Oct. 4, 1917, 23; "Newsboy Sent to Jail for Crying 'Fake' Extra," *Chicago Tribune*, Mar. 20, 1918, 6; "Of Interest to Circulators," *Editor & Publisher* 51, no. 6 (July 20, 1918): 37.

40. Elsa Wertheim, "Children in Industry and the Street Trades," *Journal of American Institute of Criminal Law and Criminology* 8 (July 1917), 284; "Newsboy Charges Von Mohr with Assault," *Salt Lake Telegram*, Aug. 19, 1918, 8; Wilma I. Ball, "Street Trading in Ohio," *American Child* 1, no. 1 (May 1919): 127–129; B. J. Griswold, "Rotary Club Adopts Newsboys of City," *Rotarian* 9, no. 6 (1916): 544; "To Re-establish Newsboys Club," *Editor & Publisher* 51, no 23 (Nov. 16, 1918): 24.

41. Kriste Lindenmeyer, *"A Right to Childhood": The US Children's Bureau and Child Welfare, 1912–46* (Urbana: University of Illinois Press, 1997), 71–73; Julia C. Lathrop, "The Children's Bureau in Wartime," *North American Review* 206, no. 744 (Nov. 1917): 734–746; "A Back-to-School Drive," *Outlook* 121, no. 12 (Mar. 19, 1919): 458; K. Walter Hickel, "War, Region, and Social Welfare: Federal Aid to Servicemen's Dependents in the South, 1917–1921," *Journal of American History* 87, no. 4 (Mar. 2001): 1362–1391.

42. "Urges a Newsboys' Union," *Washington Post*, Jan. 25, 1914, 12; Dwight, "Menace of Street Trading by Children," *American City* 12 (Jan. 1915): 24; Herschel H. Jones, "Unregulated Street Trading in a Typical City," NCLC Pamphlet No. 264 (July 1916), 5.

43. "Newsies Have a Union," *Labor Advocate* (Cincinnati), Nov. 11, 1916, 1; Mary Holliday Mitchell, "Child Labor," *Child Welfare in Tennessee* (Nashville, 1920), 378, 380–381, 391–393.

44. Anna Y. Reed, *Newsboy Service: A Study in Educational and Vocational Guidance* (Yonkers-on-Hudson, NY: World Book, 1917), xiv, 141; Bertha S. Adams, "Seattle's Newsboy Capitalist," *American Magazine*, Dec. 1917, 55–56.

45. Reed, *Newsboy Service*, xiv, 141; Helen Dwight, "Seattle's Scholarly Newsies," *Survey* 39 (Nov. 10, 1917), 145.

46. "Newsies Discontinue Paper," *Editor & Publisher* 51, no. 19 (Oct. 19, 1918): 8; *Twenty-sixth Annual Report of the Maryland State Board of Labor and Statistics* (1917), 59; "This Little Lady's Big Smile Lures Newsboys to High Ideals," *Baltimore Sun*, Mar. 11, 1917, M4; W. G. Shoup, "Carrier Boys and How to Treat Them," International Circulation Managers' Association, *Official Bulletin* 15, no. 3 (Nov. 1919): 3.

47. "The First Five Boys," Boys Town Hall of History exhibit, 1990. See also Hugh Reilly and Keven Warneke, *Father Flanagan's Life and Legacy* (Boys Town, NE: Boys Town Press, 2008), 49–50, and Kenneth B. Kidd, *Making American Boys: Boyology and the Feral Tale* (Minneapolis: University of Minnesota Press, 2004), 111–134.

48. Burt Thomas, "The Boy He Used to Be," *Detroit News*, Dec. 10, 1914, n.p.; Ernest P. LaJoie, *The Story of the Goodfellows* (Chicago: Reilly & Lee, 1938), 23–29; "Rich Men 'Newsies,'" *Washington Post*, Dec., 23, 1914, 4; "'Uxtra!' Mayor Calls out Old Newsboys to Corners," *Chicago Tribune*, Dec. 23, 1914, 1; "Old Newsboys' Day Planned in Chicago," *Atlanta Constitution*, Dec. 24, 1914, 9; Pete Waldmeir, "The Origins of the Goodfellows: 'No Kiddie Without a Christmas,'" *Detroit News*, n.d. Columbus, Ohio, spawned a similar group, the "Charity Newsies." See Nettie P. McGill, *Child Workers on City Streets*, Children's Bureau, Pub. No. 188 (Washington, DC: Government Printing Office, 1928): 124–125.

49. "Liberty Loan Newsboys Give Watch to Glason," *Boston Globe*, Apr. 13, 1920, 3; "Loop Newsboys on Valor Roll," *Chicago Tribune*, July 21, 1918, 4; "Has a Little Debt to Pay to the Huns," *Hartford Courant*, July 12, 1918, 8; "City Hall Newsboy Is a Soldier Now," *Hartford Courant*, June 23, 1918, 3; "Courant Newsboy Hears of Brother," *Hartford Courant*, Dec. 8, 1918, X5; "Arcadian Adventures," *Hartford Courant*, Sept. 8, 1918, 5; "Jeers Greet Few Violators of Gasless Day," *New York Tribune*, Sept. 2, 1918, 1, 5; "Spy Doubles Up from Punch of Angry Newsboy," *New York Evening Telegram*, July 2, 1918, 1.

50. Mae Biddison Benson, "Scrapping Newsies Grown to Soldiers Still 'Our Boys,'" *Fort Worth Star-Telegram*, Sept. 15, 1918, 27; "Father Dunne, Founder of Newsboys' Home, Dies," *St. Louis Globe-Democrat*, Mar. 17, 1939, 1, 7; "An Average Day at the Newsboys' Home," *Brace Memorial News*, Feb. 22, 1919, n.p., in *Newsboy* 24, nos. 9–10 (Mar.–Apr. 1986), 4–5; *Hartford Courant*, Nov. 27, 1917, 12; *New York Times*, Sept. 19, 1918, 4, and Oct. 14, 1918, 6; "2,520 'Newsies' in Service," *New York Times*, Nov. 13, 1917, 12; "Patriotic Newsboys Join the Colors," *Outlook*, Nov. 28, 1917: 503.

51. *Ladies' Home Journal*, June 1919, 22, and Jan. 1919, 82; "D.S.C. for Dead Newsboy," *New York Times*, Apr. 17, 1920, 10; "Al and W. J. Cough Up," *Oregonian*, May 16, 1924, 1; "Harding to Honor Newsboy's Memory," *New York Herald*, May 15, 1921, 3; "Scotty, a Newsboy of Brookline," *New York Herald*, May 18, 1921, 8; "Newsboy Who Died in War Honored by State and City," *New York Herald*, Oct. 29, 1921, 3; "Newsboys Honor Friend," *New York Times*, Jan. 7, 1933, 3; "Pays Tribute to Bacon," *New York Times*, Nov. 16, 1921, 12; "Benjamin Rutstein Square Dedicated," *Boston Globe*, Mar. 13, 1922, 18.

52. Edward V. Rickenbacker, *Rickenbacker* (New York: Fawcett, 1967), 15; W. David Lewis, *Eddie Rickenbacker: An American Hero in the Twentieth Century* (Baltimore: Johns Hopkins University Press, 2005), 9, 99, 641; Guillaume de Syon, "The Child in the Flying Machine: Childhood and Aviation in the First World War," in *Children and War: A Historical Anthology*, ed. James Marten (New York: New York University Press, 2002), 118, 122; Jonathan Lighter, "The Slang of the American Expeditionary Forces in Europe, 1917–1919: An Historical Glossary," *American Speech* 47, nos. 1–2 (Spring–Summer 1972): 81, 87, 89.

53. *Ginger, The Bride of Chateau Thierry* (1919), in Patricia King Hansen, ed., *The American Film Institute Catalog: Feature Films, 1911–1920* (Berkeley: University of California Press, 1988), F1:322; "Music Reviews," *Lyceum Magazine*, June 1919, 13; "Pershing, the Man, Gets Great Ovation from His Wounded at Walter Reed," *Washington Times*, Sept. 19, 1919, 4.

54. Leander, "On Reading at the Front," *Living Age* 295, no. 3824 (Oct. 20, 1917): 191; *The W.G.N.: A Handbook of Newspaper Administration* (Chicago: Tribune Co., 1922), 84; "Stars and Stripes Is Hauled Down with This Issue," *Stars and Stripes* 2, no. 19 (June 13, 1919): 5; "Newsboy Back with a Croix de Guerre," *Los Angeles Times*, Aug. 25, 1919, 112. See also Alfred Emile Cornebise, *The Stars and Stripes: Doughboy Journalism in World War I* (Westport, CT: Praeger, 1984) , and *Ranks and Columns: Armed Forces Newspapers in American Wars* (Westport, CT: Greenwood Press, 1993).

55. "Newsboys of Ships Become Gobs' Friends," *San Francisco Chronicle*, Sept. 1, 1919, SM12.

56. "Boxer Abe the Newsboy Here," *New York Times*, Sept. 13, 1913, 10; "Navy Can't Read Without Abe," *Los Angeles Times*, Feb. 1, 1928, A8; Abe Hollandersky, *The Life Story of Abe the Newsboy, Hero of a Thousand Fights* (Los Angeles: Abe the Newsboy, 1930), 2, 23, 26; *Fourth Estate*, Oct. 30, 1920, 23.

57. David M. Kennedy, *Over Here: The First World War and American Society* (New York: Oxford University Press, 1980), 189, 198; Byron Farwell, *Over There: The United States in the Great War, 1917-1918* (New York: Norton, 1999), 233; John Keegan, *The First World War* (New York: Knopf, 1999), 408; N. P. Johnson and J. Mueller, "Updating the Accounts: Global Mortality of the 1918–1920 'Spanish' Influenza Pandemic," *Bulletin of the History of Medicine* 76 (2002): 105–115; "Newesboy Flu Victim," *Topeka State Journal*, Nov. 2, 1918, 6; "Influenza Kills Aged Aristocrat of Newsboy Clan," *Chicago Tribune*, Oct. 18, 1918, 13; "Influenza Suspends Newspaper," *Washington Post*, Oct. 20, 1918, 4; Richard Collier, *The Plague of the Spanish Lady: The Influenza Pandemic of 1918-1919* (New York: Atheneum, 1974); John M. Barry, *The Great Influenza: The Story of the Deadliest Pandemic in History* (New York: Penguin Books, 2004), 348; "Notice to Chieftan Readers," *Pueblo Chieftain*, Nov. 5, 1918, 1; "'Crip' Only Help of Mother, Ailing," *San Francisco Chronicle*, June 3, 1905, 16; George Barke, "Precautions Against the Flu," *Chicago Tribune*, Dec. 20, 1918, 8; "Newsboys Have Organization All Their Own," International Circulation Managers' Association, *Official Bulletin* 15, no. 4 (Jan. 1920): 1.

58. "Newsboys Sought in Scout Campaign," *Cleveland Plain Dealer*, Dec. 20, 1917, in J. D. Robinson Scrapbook, 1905–1924, 1, Toledo Public Library; "The World and Scouting, 1910–1919," Boy Scout Stuff: A Virtual Boy Scout Museum, accessed May 22, 2014, www.virtualscoutmuseum.com/timeline.html.

59. William D. Boyce, "Memorandum Concerning How Scouting Came to America as Told by W. D. Boyce," July 14, 1926, Boy Scouts of America Headquarters, Archives, File 8-01, cited in Carolyn Ditte Wagner, "The Boy Scouts of America: A Model and a Mirror of American Society," PhD diss., Johns Hopkins University, 1979, 9–10; John I. Dean, "Scouting in America, 1910–1990," EdD diss., University of South Carolina, 1992, 22, 33–34, 66–67; Janice A. Petterchak, *Lone Scout: W. D. Boyce and American Boy Scouting* (Rochester, IL: Legacy Press, 2003), 13, 26, 93–117, 133–136.

60. Milton A. McRae, *Forty Years in Newspaperdom* (New York: Brentano's, 1924), 372–374; Wagner, "The Boy Scouts of America," 63–66, 104, 112; David I. Macleod, *Building Character in the American Boy: The Boy Scouts, YMCA, and Their Forerunners, 1870–1920* (Madison: University of Wisconsin Press, 1983), 146–147, 157; Robert Bremner, "Giving for Children and Youth," in Richard Magat, ed., *Philanthropic Giving: Studies in Varieties and Goals* (New York: Oxford University Press, 1989), 323.

61. Harry Golden, "Greetings to a Living Legend," *Life Magazine* 63, no. 3 (July 21, 1967),14; "Alleged Anarchistic Paper Sales Stopped," *San Diego Union*, Feb. 9, 1916, 9.

62. "Socialists Rebel at Emma Goldman," *New York Times*, Apr. 3, 1916, 22; "Reds and Socialists Clash," *New York Tribune*, Apr. 3, 1916, 5.

63. David Nasaw, *The Chief: The Life of William Randolph Hearst* (Boston: Houghton Mifflin, 2000), 241, 246–248.

64. *New York Tribune*, June 2, 1918, 2; "Of Interest to Circulators," *Editor & Publisher* 51, no. 7 (July 27, 1918): 36; "Newspaper Specials," *Wall Street Journal*, Sept. 27, 1918, 7, Nov. 1, 1918, 6.

65. Golden, *Right Time*, 54; Lucy Maynard Salmon, *The Newspaper and the Historian* (New York: Oxford University Press, 1923), 136; "Dealers Refuse Hearst Papers," *Los Angeles Times*, Aug. 21, 1918, 110; "Few Hearst Papers Sold," *New York Times*, Aug. 17, 1918, 14; "Arrest Hearst Newsboys," *New York Times*, Aug. 18, 1918, 7.

66. Edwin Emery and Michael Emery, *The Press and America: An Interpretive History of the Mass Media*, rev. ed. (Englewood Cliffs, NJ: Prentice Hall, 1992), 515–516; Ralph Chaplin, *Wobbly: The Rough and Tumble Story of an American Radical* (Chicago: University of Chicago Press, 1948), 219–238, 305–306; Minna Lewinson and Henry Beelte Hough, *A History of the Services Rendered to the Public by the American Press During the Year 1917* (New York: Columbia University Press, 1918), 4; "*New Yorker Staats-Zeitung v. Nolan* (1918)," in Leon Hurwitz, *Historical Dictionary of Censorship in the United States* (Westport, CT: Greenwood Press, 1985), 288–289; Carl Wittke, *The German-Language Press in America* (Lexington: University Press of Kentucky, 1957). See also Mott, *American Journalism*, 632–633; Charles V. Kinter, "The Newspaper in Two Postwar Periods," *Journal of Marketing* 13, no. 3 (Jan. 1949): 371–372; and Marshall Beuick, "The Declining Immigrant Press," *Social Forces* 6, no. 2 (Dec. 1927): 259.

67. Steven J. Diner, *A Very Different Age: Americans of the Progressive Era* (New York: Hill and Wang, 1998), 239; *Pueblo Chieftain*, June 28, 1917, 2; *Tucson Daily Citizen*, July 10, 1917, 8; "Newsdealers Go on Strike," *New York Tribune*, Jan. 27, 1918, 1; "Gotham Newsboys Called on Strike," *Los Angeles Times*, Jan. 28, 1918, 18; "Newsboy Strike Spreads to the Bronx," *New York Tribune*, Jan. 29, 1918, 11; "Rise in Price Causes Protest," *Christian Science Monitor*, Jan. 31, 1918, 7; "The High Cost of Editing," *Outlook*, Feb. 6, 1918: 206; "A.D.T. Boys Strike but Don't Tell Why," *New York Times*, Feb. 2, 1918, 15; "Messengers' Strike Gains More Recruits," *New York Times*, Feb. 3, 1918, 3.

68. "Some Newsdealers Resume Deliveries," *New York Times*, Feb. 1, 1918, 18; Louise M. Boyer to Ernest Boyer, Feb. 8, 1918. box 5, folder 51, Helen King Boyer Collection, Georgetown University Library, Special Collections.

69. *New York Sun*, Feb. 2, 1918, 14, Feb. 6, 1918, 14, Feb. 8, 1918, 14, Aug. 22, 1918, 12, Aug. 23, 1918, 12; "Newsdealers Face Loss of Licenses," *New York Times*, Feb. 2, 1918, 9; *New York Times*, Feb. 1, 1918, 8, 18, Feb. 3, 1918, 1, 4, 7; "New York Newsboys Strike," *Hartford Courant*, Jan, 27, 1918, 10; "Among New York Papers," *Hartford Courant*, Jan. 29, 1918, 12; "Newsboys' Strike Ends," *Hartford Courant*, Feb. 5, 1918, 2; "Dealer and Crowd Rout Hearst Agent," *New York Tribune*, Sept. 21, 1918, 14; "Newsboys Ask for Defence Fund," *New York Tribune*, Oct. 4, 1918, 16.

70. "Police Passive While Mob Riots and Manhandles Women and Men," *Minneapolis Journal*, July 3, 1918, 1–2.

71. Ibid.

72. "Thugs Drop Loop Rioting for Day," *Minneapolis Journal*, July 7, 1918, 1–2; "Four Agitators in Paper Riots Given 20 Day Sentences," *Minneapolis Journal*, July 8, 1918, 2; Bob Cramer, "The Road to Yesterday and Back Again," *Minneapolis Labor Review*, Aug. 6, 1964, 2.

73. "Police Failure to Halt Rioting Seen by State's Men," *Minneapolis Journal*, July 8, 1918, 7; "George 'Joe' Gites," *Minneapolis Labor Review*, Sept. 5, 1957, 4.

74. "Minister Charges Socialists with Blame for Riots," *Minneapolis Journal*, July 8, 1918, 10; Joseph Hart, "When Elections Mattered," *City Pages* 18, no. 881 (Oct. 22, 1997): 1.

75. "Police Stop Paper Sale," *Minneapolis Journal*, July 6, 1918, 2.

76. "Newspaper Price Scale Established," *Minneapolis Journal*, July 8, 1918, 1.

77. Simpson, "Seattle Newsboys," 23; Natalia Salinas-Aguila, "Seattle Union Record" (2001), Labor Press Project, Harry Bridges Center for Labor Studies, University of Washington, http://depts.washington.edu/labhist/laborpress/Union_Record_1900.shtml; "Of Interest to Circulators," *Editor & Publisher* 51, no. 8 (Aug. 3, 1918): 36.

78. Mildred Zolun, "Chicagoland Final Edition," *Chicago Tribune*, Dec. 26, 1999, 22; "City Goes Wild with Joy," *New York Times*, Nov. 8, 1918, 1; "United Press Men Sent False Cable," *New York Times*, Nov. 8, 1918, 1; "Crowds Parade in Boston," *New York Times*, Nov. 8, 1918,

3; "Nation Rejoices at War's End," *New York Times*, Nov. 12, 1918, 1; "Again We Celebrate," *New York Times*, Nov. 13, 1918, 12; "75-Year-Old 'Newsboy' Starts His 56th Year in Same Selling Spot," *Baton Route Times Advocate*, Nov. 19, 1955, 1.

79. Dean Collins, "Post Bellum," *Hustler*, Feb. 1918, 4, in Nasaw, *Children of the City*, 79–80.

Chapter 13

1. "Pen Points," *Los Angeles Times*, Mar. 3, 1929, B4; "'Jazz Age' Is Blamed for Crime," *Los Angeles Times*, Aug. 10, 1921, II1; Silas Bent, *Ballyhoo: The Voice of the Press* (New York: Boni and Liverwright, 1927); Herbert Asbury, "Year of the Big Shriek," in *Mirrors of the Year 1927–1928* (New York: Stokes, 1928), 191; Gerald Leinwand, *1927: High Tide of the 1920s* (New York: Four Walls Eight Windows, 2001), 1, 259.

2. Robert H. Ferrell, *The Presidency of Calvin Coolidge* (Lawrence: University Press of Kansas, 1998), 61; "Hammond Sponsors Newsboys' Savings," *Washington Post*, Sept. 25, 1926, 24.

3. For valuable syntheses of the era, see Frederick Lewis Allen, *Only Yesterday: An Informal History of the 1920s* (New York: Harper & Row, 1931); Lynn Dumenil, *The Modern Temper: American Culture and Society in the 1920s* (New York: Hill and Wang, 1995); David J. Goldberg, *Discontented America: The United States in the 1920s* (Baltimore: Johns Hopkins University Press, 1999); Nathan Miller, *New World Coming: The 1920s and the Making of Modern America* (Boston: Da Capo Press, 2004); and Paul V. Murphy, *The New Era: American Thought and Culture in the 1920s* (Lanham, MD: Rowman and Littlefield, 2012).

4. *Report of Maryland State Board of Labor and Statistics* (1921), 60; "Newsboy Shoots Himself Because Father Scolded," *Baltimore Sun*, Aug. 22, 1921, 1.

5. Miller, *New World Coming*, 283; Civic Federation of Dallas, *The Newsboys of Dallas: A friendly study of the boys, their work and thrift, home life and schooling and of their general character, associations, ambitions and promise of fitness, as future responsible citizens of Dallas* (Dallas: Civic Federation of Texas, 1921), 4.

6. Kriste Lindenmeyer, *"A Right to Childhood": The U.S. Children's Bureau and Child Welfare, 1912–46* (Urbana: University of Illinois Press, 1997), 103–107.

7. Lloyd A. Wilhoit, "Trapping of Hun Agents Disclosed," *Atlanta Constitution*, Feb. 23, 1919, 10; "Boys Do Big Soldier Trade," *New York Times*, Feb. 8, 1919, 13; Howard Zinn, *A People's History of the United States* (New York: Harper Colophon, 1980), 373; "Four Held in Bail in Drug Crusade," *New York Times*, Feb. 9, 1923, 16; "Dear Little Newsies of Newsless News Lose All Their Booze," *Denver Post*, Nov. 25, 1919, 1, 9; "Heavy Bonds Ordered for Whisky Sellers," *Atlanta Constitution*, Apr. 28, 1920, 10; "Autobiography of Anthony Morelos Brown, 1904–1970," prepared by Clyde Weiler Brown, 1976, 9, www.orsonprattbrown.com/martha-anthony.html.

8. William Howland Kenney, *Chicago Jazz: A Cultural History, 1904–1930* (New York: Oxford University Press, 1993), 123; "Snappy Jazz Makes Flappers Buy, Newsboy-Musician Says," *Salt Lake Telegram*, Mar. 9, 1928, 14.

9. Alfred McClung Lee, *The Daily Newspaper in America: The Evolution of a Social Experiment* (New York: Macmillan, 1937), 719, table VIII; 723, table XI; 724, table XII; 726, table XIII; "Newsboys' Idols Toppled," *New York Times*, Oct. 1, 1920, 2; "Newsies Go on Record as Condemning Players," *Washington Post*, Oct. 1, 1920, 10; *Printers' Ink*, Sept. 28, 1922, 82.

10. Thomas Fleming, *The Illusion of Victory: America in World War I* (New York: Basic Books, 2003), 307; "Penniless Soldiers Peddle," *New York Sun*, Jan. 11, 1919, 14; "War on Khaki Panhandlers," *New York Sun*, Jan. 17, 1919, 14; *More Education Pays*, NCLC Pamphlet No. 270 (Jan. 1917), 17; "Want Newsstands for Blind," *New York Sun*, Mar. 23, 1918, 3; Maurice B. Hexter, "The Newsboys of Cincinnati," *Studies from the Helen S. Trounstine Foundation 1*, no. 4 (Jan. 15, 1919): 115; "Asks Blind Newsboy Be Allowed to Keep Stand," *Cleveland Plain Dealer*, Aug. 23, 1921, 4; Richard Norton Smith, *The Colonel: The Life and Legend of Robert R. McCormick, 1880–1955* (Boston: Houghton Mifflin, 1997), 245; "Woods Asks Ban on Soldier Peddlers," *New York Sun*, Apr. 4, 1919, 8; "Woods to War on Fakers in Uniform," *New York Sun*, Apr., 29, 1919, 5; "Baker Discredits Pedlers in Uniform," *New York Sun*, Sept. 1, 1919, 14.

11. "'Gimpy' Says He Became a Robber to Patch Up Leg," *Chicago Tribune*, Apr. 7, 1919, 10.

12. Russ Stewart, "News-Stands, Chronology," 1895–1939, Herman Kogan Papers, box 58, folder 1, Newberry Library, Chicago; "Newsboys on Strike," *Atlanta Constitution*, Jan. 7, 1919, 12; "All News Vendors Must Wear Badges," *Atlanta Constitution*, June 5, 1919, 17.

13. "Machine Guns in Butte Ready to Quell Riot," *Chicago Tribune*, Feb. 11, 1919, 1; "Attack Is Made on Carriers of Post," *Anaconda Standard*, Feb. 11, 1919, 14; "Newsboys Are in the Fight for Democracy," *Butte Daily Bulletin*, Feb. 11, 1919, 2; "Theft of Papers Is Latest Effort," *Anaconda Standard*, Feb. 12, 1919, 3; "Guard Butte News Vendors; City Is Quiet," *Chicago Tribune*, Feb. 13, 1919, 5; "A Fatal Mistake," *Anaconda Standard*, Feb. 17, 1919, 4; Dale Martin, "School for Struggle: The Butte Newsboys Strikes of 1914 and 1919," *Speculator* 2, no. 2 (Summer 1985): 11.

14. "Newsboys Go on Strike," *New York Times*, Aug. 27, 1919, 2; "Newsie Strikebreakers Ignore Big Threats," *Muskegon Chronicle*, Sept. 26, 1919, 9; Up north, hawkers in Ottawa stopped circulating papers in support of striking railroad workers. "R. R. Workers Prepare Plan to End Strike," *Salt Lake Herald*, June 4, 1919, 1.

15. "Seattle to Enforce Law," *Los Angeles Times*, Feb. 7, 1919, 11; Roger Simpson, "Seattle Newsboys: How Hustler Democracy Lost to the Power of Property," *Journalism History* 18 (1992): 23; History Committee, *An Account of What Happened in Seattle and Especially in the Seattle Labor Movement, During the General Strike, February 6 to 11, 1919* (Seattle: General Strike Committee, 1919), www.flag.blackened.net/revolt/hist_texts/seattle1919_p2.html; "Soldiers Guard Seattle Plants," *Atlanta Constitution*, Feb. 8, 1919, 1; "Seattle to Face Army Rule Unless Strike Ends Today," *New York Times*, Feb. 8, 1919, 1; "Seattle Strike Off at Noon Today," *New York Times*, Feb. 11, 1919, 3; "Ole Hanson, "Ole Hanson on the Job!," *McClure's Magazine* 51, no. 4 (Apr. 1919): 15; "V-Volleys," *Chicago Tribune*, May 2, 1919, 18.

16. "Refuses to Take Back Stand Girls Back," *Boston Herald*, Oct. 19, 1920, 5; Anna Weinstock, "Boston News Stand Girls Fight for Rights," *Life and Labor* 11, no. 119 (Jan. 1921): 5–9.

17. Dale Martin, "Portrait of a Young Organizer," *Speculator* 2, no. 2 (Summer 1985): 11.

18. "S.F. Newsies Strike When Price Raised," *San Diego Union*, Feb. 3, 1921, 1; "Police Captain Struck in Newsboy Riots," *Seattle Star*, Feb. 3, 1921, 1; negatives of photographs from the 1921 newsboy strike, *Americana with Photographs and Manuscript Material*, Sale 407, Lot 74, July 9, 2009 (San Francisco: PBA Galleries, 2009), 23, www.pbagalleries.com/newsletter/407.pdf; "Get Strike Fever," *Los Angeles Times*, Sept. 28, 1921, II, 12.

19. "Newsboys Call Strike," *Los Angeles Times*, Feb. 16, 1922, 11; "Newsboys Strike for 2-Cent Paper," *New York Times*, Feb. 16, 1922, 5; "News and American Newsboys Strike," *New York Times*, Apr. 27, 1922, 2; "Strikers Beat Newsboy in City Hall Park," *New York Herald*, Apr. 27, 1922, 3; "Newsboys Continue Strike," *New York Times*, Apr. 28, 1922, 3.

20. *Kansas City Advocate*, May 15, 1922, 4; "Newsboys Strike When Ordered to Clean Up," *Kalamazoo* (MI) *Gazette*, July 18, 1922, 1.

21. "Crimson Newsboys, Dissatisfied with Standard of Living, May Strike," *Harvard Crimson*, May 7, 1926, n.p.; "Paper Deliverers Strike in Newark," *New York Times*, Oct. 13, 1928, 30; Timothy Wiese, "San Francisco Labor Activist Archie Brown," master's thesis, Sonoma State University, 1999, 18–19.

22. S. M. Reynolds, "Chicago Found to Be Center of Red Propaganda Efforts," *Baltimore Sun*, Nov. 14, 1919, 10; "The Davey Sedition Bill," HR 10650, Nov. 17, 1919; "Miles of Boys, of All Nations, to Parade Up Avenue Saturday," *New York Tribune*, Apr. 24, 1921, 12; Bud Schultz and Ruth Schultz, *The Price of Dissent: Testimonies to Political Repression in American* (Berkeley: University of California Press, 2001), 23.

23. "Newsboy Identifies Man with Shotgun," *Boston Globe*, June 26, 1920, 2; Michael M. Topp, *The Sacco and Vanzetti Case: A Brief History with Documents* (Boston: Bedford/St. Martin, 2005), 89; Bruce Watson, *Sacco and Vanzetti: The Men, the Murders, and the Judgment of Mankind* (New York: Penguin, 2008), 348; David Montgomery, "Thinking About American Workers in the 1920s," *International Labor and Working-Class History* 32 (Fall 1987): 17–18.

24. "Mercury Editor to Turn Newsboy and Dare Arrest," *Atlanta Constitution*, Apr. 5, 1926, 2; "Newsboys Check Harvard Radical Magazine Debut," *Chicago Tribune*, Mar. 22, 1929, 12; "Harvard Red," *Chicago Tribune*, Mar. 28, 1929, 14.

25. "Vilification Brings Arrest," *Los Angeles Times*, Aug. 14, 1926, n.p.; "News Vendor Gets Sniper Bullet in the Back," *Los Angeles Times*, Dec. 8, 1926, A2; Matthew Avery Sutton, *Aimee Semple*

McPherson and the Resurrection of Christian America (Cambridge, MA: Harvard University Press, 2007), 109–111.

26. "Boston Newsies Have Dinner at Billy Sunday's Expense," *Editor & Publisher 49*, no. 36 (Feb. 17, 1917): 31; "Advertising a Force in Church Expansion," *Editor & Publisher 49*, no. 52 (June 9, 1917): 35; "Newsies Sell Cartoon of Sunday; Arrested," *Chicago Examiner*, Apr. 8, 1918, 6; "Praise Shouted by Two Claiming Blindness Cures," *Atlanta Constitution*, Aug. 10, 1923, 18; Zell Miller, *They Heard Georgia Singing* (Macon, GA: Mercer University Press, 1996), 160–161.

27. "Streetcars for Churchgoers Only, Is Blue Law Chief's Aim," *New York Tribune*, Nov. 27, 1920, 1; "National Affairs: Fistibuster," *Time 9*, no. 9 (Feb. 28, 1927), 11.

28. Lee, *Daily Newspaper in America*, 719, 723–726. On the centrality of mass media and knowledge creation in this era, see Warren Susman, "Culture as Civilization: The Nineteen-Twenties," in *Culture as History: The Transformation of American Society in the Twentieth Century* (New York: Pantheon, 1984), 105–121.

29. William Allen White, *Autobiography* (New York: Macmillan, 1946), 632; "A Fictitious Public Interest," *Wall Street Journal*, Jan. 20, 1925, 1; Lee, *Daily Newspaper in America*, 268; William J. Thorn, with Mary Pat Pfeil, *Newspaper Circulation, Marketing the News* (New York: Longman, 1987), 49.

30. Simon Michael Bessie, *Jazz Journalism: The Story of the Tabloid Newspaper* (New York: Dutton, 1938), 184; Lee, *Daily Newspaper in America*, 651; Alma Whitaker, "Sextenuating Circumstances," *Los Angeles Times*, Mar. 13, 1927, K15; Will Stevens, "How to Succeed in Selling by Really Trying," *San Francisco Sunday Examiner & Chronicle*, May 1, 1966, Sec. 4, 8.

31. "Valentino on Mend," *Los Angeles Times*, Aug. 19, 1926, 1.

32. John S. Kennedy, "A Bolt from the Blue," in *Molders of Opinion*, ed. David Bulman (Milwaukee: Bruce Publishing, 1945), 155.

33. Edward H. Weiner, *Let's Go to Press: A Biography of Walter Winchell* (New York: G. P. Putnam's Son, 1955), 5, 27–28, 31; Neal Gabler, *Winchell: Gossip, Power and the Culture of Celebrity* (New York: Knopf, 1994), 17, 92.

34. "Confesses Staging Hollywood Parties," *Los Angeles Times*, June 1, 1924, B6.

35. The term "muscle journalism" is attributed to Chicago newsman Frank W. Carson. See "Frank Carson, 60, of Daily News, Dies," *New York Times*, Mar. 20, 1941, 21; Burton Rascoe, *Before I Forget* (New York: Literary Guild of America, 1937), 269; Gus Russo, *The Outfit: The Role of Chicago's Underworld in the Shaping of Modern America* (New York: Bloomsburg, 2001), 198; Jon Bekken, "Crumbs from the Publishers' Golden Tables: The Plight of the Chicago Newsboy," *Media History 6*, no. 1 (2000): 51–53; "Union Agent Slain by Chicago Gunmen," *New York Times*, July 27, 1931, 5; "Three Accused of Racketeering Among Newsboys," *Chicago Tribune*, Aug. 14, 1932, 8; *The W.G.N.: A Handbook of Newspaper Administration* (Chicago: Tribune Co., 1922), 120–124, 513.

36. Irving Bernstein, *The Lean Years: A History of the American Worker, 1920–1933* (Baltimore: Penguin Books, 1966), 194–206; Andrew Wender Cohen, *The Racketeer's Progress: Chicago and the Struggle for the Modern American Economy, 1900–1940* (Cambridge: Cambridge University Press, 2004), 62–97; Leinwand, *1927*, 142–143; Smith, *The Colonel*, 273–274; Laurence Bergreen, *Capone: The Man and the Era* (New York: Simon & Schuster, 1994), 545; Miller, *New World Coming*, 308.

37. "Why the Tribune Has the Largest Morning Daily Circulation in America," *Chicago Tribune*, Nov. 13, 1921, B2; John Cooney, *The Annenbergs: The Salvaging of a Tainted Dynasty* (New York: Simon & Schuster, 1982), 32–33; "Max Annenberg Tells of Selling News," *Chicago Tribune*, Dec. 16, 1921, 15.

38. *The W.G.N.*, 276; *Pictured Encyclopedia of the World's Greatest Newspaper* (Chicago: Tribune Co., 1928), 434–438, 478; E. R. Eastman, *These Changing Times* (New York: Macmillan, 1927), 197–199; Louis M. Lyons, *Newspaper Story: One Hundred Years of the Boston Globe* (Cambridge, MA: Harvard University Press, 1971), 97–98; Leinwand, *1927*, 13; "Great Advances Made in Circulation," *Oregonian*, Dec. 4, 1925; *When Denny Went to Towson* (Baltimore: The Sun, 1922), 9.

39. "Delivers Papers to Coolidge by Plane," *Los Angeles Times*, Mar. 20, 1926, 5; "Newsboys May Use Aeroplanes," *Daily Oklahoman*, Jan. 8, 1911, 8; "Glenn Curtiss and His Happiest Hour,"

Hartford Courant, June 15, 1911, 17; "Newsboy of the Clouds' Delivers the Call to Vallejo by Biplane," *San Francisco Call*, Apr. 4, 1912, 3; "Acts as Aerial Newsboy," *Cleveland Plain Dealer*, Aug. 30, 1912, 1; *Box Kites to Bombers: The Story of the Glenn L. Martin Company* (Baltimore: Glenn L. Martin Co., 1945), 13.

40. "Enter Flying Newsboy," *Adrian Daily Telegram*, June 9, 1919, 5; *Editor & Publisher* 52, no. 10 (Aug. 7, 1919): 30; "Texas Aerial Newsboy Graduates to Airmail," *Salt Lake Telegram*, Mar. 4, 1928, 8; Floyd J. Healey, "'Times' by Airplane," *Los Angeles Times*, Apr. 15, 1928, 1; Frank Luther Mott, *American Journalism: A History of Newspapers in the United States Through 260 Years: 1690 to 1950* (New York: MacMillan, 1950), 716–717.

41. Liz Watts, "The Flying Newsboy: A Small Daily Attempts Air Delivery," *Journalism History* 28, no. 4 (Winter 2003), 163–171; "Boy Aviator Is Killed," *New York Times*, July 19, 1934, 9.

42. Alba M. Edwards, *Children in Gainful Occupations at the Fourteenth Census of the United States*, US Dept. of Commerce, Bureau of Census (Washington, DC, 1924), 56; *Children in Gainful Occupations at the Fifteenth Census of the United States*: 1930, US Department of Commerce, Bureau of Census (Washington, DC, 1933), 8; *Child Labor Facts and Figures*, Children's Bureau, Pub. No. 197 (Washington, DC: Government Printing Office, 1933), 2; Raymond Fuller, "Child Labor in Our Cities," *Good Housekeeping* 25 (Nov. 1922), 145; Sidney D. Long, *The Cry of the Newsboy* (Kansas City, MO, 1928), n.p.; George B. Mangold, *Problems of Child Welfare*, 3rd ed. (New York: Macmillan, 1936), 303; Katharine Dupre Lumpkin and Dorothy Wolff Douglas, *Child Workers in America* (New York: Robert M. McBride, 1937), 45.

43. Marion Willoughby, *Cleveland School Children Who Sell on the Street* (Cleveland: NCLC for the Ohio Consumers' League, 1924), 18; R. F. Woodbury, Fred R. Davis, and Julia E. Chadwick, "Street Traders of Buffalo, New York, 1925: A Study Made by the Juvenile Protective Department, Children's Aid and Society for the Prevention of Cruelty to Children of Erie County, New York," *Foundation Forum* 52 (Aug. 1926): 13–14; "Round Table Discussion of Street Trades," Nov. 18, 1926, 1, NYCLC Collection, box 3, folder 4, New York State Library, Albany; "Praises Newsboys as Self-Reliant," *New York Times*, Nov. 19, 1926, 13; G. S. Dow, "The Newsboys of Denver," *Social Forces* 4, no. 2 (Dec. 1925): 331–333; "Denver Newsboys Win," *Christian Science Monitor*, Aug. 28, 1925, 1; "Street Trades Control in Toledo," *American Child* 5, no. 8 (Aug. 1923): 3; John H. Sines, "Boyhood Survey Reveals Much," *Trenton Times*, Mar. 15, 1922, 7; Harold Cary, "In the School of Crime for Boys," *Collier's* 72 (Oct. 13, 1923): 15.

44. *American Child* 1, no. 1 (May 1919): 73; "Editorial Comment on Child Labor Decision," *American Child* 4, no. 2 (Aug. 1922), 91–96; *American Child* 6, no. 12 (Dec. 1924), 2.

45. "Child Labor Amendment Favored by Newspapers," *American Child* 5, no. 10 (Oct. 1923), 1; "Newsboys Not Affected by the Child Labor Bill," *Atlanta Constitution*, Aug. 4, 1925, 4; Judith Sealander, *The Failed Century of the Child: Governing America's Young in the Twentieth Century* (Cambridge: Cambridge University Press, 2003), 150–156.

46. Grace Abbott, "The Child Labor Amendment—1," *North American Review* 220, no. 825 (Dec. 1924): 223; Anna Y. Reed, "Child-Labor Legislation: A Point of View," *Elementary School Journal* 23, no. 4 (Dec. 1922): 282.

47. McGill, *Child Workers on City Streets*, 54–64; *Ogden Standard*, June 28, 1927, 11.

48. *Child Labor in North Dakota*, Children's Bureau, Pub. No. 129 (Washington, DC: Government Printing Office, 1923), 47–51.

49. "Frees Newsie, Scolds Cop," *New York Herald*, Mar. 11, 1921, 11; "Subway Newsboy Freed," *New York Herald*, July 13, 1921, 22; Herbert Mitgang, *Once upon a Time in New York: Jimmy Walker, Franklin Roosevelt and the Last Great Battle of the Jazz Age* (New York: Simon & Schuster, 2000), 137.

50. Ruth Smiley True, *Boyhood and Lawlessness* (New York: Survey Associates, 1914), 122; "Cost $3500 to Call This Boy 'Toughest Kid in Hell's Kitchen,'" *Philadelphia Inquirer*, June 25, 1920, 1; "'Uplift' Nets Him $3500," *New Orleans Item*, June 28, 1920, 6; "The 'Tough Kid,'" *Elkhart Truth*, July 14, 1920, 4.

51. Mary Stevenson Callcott, *Child Labor Legislation in New York* (New York: Macmillan, 1931), 33 n. 10; Roy F. Woodbury, "Children in Street Work," *Family* 10, no. 3 (May 1929): 85–87; "Boy Paper Sellers Seized," *New York Times*, Oct. 29, 1927, 36.

52. "Subcommittee Votes New Child Labor Law," *Washington Post*, Feb. 7, 1928, 20; "Child Labor," *Monthly Labor Review* 28 (May 1929): 116; Frank Stricker, "Affluence for Whom?— Another Look at Prosperity and the Working Classes in the 1920s," *Labor History* 24, no. 1 (Winter 1983): 15, 20, 23. On children's social value, see Viviana A. Zelizer, *Pricing the Priceless Child: The Changing Social Value of Children* (New York: Basic Books, 1985).

53. Charles S. Meeks, "Study of the Progress of Newsboys in School," *Elementary School Journal* 24 (Feb. 1924): 430–433; McGill, *Child Workers on City Streets*, 15–16; *The Newsboys of Denver: A Report by the Committee on Education and Welfare of the City Club*, Pamphlet 5, City Club of Denver, Apr. 6, 1925.

54. Robert Dunn, *The Americanization of Labor: The Employers' Offensive Against the Trade Unions* (New York: International Publishers, 1927), 207; Michael E. Parrish, *Anxious Decades: America in Prosperity and Depression* (New York: W.W. Norton, 1992), 226; Richard Norton Smith, *The Colonel: The Life and Legend of Robert R. McCormick, 1880–1955* (Boston: Houghton Mifflin, 1997), 264; *Toledo School Children in Street Trades* (Toledo Consumers' League and the Ohio Council on Women and Children in Industry, 1922), 11; McGill, *Child Workers on City Streets*, 13–15; *The Health of a Thousand Newsboys in New York City: A Study Made in Cooperation with the Board of Education by the Heart Committee of the New York Tuberculosis and Health Association* (New York: The Committee, 1925).

55. "Scoreboards Draw 10,000 to City Hall," *New York Times*, Oct. 3, 1926, S3; "Huge Crowd Sees Game Pictured on Post Scoreboard," *Washington Post*, Oct. 6, 1924, 2; "Nip Winters in Rare Form, East Winner," *Pittsburgh Courier*, Oct. 11, 1924, 6. See also Roderick Nash, *The Nervous Generation: American Thought, 1917–1930* (Chicago: Rand McNally, 1970).

56. "Baseball Lottery Revealed," *New York Tribune*, Mar. 18, 1922, 2; Frank Smith, "Time Now Ripe to Squelch Baseball Lotteries for Year," *Chicago Tribune*, Mar. 18, 1922, 11; "Detroit Fans Out Early to Buy Opening Game Tickets," *New York Times*, Mar. 28, 1922, 24.

57. Benjamin G. Rader, *Baseball: A History of America's Game* (Urbana: University of Illinois Press, 2002). 110; "'Newsies,' Carrier Boys Will Have a Baseball League," *San Francisco Chronicle*, Sept. 4, 1922, H2; *North Louisiana Sanitarium, Inc., v. Serio et al.*, No. 3871, Court of Appeals of Louisiana, Second Circuit, 15 La. App. 123; 130 So. 646; 1939 La App. Lexis 649; "Newsboys Victorious," *Baltimore Sun*, Sept. 7, 1924, S2.

58. Ethel E. Hanks, "Children Who Trade in the Streets. A Study in Troy, New York," 1923, 14, box 31, folder 26, NYCLC Papers; Robert W. Wells, *The Milwaukee Journal: An Informal Chronicle of Its First 100 Years, 1882–1982* (Milwaukee: Milwaukee Journal, 1981), 205–206; Bill Farrell, *Cradle of Champions: Eighty Years of New York* Daily News *Golden Gloves* (Champaign, IL: Sports Publishing, 2006), 3.

59. Randy Roberts, *Jack Dempsey: The Manassa Mauler* (Urbana: University of Illinois Press, 2003), 6, 36; Roger Kahn, *A Flame of Pure Fire: Jack Dempsey and the Roaring '20s* (New York: Harcourt Brace, 1999), 94, 98–99, 158; "Puebloan Member of Mob Seeking to Lynch Slayer," *Pueblo Chieftain*, June 29, 1917, 3.

60. "Jack Dempsey to Eat Turkey with Tracy's Newsboys," *Salt Lake Telegram*, Nov. 29, 1922, 9; Sparrow McGann, "Jack Dempsey Makes Fast Friend of Little Newsboy," *Sunday Oregonian*, Aug. 28, 1921, II, 1; Ed O'Malley, "Newsies Bout a Big Success," *Los Angeles Times*, Jan. 27, 1922, III, 1; Robert Edgren, "Life of Champions Not All Roses, Says Dempsey," *Oregonian*, Dec. 31, 1922, 2; Kahn, *Flame of Pure Fire*, 125–126.

61. "Tribune Sets 1,075,000 as New Record," *Chicago Tribune*, Sept. 24, 1927, 1.

62. James B. Roberts and Alexander G. Skutt, *The Boxing Register*, 4th ed. (Ithaca, NY: McBooks Press, 2006), 74–75, 158–159, 176–177; "'Rocky Kansas' Title Won by Persistency," *Baltimore Sun*, Dec. 27, 1925, 18; William B. Shubb, "Talk of the Town," *Sacramento Bee*, 1999, D1, D4; *Los Angeles Times*, May 4, 1924, 15; "Pete Herman Regains World's Bantam Title," *Wilkes Barre Times Leader*, July 26, 1921, 17; "Heavy Champions Western Products," *Anaconda Standard*, Nov. 22, 1919, III, 2; Benjamin G. Rader, "Compensatory Sports Heroes: Ruth, Grange and Dempsey," *Journal of Popular Culture 16*, no. 41 (Spring 1983), 11–22.

63. Peter Heller, *In This Corner: Forty-Two World Champions Tell Their Stories* (New York: Da Capo Press, 1994), 99–100; *Boxing Research Organization Journal 78* (June 22, 2003), 71–81; "He 'Didn't Know No More for Some Time,'" *Los Angeles Times*, June 21, 1921, I12.

64. Cornelius Vanderbilt Jr., *Farewell to Fifth Avenue* (New York: Simon & Schuster, 1935), 65.

65. Chicago Vice Commission, *The Social Evil in Chicago: A Study of Existing Conditions, with Recommendations* (Chicago, 1911), 35–36. See also Mark Haller, "Urban Vice and Civic Reform: Chicago in the Early Twentieth Century," in *Cities in American History*, ed. Kenneth T. Jackson and Stanley K. Schultz (New York: Knopf, 1972), 290–305.

66. Elsa Wertheim, "News Alleys," *Child Labor Bulletin 6*, no. 1 (May 1917), 45.

67. F. Zeta Youmans, "Report for the Year Ending December 31, 1924," 10–11, Juvenile Protective Association Records, Juvenile Occupation Department, University of Illinois at Chicago (henceforth JPA Records), folder 12; "Child Labor—Street Trade—News Alley Investigation," May 1921–Apr. 1929, folder 84, JPA Records; P. A. Holbert, "Two Nights in the News Alley," Mar. 13 and 30, 1923, 5, folder 84, JPA Records; "Herald Examiner News Alley, Mon. Dec. 3, 1923," folder 84, JPA Records; "Special Investigation. Herald Examiner News Alley, Jan. 21, 1924," folder 84, JPA Records; Roger Freund, "Herald Examiner News Alley Investigation," Jan. 22, 23, 28, 1925, folder 84, JPA Records; and "Young Street Traders with Juvenile Court Records," ca. 1926, n.p., folder 88, JPA Records.

68. "Herald Examiner News Alley, Mon. Dec. 3, 1923," folder 84, JPA Records; Holbert, "Two Nights in the News Alley," 5, folder 84, JPA Records.

69. Ibid.

70. Ibid.

71. Ibid.

72. Clifford R. Shaw, *The Jack-Roller: A Delinquent Boy's Own Story* (1930; repr., Chicago: University of Chicago Press, 1994), ch. 7.

73. Philip Marcus, "Newsboys. When Papers Was a Penny Apiece . . . ," WPA-LC Writers' Unit, Chicago, IL, May 18, 1939, 4, Library of Congress.

74. Nels Anderson, "The Mission Mill," *American Mercury 8* (Aug. 1926): 489–491.

75. F. Zeta Youmans, "Childhood, Inc.," *Survey 52* (July 15, 1924): 462; Youmans, "Report for the Year Ending December 31, 1924," 14, folder 12, JPA Records.

76. McCormick to Miss Jessie F. Binford, July 20, 1923, and "Herald Examiner News Alley, Mon. Dec. 3, 1923," folder 84, JPA Records.

77. *Street Traders of Buffalo, New York, 1925* (Buffalo: Juvenile Protective Department, 1926), 9–10; Arthur L. Beeley, *Boys and Girls in Salt Lake City: The Results of a Survey Made for the Rotary Club and the Business and Professional Women's Club of Salt Lake City* (Salt Lake City: University of Utah, Dept. of Sociology and Social Technology, 1929), 70–72; Ben Kaplan, "A Study of Newsboys in New Orleans," master's thesis, Tulane University, 1929, 19, 24, appendix 2; "Newsies Show Regard for Mischler," *New Orleans States*, Jan. 1, 1921, 1; "Arrests to Check Fake 'Extra' Sale," *New Orleans Times-Picayune*, Feb. 19, 1932, 25.

78. Kaplan, "A Study of Newsboys in New Orleans," 19, 24, appendix 2.

79. "Herald Examiner News Alley Report by Roger Freund, Jan. 22, 1925," folder 12, JPA Records.

80. "Newsboys Now Famous," *Los Angeles Times*, Dec. 4, 1921, VIII, 3; "Leow, Once a Newsboy, Who Found Fortune in Pennies," *Washington Post*, June 1, 1924, A3; S. J. Woolf, "The Newsboy Who Became a Radio Chief," *New York Times*, Jan. 6, 1929, 85; "Yellow Cabs' Chief Retires," *Los Angeles Times*, Jan. 8, 1929, 7; *Tulsa Daily World*, Dec. 31, 1922, 22; Irving Vaughan, "Things You May Not Know About Sport Celebrities," *Chicago Tribune*, Jan. 21, 1926, 19; "Howard K. Brooks Dies at Age of 75," *New York Times*, Sept. 19, 1929, 21.

81. "Circulation Men Review Problems," *Atlanta Constitution*, June 22, 1927, 9; "Sproul New U. C. Head," *Los Angeles Times*, June 12, 1929, 1; "New Bishop of Chicago," *Chicago Tribune*, May 13, 1928, D6; "Florida Developer Drowned off Liner," *New York Times*, Oct. 14, 1926, 27; "As Others See Us," *Living Age*, Nov. 1928, 225.

82. Scott Nearing, "The Newsboy at Night in Philadelphia," *Charities and Commons 17* (Feb. 2, 1907), 784; Temple, "Jimmy Pays His Income Tax," *Cleveland Plain Dealer*, Mar. 14, 1921, 5; J. R. Shaver, Illustration 13 – No Title, *Life*, Apr. 21, 1921, 558; J. R. Shaver, "Why Not?," *Life*, May 19, 1921, 715; "Dick, the Wall Street Waif; or, From Newsboy to Stock Broker. By a Self Made Man," *Fame and Fortune Weekly. Stories of Boys Who Make Money 1168* (Feb. 17, 1928); "94-Year-Old 'Newsboy' Leaves $50,000 Estate," *New York Times*, Dec. 27, 1925, E1.

83. Douglas Martin, "Bernard Green, Newsstand Chain Founder, Dies at 91," *New York Times*, Mar. 1, 2002, A21; "Millionaires Number 11,000," *Los Angeles Times*, Sept. 12, 1926, 13;

Joseph S. Wasney, "U.S. Millionaires Number 40,000," *Atlanta Constitution*, Feb. 3, 1930, 1; Carson C. Hathaway, "Millionaire Army Has 74 Classes as 'Multi,'" *New York Times*, Oct. 3, 1926, XX 7. The US Treasury said anyone with an income of $50,000 had assets of $1,000,000.

84. Patricia Condon Johnston, "Edward Brewer: Illustrator and Portrait Painter," *Minnesota History* 47, no. 1 (Spring 1980), 2–15; *Saturday Evening Post*, Feb. 19, 1927, 159.

85. Stephen Rudd, *The Mystery of the Missing Eyebrows* (Terre Haute, IN: R. H. Gore, 1921); Paul A. Gore, *Past the Edge of Poverty: A Biography of Robert Hayes Gore, Sr.* (Fort Lauderdale, FL: R. H. Gore, 1990), 43–44.

86. Lee McCrae, "He Invests in Human Bonds," *Watertown Times*, Sept. 25, 1920, 10; "Hammond Sponsors Newsboys' Savings," *Washington Post*, Sept. 25, 1926, 24; Nov. 24, 1926, 22; "Frugal Newsboys," *Atlanta Constitution*, Feb. 20, 1927, D15.

87. "Schneider Wins Harvard Prize," *Boston Globe*, Dec. 15, 1920, 1; "Kopp Wins Newsboys' Harvard Scholarship," *Boston Globe*, Sept. 2, 1921, 20; Harry E. Burroughs, *Boys in Men's Shoes* (New York: Macmillan, 1944); *Crisis* 40, no. 10 (Oct. 1931), 346; Jerome Karabel, *The Chosen: The Hidden History of Admission and Exclusion at Harvard, Yale, and Princeton* (New York: Mariner Books, 2005).

88. George Gibbs, *Youth Triumphant* (New York: D. Appleton, 1921); "Runaway Girl Found as She Tries to Become Newsboy," *Chicago Tribune* May 16, 1928, 17; "Newsgirl to Lawyer, Immigrant's Record," *Christian Science Monitor* Jan. 31, 1923, 1.

89. *Little Orphan Annie*, in *Oakland Tribune*, Jan. 8, 1928, n.p.; Philip Schuyler, "News of Yore: Harold Gray Profiled," *Stripper's Guide*, June 14, 2007, www.strippersguide.blogspot. com/2007_06_01_archive.html.

90. Garland Anderson, *From Newsboy and Bellhop to Playwright* (1925), 7; James V. Hatch and Ted Shine, eds., *Black Theatre USA: Plays by African Americans* (New York: Free Press, 1974), 95–97.

91. Harry F. Liscomb, *The Prince of Washington Square: An Up-to-the-Minute Story* (New York: Stokes, 1925); "Newsboy Becomes a Novelist Overnight," *Afro American*, Mar. 14, 1925: A2; Eunice Hunton Carter, *Opportunity: Journal of Negro Life* 3 (Sept. 1925): 381–382; *New Yorker*, Feb. 28, 1925, 26.

92. *Dinty*, Marshall Neilan Prods., 1920; "The Reason for 'Dinty,'" *Washington Post*, Jan. 2, 1921, 48; "Society," *Coconino* (AZ) *Sun*, Sept. 9, 1921, 5; *Let 'Er Go Gallegher*, Pathé, 1928; Deac Rossell, "The Fourth Estate and the Seventh Art," in *Questioning Media Ethics*, ed. Bernard Rubin (New York: Praeger, 1978), 282. Others of this ilk are *Hush Money*, Paramount, 1921; *Her Mad Bargain*, Associated First National Pictures, 1921; *For His Sake*, Zerner Film, 1922; *How Baxter Butted In*, Warner Bros., 1925; *Youth and Adventure*, FBO, 1925; *The Cowboy Cop*, FBO, 1926; *Stepping Along*, Paramount, 1926; and *Idaho Red*, FBO, 1929.

93. Thomas Wolfe, *Look Homeward, Angel* (New York: Scribner, 1929), 117–132.

94. "Competition Between Two Ohio Newsies," *Boston Globe*, July 12, 1920, 10; "Cox Poses for Film on Rise of Newsboy," *New York Times*, Aug. 24, 1920, 3; Teresa Zumwald, "James M. Cox, Publisher," *Dayton Daily News*, 1998, accessed Jan. 17, 2009, www.daytondailynews. com/history/content/service/info/history/cox.html (no longer available online).

95. James Boyland, ed., *The World and the 20s: The Golden Years of New York's Legendary Newspaper* (New York: Dial Press, 1973), 37; Mayme Ober Peake, "Mrs. Harding, as Wife of Newspaper Owner, Has Learned to Know People," *Baltimore Sun*, May 9, 1920, 14C; "Neighbors Turnout to Greet Harding," *New York Times*, July 6, 1920, 9; Miller, *New World Coming*, 66.

96. "Hail Cox on Parade of 10,000 in Dayton," *New York Times*, July 31, 1920, 2; "Cox Poses for Film on Rise of Newsboy," *New York Times*, Aug. 24, 1920, 3; "Cox Shouts His Indignation at Saturday Post," *San Francisco Chronicle*, Oct. 25, 1920, 3; Jan Cohn, *Creating America: George Horace Lorimer and the Saturday Evening Post* (Pittsburgh, PA: University of Pittsburgh Press, 1995), 158–160.

97. "Washington Officials Home After July 4 Celebrations," *Oregonian*, July 9, 1920, 10; "Boston Newsboys Mourn President Harding," *New York Times*, Aug. 10, 1923, 3; *New York Times*, Jan. 6, 1930, 35; "Newsboys Celebrate Signing of Peace Pact in Novel Way," *Christian Science Monitor*, Jan. 19, 1929, 1; C. G. Poore, "Newsboy Club in Boston Helps Them to Careers," *New York Times*, June 16, 1929, XX7.

98. "Smith Urges Newsboys to Live Up to Spirit of Young America," *New York Tribune*, Feb. 23, 1921, 4; "Smith Eats Meal at His Old Haunt," *New York Herald*, Feb. 23, 1923, 3; "Gov. Al Smith Eats Chicken with Newsies," *Washington Post*, Feb. 24, 1925, 10; "Newsboys Aid Smith Fund," *New York Times*, Aug. 29, 1928, 3; Herbert Hoover, *Memoirs: Years of Adventure, 1874–1920* (New York: Macmillan, 1951), 17; Dexter Marshall, "New Timber in Senate," *Dallas Morning News*, Jan. 26, 1908, 7.

99. "Once Newsboy and Bootblack, Is Now Member of Congress," *Christian Science Monitor*, Dec. 17, 1924, 5; "The Newsboy Congressman," *Atlanta Constitution*, Jan. 28, 1928, G1; Rose Jacobstein, "Jacobstein Family History," unpublished archive, accessed Feb. 10, 2009, www.en.wikipedia.org/wiki/Meyer_Jacobstein. On the immigrant response to the era's racial nationalism, see Gary Gerstle, *American Crucible: Race and Nation in the Twentieth Century* (Princeton, NJ: Princeton University Press, 2001), 115–122.

100. Beverley Smith, "Thanks to Brother Gus," *American Magazine 128*, no. 6 (Dec. 1939), 84.

101. Miller, *New World Coming*, 146; "$5,000,000 Suit Filed Against Ford," *New York Times*, Feb. 2, 1921, 13; "Ford Paper Sales Curbed," *Christian Science Monitor*, Mar. 21, 1921, 2; "Toledo Bars Ford's Paper," *New York Tribune*, Mar. 24, 1921, 22; "Ford Paper Sales Barred in Chicago," *Christian Science Monitor*, Mar. 25, 1921, 1; "Ford Paper Is Not to Be Barred" and "Sale Restricted in Columbus, Ohio," *Christian Science Monitor*, Mar. 29, 1921, 1; "Ford Tests St. Louis Ban," *New York Times*, Mar. 29, 1921, 9; "Dearborn Pub. Co. v. Fitzgerald. 271 F. 479. Apr. 16, 1921," in Leon Hurwitz, *Historical Dictionary of Censorship in the United States* (Westport, CT, 1985), 83, and www.westlaw.com, 2002, 1–6; "St. Louis Officials Ordered to Court," *Christian Science Monitor*, May 2, 1921, 1; "Ford Newspaper Sellers Freed," *New York Times*, May 11, 1921, 7; "An Attack on Freedom of the Press," *Chicago Tribune*, May 12, 1921, 8; "Chief's Ban on Ford's Weekly Lifted by Writ," *Chicago Tribune*, Aug. 5, 1921, 17; "Ford Weekly Is Selling in Chicago," *Christian Science Monitor*, Aug. 16, 1921, 9; "Boys Arrested for Selling Ford Weekly," *Christian Science Monitor*, Sept. 1, 1921, 4; "Fight over Ford's Paper," *New York Times*, Sept. 2, 1921, 14; "Ford's Paper Wins Suit," *New York Times*, Sept. 9, 1921, 3; "Ford Paper Sale Again at Issue," *Christian Science Monitor*, Sept. 10, 1921, 4; Douglas Brinkley, *Wheels for the World: Henry Ford, His Company, and a Century of Progress, 1903–2003* (New York: Viking, 2003), 238, 257–267, 346; Neil Baldwin, *Henry Ford and the Jews: The Mass Production of Hate* (New York: Public Affairs, 2001), 96.

102. "Young 'Night Riders' Maltreat Newsboy," *San Francisco Chronicle*, Mar. 10, 1922, 1; Thomas R. Pegram, "Kluxing the Eighteenth Amendment: The Anti-Saloon League, the Ku Klux Klan, and the Fate of Prohibition in the 1920s," in *American Public Life and the Historical Imagination*, ed. Wendy Gamber, Michael Grossberg, and Hendrik Hartog (Notre Dame, IN: University of Notre Dame Press, 2003), 240–261.

103. "Steubenville Klan Asks State Guard," *New York Times*, Aug. 19, 1923, 2; "Ohio Klan, Defiant, Threatens Niles," *New York Times*, Nov. 4, 1924, 2; "Niles Ku Klux Klan Riot of 1924," Oral History Interview with Frank E. McDermott by Stephen Papolas, Dec. 8, 1982, Youngstown State University Oral History Project, www.digital.maag.ysu.edu:8080/jspui/handle/1989/2595.

104. Mike Jacobs, "Jazz Age Young Urban Ethnics Respond to the Klan," unpublished paper presented at Children in Urban America Conference, Marquette University, Milwaukee, May 5, 2000, 7–8.

105. "Muncie Editor Assails Judge; Newsboys Held," *Chicago Tribune*, Feb. 20, 1927, 14; John Bartlow Martin, "The Rise and Fall of D. C. Stephenson," in *Indiana History: A Book of Readings*, ed. Ralph D. Gray (Bloomington: Indiana University Press, 1994), 312. See also Robert S. Lynd and Herlen Merrell Lynd, *Middletown: A Study in Contemporary American Culture* (New York: Harcourt, Brace, 1929), 481–484.

106. "Nine Witnesses Accuse Dearth as Trial Begins," *Chicago Tribune*, Mar. 23, 1927, 3; Richard K. Tucker, *The Dragon and the Cross: The Rise and Fall of the Ku Klux Klan in Middle America* (Hamdon, CT: Archon Books, 1991), 84–87.

107. "Dearth Acquitted by Indiana Senate," *New York Times*, Apr. 2, 1927, 2; "Indiana's Dearth," *Time*, Apr. 4, 1927, n.p.; "Mayor of Muncie Wins Full Pardon," *New York Times*, Dec. 15, 1933, 19.

108. Langston Hughes, *The Big Sea* (New York: Knopf, 1940), 21–22; Arnold Rampersad, *The Life of Langston Hughes*, vol. 1, *1902–1941: I, Too, Sing America* (New York: Oxford University Press, 1986), 17.

109. William Tuttle, *Race Riot: Chicago in the Red Summer of 1919* (Urbana: University of Illinois Press, 1970), 142; Ethan Michaeli, *The Defender: How the Legendary Black Newspaper Changed America* (New York: Houghton Mifflin Harcourt, 2017), 115.

110. "75-Year-Old 'Newsboy' Starts His 56th Year in Same Selling Spot," *Baton Rouge State Times Advocate*, Nov. 19, 1955, 1; "Newsboy at One Corner . . . ," *Omaha Sunday World Herald Magazine*, Oct. 14, 1928, 7; "Whites Clash with Negroes in Near-Riot," *Baltimore Sun*, July 24, 1921, ES20; Buck Colbert Franklin, *My Life and an Era: The Autobiography of Buck Colbert Franklin*, ed. John Hope Franklin and John Whittington Franklin (Baton Rouge: Louisiana State University Press, 1997), 196.

111. Richard Wright, *Black Boy* (New York: Harper & Row, 1945), 94, 141–147; Hazel Rowley, *Richard Wright: The Life and Times* (New York: Henry Holt, 2001), 24; Janice A. Petterchak, *Lone Scout: W. D. Boyce and American Boy Scouting* (Rochester, IL: Legacy Press, 2003), 90.

112. Nettie P. McGill, *Child Workers on City Streets*, Children's Bureau, Pub. No. 188 (Washington, DC: Government Printing Office, 1928), 71; Lewis Hine, *Roland, Eleven Year Old Negro Newsboy, Newark, N.J., August 1st. 1924*, Library of Congress Collection, Hine no. 4945.

113. Benjamin Rivlin, ed., *Ralph Bunche: The Man and His Times* (New York: Holmes & Meier, 1990), xx; *Cincinnati Union*, Feb. 4, 1922, 2.

114. *New York Amsterdam News*, Nov. 23, 1927, 5.

115. Martin Dann, *The Black Press, 1827–1890: The Quest for National Identity* (New York: G. P. Putnam's Sons, 1971), 197; Henry Lewis Suggs, ed., *The Black Press in the South, 1865–1979* (Westport, CT: Greenwood Press, 1983), 46–47; Studs Terkel, *Hard Times: An Oral History of the Great Depression* (New York: Pantheon, 1970), 117; Roi Ottley, "The Lonely Warrior: The Life and Times of Robert S. Abbott," *Chicago Defender*, June 18, 1955, 2.

116. Michaeli, *The Defender*, 165; Nettie George Speedy, "My Scrap Book of Doers," *Chicago Defender*, Mar. 14, 1925, 4; Ottley, "Lonely Warrior," 2; Hayumi Higuchi, "The Billiken Club: 'Race Leaders' Educating Children (1921–1940)," *Transforming Anthropology* 13, no. 2 (Oct. 2005), 154–159.

117. Ernest F. Imhoff, "The Tragic Voyage of the Evening Sun Newsboys Band," *Baltimore Sun*, Jan. 23, 1994, 3; *Pittsburgh Courier*, Feb. 23, 1924, 5; "Lionel Hampton, 94; Former Chicago Defender Newsboy, International Ambassador of Jazz Dies," *Chicago Defender*, Sept. 3, 2002, 6; "Major Clark N. Smith Directed Defender Newsboys Band During the Early Bud Billiken Day Parade," *Chicago Defender*, Aug. 10, 2002, 23; Marian M. Ohman, "Major N. Clark Smith in Chicago," *Journal of the Illinois State Historical Society* 96, no. 1 (Spring 2003), 56; E. Diane Lyle-Smith, "Nathaniel Clark Smith (1877–1934): African American Musician, Music Educator and Composer," *Bulletin of Historical Research in Music Education* 17, no. 2 (Jan. 1996): 110–111; John Steiner, "Chicago," in *Jazz: New Perspectives on the History of Jazz*, ed. Nat Hentoff and Albert J. McCarthy (1959; repr.,. Cambridge, MA: Da Capo Press, 1975), 163.

118. David I. Macleod, *The Age of the Child: Children in America, 1890–1920* (New York: Twayne, 1998), 84; Miller, *New World*, 259; "Nation's School Bands Compete," *New York Times*, Apr. 14, 1929, 142; Edward Bailey Birge, *History of Public School Music in the United States* (Philadelphia: Oliver Ditson, 1928), 302; Gerald W. Johnson, Frank R. Kent, H. L. Mencken, and Hamilton Owens, *The Sun Papers of Baltimore, 1837–1937* (New York: Knopf, 1937), 399–400; Fred Rasmussen, "Five Newsboys Died on Burning Ship," *Baltimore Sun*, July 4, 1998, 2.

Chapter 14

1. Errol Lincoln Uys, *Riding the Rails: Teenagers on the Move During the Great Depression* (New York: Routledge, 2003), 158; Dempsey J. Travis, *An Autobiography of Black Chicago* (Chicago: Urban Research Institute, 1981), 33.

2. Alba M. Edwards, *Sixteenth Census of the United States: 1940. Population: Comparative Occupation Statistics for the United States, 1870 to 1940* (Washington, DC: Government Printing Office, 1943), 29; "Finds Newsboys Older," *New York Times*, Mar. 13, 1935, 10; *Children Engaged in Newspaper and Magazine Selling and Delivering*, Children's Bureau, Pub. No. 227 (Washington, DC: Government Printing Office, 1935), 55; "The Wall Street Crash," *New York Times*, June 5, 1932, 12.

3. Sidney Fine, *Frank Murphy: The Detroit Years* (Ann Arbor: University of Michigan Press, 1975), 268–276; Miriam Keeler, "Child Labor," *Review of Educational Research* 6, no. 2 (Apr. 1936): 239–240; "Newsboy Club's 'Vengeance Squad' Kills Lad in Detroit for Beating One of Its Members," *New York Times*, Dec. 7, 1931, 1; "Newspapers & Newsboys," *Time* 18, no. 24 (Dec. 14, 1931), 48.

4. "Press: Newsboy Labor," *Time* 23, no. 26 (June 25, 1934), 68; *The N.B.A. Handbook for Newspaper Boys* (Indianapolis: Newspaper Boys of America, 1932), 114; Frank Luther Mott, *American Journalism: A History, 1690–1960* (New York: Macmillan, 1962), 675; Edwin Emery and Michael Emery, *The Press and America* (Englewood Cliffs, NJ: Prentice Hall, 1992), 535–536, 621; Alfred McClung Lee, *The Daily Newspaper in America: The Evolution of a Social Instrument* (New York: Macmillan, 1937), 719.

5. Charles L. Allen, "The Press and Advertising," *Annals of the American Academy of Political and Social Science* 219 (Jan. 1942), 88; Caroline Bird, *The Invisible Scar: The Great Depression, and What It Did to American Life from Then Until Now* (New York: D. McKay, 1966), 61–62; Howard M. Bell, *Youth Tell Their Story: A Study of the Conditions and Attitudes of Young People in Maryland Between the Ages of 16 and 24* (Washington, DC: American Council on Education, 1938), 162–165; Robert W. Wells, *The Milwaukee Journal: An Informal Chronicle of Its First 100 Years, 1882–1982* (Milwaukee: Milwaukee Journal, 1981), 239; William B. Helmreich, *The Enduring Community: The Jews of Newark and the Metrowest* (Edison, NJ: Transaction Books, 1998), 75; J. Brooks Atkinson, "The Play," *New York Times*, Dec. 11, 1931, 34.

6. "News Excites the City," *New York Times*, Feb. 16, 1933, 2; Theodore White, *In Search of History: A Personal Adventure* (New York: Harper & Row, 1978), 8, 38; "Cash Rushed to Relieve Michigan Banks," *New York Times* Feb. 15, 1933, 1; Bird, *Invisible Scar*, 99–100; "For Money," *Time* 21, no 2 (Jan. 9, 1933), 28; Mario DeMarco, "Being a Newsie," *Good Old Days*, Nov. 1992, 35.

7. "400,000 Bail Set for Dillinger Gang," *New York Times*, Jan. 27, 1934, 3; Bonnie Parker, "The Story of Bonnie and Clyde," 1934, in *The True Story of Bonnie and Clyde: As Told by Bonnie's Mother and Clyde's Sister* (New York: Signet Books, 1968), 169; John Neal Phillips, *Running with Bonnie & Clyde: The Ten Fast Years of Ralph Fults* (Norman: University of Oklahoma Press, 2002), 219.

8. John Shidler, "Newspaper Circulation Jargon," *American Speech* 7, no. 2 (Dec. 1931): 159–160; Don G. Churchill, "A Survey by the Burroughs Newsboys Foundation," Boston, 1937, 45–47, Hattie H. Smith Papers, Schlesinger Library, Harvard University; "Newsboy Wears a Neon Sign Lighted by Pocket Battery," *Popular Mechanics* 67, no. 4 (Apr. 1937), 561; Theodore Pratt, "Our Footloose Correspondent," *New Yorker*, Feb. 5, 1938, 62; *Children Engaged in Newspaper and Magazine Selling and Delivering*, 11, 51, 4–5; "Report on Bronx Home News Hearing," Nov. 13, 1933, box 33, folder 20, NYCLC Papers; *New York Times*, June 5, 1932, 12; "Empire Building on a Paper Route," *New York Times*, June 10, 2001, sec. 3, 2; "Child Labor Ruling Postponed by NRA," *Editor & Publisher* 67, no. 6 (June 23, 1934): 7, 16; Henry Bonner McDaniel, *The American Newspaperboy: A Comparative Study of His Work and School Activities* (Los Angeles: Wetzel, 1941), 17.

9. "Boston Newsboys Sales Champions," *New York Times*, June 22, 1934, 16; Todd Alexander Postol, "Creating the American Newspaper Boy: Middle-Class Route Service and Juvenile Salesmanship in the Great Depression," *Journal of Social History* 31, no. 2 (Winter 1997): 329–332; Postol, "Masculine Guidance: Boys, Men, and Newspapers," 1930–1939," in *Boys and Their Toys: Masculinity, Technology, and Class in America*, ed. Roger Horowitz (New York: Routledge, 2001), 169–198; E. D. Hood, "Report of Newspaper Boy Committee," *Proceedings*, International Circulation Managers' Association 43rd Annual Convention, Savannah, GA, 1941, 145; McDaniel, *American Newspaperboy*, 127.

10. Postol, "Creating the American Newspaper Boy," 329, 333–334; *Proceedings*, International Circulation Managers' Association 38th Annual Convention, 1936, 91; A. Cohen, "Building Carrier Morale," International Circulation Managers' Association, *Official Bulletin*, Sept. 1931, 29.

11. Postol, "Masculine Guidance," 169; Todd Alexander Postol, "America's Press-Radio Rivalry: Circulation Mangers and Newspaper Boys During the Depression," in *Studies in Newspaper and Periodical History: 1995 Annual*, ed. Michael Harris and Tom O'Malley (Westport, CT: Greenwood Press, 1997), 159; "Grand Rapids Herald Newspaper Boy's Greeting for a Happy 1933," Collection No. 297, Grand Rapids History and Special Collections Archives, Grand Rapids Public Library.

12. William M. Camp, "Newsboy Wins Trip to Europe," *National Educational Outlook Among Negroes* 2, no. 1 (1937): 16; "30 Dailies Sponsor Soap Box Derby," *Editor & Publisher* 67, no. 20 (July 21, 1934): 25; Kriste Lindenmeyer, *The Greatest Generation Grows Up: American Childhood in the 1930s* (Chicago: Ivan R. Dee, 2005), 173; "Rise in School Age Debated in Albany," *New York Times*, Feb. 6, 1935, 21.

13. Charles W. Palmer, "The School Records of Philadelphia Newsboys," *School and Society* 32, no. 828 (Nov. 8, 1930): 645–646; Charles W. Palmer, "A Study of Part-Time Jobs for Boys," *School Review* 39, no. 9 (Nov. 1931): 678; George B. Mangold, *Problems of Child Welfare* (New York: Macmillan, 1936), 318–319; Clyde W. Taylor, "Influences of Newspaper Routes," *School Review* 49, no. 1 (Jan. 1941): 57–59; White, *In Search of History*, 39.

14. William H. Kilpatrick, "A Plea for School 'Fads,'" *New York Times*, Feb. 5, 1933, XX 4; "The Newsboys' Republic in Milwaukee Public Schools," Jan. 1, 1934, Milwaukee Public Schools Collection, MSS Collection 1680, file 30, Milwaukee County Historical Society; "Character Studies Among Newsboys in Milwaukee," *Elementary School Journal* 30, no. 5 (Jan. 1930): 332–333; *Children Engaged in Newspaper and Magazine Selling and Delivering*, 10; George W. Zorsch, "1932 Report Covering Street Trades Enforcement," 11, box 3, folder 9, NYCLC Papers. See also David Tyack, Robert Lowe, and Elisabeth Hansot, *Public Schools in Hard Times: The Great Depression and Recent Years* (Cambridge, MA: Harvard University Press, 1984).

15. *N.B.A. Handbook*, 7; "Maurice G. Lipson," *Indianapolis Star*, Nov. 25, 1980, 32; "Newsies Call on Hoover," *Pittsburgh Courier*, Jan. 3, 1930, A8; Herbert Hoover, "Message on the First Annual Patriotic Pilgrimage of Newspaper Boys of America," Oct. 1, 1930, American Presidency Project, www.presidency.ucsb.edu/ws/?pid=22370.

16. T. Earl Sullenger, "The Newsboy as a Juvenile Delinquent," *Journal of Juvenile Research* 15 (1931): 216; Chaim Towber and M. J. Rubenstein, *The Newsboy* (New York: Metro Music, 1934).

17. *Child Labor: A Publication of the White House Conference on Child Health and Protection* (New York: Century, 1932), 162; "Hilliard, William A.," BlackPast.org, accessed Sept. 20, 2009, www.blackpast.org/?q=aaw/hilliard-william-1927; *Oregonian*, Mar. 28, 1933, n.p.; Allison Davis and John Dollard, *Children of Bondage: The Personality Development of Negro Youth in the Urban South* (Washington, DC: American Council on Education, 1940), 122.

18. *Children Engaged in Newspaper and Magazine Selling and Delivering*, 19–20, 45; Lee, *Daily Newspaper in America*, 298; *Charleston News & Courier*, May 2, 1936, 12; Mary Fox, "'For Newsboys, I Like Girls,'" *American Magazine* 110 (July 1930): 80.

19. Russell Baker, *Growing Up* (New York: Congdon & Weed, 1982), 96, 151–157; Russell Baker, *The Good Times* (New York: Morrow, 1989), 7–21; Samuel Hynes, *The Growing Season: An American Boyhood Before the War* (New York: Viking Penguin, 2003), 9, 84, 100–101.

20. Lawrence Ferlinghetti, *A Coney Island of the Mind* (New York: New Directions, 1958), 60; Neeli Cherkovski, *Ferlinghetti: A Biography* (New York: Doubleday, 1979), 17.

21. Viviana A. Zelizer, *Pricing the Priceless Child: The Changing Social Value of Children* (New York: Basic Books, 1985), 73–112.

22. Churchill, "Survey by the Burroughs Newsboys Foundation," 29; Zorsch, "1932 Report Covering Street Trades Enforcement," 1–2; *Children Engaged in Newspaper and Magazine Selling and Delivering*, 14; Harry M. Shulman, *Newsboys of New York: A Study of Their Legal and Illegal Work Activities During 1931* (New York: New York Child Labor Committee, 1932), 6–7, 30; Paul D. Nelson, "Lee Lawrie, Courthouse Sculptor," 2009, Institute for Global

Citizenship, Macalester University, Staff Publications, Paper 3, accessed Nov. 5, 2016, https://digitalcommons.macalester.edu/igcstaffpub/3. On children as breadwinners, see Lizabeth Cohen, *Making a New Deal: Industrial Work in Chicago, 1919–1939* (Cambridge: Cambridge University Press, 1990), 246–249.

23. Sullender, "Newsboy as Juvenile Delinquent," 217; Shulman, "Newsboys of New York," 25.

24. Kenneth L. Kusmer, *Down and Out, on the Road: The Homeless in American History* (New York: Oxford University Press, 2002), 204; Thomas Minehan, *Boy and Girl Tramps of America* (New York: Farrar and Rinehart, 1934), 16; Mark Aldrich, *Death Rode the Rails: American Railroad Accidents and Safety, 1825–1965* (Baltimore: Johns Hopkins University Press, 2006), 264; Glen Steele, *Temporary Shelter for Homeless or Transient Persons and Travelers Aid*, Children's Bureau (Washington, DC: Government Printing Office, 1932), 44; *Children Engaged in Newspaper and Magazine Selling and Delivering*, 50–51; "Peril to Children in Crisis Stressed," *New York Times*, Dec. 14, 1932, 2.

25. "Opens New Boys' Shelter," *New York Times*, Dec. 22 1932, 4; "Boy Wanderer, 16, Finds 'Happiest Christmas,' with Farm Job Likely, at Newsboys' Dinner," *New York Times*, Dec. 26, 1933, 2; Owen R. Lovejoy, "Scores Camp Plan for Nomad Youth," *New York Times*, Feb. 16, 1933, 22; "19 Pickets Seized at Newsboy Home," *New York Times*, Oct. 14, 1934, 20; Joan M. Crouse, *The Homeless Transient in the Great Depression: New York State, 1929–1941* (Albany: State University of New York Press, 1986), 77–78. See also Roy Rosenzweig, "Organizing the Unemployed: The Early Years of the Great Depression, 1929–1933," *Radical America* 10 (July–Aug. 1976), 37–60.

26. Harry Black, *From Newsboy to Preacher: The Story of My Life* (Los Angeles, ca. 1932), 139; Edmund Ramsden, "Rats, Stress and the Built Environment," *History of the Human Sciences* 25, no. 5 (Dec. 2012): 127. See also Thomas E. Bergler, *The Juvenilization of American Christianity* (Grand Rapids, MI: Wm. B. Eerdmans, 2012).

27. Studs Terkel, *Hard Times: An Oral History of the Great Depression* (New York, Random House, 1970), 20.

28. Shulman, "Newsboys of New York," 6; Todd Alexander Postol, "Hearing the Voices of Working Children," *Labor's Heritage* 1, no. 3 (July 1989): 10.

29. *Child Labor: Report of the Subcommittee on Child Labor. White House Conference on Child Health and Protection* (New York: Century, 1932), 146; Kriste Lindenmeyer, *"A Right to Childhood": The US Children's Bureau and Child Welfare, 1912–1946* (Urbana: University of Illinois Press, 1997), 87, 164–170, 122–123; Fred Romanofsky, "Dead End Kids," Dec. 15, 1938, American Life Histories, Federal Writers' Project, Manuscript Division, Library of Congress.

30. See Richard A. Reiman, *The New Deal and American Youth: Ideas and Ideals in a Depression Decade* (Athens: University of Georgia Press, 1992); Helen Keller to Franklin Roosevelt, May 19, 1933, Legislation: Federal file, American Foundation for the Blind, cited in *Helen Keller: Selected Writings*, ed. Kim E. Nielsen (New York: New York University Press, 2005), no. 44, n.p.

31. "Johnson Lashes at Press Critics," *New York Times*, Aug. 3, 1934, 9; Margaret A. Blanchard, "Freedom of the Press and the Newspaper Code: June 1933–February 1934," *Journalism Quarterly* 54, no. 1 (1977): 40–49; Lee, *Daily Newspaper in America*, 240–250.

32. "News Men Demand 5-Day Week in Code," *New York Times*, Sept. 23, 1933, 8; "Small Newspapers Discuss Problems," *New York Times*, Apr. 25, 1934, 7.

33. *American Child* 15 (Nov. 1933), 2, cited in Walter Trattner, *Crusade for the Children: A History of the National Child Labor Committee and Child Labor Reform in America* (Chicago: Quadrangle Books, 1970), 292 n. 13; "Status of Newsboys," *New York Times*, Oct. 30, 1933, 3; "The Newspaper Boy, Article I," International Circulation Managers Association, Reston, VA, VF-L2-12.

34. Postol, "Hearing the Voices of Working Children," 9–10, 15.

35. "Text of Order and Letter by President on New Code for Newspapers," *New York Times*, Feb. 20, 1934, 8; "Press: Newsboy Labor," *Time* 23, no. 26 (June 25, 1934), 68.

36. George H. Manning, "Child Labor Ruling Postponed by NRA," *Editor & Publisher* 67, no. 7 (June 30, 1934): 7, 16; "Newsboys: New Dealers Wage War on Child Labor Provision," *News-Week* 3, no. 26 (June 30, 1934), 30; Trattner, *Crusade for the Children*, 194; "Newsboy Not

Delinquent Says Expert," *Hartford Courant*, July 28, 1934, 2; Lloyd Smith, *The Paper Route: A Training for Any Business or Profession*, 2nd ed. (Kansas City, MO: Burton, 1929), 14.

37. "Child Labor Ruling Postponed by NRA," *Editor & Publisher* 67, no. 6 (June 23, 1934): 7; "Argue 14-Year Age as Newsboy Limit," *New York Times*, June 23, 1934, 4.

38. "J. D. Barnum Heads Publishers' Group," *New York Times*, Apr. 27, 1935, 4; Dorothy Dunbar Bromley, "The Newspapers and Child Labor," *Nation* 140, no. 363 (June 30, 1935), 132; *Child Labor Facts*, NCLC Pub. No. 369 (1937), 20–21; Elisha Hanson, "The American Newspaper Publishers Association," *Public Opinion Quarterly* 2, no. 1 (Jan. 1938): 126.

39. Lindenmeyer, *"A Right to Childhood,"* 196.

40. *American Child* 15 (Nov. 1933), 2, cited in Trattner, *Crusade for the Children*, 292 n. 13; "Ratification of Child Labor Amendment by a State Legislature After Previous Rejection," *Yale Law Journal*, 47, no. 1 (Nov. 1937): 148–151; George Seldes, *Lords of the Press* (New York: Julian Messner, 1938), 34, 373; "Opposition to the Amendment," *Survey Graphic* 26, no. 1 (Jan. 15, 1937), 10–12; Bromley, "Newspapers and Child Labor," 131–132.

41. See George Seldes, *You Can't Do That!* (New York: Modern Age Books, 1938), 84–101; Emery and Emery, *Press and America*, 697, 687; "Opposition to the Amendment," *Survey Graphic* 26, no. 1 (Jan. 15, 1937), 10–12; "Newspaper Blood Money," *Christian Century*, Feb. 6, 1935, 167–168.

42. "Security Jam Ends, House Passes Bill," *New York Times*, Aug. 5, 1939, 3.

43. "Newsboy Not Employee of Publisher Within Meaning of Compensation Act," *Business Law Review* 16, no. 3 (July–Dec. 1930): 195–198; Miss Minor, "Memo on Newsboy Case," box 3, folder 6, NYCLC Papers; *Oklahoma Pub. Co. v. Greenlee*, 300 P.684, 150 Okla. 69 (Sup. Ct. Okla, 1931); *Associated Indemnity Corporation v. Industrial Acc. Commission*, 12 P.2d 1075 (Cal. Ct. App. 1932); *Hartford Accident & Indemnity Co. v. Industrial Accident Commission*, 123 Cal. App. 151, 10 P.2d 1035 (Cal. D.C. App. 1932); Marian Faas Stone, "Industrial Accidents to Employed Minors in California in 1932," *Monthly Labor Review* 39 (Nov. 1934); "Workmen's Compensation. 'Independent Contractor.' Denial of Compensation to Dependents of Newsboys," *Columbia Law Review* 35, no. 8 (Dec. 1935): 1325–1327; Charles Rohleder, *The Newspaper Boy—Merchant or Employee?* (Indianapolis: Newspaper Boys of America, 1937), 44; *Creswell v. Publishing Co.*, 204 NC 380 (1933), in *Fourth Decennial Digest* 33 (1926–36), Key No. 340; *Balinski et ux. v. Press Pub. Co. et al.*, 118 Pa. Super. 89 (1935); *Birmingham Post Co. v. Sturgeon*, 227 Ala. 162 (1933).

44. Herman Miles Somers and Anne Ramsay Somers, *Workmen's Compensation: Prevention, Insurance, and Rehabilitation of Occupational Disability* (New York: John Wiley & Sons, 1954), 57; "New Labor Laws of 1937," *American Labor Legislation Review* 27, no. 4 (Dec. 1937): 185–186; Industrial Commission of Wisconsin, "A Note on the Street Trades Law," in *Street Trades and Public Exhibition Permits, 1940 and 1941*, Dec. 21, 1942, 1; Frances Mary Albrier, *Determined Advocate for Racial Equality: An Interview Conducted by Malca Chall, 1977–78* (Berkeley: Regional Oral History Office, Bancroft Library, University of California, 1979), 215.

45. *NLRB v. Hearst Publications*, 322 US 111 (1944); Katharine Du Pre Lumpkin, "The Child Labor Provisions of the Fair Labor Standards Act," *Law and Contemporary Problems* 6, no. 3 (Summer 1939): 400–401; *Myers v. Stat Journal Co.*, C. C. H. Lab. Law Serv. 18,290 (Mich. Cir. Ct., 1938); "Test Suit by a Newsboy," *New York Times*, Dec. 10, 1938, 5; "Newsboy Is Ruled Beyond Wage Law," *New York Times*, Jan. 1, 1939, 7; "The Newsboy," *Los Angeles Times*, Apr. 19, 1939, A4.

46. "Newsboys Protest Distributing Plan," *Baltimore Sun*, Oct. 15, 1930, 28; "Newsboys' Strike Litters Streets of Pittsburgh," *Los Angeles Times*, July 20, 1933, 1; "Newsies Strike—Dailies Rob 'Em," *National Labor Tribune*, July, 20, 1933, 1, 8; "Arrests in 'Newsies' Strike Draws Protest," *Pittsburgh Courier*, July 22, 1933, 1.

47. "Afternoon Residence Delivery" (ca. 1931), 3, box 3, folder 5, NYCLC Papers; "Report on Bronx Home News Hearing," Nov. 13, 1933, box 33, folder 20, NYCLC Papers.

48. "Street Boys 'Strike' in Cleveland," *Editor & Publisher* 67, no. 2 (May 26, 1934): 32; "Strike of Newsboys Ends in Cleveland," *Editor & Publisher* 67, no. 3 (June 2, 1934): 30; "Boys and Publishers Agree on Terms," *Editor & Publisher* 67, no. 5 (June 16, 1934): 38; "Hits Papers'

Motives," *Cleveland Plain Dealer*, Oct. 28, 1934, 14; Lee, *Daily Newspaper in America*, 300; *New York Call*, June 22, 1935, 4.

49. "Striking Holyoke Newsboys Try to 'Picket' Transcript," *Springfield Republican*, Sept. 11, 1934, 2; "Newsboys' Strike Comes to Close," *Springfield Republican*, Sept. 13, 1934, 4.

50. "The Great Depression in Washington State," Labor Events Yearbook, 1936–37, www.depts. washington.edu/depress/yearbook1936.shtml; Shelden C. Menefee, "The Decline of Dave Beck," *Nation* 146, no. 13 (Mar. 26, 1938), 354–355.

51. "Newsboys Go on Strike at Some Loop Corners," *Detroit News*, Apr. 5, 1937, n.p.; Chapin Hall, "What Goes On," *Los Angeles Times*, July 3, 1937, 2; Bob Ray, "The Sports X-Ray," *Los Angeles Times*, Aug. 25, 1937, A14; "Newsboys' Strike Settled," *Springfield Republican*, Aug. 4, 1939, 4. Meanwhile in Canada, carrier boys in Sydney, Nova Scotia, successfully struck the *Halifax Herald* in September 1937 to increase payment rates. See *Toronto Clarion*, Sept. 22, 1937.

52. "Conciliator Willing to Effect Meeting in Newsboy Strike," *Cleveland Plain Dealer*, June 11, 1940, 1, 14; "Destroy Papers in Newsboys Strike," *Cleveland Plain Dealer*, June 14, 1940, 19; "Cleveland Papers End Street Sales," *Los Angeles Times*, June 19, 1940, 10; "Newsboys' Strike," *Newsweek* 16, no 3 (July 15, 1940), 42.

53. *The People v. Thomas W. Armentrout et al.*, Cr. A. No. 632, Appellate Dept., Superior Court of California, Los Angeles County, 118 Cal. App. Supp. 761; 1 P.2d 556; 1931 Cal. App. Lexis 22, July 3, 1931, decided; "Man and Union Convicted of Contempt of Court," *Los Angeles Times*, May 26, 1837, 6.

54. "Four Killed in Riot at Main Ford Plant as 3,000 Idle Fight," *New York Times*, Mar. 8, 1932, 1, 10; "Reds Are Sought in Fatal Red Riot," *New York Times*, Mar. 9, 1932, 3; Bird, *Invisible Scar*, 173–174.

55. "Arrest of Newsboy in Attempt to Halt Communist Papers," *Western Worker*, Feb. 15, 1932, 4; Harvey Schwartz, *Solidarity Stories: An Oral History of the ILWU* (Seattle: University of Washington Press, 2009), 15, 93; Mike Quin, *The Big Strike* (Olema, CA: Olema Publishing, 1949), 61.

56. "Riots Give Toledo Press Taste of War," *Editor & Publisher* 67, no. 3 (June 2, 1934): 7; Herbert Solow, "War in Minneapolis," *Nation* 139, no. 3065 (Aug. 8, 1934), 160.

57. "Guild on Strike at Wilkes-Barre," *New York Times*, Oct. 2, 1938, 12.

58. Mapheus Smith, "An Empirical Scale of Prestige Status of Occupations," *American Sociological Review* 8, no. 2 (Apr. 1943): 188.

59. Joseph Liss, "Morning Paper—A Play About Newsboys," Federal Theatre Playscript No. 21 (July 1937), 3, folder 38.288, Hallie Flanagan Papers, Vassar College. On the Popular Front, see Michael Denning, *The Cultural Front: The Laboring of American Culture in the Twentieth Century* (London: Verso, 1996), 4–21.

60. See Richard A. Reiman, *The New Deal and American Youth: Ideas and Ideals in a Depression Decade* (Athens: University of Georgia Press, 1992), 7.

61. Gregory Novikov, "*Newsboy*; an adaptation for the American League Against War and Fascism, from a poem by V. J. Jerome, as co-ordinated by the Workers Theatre," 1933, New York Public Library for the Performing Arts, reprinted in Jay Williams, *Stage Left* (New York: Charles Scribner's Sons, 1974), 90–96. See also "Workers Theater to Present New Play," *New York Amsterdam News*, Dec. 1, 1934, 10, and Bosley Crowther, "Theater of the Left," *New York Times*, Apr. 14, 1935, X 1–2. *Newsboy* debuted at the Round House in the working-class Ancoats district of Manchester in 1934.

62. William Gropper, "'Extry! Corrupt Judge in Hiding!,'" *Masses* 6 (Apr. 1931): 5.

63. Edward Brunner, "Red Funnies: The New York *Daily Worker's* 'Popular Front' Comics, 1936–1945," *American Periodicals* 17, no. 2 (2007): 188; Mathew Blake, "Woody Guthrie: A Dust Bowl Representative in the Communist Party Press," *Journalism History* 35, no. 4 (Winter 2010): 184–193; Seldes, *Lords of the Press*, 41; Lee, *Daily Newspaper in America*, 3, 258–313.

64. See Robert Sklar, *City Boys: Cagney, Bogart, Garfield* (Princeton, NJ: Princeton University Press, 1992); "Coming Pictures," *New York Times*, Feb. 28, 1932, X6; *New York Times*, Apr. 24, 1932, X 5; "The Screen," *New York Times*, Jan. 18, 1935, 29; Deac Rossell, "The Fourth Estate and the Seventh Art," in *Questioning Media Ethics*, ed. Bernard Rubin (New York: Praeger, 1978), 268; Lary May, *The Big Tomorrow: Hollywood and the Politics of the American Way*

(Chicago: University of Chicago Press, 2002), 64–84; Morris Dickstein, *Dancing in the Dark: A Cultural History of the Great Depression* (New York: W. W. Norton, 2009), 219, 227–233.

65. Bob Gilmore, *Harry Partch: A Biography* (New Haven, CT: Yale University Press, 1998), 103; S. Andrew Granade, *Harry Partch: Hobo Composer* (Rochester, NY: University of Rochester Press, 2014), 116–117, 199–200.

66. George Hulme, *Mel Tormé: A Chronicle of His Recordings, Books and Films* (Jefferson, NC: McFarland, 2000), 7; John Dunning, *On the Air: The Encyclopedia of Old-Time Radio* (New York: Oxford University Press, 1998), 99; "Edgar Bergen Dies at 75," *Variety*, Oct. 4, 1978, n.p.; Charles L. Allen, "The Press and Advertising," *Annals of the American Academy of Political and Social Science*, 219 (Jan. 1942): 89.

67. Masha Zakheim, *Coit Tower San Francisco: Its History and Art* (Volcano, CA: Volcano Press, 2009); John Jenkisson, "Former WPA Muralist Succeeds as Cartoonist," *New York World-Telegram*, Apr. 30, 1945; Emma Ross, "Mischa Richter," Provincetown Arts Registry, accessed Aug. 30, 2009, www.provincetownartistregistry.com/R/ richter_mischa.html.

68. "New York Library Waits 40 Years for These Murals," *Life*, Sept. 30, 1940, 64.

69. Shulman, "Newsboys of New York," 24.

70. William Stott, *Documentary Expression and Thirties America* (New York: Oxford University Press, 1973), 50, 212. See also Cara A. Finnegan, *Picturing Poverty: Print Culture and FSA Photographs* (Washington, DC: Smithsonian Books, 2003), and Kathleen Thompson and Hilary Mac Austin, *Children of the Depression* (Bloomington: Indiana University Press, 2001). Theodor Jung, *Newsboys Admiring Sporting Goods, Jackson, Ohio*, Apr. 1936; Ben Shahn, *Newsboy, Newark, Ohio*, Summer 1938; John Vachon, *Farm Boy Who Sells "Grit." Irwinville Farms, Georgia*, 1938; Arthur Rothstein, *Newsboy on Main Street, Montrose, Colorado*, Oct. 1939; all FSA-OWI Photograph Collection, Library of Congress.

71. James Thurber, "Voices of Revolution," *New Republic*, Mar. 25, 1936, 200–201; William Saroyan, "Resurrection of a Life" (1935), in *The Best American Short Stories of the Century*, ed., John Updike and Katrina Kenison (Boston: Houghton Mifflin, 1999), 159–168.

72. Upton Sinclair, *The Flivver King: A Story of Ford-America* (Chicago: Charles H. Kerr, 1987), 9.

73. James T. Farrell, "The Scoop," in *Can All This Grandeur Perish?* (New York: Vanguard, 1937), 130–135.

74. "The Author of the Alger Books for Boys," *New York Times*, Jan. 10, 1932, SM 21; "Blasé Age Ignores Alger Anniversary," *New York Times*, Jan. 14, 1932, 23; "Boys Today Doubt Alger's Success Code," *New York Times*, Feb. 3, 1932, 17; Warren I. Susman, "The Culture of the Thirties," in *Culture as History: The Transformation of American Society in the Twentieth Century* (New York: Pantheon Books, 1984), 165.

75. DeMarco, "Being a Newsie," 35; Frank Russo, interview by author, Santa Cruz, CA, 1989.

76. White, *In Search of History*; Baker, *Growing Up*, 152–153; Timothy B. Tyson, *Radio Free Dixie: Robert F. Williams and the Roots of Black Power* (Chapel Hill: University of North Carolina Press, 1999), 24, 195, 203.

77. "Fascists React to Rebuke," *New York Times*, Apr. 29, 1931, 10; "Madrid Bans 'Amateur' Newsboys," *New York Times*, July 10, 1934, 19; "Nazis Beat Foes in Saarbrueck," *New York Times*, Jan. 10, 1935, 6; "Reich to Check Up on Newsboys," *New York Times*, Dec. 12, 1935, 14.

78. See Bird, *Invisible Scar*; Tom Brokaw, *The Greatest Generation* (New York: Random House, 1998); and Glen H. Elder Jr., *Children of the Great Depression* (Chicago: University of Chicago Press, 1974).

79. Ferlinghetti, *Coney Island of the Mind*, 60.

Conclusion

1. "From Prince to Newsboy," *New York Sunday Journal*, Dec. 13, 1893, 27; James L. Ford, *Forty Odd Years in the Literary Shop* (New York: E. P. Dutton, 1921), 162–163; "Runaway Girl Found as She Tries to Become Newsboy," *Chicago Tribune*, May 16, 1928, 17.

2. Bureau of the Census, *Historical Statistics of the United States* (1976), table H-424.

3. New York State Department of Labor, "The Newsboy: Newspaper Trade Attracts Large Number of Youngster; Age Requirement Low," *Industrial Bulletin* 25 (Aug. 1946): 26–27.

4. "Child Labor Amendment Still Needed," *Social Service Review* 115, no. 2 (June 1941): 347; Henry Bonner McDaniel, *The American Newspaperboy: A Comparative Study of His Work and School Activities* (Los Angeles: Wetzel, 1941), 43.

5. Bill Vaughn, "Voice from the Past: When War Came to KC," *Kansas City Star*, Dec. 7, 1991, A18; Betty Jean Miller, "Former Corner Newsboys Heralded the Day's Biggest News," *St. Petersburg Times*, July 20, 1997, 12; Marcia Blackburn, "Spotlight on 100 Years of News," *Binghamton Press and Sun-Bulletin*, June 6, 2004, C1.

6. Ben Y. Tonooka, Oral History Interview by Martha Nakagawa, Feb. 6, 2012, Los Angeles, Densho Visual History Collection, http://archive.densho.org/main.aspx. See also John D. Stevens, "From Behind Barbed Wire: Freedom of the Press in World War II Japanese Centers," *Journalism Quarterly* 48 (Summer 1971): 279–287, and E. J. Friedlander, "Freedom of Press Behind Barbed Wire: Paul Yokota and the Jerome Relocation Center Newspaper," *Arkansas Historical Quarterly* 44, no. 4 (Winter 1985): 303–313.

7. E. D. Hood, 43rd Annual Convention of the International Circulation Managers' Association, 1941, 145; George Gallup, "Newsboys Retain Popular Appeal," *New York Times*, Dec. 25, 1942, 13; "Roosevelt to Newsboys," *New York Times*, Oct. 2, 1943, 11; "Topics of the Times," *New York Times*, Oct. 2, 1954, 16.

8. *Prince v. Massachusetts*, 321 U.S. 158, 166–168, 64 S.Ct. 438, 88 L.Ed. 645 (1944).

9. E. Nelson Bridwell, ed., *Shazam! From the Forties to the Seventies* (New York: Harmony Books, 1977); R. J. Vitone, "Simon & Kirby's Kids Go to War!," and Rich Morrissey, "Extra! The Newsboy Legion!," in *Jack Kirby Collector* 7, Oct. 1995, 11, 23.

10. *Saturday Evening Post*, Oct. 7, 1944, 73.

11. Arthur P. Young, "Alger at the Comics, Part 4: 'The Will to Win,'" *Newsboy*, Sept.–Oct. 2010, 3–4; "Horatio Alger Awards Presented," *Richmond Times-Dispatch*, May 14, 1948, 22; Foster Eaton, "Father Dunne's Life on Screen," *St. Louis Star-Times*, May 7, 1948.

12. "Publishers Consider Strike Compromise," *Joplin* (MO) *Globe*, Aug. 23, 1945, 12; "Kansas City Strike Ends," *New York Times*, Feb. 2, 1947, 30.

13. Marc Linder, "From Street Urchins to Little Merchants: The Juridical Transvaluation of Child Newspaper Carriers," *Temple Law Review*, Winter 1990, 847.

14. Lewis Wood, "Gives Newsboys Employe Status," *New York Times*, Apr. 25, 1944, 14; California Legislature, *Fourth Report of the Senate Fact-Finding Committee on Un-American Activities: Communist Front Organizations* (1948), 350, 224–225.

15. "Publishers Assail Procedure of WLB," *New York Times*, Apr. 28, 1944, 12; California Legislature, *Fourth Report*, 350, 224–225; Todd DiPastino, *Bill Mauldin: A Life Up Front* (New York: Norton, 2009), 217–239.

16. "A Robot Newsboy," *Maryville Daily Forum*, Sept. 24, 1945, 17; "Trolley, Bus Newspaper Service Starts Monday," *St. Paul Pioneer Press*, July 23, 1950, n.p.

17. Elliott West, *Growing Up in Twentieth Century America: A History and Reference Guide* (Westport, CT: Greenwood Press, 1996), 127, 207, 217; Jim Willis, *Surviving in the Newspaper Business: Newspaper Management in Turbulent Times* (Westport, CT: Praeger, 1988), 94–95; Joseph B. Forsee, "A Study of Fifty-Two Former Newspaperboys to Determine Effects of Carrying Newspapers," master's thesis, University of Missouri, 1950, 19–20.

18. Sol Glass, *United States Postage Stamps, 1945–1952* (West Somerville, MA, Bureau Issues Assoc. Inc., n.d.), 221–222; *Philadelphia Evening Bulletin*, Oct. 4, 1952; Donald J. Wood, *Newspaper Circulation Management—A Profession* (Oakland, CA: Newspaper Research Bureau, 1952), 35; "American Child," in *NASSP Bulletin* (National Association of Secondary-School Principals) 37, no. 248 (Jan. 1953): 256–258.

19. "Schoolboy's Coin Aids in Spy Case," *New York Times*, Sept. 22, 1957, 29 ; "2 Cited in Spy Case," *New York Times* Dec. 24, 1957, 7; "FBI History. Famous Cases. Rudolph Ivanovich Abel (Hollow Nickel Case)," accessed July 28, 2018, www.fbi.gov/libref/historic/famcases/abel.htm.

20. "Weaver Will Head Freedom Crusade," *Cleveland Plain Dealer*, Dec. 14, 1953, 11; "'Truth Dollars' Campaign Ready," *New Orleans Times-Picayune*, Jan. 16, 1955, 4; *Trenton Times*, Feb. 12, 1963, 8.

21. Sid Marks and Alban Emley, *The Newspaperboy's Hall of Fame* (Hollywood: House-Warven, 1953); "Newspaper Carrier Hall of Fame," News Media Alliance, accessed July 10, 2018, https://www.newsmediaalliance.org/research_tools/newspaper-carrier-hall-fame; Reg Manning, "A 'Youth Movement' to Be Proud Of," *Burlington Free Press*, Oct. 14, 1967, 12.

22. Emory, "All Power to the People," *Black Panther*, Berkeley, CA, Mar. 9, 1969, 20; "Young People Wanted to Sell the Black Panther," *Black Panther*, Mar. 16, 1969, 7.

23. "Disappearing Americana Includes Corner Newsboys," *Baton Rouge State Times Advocate*, Feb. 22, 1970, 28; John Tebbel, "The Changing American Newsboy," *Saturday Review*, Feb. 13, 1971, 56–58; Kurt Vonnegut Jr., *Slaughterhouse-Five or The Children's Crusade: A Duty-Dance with Death* (New York: Delacourte Press/Seymour Lawrence, 1969), 160; Studs Terkel, *Working: People Talk About What They Do All Day and How They Feel About What They Do* (New York: Pantheon, 1972), 16; Jon Bekken, "Newsboys," in *History of the Mass Media in the United States: An Encyclopedia*, ed. Margaret A. Blanchard (Chicago: Fitzroy Dearborn, 1998), 427.

24. *Warshafsky v. The Journal Co*, 216 NW 2d 197, 63 Wis. 2d 130—Wis: Supreme Court, 1974; "Recent Developments," *Journal of Family Law* 14 (1975): 162–169.

25. John Tebbel, "The Changing American Newsboy," *Saturday Review*, Feb. 21, 1971, 57; David Satter, "1,000 Mourners Fill Church for Slain Newsboy's Funeral," *Chicago Tribune*, Mar. 19, 1975, B18.

26. Paul Mokrzycki, "Lost in the Heartland: Childhood, Region, and Iowa's Missing Paperboys," *Annals of Iowa* 74, no. 1 (Winter 2015): 65.

27. Mark A. Stein, "Carriers—The Young Are Fading," *Los Angeles Times*, Apr. 10, 1987, pt. 1, 1, 30–31; Michael Freitag, "What's New in Newspaper Delivery; Paperboys Go the Way of the Dodo," *New York Times*, Mar. 22, 1987; Anne Bridgman, "Missing-Children Phenomenon Fuels School-Fingerprinting Programs," *Education Week* 3, no. 7 (Oct. 19, 1983).

28. Marc Linder, "What's Black and White and Red All Over? The Blood Tax on Newspapers," *Loyola Poverty Law Review* 3 (1997): 76–77; Marc Linder, "Hey Newsboys & Girls—Getting Injured Without Workers' Compensation Builds Character," *Nieman Reports* (Winter 1998), 62; "Carrier Fatally Stabbed," *Trenton Times*, June 11, 1993, A15; Mary Hardie, "It's a Changing World for Newspaper Carriers," *Gannetteer*, Dec. 1993, 5; Robert Neuwirth, "Quiet Tragedy: Violence Against Carriers," *Editor & Publisher*, Sept. 12, 1998: 8.

29. Neuwirth, "Quiet Tragedy," 8; "Are Newspapers Taking Advantage of Child Labor," *Stark Metropolitan Magazine*, Apr. 1988, 8–10; *The Untouchables*, "A Tale of Two Fathers," season 1, episodes 7–8, dir. by Steve De Jarnatt, written by Christopher Crowe and Richard Chapman, CBS, Feb. 14 and 21, 1993.

30. Neuwirth, "Quiet Tragedy," 8; John Bekken, "Newsboys: The Exploitation of 'Little Merchants' by the Newspaper Industry," in *Newsworkers: Toward a History of the Rank and File*, ed. Hanno Hardt and Bonnie Brennen (Minneapolis: University of Minnesota Press, 1995), 190–225; Patricia Callahan, "Delivering the News: Children Injured on Paper Routes Often Go Uninsured," *Wall Street Journal*, July 19, 2002, A1; Linder, "Hey Newsboys & Girls," 62.

31. Daniel Machalaba, "Are Newspaperboys a Vanishing Species?," *Wall Street Journal*, Mar. 31, 1981, 1; John Reilly, "Paper Route No Longer Kid Stuff," *USA Today*, Oct. 12, 1984.

32. Rolf Rykken, "Shift to Adult Carriers Continues Apace," *Presstime* 13, no. 2 (Feb. 1, 1991): 22–23; "Youth Peddling: Kids in Danger," National Consumer Leage press release, Mar. 12, 1999; Stacy A. Teicher, "Door-to-Door Sales Crews or Indentured Servants?," *Christian Science Monitor*, Apr. 5, 1999.

33. John M. McGuire, "Street Corner Sellers," *Everyday Magazine, St. Louis Post-Dispatch*, Sept. 15, 1992, 1F; Bekken, "Newsboys," 426.

34. Norma Fay Green, "Chicago's *StreetWise* at the Crossroads: A Case Study of a Newspaper to Empower the Homeless in the 1990s," in *Print Culture in a Diverse America*, ed. James P. Danky and Wayne A. Wiegand (Urbana: University of Illinois Press, 1998), 34–55.

35. Tony Rogers, "Are Newspapers Dead or Adapting in the Age of Digital News?," *ThoughtCo*, Sept. 26, 2017, https://www.thoughtco.com/adapting-in-the-age-of-digital-news-consumption-2074132.

36. "Luce Hall of Reporting Opens with Nostalgia at Smithsonian," *New York Times*, May 2, 1973, 38; Robert C. Post, *Who Owns America's Past? The Smithsonian and the Problem of History* (Baltimore: Johns Hopkins University Press, 2013), 137.
37. Aviva Chomsky, "A Newspaper Crisis Reveals Unreported Worlds," Feb. 4, 2016, TomDispatch.com, http://www.tomdispatch.com/post/176099.

NAME INDEX

Page numbers followed by *f* refer to figures.

SUBJECT INDEX

Page numbers followed by *f* refer to figures.